THE WAR
ILLUSTRATED

Hoppé

HIS MAJESTY KING GEORGE VI

THE WAR
Illustrated

Complete Record of the Conflict
by Land and Sea and in the Air

Edited by
SIR JOHN HAMMERTON

Volume One

THIS FIRST VOLUME OF THE WAR ILLUSTRATED contains the weekly issues from No. 1 to No. 20. The whole series of full-page portraits of prominent personalities in the War appearing weekly as Our War Album is here reprinted in a superior style to form an art supplement at the beginning of the volume. The General Index has been carefully compiled to facilitate ready reference to any of the literary or pictorial contents of the volume, and a glance at it will suffice to indicate the wide scope and thoroughness of our contemporary chronicle.

It is hoped to maintain the successive volumes of THE WAR ILLUSTRATED *in a similar manner, but that must depend in some degree upon the availability of the various materials essential to its production—photographs, paper, printing ink and binding boards. The Editor can at least assure his readers that no effort will be spared by himself and his publishers to provide the best that can be secured.*

Published 2000
Cover Design © 2000
TRIDENT PRESS INTERNATIONAL
ISBN 1-58279-100-7 Single Edition
ISBN 1-58279-019-1 Special Combined Edition*
*Contains Volume 1 & 2 Unabridged

Printed in Croatia

Vandyk

RT. HON. NEVILLE CHAMBERLAIN, P.C., M.P.
After striving most valiantly and earnestly for peace, the Premier has risen to fresh
heights as the leader of Britain at war. Although in 1939 he celebrated his seven-
tieth birthday, increasing years have but added to his vigour and resolution.

Fox

RT. HON. WINSTON CHURCHILL, P.C., M.P.

For forty years the man who now chuckles over the epithet of " Nazi Enemy Number One " has been one of the most prominent and most discussed of British personalities. Today, as in 1914, he has his place at the head of the Board of Admiralty.

6

Keystone

RT. HON. LESLIE HORE-BELISHA, P.C., M.P.

Secretary of State for War from May 1937 until January 1940, during his period of office
the British Army was transformed from a comparatively small establishment of volunteers
into the huge force which embodies the cream of Britain's young manhood.

Howard Coster

RT. HON. VISCOUNT HALIFAX, P.C.
During five difficult years he acted most worthily as the King-Emperor's Viceroy
in India, and since early in 1938 he has guided with the same high-minded purpose
and inflexible determination the stream of British foreign policy.

Fayer of Vienna

RT. HON. ANTHONY EDEN, P.C., M.P.

Knowing war from actual service in the field—in the Great War he held a commission in the King's Royal Rifle Corps—the Dominions Secretary has been hailed for some years past as an outstanding champion of the principles embodied in the Covenant of the League of Nations.

Vandyk

RT. HON. SIR KINGSLEY WOOD, P.C., M.P.
Dust has not settled on his laurels as Minister of Health, and today the enthusiasm
which he once displayed over such things as drains and dustbins is directed towards
the maintenance of Britain's superiority in the air.

Hay Wrightson

ADMIRAL OF THE FLEET LORD CHATFIELD, O.M.
He joined the Queen's Navy in the 1880's and during the Great War was Beatty's
Flag Captain. Now, however, he has exchanged the quarter-deck for a desk in
Whitehall, whence he directs the co-ordination of the fighting services.

Keystone

ADMIRAL OF THE FLEET SIR DUDLEY POUND

Britain's First Sea Lord fought at Jutland in command of H.M.S. Colossus, and was Commander-in-Chief of the Mediterranean Fleet during that difficult time of the wars in Abyssinia and Spain.

GENERAL VISCOUNT GORT, V.C.

In this war Britain's Expeditionary Force is commanded by a "front line soldier," for General Viscount Gort served throughout the last war as an officer in the Grenadier Guards. He won his V.C. for splendid bravery at Cambrai in September, 1918.

GENERAL SIR EDMUND IRONSIDE

Entering the Royal Artillery in 1899, he served on the Staff during the Great War, and in 1918 was Commander-in-Chief of the Allied troops engaged in the Archangel expedition. Now he holds the all-important military position of Chief of the Imperial General Staff.

Elliott & Fry

AIR CHIEF MARSHAL SIR CYRIL NEWALL
Chief of the Air Staff since 1937, he joined the army in 1905, but during the Great War
was attached to the Royal Flying Corps. In the early nineteen-thirties he commanded the
Air Force in the Middle East, and received his Air Chief Marshal's baton in 1937.

15

Bassano

RT. HON. SIR NEVILE HENDERSON, G.C.M.G.

St. Petersburg, Tokio, Rome, Paris, Constantinople, Cairo, Belgrade, Buenos Aires—to them all Diplomacy has called him. But never has he had a more difficult task than when in Berlin from 1937 to the outbreak of war he strove to convince the Nazis of Britain's earnestness.

16

Vandyk

GEN. RT. HON. JAN CHRISTIAAN SMUTS, P.C.

Great Empire statesman, famous soldier (he fought against Britain in the Boer War and for the Commonwealth in the Great War), distinguished philosopher, a principal founder of the League of Nations—he is now for the second time Prime Minister of the South African Union.

Associated Press

REAR-ADMIRAL SIR HENRY HARWOOD
Commodore of the South American Division of the Royal Navy, he displayed the true
Nelson touch when with his three light cruisers he engaged the German pocket battleship
" Graf Spee." After the action he sent the message to his men, " Thank you, boys."

Keystone

M. EDOUARD DALADIER
Bourgeois of the bourgeois, for years past he has been a dominant figure in French politics.
Premier in 1933, in 1934, and again in 1938, since the beginning of the war he has been
also Foreign Minister. Like Clemenceau in the last war he embodies the French will to win.

GENERAL M. G. GAMELIN, G.C.V.O.
Generalissimo of the Allied Armies on the Western Front, he was first taken note
of by History for his share in the direction of the Battle of the Marne. Later he saw
service as a divisional general in the line and afterwards commanded in Syria.

Planet News

GENERAL A. J. GEORGES

After service in Algeria and Morocco he was badly wounded in the Great War and later
served as Pétain's Chief of Staff in North Africa. He helped Maginot to draw up the plans
for the famous Line, and now commands the French armies of the North-East.

ADMIRAL J. F. DARLAN, G.C.V.O.
The Commander-in-Chief of the French Navy served throughout the Great War for the most part on land—in command of naval guns in France and Salonika. After the War he saw service in Chinese waters, and on the last day of 1936 was appointed Chief of the Naval Staff.

Planet News

GENERAL JOSEPH VUILLEMIN
One of France's pioneer airmen, he went into action with his squadron immediately on the outbreak of the Great War and achieved fame as an air ace. With him as Commander-in-Chief, the French Air Force may be expected to repeat the glories of 1914-1918.

Planet News

GENERAL WLADYSLAW SIKORSKI
Prime Minister and War Minister in the Polish Government in Exile and Commander-in-Chief of the new Polish army now coming into being in France, General Sikorski played a prominent part in the fight for his country's independence and was Prime Minister in 1923.

General Index to Volume One

This Index is designed to give ready reference to the whole of the literary and pictorial contents of THE WAR ILLUSTRATED. *Individual subjects and persons of importance are indexed under their own headings, while references are included to general subjects such as Poland, War in ; Finland ; France, etc. Page Numbers in italics indicate illustrations.*

Aaland Islands, Finland and, 266
——Russia and, 233, *234*, 490
Abo, U-boats built at, 628
Achilles, H.M.S., *Graf Spee* action, 505, 526, *529*
——New Zealanders in, 548, 587
Admiral Graf Spee, attack on, 505–06, 526, 540–42
———at Montevideo, 526–30, 541, *575*
———prisoners on board, 541–42
———scuttled, 527, *530*, *575*, *591*
Admiral Scheer, sinks *Clement*, *382*
Admiralty, British Board of, *471*
Aeroplanes, British, bomb U-boat, 222–23
——fighters, *423*
——hunting U-boats, *205*
——taking off from *Courageous*, *115*
——*see also* individual types
—**French,** for liaison work, *166*
——return to aerodrome, *228*
—**German,** minelayers, *435*
——wrecked, *492*
——over Poland, *132*
——silhouettes for recognition, *294–95*
——wrecked at Dalkeith, *289*
———near Warsaw, *53*
———*see also* Heinkel, Messerschmitt
—neutral, to be orange, 376
—**Polish,** crashed, *221*
—from U.S.A., speed up, 474
Africa, North, French troops from, *291*
Aga Khan, loyalty, 84
Agriculture & Fisheries, 364
Ahrens, Capt., of *Bremen*, 254, *255*
Air, Britain's supremacy in, 238
Aircraft, British manufacture, *272–73*
—German, in Poland, 62
—as minelayers, 398
Aircraft-carrier, life in, *620*
Air Defence, of Great Britain, 330–32
Air Defence Cadet Corps, *495*
Air Force, French, bring down 9 'planes, *362*
———progress, 390–91
——**German,** on both fronts, *169*
———efficiency, *632*, *633*
———in Poland, 66
———weaknesses, 94
——of nations, strength compared, *15*
——**New Zealand,** training, 587
——**Royal,** Berlin visit "a dream," 224
———Christmas menu, 499
———Coastal Command, *443*
———The Dawn Patrol, *432–33*
———fighters, *423*
———firing party, *287*
———first decorations for, *333*
———flights over Germany, 138, 187–88, 293
———French graves, *581*
———Heligoland battle, 554–55
———Heligoland raid (Dec., '39), 469
———Sir K. Wood's statement, 502
———lands in France, *235*
———life in, Western Front, *624–25*
———modern equipment, *114*
———New Zealanders in, 587
———N.C.O.s rank badges, *307*
———Operations Room, France, *546*
———as prisoners of war, 62, *159*
———propaganda raids, 138
———raids German fleet, 31
———rank badges, *282*
———reconnaissances, 187–88
————'plane brought down, 286
———rush of recruits, 62
———specialists' badges, *415*
———Supermarine "Spitfires," *65*
———in training, *243*
———and U-boats, 142
———*see* Auxiliary Air Force
——**Russian,** *91*
———women in, *457*
Air Lane, safety, for Allies, 256
Air-liner, Dutch, Germans fire on, 188
Air Raid Precautions : *see* A.R.P.
Air Raids, on civilians, futility, 461
——German, on Britain, 242, 422
———this war and last, *567*
———on British convoys, 269, 283–84
———on British ships, 143, *270*, 286
———first on Great Britain, 252, 296–97, 315–16
———on Poland, girl casualties, *225*
———rooms for viewing, 376
———on Scotland, 284–85
———on Shetlands, *383*
Air Raids and Warnings, facts about, 44
Air Raid Shelter, in kitchen, *535*
———of Soviet Embassy, London, 474
Air Raid Warden, full kit, *215*
Air Raid Warnings, in Britain, the first, *6*
Air Strength, of British Empire, 247
Ajax, H.M.S., and *Graf Spee*, 505, 526, *529*, 540
Alarm Clocks, for convoys, 532, 533
Albania, Italy annexes, 610
—political situation, 494
Albert Canal, fortification, *335*
Aldershot, Gamelin at, *40*
—machine-gun range, *8*
Alexander, A. V., 143
Alexandre Andre (ship) and *San Alberto*, 603
Algérie, French cruiser, *361*
"Alice," motor-lorry, *305*
Allen, Trevor, on the Balloon Barrage, 440
Allies, war position, Dec. 1939, 451
Alvis (trawler), U-boat and, 190
Ambulance, coach as, *10*
Ambulance Train, for rehearsal, *341*
American Farmer, S.S., and *Kafiristan*, *222*
Americans, in French army, 62
Ammunition, lift for, Maginot Line, *77*
—dump, in French farmyard, *388*
—shortage in Finland, 583
Anches, George, in *Simon Bolivar*, 412
Andrews, Boatswain, in *Cresswell*, 446
Angers, Polish Government at, 425
Anglo-French-Turkish Pact, 264–65, 274
ANT 6, Russian aircraft, *459*
Anti-aircraft, Bofors gun for, *330*
———British, *5*
————in London, *73*
————in France, *355*
————officer-observer, *227*
————science and, *364*
——Dutch, *358*
——Finnish, *486*, *577*
——fragment danger, 566
——French gunners, *189*
——German, camouflaged, *78*
Anti-aircraft Battery, British, mail, *109*
———member sleeping, *72*
——French, practising, *76*
——German, on raft, *36*
———gas masks for, *36*
——Polish, *38*, *39*
Anti-aircraft Guns, on British cruisers, *271*
———British, in France, *229*
———for British liners, *172*
———Danish, *491*
———for Dover patrol, *300*
———Finnish, *266*
———French, on dunes, *454*
———naval, preparation, *283*
———shells for, *191*
Anti-Comintern Pact, 29, 213
Anti-tank Barricade, in Maginot Line, *326*
———before Mannerheim Line, *519*
———Polish, *37*
———in Siegfried Line, *43*
Anti-tank Gun, German, in Bydgoszcz, *67*
———in Warsaw, *162*
Aquitania, R.M.S., *172*
Archibald, David, 252
Arensberg, military base, *223*
Argentina, meat from, for Britain, 384
Argyll and Sutherland Highlanders, with primitive gas masks, *276*
Ark Royal, H.M.S., with aircraft, *143*
——alleged sinking, *408*
——captures German prize, 344
——life in, 620, *621*
Arlington Court, S.S., survivors' stories, *445*
Armée de l'Air, L' : *see* Air Force, French
Armistice Day (1939), at Front, 376
———in London, *377*
———Nazi schemes for, 387–88
———the Queen's broadcast, 396, *397*
Armoured Cars, French, by roadside, *304*
——Polish, in Warsaw, *71*
——Russian, in Poland, *123*
———in Ukraine, *135*
Armstrong, cartoon by, *376*
Armstrong-Whitworth "Whitley," adventures, *539*
Army, British, battle dress, *468*
——new system for commissions, 236
——Ordnance Corps : *see* Ordnance
——proficiency badges, *415*, *479*
——rank badges, *282*, *307*
Dutch, mobilization, *334*
—of Finland, *266*
—**French,** Americans in, 62
——concert for, *324*
——entertainment for, *356*
——outpost duty, *228*
——patrols, *489*
——rations, 154
——strength, 62
—**German,** compared with 1914, 320
——facts about, 450
—**Latvian,** *233*
—of nations, strength compared, *14–15*
—of **Poland,** in field, *79*
——Hore-Belisha on, 427
Army Service Corps, Royal, horses for, *607*
Arne Kjode (ship), survivors' stories, 478
Arnoux, Alexandre, 578
A.R.P., A.F.S. and, *311*
—in Berlin, *53*
—British, *215*
——in Hackney, 310
——London rehearsal, *566*
——in L.M.S. sheds, *319*
A.R.P. (*cont.*)
——practice at Bethnal Green, *365*
——surprise practices, *249*
——women and, *44*
—in Helsinki, *464–65*
—in Paris, *90*
—in Stockholm, *268*, *491*
—in Vatican, 62
Artillery, applied science for, 364
—British, training, *218*
—French, 75's, *259*
—Polish horse, *49*
——mechanized, *21*
Artillery, Royal Regiment of, coastal defence battery, *321*
———regimental tie, 538
Asdic, meaning, 538
Ashlea, S.S., and *Graf Spee*, 541
Athenia, S.S., Churchill's alleged responsibility, 346
—German lies about, 406–07
—photographic evidence, *406*, *407*
—sinking of, *12*, 50–51
—survivors from, *50–51*, *279*
Athlone Castle, R.M.S., camouflage, 154
Atlantic Ocean, maps, *345*, *505*
Australia, Air Force of, *57*, *631*
—declaration of war, 84
—Women's Voluntary Service, London, *599*
Austria, Hitler and, 24
—mourning forbidden in, 192
Austrians, Legitimists, as Allies, 474
Auxiliary Air Force, and balloon barrage, *441*, 568
———in Borkum raid, 435
Auxiliary Fire Service, practices, *249*, *365*
———training, *311*
———village practice, *461*
Auxiliary Military Pioneer Corps, *501*
Auxiliary Territorial Service : *see* W.A.T.
Avenol, M., 538
Avro "Anson," bombers, for A.I.F., *57*

B

Bacon, ration schemes, 462
Badges, of proficiency, etc., *415*
—of rank, *282*, *307*
—of skill and qualification, *479*
Bagpipes, in France, *322*, *353*
Bahamas, loyalty, 84
Bahrain, support from, 84
Bail, Malcolm, in *San Alberto*, *603*
Baker, woman does round, *105*
Baker, J. J., *Sheaf Crest* survivor, 478
Balbo, Marshal, Balkan statement, 494
Baldwin, C. E., D.S.M., *558*, *601*
Balkan States, Italy and, *556*
——"peace bloc" in, *494*
Balloon Barrage, in Berlin, *53*
———British, humour in, *89*
————London, balloons of, *5*
————King and Queen visit, *397*
————manufacture, *184–85*, *569*
————men of, 440–41
————new developments, *568*
——French, *199*
Balloons, captive, in air defence, *78*
——German experiments, 192
—for weather conditions, *614*
Baltic States, map, *234*
——concessions to Russia, map, *431*
——Russia and, 223, 233–34, 610, 618
——strategic position, map *171*
Balts, in Gdynia, 392
Bankhead, W., Pro-Ally, 298
Barbados, loyalty, 84
Barbed Wire, against sabotage, *405*
——French patrols in, *489*
——to prevent desertion, 192
——round prison camps, 394, *395*
Barber, British, in France, *229*
Barham, H.M.S., following *Renown*, *7*
Barking Creek, A.F.S. at, *311*
Barnetson, Capt. James, of *Olivegrove*, *75*
Barrett, Flying-Officer John, receives D.F.C., *333*, *601*
Barrie, Claud, and sinking of *Athenia*, 51
Barwell, Wg. Com. P.R., D.S.C., *601*
Basutoland, loyalty, 84
Baths, for Finn soldiers, *617*
Batson, Capt., of *Heronspool*, 318
Batt, Henry Samuel, in *Simon Bolivar*, 413
Battle-cruiser, facts about, 626
Battleships, of British Navy, *107*
———facts about, 626
Bavaria, Anti-Hitler leaflets in, 480
Bechuanaland, loyalty, 84
Beck, Col., letter from Szathmary, 60
——Polish Foreign Minister, *131*
——as refugee, 232
——with Sir H. Kennard, *38*
"Bed and Breakfast," in B.E.F., *110*
Beechnuts, oil from, 310
Belgium, no black-out, 182
—defences, map, *335*
—Luxemburg's agreement with, 262
—neutrality guaranteed, *25*
Belgium (*cont.*)
—prepares to mobilise, 388
—reaffirms neutrality, 291
—stands to arms, *179*
—threatened with invasion, 334–35
—violation, in 1914, 2, 25
Bell, Capt. F. S., of *Exeter*, *529*
Benes, Dr. E., broadcast of Sept. 18, 146
Benn, Capt. W. F., *244*
Bergen, *City of Flint* at, *349*
Berlin, A.R.P. in, *54*
—black-out in, *127*
—Bolshevist slogans in, 160
—children for farm work, 160
—English church in, 154
—exhibition of war loot, 320
—fuel rationing in, 376
—Hitler's peace speech, *246*
—Jew shops wrecked in, *120*
—R.A.F. over, 293
—Reichstag deputies in, *30*
—Winter Relief Fund in, *277*
Bessarabia, Rumania acquires, 136
—Russia's designs on, 494
Besson, Dr. William, in *Simon Bolivar*, 412
Bethnal Green, A.R.P. practice at, *365*
Bialystok, Communist canvassers in, *392*
—for Russia, 165
—street in old town, *101*
Biard, Capt. H. C., in aircraft-carrier, 620
Bickford, Lt.-Com. E. O. B., *523*, *601*
Biddle, Mr., on bombing of open towns, 82
Bikanir, H. H. the Maharaja, 22, 306
Birds, as gas detectors, *548*
Birdwood, Field-Marshal Lord, *216*
Blackberries, British troops picking, *73*
—tea from leaves, 224
Blackburn "Shark," *371*
Blackburn "Skua," dive bomber, *620*
Blackheath, caves as shelters, 310
Blackhill (ship), sunk, *398*
Black-out, Anti-Nazi uses, 217
——in Cologne, 288
——of convoy ships, 532
——dog's coat for, *89*
——in Germany, laws about, 94
——in Great Britain, *127*
——heroes of, *623*
——lesson from 1918, 215
——in London, *152*, *319*
——none in Belgium, 182
——in Paris, modification, 339
——white accessories in, 182
Black-out Man, new industry, *147*
Blackpool, evacuated children at, *11*
Black Sea, Turkey's guard over, 216
Blackstone, Sir William, on Navy, 16
"Black Velvet," King and Queen at, *506*
Blagrove, Rear Adm. H. E. C., death, *251*
Blaney, Maj.-Gen. Sir Thomas, 329
Blaskowitz, Gen., *194*, *230*
Blighty, magazine, re-issue, 182
Blimp, meaning, 538
Bliss, William, poems by, 544, 608
Blockade, British, of Germany, 278–79, 472
——effect, 600
——enforcing, 202–03
——striking balance, 596
—German, of Great Britain, 302
———Schacht and, 256
—technical meaning, 434
Blomberg, Field-Marshal von, 250
Blue Book, as best-seller, 150
——meaning, 434
Boche, meaning, 528
Boeing Bombers, American aircraft, *298*
Bofors, anti-aircraft gun, *330*
Bohemia, Hitler and, 24
Bolsheviks, Hitler on, 212
Bolshevism, Hitler's hatred of, 29
—Italian view, 556
—Mussolini and, 213
Bombers, British, fight German fighters, 636
—German, for examination, *418*
——in Poland, *82*
———children watching, *99*
——starting dive, *283*
—Russian, *91*
——brought down by Finns, *486*
——over Helsinki, *465*
Bombing, German training in, *633*
Bombs, British manufacture, *367*
—carried by Fairey "Swordfish," *269*
—first on Great Britain, 383
—loaded on German 'plane, *52*, *53*
—messages in, Warsaw, 62
See High Explosive ; Incendiary
Booby Trap, German, *489*
Booth, Sgt.-Observer, taken prisoner, 159
Boothby, Claude, in *Arlington Court*, 445
Borkum, British raid on, 435
—map, *435*
Bosnia (ship), torpedoed, *74*, *87*
Bosporus, from Istanbul quays, *264*
Boulton Paul "Defiant," *423*
Bowen, Frank C., on mines, *630*
Boyd, Air Vice-Marshal Owen, *569*
Branchitsch, Gen., reviewing troops, *327*

Bread, Russian, Finns take, 606
Breeches Buoy, use, 509, 597
Bremen, S.S., escape, 254–55
——reported whereabouts, 192
——submarine spares, 522, 523
Bren Gun, camouflage for, 291, 579
——carriers in France, 200, 304
——W.A.T. stripping, 211
Brest-Litovsk, Russia and, 133, 134, 165
Bretagne, S.S., sunk, 245, 253–54
Bretons, as sailors, 359
Bridge, blown up by Poles, 37
—guarded, India, 57
—over Maas, steel gates for, 358
—railway, over Rhine, 226
—sentry on, London, 2
Bristol "Blenheim," British 'plane, 423
——German chases, 286
——raid Borkum, 435
British Empire, gets into its stride, 329
——marshalling air strength, 247
——at outbreak of war, 57, 84
——and R.A.F., 238
British Expeditionary Force, behind lines, 261
———big guns with, 176–77
———cheers Chamberlain, 547
———Christmas with, 499
———earliest photos, 229
———eye-witness accounts, 155–56
———first arrivals in France, 110, 112–13, 118, 144–45
———flowers for, 257
———football for, 168
———French welcome for, 200
———in front line, 514–16
———resting, in France, 201
———through French eyes, 323
———transport, 235–37
————French navy and, 359
————organization, 343
British Honduras, loyalty, 84
Brno, revolt in, 125
Broadcasting, from car, Moscow, 521
—German strictures on, 22
—in Greek, 182
Broadhurst, Sqn. Ldr. H., D.C.F., 601
Brooke, Sir Alan, 369
Brown (cricketer), in Police War Reserve, 147
Brown, Vice-Adm. Sir Harold, 343
Brownrigg, Lt.-Gen. Sir Douglas, 261
Bruce, Fireman William, 372
Brünsbüttel, British raid on, 31
Bryant, W., of Clement, 382
Brzezany, Smigly Rydz born at, 69
Buchenwald, concentration camp at, 312
Buck, Samuel, of Compaganus, 573
Bugler, Polish, 34
Bulgaria, beech-nuts from, 310
—and the Dobruja, 494
Bull, George, Cresswell's skipper, 446
Burgin, Rt. Hon. Leslie, 343
Busby, Capt. John, of Kafiristan, 222
Bus Conductors, women as, 105
Bus Driver, in black-out, 623
Butcher, of Warsaw, anecdote, 253
—women as, 105
Butter, ration schemes, 462
Bydgoszcz, German anti-tank gun in, 67
—market square, 101

C

Cadiz, U-boats built at, 628
Cajander, M., Finnish Prime Minister, 428
Calcraft, E. G., photographer, 252, 253
Calinescu, M. Armand, 136, 494
Camels, ploughing with, Germany, 154
Camera Gun, for Air Arm training, 371
——for French Air Force, 390
Camouflage, for A.A. gun, 73
—for Bren gun, 291, 579
—for British lorry, 237
——'planes, 114, 239
——transport column, 112
—for Dutch gunners, 358
——trench, 358
—for Fairey "Battle," 246
—for Finnish tank, 455
—for French A.A. gun, 454
——big gun, 193
——farmhouse, 368
——75's, 259
—for German A.A. gun, 78
——trenches, 354
—for horses, 607
—in Maginot Line, 326
—natural, 560
—netting for, girls making, 447
—snow as, 521
—in snow, 456
—for Turkish tank, 265
Campinchi, M., 360
Canada (ship), sunk, 398
Canada, declares war, 84
—oil in, 598
—and R.A.F., 329
—soldiers of, 57
Canadians, arrival of first contingent, 522, 548, 549, 571–72
—and Hitler, 154
Cang, J., escape from Poland, 156, 158
Canteen, cooking for, 599
—French, 324
Canterbury Cathedral, A.R.P. in, 153
Cape Town, Ark Royal at, 621
Cardoso, Harold, describes air-fight, 354
Cargo Liner, and U-boats, 174
Carol, King of Rumania, 136
Carrier Pigeons, in Belgian army, 310
——for R.A.F. 443, 444
Carvell, Consul-General, on Dachau, 312
Casey, Mr. R. G., Australian Minister of Supply, 247, 329
——broadcast from London, 338
Cash-and-carry, meaning, 298
Castonier, Elizabeth, 348
Casualties, first British, 514
—German, in Poland, 230, 286
—Russian, in Finland, 583, 614, 616
—in surprise A.R.P. practice, 249, 566
Cavalry, British, in France, 290
—Finnish, 429
—Polish, characteristics, 20, 21
Cellulose, from potato tops, 310
Cemeteries, French, new graves, 581
Cenotaph (London), sandbagged, 153
Censorship, German, 474
Central Control Room, of Fighter Command, 331–32
Ceylon, loyalty, 84
Chamberlain, Rt. Hon. Arthur Neville, on Anglo-French-Turkish Pact, 264
———on British ultimatum, 28
———broadcast (Sept. 3, 1939), 4, 60
————(Nov. 26), 436
————message to Germany, 60
———with Churchill and Wood, 436
———on enemy air-raids, 242
———in France, 547
———with gas mask, 45
———on Germany and Finland, 594
———on Graf Spee action, 506
———head of War Cabinet, 9
———on Hitler's peace proposals, 246
———on invasion of Finland, 498
———and Munich Agreement, 25
———peace-maker, 27
———on Poles' fighting qualities, 33
———on probability of war, 28
———on the Rawalpindi's fight, 439
———on seizure of contraband, 202
———speech in Commons (Sept. 3), 60
————Sept. 13, 124
————Sept. 14, 124
————Sept. 20, 146
———in Commons (Oct. 26), 306
———Nov. 21, 434
———at Mansion House, 634
———states war aims, 404
———on "strangest of wars," 402
———with Supreme War Council, 137
———on war aims and peace aims, 466
Chamberlain, Mrs., with gas mask, 45
Chamier, Air Commodore, J. A., 495
Channel Ferry, For B.E.F., 300
Charles I, statue protected, 319
Chatfield, Rt. Hon. Adm. Lord, on Graf Spee action, 506
———broadcast (Dec. 20), 626
———in Sussex, 137
———in War Cabinet, 9
Chelmno, town hall and square, 101
Chenilette, French light tank, 140, 260
Chestnuts, roast, in France, 388
Chevalier, Maurice, in Ensa concert, 410
Children, as air-raid victims, 225, 231
—coloured gas-masks for, 182
—evacuated, help on land, 104
—evacuation of, 10, 11
—Hitler's war on, 82–83
—Polish, watching German aircraft, 99
—Tommies with, 261
China, air-raid casualties, 461
Chinese, in British Red Cross, 89
Chitral, S.S., and Rawalpindi survivors, 437, 438, 476
Cholerton, Mrs., on Helsinki air-raids, 507
Christea, Miron, Rumanian Patriarch, 136
Christian X, King of Denmark, 268
Christianity, Nazism and, 4, 574
Christmas (1939), for B.E.F., 499
——in Finland, 582, 584, 592–93
Christmas Trees, in Germany, 384
Chrobry (ship), odyssey of, 444
Churchill, Rt. Hon. Winston Spencer, on anti-submarine campaign, 142
———birthday cartoon, 493
———broadcast of Oct. 1, 180
————Nov. 12, 374–75
————Dec. 18, 522–23
———with Chamberlain and Kingsley Wood, 436
———on contraband seizure, 203
———on convoy system, 269
———on first month of war, 173
———in France, 374, 375
———on the French navy, 360
———with Gamelin in Paris, 344
———as German scapegoat, 154
———on Graf Spee, 530
———illustrated biography, 181
———and invention of tanks, 186
———message from Adm. Forbes, 143
———at microphone, 180
———Royal Oak statement, 244
———on Russian policy, 303
———second statement on U-boats, 344–45
———and sinking of Athenia, 50, 406
———survey of war (Dec. 6), 470–71
———threat to, on mine, 398, 403
———villain of piece, 346
———in War Cabinet, 9
Ciano, Count Galeazzo, 556, 594
City of Flint, S.S., and Athenia, 51
———at Halifax, N.S., 279
———odyssey, 348, 349
City of Mandalay, S.S., sunk, 316, 317
Clement, S.S., sunk, 382
Clergyman, as postman, 147
"Clergymen's Bombs," leaflets, 256
Clothing, Army, manufacture, 570
—Germany's rations, 474
Coal Mines, Silesian, Poles flood, 192
Coastal Command (R.A.F.), a day's experience, 443
——Australians with, 631
——convoy duty, 638
——diagram sketch, 533
Coastal Defence, battery for, 321
Coasting Steamer, 174
Codreanu, M. Rumanian Fascist, 136
Coffee, German ration, 126
—for Hitler, as contraband, 182, 203
Colleague (trawler), and Compaganus, 573
Collins, Lt.-Gen. D. S., with Q.M.G., 343
Cologne, black-out in, 288
Colonial Troops, French, 291
Columbus S.S., scuttling of, 564, 572
Commissions, in British Army, 236
Commonwealth Aircraft Corporation, 247
Communication Trench, French, 209
Communism, in Russia, and Fascism, 122
Community Singing, British troops 72
Compaganus (trawler), bombed, 573
Concentration Camps, White Paper on, 312
Conscientious Objector, death for, 154
Conscription, in Great Britain, 8
Conscripts, Nazi, 354
Contraband Control, distinct from blockade, 434
Contraband of War, Allies' control, 202–03
———French captures, 360
———Hitler's coffee as, 182, 203
———list, 202
———two classes, 278
Convoy, arrival, London, 463
—attacked from air, 283–84
—land, Finns capture, 615
—in North Sea, 278
—some secrets, 532–33
Convoy Duty, by British Navy, 269
——an impression, 372–73
——R.A.F. on, 638
Convoy System, against U-boats, 172
——inauguration, 142
——statistics, 373
Cook, James, captain of Athenia, 50
Cook, Mrs. M. E., 151
Cooks, British Army, in French farm, 237
——W.A.T.S. as, 263
—French army, 227
Copenhagen, flags in 268
Corbin, M., in Sussex, 137
Corsets, for warmth, Russian officer, 520
Cost of Living, in Germany, 480
Cotomatis, Capt., of Paralos, 606
Cotton, for Germany, blockade and, 279
Courageous, H.M. Aircraft-Carrier, 117
——at Gibraltar, German officers in, 117
——list of survivors from, 117
——sinking of, 115–16
Cow, in burning Polish village, 59
—for draught work, Germany, 352
Cowen, William, and Simon Bolivar, 412
Cowles, Virginia, 30
Cox, Geoffrey, on landing of B.E.F., 118
—on Russians in Finland, 604
Crabbe, Lt., broadcast, 159
Cracow, becomes German, 165
—bugle call in, 34
—Poles abandon, 37
—professors arrested, 590
—Smigly Rydz at, 69
Craigie Lea (boat), Germans bomb, 573
Crash Helmet, for tank driver, 260
Crerar, Hon. T. A., 329, 338
Cresswell (ship), survivors' stories, 445–46
Croix de Guerre, for French airmen, 362
Cross, Mr. R. H., 278
Crowder, Miss, Yorkshire survivor, 318
Cruiser, British, of Ajax class, 513
"Cruiser," tank, 595
Cumberland, H.M.S., 526, 575
Curtiss Fighters, for French air force, 362
Curzon Line, in Poland, map, 103, 165
Cutajar, Antonio, 347
Cuxhaven, British raids on (1914), 31
Czech Legion, formation, 62
——recruits for, Paris, 90, 125
Czecho-Slovakia, under German rule, 393
—Germany annexes, 610
—Hitler and, 24
—Nazi garrison in, 224
—reign of terror in, 590
—revolt in, 125
Czeremcha, station bombed, 156
Czestochowa, Germans take, 37
—monastery church in, 101
Czuma, Gen., 131

D

Dachau, concentration camp at, 312
Daehne, Capt. Wilhelm, 572
Dagenham, Golden Eagle at, 10
Dagö, as possible naval base, 170, 171
Daitz, Werner, 302
Daladier, M. Edouard, bestows Croix de Guerre, 362
——biography, 137
——broadcasts, 60, 210
——dug-out named after, 326
——guest of King, 483, 484
——with Hore-Belisha, 280
——letter to Hitler, 28
——in Sussex, 137
Dalkeith, German 'plane wrecked at, 289, 296, 315
Daniel, Capt. Henry, and Graf Spee, 591
Danzig, Free City, pictures and history, 18
—Post Office garrison surrenders, 59
—the Senate, 18
Danzig (cont.)
—signboards near, 35
Dardanelles Conference, Turkey and, 216
Darlan, Adm., Churchill with, 374
——and French naval efficiency, 360
——with Gamelin and Churchill, 344
Day, Frances, with troops, 72
Day Spring (fishing boat), rescues German airmen, 252
Dead, Russian, in Finland, 605
Dean, Basil, and the N.A.A.F.I., 500
Death, in action, Germany and, 160
Decontamination Squad, in Berlin, 53
———a member, London, 6
———station, 215
Delmer, Sefton, on Warsaw raids, 52
Denmark, compulsory service in, 268
—German patrol ships off, 302
—war fears, 490
Depth Charge, from destroyer, 299
——effect, 173
——mechanism, 207
——for U-boats, 47, 205, 627, 628
Deserters, from Germany, 62, 256
Desertion, Nazi fear of, 192
Destroyers, British, aid for Simon Bolivar, 411
——on Dover Patrol, 299–301
——hoisting depth charges, 207
——on night watch, 204–05
——patrolling North Sea, 175
——sunk, 381
——and U-boats, 106, 627
—Polish, with British Navy, 425, 476, 477
Deutschland (ship) at Brunsbüttel, 31
—and City of Flint, 348
—constructional diagram, 437
—German pocket battleship, 279
—officers entertained by Courageous, 117
—prisoners in, 381–82
—sinks Rawalpindi, 437–39
Devonport, Hore-Belisha member for, 281
Diamantis, U-boat and, 220
Diary of War, 32, 64, 96, 126, 160, 192, 224, 256, 288, 320, 352, 384, 416, 448, 480, 512, 544, 576, 608, 640
Dickson, John, Jr., on first raid over Britain, 252
Dictionary of War, 32, 64
Dietrich, Capt., and Graf Spee, 526
Dietrich, Marlene, efforts for parents, 126
Dill, Sir John, with D. of Gloucester, 369
——with Gamelin, 369
Distinguished Flying Cross, first recipients, 333
Distinguished Flying Medal, first recipient, 333
Djugashvili, Josef Vissarionovich: see Stalin
Dobruja, debatable land, 494
Dogs, black-out costume, 89, 127
—for food, Warsaw, 384
—shelter for, 310
—for war service, France, 224
———Russia, 376
Dominions, British, air pilots from, 167
——representatives in England, 329
Doran, Acting Flt.-Lieut., K.C., receives D.F.C., 333, 601
Doric Star, S.S., and Graf Spee, 540, 541
Dormitory, for evacuated business staff, 147
Dornier DO.17, German warplane, 23, 294
——shot down on Western Front, 537
——18 K. German bomber, 295
——24. caught by searchlight, 502
———German bomber, 293
——215, German bomber, 294
Dornier Flying-boat, crashed, 286
———crew rescued, 270
———brought down by N.Z. airman, 357
Dove, Capt., on Graf Spee battle, 506, 541, 542
Dover, German air view, 525
Dover Patrol, at work, 299–301
Dowding, Air Chief Marshal Sir Hugh, and British air defence, 231–32
———with Dominions representatives, 329
Downs, The, contraband base, 202
Downs, Kenneth, with French troops, 188
Drake, E. Millington, 526, 527
Draughtsmen, German shortage, 320
Drewett, W. H., in A.M.P.C., 501
Driver, British, maps for, 257
Drunkards, habitual, in Germany, 474
Drury Lane, Ensa at, 500
Duca, Ion, assassination, 136
Dudgeon, William, on air-raid, 316
Dug-out, modern, artillery officers in, 561
——named after Daladier, 326
——in Siegfried Line, 78

E

Ebes, Dr., Simon Bolivar's surgeon, 412
Eden, Rt. Hon. Anthony, broadcast speech, Sept. 11, 124
————Oct. 25, 306
——meets Canadians, 571
——portrait, 329
Edinburgh, H.M.S., firing at aeroplane, 297
——Nazi lies about, 408
Edinburgh, air-raid over, 242
Education, in Germany, 310
Edwards, Pilot Officer, taken prisoner, 159
"Eggfried Line," in London, 89
Eidanger (ship), and Bosnia, 87
Eileen Wray (trawler), 573

Eire, shipwrecked crew landed in, 220
Eisenbach (ship), as raider, 94
Electric Motor, for cars, *447*
Elephants, for ploughing, Germany, *277*
Eliot, Mrs. Walter, *151*
Elizabeth, H.M. Queen, broadcast, 396, *397*
— —head of women's services, *151*
— —on stage of Drury Lane, *500*
— —war work, *396, 397*
Embargo, U.S.A. lifts, 298
— — —first goods after, 376
Emerson, Bugler R. D., 116
Emile Miguet (ship) sunk, *318*
Ensa, first concert in France, *410*
—King and Queen with, *500*
—work, *275*
Entente Cordiale, in Maginot Line, 322–24
Entertainments National Service Association : *see* Ensa
Epp, Gen. von, 350
Erkko, M, Finnish Foreign Minister, *268*
Eros (statue) evacuated, *319*
Essegny, Charmes Military Cemetery, *581*
Essen, Rudy von, *Tajadoen* survivor, *509*
Essener National Zeitung, 291
Essex Scottish Highlanders, *247*
Estonia, pact with Soviet, 233
—Russia and, 170, *171, 618*
Ethanol, new gas, 534
Eton, playing fields for food growing, 474
Etruria (trawler), bomb damage, *559*
Europe, Central, map showing R.A.F. flights, *293*
—changes of 1939, *610*
—mastery of, Germany's aim, 404
—weather map, *451*
Evacuation, of Americans, 192
—of animals, 62
—of children, *10, 11*
— —and land work, *104*
—in Finland, *267*
—of German towns, *198*
—from Paris, 339
—Queen and, *397*
—of Strasbourg, *308–09*
Evans, Adm. Sir Edward, *249*
"Even Hitler had a Mother," 182
Everett, Cmdr. D. H., promotion, *601*
Exeter, H.M.S., and *Graf Spee*, *505*, 506, 526, *529*, 542, 575
Exports, German, Britain seizes, 472
Eye-Witness, on air-fight, 219

F

Fairey "Battle" Bombers, camouflaged, *246*
— — —a flight, *187*
— — —for reconnaissance, *238*
— — —in snow, Western Front, *624–25*
Fairey "Swordfish," on convoy duty, *269*
Fanad Head, and bombed U-boat, *635, 637*
F.A.N.Y., *44, 599*
Farm, French, ammunition dump in, *388*
— —camouflaged, *368*
— —Field Kitchens in, *237*
— —ruined, infantry in, *449*
Farm Work, for school children, 160
Fascism, anti-Communist and anti-Democratic, 416
—and Soviet Communism, 122
Fat, substitutes for, Germany, 154
Faussett, William, in the *Cresswell*, 446
Ferguson, Major, in *Terukini Maru*, 414
Fianona (ship), mined, *403*
Field Artillery, German, in Warsaw, *195*
Field Kitchen, *237, 263*
Fields, Gracie, in Ensa concert, *410*
Fifth Column, meaning, 538
Fighter Command, organization, 331
Fiji, loyalty, 84
Finland, air-service from Scotland, 376
—anti-aircraft efficiency, *557*
—Brain over Brawn in, 582–85
—climate aids resistance, 550–53
—Cox on war in, 604
—Germany the betrayer, 458
—government statement, 538
—Italian sympathies with, *557*
—map, *430*
—not Stalin's birthday present, 519–21
—reply to Russia (Nov. 28), 498
—resistance, 431, 455–57, 486–88
—Russia not "at war" with, 480
— —demands on, 233
— —invasion of, 428–30
—Russian casualties, *614*
—southern half, map, *487*
—Soviet dealings with, 223, 610
—stand against Soviet, 328
—struggle for independence, 266–67
—"Suicide Squad," 586
—war maps, *520, 583*
—women's services, *619*
Finns, ignore cold, *617*
Fire Brigade, of Polish village, *130*
See Auxiliary Fire Service
Fire Pumps, for Paris A.R.P., *90*
Fireworks, British storage, 182
First Aid Nursing Yeomanry : *see* F.A.N.Y.
First-aid Station, London baths as, *8*
Fish, temporary supply centre, *104*
Fishermen, and German airmen, *242*, 252
Fishing, development, Germany, 384
—in the Rhine, 192
Fishing Fleet, Nazi attacks on, *522, 559*, 573
Fishmonger, humorous, Bicester, *447*
Five Years' Plans, Stalin and, 460
Fleet Air Arm, constitution, *371*
— — —*Kestrel*, training station, *346*
— — —life in, *620, 621*
— — —and U-boats, 142
Fleming, Harry, of *Rawalpindi*, 476
Flight-Sergeant, British, with gunner, *293*
Floods, in Low Countries, 179, *335*
Flowers, for B.E.F., *257*
Flying-boat, British, diagram sketch, *533*
Flying Pencil Bomber : *see* Dornier DO 17
Fog-buoys, for convoy ships, 532, *533*
Food, arrival, Britain, *462, 463*
—for British troops, *263*
—conditional contraband, *278*
—for German prisoners, 394, *395*
Food Control, in Great Britain, 462
Food Supply, of Great Britain, *104*
Football, for Allied troops, *292*
—for British troops, *73*
—for German prisoners, *394*
—on Western Front, *168*
Forbes, Adm. Sir Charles, *143*, 522
Forbes, Miss J. Trefusis, *151*
Formose (ship), and the *Graf Spee*, 505
Forrest, William, arrested as spy, 189–90
Forster, Herr, on Poland, 392
Forth, Firth of, map, *242*
— —German raids on, *297*, 422
Forth Bridge, Balloon Barrage for, 568
— —Nazi lies about, 408, *409*
Fortunes, of Nazi leaders, 288
Foulkes, Maj.-Gen. C. H., on Gas attacks, 534
— —on high-explosive bombs, 566–67
— —on possible air-raids, 461
Four-Power Conference, at Stockholm, *268*
Four-wheeler, returns to London, *447*
France, Air Force, *390–91*
—B.E.F. arrives in, 112–13
— —reception in, *257*
—British food in, 154
—fighting services, *13*
—German appeals to, 310
—Hitler on, 212
—mobilization, Pattinson Knight on, 88
—Navy, 359–61
—Poles recruiting in, 182
—Polish army in, *425*
—tanks, *186*
—typical poilu, *3*
—under war conditions, *90*
—war strength, *14*
Franco, General, 29, 213
Francs-tireurs, in Poland, 67
Frank, Dr. Hans, *504*
Frank, Karl Hermann, and the Czechs, 393
Frankau, Gilbert, The Crooked Cross, 224
Frederick Charles, of Hesse, 458
Freyberg, Maj.-Gen. B. C., V.C., 587
Fricordin, meaning, 538
Friedlander, Mona, *599*
Front Line, what it is really like, 578–80
Fuel, rationing, 376
Funeral, of British airmen, in Germany, *159*.
— —seamen, Rosyth, *287*
—of French airmen, in Germany, *159*
—of *Graf Spee* sailors, *527*
—of Nazi airmen, in England, *287*
Fyfe, Hamilton, on cold in Finland, 614

G

Gainard, Capt. Joseph H., 348
Galway, *Athenia* survivors at, *12*
Galway, Lord, on *Achilles*' exploit, 548
Gambia, A.R.P. in, 567
Gamelin, Gen. Marie Gustav, biography, *40*
— —blockades Germany, 108
— —at British G.H.Q., *369*
— —with Churchill and Darlan, *344*
— —first blows in West, 76–78
— —at French G.H.Q., *199*
— —with Gort, *258, 322*
— —in Sussex, *137*
Gas, for motor-cars, *319*
—rationed in Italy, 154
—poison, German lies about, *276*, 310
— —German use, *276*
— —Russian use, 487
Gas Attacks, commonsense view, 534
Gas Chamber, popularity, 182
Gas-detectors, in London, *215*
Gas-masks, for air defence units, *331*
— —for bathers, London, *45*
— —British, in Maginot Line, *385*
— —for British gun-crew, *560–61*
— —Buna useless for, 384
— —coloured, for children, 182
— —compulsory in Reading Room, 182
— —drill with, London, *535*
— —early type, *276*
— —Eros holds, *319*
— —for German anti-aircraft, *36*
— —German civilian, *30*
— — —rifleman, *23*
— —for hop-pickers, *8*
— —for horses, 224
— —the King carries, *396*
— —of land workers, *104*
— —like Mickey Mouse, 310
— —for London police, *6*
— —for naval gunners, *283*
— —New Zealand inspection, *587*
— —of Parisian girls, *90, 339*
— —Polish, abandoned, *241*
— — —practice with, *79*
— —for Red Cross nurses, *235*
— —in Stockholm, *491*
— —use of container, 154
Gates, water-tight, for Tube tunnels, *215*
Gawsworth, John, Afterwards, 480
Gazetteer of War, 96, 146, 178, 274, 338, 466
Gdynia, becomes German, *165*
—bombarded, 36
—devastation, 392
—German troops in, *100*
—hostages shot at, 590
—in peacetime, *100*
—surrender, *100*
Geer, Jonkheer de, 358, 402
Geheime Staatspolizei : *see* Gestapo
General Headquarters, Gort's rooms, *481, 482*
Geneva, information bureau in, 62
George V, H.M. King, cards for troops (1914), *499*
George VI, H.M. King, with B.E.F., 483–84, *510*
— —on board *Royal Oak*, *251*
— —broadcast, at outbreak of war, 4
— —Christmas broadcast (1939), 549
— —decorates Navy, *558*
— — —R.A.F. heroes, *333*
— —message to Merchant Navy, 174
— —reply to peace appeal, 402
— —on stage of Drury Lane, *500*
— —visits Gort, *482*
— —war work, *396, 397*
— —welcomed by French maire, 510
Germain, José, in the *Bretagne*, 253
German Embassy, in London, prospective return, 182
German Freedom Party, activities, 217
German Freedom Station, and Munich bomb, 351
Germans, in history, 553
Germany, air losses concealed, 256
—Anti-Nazi movement in, 217
—armed forces, *23*
—balloon barrage in, 568
—betrayer of Finland, 458
—cartoons from, *248*
—consumption of alcohol in, 310
—disillusionment in, 352
—effect of British blockade, 278–79
—on eve of war, 30
—France invades, *41, 259*
—Greater, in 1939, map, *536*
—and mastery of Europe, 404
—in 1918 and 1939, maps, *612*
—pact with Russia : *see* Soviet-German Pact.
—and Partition of Poland, *165*
—people's view of war, 405
—R.A.F. flights over, *293*
—rationing in, 62
—and Russia, declaration, 178
—Russia as jackal to, 122
—in Russian cartoons, *248*
—Russian grain for, 310
—Russia's aid for, 303
—and Straits Convention, 216
—tanks, *186*
—towns evacuated, *198*
—trade routes, map, *472*
—typical soldier, *3*
—war strength, *15*
Gestapo, in conquered Poland, 392
— —Warsaw, 230, 424
—Himmler the head, *121*
—members in U-boats, 173
—and Munich bomb, *379*
Ghetto, of Warsaw, *19*
Gibraltar, a contraband base, 202
—*Courageous* at, *117*
Gifford, Sqn.Ldr. P., D.F.C., *601*
Gilmour, Sir John, convoy statistics, 373
Gipsy, H.M.S., mined, *401, 403*
Glenny, Lieut. J. E. M., receives D.S.C., *558, 601*
Gloster "Gladiator," British 'plane, *423*
Gloucester, H.R.H. Henry, Duke of, at Ensa concert, *410*
— — —in France, *261*
— — —with Gort and Dill, *369*
Gneisenau (ship), submarine sights, 522
Goebbels, Dr. Paul Josef, breaches of discipline, 416
— —gives "naked truth," 346
— —Grambert's caricature, *148*
— —radio sets for troops, 352
— —reasons for disgrace, 192
— —speech (Dec. 22), 626
— —war-maker, *26*
Goeben (ship), now the *Yavuz*, *265*
Goering, Field-Marshal Hermann, broadcast speech (Sept. 9), 62
— —and Czecho-Slovakia, 24
— —first war speech, 94, 95
— —and German Air Force, *169*
— —head of Air Force, 632
— —with Henderson and Ribbentrop, *150*
— —in Munich putsch, 350
— —private fortune, 148
— —war-maker, *26*
— —Soviet guest of honour, 376
— —in Who's Who, 154
Goga, M., Rumanian premier, 136
Gold, for Germany, from Russia, 279
—Poland's reserve, 310
— — —Rumania holds, 192
Golden Eagle (steamer), for evacuation, *10*
Goltz, Gen. Von der, in Finland, 266, *458*
Goods Wagons, to carry troops, *258*
Goodwood (ship), chief officer from 74
Goose-step, in Nazi army, *23*
Gordon Lennox, Victor, 404
Gori, Stalin's birthplace, *460*
Gort, John Standish Surtees Prendergast Vereker, Viscount, activities, *368–69*
— — biography, *111*
— —at British G.H.Q., *369*
Gort, Viscount (*cont.*)
— —Christmas message, *578*
— —Churchill with, at G.H.Q., *375*
— —at desk, *482*
— —door of room, G.H.Q., *481*
— —Duke of Gloucester with, *261, 369*
— —at Ensa concert, *410*
— —with Gamelin, *40, 258, 322*
— —Hore-Belisha's appointment, 281
— —Hore-Belisha with, *427*
— —the King visits, *482, 484, 510*
— —with Tommy, *46*
— —on tour of inspection, *292*
Goschen, Sir Edward, 25
Gospell, Ordinary Seaman, *381*
Gotenhafen, Nazi Gdynia, 392
"Gott Strafe England," 192
Graf Spee : *see* Admiral Graf Spee
Gramophone, for propaganda, 126, 217
Graveley, F/O. R.C., E.G.M., *601*
Grazia (ship), sunk, 400
Great Britain, air defence, 330–32
— —air-raids, last war and this, *567*
— —air supremacy, 238
— —cheered by Poles, *38*
— —"desperate" condition, 320, 474
— —as field of war, 416
— —first air raids on, 252, 296–97, 315–16, 383
— —food supply, 462
— —German raids on, Oct.–Nov., 422
— —German virulence against, 160, 291
— —Germany's blockade of, 302
— —minefields, East Coast, *630*
— —National Registration in, *141*
— —typical soldier, *3*
— —War Cabinet, *9*
— —war strength, *14*
— —young troops in, *72, 73*
Great War, air raids in, statistics, 461
— —causes, 2
— —Germany's defeat, *612*
— —and Poland, *103*
— —violation of Belgium, 25
Greenwood, Rt. Hon. A., message to Labour Party, 124
— —on outbreak of war, *28*
— —speech in Commons (Sept. 3), 60,
Greiser, Herr, in Danzig Senate, *18*
Greiser, Arthur, *536*
Grenadier Guards, in Paris, *389*
Griffiths, Lt. G. B. K., 603
Grimes, cartoon by, *56*
Gripenberg, G. A., 594
— —broadcast, 626
Grizodubova, Valentina, *457*
Grodno, the castle, *101*
—Russians take, 132
Grossman, Dr., in Danzig Senate, *18*
Groupes Francs, in training, *516*
Grudziadz, church at, *101*
—Germans take, 37
Grudzinski, Lt.-Comr. John, commander of *Orzel*, 511
Guards Regiments, British, in Paris, *389*
Gunners, French, *41*
—Polish, *98*
Gunnery, instruction in, for militia, *8*
Guns, Belgian, on frontier, *335*
—British anti-aircraft, *5*
— —camouflaged, *73*
— —anti-tank, in action,
— —for armed liner, *347*
— —coastal defence, *321, 342, 336–37*
— —18-pdr., under willow, *560*
— —about to fire, *560–61*
— —heavy, in France, *355*
— —howitzer, *609*
— —manufacture, *273–74*
— —naval, practising, *97*
— — —testing, *366*
— —quick-firing two-pounder, *330*
— —with rubber tires, *176–77*
—camouflage for, *326*
— —in Luxemburg, *262*
—Finn, camouflaged, *521, 552*
—French A.A., camouflaged, *454*
— —drawn by tractor, *166*
— —light, *140*
— —man-o'-war, 359
— —near Strasbourg, *193*
— —75 mm., *138*
— —105 mm., *514*
—German field, in pill-box, *140*
— —howitzer battery, *23*
— —naval, on railway, *450*
— —in Warsaw, *195*
Gustav V, King of Sweden, *268*, 306
Gwynne-Vaughan, Dame Helen, *151*, 211

H

Haakon VII, King of Norway, *268*
Hacha, Dr. Emil, *393*
Hague Convention, and mines 398, 630
Haifa, a contraband base, 202
Hair-cut, for British soldier, France, *229*
Hale, Binnie, Queen with, *500*
Halifax, Rt. Hon. Viscount, on bombing of open towns, 82
— —broadcast (Nov. 7), 370
— —speech of Dec. 5, 528
— — —in Lords (Dec. 13), 562
— —with Supreme War Council, *137*
— —in War Cabinet, *9*
Halman, K. E., in *Fanad Head*, 635
Hamburg, U-boats in harbour, *245*
—war memorial, 474
Hangoe (or Hanko), burned (1918), 458
—Finnish port, *328*
—Russians repulsed at, 431
Hankey, Maurice, Baron, *9*

Harminc, M. Milan, 178
Harris, Capt. F. C. P., Master of the *Clement*, *382*
Harris, Petty Officer Percy, of *Rawalpindi*, *439*, *475*
Harrison, Paymaster-Lieut. *Royal Oak* survivor, 251
Hartley, Capt., of *Eileen Wray*, 573
Harwood, Commodore, Sir H. H. and the *Graf Spee*, 505, *506*, *527*
— —receives K.C.B., *601*
Haugesund, *City of Flint* at, 348, *349*
Hawker "Demon," gunner in, *5*
Hawker "Hurricane," British 'plane, *114*, *423*
— —in Dawn Patrol, *432–34*
Hay-boxes, for Balloon Barrage men, 440
Heil Hitler ! salute outmoded, 94
Heimwehr, of Danzig, *18*
Heinkel Bomber, brought down at Dalkeith, *289*, *296*
— —in flight, *169*
— —mine-layer, wrecked, *492*
— —varying types, 294–95
— —wreck, in Denmark, *270*
Heinkel H E *111* **K,** German bomber, *294*
Heinkel H E *111* **S,** German bomber, *294*
Heinkel H E *115*, German bomber, *295*
Hel, capitulation, 164
Helferrich, Emil, on German trade, 472
Heligoland, air battle over (Dec. 18), 554–55
—air view, *469*
—diagrammatic map, *503*
—R.A.F. raid (Dec. '39), 469
— — —type of 'plane used, *503*
Helsinki, airport, *430*
—air-raids on, 431, *464–65*, *487*, *488*, *496–97*, 582, *584*, *585*, *592–93*
— — —eye-witness accounts, 507–08
—devastation in, *417*, *464–65*
—evacuation of, *267*
—high-explosive bomb effect, *566*
—modern city, *430*
—South Harbour, *267*
—women observers in, *619*
—wrecked church in, *487*
Henderson, Sir Nevile, "Final Report," 250
— —with Goering and Ribbentrop, *150*
— —on Nazism, 402
— —pre-war diplomatic work, *150*
Henschel Dive-bomber, dropping bombs, *169*
Henson, Leslie, and Ensa, 500
Heronspool (ship), sunk, 318
Hertzog, Gen. J. B. M., 84
Hess, Rudolf, with Hitler at Munich, *350*
— —private fortune, 148
— —war-maker, *26*
Hesselberg, Nazi sacred mountain, 574
Heybeliada Island, Turkish Naval College on, *264*
High-explosive bombs, danger, 566–67
Highlanders, buying cooking utensils, in France, *236*
—Gort with, *368*
Himmler, Heinrich, biography and character sketch, *121*
— —caricature of, *217*
— —and habitual drunkards, 474
— —and Münich bomb, 351
— —private fortune, 148
— —war-maker, *26*
History, for Czechs, limitation, 160
Hitler, Adolf, attempted assassination, 351, *379*
— —and blockade of Britain, 302
— —and bombing of open towns, 82–83
— —character, Henderson's reading, 250
— —coffee for, as contraband, 182, *203*
— —dream of domination, 61
— —entry into Warsaw, 194, *197*
— —German deification, 574
— —Germans' view of, 405
— —letter to Daladier, 28
— —on Eastern Front, *58*
— —flying over Poland, *132*
— —fourth bodyguard battalion, 182
— —and Germans in Latvia, 233
— —and the *Graf Spee*, 530
— —and Henderson, 150
— —Himmler with, *121*
— —and the Jews, *120*
— —leaving Landsberg (1924), *350*
— —losing weight, 416
— —"may he starve," 192
— —on misery, 277, 288
— —at Münich beer house (1938), *350*
— —and Netherlands neutrality, 179
— —opposition to, in Germany, 217
— —peace proposals (Oct. 1939), *246*
— —portrait for Isolationists, 256
— —probable view of war, 451
— —protective squadron, 126
— —refortifies Heligoland, 469
— —revolver practice, 384
— —rhetorical pose, *212*
— —routed at Munich (1923), 348
— —his "secret weapon" revealed, 398–99, *403*
— —on the Siegfried Line, 43
— —6 year campaign of lies, 24
— —speaking in Kroll Opera House, *24*
— —speech in Beer Cellar, Munich (Nov. 8), 370
— —speech broadcast, *277*
— — —at Danzig, Sept. 19, 146
— — —learned by school children, 160
— — —to Reichstag (Sept. 1), 60, 62
— — — —(Oct. 6), 210
— —Stalin "afraid of," 288
— —strategy lessons, 480
Hitler (*cont.*)
— —war-maker, *26*
— —welcomes Mussolini, *213*
— —in "Who's Who," 154
— —words he has eaten, 212
Hitler Calendar of Aggression, in Yugoslavia, 310
Hitler Youth, musketry practice for, 310
Hoarding, in Germany, campaign against, 154, 320
Hoare, Rt. Hon. Sir Samuel, on civilian effort, 147
— — —speech to Chelsea Conservatives, 466
— — —in War Cabinet, *9*
Holland, defences, map, *335*
—fortifies frontier, 256
—prepares for invasion, 291, *292*
—stands to arms, *179*
—threatened with invasion, 334–35, *358*
—U-boats built in, 628
Hollweg, Herr von Bethmann, 25
Holmsen, Isak, account of raid on Fleet, 286
Holsti, Rudolf, correspondence with M. Avenol, 538
Home Front, balloon manufacture, *569*
— —camouflage netting manufacture, *447*
— —food cultivation, *104*, *319*
— —horse transport returns, *183*
— —humour on, *89*, *447*
— —King and Queen inspect, *397*
— —National Registration, *141*
— —Observer Corps, *363*
— —ship building, *588–89*
— —tin hat manufacture, *563*
— —uniform manufacture, *570*
— —women's service, *104*, *105*, *151*, *211*, *599*
See also A.R.P., Auxiliary Fire Service ; Black-out ; Evacuation ; Munitions ; Rationing
Honours, of 1939, *601*
Hop-pickers, gas-masks for, *8*
Hore-Belisha, Rt. Hon. Leslie, 281
— — — —in France, *280*, *427*
— — — —Gort his Military Secretary, 111
— — — —resignation, *640*
— — — —speech in House (Nov. 22), 427
— — — —Trafalgar Day broadcast, 280
— — — —on transport of B.E.F., 235–37
— — — —in War Cabinet, *9*
Horizon Blue, compared with khaki, *229*
Horse Artillery, Polish, *49*
Horse-box, as bedroom, 182
Horses, dead, Finland, *582*
—gas masks for, 224
—return to service, *183*
—for transport, Western Front, *607*
Hospitals, British, mail for, *442*
— —evacuation of, *10*
—Finnish, bombed, *584*
— —military, first patients, *340*
— —underground, *249*
Hospital Ship, equipment, *341*
— —German, 474
Hospital Station, Polish, from air, *132*
Hospital Trains, equipment, *341*
— —Finnish, *619*
— —German, Hitler in, *58*
— —Germans bomb, 82
Hostages, shot, 590
Howitzers, British, for embarkation, *258*
— —9·2, *218*
— —in England, *609*
—French, loading, *199*
—German battery, *23*
— —behind Siegfried Line, *208*
Hoyle, A.B., destroyer survivor, 381
Huard, Mddle., *90*
Hughes, Naval Writer Tom, 116
Hull, Mr. Cordell, in consultation, *149*
Hungary, Ragged Guard in, 288
—and Rumania, 494
—war strength, *14*
Huntley, Mrs., in *Terukini Maru*, 414
Hurst, Capt., of *Arlington Court* 445
Hyderabad, Nizam of, 22, 376
Hydrogen, for Balloon Barrage, *440*, *441*
Hydrophone, British, perfection, 628

I

Ida Bukke (ship), U-boat and, *245*
Identity Card, British, *141*
Iko-Turso, Finnish submarine, *628*
Illingworth, cartoons by, *494*, *564*
"Imaginot Line," in London, *89*
Incendiarism, in Germany, 320
Incendiary Bomb, A.F.S. deals with, *311*
— —danger, 566–67
— —effect, Finland, *496–97*, *507*, *584*, *592–93*, *604*
— —in Poland, *253*
Income Tax, German, as gratitude, 320
Independence Hall, S.S., and *Yorkshire*, *316*, *317*
Independent Labour Party, messages from German Socialists, 92, 124
Independent Socialists of Germany, messages to I.L.P., 92, 124
India, bridge sentry in, *57*
—message to Poland, 84
Industrial Research, Government branch, 364
Infantry, British, equipment, *112–13*
—French, on the march, *354*
— —in ruined farmhouse, *449*
—German, in Saar village, *450*
—Polish, training in France, *425*
Informing, rewards for, Germany, 62
Injustice, Germany's fight against, 256
Invention, British, for war purposes, 364
Inverliffey (ship), sinking of, 86
Iran, oil in, 598
Iron Cross, for German war-correspondents, 376
Iron Duke, H.M.S., damaged, 242, 422
Iron Guard, numbers recant, 416
— —Rumanian Fascists, 136
Iron Ore, Swedish product, *490*
Ironside, Gen. Sir Edmund, with air and sea chiefs, *46*
— — —at Cenotaph, *377*
— — —with Lord Gort, *111*
Irvine, John K., 350
Isabella Greig (trawler), 573
Isolationists, Hitler's portrait for, 256
Istanbul, quays at, *264*
Italy, gas rationed in, 154
—German propaganda in, 63
—neutrality, 213, 556–57
—and Straits Convention, 216
—war strength, *15*
Izvestia, on Finn methods of fighting, 455

J

Jam, prevention of hoarding, Germany, 320
Japan, on German breach of faith, 22
—and Münich bomb, 474
Jaslo, gas notice at, *276*
Jean Jabot (ship), *285*
Jennings, Cmdr. R. B., promotion, *601*
Jews, Austrian, last for rations, 352
—bed-linen confiscated from, 288
—compulsory labour service for, 192
—in concentration camps, *312*
—France and, Hitler on, 212
—in German Poland, 224
—in Germany, changed opinion on, 62
—Hitler and, 120
—levy on fortunes, 352
—and national service, Palestine, 182
—Pogrom against, 380
—Polish, Nazi treatment, 392
— —trade restrictions, 352
—radios confiscated, 182
—reserve for, Poland, 416
—in Russia, Hitler on, 212
—Slovakian shops for soldiers, 160
Joffre, Marshal Césare, and Gamelin, 40
Jolly, Commander R. F., death, *242*
— —posthumous E.G.M., *601*
Junkers JU., German bombers, *295*

K

Kafiristan (ship), torpedoed, 222
Kallio, M. Kyösti, with aide-de-camp, *328*
— —broadcast, 306
— —goes to Stockholm, 267
— —with Scandinavian kings, *268*
— —in trenches, *551*
Kandalaksha, railway at, *614*
Karelian Isthmus, Mannerheim Line on, 428
— —Russian attempts in, 550–52
— —casualties in, 614
Karlsruhe, evacuated, *198*
Katowice, becomes German, 165
Kaunas, capital of Lithuania, *223*
Kawasima, engineer, *Terukini Maru*, 414
Keen, Lieut. Bernard B., R.M., *244*
Kelly, Sir Howard, on R. Plate battle, 526
Kemal, Mustapha, 216, 265
Kennard, Sir Howard, with Col. Beck, *38*
Kennedy, Capt. E. C., 437–39
Kensington Court, S.S., 156, *157*
— —rescuers' awards, *601*
Kensington Gardens, sand from, 62
Kent, H.R.H. George, D. of, *425*
Kestrel, H.M.S., recruits training at, *371*
— —"sunk" by Nazis, *346*, 376
Khaki, compared with horizon blue, *229*
Khimi Reservoir, Russian sailors in, *459*
Kiel, revolt precautions in, 474
Kiel Canal, air view, *85*
— —British raid on, 31
— — —eye-witness stories, 85–86
— —map of area, *31*
Kiel Harbour, Grand Admiral Raeder in, *173*
— —U-boat submerging in, *118*
Kiev, Poland takes (1920), 103
King, Right Hon. W. S. Mackenzie, 84
Kingston-on-Thames, gas chamber 182,
— —woman in butcher's shop, *105*
Kingswood, scrap metal from, *535*
Kinloss, aerodrome, Nazi photo, *525*
Kirkwall, contraband base, 202
Kirov, Russian cruiser, *459*
Kirunavara Mines, Sweden, *490*
Kleber, Gen., at Kock, 196
Knatchbull-Hugessen, Sir Hughe, *264*
Knickerbocker, H. R., on Nazi fortunes abroad, 148
Knight, H. Pattinson, 88
Knights of Truth, in S. Africa, 474
Knitting, by grandfather, *535*
Knot, nautical, 626
Knute Nelson, S.S., and *Athenia*, 12, *50*, *51*
Koch, Herr, 22, 602
Kock, Poles surrender at, 196
Koeln, German cruiser, *523*
Koht. M., Norwegian Foreign Minister, *268*
Kollupailo, M. Ignacy, from *Chrobry*, *444*
Koscianski, Maj., *93*
Kosciusko, Taddeuz, monument blown up, 504
Kosciusko (*cont.*)
— —Polish patriot, 102
Kovno : *See* Kaunas
Krakow : *See* Cracow
Krivitsky, W. G., on Stalin, 602
Kuresaar : *See* Arensburg
Kutno, train bombed at, 53
Kuusinen, Otto, leads Finnish puppet government, 431

L

Labour Corps, German, Poles in, *98*
Ladoga, L., fighting on, 486, 487
Lamm, Gustave, killed in Dutch air-liner, 188
Lammermoor Hills, German 'plane crashed on, 350
Landra, Prof., at Sachsenhausen, *312*
Landsberg, Hitler leaving, *350*
Lang, Albert, on sinking of *Inverliffey*, 86
Langman, Dr. Otto, and *Graf Spee*, 527
Langsdorf, Capt. Hans, of *Graf Spee*, 526, 530, *540*
— —suicide, 575
— —tribute to British, 542
Larder, British, stocking, *462*
Latvia, Germans in, Hitler's demands, 233
—Russia and, 170, *171*, 618
—services in, *233*
—terms with Stalin, 233
Laudrien, Gen., Hore-Belisha with, *280*
Lausanne, Treaty of, Turkey and, 216
Lawrence, T. E., Finnish counterpart, 586
Leaflets, Finn, on Leningrad, 488
—German, in Arabic, 480
—R.A.F., "clergyman's bombs," 256
— —effect, 293
— —German hatred, 192
— —over Germany, *56*
— —sold for Red Cross, 256
— —text, *92*
— —on three years' war, 178
League of Nations, expels Russia, 521
— — —and Finland, 266, 488
— — —Hitler and, 24
— — —resolution on Russia, 562
Leave, from France, first arrivals, *517*
Lebrun, President Albert, guest of King, 483, *484*
— —reply to Netherlands' peace appeal, 402
Ledbetter, Royston A., *Rawalpindi* survivor, 476
Lee, Armistead, in *American Farmer*, 222
Lee, Frederick, in the *Cresswell*, 446
Leipzig (ship) torpedoed, 522
Lenin, statue in Kremlin, *303*
Leningrad, Finn leaflets on, 488
Leningrad-Murmansk Rly., Finns cut, 586
Leopold III, K. of the Belgians, appeals for peace, *27*, 28, 334–35, 370
— — — —Allies' replies, 402
— —broadcast to U.S.A., 338
— —reaffirms Belgian neutrality, 291
Letters, for British and French troops, *109*
—B.E.F. writing, *237*
Letts, patriotism, *233*
Lewis, Lieut. R. C., D.S.O., *558*, *601*
Ley, Dr. Robert, and deification of Hitler, 574
— —private fortune, 148
— —soothing broadcasts, 405
Liaison Work, French aeroplanes for, *166*
Liberty, statue of, Riga, *223*
Libre Belgique, La, 405
Lieutenant, Ella, in *Simon Bolivar*, 411
Life-belts, for British soldiers, *161*
Lifeboat, from *Simon Bolivar*, *412*
—of *Terukini Maru*, *413*, *414*
Lifeboat Institution, Royal, international thanks, 376
— — —and the war, *597*
Life-jacket, for British seaman, *372*
Lighthouse, of Hel, *164*
Lighting, for trains, *535*
Limerick, Countess of, President of British Red Cross, *151*
Lindbergh, Col., on arms embargo, 182
Lindsell, Lieut.-Gen., Sir W. G., *343*
Liner, British, gun for, *347*
Link Trainer, for R.A.F., *243*
Linlithgow, Marquess of, on Indian loyalty, 84
"Lion Has Wings," stills from, *332*
Lipinski, Col., *131*
Listening Post, Maginot Line, *545*
Lithuania, pact with Soviet, 233
—and Poland, in Middle Ages, 102
—Russia and, 170, *171*, 618
Little, Sir Charles, with *Rawalpindi* survivors, *439*, 475
Litvinov, Maxim, 602
Liverpool, German air photo, *525*
Lloyd-George, Rt. Hon. David, 181
Locarno Pact, Hitler and, 24
Lochavon, S.S., sunk, 245
Lockheed Hudson, American aircraft, *298*
Lodz, becomes German, 165
—under German occupation, 504
Lohse, Herr, fears of revolt, 474
London, Armistice Day (1939), *377*
—A.R.P. in, *215*, *249*, *566*
—before and during war, *152*
—black-out in, *319*, *623*
—bridge guard in, *2*
—crowded theatres in, 500
—evacuation of children from, *10*, *11*
—first-aid station in, *8*
—first air-raid warnings, *6*
—fish for, supply centre, *104*
—food convoy arrives, *463*

London (*cont.*)
—four-wheeler's return, *447*
—Gamelin in, *40*
—German Embassy in, 182
—horses return to, *183*
—at outbreak of war, *44, 45*
—Rhys' poem on, 320
—searchlight in, *5, 73*
—" starving," 346
—troops drilling in, *72*
—war posters in, *2*
—women replace men in, *105*
London, Midland & Scottish Rly., hospital trains, *341*
Look-out Man, in convoy, *372*
Loot, German definition, 474
—from Poland, 256
— —Berlin exhibition, 320
Loraine, Violet, Queen with, *500*
Lorries, British, carrying troops, *305*
— —by Channel Ferry, *300*
— —in France, *236*
— —motor, convoy in France, *343*
— —soldiers riding on, *129*
—Russian, with bread, *606*
— —Finns take, *605*
Lotta Svard, Finnish National Service, *619*
Loud-speaker, German, machine-gunned, 310
Louis Ferdinand, Prince, Prussian pretender, 310
Louis Scheid (ship), 508-09
Louisiane, S.S., sunk, 245
Low, David, cartoons by *29, 128, 214, 314, 543*
Löwenthal, evacuated, *198*
Lublin, becomes German, 165
Lubricants, absolute contraband, *278*
Lucio, " The Secret Weapon," 416
Ludendorff, Eric von, and Finland, 458
— —in Münich " putsch," 350
Luftwaffe : *See* Air Force, German
Lukasiewicz, M., Polish ambassador in Paris, 182
Lulea, Swedish port, *490*
Luukkonen, Miss Fanni, *619*
Luxemburg, fears for neutrality, 262
—fighting watched from, 182
—official language, 256
Lwow, bombing of, 222
—for Russia, 165
—Rydz' victory at (1919), 69

M

Maas R., and Dutch defence, *335*
— —steel gates for bridge, *358*
McCann, Lady, *599*
M'Ewan, John, and sinking of *Athenia*, 51
Machine-gunners, German, in air, *187*
— —by parachute, *55*
— —Polish, *67*
— —Turkish, *265*
Machine-gun Post, cellar as, *386*
Machine-guns, of British fighters, 332
— —captured German, *227*
— —Finnish, on ski, *455*
— —German, electrically controlled, 94
— — —in Siegfried Line, *420*
— —range for, Aldershot, *8*
— —Russian, *91*
— — —Finns take, *616*
Macintosh, for British troops, *322*
McNaughten, Maj.-Gen., and 1st Canadian contingent, 571
McPherson, Flying Officer Andrew, receives D.F.C., *333, 601*
Maeki, Taisto, Finnish athlete, 266
Maestricht, Dutch troops at, *334*
Magdapur (ship) sinking of, *75*, 86
Maginot, André, designed Maginot Line, 42
Maginot Line, *42*
— —activity behind, *138, 140*
— —birds for gas detection, *548*
— —British in, *385, 387*
— —Entente Cordiale in, 322–24
— —first British troops in, 484
— —food and rest in, *516*
— —forward listening post, *545*
— —Hore-Belisha on, *427*
— —maps, *42, 139, 419*
— —scenes in, *77*
— —section of main forts, *426*
Maginot Medal, for George VI, 484
Magna Carta, copy in Washington, 474
Majorities, in Poland, 22
Makeig-Jones, Capt. W. T., of *Courageous*, 116, *117*
Malta, loyalty, 84
Manchester, women bus conductors in, *105*
Manganese, for Germany, from Russia, 279
Manifest, of coffee cargo, *203*
Mannerheim, Field-Marshal Baron Carl Gustav, " Defender of Finland," *428*, 431
— — —Finn C.-in-C., *266*
— — —patriot, 458
— — —with staff, *457*
— — —von der Goltz with, *458*
Mannerheim Line, Finnish fortification, 487
— —gun emplacement in, *551*
— —rifle pit in, *550*
Maps, in case, for British driver, *257*
—commandeered in Germany, 310
Marchant, Vincent, *Royal Oak* survivor, 251
Margarine, British production, 462
Marie-Adelaide, ex-Grand-Duchess of Luxemburg, 262
Mariehamn, capital of Aaland Islands, *234*
Marne, 1st battle of, Gamelin and, 40
Marriage, at distance, in Germany, 376
—" Mein Kampf " and, *212*
Marschall, Rear-Adm., and the *Rawalpindi*, 437
Marsden-Smedley, Hester, at Siegfried Line, 158
Marseilles, profiteering in, 224
Martindale, Nancy, on bombing of Lwow, 221–22
Mary, Queen, cards for troops (1914), *499*
Masaryk, Jan, 590
Massey, Right Hon. Vincent, meets Canadians, 571
— —at R.A.F. Fighter Command, *329*
Massigli, M., and Turkish Pact, *264*
Mastiff, H.M. Minelayer, sunk, 399, *403*
Mathews, Mrs. Laughton, *151*
Matukura, Capt., of *Terukini Maru*, *413*
Mauretania, R.M.S., A.A. guns on, *172*
Maurois, André, and Col. Bramble, 376
Max, Burgomaster Adolph, death, *334*, 335
Maxwell, Mary, 53
Meat, for Britain, from Argentine, 384
—cutting up, by A.T.S., *263*
—German ration, 126
—none in Münich, 288
Mechanized Unit, British, at field kitchen, *237*
— —Nazi, in Poland, *230*
Medical Research, Gov. branch, 364
" Mein Kampf," amended editions, 192
— —confiscated in Prague, 352
— —for house protection, *89*
— —on lying propaganda, 406
— —Nazi bible, 61
— —as wedding gift, *212*
Melbourne, aircraft factory in, *247*
Memel, Hitler and, 24
—Lithuania and, 170
—receiving sets seized, 154
Menzies, Right Hon. R. G., on Australian loyalty, 84
—broadcast (Dec. 20), 594
—Christmas broadcast, 548
Merchant Cruiser, Armed, facts about, 626
Merchant Navy, British, armed, 142, *347*
— — —badge of, *470*
— — —in both Wars, 172
— — —doggedness, 182
— — —King's message to, 174
— — —types, *372*
Merchant Ships, Armed, facts about, 626
— —German, orders, 320
Messerschmitt Fighters, captured, 238
— —shot down, *169, 362*
— —ME109, German bomber, *295, 632*
— — —in Heligoland battle, 554–55
— —ME110, German bomber, *295, 636*
— — —in Heligoland battle, 554–55
Mess-room, German, underground, *450*
Metal, German sources, 474
Metro, Paris, woman conductor on, *105*
Michael, Crown Prince of Rumania, reviewing troops, *136*
Michalowski, Count Joseph, wife killed by tank, 508
Mickiewicz, Miss Jadwiga, from *Chrobry*, *444*
Middlesex Hospital, A.R.P. in, *45*
Midsummer, Baltic festival, *574*
Milch, Gen., and German Air Force, *169*
Militia, British, gunnery instruction for, *8*
Milne, A. A., Par Nobile Fratrum, 512
Minefields, in North Sea, chart, *398*
Mine-laying 'Planes, measures against, 435
— —searchlight catches, *502*
— —wrecked near Sheringham, *492*
Mines, detection from air, 269
—detonated by gun-fire, *119, 403*
—facts about, 630
—floating, Germany's use, *398–99, 400–01*
—in front of Siegfried Line, 320
—land, detection, 580
— —in Finland, 455
— —French examining, *227*
— —in No-man's Land, *452*
—magnetic, Churchill on, 470
— —Germany's use, 398, *399, 403*
— —measures against, *435*, 472
—washed ashore, *493*
Minesweepers, Admiralty calls for, 399
—King inspects, *558*
—trawler as, with paravane, *119*
Mine-sweeping, Churchill on, 470
Ministry of Information, on Goering's speech, 94
— — —statement on Poland, 274
— — — —on Russia and Poland, 146
Minorities, German, no desire to return, 384
Mirrors, pocket, for air pilots, 474
Mistletoe, for B.E.F., *499*
Mlawa, Germans take, 37
Modlin, Germans bombing, *196*
—surrender, 164
Mohawk, H.M.S., air-raid casualties, *242*
Moll, Capt. J., in Dutch air-liner, *188*
Molotov, M., address to Supreme Soviet Council, 338
—broadcast (Nov. 29), 498
— —on Poland, 122
—on Finland, 328
—and invasion of Finland, 428, 430
—to Moscow Soviet (Nov. 6), 370
—reply to League of Nations, 538
—speech of Oct. 31, *303*
Montague, E. A., 510
Montevideo, *Graf Spee* at, 505, *506, 526, 528–29, 541*
—harbour, *527*
Montreux Convention, and Turkey, 264
Montserrat, loyalty, 84
Moravia, Hitler and, 24
Moray Firth, " coastal fort " of, *524*
Morrison, Herbert, M.P., broadcast (Nov. 27), 466
— —on evacuation of children, 11
Morrison, W. S., Food Controller, *462*
Moscicki, Ignace, *98*, 232
Moscow, broadcast from car, *521*
—as diplomatic centre, 170–71
—German radio from, 288
—Supreme Soviet Council in, *303*
Moselle R., bridge destroyed, *262*
Motor-bus, gas-driven, *535*
— —Helsinki, destroyed, *507*, 508
— —Warsaw surrender in, *230*
Motor-car, drawn by horse, *183*
— —electric motor for, *447*
— —gas for, *319*
Motor-cycle Corps, French, *236*
Mourning, forbidden in Austria, 192
Mud, B.E.F. in, *515*
Muhammad Zafrullah Khan, Sir, *329*
Mules, drawing French guns, *140*
—for transport, Western Front, *607*
Muleteer, Turkish, *265*
Munch, M., Danish Foreign Minister, *268*
Munich, beer hall at, *351*
—bomb at, 351, *379*
— —Japan's interest, 474
—on eve of war, 53
—no meat in, 288
Munich Agreement, 25
— —Daladier and, 1?7
— —Mussolini and, *213*
— —respite after, 610
Munich Putsch (1923), eye-witness account, 348
Munitions, manufacture, *191*
Murmansk, *Bremen* at, 254
—Finn air-raids on, 457, 488
—map, *279*
Murtha, J., account of air-raid, 284
Music, for British troops, *275*
Mussolini, Benito, and Albania, 610
— —neutral policy, 213, 556–57
— —peace-maker, *27*
— —welcomed by Hitler, *213*
Mustard Gas, in Poland, 276
— — potency, 534

N

N.A.A.F.I., organization, 500
Napoleon I, and blockade of Britain, 302
— — and invasion of Britain, 363
Narva R., railway bridge over, *223*
National Registration, in Great Britain, *141*
Naval Eye-Witness, submarine saga, 206-07
Naval Reserve, Royal, members at Waterloo, *4*
Navigation Officer, in British destroyer, *204*
Navies, of nations, strength compared, *15*
Navy, French, 359–61
— —on patrol duty, 360
—German, British raid on, 31
—**Norwegian**, *491*
—Royal, A.A. guns in, *271*
— —badges of rank, *282, 307*
— —battleships, *107*
— —convoy duty, 269, 372–73
— —diagrammatic picture, *16–17*
— —fight against U-boats, *106*, 172–75
— —German air raid on, *143*
— —Germany's boast, 352
— —gunnery practice, *97*
— —proficiency badges, *415, 479*
— —U-boat account, *245*
—**Russian**, *91*
— —personnel, *459*
— —seamen exercising, *135*
—**Turkish**, *264, 265*
Navy, Army and Air Force Institutes : *see* N.A.A.F.I.
Nazi Party, programme of, 61
Nazism, and the German character, 4
Neilson, A., on Rosyth air-raid, 315
Nelson, H.M.S., following *Renown*, *7*
Nepal, loyalty, 84
Nesworthy, G. S., *Sheaf Crest* survivor, 476
Netting, for camouflage, *237*
— — —British appeal, 310
— — —girls making, *447*
— — —of French 75's, *259*
Network, steel, for aerodrome runway, *239*
Neuester Nachrichten, map from, *346*
Neugebauer, Gen. Norvid, *131*
Neunkirchen, general view, *41*
Neurath, Baron von, 24, 393
Neutral Countries, views on war (Dec. 1939), 454
Neutrality, U.S. declaration of, *149*
Neutrality Bill, American, passed, 298
Newall, Air Chief Marshal Sir Cyril, at Cenotaph, *377*
— — —with Ironside and Pound, *46*
New Forest, ponies, protection, 376
Newfoundland, loyalty, 84
—recruiting in, 376
Newspapers, on sale, Washington, *149*
—use in black-out, *127*
New Year, British welcome to, 547–48
New York, anti-aircraft guns for, 182
— —A.R.P. in, 126
New York Times, on Russia and Finland, 430
New Zealand, declaration of war, 84
— —help from, *587*
— —and R.A.F., 329
New Zealander, in Air Force, adventures, 539
Nichols, Com. R. F., of *Royal Oak*, *244*
Nicolson, Hon. Harold, 22
Niehoff, Lieut. Rolf, German airman, *315*
Niemen R., at Grodno, *101*
— —Rydz' victory on, 69
Nigeria, loyalty, 84
Night Blindness, vitamins for, 474
Night Hawk (trawler), and *Arne Kjode*, survivors, 478
No-man's-land, mines laid and exploding, *452*
— — —modern scene, 76–77
Non-commissioned Officers, British, rank badges, *307*
Normandie, R.M.S., possible aircraft carrier, 352
North Sea, British cruiser patrolling, *513*
— —convoys in, *278, 373*
— —destroyer patrol in, *175*
— —German bomber brought down, *270*
— —minefields in, chart, *398*
— —naval officers' dress in, *532*
— —Nazi mastery, map, *346*
North Shields, camouflage netting at, *447*
Norway, war fears, 491
Nowak, Col., flight from Warsaw, 221
Nuffield, Lord, and " Blighty," 182
Nuremberg, Nazi demonstration at, *1*
Nurmi, Paavo, Finnish runner, 266
" Nurse Edith Cavell," shown in Washington, 94
Nurses, British, distributing mail, *442*
— —in France, *201*
— —helped by sailor, *166*
— —at hospital concert, *340*
— —in hospital ship, *341*
— —R.A.F. and, *235*
Nykoff, M., with M. Paasikivi, *267*

O

Observation Post, French, *516*
— — —commanding Westwall, *260*
— —German, *580*
Observer Corps, British, work, *363*
October Revolution, Soviet battleship, *135*
Oesel, Arensberg on, *223*
—as possible naval base, 171
Ohqvist, Gen., with Mannerheim, *457*
Oil, British loss and gain, 142
—German shortage, 632
—for Germany, from Russia, 279
—war essential, *598*
Olaf Tryggvason (ship), and *City of Flint*, 348, *349*
Old Masters, Germany sells, 376
Olivegrove (ship), sinking of, *75, 86*, 87
Oliver, Dame Beryl, head of V.A.D., *151*
Oman, support from, 84
Opletal, Jan, death, 393
Orange, colour for neutral 'planes, 376
Orbay, Gen., with Turkish mission, *216*
Order in Council (Nov. 27), and German exports, 472
Ordnance, King inspects, *397*
Ordnance Corps, Royal Army, munition output, 366–67
— — — —supplies uniform, *570*
Orkneys, air-raids on, 422
Oropesa Floats, for minesweepers *399*
— —origin of name, 538
Orzel, Polish submarine, story, 511
Osipenko, Capt. Polena, Russian airwoman, *457*
Osterman, Lieut. Gen., Finn C.-in-C., *428*
— —with Mannerheim, *457*
Ottawa, Empire conference at, 329
Outpost Duty, French soldiers on, *228*
Ouvry, Lieut.-Com. J. G. D., receives D.S.O., *558, 601*
Oxley, H.M.S., lost, 344
Oxygen Apparatus, for air pilots, *114*

P

Paasikivi, Dr. J. K., Finnish Minister at Stockholm, *267*
— —leads Finnish delegation, 223, 233
Paasonen, Col., Finnish statesman, *267*
Page, Coxswain S. H., *597*
Page-Croft, Sir Henry, on air-raids, 44
Paldiski, Finns bomb, 488
Palestine, loyalty, 84, 182
Pamphlets, Germans drop, 418
—British propaganda : *see* Leaflets.
Panagos, Capt., skipper of *Diamantis*, *220*
Papalemos (ship), *Clement's* crew transferred to, 382
Papen, Herr Franz von, 264
Parachutes, German soldiers dropped by, *55*
—testing silk for, *243*
—in use, *219*
Paralos (ship), sunk, 606
Paravane, in French cruiser, *361*
—for minesweepers, 399
—use, *119*
Parcel, for B.E.F., tidying, *442*
Paris, black-out in, *623*
—Czech volunteers in, *125*
—French troops in, 14 July, *13*
—Guards' Regiments in, *389*
—under war conditions, *90, 339*
—women replace men in, *105*

Parker, Louis N., poem by, 192
Parkes, Dr. Oscar, panorama of Imperial Navy, 16–17
Parry, Capt., of Achilles, 529
— —receives C.B., 601
Partridge, Sir Bernard, cartoons by, 61, 182, 310, 474, 493, 512, 544, 608, 639
Partridge, George, in Arlington Court, 445
Pavis, G., sketches by, 323
Peace Aims, Chamberlain on, 436
Peace Front, Turkey and, 216
Peace Offensive, Chamberlain and, 246
Pearson, H., of Arlington Court, 445
Pedersen, Capt., H. A., of American Farmer, 222
Pertinax, on Gen. Gamelin, 40
Pétain, Gen. Henri Philippe, 140
Petrol, high price for, Poland, 224
—rationing, fashion results, 126
Petsamo, ceded to Finland, 328
—destroyed, 519
—fighting in, 486
—Russians driven from, 431
—sea shore near, 457
Philipps, R., in Independence Hall, 316
Phillips, Lieut.-Com. G. C., of Ursula, 523
— —receives D.S.O., 601
Phillips, Gordon : see Lucio
Phillips, T. G., of Stanholme, 636
Photographers, Iron Cross for, 376
Photography, lies by, 408, 409
—propaganda by, 524–25
Phyllisia (trawler), and Cresswell, 446
Piano-accordion, in British Army, 275
Pigs, German, in Luxemburg, 262
—as watch-dogs, 376
Pilate, Pontius, "first pacifist," 480
Pill-box, German, field gun in, 140
— —French, on Western Front, 611
Pilots, British, equipment, 343
— —at training course, 167
Pilsen, Czech revolution in, 125
Pilsudski, Marshal Joseph, home, 70
— —as Polish president, 103
— —saying of, 22
— —and Smigly Rydz, 69
Pinkerton, Sqn.-Ldr. G. C., D.F.C., 601
Pirmasens, evacuated, 198
Pistols, automatic, of French army, 418
Pius XII, Pope, 27
— —address to College of Cardinals, 626
— —speech to Polish deputation, 210
Playfair, Air Vice-Marshal, P. H. L., 246
Ploughing, by elephants, Germany, 277
Plum Puddings, for B.E.F., 499
Pocock, Jack, and destroyer's crew, 381
Poilus, conditions of service, 326
—entertainments for, 356
—in ruined building, 489
See Army, French
Poland, army in field, 48–49, 79
—before and after Great War, maps, 103
—birth-rate, 22
—campaign in, a "strafe," 288
—Cang's escape from, 156
—communiqué on Russian invasion, 146
—defeat, 240–41, 392
— —price of, 230–32
—dogged fighting in, 130–33
—end of first phase, 98–100
—fight for freedom, 66–68
—final surrender, 194–96
—Fourth Partition, 165
—in France, 425
—German advance in, map, 68
— —behaviour in, 504
— —invasion of, 36–37, 610
— —line, Sept. 20, 1939, map, 100
— —persecution in, 590
— —poets for, 310
—Germans in, 59
—German terrorism in, 508
—Germany's strength against, 62
—girls killed in potato field, 225
—gold reserve, 310
—history, 102–03
—Hitler and, 24
—infantry on march, 33
—a Jig-Saw, 536
—loot from, 256, 320
—M. of I.'s statement on, 274
—oil from, 279
—outbreak of war in, 20–21
—partition of 1939, map, 103
—Red Army in, 91
—religious instruction forbidden, 310
—Russia and (since 1920), 170
—Russia invades, 122, 610
—Russian armoured cars in, 123
—Stalin and, 460
—typical soldiers, 3, 37
—war strength, 14
Poles, in France, recruiting, 182
—in German labour corps, 98
—Germans shoot civilians, 126
—for Russian industry, 352
Police, in German provision shops, 62
—in London, air raid warning, 6
—in Paris, in black-out, 623
Pollard, L., in Sea Venture, 348
Pollock, 2nd Lt., grave, 581
Poniatowski, Joseph Anton, Prince, 102
Ponies, New Forest, protection, 376
Pontoon Bridge, over Rhine, from air, 226
Poole, Capt. Walter H., in Bosnia, 87
Poppies, for Armistice Day, 376
Portobello, German airmen buried at, 287
Post, for British and French troops, 109
Post, Evert, on Bremen's escape, 254
Posters, in London, 2, 44
—for Polish mobilization, 38
Postman, parson as, 147
Post Office, for Army mail, 442
Potatoes, cellulose from tops, 310
—less acreage, Germany, 480
Potato Field, Polish, air-raid casualties, 225
Potez 662, French warplane, 13
Pottinger, Capt., of the Ashlea, 541
— —at Langsdorf's funeral, 575
Pound, Adm. Sir Dudley, at Cenotaph, 377
— — —Churchill on, 522
— — —with Ironside and Newall, 46
Pownall, Lieut.-Gen., 375
Poznan, becomes German, 165
—German terrorism in, 508
Praga, child amid devastation of, 231
Prague, under German rule, 393
—"Mein Kampf" confiscated in, 352
"Pravda," on Finn methods of fighting, 455
—on M. Cajander, 428
—Stalin editor, 460
Predictor, for anti-aircraft battery, 364
—British, in France, 355
Preece, Sydney G., in Simon Bolivar, 412
Prendergast, Maurice, on U-boats, 628
President Harding, S.S., rescues by, 318
Press, British, Henderson on, 402
Price, G. Ward, on our adversaries, 320
Priday, Cpl. Thomas, first British soldier killed, 578
Priests, Polish, Nazi treatment, 590
Princess Royal, H.R.H., gifts for troops, 499
Prisoners of War, bureau for, Geneva, 62
— —German, Downs on, 188
— — —in England, 313, 394–95
— — —in France, 352
— — —of French, 454
— — —interrogation, 454
— — —luck of, 182
— — —in Warsaw, 99
— —Polish, in cage, 102
— — —for German agriculture, 352
— — —Germans use, 192
— — —on land, 392
— — —as slaves, 504
— — —from Westerplatte, 93
— —Russian, of Finns, 550, 582, 604, 605
Profiteering, in Marseilles, 224
Propaganda, German, gas lie, 276
— —lying, 406–09
— —photographic, 524–25
— —silence for, 154
— —pictorial, 63
— —by schoolchildren, 384
— —some tales, 346
— —weariness of, 160
—Russian, in Poland, 132–33, 134
Propaganda Raids, British, over Germany, 56, 138
See Leaflets.
Prussia, small population, 22
Przemysl, for Russia, 165
Pussbach, Lieut. Hans, 348
Puttlingen, evacuated, 198

Q

Q Department, 343
Quartermaster-General, duties, 343
Quatorze Juillet, French parade on, 13
Queensferry, South, front seats for air-raids, 376

R

Rabbit, killed by German bomb, 383
Racecourse, as internment camp, 182
Raczynski, Count Edward, British broadcast, 92
— — —note to British Government, 178
— — —Polish ambassador, London, 131
Radio, amateur British stations close, 182
—for Balloon Barrage men, 440
—birth announcements by, 288
—in British flying boat, 444
—for Finn "Suicide Squadron," 586
—in Fleet Air Arm, 371
—in Germany, decoy advertisement, 320
— —Jews' sets confiscated, 182
— —receiving sets seized, 22, 154
— —secret, 224
Radio Commentator, Finn, 585
Radio Sets, for German troops, 352
Radium, protection for, 376
Radomsko, Germans take, 37
Raeder, Grand Admiral, 173
Raemakers, Louis, cartoon by, 214
R.A.F. : see Air Force, Royal
Raft, German A.-A. battery on, 36
—Polish, crossing river, 66
Ragged Guard, in Hungary, 288
Raiders, German ships as, 94
Railway, German, sabotage fear, 405
— —for gun-transport, 450
Railway Coach, Polish, bombed, 158
Railway Station, French, British troops at, 304
Rain, B.E.F. in, 322
—Rumania prays for, 384
Rakov, Russian tank in, 135
Ramrod, for heavy artillery, 218
Ramsgate, air raid shelter in cliffs, 447
Range-finder, Finn, 577
— —French, in use, 355
— —for Polish anti-aircraft gun, 38
Rank Badges, British Navy, Army and Air Force, 282
— —of British N.C.O.'s, 307
Raskova, Senior Lieut. Marina, Russian airwoman, 457
Ration Cards, German, scope, 22
Rationing, of fuel, British and German, 376
—of gas, Italy, 154
—in Germany, 62
— —quantities, 126
— —significance, 250
—social value, 182
Rations, British, preparation and distribution, 263
—daily allowance for British troops, 263
—Front Line distribution, 578
—German, New York tries, 256
—Germans bringing, 580
—for German soldiers, 182
Rauschning, Dr. Hermann, 602
Rawalpindi, S.S., sunk, 437–39, 475–76
Raymond, Ernest, poem by, 160
Reading, Christmas puddings at, 499
Reading, Stella, Marchioness of, and Women's Voluntary Service, 151
Reaping, by Women's Land Army, 44
Red Cross, for ships and trains, 341
Red Cross, International, in Poland, Germany hinders, 416
Red Cross Society, leaflets sold for, 256
— — —uniform for canteen workers, 324
Refrigerator Ship, and U-boats, 174
Refugees, Polish, 68
Regent Tiger (ship), sinking of, 86, 285
Register Office, sandbagged, Wandsworth, 62
Registration, National, Great Britain, 141
Reichstag, and Hitler's peace speech, 246
Reidy, Marine M., on sinking of Courageous, 115–16
Reitz, Col. Deneys, broadcast from London, 338
— —in England, 329
Religion, forbidden in Poland, 310
Rennell, Lord, The Voice of the Empire, 288
Renown, H.M.S., leading Fleet, 7
Reprisals, commercial, against Germany, 434
Reservists, French, 227
—German, description, 22
Restaurants, German, restrictions, 160
Revetting, British trench, 421
Reynaud, M. Paul, broadcast, 434
— —finance speech (Dec. 13), 562
Rhine, R., fishing in, 192
— —French end of bridge over, 199
— —French troops on, 209
— —Kehl bridge over, 309
— —The New Watch on, 108, 613
— —pontoon bridge over, 226
— —railway bridge over, 226
Rhodesia, Northern, loyalty, 84
Rhys, Ernest, poem by, 320
Ribbentrop, Joachim von, Danzig speech, 306
— —with Henderson and Goering, 150
— —preface to German White Book, 562
— —private fortune, 148
— —"slave of Stalin," 384
— —and Soviet-German pact, 29, 460
— —Soviet guest of honour, 376
— —speech stopped by R.A.F., 293
— —war-maker, 26
— —in Who's Who, 154
Richards, Ben, rescues destroyer's crew, 381
Richards, Rev. R. D., as postman, 147
Riddell-Webster, Maj.-Gen. T. S., 343
Riflemen, Finn, on ski, 456
Rifle Pit, in Mannerheim Line, 550
Rifles, Finn, 616
—French automatic, 228
—repairs to, 467
—Russian, Finns take, 616
Riga, statue of Liberty at, 223
Rio de Janeiro, Ark Royal at, 621
Riverdale, Lord, 247
River Plate, Battle of, 526–30, 575
— —estuary, map, 530
Road, mined, procedure, 452–53
Roadsweepers, women as, Paris, 105
Robb, John, skipper of Craigie Lea, 573
Roberts, Capt., of President Harding, 318
Robertson (cricketer), in Police War Reserve, 147
Robinson, Charles, trawler skipper, 190
Robinson, Wyndham, cartoons by, 128, 148, 214
Rocket Apparatus for lifeboat, 597
Rodney, H.M.S., following Renown, 7
Roederink, J. B., captain of Tajadoen, 508–09
Roman (trawler), and U-boat, 87
Roman Catholics, German persecution, 62
Rome, sympathy with Finland, 557
Rome-Berlin Axis, origin, 213
Roosevelt, President Franklin D., and arms embargo repeal, 149, 178, 298
— — —on invasion of Finland, 498
— — —offers mediation for Finland, 430
— — —peace-maker, 27, 28
Rosenberg, Alfred, his "Myth of the 20th Century," 61
— —and the new paganism, 574
Rosyth, German raids on, 242, 315
—sailors' funeral at, 287
Roundabout, black-out dangers, 127
Royal Air Force : see Air Force
Royal Engineers, and Army Post Office, 442
— — —British type, 3
Royal Marines, rank badges, 282
Royal Oak, H.M.S., Churchill's statement, 344
— — —sunk, 244, 251
Rubber, for Germany, blockade and, 279
Rubber Boat, for German airmen, 284–85
Rudyard Kipling (trawler), sunk, 190
Rumania, army, 136
—Polish refugees in, 100, 230
—political situation, 494
—prays for rain, 384
—premier assassinated, 136
—Russia and, 171
—specialists called up in, 154
—war strength, 14
Rummel, Gen., and Col. Nowak, 221
Runeberg, J. L., Finn poet, 619
Russell, Able-Seaman F., 439, 475
Russia, and Baltic States, 233–34, 431, 618
—and British blockade, 279
—in cartoons, 248, 543, 639
—communism, Germans on, 192
—dogs for service in, 376
—as European power, 135
—expelled from League, 521, 562
—and Finland, 266–67
—Finland's stand against, 328, 486–88
—and Germany, 122, 178
—and Germany's Baltic trade, 416
—Germany's pact with : See Soviet-German Pact
—grain for Germany, 310
—Hitler on, 212
—Hitler's possible thoughts, 451
—invades Poland, 66–68, 98, 610
— —Finland, 428–31
—Navy and Air Force, 459
—new footholds in Baltic, 223
—note to Polish Ambassador, 122
—oil in, 598
—and partitioning of Poland, 132–34, 165
—and Poland, in history, 102
— — —(since 1920), 170
—Polish labour for, 352
—riddle of, 303
—tanks, crossing river, 186
—treatment of conquered Poland, 392
—Turkey and, 216
— —abortive negotiations, 264
—war strength, 15, 91
Russians, poor equipment, 550, 552
—surrender, 582
Rutkowska, Nurse Helena, 444
Rydz, Marshal Smigly, biography, 69
— —and defence of Westerplatte, 35
— —Polish generalissimo, 20
— —portrait on poster, 38
— —as refugee, 232
Ryti, Dr. Risto, broadcast, 488
— —Finn Prime Minister, 431
— —and Finn resistance, 457

S

Saar, French advance into, map, 168
— —attacks in, map, 76
—sketch map of region, 41
—village under fire, 450
Saarbruecken, air view, 41
—civilians evacuate, 166, 198
Saaremaa : see Oesel
Saarlouis, evacuated, 198
Sabotage, in Austria, 384
—bad work as, 224
—precautions against, Germany, 405
Sachsenhausen, Prof. Landra at, 312
Saldiray, Turkish submarine, 265
Salisbury Cathedral, "looted," 384
Salla, Russian convoy captured at, 615
Salmijaervi, Finns destroy mines, 519
—Russians bomb, 457
Salmon, H.M.S., exploits, 522, 523
San Alberto, tanker, 603
San Calisto, tanker, 603
Sandbags, for British Government, 310
—in London, 8, 152, 153
—in Paris, 90, 339
—for register office, Wandsworth, 62
—for Scots' trenches, 368
—for street barricade, 386
—use, 153
Sandler, M., Swedish Minister, 268
Sarajoglu, M., and Russia, 264
— —Turkish Foreign Minister, 216
Sausages, captured by Finns, 615
S B, Soviet bomber, brought down, 520
Scandinavia, German spies in, 352
—Germany's dependence on, 600
—rulers in counsel, 268
—war fears, 490–91
Scapa Flow, air raids on, 242
— —map, 244
Schacht, Dr., plans blockade, 256
Scharnhorst (ship), submarine sights, 522
Schirach, Baldur von, medically unfit, 384
Schleicher, Flieger, buried, 287
Schleswig-Holstein (ship), 35, 93
Schneeberg, Germans occupy, 228
Schofield, Capt. J., 156
Schumacher, Wing-Com., 555
Schuschnigg, Dr. Kurt, 126
Schutz-Staffeln, Himmler the head, 121
Schwarze Korps (newspaper), 376
Science, popular, German demand, 352
—for war purposes, Great Britain, 364
Scotland, air-service to Finland, 376
—German 'plane approaching, 622
Scottish Regiment, with pipe band in France, 353
— —revetting trench, 421
See Highlanders
Scraps of Paper, the Two, 25
Scuttling, method, 626
Sealed Orders, officers studying, 372
Seaplane, as minelayer, 398
—rescue by, 156, 157
—and ship's S O S, 443

Searchlights, in British air-defence, *331*, *364*
—on Dornier DO 24, *502*
—in London, *5*, *73*
Sea Venture (freighter), sunk, 347
Secret Weapon, of Hitler, 398–99, *403*
Selter, Karl, Estonian Minister, 171
Sentry, British, with gas mask, *385*
—Finn, in snow, *550*
—German, in Siegfried Line, *613*
—Russian, at Vilna aerodrome, *221*
Serenity (collier), survivors, *573*
Sewing, no materials for, Germany, 474
Seydam, Dr. Reyfik, *264*
Seydel, Unter-offizier, buried in England, *287*
Shampoo Lotion, as soap, Germany, 384
Shaving Soap, rationed in Germany, 182
Sheaf Crest (collier), survivors' stories, 476–78
Sheep, S. Africa's gift, 376
Sheets, material for, Germany, 22
Shelley, George, Shadows on Lake, 448
Shells, for A.-A guns, manufacture, *191*
—British, manufacture, 366, *367*
Sheringham, German minelayer wrecked at, *492*
Shetland Islands, air-raids on, *422*
— —bombs on, *383*
Shipbuilding, in Great Britain, *588–89*
Shipping, British and neutral losses, *470*, *471*
—British losses (Sept.–Dec.), 596
—Debits and Credits, *302*, *345*, *471*, *596*
Shock Troops, in Siegfried Line, 288
Short "Sunderland," for Australian Air Force, *631*
— —on convoy duty, *638*
Shoes, German expedients, 384
—illegal selling, Germany, 474
Sibelius, Jan, a Finn, 266
Sidor, Dr. Karl, Slovak leader, *125*
Siege, State of, technical meaning, 434
Siegfried Line, *43*
— —air-fight over, 219–20
— —floods in, 288, 474
— —forts in, *327*
— —French advance towards, 158
— — —attack on, 76–78
— — —guns bombarding, *193*
— —German howitzer in action, *208*
— —Germans strengthen, 199
— —illness in, 192, 416
— —maps, *42*, *139*, *419*
— —minefields in front, 320
— —R.A.F. photograph, 168
— — —reconnoitres, 200, 238
— —scenes in, *78*, *208*, *420*
— —second projected, 480
— —sentry in, *613*
— —snow in, *548*
— —sorties from, 288
— —weakness, 62
Signallers, of anti-aircraft battery, *73*
Sikorski, Gen., with Duke of Kent, *425*
— —leaves Paris for Angers, *425*
— —on occupation of Poland, 504
— —and *Orzel* crew, 511
— —on Poland's resurrection, 425
— —with Polish Army in France, *425*
Silk, for parachutes, testing, *243*
Simon, Right Hon. Sir John, broadcast (Nov. 22), 434
— —in War Cabinet, *9*
Simon Bolivar, S.S., sunk, *378*, 398, *400*, 411–13
Simpson, P.O. Frank, of *Rawalpindi*, *475*
Sind Province, loyal message, 84
Sing-songs, for British troops, *275*
— —for R.A.F., *624*
Skates, Finns fight on, 582
Skis, for Finn machine-gun, *455*
—Finn riflemen on, *456*, *552*, 586
—Russian troops on, *456*
Skoda Armament Works, in Pilsen, *125*
Slattery, Aircraftman, taken prisoner, 159
Sliedricht (ship), survivors' stories, 478
Slovakia, Hlinka Guard in, 310
—Jewish shops for soldiers, 160
—textile plant destroyed in, 62
Small Arms, British manufacture, *467*
Smallbones, Miss Irene, *380*
Smallbones, R. T., on Jewish pogrom, *380*
— —on German concentration camps, 312
Smith, Flight-Lt. Thurston, and *Kensington Court*, *157*
— —receives D.F.C., *333*, *601*
Smoke Flares, for convoy ships, 532
Smoke Screen, French tank under, *13*
— —Germans first use, Western Front, 418
— —for parachuted soldiers, *55*
Smuts, Right Hon. Jan C., becomes S. African Prime Minister, 84
— —message to S. African people, 124
— —speech in Parliament (Sept. 4), 92
Snow, in Finland, *456*
— —uses, *521*
—on Western Front, *548*, *579*, *624–25*
Soap, German shortage, 22, 480
—shampoo lotion as, Germany, 384
—substitutes rationed, Germany, 416
Soho, German café in, 182
Soldiers, of combatants, types, *3*
Sorters, in Army Post Office, *442*
Sosnowski, Gen., Polish general, *131*
Sound Locator, in air defence, *331*
— —for Observer Corps, 363
Sound-ranger, scientific instrument, 364
South Africa, declares war, 84
South Africa (*cont.*)
— —gift of sheep from, 376
— —"Knights of Truth" in, 474
— —training airmen in, 329
Southampton, H.M.S., damaged in air raid, 242
Southend, lifeboat crew, *597*
Southern Cross, S.Y., and *Athenia*, 12, 51
Soviet-German Pact, *29*
— — —effect on Mussolini, 213
— — —Stalin and, 460
— — —Storm troopers revolt, 320
— — —suggested reasons for, 602
Spain, air-raid casualties in, 461
—neutrality, 22
Specialists, R.A.F., badges, *415*
—Rumanian, called up, 154
Spiders, use of webs, 343
Spies, German, in neutral ports, 224
— —in Scandinavia, 352
Spirfanger (ship), 445
Spying domestic, in Germany, 384
Spun-wood, for German clothes, 22
Squadron, in Air Force, 538
Squire, Sir John, To the Dead, 384
S.S. : *see* Schutz-Staffeln
Stables, British soldiers resting in, *201*
Staehelin, Dr. Rudolf, and gas lie, 276
Stalin, Joseph, "afraid" of Hitler, 288
— —and the Baltic, 233–34
— —biography and character, *460*
— —birthday eulogy 550
— —birthday present fails, 519–21
— —Bolshevism, 303
— —caricature from "Vu," *29*
— —and Finland, 266–67, 428–30
— —and German conquest of Poland, 122
— —and Poland, 98
— —portraits for Poland, 192
— — —with transport column, *605*
— —possible view of war, 451
— —shakes hands with Ribbentrop, *29*
— —Tanner saves, 310
— —with Voroshilov, *460*
— —wish to forestall Hitler, 256
Stamer, Capt., scuttled *Watussi*, 542
Stanholme, S.S., torpedoed, 636
Starace, Gen., with Mussolini, *557*
Starhemberg, Prince von, deprived of citizenship, 384
— —to form Austrian Legion, 160
Star of David, worn by Jews, *312*
Starzynski, M. Stephan, broadcast, 99
— —on capitulation of Warsaw, 164
— —mayor of Warsaw, *131*
Steed, Wickham, letter to "Times," 178
Steel, British manufacture, 366, *367*
—for reinforcement, Siegfried Line, *78*
—for wedding-rings, Germany, 376
Steel Helmet, for bather, London, *45*
— —French type, *355*
— —for London police, *6*
— —manufacture, *563*
— —Polish, abandoned, *241*
— —for programme money, *324*
— —for Red Cross nurses, *235*
Stepney, children evacuated from, *11*
Stockholm, A.R.P. in, *491*
—air-raid shelter in, *268*
—views of, *473*
Stockings, rationed in Germany, 384
Stonegate (ship), crew in *Deutschland*, 381
—passengers in *City of Flint*, 348
Storm Troopers, German, at Nuremberg, *1*
— —revolt, 320
Stowe, Leland, on Russian troops, 550
Straits Convention, signed, 216
Strasbourg, D. of Windsor at, *325*
—evacuation, 108, 308–09
—views of, *303–09*
Streatham, children evacuated from, *10*
Streicher, Julius, Jew-baiter, *120*
— —and the Nazi Church, 574
Strength Through Joy, hospital ships, 474
Stretcher-bearer, Finnish, *593*
— —Polish, *98*
Strikes, in Germany, 154
Stubbs, Capt., of *Doric Star*, *540*, 541
Submarines, British, best week, 522–23
— —"Ursula" class, diagram, *629*
— —fight for life, 206–07
—Finnish, *628*
—German : *see* U-boats
—Polish : *see Orzel* ; *Zbik*
—Turkish, *265*
Sudbury, A.F.S. at, *311*
Sudeten Germans, and Czechs, 393
Sugar, no British rationing, 462
Suicide, in Germany, 352
Suicide Squad, of Finland, 586,
Sunderland Flying-boat, diagram, *533*
Supermarine "Spitfires," above clouds, *65*
Supply, Ministry of, organization, 343
Supply Train, Russian, wiped out, 582
Supreme Soviet Council, Molotov's speech to, *303*
Surtees, Robert, Gort's grandfather, 111
Sussex, German 'plane over, 422
Suursaari, Aaland Islands, *234*
Swailes, Helen, in *Terukini Maru*, *414*
Swanney, James, fisherman, killed, 573
Swastika, facts about, 538
Swaziland, loyalty, 84
Sweden, and the Aaland Islands, 266
—war fears, 490–91
Swinton, Maj.-Gen. Sir Ernest, broadcast, 324
— —invented tanks, 186
Switzerland, barbed wire defences, *292*
—merchant fleet for, 474
Sword, Russian, as souvenir, *519*
Szathmary, Dr., letter to Col. Beck, 60

T

Tabor, revolt in, *125*
Tacoma (ship) and *Graf Spee*, 527, *529*, *541*
Tajadoen (ship), survivors' stories, 508–10
Tallinn, capital of Estonia, *223*
—*Orzel* at, 511
Tanganyika, loyalty, 84
Tank (water) emergency, *215*
Tanker, function, *174*
Tanks, British, German, Soviet and French, *186*
— —details, *595*
— —and overturned van, *518*
— —by roadside, *110*
—Finnish, *455*
—French, *76*, 77, *108*
— —Chenilette, *140*, *260*
— —miniature, *489*
— —under smoke screen, *13*
—German, kills woman, 508
— —Polish women destroy, 126
—Polish, *48*
— —moving forward, *79*
— —under observation, *66*
—Russian, lie to Poles, 126
— —light, wrecked, *586*
— —in Rakov, *135*
Tank Traps : *see* Anti-tank Barricades
Tanner, M. Vaino, Finnish Minister, *455*
— —saves Stalin's life, 310
Tauna, Finn bath, *617*
Tavela, Gen., 586
TB3, Russian aircraft, *459*
Tchakmak, Marshal, *264*
Tea, from blackberry leaves, 224
—British control, 462
—for R.A.F., Western Front, *624–25*
Techel, Dr., and U-boats, 628
Telephone, regulations, Germany, 416
Telescope, from "former German officer," 376
Terijoki, bridge at, *430*
—puppet government at, 431, 457
Territorial Army, Hore-Belisha with, *281*
Terry, Lieut. Anthony, of *Royal Oak*, *244*
Terukuni Maru, S.S., *400–01*, 413–14
Thames, R., balloon barrage, *568*, *569*
Thames Haven, German photographs, *524*
Theatre, for French troops, *356*
—London, in wartime, *500*
Thomas, Bert, cartoon by, *128*
Thomas, A/Sgt. C., grave, *581*
Thomas, George, 284
Thomas, Jack, in *Independence Hall*, 316
Thomason, Albert, trawler skipper, 190
Throwers, for depth charges, *207*
Thyssen, Dr. Fritz, alleged flight, 256
Tin Hat : *see* Steel Helmet
Tires, German, confiscated, 154
—old, uses, 480
—rubber, for British heavy gun, *176–77*
Tolva, L., Russian casualties at, 614
Tonga, loyalty, 84
Torpedoes, from British destroyer, *106*
—manufacture, *531*
—tubes for, on destroyer, *207*
Torpedo Boat, Motor, British, *106*
Toupolev, A. N., aircraft designer, *459*
Tractor, for French gun, *166*
— —tanks, *186*
—Turkish, camouflaged, *265*
Trains, Polish, bombed by Nazis, *163*
—refugee, bombing of, 53
Tram-car, wrecked, in Warsaw, *232*
Tram-conductor, woman, Germany, *277*
Tramp Steamer, function, *174*
Transjordan, supports Britain, 84
Transport, British, camouflage for, *237*
—German, in Poland, *59*
—Polish, crossing Vistula, *66*
—Turkish, mules for, *265*
Transport Column, British mechanized, *112*
— —Polish, wrecked, *102*
— —Russian, Finns take, *605*, 606
Transport Service, private car in, *147*
Trawlers, as minesweepers, *119*
—U-boats and, 87, 172, *190*
Trenches, British, pumping out, *485*
— —soldiers revetting face, *421*
—citizens digging, Warsaw, *70*
—Dutch, camouflaged, *358*
—in Finland, *267*
—King leaving, *483*
—Nazis camouflaging, *354*
—in Poland, *79*
—Polish, from air, *132*
—on Swedish frontier, *491*
Trench Mortar, Hore-Belisha inspects, *281*
Tresteill, Joan, *Simon Bolivar* survivor *378*
Trinidad, loyalty, 84
Troopship, soldiers in life-belts, *161*
Troop Train, French, 88
Trotsky, Leon, on Stalin and Hitler, 288
Trousers, Russian, camouflaged, *617*
Truth, Goebbels on, 480
Turkey, guards Black Sea, 216
—our new Ally, 264–65
—war strength, 14
Turku, bombed, *584*
Turnbull, Miss, helps Jews, 380
Tuscaloosa, U.S.S., and *Columbus*, 572
Tweed, Col. T. F., 30
Tweedie, John, of *Isabella Greig*, 573
Tweedsmuir, Lord, *84*

U

U 35, and *Diamantis*, *220*
U 36, at rest on surface, *446*
U 39, submerging, *446*
U-boats, apologetic commanders, 310
—bombed from air, 118, 222–23, *635*, *637*
—captain captured, 253–54
—Churchill's second statement, 344–45
—convoys as protection against, 269
—destroyed by depth charge, *47*
—destroyers' watch for, 204–05
—Dover Patrol and, 299–301
—French navy and, 360
—at Hamburg, *245*
—humane commanders, 196, 446
—life in, pictures, *173*, *627*
—meaning of name, 434
—methods of combating, 172–75
—as minelayers, 398, *399*, 630
—Navy's fight against, *106*
—officer's sentiment, 320
—prisoners from, *313*, 394, *395*
—sinking of, *299*, *627*
—submerging, Kiel Harbour, *118*
—tonnage sunk by, *302*
—torpedoes *Bosnia*, *74*
—training in, *245*
—work of, *74–75*
U-boat War, measures against, 142
Uebelhör, on mastery of Poland, 504
Uganda, loyalty, 84
Ukraine, Russia in, *135*
Uniform, British manufacture of, *570*
Union Castle Line, liner of, *174*
United States of America, aeroplane industry speed up, 474
— — —first reaction to war, *149*
— — —Leopold III's broadcast to, 338
— — —oil production, 598
— — —passes Neutrality Bill, 298
— — —war strength, *15*
United States Lines, wants British sailors, 376
Unruh, Rear-Adm., 164
Ursula, H.M.S., exploits, 522, *523*
— —sectional diagram, *629*

V

Valiant, H.M.S., following *Renown*, *7*
Van, overturned, British help with, *518*
Vatican, A.R.P. in, 62
Vearncombe, Able Seaman A. L., receives D.S.M., *558*, *601*
Veltman, L., in *Simon Bolivar*, 411
Venezuela, oil in, 598
Venning, Lt.-Gen. Sir Walter, Quarter-master-General, *343*
Vercel, Roger, black-out lesson, 215
Vermont S.S., U-boat and, 310
Vernon, H.M.S., decorations for, *558*
Vickers, Messrs, small arms manufacturers, *467*
Vickers., Sgt. Observer J., Médaille Militaire, *601*
Vickers-Armstrong "Wellington," *7*, *503*
— — —in Heligoland air battle, 554–55
Vickers-Supermarine "Spitfire," British 'plane, *423*
— — —manufacture, *272–73*
Victoria Cross, Gort wins, 111
Vienna, empty baskets in, 376
—Jew-baiting in, *120*
Viipuri, bomb damage, *521*
—raids on, 582, *584*
Village, Polish, German terrorism in, *80–81*
—ruined, Western Front, *418*
Villard, Oswald Garrison, 632
Vilna, bombing of, *83*
Vistula R., becomes German, 165
— —Polish transport crossing, *66*
— —Warsaw on, *19*
Vivian, Sir Sylvanus, *141*
Völklingen, air photo, *226*
Voorspuiy, Capt. H., of *Simon Bolivar*, 412
Voroshilov, Klement, Russian minister, *122*
— —with Stalin, *460*

W

Wales, Prince of : *see* Windsor, Duke of
Walker, Peter, 252
Wallenius, Gen., Finn general, *582*, 583
Wandsworth, register office, 62
War, Diary of : *see* Diary
War Aims, Chamberlain on, 404, *436*
War Cabinet, of Great Britain, *9*
War-correspondents, Iron Cross for, 376
Warndt Forest, French clear, 77
— —scene in, *108*
Warning ! Text of leaflet, 56, *92*
Warrant Officers, British, rank badges, *307*
Warsaw, air-raids on, 221, *222*
—bomb damage, *52*
—bombing of, 82–83
—Col. Nowak's flight from, 221
—crowds cheering England in, *38*
—devastation, *232*, 310, 392
— —problems, 230
—dogs as food, 384
—during air-raid, *164*
—first raids on, Delmer's account, 52
—German guns in, *195*
—Germans advancing on, *99*
— —bomb, 37
— —troops enter, *240*
—last days of defence, 130
—last train to Rumania, *189*
—messages to, in bombs, 62
—not to be rebuilt, 288
—photographing raids on, 252–53
—picture map, *133*

Warsaw (cont.)
—Poles march out, 241
—Polish armoured cars in, 71
—refugees from, 424
—siege and fall, 162–64
—street barricades in, 196
—three views, 19
—trench digging in, 70
—water shortage in, 320
—woman in ruined home, 99
Warsaw, Grand Duchy of, history, 102
War Strength, of the nations, 14–15
War Weariness, in Germany, 256
Washington, S.S., and *Olivegrove,* 75, 86
Washington, anti-German sympathies 94
—notice in front of Capitol, 149
—war scenes in, 149
Watch on the Rhine, The New, 108
Water, shortage in Warsaw, 320
Waterloo Station, navy and army at, 4
Waterson, Mr. F. S., 329
W.A.T.S., as cooks, 263
—duties, 211
Watson, Chief Officer William, 87
Watussi, S.S., scuttled, 542
Wavel, Lt.-Gen. Sir A. P., 264
Weather, European map 451
—forecast, balloon for, 614
Wedding Rings, of steel, Germany, 376
Wetzsacker, Baron von, 150
Wells, H. G., in causes of Great War, 2
Wells, John Desmond, 116
Welsh Guards, in Paris, 389
Wensvoort, Cristina, 378
"We're Going to Hang our Washing," etc., Nazi view, 256
Wernik, Miss Bronislawa, 444
Western Front, air battles on, 166–68, 354
—all quiet on, 258–60
—approach of winter on, 291–92
—British football match, 168
—delayed action on, 386–88
—early activity on, 138–40

Western Front (cont.)
—French and German front lines, 326–27
—French bring down 9 'planes, 362
—frost on, 611
—Germans' disappointment, 288
—horse and mule on, 607
— — —life on, 624–25
—mysterious warfare, 199–200
—R.A.F. Operations Room, 246
— — —life on, 578–80
— — —photographs, 226
—relief map, 419
—waiting for Zero Hour, 227–28
—war zone, map, 139
—winter raids on, 418
Westerplatte, defences, 18
—defence of, 35
— —map, 35
Westmacott, Paymaster Sub.-Lt. S. F., *Courageous* survivor, 116
Westminster, A.R.P. practice in, 365
Westminster Hospital, radium protection, 376
Westwall : *see* Siegfried Line
Westwood, car drawn by horse at, 183
Weygand, Gen. Maxime, and Turkish Pact, 264
Weymouth, contraband base, 202
Weymouth Bay, *Royal Oak* in, 251
Whitby, German airman at, 284
White, for black-out wear, 182, 623
—as camouflage, Finland, 552, 577, 586
White Book, of Finnish Government, 562
—German, on prelude to war, 562
White Paper, on German concentration camps, 312
— —meaning, 434
Whiteway, Mr., in *Terukini Maru,* 414
Wilhelm II, allowance stopped, 256
— —compared with Hitler, 61
Wilhelmina, Queen, appeals for peace, 27, 334–35, 370

Wilhelmina, Queen (cont.)
— —Allies' replies, 402
Wilhelmshaven, British airmen killed at, 159
— —raid on, 31, 85
Willits, Sergeant W. E., receives D.F.M., 333, 601
Willow Tree, as camouflage, 560
Wilno, capital of Lithuania, 170
—for Russia, 165
—Russians enter, 170
—transferred to Lithuania, 233, 618
Wilson, Telegraphist Aspinall, 206
Wilson, "Tiny," Canadian Army cook 571
Wilson, President T. Woodrow, 103
Windsor, Ont., Essex Scottish Highlanders at, 247
Windsor, H.R.H. Edward, Duke of, in France, 261, 292
— —in last war and this, 325
Wine Merchant, British troops help, 518
Winter, first of war, 451–54
Winter Relief Fund, in Berlin, 277
Wireless : *see* Radio
Wireless Operator, of R.A.F., 246
Wirraway Aeroplanes, manufacture, 247
Wishful Thinking dangers, 622
Wisters, J. H., in *Simon Bolivar,* 412
Wolfe, Humbert, Dachau, 576
— —on loss of *Courageous,* 116
— —"1939," 126
— —The Shroud of Gold, 352
— —Silence and the Black-out, 534
Wolfram, contraband, 203
Women, as balloon makers, 184
—and national service, 44
—organization, Germany, 480
—replace men, Germany, 277
— — —London and Paris, 105
—rush to volunteer, 22
—in Russian Air Force, 457
—war services, 151, 599
— — —Finland, 619

Women's Land Army, reaping, 44
— —training, Sussex, 104
Wood, Right Hon. Sir Kingsley, on Britain's air supremacy, 238
— —with Chamberlain and Churchill, 436
—on Dominions' air effort, 247
—on R.A.F. over Berlin, 293
—statement of Dec. 12, 502
—in War Cabinet, 9
Wood, William, return from Germany, 30
Woodhouse, Capt. C. H. L., of *Ajax,* 529
—receives C.B., 601
Work, hours of, Germany, 154
Working Party, in London street, 45
Wounded, British, the first, 340
—Finnish, 593
—transport of, 341
—training for commissions 599
W.R.N.S., King inspects, 558
Wykeham-Martin, Lieut. M., F., D.S.C. 601
Wynoldt, Anny, air hostess, 188

Y

Yavuz, Turkish battle cruiser, 265
Yeomanry, man howitzers, 609
York, Archbishop of, broadcast, 210
Yorkshire, S.S., sunk, 316, 317
Yssel, R., and Dutch defence, 335
Yugoslavia, "Hitler Calendar of Aggression" in, 310

Z

Zbik, Polish submarine, 132
Zec, cartoons by, 128, 214, 312, 460, 543, 602, 639
Zeppelins, for Russo-German goods transport, 192
Zero Hour, waiting for, Western Front, 227–28
Zoo, food problems in, 310

List of Maps and Plans

Atlantic Ocean, N., shipping routes and traffic, pre-war, 345
— —N. Sea, pre-war trade routes, 472
— —S., *Graf Spee* battle, 505
Balkans, spheres of influence, 556
Baltic to Black Sea, 171
Baltic and Scandinavia, concessions to Russia, 234
— —Russo-Finnish conflict, 431
Czecho-Slovakia, scene of revolt, 125
Danzig, Westerplatte, 35
Europe, Wartime, Supplement, Vol. 1, No. 1
—influence of weather on operations, 451
—Central, all war areas, Supplement, Vol. 1, No. 3
— — —areas flown over by R.A.F., 293
—N.W. (Murmansk), 279
— — —route of *City of Flint,* 349
Finland, physical features, 487
—Russian claims, 431
—and Scandinavia, 234
—war areas, 430, 520,

Finland (cont.)
—war areas four fronts, 583
Firth of Forth, German raids, 242, 409
France, German frontier, relief map, 419
German Maps circulated during Great War, 404
Germany, area flown over by R.A.F., 293
—French frontier, contour map, 419
—Greater, Nov., 1939, 536
—pre-war import trade routes, 472
Great Britain, air-raids, 1914–18 and 1939, 567
Heligoland Bay, 31
Holland and Belgium, defences, 335
Maginot Line and Siegfried Line, 42, Sup. Vol. 1, No. 3
Murmansk, 279
North Sea, German map, 346
— —minefields, 398
— —and Shetlands, 383
Oil, World centres and routes, 598
Poland, the Corridor, Danzig, E. Prussia, etc., Supp. Vol. 1, No. 1
—German progress early Sept., 68

Poland (cont.)
—line reached by Germans, Sept. 20, 100
—1914, 1919–20, and 1939, 103
—1914 boundaries : Curzon Line : Nazi and Soviet line, Sept. 29, 165
Rawalpindi, scene of battle, 437
Rhine, Supp. Vol 1, No. 3
River Plate, *Graf Spee* battle, 505
— —scuttled, 530
Russia, and neighbouring countries, 171
—claims on Finland, 431
Saar, French advances, 168
Saar Basin, 41
Scandinavia, 171, 234, 431
Scapa Flow, 244
Shetland Isles, 383
Siegfried Line and Maginot Line, 42
Warsaw, bombing, 133
Western Front, first action, 76
— —Moselle and Rhine, Supp. Vol 1, No. 3
— —common frontier, 139
— —relief map, 419

Errata and Addenda

Page 4. Column 3 (Poland). *For* "Planes, 1,500" *read* "Planes, 2,500."
" **38.** Centre photograph. Inscription on banner should read "Niech zyje Anglia." Bottom caption, lines 3 and 4, *for* "By order . . . one hour" *read* "In the event of war every man, without regard to age, and every woman, will be soldiers."
" **111.** Column 1, line 6, delete "Plumer ;" line 24, *for* "three" *read* "two"; line 25, *for* "four" *read* "three."
" **121.** Caption of lower photo should read: "In this photograph of the Fuehrer in Poland, studying a map of the battlefields, the Gestapo chief is seen extreme right."
" **136.** Column 2, lines 2 to 5 below picture of car, *for* "in return . . . . . . on" *read* "despite many considerations to continue in neutrality, her rulers decided to throw in their lot with ;" line 7, *for* "two days" *read* "having just"; line 8, delete "she"; line 9 *for* "and" *read* "she."

Page 136. Col. 2, line 2 above lower picture, *for* "managed to . . . . . . Bessarabia" *read* "secured the Russian territory of Bessarabia, in all which territories large numbers of Rumans have had their homes for centuries." Col. 3, line 1, insert "also" before "been"; line 2, delete "exceedingly"; line 4, *for* "adventures" *read* "decisions"; line 5, delete "and riddled with corruption." Lines 16 and 15 from bottom, delete "many of his followers were also sent to gaol."
" **151.** Top caption, line 3. *For* "Elliot" *read* "Elliott."
" **175.** Caption. Line 1, *for* "destroyers" *read* "destroyers and light cruisers"; line 2, *for* "destroyers" *read* "a light cruiser and a destroyer."
" **208.** Line 3 of caption. *For* "his rifle" *read* "a light machine-gun."
" **211.** Top left caption. *For* "a Bren gun" *read* "an anti-tank rifle."
" **215.** Top right caption. Last line should read : "comes into contact with it."

Page 218. Lines 3 and 4 of caption. *For* "clean out . . . . . . photograph" *read* "press the charge home before firing."
" **220.** Line 2 of caption. For "the crew" *read* "the crew of the sunk vessel."
" **242.** Column 3, line 17, *for* 246, *read* 244.
" **276.** Left caption, line 3. *For* "Argyle," *read* "Argyll."
" **307.** Caption to 15th illustration should read: "All other 2nd class Warrant Officers." Caption to 16th illustration should read "Warrant Officers, Class III." Leading Aircraftman (last illustration) is not an N.C.O. rank.
" **313.** Last sentence of centre caption. *Read* "In the second National Defence men are digging a shelter."
" **348.** Col. 3, lines 3 and 4, *read* "the mine-layer 'Olav Tryggvason.'"
" **353.** Caption, line 1. *For* "a Scottish" *read* "an Irish." *For* last sentence *read* "It will be noticed that the pipes have only two drones, whereas Scottish war pipes have three."

Page 361. Caption, line 2. *For* "one of her guns" *read* "one of her boats."
" **370.** Bottom of column 1. Add "As Sovereigns of two neutral States, having good relations with all their neighbours, we are ready to offer them our good offices."
" **455.** In caption, for "Valno" *read* "Valno."
" **476.** In caption, *for* "Emilie Miguel" *read* "Emile Miguet." Bottom photograph. The photograph shows a British destroyer.
" **489.** Top caption. *For* "These small landships are manned by one man," *read* "The French tank illustrated has a crew of at least two men."
" **501.** First line, *for* "November 10, 1939," *read* "October 26, 1939."
" **514.** Line 2 of caption. *For* "Equivalent to 3½-in.," *read* "Equivalent to about 4½-in."
" **523.** Line 3 of top left caption. *For* "8-in. torpedo tubes" *read* "21-in. torpedo tubes."
" **544.** Column 3, line 14 from bottom. *For* "Columbia" *read* "Columbus."

Vol. 1.   A Permanent Picture Record of the Second Great War   No. 1.

Red-letter days in the Nazi calendar are the gigantic demonstrations of military might and hysterical fervour held at Nuremberg. As shown in this photograph, the ceremony resembles a mighty communion, in which massed ranks of hundreds of thousands of worshippers of a God of Blood and Iron receive the Nazi " Sacrament " from their Leader. These are the storm troopers—poor devils—bred for Nazi cannon-fodder.

Photo, Associated Press

Why We Are At War

Confronted by the record in other pages of the things Hitler has said and the things he has done, the reader will be in small doubt as to the immediate reasons which have compelled Britain to go to war. Now in this chapter we are given a revelation of the principle that we are fighting—the principle that Might is Right.

Fully-equipped with his steel helmet, gas mask and fixed bayonet, this sentry keeps guard over a London railway bridge.

WHEN Britain went to war in 1914 many reasons were advanced for the tremendous step. The primary cause of the War, of course, was the invasion of Belgium, whose integrity and independence we had been pledged to defend since the Belgian kingdom had come into existence. Of the tens of thousands, the hundreds of thousands, who stormed the doors of the recruiting stations in those early days of war twenty-five years ago, the great majority had left their homes and jobs because of their resolve to avenge the violation of an innocent little people by the Prussian bully.

Another reason was Anglo-German rivalry in the field of commerce and in the sphere of world politics. This rivalry was something more than a clash of interest; rather it was a conflict of principle. Even at the beginning of the War it was realised that Britain was fighting for Democracy against Autocracy in general and Prussian imperialistic militarism in particular. "We are fighting Germany," wrote H. G. Wells in the first number of THE WAR ILLUSTRATED, published on August 22, 1914. "But we are fighting without any hatred of the German people. We do not intend to destroy either their freedom or their unity. But we have to destroy an evil system of government and the mental and material corruption that has got hold of the German imagination and taken possession of German life .... And also we have to learn from the failure of that victory to avoid a vindictive triumph."

"Prussian Militarism," continued Mr. Wells, "is an intolerable nuisance in the earth. Ever since the crushing of the French in 1871 the evil thing has grown and cast its spreading shadow over Europe ... But now at last we shake ourselves free and turn upon this boasting wickedness to rid the world of it. The whole world is tired of it. And ' Gott,' Gott so perpetually invoked—Gott indeed must be very tired of it."

If the world was tired of it in 1914, it was still more tired of it in 1918, after a struggle in which all the resources of the greatest nations had been exhausted in an orgy of destruction and, more appalling still, the blood of millions of the best and bravest had been poured out on the battlefield. When the "Cease fire" sounded on that Armistice Day in 1918, there was little carefree jubilation, practically nothing of the nature of triumphing over a vanquished foe. In every nation there was one thought uppermost in the minds of the people—the thought that they were at last awaking from a nightmare of unrelieved horror. In all countries, too, it was said, and said with hard determination, that this evil thing which had come upon the world must and should be exorcised now and for evermore.

Was Prussianism Smashed ?

And on the face of it, it seemed indeed that Prussian militarism had not only been defeated but had been completely smashed. Kaiserism and all that it stood for was kicked into the gutter by the German troops and populace as they realized the bitterness of defeat and endured the humiliations of the Peace.

They had entered the war with the most confident hopes of glory and easy conquest; when it was ended theirs was a country through which stalked relentlessly the spectres of famine and revolution. Even the victorious powers were in little better plight. They had won—but at what a price !

So it was that in 1919 men of good will everywhere strove to build a new world from which the spirit of militarism and all those vilenesses which are best expressed by the word "Prussianism" had been completely banished—and for ever. Gradually Europe and the world settled

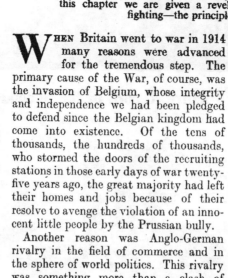

On the evening of Saturday, September 2, the newspaper placards told the London crowds that war, if it had not actually begun, was but a matter of a few hours. The armed forces of the Crown mobilized, and (even more significant for those who remembered the rape of Belgium a quarter of a century before) the invasion of Poland—these removed the last shred of hope that even yet peace might be preserved.

Photos, Wide World

Types of the Men Who Fight and Suffer

Briton, Frenchman, German and Pole—here are typical soldiers destined to play their part in the struggle of 1939. Cheerfully smiling, is the R.E. sergeant, like his predecessor of 1914–1918, confident in his cause and his leaders. The poilu stands ready in his new equipment. Below right, the Polish soldier is the epitome of sturdy valour; while the young Germans no doubt remember that they are " Jerry's " sons.

Photos, Keystone, Wide World, L.E.A., Paul Popper

down from the strain and loss of the great war. The material losses were largely repaired, though, alas, the gaps in the generations could never be filled. In Germany there were signs of the firm foundations of a new order—an order of true liberalism, of toleration, and enlightened, peace-loving and peace-ensuing democracy.

With what apprehension, then, and later with what horror, did the outside world discern the phoenix-like growth in Germany of something which was all too plainly akin to the Prussianism which it was believed the war had finally killed !

Some would blame this rebirth of a thing essentially ugly and evil upon the great slump which deprived Germany of her economic and financial supports. Others have it that there is something essentially militaristic in the German spirit. Yet others adopt the kinder—and,

let us hope, truer—view that the average German is one who is constitutionally better fitted to be led rather than to play an active part in a political system which can only function properly if all, or at least the majority, of the citizens are prepared to make their contribution to its proper working.

The German, in a word, has a passion for regimentation ; he loves order, and is not at all averse to being ordered about. In the cold air of the Weimar republic he felt it difficult to breathe ; it demanded of him a knowledge, a spirit of toleration, a willingness to take part in dull and uninteresting work, which he found it difficult to afford in an age of scarcity and insecurity.

Nazism removed from him the necessity of taking thought. He willingly gave up those rights and liberties which are regarded as the very life-blood of British citizenship. He gladly agreed to sink his individuality in that of the mass ; he concurred in that final stage of self-stultification, the subordination of the individual to the totalitarian god— the all-powerful, allegedly all-knowing, supposedly all-wise State.

Hypnotized and deluded by the messianic promises of the Leader, his conscience stifled by the assertions of the new ideology, his reason deafened by the clamour of the drums—the German

abandoned his interest in politics to the men of the Nazi machine—men who, to the world at large, came to resemble ever more closely the gangsters of the American underworld. All that spoke of the liberal Germany of Stresemann— let alone of the Germany of Goethe and Schiller, Kant and Mendelssohn—was spurned with contumely. Christianity was assailed, and the crude paganism of the old Teutons was officially resurrected.

At first the world outside refused to believe that the Germany which had travailed so hardly in 1919 was so soon lying on its deathbed. But it was not long before the last illusions were crushed beneath the hammer-blows of Nazi might. In the reoccupation of the Rhineland, the reintroduction of conscription, the creation of an air force ; in the cruel bullying and eventual seizure of Austria ; in the successful

dismemberment and final engorging of the democratic republic of Czecho-Slovakia ; finally in the onslaught upon a Poland which had committed the greatest crime in the Nazi calendar—refusal to submit to the most outrageous demands presented at the point of the pistol—in all these the one argument used was FORCE.

As Mr. Chamberlain declared in his noble pronouncement over the wireless Hitler's " action shows convincingly that there is no chance of expecting that this man will ever give up his practice of using force to gain his will. He can only be stopped by force."

When historians come to write the record of these momentous days and weeks, they will no doubt have to say that there were many other reasons why Britain took up a sword for the second time against Germany. For us, living in this critical moment, the situation is plain. The things we are fighting against are, to quote Mr. Chamberlain again, " the evil things—brute force, bad faith, injustice, oppression and persecution."

In 1939, as in 1914, the enemy is the same. Then we called it by the name of Prussian Militarism : today we know it as Nazism. Under whatever name it is a foul growth, something to be cut out of the body of the nations.

And that we shall most surely do, if, in the words of the King, we " stand calm, firm and united "—if we " do the right as we see the right, and reverently commit our cause to God."

As Britain drew nearer to the hour of war, men in uniform appeared in ever increasing numbers. These photos, taken at Waterloo on the day of mobilization, show naval reservists stepping out to join the train for Portsmouth, and (below) a group of Army N.C.O.s getting ready to march off.

Photos, Keystone, Sport and General

How We Fight the Raiders from the Skies

In the turret of his Hawker " Demon " fighter this warrior of the skies sights his gun.

For hours and days before the actual commencement of hostilities the anti-aircraft defences of Britain were manned and fully equipped. Top right, a gun crew makes ready for action. Middle, a London searchlight probes the night sky. Bottom, balloons of the R.A.F. balloon barrage, a most impressive and reassuring sight, being sent up.   *Photos, Chas. E. Brown, Associated Press and Fox*

Britain's First Air Raid Warnings

A police constable wearing steel helmet and carrying his gas mask gives the warning by blowing his whistle.

Half an hour after the war began, Britain received her first air raid warning. Everywhere in London and the southern and eastern counties the sirens wailed their note of warning.

Surprised and hardly believing, the people listened. There was not the slightest sign of panic. The Air Raid Wardens repeated the warning on their whistles, and the people proceeded at once in the most orderly fashion to their shelters. Auxiliary firemen put on their uniforms in readiness for any emergency.

In a few minutes the "All Clear" was sounded, but it was only some hours later that the Air Ministry announced that a strange aircraft had been observed approaching the south coast, and as its identity could not be readily determined, the air raid warning was given. It thus provided excellent practice so that further warnings were received with the same sang-froid.

The photograph above shows Londoners trooping cheerfully into an underground shelter when the first warning was given half an hour after the outbreak of war. Left, a member of a decontamination squad tells a householder to go indoors, and right, a policeman shows the "all clear" notice.

Photos, Topical, Wide World, Associated Press.

Britain is at Full Strength by Air Land and Sea

Amongst the most powerful of Britain's bombing 'planes are twin-engined Vickers Wellington, seen here in flight.

I N the Crisis of 1938—that crisis which had its origin in German aggression against Czecho-Slovakia and its outcome in the Munich Conference which dismembered the little republic—Britain's material preparations were supposed by some to have fallen short of what would be required to support her readiness of spirit. For years she had believed, and acted on the belief, that the nations were resolved, in the light of the bitter experience of the Great War of 1914-1918, that war as an instrument of national policy should be abandoned. The unscrupulous conduct of Nazi Germany, however, in attacking her peaceful neighbours led to Britain's realization of her true character and aims, and when Poland's turn had come to receive the German onslaught, "ready, aye ready" was the watchword, and in the armed forces, the civilian defence organizations, and the ranks of the population as a whole, the signs of alert resolution were much in evidence.

Sweeping through the seas in splendid majesty come some of the greatest vessels in the British navy—the battle-cruiser Renown, the battleships Barham, Valiant, Rodney, and Nelson. Floating fortresses of steel and armament, they are manned by men possessed of the same spirit as that which nerved Nelson and Drake and the other gallant sea-dogs of the past. The smaller picture in this page shows an anti-tank gun in action.

Britain's Home Defences Were All Ready

Men of an infantry regiment on the machine-gun range at Aldershot. In this war more even than in the last the machine-gun is the principal instrument of mobile fire-power.

IN the interval that elapsed between the Crisis of September 1938 and that of a year later, Britain made vast strides in preparing for that war which all men of good will still believed might, and should, be averted. Conscription was introduced—an unprecedented step in peace-time so far as this country is concerned ; the Territorial Army was brought up to full strength and then doubled ; and in the field of A.R.P. gas-masks were distributed to all and shelters constructed in which the people might take refuge from air attack.

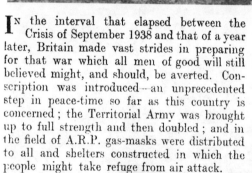

Here we have three pictures out of many illustrative of Britain's readiness to meet the emergency. Top left, even the hop-pickers went into the Kentish fields with their gas-masks. Centre, some of the new militiamen making the acquaintance in camp of a big gun. Below, baths in North London converted into a first-aid station, sandbagged as a safeguard against air attack.

Photos. Wide World. Topical and Fox

Britain's War Cabinet

Our Fate is in Their Hands

Rt. Hon. NEVILLE CHAMBERLAIN, P.C., M.P. Born in 1869, second son of Joseph Chamberlain, our Prime Minister was appointed Director-General of National Service in 1916. Postmaster-General in 1922, he was Minister of Health in three governments and Chancellor of the Exchequer in two before he succeeded Mr. Baldwin as Prime Minister and First Lord of the Treasury in 1937.

Rt. Hon. Admiral of the Fleet LORD CHATFIELD (right). Born in 1873, he entered the Navy in 1886. During the Great War he served as Flag Captain to Beatty in H.M.S. Lion during the action off Heligoland in 1914, the Dogger Bank action in 1915, and the Battle of Jutland in 1916. After commanding the Atlantic and Mediterranean Fleets, he became Chief of the Naval Staff in 1933 and in 1939 was appointed Minister for Co-Ordination of Defence.

Rt. Hon. LORD HANKEY (centre left). Born in 1877, Maurice Hankey during the Great War was Secretary of the War Cabinet and of the Imperial War Cabinet. Raised to the peerage in 1939, he became Minister without Portfolio in September 1939.

Rt. Hon. Sir KINGSLEY WOOD, M.P. (centre right). Secretary of State for Air since 1938, he was previously Postmaster-General and Minister of Health. He was born in 1881, and has been M.P. for Woolwich West since 1918.

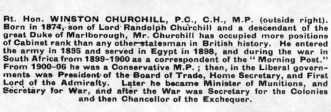

Rt. Hon. WINSTON CHURCHILL, P.C., C.H., M.P. (outside right). Born in 1874, son of Lord Randolph Churchill and a descendant of the great Duke of Marlborough, Mr. Churchill has occupied more positions of Cabinet rank than any other statesman in British history. He entered the army in 1895 and served in Egypt in 1898, and during the war in South Africa from 1899-1900 as a correspondent of the " Morning Post." From 1900-06 he was a Conservative M.P. ; then, in the Liberal governments was President of the Board of Trade, Home Secretary, and First Lord of the Admiralty. Later he became Minister of Munitions, and Secretary for War, and after the War was Secretary for the Colonies and then Chancellor of the Exchequer.

Rt. Hon. Sir SAMUEL HOARE (left). Born in 1880, he was Air Secretary in 1922, Secretary for India in 1931, and for Foreign Affairs in 1935. Home Secretary in 1937, in 1939 he became Lord Privy Seal.

Rt. Hon. LESLIE HORE-BELISHA, P.C., M.P. (centre). Secretary of State for War since 1937. He was Minister of Transport from 1934-37.

Rt. Hon. VISCOUNT HALIFAX, P.C. (right). Born in 1881, Edward Wood was appointed Viceroy of India in 1926 and elevated to the peerage as Baron Irwin. Returning in 1931, he is now Secretary of State for Foreign Affairs.

Rt. Hon. Sir JOHN SIMON (outside right). He became Foreign Secretary in 1931, Home Secretary in 1935, and Chancellor of the Exchequer in 1937.

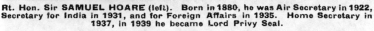

Photos, Wide World, Topical, Keystone, Bassano, Vandyk

The Children's Trek to Safety:

Among Britain's emergency preparations was the evacuation of large numbers of children, mothers, and sick and infirm folk from the overcrowded cities. These pictures illustrate the great move proceeding "according to plan."

The first stage to safety for many children was down an escalator to the Underground.

Photos, Keystone, L.N.A. and Fox Photos

Long before the state of emergency was declared, plans for the evacuation of urban children had been framed with the most careful precision. When "zero hour" came school-teachers marched with their classes to the trains, buses, coaches and steamers that had been provided for their transport, and without a hitch the vast exodus was carried through to a triumphant conclusion. By Saturday evening, the first day of the move, hundreds of thousands of boys and girls were settling down in their new homes in country villages and towns far removed from the danger zones in the congested cities.

In the top photograph hospital patients well enough to travel are being taken in one of the familiar "Green Line" coaches to peace and safety. In centre photograph mothers and children, with father carrying the baby, start out from Streatham on the first stage of their journey. Happiest of all, perhaps, were some thousands of children who made the journey to their new homes by steamer. Above, children are embarking on the Golden Eagle at Dagenham for transport to a safety zone.

A Triumph of British Civilian Organization

London children learn that ring-a-roses is an even happier game amid grass and trees than it is on an asphalt playground.

IN the four days ending Monday, Sept. 4, 650,000 schoolchildren and others were evacuated from Greater London. No tribute was more highly earned than that paid by Mr. Herbert Morrison, M.P., Leader of the L.C.C., to the splendid behaviour and bearing of the thousands of Londoners who had been concerned in the evacuation in various ways. In the great cities of the Provinces, too, there was the same story to tell of careful planning and complete success.

Evacuation of children north and south is shown in these two photographs. Left, three happy youngsters from Stepney, out of bed at 5 a.m., labelled and carrying full equipment, are ready for a great adventure. Right, children from a Northern evacuation area are being handed over to their temporary parents at Blackpool by those who have marshalled them from their homes. At the other end of their journey the children had a reception that justified their high hopes.

Photos: Keystone, Fox Photos and L.N.A.

The Dastardly Sinking of the 'Athenia'

Hardly had the world realized that war had again begun when it received with a thrill of horror the news that the German U-boats had claimed their first victim. Without a word of warning, a passenger liner was torpedoed and sent to the bottom, 200 miles from land. The crime is described below and in a later page.

O N the night of Sunday, September 3rd—the first night of the war, so far as Britain was concerned—the moon, rising above the sea some 200 miles beyond the Irish coast, looked down upon a scene of horror such as had not been witnessed since the close of the Great War. In the silvery waters a ship, mortally stricken, was sinking, while the sea about her was illumined by the flares borne by the boats lowered from her doomed shape.

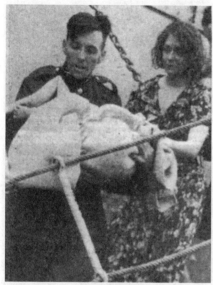

Pathetic scenes were witnessed at Galway as the Athenia survivors were landed.

A few minutes before, the Athenia had been pursuing a steady course en route from Belfast to Montreal. Her 1,400 passengers had been seated in the lounges or at the dinner tables, talking about the war which had so suddenly come upon the world, and fondly anticipating the reunion with their relatives and friends which they confidently expected in the course of a few days. Among them were several hundred Americans returning from their curtailed visits to London or Paris, and also many refugees who, fleeing from the terror on the Continent, were seeking in the New World that peace and security which had been denied them in their homeland.

Suddenly, as dusk fell, the ship shivered beneath a shock. Few could have guessed the cause of the explosion, but without a trace of panic passengers proceeded to their lifeboat stations.

They were not left long in doubt. According to several of the survivors who reported their experiences the next day, they saw a short distance away, emerging from the waters, the sinister hull of a submarine; it turned a gun on the ship and fired at her wireless . . . Within a few hours, then, of the opening of the war, the German U-boats had made their reappearance.

There ensued a succession of horrors, illumined by many a flash of human bravery and endurance. One by one the boats were lowered into the sea. In the hurry of the moment—perchance owing, too, to the list of the sinking vessel—some capsized, throwing their human load into the waters. From all sides came desperate shouts for help.

Meanwhile the ship's S O S signals had been received, and many a vessel hurried forthwith to the Athenia's rescue. About 2.30 on the Monday morning the steam yacht Southern Cross arrived and found that already the merchantman Knute Nelson was standing by and had rescued a number of passengers. Somewhat later three English destroyers dashed up at top speed and took part in the rescue operations.

All through the night and the hours of morning the Athenia settled in the water. At 10 a.m. her bow thrust itself into the air; then she sank into those waters which twenty years before had formed a grave for so many brave British ships.

When the survivors were landed they had much to tell of heroism of all who had played a great part in the ordeal.

"Marvellous crew, heroic passengers, perfect morale," was the general verdict. Yet they had, too, many stories to tell that were heartrending in their stark simplicity.

"One lifeboat turned turtle nearing the stern," said a message from the Southern Cross, "Our seamen rescued most. A man stood on the keel and dragged the drowning ones from the water. A young woman pulled from the water sat for a moment quietly in the rescue boat and then, screaming "My baby!" leaped into the sea.

"One boat was swamped near our bow. All hands were engaged in hauling aboard those from another one and we were helpless to save. Their screams were heartrending.

"Lifeboats were crammed to the danger point, many filling with water and people sitting waist deep.

"Many of the passengers were injured," went on the statement, "some seriously. A Russian Jewish couple, starting a new life in the United States, saw their two young sons drown when the boat capsized at the stern. . . .

"While the boats manoeuvred to come alongside a great school of whales plunged around them. Many women rowed along with the men 8–10 hours—many with clothing torn off, black with grease, barefooted, penniless, but answering with a smile after a night of horror without precedent."

The first victim of the German submarines in the war, T.S.S. Athenia was owned by Donaldson Atlantic Line, Ltd., of Glasgow, and was of 13,581 tons. She was built by Fairfields, of Glasgow, in 1923, and had recently been reconditioned and reconstructed on a large scale. She plied between Glasgow and Montreal.

France Takes Up The Challenge

Above is one of the latest type of French military aircraft, a Potez 662, with which France meets Germany's challenge in the air. Left is a French light tank advancing under the protection of a smoke screen.

Steel-helmeted and clad in the war-time uniform of horizon blue, these soldiers of France are marching through Paris during the 14th of July celebrations this year. The peace-time establishment of the French Army in 1938 was 676,000, but when, first, the manning of the Maginot Line, and then general mobilization was ordered, that figure was multiplied many times.

Photos, Planet News

War Strengths of the Allies and European Neutrals

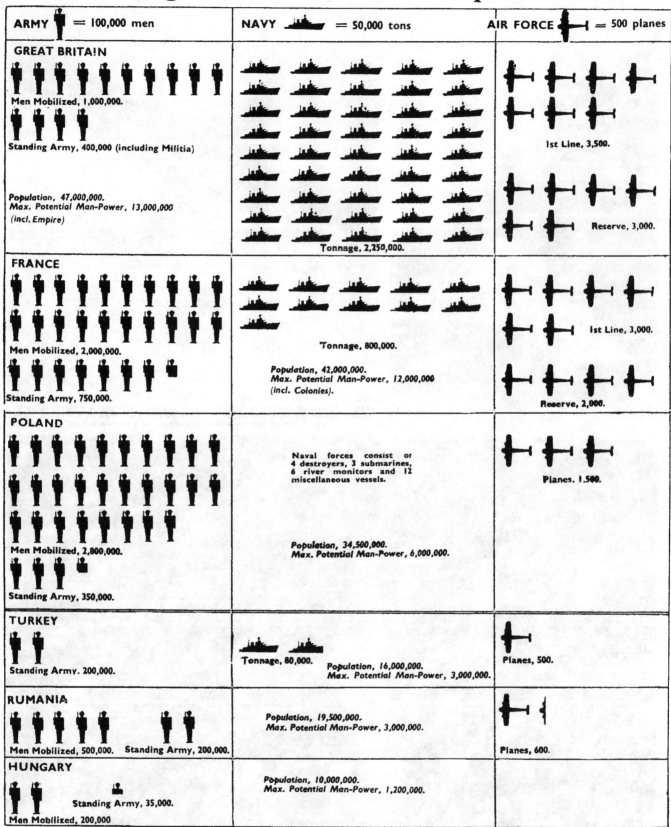

ARMY = 100,000 men   **NAVY** = 50,000 tons   **AIR FORCE** = 500 planes

GREAT BRITAIN

Men Mobilized, 1,000,000.

Standing Army, 400,000 (including Militia)

Population, 47,000,000.
Max. Potential Man-Power, 13,000,000
(incl. Empire)

Tonnage, 2,250,000.

1st Line, 3,500.

Reserve, 3,000.

FRANCE

Men Mobilized, 2,000,000.

Standing Army, 750,000.

Tonnage, 800,000.

Population, 42,000,000.
Max. Potential Man-Power, 12,000,000
(incl. Colonies).

1st Line, 3,000.

Reserve, 2,000.

POLAND

Men Mobilized, 2,800,000.

Standing Army, 350,000.

Naval forces consist of
4 destroyers, 3 submarines,
6 river monitors and 12
miscellaneous vessels.

Population, 34,500,000.
Max. Potential Man-Power, 6,000,000.

Planes, 1,500.

TURKEY

Standing Army, 200,000.

Tonnage, 80,000.   Population, 16,000,000.
Max. Potential Man-Power, 3,000,000.

Planes, 500.

RUMANIA

Men Mobilized, 500,000.   Standing Army, 200,000.

Population, 19,500,000.
Max. Potential Man-Power, 3,000,000.

Planes, 600.

HUNGARY

Standing Army, 35,000.

Men Mobilized, 200,000

Population, 10,000,000.
Max. Potential Man-Power, 1,200,000.

The picture diagrams given in the charts on these two pages show at a
glance the comparative fighting strengths by land, sea and air of the
countries illustrated. Each complete figure represents 100,000 men,
each ship 50,000 tons and each aeroplane 500 'planes.

Germany, Italy, Soviet Russia and the U.S.A.

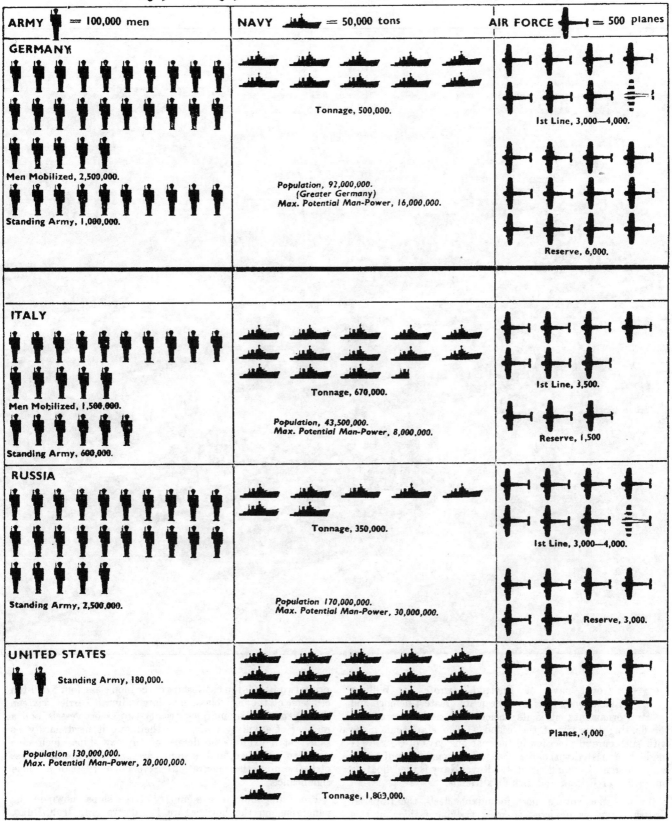

ARMY 👤 = 100,000 men

NAVY 🚢 = 50,000 tons

AIR FORCE ✈ = 500 planes

GERMANY

Men Mobilized, 2,500,000.

Standing Army, 1,000,000.

Tonnage, 500,000.

Population, 92,000,000.
(Greater Germany)
Max. Potential Man-Power, 16,000,000.

1st Line, 3,000—4,000.

Reserve, 6,000.

ITALY

Men Mobilized, 1,500,000.

Standing Army, 600,000.

Tonnage, 670,000.

Population, 43,500,000.
Max. Potential Man-Power, 8,000,000.

1st Line, 3,500.

Reserve, 1,500.

RUSSIA

Standing Army, 2,500,000.

Tonnage, 350,000.

Population 170,000,000.
Max. Potential Man-Power, 30,000,000.

1st Line, 3,000—4,000.

Reserve, 3,000.

UNITED STATES

Standing Army, 180,000.

Population 130,000,000.
Max. Potential Man-Power, 20,000,000.

Tonnage, 1,800,000.

Planes, 4,000.

Top, we see the strength of the German Reich (Greater Germany).
Next, her associated (but neutral) Axis power, Italy. Below are Soviet
Russia and the U.S.A. Exact figures of the fighting forces are not
available, but careful calculations provide serviceable comparisons.

BRITAIN'S ROYAL NAVY—The Floating

" THE royal navy of England," wrote Sir William Blackstone, "has ever been its greatest defence and ornament; it is its ancient and natural strength; the floating bulwark of the island." The statement made with such careful precision in the spacious days of George III might be repeated without a change in phrase or word today when George VI is king. Still the Royal Navy is the "floating bulwark" of Britain and Britain's friends.

What is the world's most formidable fleet—the Imperial British Navy—is depicted in most striking fashion in this panorama specially drawn for "The Daily Telegraph" by Dr. Oscar Parkes, the naval artist, and reproduced here through the courtesy of that newspaper. Most of the vessels depicted have already taken their place in the fighting line on the seven seas, and the remainder are approaching completion.

It should be noted that the illustration does not include any vessels of the 1939 construction programme, which com-

prises two 40,000-ton battleships of the Lion class, four 8,000-ton cruisers of the Fiji class, one large aircraft-carrier, sixteen destroyers, four submarines, twenty-two escort vessels, and a number of auxiliary craft. Furthermore, it need hardly be said that it exhibits no details of any new ships which have not been published, and in some cases, such as the Lion class of battleships, the illustrations have no more than a token significance.

Proceeding now to a summary of the ships shown in the panorama, on the horizon are 171 destroyers; **Iron Duke,** Jellicoe's flagship at the battle of Jutland (shown in the middle above the top line of ships in the left-hand section of the drawing), and depot ships.

A—51 minesweepers and patrol vessels.
B—39 escort vessels and two netlayers, Guardian (25) and Protector (26).

Next (**C, D, E, F**) ride serried columns of cruisers ranging from a few survivors of the Great War, of 1914–1918 programme, to the very latest types, e.g. the 10,000-ton Belfast

rk and Sure Shield of Our Land and Race

and Edinburgh, the 9,100-ton Southampton class, the 8,000-ton Fijis (which, despite very moderate size, mount twelve 6-in. guns), and the small but exceptionally powerful cruisers of the Dido group. On these cruisers largely depends the responsibility of ensuring the safety of our trade routes in war-time.

The cruisers in line **C** are—1, **Despatch**; 2, **Diomede**; 3, **Delhi**; 4, **Dunedin**; 5, **Durban**; 6, **Danae**; 7, **Dauntless**; 8, **Dragon**; 9, **Enterprise**; 10, **Emerald**; 11, **Adventure** (minelayer); 12, **Cardiff**; 13, **Calcutta**; 14, **Carlisle**; 15, **Capetown**; 16, **Curlew**; 17, **Coventry**; 18, **Cairo**; 19, **Curacoa**; 20, **Colombo**; 21, **Ceres**; 22, **Caradoc**; 23, **Calypso**; 24, **Caledon.**

In line **D** all the cruisers are building excepting Edinburgh, Belfast, and Adelaide.

The next line, **G**, comprises battleships and carriers (all building). Two new battleships of the Lion class, each of 40,000 tons (to be armed with 16-in. guns): these were recently laid down; the five almost equally powerful ships of the King George V type (35,000 tons, ten 14-in. guns), launched this year; and the huge 23,000 tons group of aircraft-carriers known as the Illustrious class—**Illustrious, Victorious, Formidable, Indomitable** and **Implacable**—each capable of taking to sea between sixty and seventy aircraft.

H—In this line are the five Queen Elizabeth battleships which have been practically rebuilt: **Warspite, Malaya, Barham, Valiant** and **Queen Elizabeth**; the aircraft-carriers **Ark Royal, Furious, Courageous, Glorious, Eagle,** and other smaller vessels of the same type.

I—Here will be observed the outlines of the battleships **Nelson** and **Rodney**, the five sister ships of the Royal Sovereign class: **Royal Sovereign, Royal Oak, Revenge, Resolution,** and **Ramillies**—with the battle-cruiser **Hood** (still the world's largest man-of-war, 42,100 tons), and her modernized consorts **Repulse** and **Renown**, and submarines and monitors.

J—Patrol vessels, destroyers, escort vessels and gunboats.
K—Escort vessels, minesweepers and minelayers.

The personnel of this mighty force reaches an establishment of about 135,000, a figure unmatched by any other navy in the world, and it may be said in every confidence that, though our ships are no longer " hearts of oak," still today, as in all the centuries of the past, " hearts of oak are our men."

Drawing reproduced by permission of " The Daily Telegraph "

Danzig and the Men Who Betrayed It

Above is the scene at a sitting of the Senate of the Free City of Danzig, a body consisting of 12 members, the highest State authority, which was eventually usurped by the Nazi party. In this photograph are Herr Greiser, Dr. Grossman, and other Senators.

Situated at the mouth of the Vistula, great river of Eastern Europe, stands Danzig, the city which was the final objective in Hitler's campaign of aggression. For centuries it has been a centre of economic life. Danes, Pomeranians, Prussians, Brandenburgers and Teutonic Knights have held it in turn, but from the Middle Ages until the infamous partitions of Poland at the close of the 18th century, it was a Free City under Polish control. With truth did Frederick of Prussia declare that he who ruled in Danzig was more the king of Poland than the sovereign in Warsaw.

For a short time during the Napoleonic age it was a dukedom, but with the collapse of Napoleon's empire it was returned to Prussia. It was the capital of West Prussia until 1919. At Versailles the treaty-makers resolved that the ancient Free City centre should be re-established under the League of Nations.

Above, left, is a main street in Danzig showing Nazi flags flying from most of the buildings in August, as a result of the National Socialist domination of the city. Centre, two men of the Danzig Heimwehr stand beneath the true flag of the " Free City," before its independence was destroyed. Below, right, is a portion of the defences of Westerplatte, near Danzig, which was so heroically defended by the Poles.

Photos, Keystone, Wide World

Warsaw: First Victim of the New Nazi Ruthlessness

Situated on the left bank of the Vistula, Poland's capital city boasts of many splendid buildings, relics of the country's past or creations of the bustling present. Above we have a view of the city as one approaches from **Praga**, the suburb on the opposite bank.

For most of the world the news of the bombing of Warsaw was the first indication that Germany had rejected the method of conciliation and had let loose the thunderbolt of war. These pictures show (left) one of the fine new buildings in the Napoleon Platz, and (right) a scene in the Ghetto.

Photo, Wide World, Dorien Leigh & Wide World

Poland Resolute Against the German Might

IF you want a symbol of Poland in arms you will find it not in speeding aircraft, marching masses of infantry, rumbling tanks and mechanized artillery, but in a trooper of the national cavalry. Alert, swift-moving, ready for every eventuality, quick to seize every change in a changing situation—such is the man and the men on whom Poland depends in her hour of supreme crisis.

Poland's horsemen have ever been famous for their dash and gallantry, and their prowess is recorded in letters of gold in their country's history. Today, as always in the past, Poland's cavalry is the backbone of her army.

If it is thought strange that in this age of petrol and machinery a nation should rely for the mobility of its armed forces on the horse, we should take a look at the map. Physically speaking, indeed, Poland has no well-marked boundaries save in the south-west, where a range of mountains separates her from Slovakia.

Marshal Smigly Rydz, the Generalissimo of the Polish Army, is a soldier of international reputation to whose great abilities the efficiency and preparedness of the Army are due. He has been nominated by President Moscicki as his successor should the office become vacant before the end of the war.

equal to none. In the air the excellence of her position is not so marked, but even so her air force has an estimated strength of 2,500 planes, and in particular the Polish standard bomber can carry 2½ tons at a top speed of over 300 miles per hour.

The Polish army actually numbers just over a quarter of a million men, but there are three million trained reserves. Furthermore, owing to the extraordinary youthfulness of the Polish population as a whole, the country could ultimately mobilize an army of six million men of military age.

Although Poland is presumed to possess nothing in the nature of a Maginot or Siegfried Line, practically all her big towns are armed camps or the centres of fortified systems.

Elsewhere her boundaries are drawn across a vast plain largely roadless, and marked in many a place by lakes, woods and great expanses of marshland. In the midst of such watery wastes mechanical fortresses, stiff with guns and heavy with armament, might well be worse than useless. Their speed would be cut down to a minimum, and the danger of bogging would confront them at every turn. How different, however, is the position of a cavalry force in such a region—a force which can take advantage of every little area of firm ground! Poland's cavalry, equipped with sword, lance and machine-guns, is said by some best qualified to know to be the best in Europe.

But Poland has not neglected her other arms. She has tanks of excellent quality and high performance, and her infantry —recruited from a race of hard-working, long-enduring peasants—can march 30 to 40 miles a day, and have a courage

Poland mobilized with a complete calmness that was the surest sign of the stern determination of every Pole to fight and win. In the top photograph young Poles are reading the proclamation that calls them to the colours, while in the lower one a young Polish woman slips an " emergency ration " into her husband's pocket as he goes off to the front.

Photos, Keystone, and Planet News

A "flying unit" of the Polish Army is seen above moving up to the front on August 28, when Hitler had already begun to provoke those "frontier incidents" which disclosed his real intentions towards the Polish State.

Forts and armaments and huge resources in man power are not everything, however. There must in addition be that indefinable something that we very inadequately suggest when we use the word *morale*. Where that something resides is difficult to define, but at least it may be said to be personified in the country's leaders—in those men who have the control of the Republic. Poland is particularly fortunate in that her leaders at the present hour of testing are all men who have been through the fires of adversity and know from actual experience what war means, how it should be carried on, and how victory may be won. Pilsudski, the father of the Republic, is dead, but his mantle has fallen upon his able lieutenant, Marshal Smigly Rydz, who today, as Inspector-General of the forces, is in effect the supreme controller of Poland's destinies in peace and war. Surrounding him are many men of great ability and courage.

Surveying, then, the armed forces with which Poland is meeting the furious menace from beyond her borders, remembering her past history of vicissitudes crowned by ultimate triumph, and realizing the inspiration afforded by tried and trusted leaders, we may well believe that she may face the brutal challenge to her existence with the confidence born of material strength and spiritual resolve.

The two photographs above show Poland's preparedness. In that in the middle of the page heavy mechanized artillery is moving into action. Immediately above is a magnificent array of Polish cavalry. The Poles are great horsemen and Poland is a great horse-breeding country. Early in the war the Polish cavalry achieved conspicuous success against the invaders of their country. Though cavalry is still an important part of the Polish Army, it is retained only because of special conditions, and mechanization has been carried out in every branch where it is advantageous.

Photos, Wide World, Associated Press and Planet News

ODD FACTS ABOUT THE WAR

Grey Hairs for the Firing Line

" I watched columns of older reservists march to the trains that were to carry them to points near the Polish border. There was no flag waving, no military bands. The men shambled along dejectedly. Bald heads were seen all along the line, and no one in the ranks was without greying hair. One man in five seemed to have a snow-white head."

(Berlin Correspondent in *News Chronicle*, August 28.)

Death Penalty Threat

The German broadcasting stations announced as soon as war began that it was a punishable offence to listen-in to French broadcasting stations.

Anyone doing so, or passing on information picked up from French broadcasts, was liable to a death penalty, it was announced.

German Radio Sets Confiscated

All radio sets in Germany have been banned and will be confiscated, with the exception of the small "people's sets," which can only get local stations.

Heil Frieden !

There were remarkable scenes at Liverpool Street Station on August 26 when four trains carrying nearly 800 people left for the Continent. Altogether, between 1,500 and 1,800 foreigners left during the day. Most of them were Germans who had been advised by their Embassy to leave.

The one topic of conversation as the trains stood waiting in the platforms was the common hope for peace. There were no cries of " Heil Hitler " as the train drew out. Instead, there were calls of " Heil Frieden "— hail peace.

Ration Cards in Germany

Rationing of many foodstuffs, as well as of textiles and boots and shoes, was introduced by decree on August 27, and cards have been distributed throughout Germany.

Food will be distributed in the following quantities per head each week : Meat, 25 oz. ; butter, margarine or oil, 15 oz. ; sugar, 10 oz. ; jam, 4 oz. ; coffee or coffee substitute, 2 oz. ; tea substitute, ¾ oz. ; milk, 2½ pints ; and soap, 1 oz.

Eggs, potatoes and bread, which are on the cards, are not strictly controlled for the moment. Cocoa is also free.

Women Rush to Join Up

A one-way traffic system had to be put into operation in the corridors at the Women's Voluntary Service headquarters in S.W. London because of the rush of the women to join up.

Woes of the Hausfrau

" The German woman wears clothes made of ' spun-wood,' that is to say, artificial wool made from wood pulp. A skirt looked nice enough until you had sat on it for an hour or two, but then there were creases like railway lines. And woe betide a ' spun-wood ' suit that got caught in the rain ! Sheets are a problem in Germany today ; wash them gently and all is well, but boil them—and they become soup ! The girls in the shops warn you not to iron these sheets and dresses with an over-hot iron, and on no account to boil them."

(An Englishwoman resident in Berlin—in *Daily Mail*, August 29, 1939.)

Don't Forget the Poor Majorities !

It has become a widespread habit in post-War Europe to give more attention to minorities than to the poor old majorities, which, after all, are also there. Of the 35,000,000 of Poland, 25,000,000 are the purely Polish majority. Of the remainder, most are Jews and Ukrainians, who hate the Nazi menace as least as much as the Poles themselves.

(A. T. Lutoslawski, in *Daily Mail*, Aug. 23.)

Pilsudski said—

To be vanquished and not surrender is victory.

He Wants to Understand Us !

" The Chancellor has courageously put aside the encirclement machinery and has once more revealed the wider background which culminates in the untiring endeavour for a lasting Anglo-German understanding."

(*Hamburger Fremdenblatt*.)

Poland, Nation of Youth

Poland has now a population of 35,000,000, an increase of 8½ million (nearly half a million a year) since the Great War. Of European countries this is by far the highest birth-rate. As a consequence Poland has a very low average age.

India's Loyalty

Leading Indian Princes have offered to place at the disposal of the King-Emperor all the resources of their States.

The Maharaja of Bikaner stated :

" It can safely be predicted that the Princes of India will rally like one man round their beloved King-Emperor and stand solid behind the Empire should war unfortunately break out."

The Viceroy, the Marquess of Linlithgow, has received from the rulers of States in all parts of India assurances of loyalty in the event of war.

The first ruler to place his troops and resources unreservedly at the disposal of the King-Emperor was the wealthy Nizam of Hyderabad, whose State is as large as Italy. Others who followed included the Maharajas of Travancore, Kashmir, Bikaner, Kapurthala and Jind.

The Nawab of Rampur, who recalls the example of his forefathers at the time of the Indian Mutiny and the Great War, proudly offers his personal services as a soldier.

Wish Fulfilment ?

A loose-leaf atlas is widely advertised in Germany. Purchasers are given coupons which entitle them to free new maps of greater Germany when the boundaries are altered. (*Sunday Express*.)

Mind the Pitch !

One of the nicest of A.R.P. stories has cropped up. It illustrates this England, this British way of doing things.

In a certain suburb, an A.R.P. expert with wide experience of trench and bomb shelter systems noticed some young men digging a straight trench alongside some playing fields. It was to be a refuge in case of sudden air raids.

My friend pointed out that the blast of a bomb at either end of the trench would immediately kill all occupants. He told them that the best way to construct such a trench would be to use the traverse or gridiron system. One of the diggers thought for a moment, then replied :

" But, old boy, that would spoil the football pitch ! " (*Star*.)

Nazi Cold-bloodedness

" It is the crowded quarters which will suffer the most from bombing. Those quarters, however, are inhabited by those who have not succeeded in life—the refuse of the community in fact, which would be well rid of them. Besides, the explosions of the bombs will inevitably cause many cases of madness. The person whose nervous system is deficient will not be able to survive the shock. In this way, bombing will help us to discover the neurasthenics in our community and to remove them from social life."

Archiv der Gesellschaft für Rassenbiologie, Berlin (Race-biology laboratory).

(*News Review*, August 18, 1938.)

Japan is Shocked

Japan is not inclined to arraign or condemn Germany, who is dead to moral sense and who justifies any Machiavellian makeshift for safeguarding her national existence.

It would be the height of folly for Japan to attempt to blame such a country for a breach of faith. (*Chugai Shogyo Shimpo*)

Man Goes Back to the Melting Pot

" By some power deeply seated in our nature and over which we seem to be powerless, we, after two centuries of enlightenment, have been thrust back, with all our load of knowledge and equipment upon us, into a dark age which will require deep thinking, resolute action, endurance and courage if the world is to find a fortunate exodus from the Egypt in which it now is."

(Sir Arthur Keith in *Sunday Times*, Aug. 27.)

Plenty of " Living Space " in Prussia !

Herr Koch, Nazi district leader in East Prussia, has declared that his province, whose present population is 2,500,000, needs an increase of 2,000,000 inhabitants. This, in spite of the fact that, since 1933, several hundred thousand workers have been brought in to staff the 157 new factories established during the same period.

Germans Mustn't Get Dirty !

The new German rationing regulations issued on August 29 extend to many household commodities. For instance, one stick of shaving soap must last five months, while all toilet soap has to be reserved for infants under two and for those in unavoidably dirty occupations. The general public is warned to avoid getting dirty unnecessarily.

That Sinking Feeling

" The Germans have always known that they are expert in violence but amateurs in psychology. This knowledge tempts them to bluff and bluster in hope of assuaging the pangs of self-distrust. Thus, even while they rejoice at Herr von Ribbentrop's diplomatic victory, they will retain an uneasy feeling inside."

(Harold Nicolson, M.P., in *The Times*, August 30.)

Chamberlain Loquitur

I labour for peace, but when I speak unto them thereof, they make them ready for battle—(Psalm 120).

Britain's Agriculture

As far as agriculture is concerned, Great Britain is in a vastly better position than she was in 1914. We have about a million more cattle, 1,250,000 more sheep, 1,300,000 more pigs, and many millions more poultry than we had then.

Moreover, by skilful breeding and feeding, the production per animal has been greatly increased, cows, for example, yielding at least 50 per cent more milk than in 1914.

Our 4,000 acres of sugar beet in 1914 has grown to 345,000 acres. 18 sugar beet factories last season produced nearly 6 million cwt. of sugar.

The number of farm horses has decreased, but their place has been taken by about 50,000 land tractors and hundreds of thousands of lorries.

Spain Keeps Out

Italian hopes that Spain might serve her as a base, or even as an ally, have foundered. Germany's cynical embrace of the Bolsheviks, who organized and largely reinforced the Spanish Revolution, has so shocked the new Nationalist Government of Spain that its sentiments towards both its recent allies have become " A plague on both your houses."—

(*Daily Mail*.)

The Armed Forces of Germany Advance

This gas-masked German rifleman has been dropped from a 'plane by parachute. Many such men were landed behind the lines in the invasion of Poland.

In the army of Nazi Germany as in that of the Kaiser the infantry march the goose-step way.

Rumbling over the roadless plain (left) goes one of the guns of a German heavy howitzer battery, its crew riding in comfort on the limber. In the picture on the right we see the new German bombing 'planes—the twin-engined all-metal Dornier DO.17, well named the "flying pencil." Note the bomb-aimer's compartment in the floor of the nose.

Photos, Camera Talks and Associated Press

HITLER'S SIX-YEAR CAMPAIGN OF LIES

No British statesman knows Hitler so well as Mr. Chamberlain, and we have it on his authority that Hitler's "word is, for us, not worth the paper it is written on." Below are some of the most outstanding instances of the Fuehrer's breaches of faith.

Amongst the last pictures to leave Germany before the war is this, Hitler addressing the Reichstag in the Kroll Opera House, Berlin.
Wide World

1933

May 17. In a Speech to the Reichstag, Hitler said :

Germany will tread no other path than that laid down by the treaties. The German Government will discuss all political and economic questions only within the framework and through the treaties. The German people have no thought of invading any country. **On October 14 Germany left the League and the Disarmament Conference.**

On March 10, 1935, General Goering made known the existence of a German Air Force, the constitution of which had been forbidden by the Peace Treaty.
On March 16, 1935, Hitler decreed Conscription in Germany, also forbidden by the Peace Treaty.

1934

Jan. 30. From Hitler's Speech in the Reichstag :

After this question (the Saar) has been settled the German Government is ready to accept not only the letter but also the spirit of the Locarno Pact. **In March, 1936, Germany denounced the Locarno Pact by reoccupying the demilitarized zone of the Rhineland.**

1935

May 21. In a Speech to the Reichstag, Hitler declared :

The German Government has broken away from the discriminatory articles of the Treaty, but it herewith solemnly declares that these measures relate exclusively to the points which involve moral and material discrimination against her people. It will therefore respect unconditionally the articles concerning the mutual relations of nations in other respects, **including the territorial provisions, and** will bring about the revisions inevitable in the course of time **only by the method of peaceful understandings.**

1936

Jan. 30. In a Speech at Berlin, Hitler said :

Germany will be a lover of peace such as only a peace-loving nation can be.

March 7 :
Germany denounced the Treaty of Locarno and reoccupied the demilitarized Rhineland zone.

On the same day, Hitler declared to the Reichstag :

Germany will never break the peace of Europe. After three years I can regard the struggle for German equality as concluded today. We have no territorial demands to make in Europe.

We are aware, above all, that all the causes of tension which arise as a result either of faulty territorial provisions or of a disproportion between the size of populations and their living space **cannot be solved by means of war in Europe.** At the same time we hope that human wisdom will help to mitigate the painful effects of these conditions and to remove causes of tension **by way of gradual evolutionary development in peaceful collaboration.**

1937

Jan. 30. In a Speech to the Reichstag, Hitler declared :

The period of so-called surprises is now over . . . **PEACE IS OUR DEAREST TREASURE.** . . . As an equal state Germany is conscious of its European task to co-operate loyally in removing the problems which affect us and other nations.

1938

In the agreement reached with Dr. Schuschnigg at Berchtesgaden on Feb. 12, Hitler reaffirmed his recognition of Austrian sovereignty, already expressed in the Austro-German Agreement of July, 1936.
On March 11, Germany annexed Austria.
The disparity between the declarations of May 21, 1935, and the events of March 11, 1938, prompted M. Mastny, the Czecho-Slovak Minister in Berlin, to convey to Field-Marshal Goering on the same evening the apprehensions of the Czecho-Slovak Government. Field-Marshal Goering immediately assured him that Germany had no hostile intentions against Czecho-Slovakia. "I give you my word of honour," he said, "and I can add that we wish only for better relations."
On March 12 Baron von Neurath informed M. Mastny officially in the name of the Reich Chancellor that Germany had no hostile intentions towards Czecho-Slovakia. He alluded to the interest taken by Germany in the Sudeten Germans, but at the same time expressed the hope that "this domestic question of the Czecho-Slovak State" might be satisfactorily settled.
Baron von Neurath also referred to the Treaty of Arbitration concluded in 1925 between Germany and Czecho-Slovakia as part of the Locarno Pacts. This treaty had been specifically recognized as still valid by the Reich after the Locarno Pacts were disavowed by Herr Hitler. An attempt was later made by the Czecho-Slovak Government to invoke it, but it was then denied in Germany that it was still binding.

On March 13 M. Mastny received a fifth assurance from Field-Marshal Goering that Germany had no hostile intentions against Czecho-Slovakia. With the consent of the German Government these assurances were communicated by Mr. Chamberlain to the House of Commons on March 14.
On Sept. 24 Germany sent her seven-day ultimatum to Czecho-Slovakia, which led to the Munich Conference of Sept. 29/30.

Sept. 26. Speaking in Berlin, Hitler said :

And now the last problem which must be solved confronts us. It [i.e. the claim for the Sudeten lands] is the last territorial claim that I have to make in Europe, but it is one I will not renounce . . . I assured Mr. Chamberlain that after this there would be no more international problems. I promised afterwards that if Herr Benes would settle peacefully his problems with the other minorities, I would even guarantee the new Czech State. We do not want any Czechs. Our demand for the Sudetens is, however, irrevocable.

Oct. 9. Speaking at Saarbrücken, Hitler said :

Now as a strong State we can be ready at any time to pursue a policy of understanding with surrounding States. We can do this because we want nothing from them. We have no wishes, no claims. We want peace.

1939

Jan. 30. Speaking in the Reichstag, Hitler said :

Only the warmongers think there will be a war. I think there will be a long period of peace.
On March 15 Bohemia and Moravia were declared German protectorates, after a threat that otherwise Prague would be mercilessly bombed.
On March 23 it was announced that Memel had returned to Germany.

After Czecho-Slovakia and Memelland came the turn of Poland. After the signing of a non-aggression pact with Poland in January, 1934, Hitler had said:

I sincerely hope that our new understanding will mean that **Germany and Poland have definitely abandoned all idea of a resort to arms,** not for ten years only, but for ever . . .

Furthermore, in May 1935, he declared :

Germany has reached a non-aggression pact with Poland which she will keep blindly, and which she hopes will be prolonged constantly, and will lead to more and more friendly relations . . . **Germany has nothing to gain by a European war. We want peace . . .**

Again on February 22, 1938, in a speech to the Reichstag, he stated :

We are sincerely satisfied about the friendly rapprochement which has taken place in recent years between ourselves and Poland . . . Since the League has ceased its disturbing interference in Danzig, this most critical spot for the peace of Europe has lost its danger. Poland respects German claims on Danzig, and the Free City and Germany respect Polish rights.

Nevertheless, on Sept. 1, 1939, Danzig was declared part of the German Reich and POLAND WAS INVADED BY GERMANY.

THE TWO 'SCRAPS OF PAPER'

One ' scrap of paper ' brought Britain into the last war—a written engagement that Germany refused to believe that Britain would keep. Another, signed only in September, 1938, was the ' No More War ' Anglo-German declaration, now thrown on to the scrap-heap of false hopes and broken promises.

ON the evening of August 4, 1914, Germany's Chancellor and Britain's Ambassador in Berlin met at the Chancellery to discuss the situation which had arisen as the result of German violation of Belgian territory. German troops had crossed the frontier that very morning ; Britain, true to her pledged word, had delivered what was in effect an ultimatum making it plain to the Imperial Government that unless they gave an assurance by 12 o'clock that night that they would proceed no farther with their violation of the Belgian frontier and stop the advance of their invading army, she would be forced to take such steps as her engagements required.

Herr von Bethmann Hollweg was agitated, even distraught. Sir Edward Goschen, too, was excited. Both felt themselves to be in the grip of a fast-moving fate. As soon as Goschen entered

everything "had tumbled down like a house of cards."

Sir Edward Goschen retorted that if the Chancellor wished him to understand that for strategical reasons it was a matter of life and death to Germany to advance through Belgium and so violate the latter's neutrality, so it was a matter of life and death for the honour of Great Britain that she should keep her solemn engagement to do her utmost to defend Belgium's neutrality if attacked. That solemn compact simply had to be kept, or what confidence could anyone have in engagements given by Great Britain in the future ?

When Belgium Was Violated

There was no need to say what that " solemn compact " was. Bethmann Hollweg, from his long experience as German Chancellor, could not but be well aware of the existence of the Treaty of April 19, 1839, which, establishing peace between Holland and Belgium, also declared Belgium's status as an independent and permanently neutral kingdom. To that Treaty were appended the

signatures of the representatives of Great Britain, France, Prussia, Russia and Austria. By the very first article of the Treaty the five Powers guaranteed the neutrality of Belgium.

Signed and ratified in good faith, honourably maintained for three-quarters of a century, this was the pact which Bethmann Hollweg scornfully referred to as " a scrap of paper."

' No More War '

During the Crisis of 1938, the first act in the tragic drama of Czecho-Slovakia's downfall, Germany and Britain were once again within an ace of war, when for a space peace was saved. The Prime Minister came back from Munich, and as he issued from his 'plane at Heston on September 30 he waved a piece of paper to the cheering crowd that greeted him. This paper bore the words : " We are resolved that the method of consultation shall be the method adopted to deal with any other questions that may concern our two countries, and we are determined to continue our efforts to remove possible sources of difference and thus to contribute to assure the peace of Europe," and to it were attached the signatures of Adolf Hitler and Neville Chamberlain.

But after 1938 came 1939 ; after Munich, Prague ; after Prague, Danzig . . .

And thus the " No more war " promise of September 1938 is just another scrap of paper. When shall the word of a German ever again be trusted ?

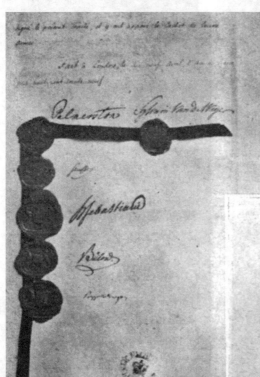

the Chancellery, the German Chancellor began a harangue which lasted for some twenty minutes. He said " that the step taken by the British Government was terrible ; just for a word, a mere word—' neutrality,' a word which in war-time had so often been disregarded—just for *a scrap of paper* Great Britain was going to make war on a kindred nation who desired nothing better than to be friends with her."

For years, he continued, he had directed his policy towards a better understanding between Germany and Britain, and now

We, the German Führer and Chancellor and the British Prime Minister, have had a further meeting today and are agreed in recognising that the question of Anglo-German relations is of the first importance for the two countries and for Europe.

We regard the agreement signed last night and the Anglo-German Naval Agreement as symbolic of the desire of our two peoples never to go to war with one another again.

We are resolved that the method of consultation shall be the method adopted to deal with any other questions that may concern our two countries, and we are determined to continue our efforts to remove possible sources of difference and thus to contribute to assure the peace of Europe.

September 30. 1938.

Here are illustrated the two "Scraps of Paper" referred to above. The first is the Treaty of April 19, 1839, guaranteeing the neutrality of Belgium ; among the signatures may be seen those of Lord Palmerston, Britain's representative, and Bülow, who signed for Prussia. On the right is the document which Mr. Neville Chamberlain brought back from the Munich Conference ; above the Premier's signature is that of Adolf Hitler. Both documents were treated as mere scraps of paper when it suited Germany to do so.

*Right-hand photo,
Wide World*

These Men Sought War

Paul Joseph Goebbels, Reich Minister of Propaganda and supreme master of German press and radio. He practises his master's doctrine, "The bigger the lie the greater its value."

Joachim von Ribbentrop, Germany's Foreign Minister, was for a time the Reich's Ambassador at the Court of St. James's.

Adolf Hitler, born an Austrian, became the apostle of Pan-Germanism. Chancellor of the Reich since 1933 he has established his power on the doctrine of the Mailed Fist. (Below) Party leader Rudolph Hess has from the early days of the Nazi movement been Hitler's most trusted adherent.

Field-Marshal Hermann Goering was recently nominated by Hitler to be his successor as Fuehrer of the German Reich.

Photos, Wide World, Associated Press, Mondiale

Heinrich Himmler is the dreaded head of Hitler's secret police, the Gestapo. His system of espionage reaches into every house in Germany.

And These Are They Who Sought Peace

King Leopold of the Belgians broadcast a memorable appeal for sanity and reason to the whole world.

Neville Chamberlain, Britain's Prime Minister, comes first among those who made a noble stand for peace.

Pope Pius XII exerted all his great spiritual authority in appeals for "justice and charity."

Signor Mussolini, speaking for Italy, made great efforts for appeasement until the last moment.

Queen Wilhelmina of Holland joined in the appeal of King Albert and the Oslo Powers to Hitler.

In 1939, as in 1938, President Roosevelt voiced the feelings of America in his appeals to Germany.

Photos: Wide World & Speaight

WORDS THAT HISTORY WILL REMEMBER

A Record of the Vital Declarations and Solemn Statements of the World's Leaders

Wednesday, Aug. 23, 1939
King Leopold of the Belgians :

Broadcasting in the name of the King of Denmark, the President of Finland, the Grand Duchess of Luxemburg, the King of Norway, the Queen of Holland, and the King of Sweden he said :

"The world is living in such a period of tension that there is a risk that all international cooperation should become impossible. . . . Lack of confidence reigns everywhere. But there is no people which wants to send its children to their deaths. . . .

"We want peace with respect for the rights of all nations. It is our wish that the differences between nations should be submitted to conciliation in a spirit of goodwill. . . . Let those in whose hands rests the destiny of the peoples apply themselves to settle peacefully the differences which separate them."

After the announcement of the German-Soviet Pact the British Cabinet announced that " such an event would in no way affect their obligation to Poland which they have repeatedly stated in public and which they are determined to fulfil."

Thursday, Aug. 24
Mr. Chamberlain in House of Commons :

"The international position has steadily deteriorated, until today we find ourselves confronted with the imminent peril of war. . . . Nothing that we have done, or that we propose to do, menaces the legitimate interests of Germany. It is no act of menace to prepare to help friends to defend themselves against force. . . .

"War between our two countries, admitted on all sides to be the greatest calamity that could occur, is not desired either by our own people or the German people. We do not think of asking Germany to sacrifice her national interests, but we cannot agree that national interests can only be secured by the shedding of blood or the destruction of the independence of other states. . . .

"We want to see established an international order based upon mutual understanding and mutual confidence, and we cannot build such an order unless it conforms to certain principles which are essential to the establishment of confidence and trust. These principles must include the observance of international undertakings when they have once been entered into, and the renunciation of force in the settlement of differences. . . .

"If, despite all our efforts to find the way of peace, we find ourselves forced to embark upon a struggle which is bound to be fraught with suffering and misery for all mankind and the end of which no man can foresee, if that should happen, we shall not be fighting for the political future of a far-away city in a foreign land ; we shall be fighting for the preservation of those principles of which I have spoken, the destruction of which would involve the destruction of all possibility of peace and security for the peoples of the world. . . .

The Rt. Hon. Arthur Greenwood in House of Commons :

". . . The peril of war comes not from us. No democratic country will make war, but Britain, with others, will defend their own liberties and the liberties of those who are threatened by force, realizing that a threat to the liberty of one is a threat to the liberty of all. The aggressor must know that in our view liberty, like peace, is indivisible. . . ."

Friday, Aug. 25
President Roosevelt's appeal to Hitler :

"To the message which I sent you last April

I have received no reply, but because my confident belief that the cause of world peace—which is the cause of humanity itself—rises above all other considerations, I am again addressing myself to you, with the hope that the war which impends and the consequent disaster to all peoples may yet be averted. . . .

"The people of the United States are as one in their opposition to policies of military conquest and domination. They are as one in rejecting the thesis that any ruler or any people possess the right to achieve their ends or objectives through the taking of action which will plunge countless millions into war, and which will bring distress and suffering to every nation of the world, belligerent and neutral, when such ends and objectives, so far as they are just and reasonable, can be satisfied through the processes of peaceful negotiation or by resort to judicial arbitration. . . ."

Saturday, Aug. 26
President Roosevelt's second appeal to Hitler :

"Countless human lives can yet be saved, and hope may still be restored that the nations of the modern world may even now construct the foundation for a peaceful and happier relationship if you and the Government of the German Reich will agree to the pacific means of settlement accepted by the Government of Poland."

M. Daladier's Letter to Herr Hitler :

". . . up to the present there has been nothing which could prevent a peaceful solution of the international crisis with honour and dignity for all people if there is an equal will to peace on both sides. . . ."

Herr Hitler's Letter to M. Daladier :

"Danzig and the Corridor must return to Germany. The Macedonian conditions at our Eastern frontier must be removed. I see no way of being able to persuade Poland, which shields itself from attack under the protection of its guarantees, to accept a peaceful solution. But I would despair of an honourable future for my people if, in such circumstances, we were not determined to solve the question in one way or another."

Nothing in the Commons debate on September 1 gave such intense satisfaction as the forthright speech of Mr. Arthur Greenwood, Acting Leader of the official Labour Opposition.

Tuesday, Aug. 29
Mr. Chamberlain in the Commons :

"The British people are said sometimes to be slow to make up their minds, but having made them up they do not readily let go."

Friday, Sept. 1
Mr. Chamberlain in the Commons :

"No one, I think, can say that the Government could have done more to try and keep open the way for an honourable and equitable settlement of the dispute between Germany and Poland. Nor have we neglected any means of making it crystal clear to the German Government that if they insisted on using force again in the manner in which they had used it in the past we were resolved to oppose them by force. Now that all the relevant documents are being made public we shall stand at the bar of history knowing that the responsibility for this terrible catastrophe lies on the shoulders of one man. The German Chancellor has not hesitated to plunge the world into misery in order to serve his own senseless ambition. . . .

"It appears to the Governments of the United Kingdom and France that by their action the German Government have created conditions—namely, an aggressive act of force against Polish territory which threatens the independence of Poland—calling for the implementation by the Governments of the United Kingdom and France of the undertaking given to Poland.

"Unless the German Government are prepared to give his Majesty's Government satisfactory assurances that the German Government have suspended all aggressive action against Poland, and are prepared promptly to withdraw their forces from Polish territory, his Majesty's Government in the United Kingdom will, without hesitation, fulfil their obligation to Poland. . . .

"We have no quarrel with the German people except that they allow themselves to be governed by a Nazi government. As long as that government exists and pursues the methods it has so persistently followed during the last two years there will be no peace in Europe. . . ."

The Rt. Hon. Arthur Greenwood in House of Commons :

". . . I now reaffirm for the third time in this House during the present crisis that British labour stands by its pledged word. At whatever cost, in the interests of the liberty of the world in the future we are to use all our resources to defend ourselves and others against aggression. . . .

"Herr Hitler has put himself grievously in the wrong. He has become the arch-enemy of mankind. He has been guilty, not merely of the basest and gravest treachery to this Government and this people, but he has been guilty of the basest treachery to all peoples to whom in the past he has given promises.

"I never thought that I should quote from a document of which Herr Hitler was the author, with approval, but in the proclamation to the army which he issued at six o'clock this morning, he said : ' In order to put an end to this lunacy I have no other choice than to meet force with force from now on. . . .'

"I was glad when the Prime Minister used words which I have used in our official declaration—' We have no quarrel with the German people,' but while we have no passion against the people we shall enter this struggle with a grim determination to overthrow and destroy that system of government which has trampled on freedom, crucified men and women, and which has brought the world back to the jack-boot of the old Prussian régime."

[*Further Declarations and Statements appear in later pages.*]

Slavs and Slaves Shake Hands

In a last effort at intimidation, Hitler broke completely with his traditional policy and allied himself with the " Bolshevik murderers " he had so often denounced.

Josef Stalin, Secretary-General of the Russian Communist Party, as seen by the cartoonist of ' Vu,' the Paris journal.

For years—since, indeed, the launching of the Nazi Party—Hitler, by written word and word of mouth, has declared in the most unequivocal fashion, the irreconcilability of German Nazism and Russian Bolshevism.

Turning the pages of " Mein Kampf," you will not go far before you find some expression of the Fuehrer's hatred of all that Bolshevism is and stands for. With passionate fervour he warns the German people never to forget that the pestilence which rots Russia is one that hangs perpetually over Germany, too. He paints the Bolshevists as vile and bloody tyrants—men who, favoured by circumstances, in a tragic hour for Russia, for Europe and for humanity, were enabled to overrun a great State, massacring in the process millions of their countrymen. Never (he says) in the whole of history,

has there been a terror so horrible as that which was set up in Russia. And it goes without question that directing this Terror are members of that race which combines the most bestial cruelty with enormous skill in lying—the Jews !

In his speeches, too, Hitler has been at no pains to give expression to the belief that Nazism and Bolshevism are ideological opposites. At Nuremberg, in September, 1936, he said that : " We see in Bolshevism a bestial, mad doctrine which is a threat to us. In the past Bolshevism tried to work on our territory just as it is now trying to push its military forces ever closer to our frontiers. We exterminated Bolshevism on our own ground. We warded off the attempt to infect Germany from Moscow."

On February 22, 1938, he said that with one country " we have refused to enter into relations. That State is

Soviet Russia. We see in Bolshevism the incarnation of human destructive forces." At the Nuremberg Congress of 1938 he declared that " the danger of Bolshevist destruction in other nations is towering over our world more menacingly than ever."

The Anti-Comintern Pact made by Germany, first with Japan and then later with Italy as well, was regarded in Moscow as a direct threat to Soviet Russia. In the Spanish Civil War German airmen, troops, and technicians helped General Franco to save Spain from what Hitler declared in his address to the returning warriors was " the fire of a revolution fanned by international forces, which was intended to lay not only Spain, but Europe, in dust and ashes."

We can thus understand the gasp of amazement which went round the world when on August 21, 1939, it was an-

WHIPHAND

Low's masterly cartoon in the London " Evening Standard " well suggests the way in which the blindfolded German masses are being driven by Hitler like slaves to the slaughter. Below, Stalin and von Ribbentrop are shaking hands after they had signed the German-Soviet Pact— the Pact in which two great peoples were treated as mere pawns in the game of high politics.

nounced that Germany and Russia were to sign a pact of non-aggression, and that von Ribbentrop would proceed to Moscow on August 23 for that purpose.

So complete a reversal of policy was almost without precedent in history.

Some said that the Pact demonstrated that Nazism and Bolshevism were but different faces of the same thing. Others saw in it a clumsy attempt by the Nazi diplomatists to frighten Britain and France from implementing their agreements with Poland.

If this were indeed the reason, it failed in its object. The Nazis forgot that to the Democracies treaties are solemn obligations, and policy has its foundations in something more substantial than the shifting sands of a temporizing diplomacy.

Germany on the Eve of the Nazi Betrayal

WHEN, a week before the invasion of Poland, the correspondents of the British Press were withdrawn from Berlin, a curtain descended upon Germany, cutting it off, as it were, from the outside world. Occasionally it was moved by the breath of rumour, but it was lifted only when a traveller returned to Britain with the stories of what he had heard and seen.

Judging from these first-hand reports, Germany was not so much surprised at learning that she was on the verge of war as stunned. " People with anxious faces stood at street corners talking in whispers," said Mr. William Hood, who reached London after a 42-hour train journey from Munich. " During the previous two weeks no one seemed to believe that war with Britain would really come. The sudden darkening of the city, the train delays, and finally the news of mobilization, came as a shock to people informed of world events only by state-controlled newspapers and radio."

Colonel T. F. Tweed, Mr. Lloyd George's political officer, who returned to England after a 3,000 mile tour of Germany and Austria, said that " the most eloquent summing-up of the situation was made by a professor at an ancient university town with the remark : ' The German people do not wish for war, but no longer do we decide such things for ourselves ! ' "

The most vivid picture of Germany on the eve of war was given by Miss Virginia Cowles, special correspondent of the " Sunday Times," who left Germany on the afternoon of Saturday, September 2nd, after a flying visit to Berlin. Writing on that day she said that the great majority of the German people did not even then believe that the German attack on Poland

would lead to a world war. The morning papers had carried no news of the British and French ultimatum, but had printed only some obscure paragraphs referring to the general mobilization. When she crossed into Holland from Germany at noon, not one of the throng of Germans on the platform was aware of the probability that in a few hours Germany would be at war with Britain and France.

A black-out on the preceding night had flung a heavy cloak of war over Berlin, but there was still a general feeling that Hitler would pull off the Polish coup just as he had done in the case of the Anschluss and the dismemberment of Czechoslovakia.

Hitler's announcement in the Reichstag that Danzig was now German created an atmosphere of unmistakable alarm, and his radio address in which he declared his

intention of subduing Poland by force was greeted by a surprising lack of enthusiasm. Only two or three hundred people gathered in the square before the Chancellery to cheer him as he appeared on the balcony dressed for the first time in the field grey of the German Army, his face tense and unsmiling.

" We got back to the hotel," says Miss Cowles, " to find waiters and porters whispering together in low, strained voices. When I asked one of the men if he was not aware of the fact that Germany had precipitated a world war, he looked at me in despair, and said, ' Mein Gott, I hope not ; I had four years in the last one and that was enough ! ' "

As she left Berlin, Miss Cowles carried with her an impression of a city which was like an armed camp—a city whose foreboding atmosphere was accentuated by the silhouettes of men mounting the anti-aircraft guns on the roofs.

" We roared towards Cologne through a silent and darkened Germany in which all the lights were extinguished and the blinds had been drawn." The Germans in the compartment were only mildly apprehensive. One of them explained that Britain would not be so foolish as to risk a world war ; suggestively he drew his finger across his neck and said, " After we cut Poland's throat we will all settle down to peace."

His attitude of easy optimism was, however, the exception.

" One's reaction of Germany on the eve of a great war," concluded Miss Cowles, " is that one is torn between pity and horror. One is struck by the tragedy of a great people living in a vacuum of ignorance, and appalled by the gangster philosophy of the Third Reich."

Above, the Reichstag Deputies are seen assembled in the Ambassadors' Hall of the New Chancellery in Berlin on August 27, acclaiming the Fuehrer when he made his last warlike speech four days before he invaded Poland. The top photograph shows the type of gas mask now used by the civil population of Germany.

Photo, Wide World

The Audacious Raid—R.A.F. Bombs German Fleet

Hardly had a state of war between Britain and Germany come into operation when on Sept. 4 the R.A.F. began its offensive. Sweeping across the North Sea, bombers raided the German fleet and did damage to an extent surpassing far that which would have satisfied their most ardent hopes.

DISPLAYING that audacity and dash which characterized their predecessors of the last war, the R.A.F. commenced hostilities against Germany with a lightning raid on the German fleet in its harbours at Wilhelmshaven, Cuxhaven and Brunsbuttel at the entrance of the Kiel Canal.

Their work was well done, for the official communiqué issued after their exploit records that several direct hits with heavy bombs were registered on a German battleship in Schilling Roads, off Wilhelmshaven, which resulted in severe damage, while at Brunsbuttel the attack was carried out on a battleship lying alongside the mole, again causing heavy damage. It should be added that the operation was carried out in very unfavourable weather conditions, and that the attacking aircraft had to meet both air attack and heavily concentrated anti-aircraft fire. Small wonder that in the circumstances some of the raiders failed to return.

The daring exploit reminds us of one of the first of the innumerable gallant episodes in the history of Britain's airforce. It was on Christmas Day of 1914 that nine British seaplanes, with some submarines in support, made a raid on the German base at Cuxhaven. So small and low-powered were the seaplanes of those days that they could not be relied upon to fly across the North Sea, let alone take with them a supply of bombs, however light. Hence the 'planes were carried most of the way across the water in three cross-Channel steamers, Engadine, Riviera and Empress, each of which had been fitted up to carry seaplanes.

By 6 a.m. on Christmas morning, the little flotilla had reached a position twelve miles north of Heligoland, and an hour later seven of the seaplanes flew off to their destinations. The other two, however, failed to take off, and their flights were consequently abandoned.

The remaining five sped across the sea to the German coast. Heavy frost and fog on land made bombing difficult, and what was worse, by the time the missiles had been dropped upon the objectives, fuel was running short. The attacking 'planes turned about to return to their parent ships. Only three of the pilots returned at once, though the others were picked up later—three by a British submarine and another by a trawler.

This air attack was not directed against the German High Seas Fleet, for such small bombers, however intrepidly flown, could not hope to damage to any worthwhile extent the enormous fleet that Germany had built in readiness for "Der Tag." The actual objective was to destroy Zeppelins—then the only enemy aircraft that could reach England and return—some of which were housed in sheds at Cuxhaven. A reconnaissance of German harbours was another object, and in this the raid was more successful than in destroying the Zeppelins.

Today it is a very different story, for serious damage to two ships out of a fleet that can boast only two battleships of 26,000 tons and three "pocket battleships" of 10,000 tons each, may justifiably be described as a major naval disaster.

Here is the scene of the first exploit of the R.A.F. in the war—the Kiel Canal. The photograph was taken from the deck of a German warship, perchance one of the vessels which were seriously damaged by the bombs dropped by the audacious invaders.
Photos, Keystone and E.N.A.

Above is the Deutschland at Brunsbuttel. She is one of the "pocket battleships" of 10,000 tons which Germany laid down in 1929. She is armed with nine 11-inch and twelve 6-inch guns. Left, a map of the area and places raided on Sept. 4, 1939.

Our Diary of the War

Wednesday, August 23, 1939

German-Soviet Pact of Non-Aggression signed in Moscow by Von Ribbentrop and Molotoff, in presence of Stalin.

Sir Nevile Henderson, British Ambassador to Germany, delivered to Hitler a message from the British Government and a personal letter from the Prime Minister.

King Leopold of Belgium broadcast an appeal for peace to all nations on behalf of seven small states.

Thursday, August 24

The King arrived in London from Balmoral and held a Privy Council.

Parliament met and passed the Emergency Powers (Defence) Act.

President Roosevelt sent an appeal to King Victor Emmanuel, urging the calling of a peace conference.

The Pope broadcast an appeal for peace.

Von Ribbentrop returned from Moscow and immediately saw Hitler.

British subjects warned to leave Germany.

Herr Forster proclaimed himself Head of the State of Danzig.

Friday, August 25

Sir Nevile Henderson called on Hitler at the latter's request, as also did French, Italian and Japanese envoys.

Hitler cancelled Tannenberg celebrations.

Anglo-Polish Agreement of Mutual Assistance signed in London.

Mussolini was twice in telephonic communication with Hitler.

President Roosevelt sent messages to Hitler and Polish President urging settlement of differences by direct negotiation, arbitration or conciliation at the hands of a disinterested Power.

Germans advised by their Embassy to leave Great Britain.

German merchant ships ordered by their Government to remain in or return to German ports.

Saturday, August 26

Sir Nevile Henderson flew to London with a message from Hitler. The reply was considered at a meeting of the Cabinet at which Sir Nevile was present.

Hitler received the French Ambassador after day of consultation with his advisers.

The Nazi Party "Congress of Peace" at Nuremberg was cancelled.

Germany gave assurances of respect for the frontiers of Belgium, Holland and Switzerland.

Further messages exchanged between Hitler and Mussolini.

Roosevelt made a second appeal to Hitler for the maintenance of peace, enclosing the reply from the Polish President.

Sunday, August 27

The Cabinet met to consider the reply to Hitler's proposals.

Hitler rejected a proposal from M. Daladier that one more attempt should be made at direct negotiation between Germany and Poland. At the conclusion of the letter Hitler made the clear demand that Danzig and the Corridor must return to the Reich.

Rationing introduced in Germany.

Admiralty assumed control of British merchant shipping.

The entire German-Polish frontier was closed to railway traffic.

Stated that France now had about 3,000,000 men under arms.

Monday, August 28

British Government's reply to Hitler was delivered to him by Sir Nevile Henderson.

Defence Regulations, made under the Emergency Powers (Defence) Act, were issued by the Stationery Office.

The Mediterranean was closed to British ships on orders from the Admiralty.

Government of Holland ordered the mobilization of the Army and Navy.

Fall of Japanese Cabinet.

Tuesday, August 29

Hitler handed to Sir Nevile Henderson his reply to the British note, making at the same time verbal explanations. The reply was immediately transmitted in code to London. It was stated in Berlin that the British proposal of direct negotiation between Germany and Poland had been accepted provided that a Polish plenipotentiary arrived in Berlin within 24 hours.

At a brief sitting of both Houses of Parliament, statements on the crisis were made by Lord Halifax and the Prime Minister.

Germany occupied Slovakia as a "protection" from the Poles. Poland issued a protest.

The diplomatic representatives of Great Britain, France and Poland accepted an offer of mediation made jointly by Queen Wilhelmina and King Leopold.

Wednesday, August 30

The Poles declined to send a plenipotentiary under menace.

The Cabinet considered Hitler's last communication and sent a reply to Berlin, which was handed to Von Ribbentrop shortly after midnight by Sir Nevile Henderson.

Hitler issued a decree setting up a Council of Ministers for the Defence of the State. Field-Marshal Goering was appointed chairman and invested with very wide powers.

Thursday, August 31

The Soviet-German Pact was ratified by the Supreme Council in Moscow.

The German Government broadcast a 16-point plan for a settlement with Poland. In spite of the fact that this was the first time that the Polish Government heard of them, it was stated that the German Government had waited in vain two days for the arrival of a Polish negotiator, and therefore considered that the proposals had been rejected.

British Fleet mobilized.

French railways under military control.

The Pope made a new peace appeal, notes being handed to all envoys of foreign countries attached to the Holy See.

Friday, September 1, 1939

Poland was invaded by German forces from East Prussia, Slovakia and the main body of the Reich in the early morning. No declaration of war had been made.

Britain and France delivered final warnings to Hitler to withdraw from Poland.

General mobilization proclaimed in Britain and France.

Statements on the German invasion of Poland were made in both Houses of Parliament. In the Commons war credits totalling £500,000,000 were voted. A number of emergency measures were passed through all their stages.

President Roosevelt appealed to Great Britain, France, Italy, Poland and Germany to refrain from bombing civilians and unfortified towns, and received assurances from Britain, France and Poland. Italy replied that she was not concerned, as she was remaining neutral.

Hitler, addressing the Reichstag, gave his reasons for the invasion of Poland, and subsequently a Bill entitled "The Law for the Reunion of Danzig with the German Reich" was passed with acclamation.

The evacuation of British school children from exposed and congested areas was begun, and nearly 500,000 were moved.

The Government took over control of the railways.

Saturday, September 2

Mr. Chamberlain announced in the House of Commons that Germany's delay in replying to the British warning might be due to consideration of a proposal, put forward by Mussolini, for a Five-Power Conference.

The British and French Governments consulted on the question of a time limit for Hitler's reply.

Bill for compulsory military service between the ages of 18 and 41 passed.

Fighting in Poland increased in intensity. Warsaw was bombed six times.

Hitler sent a favourable answer to Roosevelt's appeal against bombing open towns.

British Government received pledges of support from Canada, Australia and New Zealand and from 46 Indian rulers.

Berlin officially denied that either gas or incendiary bombs had been used during raids on Polish towns.

Sunday, September 3

A final British note was presented in Berlin at 9 a.m. giving Hitler until 11 a.m. to give an undertaking to withdraw his troops from Poland.

At 11.15 Mr. Chamberlain, in a broadcast to the nation, stated that "no such undertaking had been received and that consequently this country is at war with Germany."

The French ultimatum, presented at 12.30 p.m., expired at 5 p.m.

The German reply rejected the stipulations that German troops should withdraw from Poland, and accused the British Government of forcing the war on Germany.

Fierce fighting on both Polish fronts.

A War Cabinet of nine members was created, to include Mr. Churchill as First Lord of the Admiralty.

The King broadcast a message to his peoples.

Hitler left Berlin to assume command on the Eastern front.

German submarine torpedoed and sank without warning the British liner *Athenia*, 200 miles north-west of Ireland.

Roosevelt announced that U.S.A. would remain neutral.

Mr. de Valera announced that Eire would remain neutral.

Australia and New Zealand declared war on Germany.

Pronunciation of Polish Names

The correct pronunciation of Polish names is a matter of difficulty and frequent difference of opinion. Here from time to time we shall give the best approximate equivalents in English sounds of names of persons and places of immediate interest. Note that the stress is always on the last syllable but one.

Moscicki	..	..	*mosh-tsee-ski*	Katowice	*ka-to-vee-che*
Smigly-Rydz	..	..	*shmig-li ridz*	Westerplatte ..	*ves-ter-pla-te*
Skladkowski	..	..	*skwad-kof-ski*	Grudziadz ..	*groo-jonts*
Kasprzycki	..	..	*kasp-zheet-ski*	Cracow ..	*kra-kof*
Jaroslaw	..	..	*ya-ros-waf*	Czestochowa ..	*chan-sto-ho-va*
Dzialdowo	..	..	*jal-do-vo*	Chojnice ..	*hoy-neet-se*

SPECIAL SUPPLEMENT

The War Illustrated

Reference Maps

of

WARTIME EUROPE

Presented with No. One
of The War Illustrated

In this Supplement we present a large-scale map of Europe as it was at the outbreak of the War of 1939. This map (based by courtesy of " The Daily Telegraph " on one copyright by that newspaper) indicates the combatant Powers. Greater Germany, the Third Reich, is shown with a heavily shaded border, and includes all the countries and territories which have been added by force, or by threat of force, since the rape of Austria in 1938. Italy and Russia, which are in alliance or association with Germany, are shown with a light tint border. Panels in appropriate positions in the map give figures of the men mobilized, naval tonnage, aeroplanes and population of the seven countries directly concerned. For full details and comparisons in the form of picture diagrams of the fighting forces of the Allies, Germany, and other Powers, see pages 14 and 15.

It is of interest to note that the air distances between the various capitals and important towns on the Continent are as shown in the table below.

Approximate Air Mileage Between Capitals and Principal Towns

LONDON to:

Paris	205
Berlin	600
Cologne	310
Frankfort	400
Vienna	800
Prague	650
Lyons	480
Marseilles	660
Warsaw	950
Hamburg	460
Hanover	440
Rome	920
Budapest	920
Moscow	1,650
Belgrade	1,150

BERLIN to:

Rome	750
Prague	175
Budapest	450
Vienna	500
Bucharest	850

PARIS to:

Berlin	600
Amsterdam	260
Rome	700
Prague	580
Vienna	650
Warsaw	850
Leningrad	1,350
Moscow	1,600

ROME to:

Prague	600
Vienna	240

LENINGRAD to:

Moscow	400
Warsaw	600
Bucharest	1,100
Budapest	950
Berlin	850
Belgrade	1,100
Prague	1,000

On the last page of this Supplement is printed a special map of Poland on a large scale which includes the places of importance in the military campaign. Arrows indicate the main lines of the German invasion.

Based upon Maps prepared by Geographia Ltd., reproduced
by courtesy of " The Daily Telegraph."

'The War Illustrated' Map of WARTIME EUROPE

Prepared by Geographia, Ltd.

English Miles

Former Boundary of Czechoslovakia (PRE-MUNICH)

GREAT BRITAIN
Mobilized ... 1,000,000
Naval Tonnage ... 2,250,000
Aeroplanes ... 1st 3,500
Res. 3,000
Population ... 47,000,000

GERMANY
Mobilized ... 2,500,000
Naval Tonnage ... 500,000
Aeroplanes 1st 3,000 4,000
Pop.(Gtr. Germany) 92,000,000

FRANCE
Mobilized ... 2,000,000
Naval Tonnage ... 800,000
Aeroplanes ... 1st 3,000
Res. 2,000
Population ... 42,000,000

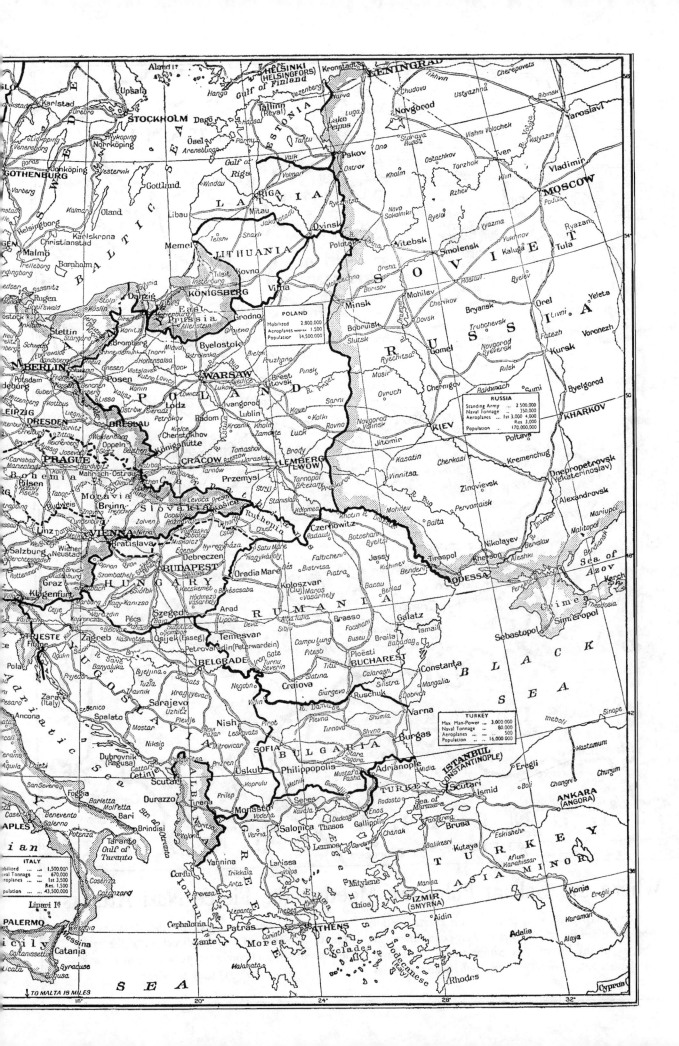

Where the Gallant Poles are Meeting the Fierce Nazi Attacks

This map is an enlargement with greater detail of the section of the main European map in pages ii and iii of this Supplement. It shows Poland, the Corridor west of Danzig, East Prussia, and the countries on the borders of Poland. Arrows indicate the direction of the early German attacks. Danzig territory is shown black.

Courtesy of "The Daily Telegraph"

Vol. 1 ## A Permanent Picture Record of the Second Great War **No. 2**

Carrying their rifles and machine-guns, these Polish infantrymen are typical of the army which is resisting the German invasion. "The Polish soldier," said Mr. Neville Chamberlain, "has ever shown himself to be a courageous and determined fighter, and today he is worthily maintaining this tradition. Against overwhelming superiority in the air, outnumbered and out-gunned, he is contesting every yard of the German advance."

Photo, Keystone

To Arms! Poland's Fair Lands are Invaded

Photo, Keystone

Iɴ the higher of the two towers of the old Gothic church of St. Mary in Krakow, rising 250 feet above the medieval houses, stands a sentry-box from which is sounded every hour a bugle call—a call which is suddenly interrupted. This "broken note" keeps ever fresh and green the memory of the brave Polish bugler who, in 1241, warned the inhabitants of the city of the impending approach of the Tartar hordes, and as he warned them, ere his call could be completed, fell dead with his throat pierced through by an arrow from a Tartar bow. But Krakow had heard the warning, and the invaders were repulsed with heavy loss.

In the seven hundred years which have passed since then, the bugle many a time has sounded the call to meet Poland's foes. Enemy after enemy has marched across the country's fair face, has ravaged and destroyed—and has at last been defeated and driven out.

Today the call sounds again. A new foe has swept across the frontier —this time from the west. Against tremendous odds the Polish army has fallen back, and Krakow hears once more the tread of enemy feet through her streets. But the indomitable spirit of the army, of the people, remains unsubdued.

In the past the Poles have survived invasion after invasion, internal intrigue and foreign war, partition by brute force and revolt savagely suppressed. Out of their present trials they will emerge—not alas! unscathed—but crowned with the laurels of victory.

Poland is not yet lost
While we are still living
That which foreign violence from us
  grasped
We shall re-take by the sword.

**From the Polish
National Anthem**

Magnificent Heroism of the Poles at Westerplatte

In accordance with a clause in the Treaty of Versailles, the Poles were allowed to establish a military base or munitions dump at Westerplatte, at the entrance of the harbour of the Free City of Danzig. The situation of Westerplatte between the Vistula and the Baltic is indicated in the adjoining sketch map, and above and below are photographs of the post.

Two signboards near Danzig. Who, before September 1, had heard of Westerplatte? Then, however, it became a synonym for Polish tenacity.

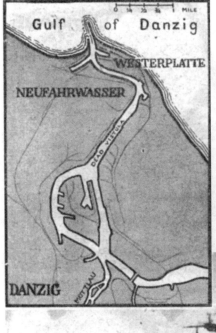

W HEN on the morning of September 1, 1939, Danzig was declared part of the German Reich, the company of Poles garrisoning Westerplatte refused to surrender, and for days they staunchly resisted furious attacks by enormously superior German forces operating by land, sea and air. "Soldiers of the Westerplatte," Marshal Smigly Rydz addressed them from Warsaw, "fight! You are fighting the fight of Poland. Poland watches your gallant struggle with pride. Fight for Poland to the last man." Not until the morning of September 7 did they submit.

In this dramatic photograph the German cruiser Schleswig-Holstein is seen bombarding a handful of Poles who, with the gallant audacity of their race, resisted for a week the furious onslaught of the German invaders. It was estimated that the land forces alone of the attackers amounted to a division, whereas the defenders numbered but a company all told. Not only by land and sea was the attack delivered; bombs were rained down from German 'planes, and the photograph was taken just after a bomb had been dropped.

Photos, Wide World, Paul Popper and Planet News

Retreat—But Fighting All the Way :

At the opening of the War the principal scene of operations was Poland, and here we give a picture-story account of the initial phase of that country's invasion by the armies of Nazi Germany.

This gas-masked spotter for a German anti-aircraft battery—such as is seen mounted on a raft in the photo on the right—searches the skies for signs of approaching Polish planes.

IT was at 5.30 on the morning of Friday, September 1, 1939, that the world was deeply shocked to learn Germany had begun hostilities with Poland by air attacks on Katowice, Krakow, and Teschen. There was no formal declaration of war, and the first indication that the Poles had that a state of war existed was the bombs which were rained down on their towns and means of communication. This was Hitler's first instalment of the " lesson " that he proposed, as he said, to teach the Poles.

Following the unheralded air attack, German troops entered Poland in many places, and by the evening it was reported that fighting was going on along practically the whole of the German-Polish frontier and Poland's frontier with Slovakia, now in German occupation. The main attack, however, was in the north, where armies advancing from Pomerania and East Prussia strove to cut off the Polish Corridor. At the same time there was an extensive drive into Upper Silesia, one of the principal centres of Polish industrial production.

Everywhere the Poles were outnumbered in troops and guns and 'planes. Fighting fiercely, they fell back to defensive positions which had already been prepared. There was fighting in Danzig, where the Polish officials had made a brave but vain stand at the post office and railway station ; and at Westerplatte, at the entrance of the harbour, a company of Polish soldiers refused to surrender. Gdynia, Poland's port on the Baltic, was bombarded from sea and air ; and

In the early hours of September 1, 1939, the first troops of the German army crossed the frontier in their invasion of Poland. The photograph above is one of the first to reach London from the scene of war, and shows a detachment of German soldiers marching along a main road in the invaded territory. The men, it will be seen, are little more than boys; and some, at least, of them are happily smiling.

Photos, Wide World and Planet News

Poland's Heroic Defence of Her Historic Land

Although heavily outnumbered and possessed of nothing comparable with the immense weight of armaments and mechanized material employed by the invaders, the Polish troops defended their homeland with the utmost tenacity. Step by step they contested the advance, and their cavalry broke through and harried the fast-lengthening lines of communication. Here are typical Polish troops on the move.

Photo, Planet News

in the cour e of the day Warsaw, the capital, was bombed six times by German 'planes:

The next day the news that Great Britain and France had declared war on the German aggressor was received with transports of joy in Poland, but its effect on the invader was to make him press on with ever greater pertinacity, with a view, no doubt, to crushing the Polish opposition before Poland's allies could bring effective help. On the country roads there was a continuous stream of troops going to the front, and another in the reverse direction of refugees from the towns which were being subjected to all the horrors of armed invasion. Here and there Polish cavalry promptly counter-attacked with good effect, but the fine weather and flat terrain were both to the advantage of the German mechanized armament and transports.

Three days after the invasion began, the Germans claimed the capture, after repeated bombings, of Czestochowa, the " Polish Lourdes," and Radomsko in Silesia, while in the north they claimed to have reached the Vistula and so to have cut off the Corridor from the Polish interior. Shortly afterwards German troops were stated to have captured Grudziadz (Graudenz) and Mlawa on the East Prussia side. Rapidly pressing on in the south-west, the Germans compelled the abandonment of Krakow and were converging on Warsaw. On September 6 the Polish government decided to remove the capital eastwards.

At the end of the first week of the war the Germans had seized almost the whole of Polish territory to the west of Warsaw, and they were converging on the capital from north, south, and west. Krakow had definitely fallen ; so, too, had Lodz, Tomaszow, Poznan, Torun, Grudziadz and Bydgoszcz (Bromberg). Moreover, the capital was so closely invested that there were reports of heavy fighting in the streets of the suburbs. Broadcasts, professing to emanate from the Warsaw wireless stations, later proved to be another instance of a German coup that failed.

Almost everywhere the Poles were in retreat : yet, despite the terrible pounding they had received from the German guns and 'planes, they showed no signs of demoralization. The enemy could claim comparatively few prisoners and it was admitted that the Polish army was not only intact, but was taking up strong positions on the country's traditional line of defence—that formed by the rivers Vistula, Bug, and San.

In their advance into Poland the Germans relied very largely on their tanks, an arm in which they had an immense superiority over the defending Poles. Even so, however, the Poles were not to be outdone, and they constructed in their defensive lines a large number of tank traps such as that illustrated on the left above. Composed of huge iron girders clamped together, these traps halted the progress of many a tank and so enabled them to be put out of action by the Polish anti-tank guns. Right, a large bridge blown up by the Poles in their retreat.

Photos, Planet News and Wide World

Warsaw, The Heart of Poland Beats True

Left, Colonel Beck, the Polish Foreign Minister, is shaking hands with Sir Howard Kennard, the British Ambassador, on the balcony of the Embassy at Warsaw after Britain had declared war. Below, crowds march through Warsaw with a banner bearing the inscription, "Cheers for England." Right, Polish soldiers with an anti-aircraft gun rangefinder.

The impressive poster reproduced above announces the successful mobilization of Poland's armed forces and illustrates, too, the country's strength in men, aircraft, guns and tanks. On the right is a portrait of the commander-in-chief of the Polish Army, Marshal Smigly Rydz. The literal translation of the wording is : " By order of the President of the Republic, M. Moscicki, and the War Minister, General Kasprzycki, general mobilization throughout Poland was declared. One hundred thousand men joined the regiments within one hour."
The slogan of the poster is : " Force which with strength attacks must be repulsed with equal strength."

Photos, Wide World, Plan News and Keystone.

On the Qui Vive for the German Raiders

Within a few hours of the opening of hostilities German 'planes were reported to have bombed Warsaw, and in the course of the next week the capital was again frequently bombed and a great number of other towns—many of which could not by any straining of words be called military objectives—were subjected to aerial bombardment. In the course of the invasion a great part was played by the German air force, in army co-operation work as well as in bombing raids on roads, bridges, and other targets. The Poles for their part were by no means inactive. In particular their anti-aircraft guns—one of which is seen here—brought down a number of invading 'planes.

Gamelin—Man of the Moment

Just as in the last war the French people looked up to " Papa " Joffre and to Foch, the Supreme Generalissimo, so today they put their trust in General Gamelin, who has the control of all the armed forces—on land and sea and in the air—of the Republic.

GENERAL MARIE GUSTAV GAMELIN was born in Paris in 1872, shortly after the France of the Second Empire had crashed into bloody ruin at Sedan. It is said that, as a child, he played with toy soldiers in his nursery, and today, when he attends a meeting of the Supreme War Council, he sometimes glances across the road at the house in which he was born.

The blood of soldiers flows in his veins, although in his early days he wanted to be a painter, and still today he is something more than a dabbler in water-colours. From the military academy at St. Cyr, the French Sandhurst, he went to the Chasseurs, and after a term of

service in Africa became military secretary to Joffre.

At the outbreak of the Great War in August 1914, he held a position on the Operations Branch of Joffre's staff. What happened then may be told in the words of " Pertinax," the distinguished French journalist, writing in the columns of the " Daily Telegraph " :

On the evening of August 25 there was a discussion regarding the proper course to adopt in order to stop the movement of the German army, then pointing towards the valley of the Oise and Paris, and threatening to outflank the French line on their left.

General Berthelot, Deputy Chief of the General Staff, declared himself in favour of a counter-attack directed towards the north-west and aimed at the inner (i.e. left) front of the enemy right wing, which was opposite the British divisions. As against this, Gamelin, speaking for the Operations Branch, maintained that the blow should be delivered externally, and the invader taken in the rear by an army gathered in the region of Paris and advancing north-eastwards. Joffre decided in favour of Gamelin, who drew up Order No. 2—the seed of the Victory of the Marne.

The operation, however, was not to be put into action before the French armies had retreated behind the Seine. On the morning of September 4, when the Operations Branch met, Gamelin, examining the map on which the positions of the various Corps were laid out, observed that they " capped " the German effectives—in other words, that a sort of circle seemed to be sketched automatically round them.

The favourable opportunity offered itself ; it was worth seizing without delay. The attack must be made at once, and the proposed recovery along the Seine put aside. Such is the story of the Order No. 6 of September 4, the order which led to victory—again the work of Gamelin's pen.

In the spring of 1918 he decided to leave the French G.H.Q. for the field, and he was given command of a Brigade of Light Infantry (Chasseurs) in Alsace, and later of the 9th Division. At the time of the great March offensive of 1918 Gamelin's single division held a front— if front it may be called—which gradually spread over eleven miles. In those terrible days of defeat and retreat, he was one of the last to yield ground.

After the war he held a command in Syria, and there again he achieved victory for France at a most critical moment, when with 5,000 men he annihilated a fanatical mob of 100,000 Druses.

Small of stature, with pink cheeks, reddish hair, steel-blue eyes and a crisp white moustache, he is a typical French soldier. He is always meticulously turned-out, with his many ribbons displayed and medals in his buttonhole. His favourite phrase is reported to be, " I am a philosopher." As Joffre said after the battle of the Marne, in which Gamelin had, as we have seen, played so valuable a part : " If this be philosophy, it is time that all generals were philosophers."

On several occasions General Gamelin, French Generalissimo, has paid official visits to England, particularly since it became apparent that the Franco-British cooperation of 1914-1918 might have to be repeated in face of the menace of Nazi aggression. Top, meeting General Lord Gort at Victoria Station, London, in the summer of 1939, and below, at Aldershot.

Photos, Keystone

Nazi Germany Feels the Invader's Tread

For some days after the outbreak of war it was "All Quiet on the Western Front," and when on September 4 the curtain was lifted by the French communique No. 1, it was to say that "Operations have been begun by the whole of the land, sea and air forces." In the days that followed it was officially announced that the French army had crossed the frontier in many places and that they were engaged in destroying the outworks of the Siegfried Line in "No Man's Land."

It was on the front between the Rhine and the Moselle that the French began the attack mentioned in their communiqué of September 4. As will be seen from the sketch map at the top of the page the sector includes the Saar basin, that district of Germany which from the end of the Great War in 1918 until 1935 was controlled by a Commission representing the League of Nations. In the district are Saarbruecken (bottom photo) and Neunkirchen (centre). Top, gunners of the French army which carried the war into the enemy's territory.

Photos: The Times, Topical and L.N.A.

'They Shall Not Pass!'—Thanks to Maginot

Top: These French soldiers, armed with light and heavy machine-guns and automatic rifles, are garrisoning one of the many strong points in the Maginot Line. The lower photograph shows great guns pointed menacingly towards the east. Below, left, soldiers leaving a fort entrance after their turn of duty.

FRANCE'S famous slogan of 1914–1918 is recalled in the statement that in the war of 1939 the fighting will be carried on on the German side of the frontier. That this is so is largely due to the work of André Maginot, the ex-serviceman who, as French minister of war, was responsible for the vast system of concrete and steel fortifications, above ground and below, which in honour of its initiator is called the Maginot Line.

What has been described as the greatest defence system ever built, the Maginot Line runs from Dunkirk to Switzerland, but its most important and strongest section is the lower half, from Luxemburg, eastward to the Rhine and thence along the great river to Basle. Its route is marked black in the sketch map above; facing it, shown shaded, is the German Siegfried Line, far inferior to it in plan and execution.

Photos, "March of Time," and map, courtesy of " The Daily Telegraph"

Germany's Vaunted Western Wall

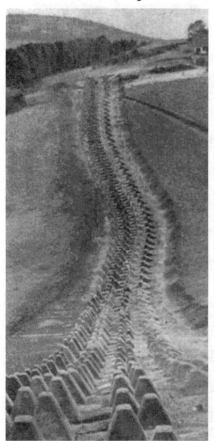

Built of heavily reinforced concrete with loopholes for machine-guns, this is one of the "air protection" towers with which the Siegfried Line is dotted.

Stretching in broad lines are cunningly devised anti-tank barricades, firmly anchored, f pyramid-shaped concrete ridges which foul the driving tracks of tanks.

Iɴ the summer of 1938 work was begun in real earnest on the construction of a vast system of fortifications on Germany's Western Front called the Siegfried Line. At Nuremberg on September 12, 1938, Hitler said that 278,000 workmen were then employed and boasted that before the following winter the vast wall of steel and concrete laid out in three, and partly in four lines of a total depth of up to 50 kilometres, with 17,000 concrete turrets, would be finished.

Taken within the Siegfried system of fortifications, on the German Western Front, this photograph shows Nazi troops about to set off to take their place in the concrete emplacements. In the background may be discerned evidences of building construction still in progress, for, unlike the Maginot Line on the opposing slopes, the Siegfried Line is but a recent and still uncompleted addition to the defences of the Reich.

Photos, Camera Talks and Keystone

In the Hour of Britain's Need and Danger

In the hour of national emergency and danger, religion makes an insistent appeal. This poster speaks for itself; it appeared on a notice-board outside a church in a south London suburb.

Nothing in the hour of crisis evoked such widespread and heartfelt admiration as the fine spirit displayed by the women who rallied to their country's service. Top, recruits to the Women's Land Army are cutting corn on a farm in Kent with a tractor-drawn reaper. Left above, lorry drivers of the First Aid Nursing Yeomanry (F.A.N.Y.) receiving a lesson. Adjoining, two London women air-raid workers, garbed in protective equipment, are on duty.

Air Raids and Warnings : Facts to Remember

From a letter to "The Times" by Brig.-Gen. Sir Henry Page-Croft, M.P., dated September 6.

Sir,—It is important that the technique of meeting enemy air raids should be as perfect as possible, and it is desirable that all citizens of London should realise that there is no possible danger to themselves from bombs until our anti-aircraft guns have been very definitely heard to be firing. The only possible exception to this would be in very rough or very cloudy weather should an enemy aircraft succeed in penetrating our magnificent defences without being observed.

We may take it, therefore, as almost certain that no citizen is in any danger until gun-fire has been heard. This gun-fire will be unmistakable, as there will be many short, sharp, loud barks from the guns, and if we are wise we will regard this as a joyous sound in that it indicates that our defences, so admirable in their preparation, are all at work. Shelter should, of course, be taken from the danger of splinters or fuses from our own shells when firing starts.

Citizens should also remember that should a bomber penetrate the defences

there will probably be at least 50 British anti-aircraft gun reports to one enemy bomb, and it is important that all should realise the loud friendly sound of the anti-aircraft fire as opposed to what will be a comparatively rare, deep, muffled rumbling of an exploding bomb.

The next thing we have to remember is that in the vastness of London the odds against a bomb reaching one's own immediate neighbourhood are very great, and to recall the comforting thought that in the whole three years of the war in Spain the total deaths of civilians from air attacks in no way equalled the number of deaths on the road in England due to motor-car accidents, while the number of injured in that prolonged war was only a small fraction of injured on our roads in a single year.

Once these facts are appreciated, it then remains important that Hitler should disturb our normal lives as little as possible, and it may be hoped, with improved experience, all-clear signals may come through more speedily. . . .

Yours, &c., HENRY PAGE-CROFT.

Standing in front of a shop window crisscrossed with white paper as a protection against flying glass, this newspaper seller's poster gives the tidings that our man-power will be fully mobilized.

Photos, Keystone, L.N.A., Fox, and Universal

These Were Ready on the Civilian Front

In times of war and crisis hospitals must continue in their healing work. Here are nurses of Middlesex Hospital, London, using mattresses to block up the windows as an air raid precaution.

NEVER has London transformed itself so completely and so suddenly as in the days immediately following Britain's declaration of war against Germany. In the Crisis of September of the year before Londoners had seen many preparations of a warlike character, but these were far outdone by those signs of war which were now to be seen on every hand. Many of the tube stations were closed; great heaps of sandbags appeared before the Government buildings and the larger offices and other places of importance; on every hand were seen signs indicating air raid shelters and auxiliary fire brigade stations, and one and all carried the little cardboard box containing his or her gas mask.

In the top photograph in this page women of London's East End are spending belated hours of summer in the open air making sandbags for use in national defence. The girls at the Serpentine lido in Hyde Park, seen in the lower left photo, are typical war-time bathing belles, 1939 pattern. The little fellow in the middle picture, though ready for all emergencies, is still determined to keep cool. On the right below we see Mr. and Mrs. Chamberlain walking across Horse Guards Parade on their return from their usual morning "constitutional" in St. James's Park.

Photos, Planet News, " Daily Mirror," and Keystone

Britain's Commanders by Land, Sea and Air

Above, General Sir Edmund Ironside, Air Chief Marshal Sir Cyril Newall and Admiral Sir Dudley Pound. Left, General Viscount Gort, V.C. — walking behind a Tommy who is blissfully unaware of the C.-in-C. !

Photos, Keystone and Fox

I N this war the leaders of Britain's fighting forces are all men who rendered distinguished service in the Great War of 1914–1918. Admiral Sir Dudley Pound, the First Sea Lord, was in command of H.M.S. Colossus at Jutland and has since commanded the Mediterranean Fleet. General Viscount Gort entered the Army in 1905. In France he won the M.C., the D.S.O. with two bars, and finally, in 1918, the V.C. Appointed Chief of the Imperial General Staff in 1937, he is now Commander-in-Chief of the British Expeditionary Force. The new C.I.G.S. is General Sir Edmund Ironside, who also has an inspiring war record. An infantry brigadier in France, he became Commander-in-Chief of the Allied troops at Archangel.

Air Chief Marshal Sir Cyril Newall has been Chief of the Air Staff since 1937.

When A U-boat Meets Its Doom

The first task of the Navy on the outbreak of war was to deal with the unrestricted submarine warfare which the Nazis entered upon in the vain hope of cutting off Britain's food supplies. Depth charges which proved so effective in dealing with U-boats in the last war are being used. When an enemy submarine is located, depth charges quickly dispose of it. These are cylindrical drums containing a high explosive, the detonating apparatus being actuated by the increasing pressure of water as the charges sink. When one explodes a huge column of water as seen above rises. Many depth charges are unloaded when a submarine is located, and each one is effective for nearly a hundred yards round the spot where it is dropped. Oil rising to the surface shows that the attack has been successful.

Photo, Fox

Poland's Army Takes the Field: These Are

In the photographs in this and the facing page we have glimpses of the Polish army as it is today. Above, a section of Polish infantry is advan-
under cover of smoke shells during manoeuvres carried out shortly before the war began. Below, a long line of Polish tanks is seen advancing in forma-
near the Polish-German frontier.

In peace-time the Polish army numbers somewhat more than a quarter of a million trained men, but there are in addition three million trained reser-
Furthermore, owing to the remarkable youthfulness of the Polish population, an army of six million could ultimately be mobilized. As the crisis
Danzig developed, the Polish authorities called up various classes of reservists; and shortly before the opening of hostilities all men up to the age of
had been called to the colours. It was estimated when the first shots were fired that the total Poland had under arms was about 2,800,000.

Photos, Keystone

n Who, Undismayed, Fought the Nazi Hordes

g to the nature of the Polish terrain—composed as it is for the most part of far-spreading plains interspersed with huge tracts of roadless marshland horse plays a far larger part in the army of Poland than in that of most of the other nations of Europe. Above, we see a Polish horse artillery battery galloping into action ; and below, the guns are moving into new positions.

for more than a hundred years—since, indeed, the days of Napoleon when the Duchy of Warsaw was resurrected as a component of the Napoleonic pire—has the country of Poland put into the field a really national army. During the Great War of 1914-18 many hundreds of thousands of Poles ed their part on the battlefields, but for the most part as soldiers of the warring empires—of Germany, Austria-Hungary, or Russia as the case might Only in the concluding months of the war did something in the nature of a truly Polish army develop—that army which, vastly increased in numbers and equipped with many of the new weapons of military action, set out in September, 1939, to meet the German onset.

We Were Victims of Nazi Frightfulness

In an earlier page (see page 12) we have already given some particulars of the dastardly sinking of the "Athenia," first victim of Nazi frightfulness on the high seas. Below is an amplified account supported by a number of first-hand survivors' stories

WHEN Mr. Winston Churchill, answering from his place on the Treasury Bench in the House of Commons questions directed to that Board of Admiralty of which he was head more than twenty years before—rose to make his second statement regarding the sinking of the "Athenia," he declared that it was now clearly established that the disaster was due to an attack without warning by a submarine.

"At 7.45 p.m. local time," he proceeded, "on the night of Sunday, September 3, a torpedo struck the ship abaft the engine-room on the port-side, when she was 250 miles north-west of the coast of Ireland. Soon after the torpedo struck the ship the submarine came to the surface and fired a shell which exploded on the middle deck. The submarine cruised around the sinking ship and was seen by numerous persons, including American survivors, a considerable number of whom—I think 12 or more—have given affidavits to this effect."

After a statement concerning the number of survivors who had been picked up by the rescue ships, the First Lord of the Admiralty went on to deny that the "Athenia" was defensively armed; on the contrary, not only did she carry no guns, but her decks had not even been strengthened for this purpose. A little later in the sitting Mr. Churchill said that it was quite clear that before the "Athenia" left on her peaceful mission, and before war was declared, the submarine must already have taken up her position waiting to pick up a prey.

Of the witnesses mentioned by Mr. Churchill to the fact that the "Athenia" was torpedoed, the first was the captain of the ship, Captain James Cook, who, in a statement, declared emphatically that: "There is no doubt about it, my ship was torpedoed. The passengers were at dinner at about 7.30 when the

Torpedoed without warning off the Irish coast, some 200 miles from the nearest land, the "Athenia" was the first victim of the Nazi U-boat campaign. These dramatic photographs show (above) a group of rescued officers on board the "Knute Nelson," a Norwegian merchantman which saved 430 people, watching their doomed vessel settling down in the water. (Top) A later view of the sinking "Athenia".

Photos : "Daily Telegraph."

They Were Survivors from the 'Athenia'

In the work of rescue of the survivors of the "Athenia," a prominent part was played by the Knute Nelson. Above, survivors just about to pass down her gangway; below, some of the injured

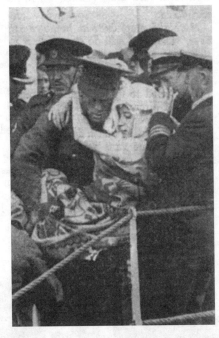

Photos, Fox and Wide World

torpedo struck the ship and the explosion killed several of them. The torpedo went right through the ship to the engine-room. It completely wrecked the galley. The submarine fired a torpedo and rose above the surface and fired a shell which was aimed at the destruction of the wireless equipment, but it missed its mark."

An officer of the " Athenia " said he saw the periscope of a submarine clearly, and also a line coming along the water as the torpedo approached the ship. Several members of the crew testified to the same fact. John M'Ewan said : " There was a great deal of smoke where the torpedo struck the ship, but through the smoke we could see the submarine break surface, and then, before we knew where we were, the commander had turned a gun on us."

Claud Barrie, a bedroom steward, said that he was in the pantry helping the waiters when there was a violent explosion. " The lights went out, the ship gave a lurch. I am an old soldier, and at once smelt cordite. ' It can't be,' I thought to myself, but my mate said, ' The swine has hit us.' The ship suddenly took a list. We ran to the alley-ways to warn our passengers and then up on deck in time to see the periscope of the submarine disappear."

Then one of the Czech refugee boys on board described in graphic fashion how he saw a submarine suddenly come up some distance away. " There was a column of water near the ship, and a black thing like a cigar shot over the sea towards us. There was a bang, and then I saw men on the submarine turn a gun and fire it."

In the light of statements such as these, it is difficult to understand the pertinacity with which the German authorities maintain that the " Athenia " could not have been sunk by a German

submarine, and that if it had been sunk by a submarine at all it was probably a British one !

In our earlier account of the torpedoing of the ship we gave an impression of the terrible hours that followed, as the boats overloaded with passengers rowed here and there across the open sea. When the survivors were landed by the rescue ships—the three destroyers, the Norwegian merchantman " Knute Nelson," the Swedish yacht " Southern Cross," and the American steamer " City of Flint " —at Galway and Greenock, there were heart rending scenes. Many were so injured that they were hurried by waiting ambulances to hospital; most of the others who were able to go to the hotels had black eyes, cut cheeks, bruised arms and legs. Some had been injured when

lifeboats were caught in a swell and dashed against the side of a rescue ship : others had crashed into bulkheads as they hurried to lifeboats or made for the boat stations. Several of those who were picked up died before landing.

Many of the women and children were in clothes borrowed from men in the destroyers; several had still their night-clothes on with a sailor's greatcoat thrown over them. Some were in stoker's uniform and wore sailor's boots. Two or three little boys were dressed in sailor's uniform.

Not for some days was it possible to estimate the full extent of the disaster in terms of human lives. Then it was stated that the " Athenia " had on board 1,418 persons, of whom over 300 were Americans, and of this total 128 were unaccounted for after the disaster.

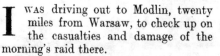

I WAS THERE ! (Continued)

I Saw the First Raids on Warsaw

By Sefton Delmer

Among the few correspondents who were able to send first-hand narratives of the opening phases of the war was Mr. Sefton Delmer. Below is his account of the first bombings of Warsaw by the German raiders reprinted from the "Sunday Express" of September 3rd.

Mr. Sefton Delmer, Special Correspondent of the "Sunday Express," whose vivid account of the bombing of Warsaw is given in this page.
Photo, " Daily Express "

I WAS driving out to Modlin, twenty miles from Warsaw, to check up on the casualties and damage of the morning's raid there.

Just across the Vistula I sighted the first group of raiders, four German bombers, being headed off from the bridge by Polish fighters. The fighters were driving them right on to Polish anti-aircraft gun fire.

Truly it was superb shooting the Polish batteries were putting up, and sure enough it told.

I saw one German machine come heading earthwards like a great black arrow. A moment later a second followed on the left. Two black clouds of smoke half a mile from each other showed where they had fallen.

More and more German bombers came over. Though I still do not think it was real mass stuff, there was one group of six triple-engined bombers with three escort planes above and behind them.

They tried to fly through a barrage of black anti-aircraft shrapnel—then suddenly the guns were silent and high out of the sky silver-glinting Polish fighters swooped down, machine guns going full out.

They swept down past the Germans. The Germans opened formation, then as the anti-aircraft fire started up again, they wheeled and bombs dropped harmlessly, judged by the cloud of smoke I saw coming up from riverside fields.

Farther on a cottage was burning. A bomb had set it on fire.

Behind this group had come another group of 'planes diving in circus. There was furious bombing. What they were after I do not know. Perhaps it was the bridge. But within a second the fighters were on their tails and the circus were forced to beat it.

By the roadside stood a fair-haired girl weeping beside her two little blond children, a boy and girl. She frantically waved at us. "Take me back to Warsaw, I can't stand it here any longer," she pleaded.

Somehow we piled them all in. The burning house was their country cottage. She had come out with them in the four o'clock bus this afternoon to have them safe outside Warsaw.

As I put them down at the first waiting tram, an air-raid warden rushed up to show us a " bit of bomb," his first. It was a fragment of shrapnel.

Driving back to Warsaw an hour and a half after the raid began, the alarm was still on. Behind us out in the country, the anti-aircraft guns firing away stopped the last wave of German afternoon raiders.

No bomb had fallen in Warsaw. Fire brigades and ambulances were standing by unwanted, but a bomb had fallen on the Jewish Children's Hospital fifteen miles from Warsaw. Fourteen children were killed and many more were wounded. Three nurses also were killed.

In the opening phase of the War, Warsaw, Poland's capital on the Vistula, was subjected to a succession of air raids by German warplanes. On the left is a huge crater made by a bomb from a German raider in one of the suburbs ; and on the right is an almost completely destroyed block of flats in the Kolo district. Above left, loading bombs on a German warplane, preparatory to setting out for a raid on a Polish town.

Photos, Planet News, Associated Press and Wide World

How Our Refugee Train Was Bombed
By a Survivor

One of the most terrible incidents of Friday, September 1, 1939, was the bombing by German 'planes of a train filled with refugees at Kutno, east of Warsaw. Here is an eye-witness account as given by a survivor to the correspondent of the "Daily Telegraph."

I LEFT Gdynia for Warsaw on Thursday, via Torun and Kutno. The train consisted of about 30 passenger coaches and three or four goods vans in the rear, drawn by two engines.

The occupants of the train were the wives and children of civil servants, officers and railway employees of the frontier zone, evacuating inland. A few soldiers, officers and reservists were also on the train.

Leaving Kutno at six a.m. on Friday, I saw six two-engined bombers flying low above the Warsaw line. The passengers watched calmly, believing that air exercises were in progress.

Suddenly we heard a detonation and a shower of machine-gun bullets struck the sides and roofs of the carriages, wounding many of the crowded passengers. The train jerked violently and stopped.

Civilians and reservists, women and children jumped through the doors and windows into a ploughed field on one side and into a wet meadow on the other. The 'planes flew over, described a circle and returned, sending a new shower of bullets into the panic-stricken crowd. The 'planes then departed.

Near the end of the train we heard moans from badly wounded soldiers— more than ten of them—in a third-class Pullman. They were literally cut to pieces with bullets and glass.

Farther on a goods van had been split in two and the bodies of eight soldiers thrown out on the roof by an explosion. Alongside the train in the ploughed field we saw 20 unexploded 100-kilogram gas bombs.

As an ex-Great War soldier, I suggest that the failure of these bombs was due to the fact that they had been dropped from a low altitude and to the fact that the soil in the field was soft.

I was too overwhelmed by the sudden attack to note the exact casualties, but I saw more than ten bodies and many more than ten wounded. I can state definitely that the airmen were flying so low that they must have known that they were massacring defenceless people.

I Was in Munich on the Eve of War
By Mary Maxwell

How the German people were led blindfold into the war was told in page 30. Here is a further picture of Germany on the eve of war by Miss Mary Maxwell, writing in the "Sunday Express."

JUST over a week ago I returned from a visit to friends in Munich.

All the people I met in Germany were unanimous that England would never fight. They have no means of knowing the real truth.

It was clear that war was the last thing any one wanted; that was true of every class, from the soldiers I talked to at a village dance, to my friend's father, a retired general from the Prussian Guards. He said : "If war comes, then we shall lose because we are half-starved already. We all know that."

The food is bad and scarce, and clothing materials are also very poor in quality. This week more stringent rationing has been introduced; it was bad enough before. Butter and milk were closely rationed and no extra was obtainable for visitors. The meat was chiefly pork and veal. Even this was not always obtainable, and the usual diet was sausage.

The people do not look so healthy as they did—gone are the fat tummies of the caricatures, the round red faces. They look thin and worried.

Vegetables are still fairly plentiful, but the bread is coarse and unappetising.

The Press campaign against England has been very bitter for the last two years, and her "decadence" has been so well rammed home that the German people really believe it is true and that she can no longer be counted as a world Power.

Hitler is still a god in Germany. He has done much that is good for Germany. He has restored their national pride, given them great arterial roads, cleared the slums. But unless he gives them peace and better living conditions there will be open revolution in Germany and Hitler will disappear.

He can make war on Poland, but his people are not behind him and already his end is in sight.

In their drive into Poland the Germans employed a very large proportion of their air force— some estimates put it at 80 per cent of the total. Hundreds of the German warplanes were brought down by the Polish fighters and anti-aircraft guns; one such near Warsaw is shown in the lower photo. Upper left, a German bomber is being re-loaded.

Photos, Associated Press and Planet News

There's A.R.P. in Germany, Too

Taken near Berlin, this photograph shows three balloons of the German capital's balloon barrage ascending during training. Below, a decontamination squad salvaging a 'plane which it had been arranged should "crash" in Berlin during an A.R.P. practice. On the right is a fully-equipped member of a German decontamination squad.

Faced by the same menace from the air as that which has preoccupied the minds of Britain's defence chiefs during the past few years, Germany has developed her own A.R.P. organization which reproduces many of the defence practices which have been carried out in our own country. Gas masks have been produced on a large scale, and have been distributed to those who can buy them; A.R.P. wardens, decontamination squads, auxiliary firemen and the like have been enlisted and trained; and up above float balloon barrages.

Nazi Soldiers Dropped from the Clouds

One of the most novel features of the present fighting in Poland is the employment by the Nazis of soldiers dropped from aeroplanes by parachute immediately behind the opposing lines. Above, the parachuted soldiers are running forward protected by a smoke screen to positions from where they can attack the enemy in rear or in flank.

This photograph shows a company of machine-gunners fully equipped, parachuting simultaneously from a squadron of aeroplanes, and ready to go into action immediately they land. In the early days of the fighting in Poland a number of these Nazi parachutists were alleged to be dressed in Polish uniforms in order to facilitate their work of sabotage, and on capture they were treated with the short shrift usually given to saboteurs.

Photos, Mondiale and Camera Talks

NOT BOMBS BUT LEAFLETS FOR GERMANS

The large-scale propaganda raids by the Royal Air Force over German territory during the five nights,
September 3rd to 8th, constituted an imaginative effort that appealed strongly to the whole world. It so
annoyed the Nazi authorities that they are said to have declared that bombs would have been preferred.

Nothing in the opening stage of the war was more finely conceived or executed than the pamphlet raids made by the R.A.F. over Germany.

Night after night in the first week of the struggle, units of the bombing command, in the course of extensive reconnaissance flights over a wide area of northern and western Germany, including the vitally important Ruhr district, dropped, in the first three raids alone, a total of some 12,000,000 copies (over 25 tons) of the note to the German people reproduced here.

We can imagine the 'planes crossing the sea in the hours of night and then climbing high above a blacked-out Germany. We can visualize the beams of the searchlights savagely stabbing the sky, and the stars momentarily blotted out by the bursts of the exploding anti-aircraft shells. Everywhere below there must have been intense activity and widespread apprehension.

Warning: A Message From Great Britain

German Men and Women : "The Government of the Reich have, with cold deliberation, forced war upon Great Britain. They have done so knowing that it must involve mankind in a calamity worse than that of 1914. The assurances of peaceful intentions the Fuehrer gave to you and to the world in April have proved as worthless as his words at the Sportpalast last September, when he said : 'We have no more territorial claims to make in Europe.'

"Never has government ordered subjects to their death with less excuse. This war is utterly unnecessary. Germany was in no way threatened or deprived of justice.

"Was she not allowed to re-enter the Rhineland, to achieve the Anschluss, and to take back the Sudeten Germans in peace ? Neither we nor any other nation would have sought to limit her advance so long as she did not violate independent non-German peoples.

"Every German ambition—just to others —might have been satisfied through friendly negotiation.

"President Roosevelt offered you both peace with honour and the prospect of prosperity. Instead, your rulers have condemned you to the massacre, miseries and privations of a war they cannot ever hope to win.

"It is not us, but you they have deceived. For years their iron censorship has kept from you truths that even uncivilised peoples know.

"It has imprisoned your minds in, as it were, a concentration camp. Otherwise they would not have dared to misrepresent the combination of peaceful peoples to secure peace as hostile encirclement.

"We have no enmity against you the German people.

"This censorship has also concealed from you that you have not the means to sustain protracted warfare. Despite crushing taxation, you are on the verge of bankruptcy.

"Our resources and those of our Allies, in men, arms and supplies are immense. We are too strong to break by blows and we could wear you down inexorably.

"You, the German people, can, if you will, insist on peace at any time. We also desire peace, and are prepared to conclude it with any peace-loving government in Germany."

" One million one hundred and two—one million one hundred and three—one million . . ."
Cartoon by Grimes. Reproduced by permission from " The Star."

Then down from the sky, instead of the bombs which had been nervously feared, there slowly dropped a gentle rain of *leaflets*.

We may see them being picked up in the light of early morning. Here, perhaps, it was a Westphalian miner who put one under his helmet as he trudged home from his night shift. There it may have been a Hanoverian peasant who, with a surreptitious glance, hid the message beneath a hummock. Some, perhaps, were retrieved by Fraus and Fräuleins on their way to factory or office desk. Others, let us hope, were captured by members of the Nazi party and were at least glanced at before they were committed to the flames.

The message they bore was one not of fierce hatred and wholesale condemnation, but of reason and of common-sense appeal. There can have been few who did not glance up at the sky from which these messages from Britain had come— glance up and think that it might not have been a leaflet that descended from the night sky, but a death-dealing bomb.

Reports from Germany and from neutral observers state that this bombardment by pamphlet was received with amazement. Guns, bombs, tanks, machine-guns are powerful enough in all conscience, but still the most powerful thing in this world of ours is an Idea. Ideas may reach far beyond the range of guns and 'planes. Nazism itself is an idea—an essentially evil idea —in action. It may well be that the proud and boasting impregnable fortress of Nazism may be brought to the ground by that other Idea which, in the opening hours of the war, made such a successful invasion of the Reich.

The Empire Rallies to the Motherland

Typical of the new Australian Air Force, many of whose machines are now manufactured in the Dominion, are these two Avro Anson bombers seen over the tail of a third machine.

Nothing can have come as a greater surprise to Hitler and his henchmen than the attitude of the British Empire to the Motherland in her hour of trial. With a complete misunderstanding of the mentality of those peoples of many countries bound together by their love of liberty and their free allegiance to the Throne, there had been a hope in Berlin that at least some of those far-off lands would lend nothing but moral support to Britain's cause. Disillusionment came swiftly to the Nazis, however, for within a few days the great Dominions and the Indian Empire had declared war against Nazi Germany. From " down under " came the word that Australia will be there, and New Zealand, too. Then with dramatic suddenness South Africa and Canada rallied to the Motherland.

Some of Canada's soldiers, eager now as in 1914 to serve the Empire, are seen in the centre photograph; they are members of the Halifax local militia on their way to take up their war station in the forts on McNab Island in Halifax Harbour. The statuesque figure of an Indian sentry guarding a railway bridge affords yet another striking exemplification of the unity of the Empire, when confronted with the Nazi challenge.

Photos, Wide World and Sport and General

The War-Maker Goes to the Eastern Front

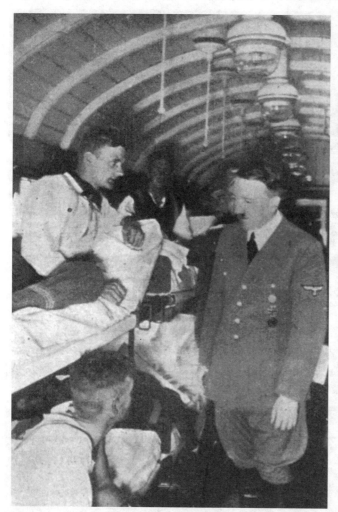

Here is the first picture of Herr Hitler at the war. He is watching his troops in action from a camouflaged observation post in Poland. Below, the Leader, wearing his new uniform on which appears the military eagle instead of the Swastika, is signing a proclamation to the German people. On the left he is visiting Nazi wounded in a hospital train.

IN his speech to the Reichstag on September 1, Herr Hitler declared : "I am from now on just first soldier of the German Reich. I have once more put on that coat that was the most sacred and dear to me. I will not take it off again until victory is secured, or I will not survive the outcome."

This photograph, received from a German source, bears the following caption in German : "The Leader with his soldiers on the Vistula. To the great and pleasant surprise of his soldiers, the Leader and Supreme Commander of the armed forces appeared unexpectedly amongst his troops whilst they crossed the Vistula. He was in the front line and was greeted with great enthusiasm." Despite this statement, however, it may be noted that few of the soldiers are wearing war kit.

Photos, Associated Press. Wide World, and Keystone

With the German Army in their Polish Drive

Breathing all the ineffable sadness of war is this photo of German artillery rushing through a burning Polish village, watched by the cow of some unhappy peasant who has been driven from his home.

After holding out heroically in the Danzig Post Office, the little garrison of Polish officials and soldiers were at last compelled to surrender. Above we see them being escorted into a German army lorry holding their hands behind their heads in submission. Centre, German transports wellnigh bogged during their advance; right, searching a captured village.

Photos, Associated Press and Wide World

WORDS THAT HISTORY WILL REMEMBER

A Record of the Declarations and Solemn Statements of the World's Leaders

(*Continued from page 28*)

Friday, Sept. 1

Hitler in a speech to the Reichstag :

" I am determined to solve (1) the Danzig question, (2) the question of the Corridor, and (3) to see to it that a change is made in the relationship between Germany and Poland that shall ensure a peaceful co-existence. In this I am resolved to continue the fight until either the present Polish Government is willing to bring about this change or until another Polish Government is ready to do so. . . .

When statesmen in the West declare that this affects their interests, I can only regret such a declaration. It cannot for a moment make me hesitate to fulfil my duty.

Germany has no interests in the West, and our Western Wall is for all time the frontier of the Reich on the West. Moreover, we have no aims of any kind there for the future. This attitude on the part of the Reich will not change. . . .

I will not war against women and children. I have ordered my Air Force to restrict itself to attacks on military objectives. If, however, the enemy thinks he can from that draw carte blanche on his side to fight by the other methods, he will receive an answer that will deprive him of hearing and sight.

This night for the first time Polish regular soldiers fired on our own territory. And, from now on, bombs will be met with bombs. Whoever fights with poison gas will be fought with poison gas. Whoever departs from the rules of humane warfare can only expect that we shall do the same.

I will continue this struggle, no matter against whom, until the safety of the Reich and its rights are secured. . . .

I am from now on just First Soldier of the German Reich. I have once more put on that coat that was the most sacred and dear to me. I will not take it off again until victory is secured, or I will not survive the outcome. . . .

" If our will is so strong that no hardship or suffering can subdue it, then our will and our German might will prevail."

Saturday, Sept. 2

Dr. Szathmary, Minister of the Slovak Republic in Warsaw, to Colonel Beck, Polish Foreign Minister :

" In the name of the Slovak people and its representatives who, under the pressure of the Third Reich, have been reduced to silence and have been reproached for penetrations exclusively in the interests of Germany, I protest against

" The brutal disarmament of the Slovak Army,

" The arbitrary occupation of Slovakia by the troops of the Third Reich,

" The use of Slovakia as a base for warlike action against the brotherly Polish people.

" The Slovak people associates itself with armed resistance against the aggressor to regain its freedom in collaboration with the civilized nations of the world and in order that it may freely decide its own destiny."

Sunday, Sept. 3

Mr. Chamberlain broadcasting from Downing Street :

" This morning the British Ambassador in Berlin handed the German Government a final Note stating that unless we heard from them by 11 o'clock that they were prepared at once to withdraw their troops from Poland a state of war would exist between us. I have to tell you now that no such undertaking has been received and that consequently this country is at war with Germany.

" You can imagine what a bitter blow it is to me that all my long struggle to win peace

has failed. . . . Up to the last it would have been quite possible to have arranged a peaceful and honourable settlement between Germany and Poland, but Hitler would not have it. . .

" His action shows convincingly that there is no chance of expecting that this man will ever give up his practice of using force to gain his will. He can only be stopped by force. We and France are today in fulfilment of our obligations going to the aid of Poland. . . We have a clear conscience. We have done all that any country could do to establish peace. . . .

" It is the evil things that we shall be fighting against—brute force, bad faith, injustice, oppression and persecution—and against them I am certain that the right will prevail."

Mr. Chamberlain in House of Commons :

" . . . This country is now at war with Germany. . . It is a sad day for all of us. For none is it sadder than for me. Everything that I worked for, everything that I had hoped for, everything that I believed in during my public life has crashed into ruins this morning. . . .

" I trust I may live to see the day when Hitlerism has been destroyed and a restored and liberated Europe has been re-established."

Rt. Hon. A. Greenwood :

" . . . . The intolerable agony and suspense from which all of us have suffered is over. We now know the worst. The hated word ' War ' has been spoken by Britain in fulfilment of her pledged word and unbreakable intention to defend the liberties of Europe. . . . May the war be swift and short and the peace which follows stand proudly for ever on the shattered ruins of an evil name."

M. Daladier in a broadcast :

" The responsibility for the bloodshed rests wholly on the Hitlerite Government. The fate of peace was in the hands of Hitler. He has willed war. . . . By standing up against the most horrible of all tyrannies and by making good our word, we are fighting to defend our land, our homes and our liberty. . . ."

H.M. the King in a broadcast :

" In this grave hour, perhaps the most fateful in our history, I send to every household of my peoples, both at home and overseas, this message, spoken with the same depth of feeling for each one of you as if I were able to cross your threshold and speak to you myself.

" For the second time in the lives of most of us we are at war. Over and over again we have tried to find a peaceful way out of the differences between ourselves and those who are now our enemies. But it has been in vain.

" We have been forced into a conflict. For we are called, with our Allies, to meet the challenge of a principle which, if it were to prevail, would be fatal to any civilized order in the world.

" It is the principle which permits a State, in the selfish pursuit of power, to disregard its treaties and its solemn pledges ; which sanctions the use of force, or threat of force, against the Sovereignty and independence of other States.

" Such a principle, stripped of all disguise, is surely the mere primitive doctrine that might is right ; and if this principle were established throughout the world, the freedom of our own country and of the whole British Commonwealth of Nations would be in danger.

" But far more than this—the peoples of the world would be kept in the bondage of fear, and all hopes of settled peace and of the security

of justice and liberty among nations would be ended.

" This is the ultimate issue which confronts us. For the sake of all that we ourselves hold dear, and of the world's order and peace, it is unthinkable that we should refuse to meet the challenge.

" It is to this high purpose that I now call my people at home and my peoples across the Seas, who will make our cause their own.

" I ask them to stand calm, firm and united in this time of trial. The task will be hard. There may be dark days ahead, and war can no longer be confined to the battlefield. But we can only do the right as we see the right, and reverently commit our cause to God.

" If one and all we keep resolutely faithful to it, ready for whatever service or sacrifice it may demand, then, with God's help, we shall prevail.

" May He bless and keep us all."

Monday, Sept. 4

Message broadcast by the Prime Minister to the German nation.

" German people !

" Your country and mine are now at war. Your Government has bombed and invaded the free and independent State of Poland, which this country is in honour bound to defend. . . .

" You are told by your Government that you are fighting because Poland rejected your Leader's offer and resorted to force. What are the facts ?

" The so-called ' offer ' was made to the Polish Ambassador in Berlin on Thursday evening, two hours before the announcement by your Government that it had been ' rejected.' So far from having been rejected, there had been no time even to consider it. . . .

" You may ask why Great Britain is concerned. We are concerned because we gave our word of honour to defend Poland against aggression.

" Why did we feel it necessary to pledge ourselves to defend this Eastern Power when our interests lie in the West, and when your Leader has said he has no interest in the West ? The answer is that—and I regret to have to say it—nobody in this country any longer places any trust in your Leader's word.

" He gave his word that he would respect the Locarno Treaty ; **he broke it.**

" He gave his word that he neither wished nor intended to annex Austria ; **he broke it.**

" He declared that he would not incorporate the Czechs in the Reich ; **he did so.**

" He gave his word after Munich that he had no further territorial demands in Europe ; **he broke it.**

" He gave his word that he wanted no Polish Provinces ; **he broke it.**

" He has sworn to you for years that he was the mortal enemy of Bolshevism ; **he is now its ally.**

" Can you wonder that his word is, for us, not worth the paper it is written on ?

" The German-Soviet Pact was a cynical volte-face, designed to shatter the Peace Front against aggression. This gamble failed. The Peace Front stands firm. Your Leader is now sacrificing you, the German people, to the still more monstrous gamble of a war, to extricate himself from the impossible position into which he has led himself and you.

" **In this war we are not fighting against you, the German people,** for whom we have no bitter feeling, but against a tyrannous and forsworn regime, which has betrayed not only its own people, but the whole of Western civilization, and all that you and we hold dear."

HITLER'S FANTASY OF IMPERIAL DOMINATION

" The German Chancellor," said Mr. Chamberlain in the House of Commons on September 1, " has not hesitated to plunge the world into misery in order to serve his own senseless ambition." What form that ambition takes is described below.

JUST as in 1914 Kaiser Wilhelm and his fellow Pan-Germans planned and worked for a German empire which should stretch from the North Sea to Baghdad and possibly far beyond, so Hitler dreams of a great Nazi dominion. Under Hitler, however, the *Drang nach Sued-Osten* (the drive to the south-east) of the Berlin-Baghdad railway, of Mitteleuropa, has been reinforced by a religious urge.

Like the Kaiser, Hitler believes that he is inspired by God—the " good old German god " of whom we heard so much in the last war—but he displays a mystical fanaticism which would have been altogether alien to the character of the Kaiser, brought up as he was on the lines of Victorian evangelicalism. Hitler sees himself as the captain of a crusade aiming at the domination of Europe's lesser breeds by men of the pure Nordic or Aryan race. With fanatical fervour he has preached his gospel from a thousand platforms and in all the seven hundred pages of " Mein Kampf " —that book which has been well described as the bible of Nazism, which is to be found at the right hand of every Nazi official, and which is put into the hands of every newly-married couple in the Nazi Reich.

There is imperialism enough in all conscience in " Mein Kampf," but it is still more clearly in evidence in that book which has been called the New Testament of Nazism—" The Myth of the Twentieth Century," published in 1930 by Alfred Rosenberg, the Russian refugee of German extraction who greatly influenced Hitler in his most impressionable early years, and who has become the priest and prophet of Pan - German Aryanism.

In this remarkable effusion, which is now in its 110th edition and of which more than half a million copies have been sold, Rosenberg visualises a German empire which shall include not only Germany but all the adjacent lands in which there is a German or an Aryan population. First Austria, he prophesied, would come into the fold, and next the Sudeten Germans; somewhat later the Teutons of Alsace-Lorraine, Switzerland,

Luxemburg, Belgium, Holland, Poland, Lithuania, Russia and Hungary will follow suit. Sometimes the union will be effected voluntarily; sometimes force of arms will be necessary. But no obstacle, however great, can stop this growth of Germany as the imperial power of central and south-eastern Europe.

Not only the German-speaking parts of the Continent are to come under the Reich. The Germans will play their part as the supermen of Nietsche's creed, and they will have as their willing and devoted slaves many other races on their border lands. Denmark, Sweden, Norway, and Finland are to form a " Northern Germanic Federation "; Jugoslavia, Rumania, and Bulgaria are to constitute the " Balkan Protectorate ", Lithuania, Latvia, and Esthonia are to be a " Baltic Dominion "; and, finally, the Russian Ukraine, together with Ruthenia and the Polish Ukraine, will form the vast " Ukrainian Dominion."

More Room for Germans!

" We demand land and soil (colonies) for the nourishment of our people and the settlement of our surplus population," declares the third article of the original programme of the Nazi party, issued in

1920, four years before the birth of " Mein Kampf "; and in " Mein Kampf " Hitler urges again and again the German right to unhampered expansion. Before the end of the twentieth century, he says, the world shall see 250 million Germans flourishing in the heart of the European continent. Nazi Germany's appetite for colonial expansion will not be sated until her bounds extend from the Atlantic and the English Channel to the Black Sea, from the Baltic to the Mediterranean.

" Then the plough will be the sword," runs a passage in " Mein Kampf," " and out of the tears of war will grow the harvest of future days."

The Plan in Operation

Step by step the great dream, fantastic though it may appear, has been carried into realisation. Austria has returned to the Reich as Hitler and Rosenberg declared it should and would; the Sudeten Germans have returned, too, and Czechoslovakia was wiped out in the process; the Germans in Memel and Danzig and the Tyrol have all returned or are returning by one way or another to their " homeland."

Then somewhere, somehow, the plan has gone wrong. Instead of executing the *Drang nach Sued-Osten* to the oilfields of Rumania and the rich corn lands of the Ukraine, Hitler has flung his legions against Poland, which up to now has played very little part in the dreams of Pan-Germanism; in the map illustrating Rosenberg's scheme of German expansion, for instance, practically the whole of Poland—including even the Corridor—is left outside the imperial limits.

Moreover, in one of his most cynical moments, Hitler has shaken hands with Moscow, with that Bolshevik monster whom he has so often and so violently denounced, and so closed the door, for the time, at least, on his expansion towards the south-east.

The Kaiser in his day made a similar move. Just as Hitler has attacked Poland, so the last of the Hohenzollerns in 1914 swept through Belgium. And Hitler should have remembered that then Britain stood by Belgium. . . . He should have thought of that—and thought again.

The Crystal Gazer
From the cartoon by Sir Bernard Partridge, by permission of the Proprietors of Punch

ODD FACTS ABOUT THE WAR

Life Among the Nazis

An Englishwoman, until recently resident in Berlin, says : " At first it was rather fun to join the rush of Berlin hausfraus every morning in the quest for butter and coffee. If you wanted something really tasty you had to get up earlier than anyone else and storm the big market halls with your shopping basket and a powerful line in persuasive language. . . For years we have been rationed to seven ounces of butter a week for each person. Since the beginning of this year we have had four and a half ounces of coffee a week, unless you were absent when the coffee registration forms were sent out. In that case you just did without, or relied on friends bringing a packet from London, Prague or Denmark. Now that the food tickets have been issued, the German housewife can expect even less."

Air-Minded Youth

In the five months April to August, 1939, the total number of pilots, observers, airmen and boys recruited by the R.A.F. was 17,755, compared with 9,714 for the corresponding period of last year.

Feeling the Pinch Already

Travellers arriving in Copenhagen stated that in Berlin police had been posted in provision shops in order to prevent customers from being served with the full amount of food to which the rationing scheme entitled them.

Dictators Become Governors

It is reported from Philadelphia that heads of the lodges of the Loyal Order of the Moose are to relinquish their title of " Dictator " in favour of that of " Governor," because political events in Europe have brought the former into such disrepute.

Bombs That Failed to Burst

It has been reported that two out of three of the bombs used in the first air raids on Warsaw did not explode. On examination they were found to contain, instead of high explosive, slips of paper bearing the words, " We are with you in spirit," and signed " Workers of the Skoda Arms Factory, Czecho-Slovakia."

(*Sunday Express,* September 3, 1939.)

United Against Aggression

Men of every nationality are enrolling under the French colours. An American division may be formed, and it is claimed that 10,000 Americans have already applied to join it.

No Repairs Undertaken

By a German A.R.P. order, all windows are to be kept open in the event of an air raid, since window-panes might be smashed by the blast of exploding bombs, and it would be impossible in wartime, because of lack of material, to repair them.

Straws in the Wind ?

According to the Copenhagen newspaper, *Berlingske Tidende,* the yellow benches in the Berlin parks labelled " For Jews Only " have had these notices removed, and have been repainted green. Moreover, the sign, " Jews Not Wanted " has been removed from a number of shops.

The Eater Eaten

" Everything includes itself in power,
Power into will, will into appetite,
And appetite, a universal wolf,
So doubly seconded with will and power,
Must make itself a universal prey,
And last eat up itself."

(Shakespeare—*Troilus and Cressida.*)

Hitler Speaks

" I will not wage war against women and children ; I have ordered my air-force to attack only military objectives. . . . If necessary I will sacrifice all. I do not desire that any German shall do other than I do. I do not want to be anything but a front soldier of the Reich."

(From speech in Reichstag, September 1, 1939.)

Class-Conscious Germany

" Mr. Chamberlain dares to say in these leaflets that Britain is fighting for right against might, but when a million and a half Germans are tormented by a common nation like the Poles, we shall not be deterred from our duty by the British Government."

(Goering in speech broadcast September 9, 1939.)

German Artists Thank Britain

The Executive Committee of the Free German League of Culture in England issued a statement in which they thanked the British people for the hospitality and help given to them and to their cultural activities in this country. The statement added : " The German artists, scientists and all those who stood up for cultural freedom were among the first victims of Nazi barbarism."

War Prisoners

The International Committee of the Red Cross at Geneva have informed the Governments of belligerent States, and of several neutral States, that they are preparing to open a central agency in Geneva for information regarding prisoners of war.

Czech Legion

It was stated by the Ministry of Information that a Czech Legion is being formed in London. Circulars in connexion with the movement bear the signature of Dr. Benes.

Through the Sandbags

Workmen piling up sandbags inside the entrance to Wandsworth Town Hall have had part of their time taken up in ushering couples through a labyrinth of sandbagged walls to the register office. " We've been leading them to matrimony since 7 o'clock this morning," said a sturdy Cockney one day. (*Star*)

Love Me, Love My Dog

More than 500 animals—mostly dogs, cats, rabbits and guinea-pigs—have been evacuated from 69 schools in the Metropolitan area by the R.S.P.C.A., who will maintain them, all separately labelled, at two animal care centres in the country.

Where Does the Sand Come From ?

One of the chief sources of supply for London sandbags is Kensington Gardens, for here, under the turf, lie quantities of sand dumped after the Great Exhibition of 1851. Hampstead Heath and the Royal Parks furnish further supplies, and the sand deposits on the East Coast are also being drawn upon.

A. R. P. in the Vatican

For the first time in history gas masks have been distributed to the Swiss Guards, the Papal Gendarmes, and other employees of the Vatican State. Dim blue lights have been installed.

Crisis Film for Posterity

Among the 2,000,000 feet of films removed to a cave " somewhere in Sussex " from London National Film Library were newsreel shots of the Crisis. They will go down in history to show future generations how Britain stood up calmly to the war threat in August, 1939.

It is Said That . .

All dancing, both public and private, has been banned from Germany. In addition to heavy taxes on all luxuries, a new tax has been announced, levying from 2½ to 10 per cent. on the income of town councils and public service companies.

Travellers arriving in Brussels state that women in the queues outside food-shops in Berlin are patient almost to the point of apathy, as they wait for the few ounces of meat, fat or coffee allowed them by their ration cards.

The big shops in Berlin remain open, although they are forbidden to sell the greater part of their wares.

A fee of five marks (8s. 4d.) is being paid in Germany to anyone informing on people expressing disaffection.

The Germans have had less time to prepare their Siegfried Line than the French have had to construct the Maginot Line. It may be, therefore, that there are some weaknesses in the Siegfried Line.

The French Army is now approaching a strength of 5,000,000 men. It will soon be at full fighting power, with more than 6,000,000 fully-trained and equipped soldiers.

A German has been executed in Berlin because he " refused to co-operate in safety measures for the protection of the Reich."

Foreign volunteers of all nationalities residing in France, asking to be enlisted, are arriving in increasing numbers over the entire country.

The President and Government of Nazi-controlled Bohemia and Moravia have warned subjects that if they join any military organization formed abroad they will be regarded as having committed high treason, and will be liable to very heavy penalties.

About 80 per cent. of Germany's air force and 70 per cent. of her land forces have been employed on the Polish front.

The crew of a British bomber was captured on Saturday near Ueberstedt in Thuringia, a province bordering Bavaria. This is the first indication that R.A.F. planes have penetrated right into the heart of Germany. (*Berlin broadcast*)

The greatest textile plant in Slovakia has been completely destroyed by explosion and fire. (*Moscow broadcast*)

From Zurich it is reported that persecution of Catholics in Germany has begun again. (*Paris broadcast*)

Goering's speech, as well as the over-hasty announcement of the capture of Warsaw, produced the worst impression upon the German public. (*Amsterdam broadcast*)

So far the war has gone according to plan. The Polish General Staff never envisaged the possibility of a prolonged defence of the western provinces, and contemplated that its main resistance would be opened on the line of the rivers Bug and Vistula, thus leaving a third of Poland in German hands.

The German mastery of the air is responsible for the unexpected tempo of the advance. The reported arrival of British aeroplanes in considerable numbers may help to provide the remedy. The dry, sunny weather has favoured the " lightning war." The Poles pray for rain.

A German officer and 20 German soldiers deserted on the Western Front, according to the Official News Bulletin of September 12th.

" If a pontoon bridge were thrown across the Rhine, thousands more of my comrades would cross it," said the officer.

Puerile Propaganda of the Nazi Peace-Breakers

THE nice Nazi officers (top), arrived at Zoppot to engage in the slaughter of the Poles, at once write home to their dear families, while (left) the poor persecuted Germans of the Corridor (a boy and girl!) run to the shelter of a German car, and a brave mother with her baby jumps the barbed wire on Eastern Poland to be rescued by a good East Prussian frontier guard, and yet another traverses Polish swamps to gain the friendly firm soil of the Reich. Laughable were it not lamentable.

Italy, fortunately for the world and herself, has not " marched " with her Axis partner. But Italians are still assaulted with Goebbels preposterous propaganda to camouflage the war guilt of Hitler, as these pictures—so childishly posed!—demonstrate. They are reproduced from the latest number of *Tempo*, a Milan illustrated weekly, just sent to our Editor.

Our Diary of the War

Monday, September 4.

Fleet blockade began.

In the course of an extensive reconnaissance of Northern and Western Germany during the night of September 3–4, R.A.F. aircraft dropped more than 6,000,000 copies of a note to the German people.

R.A.F. carried out an evening raid on Wilhelmshafen and Brünsbuttel. Two German battleships heavily damaged.

Heavy fighting on the Polish fronts, and the Poles claimed the recovery of several towns in the north-west, but admitted the loss of Czestochowa, near the upper Silesian frontier. More air raids over Warsaw.

France started operations on land, sea and air.

Evacuation of 650,000 children and adults from London completed.

Mr. Chamberlain broadcast a message in German to the German people in which he made it clear that Britain's quarrel is with the German régime, not with the people.

Egypt broke off diplomatic relations with Germany.

Japan decided upon neutrality.

German income tax increased 50 per cent.

Tuesday, September 5.

Warsaw admitted loss of several important towns south of the Corridor.

British aircraft carried out an extensive reconnaissance over the Ruhr and dropped more than 3,000,000 copies of the note to the German people.

President Roosevelt proclaimed American neutrality.

Jugoslavia announced her neutrality.

Argentina and Chile officially declared their neutrality.

British cargo steamer Bosnia sunk in Atlantic.

Three German ships, which might have become raiders, sunk, also in Atlantic.

Wednesday, September 6.

Enemy aeroplanes made a reconnaissance off the East Coast, but turned back before British fighter machines could make contact.

French troops penetrated German territory in the direction of Saarbrucken. Contact between the two armies established along the 125-miles frontier from the Rhine to the Moselle, on boundary of Luxemburg.

Polish Government left Warsaw for Lublin. Heavy fighting in Poland. Germans claimed that Krakow had been captured.

German aircraft crossed the French frontier and wheeled towards Paris, but were intercepted by French fighters.

By the passing of the Armed Forces (Conditions of Service) Act all units of the Regular Army, Territorial Army, Militia, and other auxiliary forces were merged into a single entity, the British Army.

A third successful reconnaissance was made by R.A.F. aircraft over Germany (September 5–6), and further copies of the note to the German people were dropped.

It was officially stated that South Africa was at war with Germany. General Smuts formed a new Cabinet.

Spain declared her neutrality.

Australia called up the first 10,000 of her militia.

Thursday, September 7.

French communiqués announced further advances into German territory, where reinforcements had been brought up to meet them.

Fierce fighting on two main fronts in Poland. The Germans claimed to have reached Pultusk, 30 miles north of Warsaw.

Attempts were made to torpedo the Dutch steamship Batavia in which, escorted by destroyers, Sir Nevile Henderson and his Embassy staff were returning to England.

Attacks on German submarines continued.

Iraq severed relations with Germany.

Jugoslav mobilization ordered.

Panama Canal under military control.

Garrison at Westerplatte, near Danzig, surrendered after a long and gallant resistance.

British freighter "Olivegrove" torpedoed some 200 miles north-west of Spanish coast.

Eire Government called up first line volunteers. The Army Reserve had already been mobilized.

Friday, September 8.

Paris reported that Germany had rushed six divisions from Poland to the Saar. Saarbrucken and other towns in the area had been evacuated. About 600 French tanks were leading the French attack.

German High Command claimed to have entered Warsaw, but this was denied by the Polish Government. An official Polish communiqué admitted the retreat of Polish troops in the Lodz, Ptrkow and Rozany regions south-west of Warsaw, and in the Pultusk area north of the capital.

British steamer "Manaar" shelled and sunk by enemy submarines in the Atlantic.

Both the Navy and the R.A.F. engaged in a great U-boat hunt. German merchant ships fleeing to neutral ports.

Fourth reconnaissance flight by R.A.F. over Germany to distribute copies of the note to the German people.

British and French aircraft reported to be on their way to the Polish front.

Reported shortage of food on the Siegfried Line.

Evacuation of patients from great voluntary hospitals completed, releasing about 200,000 beds for air-raid casualties.

Polish Mission under General Norvid-Neugebauer arrived in London.

Saturday, September 9

The War Cabinet announced that their policy was based on the assumption that the war will last for three years or more.

The French Command reported that an attack by one of their divisions on the Western front has secured important gains. The greater part of the Warndt Forest, an important coal-producing area, was in French hands.

The torpedoing of three more merchant ships—two British and one French—was reported. The Ministry of Information stated that it was evident that German submarine commanders had been ordered to sink on sight and without warning.

A fifth R.A.F. reconnaissance flight over Germany was made, leaflets being dropped over Cassel and other areas in Central Germany. Having inadvertently crossed a part of Belgian territory, some British aeroplanes became engaged with Belgian fighter machines. Apologies were later offered to the Belgian Government.

It was officially announced that, since the Duke of Kent had assumed a naval appointment for the duration of the war, Lord Gowrie would continue in office as Governor-General of Australia.

Field-Marshal Goering broadcast from a Berlin armament factory what was tantamount to an appeal for peace.

Sunday, September 10

The Polish General Staff announced that the Germans had withdrawn from the immediate neighbourhood of Warsaw. Fifteen bombing raids were carried out over the capital.

A statement was broadcast in Germany from Hitler's headquarters that the German advance was being slowed for the consolidation of the conquered territory.

Canada declared war on Germany.

German torpedo-boat hit a mine at the entrance to the Baltic and sank immediately.

OUR WAR DICTIONARY

Beck, Jozef (b. 1894). Polish statesman and soldier; Foreign Minister since 1932.

Brauchitsch (*Browch-itch*), **Walther Von** (b. 1882). German general; Commander-in-Chief of the Army since February, 1938; directly responsible to Herr Hitler.

Czestochowa (*Ches-to-hō-va*). Holy City of the Poles, containing an image of the Virgin, in normal times attracting thousands of pilgrims; only 20 miles from German frontier; pop. 136,000.

Gdynia (*Ge-di-nya*). Polish seaport on Corridor, chief outlet for seaborne trade; built since Great War to rival Danzig; pop. now 114,000.

Kasprzycki (*Kasp-zhee-ski*), **Tadeusz.** Polish soldier and statesman; appointed War Minister after the death of Pilsudski in 1935.

Katowice (*Kat-o-vee-che*). Polish town, on frontier of German Silesia; awarded to Poland in 1921; centre of important industrial and coal area; pop. 133,000.

Kennard, Sir Howard (b. 1878). British Ambassador to Poland since 1935; formerly Minister in Yugoslavia, Sweden, and Switzerland.

Krakow (or Cracow) (*Kra-kof*). Polish city on river Vistula, 160 miles S. of Warsaw; the old capital, it is a busy commercial centre and has a fine cathedral, castle, and university; pop. 255,000.

Maginot (*Mazh-i-no*), **André** (1877–1932). French statesman; Minister of War, 1924 and 1929–32; during second term initiated work on famous Maginot Line.

Moscicki (*Mosh-tsee-ski*), **Ignace** (b. 1867). Polish statesman; elected President in 1926 and re-elected, 1933.

Saarbruecken. Chief town of the Saarland Territory, Germany, on r. Saar; scene of first action in Franco-Prussian War, 1870; occupied by Allies in 1919; pop. 130,686.

Saarland. Territory of Franco-German border, awarded to Germany after plebiscite in 1935; rich coalfields; area 738 sq. miles; pop. 812,000.

Siegfried. Hero of German legend; immortalized in Wagner's operas, in which he slays the dragon Fafnir and performs many mighty deeds before being slain by his rival Hagen. Name given to German line of Western defences.

Smigly-Rydz (*Shmig-li ridz*), **Edward** (b. 1886). Polish soldier; Inspector-General and Marshal (since 1936) of Polish Army; since death of Pilsudski virtual dictator and officially ranking next after President.

Vol. 1   A Permanent Picture Record of the Second Great War   No. 3

Already it is clear that the pilots of the Royal Air Force in 1939 are imbued with the same indomitable spirit as the young men whose gallant deeds between 1914 and 1918 have written an imperishable page in the annals of British heroism. Moreover, the Air Force today has aeroplanes of unrivalled quality. Here we see, high above the clouds, three of its crack machines. Supermarine Spitfires, they can climb to a height of 11,000 feet in 4·8 minutes, and their speed of 362 miles per hour makes them the fastest machines in the world.

R.A.F. Official Photograph, Crown Copyright Reserved

Poland's Stand for Freedom:

Here we tell the story of the brutal invasion of Western and Southern Poland during the second week of the war. It was supported without ruth or scruple by at least 80 per cent of the world's strongest single air force and three-quarters of the Nazi land forces. The Russian invasion on September 17 brought the campaign to an effective close.

Ten days after the opening of the War, practically the whole of Poland lying to the west of Warsaw was in the hands of the Nazi invaders. The Polish Corridor, the western plains, and the "industrial triangle" of Polish Silesia and Cracow had all been overrun, and in the south the German divisions were pressing on towards Lwow with a view to seizing the oilfield on the Carpathian slopes and cutting Poland's communications with Rumania. To the west of Warsaw,

however, there still existed a considerable salient held by the Polish army entrusted with the defence of the capital.

According to all reports, the German general staff had expected that the advance to the gates of Warsaw would take four weeks. That their progress was far more rapid is due in the first place to the fine weather, and secondly to the German army's mechanized forces. Along the roads and lanes and even across the open country the armoured cars and tanks were able to make quite good going. The retreating defenders were given no rest. Harried out of one line of defence, they were pursued and often outflanked before they had time to consolidate themselves in fresh positions.

Furthermore, the German High Command flung against the Poles practically the whole weight of their air force. At first they made a pretence of not bombing open towns but only places of military importance, such as entrenchments, munition dumps, railway stations, and the like. As the struggle increased in intensity, however, and the Poles, while retreating, refused to surrender, the German airmen did not hesitate to drop their bombs on places which were not militarily defended. In a communiqué issued by the Polish Embassy in London, it was announced that even at the very commencement of the war, Warsaw, Bialystok, Bydgoszcz, Czestochowa, Gdynia, Grudziadz, Poznan, Tomaszow, Torun, Wilno, and many other open towns had all been bombed by the German air force, and that on September 11 the Germans began the methodical bombing of open towns far removed from the battle zone, employing this barbarous

Top left, Polish troops are seen in a trench watching a tank that has been in contact with the enemy. In the centre photograph German troops are crossing a river in a collapsible leather raft. In the photograph immediately above German troops are laboriously ferrying their transport across the Vistula, the Poles having destroyed all the bridges before taking up new positions.

Photos, Wide World and Planet News

Her Fight for Existence Against Fearful Odds

method of warfare with a view to paralysing the very life of the country.

Nevertheless, the Polish army, though it was in retreat, was still intact and as yet not demoralized. Again and again the Poles turned upon the invaders and drove them back despite the heavy shelling and bombing that they were compelled to endure with little chance of making any effective reply. It was well understood that the Polish High Command had long realized that it would be impossible to make any really effective stand against a German army equipped with all the very latest machinery of warfare in the open plains of Western Poland. All that they could hope to do would be to withdraw their forces as slowly and in as orderly a fashion as possible to lines already prepared beyond the Vistula. This they succeeded in doing, though with heavy loss and some disorganization. And however necessary the retreat may have appeared to those in charge of Poland's destiny, the Polish population were

stunned by the rapidity and extent of the disaster which had come upon them. As the invaders clattered through their towns and villages they retired to their houses, bolting the doors and shuttering the windows. With hate burning in their eyes they watched them pass, and they cursed them with the heaviest curses known to their vocabulary. Small wonder that some snatched up their ancient guns from the chimney-corner and as francs-tireurs played their part against the merciless aggressor who was sweeping through their country with fire and sword.

Back, then, went the Poles, resisting still with dogged bravery, but wellnigh overwhelmed by the weight of men and armament ranged against them. Arrived on the traditional line of defence on the country's great rivers, the defending army rallied and dug itself in. Attacks by the Germans were fiercely repulsed, and, moreover, the Polish forces in the salient before Warsaw were reported to have escaped from the German pincers and rejoined the main army on the Vistula.

For a day or two the situation seemed to have taken a definite turn for the better. Warsaw breathed again as the Nazi troops who had penetrated to the suburbs were ejected and pushed back several miles. But held as they were before the capital, the Germans developed

The gallant Polish machine-gunner seen in the top photograph is typical of the fine young manhood that fills the Polish Army. Below, is a German anti-tank gun in position during the street fighting that preceded the occupation of Bydgoszcz (Bromberg) on September 5.

Photos, Associated Press and Planet News

Poland is Stabbed in the Back by Russia

The sad plight which came to the people of Northern France and Belgium in 1914 has now come to the people of Poland. Above, a family driven from their home are setting forth to seek safety; the car camouflaged with tree branches that they are passing belongs to the ruthless invaders. In the first weeks of the war a great host of peasants were dispossessed of their all and forced into the wilderness, hungry and homeless.

Photo, Planet News

a further thrust from the north-east which very shortly carried their outposts across the river Bug. Surrounded already on three sides, Warsaw was now threatened from the east, and such was the weight of the Nazi numbers, such the quantity of their mechanized forces, such the preponderance of their airmen, that the Polish line along the Vistula and the Bug began to give way.

Then it was that the Polish front disintegrated. The orderly retreat became a rout. The line of battle developed into a confused medley of raids and skirmishes as the German motorized columns pushed far ahead of their infantry and penetrated to near Bresc Litewski (Brest Litovsk), Przemysl, and Lwow (Lemberg).

Mown down by the fire of the tanks, machine-gunned from the air, even the smallest concentration of Polish troops was spotted by the Nazi 'planes and blown to pieces or dispersed. The Poles resisted with fierce courage, but their tanks and artillery were all out of action, their aerodromes bombed into nothingness, their aeroplanes shot down or immobilized for want of petrol. Wireless communication, too, had broken down, with the result that the Polish High Command was out of touch with much of the battle-front. Time after time it moved its location, only to be mercilessly chased and bombed afresh.

So the struggle developed until a fortnight after the war began Poland was practically overrun by the enemy, Warsaw was on the verge of surrender to escape the bombardment with which it was threatened, and the frontier with Rumania was practically closed by the German flying columns. This was the moment chosen by Soviet Russia to order her troops to cross the frontier and take what was left of the Polish armies in the rear.

On the morning of Sunday, September 17, the vanguard of the " Workers' and Peasants' Red Army " invaded Poland at a number of points between Latvia and Rumania. Local forces of Poles tried to stem their onset, but the invaders were in such overwhelming numbers that at midnight the first Soviet communiqué announced that the Russian army had advanced more than 30 miles into Poland and had occupied, with but little fighting, a number of towns. This stab in the back completely put the finishing touches to Poland's military collapse.

This map above shows the progress made by the German army between September 8 and 18. The broken line is the front at the earlier date, and the dotted line that ten days later.

Marshal Smigly Rydz–Poland's Leader

Poland's captain in her heroic fight against Nazi aggression is
a man who already on many a hard-fought field has shown his
mettle as the commander of men.

Here we see Marshal Smigly Rydz trans-
acting State business at his desk in his
home.
Photo, Keystone

"I F anything should happen to me," old Marshal Pilsudski, father of modern Poland, told President Moscicki, " Rydz will replace me in the army." A year later Pilsudski was dead, and within a few hours of his passing the President appointed General Smigly Rydz Inspector-General, in other words, the Commander-in-Chief of the Polish army. That was on May 12, 1935, and the four years which have since elapsed did much to strengthen still further the ties binding the Marshal and the people whom he leads.

Edward Rydz was born at Brzezany in south-east Poland in 1886, and in his youth he was an art student at Cracow ; in that city's art gallery hangs a picture of our Houses of Parliament which he painted from the Embankment. Ere long, however, he was drawn into politics, and became an ardent disciple of Joseph Pilsudski. He was one of the first to join Pilsudski's semi-military organization, and during the Great War he played a distinguished part as an officer in the Polish legion. A colonel in 1916, in the following year he was appointed by Pilsudski to command the

army which was being formed in secret ready for the day when Poland would be able to strike a blow for her own independence. When Pilsudski was imprisoned Rydz carried on, and after the Armistice, when Poland was in a state of indescribable chaos as a result of the withdrawal of the alien armies which for years had been battling on her soil, it was entirely due to Rydz and his Polish military organization that order was re-established and the foreign invaders were repatriated. When, on November 10, 1918, Pilsudski returned in triumph to Warsaw, his first act was to make Rydz a general.

Defeating the Bolsheviks

In 1919 General Rydz lead the Polish army which saved the independence of Latvia and freed Wilno from the Russians. During the war with the Soviets General Rydz commanded the Polish army which swept through the Ukraine and captured Kiev, and when, in 1920, the tide turned and the Russians invaded Poland, it was Rydz who defeated the attack of Budienny's cavalry at Lwow. In August of that fateful year, when the Russians

were at the very gates of Warsaw and it seemed as if Europe were about to be submerged beneath a wave of Bolshevism, it was Rydz who led the centre of the Polish army to complete victory. In the last battle of the war, fought on the Niemen shortly afterwards, Smigly Rydz was again the commander of the triumphant Poles.

After the war with Russia Rydz co-operated whole-heartedly with Pilsudski. in the rebuilding of the Polish state, and on the Marshal's death he was appointed a marshal and designated the first person in Poland next to the President. His position as head of the army—that army to which Poland's independence is due and by which it has always been maintained—makes him in effect the leader of his country.

Trust in the Army

His belief in the necessity for a strong army is grounded in a study of his country's history as well as in the grim experience of today. " Poland's pathway has not been strewn with roses," he said once. " Although we honestly desire to live with the whole world in peace and concord, we remember the bitter past which proved that the fate of nations is decided by war. . . . In order to be able to devote oneself to art and learning, to cultivate civic and social virtues, to spend the Christmas holiday in pious repose, to muse how to build best our State and apply the wisest means towards that end —a strong and valiant army is necessary."

" In his company," said Pilsudski once of Smigly Rydz, " I always felt the atmosphere of calm and security." Never had the Pol sh people so needed a man of this character as in those early days of September 1939, when Poland was submerged by the full tide of Nazi aggression.

Marshal Smigly Rydz is seen above arriving at Cracow on August 8, 1939, to pay tribute to another famous hero in Poland's fong struggle for freedom, Marshal Pilsudski.   On that day 25 years ago Pilsudski marched into Cracow at the head of his Polish legionaries.
Photo, Keystone

Warsaw Was in the Front Line of Fighting

JUST as the Nazi attack on Poland was launched, Herr Hitler declared that he had given orders that his air force should restrict itself to attacks on military objectives. The war was not many hours old, however, before many a Polish city was being subjected to a hail of bomb and shell, and little more than a week had passed when the German High Command blandly stated that, with a view to crushing the obstinate civilian resistance, open towns and villages would henceforth be bombarded without further scruples. Thus, on land as on sea, there was launched by the Nazis a campaign of unrestricted "frightfulness" which rivalled in all its horror the worst features of the Great War that ended in 1918. In one respect, indeed, the present struggle is far worse for indiscriminate air bombing such as has been used in Poland has brought the whole civilian populace into the front line.

Among the buildings in Warsaw reported damaged by Nazi bombs was Belvedere, the former residence of Marshal Pilsudski.

Time and again Warsaw has been bombed by Nazi raiders. Above is the damage done by one German bomb in the heart of the city. While some of the citizens were engaged in clearing away the debris others marched to the outskirts to dig trenches (top, bottom right).
Photos : Sport and General, Associated Press and Planet News.

When the Poles Still Held their Capital

Though the Polish army was not so fully mechanized as the German, it had tanks and armoured cars of first-class workmanship which were handled by the soldiers with the greatest skill and daring. Above, a number of small armoured cars are seen passing through the outskirts of Warsaw on their way to meet the enemy. Such little machines are valuable for reconnaissance work and in establishing contacts.

Photo, Planet News

Young Britain Puts on Khaki

Somewhere in England Miss Frances Day gave a much appreciated entertainment to the troops, and then witnessed an entirely unmilitary "march past" of fatigue parties.

Wartime troops have come to a halt in a street in the City of London, watched with admiration and perhaps envy by those who are still in "civvies."

The young soldiers of 1939, like those of 1914–18, show their cheerful spirit in community singing. These lads, on a route march, have plenty of breath left for a sing-song.

The soldiers of the 1939 Army want to be smart, but the proper adjustment of their equipment requires some skill. Above, left, a new recruit is being shown just how it should all be done. There are peaceful hours even in wartime and, right, a member of an anti-aircraft battery in Kent takes "forty winks" and forgets Hitler.

Photos, Central Press, Keystone, Planet News and Fox

'Somewhere in England'   They Were at War

Men from an anti-aircraft battery somewhere in Kent are blackberrying on a neighbouring common, and find the early rain and late sun have provided an excellent crop.

Top, an anti-aircraft searchlight in London illuminating the sky. In that immediately above a camouflaged anti-aircraft gun, also "somewhere in London," is seen.

London is ringed by anti-aircraft batteries manned in many cases by young Territorials who have learnt in their spare time to serve their country in war. In the photograph centre right signallers of an anti-aircraft battery are operating a telephone at night. In daytime, as the photograph immediately above shows, a football makes the young troops happy.

Photos, Wide World and Central Press

Nazi Submarines Engage in Ocean-Wide Piracy

Above is the Cunard Line cargo steamer Bosnia after she had been torpedoed and set on fire by the U-boat seen in the photograph below. Both photographs were taken from the Norwegian tanker Eidanger, which rescued the Bosnia's crew.

Urged on by the necessity of striking as heavy a blow as possible at Britain's merchant fleet before the defensive tactics could be developed, the German naval authorities sent out to all seas every possible submarine about a month before the actual opening of hostilities. Germany started rebuilding her notorious U-boats in 1935, and up to April last, when the Anglo-German Naval Agreement was denounced by Hitler, 71 submarines were built or under construction. Since then 28 more are understood to have been begun, and no doubt the German naval yards are busy with further boats. Further examples of U-boat piracy with eye-witness stories appear in our "I Was There" section, pages 85–87.

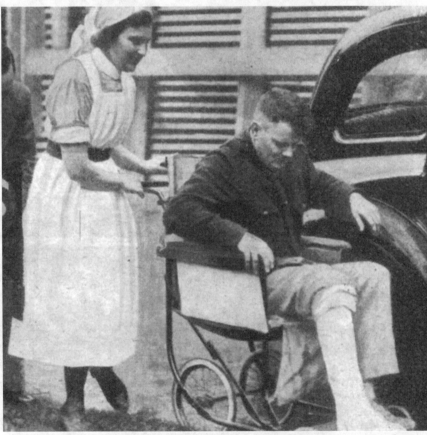

Here we see the chief officer of the Goodwood, who was injured when the ship was torpedoed, being wheeled from hospital. The heroic behaviour of captain, officers and crew of this victim of the U-boats fully upheld the finest traditions of the sea.

Photo, Associated Press

Some Victims of the Early U-Boat Campaign

Such U-boats as those seen above are making what was Germany's last desperate bid for victory in 1917, but is their first bid now.

One of the early tragic results was the sinking of the trader "Olivegrove" 200 miles off the coast of Spain. The crew were ordered by the submarine's commander to take to their boats, and were towed until the American liner "Washington" was sighted, when they were cast off and the submarine submerged (see page 87). Centre, right, one of the "Olivegrove's" boats is coming alongside the "Washington." Centre, left, Captain James Barnetson of the "Olivegrove" is seen on board the "Washington." Bottom, survivors of the "Magdapur," several of them injured, are being landed from a lifeboat. A personal narrative of the sinking of the ship is in page 88.

Gamelin's Hammer Blow at Nazi Western Forts

Where Britain and France struck their first blow against the Reich.

Properly shrouded, for military reasons, in obscurity though they were, enough was disclosed of the French military operations in the first weeks of war to realize that the attack on the Nazi lines of defence was being pushed ahead, and that from the outset Germany had been invaded and a definite threat was being developed against her famous Siegfried Line.

FOR some days after France and Britain declared war on Germany there was no news of fighting on the Western Front. In Poland the Nazi forces were rapidly making progress towards Warsaw, but where France and Germany meet it seemed that the great garrisons of the Maginot and Siegfried Lines rested immobile, watching and waiting for the first move from either side. Not a gun was fired, not a bomb was dropped ; it was, indeed, " All quiet on the Western front."

When the French issued their first war communiqué on September 4, it merely stated that operations had begun by " the whole land, sea and air forces," and, later on the same night, it was added that contacts had been progressively made on the front and that aerial forces were proceeding with the necessary reconnaissances. The communiqués issued in the days that followed were couched in similarly laconic terms, and conveyed little information beyond the fact that the French forces were engaged in occupying the territory which lies between the Maginot and Siegfried Lines.

This " No man's land " is very different from that which was so described in the Great War of 1914–1918. Instead of vast expanses of shell-pocked waste, where towns and villages, roads and streams, had been all obliterated and merged into one foul and evil-smelling whole, there is a picturesque countryside, hilly and well-wooded, dotted with villages and with numerous signs of industrial activity.

Through this difficult country—difficult in the military sense—the French now gingerly proceeded. There was nothing in the nature of a break through, for there were no fortified lines to break through. Rather it was a question of " mopping up "—destroying machine-gun nests and flattening acres of barbed wire with those massive tanks of which the French army is so justly proud ; of battering the concrete posts with heavy gun fire, of discovering and rendering harmless the numerous tank traps with which the whole district was strewn.

Probably the number of troops engaged in these preliminary operations was quite small. Unlike the Great War, which opened as a war of movement and then, after a few months, developed into a war between huge armies occupying heavily fortified positions, the war of 1939 opened between armies already entrenched behind the most massive fortifications that the skill of military engineers could devise and the labour of hundreds of thousands of workpeople could bring into being.

Some ten days or a fortnight after the campaign began it was possible to get some understanding of the method of operation, and of the results

In the upper photograph men of an anti-aircraft battery are practising loading before moving up to the Maginot Line. The other picture shows huge tanks similar to those that constitute the formidable spearhead to the French attack.

Photos Keystone and Associated Press

In the Maginot Line—France's Base of Attack

achieved. Along the whole 90 miles' front between the Moselle and the Rhine the French had carried the war into the enemy's country. The "No man's land" between the Maginot and Siegfried Lines had been practically cleared by the French mopping-up parties, and the invaders were now in contact with the advanced field works of the main German fortifications. So successful had been the operations isolated, and there were reports to the effect that the civilian population had been evacuated. The Warndt Forest to the west of the town had been cleared of German machine-gunners, and far behind the enemy lines road junctions and railways had been heavily bombed from the air and shelled by the great guns in the Maginot emplacements. In the air operations, though not as yet in those conducted on the ground, units of the British Expeditionary Force were already playing a conspicuous part.

The brunt of the attack seems to have fallen, however, on the French tanks—huge armoured fortresses weighing 70 tons apiece, and whose armament includes one of the famous 75 mm. guns slung below the tractors. On September 14 observers in Luxemburg watched eight of these tanks making their way towards the German lines. As they advanced the German outposts were compelled to withdraw, and engineers blew up the railway line in their efforts to stem the advance of the monstrous engines of war.

The roar of battle could be heard in the streets of the city of Luxemburg, many miles away, and it was obvious that the struggle, hitherto a matter of outposts, of long-range artillery fire, of bombing raids, was developing an unprecedented intensity.

Here we have two further photographs of scenes in the Maginot Line. Top, French soldiers are exercising in an underground passage ; below, an ammunition lift is being sent up to the guns from a magazine beneath.
Photos, Sport and General

The Great Siegfried Line is Threatened

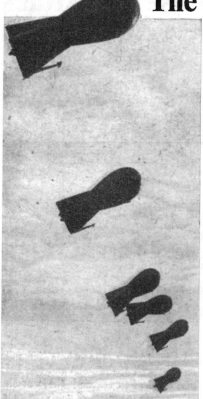

These captive balloons carry listening apparatus to detect the approach of enemy aeroplanes.

Top right, an anti-aircraft gun is being camouflaged. Centre, the framework of steel reinforcement for a concrete strong-point.

Here a deep dug-out is being constructed after the engineers have decided on a suitable position. The construction of the Siegfried Line, officially known as the Westwall, was only begun in July 1938, while work on the Maginot Line was started ten years earlier.

ALTHOUGH for more than a year some hundreds of thousands of engineers and workmen had been engaged on the construction of the Siegfried Line, Germany's western wall of defence was far from completed when war broke out. The work was pushed on with all speed, but it is hardly surprising that there were reports of criticisms by German soldiers who were stationed in the Line. According to these statements received through neutral sources, the ventilation was so bad that the air in the dug-outs was foul, and the more heavily protected dug-outs were not yet habitable—in some cases only the foundations had been laid.

Furthermore, those dug-outs which had been completed were crammed with munitions, and the garrison were in consequence exposed in open trenches to the terrible bombardment of the French artillery and aircraft. Food supply difficulties were also experienced. Semi-official French sources stated that the first heavy bombardments showed that the concrete of the fortifications was inferior.

Poland's 'Brave and Resolute' Army in the Field

IT was an official German commentator who said that
"it would be a mistake to think that the German
army has an easy task in Poland. This war is not a 'walk-
over.' The German army has to meet a brave and resolute
enemy." Since that statement was issued, the German war
machine has overwhelmed the Polish armies in the field and
has captured practically every important centre of resistance.
Nevertheless, the Nazi tribute to the quality of the Polish
troops is unaffected by the outcome of the battle.

In the top photograph Polish troops are moving forward to take up positions in advance trenches in front of Warsaw on September 12.
Middle right, Polish tanks are moving forward preparatory to taking part in an attack on the enemy lines. In the photograph immediately
above, Polish infantry are having some last-minute practice with gas masks before going into action.

Photos, Planet News and Wide World

Nazi Terrorism in Poland Knew No Mercy or Lim

tler's Plighted Word Broken Yet Again

This remarkable photograph brings home forcibly the sufferings of the Polish people and the callous cruelty of the invaders. A German staff car and some dispatch riders are halted in a Polish village while an officer observes the effect of incendiary bombs and shells. This happened before Hitler, maddened by the Polish resistance, ordered the ruthless bombing of open towns and villages. Thus, though he had promised at this time to refrain from making war on civilians, he had actually already perjured himself once more.

Photo, Associated Press

tler's Plighted Word Broken Yet Again

Murder Most Foul from the Air

In earlier pages (24 and 60) there appear clear and ample statements and examples of Hitler's declared policy of the grand lie—"the bigger the lie the greater its value." Here is presented the most heinous of all his broken words. Other photographs appear opposite.

This boy's mother was killed and he was buried alive for 12 hours by a Nazi bomb on Warsaw.
Photo, Associated Press.

" I WILL not war against women and children," said Herr Hitler in his speech to the Reichstag meeting in Berlin just as his legions were thrusting their way across the Polish frontier. "I have ordered my air force to restrict itself to attacks on military objectives."

Such was the Fuehrer's declaration— a declaration which was paralleled by his reply to President Roosevelt's appeal not to bomb civilian populations and unfortified cities in which he stated that he "agreed unconditionally to the proposal." The sentiment was irreproachable, but, alas, it was belied by the event.

A statement issued by the Polish Embassy in London on September 13 gave a list of towns which, even before Britain and France declared war on Germany, had been bombed by German aeroplanes—a list which included not only Warsaw, but all the principal centres of Polish industrial life.

"Since September 3," the statement went on, "scores of Polish towns and even villages have been raided by German bombers. Warsaw was raided repeatedly every day, and even residential quarters and working-class districts suffered grievously from deliberate bombing. The casualties among the civilians, especially among women and children between September 1 and September 3, amounted, according to official figures, to over 1,500 killed and many thousands wounded. Furthermore," the statement went on, "during the last two days the Germans began the methodical bombing of open towns far removed from the battle zone."

If the Polish Ambassador be regarded as a prejudiced witness, the same cannot be said of the United States Ambassador in Poland, who, in a telegram to the Department of State in Washington, gave a vivid picture of the bombing by Nazi airmen of the small town in which he and other members of the diplomatic corps in Warsaw had taken refuge.

"This place, a defenceless open village, was bombed at 11 a.m. today by a flight of four German 'planes, which dropped at least 12 bombs, not only on the outskirts but also along the main street 300 yards from this Embassy."

In a further telegram, Mr. Biddle declared that :

"In my opinion, the German forces are taking advantage of every opportunity without regard to the danger to the civilian population which may be involved. It is also evident that the German bombers are releasing the bombs which they carry even when in doubt as to the identity of their objectives."

He referred to the bombing of a clearly marked hospital train in Warsaw station, and the wiping out of a detachment of twelve Girl Guides in their hut. Among the other instances cited by the Ambassador were :

"attacks on my villa and that of my neighbour ; a heavy attack on modern apartment buildings in the suburbs of Warsaw situated one kilometre from military barracks ; the destruction of a sanatorium involving the death of ten children in woods near Otwock, and the bombing of a refugee train on the way from Kutno."

In the face of such indubitable proofs of the most flagrant violation of Herr Hitler's professed concern that his 'planes should spare women and children, the world learnt with a shrug of pardonable cynicism that the German High Command had announced that open towns, villages and hamlets were henceforth to be bombed and shelled, in order to break what they called the obstinate resistance of the civilian population. The excuse given by the German official news agency was that women, old men and children were erecting traps and organizing a guerilla warfare against Nazi troops.

Lord Halifax, Britain's Foreign Secretary, was not slow in replying to this further chapter in Nazi Germany's campaign of frightfulness. If the statement were true, he declared in the House of Lords, that the German High Command were intending to throw off all restraint in their air bombing, then :

"It would seem to be in direct contradiction to the statement of purpose expressed by the German Chancellor in his Reichstag speech, when he disclaimed any desire to make war on women and children. . . . Whatever may be the rights of belligerent armies as against francs-tireurs, there can be no sort of justification for what must be indiscriminate bombardment, whether from the sea or air, of the civilian population. The British Government must hold themselves completely free if such restraint is not in fact observed to take such action as they may deem appropriate."

Hitler himself is the grand franc-tireur.

Centre, a Polish soldier is seen with his wife and child, both of whom may be victims of Nazi fury while he is fighting. Immediately above, Nazi bombers are preparing for war on women and children.
Photos, Planet News and Wide World

This is the Way Nazis Made War

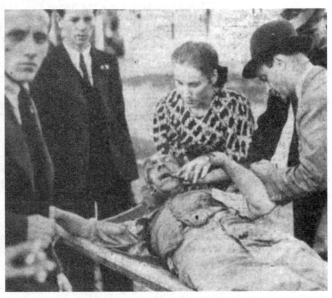

Above, a woman suffering from shock is being helped away. Right, a badly-injured civilian is receiving first-aid. All through the days of intensive bombing from the air the people of Warsaw showed remarkable courage in working in the open among the injured.
Photos, Planet News

IN the light of photographs such as these, what becomes of Herr Hitler's declaration to the Reichstag on September 1, that he would not wage war against women and children ? All the accounts from the scene of battle in Poland are agreed in stating that from the outset the Nazi airmen paid small regard to the safety of the civilian population ; and after the first few days of war even the mask of humanitarianism was thrown aside, and the air terror was developed with a view to crushing the Polish resistance. Far behind the battle zone, towns and villages were bombed by the raiding 'planes : crowds doing their Saturday shopping in the market-places of peaceful villages were machine-gunned from the air ; and on the great towns—Warsaw in particular—were dropped many tons of bombs. According to Polish broadcasts, 400 bombs were dropped on Vilna alone in one day and a total of 20,000 civilian deaths was estimated up to September 17.

In this page we give incontestable evidence that the civilian population of Warsaw was unmercifully bombed from the air. Above, working-class dwellings are on fire as a result of the dropping of incendiary bombs. The photographer who took the pictures was wounded while doing so. He said that the German bombing 'planes passed over the city with systematic regularity in their work of destruction.

THE EMPIRE'S HELP IN FIGHTING HITLER

When Britain is at war the British Commonwealth is at war, too. Hardly had Britain taken up the challenge thrown down by the Nazi aggressors when member after member of the great family of nations of which she is the head hastened to offer her their unstinted support in men, money, and materials.

O N the very day, September 3, 1939, that Britain declared war on Germany, Mr. R. G. Menzies, Prime Minister of the Commonwealth of Australia, in a broadcast to the Australian people declared that "there is unity in the Empire ranks—one King, one flag, one cause. We stand with Britain."

On the same day New Zealand hastened to make it plain that she, too, stood shoulder to shoulder with Britain and her fellow Dominions. New Zealand's fullest co-operation was promised by Mr. Fraser, acting Prime Minister, in a broadcast to the nation, and it was stated that the British Government had been informed that New Zealand concurred entirely with her determination to honour her pledged word. A week later the decision was announced to raise a special military force to serve within or beyond New Zealand.

Canada, too, was quick in making it plain where she stood. Mr. Mackenzie King, the Prime Minister, in a broadcast speech, to the nation on the first Sunday evening of the war, referred to the King's broadcast from London, in which he had appealed to all to make this their own fight to destroy once for all the doctrine that might is right. "Canada," said Mr. Mackenzie King, " has already answered that call." He went on to say that the Canadian parliament was to be called immediately, and that war measures were to be put in operation. "There is no home in Canada," he added, " and no man, woman or child whose life is not bound up with this struggle." On September 10 a state of war between the German Reich and His Majesty's Dominion of Canada was declared to exist. In his speech in the House Mr.

Mackenzie King said that Canada's liberties came from "those men in England and France who never hesitated to lay down their lives when their freedom was threatened."

Measures of economic, naval and air co-operation were immediately instituted, and, as "down under," huge sums were voted for war purposes.

In South Africa there was at first an attempt by the Prime Minister, General Hertzog, to declare the Union's neutrality in the struggle, but anti-Hitler, anti-Nazi opinion in his cabinet, as in Parliament and amongst the South African people as a whole, proved too strong. The Prime Minister resigned, and his place was taken by General Smuts, the famous

soldier-statesman who had captained South Africa in the last war.

From India, too, there came a stream of offers of service. " Nothing could be more significant," said Lord Linlithgow, the Viceroy, " than the unanimity of approach of all in India—princes, leaders, great political parties, the ordinary man and woman—or of their political contributions, and the offers of personal service which have already reached me from the princes and people of India."

So from all the British Crown Colonies, the Protectorates, the Mandated Territories, in every corner of the globe, the answer came in no uncertain voice : " Where the Motherland stands, there her children stand beside her."

THE EMPIRE STANDS TO ARMS!

Australia declared war, Sept. 3rd.
New Zealand went to war, Sept. 3rd.
Men of **Newfoundland** rushed to enlist, Sept. 4th.
Nepal offered troops, Sept. 4th.
Queen of **Tonga** put all resources at Britain's support, Sept. 4th.
Legislative Council of **Malta** reaffirmed people's loyalty, Sept. 5th.
State Council of **Ceylon** declared wholehearted support, Sept. 5th.
Emir of **Transjordan** telegraphed offering support, Sept. 5th.
Bahamas declared loyalty, Sept. 5th.
Legislative Council of **Fiji** declared loyalty and devotion, Sept. 5th.
South Africa declared war, Sept. 6th.
Governor of **Sind Province, India,** sent loyal message, Sept. 8th.
More than 50 princes of **India** had declared loyalty by Sept. 9th.
Canada declared war, Sept. 10th.
Arabs and Jews of **Palestine** had responded in support of Britain by Sept. 10th.
Message of support from Sultan of **Oman,**

Sheikh of **Bahrain,** etc., by Sept. 10th.
Legislative Council of **Tanganyika's** loyal readiness reported, Sept. 10th.
Natives of **Nigeria** declared loyalty, Sept. 10th.
Legislative Assembly of **British Honduras** passed loyal resolution, Sept. 11th.
Governor of **Northern Rhodesia** conveyed loyal messages on behalf of native chiefs, Sept. 11th.
Upper House of Central Legislature of **India** sent a message of admiration to Poland, Sept. 12th.
Aga Khan placed his services at disposal of Government of **India,** Sept. 12th.
Trinidad and **Montserrat** passed resolutions of loyalty, Sept. 12th.
House of Assembly of **Barbados** passed address of loyalty, Sept. 14th.
Kabaka of Buganda sent through Governor of **Uganda** loyal message, Sept. 14th.
High Commissioner for **Basutoland, Bechuanaland,** and **Swaziland** sent loyal resolution on behalf of Swazi nations, Sept. 6th.

Above is the scene in the Senate Chamber of the Canadian Houses of Parliament on September 7, when both houses met in a special session. Lord Tweedsmuir, the Governor-General, is reading the speech from the Throne asking the house to provide for war expenditure.

Photo, Planet News

In this Section we present week by week a collection of personal accounts of war experiences. They are selected on the same basis as those of the long series dealing with the first Great War which appeared in " I Was There," published under the same Editorship in 1938-39.

How We Bombed the Nazi Ships at Kiel

Dramatic first-hand accounts of the R.A.F. raid on the German naval bases near the Kiel Canal—the first British air action of the War—are reprinted below. In issuing the stories to the Press, the Ministry of Information stated that the pilots and crews of the aircraft engaged were drawn from Britain, Canada, Australia, New Zealand and Eire.

THE leader of the first flight to reach its objective had as his navigator a Canadian.

"We started for Wilhelmshaven at 4 p.m. on September 4," said the leader. "When we left, the afternoon was fine, but as we flew we ran into foul weather with heavy, continuous rain.

"We reached Wilhelmshaven after two hours of flying. As we turned on our last course, five minutes away from Wilhelmshaven, the weather cleared for a few minutes. Breaking the flight formation we flew singly into the Schilling Roads.

"We could see a German warship taking on stores from two tenders at her stern. We could even see some washing hanging on a line. Undaunted by the washing we proceeded to bomb the battleship.

"Flying at 100 feet above mast height, all three aircraft in the flight converged on her. I flew straight ahead. The pilot of the second aircraft came across from one side, and the third crossed from the other side.

When we flew on the top of the battleship we could see the crews running fast to their stations. We dropped our bombs.

"The second pilot, flying behind, saw two hit. We came round, and the ship's pom-pom guns began to fire as we headed for home. My navigator saw shells bursting almost on the tail of the aircraft."

The second pilot, swooping across, took a photograph just before dropping his first bomb, and it was found to be very blurred owing to the weather conditions. By now the sky had clouded over again. The aircraft were driving through blinding rain. As this bomber turned on the homeward course the navigator noticed machine-gun tracer bullets nipping past the port wing tip. They looked like small blue electric sparks.

As the pilot of the third aircraft skimmed in his turn towards the warship, he saw the first bomb drop from the second bomber. "To me," he said, "it appeared to drop dead amidships."

By now the battleship's crew were all at action stations, and the third pilot got, as he said, "some hot stuff." This pilot dropped his bombs and made a half circuit round the battleship. Wheeling he noticed three bursts of A.A. fire at the leader's machine.

BY 7.30 p.m. the flight were back at their station.

Another vivid account was given by the officers and crew of aircraft from another squadron which took part in the raids in the Kiel area.

One of the aircraft was hit several times both by shells and bullets, but returned home safely, although two of the petrol tanks were punctured. The remaining two bombers were not hit.

"We set out in fine weather," said the leader of this attack. "We were flying at 2,000 feet, but we soon ran into a belt of cloud and came down to 300 feet. In the thick mist, one pilot became separated from the others, but he took up station again after ten minutes or so.

"We were near the German coast when half a dozen enemy fighters came out to engage us.

" A game of hide and seek in the clouds followed and our craft were successful in eluding their pursuers and left them behind.

"Conditions grew worse and there was heavy rain for an hour. Then the weather improved and my bombers gained height, giving a wide berth to all the islands along the German coast. We observed considerable activity by enemy merchant shipping.

"We made our landfall accurately and flew up the Elbe estuary until we sighted a number of German naval vessels. We were then flying at 6,000 feet under a thin layer of cloud.

"The enemy held his fire until we were almost over our target.

The Kiel Canal is here seen from the air, and the airmen who took part in the raid may well have had much the same view as this. In the centre are the new locks, about 1,200 feet long and nearly 50 feet wide.   *Photo, E.N.A.*

86   *The War Illustrated*   September 30th, 1939

|||||||||||||||||||||||||||||||||||||||||||||||||||||||||||||||||||||||||||||||||||| I WAS THERE! ||||||||||||||||||||||||||||||||||||||||||||||||||||||||||||||||||||||||||||||||||||||||||

" Then suddenly he opened with every gun he could bring to bear on us ; it was terrific, especially the firing from the big ships, which seemed to carry seven anti-aircraft guns on either beam.

" You could watch the tracer shells rising after the flash of the gun in spirals and follow the whole of their course. We made our aircraft as difficult targets as we could by manoeuvring. We then straightened out and dropped our bombs.

" At once we rose up into the clouds with the shells bursting round us and made for home, after an effective smack at the enemy. Our flight all returned home safely."

The leading aircraft was hit by a shell which almost singed the trousers of the wireless operator. Two of the petrol tanks were perforated and several bits of

fuselage shot away, but in spite of everything it made its home station safely and landed without incident.

Other aircraft taking part in the raid returned independently. Two of them sighted a submarine making for Germany on the surface at high speed as was shown by her wake.

At the sight of the British aeroplanes she dived precipitately. An observer thought she left smoke behind her.

As all the bombs had been dropped on the objectives in Germany, unfortunately not one was left, otherwise she would have been an easy victim. Another bomber passed right over the top of the Heligoland fortifications, but was unmolested either by fighters or anti-aircraft fire.

injured, who were rushed to the homes of fisherfolk and given clothes and a hot meal.

The survivors were loth to talk about their terrible experience, but one of them said : " There was a terrific explosion amidships and then the boat listed. We were all thrown from our seats. I heard no warning."

Another victim of the U-boats during the same week was the British tanker " Regent Tiger " (10,176 tons). " It was a terrifying spectacle after the torpedo had struck," said one of the ship's officers. " There was an explosion, and flames 1,000 feet high roared into the sky. We were in two ship's lifeboats about 300 to 400 yards away, but at that distance the fumes were suffocating and the heat unbearable. The tanks of our ship were filled with petrol. As the fire spread the tanks blew up. We have since heard that the tanker is still ablaze and the sea around her."

We Were Victims of the Nazi U-Boats

Having taken up their positions in the High Seas days and weeks before War was declared, the German U-boats were able to sink quite a number of British merchant-vessels before the convoy system could be instituted.   What British holidaymakers saw of the sinking of the " Magdapur " is told below, and the account is followed by stories of other sinkings reported in " The Daily Telegraph " and " The Sunday Times."

When the Liverpool steamship " Magdapur " (8,640 tons) was torpedoed by a German U-boat on Sunday, September 10, thousands of holidaymakers at a British seaside resort saw from the beach the ship go down.

Following a loud explosion which rocked many of the buildings on shore, a

column of water shot into the air alongside the steamer. Two hours later she had gone to the bottom. Two ships took off the crew, most of whom were Lascars, and 70 of the survivors were brought ashore by the coast lifeboat. When news of the sinking spread, the local A.R.P. services were mobilized to deal with the

The " Inverliffey " was another British tanker sunk by a German submarine—this time in the open sea of the Atlantic. Third Officer Albert Lang had this thrilling story to tell when he landed in England.

" It was about one o'clock in the afternoon," he said, " when a submarine fired at us. We sent out an S O S and tried to get away, but shells continued to burst all around us.

" We had a crew of forty on board. We lowered the boats as soon as we could. The captain and several of the officers left in the last boat. There were eight of us in this boat, and as we rowed away the submarine fired into the ' Inverliffey' amidships. She went up with a roar.

" Flames and smoke went up 500 or 600 feet. We rowed for our lives until we could row no more, and when we thought we were done the commander of the submarine steered his ship alongside and told us we could stand round the conning-tower. We were nearly waist-deep in water.

" The submarine commander said that if any British warships turned up he would have to submerge and leave us. This would have meant that we should have been struggling in the water with no boats near.

" No sooner had we all got on to the submarine than it got up speed and took us out of danger.

" The commander, a young man, treated us decently. The submarine cruised away until we got near one of our own lifeboats. Then the captain waved his hand in farewell, submerged his ship, and we swam to the boat.

" Some hours later we were picked up, and afterwards transferred to another vessel."

The sinking of the " Olivegrove " took place at 9 o'clock at night.   Above, survivors are coming alongside the U.S. liner " Washington " in one of the ship's boats.   Other photographs of the sinking of the " Olivegrove " are in page 75.

Photo. Keystone

September 30th, 1939　　　　　　　　　　　　　　The War Illustrated　　　　　　　　　　　　　　87

IIIIIIIIIIIIIIIIIIIIIIIIIIIIIIIIIIIIIIIIIIIIIIIIIIIIIIIIIIIII **I WAS THERE!** IIIIIIIIIIIIIIIIIIIIIIIIIIIIIIIIIIIIIIIIIIIIIIIIIIIIIIIIIIIII

This remarkable photograph shows the explosion which immediately preceded the disappearance of the **Bosnia**. It was taken by a survivor of the torpedoed ship's crew from the deck of the Norwegian tanker Eidanger. Other photographs are in page 76.

Photo, Associated Press

THE story of the sinking on September 7 of the "Olivegrove" (Glasgow freighter, 4,060 tons) comes from the lips of Chief-Officer William Watson.

Mr. Wilson, who was torpedoed at the Dardanelles in the last war, said that after the submarine had fired a shot across the "Olivegrove's" bows and signalled to her to abandon ship, the crew of 33 were given 20 minutes to get the lifeboats away.

"Everything was done in a leisurely way," he said, "as if the submarine had a week to do the job.

"The submarine commander hailed our two lifeboats to come alongside, and in perfect English he gave us our course to land. Nevertheless, he kept following us for nearly three hours. Then he came alongside, and, still very courteous, told us : 'There is a vessel coming to your assistance. I thank you.'

"Half an hour later we were taken on board the rescue ship, which was the American liner Washington."

When Mr. Wilson's lifeboat was bobbing in the sea beside the submarine after the ship had been sunk he was able to judge from the "grass"—marine growth—on the plating of the U-boat that she had been away from her home port for about a month—long before war was declared.

He added : "And from what I could see of the crew as they stood round the conning-tower they were all pretty 'jumpy,' dejected and shabbily dressed. The name on their hatbands was so faded that it was unreadable."

Cathil Maclean, an 18-year-old member of the crew, said :

"The commander—he seemed to be a man under 30, and, like the rest of the crew, had a long beard—told us to set a course for the north and we would be picked up by a liner. Later he fired a rocket to the "Washington" notifying her of our position."

WHEN the captain and 31 members of the crew and the solitary passenger of the Cunard White Star steamer "Bosnia" were landed at Lisbon, they had a tale to tell of stern ruthlessness on the part of the U-boat which sent their ship to the bottom.

The ship was stopped off the Portuguese coast by two warning shots. The crew were permitted to leave in the lifeboats but they were forbidden to take anything with them. Captain Walter H. Poole, however, the master, who is a veteran of the Great War, managed to salve his binoculars. As soon as they had entered the boats, the submarine torpedoed the "Bosnia." Some of the eye-witnesses said that just before the U-boat submerged her captain bowed and saluted his victims and their doomed vessel. Fortunately a Norwegian vessel, the "Eidanger," was in the vicinity and the survivors were picked up and landed safely.

Our Trawlers Met a U-Boat

When peacefully engaged in reaping the harvest of the sea, several British trawlers encountered German U-boats in the early days of the war. Below we print accounts of two such incidents, reprinted from the "News Chronicle" and the "Daily Herald."

"WE were steaming along in the darkness," one of the crew of the British steam trawler "Roman " said, "when suddenly lights of a vessel low down in the water were switched on.

"The mate dropped one of the wheelhouse windows and said to me : 'That's no trawler.'

"Looking through the binoculars, he asked : 'Have you ever seen a submarine ?' I replied : 'Only in dock.'

"'Then take a look at this,' he replied.

"Next minute we saw the outline of a submarine.

"She was only about 150 yards away.

"To prove we were a fishing vessel, we switched on all our deck lights, but for a quarter of an hour the submarine continually 'stemmed us' (kept abreast).

"Wondering what was going to happen we kept on steaming.

"I shouted down the engine room to one of the engineers : 'Ike, come and look up here.'

"The engineer climbed the ladder and I pointed to the submarine.

"All he said was : 'Crikey, why didn't you tell me before ? This is the first submarine I've seen.'

"It seemed a silly game we were playing.

"No one on the submarine hailed us and we never spoke to them, and eventually the submarine straightened out and steamed away nor'-east.

"All her lights were switched off as soon as she fell astern of us."

" We heaved a sigh of relief, of course, when the submarine departed, but we were too surprised by her sudden appearance to get in a panic."

O UR second story tells how seven unarmed trawlers risked destruction in order to save an eighth trawler which was menaced by a German submarine.

" All the eight vessels were fishing together," one of the skippers said

when the boats returned to port. " On the horizon appeared what we thought was a fishing smack.

" Our binoculars proved it to be a submarine. Several vessels chopped away their gear and we made off. The eighth trawler broke down and fell behind. If we had left her she would probably have been sunk, so all seven of us turned round. We went back, formed an escort, and the danger was over."

Sketchy black-out regulations were already in force, and nobody, except officials, could use the telephone, even to ring up in their own townships.

The route chosen took us diagonally across the famous Beauce, where on our run down a fortnight earlier a sea of golden corn stretched as far as the eye could see for well over 200 miles, with an occasional vast farmstead, like an oasis in a desert of plenty.

Already, the fields had been swept bare, the corn was threshed, and in various spots emergency flying fields had sprung up overnight.

At the townships that we could not avoid, farmers were delivering up their horses, while their womenfolk carried on the land work with oxen, and often with cows. At the various points of mobilization troops grinned and yelled salutations, and waved to us when they spotted our Union Jack.

Now the roads were beginning to show evidence of the evacuation of Paris. Every few hundred yards one met cars laden to capacity with people and luggage. Bundles were tied on to the wings, mattresses covered huge packages on the roofs, and, as often as not, a cycle was tied on to the radiators.

Everybody seemed astounded to find a private car travelling in the opposite direction, until they spotted that we were British folk scurrying back home. Recognition brought joyful little tootles on sirens, to which we responded as long as we were within hearing distance.

One old fellow, as he approached us, signalled us to stop, and insisted on our drinking wine with him and his family by the roadside.

At Mantes, one street was completely blocked with horses. Officials were busy checking to make sure that every available animal had been delivered, and country-women were returning home in cars of ancient vintage, but of surprisingly good performance.

Yet here, as everywhere, no upheaval of life was apparent. One would have thought that everything was quite normal, that the people were carrying on the routine to which they had been accustomed for years.

Once in Northern France things began to change and progress became more difficult, with long lines of transport on the roads, and huge convoys being organized with military precision in the streets of towns to which the troops— wearing their everyday civilian clothes— were reporting.

Here, too, every bridge across river or railway was guarded by two armed sentries, and there was apparent a certain tension, a feeling of waiting for something big to happen—but waiting quite calmly, with complete confidence, mingled with a determination to get on with the job and see it through.

I Saw the Frenchmen Called Up

Isolated in a farm in the French mountains, the writer of this contribution, H. Pattinson Knight, turned his car England-wards through a France in the throes of mobilization. The story is reprinted from the London " Star " of September 11.

B URIED from the outside world on a farm in the heart of the Puy de Dome, miles away from the nearest town, it was only on the eve of war, by the arrival of an official to commandeer horses, that I learned of recent momentous happenings.

Motoring over the mountain track, we reached La Bourboule for more detailed information, and we were at lunch when orders for general mobilization came over the wireless.

By the time we had finished our meal, the restaurant and hotel to which it was

was saying that the job had got to be done, and, in any case, it meant the end of Hitler's régime.

The official announcement of general mobilization was made, as usual, in French towns, by the local town-crier, after beating a tattoo on a kettle-drum. The fellow at La Bourboule made use of a bicycle to get around.

On a carrier over the front wheel he had mounted his drum, and all he had to do to draw attention was to turn a little handle that controlled the drumsticks. After listening to him, the little crowds

The fine spirit with which the young French soldiers joined up is described in this page. Above, a troop train crowded with the flower of the youth of France moves eastward from Paris. Such scenes have been enacted all over France.

Photo, Wide World

attached were being stripped of carpets and made ready for their war-time uses · the staff was being paid off, and a full inventory being taken. Incidentally, I learned that only one teaspoon could not be accounted for !

Yet, there seemed to be no hurry. Everybody knew his or her job—both peace-time and war-time—and got on with it without any fuss. There was no flag-wagging, no cheering.

On the other hand, there was no depression, and no long faces. Everybody

quietly dispersed without the least excitement.

The casino announced by loudspeaker that it would remain open to visitors that afternoon. It became a bigger meeting place than ever for a few hours. The terrace was crowded with people sipping their drinks, and everybody appeared eager to have a last flutter at the tables.

That night there was hardly a man of military age to be seen anywhere. They slipped away quietly, in small batches, and no one saw them set forth on their crusade.

Every War Has Its Lighter Side

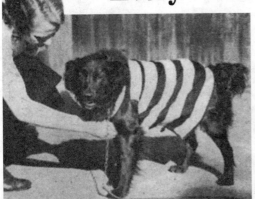

Above is one way of minimizing the disadvantage at which a black dog stands in a black-out.

This London balloon barrage team has found a really good use for Berchtesgaden as a " Funkhof."

In the middle photograph above, the Siegfried Line becomes as unsubstantial as a fried egg, while the Maginot Line shows imagination in its privacy. The Chinese gentleman above walking in London is doing his bit in the British Red Cross, but the sunshade would doubtless be discarded in an air raid. Right, an early edition of Hitler's " Mein Kampf," among other books, is being used as a substitute for sand-bags to protect the roof of a London building.

Photos, Keystone, Central Press and "Daily Mirror"

In Wartime France

Above, French women of all ages are interviewing Mlle. Huard, head of the recruiting department for volunteers for every sort of service.

These twelve trailer fire pumps drawn up for inspection are part of the Paris A.R.P. or Defense Contre-Arienne. As in London, wartime services have been formed to deal with the results of air raids, though owing to the calls of the army most of them are over military age.

PARIS, like every other capital of the belligerent countries, is " blacked out " at night, though not so completely as London. But though the streets may be dark, Paris is not downhearted. The cafés and restaurants that are still open are almost as full as usual and conversation is animated, for French men and women love to exchange views and to hear news by word of mouth. Moreover, in times of crisis the Frenchman feels the need of the company of his fellows more than ever. Paris by day, as the photographs in this page prove, shows many signs that the country is at war ; but French men and women when once their country is in danger face the future with a calm dignity, and indifference to hardship, going about their daily work unperturbed.

The complete mobilization of the army taking all men of military age has caused far more difficulties in business than in London, but Frenchwomen have filled many gaps.

Like London's girls, Parisiennes carry gas masks. Like them, too, they keep smiling, as these two mademoiselles on their way to work show.

Paris has taken the fullest precautions against air raids, and, left, workmen are piling sandbags to protect the Opera House. Right, Czech refugees in Paris are lining up to enlist in the Czech Legion, so that they may strike a blow for their country's freedom.

Photos, Topical, Wide World and Associated Press

Red Russia's Weight in the Scales of War

Though this Russian sailor is serving a formidable looking anti-aircraft machine-gun, the Red Fleet, with the possible exception of the submarine fleet is almost negligible. Below are bombers of the Soviet air fleet.

With fixed bayonets and machine-guns these soldiers of the Red Army are taking part in manoeuvres near Moscow. Their equipment is obviously based on the German model.

Photos, Planet News

THE exact numbers of the Red Army are not accurately known, but the last official figures given in January 1938 state that the strength of the army was about 1,100,000. Since then, however, there has been a considerable expansion until the total strength is now estimated at about 2,500,000. Against this number has to be set the fact that lack of railway communications and the bad state of the roads must immobilize a large proportion of the Russian forces in time of war. On paper, at least, the Russian Air Force is formidable, with its stated total of nearly 7,000 machines. As regards the Russian Navy, no battleships have been built since 1911, but reports give a good impression of the Soviet service.

On September 17 Soviet troops began the invasion of Eastern Poland, and by midnight the Red Army was more than 30 miles over the frontier. One of the first invading contingents of Red infantry is here seen marching towards the frontier.

WORDS THAT HISTORY WILL REMEMBER

A Select Weekly Record of the Most Important War Declarations and Statements

Sunday, September 3

Leaflet distributed by Royal Air Force in W. and N. Germany :

"Deliberately and coldly the Government of the Reich has forced war upon England.

Never before has any Government driven its citizens to death on such futile pretexts. This war is perfectly unnecessary.

The soil and the rights of Germany were menaced from no side at all. Nobody hindered the reoccupation of the Rhineland, nor the completion of the Anschluss or the bloodless linking of the Sudetenland with the Reich.

Neither England nor any other Powers attempted to check the rebuilding of the Reich, so long as the Reich did not forcefully crush the independence of non-German nations.

All German demands could have been considered as long as they were justified. . . .

Instead of that your Government has sentenced you to a bath of blood, to distress, and to a war that you cannot hope to win. We have not been betrayed : you Germans have been betrayed. During many years, a reckless censorship has hidden the truth from you, a truth that even uncivilized nations knew.

We and our allies have at our disposal considerable reserves. We are too strong to be broken. We can fight against you until you are entirely exhausted. You, people of Germany, now, and at any moment, have the right to make peace. We, too, hope for peace, and we are already prepared to conclude peace with any German Government which has a sincere determination for peace."

Monday, September 4

General Smuts, speaking in the Parliament of the Union of South Africa :

"General Hertzog has said this matter of Danzig is a Polish affair with which South Africa has nothing to do. But I am profoundly convinced that although Danzig and the Polish corridor were the immediate occasion of war, the real issue goes far beyond Danzig and Poland and touches South Africa.

"General Hertzog has made a statement which I regard as resembling a complete justification of Herr Hitler. I do not think that the people of the Union, in their vital interest as South Africans, could hope to justify that view. Nothing could be more fatal for South Africa, poor as it is in defence, and rich as it is in resources, to dissociate itself directly or indirectly from its friends in the Commonwealth.

"It is not only a question of loyalty and self-respect—which I assume we all feel deeply ; it is a question of importance and of the deepest interest to the future of South Africa.

"If we dissociate ourselves deliberately and conspicuously from the line of action taken by the other members of the Commonwealth, we are going to get what we deserve, and the day will come—and it will not be far off—when the same treatment will be applied to us. And when the day of trouble comes—and it will come as surely as you are seated here—when the German demand for the return of South-West Africa is made at the point of the bayonet, we shall stand alone. . . ."

Declaration by the British Labour Party to the Czecho-Slovak peoples, broadcast in their own language by secret means.

"Being in close contact with their Czecho-Slovak friends now outside their country, the Labour Party is well aware of the sufferings of the Czecho-Slovak peoples.

"Now is the time to put an end to the brutal violence endangering all Europe. We are calling from London to Prague and Bratislava. We are calling all workers of Czecho-Slovakia.

"Remain firm. Keep your hearts strong in the new wave of violence. Remain true to the deeds and principles of the great Thomas Masaryk. The hour of your liberation is near."

Tuesday, September 5

Message to the Independent Labour Party from the Independent Socialists of Germany, smuggled across the frontiers at great risk to its bearers :

"In the moment before the cannons speak, before the world faces horror and slaughter, we send our message to you. The German workers do not want this war, the German peasants do not want war.

"We love Germany, the country where we have been born and educated, but we have nothing in common with the present régime.

"In our illegal pamphlets, spread even among the fortification workers watched by the Gestapo, we have protested against the occupation of Austria against the annexation of Czecho-Slovakia, against Hitler's policy of aggression and war.

"This war is not our war, this fight is not our fight. Our common Fatherland is humanity."

Saturday, September 9

From the Broadcast to the British people made by the Polish Ambassador in London, Count Edward Raczynski :

"September 1 will go down in history as a day of shame for the brutal aggressors, and as the opening of a new chapter in the life of Europe.

"Since that day my country has been incessantly battered by practically the whole of the German army and continuously bombed by its entire air force. The losses suffered by Poland in territory and economic resources are certainly great, and owing to the crushing superiority of the enemy in equipment the Polish armies did not have as yet a chance of making full use of their skill and daring of manoeuvre.

"But our resistance has not been broken. Reserves are called up, the troops are occupying new positions and the fighting goes on. The day of aggression was fixed by the enemy beforehand, with ruthless precision. It was known to be planned for the beginning of September and some excuse or other had to be found by that time. When Nazi Germany struck at Poland with all her might, Poland had no choice but to take up arms in defence of her independence.

"The one excuse invented by the fertile brain of the German Fuehrer was the alleged maltreatment of the German minority in Polish lands. The excuse is poor and the accusation a slander. All who knew the position of the German minority in Poland, small in numbers but enjoying an important status due to its money power and to the spirit of tolerance displayed by Poland, stand amazed at the impudence of German mendacity. And this impudence shows no signs of abating.

"May I take this opportunity to utter, before the whole civilized world, the most solemn protest against the calumnies with which the aggressor attempts to besmirch the good name of the Polish nation ? . . .

"It seems the simplest thing that could be done to defend the homes of Poland against a cruel and unscrupulous aggressor. And yet, by doing it, Poland turned a new leaf in recent European history, for Poland was the first nation which dared to defy Hitler's challenge and meet his attack with fire. This act of courage was a great service rendered to all the free nations of the world.

"The time was bound to come when the Nazi methods of extortion would meet with strong resistance. But the fact is that Poland was the first nation to do it, and she accepted an unequal struggle rather than join the ranks of those who allowed themselves to be the victims of Nazi blackmail. . . ."

Third Leaflet distributed by the R.A.F. over Central Germany.   *TRANSLATION*

WARNUNG!

England an das deutsche Volk

Die Nazi-Regierung hat, trotz der Bemühungen der führenden Großmächte, die Welt in einen Krieg gestürzt.

Dieser Krieg ist ein Verbrechen. Das deutsche Volk muß zwischen dem Vorwand, den seine Regierung benutzt, um den Krieg vom Zaun zu brechen und den Grundsätzen, die England und Frankreich zur Verteidigung Polens zwingen, ganz klar unterscheiden.

Von Anfang an hat die englische Regierung erklärt, daß an der polnischen Frage nichts ist, was einen europäischen Krieg mit allen seinen tragischen Folgen rechtfertigen kann.

Fünf Monate nach dem Münchener Vertrag wurde die Selbständigkeit der Tschechoslovakei brutal zertreten. Wenn Polen nicht auch von dem gleichen Schicksal ereilt werden soll, dann müßten wir darauf bestehen, daß friedliche Verhandlungsmethoden nicht durch Gewaltandrohungen unmöglich gemacht werden, daß die zu treffende Abmachung der Lebensrechte Polens gewährleistet und auch ehrlich gehalten wird. Ein Diktat können wir weder zulassen noch annehmen.

Wenn Herr Hitler glaubte, die englische Regierung werde aus Angst vor dem Kriege die Polen im Stich lassen, so hat er sich schwer getäuscht. Erstens bricht England sein einmal gegebenes Wort nicht. Außerdem ist es aber Zeit, der brutalen Gewalt, die die Nazi-Regierung der Welt aufzwingen will, ein deutsches Halt zu bieten.

Mit diesem Krieg stellt sich der Reichskanzler gegen den unbeugsamen Willen der englischen Regierung, einen Willen, hinter dem nicht nur die gesamten Hilfsquellen und Mittel des englischen

WARNING
England to the German People

The Nazi régime has, in spite of the endeavours of the leading great Powers, plunged the world into war.

This war is a crime. The German people must quite clearly distinguish between the pretexts employed by its government so as to unleash war and the principles which have forced England and France to defend Poland.

From the very beginning the English government has made it clear that the Polish question is not one which can justify a European war with all its tragic consequences.

Five months after the Munich Agreement the independence of Czecho-Slovakia was brutally trodden underfoot. So that Poland shall not also suffer the same fate, we must insist that peaceful methods of negotiation shall not be rendered impossible through threats of force, and that in the negotiations which are requisite the Poles' right to live must be guaranteed and honourably kept. We cannot accept or admit a Diktat.

If Herr Hitler believes that the English government, out of fear of war, will allow the Poles to be left in the lurch, then he has been deceiving himself. In the first place England will not break her pledged word. Furthermore, it is high time that the brutal force with which the Nazi régime strives to dominate the World should be halted.

Through this war the German Chancellor places himself against the unbending resolution of the English government, a resolution which has behind it not only the resources and means of the whole English Commonwealth, but also a union of other great Powers. It is a question of the salvation of human freedom and the right of free peoples to live free.

Up to the very last moment the Pope, the President of the United States and the King of the Belgians, in the name of Belgium, Holland, Luxemburg, Denmark, Sweden, Norway and Finland, made fruitless appeals to your Nazi government, urgently requesting that negotiations should be resumed in the place of war.

Now a catastrophe has broken out upon you in that the Reich finds itself isolated from the community of civilised peoples, without any support save that of Communist Russia.

You cannot win this war. Against you are arrayed resources and materials far greater than your own.

For years you have been subjected to the most stringent censorship, and by means of an incredible system of secret police and informers the truth has been withheld from you.

Against you stands the united strength of the free peoples, who with open eyes will fight for freedom to the last.

This war is as repulsive to us as it is to you, but do not forget that England, once forced into war, will wage it unwaveringly to the end. England's nerves are strong, her resources inexhaustible. We will not relent.

End of a Glorious Stand

No more gallant stand has ever been made in the history of warfare than that of the garrison of the Polish fort of Westerplatte on the outskirts of Danzig, where a handful of Poles withstood furious attacks by land forces and bombardment by the battleship Schleswig-Holstein for six days. Some idea of what they endured can be gathered from the photograph (left) and that below (right).

The name of Major Koscianski, seen above, who commanded the Polish garrison at Westerplatte will stand in the roll of Poland's heroic soldiers.

Above, the Nazi flag is flying, over the shattered remains of the fort at Westerplatte after the surrender.

Left are Polish prisoners just after surrendering to the captain of the Schleswig-Holstein, seen at their head. Above, German soldiers are examining the havoc they have wrought.

Photos, Associated Press, Keystone and Central News

GOERING'S COLD CHEER FOR NAZIS

Designated by Hitler as heir-apparent to the Leadership of the Reich,
Marshal Goering's pronouncements may be taken as a true reflection
of the official Nazi standpoint.   Here is his first war-time speech.

NOT long ago Goering told the German people that they could not have both guns and butter.... When he addressed the workers in an armament factory in Berlin on September 9 he had to tell them in effect that now the guns were going off there would be still harder times for the German people.

He began his speech with an almost plaintive reference to Britain, which had come to the support of Poland—" a little State that has been inflated in the last few years as one blows up ridiculous little rubber figures." He went on :

"We have never harmed British interests. We have even recognized her dominion over a fifth of the world. But really England is not in the least concerned with Poland. The Poles are to them of as little interest as perhaps the Turks. For Britain there is nothing important in the world but herself.

"What is the situation in Poland, the scene of war ? The Polish army will never emerge again from the German embrace. We can hope that within 14 days of beginning the chief things will be achieved, and in a few weeks more the last work of cleaning up will be finished. We estimate that the whole campaign to the last clearing up will not last more than four weeks.

"If the British aeroplanes fly at tremendous heights at night and drop their ridiculous propaganda on German territory, I have nothing against it. But take care if the leaflets are succeeded by one bomb. Then reprisals will follow and will be carried out as in Poland ...

"Germany, they say, is mortally vulnerable in the economic and internal spheres. When I started the Four-Year Plan I did it with the object of forming a protection that cannot be defeated, and today I can say that Germany is the best armed State in the world. We possess all that we need to defeat our enemies. They have more gold, copper, and lead, but we have more workers, more men. That is decisive. And our production of aeroplanes and guns is still far greater than that of our enemies ...

Nazi Ideas of Honourable Peace

"You (Mr. Chamberlain) cannot doubt the will for peace of the German people. It is great and deep and the peace-will of the Fuehrer is very deep. We wish for peace and are ready for peace. It rests with you, Mr. Chamberlain. Will you give the word for life or death ? Then give it and we will take the offer. But never again shall there be a Versailles. We are ready for an honourable peace, but we will fight to the utmost if there is no peace.

"I Know Things Will Get Worse "

"I know there are many things that will get worse. There is, for example, the question of substitute materials. I admit that the suit of substitute material is not so good as a real one, especially since we have made the latest fibre from potato plant. But that is not the point. It is no longer a question of the life of the individual but of the nation. I know that war soap is not as good as peace soap and often there is no soap at all. But then we must just have dirty hands ...

"I can understand how depressed many of you are when you think of the World War. And many say that it will be the same again as it was then. But the situation is not the same ...

"I must ask hard and difficult sacrifices of you. You must understand that it cannot be otherwise. You must also understand that at the beginning everything does not go as well as it should. The most important thing is bread, and we have seen to it that there is enough. Of meat, it can be said that we eat far too much

of it in any case. With less meat we shall get thinner and so need less material for a suit. That is an advantage.

"You shall always be told the truth in this war. Maybe that at the front there is a serious reverse—that must not be hidden from you. If listening to foreign radio stations is heavily punished, it is not because we fear them but because it is dishonourable to listen to the dirty tirades of foreign countries ...

"We are prepared for an acceptable peace and equally determined to fight to the last under the Leader, who for many years has raised up the German people. Shall we be parted from such a Leader at the wish of Great Britain ? It is too monstrous to speak of it. We want peace, but peace at the price of our Leader is not to be thought of. To destroy our Leader is to destroy the German nation. Germany is Hitler, and Hitler is Germany."

Germany's Bankrupt Policy

REPLYING to this tirade, the British Ministry of Information said that in official circles it is regarded that Goering's speech revealed the bankruptcy of Nazi policy. It read :

"It is considered in official circles that Field-Marshal Goering's speech revealed the bankruptcy of German policy.

"Herr Hitler has made many promises to foreign countries : none of them has been kept.

"It is therefore not surprising that no confidence is placed in any assurance he may give, and Great Britain is therefore justified in requiring that peace should be concluded with a German Government whose word may be trusted.

"But the German Government has also misled the German people who were promised ' peace and honour.' They have not got peace because the German Government has deliberately pursued a policy of violence which has made war inevitable. They have not got honour because the world recognizes the crudity and falseness of the German Government's charges against Poland.

"The ' sickening technique,' as the Prime Minister called it, has become too familiar.

Field-Marshal Goering, a German air-ace, is head of the Nazi Council of Six.
Photo, Associated Press

"Great Britain is fighting for a return to decency in international relations. Until this is achieved no country is safe. Germany may say that she has no aims in the West, but the tale of limited German territorial ambitions has been told too often to inspire the slightest confidence.

"Great Britain does not desire another Versailles, as Field-Marshal Goering falsely alleges, nor the collapse of Germany, but a just and enduring peace with any honourable German Government.

"As regards the economic situation, Field-Marshal Goering's remarks can have brought little comfort to his hearers, who already, even before the outbreak of war, have been reduced to such meagre rations.

"What is to be said of a Government which frivolously embarks on an unnecessary war in economic conditions the gravity of which even Field-Marshal Goering's optimism does not venture to conceal from an audience which is only too well aware of the facts ? "

It Is Said That ...

There is growing German anxiety at the apparently early failure of their air force. Rapidly-mounting casualty lists and the few 'planes which return after raids on France are making a profound impression in Berlin.

It is being realized that many German pilots are too young and inexperienced. From Washington comes a statement that Germany is killing at least three pilots under training each week.   *(Reuter)*

In Western Germany the words " Heil, Hitler ! " are rapidly going out as a greeting. People are going back to the pre-Nazi salutation of " Gruss Gott ! "

At Aachen, Cologne, and Crefeld, travellers said that the police have had to disperse angry food queues ; at Aachen and Düsseldorf they broke up groups of women and children demonstrating against the departure of soldiers for the Front.

In Germany salaries are being reduced and no overtime is paid for night or Sunday work. Residents must make room for refugees, and are advised to feed rabbits and goats on materials left over from the kitchen.

Berlin tailors have issued a manifesto asking the population to hunt up old clothes capable of being refashioned.

According to a report from Panama, the German cargo boat *Eisenbach*, 4,177 tons, sailed from Corinto, the principal seaport of Nicaragua, on the Pacific coast. Gun ports—holes for guns—had been cut with oxy-acetylene apparatus. Other German ships, it is stated, are being fitted out as privateers in ports on the west coast of South and Central America.

A feature of the German offensive on the Western Front is the use of machine-guns operated electrically by remote control.

Under a decree published by the Ministerial Council for the Reich Defence, any person committing robbery, larceny or violence under cover of a black-out or an air-raid warning will be liable to sentences ranging from long terms of imprisonment to death.

Americans arriving in Copenhagen from Berlin were partially stripped at the frontier. The women were made to remove stockings, shoes, dresses and other garments. All luggage was inspected minutely, even sticks of shaving soap being taken from their cases.

A crowded theatre repeatedly hissed the scenes of German troops marching victoriously through Belgium in the Great War when the film " Nurse Edith Cavell " was given its first presentation in Washington.

Sound and Fury Against Britain

On September 9, Field-Marshal Goering, speaking in a Berlin armament factory, devoted some of his speech to some criticism and harsh words of Britain and her Prime Minister. He mingled defiance with pleas for peace, but warned the German people that they must be prepared to make " hard and difficult sacrifices."

Photo, Keystone

OUR DIARY OF THE WAR

Monday, September 11

German attack on Warsaw checked; attacking troops retired to outskirts. Polish broadcasts continued from the capital in spite of Nazi interference on the same wavelength. In the south of Poland the German advance aimed at Lwow was held up.

French attacks made substantial progress on a 12-mile front east of the Saar. There were bayonet charges by the French in the sector between Merzig, 22 miles south of Trier, and the Moselle, and air raids on troop concentrations behind the Siegfried Line.

It was reported that R.A.F. 'planes carried out a raid early on September 9 on the island of Sylt, site of a big German air base, off the west coast of Schleswig-Holstein.

The Polish Government moved their headquarters to Brzesc-Litewski (Brest-Litovsk), 115 miles east of Warsaw.

The King opened the fund of the British Red Cross and Order of St. John with a gift of £5,000.

The British Government issued, through the Ministry of Information, a declaration of policy, in which it was stated that Britain would make peace only with a German Government whose word could be trusted, and that therefore no peace was possible with Hitler.

A message to India from the King-Emperor was read by the Viceroy to the Central Legislature in Simla.

Tuesday, September 12

A meeting of the Supreme War Council was held in France, attended by Mr. Chamberlain and Lord Chatfield for Great Britain, and M. Daladier and General Gamelin for France.

The French made further progress in their advance in the region of the Saar. There was a strong reaction by the enemy.

British troops received a warm welcome in France. It was reported that R.A.F. contingents had been stationed in France for some time.

The Poles took advantage of the pause in the German attack on Warsaw to consolidate their principal lines of defence. The main German force was held up at Modlin, on the north bank of the Vistula, 15 miles from the capital. Other German attacks in Poland were to the north-east, towards Bialystok, and from the south across the San River.

The German High Command claimed that Polish troops trapped in the area west of the Vistula had failed to break through, and that the equipment of four Polish divisions had been captured.

A German submarine stopped and searched the American freighter "Wacosta" off the coast of Ireland.

Four more British cargo vessels were reported sunk by U-boats, namely, "Inverliffey," "Firby," "Blairlogie" and "Gartavon." A Finnish barque, "Olivebank," was sunk by a drifting mine in the North Sea.

It was announced that, owing to doubts about the permanence of neutrality, almost all German residents in Eire had left for Germany.

Wednesday, September 13

The German High Command announced that, in order to crush civilian resistance, open towns and villages in Poland will henceforth be bombed and shelled.

Lord Halifax stated in the House of Lords that if such action were taken by the Germans, the British Government would hold themselves free "to take such action as they might deem appropriate."

According to statements issued by the Polish Embassy in London and by the American Ambassador in Poland, German aeroplanes have for some time been bombing civilians in Poland.

German advance on Warsaw still held up, but encircling movements were made round the Polish position. Attacks on Modlin and Lwow had been repulsed, but east of Warsaw Polish forces had withdrawn under heavy pressure.

Paris reported that French troops had improved the whole of the positions taken in the course of the last few days.

French War Cabinet was formed, with M. Daladier as Prime Minister, Foreign Minister and War Minister.

Mr. Chamberlain gave Parliament a second survey of the progress of the War.

It was reported from Brussels that Hitler had issued an appeal to all doctors, engineers and other technical experts, whatever their race, who had fled from Germany, to return, with the promise that fortunes confiscated from such refugees would be restored.

Thursday, September 14

Germany claimed to have captured Gdynia and to be making rapid progress in the encircling of Warsaw. Polish reinforcements were hurried to Lwow, where the enemy's aim is to seize important oilfields and to cut communications with Rumania.

The French launched a new offensive on the extreme north of the common frontier with Germany. There was also a heavy artillery duel in the region of Saarbruecken.

Two British merchant ships, "Vancouver City" and "British Influence," sunk.

The official Kremlin organ, "Pravda" attributed what it termed Poland's "military débâcle" mainly to her brutal oppression of her minorities, especially the Polish Ukrainians and the White Russians.

In the House of Commons Mr. Chamberlain stated that no British Government would ever resort to deliberate attacks on women and children for the mere purpose of terrorism.

Lord Halifax announced in the House of Lords that the British Government had received a notification from the German Government that it would for the duration of the War observe the Geneva protocol prohibiting the use of poison gas and bacteriological methods of warfare.

Friday, September 15

A Polish communiqué declared that an attack on Lwow by German motorised forces had been repulsed. German troops crossed the frontier from East Prussia near Suvalki. The Germans claimed to have surrounded Warsaw; also to have occupied most of the Polish oilfields.

Poland stated that Germany had begun a ruthless campaign of bombing open towns.

On the Western Front a strong French force reached the outposts of the Siegfried Line.

It was reported that the situation in Palestine had markedly improved since the outbreak of war, and that Jews and Arabs were co-operating against the common danger.

The Australian Cabinet decided to raise immediately an initial volunteer force of 20,000 for service in Australia or overseas.

The Ministry of Information announced that vast seizures of goods intended for Germany, including 28,000 tons of petroleum, had been made by the British Contraband Control.

Saturday, September 16

Germany claimed to have captured Przemysl and Bialystok. The struggle for Warsaw and Brest-Litovsk continued.

French troops advanced still farther on the 40-mile front from Luxemburg frontier to 12 miles east of Saarbruecken.

A Soviet-Japanese armistice on the Manchukuo-Mongolia frontier was arranged in Moscow.

Four vessels—"Fanad Head," "Davara," "Rudyard Kipling" and "Cheyenne"—sunk by U-boats. The Belgian steamer "Alex van Opstal" was sunk near Weymouth by either a submarine or a mine dropped by an enemy minelayer.

Sunday, September 17

Soviet troops invaded Poland without warning along the whole length of the frontier, ostensibly to protect the population of Western Ukraine and Western White Russia. A Note to this effect was handed to the Polish Ambassador in Moscow, and copies of the Note to the representatives of all States with which Russia maintains diplomatic relations. A broadcast later from Moscow repeated this declaration of "protection," and added that the invasion of Poland would open a new road for the world-wide triumph of the Communist creed.

The Polish front collapsed under crushing German attacks. Germany claimed to have taken Brest-Litovsk. The Polish Government was stated to have removed to Kuty, near the Rumanian frontier; some members of it crossed into Rumania.

Germany presented terms for the surrender of Warsaw.

German attacks on the Western frontier were repulsed with loss. The French High Command recorded the arrival of large German reinforcements from Poland.

OUR WAR GAZETTEER

Brzesc-Litewski (*Bjest-Litev-ski*). Town on r. Bug, 100 miles E. of Warsaw; pop. 50,000. Known also as Brest-Litovsk, this name was given to treaty signed here, March 3, 1918, between Germany and Russia.

Bug (*Boog*). Polish river. Rises near Lwow in S.E., passes through Brzesc-Litewski, and joins Vistula 21 miles below Warsaw; of great strategic importance in defence of that city. 440 miles long.

Bydgoszcz (*Bid-goshts*). The former German Bromberg. Polish city and trade centre on main lines of communication, at gateway to Corridor; pop. 137,000.

Lodz (*Wodj*). Poland's second city, 73 miles S.W. of Warsaw; growth due to textile industry; severely damaged in Great War; pop. 665,000.

Lwow (*Lvov*). Polish city, the German Lemberg (former capital of Austrian Silesia). The commercial centre of the S.E.; held by Russians, 1914-15; pop. to-day, 318,000.

Narew (*Narev*). Polish river, part of the natural defence system of the country; rises in the N.E. and flows 200 miles to join the Bug 18 miles N. of Warsaw.

Neunkirchen (*Noyn-kirch-en*). Town in the Saarland, Germany, immediately N.E. of Saarbruecken; great ironworks and coal trade; scene of disastrous gasometer explosion in February, 1933; pop. 39,000.

Przemysl (*Pjemishl*). Polish town on r. San, 60 miles W. of Lwow; scene of continual fighting in Great War when it was Austrian fortress; pop. 51,000.

Sylt. German fortified island in N. Frisian group, lying immediately off W. end of Danish frontier; connected to mainland by Hindenburg Dam; 39 sq. m.

Vistula. (German Weichsel). Poland's greatest river. Rises in extreme S.W. of country: flows 630 miles N. through Krakow, Warsaw, Plock, Torun; enters Baltic at Danzig.

SECOND MAP SUPPLEMENT

The War Illustrated

Reference Maps

of

CENTRAL EUROPE

and

THE WESTERN FRONT

Presented with No. Three
of The War Illustrated

THE large-scale maps given in this Second Supplement cover the whole of the war areas in the East and West at this date. The map of Central Europe in the centre pages shows the whole of Germany and Poland and Western Russia with the countries on their borders which are closely concerned and may at any moment be directly affected by the aggressive actions of Nazi Germany and Soviet Russia. They include: on the north, Denmark and the independent states of Latvia (part) and Lithuania; on the south, Rumania and Hungary, Italy (part), Switzerland, Belgium, Luxemburg and Holland (parts). All these states have declared that it is their intention to remain neutral. This map is reproduced by courtesy of " The Daily Telegraph," by whom it is copyrighted. The map of the Western Front in the fourth page of this Supplement includes the places and districts affected by the French offensive against the Siegfried Line according to the latest bulletins.

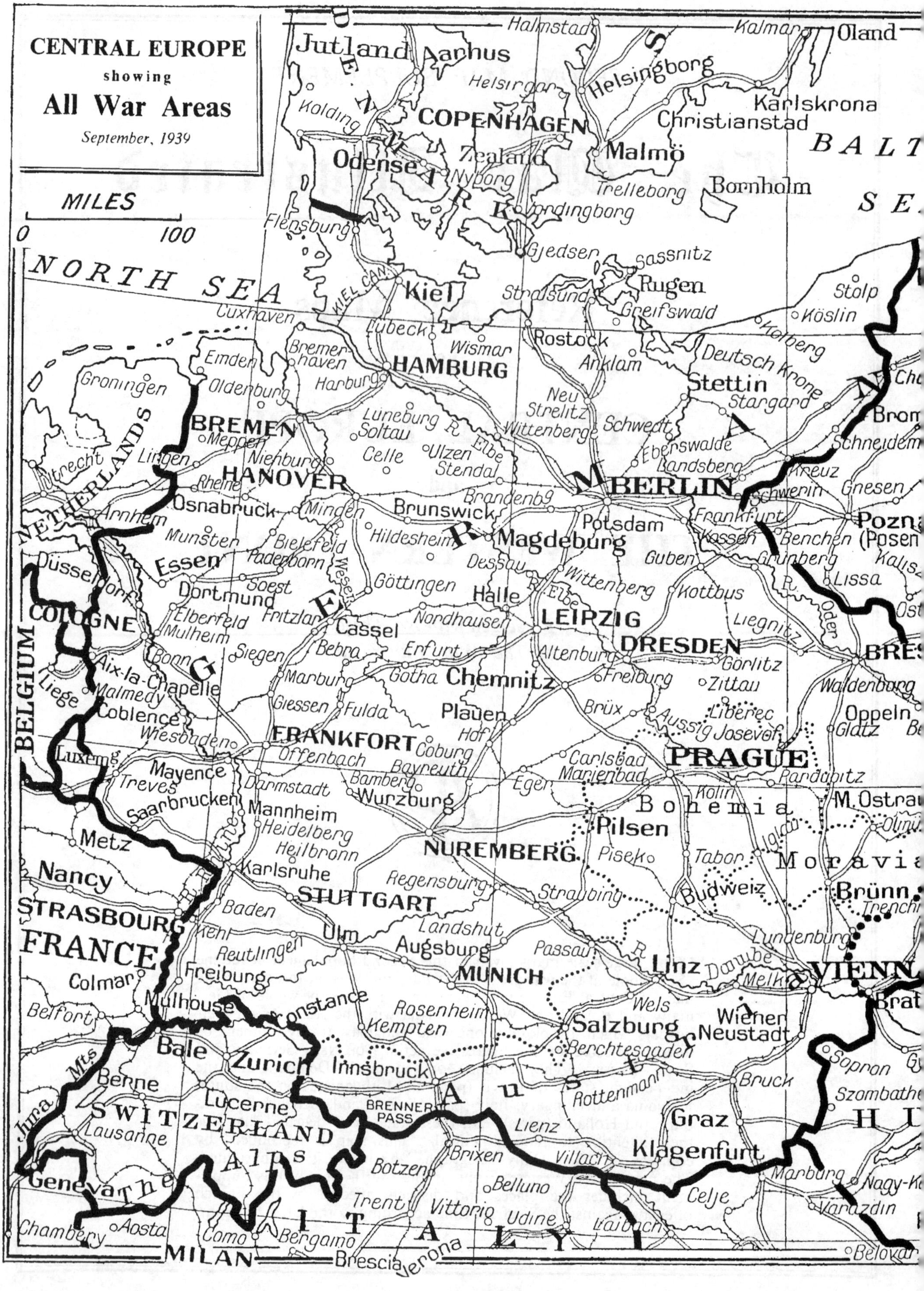
CENTRAL EUROPE
showing
All War Areas
September, 1939
MILES
0
100
NORTH SEA
BALT
SE
Jutland
Aarhus
DENMARK
Kolding
Odense
COPENHAGEN
Zealand
Nyborg
Vordingborg
Helsingor
Halmstad
Helsingborg
Kalmar
Oland
Karlskrona
Christianstad
Malmö
Trelleborg
Bornholm
Flensburg
Gjedsen
Sassnitz
Rugen
Stralsund
Greifswald
Kiel
KIEL CAN.
Cuxhaven
Lubeck
Wismar
Rostock
Anklam
Stolp
Köslin
Kolberg
Deutsch Krone
Stettin
Stargard
Bremer-haven
Emden
Groningen
Oldenburg
Harburg
HAMBURG
Neu Strelitz
Wittenberge
Schwedt
Eberswalde
Landsberg
Schneidem
Brom
Chc
NETHERLANDS
Utrecht
Lingen
BREMEN
Meppen
Nienburg
Luneburg
Soltau
Celle
Ulzen
Stendal
Elbe
HANOVER
Rheine
Osnabruck
Minden
Brunswick
Brandenbg
BERLIN
Potsdam
Frankfurt
Schwerin
Kreuz
Gnesen
Posen
Arnhem
Munster
Bielefeld
Hildesheim
Magdeburg
Kossen
Benchen
Grunberg
Guben
Essen
Paderborn
Dessau
Wittenberg
Kottbus
Lissa
Düsseldorf
Dortmund
Soest
Weser
Göttingen
Halle
Oder
COLOGNE
Elberfeld
Mulheim
Fritzlar
Cassel
Nordhausen
LEIPZIG
Liegnitz
BELGIUM
Bonn
Siegen
Bebra
Erfurt
Altenburg
DRESDEN
Görlitz
BRES
Liege
Aix-la-Chapelle
Malmedy
Marburg
Gotha
Chemnitz
Freiburg
Zittau
Waldenburg
Coblence
Giessen
Fulda
Plauen
Brüx
Aussig
Liberec
Josevof
Oppeln
Glatz
Wiesbaden
FRANKFORT
Hof
Coburg
Luxemg
Offenbach
Bayreuth
Carlsbad
Marienbad
PRAGUE
Pardubitz
Mayence
Treves
Darmstadt
Bamberg
Wurzburg
Eger
Kolin
Bohemia
M. Ostrau
Saarbrucken
Mannheim
Heidelberg
Pilsen
Metz
Heilbronn
NUREMBERG
Pisek
Tabor
Iglau
Moravia
Nancy
Karlsruhe
Regensburg
STRASBOURG
STUTTGART
Straubing
Budweiz
Brünn
Baden
FRANCE
Kehl
Ulm
Landshut
Passau
Lundenburg
Reutlingen
Augsburg
Colmar
Freiburg
MUNICH
Linz
Danube
Melk
VIENN
Belfort
Mulhouse
Constance
Rosenheim
Wels
Kempten
Salzburg
Wiener Neustadt
Brat
Bale
Zurich
Innsbruck
Berchtesgaden
Sopron
Berne
Lucerne
Austria
Bruck
Rottenmann
Szombathe
SWITZERLAND
BRENNER PASS
Jura Mts
Lausanne
Alps
Lienz
Graz
Brixen
Villach
Klagenfurt
Geneva
The
Botzen
Belluno
Marburg
Nagy-K
Trent
Vittorio
Udine
Celje
Varazdin
Chambery
Aosta
Como
Bergamo
ITALY
Laibach
MILAN
Brescia
Verona
Belovar

THE WESTERN FRONT: THE MOSELLE AND THE RHINE

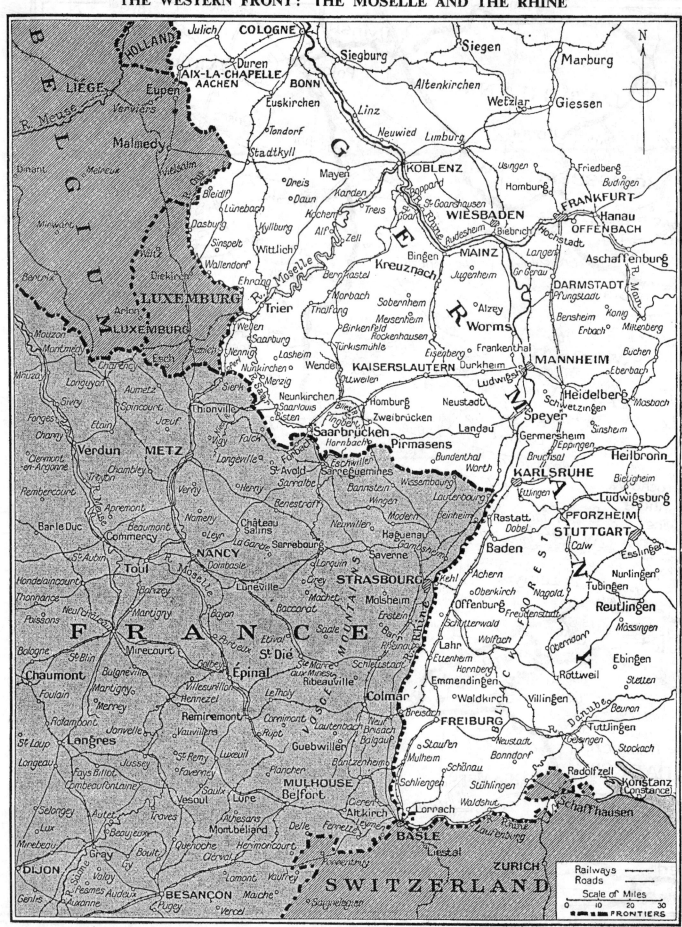

Vol. 1   A Permanent Picture Record of the Second Great War   No. 4

There can be nothing more awe-inspiring as a demonstration of naval might than the firing of a salvo by one of the giant battleships of the Navy of today such as is seen in this photograph. It was taken during battle practice in peacetime.

Photo, Charles E. Brown

Poland: The First Phase Ends

After fighting for nearly three weeks against tremendous odds—of numbers, equipment, and air power—the Polish armies were at last overthrown. Their collapse was rendered inevitable by the last-minute intervention of Soviet Russia.

Ignace Moscicki, head of the Polish State in its darkest hours, has been President since 1926.

and resource, and it was hoped that they might be able to hold out until the coming of winter, with its concomitant, that Polish mud which crippled so effectively Napoleon's scheme of empire.

The final stroke was a stab in the back. Russia, which for some days past had been displaying an ominous interest in the fate of its blood-brothers the White Russians and Ukrainians in Poland, now decided that the moment had come to intervene. Without troubling to declare war, Stalin ordered the Red Army to advance across the frontier, and in the course of a few hours huge successes were claimed by the Moscow radio.

Warsaw, the capital, still held out despite the threats of the beleaguerers that unless it surrendered it would be treated as a military objective. To the north the fortress of Modlin kept up a spirited resistance, and it was reported that the garrisons in Brest-Litovsk and Lwow had

also refused to surrender. As swiftly as the two invading armies could march—and their speed, be it remembered, was not that of foot-slogging infantry but of motorized columns—the gap between the Nazi and Soviet armies was rapidly closed. Attacked on both sides, the Polish armies continued to resist as long as possible, and particularly about Kutno, in the salient

Aᴛ the end of the first two weeks of war the Germans in their invasion of Poland had occupied the whole of the western portion of the country with the exception of a small salient opposite Warsaw, and they had crossed those rivers which it had been hoped would have provided the Poles with a line of defence on which they could have dug in for the winter. The situation was obviously critical, as the Polish front gave indubitable signs of cracking; indeed, in many places it had been penetrated by the German motorized columns, who had, for instance—at least, so it was claimed by the German wireless—occupied Brest-Litovsk and Lwow, and had almost succeeded in cutting Poland's communications with Rumania.

Nevertheless, the battle did not seem to be quite lost, for the Poles were fighting with their traditional bravery

The Nazi invaders did not hesitate to impress Polish civilians into their Labour Corps. Some of them are seen centre, left. Centre, right, is a Polish stretcher-bearer. Below, Polish gunners in action against the German invaders.
Photos, Planet News, Wide World, and Keystone

Pathos and Terror of the Last Days in Warsaw

This photograph of heartrending pathos shows a Polish mother searching the ruins of her home, bombed by the Nazis, in the hope of salving a few belongings. This scene could be multiplied many hundreds of times in the three weeks of Poland's tragedy.

Photo, Fox

I<small>N</small> an "appeal to the civilized world," the Lord Mayor of Warsaw, M. Starzynski, broadcast on September 19:

"These Polish men, women and children are not dying in vain, but they are dying not only for the freedom of their own country, but for the freedom of Europe. We know that our friends want to help us and will help us. Our lives may be in danger now, but our souls are undisturbed. We shall fight to the last man if we have to go down fighting. We shall stand at our post imbued with holy faith in our ultimate victory even in this dark hour. The day will come . "

Top left, German prisoners taken by the Poles are at exercise in Warsaw. Centre, Nazi troops are attempting an advance in a suburb of Warsaw. Below, a group of Polish boys, inured to terrorism, look up at departing Nazi bombers. One has already been wounded.

Photos, Planet News and Associated Press

Poland, showing the line reached by the Germans on September 20, 1939. Its extreme limit is marked by the dotted line. The arrows indicate the direction of the Russian advance.

west of Warsaw, the Germans had to confess that they were engaged in " one of the greatest battles of extermination of all time." Nevertheless, the enemy were able to claim a total of over 100,000 prisoners, and the Polish casualties were also said to be extraordinarily high—owing, no doubt, to the ruthlessness with which the German armoured car and machine-gun detachments mowed down the Polish infantry.

By September 21 serious resistance in Poland had almost entirely collapsed, fighting continuing hardly anywhere but near Modlin and in Warsaw. The Germans had reached the line of Bialystok, Brest-Litovsk, Lwow and Stryz, and at Brest-Litovsk and various other places on the front Nazi and Soviet troops were actually in peaceful contact. Gdynia, after resisting for more than a fortnight, had fallen at last. In the south the troops of the Red Army continued to advance until they had occupied the whole of the Polish Ukraine, and cut Poland off from Rumania and Hungary. Until the frontier was closed a stream of Polish troops, airmen and civilians poured into Rumania, trudging along the country roads side by side with lorries, motor-ambulances, tanks, armoured cars, steam-rollers, light artillery, and bullet-marked motor-cars.

Poland, militarily speaking, was down and out. There was truth in Hitler's claim that the Polish war was over.

A few years ago Gdynia was little more than a fishing village, but the Poles not only constructed a great port but built around it a flourishing watering-place. Here we see the promenade in peace-time, while in the adjoining photo German troops are marching through one of the city's fine streets. Centre, is the scene of the surrender of the city on September 14 to a German general when it had been cut off from the Polish army.

Photos, Mondiale, Keystone and Associated Press

Bombs Have Battered These Open Polish Towns

The Polish Embassy in London stated that "up to September 3, that is, the day on which Great Britain and France found themselves at war with Germany, 30 open cities and towns had been bombed." Here are views of six of them as they were in peacetime. (1) The great monastery church in Czestochowa, now destroyed. (2) The market square in Bydgoszcz. (3) The castle at Grodno from the Niemen. (4) The ancient church at Grudziadz. (5) A street in the old town of Bialystok. (6) The town hall and market square at Chelmno.

Photos, E.N.A.

Poland Has Died Before ---To Rise Again

Flushed with victory, the Nazi warlords and their Soviet abettors in the rape of Poland have
partitioned their prey, just as did the imperialist robbers of a century and a half ago.   But the
pages of history give us reason to believe that the crime of 1939 will be no more successful
than that of 1795.

No country in Europe has suffered, and survived, so many surgical operations of the most drastic description as Poland. Hardly had she emerged from the mists which shroud her origin, when she suffered her first partition into a number of small principalities. During the Middle Ages, however, Poland recovered her unity, and, allied with Lithuania, became one of the great States of the Continent—for centuries, indeed, she was a bulwark of western civilization against the inroads of the Tartars, the Turks, and the Muscovites.

With the dawn of the modern age, however, a period of decline set in for Poland. Her system of elective monarchy led to the interference in her internal affairs by outside States, and her parliamentary government was rendered useless by the fact that in the Diet every decision had to be by unanimous vote ! In the 18th century Poland's weakness became apparent to the world, and in due course she became the prey of the three neighbouring States.

It was in 1772 that Prussia, Russia, and Austria made what is called in history the First Partition of Poland.

By this act of international brigandage Poland was deprived of about one-fifth of her population and one-fourth of her territory.

Twenty-one years later the Second Partition of Poland reduced the state to about one-third of its original dimensions. In vain the Poles under Poniatowski and Kosciusko resisted the troops of Prussia and Russia sent to seize the spoil, and in 1795 the Third Partition wiped Poland from the map altogether.

During the Napoleonic Age a Grand Duchy of Warsaw was created, chiefly out of the Prussian share of Poland, but this was suppressed in 1815 by the Congress of Vienna. Posen was then left to Prussia ; Austria retained Galicia ; the eastern borderlands were incorporated with Russia, and Central Poland was constituted as the so-called Congress kingdom under the Tsar of Russia as King of Poland.

Following an unsuccessful military revolt in Warsaw in 1830, the Tsarist regime began the systematic Russification of Poland. This was intensified after a second rising, equally unsuccessful, in 1863. All self-government in Congress Poland was suppressed ; a rigorous censorship was maintained ; and the whole system of education was Russified with a view to destroying the Poles' sense of nationality and even rendering the use of their language obsolete. Readers of Madame Curie's life will remember

The Poles defending their country's soil and honour fought with such desperate valour that but few fell into enemy hands. In the top photograph Polish prisoners are seen in a " cage " to which they have been marched immediately after capture. In the lower photograph are the broken remains of a Polish transport column caught by enemy artillery and completely wrecked.

Photos, Central Press

Top left, Poland as it was before the Great War—partly German, partly Russian, and partly Austrian. Lower left, Poland as it was after the Treaty of Versailles, with the boundaries marked by the "Curzon Line" of 1920. Right, the new partition arranged this year by Hitler and Stalin, as announced in a joint communiqué issued on September 22, by Germany and Russia.

that it was under these conditions that she spent her early years in Warsaw. In Prussian and Austrian Poland the repression was not so severe, but every effort was made to damp Polish national feeling.

For a hundred years and more Poland was a mere geographical expression. Nevertheless, the spirit of her people was kept alive by the passionate propaganda of the Polish writers and artists, by revolutionaries, and by the heroes of the ill-starred insurrectionary movements.

Then came the Great War, during which Poland was the battleground of the eastern front. In 1916 Germany and Austria-Hungary held out the prospect of the restoration of an independent Poland, and in 1917 the new Russian government promised to set about the creation of a new Polish State. Already President Wilson, in his peace message of January 22, 1917, had referred to a "united, independent and autonomous Poland"—a peace aim of the Allies.

In October, 1918, a free and united Poland was proclaimed; and on November 11—our Armistice Day—the Poles set up an independent government in Warsaw, with Pilsudski as its head.

By the Treaty of Versailles of 1919 the complete independence of Poland was recognized. But the question of the boundaries of the new State required years for its solution. Particularly difficult was the determination of the boundary with Russia. The Curzon Line of December 8, 1919—so-named after

Marquess Curzon, Britain's Foreign Secretary at the time—attempted to make Poland's eastern frontier coincide with the ethnographical frontier, but in the following year Poland carried it far to the east when she invaded Russia and captured Kiev. Then the Soviet army rallied, and the Poles were driven back to the gates of Warsaw. The counter-offensive under Pilsudski reversed the situation again, and the new eastern frontier of Poland was drawn so as to correspond roughly with the frontier left after the Second Partition in 1793.

With minor modifications Poland's boundaries then remained as they had been settled by the treaty-makers in the early post-war years. Then, in 1939, Germany and Russia, the heirs of the partitioning powers of the 18th century, decided upon a fourth partition of Poland.

But just as surely as Poland was restored to the company of nations in 1919, so we may well believe that in good time she will have a glorious resurrection from the martyr's grave into which she has been thrown by the brutal aggression of her traditional foes.

In this war, as in the last one, the soldier's most welcome luxury is a cigarette. Here a Polish soldier gives a light to a comrade from his own "fag," for matches as well as tobacco have to be carefully husbanded in wartime.

Britain Won't Go Hungry in this War

On land bordering a L.P.T.B. railway track an employee tends a giant cabbage.

THERE was an immediate response to the Government's appeal to farmers and gardeners to produce more food. The Women's Land Army got to work without delay in the first days of the war. Children evacuated to the country did any job on the farms for which they were suitable, from garnering potatoes in one place to helping to exterminate a plague of caterpillars in another. All the delays connected with food supplies in the early days were caused by transport difficulties and not by any food shortage ; and though ration cards were announced these were only to ensure equality of distribution and the prevention of waste.

These recruits for the Women's Land Army are undergoing training in farm work at an agricultural college in Sussex.

The Government's resolve to prepare for a three years' war has necessitated modifications in food distribution as well as intensive efforts to increase production. Centre, left, is one of the temporary centres of fish supply in a country town just outside London. In the photograph below evacuated children are helping with the gathering of the potato crop. Their gas masks are handy.

Photos, Fox and Topical

Women Take Over in Paris and London

This woman conductor shows herself efficient on the Paris Metro. Right are some of the first women bus conductors going on duty at Manchester.

Unusual occupations come to women in wartime. Here a smart young lady has replaced a butcher in a shop at Kingston-on-Thames, while below a woman has taken on her husband's job as a baker's roundsman.

IN the last war the women of all the Allied—and enemy—countries proved that when their menfolk went to war there was hardly a man's job that they could not do, and do well. This time the response of the women has been equally fine. In France, where, when general mobilization is ordered, the vast majority of Frenchmen are called to the colours, women are soon required to do their part. Obviously in Great Britain, where the calling up of men proceeds more slowly, the mobilization of "woman power" is slower, but, as Queen Mary's message of appreciation to her countrywomen showed, every call to British womanhood to help has been abundantly met so far, and it will be to the end.

In Paris women roadsweepers have already made their appearance, and with their besom brooms make a clean sweep of the streets.

Photos, L.N.A., Topical & Keystone

Winning the Fight Against U-Boats

SINCE the last war the means of dealing with the submarine menace have been greatly improved and new devices for locating them, undreamed of in 1918, are now available. The brunt of the anti-submarine warfare falls upon the destroyers, a class of ship originally developed to deal with a type of now obsolete torpedo boats, and therefore known as "torpedo boat destroyers." They have now earned the proud distinction of being U-boat destroyers.

The fine body of men above are young sailors marching to take up their wartime duties. Such men as these hunt the U-boats with unceasing vigilance.

One of the latest types of motor torpedo boats developed since the last war.

The destroyers' duties include patrolling the shipping routes and convoying merchant ships. Their extreme handiness makes them particularly valuable for this work, and above, right, a destroyer is making a complete turn in little more than its own length. Above, one of Britain's destroyers is firing an above-water torpedo during practice. The newer destroyers of the Royal Navy are both larger and more heavily armed than earlier types.

Photos, Charles E. Brown, Fox and Keystone

Floating Strongholds of British Sea Power

Though the battleships and battle cruisers of today may lack the picturesqueness that characterized the men-of-war of long ago, there could not be a more impressive embodiment of sea power than they present. Here some of the most modern ships of the Royal Navy are seen lying stem to stern. The turrets with the great superstructure above make them appear, as they are, veritable towers of strength.

Photo, Keystone

The New Watch on the Rhine

For the third week in succession the French and German communiqués were agreed on the fact that there had been no fighting on the grand scale on the Western Front. But the artillery and other preparations for the decisive day of battle went on.

A part of the Forest of Warndt, near Saar-bruecken, in which the first French successes were secured.
Photo, L.N.A.

IN the opening stage of the war all eyes were turned on Poland, where the German military machine was engaged in *Blitz-Krieg*—lightning war—with a view to ending as soon as possible, and with not the least regard for what may be called the decencies of warfare, the resistance of the Polish army and people. Meanwhile, on the Western Front there was little to report—at least, very little was reported. On each side of the frontier between Germany and France was mobilized an army of several millions of men, occupying a defensive position which, though called a "line," is really a huge fortified area many miles in depth.

For a week or two the Paris communiqués let it be understood that the French troops were advancing in the most careful and methodical manner across the no-man's-land between the Maginot and Siegfried lines. Their progress had in it nothing that was spectacular; it was just a grim process of mopping-up machine-gun positions, destroying tank traps, and wiping out the forward positions of the Nazi infantry.

By the middle of the third week of the war the communiqués had become even less revealing, and there were many who felt that either the press censorship was operating far too severely, or else the Allied commanders were taking an unconscionable time in getting to grips with the enemy.

Such views, however, were short-sighted, to say the least. All who had any real knowledge of the fortified systems on the Western Front knew full well that the first phase of the war must necessarily be one of slow consolidation of quite minor gains.

But though there was little in the French approach to make a good newspaper story, the army was playing a very definite part in preparing the way for victory. Far behind the German lines the roads and railways were plastered by the French artillery, and the concentrations of troops—including those brought in haste from the Polish front—were subjected to aerial bombing. Then, over the whole front of nearly a hundred miles from the Moselle to the Rhine, the Nazi High Command was held on fenterhooks wondering where the next blow in the Allied attack might fall. The German troops were kept hard at it marching here and there, and digging trenches behind the line; the German population was evacuated from many a village and town in the war zone, and the news they had to carry back to the interior of Germany can hardly have contributed to the support of the home front; aerial reconnaissances above the German lines caused the defending air force to take the air and so use up in futile manoeuvring much of its petrol; in the artillery duels, too, a considerable quantity of the Nazi stores of big gun ammunition must have been expended in an altogether futile fashion.

In other words, Gamelin was engaged in a military blockade of Germany. Just as the British Navy was preventing Germany from receiving the contraband of war, so on shore the French tactics resulted in considerable inroads being made into the German stocks of petrol, oil, metals and explosives—all war material which, as the struggle wore on, Germany must find it increasingly difficult to replace. It was a French general who made a broadcast statement on September 19 to the effect that for the Allies to seek a quick (and costly) decision on the West would be a profound mistake.

Meanwhile, millions of men waited on the event. There was such a watch on the Rhine as had never been kept before in all the ages of history. Perhaps the most illuminating commentary on the situation was the report that Strasbourg, the beautiful capital of Alsace, had been abandoned by all but a thousand of its normal 200,000 inhabitants; and that, at night, through the city's silent and empty streets, there was no movement save that of the French patrols, who, every now and again, broke the silence with their rifles as they dispatched a stray cat or a dog which had been abandoned by a careless owner to its fate.

Here one of the big French tanks such as took part in the attack on the Forest of Warndt is seen. Top, it is in the open followed by infantrymen. Below, it is climbing a steep bank after making a successful crossing of a stream.
Photos, Associated Press

The Best War News Is a Letter From Home

To the soldier on active service the greatest of all joys is a letter from home. In the top photograph members of an anti-aircraft battery somewhere in Kent are eagerly receiving the latest news from their loved ones, while below a French Army postmaster is distributing letters to men just behind the line. A distinguished military writer has said that it was the letters from home that won the last war—letters to German troops telling them of unendurable privations their own folk were suffering. History may yet repeat itself in Nazi Germany.

Photos, Associated Press and Central Press

The Lads of '39 off to the Western Front

This photograph of men of the British Expeditionary Force in a lorry in France has an historic importance, for it was the first to be published of the B.E.F. in France.

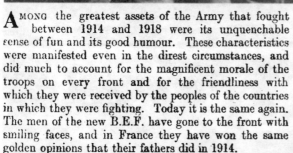

AMONG the greatest assets of the Army that fought between 1914 and 1918 were its unquenchable sense of fun and its good humour. These characteristics were manifested even in the direst circumstances, and did much to account for the magnificent morale of the troops on every front and for the friendliness with which they were received by the peoples of the countries in which they were fighting. Today it is the same again. The men of the new B.E.F. have gone to the front with smiling faces, and in France they have won the same golden opinions that their fathers did in 1914.

The cheery humour of the B.E.F. is exemplified in the photograph at the top by the man who carries his bed and breakfast with him. The recent photograph shows a scene now to be met with in every part of Britain—troops on the march. Here light tanks are drawn up by the roadside while their crews take a meal. In the bottom photograph the men in a troop train are waving to a few spectators as they pass through a wayside station on their way to join their fellows " Somewhere in France."

Photos, Associated Press, Wide World and Paramount News Reel

'Tiger' Gort—Commander-in-Chief, B.E.F.

The leader of Britain's Expeditionary Force in France is one of the heroes of the last war.
Below, in brief compass, is the record of what General Lord Gort has managed to contrive
in his fifty-three years of life.

UNLIKE the army which Britain sent to France in 1914, the Expeditionary Force which crossed the Channel the other day is captained by an infantryman. French, Haig, Smith-Dorrien, Byng, Allenby, Plumer—all were cavalrymen and had been brought up in the old cavalry tradition. General Lord Gort, however, has every claim to be regarded as one of the foot-sloggers—the P.B.I. of soldiers' parlance of the last war.

John Standish Surtees Prendergast Vereker was born in 1886, and succeeded his father as sixth Viscount Gort in 1902. As befitted the descendant of a long line of soldiers, young Gort, after leaving Harrow, passed through Sandhurst and at nineteen obtained a commission in the Grenadier Guards.

When war broke out in 1914 he was a captain ; two years later he was a brevet-major, acting lieutenant-colonel. He won the Military Cross in 1915 and the D.S.O. in 1917—the latter with three bars, representing four individual acts of bravery justifying its award. In September, 1918, he won the highest and most coveted of all military decorations, the Victoria Cross.

How He Won the V.C.

This he gained " for most conspicuous bravery, skilful leading, and devotion to duty during the attack of the Guards Division on September 27th, 1918, across the Canal du Nord, near Flesquières, when in command of the 1st Battalion Grenadier Guards, the leading battalion of the 3rd Guards Brigade."

" Under heavy artillery and machine-gun fire," continues the official record in the "London Gazette," " he led his battalion with great skill and determination to the ' forming-up ' ground, where very severe fire from artillery and machine-guns was again encountered.

" Although wounded, he quickly grasped the situation, directed a platoon to proceed down a sunken road to make a flanking attack, and, under terrific fire, went across open ground to obtain the assistance of a tank, which he personally led and directed to the best possible advantage. While thus fearlessly exposing himself he was again severely wounded by a shell. Notwithstanding considerable loss of blood, after lying on a stretcher for a while, he insisted on getting up and personally directing the further attack. By his magnificent example of devotion to duty and utter disregard of personal safety all ranks were inspired to exert themselves to the utmost, and the attack resulted in the capture of over 200 prisoners, two batteries of field guns, and numerous machine-guns. Lieutenant-Colonel Viscount Gort then proceeded to organize the defence of the captured position until he collapsed ; even then he refused to leave the field until he had seen the ' success signal ' go up on the final objective.

" The successful advance of the battalion was mainly due to the valour, devotion and leadership of this very gallant officer."

After the War he continued to make rapid progress in the military hierarchy.

A colonel in 1926, he was Director of Military Training in India from 1932 to 1936, when he came home to take up the post of Commandant of the Staff College at Camberley. By this time he was a major-general, and in 1937 he was appointed Military Secretary to Mr. Leslie Hore-Belisha, Secretary of State for War.

It is said that the meeting between the statesman and the soldier was one of dramatic suddenness. According to the story, Gort was ski-ing in Switzerland, when coming down a mountain he collided violently with another skier. Said the victim, " Who the hell are you ? " Replied the other, " Gort." Thus informally introduced, Gort and Hore-Belisha became fast friends, and he was an obvious choice for the post of Military Secretary when it fell vacant.

High Merit—Quick Promotion

Promoted lieutenant-general, he justified to the hilt the confidence reposed in him, and there was not a murmur of criticism when in December 1937, jumping clean over the heads of ninety senior officers, he received the appointment of Chief of the Imperial General Staff. Two or three days later he was raised to the rank of full general. Then, on September 4, 1939, he was designated Commander-in-Chief of the Expeditionary Force which Britain was preparing to send overseas to fight side by side with the army of her French ally.

Essentially a fighter, he is also one of the military intelligentsia. He is a sportsman, too, one who hunts and yachts and flies his own aeroplane ; here, perhaps, we have a case of heredity will out, for his grandfather on the maternal side was Robert Surtees, author of that series of inimitable sporting novels of which Mr. Jorrocks, grocer and sportsman, is the chief character.

But perhaps the most important thing to be said about Gort is that he is a soldier who has had actual experience of modern war under the most trying conditions. As he studies his maps and makes his plans in the British H.Q. somewhere in France, he will always have before him the most vivid recollection and complete understanding of what it means to be in the front line during the battle. He can never demand of a man a degree of courage, a depth of endurance, a height of resolution, beyond those which he himself has shown.

Britain's fighting forces by land are in the safe hands of these two great soldiers, Viscount Gort, Commander-in-Chief of the B.E.F., left, and General Sir Edmund Ironside, Chief of the Imperial General Staff, right.
Photo, Topical

Britain's Effort Gains Speed—
Her First Troops Go Abroad

On September 12 it was officially announced that British troops were in France, but that they had not been in action as yet. The men were taken to a southern port by railway, having marched from camp or barrack to the station at which they were to entrain. Troop trains arrived at the port in quick succession from many parts of England and Scotland. There a fleet of transports consisting of ships of many sizes was ready to embark the troops, and the journey across the Channel to France was made without a hitch. The mechanized units mostly made the journey to the port of embarkation by road. No figures were given of the number of men and amount of war material transported, but the task of transportation must obviously have been one of great magnitude. The ease and celerity with which it was carried out speak volumes for the perfection of the organization in London and the Military Commands behind it.

Photos, Paramount News Reel

The photographs in this and the facing page show the troops and transport of the new B.E.F. somewhere in England. The column of infantry (above) wear already their steel helmets, and with the donning of " battle dress " puttees have been discarded. The mechanized transport column (left) is painted with the elaborate camouflage which long and careful experiment has shown to be most effective.

THE secret of the departure of the British Expeditionary Force for France was extraordinarily well kept, and not until it had safely crossed the Channel was any official announcement of the departure made. Yet there were some who knew. The people of a port in the south of England were the first to realize what was happening. The number of trains passing towards the docks increased tremendously. By night and day the streets resounded to the rattle of Army lorries and tractors, while now and again in the bright September sunshine a long line of infantry coming from within marching distance of the port passed towards the docks.

When the British Expeditionary Force landed in France in August, 1914, its equipment was very different from that of the Army of today. Mechanization had then hardly begun. Most of the artillery and transport and even many of the ambulances, were horse-drawn. In the Army Service Corps there were a certain number of motor transport wagons which were later supplemented by motor-lorries and vans commandeered from private firms, while for the transport of troops many London omnibuses were taken off the streets and sent to France. With the original B.E.F. went a Cavalry Division and Horse Artillery, but today, with a few exceptions, all the British cavalry regiments and artillery are mechanized units, and weapons unthought of 25 years ago are employed. Transport is also completely mechanized.

THE change in the equipment of the infantry is striking. In the last war steel helmets were not issued until the end of 1915. The horror of gas was to come later, so that no gas masks were carried. Yet the total weight of equipment carried by an infantryman was even then heavy, and by June, 1916, it had risen to about 66 lb., which made it difficult to get out of a trench or to move much quicker than a slow walk or to lie down or rise with any speed. This photograph gives some idea of how completely things have changed.

British Knights of the Air

Hawker Hurricane single-seater fighters such as those seen above and below are among the fastest machines in the British or any other Air Force of today.

THE Fighter Command, R.A.F., consists of home defence squadrons equipped with aircraft specially designed to intercept raiders at the earliest possible moment. Such aircraft must necessarily be enormously powerful and capable of outstanding performances in climb, speed and manoeuvrability. Their armament, too, must be deadly, and the five-mile-a-minute Hurricanes seen in this page each have in the wings eight fixed machine-guns, aimed by directing the aeroplane at its target. A feature of the Hurricane, now general in aircraft design, is the retractable under-carriage, the landing wheels being withdrawn into the wings, adding appreciably to the speed. All fighters and bombers are now camouflaged in the green and brown " shadow shading."

The equipment of air pilots is necessarily elaborate, for at the height to which they climb the air is so rarefied that an oxygen cylinder and mouthpiece have to be worn. In the top right photograph this apparatus is being inspected. Below is the scene at an aerodrome when an alarm has been given and the pilots with their full equipment race to their machines.

Eye Witness Stories of Episodes
and Adventures in the
Second Great War

In this Section we present week by week a collection of personal accounts of war experiences. They are selected on the same basis as those of the long series dealing with the first Great War which appeared in " I Was There," published under the same Editorship in 1938-39.

I Jumped from the Sinking "Courageous"

Exclusive to THE WAR ILLUSTRATED is this first-hand story of the sinking of H.M. Aircraft-Carrier "Courageous" on September 17. It is told by R.F.R. 1572 Marine M. Reidy, who was called up from his job in the machine-room of The Amalgamated Press when the reserve fleet was mobilized at the end of July.

" A T five to eight I was on the flight deck. The submarine attacked us broadside. We were struck about five to eight, and she had disappeared about a quarter past.

" The destroyer behind us came abreast and dropped depth charges. After one of these the submarine came up out of the water. This was before we had abandoned the ship. We saw the submarine blown out of the water. Every-

body cheered. I am firmly convinced that she was sunk.

" Following the two explosions, ' Courageous' took a definite list to port. I jumped from the flight deck on to the C.P. (control position) platform and waited a while for orders and to see what would happen. The next order came about five minutes after the torpedoing. It was ' Abandon Ship,' sent by word of mouth along the decks. The broadcast which normally gives orders had been ruined, so the order was passed from man to man. The only boat they could get out was the cutter, and directly they got down to the water she sank. Then they lowered the motor-boat on the after end of the port side. The marines ran out from the mess deck, and directly the order came through ' Abandon Ship,' most of us jumped right over. The rafts were cut adrift and some of the men jumped on to them. But

I was a strong swimmer, so I swam. Some of the chaps made the mistake of running up the starboard side, but as it got higher and higher they found they could not jump into the sea, and some started to run down the flight deck. A lot must have lost their lives that way.

" The engines did not stop directly ' Courageous' was hit, and we ran on for a good couple of hundred yards. I wondered at first whether she was really very seriously hit as she did not stop. The explosion partly collapsed the bridge, because it hit just under the bridge.

" Some of the men kept their money in their pockets and left their trousers on. When we all jumped over the side these men got away so far and then found that they could not keep up with their trousers on. Then they tried to kick them off and

could not do so. Several were drowned in this way. There were plenty of logs of wood floating round and rafts and the motor-boat, but I just swam till I saw that everybody near me had something, because I had no fear at all. I knew I was a good swimmer. When they all had one I grabbed a log.

" The Captain of the destroyer manoeuvred his ship so that the rollers were breaking against it and rolling the men down towards her, and then he threw ladders and ropes and hauled the men up as they came towards him. Some of the crew dived off the side of their ship and pulled up exhausted men.

" When I entered the water the destroyer was about 1½ miles away, but when ' Courageous' went down she gradually closed in, although she was afraid to move her screws in case some poor fellows got caught in them. Another

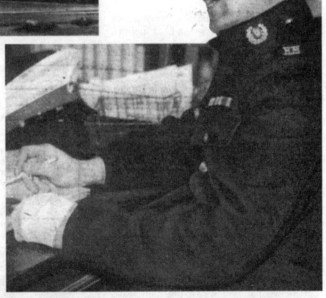

Above is Marine M. Reidy, an Amalgamated Press printer, photographed in the office of " The War Illustrated," four days after the sinking of H.M.S. " Courageous." Above, from the flight deck of the " Courageous," an aeroplane is taking off.
Photos, Fox and Topical, Copyright A.P. Ltd.

destroyer was dropping depth charges until they were sure the submarine was gone. A Dutch and an American ship were also in the vicinity and helped to pick up the survivors.

"I got into the water at ten past eight and was picked up about 9.15.

"I should like to pay a special tribute to the captain of the destroyer for his fine seamanship in keeping his ship to the rollers, and to the seamen for the way in which they worked to rescue us. They emptied their kit-bags for us, and I was dressed in two blankets strapped round me with a belt and an oilskin jacket when I arrived on shore."

We Were on 'Courageous' When She Was Hit

The first loss sustained by the Navy in the war was the sinking of the aircraft carrier " Courageous " by a German submarine on Sunday night, September 17. Below are survivors' accounts of the catastrophe reprinted by the courtesy of " The Daily Telegraph."

PAYMASTER SUB-LIEUT. I. F. WESTMACOTT, the Captain's secretary, was having his supper in the "Courageous" when he heard two explosions which seemed to lift the ship.

" All lights went out and crockery fell over," he continued. " I got out of the wardroom and made my way to the seaplane platform on top of the quarter deck. People waiting there did not seem to realise that the ship would sink so soon. Suddenly an order was given for everyone to get into the water. Some men went to the floats and others got boats out. I stripped and jumped into the water. I was in it about 40 minutes, swimming all the time, until I reached one of the destroyers.

" Everybody behaved with calm, and the men cracked jokes. There was no panic or disorder."

Almost immediately after the attack the "Courageous" began to list to port, and within five minutes the captain gave orders to abandon her.

" Her bows submerged, her stern cocked up into the air, and she foundered within 15 to 20 minutes of being hit.

" Some of the boats on the starboard side were got out, but those on the port side could not be used as she heeled too quickly.

" There were two distinct bangs at an interval of perhaps a second. I believe there were a few minor explosions when she actually foundered. Part of the ship's crew were below decks at the time."

ONE of the youngest survivors is Bugler R. D. Emerson, of the Royal Marines, aged 15, and only 5 ft. in height. When the ship was struck he went on the flight deck, took off his bugle and tied it to the ship's rail. Then he undressed, clambered down the starboard side and struck out for a raft.

" Our destroyers were dropping depth charges," he said, " and within a few minutes we saw the submarine blown up. There was no doubt about it. The conning tower broke one way and the stern was blown another and oil shot up from the water. We all cheered.

" As we paddled away the men sang, ' Heigh ho, it's off to work we go.' We had not got far when the ' Courageous ' went down with 200 men on board."

ONE of the most dramatic accounts was given by Naval Writer Tom Hughes, 18, of St. Anne's.

When the first explosion occurred, he said, he was in the canteen. He made a rush for the deck, and as he was going up the companion-way there was another explosion and a sheet of flame. He found men were throwing overboard pieces of wood, oars and anything that would float.

As an officer gave the order, " Swim for it," he clambered down a rope and dropped into the sea, which was " so thick with oil that we might have been swimming in treacle." He reached a raft, and was eventually taken aboard a destroyer.

" When we realized we had been torpedoed," said Naval Writer Hughes, " our men were so infuriated that they threw overboard depth charges in an effort to sink the U-boat.

" I was swimming when I heard a dull roar. Suddenly the submarine lifted clean out of the water and fell back like a stone. There is no doubt she was sunk.

" Hundreds of us who were struggling in the water for our lives raised a cheer. While we were swimming someone shouted, ' Are we downhearted ? ' and there was a resounding ' No ! ' in reply."

Hughes said one of his most vivid recollections was that as he was in the water he caught a glimpse of the commander of the "Courageous," Capt. Makeig-Jones, standing at the salute on

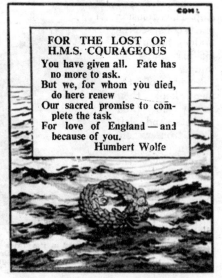

FOR THE LOST OF
H.M.S. COURAGEOUS
You have given all. Fate has
no more to ask.
But we, for whom you died,
do here renew
Our sacred promise to com-
plete the task
For love of England — and
because of you.
          Humbert Wolfe

the bridge as the vessel took her final plunge.

" As for myself, I just swam and swam. Those three hours in the water seemed much longer. I must pay tribute to the handling of the destroyer that saved us. She was so navigated that the swell created by her progress helped us to swim towards her.

" As I got fairly near her a fellow swam alongside me and said ' Help me.' I gripped him by the hair and when a man off the destroyer caught me to pull me aboard I was still hanging on. That chap's long absence from the barber's saved his life.

" Another impression which will live in my memory is that of a Royal Marine sergeant who seemed to cover an enormous distance swimming from man to man and making such remarks as ' Keep going, my lad, and you will be all right. Keep your heart and your head up.' There were heroes in plenty, but that sergeant was the greatest I saw."

JOHN DESMOND WELLS, aged 16, a boy seaman, of Seaton, Devon, said he was reading in his hammock waiting to go on duty when an explosion stunned him.

" After groping about I managed to get to the upper deck," he added. " Many men were running about but there was no panic.

" I slid down a blister [a form of protection on the ship's side] to within six feet of the water and stayed there for 10 minutes. Other men did the same.

" It was apparent that the ship was sinking, her bows being already nearly under water. I jumped clear and swam in the direction of a destroyer which was standing about a mile off. There were also two other destroyers and two merchant vessels."

Wells said that at no time was there any panic, and when the men were in the water they sang " Roll Up the Barrel."

A 17-YEAR-OLD Exeter survivor said: " I helped to lower a boat which got stuck, and a couple of us climbed down over the side of the ship to push her off.

" About 30 men were in her, but there was a rush of water into her stern as she reached the sea. She sank and the men were forced to swim.

" Meanwhile, I waited on deck and smoked a cigarette. Then I heard a shout, ' Every man for himself,' and I went down the ship's side on a rope.

" I reached a float with a number of men on it and they helped me aboard. Everybody was cheerful. Somebody said, ' Let's have a song, boys,' and we struck up ' Rolling Home ' and ' Show Me the Way To Go Home.' After about 45 minutes a destroyer came alongside, and she was handled so beautifully that she hardly disturbed the float."

'Courageous'—the Navy's First Wartime Loss

Above, the list of survivors of H.M.S. "Courageous" is being studied by those who had relations or friends on board. Left is the commanding officer, Captain W. T. Makeig-Jones, R.N., who went down with his ship while saluting the flag.

Photos, Wide World, Sport & General, Fox Photos, and Charles E. Brown

The "Courageous" (centre) was built as a shallow draft cruiser in 1915-16 to operate in the Baltic, and was afterwards converted into an aircraft carrier. The lower photograph was taken in 1937 at Gibraltar, when officers of the German battleship "Deutschland" were being entertained by the officers of the "Courageous." The officer at the piano is a German—and so was the man who launched the torpedo that sank her!

IIIIIIIIIIIIIIIIIIIIIIIIIIIIIIIIIIIIIIIIIIIIIIIIIIIIIIIIIIIII **I WAS THERE!** IIIIIIIIIIIIIIIIIIIIIIIIIIIIIIIIIIIIIIIIIIIIIIIIIIIIIIIIIIIIIIIIIIIIIIIIIIIIIIIIIIIIIIIIIIIIII

'Tommy' Lands in France Again

On September 11 it was announced that a British Expeditionary Force had been conveyed across the Channel without the loss of a single man. Here is the story of the landing of the British troops in France, as reported in the " Daily Express " by Geoffrey Cox.

IN a Channel port I have been watching columns of steel-helmeted British troops landing quietly and smoothly as if on manoeuvres, and tramping over the cobbles from the ships to their billets.

At street corners and house doors French people crowded to watch them, sometimes clapping, sometimes breaking into " Vive les Anglais."

But the landing of these Young Contemptibles was no affair of flags or flower throwing. This is ruled out by the need for secrecy in these days of air raids.

The attitude of the men seems to be : " We're here to do a job we think worth doing and we don't want any unnecessary fuss."

The French, too, share this feeling of not wishing for heroics, but the people of this port were moved by the sight of the khaki columns landing on their soil once more.

One old Frenchman who had been standing silent suddenly rushed forward to seize the hand of a great, gaunt Highlander heading a platoon.

He shook it, tears streaming from his eyes. The Highlander grinned, then carried on marching.

Out in the grey Channel I saw the dark shapes of the British and French destroyers which had escorted the latest ships to the port.

Above floated an observation balloon, scanning the port approaches for submarines. From the coastal forts great guns pointed out to sea, covering the approaches from England. Not a man was lost on this crossing.

Through the gate of their temporary barracks swung a detachment of sappers, shovels on shoulder.

Other troops, waiting for trains and lorries, crammed the bakers', the wine-shops and tobacconists'. Veterans of the last war acted as interpreters, but little interpretation was needed.

These men were taken right into French life. I saw infantrymen sitting on doorsteps like the members of any French family, with babies sitting on their knees, while hordes of little boys examined their buttons, caps and uniforms.

These men displayed the same attitude as the French towards this war—a quiet determination to see crushed once and for all this thing which has disturbed our natural life. One man told me : " A fortnight ago I was working on a building job in a remote part of Devon. I would never have believed I should find myself in France now." Two of them wore stripes from the last war.

While we were talking a whistle blew, the motor-cyclists hopped on their cycles, slung their rifles over their backs, and off went these troops, moving through villages and small towns and getting the warmest French welcome.

The troops wave back and move steadily on under the poplar trees lining the roads.

In the narrow streets of the old port town, the British troops were already completely at home. Infantrymen wearing the new battle-dress, white-belted military police, red hat-banded staff officers carrying canes, sergeants wearing the old style flat forage caps, strolled along and looked at the shop windows. Army nurses, with red-white-and-blue hatbands and with steel helmets slung over their arms, sat in their grey uniforms in the corner of a restaurant eating lunch.

The French are greatly struck by the easy air of confidence of these men, and the excellence of their bearing and equipment. An American military expert who was with me was most impressed with the calibre of this army, which he considers is probably the best fitted out in the world.

All the people of this port who remember 1914 said there was a great difference in attitude. A woman keeping a café on the port side said to me : " Then they came laughing and keen for adventure. Now they come determined to tackle the difficult job that is ahead, knowing that it is worth tackling. You tell the Old Contemptibles I've seen their sons today and they're worthy of them."

I Bombed a U-Boat from the Air

The sinking of a German submarine by a young South African pilot, laconically announced by the Ministry of Information, has stirred the imagination of the British people. Below is his own modest account of the achievement reprinted by permission from " The Daily Telegraph."

I SIGHTED the submarine on the surface and two miles away.

It was travelling pretty fast—at about 12 knots—in an easterly direction.

I took cover in a cloud to approach the submarine from astern. As I came out of the cloud, flying at 1,500 feet, I tried with my binoculars to identify the submarine. Flying closer I saw those characteristics which made me sure she was a German.

To make absolutely certain I fired some rounds of ammunition near her to give her a chance to identify herself.

She did not, so I proceeded to dive, at the same time firing my front gun at someone wearing a white hat who was standing on the conning tower.

At 500 feet the man on the conning tower disappeared and the submarine started to dive. By the time I dropped my first salvo of bombs, the nearest of which hit the water 15 or 20 yards directly ahead, the submarine was half under water.

The explosion of the bombs blew her back to the surface. That gave me time to turn round, and I then carried out an attack from the port beam.

The nearest bomb of my second salvo landed 6 feet to the side of the conning tower. It was a direct hit on the submarine's port side and there was a colossal explosion and her whole stern lifted out of the water. She dived into the sea at an angle of 30 deg.

For 20 minutes afterwards I remained over the spot watching the large whirlpools caused by escaping air coming to the surface of the water. By that time I assumed the submarine to be out of action on the bottom of the sea and returned to my base.

The U-boat seen in this photograph is just submerging in Kiel Harbour. It is approximately in the same position as was the submarine whose sinking is described by a South African airman in this page when he dropped his first salvo of bombs.
Photo, Sport and General

Paravanes Spell Safety in a Minefield

ONE of the most valuable inventions perfected during the last war was the paravane, which made it possible for ships of deep draught to pass through minefields in comparative safety. The apparatus consists of a torpedo-shaped body fitted with various devices to ensure that it keeps a straight course and maintains a certain depth. Paravanes are used in pairs, one being towed on either side of the ship. The tow-line is fitted with an apparatus that cuts through the mooring line of any anchored mine it encounters. The mine then floats to the surface and is exploded by rifle or gun fire. A pair of paravanes renders a ship practically immune from injury, even when passing through a field thickly sown with mines. The paravane was not perfected until the closing months of 1918, but it was then so effective that after September, 1918, only two ships, both light cruisers, were struck by mines, one of them in the Baltic after the Armistice. It is believed that the Germans never knew the secret of the device that had rendered their minefields ineffective until long after the war.

The paravane is used also by minesweepers. Most of the minesweeping in the last war was done by fishermen, among whom were men of sixty years of age or more. During the crisis of September, 1938, a volunteer minesweeping service was formed, and old trawlers were taken over to give the men training in this form of work.

This paravane is being slung out from the deck of a minesweeping trawler by naval ratings. Trawlers, on account of their shallow draught, are most useful for this work, minefields being laid many feet below the surface.

A paravane is taking the water, and as soon as the tow-line becomes taut the ingenious apparatus with which it is fitted will cause it to submerge to the required depth. Left, a naval rating is shooting at a mine cut adrift by the paravane.

Photos, Keystone

Hitler's S O S to the Jews

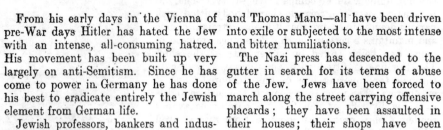

One of the most illuminating sidelights on Nazi Germany's readiness or otherwise for the waging of a long war was the appeal to the banished Jews to come back and work for the country which, under Hitler's leadership, cast them out with every kind of ignominy.

From his early days in the Vienna of pre-War days Hitler has hated the Jew with an intense, all-consuming hatred. His movement has been built up very largely on anti-Semitism. Since he has come to power in Germany he has done his best to eradicate entirely the Jewish element from German life.

Jewish professors, bankers and industrialists, Jewish journalists, artists and musicians, Jews of insignificant place and name and Jews whom the world at large has delighted to honour—such Jews as Einstein, Ehrlich, Bruno Walter, Freud, and Thomas Mann—all have been driven into exile or subjected to the most intense and bitter humiliations.

The Nazi press has descended to the gutter in search for its terms of abuse of the Jew. Jews have been forced to march along the street carrying offensive placards; they have been assaulted in their houses; their shops have been picketed by Nazis. One of the first things the Nazi conquerors did in Vienna was to compel members of the Jewish intelligentsia to go down on their knees and scrub the streets.

Julius Streicher, arch-instigator of the persecution of Jews in Germany, was said to be in disgrace after war broke out.
Photo, Associated Press

"WHO is the enemy of the German race? Who sapped the strength of the German people in the War and ensured their collapse at the end of it? Who as capitalist exploits the worker? Who as Communist inflames and then betrays him? Who corrupts and corrodes the nations with his vile and vulgar pseudo-culture? Who is the enemy of the entire human society?" These are some of the questions posed in Hitler's "Mein Kampf." He gives the answer, and in every case it is the same—*the Jew!*

No task has been too degrading for the Nazi taskmasters to set the Jews of Germany, no abuse has been too foul, no accusation too revolting. Julius Streicher's "Der Stürmer" built up a weekly circulation of 500,000 on pornography and blackmail of the Jewish people.

Yet only a few days after war broke out in 1939, posters were displayed in the German consulate in Antwerp urging all doctors, engineers and other technical experts of German nationality, *no matter what their race,* to return home and work for Germany again. The posters went on to promise that the fortunes which had been confiscated from such refugees would be restored if only they returned now in the hour of Germany's need.

But the Jews have long memories, and in that vast, world-wide front which has been built up against Hitlerism those Jews who were once a mainstay of German prosperity are finding their place. "We are anxious to put all our skill and knowledge at the service of those who are fighting the Nazis" said one Jewish spokesman.

These two photographs show scenes during the Nazi maltreatment of the Jews. Top, elderly Jews in Vienna are forced to go on their hands and knees and scrub the streets while jeering young Germans look on. In the lower photograph is a Jewish shop in Berlin wrecked during a pogrom instituted by the Nazis.

Himmler—The Man Germany Fears

In the circle of Nazi chiefs, Heinrich Himmler occupies a unique place, and particularly since war began has the importance of this arch-spy, super-terrorist of the Nazi people become clear for all to see.

Heinrich Himmler is chief of the S.S. (the Black Guards) and of the Gestapo, which together keep Germany quiet.
Photo, Associated Press

I F there is one man in Nazi Germany whom everybody fears it is Heinrich Himmler, the chief of the two great terroristic organizations, the Gestapo and the S.S.

Of lowly birth, and in early days a school-teacher, he early allied himself with Hitler and was the Fuehrer's standard-bearer during the unsuccessful Munich putsch of 1923. Since 1929 he has been commander of the S.S. (*Schutz-Staffeln*, defence corps), the black-uniformed private army which is so much in evidence in the Nazi Reich. These Black Guards are the army of the home front; 200,000 of them are trained as regular soldiers, serve for seven years, and live in barracks. They are selected with particular care, for it is intended that they should constitute a kind of Praetorian Guard such as surrounded the emperors of imperial Rome, or the janissaries of the sultan at Constantinople. Trained in special schools set up in castles in various parts of the Reich, they are permitted to marry only after a thorough investigation of the pedigree of the proposed bride. They are even forbidden to smoke. It is said that two of the Black Guards are always in attendance on Herr Hitler to protect his life with their own; even when he sleeps one is on guard inside the room while the other keeps watch between the double doors leading to it.

As commander of the Black Guards, as the person primarily responsible for the safety of the Fuehrer, Himmler wields a tremendous power, but the hate which he inspires is due to his position as chief of the Gestapo (*Geheime Staatspolizei*, secret police). He is the Fouché of the Nazi régime, and he performs his duties with an efficiency of the most sinister kind. His agents—spies is the better word—are everywhere. The concierges of most of the great apartment houses with which the German cities are filled are suspected of being in his pay, and he has informers (not to say, *agents provocateurs*) in all the factories and big business houses, in the universities and the schools, in newspaper-offices and in the beer halls. So widespread are the ramifications of his spy system that conversation in Germany is becoming a lost art, for even the most careless gossip may be reported by the Gestapo and call down upon the unhappy speaker's head the most dire consequences. For lapses of speech as well as of conduct the doors of the concentration camp are ever open—and the concentration camps are under Himmler's control.

With typically Teutonic efficiency and zeal he has built up a colossal card index system recording the names and particulars of all those persons in every rank of life who are suspected of being even lukewarm in their attachment to the Nazi system. No one knows how many millions of the German people are included in this vast dossier—and it is not intended that anybody should know.

To Himmler's headquarters are reported the names of all those who in the heat of the moment have let out an unguarded statement, or those who are believed to be not satisfied with the news given by the German official wireless, but in the silent darkness of their own homes listen in to the news bulletins given over the air by Paris and Brussels, Moscow and London. When you put through a telephone-call in Germany you can never be sure that an agent of the Gestapo is not tapping the line; and when you open your letters at the breakfast-table you have an uneasy feeling that someone has opened them before you.

Fearful in peacetime, Himmler casts an even more monstrous shadow now that Germany is at war. By his regimentation of the home front, he strives to maintain the people's morale. But it may be doubted whether morale can flourish in the forcing-bed of terrorism.

In appearance Himmler is the typical German bureaucrat; some people would call him insignificant—until they look into his eyes. He is by no means a great speaker—indeed, he is not a believer in speeches, but rather in action of the underground variety. Essentially he is an organiser, a ferreter-out of secrets, one who has an excellent ear and nose for the slightest suggestion of disaffection. Although those who have made his personal acquaintance aver that he has considerable charm, it is probably true to say that he has no friends, for even Hitler may wonder if his allegiance to him is based on personal affection or on cool calculation. During the "blood purge" of June 30, 1934, it was Himmler's Black Guards who despatched in cold blood Roehm and scores —perhaps hundreds—of the Nazi personnel whose continued existence their Fuehrer had decided was inconvenient to the maintenance of his power.

Those who hold high place in the Nazi movement today may well remember the callous competence displayed by Himmler and his agents in the mass executions. Master spy, executioner in chief—no wonder Himmler is hated and feared.

The first care of Himmler is to guard Hitler's life, and he is constantly near him. The two are here seen together in Poland, studying a map of the battlefields.
Photo, International Graphic Press

THE SOVIET PLAYS 'JACKAL TO THE NAZI LION'

Russia's unprovoked aggression on an unoffending neighbour, struggling for her
life made a most unfavourable impression on world opinion, and gave rise to a flood
of speculation as to the motives which impelled the move.

AT four o'clock in the morning of Sunday, September 17, 1939, large bodies of troops of the Red Army crossed the frontier of Poland at many points, and proceeded to attack the Polish armies, then fighting desperately for their existence against the overwhelming numbers of the Nazi invaders. Taken thus in the rear, the Polish front rapidly disintegrated, and in the course of a few hours practically the whole of Poland had been successfully overrun by the combined armies of Germany and Soviet Russia.

Although the way for this extraordinary development had been paved by the German-Soviet Non-Aggression Pact, signed in Moscow on August 23, the world received the news with a thrill of disgusted horror. That the alleged ideological opposites should agree on a non-aggression pact was one thing; for the Soviet to act, in the words of an American commentator, " as the jackal to the Nazi lion," was quite another.

The ostensible reasons for Russia's military invasion were given in the Soviet note handed to the Polish Ambassador in Moscow by Assistant Foreign Commissar Potemkin on behalf of Premier Molotoff at about the same time as the first Russian troops crossed the frontier.

' Poland has Ceased to Exist '

The note read as follows :

The Polish-German war has shown the internal bankruptcy of the Polish State.

During the course of ten days' hostilities, Poland has lost all her industrial areas and cultural centres. Warsaw, as the capital of Poland, no longer exists. The Polish Government has disintegrated and no longer shows any sign of life.

This means that the Polish State and its Government have, in point of fact, ceased to exist. In the same way, the Agreements concluded between the U.S.S.R. and Poland have ceased to operate.

Left to her own devices and bereft of leadership, Poland has become a suitable field for all manner of hazards and surprises, which may constitute a threat to the U.S.S.R. For these reasons the Soviet Government, which has hitherto been neutral, cannot any longer preserve a neutral attitude towards these facts.

The Soviet Government also cannot view with indifference the fact that the kindred Ukrainian and White Russian people who live on Polish territory and who are at the mercy of fate should be left defenceless.

In the circumstances, the Soviet Government has directed the High Command of the Red Army to order the troops to cross the frontier and take under their protection the life and property of the population of Western Ukraine and Western White Russia.

At the same time the Soviet Government propose to take all measures to extricate the Polish people from the unfortunate war into which it was dragged by its unwise leaders, and to enable it to live a peaceful life.

In a broadcast to the Soviet people delivered at 9.30 a.m. the same day, M. Molotoff declared that the events arising out of the Polish-German war had revealed the internal insolvency and obvious impotence of the Polish State. After repeating his statement concerning Poland's loss of her industrial and cultural centres, M. Molotoff went on to say that the population of Poland had been abandoned by their ill-starred leaders to their fate, and that the Polish State and its government had virtually ceased to exist.

"In view of this state of affairs," he proceeded, " the treaties concluded between the Soviet Union and Poland have ceased to operate. A situation has arisen in Poland which demands of the Soviet Government special concern for the security of its State. Poland has become a fertile field for any accidental and unexpected contingency which may create a menace to the Soviet Union. . . Nor can it be demanded of

**Klement Voroshilov has the official title
of the People's Commissar for Military
and Naval Affairs.**
Photo, E.N.A.

the Soviet Government that it should remain indifferent to the fate of its blood brothers the Ukrainian and White Russians inhabiting Poland, who even formerly were nations without any rights, and who have now been entirely abandoned to their fate. The Soviet Government deems it its sacred duty to extend the hand of assistance to them."

If these be what psychologists call good reasons for Russia's intervention, the real reasons may have been far different. For more than twenty years Russia had looked on in apparent indifference to the fate of her " blood brothers " beyond the Soviet borders. What now stimulated her energetic intervention was much more likely the rapid advance of the German army across the quivering carcase of Poland.

" Stalin," said " The Daily Telegraph," " cannot watch the German steam-roller crashing over prostrate Poland without an uneasy suspicion that the driver may forget to stop. Stalin has presumably read ' Mein Kampf.' If so, he has

no doubt noted Herr Hitler's conviction that Germany's true field of expansion is to the eastward ; what he covets most in Europe is the granary of the Ukraine. Like most monomaniacs, Herr Hitler has been true to himself if nothing else ; and there is point in M. Molotoff's insistence that Poland's White Russians and Ukrainians are under Red protection."

This argument is based on the assumption that Hitler remains a National Socialist and Stalin a Communist, but a situation may well be envisaged in which the ideological line of separation is completely erased. Indeed, for some time past there have been some critics who have asserted that the present Soviet régime is most certainly not Communism, but has many points of resemblance with State Capitalism of the Fascist variety. Some have gone further, and say that Stalin has become infected with the virus of imperialism, and is now prepared to play the game of power politics with the best.

' Triumph of Communism '

On the other hand, those who still cling to a belief in Soviet consistency find consolation in a statement broadcast from Moscow late in the evening of September 17, which declared that the Soviet action in invading Poland was aimed not only at the protection of the White Russian and Ukrainian minority in Poland, but at the opening of a new road for the worldwide triumph of that Communist creed whose spread was arrested by Pilsudski at the gates of Warsaw in 1920 and by the " Fascist state of Poland " in subsequent years.

Whatever the reason for Stalin's unleashing of his legions, there was no hesitation once the order had been given to march. Led by Voroshiloff, the Soviet Marshal, the Red armies poured across the frontier in a vast flood, seemingly determined to occupy as much Polish territory as possible before still further appropriations could be made by the Nazis. Particularly in south Poland a race developed between the German and Russian troops to obtain possession of the rich oilfield between Lwow and the Carpathians.

Perhaps it is this scramble for Polish territory which gives the key to the situation. It is hardly to be doubted that in the talks which led up to the German-Soviet Pact a month before, some partition of Poland had been resolved upon, and it may well have been decided that the German approach to a given line should be the signal for Russian intervention. The Nazis made speedier progress than had been anticipated, and Stalin may well have feared that unless he made haste Germany would have no hesitation in occupying territory which according to the agreement was to form part of Russia's share of the spoils.

Beginning of the Great Russian Betrayal of Poland

Here we see Russian armoured cars entering the territory of a country with which the U.S.S.R. had signed a non-aggression pact. The full military value of the mechanized Soviet army has yet to be proved. The effort to turn Russia from an agricultural country into a manufacturing one was not wholly successful, for the Russian does not take kindly to mechanical things.

Photo, Planet News

WORDS THAT HISTORY WILL REMEMBER

A Select Record from Week to Week of Important War Declarations and Statements

(Continued from page 92)

Monday, September 11

Mr. Anthony Eden, Secretary of State for the Dominions, in a broadcast address relayed to the United States and to the Empire :

" You may remember the famous story of the Roman envoys who went to Carthage before the 'First Punic War. Confronted by the Carthaginian Senate their spokesman said : ' I have here two gifts, peace and war, take which you choose.' No such grim alternative was given to Herr Hitler. Every inducement was offered him to enter the way of peaceful negotiation. The Polish Government had accepted the principle of negotiation. Herr Hitler deliberately and with set purpose made negotiation impossible. Instead, he chose to embark upon a war of naked aggression, and this country and France have in consequence fulfilled their undertaking to Poland. . . .

" The German Chancellor carried cynical dissimulation so far as finally to invade Poland because Poland had failed to accept peace proposals which she had never even received from the German Government. There has never been a more flagrant mockery of international good faith.

" Poland was ready to negotiate, as Czecho-Slovakia was ready to negotiate a year ago. Herr Hitler has preferred force. He has made the choice ; he must suffer the decision. For us now there will be no turning back. We have no quarrel with the German people, but there can be no lasting peace until Nazism and all it stands for, in oppression, cruelty, and broken faith, is banished from the earth. This is an issue that admits of no compromise. . . .

" Herr Hitler has claimed that his sole aim was to remedy the injustices of the Treaty of Versailles, which, he contended, was the root of all evil. This it was, we are told, which had forced him to build his colossal armaments, to march his legions into Austria, to imprison its Chancellor, to absorb Austria into the German Reich. This it was that compelled him to break faith with the British and French Governments, and, despite his pledge, so recently and so solemnly reaffirmed, to invade and subdue Czecho-Slovakia and to attempt to reduce her people to the status of hewers of wood and drawers of water.

" This it was that left Herr Hitler—we are assured—with no alternative but to turn against Poland, with whom some five years ago he had solemnly signed a pact which was to run for 10 years.

" Faced with such a catalogue of broken vows and discarded pledges, how is it possible to escape the conclusion that the Treaty of Versailles was not a grievance to redress but a pretext for the use of force ? Five times in the last 80 years the rulers of Germany have embarked with only the slightest pretext upon a war of aggression. Against peaceful Denmark in 1864, against Austria in 1866, against France in 1870, against the whole world in 1914 to 1918, and now against France, Poland, and Great Britain in 1939.

" With such a record her present rulers, had they been honest and sincere, might well have thought that they should accept to negotiate with nations who wanted nothing more than to live at peace with Germany, and who, as the documents which have been published show, excluded no subjects from peaceful discussion.

" Herr Hitler and his Nazi associates would have none of it. Flouting all the lessons of history, ignoring or deriding even their own country's experience of British character, they preferred yet once more the path of lawlessness, the path of misery and of bloodshed, the path of anarchy and want. Let the Nazi leaders ask themselves now to what destiny they are leading the German people.

" Our conscience is clear. Our memory is long, and our determination is unshaken.

" Let there be no mistake about this. Our determination to see this war through to the end is unshaken. We must make it clear to the Nazi leaders, and if we can to the German people, that this country, as the Prime Minister said, has not gone to war about the fate of a far-away city in a foreign land. We have decided to fight to show that aggression does not pay, and the German people must realize that this country means to go on fighting until that goal is reached.· . . ."

General Smuts in a message to the people of South Africa :

" Germany's policy of force extends to her former colonies. The oldest and the foremost of these is South-West Africa. This constitutes a threatening danger to the Union. If she remains neutral, South Africa cannot expect the help of other Powers, including Great Britain, when she is attacked over a Mandate which has 20,000 Afrikaners among its population. It would be a breach of faith to leave these people to the danger of falling under such a hell as the Nazi regime.

" Moreover, this is no time for displaying our separateness from the Commonwealth, which is our best friend and customer. In taking sides against Germany the Union is also participating in a struggle which touches deeply the basis of Christian values and our most valued political and civic rights."

Tuesday, September 12

Second message from the Independent Socialists of Germany to the British Independent Labour Party, smuggled through a neutral country :

" The Gestapo, the German secret service, is now in control over the workers in Germany. The fortifications workers, who have been forced to leave their homes and their families, are watched by the Gestapo. Storm troopers and blackshirts see that no revolutionary word is spoken. Guards drive them to work for long hours without a chance of rest.

" This is a pamphlet which our fortifications workers are spreading in spite of the persecution of the Gestapo ; in spite of the terror of Hitler's storm troopers :

" ' Comrades of the —— ; fight from canteen to canteen. Fight against Hitler's policy of aggression and war. We want shorter hours and more food. Give us butter and bacon, eggs and fat. We do not want war. We want to return to our families.'

" In spite of the terror of the Gestapo, the illegal fight goes on in Germany. Starved, exhausted, and persecuted, we and our comrades will win the battle for Socialism, inside or outside the frontier, in peace or in war, in liberty or in prison. The fight goes on to the last breath."

Wednesday, September 13

Mr. Chamberlain in the House of Commons :

" The people of France and the people of Great Britain are alike determined not only to honour to the full their obligations to Poland, but also to put an end once for all to the intolerable strain of living under the perpetual threat of Nazi aggression. Our French allies are, like ourselves, a peace-loving people, but they are no less convinced than are we that there can be no peace until the menace of Hitlerism has been finally removed. *Il faut en finir.*"

Thursday, September 14

Mr. Chamberlain in the House of Commons :

" His Majesty's Government have noted this announcement [the German decision to bomb open towns], which on the face of it is in flat contradiction of the German Chancellor's recent statement to the Reichstag when he disclaimed any desire to make war on women and children.

" The restrictions we—like the French— have imposed upon the operations of our own Forces were based upon the condition of similar restraint being observed by our opponents, and H.M. Government must, of course, hold themselves free, if such restraint is not in fact observed, to take such action as they may deem appropriate.

" But I wish to add that, whatever be the length to which others may go, H.M. Government will never resort to deliberate attack on women, children and other civilians for purposes of mere terrorism. . . .

Monday, September 18

Rt. Hon. A. Greenwood in a message to the Labour Party :

I realize to the full the feelings of members of the Labour Movement about yesterday's news.

The U.S.S.R. has invaded Poland. She has done so on grounds which cannot be justified and which have been used previously by Hitler as excuses for his monstrous outrages.

No one can foretell what may happen next. It is idle to speculate, but what we must do is to face realities. The new situation, however it may develop, will gravely increase our difficulties.

It is folly to pretend otherwise. The struggle will be sterner, but whatever may befall cannot alter the issue by one iota.

The British working-class Movement has adopted a definite and unalterable attitude against aggression wherever and by whomsoever it is committed.

It has accepted the challenge thrown out by Germany. It will not now turn its back on the Polish people who are the latest victims of aggression, alas, on two fronts.

However the forces of the world may be aligned in the immediate future, the spirit of those who stand unflinchingly for freedom will be victorious.

Therefore I say, do not let base passions get the better of steady judgement.

Do not let hatred obscure our minds and deflect us for one moment from the greatest task in the history of mankind—the final downfall of overlordism, dictatorship and tyranny. It may be that in the ebb and flow of war Poland will for a time be wiped off the map of Europe, but there will be a glorious resurrection.

Labour says to the Poles, therefore, bitter and tragic though your struggle may be, we will not desert you. We cannot desert the basic principle of our Movement without being traitors to ourselves.

We shall never be guilty of treachery. Loyalty to a cause is in every fibre of our being. Our message of hope to Poland is that in the days to come she will stand as an imperishable monument to steadfastness and faith in freedom when dictatorships have been swept from the face of the earth.

With Poland's rise from the ashes of the war in full-fledged freedom there will also come freedom for other peoples now dwelling in the dark shadows of cruelty and oppression.

Czechs Raise Standard of Revolt

Dr. Karl Sidor, leader of a small independent force which has been maintaining guerilla warfare against the Nazis in the Slovak mountains.

"PROTECTED" by the Nazi Reich since the spring of 1939, Czecho-Slovakia has become ever more restive under alien domination. With the military occupation of the country consequent upon the invasion of Poland, the temper of the Czechs was tried to breaking-point, and on Sunday, September 17, a revolutionary movement broke out. From Bohemia and Moravia the revolt spread to Slovakia, and despite the most ruthless measures taken by the army of occupation the fight of the oppressed peoples, driven to desperation, went on with determination and courage. Thousands of arrests were made, and hundreds of demonstrators and insurgents were shot. Still the fight went on, and it became clear even to the Nazis that the rising, though premature, symbolized a nation's determination to win liberty or die.

One of the cities of the former Czecho-Slovakia in which the revolutionary movement broke out in September, 1939, was Pilsen. Famed for its breweries, it is also the site of the Skoda great armament works (above).

Tabor, in Bohemia (above), and Brno (top right), capital of Moravia, are two of the towns mentioned as the scene of revolt against the Nazi suzerain. The map on left shows these and other centres affected.

As soon as war broke out between France and Germany the very large Czech colony in the Republic rallied as one man to the cause of freedom. Crowds of young men flocked to the Czecho-Slovak Legation in Paris (below) with a view to enlisting in the Czech legion then being formed. For though the fight be on the Rhine, Czecho-Slovakia's ultimate liberty is one of the causes at stake.

Photos, Associated Press E.N.A., Wide World

OUR DIARY OF THE WAR

Monday, September 18

Soviet and German troops met near Brest-Litovsk. In a joint communiqué the two Governments announced their intention of restoring order in Poland.

Soviet troops also reached Vilna in the north and occupied the Rumano-Polish frontier in the south.

Attack on Warsaw resumed.

Polish Government having crossed the frontier into Rumania, together with numberless refugees, the Rumanian frontier closed.

Japanese Press reports from Rome were to the effect that Hitler was bringing pressure to bear on Russia to abandon her support of China.

French troops advanced within three miles of Saarbruecken and Zweibruecken.

British **Aircraft Carrier "Courageous"** was sunk by an enemy submarine on the night of September 17, with the loss of 518 members of her crew. The submarine was believed to have been sunk later by destroyers.

Two **R.A.F. flying-boats** rescued the crew of the British steamer "Kensington Court," sunk by a U-boat in the Atlantic.

The **Duke of Windsor** assumed the rank of Major-General on taking up a Staff appointment abroad.

Lord Camrose appointed chief assistant to Lord Macmillan, Minister of Information.

Tuesday, September 19

Soviet troops occupied Vilna, advanced beyond Brest-Litovsk, and, in the South, reached the Hungarian frontier.

Hitler entered Danzig at noon, and later broadcast a speech defending his action in Poland and his policy towards Russia.

On the **Western Front**, German attacks between the district east of the Moselle and the region of Bitsch were repulsed.

Wednesday, September 20

Fierce fighting west of Warsaw in what the Germans termed a **battle of extermination.** They claimed to have taken 105,000 prisoners, and also to have captured Gdynia.

The **Soviet** army reached Lwow, said to have been conceded to them by Germany.

A **revolt in Czecho-Slovakia**, which first broke out on Sunday, continued to spread in spite of ruthless repressive measures. Mass executions were reported.

The **French Council of Ministers** met and approved the "military, economic and financial measures for pursuing the conduct of the War until final victory."

On the **Western Front** a period of comparative calm was reported.

H.M.S. "Kittiwake" struck a mine in the English Channel. Five members of the crew were missing, believed killed, and two injured.

In the House of Commons **Mr. Chamberlain** made the third of his weekly reviews of the War situation.

The **Canadian Cabinet** decided to raise immediately an expeditionary force of 20,000 for service overseas.

Australia offered to Britain the complete personnel of four bomber squadrons and two squadrons of two-seater fighting 'planes.

Contraband goods to the value of £500,000 were reported to have been intercepted on their way to Germany during the week ending September 16.

Details of the **private fortunes**, totalling over £3,000,000, accumulated abroad by seven Nazi leaders, were published by leading New York papers.

Thursday, September 21

M. Calinescu, Rumanian Prime Minister, was assassinated in Bucharest by members of the Iron Guard. General George Angeseanu appointed to succeed him.

President Roosevelt addressed Congress on the Neutrality Statutes, urging the repeal of the arms embargo.

The **Poles** continued to resist in Warsaw, Modlin and other areas, despite ruthless bombing attacks.

Germany claimed that the southern Polish army had surrendered.

On the **Western Front** there was an increase of air activity by both the French and British.

THE POETS & THE WAR

1

1939

By Humbert Wolfe

It darkens. In the marsh the Goth and Vandal
Have set their camp-fires burning.
England waits,
Half-hushed, the loud abominable scandal
of death that flies by night. Hell's at the gates.

Who mans the gate? Already the dreadful hand
Has loosed the bolt: the battle-flags unfurled
Begin to taint the wind. Answer, who stand
To make their breast the rampart of the world?

Who stands in the gate? What answer, Englishmen?
We answer, waiting not on how or why,
"We are here, freedom. Grant us once again
The will to suffer, and the right to die."

The Observer.

The British Government set up a Council of ten members to organize the **supply of munitions.**

Diplomatic exchanges preceding the outbreak of war were recorded and issued in a Government Blue Book.

Friday, September 22

Warsaw still holding out.

General von Fritsch, former Commander-in-Chief of the German Army, killed in action outside Warsaw.

That the **German army** has now lost 150,000 men was maintained by M. Giradoux, French Commissioner-General for Information, in a broadcast from Paris.

Reports from the **Western Front** stated that French detachments had reached the outskirts of Zweibruecken, in the Siegfried Line.

Steamer **"Arkleside"** reported sunk by U-boat.

A **Grimsby trawler** was reported to have sunk by accident an enemy submarine for which two British warships were searching.

The **assassins** of the Rumanian Prime Minister, and many other members of the Iron Guard, were executed in Bucharest.

The **Allied Supreme War Council** met "somewhere in Sussex."

Saturday, September 23

Polish troops still resisted desperately near Modlin, north-west of Warsaw, and in the capital itself. In South-East Poland the Germans claimed to have captured Lwow.

German High Command announced that 450,000 Polish prisoners had been taken to date, and 800 aeroplanes destroyed or captured.

Mussolini, in a speech to Fascist leaders at Rome, declared that the moment had come to cease hostilities, since Poland was now liquidated and Europe not yet effectively at war.

Two **Finnish steamers,** "Martti-Ragnar" and "Walma," sunk by U-boats.

Sunday, September 24

Bombardment of Warsaw continued incessantly. German troops claimed to have crossed the Vistula between Modlin and Warsaw, thus cutting off the latter.

On the **Western Front** local attacks by the enemy were repulsed. Several successful air actions were fought.

It was stated that the **British Expeditionary Force** in France was still moving up to its positions preparatory to going into action.

Swedish steamer "Gertrud Blatt" sunk by German submarine.

British cargo boat "Hazelside" was sunk without warning during the night by an enemy submarine. Twenty three of the crew were picked up six hours later by a fishing boat, but eleven were reported missing.

Oil wells at Drohobycz, centre of the Galician oilfields, were taken over by Soviet troops.

It is Said That . . .

New York police are making a minute survey of cellars in the city's office buildings for possible use in air raids.

A rumour current in Paris was to the effect that the ex-Chancellor of Austria, Dr. Schuschnigg, has been shot.

Gramophone records of pledges given by Hitler in his public speeches have been broadcast from France—and jammed by the Germans!

Hitler's protective squadron in his flights to the Front consists of one saloon aeroplane, five transport 'planes, 15 chasers, 18 scouts, and one refuelling 'plane.
("*Freedom*" *Station Broadcast.*)

One result of petrol rationing is that Mayfair fashion houses are designing cycling skirts for their patrons.

Of thirty-four "Hitlers" in a lunatic asylum in the Saar district, only twelve maintained this identity when evacuated.

Handbags designed to hold a miniature first-aid kit, tiny pocket torch, powder, lipstick, and gas mask, are selling in Paris.

A caravan of Russian tanks invading Poland announced to cheering crowds: "We have come to fight the Germans."

Three German tanks were caught unawares by Polish women, who drenched them with petrol and set them alight.

In one Polish village whose inhabitants, it was alleged, had fired on the Germans, every twelfth woman, child and old man was shot.

Marlene Dietrich has failed to get her parents out of Germany. Her father, a Prussian officer in the last war, now lives in retirement in Potsdam.

The German government has appealed for nettles as these are "urgently needed as an important textile material."

The weekly ration of meat in Germany is now a fraction over one pound.

The coffee ration has again been cut; it is now only 20 grammes (little more than half an ounce) per person per week.

Making the Best of a Black Business

AFTER many hundreds of years Great Britain once more knows a curfew, for at sunset, nearly an hour before it is completely dark, all lights must be put out or screened, while street lamps are never lit. Even in remote country places this regulation has been strictly observed, though in small towns and villages not usually well lit the difficulties of pedestrians and motorists have been far less than in the big cities. Such safety devices as those seen in three of these photographs have helped to make the path of the pedestrian safe.

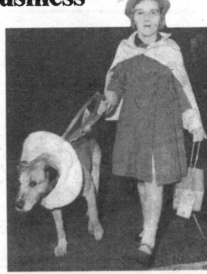

This small girl wears a white cloak and her dog has a white collar for safety's sake.

All possible precautions have been taken by this man and woman, even to white stripes round an umbrella.

As a result of the black-out, some of the devices so useful in peacetime in making the roads safe have now become a positive danger. This car was found abandoned the morning after colliding with the posts of a "roundabout" island.

Since the outbreak of war Great Britain, France, Poland, and Germany have had a complete black-out every night in their capitals and over large areas in the provinces. Left, is one of the principal streets of Berlin photographed at dusk, when usually it would be a blaze of light. Right, a woman in South London makes safety doubly sure by wearing a white coat and carrying a newspaper.

Photos, Sport & General, Fox Photos, and Central Press

Cartoon Commentary on the Conflict

"BOMB THEM, BURN THEM, GAS THEM, ENGLAND··BUT SPARE THEM **THIS**"

From the " Star "

HEILY RUSSIA

From the " Star "

A.R.P. IN GERMANY

THE CARTOON is of the highest value in graphically registering public opinion on events of urgent interest. With a swiftness far beyond the pen of the pithiest writer, the pencil of a gifted cartoonist can tell a whole story and comment upon it so that it passes to the mind of the beholder in a flash. From time to time we intend to offer our readers a choice from the most striking cartoons of the day.

From the " Evening Standard "

GERMAN MURDERER: It's all right—he's dead now!
RUSSIAN BODYSNATCHER: Then I shall rob the corpse—fearlessly!

From the " Daily Mirror "

STRANGE BEDFELLOWS

From the " Evening News "

The WAR ILLUSTRATED

Vol. 1   A Permanent Picture Record of the Second Great War   No. 5

In 1939, as in 1914, the motto of the British Army is " Tails up." These young men having a cheery ride on an Army lorry are typical of the Army of today. Regular soldiers of the peacetime Army, Territorials, including many men who served in the last war, and the Militiamen —all have made an excellent impression at home and in France, and have shown that they are worthy successors of the men of 1914-1918.

Photo, Associated Press

Poland Fought On, 'Bloody But Unbowed'

Although the Nazi joy-bells were ringing over the end of the war with Poland, the army and people of the land so ruthlessly and treacherously invaded still here and there, and particularly in Warsaw the capital, put up an heroic resistance which evoked the admiration of the whole civilized world. But the inevitable day of surrender came.

THREE weeks after the armies of the Reich crossed the Polish frontier in their war of invasion, the German High Command was able to claim that the Polish campaign was over. "In a series of battles of extermination," read the German communiqué,

"of which the greatest and most decisive was in the Vistula curve, the Polish army numbering a million men has been defeated, taken prisoner, or scattered. Not a single Polish active or reserve division, not a single independent brigade, has escaped this fate. Only fractions of single bands escaped immediate annihilation by fleeing into the marshy territory in East Poland. There they were defeated by Soviet troops." Only in Warsaw, Modlin, and on the peninsula of Hela in the extreme north of Poland near Gdynia were there still small sections of the Polish army fighting on; and these claimed the communiqué, "are in hopeless positions."

Warsaw's Heroic Defence

While the Polish authorities in Warsaw claimed that resistance was still proceeding in some parts of the country additional to those mentioned in the German communiqué, it was obvious that the Polish front had completely disintegrated. The war, from being one of movement on a vast scale, had now degenerated into one of guerilla actions. It was at Warsaw, the capital, that the

Polish resistance was finally crystallized. Scornfully refusing all demands for surrender, the Polish garrison and populace combined in presenting a firm front to the beleaguerers. Day after day the Germans bombed and shelled the city. On September 26 it was reported that the entire business centre of the city was in flames following almost continuous shelling and dive-bombing by the Nazi 'planes. On the previous Sunday, according to a communiqué issued by the Warsaw command, over a thousand civilians were reported killed, and four churches and three hospitals filled with wounded were destroyed. The communiqué went on to say that there were no longer any buildings in Warsaw remaining intact, and not a house in which there had not been a victim of the Nazi bombs or shells. Furthermore, within the previous twenty-four hours about a hundred fires had broken out following the launching upon the city of a hail of incendiary bombs. Yet, bombed and shelled without intermission, the garrison and populace kept a good heart. "The morale of the army and populace is excellent," said one communiqué and

The horror of the Nazi onslaught on the civilian population of Poland is brought home with poignant reality in these photographs. In one we see a Polish woman praying among the ruins of her home for her husband and children killed in an air raid; in the other the primitive fire brigade of a small Polish village is trying vainly to cope with the flames that incendiary bombs have started.

Photos, Keystone

They Stood by Poland to the End

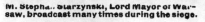

M. Stephan Starzynski, Lord Mayor of Warsaw, broadcast many times during the siege.

To Count Raczynski, left, the Polish Ambassador in London, fell the task of putting Poland's case to the British Government. Colonel Beck, right, Poland's Foreign Minister, worked indefatigably for conciliation until the last moment.

A MONG the many appealing messages to the world broadcast from the still defiant Warsaw was this by M. Starzynski, Lord Mayor of the city, on September 21:

' I want the whole civilized world to know what the Nazi Government means by humanitarian war. Yesterday in the early hours of the morning seven of our hospitals were bombed, among many other buildings, with terrible results. Soldiers wounded on the battlefield were killed in their beds. Many civilians, among them women and children, were killed outright or buried under the ruins. But the most barbaric crime was committed on the Red Cross Hospital, which had the Red Cross flags flying from the windows. Several hundred wounded Polish soldiers were there.''

Here in this page are portrayed some of those who stood in the forefront of the Polish nation in its hour of deepest trial. Left to right are General Norvid Neugebauer, who led the Polish Military Mission that arrived in London on September 8; General Sosnowski, Inspector-General of the Polish Army and the leader of the nation's final resistance; General Czuma, who commanded the Polish garrison of Warsaw in its heroic stand; and Colonel Lipinski, who broadcast the story of Warsaw's last days.

Photos, Fox, Wide World, Vandyk, and Planet News

The crew of the Polish submarine Zbik (" Wild Cat ") made a remarkable voyage to save their ship from capture by the Germans. When she arrived at the Swedish island of Sandhamn she had been at sea for 42 days and the crew were half starved.
Photo, Keystone

their best to hold up the invaders, but they were swamped by the Russian masses. At Grodno the Poles put up a desperate resistance, but the town was eventually carried and the officers of the Polish garrison were mercilessly slain. In some parts the Red Army seems to have encountered little resistance, and it was said that the vanguard always invited surrender before opening fire. From several places it was reported that the Soviet tanks and infantry announced that they were coming as liberators of the Polish people, "to defend them against the Nazis."

Indeed, there were two Russian invasions of Poland. The first consisted of the Red Army. The second comprised about 3,000 actors, musicians, poets, journalists, printers, type-setters and

"the defence of Warsaw continues." The German forces ringed the once proud and beautiful city, now reduced to a smoking shambles, and from time to time made desperate raids into the suburbs with their tanks and armoured cars, only to be held up by the trenches and barricades which the citizens had prepared a fortnight before. Not until September 27 could the Nazi wireless announce, so as to be believed by the world, that the collapse of long-sustained Warsaw's resistance was at hand.

While the German troops were advancing to, or retiring on, the demarcation line agreed upon with the Soviet, the Red Army was continuing its march into Poland. Small groups of Polish troops did

This German aeroplane, viewed from a fellow 'plane, is one of a fighter formation flying over Poland. Such machines were used to escort the bombers that rained death on Warsaw
Photos, Associated Press and Wide World

The photograph above was taken from a German aeroplane flying over a Polish Red Cross hospital station. The zigzag line is a trench. Right, Hitler is looking down at devastated Poland from the window of his private aeroplane.

Warsaw Bombed & Burned to a Smoking Shambles

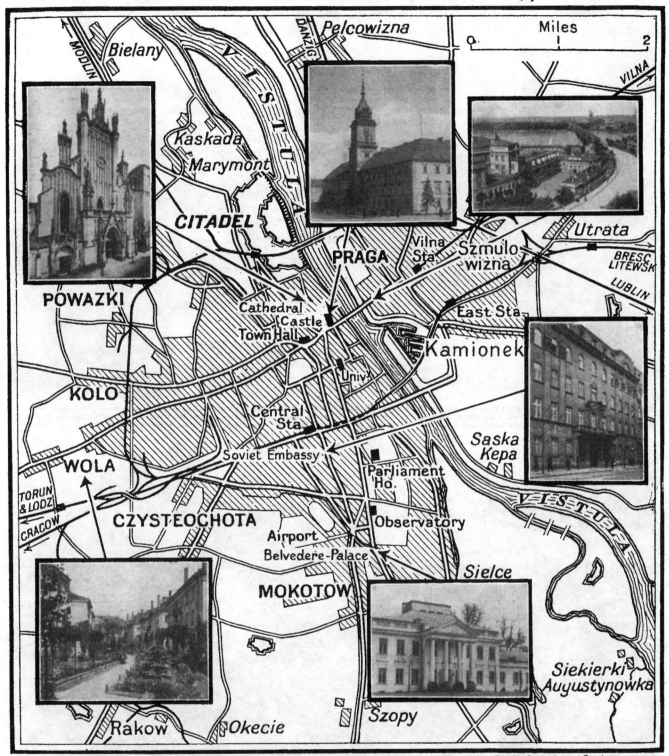

In the picture map above the principal districts and some of the finest buildings in Warsaw are shown. On the Cathedral of St. John a bomb was dropped during Mass and the roof fell on the congregation. The Zamek Palace, the home of the President, is believed to have been destroyed. In the suburb of Praga heavy fighting took place. The photograph shows the Kierbedz Bridge connecting Praga with Warsaw. The Soviet Embassy was not exempt. The Belvedere Palace, once the home of Marshal Pilsudski, was destroyed. In the suburb of Wola the Poles put up a strenuous resistance.

Photos, E.N.A., Topical, and Planet News.   Map by courtesy of " The Times "

cinema-operators. This second army was armed not with rifles and machine-guns, but with a million photographs of Stalin and thousands of copies of Russian newspapers extolling the virtues and benefits of the Soviet regime. As they followed in the wake of the Red army, the 3,000 propagandists distributed the photographs and newspapers, and then pro-

ceeded to open theatres, give concerts and film shows, and set up newspapers and pamphlets in the Polish tongue.

A rather grim accompaniment of this second invasion was the shooting (or "liquidation," to use the officially accepted term) of the official elements and the middle-classes of the conquered country. Just a week after Russia's invasion of

Poland began German and Soviet troops formally met at Brest-Litovsk—a name of ill omen in the early history of the Soviet State, for there it was that Russia signed the humiliating treaty of 1918—and the Germans formally handed over the town and fortress to the Red army. The exchange of courtesies was watched by a large but silent crowd.

With the Red Army in Its March through Poland

At Brest-Litovsk in 1918 the infant Soviet Republic signed a humiliating treaty with Germany; twenty-one years later it was in this same Polish city that the troops of Red Russia, now one of the great powers of the world, greeted the soldiers of Nazi Germany. The photo above shows a parade in Brest-Litovsk after the two forces had met. German and Soviet officers are saluting, while members of the rank and file look on.

Crossing the Polish frontier on September 17, the Soviet armies rapidly overran the eastern portion of Poland. In many places they gave out that they were coming as "liberators" of the Ukrainians and White Russians—those peoples of Poland whom Soviet Russia claims as "blood brothers." Behind the invading troops marched a body of Soviet propagandists who proceeded to distribute a quantity of literature, in which the Soviet system was lauded. This photograph shows copies of the Moscow newspapers being handed out near Wilno.

Soviet Power in the Ukraine, Baltic and Poland

ONE of the most marked features of the War has been the sudden comeback of Soviet Russia as a European great power. For years it had seemed as if the Kremlin had eyes only for Asia ; with the collapse of Poland imminent, however, Stalin decided that the time was ripe for the recovery of those peoples of Poland whom he styles the blood brothers of the Russians. As a result of the brief campaign and of the subsequent negotiations, Russia secured a large proportion of the Polish land and people.

In this page we have illustrated some of the weighty arguments which enabled Russia to take so large a portion of the Polish conquest. At the top of the page a Russian armoured car is seen crossing a river on the borders of the Ukraine, and the bottom picture is of a Russian tank passing through Rakov in the march through Poland. The centre illustration is of naval interest as it shows Soviet seamen doing "physical jerks" on board the battleship "October Revolution."—the name refers to the Bolshevik rising of 1917—in Baltic waters.

Rumania's Premier Pays The Price

When King Carol visited Hitler in November, 1938, he is believed to have refused to moderate his hostility towards the German-inspired and -financed Nazi movement in Rumania, the Iron Guard. On September 21, 1939, his Premier, M. Calinescu, was slain by Rumanian Nazi terrorists.

So yet another blood-stained page was turned in Rumania's history. Ever since the Great War Rumania has shown marked signs of political instability. Perhaps this may be attributed to the Latin temperament of the people, or it may be due to the fact that Rumania is still very young. Her independence as a modern State dates from only 1879.

During the first two years of the Great

Armand Calinescu, Premier of Rumania, was assassinated by men of the Iron Guard on September 21, 1939. Right is the scene a few minutes after this brutal act. The wooden cart was placed in the road to force the Premier's car close to the kerb. The bullet holes in the glass are clearly visible.

E.N.A. and Associated Press

O UT of the gates of the Royal Palace of Cotroceni, near Bucharest, sped the motor-car of M. Armand Calinescu, Rumania's Premier. Suddenly the chauffeur, observing a cart on the side of the road, made a swerve. The car skidded, hit the kerb, and swung round across the road. Then, simultaneously, a number of men from both sides of the road discharged their automatic pistols at the Premier and his bodyguard of detectives.

The assassination committed, the murderers jumped into three cars and drove furiously to the Bucharest wireless station. There they shot the doorkeeper and forced their way into the broadcasting studio. The gramophone record which was being played came to a sudden end, and listeners were horrified to hear the words screamed into the microphone : " The death sentence on Calinescu has been executed and the legionaries are revenged." Before the announcement could be continued the interrupter was overpowered and he and his fellow-assassins were arrested.

Late on the evening of the same day—Thursday, September 21, 1939—the captured terrorists were lined up on the scene of M. Calinescu's assassination and in full view of a great crowd were shot dead by gendarmes. The corpses, covered with a banner bearing the words, " This is the fate which will overtake all future assassins who betray their country," were left lying in the street for 24 hours.

War she played a neutral hand, but in 1916, in return for promises of vast territorial gains at the expense of her neighbours, she was induced to come in on the Allied side. In a very short time she was completely overrun by the Austro-German armies, but two days before the Armistice she declared war anew on the Central Powers, and was thus able to claim a place among the treaty-makers as one of the victorious powers.

As the reward for her intervention she was granted a huge tract of Hungarian territory—Transylvania, Bukovina, and the Banat of Temesvar. She also managed to secure the Russian territory of Bessarabia.

Rumania's post-war record has been exceedingly chequered. Apart from the dynastic troubles associated with King Carol's matrimonial adventures, she has been torn by political faction and riddled with corruption. Early in 1938 King Carol dismissed the Premier, M. Goga, and appointed in his stead the patriarch Miron Christea ; the king, himself, however, was in effect dictator. In this ministry M. Calinescu was Minister for the Interior, and among the tasks with which he was entrusted was the suppression of the Rumanian Fascist movement, the Iron Guard.

The Iron Guards were fierce anti-Semites with pro-Nazi sympathies, and were responsible for many acts of terrorism, including the assassination of Ion Duca, the then Prime Minister, in 1934. When the Iron Guards were suppressed by Carol and Calinescu they were reconstituted as the " All for the Fatherland Party." Change in name did not indicate any change of policy, however, and in May, 1938, their leader, M. Codreanu, was sentenced to ten years' imprisonment for plotting against the social order and preparing to revolt ; many of his followers were also sent to gaol. Still the agitation continued, until in November, 1938, Codreanu and thirteen of his chief supporters, when being conveyed from one prison to another, were shot by their guards " while attempting to escape."

That a few of the Iron Guard terrorists were left at large is evidenced by the brutal assassination of M. Calinescu. In the light of the Fascist aims and openly admitted pro-Nazi sympathies of the Iron Guard, it was a little naïve of the German broadcast announcer to state that " Calinescu was a thorn in England's flesh. This bloody deed was England's work " !

Rumania has an army with a peacetime establishment of about 13,000 officers and 147,000 other ranks. It has been largely mechanized of recent years, and above, King Carol, accompanied by Prince Michael, is shown reviewing a mechanized unit.

Photo, Press Topics

Daladier, the Strong Man of France

France's Prime Minister, Minister of War and National Defence, is one who
for years past has played a prominent part in the political life of the great
Republic. Here we are told something of his career. He first became
Premier on the day in 1933 that saw Hitler appointed Reich Chancellor.

A BOURGEOIS — there you have Edouard Daladier in one word. Born in 1884, the son of a baker, he was educated at Lyons, and before the Great War was a secondary-school teacher. He served at the front, won the Croix de Guerre and the Légion d'Honneur, and at the Armistice was a captain. Entering the Chamber of Deputies in 1919 as the Radical-Socialist member for Vaucluse in Provence, he first achieved ministerial rank in the Herriot cabinet of 1924, when he was appointed Minister for the Colonies. In the next year Painlevé made him Minister for War, and during the next few years he served under Briand, Steeg, Herriot and Paul-Boncour. Then, on January 31, 1933, a few hours after Hindenburg appointed Hitler Chancellor of the German Reich, Daladier became Prime Minister of the French Republic.

Daladier's first cabinet lasted some ten months, but after a period of office as Minister of War under Chautemps, he was Premier for a few days in 1934 when the Stavisky scandal was at its height.

From 1936 he was Minister of War in several Popular Front governments, and on April 10, 1938, following the downfall of M. Blum's cabinet, he became Prime Minister for the third time. In the autumn of that year he held France's helm steady through the crisis over Czecho-Slovakia. He was one of the four "Men of Munich," and to his credit let it be said that in circumstances of unprecedented difficulty he succeeded in keeping his head. It is on record that at Munich, while the Fuehrer contented himself with a glass of Rhine wine, Mussolini nibbled occasionally at a sandwich, and Mr. Chamberlain ate sparingly, only the Frenchman consumed his ordinary meal—a hot dish, salad, cheese and coffee.

Like Mr. Chamberlain, he was received on his return from Munich with transports of joy, but it was not long before, in Paris as in London, the Munich settlement was denounced as a shameful surrender. Nevertheless, Daladier continued to ride the storm. At the Radical-Socialist Congress at Marseilles he vigorously defended his conduct—"the Munich Agreement," he maintained, "was an act of reason," and he went on to claim that "we have maintained peace and the dignity of France. These we are determined to preserve."

On March 17, 1939, following upon the German seizure of the rump state of Czecho-Slovakia, his government was granted extraordinary powers for the reinforcement of national defence. Speaking before the Senate M. Daladier declared that "we find ourselves faced with a grave situation which may rapidly become dramatic. This we must meet courageously. We are going to show Europe," he said, "that we are standing with our backs to the wall. We are embarking on the task of assuring the safety of the nation and the salvation of the Republic."

As the year went on and the situation worsened, the Prime Minister still dominated the political scene. His sturdy personality seemed to embody the French will to resist the menace to her security and the future of western culture.

From the rostrum in the Chamber and through the microphone Daladier appealed to Frenchmen to bury their differences and to save their country and the world by their labours and sacrifices. Just before the war broke out he told his people that "in these solemn hours for the destiny of the world we all hope and believe that wisdom and good sense will finally triumph. But should all our efforts be in vain we appeal to you, French women and French men, to your courage and to your determination, not to submit to slavery." Well is it for France that in her hour of greatest danger she has such a man as Daladier for her chosen leader.

On September 22, 1939, the Supreme War Council of the Allies met in a Sussex town hall in a room adjoining the council chamber. Here are the members leaving the building. (1) General Gamelin, Commander-in-Chief of the French Army ; (2) Lord Chatfield, Minister for Co-ordination of Defence ; (3) Viscount Halifax, Britain's Foreign Secretary ; (4) the Prime Minister, Mr. Neville Chamberlain ; (5) M. Corbin, French Foreign Minister ; (6) M. Daladier, Premier of France.

Photo, Topical

Watch and Ward on the West

Week after week the watch on the Rhine goes on, as the world's greatest armies face each other in alert expectancy from their fastnesses in the fortified zones. Day by day the French forces, aided by Allied air reconnaissances, make local advances and consolidate their footing in German territory.

A battery of the famous French 75 mm. guns moving forward behind the Maginot Line.

Photos, Associated Press and Keystone

A FTER a silence of three weeks, on Sept. 24 the French guns in the sector running for a hundred miles from Lauterbourg, where the Franco-German frontier makes a right-angle bend to the Swiss frontier close to Basle, suddenly blazed into activity.

Thus the whole of the Western Front became an active war zone. Between the Moselle and the Rhine the French continued their penetrating tactics, pushing forward their infantry into advanced positions, bringing up their guns as the line was consolidated, and beating off the counter-attacks which from time to time were delivered by the troops occupying the forward positions of the Siegfried Line.

In the skies above, the French aeroplanes were engaged in making the most careful reconnaissance of the German positions. From time to time German fighters buzzed about their 'planes like a cloud of angry hornets, but the French fighters had no difficulty in protecting their charges. Indeed, as the war went on it became more and more plain that the French fighting 'planes were far superior in performance to those of the enemy, and it was stated with satisfaction in Paris that "the aces of 1914 have found worthy successors."

Even the Italian papers were not slow in paying tribute to the marked superiority of the French air force over that of the Nazis. We may suppose that the R.A.F. had also its share in the aerial reconnaissances, and its success in its propaganda raids over German territory was demonstrated time and again. Millions of leaflets warning the German people of the deadly consequences of "Hitler's war" if it were prolonged were showered upon the great centres of population in western and central Germany. Despite the heavy penalties decreed by the Nazi authorities against any citizen of the Reich who should be so ill-advised as to pick up one of the leaflets, let alone read it, there can be no doubt that these messages from the skies—messages which, as the leaflet itself pointed out, might well have been bombs—had a considerable moral effect.

Apart from small-scale raids, aerial reconnaissances and artillery duels, there continued to be little to report from the

Very different scenes are being enacted today in north-east France from those which were witnessed in the autumn of 1914, when ruin and desolation spread far and wide before the onrush of the German army. Now it lies safe behind the Maginot Line, and such a sight as this is very heartening to the civilian population. A French infantry regiment is drawn up by the roadside in a small town before moving off to the front.

The War Zone of the Western Front

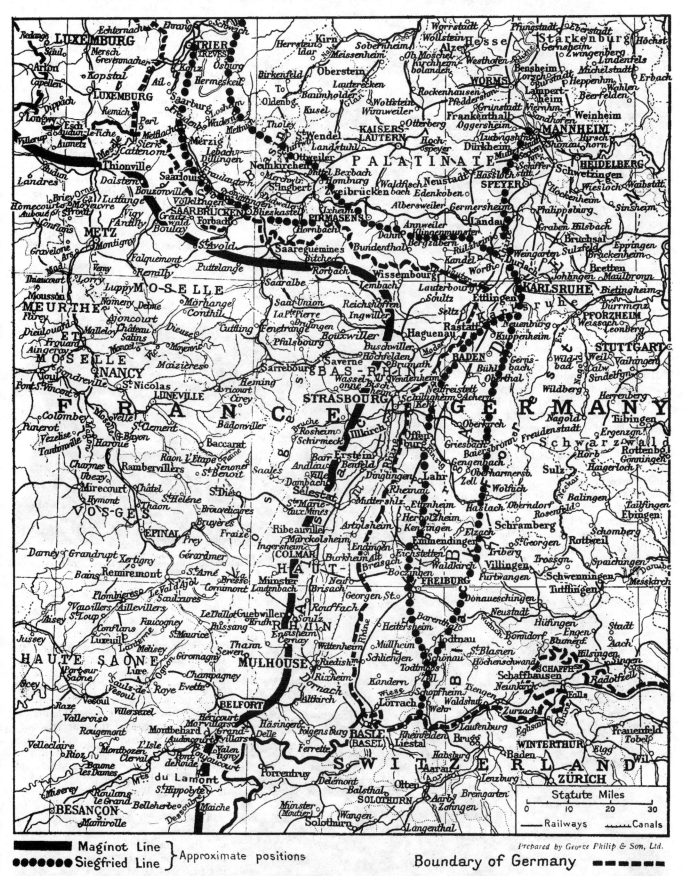

▬▬▬ Maginot Line
●●●●● Siegfried Line } Approximate positions

Prepared by George Philip & Son, Ltd.

Boundary of Germany ▬ ▬ ▬ ▬

Here we see the war zone of the Western Front—the common frontier of the belligerents, France and Germany, stretching from Luxemburg to its fellow neutral, Switzerland, in the south. Throughout its length runs a double line of fortifications—France's Maginot Line and, only a few miles away, Germany's Westwall, the Siegfried Line. Along more than half the front the opposing lines are separated by the deep valley of the Rhine, but between Rhine and Moselle lies the Saar basin, the scene of the opening fighting of 1939. In the map are the names of many, a place where Frank and Teuton have fought in their age-old rivalry of race and culture. Note that from Basle to Wissembourg in the north the Germany boundary runs along the Rhine.

frontier. Such a combination of obstacles may well cause them to think again.

So far as the Allied strategy is concerned, it seems in these early weeks of war that they are resolved to adopt an attitude of watchful waiting. After all, time is on the side of the democracies. They have very large armies of well-trained men and huge reserves of war material, whereas the German army has suffered heavy losses in the Polish campaign with consequent heavy inroads on the supplies of petrol and ammunition.

As "Scrutator" has written in the "Sunday Times," "Victory in war consists not in inflicting loss on the enemy, or even in the ratio of losses inflicted and received, but in convincing the enemy that he cannot possibly win. Already the Germans are half convinced that they cannot win a long war. If they

Western Front. From Holland there came stories of a great aircraft concentration at Aachen, and of troop movements on a large scale. Some of these movements seemed to indicate that the German High Command was meditating an attempt at turning the flank of the Anglo-French line by developing an attack through the "Maastricht appendix," that small outlying portion of Holland between Aachen and the Belgian frontier, and Belgium south of Brussels. The possibility of such a repetition of the strategy of 1914 is recognized as it must become increasingly apparent to the Germans that their only chance of winning the war is by a lightning stroke in the West similar to that which was so successful in Poland.

But before the Germans can turn the flank of the Allied positions they must overcome the resistance of the Dutch and Belgian armies, and then conquer the northern section of the Maginot Line which lies behind the Franco-Belgian

In the top photograph are French light guns drawn by mules. The photograph just above shows a French "Chenilette" or light tank being unloaded from a lorry. They can be moved thus from one part of the front to another.
Photos, Keystone and Associated Press

were not, they would not be so obviously anxious to shirk a military issue in the West. If, therefore, we continue for any considerable time without serious check, we are already half-way to victory. To try to force the issue is to encourage the enemy. On the other hand, if we keep up steady pressure and occasionally bring off a surprise, we play on the enemy's fears to bring about his defeat. He sees the vista of the war gradually lengthen, the chances of our making serious mistakes slowly disappear, and his own risks increase as the war lengthens." This is the policy of Pétain in the Great War rather than of Foch, but, "Scrutator" proceeded, "Pétain was not less of a general because he was more careful to conserve his resources and the lives of his men." Certainly, if this be the strategy which commends itself to the Allied High Command, we shall avoid all risk of repeating the disastrous mistakes and colossal losses which are associated with the names of Somme and Passchendaele.

During the last week of September, 1939, a fierce duel took place between the French and German artillery on the frontier from Lauterbourg to Switzerland. Above is a German field gun in a concrete pill box forming a miniature fortress on this line.
Photo, Fox

How the People Were Numbered

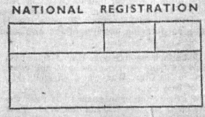

NATIONAL REGISTRATION

1. This Identity Card must be carefully preserved. You may need it under conditions of national emergency for important purposes. You must not lose it or allow it to be stolen. If, nevertheless, it is stolen or completely lost, you must report the fact in person at any local National Registration Office.

2. You may have to show your Identity Card to persons who are authorised by law to ask you to produce it.

3. You must not allow your Identity Card to pass into the hands of unauthorised persons or strangers. Every grown up person should be responsible for the keeping of his or her Identity Card. The Identity Card of a child should be kept by the parent or guardian or person in charge of the child for the time being.

4. Anyone finding this Card must hand it in at a Police Station or National Registration Office.

NATIONAL REGISTRATION

DO NOTHING WITH THIS PART UNTIL YOU ARE TOLD

Full Postal Address of Above Person :—

(Signed)

Date

Sir Sylvanus Vivian, who organized the National Register, has been Registrar-General since 1921.

The National Register taken on September 29 not only formed the basis for the issue of ration cards, but was also valuable in mobilizing the man and woman power of the country to the greatest advantage. About 65,000 enumerators were employed, and all received instructions enabling them to deal with questions raised by householders, to whom they delivered in person the identity cards for each man, woman and child in the house.

Top, left, is an identity card. Above, enumerators are being given final instructions, while on the right identity cards are being stamped ready for issue by the enumerators.
Photos, Fox and L.N.A.

HOW BRITAIN IS WINNING THE U-BOAT WAR

Remarking how strange a thing it was for him to sit at the Admiralty again after a quarter of a century and find himself " moving over the same course against the same enemy," Mr. Winston Churchill on September 26 gave the House of Commons this spirited and highly encouraging account of the anti-submarine campaign.

MR. CHURCHILL began by saying that the war at sea opened with some intensity. Then he reviewed in masterly fashion the various aspects of the campaign, extracts from his speech being printed here.

All our ships were going about the world in the ordinary way when they were set upon by lurking U-boats carefully posted beforehand. In the first week our losses in tonnage were half the weekly losses of the month of April, 1917, which was the peak year of the U-boat attack in the late war.

That was a very serious proportion. We immediately replied in three ways. First, we set in motion the convoy system. This could be very quickly done for all the outgoing ships, but it took a fortnight to organize from the other end a convoy of homeward-bound ships. This convoy system is now in full operation both ways.

The convoy system is a good and well-tried defence against U-boat attack, but no one can pretend that it is a complete defence. Some degree of risk and a steady proportion of losses must be expected.

There are also other forms of attack besides U-boats—attack by surface craft and attack from the air—against which we must be upon our guard. Every precaution is being made to cope with such attack, but we cannot guarantee immunity. We must expect further losses.

Arming the Mercantile Marine

OUR second reply to the U-boat attack is to arm all our merchant vessels and fast liners with defensive armament both against the U-boat and the aeroplane. For a fortnight past armed ships have been continually leaving the harbours of this island in large numbers. Some go in convoy, some go independently. This applies not only to the United Kingdom but to our ports all over the world.

Thus, in a short time, **the immense mercantile marine of the British Empire will be armed.** As we usually have 2,000 ships in salt water every day, this is a considerable operation.

All the guns and equipment are ready at the various arming stations, together with a proportion of trained gunners to man them and give instruction . . .

Our third reply is, of course, the British attack upon the U-boat. This is being delivered with the utmost vigour and intensity.

A large number of attacks have been made by our flotillas and hunting craft. There are, of course, many false alarms, some of them of a comical character, but it is no exaggeration to say that attacks upon German U-boats have been five or six times as numerous as in any equal period in the Great War, when, after all, they did not beat us.

The Prime Minister mentioned last week the figure of six or seven U-boats destroyed. That was, as he said, probably an under-estimate, and since then we had some fruitful days.

One-Tenth of U-Boat Strength Destroyed

BUT even taking six or seven as a safe figure, that is **one-tenth of the total enemy submarine fleet destroyed during the first fortnight of the war,** and it is probably a quarter, or perhaps even a third, of all U-boats which are being actively employed. All these vessels— those sunk and those which have escaped—have subjected themselves to what is said to be the most trying ordeal any man can undergo in war-time. A large proportion never return home, and those who do have grim tales to tell.

The British attack upon the U-boats is only just beginning. Our hunting forces are getting stronger every day. By the end of October we expect to have three times the hunting forces which operated at the outbreak of war, while at the same time the number of targets open to U-boats upon the vast expanse of the seas and oceans will be greatly reduced by the use of convoys, and the U-boats' means of attacking them will become heavily clogged and fettered.

In all this very keen and stern warfare the Royal Air Force and Fleet Air Arm have played an important part, both in directing and hunting destroyers upon their quarry and in actually attacking it themselves.

It was to bridge the gap between what we had ready at the beginning and what we have ready now that the Admiralty decided to use the aircraft carriers with some freedom in order to bring in the unarmed, unorganized, unconvoyed traffic which was then approaching our shores in large numbers . . .

IN the first week our losses by U-boat sinkings amounted to 65,000 tons, in the second to 46,000 tons, and in the third to 21,000 tons. In the last six days we have lost 9,000 tons . . .

Meanwhile, the whole vast business of our world-wide trade continues without appreciable diminution or interruption. Great convoys of troops are escorted to their various destinations. The enemy ships and commerce have been swept from the seas. **Over 2,000,000 tons of German shipping is sheltering in German or interned in neutral harbours.**

Our system of contraband and control is being perfected, and so far as the first fortnight of the war is concerned we have actually arrested, seized and converted to our own use **67,000 tons more German merchandise than have been sunk in ships of our own.**

Even in oil, where we were unlucky in losing some tankers, we have lost 60,000 tons in the first fortnight and have gained 50,000 tons from the enemy, apart from the enormous additional stores brought safely in in the ordinary way.

Again I reiterate my caution against over-sanguine deductions. We have, however, in fact got more supplies in this war, this afternoon, than we should have had if no war had been declared and if no U-boats had come into action. I am not going beyond the limits of prudent statement when I say that at that rate it will take a long time to starve us out.

Hard and Bitter U-Boat War

NOW I must speak about the character of this warfare. From time to time the German U-boat commanders have tried their best to behave with humanity. We have seen them give good warning and also endeavour to help the crews to find their way to port.

One German captain signalled to me personally the position in which the British ship was sunk, and urged that rescue should be sent. He signed his message " German submarine."

I was in doubt at the time to what address I should direct the reply. However, he is now in our hands, and is treated with all consideration.

But many cruel and ruthless acts have been done, continued Mr. Churchill. There was the "Athenia" . . . . There was the "Hazelside," 12 of whose sailors were killed by surprise gunfire in an ordinary ship, whose captain died in so gallant a fashion, going down with his vessel.

We cannot at all recognize this type of warfare as other than contrary to all the long-accepted traditions of the sea and to the laws of war to which the Germans have in recent years so lustily subscribed. . . .

In all the far-reaching control that we ourselves are exercising upon the movements of contraband no neutral ship has ever been put in danger and no law recognized among civilized nations has been contravened. Even when German ships have deliberately sunk themselves we have so far succeeded in rescuing their crews.

SUCH is the U-boat war, hard, widespread and bitter, a war of groping and drowning, a war of ambuscade and stratagem, a war of science and seamanship.

All the more we respect the resolute spirit of the officers and men of the mercantile marine, who put to sea with alacrity, sure that they are discharging a duty indispensable to the life of their island home. . . .

Tonnage Sunk by U-Boats

= 10,000 Tons

1ST WEEK

2ND WEEK

3RD WEEK

4TH WEEK

U-Boats in Commission
(Approximate number, August 1939)

= U-Boats Sunk
Sept 3 to Sept 17, 1939

Tonnage (goods) Seized and Lost during first Four Weeks of War

= 10,000 Tons

CAPTURED   LOST

Goods seized include :	Petroleum products ·	Tons 76,003
	Iron ore ·	88,003
	Manganese ore	44,003

Battleships Beat the Bombers

The first surface naval engagement of the war was a raid by Nazi warplanes on a section of Britain's Navy, on patrol in the North Sea. The Germans claimed it as a famous victory until Mr. Churchill effectively pricked the bubble of their lie.

Admiral Sir Charles Forbes, now Commander-in-Chief of the Home Fleet, won the D.S.O. at the battle of Jutland in 1916.
Photo, Wide World

SHORTLY before war broke out the Home Fleet sailed literally into the blue, and for nearly a month not a word was heard of its activities. From time to time there were reports of heavy gunfire heard in the North Sea, but the first real news of an engagement in which the capital ships of the British Navy were involved was contained in a message to the Admiralty from Sir Charles Forbes, Commander-in-Chief of the Home Fleet.

Giving the news to the House of Commons on the afternoon of September 28, Mr. Winston Churchill, First Lord of the Admiralty, read the radio message from Sir Charles, as follows :

"Yesterday afternoon, in the middle of the North Sea, a squadron of British capital ships, an aircraft carrier, cruisers and destroyers were attacked by about 20 German aircraft.

"No British ship was hit and no British casualties were incurred.

"A German flying-boat was shot down and another badly damaged."

On the same day the German wireless issued *their* account of the action. "German air forces," it ran, "successfully attacked British naval forces, battleships, aircraft carriers, cruisers and destroyers in the central North Sea yesterday. Apart from an aircraft carrier, which was destroyed, several heavy hits were made on a battleship. Our aeroplanes did not suffer any losses."

Following the statement, Mr. A. V. Alexander expressed the "hope that the public who listen in to English broadcasts from Germany will take this as an example of the veracity of their statements."

When the laughter at this thrust at Nazi propaganda had subsided, Mr. Churchill got on to his feet again. "I agree," he said, "and I might have added that another German aircraft came down and we sent out a destroyer to collect her. Her crew of four have been brought in as prisoners." This further verification of the accuracy of the British report was received with loud cheers. Once again, a Nazi statement had been shown to be—well, a "terminological inexactitude," to recall Mr. Churchill's famous phrase of years ago.

Further details of the engagement were made available later. It seems that a British submarine which had been damaged in an action with German forces was returning to its base, covered by a naval squadron, when the German machines delivered their assault. A certain amount of cloud at about 12,000 feet had screened their approach, and they made their attack through a break in the cloud with throttles full open. Such a power dive attack is perhaps the most dangerous to which a big ship may be exposed, and it reflects great credit on the anti-aircraft defences of the fleet that the 'planes were beaten off with such heavy loss. Here was a target of some 17 ships—and not a single one was hit !

When, in the action described in this page, a number of German aircraft delivered an attack on a British squadron off the coast of Norway, among the results claimed, without a shadow of justification, was the destruction of an aircraft carrier. In this photograph we see one of the Navy's complement of aircraft carriers—the 22,000-ton H.M.S. Ark Royal, mentioned in the German claims. Flying above her are some of her complement of aeroplanes. They have just taken off from the huge flight deck.
Photo, Charles Brown

From 'Somewhere in England' to 'Somewhere in

': 1939 Echoes the Story of 1914

JUST TWENTY-FIVE YEARS AFTER
the " Old Contemptibles " landed at
Boulogne, Havre, and Rouen, the British
Expeditionary Force of 1939 disembarked
at ports " somewhere in France." At first
sight this official photograph of the khaki-
clad soldiers pouring down the gangways
and assembling on the cobbled quays
might well have been taken in 1914, but
closer inspection, revealing the steel
helmets and service respirators, would
demonstrate that this is indeed the army
of 1939 that is going to war. If further
indications were sought of the changes
wrought by the passing of a quarter of a
century, they would be found in the huge
tanks that clattered and rumbled off the
boats, the armoured cars, the mass of
motor transport, and the anti-aircraft
gun guarding the quay. Yet, though the
machinery and the equipment of war
change with the passing years, the spirit
of the men themselves is as fine and true
in 1939 as in 1914 or, for that matter, in
1815 or 1415.

WORDS THAT HISTORY WILL REMEMBER

A Select Record from Week to Week of Important War Declarations and Statements

(Continued from page 124)

Monday, September 18

Communiqué issued by Polish Government at Kuty :

The Polish Ambassador in Moscow declined to accept the Soviet Note sent to him yesterday. The Polish Government approved the action of its Ambassador, who asked for his passports.

The Polish Government protests strongly against the unilateral action of Russia in breaking her non-aggression pact with Poland, and also against the invasion of Polish territory, which was undertaken when the whole Polish nation was struggling with all its might against the German aggressor.

The Polish Government parries the reasons given in the Soviet Note with the statement that the Polish Government is carrying out its duties normally and the Polish army is strugling with success against the enemy.

If the Soviet Government complains that it lacked contact with the Polish Government, the fault is its own, as the Soviet Ambassador left Poland while the whole of the remainder of the diplomatic corps maintained contact with the Polish Government without interruption.

Statement issued by the Ministry of Information :

The British Government have considered the situation created by the attack upon Poland ordered by the Soviet Government.

This attack made upon our ally at a moment when she is prostrate in face of overwhelming forces brought against her by Germany cannot, in the view of his Majesty's Government, be justified by the arguments put forward by the Soviet Government.

The full implication of these events is not yet apparent, but his Majesty's Government take the opportunity of stating that nothing that has occurred can make any difference to the determination of his Majesty's Government, with the full support of the country, to fulfil their obligations to Poland, and to prosecute the war with all energy until their objectives have been achieved.

Tuesday, September 19

Hitler in a speech at Danzig :

I tried to find a solution. I submitted proposals orally to those in power in Poland at that time. They knew these proposals—they were more than moderate. I do not know in what state of mind the Polish Government could have been to reject such proposals.

You know the developments of those days in August. I believe it would have been possible to avoid war were it not for the British guarantee and the incitement of these apostles of war.

As you know, I have ordered our air force most strictly to limit themselves only to military objectives. But our opponents in east and west must not take advantage of this. In future we shall take an eye for an eye, and for every bomb we shall answer with five bombs.

We have seen that in England this co-operation between Germany and Russia has been regarded as a crime.

To these western outbursts I give this answer : Russia remains what she is, namely, Bolshevik, and Germany remains what she is, namely National Socialist. But neither the Russian nor the German Government wants to be drawn into war in the interests of the Western Democracies.

Germany's political aims are limited. We shall come to an understanding with Russia about this, as she is the nearest neighbour whom this affects. We shall never go to war about this, because German aspirations are limited. England ought really to welcome an agreement between Germany and Russia, because such an agreement sets at rest England's fears of unlimited German expansion.

I have no war aims against England and France. I have tried to maintain peace between these countries and to establish friendly relations between the English and the German nations. Poland will never arise again in the form laid down by the Versailles Treaty Not only Germany, but also Russia guarantees this.

If England now continues the war she reveals her real aims, that she wants war against the German Government, and I have the honour to stand here as representative of this regime. It is for me the greatest honour to be regarded in that way.

When England says that the war will last three years, then I can only say that I am sorry for France. If it lasts three years the word capitulation will not arise on our side, nor in the fourth, fifth, sixth and seventh years.

About one thing there can be no doubt— we are taking up the challenge.

Dr. Benes, in a broadcast address to the Czecho-Slovak people :

The mad barbarism of Nazi Germany in Czecho-Slovakia, Poland, and even in Germany itself shows that the Nazi leaders are fully aware that their regime is nearly at an end. They are therefore taking their revenge, dealing blows right and left, and raging in a senseless manner against their own countrymen and the rest of Europe.

The peoples of the whole world are rising, and will continue to rise, to defend with their lives your freedom as well as their own. Today we are sure that Czecho-Slovakia will rise to her old frontiers of a thousand years ago. You, Czecho-Slovak people, must be among the first and most valorous in the fight.

All of us must today be ready to sacrifice even our lives for our country and for our honour. Do not forget that the tyrannical oppressor, who is in an unfamiliar environment, cannot in the end have either the moral strength or the material means to meet your united force and your relentless determination. Your steadiness and resolution will prevent the violent forces of Nazism from attaining their object, the enslaving and obliteration of the Czecho-Slovak people.

Today the retreat from the tyranny of Nazism is ended. In France, in England, and in the Allied States, millions of men and millions of tons of material are ready to strike a decisive blow against the German danger that is menacing the world.

Your place, Czecho-Slovak citizens, is today in the front line. The whole world is looking to you, recognizing your determined resistance, and is expecting that, day after day, you will deal hard blows at your enemy.

Throughout the whole country, from the last village up to Prague, in every workshop, in every enterprise, wherever you are, you must continue to carry on this struggle. There must be no place in the whole of our Czecho-Slovak country which will not show evidence of your holy determination to bear every sacrifice for your country. . . .

Wednesday, September 20

Mr. Chamberlain in House of Commons :

Against the background of these events Herr Hitler chose yesterday to address another speech to the world. It is not our way in this country to speak with boasts and threats. Perhaps for that very reason the German leaders have difficulty in understanding us, but in such comments as I have to make on the Chancellor's speech I shall not depart from our custom of speaking soberly and quietly.

The speech which Herr Hitler made yesterday at Danzig does not change the situation.

It gave an account of recent events which we cannot accept as accurate, and, as the commentary broadcast by the B.B.C. last night clearly showed, it contained certain assurances of the kind which in recent years Herr Hitler has repudiated when it suited his purpose. . . .

Herr Hitler says much in his speech about the humane methods by which he has waged war. I can only say that methods are not made humane by calling them so, and that the accounts of German bombing of open towns and machine-gunning of refugees have shocked the whole world. What I have sought for in his speech in vain is one single word to show that Herr Hitler remembers the brave men who have already lost their lives in this quarrel of his own making, or their wives and children who have been bereft for ever of the head of the family because of their leader's lust for power which had to be satisfied.

I have only one general comment to make. Our general purpose in this struggle is well known. It is to redeem Europe from the perpetual and recurring fear of German aggression and enable the peoples of Europe to preserve their independence and their liberties. . . . .

OUR WAR GAZETTEER

Bessarabia. Eastern part of Kingdom of Rumania, between Dniester and Pruth rivers and Black Sea ; great wheat-growing district ; Russian territory before Great War ; area 17,146 sq. m.

Bialystok (*Bia-wis-tok*). Town of N. central Poland ; a great industrial centre ; pop. 91,100.

Brno (*Bre-no'*). (Ger. Bruenn.) Capital city of Moravia, now in German Protectorate ; armament works gave name to Bren machine-gun ; pop. 291,000.

Cernautzi (*Chair-nout-zi*). (Ger. Czernowitz.) Town of Rumania on r. Pruth, close to Polish frontier ; until 1918 capital of Austrian province (Bukovina) ; pop. 110,000.

Esbjerg (*Es-byairg*). Seaport of Denmark on N.W. coast of Jutland ; Danish end of passenger and freight lines to England ; pop. 30 700.

Estonia. Republic on Baltic formed in 1918 ; previously in Russia ; capital Tallinn ; area 18,350 sq. m. ; pop. 1,131,000.

Friedrichshafen. Town on Lake Constance, in Germany (but close to Switzerland) ; Zeppelin airship and Dornier aeroplane works ; pop. 11,500.

Luxemburg. Independent Grand Duchy between Belgium, France, and Germany ; important mining district ; in German hands during Great War ; pop. 296,700.

Saarlautern (French Saarlouis). Town of the Saarland, Germany ; coalmining pop. 30,680.

Tallinn (Ger. Reval). Capital and chief seaport of Estonia, at mouth of Gulf of Finland ; pop. 146,400.

Tarnopol. Town of S.E. Poland, 76 miles from Lwow ; captured by Germans in 1917 ; pop. 35,900.

Wilno (or Vilna). City of N.E. Poland, seized by Poles in 1923, but still regarded by Lithuanians as their capital ; pop. 208,000.

Zweibruecken (*Zvy-brewcken*). Town of Bavaria, Germany, 10 miles from French frontier ; manufac. centre ; pop. 15,000.

Mr. Briton'll See It Through

Unexpected duties are falling on many men. Left, the Rev. R. D. Richards, of Horsmonden, Kent, is doing duty as an auxiliary postman. Above are Brown and Robertson, the Middlesex opening batsmen, now in the Police War Reserve.

Photos, Topham, Fox, Sport & General, Photo Service

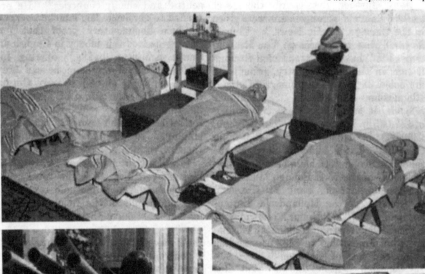

In a broadcast on September 22, Sir Samuel Hoare, Lord Privy Seal, exhorted the country to face the difficulties created by the war with cheerful confidence. "Our war effort," he went on, "is to be the maximum effort of the whole country. It will not be less than our war effort in 1918. In such an effort there will be no room for idle hands." The photographs in this page show how the people already realize this and are doing any wartime job that comes along with a will. To the spirit that inspires them Sir Samuel Hoare proceeded to pay tribute : "As a Minister of the Crown," he said, "I see the typists, the telephone girls, the Post Office officials, the messengers working as if they were the Prime Minister himself in their determination to help their country in the hour of need."

Some of the staff of a big business evacuated to Buckinghamshire are seen, centre left, in their dormitory. Left, an itinerant "black-out" man cries his wares. Above, a private car now in transport service carries a big load from Covent Garden.

Nazi Gangsters Bank the 'Swag'

These revelations concerning the disposition of the private fortunes of Herr Hitler's leading henchmen indicate that, so far from sharing their Fuehrer's confident expectations of victory, the Nazi chiefs prepared for a rainy day by placing huge sums abroad.

A Frenchman's "speaking likeness" of Dr. Joseph Goebbels, the most hateful personality thrown up in Nazi Germany. He has stolen nearly a million of his countrymen's money! His name will be as a stench for generations to come.
Caricature by Grambert of "Vu"

THE Germans have had to pay a heavy price for Nazism. They have submitted to a stern discipline, and have suffered grievous privations. They bear a crushing burden of taxation; they live in a world of high prices and short rations, long hours and low wages. They have been told that they cannot have both guns and butter—and they have swallowed the statement in the belief that the Nazis were laying the foundations of a greater and happier Reich.

Yet that system which has spelt hardships and even penury for the great mass of the German people has obviously provided the Nazi chiefs with the wherewithal of a highly expensive, if not cultured, existence. Not even his most ardent admirer would maintain that Field-Marshal Goering has the presence of one who lives a Spartan existence; and from time to time there have been many reports of the ostentatious way of life of other members of the inner circle of Nazism. Now, at a time when the Germans are being urged to tighten their belts still more, comes the most complete exposure of Herr Hitler's trusted lieutenants in the form of an analysis of their personal finances published in several of the leading American newspapers on September 21, and since then given worldwide publicity.

It was stated that information collected by "an organization of world-wide repute whose resources are literally legion in number" showed that Ribbentrop, Goebbels, Goering, Hess, Ley and Himmler had between them deposited cash and securities abroad to the total of £3,334,000 and had taken out life insurance policies in foreign currencies to the total value of £3,640,600. The respective amounts were given as follows:

Sums Sent Abroad

Von Ribbentrop, Foreign Minister and former Ambassador to London : **£1,948,000** in cash and securities and including insurance policies on the lives of himself, his wife and son to the value of £1,315,000.

Dr. Goebbels, Propaganda Minister : **£1,798,000**—cash and securities £927,000, the balance life insurance policies in respect of himself and his wife.

Field-Marshal Goering: £1,501,400—£715,000 in cash and securities, balance in insurance policies for himself and his wife.

Herr Hess, Hitler's deputy : **£801,500,** of which £449,000 is in cash and negotiable paper.

Herr Himmler, head of the Gestapo, one of whose chief duties is the hunting down and severe punishment of persons who have hidden cash and foreign securities : **£400,000** in cash and securities, plus £127,500 in life insurance policies.

Dr. Ley, Leader of the Labour Front : **£378,200,** of which £210,000 is in cash.

Many further details of the Nazi leaders' financial arrangements were given in the Chicago "Daily News." Thus it declared that insurances on Von Ribbentrop's life " have been transacted through friends in the wine industry, principally domiciled in Alsace-Lorraine, at Colmar, Ricquewhir and Mainz. Insurance policies, it is added, have face values of £17,045 in France, £68,000 in Belgium, £350,000 in Holland and £742,000 in Germany. Large sums of foreign currency are declared to have been deposited on behalf of the Nazi Foreign Minister in the Amsterdamsche bank at Haarlem, in Holland, at the Hollandsche Buitenlandbank at The Hague, and at the Banca della Svizzera Italiana at Zürich, the total amounting to £633,000 sterling at pre-war rate of exchange."

"Whether Hitler knows that his helpers have been preparing for bad weather," continues the Chicago "Daily News," "is unknown. The fact that he himself has had faith enough to restrict his investments to Nazi Germany indicates that he may have expected his disciples to do likewise."

The revelations of this monstrous plunder of the deluded German people created a worldwide stir, and it is not surprising that Dr. Goebbels hastened to make a denial of the charges, so far, at least, as he was concerned.

Addressing foreign press representatives in Berlin, on September 24, the Reich Minister of Propaganda said : " The most shameful reproach which can be made against a statesman is that he can be bribed, that he has regulated his policy for material advantage, that, when his people are at war, he knows no better than to transfer his money abroad to cover himself in the event of the war being lost."

He attacked one of the journalists who published the unsavoury details. "The American journalist, Mr. H. R. Knickerbocker," he said, " has spread through an American Press agency the libel that six of the German National Socialist leaders have transferred large fortunes abroad, depositing them in the banks of neutral and enemy countries." He proceeded to challenge Mr. Knickerbocker to produce documentary proof that " we have deposited this money in English and South American banks," offering him " 10 per cent of any sum he can prove has been sent abroad by any German statesman in the form of currency or insurance policies." Mr. Knickerbocker forthwith gave the names of the persons employed by the Nazi chiefs to make their investments.

It will require more than Dr. Goebbels' blustering denials to shake the faith of non-German people in these revelations, and the people of the Reich themselves may at least have their doubts. As the " Daily Telegraph " says, "If a half of these specific allegations is true the world is confronted with a spectacle of political graft beside which the record of gangsters like Al Capone pales into insignificance."

From the cartoon by Wyndham Robinson, by courtesy of " The Star"

America's First Reactions to the European War

Rush for newspapers in Washington when news of the invasion of Poland came through.

The hatch-covers of the "Washington" being painted with the Stars and Stripes, as a precaution against aerial attacks.

Pʀᴇsɪᴅᴇɴᴛ Rᴏᴏsᴇᴠᴇʟᴛ made a personal appeal to Congress on September 21 to repeal the arms embargo of the Neutrality Act. If this were done, belligerents would be able to buy arms and munitions in the United States, and take them overseas in their own ships on "cash and carry" terms. In addition, the President proposed to restrict the entry of American ships and passengers into "combat areas." Moreover, other American products could be acquired only under 90 days' non-renewable credits.

Left, Mr. Cordell Hull, U.S. Secretary of State, is in consultation with his advisers about the repatriation of American citizens in Europe. Above is the last page of the U.S. declaration of neutrality with the signatures of President Roosevelt and Mr. Cordell Hull. In front of the Capitol, Washington, the young people, right, have put up a notice of the declaration of war, and cluster round a portable wireless set to hear the latest news.

Photos. Topical and Keystone

SIR NEVILE AMONG THE NAZIS

The first " best-seller " of the war was the Government Blue Book covering the
diplomatic exchanges between Britain and Germany just before war was declared.
Below we print some of the more important passages from this vital document.

IN the catalogue of Government publications it is listed as Cmd. 6106—Documents concerning German-Polish relations and the outbreak of hostilities between Great Britain and Germany on September 3, 1939. So prosaic a title fails to suggest the wealth of human interest contained between the book's blue covers. It is a record of vital conversations, a picture of the clash of personalities. It is in very deed the raw material of history.

Opening with the text of the German-Polish agreement of 1934, that agreement which Hitler later described as " of greater importance to the peace of Europe than all the chattering in the temple of the League of Nations at Geneva," the book goes on to describe an interview between Sir Nevile Henderson, Britain's Ambas-

flashes which contribute so greatly to the interest of the record.

"Though I was in a hurry," reports Sir Nevile, " Field-Marshal Goering insisted on showing me with much pride the great structural alterations which he is making to the house at Karinhall and which include a new dining-room to hold an incredible number of guests and to be all of marble and hung with tapestries. He mentioned incidentally that the rebuilding would not be completed before November. He also produced with pride drawings of the tapestries, mostly representing naked ladies labelled with the names of various virtues, such as Goodness, Mercy, Purity, etc. I told him that they looked at least pacific, but that I failed to see Patience among them."

By August the international situation had gravely deteriorated, or, as Baron von Weizsacker, the German State Secretary, told Sir Nevile Henderson, " the bottle is full to the top." In his report to Lord Halifax, Sir Nevile said that the

so far as I know, broken our word. We could not do so now and remain Britain." The Ambassador added, " during the whole of this first conversation Herr Hitler was excitable and uncompromising. He made no long speeches, but his language was violent and exaggerated both as regards England and Poland."

When the interview was resumed Herr Hitler was quite calm and never raised his voice once.

" I spoke of the tragedy of war and of his immense responsibility," said Sir Nevile, " but his answer was that it would be all England's fault. I refuted this, only to learn from him that England was determined to destroy and exterminate Germany. He was, he said, 50 years old ; he preferred war now to when he would be 55 or 60. I told him that it was absurd to talk of extermination. Nations could not be exterminated, and a peaceful and prosperous Germany was a British interest. His answer was that it was England who was fighting for lesser races, whereas he was fighting only for Germany ; the Germans would this time fight to the last man ; it would have been different in 1914 if he had been Chancellor then."

There was a further interview between Sir Nevile Henderson and the Fuehrer on August 28, at which the British Ambassador again emphasized that Britain could not and would not break her word.

" I quoted a passage from a German book, which Herr Hitler had read, about Marshal Blücher's exhortation to his troops when hurrying to the support of Wellington at Waterloo : ' Forward, my children, I have given my word to my brother Wellington, and you cannot wish me to break it.' Herr Hitler at once intervened to say that things were different 125 years ago. I said not so far as England was concerned."

So the Crisis became more acute and Sir Nevile Henderson had to cable to Lord Halifax that Herr Hitler was becoming ever less reasonable. There was a stormy interview on August 30, between Sir Nevile and Herr von Ribbentrop, at which the latter used language to which Sir Nevile " mildly retorted that I was surprised to hear such language from a Minister for Foreign Affairs." " I must tell you," Sir Nevile wrote to Lord Halifax, " that Herr von Ribbentrop's whole demeanour during an unpleasant interview was aping Herr Hitler at his worst."

Just before leaving Herr von Ribbentrop, after he had handed him Britain's official warning, Sir Nevile reported to the chief that, " I told him that his attitude on that occasion had been most unhelpful and had effectively prevented me from making a last effort for peace, and that I greatly deplored it. He was courteous and polite this evening. I am inclined to believe that Herr Hitler's answer will be an attempt to avoid war with Great Britain and France, but not likely to be one which we can accept." A few hours later Britain and Germany were at war.

Sir Nevile Henderson, British Ambassador to Germany, is here seen talking to Field-Marshal Goering, left; and Herr von Ribbentrop, centre, at a reception in Berlin before the war clouds gathered. Sir Nevile is wearing the gold-braided uniform of a British Ambassador.

Photo, Wide World

sador in Berlin, and Field-Marshal Goering, in May of this year. Sir Nevile says that he warned the Field-Marshal of the consequences of Hitler yielding to the advice of his " wild men," whereupon Goering, changing the subject, complained that his holiday at San Remo had been spoiled owing to the unexpected amount of work which had been thrust upon him.

As the interview proceeded, " the Field-Marshal used all the language which might be expected in reply to a statement that Germany was bound to be defeated." In fact, he gave the Ambassador the impression, by somewhat overstating his case, of considerably less confidence than he had previously expressed.

Then we have one of those personal

Baron was of the opinion that Germany did not, would not, and could not believe that Britain would fight under all circumstances, whatever folly Poland might commit.

" I told Baron von Weizsacker," wrote Sir Nevile, " that this was a very dangerous theory, and sounded like Herr von Ribbentrop, who had never been able to understand the British mentality." It was at this interview that the Baron observed that the situation in one respect was " even worse than last year, as Mr. Chamberlain could not again come out to Germany."

On August 23 Sir Nevile Henderson had an interview with Herr Hitler at Berchtesgaden, at which he told him that " throughout the centuries we have never.

Women Leaders in the Nation's Effort

H.M. The Queen, Commandant-in-Chief of the Women's Navy, Army and Air Force Services.

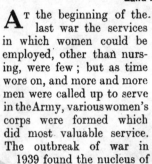

Dame Beryl Oliver, left, wife of Admiral of the Fleet Sir Henry Oliver, is chief of the Voluntary Aid Detachments. Mrs. Walter Eliot, right, is Chairman of the London Committee of the Women's Land Army.

Dame Helen Gwynne Vaughan, Director of the Auxiliary Territorial Service.

Miss J. Trefusis Forbes, Senior Controller of the Women's Auxiliary Air Force.

At the beginning of the last war the services in which women could be employed, other than nursing, were few ; but as time wore on, and more and more men were called up to serve in the Army, various women's corps were formed which did most valuable service. The outbreak of war in 1939 found the nucleus of these services already in existence, and every call for volunteers was abundantly met. As in the last war, too, thousands of women serve their country in other ways.

Stella, Marchioness of Reading, Chairman of the Women's Voluntary Service.

Left to right are Mrs. Laughton Mathews, Director of the Women's Royal Naval Air Service ; Mrs. M. E. Cook, Commandant of the Women's Mechanised Transport Corps ; and the Countess of Limerick, President of the British Red Cross Society. Many of these women leaders of the nation's effort gained experience of the various branches of work in which they are now engaged during the last war, and have patriotically come forward to lead the younger generation in the services in which they themselves won distinction between 1914 and 1918.

Changes in the London Scene: Then and Now

Strange transformations have come over many of London's business buildings. The fronts are piled high with sandbags, and the ground floors of a number have been converted to A.R.P. use. Top left is the roof of a famous city business house as it was before the war, with girls of the staff using it as a roof garden. Right, is the same roof in wartime with male members of the staff covering skylights with sandbags.

Photos, Fox

LONDONERS have accepted with characteristic good humour the stringent black-out regulations to which their city, like others, is subjected. During the first few days of war some of them sinned, not against the light, but against the dark, by allowing shafts of light to shine from their windows. In practically every case the offence was caused only by inadvertence, and defects were soon put right. At first, too, pedestrians had considerable difficulty in negotiating the traffic, but when the rationing of petrol cut down the traffic to the extent shown in the centre photographs, the dangers of darkness were considerably lessened. Other contrasts of war and peace are presented in this page.

Fleet Street, usually one of the most crowded of City thoroughfares, after a few days of war had a weekday appearance such as it used to have only on Sundays. Left, we see the "street of ink" in pre-war days, and right, in wartime.

Photos, Wide World

Trial black-outs were made in several districts of London before the war. The bottom left-hand photograph in this page shows Ludgate Hill as it was normally at night. Next it is the same scene during a practice black-out in August. The ribbons of light are made by passing cars, but one street lamp still lights up a wide area owing to its timing mechanism having failed.

Photos, Associated Press

There is Safety in Sandbags

This sandbagged figure of a Rifleman of 1800 forms part of the Rifle Brigade Memorial in Grosvenor Gardens, London.

A s a precaution against air raids London and many other large towns have used thousands of sandbags to protect buildings and national monuments. By a sad stroke of irony some of the structures that have had to be protected in this war are, as three of the photographs in this page show, memorials to those who fell in the last war— "the War to end War." Much of the sand used for London's remarkable earthworks has been dug from commons and open spaces. The task of filling the sandbags was a gigantic one and many public authorities asked for volunteers to help in the work. The response was admirable.

The impressive figures that stand beside the Royal Artillery Memorial in London take on a more warlike aspect.

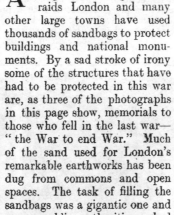

All that is portable has been removed from public buildings and placed in safety, and everything possible has been done to safeguard buildings and national monuments. Left, quantities of earth are being brought into the nave of Canterbury Cathedral to convert the crypt into an air raid shelter. Right is the Cenotaph in Whitehall seen from behind a barricade of sandbags, associating this war with the last one.

Photos, Keystone, Planet News, Topical and Associated Press

ODD FACTS ABOUT THE WAR

He Gave Hitler Orders

A former Austrian army officer, who claims that he often gave orders to Hitler during the Great War, has enlisted for active service with Canada's defence forces. He is now a naturalized Canadian.

Berlin's English Church

The English church in Berlin, which never missed a service during the years 1914-1918, is to remain open for as long as possible. The English chaplain has been ordered to leave Germany, but services will be carried on with the assistance of an American Episcopalian priest.

Pray Silence for . . .

Men eating in Berlin restaurants were arrested and sent to gaol because they talked loudly during a propaganda broadcast.

Camels Join Up

Camels are drawing ploughs across fields in Northern Germany. They formerly belonged to Hagenbeck's Circus, the owner of which has placed all his animals at the disposal of the State. Elephants are also being trained to plough.

Italy Rations Gas

The household consumption of gas in Italy is limited from September 21 to seven hours daily.

Rumania Calls Up Specialists

Specialists are being called up to the Rumanian colours. Various Ministries have been ordered to draw up lists of indispensable persons.

Memel Cannot Listen In

All radio receiving-sets in Memel territory, which was seized from Lithuania by Germany in March, have been sealed by the German authorities.

Dyeing to Enlist

At Calgary the patriotic effort of a veteran of the South African and Great Wars to enlist was frustrated by the heat of the room in which he was being examined. Soon after entering the room he began to perspire, and shoe polish which he had used to dye his grey hair began to trickle down his forehead. A rigid cross-examination about his age followed, and when it was discovered to be 77 he was rejected.

(*Times* Ottawa Correspondent)

Strikes at German Factory

The Ministry of Information stated that two strikes were reported to have taken place in the Opel works in Ruesselheim. Both were followed by a number of arrests.

No More Joy-riding

The German Minister of Economics announced that all rubber tires, except those for vehicles expressly permitted to continue to operate, are to be confiscated by the State. Tires already mounted on vehicles must be reported to the authorities, and must be kept in their present condition.

New Style Hand-bag

A gas-mask cardboard container, picked up in a Suffolk village street, was found to contain: Some knitting, a ball of wool, a powder compact, lipstick, a mirror, a handkerchief, some letters, a folder containing snapshots, chocolate--and the gas-mask.

Germany's Nervous Home Front

The Gestapo has organized a strict spy system to catch all people spreading rumours. Several death penalties have been carried out. Police charged a crowd in Prague because they cheered Polish prisoners.

First German 'Conchie'

For failing to carry out his military duties, the first passive resister in Germany has been shot. He was described as a "fanatical member" of the Society of Earnest Bible Students.

Tracking Down Food Hoarders

Germany is prosecuting a vigorous campaign against food hoarders. The *Times* correspondent in Rotterdam reports that searchers discovered in one household 80 tins of condensed milk, 70 of which were confiscated. For some months it has been practically impossible to buy condensed milk in Germany.

Overtime Not Counted

Goering's War Cabinet has abolished the regulations governing adult labour conditions. The working day for men over 16 and for all women has now been extended to 10 hours, although the working week will not exceed 56 hours.

Air Raid Modes

Suggestions for women's night raid wear include slacks and a sweater to pull over one's pyjamas, and a floor-length "house-gown" with long zipp fastener. Some smart lines in gas-mask containers have been seen: black velvet cases piped in colour, with a pocket holding purse, powder and lipstick; and one in beige material to match the wearer's suit, and held by a broad apple-green ribbon.

Registered: "Name, J. Bull. Occupation, Seeing it Through."
From the cartoon by E. H. Shepard.

Reproduced by permission of the Proprietors of "Punch"

Hitler in 'Who's Who'

From Wilhelmstrasse 77, Berlin W.8, as he unpretentiously describes his Chancellery in the publication, Hitler sent to the editor of "Who's Who" a revised proof a few weeks ago for the 1940 edition. In spite of the war, he will continue to occupy 30 lines in that work of reference. That is four lines more than Mr. Chamberlain takes.

Ribbentrop in 'Who's Who'

Both Goering and Ribbentrop will keep the Fuehrer company. The latter made several additions to the proof sent to him in June. He added to his credit the annexations of Bohemia, Moravia and Memel. While he may regret having returned the proof too early to include the Soviet Pact among his achievements, he can congratulate himself on having had the foresight to omit any reference to the anti-Comintern Pact in the current issue.

(Daily Telegraph)

Black-out Watches

Jewellers throughout the country report a boom in luminous watches as a result of the black-out. Those favoured most hang round the neck on a long leather "chain."

No Kickshaws

In France, restaurants have adapted their menus to the British taste. Bacon and eggs, "rosbif," and fish and chips are now served wherever British soldiers pass.

Fat Substitutes

The "Frankfurter Zeitung" states that Germany normally uses between 350,000 and 400,000 tons of fat annually. The German Dye Trust is preparing a special fat-substitute for use in medicines and ointments instead of pure fat.

Amateur Artists

Passengers in the liner "Athlone Castle" helped the crew to camouflage the ship when the outbreak of war was announced during the voyage home from Capetown.

Poor Mr. Churchill !

A German broadcast alleges that three Poles arrested at Czestochowa, near the famous shrine of the Black Virgin, carrying incendiary materials, admitted that they had been bribed by an English-speaking man to set fire to the shrine and the monastery. "This," added the broadcast, "is another example of Mr. Churchill's policy that in war every crime is justified."

Well-fed Poilu

French army rations allow each soldier per day: 10 to 12 ounces of meat; one to three ounces of vegetables; nine ounces of bread; one and a half ounces of coffee; two pints of wine for men in the front line, and one pint for those behind it.

Black-out Wear

The Men's Wear Council has shown some striking black-out fashions. They include sleeveless white jackets, which are easy to slip on and off, and can be folded to carry in the pocket.

Free Attention

A notice in a hairdresser's window in Stepney reads: "Hitler will be shaved free." In small type the notice adds: "With an extra sharp razor."

I Went Across with the 'New Contemptibles'

That men of the British Expeditionary Force had landed in France was freely rumoured before being announced on September 11 by the Ministry of Information officially. Here is a vivid account, reprinted from "The Sunday Times," of the arrival at a French port of a British troop transport.

EVERY day iron-grey troop transports slip inconspicuously into the harbour here, bringing fresh contingents of British soldiers for service in France.

Our particular convoy, like all its predecessors, successfully outwitted the enemy U-boats and mines, and reached its destination with the punctuality of a cross-Channel steamer.

As we slipped out of harbour in England two of the transports were sailing neck and neck, and the troops immediately turned it into a race. They crowded to the side and yelled jokes and good-humoured insults across to one another. One ship struck up "Tipperary" and the other promptly replied with "Mademoiselle from Armentières."

On board a family atmosphere was created immediately. The decks and saloons, where peacetime passengers had whiled away the voyage, were now crammed to capacity with 1,500 soldiers in holiday mood.

Many were reading the last English newspapers they would see for days. There was a babel of accents and dialects, a cross-section of England. An eloquent Cockney ordered a group of soft-voiced Midlanders out of the way as he staggered by with a bucketful of very strong, sweet tea.

The men began to sort themselves out and settle down for the voyage. Orders were issued that lifebelts must be worn, and soon everyone was exchanging notes about the manner in which they were to be adjusted. "When you jump into the water, hold the belt with your hands, or you will break your neck," said those who knew.

Among the officers and men the conversation ran on much the same lines: "Where are we going, what are we going to do?" and so on. Many remembered their families, and there was a rush for paper and pencils when a notice went up saying that letters might be posted on board.

Here and there about the ship there were impromptu concerts. Some of the singing was rather tentative, for the songs of this war have not yet been decided on. The songs of twenty-five years ago are still the favourites.

We picked up our escort of destroyers, and all the way across they hovered around us, shepherding us among the dangers of the Channel. The officers gathered in the smoking-room to hear orders issued.

When the French coast became clearly visible the troops crowded to the side to catch what was, for many of them, their first glimpse of foreign parts. One by one the four transports slipped into the French harbour. The destroyers turned round and set off home to collect the next batch. The voyage was over. Another convoy had arrived safely.

Before going on to their bases, the British soldiers generally manage to do some intensive sightseeing and shopping at the port where they arrive. Every day fresh shiploads swarm through the streets enjoying the new experience.

"Looks quite like England," say many of them when they gaze at the town from the sea, but when they get among the shops they find that the resemblance ends. The fact that French traffic keeps to the right is usually the first curiosity to be noticed—often at the cost of nearly being run over. At the cross-roads British soldiers are having the novel experience of directing the Continental traffic.

Shopping consists of pointing at what you want, tendering your largest bank-note, and receiving the change the shopkeeper gives you, or alternatively you can hold out a handful of coins and let the shopkeeper take what he wants.

The inhabitants regard their British customers with indulgent smiles, for business is good. Many have hastened to put up signs saying "English spoken," though this is often overstating the case. One shop adds "Same prices for English and French people." In particular the old women who sell chip-potatoes at stalls in the streets are doing a roaring trade.

Every now and then a troop train departs, the windows crammed with cheering soldiers. They have no idea where they are going, but this does not dampen their spirits.

On the outskirts of the town there is

These young British soldiers are giving a farewell cheer before leaving for France. Of such men an American observer said, "They have the comfortable assurance that the British never lose."

Photo, Associated Press

156   *The War Illustrated*   October 14th, 1939

|||||||||||||||||||||||||||||||||||||||||||||||||||||||||||||||||||| **I WAS THERE!** ||||||||||||||||||||||||||||||||||||||||||||||||||||||||||||||||||||

a transit camp at present largely occupied by a famous infantry regiment. When the British took it over the accommodation was not ideal, but now there is a home-like atmosphere. Outside on the grass the inevitable strong tea is constantly being brewed. On every bush freshly washed socks and underwear are hung out to dry.

An adjoining field has been scarred with trenches for A.R.P. purposes. Altogether the troops are enjoying their first impressions of France. Nor does their good humour desert them as they lie on the floor of the station waiting-room, making themselves as comfortable as may be until the time comes for their train to leave.

able to ferry the men across two or three at a time."

The pilot commanding the other flying-boat was a 25-year-old flight-lieutenant from Leigh-on-Sea, Essex.

"When we arrived," he said, "we saw the other aircraft on the water and had a darn good look round for the submarine. We saw that the other 'plane was making attempts to take off the men. Quite obviously there were a lot, and so we decided to go down.

"In the meantime another aircraft arrived, and we signalled it to look out for the submarine. We took off 14 men."

One of the crew of the second flying-boat was a young South African, who was second pilot.

"We were patrolling quite independently," said one of the pilots. "The ship sank while the remainder of the crew were getting into a position to be taken off by us. The rescue was not very difficult."

Here Captain Schofield interposed with the remark :

"It was not difficult because they were efficient. There was a swell on the sea at the time." Then he concluded with the assertion, "If all the officers and men of the R.A.F. are like these young fellows who rescued us, then England has nothing to fear."

We Were Saved by R.A.F. Flying Boats

Here, reprinted from "The Daily Telegraph," is a story that has thrilled the world. It is a joint account of the rescue of the crew of the "Kensington Court," told first by the master, Capt. J. Schofield, and then by the R.A.F. pilots who effected it.

CAPTAIN SCHOFIELD said that his ship, the 4,863-ton S.S. "Kensington Court," which was bound for Birkenhead from the Argentine with a cargo of wheat, sent out an S O S when a U-boat appeared and attacked them without warning. They turned the vessel's stern to the submarine, which kept firing at them from a range of about a mile.

"After she had fired about five shots," he said, "she came very close to the ship's stern and I decided it was time to stop the ship. I gave three blasts on the whistle and the crew took to the boats.

"One of the boats was lost. Shortly after we got away in the port boat there was a big explosion in the starboard well. We did not know whether it was a torpedo or shell. We started rowing away and soon afterwards sighted an aeroplane.

"I said : 'This has come in reply to our S O S.' Everybody was pleased and we all started to cheer. Still, we did not think it was possible for them to rescue us that way.

"We thought they would give a signal to a warship or something like that. When the first 'plane alighted on the water and someone signalled to us from the wing we began to realize that they were going to take us on board.

"There was a second 'plane there. We told the officer that there were 34 of us, and he said he would take about 20 and the other 'plane would take the rest.

"While we were getting on board a third 'plane came over and flew round. We wondered how they would get us on board, because the sea was choppy, but a door in the side of the flying-boat opened and a small collapsible boat was pushed out.

"It was all very remarkable to us. It was the modern method of rescue and we had never had any experience like it. When we got on board they gave us cups of tea and cigarettes."

Captain Schofield said that they sighted the first 'plane half an hour after they took to the boats. The submarine steamed away after seeing that the ship was settling. She had left before the 'planes arrived.

"The submarine," he declared, "gave

no warning at all that she was going to sink us. The first shot she fired was straight at the ship, and it was an explosive shell. We saw the submarine for a few minutes before she opened fire."

The pilot of the first machine on the spot, a 23-year-old flight-lieutenant, whose home is in Wimbledon, explained that they picked up Captain Schofield's S O S while they were in the air on patrol duty.

"We at once set our course for the spot indicated," he said, "and eventually found the ' Kensington Court ' sinking.

"We alighted and, after signalling the men in the boat, blew up our rubber dinghy and pushed it out with a line to each end, and by this means we were

How We Escaped From Poland

As the Germans approached Warsaw there was an increasing exodus from the capital. This personal account of dangers endured on the way to Rumania by 1,500 refugees was sent by Mr. J. Cang, "News Chronicle" Warsaw correspondent, to his paper.

THE foreign diplomats, journalists and officials were still sitting in Warsaw's fashionable cafés talking about a long war when they learned that they must pack and depart within a few hours.

Very few managed to take anything with them. My family and myself went, leaving everything behind.

So big was the rush out from Warsaw that it took over an hour to cross the Vistula Bridge towards the Eastern station, where a train was supposed to be waiting for us. It took three hours to find the carriages. The station represented the worst confusion imaginable, mothers shouting in the dark for their children, husbands for wives, children weeping for their parents, all fearing a repetition of the raids which a day earlier had bombarded the same station, killing many.

The train was composed of fourteen carriages carrying officials from the Ministry of War, the Ministry of Justice, of the Interior, of Foreign Affairs, Social and Public Works, Education and the Senate. It was originally destined for Lublin, the first halt of the evacuated Polish Government. But the direct route was impossible owing to the damaged railway line at Deblin. We were taken

a roundabout way, subjecting about 1,500 men, women and children in the train to the worst ordeal imaginable.

The first encounter with a German bomber was about 60 miles north of Warsaw. The bomber flew over the train at a low altitude, causing indescribable panic. Passengers jumped out of the carriages and ran into the fields and woods seeking any available shelter. But the bomber hurried on to the junction station in front of us, where, 20 minutes later, we ran into real hell.

Soon we reached the station called Czeremcha. Three German bombers arrived before we had time to look for shelter, and over fifty bombs were dropped, including several incendiary bombs. No shelters were available. Women, men and children clung to trees, knelt praying in the open fields, hid in the ditches near the road, whilst bombers came in still larger numbers, attacking fiercely the railway junction. I am not sure even now which noise was the more terrifying, women and children or the explosion of the bombs.

I saw a mother lying with her baby in a crater made by a bomb during one of the earlier German attacks on the same station. My own little boy, aged

IIIIIIIIIIIIIIIIIIIIIIIIIIIIIIIIIIIIII **I WAS THERE!** IIIIIIIIIIIIIIIIIIIIIIIIIIIIIIIIIIIIII

The First Rescue by Seaplane in Naval History

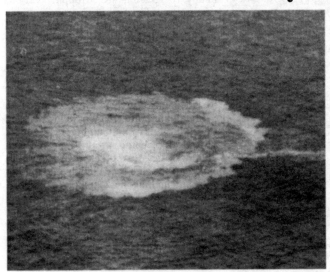

The last of the "Kensington Court," a circle of foam, is here photographed from one of the rescuing seaplanes.

THE story of the rescue of the officers and crew of the S.S. "Kensington Court" adds a remarkable page to the history of the R.A.F. The ship, on her way from Argentina to Birkenhead, was stopped by fire from a U-boat when nearing the English coast and 34 men were compelled to leave her. An SOS had been sent out before the "Kensington Court" sank, and soon after the overloaded boat carrying 34 had pushed off, a flying-boat appeared and alighted near by, followed soon after by a second. Eventually all 34 men were transferred to a collapsible rubber boat launched by one of the 'planes and carried to the aircraft. A few hours later they were safe in England. The first-hand story of this amazing rescue is given in the opposite page.

Top, right, are Captain Schofield of the "Kensington Court" with Flight-Lt. Thurston Smith (centre) and his fellow R.A.F. officer who effected the rescue here described. Centre, the ship's boat with the crew on board is nearing one of the seaplanes, while the "Kensington Court" is seen in the background with her bows already under water. Below is another view of the lifeboat as it drew near the rescuing flying-boats. A part of the wing of one of them can be seen on the right of the centre photograph.

Photos, Photographic News Agency and Planet News

Among the most dastardly acts of the Nazis in Poland was the bombing of trains carrying women and children refugees. This twisted metal work was all that remained of one coach after such an attack. The loss of life can be imagined
Photo. Keystone

four, who had gone through over thirty air raids in Warsaw, clung to my knees weeping, calling: "Daddy, dear, tell them to stop bombing."

Before we left our ditches we were bombed again and again, each time with greater ferocity and determination. Surprisingly, this station linking north-east Poland with the capital was entirely unprotected, so that the German 'planes did their destructive work without risk.

The stationmaster, worn out after enduring about 30 air raids, remained calmly on duty and managed to keep his eye on my little boy, who was wandering about scanning the sky to see whether the bombers were coming back.

The bombers obviously had not aimed at the passengers, but were attempting to destroy the junctions so as to hinder transport. Otherwise, not a few, but all would have been killed. Our ordeal was not over. It began again when more bombers arrived and hovered over the ghost train. Time after time passengers left the carriages in terror and hid in fields, woods and ditches. Once, when the bombers reappeared overhead, women and children escaped by lying down in swamps inches deep in water until the 'planes had passed.

So terrified became the passengers that the slightest noise caused people to jump from the train. At each station one saw passengers, unable to bear the strain any longer, disappear into the woods and not emerge again. A judge in Poland's highest tribunal, who travelled in the same carriage with me, left the train with his wife, preferring to remain in the fields rather than continue the journey

After each bombing fewer passengers remained in the train. Those who remained had their nerves shattered, particularly the women and children. Food and water were completely unobtainable, and people were fainting from exhaustion. The most pitiable sight was the little white-faced, terror-stricken

children seeking to hide themselves to escape the bombing. Their cries are still ringing in my ears.

For four days the train wandered from place to place, unable to reach Lublin because the town had been heavily bombed. The train was diverted

to Chelm Kowel, later to Luck, and finally to Krzemieniec, dropping various ministerial officers on the way. Soon over Krzemieniec the German bombers appeared, too, and dropped ten bombs, killing 31 people.

Unable to obtain other means of transport, many people hired plain peasant carts to take them out of Krzemieniec farther away towards the Rumanian border. We followed them. For three days and nights we wandered by road, keeping away from the main highways in fear of enemy 'planes, but even on the side roads the 'planes followed us, but making no attempt to bomb us. We met tens of thousands of refugees fleeing before the Germans without knowing where they were going. Many frontier zones were suddenly closed to refugees and people were running from place to place in search of refuge, like mice in a trap. We met refugees from Silesia and Galicia who had walked for 500 miles, and were looking like skeletons. They had lost all human appearance.

After two days in Zaleszczyki we managed to cross into Rumania about an hour before the frontier closed.

I Saw Fighting from a Foreign Frontier

Here is the first eye-witness battle story from the Western Front written by Hester Marsden-Smedley, "Sunday Express" woman reporter. She stood under fire in a sandbagged sap at Schengen, just inside the Luxemburg frontier, and watched the French advance towards the Siegfried Line.

STANDING amid the near-ripe vines which make the famous Moselle wine, I have been watching fierce fighting in this three-cornered country where Germany, France and Luxemburg meet.

French tanks left the German village of Perl and clambered up the hill. The bombardment was two kilometres away from where I was standing, the objective being an observation tower in a fortified wood. There were great puffs of black smoke over the wood, the sound following seconds later, echoing and shaking through the valleys.

After each ten minutes of heavy firing there followed quick, fierce, machine-gun fire. The ground a few yards beyond the river was suddenly rent by shells. A house in the German village of Salmdorf blew sky-high, probably an ammunition store.

Judging by the position of the firing the French are advancing. I watch intently as I lean comfortably against "neutral" sandbags which block the frontier bridge across the Moselle. Behind me lies Luxemburg, the "Pocket State" with its "army" of 300 volunteers, its fairy-tale towns perched upon the hills, and its fruitful vineyards. A few yards to the south-east is France. Immediately across the bridge—Germany. The Luxemburg Customs officer, out of a job for the moment, for there is little

frontier traffic, tells me that he watched the French, a few days before, penetrate along the railway line opposite. There had been hand to hand fighting. Then the French had gone back—"not retreated" he emphasized—just gone back.

As he spoke he gripped my collar and pushed me down. I swallowed a mouthful of sand as the world burst about my ears.

I peeped cautiously round the sandbags. A mine had exploded in the middle of the permanent way across the river. Whether one of their own or a present left by the French I could not say. We all thought it was a present.

In a few moments I saw the guard across the river doubled, and a machine-gun mounted upon the bridge with its squad of grey-uniformed, tin-hatted men.

I turned across the peaceful Luxemburg roads to the southern edge of the Grand Duchy.

My ears still humming from the Schengen explosion grew worse. A peasant driving his cattle in said tersely: "C'est le canon."

Away over there lies the Maginot Line. Beyond it the Siegfried. Beyond that the Saar Valley with its rich coalfields. In good time we will be old exactly what is happening.

But I know that there is fierce activity. I know, too, from what the people who cross over tell me, the story of the tenacity and power of the French.

There Is Still Chivalry Between Fighting Airmen

IN the last war British and German airmen gave signs of a sincere mutual respect, and the "dog fights," when opposing squadrons engaged one another, provided many an opportunity for the display of knightly courage on either side. Airmen who died within enemy lines were accorded funerals with full military honours, and sometimes fighting 'planes flew over the spot at which a chivalrous foe had been brought down and dropped a wreath in his memory. Photographs in this page, and the story of the fair treatment accorded to the British airmen taken prisoner in the Wilhelmsaven raid, show that this spirit is not yet dead.

One of the prisoners taken during the Royal Air Force raid on Wilhelmshaven is here seen standing beside the microphone while he was being questioned by a German officer on his experiences.

German airmen are standing by the graveside during the funeral of two French airmen brought down behind the German lines near Saarbruecken during the fighting on the Western Front.

Photos   Planet News, Wide World and Associated Press.

ON September 15, 1939, a German broadcast from Zeesen gave what purported to be an interview with three British airmen in the Naval Hospital at Westermuende, near Bremerhaven. Their names were given as Pilot Officer Edwards, from New Zealand; Aircraftman Slattery, from Tipperary; and Sgt.-Observer Booth, from Yorkshire. The interview was conducted by a Lieutenant Crabbe, who was stated to have shot down the 'planes; and the broadcast was rendered in German and English. The questions asked by Lieutenant Crabbe were chiefly directed to the personal comfort and well-being of the prisoners. The last question he asked Pilot Officer Edwards was, "How are you being treated?" He explained that this question would interest listeners most, even "way back at home," for he hoped the answer would be transmitted to New Zealand. The answer given was, "I have been treated very well indeed. Just as a German officer, except that I am naturally under observation." Sgt.-Observer Booth said that so far the treatment was all right, and added that he was "not dying of starvation." Aircraftman Slattery, who was suffering from a broken jaw, is said to have replied, "I have nothing to say of the Germans but kindness."

Here is the scene at the burial of three British airmen who lost their lives during the Wilhelmshaven raid. The coffins are draped in a White Ensign, and a German naval officer is reading the burial service.

OUR DIARY OF THE WAR

Monday, September 25

Polish resistance continued in Warsaw and Modlin, with appalling loss of life and destruction to buildings.

French artillery began first bombardment of Rhine fortifications. There were air battles in the Saar region.

Zeppelin base at Friedrichshafen, near Swiss frontier, was stated to have been bombed by French aircraft.

Reported that further reconnaissance flights had taken place over Western Germany on Sept. 24 and during the night. As before, copies of a leaflet were dropped. Attacks by enemy fighters were beaten off.

Sabotage was stated to be the cause of explosions which occurred in many German factories.

President Moscicki and Marshal Smigly-Rydz, interned in Rumania.

Swedish steamer " Silesia " torpedoed off Stavanger.

All German women between the ages of 17 and 25 are to be conscripted for " obligatory national labour service."

Turkish Foreign Minister, M. Saradjoglu, arrived at Moscow.

Tuesday, September 26

German attack on Warsaw renewed.

On the Western Front there was a continuation of intense artillery fire, and local infantry engagements took place.

Hitler returned to Berlin from the Eastern Front and held a conference with his ministers.

Mr. Chamberlain gave to the House of Commons his fourth review of the progress of the War.

Mr. Churchill reviewed the progress and success of the campaign against U-boats.

Twenty German aircraft attempted to bomb a squadron of the Home Fleet in the North Sea, but were driven off with two 'planes destroyed and one badly damaged. No battleship was hit and there were no British casualties.

Thirty-two survivors of the British ship " Royal Sceptre," torpedoed on Sept. 6, who had been given up for lost, arrived at Bahia, Brazil, on board the British freighter " Browning."

Wednesday, September 27

Warsaw announced that surrender had been agreed upon and that conditions were being negotiated. It was reported that the Poles were still holding out at Modlin and on the Hel Peninsula, overlooking Danzig.

Ribbentrop arrived in Moscow at the head of a delegation to discuss matters connected with Poland.

From the Western Front it was reported that Germany was massing troops in the Rhineland. Minor attacks by the enemy were repulsed.

French and British aircraft, working in co-operation, brought down several enemy fighters. R.A.F. aircraft carried out further reconnaissance flights into Germany and on the Western Front.

War Budget introduced by Sir John Simon in the House of Commons. The principal feature was an increase of income tax from 5s. 6d. to 7s. 6d.

Soviet Steamer " Metallist " was sunk by an unknown submarine off the coast of Estonia.

Slovak authorities ordered a partial demobilization.

French Admiralty announced that war contraband seized up to Sept. 25 totalled over 100,000 tons, including 24,000 tons of liquid fuel.

Communist Party premises in Paris were searched and sealed up by the French police.

Thursday, September 28

Negotiations for surrender of Warsaw and the fortress of Modlin in progress.

French troops advanced to near the Saar river. There was a heavy artillery engagement near the Luxemburg frontier.

Conversations between Ribbentrop, Molotov and Stalin continued in Moscow.

Swedish cargo boat " Nyland " sunk by U-boat off Stavanger.

THE POETS & THE WAR

II

THE FREE PEOPLES RISE

SEPTEMBER, 1939
BY ERNEST RAYMOND

We were late upon our feet, because our
   limbs and wills were free
And none could make us stand and arm
   but those who made us see ;
But now we see the menace in the quiet
   summer sky ;
We stand, the men the ages freed, to order
   our reply ; ·
We tarried in our standing ; so be it :
   this was best,
For we, so free to rise at will, shall be
   the last to rest.

We take our past upon us, and the burden
   of its fame.
Our past has called its mortgage in, and
   we shall meet the claim.
The future has foreclosed on us. It calls
   for our arrears ;
Ten thousand voices call for them from
   out ten thousands years :
And we, the freemen, answer, " Peace.
   The hour is overdue ;
We're risen for your ransom . we come
   and are not few."
—*The Sunday Times.*

Germany claimed that the U-boat that sank " Courageous " had returned to Wilhelmshaven.

Two Norwegian steamers, " Jern " and " Haugesund," sunk by enemy action.

Friday, September 29

Molotov and **Ribbentrop** signed a treaty in Moscow, by which Poland was completely abolished, and new and permanent Russo-German frontiers established. The

terms included a denial of the right of interference by any third Power, and a declaration that the war should now stop.

Estonia became virtually a Soviet protectorate by the signing of a ten-year mutual assistance pact and trade agreement. By this pact Russia gets the right to maintain naval bases on the Baltic.

There was an unsuccessful German attack on Saarbruecken.

Units of the R.A.F. carried out attacks on ships of the German Fleet in Heligoland Bight. In spite of formidable anti-aircraft fire, the attacks were pressed home at a low altitude.

A Turkish military mission, headed by Gen. Kiazim Orbay, left Ankara for London.

Norwegian steamer " Takstaas " sunk by U-boat.

Saturday, September 30

M. Moscicki resigned the Presidency of Poland. A statement from the Polish Embassy in Paris announced the constitution of a new Polish Government, with M. Raczkiewicz as President, and General Sikorski as Premier and Minister of War.

Warsaw garrison began to leave the city.

Successful reconnaissance flights were carried out by the R.A.F. over Germany. Five British aircraft, reconnoitring on the Western Front, engaged in an air battle with 15 German fighters at a height of 20,000 feet over enemy territory, and suffered some casualties.

The Air Ministry announced that R.A.F. pilots had flown at a height of only 600 feet above the Siegfried Line and made a valuable photographic survey of gun emplacements and other defences.

Danish steamer " Vendia " sunk by a U-boat off The Scaw.

Sunday, October 1

Garrison of Hel Peninsula surrendered.

The French Command reported an advance on a mile-long front west of Saarlouis. There were fierce air engagements between the Franco-British and German forces.

Count Ciano in Berlin. The Italian Foreign Minister had interviews with Ribbentrop and Hitler.

A Royal Proclamation calling up all men over 20 years of age and under 22 was made.

M. Sarajoglu, Turkish Foreign Minister, had an interview with Molotov in Moscow.

NOTE. The poem ' For the Lost of H.M.S. Courageous," G. Humbert Wolfe in page 116, is printed by courtesy of Mr. Wolfe and " The Daily Sketch."

It Is Said That . . .

German restaurants may no longer offer more than four " warm one-pot or served-on-the-plate dishes."

Since the Soviet alliance Berlin police have been busy removing slogans on pillars, worded : " Red Front ! Down Hitler, Stalin ! Long Live Trotsky."

Czech history books are to be destroyed.

Czechs may not read any history except that prescribed by the Nazis.

Secondary school-children of Berlin have been " called up " to do farm work.

Boys up to the age of 16 are paid 6d. a day.

Germany is ready to sacrifice 200 bombers to sink one British battleship. .*Berlin newspaper.*

Prince Starhemberg, former Vice-Chancellor of Austria, is seeking permission to raise an Austrian Legion to fight for France.

All Jewish shops in Slovakia have been handed over to returning soldiers as a reward for their participation in the war.

Rationing, the Gestapo terror and memories of how the last war ended are reasons for German lack of enthusiasm for " Hitler's War."

Innumerable field cards have been received at the German broadcast studios from soldiers weary of interminable propaganda.

Hearing that a German tanker in Boston Harbour was short of rations, the crew of a British liner sent over a side of beef. " Germans or not," explained the British mate, " they have got to eat."

German schoolchildren have to learn by heart passages of Hitler's Danzig speech, especially those directed against Britain.

There is no word of abuse of France in the German newspapers, the virulence of propaganda being directed against Britain.

German cards sent to parents and wives notifying them of the deaths of their sons or husbands, are set out as follows : (1) Your son (or husband) will not return home. (2) Heil Hitler !

Vol. 1   A Permanent Picture Record of the Second Great War   No. 6

Aboard the troopship which is carrying them across the Channel, these British soldiers have donned the life-saving gear which will keep them afloat if a U-boat's torpedo should make them take to the water.   During the dispatch of the new British Expeditionary Force to France in September, 1939, not a single life was lost through enemy action, so thorough and unsleeping was the watch kept by the vessels of the Royal Navy entrusted with the guardianship of the troop-carrying fleet.

British Official Photograph: Crown Copyright Reserved

Epic Siege and Fall of Warsaw

History records many a siege sustained against tremendous odds, and to the most glorious of these must now be added that of Warsaw. For nearly three weeks Poland's capital city withstood the furious might of the German invader, and only capitulated when all but honour was lost.

Stunned by the disaster, this Polish farmer stands at the door of his homestead after it had been bombed by the Nazis.
Photo, Keystone

AFTER they had bombed and shelled Warsaw for nearly three weeks, the German High Command on September 27 announced that in future the city would be regarded as a military objective. At the outbreak of war, said their communiqué, Warsaw had been considered as an open town and respected accordingly, but it had now been transformed into a fortress by the measures of the commander, who had restored the old forts and armed part of the civil population . . .

The statement was accompanied by an intensification of the attack, and the first line of forts in the north of the city and the second line of those in the south were captured by the besiegers. Following these assaults the Polish commander offered to surrender the town.

The news of the armistice was conveyed to the world in the following message broadcast from Warsaw on September 28 : " After 20 days of heroic defence, after practically the destruction of half the city, and after the destruction

After the main Polish armies had fallen back a few heroic soldiers still held out. Here Nazis are firing on a house in a Warsaw suburb already in flames in which Polish soldiers may be in hiding. Centre right, a party of German soldiers have brought an anti-tank gun into operation against Polish stragglers.

Photos, Associated Press

of the waterworks, the electric plant and other public utility services, the military authorities have decided that these disasters, coupled with the lack of ammunition and the impossibility of obtaining early assistance from the Allies, make it futile to defend the city further, involving as it would the risk of pestilential diseases as well as the entire destruction of the city, the heroic defence of which will certainly pass into history. An armistice has, therefore, been agreed upon since noon, and the conditions for the capitulation are now being discussed. The most honourable terms are being demanded by the Warsaw military authorities."

For some days past conditions in the capital had been indescribably terrible. Refugees who arrived in Hungary stated that so many people had been killed in the city streets that the task of removing the corpses had been abandoned. The supplies of food and water had given out. All the principal churches and public buildings were in ruins. Nine hospitals filled with wounded were reported to have been destroyed. The smoke and dust with which the streets were filled made breathing almost impossible.

High-Explosive Bombs Do Their Fell Work

These two remarkable photographs show a Polish goods train that has been attacked from the air by Nazi bombers. High-explosive bombs weighing 520 lb. were used and the two huge craters and the twisted rails testify to their power. It was in this way that the Nazis attacked trains carrying Polish refugee women and children away from the battle zone.

Photos, Mondiale

Reports from Budapest on September 28 stated that more than 3,000 persons, most of them women and children, had been killed in the previous twenty-four hours, and 500 fires were in progress.

In one of the last communiqués issued by the Warsaw Defence Command it was announced that fire had destroyed the food centres, and the lack of food was being cruelly felt. The number of wounded was then 16,000 soldiers and 20,000 civilians, but it was impossible to establish the exact number of dead and wounded owing to the bombardment and complete destruction of several of the hospitals. "On a number of occasions," the communiqué went on, "the wounded have had to be moved from one place to another. The conditions of hygiene are worsening daily and there is an imminent threat of epidemics."

Nevertheless, "in spite of so many misfortunes, the moral strength of the population remains unshakable. The soldiers defending the capital remain doggedly at their posts. They have shown themselves superior to the enemy wherever they have not been crushed by the superiority of technical means of fighting."

Following the announcement of the armistice from the Warsaw garrison, the German wireless stated that the city had capitulated unconditionally and would be handed over on September 29. It was not until Sunday, October 1, however, that the first representatives of the German army occupied the suburb of Praga.

In the next few days they extended their hold on the city and disarmed the Polish garrison of some 120,000 men. They were received with a death-like calm, and there was no sound save the tramp of the soldiers' feet as they quitted the city which they had defended so long and with such gallantry. The conquerors had posted armoured cars and tanks at the most important points, but they were not needed. Even they had to admit that the Poles in their hour of defeat conducted themselves like brave men, and, having laid down their arms, marched out to the prison-camps without a sign of battle weariness or demoralization, but with quick and steady step, led by their own officers in unbroken order.

As soon as they had left, scavengers and demolition squads worked furiously to clear away the ruins in readiness for the Fuehrer's triumphal entry.

A few hours before Warsaw surrendered Modlin had agreed to capitulate ; and on October 1 the gallant little garrison of Hela—4,000 men under Rear-Admiral von Unruh, described by the German official news agency as the last bastion of Polish defence—also laid down its arms. It had held out against attack from sea, land, and air for thirty days.

Organized Polish resistance had come to an end. But the fight had not, surely, been in vain. " I confidently hope," said the Mayor of Warsaw, M. Starzynsky, in reply to a radio message from the Mayor of Verdun—that French city which during the Great War withstood for so long the whole might of the German military machine—" that the defence of Warsaw has played a useful part in this inhuman war forced upon the peoples of Europe by the German spirit of domination and barbarism."

On October 1 the last Polish stronghold fell to the Nazis. It was on the Peninsula of Hel or Hela, the lighthouse of which is seen top left. The remarkable photo above was taken in Warsaw during a Nazi air raid, and the smoke from the fires caused by incendiary bombs can be seen rising in the background. Close to the left-hand lamp standard a smoke ring which such bombs always make is visible. The horses have been unharnessed, and some of them reversed in the shafts of the carts as a precaution against bolting.

Photos, E.N.A. and Planet News

How Russia and Germany Shared the Spoil

Following upon Poland's military collapse, Nazi Germany and Soviet Russia proceeded to divide the conquered land. Below we give an analysis of the results of this
Fourth Partition of Poland which, like its infamous predecessors, paid not the
slightest attention to the wishes of the people.

Twice in one week was Poland partitioned. According to the German-Soviet communiqué issued on September 22, six days after the Soviet invasion of Poland began, the line of demarcation between Germany and Russia was to follow the rivers Pissa, Narew, Vistula, and San. It transpired, however, that this line was provisional, and what was announced as the final frontier between the two States was given in an official Soviet communiqué issued on September 29. Beginning at the southernmost corner of Lithuania, the line runs in a generally westerly direction along the East Prussian frontier to the river Pissa, and then south along the river Narew to Ostroleka, from where it bears to the east along the river Bug to Brest-Litovsk. Following the river south to Chrystynopol, it there turns west just north of Przemysl to the river San, and thence up to the San's source in the Carpathians on the Ruthenian frontier.

By this "final partition" of Poland the Vistula becomes a completely German river, and Warsaw, too, which by the partition of a few days before was to be divided between the two States, now becomes entirely German. With regard to the population, it may be noted that in the territory annexed by Germany there are approximately 18,000,000 Poles, 2,250,000 Jews, and 750,000 Germans and others, whereas the territory annexed by Russia has only 5,000,000 Poles and 1,000,000 Jews (representing what may be called the alien element) and 6,000,000 Ukrainians and 2,000,000 White Russians and Lithuanians—peoples who are claimed by the Russians as "blood brothers."

As mentioned above, Warsaw becomes German. Of the other great cities Germany also receives Gdynia, largest port on the Baltic and the pride of post-war Poland; Lodz, sometimes called the Manchester of Poland, famous for the manufacture of chemicals, beer, machinery, silk and textiles; Cracow, the centre of Polish culture and also a manufacturing city; Katowice, the chief town of the Silesian coalfields, with many iron works, foundries, and machine-shops; Lublin, where there are big armament works; and Poznan, in the heart of the great agricultural region of Western Poland.

For her part Soviet Russia receives Brest-Litovsk, an important centre of communications; Lwow, famous for its manufacture of machinery and ironware; Bialystok, which may be called the Bradford of Poland; Przemysl, chief town of a petroleum producing area;

and Wilno, a grain and timber exporting centre. While Germany obtains all the coalmines and the heavy industrial area Russia has managed to secure nearly all the oilfields in Galicia. The main metallurgical and armament-producing centres—Warsaw, Lodz, Bydgoszcz (Bromberg), Poznan, Sandomierz and Radom—go to Germany, and so do two of the three main textile-producing centres—Lodz and Piotrkow. The third, Bialystok, is allocated to Russia.

Germany's Poor Bargain

These results, however satisfactory they may appear to the men in charge of the German military machine—and even they must have looked glum when they were obliged to withdraw their troops from the territory about Lwow which they had conquered in order that it might be occupied by the Soviet army— can hardly seem so pleasing to the German industrialists or to the underfed and overworked populace of the Reich. Germany, the greatest industrialized nation of the Continent, has now appro-

priated further highly industrialized areas whose factories and workshops, now that the export markets are closed by the British blockade, must inevitably compete with those established in the Reich.

What Germany wants is food and raw materials. The newly acquired agricultural districts in west Poland can hardly produce more food than is required to feed the native population, and it is Russia that has seized those raw materials of which she has already enough, and Nazi Germany far less than enough.

Moreover, for years past the German public has been educated to believe that the *Drang nach Sued-Osten* would result in the inclusion within the Reich's frontiers of the vast cornlands of the Ukraine and the rich oilfields of Galicia. Now, however, the way to both oil and corn is barred by a frowning frontier of Soviet tanks and bayonets, for the whole of the former Polish frontier with Rumania and Ruthenia is now Russian.

The result of the partition of Poland seems to show that Stalin held all the trump cards.

On this map of Poland are shown the boundaries of 1914; the Curzon Line of 1919; the boundaries of the Republic as it existed on the outbreak of war in 1939; and the line of demarcation agreed upon by the Nazi and Soviet invaders on September 29 of that year. The map also shows the distribution of peoples.

Aerial Battles in the West

Bearing in mind the fact that on the West the war is being carried on by
armies occupying great fortified systems, the gains made by the French in
the first month of hostilities are encouraging, to say no more. Particularly
in the air was the Allied supremacy increasingly made manifest.

A British nurse arriving in France gets a
helping hand with her kit from a "matelot"
—the French word for sailor.
Photo, British Official, Crown Copyright

Nied valley and, in the Hornbach
and Hardt mountains, the advance
was in the neighbourhood of two
miles; while in the Lauter valley
and south of Saarbruecken before
the heights of Spicheren, the gains
recorded were between 500 yards
to a mile. Some fifty villages on
German soil were now in French
hands.

Along the whole Rhine–Moselle front
the Germans were pushed back until the
Maginot Line in that region was no longer
within range of most of the enemy guns.
Thus, although there were no spectacular
advances, such as from time to time broke
the monotony of trench warfare in the

last war, the French made gains of the
most solid and valuable description. As
their High Command had promised at the
very opening of hostilities; all the fighting
had been on the German side of the
frontier.

Saarbruecken was still, nominally at
least, in German hands, though its population had been long evacuated, and, as
one French military commentator said:
"It was ready to fall like a ripe fruit
which the tree cannot hold." Surrounded
on three sides, it was dominated by the
French guns; indeed, the French batteries now so commanded the Saar mining
region that the German Command ordered
complete evacuation of the civilian

A MONTH after the war began more
than 150 square miles of German
territory on the west were in the
occupation of French troops. In the
Warndt Forest region—that region from
which the French engineers collected
3,000 mines, after their Moroccan comrades had carried the last enemy outposts
at the point of the bayonet—the advance
amounted to at least eight miles beyond
the frontier. In the Moselle region, the

In addition to the French first line aeroplanes many others of older pattern are employed behind the lines. The pair of machines in the
upper photograph are some of those used for liaison work between the various aerodromes in Northern France. In the lower photograph,
taken with the French army, a tractor is drawing a heavy gun into position.
Photos, Planet News

The Possible Aces of Tomorrow's Air War

The pilots in this group, studying their route before taking off, include representatives of the Dominions. From the very first days of war the Empire has made a brave show in the ranks of those writing new and glorious pages in the history of our Air Force. The men seen above are on an advanced training course with twin-engined aircraft, and they provide reinforcement pilots for squadrons already in the battle line

Photo, Planet News

Making Themselves at Home on the Western Front

The football season in France opened soon after the first troops of the British Expeditionary Force crossed the Channel. In this photograph a match is in progress behind the lines. In the map on the left the French advances into German territory on the Saar are shown in black. The Maginot and Siegfried lines are shaded.

Photo, British Official, Crown Copyright.   Map by courtesy of " News Chronicle "

population. The coal-mines, so valuable to Germany in peacetime, and still more valuable in time of war, were rendered unworkable. If the attack were not pushed home at Saarbruecken it was probably because the French anticipated a counter-attack on a large scale, and preferred to await it in the positions which they had carefully prepared.

All through these operations the French conserved their man power to the utmost, keeping casualties down to the minimum, while the Germans for their part lost heavily in counter-attacks which were invariably dissipated by the deadly fire of the French guns.

In the air there was marked activity. Day after day French and British aero-planes flew over the German defences, and from a low altitude took photographs of the Siegfried Line—photographs which were invaluable to the artillery. Almost every day the communiqués, both French and German, contained reports of air fighting. The fighting spirit of the Allied airmen was proved to be of the very highest quality, and it was soon demonstrated that in the matter of 'planes, too, the Allies need fear no comparison with the much-vaunted German Messerschmitts.

From time to time descriptions of air battles over the German line were allowed to appear in the French press. In one of these battles two French observation 'planes were sent out with an escort of nine fighters. They were above the Siegfried Line when fifteen German fighters suddenly dived out of the sky on the French formation. A furious dog-fight ensued, in the course of which seven of the German 'planes were brought down as compared with only three lost by the French. The report concluded with the statement that both the observation 'planes returned to the base bearing the results of their reconnaissance.

Meanwhile, the British Expeditionary Force was steadily crossing the Channel into France. The roads to the east were crowded with marching troops and with great convoys of tanks, armoured cars, transport wagons, field kitchens and the like. The British troops had not as yet been in action, but their presence on French soil was an immense encouragement to the French Government and people. It was generally understood that the B.E.F. was being held in readiness behind the line to meet any such move as a German advance through Belgium.

German Air Weapon at Work East and West

The violent end of one of Germany's much-vaunted Messerschmitt fighters, shot down by French anti-aircraft fire on the Western Front.

R.A.F. Official Photograph: Crown Copyright Reserved

A German flying officer in his warplane poring over the map before plotting his course.

THE German Luftwaffe—literally " air weapon "—has been built up by Field-Marshal Goering and General Milch into a formidable force both in size and quality. Germany was forbidden to possess any air force under the provisions of the Versailles Treaty (1919), and for many years she concentrated on commercial flying and gliding. With the advent to power of the Nazis, however, a fighting force was established, at first in secret ; its existence was officially admitted by Goering in March, 1934. Development since then has been rapid.

Immediately above is a photograph taken from one of a formation of German Heinkel twin-engined bombers, actually en route for its objective—military or otherwise—in Poland. This type of bomber has, it will be noted, a defensive gun position below the fuselage, with two machine-guns covering a wide field of fire. Above, right, is a Henschel dive-bomber—another standard type—dropping practice bombs. The usual method is for the latter to be released as the aeroplane pulls out of its dive.

Photo, Mondiale

Uneasy Neighbours of the Soviet Power:

As a result of Russia's intervention in Poland, diplomatic activity of the most intense kind
centred about Moscow. Only a few weeks before, all roads seemed to lead to Hitler's
eyrie at Berchtesgaden, but now it was to Stalin's bureau in the Kremlin that the
ministers of Europe flocked.

WHEN in 1920 their armies were defeated by the Poles before the gates of Warsaw, the Russians retreated behind their frontier, and for nearly twenty years played little part in the affairs of Europe. The Kremlin, it was said, had gone Asiatic. Following the Nazi invasion of Poland in September, 1939, however, Russia seemed to have become once again aware of the existence of the great and busy continent lying to the west. Stalin developed an imperialist urge, for whatever motive; and as soon as the Polish resistance showed signs of collapse and the whole country seemed on the verge of being overrun by the Nazi invaders, the Russian dictator ordered his troops to march. In the course of a week Russia recaptured all and more of the territory she had lost to the Poles in 1920, and Moscow achieved overnight the position of the diplomatic centre of Europe.

It was hardly surprising that Russia's determined intervention in Poland should give rise to nervousness in the other states bordering her on the west. Nor, indeed, were their fears groundless, for from the Baltic to the Black Sea there were reports of Russian moves of one kind or another.

The first to feel the weight of the new Russia's hand were the Baltic States—Estonia, Latvia and Lithuania. With Finland to the north, these little states were all before 1917 part of the Tsar's realm, and they all came into independent existence in the period of disorganization which ensued upon the proclamation of the Russian republic. All are strongly democratic in principle, though not always in practice, and their social and economic arrangements reveal strong equalitarian tendencies. For the most part their peoples live lives of rural simplicity, drawing their subsistence from the products of their fields and forests, and receiving manufactured goods from overseas, largely from Britain, in exchange for their butter and eggs; bacon and timber. Politically, they are little concerned with the outside world; since their establishment they have striven to live at peace with their neighbours, and of the three only Lithuania has been involved in disputes with other countries —with Poland over the occupation of Wilno, Lithuania's ancient capital, and with Germany over Memel, which she was compelled to return to the Reich on March 22, 1939.

But in the new Europe which came

One of the first places to be occupied by the Soviet troops after they crossed the frontier was Wilno, or Vilna, and here we see the Red army entering the city in triumph on September 19, 1939. The upper photograph illustrates another phase of Soviet expansion; it was taken in the Estonian island of Dagö, which in the Soviet-Estonian Pact of September 29 was mentioned as a possible base for Soviet ships and aircraft.

Photos, Associated Press and E.N.A.

On Frontiers From Baltic to Black Sea

into being following the Munich Settlement, these little Baltic lands assumed a fresh importance owing to their situation between Nazi Germany and Soviet Russia. In the summer of 1939 the negotiations between Britain and France on the one hand and Russia on the other encountered a formidable stumbling block in Russia's demand that the other powers should guarantee the independence of Estonia, Latvia and Lithuania in return for Russia's guarantee of Poland and Rumania. In the event it was Germany that made the pact with Russia.

Following the sinking of a Soviet steamer by an unknown submarine off the Estonian coast, Russia showed what is traditionally known as the strong hand. M. Karl Selter, the Estonian Foreign Minister, proceeded to Moscow, ostensibly to negotiate a new trade treaty. When the result of the deliberations was announced, however, it was found that not only had a new trade agreement been signed, but a pact of mutual assistance as well. According to this pact the two contracting parties, Estonia and Russia, undertook to render each other every assistance, including military assistance, in the event of direct aggression or the menace of aggression arising on the part of any great European power, whether made by way of the Baltic or across the territory of Latvia. Furthermore, the Soviet undertook to render to the Estonian army assistance in armaments.

Still more important, the Estonian Republic assured the Soviet Union of the right to maintain naval bases and to lease aerodromes at reasonable prices on the Estonian islands of Dagö and Ösel. In effect, as a result of the pact, Estonia became a protectorate of Russia. Moreover, Russia now obtained ice-free ports on the west, and thus was enabled to challenge the Nazi conception of the Baltic as a German lake.

In a few days the Foreign Ministers of Latvia and Lithuania arrived in Moscow on a mission similar to that of their Estonian confrère.

Turning now to Rumania, here again there was widespread concern at the extraordinary revival of Russia's power in Europe. Rumania, like the Baltic States, had profited by the collapse of Tsarism; indeed, for her seizure of Bessarabia in 1917 there was no such justification as could be claimed by those who in the north seceded from Russia and erected the Baltic republics. Reports from Rumania showed that large numbers of troops were being moved to the Bessarabian frontiers, and although it was claimed officially that the relations between the countries were cordial, correspondents on the spot declared that there was no communication between the two banks of the Dniester.

For more than a thousand miles the U.S.S.R. (Union of Socialist Soviet Republics) faces the state system of eastern Europe. Following the four Baltic republics—Finland, Estonia, Latvia and Lithuania—comes East Prussia. Next is what, until its partition between Germany and Russia in 1939, was the independent republic of Poland. Adjoining Poland is Slovakia, now a German protectorate; Ruthenia, part of Hungary; and Rumania. Beyond Rumania proper lies Bessarabia which was seized by Rumania in 1917, and south are the other Black Sea countries of Bulgaria and Turkey on both sides of the Bosporus.

Methods that Will Beat U-Boats

No experience gained in the last war proved more valuable in 1939
than the adaptation of the convoy system to modern conditions.
Within five weeks it had played a great part in defeating
unrestricted submarine warfare.

The newest Cunard Liner, "Mauretania,"
now mounts three anti-aircraft guns, one
of which is on the stern.

Photo, Planet News

A GREAT part in winning the last war was played by the men of the Mercantile Marine, as it was then called, and it is already obvious that the sons and grandsons of the gallant British seamen and fishermen of 1914–18 can show equal gallantry, equal fear-lessness and equal devotion to duty.

The men of 1914–18 had a signal recognition of their services when in 1928 King George V created the new office of Master of the Merchant Marine and Fisheries and appointed the Prince of Wales to be its first Master.

The men of the Merchant Navy and Fisheries went through a severe testing time at the outbreak of the new war. Over 2,000 British ships were then at sea, ranging from trawlers to ocean liners, and none had any defence against U-boats. The Nazis had made full preparations for taking the utmost advantage of this situation. They had placed big sub-marines along the main routes of sea traffic, while smaller U-boats in waters nearer home were ready to pounce upon anything from a trawler to an ocean liner.

No Seamen Refused

In these circumstances it was not surprising that the toll of merchant shipping was heavy : 65,000 tons were sunk in the first week, but the tonnage sunk decreased rapidly to 9,000 tons in the fourth week and nil in the fifth. Yet during the first few weeks, when the losses were at their heaviest, no British seamen refused to sail without escort. In ships great and small these worthy descendants of the great British sailors of the past took their lives in their hands, realizing that on them no less than on the men of the Royal Navy the safety of the country and final victory depended.

It is gratifying to know that they had not to run these fearful risks for long. The last war had fully proved that the best means of dealing with the submarine menace was the convoy system, and immediate steps were taken to bring it into operation again.

The essence of this system is that merchant ships both inward and outward bound should assemble at some port out-side the danger zone, and that from that point they should be escorted by warships —light cruisers and destroyers—to their destination. There may perhaps be 40 or 50 merchant ships in a convoy, marshalled in columns with the protective screen of warships around them. One of the difficulties of the convoy system is that the speed of the whole fleet of ships can be no greater than that of the slowest, and the difference in speed between the fastest and the slowest may be very considerable. It is essential, if the convoy is to be effective and if the fewest possible number of warships is to be employed to protect it, that all the merchant ships should keep station, that is, follow one another in exact lines, keeping an equal distance apart.

When the system was first introduced in 1917 it was feared that merchant sea-men, being unused to such manoeuvres, might not be able to " keep station " with absolute accuracy. To the surprise and admiration of the Royal Navy this fear proved groundless. The skippers of the Merchant Navy, handling ships of widely varying size, speed and design, kept station with an accuracy which was beyond criticism. That example of the fine seamanship of the Merchant Navy is again proving of incalculable value in fighting the submarine menace.

The fishermen no less than the officers and men of the Merchant Navy deserve their tribute, but those who are still employed in trawling, while they make an invaluable contribution to Britain's food supplies, have had to face unexpected dangers, for on September 26 Mr. Winston Churchill explained in the House of Commons that, failing in their object of seriously interfering with British shipping, the U-boats had turned their attention to neutral shipping and the " humble British trawlers." The " humble trawlers " have gone to sea just the same.

Contraband of War

The day-to-day work of the Navy is not only concerned with the protection of the convoys and the hunting of the U-boat, but also with the control of neutral shipping. By International Law every enemy ship and its cargo is a legitimate prize. That does not, however, apply to neutral ships. It is the right of a belligerent power to stop and examine every neutral ship to ensure that it is not carrying to enemy ports contraband of war. Under that term are included as definitely contraband all articles or commodities the use of which is obviously for warlike purposes. It is the duty of the ships of the Royal Navy to examine all neutral ships, which may sometimes necessitate their being taken into British ports for examination.

The possibility that U-boats might have found bases in South America and operate off the North American coast had to be guarded against. In this photograph the Cunard liner "Aquitania," seen from the air with guns mounted aft, is steering a zigzag course as a precaution, though she is within 50 miles of New York.

Photo, Associated Press

For H.M. Navy's 'Constant Care'

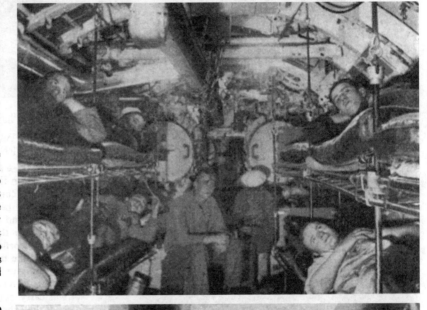

Left, the crew of a U-boat on the conning tower. Above, is a U-boat photographed from the deck of an American ship she had held up.

IN his vivid broadcast on " The First Month of the War " Mr. Winston Churchill declared that " the U-boats may be safely left to the care and constant attention of the British Navy." Prisoners taken from German submarines have testified to the terrible effects of depth charges dropped from destroyers, for even when they do not make a direct hit the explosion wrecks important mechanism and compels the boat to rise to the surface. But it is not only the Royal Navy that the crews of U-boats have to fear, for they have internal enemies as well. It has been revealed that one member of each crew, unknown to the others, is a Gestapo man, whose duty it is to spy on his shipmates and to denounce to the authorities on returning to port any one of them who has spoken an indiscreet word about the Nazi regime. The Nazis no doubt remember that in 1918 the first signs of serious disaffection in Germany's armed forces appeared in her navy

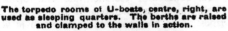

The torpedo rooms of U-boats, centre, right, are used as sleeping quarters. The berths are raised and clamped to the walls in action.

Petty officers of a U-boat, left, are holding an instruction class in the battery chamber. The submarine is propelled electrically when submerged. Above, Grand Admiral Raeder, commanding the German Navy, is addressing U-boat crews in Kiel harbour.
Photos, Mondiale, Keystone and Central Press

They Defy the U-Boats—and So Britain Lives

A T the beginning of the war the King sent the following message to the British Merchant Navy and British Fishing Fleets :

" In these anxious days, I would like to express to all officers and men in the British Merchant Navy and the British Fishing Fleets my confidence in their unflinching determination to play their vital part in defence. To each one I would say, Yours is a task no less essential to my people's existence than that allotted to the Navy, Army and Air Force. Upon you the nation depends for much of its foodstuffs and raw materials and for the transport of its troops overseas. You have a long and glorious history, and I am proud to bear the title Master of the Merchant Navy and Fishing Fleets. I know that you will carry out your duties with resolution and with fortitude, and that the high, chivalrous traditions of your calling are safe in your hands. God keep you and prosper you in your great task."

Here are some of the chief types of merchant ships that defy the U-boats. (1) A small tramp steamer such as plies round the coast and to Continental ports. (2) A tanker which brings home Britain's supplies of oil. (3) A small coasting steamer, whose funnel can be lowered to pass under bridges. She carries a gun aft. (4) A refrigerator ship that carries meat cargoes to Britain from Australia and South America. (5) A "luxury" passenger liner of the Union Castle line. (6) A cargo liner which carries mixed cargoes on regular routes and a few passengers.

Photos, Wide World, Keystone. Alfieri. Nautical Photo Agency, Union Castle Line, and Topical

In Fair Weather and Foul the Search Goes On

Most of the work of tracking and disabling U-boats is done by the destroyers, and day and night the work of searching for the Nazi pirate ships goes on. Here destroyers are patrolling the North Sea in heavy weather. They are by no means comfortable ships in rough seas. for the decks are constantly swept by waves and spray when they are moving at any speed.

Photo, Fox

'Force Will Be Met By Force'— Big Guns D

Some very big guns have gone with the British Expeditionary Force to France. Above, one of them is seen while the gun crew were undergoing intensive training for active service. An interesting point about it is the massive rubber tires, which greatly facilitate its movement over heavy roads. German guns also have such tires, but they are made of synthetic rubber, the life of which is very short.

e Nazi Artillery and Batter the Siegfried Line

It was announced on September 20 from Paris that during artillery actions, which had been very heavy, French guns again and again proved themselves superior to the German field artillery of equal calibre, which they outranged. This has proved extremely valuable in counter-battery work, the French artillery having swept with its fire a vast area from which the Germans have been forced to withdraw their guns.

WORDS THAT HISTORY WILL REMEMBER

A Select Record from Week to Week of Important War Declarations and Statements

(*Continued from page 146*)

Thursday, September 21

PRESIDENT ROOSEVELT in an address to Congress appealing for the lifting of the Arms Embargo contained in the Neutrality Statutes :

For many years the primary purpose of our foreign policy has been that this nation and this Government should strive to the utmost to aid in avoiding war among nations, but if and when war unhappily comes the Government and the nation must exert every possible effort to avoid being drawn into the war. . . .

There has been sufficient realism in the United States to see how close to our own shores came the dangerous paths which were being followed on other continents. Last January I told Congress that a war which threatened to envelop the world in flames had been averted, but it has become increasingly clear that peace is not assured. . . . And last January also I spoke to this Congress of the need for further warning of new threats of conquest, military and economic, a challenge to religion, to democracy, and to international good faith. . . . I also said: "We have learned that when we deliberately try to legislate neutrality our neutrality may operate unevenly and unfairly, may actually give aid to an aggressor and deny it to the victim."

The instinct of self-preservation should warn us not to let that happen any more. And it was because of what I foresaw last January from watching the trend of foreign affairs and their probable effect upon us that I recommended to the Congress in July of this year that changes be enacted in our neutrality laws. The essentials for American peace, American peace in this war-torn world, have not changed since last January or last July, and that is why I ask you again to re-examine our own legislation. . . .

The embargo provisions as they exist today prevent the sale to a belligerent by an American factory of any completed implements of war, but they allow the sale of many types of uncompleted implements of war as well as all kinds of general material and supplies. They furthermore allow such products of industry and agriculture to be taken in American flag ships to belligerent nations. There in itself under the present law lies definite danger to our neutrality and our peace. . . .

I seek a greater consistency through the repeal of the embargo provisions and a return to normal law. I seek the re-enactment of the historical and traditional American policy which, except for the disastrous interlude of the embargo and non-intercourse laws more than a century and a quarter ago, has served us well from the very beginning of our constitutional existence.

It has been erroneously said that a return to that policy might bring us nearer to war. I give to you my deep and unalterable conviction based on years of experience as a worker in the field of international peace that by the repeal of the embargo the United States will more probably remain at peace than if the law remains as it stands today. . . .

Sunday, September 24

Translation of a further LEAFLET dropped by the R.A.F. over Germany :

To the German people :

Germans, note that in spite of German blood which has been shed in the Polish war :

1. Your Government's hope of successful lightning war has been destroyed by the British War Cabinet's decision to prepare for a three years' war.

2. The French Army crossed the frontier into Germany on Sept. 6, or four days before German official sources admitted it. In the west, British troops are already standing shoulder to shoulder with their French allies.

3. The British and French Fleets have swept German merchant shipping from the oceans. Therefore your supplies of a whole range of essential war materials, such as petrol, copper, nickel, rubber, cotton, wool and fats, are almost gone.

You can no longer rely, as you did in the last war, upon neutral supplies because your Government cannot pay for them.

4. Night after night the British Air Force has demonstrated its power by flights far into German territory.

Germans, note !

Tuesday, September 26

M. MILAN HARMINC, Slovak Consul in London, in a communication to the Foreign Office :

The whole of Slovakia is occupied by Nazi armed forces. The voice of the Slovak people has been temporarily silenced by the ruthless abrogation of all treaties and agreements.

In the name of Slovakia I solemnly protest against this shameful betrayal, and declare that the aim and ideals of Great Britain and France are identical with those of my sorely tried people.

Mr. WICKHAM STEED in a letter to "The Times" :

As the war goes on our own people and the people of France may need an ideal more positive and sustaining than "the destruction of Hitlerism.". . . Today we are not so much allied as united. In this union lies our strength, for Great Britain is now, irrevocably, part of Europe. The "Oslo" neutrals are striving towards closer co-operation if not actual union. Is it "Utopian" to see in these things the beginnings of a movement towards a greater unity in which unlimited national sovereignties will be subordinated to common needs ? If not, this war should help to foster the international solidarity in withstanding war and creating peace that may, one day, give the German people a chance to enter, as equals, a union of nations democratically self-governed and banded together not only against lawless violence but for the mutual helpfulness which is peace.

I submit that British policy should aim at these things. To frame and to proclaim such a policy would be the most powerful propaganda.

Thursday, September 28

Declaration of the SOVIET and GERMAN Governments accompanying the Articles of Agreement comprised in the Soviet-German Pact :

The German Government and the Government of the U.S.S.R., by the treaty signed today, having finally settled questions that arose as a result of the dissolution of the Polish State, and having thereby created a firm foundation for a lasting peace in Eastern Europe, in mutual agreement express the opinion that the liquidation of the present war between Germany on the one hand and Great Britain on the other (*sic*) is in the interest of all nations.

Therefore both Governments will direct their common efforts, if necessary in accord with other friendly Powers, in order to attain this aim as early as possible.

If, however, these efforts of both Governments remain futile, it will be established thereby that Great Britain and France bear the responsibility for the continuation of war, and in the event of the continuation of the war the Governments of Germany and the U.S.S.R. will consult each other on the necessary measures.

Saturday, September 30

M. RACZYNSKI, Polish Ambassador, in a Note to the British Government :

I raise in the name of the Polish Government the most formal and most solemn protest against the plot hatched between Berlin and Moscow in disregard of all international obligations and of all principles of morality.

Poland shall never recognize this act of violence, and, fortified by the justice of her case, she shall never cease to struggle until her territories have been liberated from the invaders and her legitimate rights fully re-established.

OUR WAR GAZETTEER

Aachen (Fr. Aix-la-Chapelle). City of Germany, near Belgian and Dutch frontiers ; has famous cathedral and town hall ; on large coalfield and international rlys. ; also a great manufacturing centre ; pop. 162,000.

Grodno. Town of N.E. Poland, regarded by Lithuanians as in their country ; on r. Niemen and a main rly. junction ; pop. 49,700.

Heligoland. German island fortress in North Sea, guards naval bases and entrance to Kiel Canal ; 44 miles from mouth of Elbe ; taken from Denmark by Britain in 1807, ceded to Germany in 1890 ; fortifications at one time dismantled according to Versailles Treaty (1919) ; area only 1/5 sq. m.

Moscow. Capital city of U.S.S.R. (Russia) from 1480 to 1703 and since 1918 ; on r. Moskva and new national canal system ; pop. 4,137,000.

Moselle. River, tributary of Rhine ; rises in Vosges Mts., France, flows N. and E. through Lorraine and into Germany ; joins Rhine at Coblenz after course of 320 miles.

Potsdam. Town of Prussia, Germany, 16 m. S.W. of Berlin ; famous palaces include Sans Souci, built by Frederick the Great ; a military centre ; pop. 79,000.

Riga. Capital and chief seaport of Latvia ; on Baltic at mouth of r. Dvina ; pop. 385,000.

Slovakia. German "Protectorate" and central portion of former Czecho-Slovakia ; nominally independent, but occupied since March 1939 by German troops ; capital Bratislava ; area 14,700 sq. m. ; pop. 2,450,000.

Ukraine. Republic of S.W. Russia, a member State of U.S.S.R. ; great wheat-growing and steel and iron producing area ; cap. Kiev ; area 166,368 sq. m. ; pop. 30,960,000 ; Ukrainian minorities also in Poland, Hungary, etc.

White Russia (or Byelo-Russia). Soviet republic of W. Russia, also bordering Poland ; cap. Minsk ; area 48,940 sq. m. ; pop. 5,567,000.

Wissembourg. Town of E. France ; on German frontier between Maginot and Siegfried Lines ; scene of French defeat by Germans in 1870 ; pop. 5,000.

Dutch and Belgians on the Alert

Between France and Germany lie Belgium, the cockpit of Europe, and Holland. Both countries have received assurances from the Nazi Government that their neutrality will not be challenged, but, none the less, they are taking every precaution.

WITHIN a month of the opening of hostilities Poland lay prostrate beneath the heel of the invader. The German method of making war had proved its success. A vast army of mechanized artillery and transport, supported and very often preceded by hosts of warplanes, had wiped out what had claim to be regarded as by no means the least of Europe's armies. Following the surrender of Warsaw there came a breathing space, when the question on everybody's lips was, "Where will the next blow fall?"

In view of the immense strength of the French fortifications in the west, it was regarded as unlikely, to say the least, that the German High Command would order a frontal attack on the Maginot Line. It was argued that, rather than run the risk of losing several hundreds of thousands of men, the Nazis would be much more likely to launch a war of movement such as they had just completed in Poland. In 1914 the Kaiser's war-lords decided on the violation of Belgian neutrality, and their Nazi successors in 1939 might well repeat the stroke.

True, as recently as August 26 Hitler had repeated to the Belgian Government and to the Dutch his resolve to respect the neutrality of the one country and the other. But, confronted with the choice between certain loss and almost certain victory, one could hardly expect him to hesitate long over the tearing up of but another scrap of paper.

Certainly, the Dutch and the Belgians were alive to the dangers of the situation.

Following the report of concentrations of German troops and aeroplanes at Aachen, where the frontiers of Holland, Belgium and Germany meet, the two kingdoms decided upon the partial flooding of their main defence systems.

The Dutch commenced by flooding a small zone near Utrecht which guards the great port of Amsterdam—possibly coveted by the Germans as a submarine or air base against England—and steps were also taken to have the flood-gates ready from the Zuyder Zee across country to the Rhine at Arnhem.

The Belgians for their part flooded the lowlands north of the Albert Canal between Antwerp and Maastricht, evidently fearing an attack through the "Maastricht appendix" of Holland. The whole area between the Meuse and the Dutch and German frontiers could be flooded in an emergency, and in the artificial lakes so formed the great fortresses would stand out like islands.

In the last war the Belgians found flooding constituted a most effective defence measure, and in recent years they have perfected a system in which artillery and water are combined to excellent advantage. The flooding of vast areas with sea water involves, of course, the loss of much valuable farmland and of many villages; but, nevertheless, in the Low Countries it is regarded as the cheapest method of achieving national security.

Not that the Belgians and Dutch do not put trust in their armed forces. Both of the little democracies have armies which, though in point of numbers

The Dutch Commander-in-Chief inspects the preparations made to inundate a large area of the country in case of invasion.

they cannot compare with those of Germany and France, are still formidable.

In the event, then, of the German High Command resolving to attempt a repetition of the strategy of 1914, their armies would have to overcome the opposition—first, of the fortresses on the Dutch and Belgian frontier; next, of the water defences which have been prepared in the rear of the fortified lines, and which are dotted with forts and strong-points; and thirdly, the resistance of the Belgian and Dutch field armies. Even if all these hurdles were taken in their stride, the invaders would then find themselves confronted by the northern section of the Maginot Line, just within the Franco-Belgian frontier. And if this, too, were carried? Then they would have to meet the shock of Britain's Expeditionary Force.

Belgium has taken steps to increase and strengthen her frontier defences against a possible Nazi violation of her neutrality. Left, long rows of steel railwaylines driven deep in the ground form a serious obstacle for tanks to overcome. Running parallel with them are barbed wire entanglements. Right is a concrete frontier strong-point on the top of which is a machine-gun turret.

Photos, Wide World, Sport & General and Keystone

FIRST LORD'S TONIC FOR THE NATION

Reproduced below are the principal passages from Mr. Winston Churchill's eagerly
awaited broadcast speech of October 1st—the speech, as one American paper commented, which was worth " batteries of artillery " to the Allied cause.

THE British Empire and the French Republic
have been at war with Nazi Germany
for a month tonight. We have not yet
come at all to the severity of fighting which is
to be expected but three important things
have happened.

First Poland has been again overrun by
two of the great Powers which held her in bondage for 150 years, but were unable to conquer the
spirit of the Polish nation.

The heroic defence of Warsaw shows that the
soul of Poland is indestructible, and that she
will rise again like a rock, which may for a spell
be submerged by a tidal wave, but which
remains a rock.

What is the second event of this first
month ? It is, of course, the assertion of the
power of Russia. Russia has pursued a cold
policy of self-interest.

We could have wished that the Russian
armies should be standing on their present line
as the friends and allies of Poland, instead of as
invaders.

But that the Russian armies should stand on
this line was clearly necessary for the safety of
Russia against the Nazi menace.

When Herr von Ribbentrop was summoned to
Moscow last week it was to learn the fact, and
to accept the fact, that the Nazi designs upon
the Baltic States and upon the Ukraine must
come to a dead stop.

Triple Community of Interests

I CANNOT forecast to you the action of Russia.
It is a riddle wrapped in mystery inside an
enigma ; but perhaps there is a key. That key
is Russian national interest.

It cannot be in accordance with the interest
or safety of Russia that Nazi Germany should
plant itself upon the shores of the Black Sea, or
that it should overrun the Balkan States and
subjugate the Slavonic peoples of south-eastern
Europe. That would be contrary to the
historic life-interests of Russia.

But in this quarter of the world, the south-
east of Europe, these interests of Russia fall
into the same channel as the interests of Britain
and France. None of these three Powers can
afford to see Rumania, Yugoslavia, Bulgaria, and,
above all, Turkey, put under the German heel.

**Through the fog of confusion and uncertainty
we may discern quite plainly the community of
interests which exist between England, France
and Russia to prevent the Germans carrying the
flames of war into the Balkans and Turkey.**

Thus—at some risk of being proved wrong by
events—I will proclaim tonight my conviction
that the second great fact of the first month of
the war is that Hitler, and all that Hitler stands
for, have been and are being warned off the
east and the south-east of Europe.

WHAT is the third event ? Here I speak as
First Lord of the Admiralty with especial
caution. It would seem that the U-boat attack
upon the life of the British Isles has not so
far proved successful.

It is true that when they sprang out upon us
and we were going about our ordinary business,
with 2,000 ships in constant movement every
day upon the seas, they managed to do some
serious damage. But the Royal Navy has
immediately attacked the U-boats, and is
hunting them night and day. . . .

And it looks tonight very much as if it is the
U-boats who are feeling the weather, and
not the Royal Navy or the world-wide commerce of Britain. . . . During the first month of
the war we have captured by our efficient contraband control 150,000 tons more German
merchandise—food, oil, minerals, and other
commodities—for our own benefit than we have
lost by all the U-boat sinkings put together.

We are told that all the U-boats have gone
ome to tell their master about their exploits

and their experiences. But that is not true,
because every day, even on Sundays, we are
attacking them upon the approaches to the
British Isles. Some undoubtedly have preferred
to go off and sink the unprotected neutral ships
of Norway and Sweden.

I hope the day will come when the Admiralty
will be able to invite ships of all nations to join
the British convoys and insure them on their
voyages at a reasonable rate.

We must, of course, expect that the U-boat
attack upon the sea-borne commerce of the
world will be renewed presently on a greater
scale. We hope, however, that by the end of
October we shall have three times as many
hunting-craft at work as we had at the beginning
of the war ; and I can assure you by the measures we have taken we hope that our means of
putting down this pest will grow continually.
We are taking great care about that.

Therefore, to sum up the results of the first
month, let us say that Poland has been overrun,
but will rise again ; that Russia has warned
Hitler off his Eastern dreams ; and that the
U-boats may be safely left to the care and
constant attention of the British Navy.

Now I wish to speak about what is happening
in our own island. When a peaceful democracy
is suddenly made to fight for its life, there must
be a lot of trouble and hardship in turning over
from peace to war.

His Majesty's Government is unitedly resolved to make the maximum effort of which the
British nation is capable, and to persevere,
whatever may happen, until decisive victory is
gained.

**Meanwhile patriotic men and women, and
those who understand the high causes in human
fortunes which are at stake, must not only rise
above fear, they must also rise above inconvenience and boredom.**

Parliament will be kept in session and all
grievances or muddles or scandals, if such there
are, can be freely ventilated there. In past times
the House of Commons has proved itself an
instrument of national will-power capable of
waging stern wars.

In other fields a large army has already gone

**Mr. Winston Churchill is here seen at the
microphone making his historic broadcast.**
Photo, P.N.A.

to France. British armies upon the scale of the
effort of the Great War are in preparation.
The British people are determined to stand in
the line with the splendid army of the French
Republic, and share with them, as fast and as
early as we can, whatever may be coming
towards us both.

It may be that great ordeals may be coming
to us in this island from the air. We shall
do our best to give a good account of ourselves,
and we must always remember that the command of the seas will enable us to bring
the immense resources of Canada and the
New World into play as a decisive, ultimate
air factor beyond the reach of what we have to
give and take over here.

Hitler Began It—We End It

DIRECTIONS have been given by the Government to prepare for a war of at least three
years. That does not mean that victory may
not be gained in a short time. How soon it will
be gained depends upon how long Herr Hitler
and his group of wicked men, whose hands are
stained with blood and soiled with corruption,
can keep their grip upon the docile unhappy
German people.

**It was for Hitler to say when the war would
begin, but it is not for him or his successors to
say when it will end.**

**It began when he wanted it, and it will end
only when we are convinced that he has had
enough.**

The Prime Minister has stated our war aims
in terms which cannot be bettered, and which
cannot be too often repeated : "To redeem
Europe from the perpetual and recurring fear
of German aggression, and enable the peoples
of Europe to preserve their independence and
their liberties." That is what the British and
French nations are fighting for. . . .

Now we have begun ; now we are going on ;
now with the help of God and all that is
meant thereby, and with the conviction that
we are the defenders of civilization and freedom,
we are going on, and we are going to go on to
the end. . . .

HERE I am in the same post as I was twenty-
five years ago. Rough times lie ahead,
but how different is the scene from that of
October, 1914 : Then the French front, with its
British assistance seemed to be about to break
under the terrible impact of German Imperialism.
Then Russia had been laid low at Tannenberg.
Then the whole might of the Austro-Hungarian
Empire was in battle against us. Then the
brave, warlike Turks were about to join our
enemies. Then we had to be ready night and
day to fight a decisive sea battle with a formidable German Fleet almost in many respects the
equal of our own.

We faced those adverse conditions then.
We have nothing worse to face tonight. In
those days of 1914, also, Italy was neutral,
but we did not know the reason for her neutrality
then. It was only later on that we learned
that, by a secret clause in the original Treaty of
Triple Alliance, Italy had expressly reserved to
herself the right to stand aside from any
war which brought her into conflict with Great
Britain.

**Much has happened since then, misunder-
standings and disputes have arisen, but all the
more do we appreciate in England the reasons
why this great and friendly nation of Italy, with
whom we have never been at war, has not seen
fit to enter the struggle.**

I do not understand what lies before us, but I
must say this : I cannot doubt we have the
strength to carry a good cause forward, and to
break down the barriers which stand between
the wage-earning masses of every land and a free
and more abundant daily life. . . .

Winston Churchill, 'Nazi Enemy No. 1'

The beginning of this war, as of that of 1914, finds Winston Churchill at his desk in the Admiralty. Many pages would be required to do justice to the First Lord's career, but here are the most important facts about the man who, for forty years, has never been far from the public eye.

No statesman in British history has held so many positions of high Cabinet rank as the man who today, as twenty-five years ago, is Britain's First Lord of the Admiralty.

Winston Spencer Churchill comes of a great family, bears a great name. He is a direct descendant of the famous Duke of Marlborough, the victor of Blenheim, and son of one of the most prominent politicians of the Victorian era and of an American mother famed for her beauty and intellect. He was born in 1874, and after Harrow and Sandhurst obtained a commission in the 4th Hussars. It was, however, as "The Daily Telegraph" war correspondent in the Sudan in 1898 that he first came into public notice, and he "hit the headlines" in 1899 with a dramatic escape from captivity in a Boer armoured train.

A few years later came his spectacular incursion into politics. Abandoning the Conservatism of his youth, he became a Liberal in time to share in the triumph o 1906. Hardly had North-west Manchester enabled him to add the letters M.P. to his name when Campbell-Bannerman, the new Liberal premier, appointed him Under-Secretary for the Colonies. Under Asquith his rise was rapid— President of the Board of Trade, Home Secretary and, in 1911, First Lord of the Admiralty. He was at the Admiralty when war began, and to his foresight may be largely attributed the readiness of

Britain's fleet in that hour of great emergency.

During the War he had his hours of high success and his periods of eclipse. In the public mind he was held responsible for the failure of the expeditions to Antwerp and Gallipoli, although subsequent history has tended to reverse the unfavourable verdict of the moment.

For some years his fortunes were closely linked to those of Mr. Lloyd George, and in the later coalitions he was in turn Minister for Munitions, Secretary for War and for the Colonies.

In the South African War of 1899 Lt. Churchill, of the South African Light Horse, saw a good deal of the fighting, and had besides a spell of captivity in a Boer prison at Pretoria.

When the coalition fell in 1922 Churchill also suffered defeat. By the end of 1924, however, he was not only back in the House of Commons, but had a seat on the Treasury Bench as Chancellor of the Exchequer, this time in the Conservative administration of Mr. (now Earl) Baldwin.

When the National Government was formed in 1931 Churchill's name was missing from the Cabinet list, and during the years that followed there was no more pertinent and pertinacious critic of the Government's policy in India and international affairs than he. From the beginning he preached resistance to the Nazis, and it is not surprising that today the German wireless seems to regard Mr. Churchill as Nazi Enemy No. 1.

Mention might be made of many another facet of Mr. Churchill's varied existence. His skill as a bricklayer, for instance, has entitled him to membership of the bricklayers' union, and as a journalist and author he has won widespread recognition. Many people, indeed, who take little interest in politics and know nothing of Churchill's achievements as a Cabinet Minister, know him primarily as the author of brilliant biographies of his ancestor, the Duke of Marlborough, and of his father, Lord Randolph Churchill, and still more of "The World Crisis," the book in which he gives a vivid account of the great and eventful period covered by the years just before and during the Great War.

Now today, after years in the political wilderness—years during which he was that by no means generally welcome person, the caustic critic—he has returned to high office, called back by the voice of the man in the street, just as was Kitchener in 1914. His political knowledge, his vast administrative experience, his eloquence and his resolution —all are assets of incomparable value to Britain and Britain's cause.

In 1909, when the centre photograph was taken, Mr. Churchill was one of the rising lights of the Liberal party ; he was then President of the Board of Trade in Mr. Asquith's ministry. The photograph shows him accompanying a military officer on manoeuvres in Germany as the guest of the Kaiser. In the lower photograph Mr. Churchill is seated at his desk in his home, Chartwell Manor, near Westerham, Kent.
Photos, "Daily Mirror" and Topical

ODD FACTS ABOUT THE WAR
Worth Noting Today and Re-reading in Years to Come

" Even Hitler " . . .

Before the war the Lord Chamberlain refused to license for public performance a song called " Even Hitler Had a Mother." This ban has now been removed.

A Seat in the Stalls

The high ground near Schengen, in Luxemburg, provides a front seat for the crowds of visitors who arrive there to watch the fighting about a mile away

Under the Stamp

A letter received by English friends of a resident in Germany stated that the food was good and that they must not worry about her The letter concluded : " Tell B— to take the stamp off this envelope for his collection " Underneath the stamp were found the words : " We are starving.

In a Soho Café

Every day in London's best-known German café blond Germans are to be seen enjoying meals such as they would never know in their native land today One of them remarked : " I have been two years in Britain The longer I stayed the more I liked it ; so I never went home to Stuttgart. I never knew how much I hated Nazi-ism until I came to this country. People are decent and civilized here."

A.R.P in the B.M.

The Reading Room of the British Museum was never very easy to enter. Today not only must one have a reader's ticket, but no person will be admitted unless he carries a gas-mask.

Horse-box Bedrooms

A racecourse on the outskirts of Paris has been turned into an internment camp for Germans and Austrians. The Germans are accommodated on the paddock side, and sleep in the horse-boxes The Austrians' quarters are in the popular enclosure, and they are sleeping in the totalisator.

Increased Visibility

It has been proved that persons wearing or carrying some white addition to their clothes are visible at night, even when 20 yards away Hence the growing popularity of white gloves, white walking-sticks, scarves, and gas-mask containers.

" Not so Hard "

When a number of German officers arrived at a prison camp in England, a woman in a small group of spectators called out : " Hard luck, mate." One of the prisoners promptly retorted : " Not so hard ! "

Coloured Gas-masks

Gas-masks for children will soon be available in pastel shades. This, it is thought, will make them less repellent to their wearers.

Not for Every Day

After describing the products of Nazi field kitchens, a German press correspondent noted : "Other features of the soldiers' menus include tobacco, snuff, chocolates, sweets and strengthening drinks." But he added : " Of course, they are only given to soldiers who are subject to severe nerve strain."

New York Takes Precautions

The Federal Government has been asked to provide at least 200 anti-aircraft guns for the defence of New York against possible surprise attacks.

Hitler's Coffee

Among the consignments seized by the Contraband Committee, and coming up for judgement by the Prize Court, were 20 bags of coffee, weighing more than two tons, sent from Aden to Hamburg as a gift to Hitler from the King of the Yemen.

Polish Army in France

The Polish Ambassador in Paris, M. Lukasiewicz, has issued a proclamation calling upon all Poles between the ages of 17 and 45 to report to their nearest town hall.

Friendship Through Shaving

A Nazi broadcaster was trying to console his audience for the introduction of rationing. He said : " Ration cards help enormously to draw people nearer to each other. For example, now when we want a shave we have first to approach the mayor to get a ticket allowing us to buy shaving cream. Even the State takes an interest in the growth of our beard."

Gone to Berlin ; Back Soon

At the side door of the deserted German Embassy in London, a wooden notice inscribed " Special Division, Swiss Legation " is nailed over the brass plate announcing " Deutsche Botschaft." A policeman who enquired why the brass plate was not removed altogether was informed : " They told us to leave it ; they expected to be back before long." *(Daily Telegraph)*

Ready for Victory Celebrations

Many millions of fireworks which were ready for Guy Fawkes Day are being stored away in bomb-proof magazines, and will be available for victory celebrations.

Popularity of Gas Tests

At Kingston-on-Thames people queue up daily at the entrance to the gas chamber, opened for the purpose of letting them test the efficiency of their respirators. It was stated that people arrived somewhat nervously but left full of confidence.

Lindbergh on Arms Embargo

Colonel Lindbergh, hitherto a member of the isolationist school, now states that he is a convert to the lifting of the U.S. arms embargo.

No Radio for Jews

The confiscation of wireless sets owned by Jews in Germany has begun.

No Black-out in Belgium

All Belgian towns are to maintain their usual street lighting throughout the night. By day a big letter B in white canvas will be laid on the ground between the frontier and neighbouring villages.

Loyal Arabs

A message that the Palestinian Arabs will " abstain from all acts which could impede France or reflect on her interests " has been sent to the High Commissioner of Syria by the Grand Mufti of Jerusalem.

Defiance to U-Boats

Although some 150,000 tons of British shipping have been sunk, sometimes without warning, no British crew has refused to put to sea.

Possible False Alarm

The Shofar, the horn sounded by rabbis on the Day of Atonement, was silenced this year, in case it might be taken for an air-raid warning.

Radio Amateurs Close Down

Two thousand British amateur transmitting stations, as well as several hundreds operated by the Navy's Wireless Reserve, have become silent for the duration of the war.

" Blighty " Again

This weekly magazine, which was issued to the Services during the Great War, is to reappear on October 21. The cost of the first issue is being borne by Lord Nuffield.

Help in Palestine

Nearly 120,000 Jewish men and women, that is, a quarter of the entire Jewish population, registered for service in local defence and auxiliary services of the British Army in Palestine.

News in Greek

The B.B.C. is now broadcasting regular bulletins in Greek. This makes the thirteenth foreign language now being used by the British studios.

Taking Care of Hitler

A new battalion of bodyguards, the fourth, to accompany and protect Hitler during his visits to the Front, has been organized.

THE LITTLE RED FATHER. " Heil Kamerad ! Now that I've dealt with Poland, tell me what peace terms I am to dictate to the Democracies."

From the cartoon by Sir Bernard Partridge. By permission of the Proprietors of " Punch "

The Good Old Horse Comes Back

This horse had a rope halter by which it could be led in a black-out by a man walking beside it.

When her car was laid up owing to the petrol restriction, this lady did her weekly shopping on horseback.

In towns more than in the country the carriages of pre-car days proved more difficult to come by. This motorist, a tradesman in Westwood, Thanet, solved the problem by reducing his car to one horse-power.

HORSES, which for many years had been slowly disappearing from the London streets, had a remarkable " comeback " when the rationing of petrol took effect. On certain thoroughfares they had been altogether banned, but on September 27 the Minister of Transport announced that the ban would be lifted for the time being in view of the shortage of petrol and the consequent reduction in the number of motor vehicles available. In London it was chiefly for drawing transport vehicles that horses reappeared, but in the country many a pony trap and dog-cart were once more on the roads after being regarded for years only as lumber.

Such a scene as this at a traffic stop became quite common almost immediately after the rationing of petrol took effect, for cars were few on the streets and every horse-drawn van available was in use. At the beginning of the last war the case was very different. Petrol was not rationed, but the motor had not become nearly so general as of recent years. The horse was the mainstay of transport, and as the Army required very many horses for cavalry and transport many animals were requisitioned by the Government.

Photos, Universal Pictorial Press, B.I.P. Topical and Photopress

Women's Work That Guards the Home Skies

Making the envelope of a barrage kite balloon is the highly skilled work of these girls kneeling on the factory floor.

The making of the barrage balloons is largely done by women. In the centre photograph girls are at their machines in the sewing department with a specimen of their finished handiwork in the background. Above, left, some of the balloons are seen in a giant hangar. Right, some of these giant "sausages" are being taken out into the open to undergo their final trial for airworthiness.

Photos, Central Press

Silent Sentries Await the Raiders

WHEN the first air-raid warning sounded in London—later it came out that it was a lone machine carrying a high French official that caused all the pother—the people looked up with cheerful confidence at the balloons floating in the sky above their heads. Indeed, it is no exaggeration to say that they were amazed at the number of balloons forming the defensive network. There was a balloon barrage in the Great War, but it was a very small-scale affair, and the balloons were interconnected by a curtain of cables. Today, each balloon is a separate unit, rising from a mobile lorry on a single steel cable of great strength. The position of these units can be quickly changed when once the balloon has been grounded and deflated.

Although the photographs in this page all show balloons near ground level, these hydrogen-filled craft can be raised to a height of several thousand feet. The theory is that enemy warplanes, afraid of striking the cables—which are almost invisible—will be forced to fly above the barrage at a height where our anti-aircraft guns and fighters can deal with them. The close-up views above show clearly the three air-filled fins that steady the craft in the air.

The Tank Idea Triumphs Again

Some of the latest type of British tanks are here seen during manoeuvres. They are advancing towards a distant objective, so the pilot can therefore look out through the open conning tower. In battle this would be closed and the course would be directed by observation through a slot in the front of the tank.

It was on a September morning in 1916 during the Battle of the Somme that the first tanks lumbered across No Man's Land from the British lines and charged down upon the panic-stricken Germans. The enemy were quick to copy the British invention, and in 1939 the Nazis employed a very large number of tanks in their onslaught upon Poland. It is perhaps not too much to say that the striking and speedy success of the invaders was very largely due to their employment of those machines which proceeded from the fertile brain of Lt.-Col. E. D. Swinton, forcefully backed by Mr. Winston Churchill, in the early days of the Great War

An interesting development made by the Soviet army is the amphibian tank which can cross shallow rivers. In the centre photograph two of them are almost under water, looking more like submarines than tanks. Below, left, is one of the latest type of German tanks used with deadly effect against the Poles. Right, French tanks and tractors are being taken towards the front in the Maginot Line zone by train.

Photos, Fox, Planet News and Sport & General

'Old Hitler Gave Me a Headache'

During reconnaissance flights made by the R.A.F. on the Western
Front numberless "dog-fights" with German aircraft took place.
One of the most thrilling of these, when five R.A.F. machines
encountered 15 Messerschmitt fighters, was described in a Ministry
of Information bulletin on October 1.

THE wounded navigator of the
squadron-leader's 'plane summed
up the fight and the feelings of
the crew when he said, "Old Hitler's
given me a bit of a headache, but that's
nothing to what we'll give him."

Orders had been given for an R.A.F.
patrol to reconnoitre a position behind
the German line in the most strongly
defended part of the Saar. Anti-aircraft
batteries put up a fierce barrage, but the
British aircraft went through it successfully.

When well over the frontier, at a height
of over 20,000 ft., the squadron-leader
sighted the enemy. Out from behind a
bank of cloud came nine Messerschmitt
fighters. They approached from directly
ahead, flying 2,000 ft. higher. Away on
the right another six swooped to attack.
Breaking formation, the Germans concentrated mass fire on each British
machine in turn.

Three of our machines were shot down.
Another made a forced landing, but out
of the 12 men forming the crews eight
were seen to escape by parachute.

The squadron-leader alone was left,
but he flew on just the same to finish
his job. Dodging, side-slipping and
banking, he got away from the concentrated enemy fire, but held the course

set for the reconnaissance. Meanwhile,
in the tail of the aircraft the air-gunner
kept up a steady fire. A stream of bullets
hit the engine of the leading Messerschmitt. The enemy machine swerved,
and in a second burst into flames and
plunged to earth. Keeping up his fire,
the gunner landed further bursts into a
second fighter. With black smoke pouring from the nose it went down in a spin.
Two hundred and fifty rounds of ammunition had accounted for two enemy
aircraft. Shaken by the gunner's steady
and accurate fire, the 13 remaining
Germans gave up the fight.

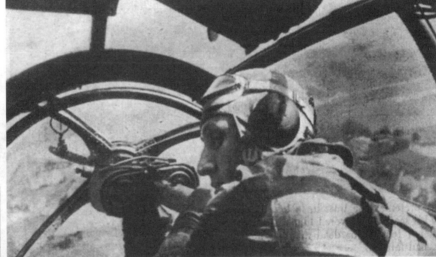

The navigator, the third member of
the crew, kept his pilot on the homeward course, though his instruments
were smashed and he himself was wounded
in the forehead.

The aircraft, when it landed, had 80
bullet holes in the fabric, the ailerons
and rudder were damaged, both petrol
tanks were burst and flooding the inside
of the fuselage with petrol and fumes. As
they crossed the frontier the engine
failed. From the starboard tank petrol
poured through a bullet hole each time the
aircraft banked, but by stopping up the
hole with his handkerchief the pilot was
able to save enough petrol to get home.

As the machine touched down it spun
in a circle, cartwheeled over on one
wing and caught fire. The navigator
was flung out on his head with his clothes
on fire. The gunner was jammed inside,
but the navigator hauled him out and
smothered his blazing coat with bare
hands. The squadron-leader had been
flung clear and was picked up dazed but
not seriously hurt.

**Fairey Battle bombers—a flight of which are seen in the lower photograph—were the type of
R.A.F. aircraft involved in the air combat described in this page. The other photograph shows
a German machine-gunner on the alert.**
Photos. Wide World and Fox

I WAS THERE!

I Saw an Air-Liner Passenger Shot

On September 26 a Dutch air-liner flying from Malmo to Amsterdam was attacked in error by a German seaplane, and one of the passengers, Mr. Gustave Lamm, a Swedish engineer, was killed by machine-gun fire. The heroine of the incident was the Dutch stewardess, Anny Wynoldt, whose story is reprinted here by the courtesy of the " Daily Express."

I HEARD rattling on the 'plane, and I hurried to Pilot Moll to ask him what was wrong.

The rattling was caused by German bullets. More came as I was on my way to the pilot, and one of these hit Mr. Lamm.

of rattling, and bullets flew round me. Some of the passengers smelled burning. I said it was a small defect in the machine.

Nobody else knew that the machine had been struck by fifty bullets. The passengers knew nothing of the attack until we landed.

These photographs illustrate the tragic incident off Denmark when a Dutch air-liner was fired on by a German military 'plane. The "air hostess" (Miss Wynoldt), whose account is given in this page, is in the centre of the group below. Second from right is the Captain, J. J. Moll, famed for his part in the 1934 air race to Melbourne. The liner involved—an American type—is seen top left; top right, bullet-holes in the fuselage.

Photos, Associated Press and Wide World

I pretended he was ill, laid him back in his seat, and covered him with a rug. Then I tended the dead man as though he had fainted.

I gave the other passengers papers and books, and talked to them about everyday things with a smile on my face, but with death in my heart, because I was the only one who knew what had happened.

When passengers asked me about the rattling, I said the aerials had got loose.

I had a terrible moment when I went into the pantry. There was another burst

With the French Troops in Germany

Towards the end of September the French had advanced into the " No Man's Land " in front of the Maginot Line, and had penetrated into German territory at several points. Mr. Kenneth Downs, a " Daily Express " special correspondent, one of the first group of newspapermen to visit the front lines on the Western Front, tells of the fine spirit of the French troops.

THIS dispatch is being written at a spot east of the Franco-German frontier which I am not at liberty to disclose, but it is where actual hostilities are in progress.

I have already witnessed an action along the front. I picked up a box of German matches and a French corporal gave me an abandoned Nazi flag he had

taken as a souvenir. I have heard intermittent firing up in the front lines throughout the day, and it is continuing now that dusk is beginning to fall.

A French observation balloon was brought down by a German 'plane a few minutes before arrival at our point of the frontier, but the French observer parachuted to safety.

At another point near the border we saw French anti-aircrafters in action against three German reconnaissance 'planes flying very high. The 'planes fled from range as black streaks and white puffs from two types of anti-aircraft shells appeared magically in the skies.

I understand that one of these 'planes was brought down at another point.

My real thrill of the day was witnessing the bringing in of a captured German officer. I just glimpsed him as he was rushed up in a tiny car to a point behind the lines and turned over to a French colonel of the Intelligence service and whisked from view.

But I saw him long enough to notice his glum features. He wore a peaked officer's cap on straw-blond hair, a field green overcoat and high quality boots. I judged him to be at least a captain. . .

On the French side general mobilization is complete. I thought I knew what mobilization meant, but when I actually glimpsed it I was completely staggered by its proportions.

Naturally I cannot disclose the names, but I can say I have seen troops from all parts of France and from all parts of the French Empire and of all military ages.

I was greatly impressed by the deadly businesslike attitude of the troops. They look good and tough.

In Spain, wherever I passed troops who were not fighting they were always singing or indulging in some sort of horseplay. I saw none of this today. The troops we passed in villages, camps or on roads were lynx-eyed, expressionless, with no illusions about what was coming, but believe me they are ready for it.

A lieutenant-colonel of the Second Bureau said : " The troops are the best I have ever seen. Theirs is a much healthier attitude than the 1914 ' On to Berlin ' nonsense. They know what it means this time. They are angry and they mean business."

French anti-aircraft gunners are here seen at the alert behind their gun, in its emplacement somewhere in the vicinity of the Maginot Line. Their appearance bears out the tribute paid to the French troops in this page : " they are angry, they mean business."
Photo, Topical

Officers and men everywhere confirmed that the German prisoners captured during the first days were completely bewildered, hardly knowing that war existed or what they were fighting about.

to carry us farther on. Then we decided to return to Rumania, hire a taxi and try our luck at the neighbouring frontier post of Zaleszczyki.

It was dark when our taxi, with lights out, crossed the bridge over the Dniester and came to a halt at the Zaleszczyki barrier. And there, to our utter dismay, who should be waiting to receive us but the bearded sleuth from Sniatyn.

" Aha," he exclaimed with stage-villainish glee, as he flashed his torch in our faces, " we meet again ! " Then, turning to a group of frontier guards, who had come up behind him, he coolly denounced us as spies.

Cowards die many times before their death. Call me a coward if you like, but if ever I felt dead and done for it was then. To be suspected as a spy was bad enough ; to be denounced as one was infinitely worse.

There had been so many cases where the police shot first and inquired afterwards—if they troubled to inquire at all.

They dragged us from the taxi, stuck revolvers in our backs, shouted " Hands up ! " and marched us to the parapet of the bridge.

The Dniester sounded very far below. A long drop.

The bearded man, who had vanished in the darkness, now reappeared with the chief of police, who began to shout at us in Polish :

" You speak German, don't you ? "

" Not a word," we both lied. " Only English and French."

A man who spoke very broken English was brought along to interrogate us. After a few questions and answers he said to me, " If you are really English, why do you speak English so badly ? "

They Arrested Me as a German Spy

Crossing the frontier into Rumania in the wake of the retreating Polish Government and the diplomatic corps came the newspaper correspondents. Among them was William Forrest, of the " News Chronicle," who tells how, in the general panic, he and an American colleague were held on suspicion of espionage.

THE scope and the accuracy of the German bombing in Poland said much for the work of the enemy spies. No wonder there was something approaching spy mania behind the Polish lines. . . .

Vigilance was greatest along the frontier. When I re-entered Poland at Sniatyn along with an American colleague we came under the suspicious eye of a

big plain-clothes detective with a bushy, brown beard. Mysterious visitors called at our hotel during the night, quizzed the landlord about our movements, and then disappeared. When we telephoned we were forbidden to speak in any language but Polish.

Three days passed in this fashion, what time we hunted in vain for petrol

Carrying Government officials, the last train to leave Warsaw for Rumania was bombed and machine-gunned fourteen times by the Nazis on its way to the frontier. Above, the train is seen halted with the passengers who left it during one of the raids waiting to re-embark when the raiders had passed.
Photo, Planet News

Was it my Scots accent, or what ? Alas, that a rolling " r " should be my undoing '

Turning to the police, my critic expressed his doubts concerning me. I felt the revolver again, pressed against my back, and said my last prayer.

The police chief, thin-lipped, grey-eyed, a man without pity, kept us waiting in an agony of suspense and then rapped out an order which we did not understand.

Our taxi drove up and, still at the point of the revolver, we were pushed inside and driven to the police-station.

It took us four hours, during which our papers and effects were subjected to a microscopic examination, to convince them of our innocence. And in the end it was not our passports—which might have been forged—but some flattering references to ourselves clipped from a Warsaw newspaper that turned the scales in our favour.

Most of the " grilling " was done by candlelight, for the electricity suddenly failed, and while our own fate was still in the balance we heard the police in the room next door beating up another prisoner.

But after our innocence was established how charming they all became. Profuse apologies ; refreshments ; and two beds for the night.

Twenty-four hours later the Russians were marching on Zaleszczyki, and the man with the beard, the police chief and his men, and the detectives who examined us, were all fleeing across the bridge into Rumania. . . .

All U-Boat Commanders Are Not So Callous

From innumerable records of German ruthlessness, it is pleasant to turn aside and read again these stories of two U-boat commanders who, while carrying out their stern duty, treated with humanity and kindness the crews of the little British trawlers who were at their mercy.

M R. CHARLES ROBINSON, master of the 333-ton Fleetwood trawler " Rudyard Kipling," gave the following account, reprinted by the courtesy of the " News Chronicle," of the sinking of his ship in the Atlantic :

" We were busy trawling on Saturday night when the bos'n shouted, ' Submarine to starboard.' The submarine signalled ' Abandon Trawler,' and we had no option but to take to our boat.

" The submarine came near and took on board my crew. Five Germans then got into our boat and rowed to the trawler. They took possession of all fresh provisions, including two boxes of fish, and also ' rescued ' the ship's cat.

" Then two time bombs were placed at the trawler's water line and the boat then set off for the submarine. When the boat had come 300 yards, the ' Rudyard Kipling ' blew up and sank.

" The trawler crew were then accommodated in the submarine and, taking the small boat in tow, the submarine started for land. We were all supplied with greatcoats by the submarine crew, and when the commander found that one of my men was without a coat, he took off his own and handed it to him.

" We were supplied with hot soup and cigars, and an hour later a ration of rum was served. This was repeated two hours later.

" At 3.45 a.m. today, the submarine stopped and the commander ordered us to get into the small boat. We had then been eight hours in the U-boat.

" The submarine stood by until the boat was baled dry. Then the U-boat crew waved us goodbye and the vessel submerged.

" We reached the shore at 9 a.m."

H ERE is the story of an encounter with an enemy submarine whose commander changed his mind, related by Mr. Albert Thomason, skipper of the trawler " Alvis," when eventually she reached port. It is reprinted here by courtesy of the " Evening News."

" At 1.20 in the afternoon I saw a shell drop short of the ship and then I saw a German U-boat.

" The commander waved to us from his conning tower to abandon ship. I ordered the crew to get a boat overboard and we pulled well clear of the trawler.

" The submarine commander ordered us alongside and told me to come on board. He extended his hand and said, ' Good afternoon, captain.' .

" We shook hands and he said, ' I am sorry, I will have to sink your ship.' He asked me if there were any more men in the Alvis ' and if that was the only boat we had.

" They handed cigarettes round to my boat crew and then the commander sent us back to the trawler with a German working party under the lieutenant.

" The Germans threw over the side half the wireless and smashed the rest with a big hammer.

" They also smashed the dynamo in the engine-room. They did not take any provisions and they did not touch the fish we had on board.

" The lieutenant asked for one of our lifebuoys for a souvenir, and we shook hands through the ring of the buoy.

" The commander sent a bottle of gin across, with his compliments. I asked for his name, but he sent a message that he regretted he was unable to tell me.

" The crew had a good growth of beard as if they had been at sea for some time, but they were well dressed and well fed."

Another member of the crew said : " The Germans told us to go back to our ship as they did not think we would be safe, 13 of us, in that boat."

One of the North Sea trawlers, which in this war, as in the last, are playing a very gallant part at sea, is seen above. In this page the skipper of a trawler tells the story of his humane treatment by a U-boat commander. Such treatment, unfortunately, has not been general.
Photo, Wide World

Million A.A. Shells in the Making

Shell cases for 3·7 in. anti-aircraft guns are being weighed in this photograph. Each one must be of the exact weight specified.

In the photograph top right the interior of 3·7 in. shells is being examined with a bright light. Centre, right, shell cases are being placed on a conveyor after being dried by compressed air. Immediately above is a huge store of shell cases ready to be sent to the filling factory.

Photos, P.N.A.

THE photographs in this page were taken at a factory in the Midlands converted from commercial purposes to the production of munitions. In this factory only 3·7 anti-aircraft shells are made, and it has a capacity of 1,000,000 shells a year. There are many munition factories in the industrial areas of the United Kingdom, some of them, like this one, originally built and equipped for commercial work, but speedily adapted to the purposes of war, while others have been specially built and equipped with new machinery. A striking feature of modern munition works is the ease with which the machinery is operated. The various processes are almost automatic, so that in a few weeks men with no previous experience of such work can acquire all the necessary skill and turn out first-class work. The adjusting and maintenance of the machines are, of course, done by some of the most skilled mechanics.

OUR DIARY OF THE WAR

Monday, October 2

M. Munters, Latvian Foreign Minister, arrived in Moscow at the invitation of Molotov.

A Soviet military mission arrived in Tallinn, Estonia, to discuss mutual relations.

That **R.A.F. 'planes flew over Berlin** during a night reconnaissance flight was reported by the Air Ministry.

The French High Command reported that local enemy attacks had been repulsed.

U.S. Senate opened the debate on the Neutrality Bill.

British freighter " Clement " reported to have been sunk by a German armed raider or a vessel termed a " cruiser."

Belgian steamer " Suzon " sunk during Sunday night by a U-boat.

Swedish steamer " Gun " reported sunk in the Skagerak by a U-boat.

Twenty-three tribunals began to deal with the 50,000 enemy aliens registered in the London area.

Tuesday, October 3

Count Ciano returned from Berlin and reported to the Italian Cabinet.

Mr. Chamberlain stated in the House of Commons that nothing in the German " peace offensive " could modify the attitude which Great Britain had felt it right to take.

German territory occupied by the French was announced by the French High Command to total 154 square miles.

M. Sarajoglu, Turkish Foreign Minister, still in Moscow and stated to be awaiting instructions from Ankara on the proposals of the Soviet Government.

The Turkish military mission arrived in London and began discussions on matters of common interest to Great Britain and Turkey.

The Lithuanian Foreign Minister, M. Urbsys, arrived in Moscow at the invitation of Molotov.

It was reported that a Dominican coast-guard cutter, caught refuelling a U-boat, had been sunk by a French cruiser.

Wednesday, October 4

German Reichstag summoned to meet on Friday.

Karlsruhe said to have been evacuated, the seventh German city behind the Siegfried Line to be converted into a military base.

Minor enemy attacks on the Western Front were repulsed.

German High Command reported that fighting was still taking place against isolated Polish detachments near the line of demarcation.

Italy maintained complete silence on the subject of the Hitler-Ciano meeting in Berlin.

Mr. Eden announced that the Dominion Governments are each sending a Cabinet Minister to London to confer with the British Government on the co-ordination of resources.

The crew of a Greek ship, " Diamantis," which had been torpedoed the day before, were landed by the U-boat on the west coast of Ireland.

Reported that Germans had captured four Swedish steamers in the Baltic.

British steamer " Glen Farg " sunk by U-boat.

Thursday, October 5

French Command reported a 7-hour battle in the Moselle Valley.

Hitler flew to Warsaw to review Nazi troops who had taken part in the siege.

A pact of mutual assistance between the Soviet Union and Latvia was signed in Moscow.

Soviet-Turkish talks reported to be held up.

French submarine arrived safely in port with a German merchant ship captured 1,000 miles from the coast.

Washington announced that a warning of the imminent sinking, in the same manner as the " Athenia," of the American steamer " Iroquois," had been received from the head of the German navy.

Mr. Chamberlain consulted with T.U.C. leaders on war work control.

THE POETS & THE WAR
III
FATHERS AND SONS

By LOUIS N. PARKER

Comrades, though no bugle sound,
  Though you hear no tramp of feet,
Feel no shaking of the ground,
  Nor the drum's inspiring beat,
We, who marched the selfsame way
  Long ago in manhood's pride,
We are with you here to-day,
  Marching at your side.

We are nought and less than nought,
  Airy shapes you cannot see,
Shadows of a wistful thought,
  Waifs of waning memory :
You, the sons of tragic years,
  Had no father's hand as guide,
We, while you were born in tears,
  Fought for you, and died.

Now the love you never knew
  Round your hearts its yearning pours,
We, your fathers, watching you,
  Send our spirits into yours ;
Ah, fulfil what we began,
  Thrust the gates of Freedom wide !
With your fathers to a man
  Marching at your side.

—*The Times.*

Ministry of Information issued the account of the escape and safe return of a British submarine practically disabled by enemy depth charges.

Swedish Government announced that 100 cargo steamers would be armed for coastal patrol.

Friday, October 6

The Admiralty made a strong protest against the " warning " by Admiral Raeder with regard to the American steamer " Iroquois." Washington reported that U.S. destroyers had been sent to meet the vessel as a precautionary measure.

Hitler announced his " peace " plan to the Reichstag. It included the proposal that a conference should be held to discuss questions arising out of the " collapse " of Poland, Germany's claims to colonies and the limiting of armaments.

A statement was later issued on the authority of the British Government that, although his proposals were " vague and obscure," they would be carefully examined, but that something more than words would be required from the German Government to establish confidence in Europe.

A conference of the Allied Commands was held in France.

Saturday October 7

Twelve German raids on the Western Front were repulsed during the night and early morning.

There was a series of artillery action on both sides between the Moselle and the Saar.

Dutch steamer " Binnendijk," bound from New York to Rotterdam, sunk by unrecognized means in English Channel.

Red Cross and St. John Fund for the Sick and Wounded reached the quarter million mark.

Reported that the £5,000,000 British loan to Poland was being used for war purposes by the Polish Government recently established in France.

Sunday, October 8

H.M. the King returned from a two-day visit to the Home Fleet.

Nazi trade delegation arrived in Moscow.

German flying boat brought down after a combat with a North Sea R.A.F. patrol.

Paris reported that French artillery were engaged in repulsing German patrol attacks, chiefly to the south-east of Zweibruecken.

Finland, under pressure, decided to send a delegate to Moscow to discuss political and economic problems.

Canada announced that a division of 20,000 men would leave for overseas early next year.

It is Said That . . .

Compulsory labour service for Jews in Germany is to be introduced.

No bombs could be more hated by the Nazis than leaflets dropped by the R.A.F.

Before evacuating Upper Silesia the Polish authorities inundated the coal mines.

Half of Poland's gold is being held temporarily by Rumania against the cost of accommodating refugees.

German authorities have had barbed wire erected all along the frontier to prevent mass desertions by Nazi soldiers.

The employment of over 500,000 Polish prisoners has greatly eased labour difficulties in German industry and agriculture.

The reported disgrace of Goebbels is said to be because he alone advised against Germany going to war.

Explaining the Soviet-German pact, Nazis stated : " Russia is no longer Communist. The last Reds have been ejected or shot."

The elusive German liner " Bremen " has been seen at the Russian Arctic port of Murmansk.

German soldiers, begging for food over the Dutch frontier, have been given it with the remark : " Eat, but may Hitler starve ! "

The Germans are experimenting with captive balloons that can be exploded from the ground and destroy near-by aircraft.

Since the alliance with Russia, amended editions of " Mein Kampf " are being hurriedly prepared.

About 10,000 Americans have been evacuated from the United Kingdom to U.S.A. and Canada since August 24.

" Gott Strafe England ! " has replaced " Heil Hitler ! " as a greeting between Germans, according to a Copenhagen paper.

Five hundred thousand portraits of Stalin have been sent from Moscow into the newly-occupied Polish territory.

French and German soldiers have been seen fishing on opposite banks of the Rhine. No shots were fired from either side.

A Basle report states that 25 per cent of the men in the Siegfried Line are ill with angina and rheumatism.

Germany is arranging to run a Zeppelin service for the transport of raw materials from Russia to German industrial centres.

Resentment is growing among the civil population of Austria, especially at Graz, where relatives of soldiers killed in action were ordered not to wear mourning.

The WAR ILLUSTRATED

Vol. 1   A Permanent Picture Record of the Second Great War   **No. 7**

Some very big guns are employed by the French army in the artillery duels that are constantly taking place on the Western Front. This huge piece of artillery, so cleverly camouflaged that from the air it might appear to be a tree trunk, is in action near Strasbourg, pounding the Siegfried Line, which from Basle to Karlsruhe lies on the right bank of the Rhine.

Photo, Central Press, British Movietone News

Poland Under the Heel of the Conqueror

Little more than a month after the first act of war, the Fuehrer of the Nazi Reich
entered Poland's capital as a conqueror. At almost the same hour the last of
the scattered outposts of Polish resistance hoisted the white flag of surrender.

ON October 5, while the smoke was
still rising from the ruins of the
city so terribly ravaged by his
bombers and artillery, the Fuehrer made
his triumphal entry into Warsaw. For
some days before men and women of the
civilian population had been conscripted
to help the labour corps of the invaders in
cleaning up the place. The streets had
been swept, the debris piled in heaps, and
the more dangerous structures demolished.
Nazi taskmasters had also seen to it that
such inscriptions as "Death to the
German invaders," scribbled on the
bare walls, were obliterated, and others—
"Death to Poland," for instance—substituted. Then the Gestapo had made, of
course, a most careful round-up of all the
dangerous or suspicious elements.

The Fuehrer travelled from Berlin to
Warsaw by air, and after inspecting the

guard of honour at the air-port he drove
into the city to the Plac Wolnosci,
situated in the diplomatic quarter. The
immediate neighbourhood was decorated
with green garlands, and there was little
to remind the conqueror of the havoc
that the siege had wrought. From those
sections of the city, the suburbs and the
business quarter, where the destruction
had been most terrible, the parade was
carefully shepherded.

At the close of the proceedings, the
Fuehrer issued an Order of the Day,
thanking the troops which had been
engaged in the Polish conquest. It read:

"On September 1 you fell into line, in compliance with my orders, to protect our Reich
against the Polish attack. In exemplary comradeship between army, air force and navy you
have fulfilled your task. You have fought
courageously and valiantly.

"Today I was able to greet the troops that
have participated in the conquest of Warsaw.
This day concludes a combat in keeping with the
best traditions of German soldiery. Together
with me the German people proudly thank you.
In unshakable confidence the nation again looks
to its armed forces and its leaders.

"We remember our dead who, like the 2,000,000
dead of the Great War, sacrificed their lives that
Germany might live. Under banners fluttering
in proud joy everywhere in Germany we stand
together more closely than ever and are tighten-
ing our helmet bands. . . . "

In his speech in the Reichstag the next
day, Hitler announced that Germany's
losses in the Polish campaign had been
10,572 killed, 30,322 wounded, and 3,400
missing. "With the fall of the fortresses
of Warsaw and Modlin," the Fuehrer
went on, "and the surrender of Hela,
the Polish campaign is ended." The result
of the struggle had been the complete
destruction of all the Polish armies.
"Now," he added, "694,000 prisoners
have begun to march towards Berlin."
A little later he paid a tribute to the
German navy which had carried out its

Incidents in the tragedy of the surrender of Warsaw are shown in the three photographs above. Top photograph, General Blaskowitz, commander of the Nazi forces that took the city, is giving instructions to a Polish general. Centre, Polish representatives are receiving the
conditions of surrender after the white flag had been hoisted over the city. In the bottom picture Nazi riflemen, occupying a point of vantage
near the capital, are picking off stragglers of the Polish army as they leave the doomed city.

Photos, Keystone and Wide World

Nazi Guns in Stricken Warsaw's Ruined Streets

Through an archway giving on a street in Warsaw we have a vision of what war means to a conquered people. Nazi field artillery entering the city is passing a house that was so badly damaged during the aerial bombardment that only the shell remains. A couple of passers-by stand in front of this relic of relentless warfare against civilians, and watch with apparent indifference a march past meant as an impressive military demonstration to overawe the conquered city.

Photo, Associated Press

The Warsaw garrison fought to the last, and here they have put up one of those street barricades that represent the forlorn hope of defenders. But the doom of the city is already sealed, for against the sky clouds of smoke can be seen rising from fires caused by incendiary bombs.

before had been set high above them in the social scale.

Such Robin Hood tactics, however, did little to ingratiate the conquerors with the conquered, and the bad feeling was intensified by the conduct of members of the German minorities in Poland, who openly gloated over the triumph of the invaders, and of the officers—many of them were very young and quite fresh to service conditions—who were creating what was described as a reign of terror in the country districts, seizing the crops and any provisions on which they could lay their hands.

Everywhere, moreover, there were the agents of the Gestapo looking for those who refused to disclose stores of food and fuel, and those suspected of still being patriotic after all their city and country had gone through.

duties in the " battles " around Wester-platte, Gdynia, Oxhoetf, and Hela.

Shortly before, the German High Command had announced the surrender of the last remnant of the Polish Army—a little force of some 8,000 men who had held out at Kock, east of Deblin, to the south-east of Warsaw, under General Kleber.

While the carefully-groomed German soldiers were goose-stepping in triumph past the Fuehrer, in another quarter of Warsaw troops of the disarmed garrison were still trudging on their way to the prison camps. A little more than a month before, the city they were leaving had been their country's pride, the home of a million people. Now it was half destroyed ; its streets were strewn with the rubbish of its palaces and humble homes alike ; many of its great buildings were little more than shells, smoke-blackened and bomb-shattered ; great numbers of its people had suffered a terrible death.

Through the ruined streets, as soon as dark fell, prowled bands of looters. The worst of the plunderers, indeed, did not have to wait till nightfall, for in their rapine they were acting under the orders of the conquerors, breaking open the closed homes and shuttered shops, and stealing from them valuable furniture, paintings and bric-à-brac to be dispatched to the Reich as spoils of war.

There were strange tales of members of the Warsaw underworld having been patronized by the Nazi conquerors—of being fed and clothed with the good things torn from those who until a few days

The fortress of Modlin made a gallant stand against the Nazis, but eventually surrendered, negotiations being opened on September 27. In this photograph German bombers are making an onslaught on the position to prepare for an infantry attack. On the right of the column of smoke that rises from the bombs, is a portion of the fortress.

Photos, Mondiale

Sorry 'Triumph' in a City of the Dead

On October 5 Hitler visited Warsaw and watched the triumphal march of Nazi troops in the Plac Wolnosci, which by a strange irony means " Freedom Square." This photograph shows troops converging on the saluting base along the Aleja Ujazdowska, in the aristocratic quarter of Warsaw, and the one which had been least damaged by the fury of war. The streets were lined with troops, but the entire absence of civilians was an eloquent reminder that Warsaw was to them a city of the dead. In the foreground is the Three Crosses church with soldiers on the roof to guard against possible " incidents."

Photo. Associated Press

German Towns Whose Citizens Have Had to Quit

Here in this page are pictures of some of the towns in Western Germany which were evacuated following French attacks. All of them are important industrial or mining centres which the Germans can ill afford to lose. (1) Saarlouis is a coal-mining centre. (2) Pirmasens has as its chief industry the manufacture of boots and shoes. (3) Löwenthal is a mining district. The sloping shaft of a pit is seen. (4) Karlsruhe has important locomotive and rolling-stock works. (5) Puttlingen lies a few miles north of Saarbruecken, and is a mining town. (6) Saarbruecken, a coal-mining centre, was the first big German town to be menaced by the French.

Photos, Wide World, E.N.A. and G.P.A.

'A Very Curious War' in the West

Preparation rather than action continued to be the keynote of the war on the Western Front. From behind their fortified lines the two belligerents watched every move made by the enemy—watched each stroke and sought to meet it by some counter-measure.

"THIS is a very curious war." The expression was often on the lips of those who remembered the conditions of 1914–1918 and compared them with those which prevailed during the first six weeks of the war of 1939. Still there was no sign of a struggle on the grand scale. Week after week went by, and still the war on the Western Front was an affair of outpost engagements, of patrols pushed out into No Man's Land, of long-range artillery duels, of aerial reconnaissances and of an occasional "dog-fight" above the lines. Only once or twice in those early weeks did French and Germans come to grips, and then there were reports of fierce fighting with the bayonet in the darkness split by the flashes of the guns.

On the whole there was little activity such as would make a good story for the newspapers. Both sides were sending out feelers in preparation for the struggle which might come tomorrow or the day after, or possibly weeks or months hence.

The Tale of Casualties

The fact that only small forces had been engaged was evidenced by the smallness of the casualties. Thus during the first month the German casualties in killed and wounded were estimated at about 3,000, with some 150 prisoners; while the French losses were probably smaller. In the last war such casualties might have been incurred in what the communiqués would have called a quiet day!

On the German side of the front there was still considerable activity in strengthening the defences constituting the Siegfried Line. Reports from neutral observers told of mysterious screens, of freshly-erected pill boxes, of fields scarred with newly-dug trenches. Now and again there were stories of troop concentrations, especially behind the Belgian frontier, and reports continued to come in of a large number of aircraft stationed in the neighbourhood of Aachen. Particularly in the north, where the Siegfried Line faces Belgium and stretches away towards the Dutch frontier, the evidences of strengthening with civilian labour were

The French end of a bridge across the upper Rhine is guarded by a soldier in a sand-bagged look-out.
Photo, Pathé Gazette

The French barrage balloon in the centre photograph has a corrugated case to help in keeping its nose to the wind. In the photograph below left, French gunners are loading a howitzer during a bombardment of the German lines. Next it is a scene outside the French General Headquarters. General Gamelin, the figure on the left of the photograph, is leaving his car after a tour of inspection.
Photos, Topical and Keystone

warned over the telephone from Coblenz of their approach. So, unscathed, the British warplanes held on along the Belgian border and on to where the Rhine turns west into Holland. There, as the weather was too bad for them to make further observations, they flew on to the North Sea coast of Germany; and thence, carefully avoiding flying over neutral Holland, made for the landing-field previously arranged for their reception in England.

Meanwhile, the other two aeroplanes in the reconnaissance had been favoured by better weather, and had returned to their aerodrome in France with a set of photographs of the utmost value for any future attack.

most marked. What this activity portended no observer could be sure. It could hardly be that the Germans anticipated an Allied attack on the Reich through the neutral countries, though the possibility of such a stroke might be held out to the German people as an incentive to their zeal. Other observers hinted that the Nazi High Command was still toying with the idea of turning the flank of the French in the Saar past Maastricht and Brussels, in which case the northern section of the Siegfried Line would constitute the pivot on which the army of invasion would turn.

R.A.F. Above the Siegfried Line

Following rumours of the evacuation by the Germans of Karlsruhe and many more of the towns and villages of the Rhineland, big troop movements near Aachen, significant concentrations of aircraft, and intensive building of fortifications near the Luxemburg frontier, the R.A.F. Command in France decided to carry out daylight reconnaissance flights along the entire course of the German frontier from the French front to the North Sea.

Leaving one of the secret British aerodromes " somewhere behind the Maginot Line," four machines set out in pairs. The first two got into bad weather, but through the gaps in the clouds they were able to look down on the French artillery pounding the fringes of the Siegfried Line.

The clouds, indeed, helped them on their flight, and they were able to dodge the anti-aircraft barrage at Coblenz. The shells burst all around them, but the 'planes were not hit, and they were similarly fortunate when they encountered another stormy reception above Siegburg, whose defences had been

The towns and villages of Northern France have abundant proof of the magnitude of Britain's war effort, and they are giving her soldiers a very friendly welcome. In the upper photograph a long train of Bren gun carriers is passing towards the front. Below, a Frenchwoman makes a generous distribution of grapes.

Photos, British Official, Crown Copyright

Sunshine and Rest-Time with the Troops in France

Many of the scenes which live in the memory of those who fought in France in 1914–1918 will be recalled by these photographs of troops in France in 1939. Here a happy band of soldiers have found a resting place in some disused stables. The pleasing photograph on the right shows nurses usefully filling in the time while they are off duty, while below a number of men are taking a rest after a gruelling march.

Photos, British Official, Crown Copyright

If It's Contraband It Won't Get to Germany

Day and night the blockade of Germany goes on—not by prowling submarine but by the
far more effective method of contraband control. Not a ship can reach a German port by the
North Sea unless she has passed through the thin grey line of the British navy.

STEAMING up the Channel they come, ships flying the flags of many neutral nations. Arrived off Weymouth they anchor in the Bay and each hoists to her masthead a red and white blue-bordered flag. This is the flag which signifies that she is awaiting examination by the officers of the British Contraband Control ; and the flag must remain hoisted until her cargo has been approved and the British Navy have granted her clearance papers.

Bound for ports all over Europe, the neutral ships come to Weymouth or to the other two contraband bases in British waters—Kirkwall, in the Orkneys, and the

Arrangements for boarding and examining neutral ships for contraband are made in the "boarding room" at the ports at which the ships call. Above, officers of the Royal Navy and R.N.R. are in consultation in such a room about ship movements.
Photo, P.N.A.

Downs, off Ramsgate, on the Kent Coast. In the first six weeks of the war the daily average of neutral ships arriving in Weymouth Bay for examination was twenty. Many of these were allowed to pass after a brief inspection of the ship's papers, but out of a total of 74 vessels carrying 513,000 tons of cargo, 99,300 tons of cargo were seized as they embraced consignments of iron ore, fuel oil, petrol, manganese ore, and wheat.

The actual procedure may be illustrated by an account of what happens when a neutral ship puts in at Weymouth. Her approach, whether by day or by night, is signalled from Portland to the headquarters of the contraband base and a boarding party of two officers and six men sets out in a fishing drifter to board her. After apologizing to the captain for the delay and inconvenience, the boarding

officer asks him to produce the ship's papers, manifest, bills of lading and other documents. At the same time the wireless cabin is sealed, so that no signals can be made while the ship is in the control zone.

After satisfying themselves that the cargo corresponds with what it is stated to be in the ship's papers, the boarding party goes ashore and a summary of the ship's manifest, giving details of the cargo and the passengers carried, ports of origin and destination, and so on, are sent by teleprinter to the Ministry of Economic Warfare. Usually in the course of a few hours the Ministry's consent to the ship's release is received and the boarding party goes out again to return the ship's papers to the captain, together with a certificate of naval clearance.

Only if the boarding party finds something suspicious does a search party go out to make a complete examination of the cargo. If the Ministry decides that the whole or part of the cargo is contraband, the ship is directed to proceed to a more convenient port, where the suspected cargo is taken into the custody of the Admiralty Marshal, who holds it until the Prize Court sits and comes to its decision as to its ultimate destination.

Weymouth, as mentioned above, is a voluntary base, but ships that do not call there of their own accord are intercepted by British warships and taken to the next contraband base in the Downs for examination. The third base, Kirkwall, in the Orkneys, is also a compulsory station. Thus no ship can enter the North Sea without first receiving the permission of the Royal Navy. There are also contraband bases outside British waters—for example, at Haifa, at one end of the Mediterranean, and at Gibraltar at the other.

What constitutes " contraband of war " was laid down in a Proclamation by the King issued on September 4. The list of goods, the import of which into enemy countries is completely prohibited, consists of : (a) All kinds of arms, ammunition, explosives, chemicals or appliances

suitable for use in chemical warfare ; (b) Fuel of all kinds and all contrivances for or means of transportation on land, in the water, or air ; (c) All means of communication, tools, implements, instruments, equipment, etc., necessary or convenient for carrying on hostile operations ; and (d) Coin, bullion, currency and evidences of debt. In addition to these articles constituting *absolute* contraband, there is what is called *conditional* contraband, comprising all kinds of food, foodstuffs, feed, forage, and clothing and articles and materials used in their production. These are seizable if they are obviously destined for an enemy country.

One Month's Seizures

In a typical week, the first week of October 1939, the British Contraband Control detained **25,000 tons of contraband** goods consigned to German ports. The cargoes included : 13,800 tons petroleum products ; 2,500 tons sulphur ; 1,500 tons jute ; 400 tons other fibres ; 1,500 tons feeding stuffs ; 1,300 tons oils and fats ; 1,200 tons foodstuffs ; 600 tons oilseeds ; 570 tons copper ; 430 tons other ores and metals ; 500 tons phosphates ; 320 tons timber. Quantities of other commodities were detained—copra, chemicals, cotton, wool, hides and skins, rubber, silk, gums and resins, tanning material, and ore-crushing machinery.

The tonnage of petroleum products— 13,800—is equivalent to about **3,600,000 gallons of petrol.** This amount should be added to the **24,000,000 gallons of fuel** captured by the British Contraband Control and the French Fleet in the first four weeks of war. The full effect of this seizure will be realized from the fact that a formation of fifty bombers would consume 4,000 gallons of petrol during an hour's flight.

The suppression of traffic in contraband of war must, of necessity, as Mr. Chamberlain said in his speech in the House of Commons on September 21, cause some inconvenience to neutrals, but it is Britain's intention to reduce it to a minimum.

The Prime Minister went on to claim that Britain's strict adherence to the rules of law is in striking contrast to the policy pursued by Germany. " No loss of life," he said, " has been caused by the exercise of British sea power, and no neutral property has been unlawfully detained. Germany's method of submarine warfare and the laying of mines on the high seas has already resulted in the death of many innocent victims, regardless of nationality, and in the unwarranted destruction of neutral property."

Getting a Stranglehold on Nazi Commerce

AKTIESELSKABET
DET OSTASIATISKE KOMPAGNI
(The East Asiatic Company Limited)

C O P Y   O F   M A N I F E S T .

Cargo shipped per DANISH Motor Ship   "DANMARK"   Captain E. H. CHRISTENSEN from ADEN to HAMBURG.

Shippers	Consignees	Marks & Numbers	No of Pcs	Description	Weight
Halal Shipping Co Ltd	H/O B/L OF HALAL SHIPPING Co LTD. Hodeidah	S. E. HERR HITLER PRESIDENT REPUBLIQUE GRAND ALLEMAGNE HAMBURG	20	Bags of Coffee	Kos. 2080

Aden, 12th August, 1939.

THE HALAL SHIPPING CO LTD

signed......G. PEEL

Agents of
Det Ostasiatiske Kompagni
(The East Asiatic Co Ltd)
Copenhagen

Most Germans have now to be content with coffee made from substitutes. The Fuehrer, however, must have the real thing, and here is a Danish ship's manifest disclosing a consignment of over two tons of coffee to Herr Hitler himself!

This barrel of wolfram is being removed from a ship under the direction of Naval and Customs officers. Left, officers and an armed guard going on board a ship which has been found to be carrying contraband.

BROADCASTING on October 1, on the results of the first month of war in the naval sphere, Mr. Winston Churchill, First Lord of the Admiralty, stated that, despite the large number of ships sunk in the first week of the conflict, the imports into Great Britain, thanks to the blockade, were larger than they would have been had there been no war ; in fact, during the four weeks of which he spoke, 150,000 more tons of merchandise were imported than would have entered the country in peacetime. The actual total contraband cargoes intercepted and brought into port by the British Navy during the first four weeks of the war, as stated by the Minister of Economic Warfare, was 289,000 tons. In addition, the French Navy accounted for 100,000 tons.

The ordinary procedure with neutral ships which may be carrying goods to the enemy is to conduct them under an escort of ships of the Royal Navy to a British port, where they are searched for anything which is contraband or conditional contraband. In this photograph a small paddle steamer usually employed as a pleasure boat is standing by after having put officers searching for contraband on board a foreign liner.
Photos, P.N.A.

With the Destroyers on Night Watch

In the British Navy's ceaseless watch upon the sea, one of the most important parts
is played by the destroyers, which prowl relentlessly in search of U-boats. Here we print
by permission from "The Times" a story of life in a destroyer during a night patrol.

A T midnight last night I became the first British journalist to go to sea in one of his Majesty's ships since war began. The Navy keeps its secrets, and not until I went aboard was I told that we were to form part of an escorting force.

"No. 1," the first lieutenant, shouts through a megaphone from the bridge: "Action stations." Officers and men, their wind-proof, thick coats with pointed cowls giving them the queer look of members of some strange brotherhood, quickly and quietly take up their fighting posts. One by one the control points report all correct. Torpedo tubes and guns are loaded, live shells stacked in readiness, searchlight and control circuits tested,

depth charges put into position. In wartime no ship of the Fleet sails without being prepared for instant action.

Up on the bridge the captain issues crisp commands. Gradually we gather way. It is completely dark, but we thread our way easily out of harbour to find our charge awaiting us. The only dim light is from the binnacle faintly lighting the face of the oilskinned quartermaster, who swings the ship now to port, now to starboard.

Just discernible ahead is a darker patch on the black water, and from it comes suddenly a stabbing speck of light, signalling us our course, station and speed.

"Twelve knots," says the captain, "one eight four revs." The engine telegraph clangs, the great turbines spin faster, and we and the other destroyers take up our appointed station.

Presently, when we are well out at sea, the captain orders "cruising stations" and two-thirds of the crew go below to rest before taking the later watches. But the captain remains on the bridge all night. For him there is no rest, no spell below till we are back in port again. Now, as we steam ahead, eight look-out men scan the water with big night glasses, reporting every object, every light.

There is little incident in the night watches. We pass a score or more ships, merchantmen and fishing boats, picked out black against silver now the moon has risen. Hour by hour passes as our escorting force slides almost silently, ghost-like, through the water, with scarcely a wisp of smoke from our funnels to betray our presence. At daybreak the bosun's pipe shrills, a raucous voice

shouts "Action stations," officers and men come on deck, and almost instantaneously all our armament is manned again, every gun and torpedo-tube loaded.

No enemy is in sight, but the Navy leaves nothing to chance, and it is part of the regular "drill" to test and check every part of a ship's armament and controls at dawn, just when attack is most to be expected. High above us an aircraft, out on the dawn patrol, swoops down to see our recognition markings, then, satisfied, turns away to resume her morning search of the ocean.

Half an hour later, we revert to cruising stations and soon the bustle of preparation for the men's breakfasts begins. They eat on two mess decks, seamen on one, stokers on the other. In the intervals between meals, the watch below sling their hammocks here, and sleep the contented sleep of men who must take their rest when they can find it. Six officers are in this ship, and it is a striking wartime point that the oldest of them is 54, the youngest member of the crew just over 18.

Up to now we have steamed at an average of 17 knots, zigzagging to dodge submarine attack, but when we reach our destination the escorting vessels swing round and set course for home. The captain orders more speed, and soon we are making 20 knots, sending a long, white wake behind us. This trip is ending, but in these waters destroyers are the policemen of the seas, and their work is never done. Tonight the ship will be at sea again.

The top photograph was taken on a destroyer searching for U-boats. The navigation officer is taking bearings while a naval rating stands by to transmit his orders through speaking tubes. Below are two of the destroyers engaged in searching the seas for U-boats. That in the foreground is making a turn at such a speed that it heels over sharply.

Photos, P.N.A.

By Sea and Air the Hunt for U-Boats Goes On

As soon as a submarine is spotted its fate can be sealed with reasonable certainty. Below, aeroplanes and destroyers are engaged in the hunt. Above is the final scene. A depth charge has been dropped, and while a column of water rises into the air, the warship that has made the hit steams away at full speed.

Photos, Fox and Central Press

By Sea and Air the Hunt for U-Boats Goes On

British Submarine's Gallant Fight for Life

One of the most gripping stories of the Navy in wartime is that which tells of the escape of a British submarine from the enemy patrols which hunted it from dawn to dusk. We retell it here in the words of " Naval Eye-Witness."

SINCE the surrendered German Fleet disappeared beneath the waters of Scapa Flow, theatrically scuttled by its own officers, there have been many mists over the North Sea.

One of these mists cleared recently to reveal a British submarine proceeding on patrol. Her log notes laconically that a full gale was blowing.

She observed a neutral fishing fleet riding out the gale at its nets, and dived beneath them to avoid unnecessary publicity. . . . At night she rose to the surface and her navigator, a Royal Naval Reserve Canadian Pacific man, observed the stars and fixed her position.

These uneventful happenings brought her, early one morning, to her allotted patrol area in enemy waters, and at the first hint of dawn she dived.

Shortly before breakfast the detonation of a depth charge quite close to her suggested emphatically that she was in the vicinity of enemy forces. Her captain decided to have a look at them through his periscope, and put his ballast pump in action.

Another depth charge promptly exploded much closer, blowing some of his fuses. It was unpleasantly obvious that he was being hunted. He stopped all his machinery, holding his breath, as it were, to listen.

The crew lay down to conserve valuable oxygen consumed by movement. During the next hour they counted the detonations of six explosions as the enemy groped about in search of them with sweep wires, electrically-operated bombs, and depth charges.

The submarine could do nothing except remain silent on the bottom, motionless. To relieve the monotony, it seemed good to the crew to start a 6d. sweepstake on the time at which the next explosion would shake the hull.

An able seaman moved softly down the narrow alley-way among the motionless men, booking their bets against next pay day.

The bombardment intensified. For the next hour the explosions averaged one every two minutes. They grew gradually more distant. Then there was a lull.

They Were Waiting for the End

About tea-time the strained, weary men in the submarine heard a wire scraping over the after jumping-stay. . . . They listened, tense, expectant.

A series of bumps thudded along the hull as if a giant were stamping along it in hobnailed boots.

Then what they awaited happened. A shattering explosion seemed to contract the hull of the submarine as their own hearts contracted.

All lights were extinguished, there was everywhere the crash of broken glass, and in the silence that followed the sound of water spurting and the hiss of air escaping from the high-pressure air-system.

Portable electric lights revealed enough of the catastrophe. One motor and both engines were out of action. From half a dozen leaks in the air-system air hissed as from a punctured tyre.

Working as noiselessly as possible, they contrived to restore the lighting, and stop the air leaks as best they could.

Then, the air gradually growing fouler because they had been a long time submerged, they sat or lay about waiting.

The First Lieutenant bethought him of a bottle of boiled sweets, and passed them round as a solace. It reminded someone else of a bag of peppermint-drops he possessed. He crept round the dripping spaces offering them to his shipmates, who sucked them appreciatively. The air was making breathing more difficult every minute.

In the meantime, the lieutenant in command was deciding on his course of action. As soon as he knew by the clock that darkness had fallen on the face of the sea, he mustered his little band of officers and men and told them of his decision.

To stay where they were meant to die the death of rats in a trap.

If the ballast tanks still held—and in his heart he doubted it—he intended to blow the water out of them and rise to the surface. Once there, although his ship was helpless as a log, he intended to fight to the death.

The crew accepted the alternative joyfully. Exchanging gasping jokes among themselves, they turned-to, loaded the torpedo-tubes, Lewis-gun and rifles, and stacked ammunition ready for the gun.

As a last grim measure they prepared a demolition charge to blow their ship to pieces rather than let her fall into the hands of the enemy.

Finally, when all was ready for what they believed would be their last fight, they blew the tanks and the submarine rose floundering to the surface.

In spite of their efforts to stop the leaks, enough air had escaped inside the submarine from the air cylinders to raise the pressure to a dangerous point.

Mindful of this, her captain, who is lightly built, had to guard against the danger of being blown through the hatch when it was opened. He selected a 14-stone signalman to cling to his legs and, thus " anchored," threw open the hatch.

So great was the rush of air that it blew his heavy binoculars, which hung by a strap, vertically above his head. He climbed out and looked anxiously about him. It was a clear night with a moderate swell. There was nothing in sight.

Limping Home to Port

With periscope gone, wireless smashed, communication pipes crushed as if squeezed by the fist of a giant, and engines disabled, unable to dive again and with only one motor in action, even now the prospect was grim enough.

He crawled away from the scene on his remaining motor, while the warrant engineer below began a desperate attempt to put life into his distorted and damaged machinery. Three hours after they had surfaced he reported the starboard engine ready, and two hours later the port.

They had now, thanks to this man and his devoted little staff, a fighting chance of life. With water still pouring in from the leaks, the captain gallantly made his way on the surface all night. In the dawn his wireless operator modestly reported that he had repaired the wireless. Their first thought was to send a

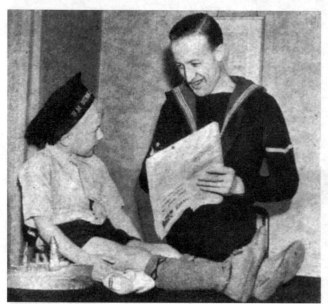

Telegraphist Aspinall Wilson, who was a wireless operator on the British submarine that limped home, tells the story to his small nephew. He spent the hours below water in repairing the installation.

Photo, Fox

These Are Always Ready for U-Boats

Depth charges are dropped overboard by mechanical "throwers" such as that seen above, which hurl them well clear of the destroyer. Left is a row of "throwers" made in Australia for the British Navy. Below, depth charges are placed in position on deck.

warning to sister submarines on patrol in the vicinity to avoid temporarily the area where trouble could be had for less than the asking.

After that, another to their base, asking for a helping hand.

Lying on the surface like a wounded duck, they saw in the afternoon a flight of enemy bombers approaching them. Wearily they again made preparations for the fight that must finish them.

The 'planes passed a couple of miles to seaward and disappeared. An hour later they returned. Once more the gun was manned, rifles distributed. The enemy disappeared again without seeing them.

The call for help brought destroyers racing across the North Sea to a rendez-vous they reached at midnight. Cruisers and an aircraft carrier appeared with the daylight and a few hours later the Fleet, terrible in its might, arrived to the support of its wounded cub.

An air attack by the enemy bombing 'planes crumpled under the anti-aircraft fire of the cruisers and the attacks of the fighters sent up by the carrier.

In due course the submarine returned to her base without further molestation.

The lieutenant in command found a letter awaiting him. It was from a relative in the country. "We hardly realize there is a war on," read the opening sentence.

He folded it reflectively and put it in his pocket to answer a little later.

Above is a scene on the deck of a destroyer at sea with depth charges being hoisted into position by means of a davit. Any warship dropping such charges does so at a speed that enables it to be some distance away before the tremendous concussion caused by the explosion is felt. On the right of the photograph can be seen some of the torpedo tubes which form the destroyer's main armament against surface vessels.

Photos, Associated Press, Central Press and Charles Brown

The Siegfried Line, the Nazis' One Hope

In the hope of checking the gradual advance of the French into her territories Germany massed the troops withdrawn from Poland behind the Siegfried Line. In the upper photograph a German howitzer is in action behind the line, but, as French artillery is markedly superior, many such big guns have been put out of action. In the photograph above, a German soldier is handing down his rifle before entering an underground passage leading to the concrete fortifications.

Photos, Fox and Keystone

The French on the Frontier and Over It

On the southern length of the western battle front the French and Germans face each other across the Rhine, which is here comparatively narrow, as can be seen in the upper photograph showing a French observation post on its banks. In the lower photograph French troops are in a communication trench. Before the Allied advance the church and war memorial were German, for this photograph was taken in German territory now occupied by the French.

Photos, Central Press, British Movietone News

WORDS THAT HISTORY WILL REMEMBER

Saturday, September 30

His Holiness POPE PIUS XII in an address to a deputation of Poles :

I am most sorrowful that hundreds of thousands of human beings were made to suffer in Poland.

We want still to hope, despite the fact that there are many reasons to believe to the contrary, on account of plans by an enemy of God which are only too well known, that Catholic life will continue with deep and fervent meaning in Poland.

In her agitated history Poland has known periods of apparent death, but she has also known many days of recovery and new life.

There are hundreds of thousands of poor human beings suffering as a result of this war against which all our efforts—as you must realize—have been persistently but fruitlessly directed for the purpose of preserving Europe and the world.

Before our eyes at this moment passes a vision of mad folly and horrible despair.

We visualize the multitude of refugees and wanderers who have lost their country and their hearts. We hear the desperate cries of mothers and brides who are weeping for their dear ones fallen on the field of battle.

We hear the lamentations of old sick men, the cries of babies who no longer have any parents, and the cries of wounded men and the death-rattle of dying people who were not all combatants.

There is one thing which has never been seen in your glorious history—an unfaithful Poland.

We will not cease to repeat that it will be possible finally through means of justice and charity—and only through these means—to restore peace to a troubled world, peace for which millions of sincere souls are lifting prayers.

Monday, October 2

His Grace the ARCHBISHOP OF YORK in a Broadcast :

. . . The Prime Minister has said that the word of Herr Hitler is not in our eyes worth the paper it is written on ; he has broken too many promises ever to be trusted again. The series of broken pledges is vividly present to all our minds, from the militarization of the Rhineland in breach of the Treaty of Locarno which he had himself reaffirmed, to the rape of Czecho-Slovakia and the device whereby he accused the Poles of rejecting proposals which had never even been submitted to them. This is a series of outrages upon foreign States. Even more fraught with shame and with unworthiness to speak for a great people like the German is the record of scandalous action at home.

It is a custom in France to use dates as the names of men and events ; Danton was proud to be called the man of the tenth of August— the date when the French Revolution entered on its final phase. Napoleon III is spoken of as the Man of December ; the reign of Louis Philippe as the July Monarchy. We should similarly think of Hitler and his colleagues as the men of the twenty-second of August, 1932 ; of the twenty-seventh of February, 1933 ; of the thirtieth of June, 1934 ; of the twenty-fifth of July, 1934 ; of the third of March, 1938 ; of the eighth of October, 1938 ; of the ninth of November, 1938.

What do these dates stand for ? On the twenty-second of August, 1932, that dreadful telegram, known as the Beuthen telegram, was published, which glorified six Nazis who trampled a helpless Communist to death in front of his mother. Those six men were on trial, and Hitler telegraphed to them, " Your freedom is our honour."

On the twenty-seventh of February, 1933, the Reichstag building was set on fire. No one doubts who started that fire ; but someone else was done to death as the culprit.

A Select Record from Week to Week of Important War Declarations and Statements

(*Continued from page* 178)

On the thirtieth of June, 1934, at least seven hundred Germans were shot in cold blood— some of the great patriots. One was a builder of the Reichswehr. Some were comrades of Hitler from the early days.

On the twenty-fifth day of July, 1934, Dollfuss was murdered. Can we acquit of guilt for this the man who set up a memorial in honour of the murderers ?

On the third of March, 1938, Pastor Niemoller was acquitted by the Law Courts and at once imprisoned in a concentration camp ; he is—so far as we know—still in a concentration camp.

On the eighth of October, 1938, the palace of Cardinal Innitzer, who had welcomed Hitler to Vienna, was sacked.

On the ninth of November, 1938, the great pogrom against the Jews took place in Germany.

The best German citizens are deeply ashamed of all these things. Many of them, because they must endure at present that their country should be governed by the criminals, would be glad to forget those dates and what took place on them. But such deeds cannot be forgotten, and those who are guilty of them are unworthy to speak and act for a great people. . . .

Friday, October 6

HERR HITLER in a speech to the Reichstag :

. . . What are the aims of the German Government with regard to the regulation of the conditions in the space west of the German-Russian line of demarcation, which has been recognized as a sphere of German interests ?

They are :

(1) To create a Reich frontier which, as has already been emphasized, corresponds to the historical, ethnographic and economic realities.

(2) To regulate the whole living space according to nationalities ; that means a solution of those nationality problems which do not always affect this space alone, but extend into practically all countries in South-Eastern Europe.

(3) In this connexion to try to solve the Jewish problem.

(4) To reconstruct economic life and traffic to the benefit of all those living in that space.

(5) To guarantee the security of that Empire space ; and

(6) To establish a new Polish State which by its structure and leadership will give a guarantee that neither a new centre of conflict directed against Germany will come into being, nor that a focus of intrigues will be created against Germany and Russia.

In addition, we must try to remove the immediate consequences arising from the war, or at least to mitigate them. . . .

If Europe wants calm and peace, then the European States ought to be grateful that Germany and Russia are prepared to transform this area of disturbance into a zone of peaceful development.

The second task, which I believe is by far the most important, should lead to the establishment not only of the feeling, but also the certainty, of European security. For this it is necessary that :

(1) There should be absolute clarity with regard to the aims of the European States in the sphere of foreign policy.

As far as Germany is concerned, it can be stated that the Reich Government is prepared to make its aims in the sphere of foreign policy perfectly clear without any reservations.

First of all, we want to say that we consider the Versailles treaty extinct, and that the German Government and with it the entire German nation see no reason and no cause for any

further revision except for the demand for such colonial possessions as are due to the Reich and correspond to it.

This means, in the first place the restoration of the German colonies. This request, let it be noted, is not dressed up in the form of an ultimatum backed by force. It is simply a claim based on political justice and economic reason.

(2) To facilitate the exchange of productions it is necessary to attain a new ordering of markets and a definitive regulation of currencies, thus removing step by step the obstacles to free trade.

(3) The most important condition for the real prosperity of European and extra-European economies is the creation of an absolutely guaranteed peace and a feeling of security among all the peoples.

This requires not only a final sanctioning of the status of Europe, but also the reduction of armaments to a reasonable and economically tolerable extent.

It is also necessary to define clearly the applicability and the use of certain modern weapons capable of striking at any time into the heart of any nation and so causing a lasting feeling of insecurity.

I do not believe there is a single responsible European statesman who does not desire at the bottom of his heart to see the prosperity of his people. The realization of this wish is only possible in the framework of the general collaboration of the nations of this Continent. The safeguarding of such collaboration must be the aim of every man who is really struggling for the benefit of his people.

To attain this aim one day the great nations of this Continent must come together and hammer out and guarantee a comprehensive agreement which will give to all a feeling of security and quiet and peace.

Tuesday, October 10

M. DALADIER, in a Broadcast to the French nation :

. . . Who will now believe that it was for a question of Danzig and the Corridor or of the fate of German minorities ?

Germany has proved that she wanted either to subjugate Poland by trickery, or defeat her by iron and the sword.

After Austria, Czecho-Slovakia ; after Czecho-Slovakia, Poland. All these conquests were but stages on the road which would have led France and Europe to the direst slavery.

I know well that today you hear talk of peace—of a German peace—a peace which would but consecrate the victories of cunning or violence and would not hinder in the least the preparation of new conquests.

Summed up, what does the latest Reichstag speech mean ? It means this :

" I have annexed Poland. I am satisfied. Let us stop fighting ; let us hold a conference to consecrate my conquests and organize peace."

We have already heard this language before. . . .

If peace is really wanted, a lasting peace which would give to every home, to every woman and child the joy of living, it is necessary first of all to appease consciences in revolt, to redress the abuses of force, to satisfy honestly the rights and interests of all peoples. . . .

If peace is really wanted—a lasting peace—it is necessary also to understand that the security of nations can only rest on reciprocal guarantees excluding all possibility of surprise and raising a barrier against all attempts at domination.

If peace is really wanted, a lasting peace, it is necessary to understand, in short, that the time has passed when territorial conquests bring welfare to the conquerors. . . .

'Wats' Carry on the Tradition of the 'Waacs'

" Come to the cook-house door, girls ! " This Section Leader—a rank corresponding to sergeant in the Army— makes sure that the " troops " will hear the call.

An unexpected place to find the A.T.S. at work is in the armoury. Here is one girl cleaning a rifle with a pull-through, and another stripping a Bren gun under the eye of an Army officer.

THE Auxiliary Territorial Service, direct descendant of the Women's Auxiliary Army Corps of the last war, was formed in September, 1938, for the carrying out of certain non-combatant duties. In a short time the " Wats " won an honoured place among Britain's volunteers, and their khaki uniform became a familiar sight in our streets and on the barrack-squares. The director of the service, Dame Helen Gwynne-Vaughan (*see* page 151), was Chief Controller of the " Waacs " during the Great War, and most of the other staff officers have had wide experience of leadership.

Above, an Army officer is watching over a group of efficient A.T.S. girls, this time arranging kit in the store, while on the right a group of qualified mechanics are attending to the engine of a staff car.

Photos, G.P.O. and Associated Press

WORDS THAT HITLER HAS EATEN

Many of those who have not read it believe that "Mein Kampf"
is a revelation of Hitler's unalterable and unaltered purpose. The
passages quoted here from Messrs. Hurst & Blackett's complete
English edition, however, are proof to the contrary.

He Has No Quarrel with France Now!

Here we see the Fuehrer in characteristic
mood—giving voice to one of these specific
utterances which match so ill with his deeds.

WHAT England has always desired, and will
continue to desire, is to prevent any
one Continental Power in Europe from
attaining a position of world importance. Therefore England wishes to maintain a definite
equilibrium of forces among the European
States ; for this equilibrium seems a necessary
condition of England's world-hegemony.

What France has always desired, and will
continue to desire, is to prevent Germany from
becoming a homogeneous Power. Therefore,
France wants to maintain a system of small
German States, whose forces would balance
one another and over which there should be
no central government. Then, by acquiring

possession of the left bank of the Rhine, she
would have fulfilled the prerequisite conditions
for the establishment and security of her
hegemony in Europe. . . . (XIII, 503–4)

**France is and will remain the implacable
enemy of Germany** It does not matter what
Governments have ruled or will rule in France,
whether Bourbon or Jacobin, Napoleonic or
Bourgeois-Democratic, Clerical Republican or
Red Bolshevik, their foreign policy will always
be directed towards acquiring possession of
the Rhine frontier and consolidating France's
position on this river by disuniting and dis-
membering Germany. . . . (XIII, 505)

IN England, and also in Italy, the contrast
between the better kind of solid statesmanship and the policy of the Jewish stock
exchange often becomes strikingly evident.

Only in France there exists today more than
ever before a profound accord between the
views of the stock exchange, controlled by the
Jews, and the chauvinistic policy pursued by
French statesmen. This identity of views
constitutes an immense danger to Germany.
And it is just for this reason that France is and
will remain by far the most dangerous enemy.
**The French people, who are becoming more and
more obsessed by negroid ideas, represent a
threatening menace to the existence of the
white race in Europe,** because they are bound up
with the Jewish campaign for world-domination.
For the contamination caused by the influx of
negroid blood on the Rhine, in the very heart
of Europe, is in accord with the sadist and
perverse lust for vengeance on the part of the

hereditary enemy of our people, just as it suits
the purpose of the cool, calculating Jew who
would use this means of introducing a process
of bastardization in the very centre of the
European continent and, by infecting the white
race with the blood of an inferior stock, would
destroy the foundations of its independent
existence.

France's activities in Europe, today, spurred
on by the French lust for vengeance and
systematically directed by the Jew, are a
criminal attack against the life of the white
race, and will one day arouse against the French
people a spirit of vengeance among a generation
which will have recognized the original sin of mankind in this racial pollution. . . . (XIII, 508–9)

FRENCH policy may make a thousand détours
on the march towards its fixed goal,
but the destruction of Germany is the end
which it always has in view as the fulfilment of
the most profound yearning and ultimate
intentions of the French. . . . As long as the
eternal conflict between France and Germany
is waged only in the form of a German defence
against the French attack, that conflict can never
be decided. . . . Only when the Germans have
taken all this fully into account will they cease
from allowing the national will-to-live to wear
itself out in merely passive defence ; but they
**will rally together for a last decisive contest
with France.** . . . Germany sees in the suppression of France nothing more than a means
which will make it possible for our people finally
to expand in another quarter. . . . (Chapter
XV, page 549).

Those "Blood-Stained Criminals," the Bolsheviks, Are Now His Allies

WE National Socialists have purposely
drawn a line through the line of conduct followed by pre-War Germany
in foreign policy. We put an end to the perpetual Germanic march towards the South and
West of Europe and turn our eyes towards the
lands of the East. . . . **But when we speak of
new territory in Europe today we must principally
think of Russia and the border States subject to
her.**

Destiny itself seems to wish to point out the
way for us here. In delivering Russia over to
Bolshevism, Fate robbed the Russian people of
that intellectual class which had once created the
Russian State and were the guarantee of its
existence. . . . This colossal Empire in the
East is ripe for dissolution. . . . (XIV, 533).

THE Russia of today, deprived of its Germanic
ruling class, is not a possible ally in the
struggle for German liberty, setting aside
entirely the inner designs of its new rulers.
From the purely military viewpoint a Russo-
German coalition waging war against Western
Europe, and probably against the whole world
on that account, would be catastrophic for us.
The struggle would have to be fought out, not
on Russian but on German territory, without
Germany being able to receive from Russia the
slightest effective support. . . . The fact of
forming an alliance with Russia would be the
signal for a new war. And the result of that
would be the end of Germany. . . .

THOSE who are in power in Russia today
have no idea of forming an honourable
alliance, or of remaining true to it, if they did.
It must never be forgotten that **the present
rulers of Russia are blood-stained criminals,** that
here we have the dregs of humanity which,
favoured by the circumstances of a tragic
moment, overran a great State, degraded and
extirpated millions of the governing classes out

of sheer blood-lust, and that now for nearly ten
years they have ruled with such a savage
tyranny as was never known before. . . . It
must not be forgotten that the international
Jew, who is today the absolute master of Russia,
does not look upon Germany as an ally, but as a
State condemned to the same doom as Russia.
One does not form an alliance with a partner
whose only aim is the destruction of his fellow-
partner. Above all,
**one does not enter into
alliances with people for
whom no treaty is
sacred ;** because they
do not move about this
earth as men of honour
and sincerity, but as the
representatives of lies
and deception, thievery
and plunder and rob-
bery. The man who
thinks that he can bind
himself by treaty with
parasites is like the tree
that believes it can
form a profitable bar-
gain with the ivy that
surrounds it.

THE menace to which
Russia once suc-
cumbed is hanging
steadily over Germany.
Only a bourgeois sim-
pleton could imagine
that Bolshevism can be
tamed. . . . In Russian
Bolshevism we ought to
recognize the kind of
attempt which is being
made by the Jew in the
twentieth century to
secure dominion over

the world. . . . How can we teach the German
worker that Bolshevism is an infamous crime
against humanity if we ally ourselves with this
infernal abortion and recognize its existence as
legitimate ? With what right shall we condemn
the members of the broad masses whose sympathies lie with a certain *Weltanschauung* if the
rulers of our State choose the representatives of
that *Weltanschauung* as their allies ? (XIV, 536).

"Mein Kampf" has become the Bible of German people and none
is allowed to escape its message. Young couples are (as shown
here) given a copy at their wedding. But if they read it, they must
find it hard sometimes to reconcile the Fuehrer's word with his deed.

Photo, Wide World

Mussolini Plays a Neutral Hand

One of the first and greatest surprises of the early days of the war was the fact that Germany's chief ally, Italy, declared her resolve to "refrain from adopting the military initiative." Below is an examination of the situation in which this development had its place.

HITLER found in Mussolini's march on Rome the inspiration of his "putsch" of 1923, and when he became Fuehrer of the German Reich, he was careful to cultivate a good understanding with the Italian Duce who might be expected already to know all that there was to know about the establishment and the running of a totalitarian regime. Mussolini, for his part, welcomed Hitler's advances more particularly as the relations between him and the Democratic Powers were becoming increasingly strained. The Abyssinian affair brought Italy almost to the verge of war with France and Britain, and even when the sanctions applied by the League of Nations states were lifted, a fresh obstacle to Italian co-operation and friendship with the Western countries was found in the civil war in Spain. When General Franco revolted against the Republican Government in the summer of 1936, Mussolini dispatched Italian troops, technicians, and vast quantities of the material of war to help the Nationalists in their fight against what Mussolini described as a Bolshevist state.

Over the Abyssinian affair the Reich had given its support to Italy, and it was probably because Mussolini was grateful for Hitler's aid and encouragement in his hour of critical need that the Rome–Berlin axis came into being, and Mussolini resolved to link Italy with Germany and Japan in the Anti-Comintern Pact. In September, 1937, Signor Mussolini visited Germany to arrange the preliminaries, and shortly after his return to Italy the

Pact was signed at the Palazzo Venezia by the Duce and Herr von Ribbentrop.

The events of 1938 cannot have been altogether pleasing to Mussolini. For many years he had regarded Austria as part of Italy's sphere of influence, and it was a distinct set-back to his policy when, in March, 1938, the German troops overran the country and faced the Italian frontier guards on the Brenner Pass. At the Munich Conference in September, Mussolini played a leading role as one of the four "Men of Munich," but in the resulting partition of Czechoslovakia Italy received not an acre of fresh territory nor any compensation whatever for the relative decline of her influence in the councils of Europe.

When the Polish question loomed on the political horizon, Mussolini made some efforts to localize the conflict, and even attempted to repeat that role of peacemaker which had won him such renown at Munich, but the most striking fact revealed in the new situation was that, when Hitler decided to march, Mussolini remained in the camp.

Italy Did Not March

For two years Germany and Italy had worked in the closest association; only as recently as May, 1939, the representatives of the two great dictatorships had begun negotiations for a definite military alliance. For long it had been assumed that when Hitler declared war, Mussolini would declare war, too. Yet on that fateful September 1, 1939, Mussolini talked but did not act.

In a telegram to Signor Mussolini thanking him for continued diplomatic support, Hitler boastingly declared : "I will not have need of military aid from Italy," but the truth may be that Italy would not have answered even had she been called.

As the days went by, various reasons were advanced for Italian inactivity. Most probably, however, it was the picture of Von Ribbentrop bending over Stalin's table and linking Germany with Bolshevik Russia that determined Mussolini to keep out of the war.

After the first month of the war of 1939, Signor Mussolini was still thinking of peaceful matters. He is here listening to an address at the opening of an art exhibition in Rome.
Photo, Associated Press

Both Mussolini and Hitler have many times in their careers fulminated against the Bolsheviks and all the wicked works and words of Bolshevism. The difference between the two may be that the former has really meant what he said.

Mussolini in many a speech has given evidence of what seems to be a sincere detestation of Bolshevism. Thus, at Palermo in 1937, he declared that : " Let it be said in the most categorical manner that we will not tolerate in the Mediterranean Bolshevism or anything of a similar nature " ; and a few weeks later, " If peace is to be lasting and fruitful, Bolshevism must be banished from Europe." As the years went by Mussolini re-affirmed time and again the identity of view of the two Totalitarian States. In May, 1939, speaking at Turin, he said : " Italy will march with Germany to give Europe that peace with justice which is among the heartfelt desires of all peoples." Among the clauses of the military alliance signed on May 22 was one which stated : " If, contrary to the wishes of the two States, it should happen that one of them is involved in hostilities, the other will give it full military support as ally."

Yet, despite these provisions and protestations, Mussolini and Mussolini's Italy did not march. Probably it is not too much to say that the same pact between Nazi Germany and Soviet Russia which knocked Tokyo off the farther end of the Rome–Berlin axis, which made Franco's Spain a neutral, which barred Germany's way to the East and made the Baltic a Russian lake—it is not too much to say that this same pact relieved the French army and the British navy of the necessity of having to wage war on a vastly extended front. Unlike Hitler, Mussolini has studied Machiavelli to such good purpose that he realizes that there are limits even to Machiavellianism.

During the crisis of September 1938 Signor Mussolini intervened to secure a peaceful solution. Above is his meeting with Hitler at Kufstein, on September 29, 1938, when the two Dictators were on their way to Munich to meet Mr. Chamberlain and M. Daladier.
Photo, Wide World

Cartoon Commentary on the Conflict

Stalin's Ally

From the " Sunday Chronicle "

Uncomfortable Grandstand   *From the " Evening Standard "*

Iɴ this page we have a second selection of the cartoonists' graphic representation of current war events. The first of them, " Stalin's Ally," is by that brilliant Dutch artist, Louis Raemaekers, whose cartoons of the martyrdom of Belgium during the last war made a profound impression on world opinion. Of the rest, three are taken from the London press and one from a Dutch journal.

FOR VALOUR?   *From the " Daily Mirror "*

"Hitler has ordered 40,000 Iron Crosses to be awarded to his troops in Poland"

*"*ACH! THESE FORTUNATE ENGLISH WHO STILL HAVE INCOMES TO TAX*"*

From the " Star "

" On the Polish Demarcation Line "
From " De Groene Amsterdammer "

These Pictures Spell A.R.P.

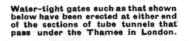

Water-tight gates such as that shown below have been erected at either end of the sections of tube tunnels that pass under the Thames in London.

In many streets gas-detectors such as this have been erected. They are coated with a substance that changes colour when gas is about, and then returns to the normal.

Air Raid Wardens are provided with an elaborate kit. It is completely gas-proof, and with a steel helmet provides as complete protection as possible for those who have to be in the open during air raids.

Photos, Central Press and Fox

A BLACK-OUT LESSON FROM 1918

"A FRIEND of mine, an airman, has told me how one night in 1918, a pitch-dark and starless night, he was searching with his squadron for Düsseldorf in the inky sea which lay below him. Nothing revealed the town. It was thought that they must be near it judging by their direction and the distance flown, but its exact situation could not be discovered. They were about to abandon their quest when a fugitive beam of light spread out, just for a second, over the blackness and then went out. A citizen of Düsseldorf had just opened and shut his door behind which lay a lighted passage. It was enough. There lay the town. The first bomb fell anywhere, lighting up the target; the others wrecked the station. See it doesn't happen here !"

Roger Vercel in " Candide " (Paris)

At hospitals and in many other buildings, decontaminating stations have been arranged. Here those caught in the open where a gas bomb has fallen would be given treatment and a change of clothing in which to go home.

One of the devices for fire-fighting that have been brought into use since Air Raid Precautions have been perfected are emergency tanks such as that seen above. The swan apparently considers that it exists for its sole benefit, but the actual purpose is to provide a water supply for fire engines should hydrants or mains be damaged. Water would then be pumped into the tanks from other sources.

Photos, Universal Pictorial Press and Topical

Turkey Guards the Black Sea

After years of virtual retirement from the European scene, Turkey assumed an ever-increasing importance following the formation of the Peace Front and the revival of Russia as a great Power.

M. Sarajoglu, the Turkish Foreign Minister, who went to Moscow to discuss the problems of the Black Sea with M. Molotov.
Photo, Wide World

In the far south-east of the Continent, where Europe looks across to Asia, lies Turkey, once one of the world's great empires and a stronghold of Moslem conservatism, but now a republic on very much restricted but at the same time very modern lines. Its importance in the political sphere is due to the fact that it contains the link between the Black Sea and the Mediterranean—the Bosporus, the Sea of Marmara, and those Dardanelles which cost the lives of so many brave men in the last war.

Demilitarizing the Straits

Despite their victory on the peninsula of Gallipoli, the Turks were hopelessly defeated by the time the Great War ended, and the resulting peace brought with it the loss of huge territories. The real nucleus of the Turkish State, however, is Anatolia or Asia Minor, and it was here that the Turkish Nationalists under Mustapha Kemal, one of the few successful Turkish generals in the Great War—he was largely responsible for the Allies' defeat at Gallipoli—rallied in the most extraordinary fashion and laid the foundations of a new State which aimed at being purely Turkish.

After much fighting the new regime was firmly established, and Mustapha Kemal, now President of the Turkish Republic, signed in 1923 the Treaty of Lausanne which restored to the Turks much more than they could have hoped to retain only a short time before.

Although they regained much territory, however, which had been occupied by the Greeks, they were compelled to accept the demilitarization of the Straits.

Thirteen years went by, and there were many changes in the political situation. Turkey had now an assured place amongst the Mediterranean countries, and she was on such good terms with Britain, France and Russia that she felt able to ask that the fortification of the Dardanelles should be made the subject of negotiation. In support of the application the Turkish Government pointed out that in 1923 the general situation of Europe from the political and military point of view was totally different. In 1936 the situation in the Black Sea was reassuring in every respect, but uncertainty had arisen in the Mediterranean, owing largely to Mussolini's strivings in the direction of a new Italian empire. At the same time naval conferences had shown a tendency towards rearmament, and there had been much development of the air arm. In the circumstances, Turkey felt that the present machinery for collective guarantees was too slow in coming into operation—in other words, she would much prefer to be in a position to depend upon her own right arm.

Following the Turkish note a Dardanelles Conference was held at Montreux, and on July 20, 1936, a new Straits Convention was signed. Among the principal clauses of the Convention was one permitting the remilitarization of the Dardanelles, and another providing that in time of war, Turkey not being a belligerent, warships should have complete liberty of passage through the Straits, but only if acting under obligations devolving from the League Covenant or "in the event of assistance being given to a State which is the victim of aggression, in virtue of a mutual assistance pact to which Turkey is a party." Further, in time of war, Turkey being a belligerent, the passage of warships through the Straits would be left entirely to the discretion of the Turkish Government, *i.e.* Turkey might close the Straits.

Italy recognized the remilitarization of the Dardanelles, but Germany officially informed Turkey that she objected to that clause which might permit the passage of Soviet battleships from the Black Sea into the Mediterranean.

Joining the Peace Front

Owing to her occupation of the key position between the two seas, Turkey was one of the first Powers approached by Britain and France when, following the collapse of the Munich settlement, they decided to establish a new Peace Front to counter Nazi aggression. On May 12, 1939, Mr. Chamberlain announced that Britain and Turkey had decided to conclude a "definitive long-term agreement of a reciprocal character in the interest of their national security," and in the next month a Franco-Turkish declaration of mutual assistance was signed in Paris.

Now, guaranteed against German aggression, Turkey further consolidated her relations with Soviet Russia, with whom, indeed, she had been on most friendly terms since the establishment of the Turkish republic. In September, 1939, the Turkish Foreign Minister, M. Sarajoglu, proceeded to Moscow to enter into negotiations with M. Molotov concerning the part which Turkey should play in the new state of affairs brought into being by the collapse of Poland.

The Turkish Military Mission to Britain arrived in London on October 3, headed by General Orbay. It was met at Waterloo Station by Field-Marshal Lord Birdwood, who was in command of the British troops fighting the Turks in Gallipoli during the Great War in 1915. The armies learned to have a mutual respect for each other, and there have since been several cordial meetings between those who led them.
Photo, Planet News

They Fight Hitler Inside Germany

For six years and more Hitler and his Nazis have done their best to smash all opposition within the Reich. They have almost succeeded—but not quite, as this brief account of the anti-Nazi underground movement shows.

S INCE Hitler came into power in 1933 Germany has become in very deed a totalitarian State. All opposition to the Nazis has been ruthlessly suppressed. Liberals have felt the iron hand of authority in the same way as Socialists, Communists, and Trade Unionists; Catholic priests have been treated with the same contemptuous firmness as the ministers of the Evangelical Church. The newspapers have been delivered up to the tender mercies of Dr. Goebbels and his henchmen; the wireless is merely the mouthpiece of Nazi officialdom; political parties have been completely banned, and all men of independent mind have been encouraged to keep their thoughts to

A mild caricature of Heinrich Himmler, chief of the Nazi spy system—but even he cannot suppress the underground movement in the Reich.

literature is illegal—is smuggled in from abroad, or is even actually printed at secret presses in Germany.

Nor is the press the only vehicle of anti-Nazi propaganda. If you purchase a gramophone record in Leipzig you may find that it begins with a Viennese waltz and ends with a series of Socialist slogans. If you passed through the gates of the Olympic Games in Berlin and purchased what looked to be the official Nazi Guidebook you might find that it also contained a vast amount of information about concentration camps, prisons, arrests and executions of the enemies of Nazism. Or, going into a bookshop, you might pick up a booklet on "First Aid in Accidents" which is really an account of the Nazi persecution of the Church, and discover that "How to Play Bridge" is really a lecture on how to carry on anti-Fascist work in Nazi organizations:

The distribution of anti-Nazi propaganda has been greatly facilitated by the black-outs imposed before and during the war. Thousands of anti-Nazi pamphlets have been distributed in the course of one night, and with the dawn the true-blue Nazi policeman is horrified to find that the wall facing him has been scribbled over with such phrases as "Down with Hitler."

The anti-Nazi movement was given a fresh impetus by the establishment of the German Freedom Party, which first sprang into prominence in April 1937, when it circulated a manifesto—a manifesto which was delivered all unwittingly by Nazi postmen. The party claims to represent all classes in Germany, all the former political parties, and the chief religious bodies. The Party's pamphlets have been delivered through the post, popped into the mouths of milk bottles standing on the doorsteps, and placed between the pages of the directories in public telephone call-boxes. It has been claimed that a million copies of one manifesto were distributed in the course of three days. As long ago as October 1937 Hitler did the Party the honour of singling it out for direct attack, declaring that it was "a foreign invention, born from a longing to see a split in our national unity."

When war came in 1939, there was no Liebknecht as in 1914 to voice in the Reichstag the opposition of the German masses to an imperialist war, but in his place there came across the air the mysterious voice of the German Freedom Party, broadcasting from some place whose exact situation Herr Himmler would very much like to know. It may be in Luxemburg, or Switzerland, or Hungary; some have said that it is as far away as Moscow; others have hinted that it may be in England. Yet others have declared that the broadcasters are risking death by speaking from some dark wood within the confines of the Reich. On October 15th it was actually stated that they were broadcasting from Cologne.

"Germany Cannot Win!"

"*Achtung! Achtung! heir spricht der Deutsche Freiheitssender!*" "Warning! Warning! The German Freedom Station calling!" No one knows who is the speaker; no one can tell how many in Germany are listening to the message. But that it is to the point and filled with danger to the Nazi regime is very evident.

"In September Hitler told the German people there would never be another 1918. Yes, Adolf Hitler, there will never be another 1918. The work will be more thorough this time. German soldiers, make yourselves ready for the hour when you turn your guns round! Women of Germany, do your duty. German youth, become the flame of the revolution which is your honour and your destiny. Close your ranks for peace, freedom and bread."

Another of the broadcasts said:

"The lightning war is a fairy tale. Nazis are preparing for a long war which will mean starvation for German people, death for the flower of our youth, destruction for our towns. The German people has no interest in either a long or a short war. It wants to live in peace. Fall of Hitler and his system is the only way to secure an honourable peace."

Hitler has silenced many voices in his time. But there is one voice that he cannot silence—that voice which through the watches of the night splits the façade of Nazi complacency with the grim warning that "Germany cannot win!"

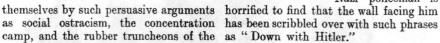

"The Man behind the Boy behind the Gun."
From the "Sydney Daily News"

themselves by such persuasive arguments as social ostracism, the concentration camp, and the rubber truncheons of the Black Guards. Spies are everywhere; indeed, Germany is the modern exemplification of the "police state" in action.

Some Still Think for Themselves

Yet, in spite of the Gestapo, the concentration camps, and the headsman's axe, there are still men in Germany who dare, not only to think for themselves, but to speak and work against the Nazi regime. Underground resistance to Hitler has been organized amongst the workers in all the big industrial centres of Germany. Sometimes these illegal groups of two or three or half a dozen persons work in isolation; more often they are linked with other groups inspired by the same political creed. In the larger factories there may be three or four of these little "cells," as they are called. Through these "cells" a quantity of illegal literature—and all anti-Nazi

Practice Makes Perfect with the Big Guns

These photographs show artillerymen being trained for work with the heavy guns.   In the top photograph practice is proceeding with a 9.2-in. howitzer, the shells of which are so costly that they are seldom fired in peacetime.   Below, the ramrod of another piece of heavy artillery is being thrown to one of the gun crew.   Ramrods are used to clean out the barrels of the guns after they have been fired, and that for the 9.2 howitzer can be seen in the top photograph.

Photos, " Daily Mirror " and Fox

Bullets Whistled Past My Parachute

This thrilling account of a three-to-one air fight over the Siegfried
Line was told to "Eye-Witness" by a gunner of the R.A.F. who
saved himself by parachute when his machine was brought down in
flames in No-man's Land.

FROM his bed in an R.A.F. medical receiving station hidden away in the woods "somewhere in France," a little Welsh air-gunner described to me an air battle over the Siegfried Line against heavy odds.

The gunner told of his remarkable escape when, after he had brought down his opponent, his own machine fell in flames.

In spite of severe burns on his face he grinned cheerfully as he took an English cigarette from me.

"We were a handful of British 'planes out on a reconnaissance flight over the Siegfried Line," he said.

"The Germans spotted us almost at once, and their A.A. batteries opened fire; but we went up well above 20,000 feet and continued our work.

"We were three in the 'plane—the pilot, the observer and myself as gunner. It was a wonderfully clear day and we could see for miles.

"Suddenly, from far down below, we saw enemy 'planes swirl up towards us. They were Messerschmitts, three formations of six each.

"We were outnumbered by more than three to one, but we prepared to give battle. The enemy began with their favourite tactics of swooping up at us from underneath, machine-gunning as they came.

"Then one of the 'planes attached itself to the tail of my machine and a terrific duel began.

"I could hear the bullets ripping through the fabric beside me. I looked round and saw the observer in a crumpled heap in his seat. He had been shot through the head.

"The enemy were using incendiary bullets, and suddenly I realized that the machine was on fire and that it was only a question of seconds before the flames reached me.

"Then, just as my clothing began to smoulder, the 'plane behind us swooped up and offered me a lovely target. I gave him all I had, and as the flames blazed into my face I just had time to see him go into a spin and disappear beneath me.

"If I had not been on fire I could easily have shot down two more. It was real

bad luck, but my pals accounted for three besides the one I hit.

"Half unconscious, I started to struggle out of my cockpit. I must have pulled the string of my parachute, for I suddenly saw it open and felt myself dragged out of the 'plane.

"I got a nasty blow on the leg from

the tail of the machine and then for a moment I suppose I fainted. Next I remember floating down while the battle continued above me.

"I knew it was Germany below me, and I began to calculate whether there was any hope of the wind carrying me over to the French lines. It seemed very doubtful.

"I saw a German aerodrome, but I could not identify it.

"Then, when I had got quite low, I heard firing and realized that bullets were whistling near me. I was above the German lines and they were shooting at me.

It was in such a parachute as this that the "little Welsh air-gunner" who tells his story in this page made his descent to earth. Parachutes, the lifebelts of the airmen, did not form part of the standard equipment in the last war, but they are now carried by every member of the crew of R.A.F. aircraft.

Photo, Keystone

220   *The War Illustrated*   October 28th, 1939

IIIIIIIIIIIIIIIIIIIIIIIIIIIIIIIIIIIIIIIIIIIIIIIIIIIIIIIIIIIIIIIIII **I WAS THERE!** IIIIIIIIIIIIIIIIIIIIIIIIIIIIIIIIIIIIIIIIIIIIIIIIIIIIIIIIIIIIIIIIII

" It was a terrible situation, but I saw that there was just a hope that I. might get right past the German lines before I landed. They went on firing at me almost until I was on the ground.

" I released my parachute and started to crawl desperately to a little thicket in the hope of hiding there. There was a wood on one side and flat country on the other, where the Germans had their lines.

" I saw the Germans leave their trenches and come running towards me. I thought I was done for, but suddenly I saw that men were running from the wood as well. I recognized them as French Algerian soldiers.

" Both sides were racing for me. Most of the French began to fire at the advanc-ing Germans, but one man came running straight towards me as hard as he could go. He picked me up, slung me over his shoulder and staggered with me into the woods.

" I was safe, but it was a very near thing. The pilot of my 'plane did not have to jump out until a little later, and he came down safely in French territory."

The little Welshman paused for a moment, then added :

" The observer must have died at once. He was shot right through the head."

The air-gunner is going back to England to get over his burns, but he expects to. return to his squadron soon.

He is not deeply impressed by his experience. " It is all in the day's work " were his parting words to me.

34 hours we came to the surface off the Irish coast at about 5.30 yesterday even-ing. A collapsible boat was lowered and again seven trips were made to the shore. The submarine remained about 50 yards off the shore, which appeared to be deserted. Immediately the submarine had taken the boat aboard she submerged and that was the last we saw of her.

" The crew waved good-bye to us. We were taken charge of by local policemen and the local people looked after us very well."

The captain said that the commander of the submarine, who appeared to be about 30, had treated them with the greatest courtesy. The crew of the submarine numbered 34.

We Were Put Ashore by a U-Boat

Here is the story told by the skipper of the Greek steamer " Diamantis " to " The Daily Telegraph " of how, on October 4, 1939, he and his men were landed in Ireland after 34 hours' hospitality in a German submarine.

WATCHED by Civic Guards who were powerless to interfere, a German U-boat appeared within 100 yards of the shore on a lonely part of the Kerry coast, Eire, landed 28 survivors of a Greek steamer which she had sunk. and then made off and submerged.

The incident took place last evening off Ventry, a hamlet overlooking a small bay near Dingle, 31 miles from Tralee.

This is close to the spot where Sir Roger Casement, the Irish rebel, was landed from a German submarine in a collapsible boat in 1916.

The 28 members of the crew of the Greek vessel, the " Diamantis," 4,990 tons, were put off in a collapsible boat belonging to the submarine.

Civic Guards, patrolling the coast, saw the submarine on the surface and hastened to the spot, but they were too late to make any attempt to detain her. While they were still some distance away the submarine stood off and submerged.

After being looked after at Dingle the crew of the " Diamantis," six of whom were suffering from shock, arrived here this evening. They later left for Holy-head.

Capt. Panagos, the master of the Greek steamer, described events to me as follows:

" When we were about 40 miles off Land's End on Tuesday the U-boat came to the surface about 1.30 p.m. The commander hailed us and we stopped. He then told us that he was going to sink the 'Diamantis.' He did not ask for our papers.

" He ordered us to abandon ship, but when he saw that the sea was so rough that our small boats could not possibly live in it he took us aboard the submarine. Four of us were taken across at a time, this necessitating seven trips as there were 28 of us. We were not allowed to take our belongings. When we got aboard the submarine three or four torpedoes were fired at our vessel and she sank in about 20 minutes.

" Many of us were wet to the skin and the submarine's crew dried our clothes and gave us hot food and cigarettes.

" Most of the members of my crew were able to sleep a little although all the time we were wishing that we were out of the submarine. The captain of the submarine spoke English and I was able to talk to him for short periods when he was off duty.

" When we had been on board for about

The submarine that sank the "Diamantis" and afterwards landed the crew at Dingle, Co. Kerry, is seen above. She is U 35, a sea-going submarine of 500 tons. The crew afterwards proceeded to England, and in the top photograph the master, Captain Panagos, is seen in London with some of the crew.

Photos, Topical

The intensive bombardment of Polish aerodromes, which was one of the Nazis' first acts of aggression against Poland, left the Poles in desperate straits for aircraft as Colonel Nowak describes in this page. Above, a Soviet sentry stands guard over a Polish aeroplane that had crashed in the aerodrome of Vilna after it had been seized by the Russians.
Photo, Planet News

We Flew From Warsaw in Makeshift 'Planes

By putting together the 1,000 parts of a dismantled Polish airplane and searching Warsaw for odd spare parts for other antiquated aircraft, Colonel Nowak, chief of the capital's air defence force, and nine other pilots escaped from the Germans, as told in an interview with a British United Press correspondent.

IN an interview Colonel Nowak said they were told by the Commander of the Defences, General Rummel, to try to get out of Warsaw. They escaped two days before the city capitulated.

"With all our aircraft destroyed and munitions running low, it became increasingly clear that Warsaw's surrender was near. General Rummel wished to save the remaining Polish pilots, including myself.

"We searched all the half-burned hangars and aviation schools and clubs for spare parts. In six days we rebuilt six makeshift aircraft—three single-seater sports 'planes, one old reconnaissance 'plane and two gliders. I was to use the reconnaissance craft—an old type.

"It had been dismantled into 1,000 parts for demonstration purposes three years ago in a flying school.

"When the airplanes were finished we had to look round for airfields. The Okecie military field was occupied by the Germans, and bitter fighting was going on at Mokotov airport, a small civil centre.

"We decided to leave on the night of September 26—the day before the Nazis claimed the surrender of the capital.

"Our infantry were ordered to clear part of the Mokotov field. Charging with bayonets and hand grenades, they drove the enemy back.

"With the other flyers I rolled the airplanes from the hangars. We started the motors. Their noise was drowned by machine-gun and artillery fire.

"As we circled Warsaw at 9,000 feet we saw the burning capital for the last time. Then we headed for freedom.

"Now I have enlisted in the Polish army on the Western front."

Miss Nancy Martindale, the English girl who was in Warsaw during the Nazi air raids.
Photo, Evening Standard

The Nazi 'Planes were Joy-Riding

Escaping from bombarded Warsaw the writer of the following personal story suffered many dangers before reaching safety. Her account of the bombing of the defenceless population of Lwow, told to "The Evening Standard" in London, makes pitiful reading.

HOW she escaped from Poland, dodging Nazi bombers, a week after the war began, was described to me in London by Miss Nancy Martindale, of Queen's Gate, Kensington.

She was in Warsaw five days after the Germans invaded Poland, and was ordered to leave. Before she did so the city was bombed four times a day.

"I was only allowed to take one small suitcase with me, because there was so little room in the two cars we managed to get," she said.

"I think we must have got the last two in Warsaw. It was pathetic to see the groups of women and children standing round the cars as we packed them. Many people were unable to obtain conveyances, but the roads were packed with old cars, bicycles, hand carts, horse carts, as well as by pedestrians leaving the city.

"We had to drive furiously the whole time, otherwise we should not have been able to cross the bridges before the Germans blew them up. We had very little food, and hardly any sleep.

"One night we slept on the floor of a village butcher's parlour. We had to start driving at four in the morning, because the raiders came over every day between 6 and 7 a.m., and we wanted to travel as many miles as possible first.

"To make matters more uncomfortable, water was terribly scarce—and non-existent for washing—and the roads were unbelievably dusty.

"Our cars got separated soon after we left Lublin, and the car I was driving ran out of petrol.

"It was impossible to buy fuel anywhere. People were offering practically all their possessions just for one gallon.

"Finally I went to a Polish colonel in the town we had reached, and he drained the tank of his own car so that we could go on. He said that no Polish man, woman or child could do enough for the English.

"At Lwow the situation was incredible. The German 'planes seemed to be joy-riding over the city. They had air raids there for five hours a day. There were no anti-aircraft guns, and no Polish aircraft at that spot to go up after the raiders.

"After three days, in which the Germans destroyed the waterworks, the station, and any factories they could see, they flew low over the houses and bombed the population indiscriminately.

"When the Germans were taken prisoners they refused to be treated at the

This aerial photograph of Warsaw was taken during one of the raids by Nazi bombers that Miss Martindale describes. The total casualties were terribly heavy, and by the time the city had surrendered, 20,000 civilians and 16,000 soldiers had been wounded.
Photo, Fox

hospitals. They insulted the doctors and tore off their bandages, saying that they would rather die for the Fatherland than be touched by a Pole."

Miss Martindale paid a tribute to the Poles. "It is hard to describe what a wonderful and courageous people they are," she said.

"While there is a mother left in Poland, the spirit of Poland is there."

I Saw a Bomber Attack a U-Boat

From a passenger on the U.S. steamer "American Farmer" comes this vivid story of the air-bombing of the German submarine which sank the Newcastle steamer "Kafiristan."

Mr. Armistead Lee, of Chatham, Virginia, said when they sighted the lifeboats belonging to the "Kafiristan" they also saw a British bomber that appeared "from nowhere as if by magic."

"The bomber," he declared, "swooped on the submarine and apparently destroyed it with a bomb. There were nine men on the deck of the submarine, but no one appeared to see the bomber coming.

"It sprayed the deck with machine-gun fire and the crews rushed to the conning-tower hatch. The submarine submerged so fast that some of those who were watching aboard the "American Farmer" thought that the hatch was not even fastened down.

"The 'plane circled and dropped a bomb. Then it circled again, dived within 15 feet of the water and dropped another bomb. We saw the submarine's bow lift. Then it slid backwards into the water.

"The bomber flew over us, and one of the fliers waved triumphantly and pointed down as if signalling that the submarine was destroyed."

Capt. John Busby, master of the

"Kafiristan," said the submarine fired a warning shot. Six out of 34 of his crew were drowned in launching the first life-boat while the "Kafiristan" was still moving.

The bomber that appeared after the "Kafiristan" had been torpedoed and took the crew of the U-boat quite unawares is seen immediately above, photographed from the U.S. liner "American Farmer," which rescued the "Kafiristan's" survivors. Above, Capt. H. A. Pedersen, of the "American Farmer," is greeting Capt. John Busby, of the "Kafiristan."
Photos, Planet News and Wide World

Russia's New Footholds in the Baltic

A train from Tallinn, Estonia's capital, is on its way to Leningrad. On the frontier archway beneath which it is passing is the Soviet slogan "Workers of the World Unite."

This railway bridge crosses the river Narva, the frontier between Estonia and Russia from the Gulf of Finland to Lake Peipus.

FOLLOWING the collapse of the Tsar's empire in 1917 Russia ceased to be a Baltic power. In 1939, however, there was a great change. Hardly had half Poland been occupied by Soviet armies when Moscow made peremptory demands on all the States which shut in Russia from the Baltic. Estonia, Latvia, and Lithuania were not slow to comply with her demands, among which was the grant of the use of several ports as air and naval bases for the Soviet's forces. Only Finland put up some show of resistance when demands for similar concessions were addressed to her from Moscow, and a delegation, lead by Dr. Paasikivi, was sent to discuss terms with Stalin and Molotov at Moscow.

Centre, is the castle of the important military base at Arensburg (or Kuresaar), on the Estonian island of Oesel (or Saaremaa), to which the U.S.S.R. was allowed by the pact of September 28 to send a large garrison. The city of Kaunas (Kovno), left, was the capital of Lithuania, while Vilna, the old capital, was included in Poland. "To fatherland and freedom" are the words inscribed on the granite base of the Statue of Liberty at Riga, seen right.

Photos, Derek Wordley, Central Press and Nick Baumann

OUR DIARY OF THE WAR

Monday, October 9

The Admiralty announced that on the previous afternoon a German naval squadron had been sighted by patrol aircraft south-west of Norway. Owing to oncoming darkness the enemy escaped.

There were **repeated actions in the North Sea** between German aircraft and British warships. No British ship was damaged.

Four British aeroplanes, flying in pairs, carried out daylight reconnaissance flights the whole way along the frontier from France to the North Sea. The first pair encountered bad weather and were assailed by anti-aircraft fire from Coblenz and Sietburg, but returned home in safety. The second pair were able to take valuable photographs.

Paris reported enemy patrol activity on either side of the valley of the Lower Nied and to the south of Saarbruecken.

For the first time, Germans made use of loudspeakers to put across propaganda from their front lines.

Dr. Juho Paasikivi, Finnish Minister in Stockholm, left Helsinki for Moscow.

Sweden decreed that men who would normally leave the army next Sunday should remain with the colours.

Count Wailaw-Grzybowski, Polish Ambassador to Moscow, and his staff left Moscow.

Soviet troops who are to occupy naval and air bases began **marching into Estonia.**

First contingent of the re-formed Czecho-Slovak army left Paris for the Western Front.

Tuesday, October 10

M. Daladier replied to Hitler's "peace" proposals in a broadcast, and stated that France would continue to fight for a definite guarantee of security in Europe.

The **work of the R.A.F.** was reviewed by Sir Kingsley Wood in the House of Commons. He announced that there would soon be 100 per cent increase in production of 'planes.

London Gazette announced that two R.A.F. officers who took part in the raid on Wilhelmshaven on September 4 had been awarded the D.F.C. These were the first decorations to be made in the present war.

Paris reported very great activity on the part of enemy reconnaissance units between the Moselle and the Saar. There was also artillery activity on both sides.

Estonian Government resigned. M. Uluots was appointed Premier, and M. Piip Foreign Secretary in the new Government.

The partial evacuation of certain towns in Finland, including Helsinki and Viborg, was begun.

Hitler opened the Winter Relief Fund campaign in Berlin.

Swedish steamer "Vistula" was reported to have been sunk by a U-boat.

Wednesday, October 11

Mr. Hore-Belisha, Secretary for War, made a statement in the House of Commons on the work of the British Army in France.

Paris reported heavier Nazi attacks on French outposts. Artillery duels of extreme violence continued.

Soviet-Lithuanian pact signed in Moscow. Vilna was restored to Lithuania in exchange for the right to establish Soviet garrisons at any point on Lithuanian soil.

M. Paasikivi, Finnish envoy, arrived in Moscow.

In all big towns in Finland machine-guns and anti-aircraft guns were being mounted. Voluntary evacuation continued.

A commercial agreement between the British and Soviet Governments was signed in London by virtue of which timber will be imported in exchange for rubber and Cornish tin.

Evacuation of Germans from the Baltic States in progress.

M. August Zaleski, Foreign Minister in the new Polish Government set up in Paris, arrived in London and consulted with the Prime Minister and Lord Halifax.

Thursday, October 12

Sharp fighting was reported from the Western Front.

THE POETS & THE WAR

IV

THE CROOKED CROSS

By Gilbert Frankau

This is the time of our testing ;
  Now, while his words still run
Hither and thither, unresting :
  "Grant but my victory won,
Grant but my new battle-stations—
These lands where I ravaged and slew—
And I will grant peace to all nations."
  Shall the Crookèd Cross conquer the
    True ?

Shall we palter and falter, forgiving
  Each wrong he has done to mankind ?
Then, indeed, were we soft with good
    living,
  Then, indeed, were we blind, and pur-
    blind,
And false to all troths that we plighted—
  Our old dead betrayed with our new—
And all hope for humanity blighted.
  Shall the Crookèd Cross wave o'er the
    True ?

Must the nations whose watchword is
    Freedom
Give ear to the cunning of Force,
  While the jackboot still tramples o'er
    Edom,
  While the Shape on the Skeleton Horse
Still grins at the work of its master—
  These corpses the bombs rent and
    blew ?
What were peace, in such case, but
    disaster ?
  Shall the Crookèd Cross haul down the
    True ?

        The Daily Mail.

Finnish-Soviet talks opened in Moscow. The American Ambassador in Moscow, Mr. Steinhardt, expressed to M. Molotov the hope that ample time would be given for these discussions.

That it would be **impossible for Great Britain to accept Hitler's proposals,** since aggression cannot be the basis of peace, and no reliance could be placed upon the promises of the present German Government, was declared by Mr. Chamberlain in the House of Commons.

It was announced that the German liner "Cap Norte" had been captured.

Government Bill to check war profiteering was introduced.

Friday, October 13

King of Sweden invited the Danish and Norwegian sovereigns and the President of Finland to a conference in Stockholm.

Three German submarines sunk by British Navy ; two were of the large ocean-going type.

Paris stated that German raiding and patrol activities had diminished.

British steamer "Heronspool" sunk by U-boat.

Sir John Gilmour appointed Minister of Shipping.

Ministry of Supply announced that three more munition factories were to be built with speed.

Saturday, October 14

Finnish delegation left Moscow to report to the Government in Helsinki.

Admiralty announced that **H.M.S. "Royal Oak"** had been sunk, presumably by a U-boat.

Two French steamers, "Louisiane" and "Bretagne," and one British, "Lochavon," sunk by enemy submarines.

Signor Bastianini, new Italian Ambassador, arrived in London.

Sunday, October 15

Paris reported that French reconnaissance units were active on the whole front. There was some reciprocal activity west of Saarlouis.

The French Command also stated that there were indications that strong concentrations of German forces were massing behind the lines.

The Admiralty issued lists of 414 survivors of H.M.S. "Royal Oak."

German-Estonian agreement for **transfer of German minority** in Estonia was signed at Tallinn.

Polish Minister in Kaunas protested to the Lithuanian Government against the incorporation of Vilna in Lithuania, on the grounds that Russia had no right to dispose of this territory.

It was reported that typhoid and cholera had broken out in Warsaw.

The first exchanges took place of British consular officials detained in Germany against German officials still in Britain.

It Is Said That . .

Unsatisfactory work in Germany is punished as sabotage.

In France dogs are being recruited for war service, chiefly for transmission of messages.

A Polish banker, anxious to leave Warsaw, paid £2,300 for 12 gallons of petrol.

"Knightly German U-boat Commanders Cleanse the Seas of Pirates."
    (*Illustrierter Beobachter.*)

German aristocrats, monarchists and other possible enemies of Nazi regime are placed in front line.

Of four deaths in action recorded in a German paper, three were of sons of noble families.

Child labour is largely employed on German farms. The average age on one farm was 12.   (*German Broadcast.*)

German spies in Swedish and Norwegian ports transmit details of sailings to U-boat commanders.

A French scientist has invented gas masks for horses.

Marseilles police closed eight shops for a month for profiteering.

Many Germans now have a second (and secret) radio set for foreign reception.

The Gestapo has ordered the withdrawal from public libraries of all books on the French Foreign Legion.

It is estimated that there are no fewer than 2,250,000 Jews in the territory annexed from Poland by the Reich.

German broadcaster defined announcement of R.A.F. 'planes over Berlin as only "a dream."

A permanent Nazi garrison of 90,000 men has been established in former Czecho-Slovakia.

Nazi broadcaster suggested that German housewives should brew tea from blackberry leaves.

Vol. 1　　A Permanent Picture Record of the Second Great War　　No. 8

In the course of his speech to the Reichstag on September 1, 1939, Hitler declared, "I will not make war on women and children." This photograph taken in a field near Warsaw shows that his words were once again falsified by the event. A ten-year-old Polish child kneels in anguish by the side of the mangled body of her elder sister after a Nazi aeroplane had swooped down and poured a rain of bullets on her and other girls and women working in the potato fields.

Photo, Wide World

Under the All-Seeing Eyes of the Royal Air Force

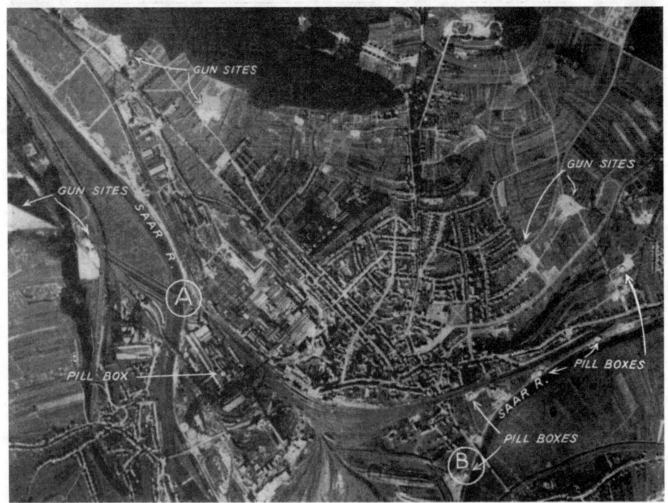

These three photographs show the results of some of the daring reconnaissance flights that the R.A.F. made on the Western Front in the first weeks of the war. That at the top of the page is of Völklingen, a mining town about 6½ miles west of Saarbruecken. It proves the remarkable degree of perfection to which aerial photography has now attained, for, though taken at a height of 20,000 feet, every landmark in the town is clearly visible in the enlarged print. The distance between the points marked A and B is about 1 mile. Bottom left is a pontoon bridge across the Rhine from which the centre pontoons have been removed by the French. This photograph was taken from a height of 600 feet. Right is a railway bridge across the Rhine; at the nearer end are gates closed as a temporary defence.

Photos, Royal Air Force: Crown Copyright Reserved

Waiting for Zero Hour in the West

An observer officer of a British anti-aircraft gun is seen above on the look-out. The gun and its crew have found a natural camouflage in a thicket.

Photo, British Official ; Crown Copyright

After many days during which there was but little to report on the Western Front, the war developed an active spurt on Oct. 16 with the launching of several German attacks on the Moselle Front.

So quiet were the opening weeks of the war that some of the German troops in the line on the Western Front did not know that there was a war on ! Such a state of affairs would have been inconceivable in the Great War, but in 1939 it was quite understandable when the armies were not occupying lines of trenches in the open but were in fact garrison troops in permanent fortifications. Moreover, their superiors had done their best to keep the German rank and file in complete ignorance of the situation, and the fact that they were at war was not realized by some until they were actually taken prisoner. Those men who came from quiet sectors of the line were told that they were on manœuvres, and that the ominous bangs which they heard on their right or left were just the results of target practice or blasting.

Taken prisoner and interrogated by their captors, these innocents were flabbergasted to learn the truth. One of the prisoners is reported to have said : " A war against France and England with the Bolsheviks as our allies ! No, that just can't be true." When assured that it *was* true, he added that " then there will be trouble. But not at first, because as Germans don't think for themselves any more it will take some time for them to realize they have been deceived. After all, Hitler got everything without war." " Poland ? " queried the interrogator. " Oh," came the reply, " that doesn't count, that was just exercising the troops."

Confronted by such an exhibition of carefully-fostered ignorance, the officers making the examination reported that the captured Nazis talked like men who, after years of living amidst savages, had at last resumed contact with civilization.

By the middle of October, however, there can have been few Germans in the vicinity of the Siegfried Line who were not aware that not only was there a war in progress, but that they were engaged in it, and very shortly might be called upon to go "over the top." French commentators said that all the signs went to show that the enemy was preparing a great offensive in which the maximum of material would be used and between 700,000 and 800,000 men. Watchers in the advanced positions of the French line reported twinkling flashlamps and the striking of matches in the opposite positions—indications of troops moving up into the forward zone, and, moreover,

French reservists are liable to be recalled to the colours up to the age of 49, but the older men are not usually sent into the front line. Upper photo, an elderly Poilu who does duty as a cook sits in his open-air kitchen to write a letter home. Bottom left, French soldiers are examining German land-mines which were discovered during a French advance and removed before they exploded. Right, a captured German machine-gun is an object of curiosity. The perforated sleeve is for cooling the barrel.

Photos, Associated Press

French soldiers are seen above on outpost duty on the Western Front. They are using an automatic rifle, supported on a rolled greatcoat, a weapon too heavy to be held to the shoulder. One magazine is in place, and the man on the left holds another ready to replace it. The bell formation of the muzzle is an anti-flash device.

heavy artillery and machine-gun fire, on the morning of October 16 the Germans launched an attack on a front of about four miles immediately to the east of the Moselle. According to the French War Communiqué No. 86, the attackers, supported by artillery fire, " occupied the height of the Schneeberg on which we had a light line of observation posts supported by land mines. Caught under our fire, the enemy attack came to a halt and they even had to withdraw to the north of Apach, into which village they had momentarily penetrated."

A further communiqué announced that " the Germans launched a second attack supported by heavy artillery in the region east of the Saar over a front of about 20 miles. Our light troops fell back fighting in accordance with their mission, but our fire held up the enemy at the prearranged line."

troops under uncertain guidance. Some of the old soldiers who peered through the murk at the moving lights may well have asked, " What would have happened to us in 1917 and 1918 if we had shown a light like that ? " Airmen returning to their headquarters from night reconnaissances reported that six or eight miles behind the line they had detected the headlights of lorries all moving towards the front, and

it was reasonable to suppose that the intermittent flashing and dimming was due to obstacles encountered on the road —unlighted vehicles and bodies of marching troops. Then, too, the photographs of the Siegfried defences, taken day after day and sometimes several times a day, gave many a clue to the expert eye.

Following reports of great activity behind the German lines accompanied by

Later it was given out that the French, in anticipation of the attack, had withdrawn from their advanced positions, leaving a quantity of mines behind them, which, as the Germans advanced, exploded and killed a large number. The Germans were reported to have employed six divisions and to have suffered more than 1,000 casualties.

So the attack collapsed, blown into nothingness by the concentrated fire of the French guns. The zero hour of the great offensive had not come—yet.

The British and French air forces early showed marked superiority over the German air force, and there was surprisingly little interference with their reconnaissance flights over the German line. Above, French aeroplanes are returning to an aerodrome after a flight over the German lines with no losses. On the ground is a machine that has just landed. The camouflage, natural and artificial, of all Allied aerodromes made it difficult to recognize them from the air when once the machines were housed.

Photos, Planet News and Keystone

They Follow in Their Fathers' Footsteps

There is a marked contrast between the colour of the British and French uniforms, as can be gathered from this photograph of two detachments of Allied soldiers passing through a French town, the British in khaki, the French in horizon blue.
Photo, Planet News

In the last war every British soldier generally managed to get a shave and a haircut even under difficult circumstances, and in the centre photograph of an Army barber at work the same desire for personal neatness is manifest in the soldiers of today. The British Army in France is not suffering those discomforts which the first B.E.F. endured in the war of 1914. The men above, photographed in October 1939, are manning an anti-aircraft gun in a field just behind the line as yet untouched by war or weather.
Photo, British Official : Crown Copyright

The Poles Pay the Price of Defeat

While the Nazi and Soviet negotiators were still haggling over the exact division of the spoils of the Polish campaign, their victim was writhing in the anguish of defeat and its horrible accompaniments.

Here on parade is a Nazi motorized unit in occupied Polish territory.
Photo, Planet News

HITLER played the role of conquering hero on October 5. He came to Warsaw, but he did not stay ; instead, he hurried back to Berlin to prepare his speech for the Reichstag, in which he claimed that the Nazi conquest of Poland had been carried out with losses which, considering what had been achieved, were a mere trifle of 44,000 killed, wounded, and missing.

(It may be remarked that, according to the "Arbeiter Zeitung," of Zürich, the real German losses in the campaign were 91,278 dead, 63,417 seriously wounded, and 84,938 slightly wounded. These figures, stated the Swiss newspaper, were based on confidential statistics drawn up by the German War Ministry. It was further reported that 190 German tanks were destroyed and 361 damaged, while the losses incurred by the German air force were 89 fighters, 216 light bombers, 107 heavy bombers, and nine observation 'planes.)

Hitler did not stay long enough in Warsaw to form any real idea of the damage caused by his essay in *Blitzkrieg*, but those officials who were entrusted with the control of the city found themselves faced with a problem of vast magnitude and baffling complexity. On a German estimate, 80 per cent of the city was in ruins. At least 16,000 people had been killed during the siege, and many of them were still unburied. The emergency hospitals were crammed with some 80,000 wounded. The water mains had been wrecked by shell fire, and the water was infected. The social system had largely broken down, and all classes of the population were on the verge of starvation. The conquerors were compelled to provide 600,000 meals a day, and also to install a number of fountains of pure water. In spite of what they could do, however, typhoid and cholera had already given signs of their dread approach.

Something like a reign of terror continued in those districts where the Gestapo succeeded in establishing itself. The spy system which had been developed to such lengths in Nazi Germany was introduced with good effect into Warsaw, and large numbers of Poles, denounced as anti-German or members of Polish patriotic societies, were arrested and dispatched to concentration camps in Germany. In the capital, as in many of the provincial towns and villages, the local citizens were compulsorily enrolled in the labour corps, and forced to work in the fields and to help clear up the abominable litter left in the wake of the machines of war.

On the Soviet side of the line of demarcation there was a terror of another kind, in which the landowners and officers, and to some extent the priests, were subjected to persecution. Many of them were murdered, and their houses

The negotiations for the surrender of Warsaw took place in a German military motor omnibus. General Blaskowitz, the Commander of the Nazi forces, is seen above, second from the left, dictating the terms. Right, Polish officers surrendering their arms.
Photos, Associated Press

and estates were plundered and confiscated. The peasants joyfully appropriated the acres whose harvests had hitherto gone to fill the barns of their masters.

But what was perhaps the most tragic act in the Polish drama was being performed in Rumania, where thousands of Poles of both sexes, of all ranks and occupations, had taken refuge. They wandered about the countryside in miserable procession, ragged and half-starved. Without homes, unable to return to their native land, nor always

Child Victims of Hitler's War of Frightfulness

The full fury of the Nazi onslaught from the air is illustrated in the two photographs in this page.   In one, taken in Praga, a suburb of Warsaw, a little figure of such infinite pathos as to move the stoniest heart sits in stunned bewilderment amidst the ruins of what was once his home. The air raid of which he was a victim destroyed twenty blocks of dwellings inhabited by the poorest class.   In the other picture another child victim has managed to save one treasured possession from the horror that has come upon him—his canary.

Photos, Wide World

Tortured Warsaw Surveys Her Wounds

The utter destruction that came to Warsaw is well seen in this photograph. A couple of German soldiers and a derelict car are the sole occupants of a once prosperous and busy street.

welcome in a country which had its own problems and to spare, they trudged through the autumn days, and at night huddled into doorways or found a bed in some lonely barn. All the worldly goods which the war had left them were contained in the pitifully small bundles which they carried on their backs or pushed before them in little handcarts.

Perhaps still more pitiable was the condition of the Polish leaders. Ex-President Moscicki found refuge in the little town of Sinaia; Colonel Beck was there too in a sanatorium. Marshal Smigly Rydz and his lady were in a palace at Craijowa; and other ministers found a temporary resting-place at Herculanee, near Turnu Severin on the Danube. •

Besides damage to buildings Warsaw suffered the almost complete destruction and immobilization of her transport services. In the centre photograph is a huge crater formed by a bomb that dropped in a main street and penetrated to the tunnel of the underground railway. But life must go on, and the first efforts to mitigate the disaster are being made. In the photograph below is another wrecked street, with a tram-car lying on its side in the roadway, having been caught by the blast of a shell, or it may have been used as a barricade.

Photos, Planet News and Associated Press

The Bolshevik Flood Reaches the Baltic

For years Hitler vociferated that Nazism was Europe's principal embankment against Bolshevism. In 1939, however, he himself opened the flood-gates by his pact with Moscow, and so made it possible for the Bolshevik tide to engulf the Baltic lands.

As the result of a practically bloodless campaign Stalin seized almost half Poland. Still he was not satisfied. Less than a month after the Red army invaded Poland, Soviet troops were massed in menacing readiness on the frontiers of the three Baltic republics of Estonia, Latvia, and Lithuania.

Estonia was the first to come to terms with her great neighbour. On September 29 a Soviet-Estonian pact of mutual assistance was signed, following which large detachments of Russian troops crossed the Estonian frontier to occupy the naval bases and aerodromes provided for in the agreement. It was stated that a permanent Russian garrison of some 25,000 men was to be maintained in the little country.

Latvia's turn came next, and on October 5 she accepted from Russia a pact on the lines of that just concluded between the Soviet and Estonia. It provided for Russian naval and air bases at the Latvian ports of Libau (Liepaja) and Windau (Ventspils), supported by coastal batteries and garrisons at various places.

Then a few days after the signing of the pact with Latvia, the Russians concluded a similar pact with Lithuania. The U.S.S.R. was granted the right to maintain in Lithuania land and air forces of a certain size, and each country guaranteed the territories of the other against aggression, besides agreeing not to participate in any alliance or coalition aimed against the other. As a solace to Lithuania's rather wounded pride, the Russians agreed that Wilno—the former capital of Lithuania which was occupied by the Poles in 1920—and Wilno district should be transferred to Lithuania.

Demands on Finland

By way of completing Russian control over the eastern Baltic Stalin now made an approach to the Finnish government, but whereas the ultimatums dispatched to Estonia, Latvia and Lithuania had called for the presence of their ministers in Moscow within twenty-four hours, no time limit was specified in the case of Finland. In fact, six days elapsed before Finland's representative, M. Paasikivi, the republic's Minister in Stockholm, appeared in Moscow. Certain demands were laid before him, and although no details were published officially, it was rumoured that they included the cession, in return for certain territory in eastern Karelia, of the islands of Tytarsaari, Lavansaari, Seiskari, and possibly Suursaari, at the entrance to Kronstadt Bay in the Gulf of Finland. It was also reported that Finland had been requested not to fortify the Aaland Islands, and that

Finland had been invited to conclude a military pact with Russia.

Whatever the result of his negotiations with Finland, however, Stalin might well congratulate himself upon his latest victory in the diplomatic war. By her occupation of the Estonian ports and the islands of Dagö and Ösel, Russia now possessed a first-class fairway from her naval base of Kronstadt into the Baltic; and her control of the Latvian ports of Windau and Libau still further ensured her domination of the sea. If, moreover, the Aaland Islands were occupied, or at least controlled by Russia, then the fact that the Baltic had ceased to be a German

lake would become still more apparent, for batteries planted on the Aaland Islands would effectually command the channel, the Gulf of Bothnia, down which the ships carrying Swedish ore from the mines at Gällivare and Kiruna have to pass— and without Swedish ore Germany would be unable to continue this war very long, or to wage another effectually.

Immediately following the establishment of Russia's protectorate over the Baltic States there came the amazing report that Herr Hitler had "invited" all the Germans resident in Latvia to "return home to the Reich," and a little later it was announced that a similar

The Letts are an intensely patriotic people, and a call for women to serve in various capacities met with an instant response. In the top photograph is a parade of women voluntary workers. The lower photograph shows a review of the Latvian army, which has a peacetime establishment of 2,200 officers and 23,000 men.

Photos, Derek Wordley and Wide World

"invitation" had been sent to the Germans in the other two Baltic republics. It seemed that arrangements had already been made for the evacuees to leave by sea, and a considerable number of ships were already anchored at Baltic ports, ready to begin the transfer of the local Germans to the Reich. In Latvia alone it was estimated that there were 60,000 persons of German blood who would be affected by the "invitation."

Several reasons were advanced for this astounding stroke of policy, but none that was official was vouchsafed. Some suggested that Hitler wanted German colonists for his newly-conquered territories in western Poland ; others thought it more likely that Stalin was determined to remove from the territory now just come under his control any potential sympathizers with his rival dictator.

In this map are shown the four countries, Finland, Estonia, Latvia and Lithuania, immediately concerned in the Soviet advance towards the Baltic, and also the Aaland Islands, part of the territory of Finland. In the map inset is the Gulf of Finland on an enlarged scale.

The Aaland Islands form one of the most important strategic points in the Baltic. Suggestions by Sweden and Finland that they should be fortified were vetoed time after time by Russia, and they once again became a bone of contention in 1939. Top, the capital of the Aaland Islands, Mariehamn. Below, the landing-place on the Finnish island of Suursaari.
Photos, Wide World and E.N.A.

Then there was a story told to the effect that Hitler had literally sold the Germans in the three Baltic States to Stalin for Russian gold. Hitler needed gold at once, in order to pay for his war supplies ordered from abroad ; Stalin had the gold, and was prepared to let Germany have it in return for the definite abandonment of the German hold on the Baltic lands. And how could that abandonment be more clearly evidenced to the world than by the withdrawal from those States of all the German-speaking peoples ?

But a week or two before Russia had put a full stop to Germany's expansion in the south-east, when across the approaches to the Ukraine she flung a protecting wall of Soviet bayonets and tanks. Now she repeated the stroke. From the Baltic, as from the Balkans, Germany was definitely "warned off."

How the New B.E.F. Went to France

In his speech to the House of Commons on October 11, 1939, Mr. Leslie Hore-Belisha,
Secretary for War, described how in the first weeks of war Britain's Expeditionary
Force was transported to France without a single casualty.

BEGINNING by saying that the British Government had more than fulfilled their undertaking to France to dispatch to that country in the event of war an Expeditionary Force of a specified dimension within a specified time, Mr. Hore-Belisha went on :

WITHIN six weeks of the outbreak of war in 1914 we had transported to France 148,000 men. Within five weeks of the outbreak of this war we had transported to France 158,000 men.

During this period we have also created our base and lines of communication organization, so as to assure the regular flow of supplies and munitions of every kind and to receive further contingents as and when we may decide to send them. The major operation is thus over, and it is possible to speak to the House with frankness. I wish it had been prudent to do so previously.

Night by night at the War Office we have waited for tidings of the arrival of the convoys. These have averaged three every night. It would have been encouraging to have shared at every stage the news as we received it with the nation so uncertain of what was transpiring and so naturally eager for reports about its Army.

The Press, like Parliament, willingly observed a reticence which in itself was a safeguard for our contingents. There is no need for further silence, and a body of war correspondents has just arrived in France with the object of keeping us all informed of day-to-day impressions and happenings.

The Brains Behind the Move

IT was a small body of specially selected officers in the War Office who, with seven confidential clerks and typists, secretly worked out every detail of this plan for moving the Army and the Royal Air Force to France. They foresaw and provided for every need : the selection of ports and docks, of roads and railways, of accommodation of all types, of rest camps and depots, of hospitals and repair shops, at every stage on both sides of the Channel. Their ingenuity, their precision and their patience would have baffled Bradshaw. . . . The Expeditionary Force has been transported to France intact without a casualty to any of its personnel.

May I describe to the House some aspects in which the task on this occasion has differed from that of 1914, although, as one watches the process, continuing with the smoothness of a machine, one finds it hard to believe that there has been a break of 25 years in the passage of these two armies ?

Then the men marched on to the ships, the horses were led, and a light derrick could lift what the soldier could not carry. In those days there were only 800 mechanized vehicles in all, and it was a rare load that exceeded two tons.

WE have already on this occasion transported to France more than 25,000 vehicles including tanks, some of them of enormous dimensions and weighing 15 tons apiece or more.

Normal shore cranes could not raise them, special ships were required to carry them and highly trained stevedores to manipulate them. Consequently, as contrasted with 1914, where ordinary vessels took men and their material together from the usual ports, in this case the men travelled separately and the heavier mechanisms had to be transported from more distant ports, where special facilities were available. The arrangements for the reunion of the troops with their material on the other side made an additional complication.

Similarly, and for other reasons also, more remote landing-places had to be selected in France, thus making the voyages much longer.

Again internally, and as a precaution against air attack, more devious internal routes were taken than in 1914. Vehicles and men were dispersed in small groups, halted in concealed areas by day and moved onwards by night.

As with transport, so with maintenance, the problem has become greater than it was a generation ago.

Every horse eats the same food and can continue, like man, to move though hungry. Vehicles come to a standstill when their tanks are empty. There are in France 50 types of vehicle, and most of them require a different grade of fuel and lubricant. Great reserves have had to be conveyed and stored. . . .

Problems of 1914 and 1939 Compared

NONE of these problems existed, except in embryo, in 1914. It was a light army that travelled then. Nearly 60 per cent of the fighting troops in 1914 were infantrymen, relying on their rifles and bayonets and two machine-guns per battalion. Now only 20 per cent of the fighting troops are infantrymen, with 50 Bren guns, 22 anti-tank rifles, and other weapons as well, with each battalion.

It will be seen by this one example how much more effectively armed with fire power is the present Expeditionary Force.

There is, however, one respect in which our Army has not altered ; its relations with our Allies, who have welcomed the men so generously, are as good humoured. The catchwords of the soldiers are as amusing. . . .

To all those who have co-operated in this military movement, to the various Government departments both in this country and in France, the gratitude of this nation is due. Especially, however, should the achievement be recorded as evidence that the maritime might of Britain is unimpaired. **The Navy has not lost its secret, and the Air Force had held its protecting wings over another element of danger.**

IT is not only to France that British soldiers have been transported. The Middle East has been strongly reinforced, and also our garrisons elsewhere, both in material and in men.

One part of our Army, however, remains stationary in this country, waiting and watching, in little groups. In isolated stations the Anti-Aircraft Units have been on guard since before this war began, and that their vigilance is not forgotten, under-estimated, or unrecognized by this country and by this House must be their great encouragement.

We have a numerous Army. In that respect we are at the outset of hostilities better situated than we were in 1914.

We had in peacetime taken a precaution, for which we must now be thankful, of instituting a system of universal military training, and thus the even flow of recruits became as well assured to us as to the Continental countries. We had the foundation on which, after the declaration of war, we could build an even more comprehensive

Down the gangway of a transport at a French port men of the Royal Air Force are bringing their baggage ashore and lending a hand to a number of Red Cross nurses, also bound towards the front. One strange point of contrast between the nurses of 1914 and those of 1939 is that today each one carries her " tin hat " and gas mask slung over her shoulders.

Photo, British Official ; Crown Copyright

Not only cooked food bought in the canteens but culinary efforts of their own go to increase the soldiers' diet. These Highlanders at a hardware shop somewhere in France are buying cooking utensils, perhaps to make some delicacies reminiscent of home. They may find that French kitchen apparatus differs in pattern from that to which they are used, but the Army amateur cook is nothing if not adaptable and resourceful.

system and we passed the National Service Act, placing under an obligation to serve all male British citizens resident in Great Britain between the ages of 18 and 41.

In peacetime also we had doubled the Territorial Field Army. Altogether we had at the disposal of the Army in this country alone, including the Reservists and the Militia, the best part of 1,000,000 men on whom we could call at the outbreak of war.

Never had the total of our armed forces in the United Kingdom approached anywhere near such a total in time of peace.

When I first introduced Army Estimates to the House in March 1938 we were preparing out of our strategic reserve five divisions—none of them upon a Continental scale. By the time of the next Army Estimates, in March this year, the Government had decided to prepare 19 divisions—all upon a Continental scale.

Subsequently the European tension increased, and in April the plan for 19 divisions became one for 32. This will not be the limit of our effort. It is plain that great calls will be made upon our man-power. How do we intend to proceed?

In the first place we have the method of calling up classes. His Majesty has already proclaimed the classes between 20 and 22.

Those within the classes proclaimed are being called up in batches, and with each batch we are taking an additional quota of volunteers. Any man desirous of being a volunteer in the Army, and being above the age of the class called up, may register his name at either a recruiting station or a Ministry of Labour office and he will be treated in exactly the same way as the classes proclaimed. . . .

There is even greater inducement now than in previous wars to join the Army in the way described. Apart from specialist appointments, virtually all commissions will be given from the ranks. It must be remembered that the nation is in arms and there is no dearth of ability in the ranks. One of the best men who has reached the top for the leader's course on the way to a commission is a labourer's son.

Every Man May Reach a Star

THE look-out for talent is continuous, and all commanding officers are instructed to search for it. In this Army the star is within every private soldier's reach. No one, however humble or exalted his birth, need be afraid that his military virtues will remain unrecognized.

More important, no one who wishes to serve in the Army need consider his status minimized by starting at the bottom of the ladder. From the ranks we shall mainly derive our junior officers.

For officers in the middle piece and for specialists we have other sources open to us. We have the Regular Army Reserve. We have the Territorial Reserve of Officers, and we also have the Army Officers' Emergency Reserve. . . .

It will be unnecessary to remind the House that it is of the essence of reserves that they are not all used up at once, and upon the assumption that this will be a three years' war, many of those with suitable qualifications will in due course have their opportunity.

The splendid women of the A.T.S., already 20,000 strong, are about to extend their service in replacement of their brothers in arms.

Cheery greetings are being exchanged between the crews of a British column of motor lorries and a French motor-cycle unit in a town behind the lines. In the last war the part played by motor-cyclists was chiefly as dispatch riders, though after a time the condition of the roads made it almost impossible for them to approach close to the front line. In all the photographs of the British and French armies that have appeared in these pages the absence of horses is very noticeable.

Photos, Planet News

Such a scene as this is usual in many an old French farmstead where only a few weeks before the harvest was being gathered in. The Army cooks with their field kitchens have taken possession of the farm, and men of a mechanized unit are lining up with their mess tins.

Further openings for the older men will be given in two new directions . . . Home Defence Battalions . . . and an Auxiliary Pioneer Corps which will take over military pioneer work, both overseas and here.

Pari passu with this pressure upon us to take men into the Army is a pressure in the reverse direction. We have tried to deal liberally with industry, whose needs we fully recognise, just as industry will recognise that an army is a skilled profession and must also, for the safety of the country, have men of specialised knowledge.

Soldiers Back to Industry

WE have temporarily released about 10,000 Regular Reservists, and will have shortly in addition have released 12,000 Territorials either temporarily or permanently. In so far as these releases are helping to accelerate and enlarge the output of our war industries, the loss will have been repaid to us.

Any words of mine that can stimulate and electrify these industries of the country which are engaged on the output of munitions to put their last ounce into the task of meeting the needs of those in the field and of hastening the

day when others can join them will, I am sure, be endorsed by the Minister of Supply. It is the output of factories making equipment and munitions for the field which will be the ultimate measure of our effort.

I will tell the House what is being done by and for the Army to train as many men as possible to become technicians, and thereby to spare industry the full drain which would otherwise be made upon it. The Army is training such men itself. The Minister of Labour has plans in mind for enabling some of his training establishments to assist in the provision of Army requirements of skilled tradesmen. With the help of the Minister of Education we hope to use the polytechnics, technical schools, and Universities for the same purpose.

Industry will doubtless in its own ways be making provision to augment its resources of skilled personnel. We can look with confidence to these developments.

In 1914 appeals were made for recruits who had neither clothing, nor equipment, nor instructors, nor accommodation, and men were taken regardless of their civilian occupations.

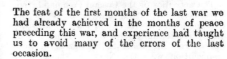

The feat of the first months of the last war we had already achieved in the months of peace preceding this war, and experience had taught us to avoid many of the errors of the last occasion.

THUS at the beginning of September we had in being an Army which was daily acquiring new strength, better cohesion, and greater efficiency.

It has been a privilege to speak of it today and to reveal that while the world was reading of the German advances into Poland British soldiers, resolved to rectify this wrong, were passing silently and in an unceasing sequence across the Channel into France. There we may think of them in their positions along a countryside whose towns, whose villages, and whose rivers are as familiar to them by memory or by tradition as their own.

How strange it is that twice in a generation men should take this journey and that sons should be treading again upon a soil made sacred by their fathers.

They are grumbling about the same things, mispronouncing the same names, making similar jokes and singing songs which seem an echo over the intervening years. And we may rest assured that they will acquit themselves with the same tenacity, courage and endurance. However long the struggle and however great the ordeal, they will, as our soldiers did before, take our arms and our cause of freedom to victory.

At the end of the day for men of the British Field Force (as it is officially known) comes a spell of relaxation. Above right, men in a farmhouse billet are doing what is the soldier's first voluntary duty—writing home. Below, men of a transport column finish work by spreading camouflage netting over their lorry.

Photos, Sport & General and British Official; Crown Copyright

Britain's Supremacy in the Air

On October 10, 1939, Sir Kingsley Wood, Secretary of State for Air, gave the House of Commons his statement on the varied and daring exploits of the R.A.F. in the first weeks of the war, and an account of the plans for further production of machines and training of personnel. For the Empire's air contribution see page 245.

Sir Kingsley Wood has been Secretary of State for Air since May 1938. He had previously proved his administrative ability as Postmaster-General and Minister of Health.

Photo, Central Press

AFTER a tribute to the preparedness and the splendid morale of the R.A.F., the Air Minister continued :

Accounts have already been given of such considerable performances of the R.A.F. as the attacks on the German Fleet and the engagements with the enemy in Germany and on the Western Front. They show that the spirit and determination of the earlier generation of our flying men have been preserved unimpaired. The men who have already been in action have indeed shown to the full their courage and efficiency. . . .

Full recognition, too, should be given to those who, though they have had to stand by at their war stations in a state of instant readiness for action by day or by night, have not yet been engaged in action with the enemy. Instant readiness is demanded, and the strain imposed has been as great as, if not greater, than if active operations were in progress. The keenness and the alertness of these officers and men are of the first order.

The activities of the Coastal Command, too, have been unremitting and strenuous in the extreme from the first day of war. Today the vastly greater range, speed, and reliability of our aircraft are being fully utilized, in close co-operation with the Navy, in the task of defeating the submarine and guiding in safety to and from our shores those merchant ships that ply the ocean.

By its very nature the work is silent and normally unspectacular. It demands continuous flying over the sea in all weathers. The magnitude of the effort of the Coastal Command may be judged by the fact that during the first four weeks of war this Command flew on reconnaissance, anti-submarine and convoy patrols a distance of approximately 1,000,000 miles and provided air escorts for over 100 convoys.

Putting the U-Boats Down

OUR air escorts have also often been able to give warning of the approach of enemy craft and of the presence of submarines from ranges which are far beyond the vision of surface craft. The result of these endeavours has been fruitful. During the first four weeks of war submarines were sighted by aircraft on 72 occasions, and 34 attacks were delivered, some of which were undoubtedly successful. . .

In the Bomber Command, apart from the larger operations upon which they have been engaged, there have been many and valuable reconnaissance flights. They have taken place day after day over German territory, and hundreds of hours of flying have been recorded. Vital military information has been gained and recorded and units have familiarized themselves with the country over which they will be called upon to operate. Day and night, reconnaissance aircraft are penetrating into the enemy's country, testing his defences and observing his movements and troop concentrations.

Survey of Siegfried Line

A COMPLETE photographic map of the Siegfried Line has been made. Many photographs, taken from only a few hundred feet above the Line, go to the composition of this map. A few days ago our aircraft, taking off from an aerodrome in France, covered the whole length of Germany from the Saar to the North Sea, flew on to Heligoland, all without serious interruptions, and then made safe landings home in England. All accounts speak as highly of the navigating skill of the pilots and crews as of their determination.

Sir Kingsley Wood then quoted from some of the detailed reports of reconnaissance pilots, illustrating the difficulties under which they worked.

The distribution of messages to the German people over large areas of enemy territory, which has been combined with successful reconnaissance work, has, I believe, been of considerable value in giving information to the people of Germany. . . .

A FTER dealing with the subject of recruiting and recording that in the first fortnight of the war over 10,000 men were accepted for service as pilots, Sir Kingsley Wood turned to the consideration of aircraft.

STARTLING claims have been made from time to time in regard to the performance of German military aircraft—particularly, for example, their fighters. The plain facts seem to be that our latest fighters are definitely better than their German counterparts. Happily, a specimen of the latest Messerschmitt fighter has fallen intact into the hands of the French, so that in regard to this aircraft at least we shall be free to test our convictions at our convenience. . . .

At the outbreak of war the rate of aircraft production represented an achievement unprecedented in this country in time of peace. Moreover, our factories are every day increasing their labour force, and the increased experience of aircraft work has already resulted in an increased output rate per man. Immediately war broke out our carefully prepared plans for greatly increased production were put into effect. They will mean in due course a rate of production more than twice the considerable figure we have now reached. . . .

Pilots in the Forefront

HIS MAJESTY KING GEORGE V, at the end of the last Great War, spoke in moving terms of the great contribution that the Empire had made in the air to victory. He recalled how the air pilots of the Empire and of Britain had ever been in the forefront of the battle, and how far-flying squadrons over home waters and foreign seas had splendidly maintained our cause.

We shall have our dangers, our ordeals, and our difficulties, but none of us doubts that when the great test comes again our airmen of today —from the Motherland and overseas—will once more record the same magnificent achievements, self-sacrifice and devotion to duty.

The first duty assigned to the Royal Air Force in France was reconnaissance over the Siegfried Line. Such aircraft as the Fairey Battles seen above are particularly valuable for this work, as they combine high speed with a steady platform for the observer and good defensive armour. Another photograph of such aircraft appears in page 187.

Photo, Wide World

Nature Conscripted to Conceal Our 'Planes

The completeness of the camouflage now used in the aerodromes in France is illustrated here. Only the distinguishing disk makes it possible to detect the aeroplane's presence.

Brushwood is extensively used for camouflage purposes at the aerodromes on the Western Front. Above can be seen the way in which a screen is built up in front of the machine when it has finished its day's work.

The centre photograph gives a close-up view of the zigzag steel network which is laid on the runways of an aerodrome. Its purpose is to prevent the wheels sinking into the mud when the machine is taking off. Grass is allowed to grow over it so that it cannot be detected from the air. Below is an example of complete camouflage. An aeroplane has its tail in a copse, and brushwood has been placed in front of it.

Photos, Associated Press, Sport & General and Keystone

Poland Bids a Temporary Farewell to Freedom

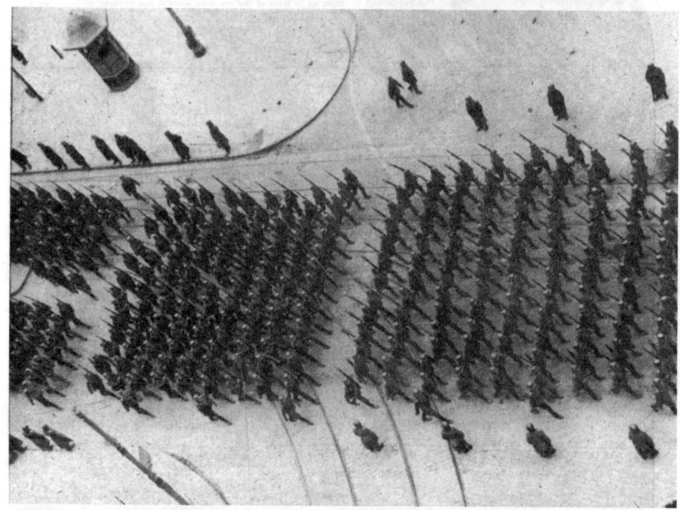

In the two photographs in this page German troops are seen entering Warsaw after the surrender of the city. To impress the inhabitants and to vaunt their martial superiority those in the top photograph were led by a band. They were among the first enemy troops in Warsaw, and they were watched by a mere handful of passers-by, stunned into indifference by the fury of the Nazi air attacks. In the lower photograph is another ineffective Nazi attempt to impress the people of Warsaw—the ceremonial march on Oct. 5, when Hitler took the salute.

Photos, Mondiale and Associated Press

After War's Tumult the Deadly Quiet of Defeat

In remarkable and pathetic contrast to the two scenes opposite is that at the top of this page. A remnant of the Polish garrison, headed by a single officer on horseback, is marching out of Warsaw before the oncoming Nazi hosts. Though no soldiers could have displayed a more gallant spirit, they show in their mien the dejection that must come even to the bravest troops when they realize that they have fought in vain. Below, is some debris of a Polish battlefield—a pile of steel helmets and gas masks cast aside when it was clear they would not be needed.

Top photograph, Wide World

Britain Takes Toll of First Air Raiders

The first air-raid warning came to Britain less than half an hour after she declared war with Germany. The first real air raid, however, was not carried out until October 16, more than six weeks later. Here we give a brief account of these first offensive operations.

Commander R. F. Jolly was in command of the " Mohawk," a destroyer which was returning to Rosyth from convoy duty on October 16. He was killed by a bomb splinter.

Photo, Sport and General

D URING the lunch hour on Monday, October 16, the beautiful gardens which run through the heart of Edinburgh were crowded with city folk reading their newspapers and enjoying their paper-bag lunches in the warm autumn sunshine.

Two o'clock had not long struck when a strange clatter in the sky drew all eyes upward. The blue was speckled with little white bursts, and in the distance there was the muffled bark of guns. It was thought at first that the anti-aircraft defences were conducting a practice shoot, but as firing developed over the Firth of Forth it was brought home to the onlookers that a real air-raid was in progress. Although no warning sirens had been heard, most of the citizens took cover. Others climbed to the roof-tops to look at what must have been one of the most stirring and strange spectacles that ever Edinburgh has witnessed in all her history.

High up in the blue German aircraft and R.A.F. machines pirouetted in a dance of death. The noise of machine-gun fire was almost continuous, and the flashes from the guns could be clearly seen. Occasionally from a distance came the dull boom of an exploding bomb.

The air-raid was carried out by twelve, or possibly more, aircraft, in waves of two or three at a time. Appearing from the east they dived down on to the ships of the Royal Navy lying in the Firth off Rosyth. One of the raiders swooped almost as low as the topmost span of the Forth Bridge, and opened fire with a machine-gun on two cruisers when flying at a height of less than 300 feet. Then it turned again towards the warships and dropped bombs, none of which hit the bridge itself.

Several bombs were dropped at Rosyth. One glanced off the cruiser "Southampton" causing slight damage near her bow, and sinking the Admiral's barge and a pinnace moored alongside. This,

incidentally, was the first hit made by German aircraft during the war upon a British ship. A second bomb fell near the destroyer "Mohawk," which was returning to harbour from convoy escort. It burst in the water, but splinters caused a number of casualties among the men on the deck of the destroyer.

The R.A.F. 'planes first made contact with the enemy off the Isle of May at the entrance to the Firth of Forth at 2.35 p.m. when they intercepted two Nazi 'planes, drove them from 4,000 feet to within a few feet of the water, and chased them out to sea. Ten minutes later another enemy aircraft was engaged over Dalkeith and sent down into the water in flames. Within a quarter of an hour a sharp combat took place off Crail and another raider crashed into the sea, its crew being rescued by fishermen. A third

This map of the Firth of Forth shows Rosyth and the surrounding area involved in the attack by German bombers on October 16.

German aircraft was destroyed in the pursuit, while a fourth was brought down in flames by anti-aircraft fire.

The raid had lasted upwards of an hour and a half, and the last of the German 'planes were speeded home at 4 p.m. when shore watchers saw two enemy aircraft flying eastward a thousand feet up, closely pursued by British fighters.

No bombs were dropped on Edinburgh, and the only civilian casualties were four people slightly injured by bullets and shrapnel. The naval casualties were seventeen killed and forty-four wounded.

The next day, Scapa Flow, the famous anchorage in the Orkneys (see map, page 246), was raided twice by German aeroplanes. In the first raid carried out by four planes at 10.30 a.m., two bombs fell near the old battleship "Iron Duke," which was somewhat damaged. One of the raiders was shot down in flames. A few hours later the second air attack was carried out by two formations of six and four aircraft, and although neither damage nor casualties were reported, the raiders were said to have suffered loss.

"We know that in the air battles which during the last two days," said Mr. Chamberlain in the House of Commons on October 18, "have been fought over our own coasts, we have destroyed eight enemy aircraft without losing a single machine of our own. We have at least the satisfaction of knowing that we have made a good beginning."

Three of the crew of four of one of the German bombers brought down over the Firth of Forth were rescued by a fishing boat. The crew of the fishing boat are here seen holding part of the equipment of the bomber's crew. One of the Germans gave a gold ring to the skipper of the boat which rescued them. (See eye-witness story in page 252.)

Photo, Central Press

The Cavalry of the Skies in Training

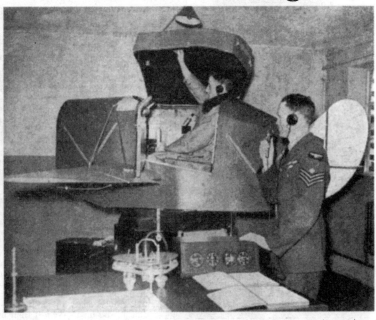

The silk of parachutes on which the lives of pilots and air crews may depend in an emergency is here seen being subjected to a most rigorous examination.

IN the repulse of the air attack on the Forth on October 16, pride of place was taken by the men of the Royal Air Force. At least two of the enemy raiders accounted for were shot down by British fighter aircraft, and the raiders were beaten off in such a way that probably not more than half returned to their base. No pilot claimed to have brought down one of the raiders single-handed; their defeat was a team job. The glory of the fight was shared by men who only a few weeks before had been going about their peacetime vocations of stockbrokers, lawyers, and sheep-farmers.

An ingenious apparatus used in the training of R.A.F. pilots is the Link Trainer, seen top right. This enables a pupil to learn the rudiments of flying solely by instruments under " blind " conditions, without leaving the ground. In the photograph immediately above are pilots who have passed through the course. They are wearing the regulation flying suit and parachute, the latter with its heavy harness and quick-release attachment. In the leggings are pockets for carrying maps.

Photos. Planet News

The Tragedy of the 'Royal Oak'

Mr. Winston Churchill stated in the House of Commons, October 17 :

"THE battleship 'Royal Oak' was sunk at anchor by a U-boat in Scapa Flow approximately at 1.30 a.m. on Oct. 14. . . .

"When we consider that during the whole course of the last war this anchorage was found to be immune from such attacks, on account of the obstacles imposed by the currents and the net barrages, this entry by a U-boat must be considered as a remarkable exploit of professional skill and daring.

"It appears probable that the U-boat fired a salvo of torpedoes at the 'Royal Oak,' of which only one hit the bow. This muffled explosion was at the time attributed to internal causes, and what is called the inflammable store, where the kerosene and other such materials are kept, was flooded. Twenty minutes later the U-boat fired three or four torpedoes, and these, striking in quick succession, caused the ship to capsize and sink. She was lying at the extreme end of the harbour, and therefore many officers and men were drowned before rescue could be organized from other vessels.

"The lists of survivors have already been made public, and I deeply regret to inform the House that upwards of eight hundred officers and men have lost their lives."

"The Admiralty immediately announced the loss of this fine ship. Serious as this loss is, it does not affect the margin of security in heavy vessels, which remains ample."

Pathetic scenes were witnessed when the lists of survivors of the "Royal Oak" were scanned by relations hoping to find their men.

Here is the boiler-room of the "Royal Oak." In such a catastrophe the engineers and stokers are in the most dangerous position in the ship.

Four of the officers who were rescued from the "Royal Oak" are seen above. They are, left to right, Captain W. F. Benn, R.N., Commander R. F. Nichols, R.N., Lieut. Anthony H. Terry, R.N., and Lieut. Bernard B. Keen, Royal Marines.
Photos, Topical, Wide World and Fox

H.M.S. "Royal Oak" was a battleship of 29,150 tons laid down in 1914. She was in action in the Battle of Jutland, but in 1934 was withdrawn from the First Battle Squadron and reconditioned at a cost of £1,000,000. She was recommissioned in 1936. She carried eight 15-in. guns, and twelve 6-in. guns as her main armament.

Scapa Flow, the land-locked Orkneys harbour, was the Grand Fleet base in 1914-18.

No Easy Passage for the U-Boats

The U-boat above sank two British ships, but the commander behaved with commendable humanity. He signalled to the Norwegian ship "Ida Bukke" then off Cape Clear, Eire, to rescue the crews and stood by until this was done. The photograph was taken by a passenger on the Norwegian ship when the crew of the U-boat gave her a parting cheer. Below, large U-boats are moored in Hamburg Harbour.

Photos, Planet News & Sport and General

Left, a German naval cadet takes the wheel while undergoing training for submarine service.
Photo, Fox

WHEN Mr. Winston Churchill spoke on October 11, 1939, in the House of Commons on the campaign against the U-boats he was able to give reassuring figures showing a steady decline in the number of British ships sunk compared with the enemy ships captured and new British tonnage launched. From 65,000 tons in the first week, sinkings fell to 5,800 tons in the fourth week. The results of the first six weeks of the war at sea, as regards Great Britain, are shown diagrammatically below. The U-boats sunk do not include those destroyed by the French. Allied losses were, however, increased about October 16 by the sinking of the British "Lochavon," 9,205 tons, and the large French steamers "Bretagne" and "Louisane."

THE NAVAL ACCOUNT
First Six Weeks of the War at Sea
September 3—October 14, 1939
(*See also diagram in page 142*)

DEBITS	CREDITS
British Merchantmen sunk	**Enemy Merchantmen captured**
174,000 Tons	29,000 Tons
The Courageous sunk Sept. 18th	**New British Ships since Sept. 3rd**
22,500 Tons	104,000 Tons
	Merchandise captured
	338,000 Tons
The Royal Oak sunk Oct. 14th	**Enemy U-boats sunk**
	Enemy U-boats damaged
29,000 Tons	18 Craft

(*Each Symbol = 35,000 tons, except Warships & U-boats*)

CHAMBERLAIN MEETS THE 'PEACE OFFENSIVE'

On October 12 the Prime Minister made his eagerly-awaited statement in the House of
Commons in reply to the " peace proposals " put forward by Herr Hitler on October 6.
The most important passages of Mr. Chamberlain's speech—in which he declared
that " acts, not words alone " must be forthcoming—are reproduced below.

THE Prime Minister began by saying that consultations had taken place with the French and the Dominion Governments regarding the terms of Herr Hitler's speech. After summing up the vain efforts of the British Government to preserve peace, Mr. Chamberlain continued :

ON Sept. 1 Herr Hitler violated the Polish frontier and invaded Poland, beating down by force of arms and machinery the resistance of the Polish nation and Army. As attested by neutral observers, Polish towns and villages were bombed and shelled into ruins ; and civilians were slaughtered wholesale, in contravention, at any rate in the later stages, of all the undertakings of which Herr Hitler now speaks with pride as though he had fulfilled them.

It is after this wanton act of aggression, which has cost so many Polish and German lives, sacrificed to satisfy his own insistence on the use of force, that the German Chancellor now puts forward his proposals. If there existed any expectation that in these proposals would be included some attempt to make amends for this grievous crime against humanity, following so soon upon the violation of the rights of the Czecho-Slovak nation, it has been doomed to disappointment. The Polish State and its leaders are covered with abuse. What the fate of that part of Poland which Herr Hitler describes as the German sphere of interest is to be does not clearly emerge from his speech, but it is evident that he regards it as a matter for the consideration of Germany alone, to be settled solely in accordance with German interests . . .

WE must take it, then, that the proposals which the German Chancellor puts forward for the establishment of what he calls " the certainty of European security " are to be based on recognition of his conquests and his right to do what he pleases with the conquered. **It would be impossible for Great Britain to accept any such basis without forfeiting her honour and abandoning her claim that international disputes should be settled by discussion and not by force.**

The passages in the speech designed to give fresh assurances to Herr Hitler's neighbours I pass over, since they will know what value should be attached to them by reference to the similar assurances he has given in the past. It would be easy to quote sentences from his speeches in 1935, 1936, and 1938 stating in the most definite terms his determination not to annex Austria or conclude an *Anschluss* with her, not to fall upon Czecho-Slovakia, and not to make any further territorial claims in Europe after the Sudetenland question had been settled in September, 1938. Nor can we pass over Herr Hitler's radical departure from the long professed principles of his policy and creed, as instanced by the inclusion in the German Reich of many millions of Poles and Czechs, despite his repeated professions to the contrary, and by the pact with the Soviet Union concluded after his repeated and violent denunciations of Bolshevism.

No Reliance on Hitler's Word

THIS repeated disregard for his word and these sudden reversals of policy bring me to the fundamental difficulty in dealing with the wider proposals in the German Chancellor's speech. The plain truth is that, **after our past experience, it is no longer possible to rely upon the unsupported word of the present German Government.** It is no part of our policy to exclude from her rightful place in Europe a Germany which will live in amity and confidence with other nations. On the contrary, we believe that no effective remedy can be found for the world's ills that does not take account of the just claims and needs of all countries, and, whenever the time may come to draw the lines of a new peace settlement, his Majesty's Government would

feel that the future would hold little hope unless such a settlement could be reached through negotiation and agreement.

It was not, therefore, with any vindictive purpose that we embarked on war, but simply in defence of freedom. It is not alone the freedom of the small nations that is at stake ; **there is also in jeopardy the peaceful existence of Great Britain, the Dominions, India, the rest of the British Empire, France, and indeed of all freedom-loving countries . . .**

His Majesty's Government know all too well that in modern war between great Powers victor and vanquished must alike suffer cruel loss. But surrender to wrongdoing would spell the extinction of all hope, and the annihilation of all those values of life which have through centuries been at once the mark and inspiration of human progress.

We seek no material advantage for ourselves ; we desire nothing from the German people which should offend their self-respect. **We are not aiming only at victory, but rather looking beyond it to the laying of a foundation of a better international system which would mean that war is not to be the inevitable lot of every succeeding generation.**

I am certain that all the peoples of Europe, including the people of Germany, long for peace —a peace which will enable them to live their lives without fear, and to devote their energies and their gifts to the development of their culture, the pursuit of their ideals, and the improvement of their material prosperity. The peace which we are determined to secure, however, must be a real and settled peace—not an uneasy truce interrupted by constant alarms and repeated threats.

Obstacles to Peace

WHAT stands in the way of such a peace ? It is the German Government, and the German Government alone, for it is they who by repeated acts of aggression have robbed all Europe of tranquillity and implanted in the hearts of all their neighbours an ever-present sense of insecurity and fear . . . .

I would sum up the attitude of his Majesty's Government as follows :

Herr Hitler rejected all suggestions for peace until he had overwhelmed Poland, as he had previously overthrown Czecho-Slovakia. Peace conditions cannot be acceptable which begin by condoning aggression.

The proposals in the German Chancellor's speech are vague and uncertain, and contain no suggestion for righting the wrongs done to Czecho-Slovakia and to Poland.

Even if Herr Hitler's proposals were more closely defined and contained suggestions to right these wrongs, it would still be necessary to ask by what practical means the German Government intend to convince the world that aggression will cease and that pledges will be kept. Past experience has shown that no reliance can be placed upon the promises of the present German Government. **Accordingly, acts—not words alone—must be forthcoming before we, the British peoples, and France, our gallant and trusted Ally, would be justified in ceasing to wage war to the utmost of our strength.**

Only when world confidence is restored will it be possible to find—as we would wish to do with the aid of all who show good will—solutions of those questions which disturb the world, which stand in the way of disarmament, retard the restoration of trade, and prevent the improvement of the well-being of the peoples. . . .

The issue is therefore plain. Either the German Government must give convincing proof of the sincerity of their desire for peace by definite acts and by the provision of effective guarantees of their intention to fulfil their undertakings, or we must persevere in our duty to the end. **It is for Germany to make her choice.**

The Reichstag, once the free parliament of the German Empire, has now become merely a machine to register Nazi decrees. Above is the meeting at which Hitler made his futile appeal for peace on October 6, at the Kroll Opera House, Berlin. The deputies are fulfilling their only function on such occasions—to give the Nazi salute and acquiesce in everything.

Photo, Keystone

Marshalling the Empire's Air Strength

In the last Great War the Dominions contributed to Britain's Air Force large numbers of skilled and courageous pilots and crews. Again today the whole strength of the Empire in the air is being marshalled, and there is no doubt that the effort of 25 years ago will be largely exceeded in the present conflict.

EVEN before war broke out the Dominions hastened to offer Britain all the assistance in their power, and as soon as the struggle began efforts were made to tap the vast resources, human and material, of the nations of the Commonwealth. Particularly was the help of the Dominions sought and received in the matter of air defence.

"Already," said Sir Kingsley Wood, Minister for Air, in the House of Commons on October 10, "the Dominions have signified their intention of making a great and powerful contribution to the common cause in relation to air defence." Sir Kingsley went on to say that the Government had put forward for consideration of the Governments in Canada, Australia and New Zealand an outline of arrangements for the rapid expansion of the air forces of the respective countries, and the Dominions had signified their ready acceptance of the proposals.

Training schools, he proceeded, would be established and maintained in each of these Dominions, but the more comprehensive and technical facilities required for advanced training, apart from those available in Great Britain, would in the main be concentrated in Canada. To the Canadian centres would proceed personnel from the more elementary schools in Australia and New Zealand and also in this country ; there they would receive, with similar personnel from Canadian schools, the advanced training designed to fit them for all service in the line.

To facilitate this large concentration of advanced air training in Canada, a technical mission headed by Lord Riverdale—better known, perhaps, as Sir Arthur Balfour, the great steel magnate—has been sent to Canada to consult there with corresponding missions from Australia and New Zealand. For various reasons the Government of the Union of South Africa prefers to train her air force personnel at home. "But," commented Sir Kingsley Wood, "the Union authorities intend to make their training as complete as possible, and to expand their air force to the fullest extent of their resources."

Meanwhile in Australia the work of aircraft production has forged ahead. "The Commonwealth aircraft factory," said Mr. R. G. Casey, the Minister of Supply, in a broadcast delivered on October 16, " is now turning out enough 'planes to rearm a squadron every three weeks." Mr. Casey went on to say that the Australian Government planned to construct aircraft on a large scale so that Australia could supply the other Dominions as well as herself. Taken in conjunction with the fact that Australia was now making her own artillery, machine-guns, armoured cars, and every type of shells and bombs, it would be seen that the Commonwealth was rapidly becoming an Empire arsenal.

Well might Sir Kingsley Wood, in concluding his speech in the House of Commons, pay a tribute to the vision and imagination of the Dominion statesmen who are responsible for these striking developments in Empire policy.

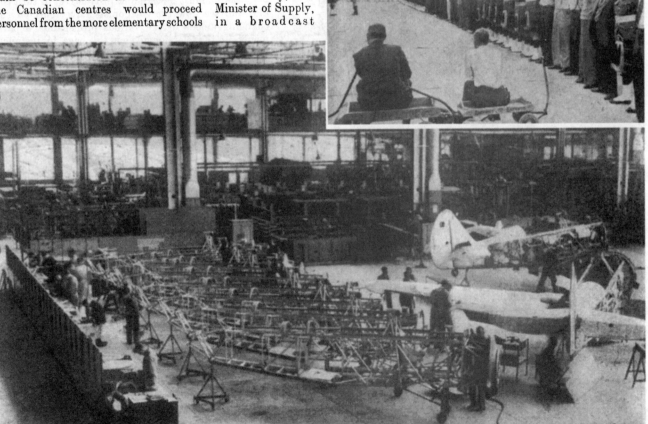

The war effort of the Dominions includes both men and material. Above, men of the Essex Scottish Highlanders are lining up at Windsor, Ontario. The regiment which is being brought up to full strength for service overseas is linked with the British Essex Regiment. Below, a scene in the Melbourne factory of the Commonwealth Aircraft Corporation, where Wirraway two-seater general-purposes craft are under construction. This is an adaptation of an American make built under licence. Machines to equip a squadron are completed every three weeks.

Photos, Sport & General and Wide World

How They Saw Each Other—'Only Yesterday'!

"Stalin (to Uncle Sam): Friend Capitalism, as I need more capital for industry I will smoke the Pipe of Peace." This cartoon appeared in the famous German comic periodical "Kladderadatsch" in 1938, when Moscow was said to be seeking American financial aid.

"A great event on a collective farm—a blade of wheat actually grows." This sarcastic pictorial comment on Russia's farming experiment appeared in the Berlin paper "Die Brennessel" before the German-Soviet Pact.

Political cartoonists are among the shock-troops of propaganda, and in all the Totalitarian States their services have been enlisted with a view to pillorying the personalities and deriding the principles associated with the opposing ideology. In Nazi Germany and Soviet Russia the cartoonists have been particularly busy, and here in this page we give further examples of this pictorial warfare conducted when the two systems were supposed to be poles apart.

But the political leopard often changes his spots, and it must be sad, and instructive, to turn the files and see how the cartoonists have reflected the changing moods of the various propaganda departments. In the selection given in this page, for instance, the cartoonists show us how Germany and Russia regarded each other—*before* the German-Soviet Pact!

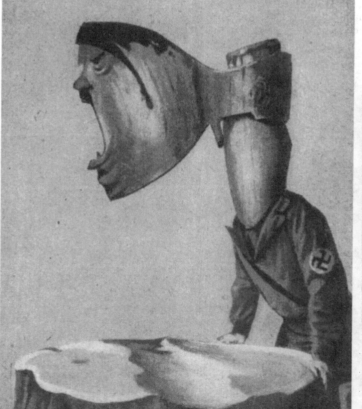

"We are one people. There is no opposition to the Third Reich," was the caption to the cartoon above, left, published in the Moscow "Krokodil." The self-explanatory cartoon above, right, appeared in the Russian daily newspaper "Izvestia." The wording on the original was, of course, in Russian. In other pages of "War Illustrated" have appeared extracts from Nazi writings and speeches against Soviet Russia. The cartoons here reproduced show that the wordy warfare was conducted pictorially as well as verbally.

Make-Believe—But Very Like the Real Thing

A first-aid party has been called upon at a moment's notice to deal with all sorts of imaginary injuries. Above, Admiral Sir Edward Evans watches their work. Right, the Auxiliary Fire Service is called upon to extinguish a fire of wood pavement blocks under the same eagle eye.
Photos, Central Press and Planet News

ADMIRAL SIR EDWARD EVANS, who won fame in the last war as "Evans of the Broke," is one of the two Commissioners for Civil Defence in the London Region. He has introduced the practice of having surprise exercises for the A.R.P. organizations in his charge instead of prearranged exercises. His method is to call on a local A.R.P. controller, inform him that an air raid is in progress, point out on a map where bombs have fallen and state the damage. The whole staff at once takes action.

In danger zones elaborate preparations to deal with casualties during air raids have been made. In one borough near the Thames estuary a complete underground bomb-proof hospital has been built. The first waiting-room is seen in the photograph above, and the strength of the structure is noticeable. In the photograph centre right, a "casualty" is being brought into the hospital during air-raid practice.
Photos, John Topham

WHEN HITLER HOISTED THE PIRATE'S FLAG

On his return to England from Berlin, Sir Nevile Henderson, Britain's Ambassador to Germany from 1937 to the declaration of war, prepared his "Final Report" (Published by H.M. Stationery Office, Cmd. 6115), from which the passages quoted below are taken.

IF the nose of Cleopatra had been shorter, said a clever French writer, the whole face of the earth would have been changed. If Field-Marshal von Blomberg had not married his typist, then world history since the spring of 1938 might have taken a very different course.

This is the opinion of no less an authority than Sir Nevile Henderson, Britain's Ambassador in Berlin, expressed in his official Report to Lord Halifax on the circumstances leading to the termination of his mission on the outbreak of the Anglo-German war. He writes that he is more than ever convinced of the major disaster which the Blomberg marriage involved, owing to the consequent elimination of the more moderate and independent of Hitler's advisers, including Blomberg himself, Baron von Neurath, and General Fritsch.

The Dictator's "Yes-Men"

"The tragedy of any dictator is that, as he goes on, his entourage steadily and inexorably deteriorates. For lack of freedom of utterance he loses the services of the best men. All opposition becomes intolerable to him. All those, therefore, who are bold enough to express opinions contrary to his views are shed one by one, and **he is in the end surrounded by mere yes-men**, whose flattery and counsels are alone endurable to him."

"WHEN a decision has to be taken," Marshal Goering told Sir Nevile once, "none of us count more than the stones on which we are standing."

No one could accuse the Ambassador of being an unkind critic of Nazism; indeed, such criticisms as there have been of Sir Nevile's mission in Berlin are from the opposite angle. In his final report he refers to the great achievements of the man who "restored to the German nation its self-respect and its disciplined orderliness." Although they were accompanied by detestably tyrannical methods, many of the Fuehrer's social reforms were carried out on highly democratic lines.

Shocked Public Opinion

"Nor was the unity of Great Germany in itself an ignoble ideal . . . It was not the incorporation of Austria and the Sudeten Germans in the Reich which so much shocked public opinion in the world as **the unscrupulous and hateful methods which Herr Hitler employed** to precipitate an incorporation which would probably have peacefully come in due course of its own volition and in accordance with the established principle of self-determination."

Yet even these methods might have been endured in a world which sought peace if Herr Hitler had been willing to accord to others the rights which he claimed for Germany. But it was not to be.

"Revolutions are like avalanches, which once set in motion cannot stop till they crash to destruction at the appointed end of their career."

The true background to the events of August 1939 was the Nazi occupation of Prague on the preceding March 15, which involved the "callous destruction of the hard and newly-won liberty of a free and independent people" and Hitler's deliberate violation by this act of the Munich Agreement which he had signed not quite six months before.

Hitler's True Colours

"Up to last March the German ship of State had flown the German national flag, and in spite of the 'sickening technique' of Nazism it was difficult not to concede to Germany the right both to control her own destiny and to benefit from those principles which were accorded to others. On March 15, by the ruthless suppression of the freedom of the Czechs, **its captain hoisted the skull and crossbones of the pirate, cynically discarded his own theory of racial purity** and appeared under his true colours as an unprincipled menace to European peace and liberty."

It must be left to history to determine whether Hitler could have acted otherwise; we cannot tell how far he himself believed in the truth of the tales of atrocities against the Germans which featured so largely in the Czech Crisis, and a year later were "rehashed up almost verbatim in regard to the Poles."

German "Will to Believe"

"Germans are prone in any case to convince themselves very readily of anything which they wish to believe. Certainly he behaved as if he did believe, and, even if one may give him the benefit of the doubt, **these reports served to inflame his resentment to the pitch which he or his extremists desired.**"

FOR a week, indeed, Herr Hitler did hold up the war. He told our Ambassador that he preferred war when he was fifty to when he was fifty-five or sixty, but his actions proved that up to the last he was hopeful of being able to detach Britain from the ranks of his enemies.

"It was not the horrors of war which deterred him," says Sir Nevile; and in another passage he gives his impression that "**the corporal of the last war was even more anxious to prove what he could do as a conquering Generalissimo in the next.**"

A NUMBER of indications—for example, the introduction on August 27 of a system for the rationing of foodstuffs and other commodities throughout Germany—go to show that the war should have begun on August 26, but Hitler hesitated in order to make one final effort to secure Britain's neutrality.

There is no reason to doubt that Herr Hitler was perfectly sincere in his desire for good relations with Great Britain. It was at Hitler's own suggestion that Sir Nevile flew to London on the very eve of war in order to put before the Cabinet Hitler's latest proposals.

"I felt it my duty to tell him quite clearly," he writes, "that my country could not possibly go back on its word to Poland, and that, however anxious we were for a better understanding with Germany, we could never reach one except on the basis of a negotiated settlement with Poland."

"THE Fuehrer," writes Sir Nevile in one of the most interesting passages in his Report,

"will prove in the future a fascinating study for the historian and the biographer with psychological leanings. Widely different explanations will be propounded, and it would be out of place and time to comment at any length in this despatch on this aspect of Herr Hitler's mentality and character. But he combined, as I fancy many Germans do, admiration for the British race with envy of their achievements and hatred of their opposition to Germany's excessive aspirations.

"It is no exaggeration to say that he assiduously courted Great Britain, both as representing the aristocracy and most successful of the Nordic races, and as constituting the only seriously dangerous obstacle to his own far-reaching plan of German domination in Europe. This is evident in 'Mein Kampf,' and, in spite of what he regarded as the constant rebuffs which he received from the British side, he persisted in his endeavours up to the last moment."

Analysing the Fuehrer

"Geniuses are strange creatures, and Hitler, among other paradoxes, **is a mixture of long-headed calculation and violent and arrogant impulse provoked by resentment.** The former drove him to seek Britain's friendship and the latter finally into war with her. Moreover, he believes his resentment to be entirely justified. He failed to realize why his military-cum-police tyranny should be repugnant to British ideals of individual and national freedom and liberty, or why he should not be allowed a free hand in Central and Eastern Europe to subjugate smaller and, as he regards them, inferior peoples to superior German rule and culture.

He believed he could buy British acquiescence in his own far-reaching schemes by offers of alliance with and guarantees for the British Empire. Such acquiescence was indispensable to the success of his ambitions and he worked unceasingly to secure it. **His great mistake was his complete failure to understand the inherent British sense of morality, humanity and freedom.**"

SO it was that on the morning of Monday, September 4, a little party—thirty men, seven women and two dogs, says Sir Nevile with a whimsical touch—left the British Embassy in Berlin on their way home. There was no sign of hostility; the streets of the capital were practically deserted.

"There was nothing to indicate the beginning of a war which is to decide whether force is to be the sole arbiter in international affairs; whether international instruments solemnly and freely entered into are to be modified, not by negotiation, but by mere unilateral repudiation; whether there is to be any faith in future in written contracts; whether the fate of a great nation and the peace of the world is to rest in the future in the hands of one man; whether small nations are to have any rights against the pretensions of States more powerful than themselves; in a word, whether government of the people by the people for the people is to continue in this world, or whether it is to be replaced by the arbitrary will and ambition of single individuals regardless of the peoples' will."

We Were Rescued from the 'Royal Oak'

In the early hours of October 14, 1939, when the battleship " Royal Oak " was torpedoed in the harbour at Scapa Flow, 810 officers and men lost their lives. Those who managed to survive the ordeal had great difficulty in reaching safety, as is shown by the following stories reprinted from the " Daily Telegraph" and " Daily Express."

VINCENT MARCHANT, 18, of Doncaster, described how he was asleep in his hammock when the first explosion occurred.

" I ran to the upper deck to see what happened," he said. " There was a second explosion twenty minutes later, followed by a third and then a fourth. By that time the ship was tilting. She was sinking rapidly.

" Remembering what happened on the ' Courageous ' and the lesson that taught us, I stripped myself of all my clothing and, tying my safety belt around my waist, dived into the water. Searchlights were playing over the surface and I could see hundreds of heads bobbing around.

" Great volumes of oil started to belch up to the surface. My eyes started to smart and the faces of all the men swimming in the water turned a greasy black. I was caught in a searchlight for several minutes and saw that two of my pals were swimming alongside me. Later, however, they had cramp and disappeared.

" A small boat passed near at hand with someone on board shouting for survivors. I ' ahoyed,' but they evidently did not hear me and the boat disappeared into the darkness.

" I swam and swam for I don't know how long, but I must have gone about a mile and half when I felt the rock under me. I scarcely remember what happened after that. It was like a nightmare.

" I have just a vague recollection of climbing up the sheer face of a cliff about 20 to 30 feet high.

" Another figure was climbing behind me, but he slipped and crashed among the rocks below. He must have been killed or drowned. I lay down on the top of the cliff and lost consciousness.

" Then I heard someone shouting from the direction of the sea. They told me not to try to climb down again as they would send someone along the top of the cliff."

Another survivor was Paymaster-Lieutenant Harrison, of Glasgow, whose birthday was just fifty-eight minutes old when the first explosion occurred. This is his story:

" I was in the mess at two minutes to one when I heard a minor explosion.

" I was just about to open a parcel from my wife—a birthday present—but I replaced the string and went up on deck.

" Three minutes after I left the mess there was a violent explosion. I was pitched forward.

" Then there came another explosion. I joined a queue and was making to go overboard on the port side when there came a fourth explosion.

" I managed to get to a canvas lifeboat, but after I had clung to it for a while another poor fellow arrived almost exhausted. I hoisted him into my grip on the boat and swam away.

" A piece of wreckage came along and I used it for swimming support. Later I bumped into a log, and with wood support under both arms I swam to a drifter and was taken aboard.

" It was a lucky birthday for me."

Lieutenant Harrison still has his birthday present. He was clinging to it when he was rescued.

Rear-Admiral H. E. C. Blagrove was among the officers lost when the " Royal Oak " went down. He had been appointed Admiral Superintendent of Chatham Dockyard as from October 2. *Photo, Keystone*

H.M.S. " Royal Oak " was one of the ships inspected by the King during his visit to the Home Fleet in Wey outh Bay, June 20-23, 1938. His Majesty is here seen coming on board the ship. The " Royal Oak " then formed part of the 2nd Battle Squadron. *Photo, L.N.A.*

What We Saw of the First Air Raid on Britain

At about half-past two in the afternoon of Monday, October 16, German 'planes began a series of bombing raids on warships in the Firth of Forth. The following eye-witness stories are reprinted from the " News Chronicle," " Daily Mail," and " Daily Express."

A THRILLING story of the shooting down of the bomber which fell in the sea off Crail was given by the crew of a fishing boat which rescued from a watery grave three of the crew of four of the German machine.

These three were landed at Port Seton, a little fishing village a few miles along the east coast from Edinburgh.

The fishing vessel was the " Day Spring," which had been fishing near the May Island and was returning to Port Seton with her catch.

Mr. John Dickson, Jnr., whose father is the skipper of the vessel, said : " About three o'clock we were returning home when we saw a large black aeroplane travelling at a high speed.

" It was being pursued by two British fighters and they made rings round it. They dived underneath it and then circled up again. They both started firing into the tail of the German.

" The German 'plane swept round in a circle and then suddenly heeled over and flopped into the sea.

" One wing struck the water first, and the machine floated for a short time. When we came up three of the crew were clinging like grim death to an air-compressed lifebuoy, and each of the men also had a lifebelt of similar construction round his chest.

" Just before the 'plane sank another black machine—a German which was smaller than the other—came down, swept low over it and then made off.

" I saw some of our fighters go after it. We threw ropes to the crew of the sinking 'plane, and when we hauled them aboard we discovered that they were all three wounded.

" They told us that another member of the crew had gone down with the 'plane.

" They were all young chaps. The man who appeared to be the senior had a bad eye injury.

" Another had been shot in the ribs, and we stretched him out on the deck. The third man had been shot in the arm and it was broken.

" The three men were very grateful for being rescued, and the leader, who spoke English fairly well, took a gold signet ring from his finger and gave it to my father for saving his life.

" ' This is a ring for saving me,' he said."

An Edinburgh commercial traveller, who spoke to the pilot when he landed, told a reporter that the German had said to him : " We were much too slow to get away from the first British fighters."

ONE of the most dramatic eye-witness stories came from a passenger in the 2.30 train from Edinburgh to Dunfermline.

Mr. David Archibald, of Dunfermline, said : " At Dalmeny we were told that an air raid was in progress and it was left to our own discretion whether we would continue the journey across the Forth Bridge. Most of us decided to continue.

" As the train travelled slowly across the bridge two 'planes, one near the south shore and one to the north shore of the Forth, appeared to dive over us and bombs were dropped near the bridge.

" A huge column of water shot up."

One of these 'planes dived so close to the water, said other watchers, that the pilot had to go under a span of the bridge to straighten out.

MR. PETER WALKER, Provost of South Queensferry, saw the whole of the raids from his house two miles away.

He said : " I heard a terrific explosion, and saw a great waterspout rising from the river into the air.

" A bomb was released, and I could plainly see it fall.

" More 'planes came over. A terrible hail of shells went up from the anti-aircraft batteries.

" It seemed as though the raiding aircraft reeled. Then they seemed to recover. Numbers of bombs fell—but all dropped into the water.

" It seemed impossible that the 'planes could live in the barrage of shrapnel put up by the anti-aircraft guns. A shot struck one 'plane and I saw part of the machine fall into the Firth.

" Our guns seemed to be aimed quite coolly, though I counted about 20 bombs when the raiders first swooped down. The 'planes were beaten off for a time, but back they came, apparently determined to bomb the Forth Bridge.

" It was only after the first bomb had been dropped—a few minutes after 3 o'clock—that I heard an air raid siren go. Just as I heard it I saw a single German 'plane coming across the river.

" I heard a number of terrific explosions, but so far as I could see no damage was done. Anti-aircraft forced this machine to retire. After a few minutes of this amazingly hot attack and equally active defence a number of speedy British fighters streaked over in pursuit of the Germans."

A VETERAN of the last war gave the following account of the raid.

" We heard a burst of machine-gun fire, followed by the sound of an anti-aircraft shell bursting. Then the siren sounded. Marines came round shouting to us to take cover, but I saw some young workmen climb up on the rooftops to watch. " We saw 'planes coming over very high, perhaps 15,000 feet. They dodged in and out of white, woolly clouds against the blue sky. One separated from the others and went on up the Forth. Anti-aircraft shells began to burst round them like bunches of grapes.

" One of the machines came plunging down, and dived into the Forth, leaving a trail of blue smoke. From 3 to 3.30 the 'planes circled overhead. I heard two heavy detonations, like bombs dropping. The ground around us was peppered with shrapnel.

" I saw the enemy 'planes rocking as the ' Archies ' burst around them.

" After a quarter of an hour another of the 'planes nose-dived, then flattened out level with the top of the Forth Bridge and disappeared seawards, followed by bursting shells.

" The other 'planes went over towards Edinburgh. Firing ceased, and British fighters appeared and criss-crossed above the Forth as though searching for something.

" Then the 'plane which had gone up the Forth reappeared, flying at about eight or ten thousand feet, right in the eye of the sun. Our fighters forced it into the barrage of anti-aircraft fire and it suddenly went into a dive, levelled out, dived again and crashed."

I Followed Warsaw Raiders with My Camera

When the war broke out, Mr. E. G. Calcraft, the author of this dramatic contribution, was in Poland taking photographs for the Planet News Ltd. and a number of his striking pictures have appeared in the pages of WAR ILLUSTRATED.

THE first I knew of the war was when the 'plane in which I was travelling from Riga to Warsaw was chased by a German single-seater scout machine, soon after we left Vilna. We were a fast 'plane and so got away, but when we arrived at Warsaw we found that there were eight bullet-holes in our machine.

In Warsaw I experienced nine air raids in three days. The people were quite calm and at first quite a number remained in the streets. I had an official permit to do so, and so I was able to watch the fighting. Not that there was very much of a fight, for though the Polish anti-aircraft guns were very good,

November 4th, 1939　　　　　*The War Illustrated*　　　　　253

IIIIIIIIIIIIIIIIIIIIIIIIIIIIIIIIIIIIIIIIIIIIIIIIIIIIIIIIIIIIIIIIIIIIIIIIIII **I WAS THERE!** IIIIIIIIIIIIIIIIIIIIIIIIIIIIIIIIIIIIIIIIIIIIIIIIIIIIIIIIIIIIIIIIIIIIIIIIIII

they seemed to fire a bit late all the time, and as for the Polish 'planes, most of them had been caught on the ground and destroyed.

On Saturday, September 2, we had raids at 6.30 in the morning, at 12 o'clock, and at 4.30. In between I took photographs of the scenes at the British Embassy, more particularly when Colonel Beck came down to see our Ambassador, Sir Howard Kennard.

The worst of the raids in my experience was the 4.30 raid on Monday afternoon. As soon as the 'planes had passed I went to the actual area where the bombs had fallen in the Praga district. The first sight I got of it was the injured and dead lying about in the street. Whole rows of houses were blazing. They belonged to working-class people, small cottages and villas, nowhere near any military objective. Even the nearest bridge across the Vistula was easily a kilometre and a half away.

Little children had been terribly cut by the glass and debris, and women were searching among the wreckage for their children. When they could not find them they just went mad, and some of them were put in police cells. Some were rolling in the streets, crying and screaming. My worst incident was when the butcher who had been killing cattle in the yard of his butcher's shop found that his twelve-year-old child was in the building which had just been hit with an incendiary bomb. I was taking a picture, and he thought that I was a German gloating over the damage. He came towards me with his axe and pinned me against the wall. Fortunately an officer saw what was happening and held

These two photographs were among those taken by Mr. Calcraft. Left, a fire caused by an incendiary bomb is being fought. The man on the right was a butcher whose 12-year-old daughter had shortly before been burned to death. Right, young girls in uniform are digging air raid trenches in Warsaw, a work in which thousands of women were employed.

Photos, Planet News

him while he explained who I was. Then he came and kissed me on both cheeks.

Another picture that sticks in my mind is when I ran up to where a bomb had fallen and saw two policemen leading an old lady away. She had been blinded by the blast of a bomb.

The 'planes were flying at about 7,000 feet. They had a trick of pretending that they were hit and coming down as low as within 400 feet of the ground, then they would suddenly straighten out and release all their bombs.

After nine raids I had had enough, especially as in one of them I got a

cracked jaw from falling debris. So I went to the Foreign Office on the Monday and got a permit to leave, and caught the 12 o'clock train that night to Riga.

Normally the journey takes eight hours, but it took me five days, and we were bombed ten times on the way. When a raid was in progress the train was stopped and we could get out or stay in it as we liked. There was no food on the train and the cackling of hens, etc., told us where to find something to eat. We waited 4½ hours at Vilna, but we were well over the frontier into Lithuania before the first of the Russians made their appearance.

Many of the photographs of the raids on Warsaw that have appeared in "The War Illustrated" were taken by Mr. E. G. Calcraft, of Planet News, seen above. He risked his life again and again to make this remarkable pictorial record.

Photo, Planet News

We Saw the U-Boat Captain a Prisoner

The French liner "Bretagne," with 360 passengers and crew, was torpedoed in the Atlantic on October 14, 1939. Fortunately, the survivors were picked up from the boats by a British warship. The following story is reprinted from the "Daily Telegraph."

THE French liner "Bretagne," with 360 passengers and crew, was torpedoed in the Atlantic on October 14, 1939. Fortunately, the loss of life was very small, as the survivors were picked up from the boats by a British warship.

How a German submarine followed in the wake of the "Bretagne" "like a shark," disabled the wireless apparatus

by gunfire and torpedoed the vessel while the passengers and crew were taking to the boats, was told by M. Jose Germain.

"At dawn on Saturday, when we were 300 miles from land, the ship's siren awakened us and we knew that we were being hunted by an enemy submarine. We tried to escape by putting on full speed and steaming a zigzag course, but the U-boat grimly followed in our wake.

The survivors of the French liner "Bretagne," which was sunk by a submarine in the Atlantic on October 14, were landed at a British port. Some of them are here seen being cared for by sailors in the traditional way of the British Navy. The "Bretagne" was a ship of 10,108 tons belonging to the Compagnie Générale Transatlantique. She carried about 360 people, including 125 passengers. Five of the crew and two passengers were killed by the explosion.

Photo, Associated Press

" Gradually it caught up with us and then circled slowly round. The tense silence was suddenly broken as the submarine opened fire without warning and shelled the ship's radio cabin, seriously wounding the operator.

" We were ordered to the boats, and the officers, by their example and efficiency, prevented any panic. In the middle of this there was a terrific explosion and the ship shivered as though her screws were racing above water. A torpedo had entered No. 2 hold and exploded.

These survivors from the "Bretagne" are waiting to be fitted out with clothes after being landed at a British port.

Photo, Sport & General

Many on board leaped over the side and were picked up by the boats. No one who jumped with a lifebelt was lost.

" For five hours we rowed until we were picked up by a British warship.

" When we were picked up we found the captain of a German U-boat on board. He had been taken prisoner not far from the spot where we were torpedoed after having sunk a British cargo boat."

How We Dodged the British Navy

One of the mysteries of the early days of the War was the disappearance of Germany's crack liner, the " Bremen," after she sailed from New York on August 30. It was eventually established that the liner had reached the Russian port of Murmansk.

ONE of the crew of the " Bremen " was Evert Post, a Dutchman who, on reaching Amsterdam, told the story of his voyage to the newspaper " Het Volk."

" After we left New York on August 30 we went at top speed," he said. " During the night we carried no lights, and no one was allowed even to light cigarettes on deck. In daytime all hands were in the lifeboats with pots of paint and long brushes, painting the hull a greyish colour. No radio reports were sent out.

" On September 3 Captain Ahrens called everybody into the saloon and told us war had broken out.

" ' I swear solemnly,' he said, ' that the English won't get me alive, nor my ship. I prefer to sink her.'

" The crew answered with ' Hochs ' and gave the Nazi salute. Next day the captain again called us together and said :

" ' Between England and Iceland, where we are now, British warships are watching every ten miles. We are in the lions' den.'

" Every day lifeboat drill was held. The forepart of the ship was evacuated, in case we ran into a mine.

" Everywhere on deck were set barrels of petrol, to be set on fire if a British warship came near.

" Everyone wore his best clothes, as we would not have been able to take any baggage into the boats with us. No one slept or undressed.

" The sailors were half-frozen while we were running between Iceland and Spitzbergen, but they did not dare to go below. On the morning of September 6 we sighted the coast of Murmansk and we all cheered. We were approached by a warship, which turned out to be Russian. We anchored in the bay, flying the company's flag, the Russian flag, and the swastika.

" We were not allowed to land, and we spent days watching films and listening to our own band.

" One day the German Minister came aboard, and told us we would go by train to Leningrad, then by ship to Kiel and Bremerhaven. We started on September 18, each of us with two parcels of bread and sausages, and had an uneventful journey."

The 'Bremen' Runs the Gauntlet from New York to the Arctic

When they heard that war was declared, the crew of the "Bremen" took an oath to sink their ship rather than let it fall into enemy hands.

As described in the story in the opposite page, all available hands were set to work in mid-Atlantic repainting the "Bremen" a dull grey.

The crack North German-Lloyd liner "Bremen" (51,731 tons) was in dock at New York just before the outbreak of war (above), but when it seemed inevitable that war was coming Capt. Ahrens, the skipper (centre), decided that his ship should run the blockade. On August 30, therefore, the great ship slipped out into the Atlantic. Some weeks later it transpired that the "Bremen" was at Murmansk, the Russian harbour within the Arctic Circle. She had arrived there on September 6, after a nerve-wracking voyage of about 4,750 miles.

Photos, Wide World

OUR DIARY OF THE WAR

Monday, October 16

German troops launched an attack on a four-mile front immediately east of the Moselle. They were halted by French gunfire. The enemy attacked later along a 20-mile front east of the Saar. French outposts retired, according to plan, to lines of defence well in front of the Maginot Line.

Two enemy air raids were carried out in the Firth of Forth. The first, a reconnaissance raid, took place between 9 a.m. and 1.30 p.m., several aircraft being seen over Rosyth.

At 2.30 p.m. a series of bombing raids began. Twelve to fourteen 'planes took part, four of which were brought down. Slight damage was done to the cruiser "Southampton," and less still to the cruiser "Edinburgh" and the destroyer "Mohawk."

R.A.F. carried out further reconnaissance flights during Sunday night over northern and central Germany, and further leaflets, printed in large type so that they could be read without being picked up, were dropped.

The Polish Embassy in Paris stated that Polish troops were still holding out against German and Russian invaders, notably at Suwalki, in the Carpathians, and in the Pripet Marshes at Bialowieza.

French steamer "Vermont" sunk by U-boat.

Paris reported the loss by torpedoing of the tanker "Emile Miguet."

Tuesday, October 17

French command reported sharp infantry engagements following the two German attacks of Monday.

Two German air attacks were made over the north of Scotland. The first raid, at 10.30 a.m., and directed at Scapa Flow, was carried out by four machines. The battleship "Iron Duke" suffered some damage. Two enemy 'planes were shot down.

The second raid, on the Orkneys, lasted from 12.30 to 2.30, and was carried out by ten 'planes. No damage was done.

Enemy aircraft were active near the east coast of Britain during the afternoon. Two were destroyed in a fight with R.A.F. All British aircraft returned safely.

Reported that the first of the two **British Army Corps in France** had taken over a section of the front.

Turkish Prime Minister announced that negotiations between Turkey and Moscow had been broken off, and that M. Sarajoglu, Foreign Minister, was returning to Ankara.

Mr. Churchill announced in the House that the "Royal Oak" was lying at anchor in Scapa Flow when she was torpedoed at 1.30 a.m. on October 14.

Norwegian steamer "Lorentz W. Hansen" reported sunk in North Atlantic.

Officers and crew of the British steamer "Sneaton" sunk by a U-boat were brought to port by a Belgian oil-tanker.

Wednesday, October 18

Paris reported great activity behind the German lines, but no renewal of the attack.

Enemy aircraft approached Scapa Flow; no bombs were dropped. They were engaged by heavy anti-aircraft fire.

The Kings of Norway and Denmark and the President of Finland arrived in Stockholm to confer with the King of Sweden.

The German Ambassador to Turkey, **von Papen, was recalled** by his Government.

General Wavell, commander of British land forces in the Middle East, and General Weygand, former chief of French General Staff, arrived in Ankara by air for talks with the Turkish General Staff.

The Admiralty announced that 24 officers and 786 men lost their lives in H.M.S. "Royal Oak," out of a complement of 81 officers and 1,153 men.

Reported that two British liners, "City of

Mandalay" and "Yorkshire," had been torpedoed in the Atlantic. U.S. steamer "Independence Hall" picked up 300 survivors.

R.A.F. aircraft made a successful night reconnaissance over north-west Germany.

Thursday, October 19

Heavy rain held up operations on the Western Front. Some German outposts were stated to be flooded.

Anglo-French Treaty with Turkey was signed at Ankara. The terms provide for mutual assistance in the event of an act of aggression by a European Power against any of the signatories, leading to war in the Mediterranean area. The Treaty has been concluded for 15 years.

Two German airmen, half the crew of a bomber shot down over the North Sea on Tuesday, drifted ashore in a collapsible rubber boat at Whitby.

German balloon, to which a long wire cable was attached, came down in a field at Cruden, Aberdeenshire.

Sir Kingsley Wood returned to London from a 2-days visit to France to inspect the R.A.F. units.

The Scandinavian monarchs and the President of Finland broadcast declarations of mutual solidarity and of Finland's determination to preserve her integrity.

Ministry of Transport announced that in September, first month of the black-out, the total number of persons killed on the roads of Great Britain was 1,130, compared with 617 in August.

During the week ending October 14, the British Contraband Control intercepted and detained 23,000 tons of goods, making a total of 338,000 tons since the beginning of its activities.

Friday, October 20

The Western Front generally was quiet. There was patrol and reconnaissance activity between the Moselle and the Saar.

German reconnaissance aircraft appeared twice over the Firth of Forth area. R.A.F. fighters took off to meet them, but the enemy 'planes disappeared before contact could be made.

King George and the President of Turkey exchanged telegrams expressing mutual satisfaction over the signing of the Treaty between Britain, France and Turkey.

Mr. R. G. Menzies, Prime Minister of Australia, announced the re-introduction in January, 1940, of compulsory military training for home service.

It was announced that Hitler had signed a decree by which 3,000,000 Jews now living in Poland will get their own territory in East Poland, with a Jewish capital at Lublin.

Saturday, October 21

A British convoy in the North Sea was attacked by twelve German raiders. They were engaged by British fighters and escort vessels, and **four enemy aircraft were brought down.** No casualties were suffered by British aircraft, nor was any damage done to the convoy or escort.

There was heavy artillery action from both sides on the Western Front.

Hitler summoned all Nazi district leaders throughout the Reich to "important consultations" in Berlin.

Finnish delegation left Helsinki for Moscow with new instructions for the resumption of negotiations with the Soviet Government.

Mr. Hore-Belisha, Minister for War, broadcast a review of the position at the end of the seventh week of conflict.

Italo-German agreement for the transfer to the Reich of German citizens in South Tyrol was signed.

German minefield patrol vessel "Este 710" struck German mines in the Baltic and sank.

Sunday, October 22

Paris reported that, apart from sporadic artillery exchanges, the Western Front had been generally calm since the French took up their new positions. No-man's-land on the Moselle-Rhine front was said to be still a sea of mud.

There were **further enemy air operations** off the East Coast of Britain. In the morning R.A.F. fighters went up to intercept unidentified aircraft flying northwards. No bombs were dropped. In the afternoon two enemy aircraft were seen over the south-east of Scotland, and **one was shot down.**

General Wavell and General Weygand left Ankara at the conclusion of successful talks with the Turkish General Staff.

It Is Said That . . .

The Luxemburg dialect is now the official language of the Grand Duchy.

Ex-Kaiser's allowance of £350 a month has been stopped by Hitler's orders.

Stalin's hurried grab at the Baltic States attributed to the wish to forestall Hitler.

A total Continental blockade of England has been planned by Dr. Schacht.

R.A.F. leaflets, drifted over Dutch frontier, were sold for Red Cross for 6s. 8d.

Youths of 18 need no longer obtain the consent of their parents to serve the Reich.

The Gestapo have confiscated all headphones; discovery of their use entails heavy penalties.

Twelve German deserters, armed and carrying a machine-gun, surrendered at the Belgian frontier.

Isolationist U.S. senators have received from unknown source photograph of Hitler with flattering inscription.

New York family tried living on Nazi war-time rations, but became in a week "morose, irritable and discontented."

Despite Nazi denials of any intention to violate Dutch territory, Dutch military authorities are pressing ahead with fortifications on their eastern frontier.

German workers are being taught Russian.

War weariness is already rife among the German population.

Germans are being kept in ignorance of their own losses in the air.

"Germany fights against injustice; England to preserve it." (*German Radio*)

Nazis call pamphlets dropped by R.A.F. "clergymen's bombs."

Loot secured in Poland far exceeds that obtained in Czecho-Slovakia.

Art treasures and valuable furniture, textiles and metals are dispatched to German homes.

"The soldier's wife is a very remarkable woman." (*Mr. Ernest Brown, Minister of Labour*)

Nazi broadcasters consider the song "We're Going to Hang Our Washing on the Siegfried Line" is in very bad taste.

Dr. Fritz Thyssen, German steel magnate and erstwhile friend and backer of Hitler, is reported to have fled from the Reich.

A secret "safety" air lane has been established between England and France, and is used by military missions, couriers and official personages.

Vol. 1   A Permanent Picture Record of the Second Great War   No. 9

The friendliness and courtesy which the British soldiers in France showed to the French people as soon as they landed brought a quick response. It here takes material form, for a young Frenchwoman is making a lavish distribution of the last autumn flowers from her garden to the khaki quartette whose car has halted near her home. Slung across the sergeant's shoulder is one of the cases of maps which are provided for most drivers of military cars in France.

Photo, P.N.A.

In Fifty Days They Didn't Drop a Bomb!

Seven weeks had passed and still the great offensive had not come. Indeed, there were some in Paris who went so far as to say that the war on the Western Front had resolved itself into a stalemate.

AFTER the first fifty days of war no fighting on the grand scale had been seen on the Western Front. As one of the great Paris newspapers put it, a "kind of half truce" was in operation, thanks to which civilian life and railway and road traffic had been able to continue almost normally on both sides of the frontier.

For a few weeks the French had engaged in offensive operations. Their line had been carried over the frontier on to

German soil, but the fighting had been entirely a matter of outpost engagements, of patrol fighting patrol in "No-man's-land," and of long-range artillery duels between the guns in the Maginot and Siegfried Lines.

Considerable progress had been made ; and that the menace of the attack was fully realized by the Nazis was evidenced by the fact that many of the towns in the war zone had been cleared of their civilian population. It had been said in the newspapers, though not in the official communiqués, that Saarbruecken was practically surrounded and could be captured at any moment, and the same fate was believed to be threatening several other of the Rhineland towns.

When the Germans delivered their long-expected counter-attack it was revealed that the French had retired from their advanced positions a fortnight before. In the French War Communiqué No. 87, issued on the night of October 17, it was stated that : "Towards the end of yesterday afternoon the Germans,

supported by heavy artillery fire, launched a second attack over a front of 18 miles in the region east of the Saar. Our light advance elements withdrew gradually as planned, but our fire held up the enemy on the pre-arranged line. In anticipation of this resumption of the German offensive the French command a fortnight ago decided to withdraw to other positions those French divisions which had taken the offensive on German territory in order indirectly to assist the Polish armies. The whole of the necessary movements were completed by October 3. After that date we had only light advance elements and a few supporting units in contact with the enemy."

The communiqué issued by the German High Command on the same day confirmed the retirement : "French troops yesterday evacuated the greater part of the German territory occupied by them in front of our fortifications. They retreated to and over the frontier."

In readiness for the attack the Germans had massed a very large number of troops,

The soldiers of 1939, like those of 1914, sometimes travel in goods wagons. They are equally ready with a piece of chalk, and "Vive la France," "Vive la England" and "Gott Strafe Hitler" are some of the inscriptions that they have chalked up.

Photo, Sport and General

After a discussion of plans, Viscount Gort, British C.-in-C., and General Gamelin, French C.-in-C., are seen above taking a stroll near headquarters. Below are British howitzers in England on their way to embarkation for the front. For easy transport the barrels are detached from the breech and carried on separate limbers.

Photos, Associated Press

French Men and French Guns on German Soil

In the course of their advance across the frontier, the French troops occupied a number of German villages. So steady and so careful was their progress that little damage was done, and from some places the civilian population was not evacuated. In the photograph above a column of French infantry is marching through one of these villages, which for the time, at least, heard the invaders' tread.

Photo, Central Press

Since the days of Napoleon, and even long before, the French army have been famed for the excellence of their artillery. In this war as in that of 1914-1918 our Allies put their trust very largely in the famous 75-mm. gun. Here we see a battery of "75's" on the Western Front in the open, but partially concealed by a network camouflage.

Photo, Topical

but most of these were not needed when it was discovered that the French were holding mere outpost lines. In their withdrawal they had carefully sown the ground with mines of various descriptions, and as the German infantry advanced, these caused heavy losses. At the same time a huge volume of fire was kept up from the line to which the French had already retired, while the guns in the Maginot Line kept up a heavy bombardment of the zone of hostilities.

The German Command had let it be known that they had no intention of endeavouring to force the French back as far as the Maginot Line; their offensive was directed merely to regain possession of German territory which had been occupied by the French in the first few weeks of war. Nowhere did German troops cross the French frontier.

Following the engagement the German High Command issued a review of operations on the Western Front since the beginning of the war. Since September 9, it stated, when the French opened hos-

The smallest type of French tank is the chenilette, and so fast and handy are they that, among other uses, they have been employed in carrying ammunition to the front. Here we see several, with their drivers standing by: they are wearing a kind of steel crash helmet.
Photo, Sport and General

tilities, no serious fighting had taken place anywhere on the front. There had been purely local fighting on the terrain between the frontier and the Westwall (Siegfried Line), and the French occupied a few German districts near the frontier between Luxemburg and Saarlautern, the Warndt Forest, and a salient south-east of Saarbruecken.

"Only in the two last-named districts which were evacuated according to plan did the enemy advance to a depth of from three to five kilometres, and with heavy losses. The rest of the territory in front of the Westwall was not occupied by the enemy.". . . Absolute quiet has reigned since the beginning of the war on the Upper Rhine from Karlsruhe to Basle. . . . There have been no bomb attacks." The communiqué concluded by saying that apart from air force casualties (169 dead, 356 wounded and 144 missing), "only one German has been killed on the Rhine front, and he by falling shrapnel from our own anti-aircraft fire!"

Thus, after seven weeks of war, the French positions were practically what they had been at the opening of hostilities. The advance, so carefully planned, so methodically executed, with such careful a regard for human life, had succeeded in its objects. The French patrols and outposts had felt their way across "No-man's land" until they fumbled, as it were, at the concrete bastions of the great Siegfried Line itself.

Having gained the information they sought, and pressure on the West being of no more avail to the Poles, the French retired, and their retirement was so carefully planned and so silently carried out that fourteen days elapsed before the opposing forces ventured to make a frontal assault. Then they moved forward in great strength, only to beat wildly in the air at an enemy who had already eluded their grasp, and on the eve of winter they settled down to consolidate themselves in a ground which had already been turned into a quagmire by the French.

One of the objects of the French advance into German territory was to observe the Siegfried Line at close quarters. Observation posts were established on high ground commanding the vaunted Nazi "Westwall," and one of these is seen above with the observers recording the results. When bad weather came, some of these observation posts were abandoned.
Photo, Associated Press

Behind the Lines with the British Field Force

With the British Army in France are two of the King's brothers. Top left is the Duke of Gloucester, Chief Liaison Officer, with Viscount Gort and Lt.-Gen. Sir Douglas Brownrigg. Above, the Duke of Windsor is being greeted by a French Officer.

The diffidence which some travellers show in speaking a foreign language does not prevail in the British Army, and the soldiers manage to make themselves understood with a few words and signs. They are particularly happy with children, as the centre photograph shows, and many French youngsters have heard from their parents, who were themselves children in the last war, that the Tommies of those days were always the children's friends. Bottom, British soldiers are on the march in a French village.

Photos, British Official ; Crown Copyright

Luxemburg Fears Again for Her Neutrality

Though great trunk railway-lines run through Luxemburg, few travellers spare more than a passing glance for the little Grand Duchy. Here are some details of the land and its people—details which are not unimportant in view of Luxemburg's position.

To most people, perhaps, Luxemburg is just a famous broadcasting station. There is, however, much more to be said about the little country, a land of woods and pasture, vineyards and orchards, which lies between France, Belgium and Germany on the southern slopes of the Ardennes.

Although it is only nine hundred and ninety-nine square miles in extent, Luxemburg ranks among the independent countries of Europe. It is a Grand Duchy, and its present ruler is the Grand Duchess Charlotte, who succeeded her sister, Marie-Adelaide, in 1919. During the Great War the Grand Duchy was overrun by the German armies, and Marie-Adelaide protested unavailingly against the occupation. Following the war political complications led to her abdication, and she died a few years later in a convent in Italy.

Before and during the Great War Luxemburg was a member of the German Zollverein, or customs union, but by a referendum held in 1919 the Luxemburg people voted in favour of an economic union with France. France, however, refused in favour of Belgium to consider the possibility of an economic union, and in 1921 Luxemburg concluded an agreement with Belgium for the economic union of the two countries. The agreement was to run for fifty years, and as a result there is no customs barrier between Luxemburg and Belgium, and Belgian currency is used in the Grand Duchy.

For the most part the Luxemburgers—there are about 300,000 of them—are farmers on a small scale. A good many, however, are employed on the railways—there are 338 miles of railway in the country owing to the fact that several of the main European lines run through it—and on the international telegraph and telephone systems.

Militarily speaking, Luxemburg does not count; its army, indeed, numbers 250 men (including 10 officers and 50 bandsmen), supported by a police force of 225. It will be understood that the Luxemburgers want nothing so much as to be allowed to remain neutral in all quarrels which distract their great neighbours, but unfortunately for their peace, geography has often ruled otherwise. In 1939, as in many a year of its storied past, Luxemburg heard beyond her frontiers the tramp of thousands of armed men; and from one corner of the little State, at Remich, the Luxemburgers and their visitors had what may be described as a grand-stand view of the fighting in No Man's Land between the Maginot and the Siegfried Lines.

Threat to Neutrality

As the war progressed, however, there were rumours of German preparations on a large scale facing the Luxemburg frontier, and the Luxemburgers grew more than a little anxious at the suggestions which were thrown out that Germany was contemplating, for the second time in twenty-five years, a violation of Luxemburg territory with a view to turning the flank of the French defences on the Rhine-Moselle frontier.

Within only a few days of the outbreak of hostilities, indeed, the neutrality of Luxemburg was violated when a dozen inhabitants of the opposite German shore swam across the Moselle and scrambled up the bank into Luxemburg, driven there by hunger. They were received, if not with open arms, at least in a mood of willing helpfulness, and were returned to Germany only after they had been given a good meal. By way of conclusion of this little story, it should be added that these violators of Luxemburg neutrality were German *pigs*!

So for the time being Luxemburg remained a little island of peaceful neutrality in an ocean of war. The frontiers on all sides were still kept open. Luxemburg peasants crossed the river as of old to work in the German vineyards, and as beneath the hedges the Luxemburgers took out their dinners, the German soldiers crowded round to read the newspapers in which they were wrapped.

Possibly from the preposterous fear that the Allies might violate the neutrality of the little principality, the Nazis severed some of the communications between Luxemburg and Germany. Left, a bridge across the River Moselle, which forms the frontier, has been blown up; and, above, a camouflage gun-screen has been erected on the heights above the river.

Photos: Associated Press

None But The Best for Britain's Army

The bill of fare is always interesting reading to the young soldiers, and no one should get up from an Army meal hungry. The sergeant-cook is here chalking up the dinner menu on a blackboard.

One of the duties of the A.T.S. is to provide cooks for the Army. Here recruits are learning from a professional how to cut up joints.

THE diet of the British troops is a generous one, and there is far more variety than was the case in 1914. The daily ration for each man is:—

Bread	.. ..	16 oz.	Potatoes	12 oz.
Meat	..	14 oz.	Bacon	3 oz.
Vegetables	..	8 oz.	Cheese	1 oz.

There are also ample allowances of margarine—including a proportion of butter—tea, milk, sugar, rice, salt, pepper and mustard. Tinned herrings and tinned salmon are also provided, while each man receives two ounces of tobacco or cigarettes and two boxes of matches a week.

Plenty of food of the best quality is one of the first requisites of an army both in training and in the front line, and a huge organization is needed to give the soldier his meals. Left, "somewhere in France," a quartermaster-lieutenant is checking up the issue of rations. Right is a midday scene in the west of England. A column on the march has halted close to the sea, and at a mobile kitchen soldiers are lining up with their mess tins all ready to receive a hot meal.

Acknowledgements as follows: Photos, Topical, Fox, P.N.A. and Photopress

Salute to Turkey, Our New Ally

In the Great War Turkey was ranged with Britain's enemies, but in
1939 the countries whose sons had warred to the death on Gallipoli
found themselves in happy union.

A naval cadet with rifle and fixed bayonet
sounding the "fall in" at Turkey's new
great Naval College on Heybeliada Island,
near Istanbul.
Photo, Keystone

ALTHOUGH Turkey and Russia remained on excellent terms, the negotiations at the Kremlin between M. Stalin and M. Molotov on the one hand, and M. Sarajoglu, Turkish Foreign Minister, on the other, reached a deadlock on October 17. Some supposed that Turkey had been asked to join a Balkan *bloc* supporting Russia and Germany; others expressed the view that Russia had demanded that Turkey should unconditionally close the Dardanelles against Allied warships—a demand which Turkey refused to grant since it was clearly incompatible with the Montreux Convention of 1936.

Whatever the reason, the negotiations were broken off and M. Sarajoglu left for home. While he was still on the way to Ankara it was announced that the Turkish treaty with France and Great Britain negotiated in the previous June would be signed forthwith.

The actual treaty was signed in Ankara at 6.30 p.m. on October 19 by the Turkish Prime Minister, Dr. Reyfik Saydam, and the British and French Ambassadors, Sir H. M. Knatchbull-Hugessen and M. Massigli. Also present at the signing were General Sir A. P. Wavell, Commander of the British Forces in the Middle East, and General Weygand, Commander-in-Chief of the French Forces in Syria, who had already started staff talks with Marshal Tchakmak, Chief of the Turkish General Staff. The treaty came into force immediately, and is valid for fifteen years. That same night Herr von Papen went back to Berlin to meet a Fuehrer enraged by the complete collapse of German foreign policy on yet another front.

The treaty is a mutual assistance pact. Britain and France will aid Turkey if an act of aggression is committed against her by a European power; Turkey will come to the aid of her allies if a European power commits an act of aggression leading to war in the Mediterranean area in which France and the United Kingdom are involved, and, moreover, will help France and the United Kingdom if they are engaged in hostilities in virtue of their guarantees to Greece and Rumania.

Announcing in the House of Commons

The signatories to the Anglo-French-Turkish Pact are seen above: (1) Sir Hughe Knatchbull-Hugessen, British Ambassador to Turkey; (2) M. Massigli, French Ambassador to Turkey; (3) Dr. Reyfik Saydam, Turkish Prime Minister. Right are the officers who took part in the staff discussions: (4) Lt.-Gen. Sir A. P. Wavell, commanding the British forces in the Middle East; (5) General Weygand, French Commander in the Near East; (6) Marshal Tchakmak, chief of the Turkish General Staff.
Photos, Russell, Wide World, E.N.A. and Planet News

the signing of the pact, the Prime Minister said it would "give the House great satisfaction to learn that our negotiations have been brought to this successful conclusion, and that seal has been set on our close and cordial relations with a country for the qualities and character of whose people we have the highest regard and admiration." In Britain and in France, and also in Turkey, the pact was generally welcomed, and Moscow regarded it with

The quays at Istanbul (Constantinople) look out over the Bosporus, which divides European
from Asiatic Turkey. The only entrance to the Black Sea, which gives access to Russia
from the Mediterranean, is through the Dardanelles, the Sea of Marmara, and the Bosporus,
all of which are commanded by Turkey.   *Photo, Dorien Leigh*

The Guardians of the Straits are Ready Now

The largest ship in the Turkish fleet is the battle-cruiser " Yavuz," above. She was the German ship " Goeben " that took refuge in Turkish waters in August 1914. The submarine " Saldiray," seen right, is one of the most powerful of the five in the Turkish navy.

benevolent detachment. As Mr. Chamberlain told the Commons, " it has been announced both from Moscow and Angora that Turkey's relations with the Soviet Government continue as in the past to rest on a foundation of friendship. In Berlin, however, the pact was reported to have created a tremendous impression, for great hopes had been reposed in von Papen's diplomacy. Hence furious attacks were made in the German press on Turkey for having

listened to the siren voices of her onetime foes.

In 1914 it was a great reverse for the Allies when Turkey decided to throw in her lot with the Central Powers ; in 1939 it was as great a victory for the Allied cause when Turkey, rejuvenated, having thrown off the shackles of a corrupt and decaying political, social, and religious system, took her place side by side with the great Western Democracies in their stand against Nazi aggression.

Turkey's revival is based on the army which Mustapha Kemal reorganized after the Great War and led to victory over the Greeks. The Turkish Army is now one of the most formidable fighting machines in the Mediterranean zone. These photographs illustrate its modern aspect left, above, machine-gunners in action ; left, below, a camouflaged tractor ; right, a muleteer of the transport.

Photos, Planet News and Keystone

Finland Resolved to Defend Her Heritage

Following Soviet Russia's diplomatic onslaught on Estonia, Latvia and Lithuania, demands were alleged to have been addressed to Finland. But Finland is a Scandinavian power, not a Baltic State, and " no surrender " was the watchword of her people.

WHEN it was announced that Finland had been invited by Stalin to send a representative to discuss political and economic questions with Russia, the little " country of a thousand lakes " prepared for the worst. Having just witnessed the capitulation of the three Baltic States, Finland felt that she, too, would now be required to enter the orbit of Moscow. In particular she feared that Russia would demand some share in the control of the Aaland Islands—those islands which, lying at the mouth of the Gulf of Bothnia, form the key to the eastern Baltic.

Finland's suspicions of Russia's intentions have plenty of justification in history. From 1809, when her centuries-old connexion with Sweden terminated, Finland was part of the Russian Empire with the Tsar ruling as Grand Duke. For many years she was permitted to enjoy a large measure of autonomy, with her own government, religion, language, educational system and army. Her liberties were severely infringed, however, in the early years of the present century when a period of intense Russification set in. There were few regrets, therefore, when the Tsarist regime crashed into ruin in 1917. The suspended constitution was at once restored, and on December 6, 1917 the sovereign independence of Finland was proclaimed. In the following year, however, fighting broke out between the Finnish Communists and Russian revolutionary troops on the one hand, and the White Guard, led by General Mannerheim, supported by a German force under Von der Goltz, on the other. Finland's War of Independence, as it is called, was short but fierce ; it lasted only four months in 1918, but it was marked by a Red terror and a White counter-terror in which some 15,000 men, women and children were reported to have been slaughtered.

Problem of the Aalands

After the collapse of Germany Mannerheim gravitated towards England and America, and in the summer of 1919 a democratic republic came into being. Peace with Soviet Russia was signed in 1920, and a little later in the same year Finland was admitted as a member of the League of Nations. In 1921 her sovereignty over the Aaland Islands, disputed by Sweden, was recognized by the League, although it was agreed that the Islands should be neutralized and demilitarized. Eighteen years later, in the period of unrest consequent upon the crisis over Czechoslovakia, Finland consulted with Sweden concerning the re-fortification of the islands, but the work had hardly commenced a year later.

Since the winning of independence the Finns (who, it should be remarked, are not Slavs like the Russians but cousins of the Magyars) have devoted all their efforts to the peaceful development of their national estate. About the size of England, Scotland and Wales, Finland is primarily an agricultural country, although so many are its lakes and so large its Arctic region, that only one-twentieth of its area is cultivated. Vast are its forests ; and timber, pulp and paper are the country's chief items of export. Most of the trade is done with Britain, though Germany is a good second.

For centuries the Finns have been proud of their national culture. In their roll of honour are famous writers and artists and, above all, musicians—Jan Sibelius, for instance. World-famous in the field of sport is Paavo Nurmi, the runner whose ten-mile record set up eleven years ago still stands, and Taisto Maeki, holder of four world records. In the field of government Finland will ever be renowned as the country which first gave its women the parliamentary franchise.

Primarily a nation of peace-lovers, the Finns have often displayed soldierly qualities of the highest order. When in October 1939, therefore, there came what seemed to be a threat to the nation's independence, the Republic flew to arms. The peacetime strength of the army is only some 30,000 men, but there is a Civilian Guard of 100,000, and reserves of one kind and another bring the total of the military forces up to some 300,000 men. Neutral observers who visited

Every Finnish citizen is liable for service in the army, the peacetime strength of which is 2,000 officers and 31,000 other ranks. Above is Marshal Mannerheim, left, the commander-in-chief. Right, a battery of Finnish anti-aircraft guns.
Photos, Keystone and Wide World

Finland in those weeks of crisis reported having seen with amazement enormous quantities of arms and munitions of the very latest patterns.

Finland was resolute, and reports that the Russian army was massing in great strength near Leningrad, only twenty-five miles from the Finnish frontier, led to no weakening in the country's will to resist. All the reservists were called up, and arrangements were made for the evacuation of Helsinki (Helsingfors in Swedish), Viipuri (Viborg), and other towns. M. J. K. Paasikivi, Finland's Minister at Stockholm and former Prime Minister, who was generally held to be best acquainted with the Russian Government, was despatched to Moscow to find out what terms Stalin was prepared to offer, and President Kallio proceeded to

The Finnish Minister at Stockholm, M. J. K. Paasikivi, is seen right in the photograph above with Colonel Paasonen, left, and M. Nykoff. In October 1939 he acted as Finland's principal representative in the discussions concerning the questions at issue with Soviet Russia.
Photo, Central Press

Finland, while still hoping for the best, did not slow down her preparations for the worst. Above, left, trenches are being dug. Women and children were evacuated from danger zones, including Helsinki, and on the right some are waiting on a railway platform to entrain.

Finland's capital, Helsinki, formerly known as Helsingfors, is one of the most beautiful cities of Northern Europe. This photograph shows the South Harbour which runs right into the heart of the city. The building in the centre is the Lutheran Church of St. Nicholas.
Photos, Topical, Wide World; Derek Wordley

Stockholm to consult with the kings of the Scandinavian countries concerning the problems of their joint interests.

Back and forth between Moscow and Helsinki travelled M. Paasikivi. Rumours were rampant to the effect that Finland was being asked to tread the same hard path as the Baltic States, but nothing official concerning the negotiations was vouchsafed to the general public.

Then on October 23 there came a report from Helsinki that Stalin's claims on Finland would be shown to be more modest than the world had hitherto supposed. According to an announcement made by the Moscow radio, Russia would now ask Finland only not to fortify the Aaland Islands, and to remove the present defences. That military alliance with Russia which had been so feared by the Finns was not, it was stated, being insisted upon; Russia would be content if Finland pledged herself not to engage in a combination of powers directed against Moscow.

Finland waited — but not for one moment did she relax her attitude of calm watchfulness and readiness for every eventuality.

Scandinavia's Rulers Take Counsel Together

The three kings of the Scandinavian countries and the President of Finland who took part in the Four-Power Conference at Stockholm on Oct. 18-19, 1939, are seen above with their Foreign Ministers. Left to right : M. Erkko, Finnish Foreign Minister ; M. Munch, Danish Foreign Minister ; President Kallio of Finland ; King Haakon VII of Norway, King Gustav V of Sweden ; King Christian X of Denmark ; M. Koht, Norwegian Foreign Minister ; and M. Sandler, Swedish Foreign Minister.

Above, the first air raid shelter is being dug in the Heotorget Square in Stockholm ; right, flags flying from the Copenhagen Stock Exchange in honour of the Conference.

Denmark, in common with other Scandinavian countries, called a number of classes to the colours as part of the precautions aimed at preserving her neutrality. Here men called up for service are lining up to report. Military training is compulsory for every able-bodied man in Denmark, even the clergy having to serve.

L INKED by ties of race and culture, history and interest, the Scandinavian countries, Sweden, Norway, and Denmark co-operated in 1939, as they did during the war of 1914–1918, but this time Finland was joined in their conclave. On October 18 and 19 the kings of Denmark, Norway and Sweden, and the President of Finland, with their Foreign Ministers, met in Stockholm to discuss the problems due to the international situation. The four Governments declared that they were " determined in close co-operation to adhere consistently to strict neutrality. Their intention is to let their attitude with regard to all problems which may occur be determined by their solicitude to uphold a neutral position in full independence." They also decided that as far as possible they should maintain traditional commercial relations and support each other in securing vital supplies for their peoples.

Convoys are Safe with the Royal Navy

In the fight against the U-boats and the air-raiders the convoy system is proving its
worth over and over again. As in the last war, so in this, the Navy is seeing that the
food-ships arrive safe home in port.

ONE of the first steps taken by the British Admiralty to counter the submarine menace was the institution of that system of convoys which proved so successful in the last war. In his first statement to the House of Commons Mr. Churchill reported that a convoy system had been organized, and was already in full operation for both outgoing ships and those homeward bound.

It may be assumed that the measures first adopted in the last war have now been well-nigh perfected. The practice is for ships to assemble at certain specified ports of departure. There the masters are called together and given instructions concerning the stations they are to keep in the convoy—a most important matter—the measures to be adopted for the black-out of their vessels, the zig-zag course to be steered, and the action expected of them if and when a U-boat is sighted.

When all the ships of the convoy have been assembled, it leaves harbour and, under an escort of cruisers, destroyers and other vessels of the British Navy, is shepherded across the ocean.

U-Boats at a Disadvantage

The advantages of the convoy system hardly need stressing. A solitary vessel attacked by a U-boat is at the raider's mercy, but when a U-boat breaks water and delivers an attack on a convoy it is the U-boat that is in the unenviable position. It may have time to fire a shell or to launch one torpedo, but that will almost surely be its last; before it has time to deliver a second attack the racing destroyers will have sent it to its grave by their depth charges. Then the crew of a vessel torpedoed in a convoy have a much better chance of rescue than if the ship were proceeding on its own.

The success of the convoy system was demonstrated even in the first few weeks of the war. The number of sinkings was at once reduced, and those ships lost were either vessels which were proceeding separately or were on their way to join a convoy.

In the last war the convoy system was so successful that 99 per cent of the ships convoyed were escorted in safety to their destinations. The present war may well repeat the successes of the

last, and this despite the fact that today the naval escort have to be prepared for an attack from air-raiders as well as one by submarines.

The first air attack on a British convoy was delivered by Nazi 'planes in the North Sea on the afternoon of Saturday, October 21—ominously enough, if the Germans had remembered it—Trafalgar Day.

Air Attack in the North Sea

During the morning enemy aeroplanes had been spotted shadowing the convoy as it steamed in two lines southward, protected by escort vessels and reconnaissance 'planes. At 12.30 three bombers dived out of the mist on to the convoy, but in the face of tremendous fire banked steeply and vanished in the distance. Half an hour later a further attack was delivered by two flights of three aeroplanes each. The leading escort vessel opened a heavy barrage which made the attackers turn away. Coming back again, they drew the fire of all the escort ships, and before they had time to retreat were engaged by a flight of British fighters which came swooping across the convoy from the land. When last seen from the convoy the raiders were disappearing into the clouds to the eastward, closely pursued by the British 'planes. It was later announced that three of the Nazi seaplanes were shot down and a fourth forced to land, but no hits were obtained on the convoy and there were no casualties. The convoy reached its destination without further molestation.

The same week-end saw the release of another story evidencing the care with which convoys are shepherded across the ocean—this time by aeroplanes of the Auxiliary Air Force. The convoy was warned by the airmen twice of drifting mines, which in each case were directly in the path of the leading ships and close to them. The airmen, who until a few weeks before had been employed in their civilian occupations, dropped smoke flares as markers within a few feet of the mines, and warned the convoy of their presence by flash-lamp signals. On the first occasion the ships' helms were thrown hard over, and the escort led the convoy on a new course. On the second occasion there was just enough time for an escorting destroyer to steam across the merchantmen's course and put the mine out of action by machine-gun fire. The sea was rough, and the detection of floating mines is always a matter requiring careful and skilled observation; yet here again the effective liaison between the convoy and its escort of ships and 'planes was strikingly demonstrated.

In the light of such convincing experience of the efficacy of our Navy's defence methods, it is not surprising that from the neutral countries, and from Scandinavia in particular, came requests for the establishment of more and larger convoys; and this despite the fact that Germany announced that neutral ships accepting a place in a British convoy were liable to be treated as enemy craft.

As emphasized by both the Prime Minister and the Air Minister, the work of the Coastal Command, R.A.F., and the Fleet Air Arm on convoy and anti-submarine patrol is exacting and "almost continuous." The Fairey Swordfish, seen above on such patrol, carries either bombs, slung in the racks seen under the wings, or a single torpedo between the widely splayed legs of the undercarriage. *Photo, Wide World*

Nazi Bombers Brought Down by British Guns

This German aeroplane, a twin-engined Heinkel bomber, is one of the two which were disabled by gunfire during the attack by the Nazis on British warships in the North Sea on October 9, and afterwards came down on Danish territory. According to the Admiralty statement, no British ship was damaged and other German aircraft may have been hit. Thus one more demonstration of the prediction that the " battle-ships would beat the bombers " was given by the Royal Navy.

Photo, Associated Press

One of the Nazi bombers shot down when attacking British warships in the North Sea on September 26 is seen in the photo above. The crew are launching their rubber boat in which some of them kept afloat until picked up.

The photograph above and that centre-right were taken during the rescue on September 26. Above, the British destroyer is approaching the enemy aircraft to pick the crew up from their rubber boat. The German machine is a Dornier flying-boat, a long-range type of aircraft similar to those which were used on Germany's air mail service across the South Atlantic.

Photos, Central Press

THE first raids by Nazi bombers on the British coasts and ships resulted in negligible damage to the targets, but in very serious losses to the attackers. The losses of the Germans in raids made in the course of a month are summarized, the numbers of 'planes brought down being given in brackets:

Sept. 26.—Attack on British warships in North Sea (2).
Oct.   9.—Attack on Navy in North Sea (4 in sea; 2 in Denmark).
Oct. 16.—Attack on warships at Rosyth (4; 3 more probable).
Oct. 17.—Raids on Scapa Flow (2).
Oct. 17.—Air fight over North Sea (2).
Oct. 21.—Attack on North Sea convoy (7).
Oct. 22.—Raids south-east Scotland (1).

Thus from the very beginning it was clearly demonstrated that warships, properly guarded and defended, had little to fear from aerial attack.

'German' Ocean—Not With These About!

This impressive line of warships are cruisers of the "Southampton" class patrolling the North Sea with their A.A. guns at the ready. They demonstrate that the Nazi claim that it is now the "German Ocean" is only one more example of vain boasting. It is this constant British patrol that has "beaten the bombers" and made the threat of air action against the navy of little effect. On patrol duty the crew are always ready to take up their battle stations and the ships are cleared for action.

Photo, Fox

The photograph above shows o
tion.   Those in the farthest lin

In the early days of the intensive N
despite the magnitude of the effort

actories Today's Effort Speeds Tomorrow's Victory

s of an aircraft factory in which Vickers-Supermarine Spitfire fighters are being built.   The long rows of machines are in various stages of construc-
stage when the tall unit is in place and the Rolls-Royce engine, which will give the machines a speed of nearly 370 miles an hour, has been fitted.
In the foreground are machines in an earlier stage of construction.
Photo, Fox

ent the German people were told that " guns are better than butter."   In Britain no one will go hungry to pay for guns or any other form of armament,
graphs give a glimpse.   That above and that left show processes in the making of a 16-in. gun such as forms the main armament of battleships.   In
e barrel is being gauged after boring, and in the second (left) the inner tube is being inserted into the barrel.
Photos, Central Press

WORDS THAT HISTORY WILL REMEMBER

A Select Record from Week to Week of Important War Declarations and Statements

(Continued from page 210)

Tuesday, October 17, 1939

Statement issued by the WAR OFFICE through the Ministry of Information :

German propaganda has endeavoured to create the impression that Poland was sacrificed by her Allies fruitlessly and that the efforts of the Polish Army contributed nothing to the Allied cause. In fact, however, Poland's contribution towards the final victory of her Allies was important, as the following points show :

(1) The casualties inflicted by Poland on the German Army were undoubtedly greater than the figures given by Hitler in his Reichstag speech. Even if German losses totalled only 150,000 casualties (a reasonable estimate), this represents a considerable wastage at the outset of what may be a long war.

(2) German losses in material also were considerable. In one attack alone they lost 83 tanks on a narrow front, and in Sosnkowski's successful counter-attack near Lwow on September 16 they are reported to have lost over 100 tanks. Losses of German aircraft were also appreciable ; and German consumption of petrol—the weakest point in her supply system —was enormous.

(3) By holding about 70 German divisions on the Eastern Front the Polish Army enabled France to complete her mobilization without disturbance.

(4) By compelling Germany to concentrate the bulk of her Air Force on the Eastern Front Poland contributed greatly to the safe transportation of the B.E.F. to France.

(5) The Polish campaign has furnished the Allies with valuable information as to the tactics developed by Germany in the use of aircraft, tanks, and motorized units.

(6) There is reason to believe that the inability of German infantry to advance without tank support against even relatively weak Polish defensive positions came as a severe shock to German formations, who are aware that the Maginot Line is an infinitely more formidable proposition. The moral of German tank personnel was also shaken by the effectiveness of even the very limited anti-tank artillery commanded by the Poles.

(7) Finally, the heroic defence of Warsaw, Modlin, etc., has given an example to the world of utmost gallantry in desperate circumstances. That example will stimulate the Allied forces in the West ; and it has always been clear that the Poles' eventual independence would have to be established by the victory of the Allies and not by the outcome of events on Polish soil.

Thursday, October 19

Translation of French text of TREATY OF MUTUAL ASSISTANCE, signed in Ankara, between France, Great Britain and Turkey :

ARTICLE 1

In the event of Turkey being involved in hostilities with a European Power in consequence of aggression by that Power against Turkey, the French Government and the Government of the United Kingdom will co-operate effectively with the Turkish Government and will lend it all aid and assistance in their power.

ARTICLE 2

(1) In the event of an act of aggression by a European Power leading to war in the Mediterranean area in which the United Kingdom and France are involved, Turkey will collaborate effectively with France and the United Kingdom and will lend them all aid and assistance in its power.

(2) In the event of an act of aggression by a European Power leading to war in the Mediterranean area in which Turkey is involved, France and the United Kingdom will collaborate effectively with Turkey and will lend it all aid and assistance in their power.

ARTICLE 3

So long as the guarantees given by France and the United Kingdom to Greece and Rumania by their respective Declarations of April 13, 1939, remain in force, Turkey will co-operate effectively with France and the United Kingdom and will lend them all aid and assistance in its power, in the event of France and the United Kingdom being engaged in hostilities in virtue of either of the said guarantees.

ARTICLE 4

In the event of France and the United Kingdom being involved in hostilities with a European Power in consequence of aggression committed by that Power against either of those States without the provisions of Articles 2 or 3 being applicable, the High Contracting Parties will immediately consult together.

It is nevertheless agreed that in such an eventuality Turkey will observe at least a benevolent neutrality towards France and the United Kingdom.

ARTICLE 5

Without prejudice to the provisions of Article 3 above, in the event of either :

(1) Aggression by a European Power against another European State which the Government of one of the High Contracting Parties had, with the approval of that State, undertaken to assist in maintaining its independence or neutrality against such aggression, or

(2) Aggression by a European Power which, while directed against another European State, constituted, in the opinion of the Government of one of the High Contracting Parties, a menace to its own security, the High Contracting Parties will immediately consult together with a view to such common action as might be considered effective.

ARTICLE 6

The present Treaty is not directed against any country, but is designed to assure France, the United Kingdom, and Turkey of mutual aid and assistance in resistance to aggression should the necessity arise.

ARTICLE 7

The provisions of the present Treaty are equally binding as bilateral obligations between Turkey and each of the two other High Contracting Parties.

ARTICLE 8

If the High Contracting Parties are engaged in hostilities in consequence of the operation of the present Treaty, they will not conclude an armistice or peace except by common agreement.

ARTICLE 9

. . . The present Treaty is concluded for a period of 15 years. . . .

PROTOCOL No. 1

The undersigned Plenipotentiaries state that their respective Governments agree that the Treaty of Mutual Assistance dated this day shall be put into force from the moment of its signature.

PROTOCOL No. 2

. . . The obligations undertaken by Turkey in virtue of the above-mentioned Treaty cannot compel that country to take action having as its effect, or involving as its consequence, entry into armed conflict with the U.S.S.R. . . .

OUR WAR GAZETTEER

Aaland (or Aland) **Islands.** Group of 300 isles at entrance to Gulf of Bothnia, belonging to Finland since 1921 ; in that year their fortification was forbidden ; Finnish and Swedish request early in 1939 for remilitarization objected to by U.S.S.R. ; home of windjammers ; a. 550 sq. m. ; pop. 27,000.

Finland. Republic of N. Europe with coastline on Baltic ; fringed by islands and dotted with lakes ; timber, abundant water power ; renowned for triumphs of long-distance athletes ; declared independent from Russia in 1917 ; cap. Helsinki ; a. 147,811 sq. m. ; pop. 3,834,000.

Forth, Firth of. River estuary on E. coast of Scotland between Fife and Lothians ; spanned at Queensferry by famous railway bridge (completed 1890), 8,295 ft. long ; also at Kincardine by new road bridge (opened 1936).

Helsinki (or Helsingfors). Capital city and chief seaport of Finland ; proposed venue of Olympic Games, 1940 ; pop. 293,000.

Karlsruhe. Town of Germany, capital of Baden State ; 6 m. E. of Rhine at point where French frontier makes sharp turn ; noted palace, museum, art gallery, etc. ; pop. 178,000.

Kronstadt. Seaport and naval base of U.S.S.R. ; on island of Kotlin in Gulf of Finland, 20 m. W. of Leningrad ; founded by Peter the Great, 1710 ; pop. 43,800.

Latvia (or Lettland). Republic on Baltic, part of Russia until 1918 ; cap. Riga ; a. 25,000 sq. m. ; pop. 1,950,000.

Liepaja (Ger. Libau). Seaport of Latvia, 150 m. W. of Riga ; excellent harbour ; pop. 57,000.

Lithuania. Republic on Baltic, independent of Russia since 1918 ; also borders Germany, who took Memel in Mar. 1939 ; cap. Kaunas, but people only recognize Vilna (now reannexed) ; approx. a. 20,000 sq. m. ; pop. 2,374,000.

Memel (or Klaipeda). Seaport now attached to E. Prussia (Germany), in district—Lithuanian since 1919—reannexed after ultimatum of Mar. 1939 ; pop. 38,545.

Rosyth. Naval base on N. (Fife) coast of Firth of Forth, Scotland, just W. of Forth Bridge ; busy only with ship-breaking from end of Gt. War to 1938.

Scapa Flow. Landlocked harbour in Orkneys, N. Scotland ; principal base of Grand Fleet during Great War ; Ger. Fleet interned here, Nov. 1918, and scuttled June, 1919.

Strasbourg (Ger. Strassburg). City of Alsace, France, just to W. of Rhine ; cathedral has famous tower and clock ; university, printing centre ; German from 1870 to 1919 ; ringed by Maginot forts ; pop. 193,000.

Ventspils (Ger. Windau). Seaport of Latvia, on Baltic ; pop. 15,000.

Sing-Songs and Stars for the Young Soldiers

After attending church parade at a camp in Sussex the troops were entertained by a concert party in which were famous stars. These members of the audience prove that even in the open air an accomplished comedian can "bring the house down."

In the last war mouth-organs were the favourite musical instrument of the troops, but it is with a piano-accordion that the young soldier in the photograph is accompanying a sing-song that is in progress in a training-camp.

It was not until February 1915 that some attempt was made to provide entertainment for the troops in the last war. This time the need was quickly recognized, and during the first two weeks of the war ENSA—Entertainments National Service Association—came into being with its headquarters at Drury Lane Theatre, London, to organize concert parties, and by September 23 ten parties were touring camps in Britain. Above is a part of the audience at a camp entertainment.

Photos, Wide World, Fox, and Topical

Nazi Poison Propaganda: The Great Gas Lie!

Stage by stage the Nazi propagandists built up the fantastic story described here—
a story which was believed might well be the prelude to the use of poison gas by the
Germans on the Western Front.

HERE is a little story told by the Germans. On September 8, when the invasion of Poland was at its height, a company of Nazi sappers were removing a barricade at a bridge on the outskirts of Jaslo in Galicia. An explosion occurred, as the result of which four sappers died and ten were injured. On investigation it was discovered that the casualties were due to mustard gas. . .

More than a month later—on October 12—the Germans stated that this gas was part of a consignment which had been supplied by Britain to the Poles, who had used it in battle.

So, at least, runs the story—a story

One of the most unpleasant surprises of the last war was the German use of poison gas, preceded by accusations of its use by the Allies. Here we see Argyle and Sutherland High-landers wearing improvised gas-masks issued on May 3, 1915.

which was immediately denied by the British Government. "No gas in any form whatsoever has been supplied at any time to Poland by Great Britain," said a Government statement issued on the evening of October 12. Following repetitions of the story the British repeated their denial on October 15. Yet, shortly afterwards, the fabrication was reproduced in a German leaflet widely circulated in neutral countries. The story was, indeed, embellished somewhat. Thus, it was said that on September 23, after the capture of Oxhoeft, near Gdynia, an ammunition dump was discovered containing a considerable quantity of mines, each holding 22 lb. of mustard gas. "Furthermore," so the German tale continued, "in an arsenal near Gdynia in which the deliveries of ammunition made by Great Britain shortly before the war were stored several thousand mustard gas mines were found to be among the war material supplied by Britain." In broadcasts, too, the Germans asserted that they had found, in various parts of Poland, depots

of mustard gas mines whose markings showed that they came from the store near Oxhoeft.

But the War Office, with full knowledge of the facts, declared that " no gas mines were shipped from Britain to Gdynia at any time." Moreover, they pointed out that there were some strange features of the story which required explanation. Although, for instance, the German wireless announced on September 16 that Nazi sappers had been killed or wounded by poison gas on September 8, and the discovery of the gas dump at Oxhoeft was stated to have been made on September 23, it was not until October 12 that Britain was accused of having supplied the gas.

Furthermore, the Swiss doctor whom the leaflet stated had diagnosed nine German wounded at Jaslo, Poland, to be suffering from mustard gas poisoning, had said nothing to substantiate the story of the discovery of a gas dump near Gdynia. When interviewed at Geneva by a representative of the London "Daily Express," the gentleman referred to, Dr. Rudolf Staehelin, of Basle, said that when he was attending a patient in Berlin, the German Government invited him to make a diagnosis of nine sick men. He im-

mediately got the impression that there was something strange about the request, but he could not refuse to go without appearing to give offence. He was taken by aeroplane to Jaslo, and from there to a hospital where he diagnosed with certainty that nine soldiers showed symptoms like those produced by Yellow Cross (mustard) gas. "I asked the circumstances in which it happened, and was taken to a bridge where they pointed out a hole produced by a bomb. I smelt lime chlorate, which is the *antidote* for Yellow Cross gas. That is all I saw there."

Moreover, in a statement to the Geneva correspondent of "The Times," the Professor declared, "I found no evidence indicating in what circumstances the poisoning had occurred. I feared that my statement would be misused for anti-British propaganda. The German Press and tracts sent by mail to neutrals pretend that a "Basle Professor of European fame has given evidence of Polish resort to gas warfare at Jaslo—which is untrue."

There the matter might be left to rest, but for the fact that when in 1915 the Germans first used poison gas, they, as it were, prepared the way by accusing the British of having already used it. On April 17, 1915, the German Wolff News Agency stated that: "Yesterday, east of Ypres, the British employed shells and bombs filled with asphyxiating gas." The statement was completely untrue, but as a sequel there came, on April 22, the death-dealing clouds of chlorine.

The British War Office, recollecting the sequence of events in 1915, suggested that something of the same kind might well be in preparation for 1939. Indeed, they asserted that " the persistent repetition of this flimsy and mendacious story, in spite of the British Government's categorical denials, clearly indicates an intention on the part of Germany to use poison gas on the Western Front in contravention of the 1925 Geneva protocol to which they are signatories."

These German photographs are supposed to substantiate the fantastic German story told in this page. Below, the crater near the bridge at Jaslo; above, a notice stated to have been found near Warsaw: "Gas. No Admittance." Such notices, however, were stated to have been issued to Polish A.R.P. wardens to mark spots where German gas bombs exploded!

'There will always be Misery,' says Hitler

All sorts of expedients have been adopted by the Nazis to conserve the precious petrol of which they have all too small a stock. Above, elephants from the famous menagerie at Hamburg are being used for ploughing. The partial disuse of farm tractors and the substitution of animals means that ploughing and other operations are performed much more slowly and at much greater cost of labour.

D URING the hard winters that are experienced in Germany the poorly-paid working classes have fared very badly under the Nazi regime, and the Winter Relief Fund, a collection to enable them to purchase even the meagre fare now obtainable in Germany, has been a regular feature ever since the Nazis came into power. How pressing is the need is proved by the fact that, on October 10, Hitler himself opened the campaign for subscriptions.

In the course of his speech the Fuehrer is reported to have said :

"One has become accustomed to the fact that the man-in-the-street has, more or less willingly, contributed to the winter relief work. I say more or less. The great majority show more willingness ; it is only a small minority who show less. We want to give each individual an insight into the real misery of many of the people. Every individual must realize that fortune and wealth have not come to all of us, nor will they. **There has always been misery ; there is misery today ; there will always be misery.**"

In a Berlin street a collection is being made for the Winter Relief Fund. Even those who cannot really afford what they give are wise to give it willingly and with a smile.

Not only the calls of the Army, but those of men for munition work and the intensive cultivation of farms made necessary by the Allied blockade have made it imperative in Germany that, whenever possible, men's work should be done by women. Above left is a woman tram conductor, a common sight in every German city. The photograph, right, provides pictorial proof of the dejection which has come upon the German people. These sad-faced and listless folk are not even cheered up by the voice of their Fuehrer to which they are listening.

Photos, Keystone, Wide World, Central Press and Planet News

Germany Must Feel the Pinch of the Blockade

With every week that passes the Allies' blockade of Germany becomes ever more stringent, and already the Reich is feeling the loss of those goods which are essential to the successful prosecution of the war.

HERR HITLER sees war in the terms of a *Blitzkrieg.* He gloats over his speeding aeroplanes, the darting movements of his motorized columns. He exults over the fact that the war in Poland has been brought to a close in just a few weeks.

Great battles may be won by lightning strokes, and many of the greatest battles which history records have been won in this way. But the last battle—that battle which, as someone has said, Britain always wins—is won by a weapon which, although slow to begin, is unremitting in its progress, and deadly in its result—the blockade.

Armies cannot march without food and shoe-leather; cannon and machine-guns cannot be made and are useless without explosives; aeroplanes cannot fly and tanks cannot charge without petrol. And it is just these things, the great raw materials of the world, that the navies of Britain and France are cutting off from the German market.

In the House of Commons on October 25 the Minister of Economic Warfare, Mr. R. H. Cross, said that the system of contraband control was operating so satisfactorily that " in general the position is that Germany is now effectively cut off from nearly all her overseas sources of supply. During the preceding week," he went on, " 128 ships were detained for examination at the British control bases at Weymouth, Kirkwall and the Downs, and the total number of ships dealt with was nearly 50 per cent more than in any previous week."

Some idea of the effectiveness of the blockade may be gathered from the figures Mr. Cross gave of the quantity of goods which had been intercepted and detained by the Contraband Control in the first six weeks of war. In the total of 338,000 tons of goods suspected of being contraband destined for Germany were: 76,500 tons of petroleum products; 65,000 tons of iron ore; 38,500 tons of manganese ore; 24,500 tons of phosphates; 21,500 tons of aluminium ore; 16,500 tons of haematite ore; 13,000 tons of copra; 10,300 tons of oilseeds.

 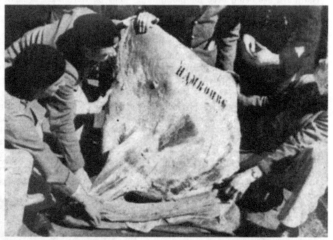

The two categories of contraband, absolute and conditional, are illustrated in these photographs of cargoes of ships captured by French patrols. That left consists of lubricants consigned to an enemy port, and clearly valuable to the fighting forces; it is therefore absolute contraband. Right is meat consigned to Hamburg. Food is conditional contraband, but an American writer has said that it is more than a possibility that all foodstuffs imported into a belligerent country will serve a military end. Hence the cargo was seized.

Photos, Courtesy of the French Embassy

Above is a convoy in the North Sea, photographed from one of the ships. It will be seen that they are spread over a wide area. On the extreme right is a tanker and next to it a destroyer, while other destroyers and merchant ships are visible on the horizon. The escorting ships steam on either side of the merchant ships, sometimes making a zigzag course. The flagship of the convoy is usually a light cruiser. The speed of the whole convoy must necessarily be the top speed of the slowest ship.   *Photo, Fox*

The Nazi economists do their best to belittle the menace of the blockade by asserting that their new-found friend, Soviet Russia, will more than make good the deficiencies resulting from the Allied blockade. For years they have held out to the German people a picture of Ukrainian fields waving with corn, of gushing oil wells, and of huge stores of minerals lying waiting to be tapped in Red Russia's soil. Now they are saying that as the result of the German-Soviet Pact of August 23, 1939, all the natural wealth with which Russia is endowed will be placed at the disposal of the Reich.

Can Russia Help?

The claim, however, will not bear examination. It is true that Russia is, potentially speaking, an immensely rich country, but there are definite limits to her productive capacity, imposed by the conditions of transport and the efficiency and the willingness of the Russian workers. In the Ukraine, often described as Europe's greatest wheatfield, there have been even of late years the most terrible famines. The Russian railway

The German 10,000-ton " pocket " battleship " Deutschland," which slipped through the British blockade of the North Sea to become a commerce raider, is shown in this photo, taken when she passed down the English Channel in April 1939. Top is the American steamer " City of Flint " arriving at Halifax, Nova Scotia, with survivors of the " Athenia " on board. On her return voyage she was captured and taken to Murmansk (shown in the map of north-west Europe, above) by the " Deutschland."

Photos, Wide World and Associated Press ; map by courtesy of the " Daily Telegraph"

and other metals, timber, rubber and textile fabrics such as cotton. Some of these Germany has and to spare—coal, and possibly timber. Iron ore she imports in huge quantities even in peace-time, and now her main channel of supply, from Sweden, is liable to be intercepted by submarine action or as the result of political complications. Further supplies of timber and small quantities of oil she may now obtain from Russia, but with regard to the latter it may be pointed out that Russia of late years has reduced her exports of oil from 6,000,000 tons in 1931 to 1,100,000 tons in 1938, and even in peacetime Germany was dependent upon foreign oil supplies to the extent of 5,000,000 tons per annum. As for the Polish oil-fields recently included in Russia's share of Poland, production had been falling for some time before the war, and it is estimated that Germany may expect to secure only half-a-million tons a year from this source.

" Ersatz " Found Wanting

Rubber and cotton are but two of the many materials which are not produced in Germany, and which are now cut off by the blockade. It is true that German chemists have produced a synthetic rubber, but like most of the *ersatz* (artificial) substances, it can hardly be compared with the real thing. With regard to metals, Russia may be able to spare some of her production of man-ganese—absolutely necessary in the manu-facture of the steel of which guns and armour are made—and some of the gold from her mines in the Urals.

As the weeks and months go by, the effect of the Allied blockade must be made increasingly manifest. Perhaps the best tribute to its real value is the counter-blockade which Germany has declared against Britain. By her sub-marine warfare, her commerce raiders, and such arrangements as the proposal that all neutral traffic from the Baltic should pass through the Kiel Canal, she hopes to bring Britain to her knees before the blockade shall have produced in Germany a repetition of 1918.

and road system are still far from approaching the standards of the West. About the Russian workers we have the evidence of many technicians that, despite their frequent enthusiasm they

fall far short of the mechanically-minded artisans of America and Britain.

In the prosecution of a war there are certain raw materials which are absolutely essential—for example, coal, oil, iron ore

Mr. Hore-Belisha Talks About the War

Delivered on the evening of Saturday, October 21, 1939—" Trafalgar Day "—this
broadcast speech by the Minister for War was widely welcomed for its clear statement
of the war's balance-sheet to date, expressed in a mood of resolute optimism.

"TONIGHT," said Mr. Hore-Belisha, " marks the close of the seventh week of the war. Hitler had fixed in advance the day of his assault, and Poland, endeavouring to resist the devastation of her homes, was harried. Her army was destroyed, but the memory of its valour is indestructible. The aggressor calculated that such swift and ruthless action in the East would intimidate the friends of Poland in the West. But it was not in the character of either France or Britain to desert an ally." Then he proceeded :

"Tomorrow will be the seventh Sunday since our Prime Minister—who had exhausted every means of conciliation—announced that

Not long before war was declared Mr. Hore-Belisha went to France to inspect the wonders of the Maginot Line. Above, he is seen on this occasion with General Laudrien and M. Daladier studying a map. In September the War Minister was in France again, at a Council of War in Paris.
Photo, Keystone

Germany had rejected our ultimatum to withdraw her troops from Poland, and that our task thenceforward had become nothing less than this—' to redeem Europe from the perpetual and recurring fear of German aggression and to enable the peoples of Europe to preserve their independence and their liberties.' That is a great task—a supreme task—and the war will not end until it is completed.

"We have settled down—each one of us—to play our appropriate part, and the virtue most required is the virtue of patience. Everybody is a participant in this war. Our confidence and our faith in the motive which inspires us are our armour on the Home Front.

Germany's Three Alternatives

"THREE courses are open to Nazi Germany : To try and smash through by land, sea and air ; to remain quiescent in the hope that we will prematurely take up the offensive against them ; or to lure us into the discussion of specious terms of peace. I will examine these courses one by one.

"Recent military experience shows that an offensive against prepared positions is unprofitable. Poland had no Maginot Line on which to withstand the heavy onslaught made against her. On the Western Front there are strong defences, and they become stronger every day. **The enemy will pay dearly for any massed attack upon them.** Our

commanders are not likely, in advance of the time that suits them, to risk unnecessarily the lives of those who compose our Armies.

"Consequently, up to the present this war has differed from our preconceptions. We thought, perhaps, that more would happen—decisive battles by land, sea and air ; on the Home Front we expected to be brought nearer and more quickly to a grim reality. There have been many, night and day, ready for action. It is, however, no disadvantage that seven weeks have passed without the need for implementing the purpose of our comprehensive preparations.

"Despite the apparent inactivity decisive developments have, in fact, occurred which should not escape our notice. The constant cry of Nazi Germany has been since its inception, ' Give us a free hand in the East.' There was a long agenda of conquests to be made in that direction. Poland was but an item. The

Baltic States were to be dominated, but from these, German nationals are now in retreat ; Russia has claimed this sphere of influence. The cornfields of the Ukraine were coveted ; Russia has made sure of this harvest. Through Poland, Nazi Germany was to have an entrance to Rumania ; this entrance has been barred—by Russia. ' Berlin-Baghdad.' Turkey alone could be the avenue to this ambition. Turkey, a brave and respected friend, stands firmly in the path. Iraq is our loyal and unshakable ally.

"NAZI Germany can assess her Eastern balance-sheet after seven weeks of war. Turning now to the West ; the expulsion of Nazi German commerce from the sea is incontrovertible. We have lost a fraction of our tonnage—less than one per cent. We still have twenty-one million tons of shipping of our own. We have lost two important ships of the Fleet. Valiant lives have been forfeited in the sea as in the air. We do not underestimate this sacrifice. **Our Auxiliary Air Force,** as one of the pilots, I hear, put it, **lost its amateur status at Rosyth this week,** and on its first opportunity, assisted by the anti-aircraft guns giving their baptism of fire, accounted for one in four of the invaders.

"With the help of the Mercantile Marine, **the British Expeditionary Force has been safely and silently carried to France.** It is the vanguard of the Great Army now training in Britain.

This, in its turn, will be increased by Militiamen in their age groups—another quarter of a million registered today—and by volunteers of all ages fit for military service. Of these we have already taken fifty thousand. I may add that our Armies will be officered almost entirely by promotions from the ranks.

"The final magnitude of our effort will depend on the extent to which factories can supply equipment and munitions for our men. **I appeal to them—to their workmen and directors—to intensify their part.**

"The Dominions are making ready their contingents to stand beside our own. They never fail to emphasize our solidarity. Their Ministers are even now arriving in London to discuss the best means of consolidating the Imperial effort. Indian troops are in position at several strategic points. India and all other parts of the Empire are anxious to take an increasing share.

"As the days pass, Nazi Germany must watch this gathering momentum and realize that Time is on the side of France, of Britain and the Empire.

What We Are Fighting For

"I WILL now speak of the third course by which the enemy may try to escape from the venture on which he started. It is the one against which we must be most carefully on our guard. No peace proposals which rely for their sanction on a broken word can be considered. Nothing but guarantees for the establishment of a new order, from which the menace of Nazi oppression is removed, can justify us in laying down our arms.

"There is something more—something greater —in this war than a combat between opposing armies ; **something more eternal than a grapple in the skies between the ' Spitfires ' of Britain and the ' Heinkels ' of Nazi Germany ;** something more desperate than a death struggle between the U-boats and the destroyers. **There is a conflict between the forces of good and the forces of evil,** and what has to be determined is which shall possess the soul of countries and of Man.

"We did not enter the fight merely to reconstitute Czechoslovakia ; nor do we fight merely to reconstitute a Polish State. Our aims are not defined by geographical frontiers ; we are concerned with the frontiers of the human spirit. **This is no war about a map. It is a war to re-establish the conditions in which nations and individuals—including (may I say?) the German nation and German individuals—can live or live again.**

Hitler's Legacy to History

"THERE can be no question of our wavering in any degree. This tyranny, whose challenge we have accepted, must, and will be, abased. Those who take up the sword are said to perish by the sword. Yet there have been those, using this weapon, who have been entitled to respect. Alexander the Great was a conqueror, but he spread the riches of Greek civilization to the Orient. Caesar was a conqueror, but he extended the justice of Roman law. Napoleon was a conqueror, but he carried some principles of enlightenment with his standards.

"**What boon does the leader of Nazi Germany bring ? What iota of happiness has he granted even to Austria, a German-speaking people ? For what will he be remembered ?** For his tortures ; for his concentration camps ; for his secret police ; for his ignoble effort to spin Europe into a web of racial hatred and religious persecution.

"Only the defeat of Nazi Germany can lighten the darkness which now shrouds our cities, and lighten the horizon for Europe and the world."

The Man Who Got the Army Ready

Youngest member of the War Cabinet, Mr. Leslie Hore-Belisha
holds the post to which Lord Kitchener gave his splendid talents in
the last war. Below we give some account of the War Minister's
career and personality.

The Secretary of State for War, Mr. Hore-
Belisha, who has already gained for himself
an outstanding position among British war
leaders.

WHEN in 1923 Leslie Hore-Belisha
stood as Parliamentary candi-
date in the Liberal interest for
Devonport his opponent, in a mood of
unguarded depreciation, is said to have
referred to him as " a little chit of a
fellow." The reply was scathing. " I
am proud to be called ' a little chit of a
fellow,' " said Mr. Hore-Belisha, " because
I am rather older than Napoleon was
when he led to victory the greatest armies
that the world has ever seen ; because I
am older than was Alexander when he
conquered the then known world ; because I am rather older than Hannibal,
probably the greatest general the world
has ever seen." Then after saying that
he was five years older than Pitt when he
first became Prime Minister, and six years
older than Mr. Gladstone when he first
became a Minister, he went on : " If you
want a monument to the achievement of
the older politicians you may find it across
the Channel. It is three hundred miles
long and a half-mile deep, and it is studded
with the tombstones of ' little chits of
fellows.' "

Captivated by his audacious manner,
his rich eloquence, and his supreme self-
confidence, the electors of Devonport
returned him at the head of the poll ; and
in not one of the elections since 1923 has
his hold on the city been really challenged.

At that time he was only twenty-eight.
His father, Mr. J. I. Belisha, a London
stockbroker, died when Leslie was five
months old, and in 1912 his mother
became the wife of Sir Adair Hore, a
leading civil servant, when her son added
her new married name to his own.

Educated at Clifton College and at St.
John's College, Oxford, he was at a university on the Continent when war broke
out in 1914. He joined up a few weeks
later in a Public Schoolboys' Battalion,
and later received a commission in the
Royal Army Service Corps. After seeing
service in France and Salonika, he was

demobilized with the rank of major. Then
he went back to Oxford, where his oratory
won him the presidency of the Union.

Answering the call of politics, he stood
unsuccessfully for Devonport in 1922, but,
as before mentioned won the seat in 1923,
and in the same year was called to the bar.
His first taste of office was in 1931 when
as a member of the Liberal National wing
of the Government hosts he was appointed Parliamentary Secretary to the
Board of Trade, which post he exchanged
in the next year for that of Financial
Secretary to the Treasury. From 1934
to 1937 he was Minister of Transport, and
his term of office was notable for the first
real attempt to reduce the road's shocking
toll of tragedies. The Belisha beacons
which stand at every principal crossing
are monuments to his organizing initiative.

New Broom at the War Office

When Mr. Neville Chamberlain formed
his first Cabinet in May, 1937, Mr. Hore-
Belisha became Secretary of State for
War, and his advent gave a new impetus
to the reorganization of the army on a
mechanized and motorized basis. Many
reforms were also carried out in the conditions of service, training, and equipment of the regulars and the territorials.
Then in April, 1939, conscription was
introduced for the first time in a Britain
not engaged in war.

Critics of his regime were many, and
their criticisms grew loud when it was

seen that he sometimes scorned the well-
tried path and preferred not only new
methods but new men. His dramatic
appointment of Lord Gort to the position
of Chief of the General Staff aroused
much comment, but the decision was
soon seen to be well justified. Those who
cavilled at the apparent unpreparedness
of the anti-aircraft defences at the time
of the Munich Crisis were also, later, prepared to admit that the Minister for War
had completely remedied the position.

Only sixteen years have passed since
Mr. Hore-Belisha caught the public ear
with his smart retort to his disparaging
critic, and in those years he has had to
encounter many a hurdle which would
have unseated a less skilful, a less daring,
rider. He is a Jew, and following the
glittering example of Disraeli, Jews in
politics are expected to be strikingly
successful where another might be permitted a modest distinction.

He is a Liberal, and there are some who,
in these days when the old Liberal party
has declined almost into nothingness,
resent the fact that so many Liberals
hold high places in the National Government. Furthermore, he is young—at
least as politicians go. Today as he sits
in the Cabinet, he is the youngest at the
table. Yet he holds one of the most
responsible positions in wartime Britain.

The " little chit of a fellow " has indeed
come some way. Who shall say how far
he may not go ?

Since 1937, when he was appointed Secretary of State for War, Mr. Hore-Belisha has lost
no opportunity of becoming fully acquainted with the men on whom the brunt of the fighting
now falls and with their equipment. Above he is seen with a Territorial battalion in
training before the war, listening to an expert explanation and demonstration of the
working of a trench mortar.

Photos, Central Press

How to tell Officers of Navy, Army and Air Force

Officers of the Royal Navy and Marines

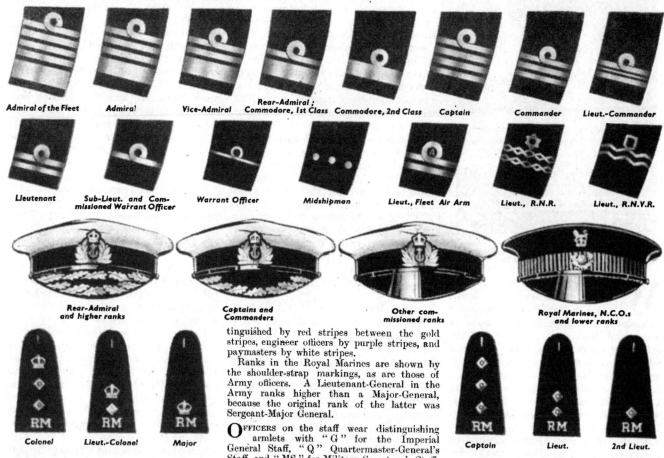

tinguished by red stripes between the gold stripes, engineer officers by purple stripes, and paymasters by white stripes.

Ranks in the Royal Marines are shown by the shoulder-strap markings, as are those of Army officers. A Lieutenant-General in the Army ranks higher than a Major-General, because the original rank of the latter was Sergeant-Major General.

OFFICERS on the staff wear distinguishing armlets with "G" for the Imperial General Staff, "Q" Quartermaster-General's Staff, and "MS" for Military Secretary's Staff. Officers attached to the War Office have an armlet half blue and half red with the Royal Crest upon it and the letters in red; the staff of Home Commands have scarlet letters on red, black and blue armlets, and area and district garrison staff officers wear green armlets with black lettering.

A qualified pilot of the R.A.F. wears a double-winged badge on his left breast, and an observer a single wing in the same position.

THOUGH many of the ranks of officers of the Army and Navy date back hundreds of years, the distinguishing badges on caps, shoulder-straps and sleeves are comparatively modern. In the Royal Navy, surgeons are dis-

Officers of the Army

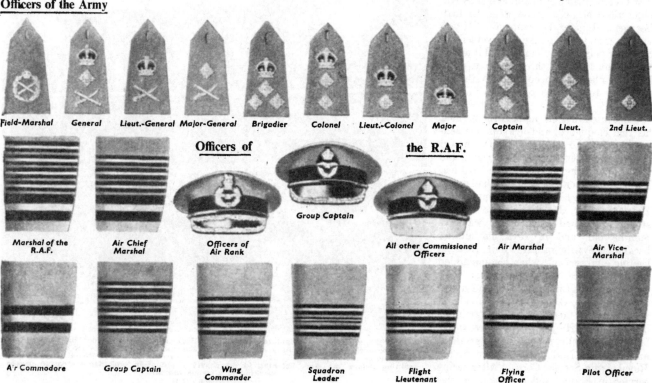

Eye Witness Stories of Episodes
and Adventures in the
Second Great War

How Our Convoy Beat the Nazi 'Planes

On October 21 Nazi warplanes swooped on a convoy of British ships in the North Sea. Eye-witnesses at sea and on shore described in vivid detail how the escorting warships and R.A.F. fighters drove off the raiders with considerable loss. The following stories are reprinted from the " Daily Telegraph " and " Daily Mail."

THE chief officer of one of the attacked ships, when he returned to his home last night, said that the convoy was attacked three times in just over two hours without the enemy registering a single hit. He saw one raider crash into

the sea after being hit by a salvo from one of the escorting British warships.

" Bombers swooped down on us as if from nowhere," he said. " I counted nine of them coming from behind a raincloud.

" They had the sun behind them, and this was an added advantage. Before I had time to realize they were enemy 'planes the guns of the warships escorting us opened fire on them.

" One of the raiders was caught by the first salvo and I saw it crash into the sea. All the other warships opened fire simultaneously, and the din was terrific. It was a remarkable sight. From both sides of the decks flame belched all along the ships.

" I am quite certain that none of our ships was hit, but from what I heard later three other enemy 'planes were brought down by R.A.F. fighters. This raid was all over in about five minutes, and then the attacking 'planes cleared off.

" About twenty minutes later four more German bombers attacked our convoy. They were fairly high, and the escorting ships fired at them straight away. Again the enemy failed to register a hit.

" One of the 'planes, to get low down, looped the loop and made a power dive at one of the warships. A bomb fell fairly close to the war vessel but caused

no damage. The warship replied with its guns and the raiders quickly disappeared.

" Later again we heard the drone of aeroplane engines, but no further attack was made on us."

The chief officer praised the efficiency of those aboard the escorting warships. At no time was there the slightest confusion and everything went off perfectly.

" As soon as the raiders appeared," he said, " the warships' guns swung into position as if someone had pressed a button. With such efficient protection we have very little to worry about as far as German air attacks at sea are concerned.

" After the last attack one of the ships escorting us moved along the convoy and signalled a message complimenting the crews of the merchant ships on having kept their stations so well during the attacks."

Clouds have helped the Nazi bombers in the raids on British shipping, concealing them from the anti-aircraft guns until they dived towards their objective. In the top photograph is a German heavy bomber starting its dive. Below, naval gunners wearing their gas masks are manning an anti-aircraft gun after receiving a warning of approaching raiders.

Photos, Mondiale and Associated Press

Sailing at the tail of the convoy was a collier, and one of its crew described what he had seen of the raids :

" Suddenly three German 'planes dropped from nowhere on to the British bomber that was in our escort. One minute the sky seemed empty, and the next they were roaring down on us.

" It was a surprise attack, but it failed. The pilot of our bomber escaped from them.

" The attack started to warm up. First came three more Nazi 'planes, then two more, from different directions.

" The escorting warships opened fire with their anti-aircraft guns, and at that moment British fighting 'planes came over.

" There were many ships in the area. Through all the fighting the convoy kept on its way."

Messroom Steward J. Murtha, of South Shields, here broke in :

" It was an amazing sight. It was impossible to tell how many of our 'planes came over, but they finished the attack in a few minutes.

" So far as I know, the only anti-aircraft fire was by the warships.

" One of the merchant ships was armed with a 12-pounder anti-aircraft gun, but it was not brought into action.

" We had our sights on one of the enemy 'planes, but we were not allowed to open fire," said Able Seaman Atkinson, who was one of the gunners.

" We were just aching to have a go, but we couldn't. I think we could have got one of the Germans, too.

" The enemy 'planes were driven off, and we saw one going south, ' fluttering ' as though badly damaged. We do not know what happened to it.

" We carried on, and all was quiet until some miles farther on, when suddenly one solitary German 'plane came diving down on the convoy.

" He was the first we saw to drop a bomb. It landed not far from one of our escorts, and sent up a fountain of water. But I don't think it did any damage.

" That was the last thing the German did. A burst of anti-aircraft fire caught him and we saw him crash into the sea some distance away. The explosion of the bomb was felt in our ship.

" We did no firing at all, but the ship next to us in the convoy used her anti-aircraft gun when the 'planes were over us. Not one of the ships in our convoy left its line."

On shore, spectators at many points saw British fighters race out to engage the enemy, and heard the crash of gunfire at sea.

During the second engagement German bombers were forced shorewards. People in the coastal district saw them desperately trying to dodge the barrage and anti-aircraft fire.

Here is the story of a rector's wife :

" We saw six German 'planes come over from the south just before noon. They appeared out of the mist. Three of them were flying so low that we could almost read the letters on them. The other three were flying high.

" Then six more German 'planes came from the north. British fighters swept up from all directions. It appeared as though they had driven the German 'planes into the range of the shore batteries, which opened fire.

" So did the guns in the escorting destroyers. The British fighters swooped and fired at the Germans. The raiders could not escape.

" One was struck by a shell, I think, from a shore battery. It screamed down into the sea, and there was a huge column of smoke.

" A little later there was a big explosion and a spout of flame from the sea.

" Then another of the German 'planes on which British fighters had been swooping fell into the sea.

" The fight went on for some time, out into the mist and back again. We heard that two more Germans had fallen into the sea farther south.

" All the time R.A.F. fighters were diving into battle. Finally the German 'planes seemed to see some chance of escape as darkness and the mist came up again.

" They swept round and raced off to sea, chased by our fighters."

Two Days at Sea in a Rubber Boat

Following the German air raids on the coast of Scotland, the collapsible rubber boats with which aeroplanes are fitted featured in several rescue stories. Here, reprinted from the " Daily Mail," is the tale of the first two Germans to reach England in such a boat.

SPECIAL Constable George Thomas, guarding a railway tunnel on the coast near Whitby, looked round and saw—a young German airman in full flying kit, clawing his way over the crest of the 150-ft. high cliffs.

Mr. Thomas ran, grasped his hands, and hauled him up.

" I am a German flyer," gasped the man in English. " My friend is below and needs help. Where am I—near the Firth of Forth ? "

Help was called, a coastguard went down the cliff on a rope, the second man was hauled up unconscious.

And that was how, after two days at sea, foodless and without water, in a tiny rubber boat, two Nazis who had tried to raid Scotland were saved.

Here is the full story of their ordeal, pieced together from the disjointed sentences which the younger man was able to speak to his rescuers before they left him in hospital.

It was on Tuesday, October 17, that their 'plane, together with another Nazi

Here one of the two Nazi airmen who had an almost miraculous escape from death when they drifted ashore at Sandsend, near Whitby, Yorkshire, after being afloat in their rubber boat for 43 hours, is being carried from Whitby hospital. The machine was brought down in the North Sea, and two other members of the crew were drowned. The rubber boats carried by aircraft are little more than very large lifebuoys.   *Photo, G.P.U.*

A heavily-laden lifeboat carrying members of the crew of the " Regent Tiger " is approaching the French steamer " Jean Jabot " that rescued them.
Photo, Associated Press

bomber, was shot down over the North Sea about five o'clock.

The crew of the other 'plane were saved, but all on board this 'plane were thought to be dead. Only two of the crew, however, had been killed.

The two survivors, the younger man wounded in the leg, managed to inflate and launch their rubber lifeboat in the heavy seas.

As they got on board, the 'plane sank— before they could get any food or drink from it.

Throughout that might they dared not sleep, for they had to paddle with their hands to keep head-on to the seas lest it capsize.

At intervals throughout the night they fired Very lights, but these apparently were not seen. Dawn came, the day passed, but there was no sight of land.

When darkness fell on Wednesday the older man was rapidly losing strength, but his injured companion managed to keep the boat steady. For two hours he sent up Very lights, but no help came.

Though he did not know it, Whitby and Runswick Bay lifeboats had put out and searched in vain.

This morning the two men dimly saw the cliffs of the Yorkshire coast. A current caught the boat and carried it shorewards. Then the tide lifted it into a rocky cove at the foot of the cliffs.

Almost at the end of his strength the wounded man dragged his companion, now almost unconscious, ashore.

Then he began the climb that ended in their capture—and safety.

This remarkable photograph, taken from the " Jean Jabot " after she had picked up the crew of the " Regent Tiger," shows the last moments of the tanker. She was torpedoed by a Nazi submarine, and the huge column of smoke arose as her cargo of 15,000 tons of petrol went up in flames. The " Regent Tiger " was sunk in the English Channel, and the " Jean Jabot " rescued 44 members of her crew.
Photo, Associated Press

The Terror of a Blazing Oil Tanker

It is a terrifying enough experience to be in a torpedoed ship, but when that ship is an oil tanker, the terror must be intensified a hundredfold. Here is the story of those who survived the sinking of the " Regent Tiger," on September 8.

THE crew and passengers of the British tanker " Regent Tiger " landed in England on September 11, having been picked up by the Belgian liner " Jean Jabot " after two-and-a-half hours in the boats.

" It was a terrifying spectacle after the torpedo had struck," said one of the ship's officers. " There was an explosion, and flames 1,000 ft. high roared into the sky. We were in two ship's lifeboats about 300 to 400 yards away, but at that distance the fumes were suffocating and the heat unbearable.

" The tanks of our ship were filled with petrol. As the fire spread the tanks blew up. We have since heard that the tanker is still ablaze and the sea around her.

" It was about 9.30 a.m. on Friday when the U-boat appeared about a quarter of a mile away from us. Four shots were fired from the submarine, two over us and two in front. We had about ten minutes in which to take to the boats."

Another member of the crew said the U-boat attempted to destroy the tanker's wireless aerial with shell fire.

" Everybody was calm, especially our three passengers," he added.

The German pilot's story of his eventful pursuit of a hedge-hopping English 'plane is described in this page. The R.A.F. machine was stated to be a Bristol Blenheim. This outstanding type, illustrated above, is a high-performance, twin-engined monoplane designed primarily for bombing, but also adapted as a fighter-bomber or as a reconnaissance type.

Photo, " Flight "

I Chased a British 'Plane Over My Home

During one of the R.A.F. reconnaissance flights over Germany, a Bristol-Bomber was brought down by a German 'plane after a thrilling aerial steeplechase over the countryside of Emsland. The German pilot, Flight-Lieutenant " K," gave his version of the encounter in the " Westfaelische Landeszeitung."

"I WAS sitting in my machine," he said, "somewhere in Ems at 10 minutes past 3 in the afternoon when an enemy scout was reported flying from the north at a height of little more than 100 ft. When the Englishman, whom I could plainly see in his machine, was flying over us I took off. A.A. artillery came into action, and to avoid this I rose to some height. The enemy swung round to westward, seeking a cloud in which to escape. He swerved sharply, lessening considerably my chances of hitting him. I followed close at his heels and, seeing that he could not shake me off, he went into a spin dive into a cloudbank about 200 metres in depth. I dived even more steeply. As I came out of the cloudbank I saw him emerge from the cloud above me.

"He again dived, and then there began a mad pursuit which almost beggars description. The Englishman was a good, adroit, and skilful airman. He utilized every unevenness in the ground, every hedge, every ditch as cover. He slipped between trees and skimmed over the houses. As I raced on I could see the smashed tree-tops silhouetted against the sky and the broken bushes flying through the air. Now and again I expected to see

him remove a roof, but with his speed of 300 kilometres an hour he jumped over every obstacle. At times we were barely 6 ft. from the ground, and even eye-witnesses thought he was down. But he went on, though escape was now out of the question.

"At last, after another volley, I saw the pilot lay his machine on the ground, and the three occupants jumped out. They had not had time to release the landing gear of the aeroplane, which was already in flames, and it simply crashed in a potato field. I circled above them and they greeted me with clasped hands, as if to say that they would like to shake hands with me after a chivalrous fight."

We Strayed Into a North Sea Battle

When five British warships were fighting a fleet of German bombers off the coast of Norway on October 9, a Norwegian fishing-boat found itself in the middle of the battle. The story told by her skipper Isak Holmsen is here reproduced from the "Daily Express."

"WE were out fishing on the Viking Bank off the coast of Norway," said Mr. Holmsen, "when we saw five warships flying the British flag bearing down on us.

"Suddenly, as though from nowhere, a great swarm of German bombers marked with the Iron Cross swooped overhead and attacked the British ships which greeted them with a terrific fire from their anti-aircraft guns. The 'planes swerved away after dropping their bombs some hundreds of yards off their targets.

"By the time the bombers dived again we were in the centre of the battle, with the British warships all round us, blazing away at the 'planes.

"Hell was let loose then for hours. Bombs seemed to fall like hail from the wheeling 'planes—like great gulls diving and roaring away into the skies again.

"Dozens of bombs dropped close to us.

"I ordered ' full speed,' and we tried to get out of the battle. We had the deck cleared ready to take off in the small boat if we were hit. But everywhere we moved the battle seemed to follow.

"The warships, zig-zagging at terrific speed as they drove off the 'planes time after time, sent up waves that nearly swamped us. And the noise of their guns deafened us.

"At last the Germans had had enough, and they turned and flew away southwards. One of my crew said he counted 150 of them.

"Not one British ship was hit—even we escaped. The warships then sailed westwards, and we were left alone in the ' battlefield.' Well, we never dreamed we'd be in the middle of a battle.

"Have you ever been in a fifteen-ton boat with warships firing all round you and 'planes dropping bombs all round you ? Some of these bombs fell only fifty yards away; and our boat rocked as if she would turn over at any minute.

"We noticed two of the German 'planes in difficulties. They were far from us, but seemed to be falling into the water, and after the warships left a big red 'plane— we could not see her markings—circled around. Maybe she was looking for these two 'planes."

The fate of some of the Nazi bombers which were believed to have been damaged by British fighters and anti-aircraft guns is not certain, but several of them came down on neutral territory. Above is one which crashed in Norway. It is a Dornier flying-boat similar to that seen in page 270.

Photo, Planet News

Friend and Foe Borne in Honour to the Grave

The bodies of the German airmen brought down during the raid on Rosyth lay in the church of St. Philip, Portobello, watched over by two policemen (top right). Then the coffins were carried to the grave and a firing-party supplied by the R.A.F. paid a last tribute to the brave enemy.

Photo, " Daily Mirror "

Above is the scene in Portobello when officers of the R.A.F. bore the coffins of the German airmen, Unter-offizier Seydel and Flieger Schleicher, to the grave. Kilted pipers played a lament.

Britain's first real air raid took place on Monday, October 16, when German 'planes attacked ships of the British Fleet lying at Rosyth. The pictures in this page illustrate the funerals of the victims of the raid : the three above of the two German officers, and below those of ten of the seventeen British naval men. Left, the procession approaching the cemetery at Rosyth ; right, a firing-party from the Royal Navy saluting their fallen comrades.

Photos, Topical, Sport & General, and Graphic Photo Union

OUR DIARY OF THE WAR

Monday, October 23

Finnish delegation, led by M. Paasikivi and accompanied by M. Tanner, Finnish Minister of Finance, arrived at Moscow to resume negotiations with Russia.

Paris reported that, after a quiet night on the Western Front, there had been **marked activity on the part of advance units,** particularly in the region west of the Saar.

Two British ships, " Sea Venture " and " Whitemantle," were reported sunk. The first was torpedoed off the north coast of Scotland ; the second lost after an explosion due either to a mine or a submarine.

U.S. steamer " **City of Flint,**" which had been **seized as contraband** by a German cruiser, was brought by a prize crew into Kola Bay, north of Murmansk, flying the Swastika.

Sir Eric Phipps, retiring British Ambassador, left Paris.

Tuesday, October 24

Raids and ambushes were reported from various parts of the Western Front, and fairly sharp engagements towards the south-eastern border of the Forest of Warndt, where a German attack on a French outpost was driven back.

Von Ribbentrop delivered **a bitter speech** at Danzig in which he accused the British Government of systematically preparing, over a period of years, to make war on Germany.

Greek steamer " Konstantinos Hadjipateras " sunk by U-boat in the North Sea.

Poland's gold reserve, amounting to more than £15,000,000, reached Paris after an eventful journey from Warsaw.

Leaders of the Finnish delegation left Moscow to consult with their Government on new proposals put forward by Stalin.

Polish Consul-General in London announced that Poles in Britain would be mobilized for service in the Polish Army in France.

Wednesday, October 25

The Air Ministry announced that reconnaissances carried out by the R.A.F. during the preceding 24 hours included **night flights over Berlin,** Magdeburg and Hamburg.

Paris reported that French troops had repulsed a German detachment in the region close to the Moselle. As a whole, conditions on the Western Front were quiet.

Five British ships were reported sunk by enemy action : " Ledbury," " Menin Ridge," and " Tafna," all in the North Atlantic ;

" Stonegate," attacked and sunk by German battleship " Deutschland " ; and " Clan Chisholm," sunk off the Spanish coast.

Thursday, October 26

Air Ministry announced that it was now known that at least **seven out of twelve German aircraft failed to return** to their base after last Saturday's attack on a British convoy in the North Sea.

There were minor encounters between contact units and artillery action on both sides at various points of the Western Front.

THE POETS & THE WAR

V

THE VOICE OF THE EMPIRE

By Lord Rennell

If my work is over and if in vain I had hoped at the close of life
That peace would fall with the evening, not passion and hate and strife,
I can still give thanks as my sun goes down for one treasure of passing worth,
The faith that was staunch to the motherland of her sons at the ends of the earth,
When she called them all into council and their splendid answer came,
Their pledge in an issue greater than conquest, profit or fame,
That peoples should live in freedom, unfettered in word or thought,
And hold the land that their fathers held and the faith that their fathers taught.
From the isles of all the oceans, from the north to the tropic sun
We have heard the homing voices, and the soul of their voice was one—
She has carried the flag of freedom over many an unplumbed wave,
Saint George's cross at the masthead, to liberate not to enslave.
She sheltered us in our childhood. We are nations now full-grown.
If Britain must draw her sword once more she shall not draw alone.
With a single voice in a common cause we bid the challenger know
We stand with the Mother Country, and where she leads we go.

—*The Times.*

Southern Rhodesia offered to maintain three air squadrons in the field on any front.

Admiralty announced that the wreck of a German submarine, containing more than 50 dead, had been washed up on Goodwin Sands.

Murmansk marine authorities ordered the release and immediate departure of the U.S. vessel " City of Flint," brought in by a German prize crew on Tuesday.

Soviet Government replied to British Government's Notes of September 6 and 11 on questions of war contraband, declining to recognize the validity of the British contraband list or the British Government's right to inspect and detain Soviet merchant ships.

It was officially confirmed in Berlin that **Hitler intended to bring back all German minorities** from all countries.

An Austrian " Freedom " radio station began sending out anti-Nazi broadcasts.

Friday, October 27

Massed concentration of German troops was reported in the Saar, along the Belgian, Dutch and Swiss frontiers, and along the German North Sea coast.

U.S. Senate passed the **Bill repealing the arms embargo provision** of the Neutrality Act.

King Leopold broadcast an address to the people of the United States in which he declared Belgium's neutrality, but stated that, if attacked, she would not hesitate to fight.

German press complained that alleged anti-Nazi propaganda in Belgian newspapers were a breach of neutrality.

German submarine sunk by French Navy in the Atlantic.

Malaya made a first contribution of £80,000 to the Red Cross and St. John Fund, thus bringing it up to over the half-million mark.

Saturday, October 28

Germans reported to have massed 65–80 divisions behind the lines from the North Sea to Switzerland.

Nazi aeroplane, attempting a reconnaissance flight over the Forth area, was **forced down east of Dalkeith** by British fighters. Two of the crew survived and were taken to Edinburgh.

Another German 'plane appeared over the Orkneys, but disappeared when fighters went up to engage it.

Air Ministry announced that R.A.F. aircraft carried out night reconnaissances over certain areas in Southern Germany. This was the first flight in severe weather. All aircraft returned.

Washington issued a protest against the attitude of the Soviet Union over the case of the " City of Flint," the whereabouts of which are at present uncertain.

Sunday, October 29

Increasing number of British heavy guns were moved into position on the Western Front.

French official communiqué reported all quiet generally during the day.

Hitler said to have taken up headquarters at Godesberg.

Himmler took over his duties as Director of Colonization in Polish territory occupied by Germans.

First contingent of Soviet troops entered Latvia to begin occupation of bases allotted by the Latvian-Soviet agreement.

It Is Said That . . .

In Cologne motor-cars are forbidden even dimmed side-lamps after dark.

The word "axis" is said to have disappeared from the Italian vocabulary.

Young Nazi officers are creating a reign of terror in Polish villages.

German officer called Polish campaign a " strafe " expedition, not a war.

" Stalin is afraid of Hitler, and he has every right to be so," says Trotsky.

Warsaw was so damaged by bombardment that it may not be completely rebuilt.

German soldiers on service now hear by radio of the arrival of babies born to their wives.

" There has always been misery ; there is misery today ; there will always be misery." (Hitler at opening of Winter Relief Fund.)

German troops in Poland were bitterly disappointed at being ordered to the Western Front ; they thought they were going home.

A traveller through Munich said that, apart from eggs, meat was unobtainable there.

Large areas of the Siegfried Line are threatened if the Rhine rises in flood.

Moscow radio programmes in German now start : " Proletarians of the World, unite ! "

Nazi authorities in Poland are confiscating bed-linen for hospitals, especially from Jews.

German casualties in Poland were eight times as great as the figure mentioned by Hitler.

Units of armoured infantry, constituting " shock troops," have made sorties from the Siegfried Line.

A group of German officers have petitioned for a commission to investigate the story of Nazi fortunes abroad.

In Germany retired State officials up to the age of 70 have been mobilized for clerical work.

An organization of volunteer guerilla fighters, " the Ragged Guard," are openly attacking Nazidom in Hungary.

Vol. 1   A Permanent Picture Record of the Second Great War   No. 10

The German reconnaissance 'plane that was shot down by R.A.F. fighters near Dalkeith on October 28 is being examined by British experts. The first enemy aircraft to be brought down on British soil, it finally struck a hillside and was severely damaged. The machine carried a crew of four, of whom two were killed and one wounded. It is a Heinkel bomber, but on this occasion carried no bombs. The man on the extreme right is examining ammunition carriers that fell off the machine when it crashed.

Photo, Associated Press

British Cavalry in France—25 Years Ago and Today

WHAT a contrast, resulting from the mechanization of the Army, is shown in these two photographs! In that above a cavalry regiment is seen in France in the autumn of 1914, while below is a so-called "cavalry" regiment in France in October, 1939. The whole of the British cavalry has now been mechanized, the exceptions being the Household Cavalry—that is, the Life Guards and Horse Guards, who perform ceremonial duties in England—the Scots Greys, who perform similar duties in Scotland, and the 1st Dragoons. Though from the spectacular point of view the disappearance of horses is regrettable, in wartime it is a change that no animal-lover can regret, for one of the tragedies of the last war was the suffering of the horses, facing with such patient courage the terrors of the battlefield, but only too often terribly injured by gunfire under circumstances that made it impossible that they could be quickly put out of their misery.

Photos, Imperial War Museum, and British Official: Crown Copyright

Allies & Neutrals Await the Nazis

From the North Sea to Switzerland, along a front of some five hundred miles, the Germans faced a formidable collection of nations—some already their enemies; others neutral—as yet.

France's North African army, which numbers nearly 200,000 men, did admirable service in the last war and is already reinforcing the French army. Above, French Colonial troops are marching towards the front.

Photo, Planet News

A s October drew to its close General Winter took over on the Western Front. Snow appeared on the upper slopes of the Vosges and the Black Forest, and the Rhine, swollen by a month of almost continuous rain, rose three feet and overflowed its banks. The "No-man's land" between the Maginot and Siegfried Lines, already churned up by the bombardments of two months of war, was now converted into something little short of a morass, and it was generally held that the sticky soil would prove an unsurmountable obstacle to the progress of tanks and other ponderous machines of modern warfare.

That the Germans had not yet given up the idea of an offensive on a large scale, however, was suggested by the reports of huge concentrations of men and 'planes all along the Western Front. According to a Rome authority Germany had 18 divisions along the French frontier, 12 along the Swiss frontier from Basle to Lake Constance, and between 75 and 80 divisions on the remainder of the front, including 31 divisions in the Palatinate between Saarbruecken and Karlsruhe. Estimating a German division at between 10,000 and 12,000 men, it will be seen that a total of more than a million men was now massed near the Westwall.

It was understood that the Fuehrer himself was in actual command of the German forces, and his appearance at Godesberg, exactly opposite the middle of the frontier between Germany and Belgium, gave rise to rumours that he was contemplating launching an attack against Belgium. In the light of such rumours, King Leopold of the Belgians made a fresh declaration of his country's neutrality, accompanied by the unequivocal warning that: "If we were attacked in violation of the solemn and definite undertakings that were given us in 1937 and were renewed at the outset of the present war, we would not hesitate to fight with the same conviction, but with forces ten times stronger."

An invasion of Belgium would almost certainly involve the Netherlands, as a little outlying portion of Holland lies right in what would be the line of advance from Aachen. But the Dutch, too, left no doubt that they were well prepared to meet any invasion.

Holland, indeed, might be expected to receive the attention of the Nazi war lords, faced with the necessity of selecting a favourable field of manoeuvre for their mechanized and motorized columns in

the depths of winter. Part of Holland, particularly the east, is of a sandy character, which the winter frosts would render firm enough for the operation of the German armoured columns. Moreover, it might well be that the Germans would find in Holland an objective quite apart from the turning of the French flank. Amsterdam would make an excellent base for submarines operating against England, and from aerodromes situated on the Dutch coast raiders might be dispatched across the North Sea with far greater ease and safety than from the aerodromes in northern Germany.

As the war drew on Hitler singled out Britain as the Reich's principal antagonist, and the Nazi wireless and press were filled with the most violent attacks on Britain and her rulers. Following Herr von Ribbentrop's speech at Danzig it was stated in Field-Marshal Goering's newspaper, "Essener National Zeitung," that: "The moment has come when the war which Britain wanted must shower down

Camouflage, which only achieved its full development on land and at sea in the later years of the last war, is now employed as a matter of course. In the centre photograph a Bren gun carrier is being "put to bed" by having camouflaged netting drawn over it. In the photograph immediately above, Nature—and the farmer—provide camouflage for a Bren gun in a sugar beet field.

Photos, British Official ✷ Crown Copyright

on the British Isles themselves. . . Now that the Fuehrer's outstretched hand has been rejected with insulting arrogance, weapons must speak." Coupled with the reports of great troop concentrations behind the line there were stories of the most fantastic description of the "terrible" weapons which Germany was about to launch against Britain.

The nature of these weapons was officially undisclosed, but one was believed to be the dropping of a large number of troops on the east coast by parachute! The neutral people to whom these stories were given out by the Nazi propaganda authorities were impressed—until it was pointed out that even if 300 machines carrying 20 soldiers each were employed in the invasion, and two-thirds managed to get through, the English defence forces would have to tackle

Viscount Gort, right, is here seen on his way to a tour of inspection of British troops near the front line in France. Among those who follow him are Major-Gen. the Duke of Windsor and an officer of a Highland regiment which later the C.-in-C. inspected.
Photo, British Official: Crown Copyright

the mere handful of 4,000 men, who would promptly be interned.

Meanwhile, on the Western Front the British Field Force, though not yet in action, was occupying a position in the front line alongside the troops of its French ally. It was reported on October 19 that some 30,000 men were actually face to face with the enemy, and far behind the lines the countryside literally bristled with British guns.

In the last war the British troops played football, but to most of their French Allies the game was something new. Now both Association and Rugby football have won popularity with the French and informal international matches are played behind the lines. Above, a British team has beaten a French team and gets the "Cup" in the form of a bunch of flowers.
Photo, Gaumont British News

Holland, having already made preparations to flood large areas should the Nazis attempt to violate her neutrality, has made further defences such as that seen above, where a soldier stands sentry over a concrete stronghold protected by steel railway lines against tanks and by barbed wire against infantry. Right, barbed wire defences are being erected in a forest clearing in Switzerland. *Photos, Keystone*

R.A.F. Rules the German Sky

Nothing can stop the R.A.F. reconnaissances and leaflet-distributing
flights over Germany—neither enemy fighters nor anti-aircraft fire,
neither the dark of a moonless night nor the most bitter cold.

**At a British aerodrome in France a Flight
Sergeant exchanges parting words with
the gunner of an R.A.F. aircraft before
the machine takes off.**
Photo, British Official, Crown Copyright

GERMANS who had tuned in to
Hamburg on the night of October
25 to hear their Foreign Minister
deliver a really full-blooded attack on
Britain were perturbed when Von Rib-
bentrop's voice was suddenly cut off.
No official reason was vouchsafed for the
shutting down, but later it came out that
R.A.F. aeroplanes had appeared over
Hamburg, Magdeburg and Berlin.

That raid which sent the Hamburg
announcer to cover was but one of a
series which began in the early hours of
the war. Week after week, on several
days in each week, the R.A.F. conducted
pamphlet raids over German territory,
upwards of 20,000,000 leaflets being
dropped from the air. The effectiveness
of this very modern method of warfare
may be gauged from the fact that the
severest penalties were at once enacted
by the Nazi authorities against those
Germans who had the hardihood to pick
up, let alone read, one of the leaflets.
But even if the pamphlets were not
read, the spectacle of the fields littered
with the white specks can hardly have
encouraged the Germans in their belief
in the invincibility of their air force.
Any one of those bits, they might well
ruefully reflect, could have been a bomb !

Raiders Over Berlin

Even Berlin, 400 miles from the Maginot
Line, behind which the nearest British
aerodromes are situated, was reached
on more than one occasion by 'planes
of the R.A.F. The Nazi authorities at
first declared that no British 'planes had
been anywhere near the capital, but
later they acknowledged that a flight
had taken place over Berlin, although it
was so harmless that the inhabitants went
on sleeping quietly and peacefully during
its progress. On which Sir Kingsley Wood
dryly commented in his House of Commons

speech : " As our airmen on their return
told of the firing and the searchlights they
encountered, we can only suppose that
the people of Berlin sleep very soundly."

Quite apart from their value as propaganda and their influence on Nazi
morale, these leaflet raids familiarized
the British airmen with the German
terrain, and also gave them invaluable
practice in long-distance flying. They
were supplemented by reconnaissance
flights which were carried on by day and
by night over the whole of the German
line and much of its hinterland.

Detectives of the Air

Peering down through the windows of
their 'planes, the lynx-eyed observers
watched for every movement, every tell-
tale change in the countryside. Troops
on the march, however swiftly they
might take cover; guns dragged to new
positions ; new pill boxes erected ; lines
of trenches freshly dug ; more acres
bearing an ugly burden of barbed wire—
none of these things passed unnoticed by
the aerial detectives. As often as not
what their eyes saw was supplemented by
the record of their cameras, and soon in
the headquarters of the Allied armies
there was a complete photographic
record of the Siegfried defences.

Pamphlet raids and reconnaissance
flights, conducted very often in the teeth

of furious enemy activity from the ground
and in the air itself, make the most
exacting demands on the airmen engaged. When it was announced, for
instance, that " On October 27 R.A.F.
'planes carried out reconnaissance flights
over certain areas of Southern Germany,"
the Air Ministry's bald announcement
gave no indication of the terrible weather
conditions prevailing during the reconnaissance. Later it was revealed that the
crews were flying in icy conditions for
most of the time, and the cold was so
intense—the temperature fell to 30 deg.
below zero—that some of the men,
although enclosed in their cabins, were
sick ; others cried out in sheer pain ;
and all were completely numbed. Their
breath froze on their goggles ; ice formed
on the fuselage and against the cabin
windows ; the control wires froze, and
had to be pulled free with stiffened
fingers every few minutes. The cold, said
one of the pilots, seeped through metal,
then through gloves and heavy clothing,
until it caused the body to ache. Followed
an almost overpowering desire to sleep,
to give up. . . .

" In an effort to keep warm you slapped
yourself and then slapped someone else.
But that was no good, it only exhausted
you. One thought persisted—there was
a job to be done. At last it was done."

**In this map of Central Europe the shaded portions indicate the areas of Germany officially
stated to have been flown over by the R.A.F. in leaflet and other raids. Wide districts of
Central and Southern Germany were also visited by both British and French air forces.**

How to Recognize German Raiders

Silhouettes of Nazi Offensive Machines

Here, in these pages, we have illustrations of the principal types of German bombing 'planes—and a couple of fighter models. With one exception they are all relative in size. Many of these warplanes have already appeared above the coasts of Britain, and more still may be recognized if further opportunities for the identification of enemy craft are afforded as the war proceeds.

Drawings in this and the opposite page taken by permission from "Flight"

JUNKERS JU 89
The largest of Germany's bombers, a four-engined type that could also be used for troop transport.

HEINKEL HE 111K
A medium-sized bomber distinguished by its elliptical wings and finely streamlined fuselage.

THE outstanding German aircraft in these pages are shown without detail —in silhouette as they would appear to an observer below. They are all to scale except the twin-engined Messerschmitt, on which we show the markings of the German Air Force. These indicate another method of identification, and consist of swastikas on the tail and black crosses on the wings and the fuselage. The Heinkel bomber shot down on October 28, 1939, had an extra set of large crosses on the inner portion of the wing. The German Air Force (Luftwaffe) is formidable, and the only real doubt cast on the equipment is its lasting quality. It is known, too, that training fatalities in Germany have been exceptionally high.

HEINKEL HE 111S
This is a development of the HE 111K, and it was one of this type that was shot down in Scotland on Oct. 28, 1939. Note the transparent nose.

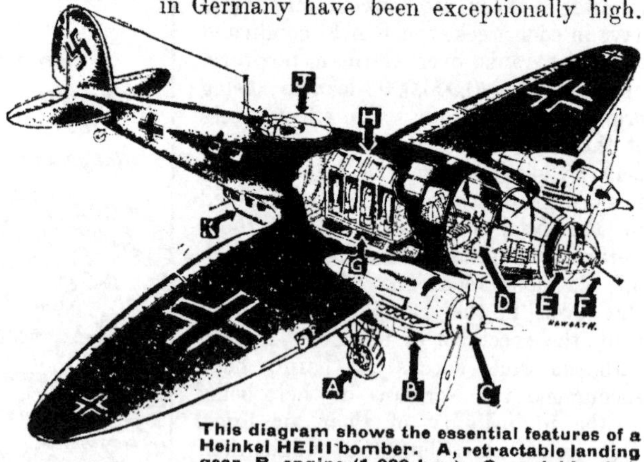

This diagram shows the essential features of a Heinkel HE111 bomber. A, retractable landing gear. B, engine (1,000 h.p.). C, variable pitch airscrew. D, pilot's control. E, bomb sights. F, J and K, machine-guns. G and H, bomb magazine.

DORNIER DO 17 AND DO 215
The "flying pencil" bomber, so called because of its slim fuselage (when seen from the side). Radial engines are sometimes fitted. The DO 215 (below right) has a redesigned nose.

JUNKERS JU 88
A new bomber seen over the Forth on Oct. 16, 1939. The two engine nacelles are of unusual design.

JUNKERS JU 87
A single-engined dive-bomber much employed in the Polish campaign. It has a distinctive " cranked " wing.

JUNKERS JU 86K
Bomber version of a well-known transport aircraft. May be fitted with diesel engines (as shown) or radials.

MESSERSCHMITT ME 109
Germany's most famed fighter. A special version holds the world's speed record. The Heinkel HE 112 (not shown) is another outstanding type in this class.

HEINKEL HE 115
A twin-float seaplane for torpedo-dropping, bombing, or reconnaissance. Employed in attack on convoy, Oct. 21, 1939.

DORNIER DO 18K AND DO 24
Tandem diesel engines (one may be seen) and sponsons (" seawings ") characterize the DO 18K reconnaissance flying boat (above) already used over the North Sea. The larger DO 24 flying boat (below) has three radial engines (as shown) or liquid-cooled units.

MESSERSCHMITT ME 110
(Above) A new heavily armed fighter-bomber that could be used for escort duty. Note— This drawing is not to scale, but is included to show typical markings.

It's Not so Easy to Bomb Britain!

Following the opening of the air offensive against Britain, much surprise
was expressed concerning the smallness of the attacking forces. The facts
given below will help to explain a puzzling phase of the war.

An R.A.F. man is here examining the bullet
holes in the reconnaissance 'plane brought
down in Scotland on October 28, the first
crash on British soil.

THE first air raids on Britain were, to put it mildly unimpressive. For years past imaginative writers had prophesied an invasion by aerial navies darkening the sky and pouring down on a terrified populace a deadly hail of gas and incendiary bombs. The reality was far different. When the raiders made their appearance they came in ones and twos or in small parties of which the largest was that of twelve or fourteen which raided Rosyth on Oct. 16. Such few bombs as they dropped were discharged on strictly military, or rather naval, targets. The civilian population were so far from being terrorized by the approach of the raiders that Edinburgh folk hardly looked up from their lunches as they heard the aerial dog-fight in progress above their heads, and those country people whom the German wireless described as—shocking indignity !—peasants seemed to be hardly more than mildly interested as they watched Nazi 'planes being pursued over their fields and house-tops by the fighters of the R.A.F. Scottish nonchalance and Northumbrian imperturbability were more than a match for the Nazi air terror.

What many people, and even some of the alleged experts, had failed to understand is that German raiding 'planes, even travelling by the shortest route, have to cover some 400 miles across the North Sea before they can arrive over the coast of Scotland ; in other words, a raider must fly the best part of a thousand miles non-stop, carrying for at least half that distance its full load of bombs, and all the time exposed to attack from surface vessels, from fighter aircraft, and

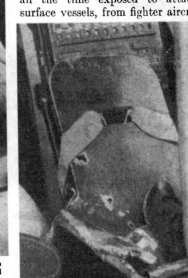

The wrecked nose of the machine after it had crashed into a hillside is seen above. Note the
insignia of the squadron or pilot.   Right is a bullet-riddled seat in the cabin, with boots and
other articles of equipment scattered about.
Photos, Associated Press, G.P.U. and British Paramount News

The news that a raider had been shot down brought many spectators, some of whom had actually witnessed the fight, to the spot (see further
eye-witness stories in page 315).   A new feature of this machine was that it had two sets of markings on the wings, a large and a small cross.   The
small bullet holes are the points at which the bullets entered the machine, and the large ones those at which they came out on the other side.
The number of these marks show the terrific fusillade to which the machine was subjected before it was brought down.

First Photograph of the First Air Raid on Britain

The dramatic photograph above, which, like that in page 299, is exclusive to **THE WAR ILLUSTRATED**, was taken on Oct. 16 during the first raid on the Firth of Forth (and Britain), of which eye-witness accounts are given in pages 242, 252 and 315. The ship that is bombarding the enemy aircraft is H.M.S. " Edinburgh," a 10,000 ton cruiser. On the extreme left is the spray thrown up by a bomb dropped by the aircraft which has fallen far wide of the mark.

Photo, Associated Press

eventually from the land defences. The range of the attacking aeroplanes is affected by the weight of the fuel and bombs it has to carry, and it should be remembered that a long sea-crossing is full of danger to landplanes, while seaplanes, which have already been employed in a number of raids, are very much slower and much more difficult to manoeuvre.

Despite the enormous strides which have been made of recent years in the development of the military aeroplane, bomb loads exceeding 2,000 pounds are rarely carried long distances (a typical bomb of standard size might weigh 112 lb. or 500 lb.). When flying at a great height, precision-aiming is very difficult if the defences are at all active, and

with dive-bombing, which is apparently favoured by the German air force, only limited accuracy is possible, and great risk is involved to the 'plane itself, which at the bottom of its dive is within short range of the guns.

Some air strategists believed in the use of a large number of bombers, maintaining that, whatever the opposition from the air or from the ground, *some* of the attackers must always penetrate the defences and reach their objectives. Against this, however, must be set the undoubted fact that one solitary machine presents the most difficult of targets for the defences.

In the first month's raids, whether the attackers came individually or in flights, the result was much the same. The

R.A.F. fighters proved themselves to be more than a match for the enemy machines, and the ground and naval anti-aircraft defences, improved out of all knowledge in recent years, and equipped with ultra-modern detecting and gun-laying equipment, put up a barrage which must have been terrifying in its deadly effect.

It is only fair to state, however, that these early raids—with the exception, perhaps, of that on the Firth of Forth—were but half-hearted affairs ; they were not so much attacks seriously planned and pushed home with determination, but " feelers," reconnaissances aimed at spying out the lie of the land and the disposition of our naval and aerial forces, and testing out the defences.

Opening the Doors to America's Limitless Arsenal

The news that the U.S.A. Congress had raised the embargo on the supply of arms
to the belligerents was hailed with relief by the Allies and with fury by Germany, while
Soviet spokesmen charged the U.S.A. with having abandoned neutrality.

WHAT was claimed in France as the second great victory of the war—the first being the Anglo-French Pact with Turkey—was the passing of the American Neutrality Bill involving the repeal of the embargo on the export of arms. The United States Senate approved the lifting of the embargo on October 28, the House of Representatives followed suit, and on November 4 the President's signature made the Bill an Act.

In August 1935 the U.S.A. passed a temporary neutrality act which forbade the export of arms and ammunition to belligerents, and authorized the President to close American ports to belligerent vessels and to proclaim that American citizens travelling in belligerent merchant ships did so at their own risk. Renewed in 1936, this legislation was put on a more permanent footing in 1937. It is the 1937 measure which has now been modified.

Under the new Act the embargo on the sale of arms to belligerent countries is repealed; but belligerent powers purchasing goods from the United States will have to pay for them before they obtain delivery (this is the famous " cash and carry " clause), and will also have to fetch them in their own ships, as American vessels are forbidden to carry goods or passengers to the belligerent countries.

Furthermore, the President is given authority to prevent Americans from travelling in ships of the belligerent countries except in accordance with rules laid down by him, and also to impose restrictions on the use of American ports by the submarines or armoured merchantmen of the belligerents.

The most important of these provisions is the first. " These embargo provisions as they exist today," said President Roosevelt in his declaration to Congress on September 20, " prevent the sale to a belligerent by an American factory of any completed implements of war. But they allow the sale of many types of uncompleted implements of war, as well as all kinds of general materials and supplies." (Thus, while a complete Curtiss Hawk or Lockheed aeroplane could not be supplied to the Allies once the war had begun, the component parts could.) Now that the Act is passed any belligerent country can buy in the United States any war stores which it has the money to pay for, and which it can take away. In theory all the warring nations are put on an equality ; Germany has an equal right to buy with France or Britain. But as Britain and France control the seas, the lifting of the embargo means in effect that the Allies are enabled to enjoy that immense advantage over

their enemy which their vastly superior sea-power warrants.

The lifting of the embargo concludes a campaign which was fought most resolutely for several weeks. Both those who under President Roosevelt's lead proposed the lifting of the embargo, and those die-hard isolationists who fought to the last to prevent its repeal, were convinced that their attitude was that which would best serve America's determination to keep out of the war.

On the one hand, it was argued that the embargo operated in favour of Germany, who, as a land power, had access to implements of war supplied by Russia, Rumania, Italy and the rest, while Britain, surrounded by water, was prevented from obtaining arms in the American market. On the other, the isolationists vehemently declared that America " could not become the arsenal for one belligerent without ultimately becoming a target for the other."

Thousands of 'Planes

The signing of the Act meant the release of at least £44 millions' worth of warplanes and military equipment ordered in America by the Allies before the war began. It was understood that between 300 and 400 aeroplanes were already crated in American ports awaiting shipment to England and France, and that orders which had been in suspense were for 2,500 or 3,000 'planes.

That the repeal went through in the end may be taken as further proof that the great mass of the American people are sympathetic to the cause of the Allies, although only a tiny fraction of Americans are prepared to urge that their country should actually go to war with Nazi Germany. But while it was again and again declared that the United States was neutral and had no intention of becoming involved in the war, it was the Speaker of the House of Representatives, Mr. W. Bankhead, who declared that "You cannot place an embargo on man's mind and heart. . . Thank God, we are still entitled to express our views and our preferences for the democratic liberties of France and Britain to the rule of the concentration camp and the firing squad."

When the new Neutrality Act was passed there were already American military aircraft ready to be delivered to the Allies on the " cash-and-carry " system. In the top photograph are twelve Lockheed Hudson reconnaissance machines standing ready on the manufacturers' aerodrome in California. Aircraft of this type were supplied in quantity to the R.A.F. before the war. Boeing bombers, known as " flying fortresses," may also be ordered from the U.S.A. Below is one of these giant aircraft in the works.

Photos, Planet News and Mondiale

One More U-Boat Has Dived to Its Doom

This unique photograph, exclusive to **THE WAR ILLUSTRATED**, is perhaps the most striking pictorial record of naval activity that has yet been published. It was taken from the deck of a liner forming part of a convoy in the English Channel after a U-boat had been seen approaching it. The submarine has dived again, but one of the escorting destroyers has just dropped a depth charge—note the ring of foam astern—on the spot where the periscope was last seen. As the charge explodes a great column of spray rises above the sea, and later oil appears on the surface, a sure sign that the charge has found its mark. The ship's boat in the foreground is swung out ready for immediate lowering.

Photo, Associated Press

The Famous Dover Patrol Carries On

Above, ships of the Dover Patrol are seen at sea keeping the ceaseless vigil that makes the Straits of Dover safe for all Allied shipping.

The Dover Patrol today has to be on the alert against air as well as submarine attacks. Here crews of anti-aircraft guns are at their stations on one of the patrolling destroyers.

Photos, Central Press

To carry the mechanized B.E.F. to France ships of many types have been pressed into service, among them the Channel ferry-boats that carried goods-wagons to France before the war. This one, seen as it sets out from an English port on the Kent coast, has a load of Army lorries on board. The first Channel ferry was operated in December 1916.

Photo, Associated Press

THE Straits of Dover give the easiest access to the Seven Seas for all the countries of Northern Europe, and the shortest sea routes from England to France are those from Dover and Folkestone to Calais and Boulogne. On these grounds it is clear that the guarding of the narrow seas is one of the Royal Navy's most important duties in time of war, and immediately on the outbreak of war the Dover Patrol came into full activity once again. Between 1914 and 1918 it did work of the utmost importance to the nation, and by their valour, endurance and resource, the men who manned its ships gained immortal fame and wrote a golden page in the history of the Royal Navy. When the naval history of this war comes to be written it will be seen that the men of the Royal Navy today have not fallen short in zeal, efficiency and bravery of those who in the last war put to their credit two of the most remarkable exploits in naval history—the raids on the German bases at Ostend and Zeebrugge.

The U-Boat Hunt Starts at Dawn

This photograph was taken at a British destroyer base just as the sun was rising. It shows the small ships putting to sea on their daily hunt for U-boats, a duty which, as Mr. Winston Churchill has said, they perform "with zeal and not without relish." By the end of October 16 enemy submarines were stated to have been sunk, while four others were believed to have been destroyed or seriously damaged. The largest British destroyers are the Tribal class, each of which is named after some native tribe such as Afridi and Bedouin. They are vessels of 1,850 tons.

Photo. Keystone

Hitler Doomed to Failure Where Napoleon Failed

Now that Britain has been elevated by the Nazi spokesmen into the position of the
" villain of the piece " we may expect an intensification of the German blockade.
Already, indeed, Hitler is threatening to attempt what Napoleon tried—and failed to do.

HELD at bay on the west by the impregnable wall of the Maginot Line, manned by the armies of France and Britain, feeling day by day the pincers closing on the vital supplies of his people, Hitler now threatens and plans an intensification of the blockade of Britain on a stupendous scale. More still, a great system of counter-blockade is contemplated by which she is to be cut off entirely from the markets of Europe.

But Napoleon tried that 130 years ago. In 1806, when he was at the height of his power, and of all the countries of Europe only Britain stood out against him, he forbade all trade between Britain and the Continent. Despite all his efforts British goods were smuggled in, however, because, though he was master on land, Britain was mistress of the seas.

Hitler is said to be a close student of Napoleon's story ; if so, he would seem to have finished his reading at 1806, for the scheme which he and his satellites now propound resembles all too closely that which ended in the disaster of 1812. From Copenhagen comes the report of the formation of " The Society for European Economic Planning and Large Scale Economics," under the leadership of Werner Daitz, an associate of Alfred Rosenberg, principal originator of the myth of Nazism. The task of the society is said to be the production of a 4-year plan involving not only Germany and Soviet Russia, but almost all the neutral States on their borders, with a view to the diversion of all trade from Great Britain either to Germany or to neutral countries. In return for this subordination of their national economics to Germany's wartime needs, the neutrals would be offered special transit and industrial facilities.

Both in the Scandinavian countries and in the Balkans there was scathing criticism of the scheme, and there were more protests at the further suggestion that Germany was about to try to compel all Scandinavian ships to use the Kiel Canal on voyages from the Baltic to the North Sea—the object being, of course, to facilitate the seizure of all cargoes which the German authorities might consider to be contraband.

Neutral indignation against Germany was still further intensified by the sinking by German submarines of a number of neutral ships in the Baltic.

While the regimentation of the neutrals hangs fire Germany's warfare on the high seas continues at high pressure.

In the first two months of the war, the German High Command have proudly claimed, the Nazi U-boats sank 115 ships of a total tonnage of 475,321 tons. This figure, however, is undoubtedly an exaggeration, as British official statistics give the total losses of merchant vessels during September and October as 91 vessels of a gross tonnage of 364,210. Of these 53 were British, 6 French and 32 neutral (8 Swedish, 7 Norwegian, 7 Finnish, 1 Danish, 1 Dutch, 1 Soviet, 2 Belgian, 4 Greek and 1 Rumanian).

The total British tonnage lost in the two months—236,843—should be compared with the 17,891,134 gross tonnage of steamships and motor ships possessed by Great Britain and Ireland in July 1939. A little calculation will show how long it would take to wipe out Britain's Mercantile Marine at the rate of sinking which has hitherto prevailed, and which, incidentally, is now on the decrease. Furthermore, in the same two months of war 61,500 tons of German shipping were captured and, even more important, new ships of a total tonnage of 104,000 went down the slipways in British shipyards. Well may Mr. Churchill say that " at this rate it will take a long time to starve us out."

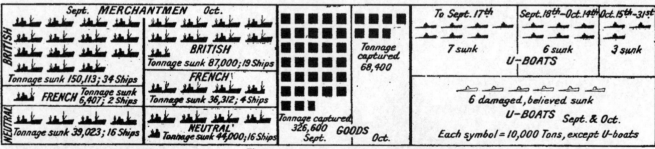

Figures are necessarily approximate and according to latest information available at time of printing.

As the diagram above shows, the Nazi U-boats have taken heavy toll of neutral ships. The two lower photographs were taken from a German patrol ship at work off the coast of Denmark when a Danish ship had been stopped to be searched for contraband. Left, the boat is being lowered, and, right, it is being rowed towards the neutral ship. *Photos, Wide World*

The Russian Riddle is Still an Enigma

Russia's words and deeds have changed the face and destinies of Europe in the few weeks since war began. Yet still the motives of the Kremlin's policy are obscured by an ideological camouflage.

M. Molotov has been prominent in the public affairs of Soviet Russia since 1917. He succeeded M. Litvinoff as Commissar of Foreign Affairs on May 3, 1939.

Photo, Planet News

" A RIDDLE wrapped in mystery inside an enigma "—that is how Mr. Winston Churchill has described Russia's policy in the war. " But perhaps," he went on, " there is a key. That key is national interest."

Certainly Soviet Russia would seem to have done very well during the first phase. With a loss to the Red army of only 731 killed and 1,862 wounded—these are the Russian official figures—she occupied nearly half Poland, and then, by a vigorously directed diplomatic onslaught backed by a substantial show of force, brought the Baltic States within her sphere of influence, and unfolded similar designs on Finland.

What next ? Stalin had reopened Russia's gateway on to Western Europe, and it was confidently expected in Nazi circles that in return for the support which Germany had granted the Soviet both in the matter of Poland and of the Baltic States, Russia would now fling her weight into the struggle against the Western Democracies. When it was announced that M. Molotov, the Soviet Prime Minister and Commissar for Foreign

Affairs, was about to give a declaration on Russian policy to the Council of the Soviet Union, Berlin expressed the confident belief that the week would be one of " decisive importance " to Germany.

Molotov's speech, however, delivered on October 31, must have considerably dashed Nazi hopes. There had been talk of Russia supplying 2,000 aeroplanes to aid Hitler's offensive in the West, but the Commissar's chief point was that Russia was to remain neutral. The Soviet's future aims, he said, were a free hand in international affairs, the continuance of the policy of neutrality, and the cessation of the war. In a most interesting passage he declared that everybody realized that there could be no question of restoring the old Poland, and that it was therefore absurd to continue the present war.

Those Aggressive Allies !

MOLOTOV even suggested that the Allies, " which but yesterday were declaiming against aggression, are in favour of continuing the war and are opposed to the conclusion of peace. The roles, as you see, are changing." In other words, he held up the Allies as the aggressors against a peace-desiring Germany and Russia ! Probably none in the subservient throng who hung on his words thought that but for the Nazi-Soviet Pact of August 23 there would probably never have been a war at all.

Proceeding, Molotov poured scorn on the declaration of the British Government that Britain's aim in the war was the " destruction of Hitlerism."

" The ruling circles of Great Britain and France " had other and more actual motives for going to war with Germany.

" These motives do not lie in any ideology but in their profoundly material interests as mighty colonial powers."

" The imperialist character of this war is obvious to anyone who wants to face realities and does not close his eyes to facts," he proceeded—and then, by a not altogether happy juxtaposition, went on to accuse the Finns of having acted in a way harmful to the cause of peace because they had refused terms dictated to them by Russia !

All this, however, is by the way. What is to the point is the support which Germany may receive from Soviet Russia. Although far from cordial in his expressions of friendship to the Reich, Molotov at least gave ground for believing that Russia is prepared to render such economic aid to Germany as lies within her power. Despite the queues of Muscovites waiting to buy shoes, clothes, milk, and meat, despite the fact that the Soviet is busily engaged in the third of its five-year plans, we may readily believe that the Russian masses will be screwed up to render out of their insufficiency some substantial aid to Germany. Gold, iron ore, oil, wheat and meat—all may be sent to the Reich in considerable quantities.

But there can be nothing more than a liaison between Nazi Germany and Bolshevik Russia. Stalin is a realist, and is careful to retain his freedom of action. If we reject the idea that he has become an imperialist after the pattern of Peter the Great, we are bound to admit that he is still a Bolshevik—and as a Bolshevik he must eagerly look forward to the coming of that day when Germany shall have been weakened to the death by her struggle with internal discontents and foreign foes.

On October 31 M. Molotov made his speech on the present situation which profoundly disappointed Nazi Germany. It was delivered to the Supreme Soviet Council, which actually meets only to applaud and register the decisions of the Soviet leaders. Above, the Supreme Council, is seen in session. Its meetings are held in one of the rooms of the Kremlin, the old fortress-palace of Moscow. Over the assembly a statue of Lenin, whose body lies just outside, dominates the scene.

Photo, Planet News.

The War of Machines on the Western Front—

The photographs in this page and that opposite afford another remarkable proof of the pitch to which mechanization has attained in the armies of today. At the top of this page French armoured cars are seen drawn up by the roadside. They now perform the duties that once fell to cavalry patrols. Immediately above is a scene at a wayside railway station in France. A train has just brought in a number of British troops, and a long line of trucks laden with Bren gun carriers, lorries and cars.

Photos, Courtesy of the French Embassy, and British Official: Crown Copyright

—Makes Foot-slogging Quite Old-fashioned !

Over the cobblestones of French villages thousands of lorries such as these have rumbled in the last few weeks while the **British Army** at the front has been steadily reinforced. This train of lorries is moving off after halting for the men's midday meal. The same tendency that was apparent in the last war to give lorries, guns and tanks names remarkable for their seeming inappropriateness has manifested itself again in this war. Thus the leading car of this column has been named " Alice."

Photo, British Official : Crown Copyright

WORDS THAT HISTORY WILL REMEMBER

A Select Record from Week to Week of Important War Declarations and Statements

(Continued from page 274)

Thursday, October 19

KING GUSTAV of Sweden and PRESIDENT KALLIO of Finland in broadcasts from the Royal Palace at Stockholm :

My invitation to this meeting was a duty I had to perform. Sweden's welfare and my warm feelings for the other Northern peoples guided me. Our consultations have confirmed the unity of the Northern Governments. We consider it vital that each of our countries should be able to pursue in absolute independence its traditional policy of impartial neutrality. We appreciate highly the warm-hearted greetings from all the rulers on the American Continent. In maintaining our neutrality we depend on the mutual support and co-operation of all countries with the same policy of neutrality as ours. I know that the Northern peoples unreservedly wish to live at peace with all nations, and are inspired by a mutual wish to live as free nations. Therefore my most heartfelt wish is that no one of the Northern countries shall be impeded in the exercise of its right independently to establish a peaceful existence. My dearest wish is that these countries may be able to co-operate to re-establish peace and settle the grave disputes now separating the belligerents. All countries long for peace and security.

PRESIDENT KALLIO said :

The Finnish people are grateful for the diplomatic support given by the Northern countries. This evidence of Northern solidarity has not stopped with words, but has found expression in action. The Finnish people know how deeply the Northern countries feel their connexion with Finland at a time when the Great Powers of Europe are at war, and when her Eastern neighbour had raised grave questions for solution by Finland. Trusting in God and their just cause, Finland's peace-loving people will defend their independence and integrity, although we only wish to live in peace in our own country. We hope that our powerful neighbour will respect the treaties which hold explicit stipulations that possible disputes shall be settled peacefully. Finland respects her obligations.

Tuesday, October 24

HERR VON RIBBENTROP, German Foreign Minister, in a speech at Danzig :

. . . Among the whole of world public opinion there is not the slightest doubt that the French people did not want this war and would rather have peace today than tomorrow, but that the war has been imposed on them by Britain by negotiations in Paris and with the French Government.

With regard to Britain, it could be proved beyond all doubt that this war against Germany had been systematically and secretly prepared for years by the present British Government . . .

The British people who, at heart, would like to live in friendship with the German people were by all possible means of propaganda and at the demand of the British Government brought to a state of hatred and panic in regard to Germany.

The aim of the British Government was by this means to bring Great Britain politically and diplomatically to the brink of an unbridgeable gulf with Germany so that it would be possible to unleash the war against Germany at whatever moment appeared most favourable to them.

This had to happen in such a way that there would be no way of retreat left open to the Government in face of its own people. This situation was brought about by Mr. Chamberlain guaranteeing Poland. That this guarantee was only an excuse is clear from the Government's declaration in the House of Commons

that it was intended to be directed only against Germany. Not the inviolability of the Polish State but armed assistance against Germany was Britain's concern.

This policy can only be understood as an expression of Britain's unceasing will to furnish herself in all circumstances—and in a not too far future—with an excuse for attacking Germany. The results of this neatly calculated British policy followed according to programme. The Poles fell into an ecstasy of megalomania.

Again the real intentions of Britain's policy were demonstrated. Instead of advising Poland to decide in favour of a still possible settlement with Germany, Britain, as we now know, incited the Poles to aggressive acts against Germany.

Britain, through a statement by her Foreign Minister, Lord Halifax, rejected Signor Mussolini's plan of September 2 for a peaceful settlement of the Polish conflict, which had been accepted by Germany and France. . . .

But the British Government showed its true face and its desire to annihilate the German people when it rejected the magnificent peace offer that the Leader made to Britain before the Reichstag on October 6, and answered it, through the mouth of the Prime Minister, Mr. Chamberlain, with abuse which called forth utter indignation throughout the whole German nation.

The Polish example has proved that it is not good to challenge Germany.

Chamberlain and his accomplices will have their eyes opened and filled with tears in due course. There will come a time, perhaps, when they will have leisure enough to contemplate whether it was good policy to reject Germany's hand of peace.

His Highness the MAHARAJA OF BIKANIR at a Durbar in honour of his 59th birthday :

We are fighting to resist aggression whether directed against ourselves or others, to break the bondage of fear daily encroaching upon the world. And we must not forget that should Hitler win this war all talk of freedom and democracy for India will vanish like thin smoke, and brute force and the doctrine that might is right will reign supreme. . .

It is my profound conviction that in these troublous times when everything is so much subjected to revolutionary changes and upheavals the great Empire over which his Imperial Majesty reigns offers the one stable element, the firm rock on which a peaceful world order could be raised, the one institution in which under a beneficent spirit of peace human effort in every direction could find its fullest realization.

Wednesday, October 25

Mr. ANTHONY EDEN, Secretary of State for Dominion Affairs, in a broadcast :

. . . The war has been in progress less than two months, but already Herr Hitler has lost the initiative. The aggressor's early advantage is spent. The road to the east is blocked by Russia or barred by Turkey. In the west every week that passes adds to the strength of the free democracies. With fast gathering momentum we swing into our stride. German attacks by air upon our Fleet, or upon our merchantmen, have failed utterly in their purpose. By comparison with the last War the

submarine has proved to be an indecisive weapon, while the percentage of losses among German U-boats has been infinitely higher. . . . The much heralded German offensive in the west still hangs fire, while winter closes in, a winter no doubt difficult for all, but infinitely to be dreaded by Germany. In all this there is encouragement for the final victory, nor has any one of us in any part of the British Commonwealth a doubt of the ultimate outcome. Strain and stresses there must be, and even moments of deep anxiety, but the issue cannot be in question. . . .

Every war is fought on two fronts. An army in the field depends on the spirit of the nation at home. The home front is not only a source of material supplies, but of spiritual inspiration. Our democracy is alive and active. That is a healthy sign. It is going to help us to win. But if this spirit is to be maintained and strengthened it is essential that we should be fully conscious of what we are fighting against, and what we are fighting for. This war has been thrust upon us and upon the world by the German Government's flagrant breaches of faith and by the German Chancellor's obsession that his will must prevail at all costs. Even so, we are not fighting against one man, nor for any given frontier, but in support of a principle. That principle is good faith between peoples, and without it there can be no peace. Nazi leaders are loud in their declarations that this war was thrust upon them. The evidence is against them, the documents have been published, the world can judge.

We believe that, when we have won through to the end, a heavy responsibility, which will also be an unrivalled opportunity, will fall to the Allied Powers. It will be our task then to give practical expression to the innermost feelings of men and women in all lands where servitude has not starved or frozen them. Those feelings are for a closer European unity and a wider world understanding, for an international order that shall be respected, for religious toleration, for the denial and not the worship of an aggressive nationalism, for liberty, security, and peace. The task will be arduous, the struggle hard fought, but if we will keep the aim steadfastly before us we cannot fail, for that aim is the aim of the better part of mankind.

Thursday, October 26

Mr. CHAMBERLAIN in the House of Commons :

I do not propose to waste the time of the House by commenting on the many details of this performance [Herr Ribbentrop's speech at Danzig]. No one in this country will be deceived by its distortions of the truth, and there is already abundant evidence that Herr von Ribbentrop has been no more successful in his attempt to mislead impartial observers in other parts of the world. Indeed I even cherish the hope that despite all suppressions and falsifications there are still some in Germany itself who see where the real truth lies.

The main thesis of the speech is that it was England and not Germany who desired and plotted for war. The whole world knows that this is not true. The whole world knows that no Government ever sought more ardently to avoid war or took greater risks to preserve peace than did the Government of this country. We have already published with complete frankness all the essential documents relating to the causes of the war. We are content to be judged by the facts and to know that the verdict of the great majority of neutral observers is in our favour.

How to Tell Non-commissioned Ranks of the Forces

Petty Officers of the Royal Navy

Petty Officer

Petty Officer Telegraphist

Regulating Petty Officer

Chief Petty Officer Artisan

Chief Stoker and Stoker Petty Officer

Leading Seaman

Chief Petty Officer cap badge

I N page 282 the distinguishing badges of officers of the Royal Navy, Army and Royal Air Force, and of naval warrant officers, are given. Here we show the badges of R.N. petty officers, and of warrant and non-commissioned officers in the other two services. The great mechanical developments that have taken place in the equipment of the Navy, the Army and the Air Force have given rise to a number of new badges that indicate in what particular work the man who wears them specializes, irrespective of rank. These will be given later. The badges in this page show standing in seniority as well as special duties. Petty officers in the Royal Navy are the equivalent of the senior N.C.O.s in the Army and are generally accounted to be the backbone of the Service.

Petty Officer cap badge

Warrant Officers and N.C.O.s of the Army

Regimental Corporal - Major (Household Cavalry), Conductor (Royal Army Ordnance Corps), and 1st Class Staff Sergeant-Major

1st Class Master Gunner

2nd Class Master Gunner

Bandmaster

All other Warrant Officers 1st Class

Master Gunner 3rd Class

Quartermaster-Sergeants ranking as Warrant Officers

All other 2nd Class Warrant Officers

Staff Sergeant

Sergeant; Corporal or Bombardier(centre); Lance Corporal or Lance Bombardier (bottom)

A LL the badges in the above two lines are of warrant officers, with the exception of those in the last square (Sgt., Cpl., and L. Cpl.). In the cavalry some of the non-commissioned officers are differently named. In the Household Cavalry a Staff Sergeant is Corporal of Horse and in other cavalry regiments Squadron Corporal-Major. Warrant officers hold a warrant of appointment as distinct from a commission. In the Army, like commissioned officers, they wear Sam Browne belts. Warrant officers in the Navy (who rank with subalterns in the Army) wear cocked hats, frock coats and swords when in full dress.

Warrant Officers and N.C.O.'s of the Royal Air Force

Warrant Officers

Flight Sergeant

Sergeant

Corporal

Leading Aircraftman

Dramatic Story of Strasbourg's Great Exodus:

The Place Kléber, named after one of Napoleon's generals who was born in Strasbourg, is seen above, left, as it was before the war and, right, as it was after the evacuation, empty except for Army lorries. The tower of the cathedral is noticeable in both photographs.

THINK of a city as big as Cardiff, much greater than Aberdeen, half as big again as Derby, from which the entire population of some 220,000 souls has been evacuated. Its thronging streets, its splendid historic square, its great railway terminus, its superbly towered Gothic cathedral, its ancient university, its once crowded quays, its numerous picturesque buildings, all echoless and deserted, left to the care of some mobile guards and a few civic officials, and to the flocks of pigeons which used to be as great an attraction to the visitor as those of Trafalgar Square or the Piazza San Marco! The only sounds of life are the whir of the wheels of the elderly guardians as they cycle on their rounds!

Strasbourg offers one of the most dramatic and emotional pictures of the War. It is France's nearest town of importance to the Rhine frontier, for the Kehl bridge which connects its suburb with the German bank of the Rhine is only two miles distant. Like the famous bridge between Tarascon and Beaucaire which is said to "divide" the two towns, the Kehl bridge now divides France and Germany. Its roadway has been dismantled and at either end strongly armed forces

Left above is the evacuation order that was posted throughout Strasbourg, and it gives instructions to the inhabitants of each ward of the city to leave their homes immediately. They are to take with them food for several days, to provide the means of transport, including vehicles and horses that have been requisitioned, and to take with them all animals and non-perishable food. In the two lower photographs the results of the evacuation are seen. Left, a street along which one of the last of the evacuees drives a cart carrying his household goods. Right is one of the city's squares of which pigeons and a Garde Mobile are now the only occupants.

Photos, E.N.A. and Courtesy of the French Embassy

Historic City of France Emptied of 220,000 Souls

The Kehl bridge across the Rhine, so called because it is on the road to Kehl, the nearest German town to the Rhine which here forms the frontier between France and Germany, is seen above. Left is the fine and impressive structure as it was in peacetime from the French end, while right is the bridge from the same viewpoint with the approach heavily sandbagged and guarded by a concrete blockhouse. Below is the once busy square in front of Strasbourg railway station, now completely deserted except for two Gardes Mobiles.

maintain a constant vigil. Here is the real stuff of drama and we are fortunate —thanks to the co-operation of the French Embassy—to be able to offer our readers these views of Strasbourg before and after evacuation.

The inhabitants scattered over France in temporary shelters have here the assurance that neither damage from the enemy action, nor from robbers or evil-doers has befallen their homes . . . despite foul lies circulated by Nazi wireless. When comes the final day of victory for the Allies it is to be hoped that the antique beauty of Strasbourg may have survived to cheer its returning townsfolk.

 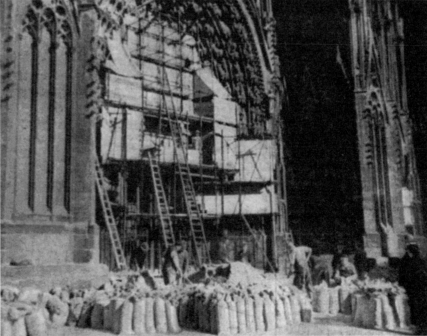

One of the wonders of Strasbourg is the astronomical clock in the south transept of the Minster, seen left. It was constructed in 1838–42 to replace one made in 1574. In the new clock some of the decorative paintings of the old clock have been used. When the clock strikes it attracts crowds of sightseers. The hours are struck on a bell by an angel while the twelve Apostles appear around the clock. The greatest care has been taken to avoid damage to the interior decorations. Protective sandbags have been used and the more delicate work is protected by a covering of plaster. Right, the protective work is seen in progress.

Photos, E.N.A. and Courtesy of the French Embassy

ODD FACTS ABOUT THE WAR

Worth Noting Today and Re-reading in Years to Come

Any Repayment ?

M. Tanner, member of the Finnish delegation to Moscow, saved Stalin's life in 1905 when the latter was a young revolutionary refugee, by protecting him from the Russian secret police.

Army Pigeons

The Belgian army has at its disposal a large contingent of carrier pigeons. During the Great War the birds rendered invaluable service, and it is possible that militarized pigeons may be needed again in emergency.

" As the Twig is Bent . . . "

The German High Command has ordered schoolteachers to educate children on more militaristic lines. The chemistry course must include lessons on chemical warfare and the use of gases. History lessons must stress German military achievements ; mathematics must include ballistics.

U-Boat Commander Apologized

When a German submarine stopped the French steamer " Vermont " by shell fire, the commander, having seen the crew safely transferred to their boats, explained : " It is not my fault I have to do this, but war is war. I am sorry."

Bulgarian Beechnuts for Germany

Germany will take unlimited quantities of beechnuts, which are rich in vegetable oil. So Bulgarian schoolchildren were given a week's holiday to gather them for export.

Slovak Reserve Army

All male Slovaks who are over 16 years of age are required to join the Hlinka Guard, thus forming a reserve army. They are to receive a thorough military training.

New Source of Cellulose

A company has been formed in Germany for the production of cellulose from potato tops. This is to be used in the paper industry.

Goebbels Closed Down

French machine-gunners trained their guns on a German propaganda loud-speaker mounted on a car near the front line—and silenced it.

Mobilizing Fishwives

The Ministry of Supply requires hundreds of thousands of nets to use in the camouflage of guns, buildings, etc., and has appealed to fishing villages for help.

More Revision of Frontiers ?

German booksellers have been ordered to hand over to the Nazi Government all maps of France, Belgium and Holland which they have in stock.

Dogs Welcome

British dog-lovers are posting on their gates copies of a notice issued by the National Canine Defence League : " You are not allowed to take your dog into an air-raid shelter, but both you and your canine friend are welcome here when a warning is given."

Future Monarch ?

The successor to the Prussian throne recognized by the Hohenzollerns is Prince Louis Ferdinand, a grandson of the ex-Kaiser and born in 1907. He is now a flight-lieutenant in the German Air Force.

Musical Guides

Members of the Remscheid (Rheinland) Philharmonic Orchestra have offered, as an inducement to timid patrons, to see them home in the black-out after the concerts.

England the Enemy

Loud-speakers the whole length of the Rhine front broadcast incessantly that Germany does not want to fight against France.

Ban on Religion

In the parts of Poland annexed by Stalin, Russian is being introduced as the main language. The teaching of religion in the schools is forbidden.

Grain for Germany

Russia has agreed to supply the Nazis with 1,000,000 tons of grain and cereals, delivery to be completed in two months.

" Hitler Calendar " in Yugoslavia

The " Hitler Calendar of Aggression," compiled by " The Times," was translated and circulated by a Yugoslav periodical, " Vidici." It met with great success, but German threats have caused " Vidici " to be suppressed.

Mickey Mouse Masks

Special " Mickey Mouse " gas-masks in various colours and having separate eye-pieces and a little nose are being made for small children who are repelled by the ordinary ones.

Food Problems at the Zoo

Penguins, who normally will eat only fish, are being fobbed off with raw meat dipped in cod-liver oil.

Another Source of Nerves

German children are getting into trouble because they have discovered that by blowing down the spout of a water-can they can imitate an air-raid siren.

Poland's Gold Reserve

The £15,000,000 brought by devious ways from the vaults of a Warsaw bank to Paris will be kept by the Polish Government to form a reserve for a restored Polish currency in the reconstituted Poland.

Keeping Up Their Spirits

The consumption of alcohol in Germany has risen 150 per cent since Hitler came into power.

Natural A.R.P. Shelters

The caves at Blackheath, which were closed in 1853, have been reopened by order of Greenwich Borough Council, who are considering their use as air-raid shelters.

Bags of Bags

An order for 500,000,000 sandbags has been placed with the Indian Jute Mills Association by the British Government.

Kultur for Poland

By request of Goebbels, a party of German poets has been touring the Polish provinces, beginning at Danzig.

The Right Spirit

Owing to the need for economy, Hackney Borough had to sack a number of its paid A.R.P. wardens. But more than half those dismissed returned to work on a voluntary basis.

Devastated Warsaw

According to Dr. Otto, German Mayor of Warsaw, over one-third of the houses have been completely destroyed, and one-fifth badly damaged. Artillery was chiefly responsible for the destruction.

Charlemagne Evacuated

Treasures of Aachen Cathedral, near the Western Front, which have been removed into the interior, include the remains of Charlemagne, who died in 814.

Poison Pens

Germany has caused leaflets to be distributed in Italy repeating the lie that poison gas was supplied by Britain to the Poles.

Nazis in Embryo

The winter programme for members of the Hitler Youth includes musketry practice for all boys of 16–18.

MR. PUNCH'S NAZI PROPAGANDA LEAFLETS
No. 1.—How the Great War Plot against Germany began: February 27, 1933
From the cartoon by Sir Bernard Partridge. By permission of the Proprietors of " Punch "

Training to Fight Enemy Fire-Makers

The Auxiliary Fire Service has undergone intensive training, and on October 29 a rehearsal of the duties they would have to perform during an air raid took place, in which 1,500 men with 300 pumps were engaged. Above, left, some of the pumps are seen in action at Barking Creek. Right, an Auxiliary Fireman is rolling up hose after the rehearsal.
Photos, Fox and G.P.U.

With the great pressure of water produced by the modern fire pumps there is a strong tendency for the nozzle to be forced upward and it takes two men to direct the jet. These two firemen (left) are playing on a derelict cottage at Sudbury which is blazing fiercely. Right, the staff of a London firm are being shown how to deal with an incendiary bomb.
Photos, Keystone and Associated Press

BEHIND THE SCENES IN NAZI PRISON CAMPS

No more terrible record of human depravity and brutality can be imagined than that given in the Government White Paper (CMD 6120) : "Papers Concerning the Treatment of German Nationals in Germany, 1938-39," selections from which follow.

SINCE the National Socialist Party attained to power in Germany there have been frequent reports of atrocities committed in the concentration camps—reports so terrible that many people refused to believe that human nature, even when stimulated by political passions of the grossest kind, could descend to such levels of cruel behaviour. That the stories were only too true, however, is evidenced by the documents now given to the world.

Here, to begin with, is an account by Mr. R. T. Smallbones, His Majesty's Consul-General at Frankfort-on-Main, of the experiences of a Jew, a well-educated man, who was arrested by the secret police during the anti-Jewish manifesta-

"In Germany there is Happiness and Beauty."—ADOLF HITLER
Cartoon by Zec, by courtesy of the " Daily Mirror."

strapped. He was then bent over a pole and his head was secured between two horizontal bars. Men were given up to fifty strokes, except in the case of promiscuous flogging inflicted for sport, and each guard was only allowed to inflict ten lashes lest his strength gave out. (Flogging was ordered for trifling offences such as not jumping to attention quickly or not obeying an order. A rabbi was flogged because he refused to sign his name on the Sabbath. He was then threatened with a second flogging. His spirit was too weak and he signed.) Some died stretched between the poles. Those who survived were kicked back into the shed. In the daytime the floggings took place in public as a warning to the others. Some went mad. They were then chained up and a sack tied round their heads to stifle their shouts.

"In present-day Germany," stated a former prisoner, "no word strikes greater terror in people's hearts than the name of Buchenwald." With good reason.

Even slight offences —drinking some water during working hours —were punished by the S.S. with loss of midday meal and with having to stand to attention for four hours during the short " free period " normally allowed on Sundays. But the main punishment was the lash. A public flogging was given for minor offences, for instance, if a prisoner was caught smoking at work. At the end of the afternoon roll-call, the numbers of the prisoners sentenced to be flogged were read out—there would be several every day—and the men were led out and bound fast to the whipping-block. The usual punishment, twenty-five strokes with a raw hide whip on the buttocks, was carried out by two hefty S.S. guards, taking turns with the

whip. A third S.S. man held the victim's jaws together to stifle any cries. Some of the older prisoners, unable to work fast, were flogged in this inhuman way for laziness. After the flogging the victim was made to take down his trousers and display his bloody stripes to an S.S. man, whose business it was to judge whether the lash had been strongly enough laid on . . .

Another punishment was that known as " tree-binding," and the guards showed great inventiveness in developing the possibilities of this torture. If only a slight offence had been committed, the prisoners would be bound to the tree in such a way that they stood facing it, and as if embracing it, their hands pinioned together. The straps that bound them would be pulled so tight that they could barely move. The guards would now play " merry-go-round " with them, that is, they would force them to make their way round and round the tree. If they could not move quickly enough it was usual to help them by kicking their ankles.

FOR the Jews arrested in south and west Germany, Dachau Camp was the place of concentration. Writes Consul-General Carvell of Munich to Lord Halifax (Jan. 5, 1939) :

Apparently the first day of captivity was one of indescribable horror, since no released prisoner has been able or willing to speak about it.

On entering the camp every prisoner had his head shaved, and was given a coarse linen prison suit with a " Star of David " stamped in yellow upon it. It seems that no other clothing was provided, even after the onset of extreme winter weather. Underclothing could, however, be bought at the canteen at a price. Two hundred to 300 persons were crowded together in huts originally built for sixty to eighty persons. Some prisoners appear to have slept on the bare boards, but most had straw. At first each person had only one thin blanket, but now some have two. The food is of the roughest kind, and the Jews receive only half the quantities allowed to the Aryan prisoners. Six persons eat out of the same dish.

To quote the introduction to the British White Paper, " under the present regime the conditions in Germany itself are reminiscent of the darkest ages in the history of man."

tions in November 1938 and taken to the Buchenwald camp, near Weimar.

On arrival they were driven with kicks and blows into a wire enclosure. (This was charged with an electric current and many were badly burnt who tried to escape. This comes from other sources.) They were then addressed by the commander of the camp, who told them what he thought about the Jews. Then every man had his hair cropped and his moustache clipped off. They had great sport with the rabbis whose religious tenets do not allow them to have their beards touched with the scissors. . . .

The camp at Buchenwald was at that time under construction and this added to the discomforts. No water was laid on and there were no latrines. The prisoners were given no water to drink the first day and never any water for washing. (My friend above referred to went for sixteen days without washing except when he collected some rain water.) On the second day my informant was given a drink of hot water, flavoured to represent coffee, and some bread. The prisoners by then were half crazy with thirst and hunger.

During the first night guards came in and picked out men at random and took them outside to be flogged. Fixed on the ground were two footplates to which the man's feet were

An attempt was made by the Nazi Government to prove that their treatment of the Jews was fair. Professor Landra, head of the Race-Politics Department of the Italian Government, was invited to visit the concentration camp at Sachsenhausen. He is seen above inspecting a number of Jewish prisoners selected from those who showed no marks of their ill-treatment. Each one wears the six-pointed Star of David to show that he is a Jew.
Photo, International Graphic Press

Britain's First Bag of Prisoners of War

The crews of a captured German tanker and cargo steamer are seen above being landed at a Scottish port. Right, the captured crew of a U-boat forced to the surface by depth charges are brought ashore.

Photos, Associated Press, Topical and G.P.U.

The final destination of all German prisoners of war is a military prison such as that seen in the photographs left and above. In the first, prisoners are at exercise in an enclosure fenced with barbed wire and watched by an armed guard. Above, they are at work building sandbag defences against air raiders from their own country.

The German airman here seen escorted by an officer with an armed guard at a railway terminus was the first Nazi air officer to be brought to London.

MANY of the German prisoners have been astonished at the conditions in Britain—so different from what they had been led to expect. The "Evening Standard" relates the following concerning the capture of the first Nazi airmen in Britain. "One young pilot officer clearly believed in the efficacy of his Fuehrer's promised 'Blitzkrieg.' 'Take good care how you handle me,' he said. . . . 'There will be a rescue party over for me in about a month, and what happens to you then will depend on the way you treat me now.' During the journey to prison camp he passed a number of artillery units on the march. On arrival he was given a large and satisfying dinner. He could remain silent no longer. 'I cannot understand it,' he said. 'At home they told us that you were defenceless and starving on account of our U-boat blockade. And here you are living like pigs in clover.'"

Cartoon Commentary on the Conflict

Earlier selections of current cartoons have appeared in pages 128, 214 and 248.

Modern Diplomacy   *From the "New York Daily News"*

Feeding Time   *From the "Daily Mail"*

H ERE are more graphic comments on the European situation. They show many contrasting moods, from the grim indictment of "The Harvest of the Moselle" to Low's brilliant "Interminable Overture" and the typically British guying of our own Government shown in "Feeding Time" by Illingworth.

Below: Left, The All-Metal Model—from the "Melbourne Argus"; centre, "Still Your Move, Adolf"—from the "Daily Mirror"; right, "The Harvest of the Moselle"—from "De Groene Amsterdammer."

Interminable Overture   *From "The Evening Standard"*

We Saw the First Air-Raid at Rosyth

Here we print a vivid, unpublished account of the bombing of British cruisers during the first air-raid on Britain written by Mr. A. Neilson, an ex-member of the R.A.F. See also the photograph in p. 297.

ON Monday, October 16, at 2.30 p.m., my wife and I chanced to be travelling slowly along a coast road on the Firth of Forth, at a point exactly opposite two cruisers, "Edinburgh" and the "Southampton."

Suddenly there was a loud cracking noise which seemed to be within the car, and which I immediately diagnosed as a broken ball-race. Again! But this time the cracking noise was a few hundred yards away and easily recognizable as machine-gun fire. I stopped the car and jumped out just in time to see a great volume of water shoot up within a few yards of one of the cruisers. "Air Raid!" I called. "Come out quick!"

The attacker had gone, but presently the cruisers started loosing their shells to a height of about 6,000 feet. Up among the white puffs of smoke my wife spotted something. "Look, there he is!" As she spoke the machine banked and came down in a fast dive from the west. Down, down he came, until directly over the Forth Bridge he released two large bombs whose course we were able to follow until they plunged into the river within a few yards of one of the cruisers.

Several times this happened, and of the bombs which were dropped I should say more than one was as near as 30 yards from one or other of the cruisers.

Certainly a lucky day for them. Right behind us in a wood an anti-aircraft battery blazed away, and as we were not more than 400 yards from the cruisers the noise was terrific, and all about us we could hear quite distinctly the orders given on the ships' loud-speakers.

As we were on rising ground and looking down on the scene we had a perfect view of the whole affair. My wife was a bit afraid to begin with, but I insisted that we were tremendously fortunate to get such a view and that we might never have such an oppor-

tunity again. I may say it was fairly obvious she was satisfied on this point – but not just in the way I intended her to be. I continued to reassure her, however, and pointed out that there was not a chance in a million of a bomb dropping near us as the marksmanship was far too good for that. The danger of shrapnel dropping on us was slight as we were too close to the guns. One large piece did, however, land within 50 yards of my car. What I did not tell her and what I dared not think about was my secret fear of what would have happened to us if one of the bombs had made a lucky hit where the raider was aiming. . . .

It was a most thrilling experience which I should not have missed for a great deal.

They Were Shot Down in the Lammermoors

A German aeroplane, attempting reconnaissance in the Firth of Forth area on October 28, 1939, was intercepted by British fighters and forced down—the first to crash on British soil. Here are first-hand impressions, reprinted from the "Observer" and the "News Chronicle," of this dramatic encounter.

SCOTTISH country folk, and particularly the 600 inhabitants of Humbie, saw British fighters chase the German 'plane which tried hard to shake them off. They saw a display of aerobatics which held them spellbound, and finally the German machine forced to earth.

Over one hundred people gathered on a high piece of ground to watch the grim contest. One of them stated: "The 'plane was brought down about two miles away. It came down on a hillside,

struck a stone wall, and even then the pilot would not give up. He tried to get the machine into the air again, and ran along the ground for about half a mile before he had to stop.

"In the air it was a fine sight. British 'planes chased the raider for several miles, and the way they looped and turned and twisted in the air as the German tried to get away was marvellous."

Another eye-witness said that a German

When the first Nazi aeroplane was brought down on British soil near Dalkeith on the morning of October 28, two of the crew were killed and the pilot was wounded, only the observer, Lieut. Rolf Niehoff, seen above left, escaping all injury. Right is a close-up view of the ammunition strewn amongst the heather. The raider is seen also in page 289 and other photographs appear in page 296.

Photos, Associated Press and British Paramount News

316   *The War Illustrated*   November 18th, 1939

||||||||||||||||||||||||||||||||||||||||||||||||||||||||||| **I WAS THERE!** |||||||||||||||||||||||||||||||||||||||||||||||||||||||||||||||

'plane came very low over the houses at Humbie.

"I heard machine-gun fire and saw a 'plane streak across the sky with British fighters in close pursuit," he added.

"The enemy 'plane was forced down and taxied across a field and then went up again very low and made for the Lammermoor Hills, where he was again forced down. The 'plane went through a wall, and then taxied along the heather and crashed into the hillside."

And the verdict of the British experts was : "A fine achievement in the circumstances."

When the machine came to a halt the pilot was assisted out by his navigator, the only uninjured member of the crew.

A policeman appeared shortly afterwards, and the pilot, speaking good English, said : "We surrender as prisoners of war. Please see to my gunners in the back of the aircraft."

But both gunners were dead.

The German pilot and his companion were taken as prisoners to Edinburgh.

Some of the 225 survivors of the liner "Yorkshire" after they had been rescued, being fed on board the American steamer "Independence Hall."
Photo, Keystone

We Watched a Duel in British Skies

On October 30, 1939, a Nazi aeroplane flew over a town on the North-East coast, just as people were going to business. A British pursuit 'plane engaged it, and the ensuing fight is vividly described below by some eye-witnesses in "The Daily Telegraph."

Aᴺ A.R.P. storekeeper told with graphic detail how the machines engaged in combat.

"I saw a big black machine," he said ; "it would not be any higher than 200 ft. and was about a hundred yards away from us. Then a smaller 'plane loomed in sight.

"The machines were so close to me that I saw the machine-gunner in the second 'plane rise in his seat as he fired a number of rounds.

"The first 'plane, up to this point, appeared to be unaware of the fact that he was being pursued, but immediately the first round was fired from the British machine the Nazi darted off at a tangent in a northern direction."

A milkman said he was going his rounds when he saw the first 'plane pass over, but he could not identify it.

"It had hardly passed over," he said, "when another 'plane came in sight. I could see the Swastika plainly because it was flying dangerously low and the roar of the engine was deafening.

"The machine was extremely lucky not to strike some of the higher buildings of the town, then it made off seawards and narrowly escaped striking the cliffs.

"Smoke could be seen belching from the machine as it made off in a northerly direction, and this at first led to the belief that the machine had crashed. However, it appears to have got away."

A graphic account of how a German 'plane, apparently the same as that over the coast a few minutes later, flew down to within about 30 ft. of a motor-bus at a spot in Northumberland was given by the only passenger in the bus.

"I had been up in the country for the week-end, and was returning in the bus," he said.

"About 8.25 a.m. I saw a large black 'plane flying very low towards us. The conductor and driver thought at first that it was a British 'plane, but I was in the Naval Air Service in the last war and believed myself that it was a German type.

"The 'plane eventually came down to within 30 ft. of us, and I could plainly see the black crosses on the underside of the wings. I thought the machine was going to land, but it followed the bus and circled overhead for about three minutes.

"At one time I thought the crew were going to open fire on us. I could see the pilot examining the bus, and it seemed to me as though he was trying to get his bearings from the destination board.

"Nothing happened, however, and eventually the machine turned and flew away. As soon as possible I reported the matter to the police."

Mr. William Dudgeon, a farmer, said, "When the 'planes passed my farm they were going towards the coast and about 200 yards apart. I saw smoke coming from the second 'plane, which I took to be a German machine.

"The engine seemed to splutter, but the machine kept going on. There was no machine-gun fire when they passed me."

The German 'plane flew so low that it nearly struck high buildings at another coast town and narrowly missed the telegraph wires. It then made off seawards and smoke was seen coming from it. People thought it would crash into the sea, but when they reached vantage points they could see no trace of it.

Stars and Stripes Went to the Rescue

On October 21, 1939, the United States ship, "Independence Hall," steamed into Bordeaux harbour crowded with the 300 people rescued from the British liners "Yorkshire" and "City of Mandalay," which had been torpedoed almost simultaneously. Poignant stories of the sinking as told by eye-witnesses are here reprinted from "The Daily Telegraph," "Surrey Comet," and Reuters.

Cᴀᴘᴛᴀɪɴ Mᴀᴄᴋᴇɴᴢɪᴇ, commander of the "Independence Hall," said :

"I heard the S O S from the 'Yorkshire,' and raced to the position given just in time to see the 'City of Mandalay' apparently standing by to help the 'Yorkshire.' But suddenly the 'City of Mandalay' herself broke in two and sank.

"It took only nine minutes for the 'City of Mandalay' to sink, but the 'Yorkshire' took forty-five minutes to sink.

"The captain of the U-boat came close and, speaking English, thanked me for saving the survivors. Then the U-boat disappeared."

Two American passengers on the "Independence Hall," Mr. R. Philipps and Mr. Jack Thomas, describing rescues from the "City of Mandalay," said :

"We were off the coast of Portugal when the steamer received an S O S from the 'Yorkshire,' which had just been sunk by a German submarine. The 'Independence Hall' went to the scene of the disaster as soon as possible, but on the way at 4 p.m. a second message was received, this time from the 'City of Mandalay,' announcing that she also was sinking. When we approached the 'City of Mandalay' a terrible spectacle confronted us. We saw the doomed steamer sink into the sea. There were four small boats packed to breaking-point. Men were swimming, and we heard the cries of children rise from the scene. Two lifeboats from the sinking ship were full of water, and the passengers were barely able to keep afloat. An expectant mother was among those rescued, but her husband was lost.

"A weeping mother sought disconsolately for her missing children. A man hoisted himself aboard holding carefully a small bundle, containing his six-months-old baby, whose mother was lost.

War Once More Against Women and Children

A swirl of water and floating wreckage marked the spot where the Bibby liner "Yorkshire" made her last plunge.

The Bibby liner "Yorkshire" was torpedoed on October 17, and sank within 14 minutes. Among her passengers were the wives and children of many soldiers returning from the East. Above is the "Yorkshire" just after the torpedo had struck, when a cloud of smoke ascended to the sky.

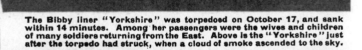

When the "Yorkshire" was sunk many lives were saved by the life belts in the use of which all the passengers had been instructed. Above, those used by the survivors of the "Yorkshire" are drying on the deck of the American steamer "Independence Hall."

The "Independence Hall" previous to picking up the survivors of the "Yorkshire" had saved 75 passengers of the "City of Mandalay." All those she rescued were landed at a French port and some of them are seen (right) coming ashore wrapped in blankets.

Photos, Keystone, Associated Press and Planet News

" The officers of the British ships were sublime. Only two of them escaped ; all the rest went down with their ships. With blood streaming down his face and although seriously wounded, the second officer of the ' Yorkshire ' coolly gave orders to abandon ship. He continued at his post with other members of the crew who perished."

AMONG the survivors of the " Yorkshire " was Miss Crowder, of Molesey. Here is her vivid account of the experience.

" The attack took place at three-thirty in the afternoon," she said. " I was asleep in my cabin at the time and was awakened when the radiator and a washbasin were hurled on to my bed.

" The first torpedo had struck us. It was immediately followed by two others. The din from the explosion was terrific —unbelievable. Seven minutes later the ship had sunk and for seven and a half hours, in an open boat, we were tossed about in a violent sea, for most of the time in the dark.

" We had all given up hope long before we saw the lights of the ' Independence Hall.'

" The most harrowing thing about it all was to see people whom you were unable to help. All the lifeboats on the starboard side were out of use, either destroyed by fire, or smashed by the concussion, and the result was that the portside boats were terribly overcrowded.

" The one I was in was built to take seventeen ; there were fifty-two of us in it, and it was a terrible thing to see people clinging to bits of wreckage, or floundering in the water, begging in vain to be taken aboard.

" And there were other terrible things.

One woman in our boat had lost her four children. She was demented with grief and we had to look after and try to console her as we tossed about hopelessly in the darkness."

It became dark at 5.30 p.m. and the seven lifeboats were tied together and from then until they were picked up five and a half hours later they sent up a flare every half-hour. High seas were running and one minute the passengers in a boat would look up and see the neighbouring boat riding high above them on a wave ; the next, it would be beneath them in a trough.

With the exception of one, who was washed overboard, all the ship's officers were lost, and two stewards took charge.

Without them and their amazing courage, Miss Crowder said, everyone would probably have been drowned. The soldiers, too, were helpful, particularly in keeping people's courage up ; they sang " The Lambeth Walk " and when the " Independence Hall " drew near, they struck up " The Yanks are Coming."

Saved One Crew While Seeking Another

Answering the call of the torpedoed French tanker " Emile Miguet," the U.S. liner " President Harding " came upon two lifeboats of the British freighter " Heronspool," and took aboard 36 victims of another U-boat attack. Below are the stories, reprinted from " The Times," related by the captains of the two vessels concerned.

THE United States liner " President Harding," her flag at half-mast for one of her crew lost overboard, docked in New York on October 21 with 596 passengers, 36 survivors from the torpedoed British freighter " Heronspool," and a crew of 300.

Captain Roberts, of the " President Harding," disclosed that it was only by chance he had been able to rescue the crew of the " Heronspool." At 7.30 p.m. on Friday, the 13th, he received a message from the French tanker " Emile Miguet," that merely said " attacked by submarine." He turned his ship back toward the position given by the tanker, which was 200 miles away. Shortly before midnight he saw lights flashing. Moving toward them he came upon two British lifeboats. Captain Batson, master of the " Heronspool," hailed the " President Harding," asked if she were British or French, and then inquired " May we come aboard ? "

" We took them aboard," Captain Roberts said, " but this was not the crew we were looking for, so we kept on until at daybreak we saw dense clouds of smoke on the horizon. That was the ' Emile Miguet ' on fire and with her decks awash. There were two British destroyers near by and we asked them if they had taken on the ' Emile Miguet's ' crew, but they said they had seen no signs of them. We circled the ship, saw no signs of life on board, and finally at 8.30 in the morning resumed our course."

Captain Batson, of the " Heronspool," said that at 6 o'clock on Friday evening he saw the " Emile Miguet " being shelled about six miles distant, so he steered away north-eastward. About 8 o'clock they heard an explosion and saw a column of water rise on the starboard beam. Half an hour later the submarine approached and signalled : " What ship ? "

" As soon as we could make him out," Captain Batson said, " we fired two shots at him, whereupon he dived. I hauled to the westward for two hours, then zigzagged. About 11 p.m. the submarine appeared in sight nearly aft. We quickly fired two shots at him in succession. He disappeared, but reappeared at midnight and fired a shot which exploded close to our starboard beam. Then we sighted him on the starboard quarter and fired at him. Then he appeared on the port quarter and again we fired."

The submarine submerged again, but soon there was a violent explosion in the forepart of the "Heronspool." She had been torpedoed. Captain Batson continued :

" We then abandoned ship in two lifeboats, and after pulling away for some distance lay to. We saw that the forepart of the ship appeared to have been blown away, and that she was listing to port. The submarine appeared in full view a short distance away 20 minutes later, but seemed not to notice us. We sighted the ' President Harding ' about 5.30 a.m., and shortly after that the ' Heronspool ' disappeared "

This photograph was taken from the deck of the " President Harding," which answered the SOS of the French tanker " V. Emile Miguet " after she had been torpedoed and was ablaze. The crew of the French ship had already been rescued before the " President Harding " came on the scene, but the American ship then had on board the crew of the torpedoed British ship " Heronspool."   *Photo, Keystone*

Mr. Briton'll See It Through

Towards the end of the last war, when petrol was scarce, coal gas carried in a bag on the roof was used as fuel. This private car was one of the first to be adapted to gas in 1939.

This driver of an L.M.S. engine combines the duties of his ordinary avocation with that of Head Warden in the locomotive sheds. It is his duty to inspect the sheds for A.R.P. To facilitate the work of shunting with dimmed lights, the buffers of locomotives are painted white. The fireman is touching them up.

The figure of Eros in the centre of Piccadilly, perhaps London's best-known piece of sculpture, was removed to a place of safety in the last war, and also in this war. During the preparations for removal a workman has given Eros his gas-mask "to hold." Left, a new recruit on the farm learns to plough; with his three co-workers he is helping to increase the 1940 harvest.

Not only air raid precautions but black-out precautions have been taken in London and every other large city. Both are illustrated in the two photographs above. That left shows hurricane lamps used in a London borough to mark the street refuges at night. They are quite invisible from above. Right, the statue of King Charles I, the finest work of its kind in London, is being encased in a wooden framework preparatory to being sandbagged. The statue stands on the south side of Trafalgar Square at the top of Whitehall.

Photos, Topical, J. H. Foy, Fox & Keystone

OUR DIARY OF THE WAR

Monday, October 30

Admiralty announced that a destroyer flotilla was in action with two German bombers south of the Dogger Bank. No damage was done to the ships.

Nazi reconnaissance 'plane was seen over the **north-east coast** of England. British fighter aircraft went up, and after a machine-gun duel the Nazi machine vanished out to sea in a cloud of smoke.

Enemy aircraft were also reported off the **south-east coast.** British 'planes went up to investigate, but did not make contact.

Paris reported activity by contact units on the whole front and local activity by artillery. French chaser and reconnaissance aircraft were intensely active.

Air Ministry announced that R.A.F. machines had made extensive reconnaissances of aerodromes in North Germany. All 'planes save one returned safely.

Crew of the British steamer " Malabar," sunk by a U-boat on Sunday, were landed.

Crews of the trawlers " St. Nidan " and " Lynx II," sunk on Friday night by a U-boat, were landed on the Scottish coast by the trawler " Lady Hogarth."

White Paper on the conditions in Nazi concentration camps was issued by the British Government.

Tuesday, October 31

Air Ministry announced the first encounter between British fighters and German bombers over French territory. One of the raiders was shot down.

Paris reported greater artillery activity on both sides. The Germans made use of their heavy guns for the first time, shelling a village eight miles behind the French lines.

M. Molotov, addressing the Supreme Council of the Soviet Union, attacked Britain for waging war on Germany, but reaffirmed the neutrality of the U.S.S.R. He gave details of the **proposals made to Finland** and stated that they had been **refused.**

Important changes were made in the Italian Cabinet, the general result being to strengthen Italy's neutrality.

It was stated that Britain had decided to recognize the Italian occupation of Albania by appointing a consul-general in Tirana.

U.S. steamer " City of Flint " reported to have arrived at Tromsœ, Norway, flying the swastika, and to have left four hours later accompanied by a Norwegian warship.

The Prime Minister of Australia announced the abandonment of the plan for an Australian expeditionary air force in favour of a general reconnaissance squadron for service in and around Great Britain.

Wednesday, November 1

Finnish delegation left Helsinki to return to Moscow.

Paris reported that German heavy artillery in and just behind the Siegfried Line had been **shelling the French fortifications** and villages several miles behind.

R.A.F. aircraft made successful reconnaissance flights over north-west Germany.

Dutch royal decree proclaimed a state of siege in certain municipalities along the frontiers and in military inundation zones.

Two decrees were sanctioned by the Swiss Federal Government which take into account the possibility of invasion of Swiss territory.

Lord Nuffield appointed Director-General of Maintenance in the Air Ministry.

Dominion Ministers and representatives of the Government of India met the Prime Minister and several members of the War Cabinet at the first of a series of conferences on Empire collaboration in wartime.

The Prime Minister of Australia announced decisions to increase the fighting power of the three services.

Thursday, November 2

H.M. the King decorated five men of the R.A.F.

President **Roosevelt's Neutrality Bill** passed by the House of Representatives.

Two German aeroplanes brought down over the Western Front by British aircraft and anti-aircraft guns in conjunction with the French.

Paris reported that French patrols had been active throughout the day between the rivers Blies and Rhine.

THE POETS & THE WAR

VI

LONDON

By ERNEST RHYS

London, the " Flower of Cities All,"
As old Dunbar once did you call,—
" Rose Royal and Original."

You that have seen beneath your sky
Long lines of men go marching by
To take the field for Liberty.

What sable pall is dropt to-night
Upon the town that shone so bright—
Shops, streets ashine and myriad light ?

And they, your peerless women, they
That are your silent soldiery,—
What fate for theirs and them may be ?

And we that are your sons of grace,—
This night we bow like one that prays,
For a man must love his mothering place,

And when the war planes hover near,
And the winged harpies swoop and lower,
We love you most, oh ! fearless flower !

—The Sunday Times

Germans now using shock troops for raids on the French lines.

German envoys to Moscow and Rome, who had been summoned to Berlin, were in consultation with Hitler.

Messages exchanged between Italy and Greece reaffirming their collaboration for peace.

Finnish delegates arrived in Moscow.

Friday, November 3

Third series of talks between Finland and Russia began. A few hours earlier, " Pravda," Russian official organ, made a violent attack upon Finland, which later was broadcast.

Roosevelt's Neutrality Bill adopted by U.S. Senate and House of Representatives.

Paris reported a quiet day on the Western Front, with a few encounters between contact units.

Admiralty announced U.S. ship " City of Flint " had been sighted proceeding southwards inside Norwegian territorial waters.

General Smuts, Prime Minister of South Africa, stated that the Union would keep its promise to defend British territories in Africa if they appealed for aid.

Allied Contraband Control organisation have now intercepted and detained over 500,000 tons of contraband suspected of being destined for Germany.

Saturday, November 4

President Roosevelt signed proclamation putting new Neutrality Bill into effect.

Huge new orders of wartime supplies were confirmed by British and French agents, and shipment was to start immediately.

Norwegian Admiralty announced that U.S. steamer **" City of Flint " arrived at Haugesund** on Friday afternoon, accompanied by two Norwegian warships, and anchored there without permission. Whereupon the **German prize crew were interned,** and the ship was now on her way to Glasgow under the American flag.

Paris reported that on both sides light reconnoitring units had been active between the Moselle and the Saar.

French cargo-boat " Baoule " reported to have been sunk in the Atlantic.

Bodies of five German sailors washed ashore in Kent.

Sunday, November 5

" City of Flint " reached Bergen.

German Government lodged a protest in Oslo against the release of the vessel and internment of the prize crew. The protest was rejected.

Finnish-Soviet negotiations continued. The delegates reported to Helsinki, asking for further instructions.

The Western Front remained quiet.

Mr. Churchill, who had gone to Paris on November 2 to discuss the work of the British and French Navies, visited British General Headquarters.

Swedish Government protested against extension of German minefields, which are now within three miles of the Swedish coast.

It Is Said That . . .

There is acute shortage of water in Warsaw ; a modicum is supplied to endless queues by German military water-carts.

" The German people do not want war. I don't want it myself. I am only carrying out my duty." (*U-boat Officer.*)

German radio station in Poland opened by telling Poles that Britain's domestic condition was growing " desperate."

Thousands of Storm Troopers are being shot because they revolted against the Soviet-German pact.

Minefields in front of the Siegfried Line are as much an obstacle to advancing Germans as to invading French.

German merchant ships have orders to scuttle themselves rather than be captured by British ships.

Incendiary fires throughout Germany are causing great anxiety, and drastic measures are dealt out to offenders.

" In the present war we have three adversaries—the Germans, the Bolsheviks and the bureaucrats." (G. Ward Price.)

The German army today is stated to be greatly inferior to the Kaiser's splendid fighting machine in 1914.

There is a grave shortage of skilled engineers, machine workers and draughtsmen in German armament factories.

War loot brought back from Poland was exhibited for two days in Berlin's main thoroughfare, Unter den Linden.

German grocers have been ordered to perforate the lids of jam jars before selling, to guard against hoarding.

Gestapo arrested those answering decoy advertisement offering " Second-hand radios capable of receiving all European stations."

German civilians have been told that the recent 50 per cent increase in income tax is an expression of their gratitude to the troops.

Vol. 1   A Permanent Picture Record of the Second Great War   No. 11

One of the guns of a coastal defence battery in the east of England is here seen in action during practice. In pages 336 and 337 a wider view of a whole battery of these guns is given. The photograph above shows the gun and the heavy concrete structure on which it is mounted. That structure contains the magazine from which shells are being passed up from hand to hand by a chain of men. Such guns are manned by men of the Royal Regiment of Artillery, into which is now merged the Royal Garrison Artillery which at one time handled all the heavier guns.

Photo, Sport and General

Entente Cordiale in the Maginot Line

While the great offensive still tarried on the Western Front, the British troops consolidated their position in the esteem and affection of their French allies and wartime hosts. The Entente Cordiale of years gone by was fortified by the camaraderie of the present.

Viscount Gort, C.-in-C. of the British Field Force, is here seen with General Gamelin, Commander-in-Chief of the Allied Armies.
Photo, British Official: Crown Copyright

IN *l'autre*, "the other," as the French have come to call the war of 1914–18, the rains of autumn drove the contending armies into the comparative inactivity of trench warfare. Again in 1939 the rains, supplemented by an early foretaste of the winter snow, had a similar effect, although in this war the men, both French and British, were not compelled to shiver in waterlogged trenches, but had quite comfortable quarters in the underground forts of the Maginot Line or in billets in the towns and villages to the rear. Maybe the Germans for their part were not quite so comfortable : if report spoke true, the concrete used in the Siegfried Line was not so waterproof as could be desired.

Relations between the French and British troops in the line were most cordial. In the sector of the front exclusively occupied by the British, and in those districts in which scattered units of the R.A.F. found their homes, the civilian population made the newcomers welcome just as they had greeted their fathers a generation before. Moreover, for many of the men in the British Field Force, France was no strange country

inhabited by foreigners speaking an unpronounceable lingo, but the land in which they had spent some of the most strenuous and never-to-be-forgotten days of their youth. As they travelled along the great poplar-lined *routes nationales*, as they halted in the *place* and clinked their glasses in the *café* on the corner or in the village *estaminet*, their minds were carried back over the years, and it seemed only yesterday that they were here with comrades whom they had known and lost. For quite a number of young men in the Field Force, their first leisure was devoted to a visit to a Great War cemetery in which lay one whose name, perhaps, they bore.

So the weeks slipped by, and still the great armies massed in the opposing fortified zones made no move. There were artillery bombardments, as when Forbach, a small French frontier town practically in the front line, was shelled for several days at the beginning of November, doubtless with a view to hampering the French communications. There was some fighting in the air, too, and on November 6 the French G.H.Q. stated in their communiqué that,

The Nazi gibe that Britain would fight to the last Frenchman is day by day being countered in France by the best of all evidence, that of ocular demonstration. In French villages the passing of a column of British soldiers marching towards the front is an everyday occurrence. Torrential rain has fallen since the B.F.F. went to France, and macintoshes have proved a useful part of the soldier's equipment, but road surfaces have vastly improved since 1914, and so the mud is not what it was. A pipe-band is playing the troops past. *Photo, British Official: Crown Copyright*

Britain's Field Force Through French Eyes

—CAMIONS BOURRÉS D'HOMMES ET DE MATÉRIEL, MOTOCYCLISTES IMPECCABLES, MITRAILLEUSES, CANONS MONTÉS SUR PNEUS, TOUT CELA DÉFILE SUR LES ROUTES DE FRANCE A UN RYTHME ACCÉLÉRÉ. DE JOYEUSES INSCRIPTIONS À LA CRAIE DÉCORENT LES VOITURES. GAIS OU SÉRIEUX SELON LEUR TEMPÉRAMENT LES SOLDATS D'OUTRE-MANCHE SALUENT AU PASSAGE LES PAYSANS DE FRANCE DONT LES FILS SONT DÉJA PARTIS.

DIMANCHE MATIN AU VILLAGE.

—ON NE CRIE PAS : AU JUS LÀ-DEDANS, MAIS : HELLO BOYS TEA IS READY !

CHEZ L'HABITANT. — ON NE PARLE PAS LA MÊME LANGUE MAIS ON SE COMPREND BIEN TOUT DE MÊME !

A L'UNIQUE BISTRO
LA BIÈRE POUR N'ÊTRE PAS "MADE IN ENGLAND" N'EN EST PAS MOINS APPRÉCIÉE

LA TOILETTE MATINALE A LA GRANDE JOIE DES ENFANTS DU PAYS.

These sketches by G. Pavis, from the French paper "Candide," are given here as showing the impression made on the French by our Army in France. The inscription under the top one reads : Lorries laden with men and material, impeccable motor-cyclists, machine-guns, guns mounted on pneumatic tires—all these are seen streaming over the roads of France in an ever-increasing rhythm. Comic inscriptions in chalk decorate the transport. Grave or gay, according to their temperament, the soldiers from across the Channel greet, as they pass by, the peasants of France, whose sons have already gone. The centre sketches show : Sunday morning in the village; "Tea up" in the barn; and Tommy overcoming the language difficulty with the local inhabitants. Bottom row : Beer, even if not "made in England," is none the less appreciated, and (right) the morning toilet is a never-ending source of joy to the local kiddies.

The French Army, like the British, can provide much of its own entertainment. Recently a French Infantry Regiment organized a most successful concert of its own in Paris. The programme-seller at the concert collected the money in a steel helmet.
Photo, Planet News

"During a violent fight, nine French fighters attacked a group of 27 German fighters. Nine of the latter were brought down, of which seven fell within our territory. Every one of our 'planes engaged in this encounter returned safely." A few days earlier news had come in of the first air battle over the British lines, in the course of which three Royal Air Force 'planes engaged several German 'planes which were attempting to make a photographic reconnaissance over the British lines. One of the German machines was riddled with bullets and finally crashed in a hedge, while a second was forced down into Belgium with smoke emerging from its tail. In this engagement the British anti-aircraft contingents gave a demonstration of remarkable efficiency.

For the most part, however, the war seemed to be at a standstill. Millions of men were ever on the alert; from Holland to Switzerland nations in arms watched every move of the armies congregated in the neighbourhood of the Siegfried Line. For the more unthinking newspaper reader the war was boring. But, as Major-General Sir Ernest Swinton so pertinently pointed out in the first of his broadcast talks on the progress of the war, "The war is not being run to provide news. And when I hear people complaining about the lack of news from France and talking about 'All quiet on the Western Front,' I say, 'Thank God that there *is* no news of battles: thank God that the commanders have learned something from 1914–1918, and that the Allied troops are not going to be thrown in haste, without due preparation, against a stone wall, or rather, a steel and concrete maze, bristling with every sort of gun.'"

More and more it came to be realized that despite the strain of keeping great armies in the field and their peoples as a whole on a war footing, Britain and France had nothing to gain by haste. Hitler, however, was in a hurry; every day that went by saw an increase in the strength of his foes and a more than corresponding diminution in Germany's lead in military preparedness. So he consulted and deliberated, planned and plotted great offensive movements. There was something not far removed from pathos in the report that the Fuehrer was taking lessons in military strategy.

The women who work the canteens and hostels that provide accommodation for French soldiers behind the lines wear the Red Cross uniform. Above is the interior of a canteen where soldiers are being served by attendants. If they stay the "poilus" are sure of comfort, and if they have to be up early to catch a train and return to duty, one of the tireless Red Cross workers will see that they are off to time.
Photo, Topical

The Duke of Windsor Sees His Second War

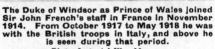

During his visit to the French Army the Duke of Windsor went as far south as Strasbourg, and he is seen above (left) taking a look at the German lines just across the Rhine. In the days spent with Britain's Allies His Royal Highness met and talked with many distinguished officers, and made acquaintance, too, with the Poilus of today. Above (right) he is meeting French Staff Officers.

Photos, Sport & General, Wide World and Topical

Further north the Duke of Windsor encountered rough weather while he was becoming fully acquainted with the positions and plans of the French Army. He is here seen with French officers during a snowstorm.

The Duke of Windsor as Prince of Wales joined Sir John French's staff in France in November 1914. From October 1917 to May 1918 he was with the British troops in Italy, and above he is seen during that period.

Photo, Imperial War Museum

Early in September the Duke of Windsor returned to England from France to offer his services to his country. On September 19 it was announced from the War Office that he had been allowed temporarily to relinquish his rank of Field-Marshal in the British Army and assume that of Major-General in order that he might take up a staff appointment with the Army in France. A few days later His Royal Highness went to France. He has since spent some time with the French Army, and is here at a march past of French troops.

Here in Their Front Line are the 'Poilus'

Day by day the reinforcement of the French Army in the Saar region goes steadily on and men and guns are piling up around the Western front. Above, left, what looks like a load of brushwood is being drawn along a road. Beneath the leaves and branches is a big gun moving towards its position. Right is such a gun ready for action with its camouflage of netting.

Photos, Courtesy of the French Embassy

FRENCH soldiers' pay is very small compared with that of their British comrades-in-arms, but on November 5 decrees effecting considerable increases in both pay and allowances were published in the "Journal Officiel," the equivalent of the "London Gazette." Until that date the French soldier received only 50 centimes a day, that is, a little over three farthings in English money. The chief increases were a 10 franc daily allowance for all ranks in the combatant zone—to be fixed each month by the Commander-in-Chief—and an increase in pay for those on daily rates, ranging from 25 centimes for a private soldier to 5 francs 90 centimes (a little over 8d.) for a sergeant-major.

Like the British Tommies, the French Poilus often give a homely touch to their wartime quarters. This dug-out has been named Ed. Daladier in honour of the French Prime Minister, and a German steel helmet and a lucky horseshoe complete its external decorations.

Photo, Planet News

The "strong point" in the Maginot Line seen left is typical of the impregnable fortresses which constitute France's frontier defence. The German High Command quailed before the idea of taking such positions by direct assault and Hitler therefore had to reconsider his plans. On the left of the photograph are steel rails driven into the ground as defences against tank attacks.

Photo,. Courtesy of the French Embassy

While Here Are Nazis in Their 'Westwall'

In the south-east the Maginot and Siegfried Lines are close together, lying on the banks of the Rhine, here comparatively narrow. Above left is a fort on the Maginot Line seen across the river from a look-out post on the Siegfried Line, such as that shown above right.

Photos, Wide World

THE whole length of the frontier between France and Germany is defended on the French side by the Maginot Line and on the German side by the Siegfried Line or Westwall. Both lines of fortifications have been extended to the French and German frontiers with Luxemburg and Belgium. There are 12,000 forts in the Siegfried Line. The defences in both cases are naturally stronger where the French and German frontiers are contiguous. The Siegfried Line has more than once been flooded by the Rhine, and it has been suggested that if Holland found it necessary to inundate part of her territory in self-defence the Siegfried Line might be flooded.

The entrance to one of the blockhouses in the Siegfried Line above gives some idea of the thickness of the walls and the great steel girders that form the framework. The German sentry is wearing a forage cap very similar to that of the British Army.

Seen right reviewing troops, General von Brauchitsch, the Commander-in-Chief of the German army, went to the Western Front when Poland had been overrun. It was rumoured that he had raised strong objections to a great offensive on the Western Front, and that he was about to be succeeded by General von Keitel.

Photos, Planet News

Finland Stands Out Against the Soviet

In earlier pages (see pages 233 and 266) some account has been given of the negotiations between Soviet Russia and Finland which were opened following the former's diplomatic successes against the Baltic States. Below, the story is carried to a later stage. A map including the places mentioned is given in page 234.

After weeks of negotiation behind closed doors, after the Finnish delegates had paid three visits to Moscow, a flood of light was thrown upon the Russian-Finnish situation by the speech of M. Molotov, Russia's Prime Minister and Commissar for Foreign Affairs, to the Supreme Council of the Soviet Union on October 31. It was towards the end of his speech that M. Molotov devoted a paragraph or two to his Government's demands on Finland.

"It was untrue," he said, "that the Soviet Government were demanding the Aaland and other islands from Finland. What she wanted was a mutual assistance pact along the lines of those negotiated with the other Baltic States. But this Finland had refused." The reason for Finland's refusal was not stated by M. Molotov, but there was little doubt that Finland had taken her stand on the maintenance of an absolute neutrality which would be inevitably compromised by any such pact as those referred to by M. Molotov.

Russia's second demand, said M. Molotov, had been that Finland should move back some kilometres from the frontier opposite Leningrad, and take part of Russian Karelia in exchange. Here it may be mentioned that the Finnish frontier is only 25 miles from Leningrad, which would therefore be within range of heavy guns mounted on Finnish soil. But any modification of the frontier in this region, however reasonable from Russia's point of view, would probably be strongly contested by the Finns, as it might involve bringing the Russian frontier to the western shores of Lake Ladoga and to the very gates of Viipuri (Viborg).

A still more serious threat to Finland was contained in M. Molotov's next statement, that Russia had "also sought to rent some islands and create naval bases in the northern part of the Gulf of Finland." Here it may be said that the exchange of certain islands in the Gulf for very much larger territory in Russian Karelia might be agreed to by the Finns, but the establishment of a Russian naval base on the Finnish mainland would be an altogether different matter. It was understood that the site the Russians had in mind was Hanko

to the Arctic to the west of Murmansk. Russia ceded Petsamo to Finland by the Treaty of Dorpat in 1920, receiving in exchange a considerable area in the isthmus of Karelia, facing Leningrad. If it were returned to Russia it would mean that Finland would be cut off from the Arctic, which in summer at least affords an alternative exit to the Baltic, and Soviet Russia would be given a common frontier with Norway.

Finland, it will be seen, was adopting an eminently reasonable attitude. She was willing to compromise wherever possible, but whereas she might cede to Russia certain of her outlying islands and even permit of some adjustment of her eastern frontier, in order to allay Russia's fears concerning Leningrad and Murmansk, she could not grant a lease of, say, Hanko without not only infringing

The President of Finland, M. Kyösti Kallio, was elected in February 1937 and recently attended the Conference of the Scandinavian States with the Kings of Denmark, Norway, and Sweden. He is seen left with one of his aides-de-camp. Above is Hanko, which Russia covets as a naval base. It is on the Finnish mainland at the northern entrance to the Baltic.
Photos, Wide World

(Hango), on the coast to the west of Helsinki and on the opposite shore of the Gulf of Finland to the islands of Dagö and Ösel, which had just been leased by Estonia under duress to the Soviet.

Another demand, one not mentioned by M. Molotov in his speech, was reported to be an exchange of territory near Petsamo (Petschenga), the port in the narrow strip of Finnish territory which reaches out

her own neutrality, but ceasing in some measure to be mistress in her own house.

In her stand against the Soviet's more extreme demands Finland was assured of the moral support of the outside world. That active support which Germany had professed to be so eager to give was not forthcoming. It was rumoured that only a few months before Germany had been advising Finland to fortify the Aaland Islands just as she advised the Estonians to fortify the islands of Dagö and Ösel—all with a view to bottling up Russia at the far end of the Gulf of Finland. Russia, however, had refused to be bottled up, and in the diplomatic tussle had proved more than a match for Nazi Germany. Fortunately for the Finns, they have never relied overmuch on outside help. In this latest crisis they hoped for the best, but in view of Russia's attitude kept on the alert.

The Empire Gets into Its Stride

Increasing practical co-operation of the Empire was one of the most marked features of the first two months of the War. Here some of the principal developments are recorded, culminating in the meeting of Empire statesmen in London.

Mr. Anthony Eden was appointed Dominions Secretary, when the Government was reconstructed on the outbreak of war. He had not held office since he resigned the Foreign Secretaryship in February 1938.

REMARKABLE evidence of Empire unity was provided by the assembly in London of Empire delegates to confer with the British Government. The plan was announced by Mr. Eden early in October, and by the end of the month they were here, including: Sir Muhammad Zafrullah Khan, a member of the Viceroy's Council, for India; Colonel Reitz, who, like Smuts and Hertzog, fought gallantly against us in the Boer War, and is now Minister of Native Affairs for South Africa; Mr. T. A. Crerar, Minister of Mines, and Air-Commodore L. S. Breadner, Senior Air Staff Officer, for Canada; the Scottish Mr. Peter Fraser, who has acted as deputy Prime Minister of New Zealand during the illness of Mr. Savage; and Mr. R. G. Casey (D.S.O. and M.C. in the last war), former Treasurer, and now Minister of Supply, for Australia. Creating an interesting precedent, the House of Commons gave the Empire delegates some reserved seats among the M.P.s, and they were able to listen with the rest of the House on November 2 to Mr. Chamberlain's welcome and his review of the Empire's effort.

Mr. Casey, as Minister of Supply, has been responsible for the militia training scheme providing for two batches of 40,000 men to be in training by the middle of November, and a special force, known as the Sixth Division, of 20,000, under Major-General Sir Thomas Blaney, for service at home or abroad. Australia joined whole-heartedly in the great scheme for establishing an Empire Air Force in Canada, where personnel could receive advanced training.

New Zealand has agreed to co-operate in this plan, and a proportion of R.A.F. trainees from Britain also will put the finishing touches to their work in Canada. On November 6 the British, Australian, New Zealand, and Canadian representatives met in conference at Ottawa to discuss details. Altogether the Dominions have about 2,000 picked men serving already in the R.A.F. in Britain and France, but the new scheme for pooling resources in Canada, and for the manufacture of equipment and 'planes in Canada, as well as the great supplies from the United States now available owing to the repeal of the arms embargo, threaten Germany with an enormous increase of Britain's power in the air within a period of six months.

Training Airmen in South Africa

On the same day as that conference in Ottawa came the report from Pretoria of a scheme, arranged with the British Government, to establish special training schools for airmen in South Africa. Not only large-scale training of pilots, observers, photographers and machine-gunners, but also the development of a big munitions output has been agreed.

Tributary forces from all parts of the Empire were being increased or newly formed by the first week of November. The Royal West African Frontier Force more than doubled; the King's African Rifles in East Africa more than trebled.

The Empire delegates over here have been shown something of what we are doing. The secrets of the air defence of Great Britain were shown on November 4 to the Ministers from the Dominions

and India. Air Chief Marshal Sir Hugh Dowding took them over the Fighter Command, and they were also taken to the Coastal Command, whose 'planes are continuously patrolling the seas to protect shipping from U-boats. An obliging U-boat was reported during their inspection. Messages coming through referred to an actual attack on a submarine in the North Sea. "From pilot of aircraft No. —, 10.48 hours. A, over enemy submarine in position," flashed the message, and then, "Submarine is diving." "Have attacked, estimate one hit." Then a detailed message describing the attack followed. Another message received described the sighting of a submarine in the Atlantic by aircraft. Next flashed a signal indicating that the 'plane had called up a destroyer to tackle the U-boat.

On November 4 the Dominion representatives, arrived in Great Britain to co-ordinate the Empire's war effort, visited the Fighter Command of the Royal Air Force. This photograph was taken during the visit. Left to right are Sir Muhammad Zafrullah Khan, India; Sir Hugh Dowding, Air Officer Commanding-in-Chief Fighter Command; Colonel Deneys Reitz, South Africa; fifth from left, Mr. F. S. Waterson, High Commissioner for South Africa; next, Mr. T. Crerar, Canada; second from right, Mr. Vincent Massey, High Commissioner for Canada.

Photo. P.N.A.

They Are Ready to Send Death Into the Skies

This remarkable-looking weapon is a quick-firing two-pounder Bofors anti-aircraft gun of Swedish design, built by licence in Great Britain. Such guns were introduced into the British Army only in 1938, but they soon formed the standard equipment of light anti-aircraft units whose job it is to deal with low-flying enemy aircraft. The general public had their first opportunity of seeing such a gun when one was drawn through the streets of London by Territorials taking part in the Lord Mayor's Show of 1938.

Photo, Topical

At the Heart of Britain's Air Defence

To the man in the street one of the surprises of the war is the splendidly efficient way in which the German raiders have been beaten off with heavy loss. But the Fighter Command, whose work is described here, have always been quietly confident.

SOMEWHERE in England there is a room like a broadcasting studio with sound-proof boxes high up in each wall. Practically the whole of the floor space is occupied by big maps of the British Isles, and around the tables sit a number of telephone operators. This room is the central control of the R.A.F. Fighter Command—that Command which is responsible for the security of Britain's millions from enemy air attack.

At its head is the Air Officer Commanding-in-Chief—Air Chief Marshal Sir Hugh Dowding, known in the Service for some unknown reason as "Stuffy." He has under his control not only the R.A.F's fighter squadrons, but also the anti-aircraft guns, sound locators,

Air Chief Marshal Sir Hugh Dowding is A.O.C.-in-C. of the Fighter Command, and as such commands the British air defences—the fighting aircraft, the A.A. guns, the searchlights, and the balloon barrage.
Photo, Vandyk

and searchlights of the Army, the balloon barrage of the Auxiliary Air Force, and the Observer Corps of volunteer watchers and listeners. Moreover, it rests with him to decide whether or not air-raid warning sirens should be sounded in any particular area, thus bringing the whole A.R.P. system into action.

To the Central Control Room the news of approaching raiders is flashed from ships, observers on the coast, and other sources, and their location is at once charted on one of the big maps. Orders are then dispatched to air stations in the presumed path of the raiders for fighters to take off and intercept the enemy, and while in the air the pilots are kept informed by radio from the Central Control Room of the direction, speed, and number of enemy raiders. Arrows marked to show the strength of the raiders are moved about the maps by a croupier's rake to mark the progress of the raid; and other defence measures—anti-aircraft guns, for example—are brought into play as the occasion demands. In this Central Control Room, then, the whole course of an air raid on the British Isles may be

The sound locator is just as important in the defensive scheme as the anti-aircraft gun or the searchlight. The great "ears" of this modern type of locator are in the hands of young militiamen, wearing respirators as they learn their drill.

This is a typical scene at one of the hundreds of searchlight camps, dotted in remote places all over Britain. The detachments are composed largely of men who were citizen soldiers of the Territorial Army until the present emergency.
Photos, Keystone

SILENCE

The Central Control of the Fighter Command, R.A.F., is the nerve-centre of our air defences. Above is the Operations Section at this secret headquarters, where messages are received and orders given. As reports come in, details of the raid, showing the route, speed, height and strength of the enemy, are plotted on the map table below the gallery.

used as escorts for a formation of bombers. Their range and endurance are short, these qualities being sacrificed to maximum speed, climbing powers, and manoeuvrability. In actual fact the modern R.A.F. fighter monoplanes are so fast that their powers of manoeuvre are less than those of the older biplane types. Britain favours the single-seater with a single engine of tremendous power, but there are two-seater fighters in the R.A.F. and in foreign air forces, and the twin-engined, heavily-armed fighter is advocated in some expert circles. The U.S.A. has two classes of fighter, the " pursuit ship " and the attack 'plane for ground " strafing."

'Feeling of Quiet Confidence'

With 'planes and men second to none, and with that extraordinarily efficient defence organization whose heart and head we have glimpsed in the Central Control Room, it is not to be wondered at that the men in charge of the Fighter Command are fully confident of their ability to deal with enemy raiders, whether they come in little parties or in veritable navies of the air. As Sir Hugh Dowding said a short time ago when concluding a broadcast speech : " I should like to leave you with a feeling of quiet confidence in our defence organization." In Service parlance, " Stuffy " is on the job.

followed with uncanny accuracy. And not only followed, for from that same room come the orders which will send some of the raiders crashing to the ground and the remainder driven off and compelled to retire, almost certainly before they have reached their targets.

Fighters Rush to the Sky Battle

Marked on the maps are the sites of the defence stations at which fighter 'planes are stationed ready to go up at any moment. An order from the Central Control Room launches into the air 'planes which, driven by more than 1,000 horse-power, hurtle through space at over 300 miles per hour. Spying the enemy raiders in the distance, they climb to engage them, and their machine-guns pour out a deadly stream of bullets. The guns are sighted by aiming the 'plane itself at the target, and are fired by the pilot pressing a button on the control stick. The stream of bullets meets at a point 500 feet ahead of the 'plane, and then broadens out to form a cone of lead. Thousands of bullets every minute are discharged by the battery of machine-guns—one gun may fire 1,200 bullets per minute—and only one of those bullets may be sufficient to send the enemy 'plane crashing to its doom.

Fighters, the fastest machines in the Air Force, are essentially defensive weapons, although they are sometimes

Here is a close-up of another table where large-scale sectional maps of districts involved come into use. Watched by the key men in the gallery above, arrows indicating the raiders' progress are moved across the map by a croupier's rake. (The photographs in this page are of studio reconstructions).
Photos from " The Lion Has Wings," courtesy of Alex. Korda

The War's First Air Heroes Decorated by the King

On November 2 the King visited a home station of the Royal Air Force and bestowed decorations on four officers and a sergeant of the R.A.F. who had displayed great gallantry in air operations during the war. Those who were honoured are seen above after receiving their decorations. They are, left to right, Flying Officer Andrew McPherson, Acting Flight Lieut. T. M. Wetherall Smith, Acting Squadron Leader K. C. Doran, Acting Flight Lieut. J. Barrett, and Sergeant W. E. Willits.   *Photos, Bippa*

THE King, in the course of a two-day tour of his Air Force, decorated the first five airmen to receive honours during this war in the great hangar of an aerodrome, in which, only a few minutes before, the full activity of the Royal Air Force in wartime had been in progress. Full accounts of the air operations for which three of these awards were given appear in other pages of THE WAR ILLUSTRATED. In page 31 is described the bombing of the Kiel Canal bases, carried out by a flight led by Acting Flt. Lt. Doran (subsequently promoted to Acting Squadron Leader). An eyewitness account is in page 85. In page 156 Captain Schofield, of the "Kensington Court," tells his own story of the rescue of his crew by flying boats commanded by Acting Flt. Lts. Smith and Barrett. Below are official statements of the awards.

FLYING OFFICER ANDREW McPHERSON, D.F.C.

Flying Officer Andrew McPherson carried out reconnaissance flights early in September, and on one occasion was forced by extremely bad weather conditions to fly close to the enemy coast at very low altitudes. These flights made possible a successful raid on enemy naval forces.

FLYING OFFICER (Acting Flight Lieut.) THURSTON MEIGGS WETHERALL SMITH, D.F.C.
FLYING OFFICER (Acting Flight Lieut.) JOHN BARRETT, D.F.C.

Acting Flight Lieut. Smith and Acting Flight Lieut. Barrett were in September, 1939, respectively in command of the first and second of three flying boats of the Coastal Command, Royal Air Force, which were engaged on patrol duty over the Atlantic when they intercepted messages from a torpedoed merchant ship— "Kensington Court." They proceeded to the scene (some 70 miles from the mainland) to undertake rescue work. A lifeboat was seen in the vicinity containing 34 men and the first aircraft alighted and took on board 20 of the crew. A thorough search for enemy submarines was made by the second aircraft which after-

wards alighted and, in spite of the heavy swell, took on board the remainder of the crew from the lifeboat.

FLYING OFFICER (Acting Flight Lieut.) KENNETH CHRISTOPHER DORAN, D.F.C.

Acting Flight Lieut. Doran early in September led an attack against an enemy cruiser. In face of heavy gunfire and under extremely bad weather conditions he pressed home a successful low attack with great determination.

SERGEANT WILLIAM EDWARD WILLITS, D.F.M.

Sergeant William Edward Willits was the second pilot and navigator of an aircraft of the Coastal Command engaged in combat with an enemy flying boat in September, 1939. During the engagement, the pilot was shot through the head and collapsed over the control column, but Sergeant Willits succeeded in obtaining control of the aircraft despite the pilot's inertness and the extremely low altitude. After the body of the pilot had been moved clear of the controls, Sergeant Willits piloted and navigated the aircraft back to the base, a distance of about 140 miles. The airman's skill and presence of mind undoubtedly saved the lives of the other members of the crew and also the aircraft.

The King is here seen decorating Sergeant Willits with the Distinguished Flying Medal.

Threatened With War They Appealed for Peace

Of all the neutral States Holland and Belgium have perhaps most cause for uneasiness
in view of their position on the flank of the Western Front. Small wonder, then, that
on November 7 the Sovereigns of the Low Countries made a fresh effort for peace.

FOLLOWING ever more circumstantial reports of the massing of German 'planes and troops opposite their frontiers, King Leopold of the Belgians and Queen Wilhelmina of Holland on the night of November 7 issued a joint peace appeal to the belligerent Powers. " At this hour of anxiety for the whole world," the telegram began, " before the war breaks out in Western Europe in all its violence, we have the conviction that it is our duty once again to raise our voice." The appeal went on to state that the two sovereigns were ready, by every means that the belligerents cared to suggest and in a spirit of friendly understanding, " to facilitate the ascertaining of the elements of an agreement to be arrived at." It was generally believed that the appeal was the result of the most severe diplomatic pressure, backed by military force, put upon the Low Countries by Germany. King Leopold and Queen Wilhelmina were well known as ardent supporters of the cause of peace, but their efforts might well have been stimulated afresh by the imminent prospect of invasion if the war continued unchecked.

Holland must present a choice morsel to the predatory Nazis. Its capture would provide Germany with air bases some hundreds of miles nearer to the British coast than those of North Germany, and also with some very convenient harbours from which their submarines might operate. So far the scheme cannot but appear most attractive to men who, having launched a war, find it exceedingly difficult to get at

grips with their main foe across the North Sea. Yet there are many drawbacks to the plan which may well make the Nazis hesitate. The aerodromes which they would hope to create on the Dutch plains could be easily attacked by British raiders, and, moreover, an approach by air would be opened up across Holland to the great German industrial district of the Ruhr. It might also be urged that the invaders would also have to face the task of supporting the Dutch population, who, of course, would be cut off from their sources of overseas supply by the British blockade.

This consideration has not, perhaps, much weight, in view of the indifference with which the German conquerors regarded the sufferings of the native population during their occupation of Belgium in the last war. Much more force would be attached to the world-wide reprobation which would be aroused by the forcible seizure of the Netherlands,

One of the national heroes of Belgium in the last war, Burgomaster Max, of Brussels, died on November 6, 1939, when his country was once again menaced by Germany.

The threatening attitude of Hitler towards Holland and Belgium led to the dramatic meeting between Queen Wilhelmina and King Leopold on November 6-7, after which they issued their peace appeal. They are seen here as the King entered his car to return to Brussels.

Photo, Wide World

The Dutch Army has been steadily prepared for all eventualities, and these troops are assembling at Maéstricht. On November 10 leave was stopped and all men on leave were recalled. The wartime establishment of the Dutch Army is about 250,000 men.

Photo, Camera Talks

and in this connexion it should be remembered that the Dutch element in the United States is very strong—President Roosevelt himself is of Dutch descent—and of our own dominions, South Africa is allied to Holland by ties of race, language, culture and old history.

Yet another consideration might be advanced—the support by land and sea, and in the air, which the British might be expected to afford to a country the maintenance of whose integrity has ever been one of the prime objects of our foreign policy. Thus it was highly significant that on the day following the peace appeal, Mr. Hore-Belisha, Secretary for War, told a private gathering of M.P.s that though Britain had sent considerable forces already to France, she still maintained enormous reserves at home.

No doubt the Germans, if they decided to launch an offensive, would hope to overrun Holland before any effectual aid could be rendered by the Allies. The Dutch army has not been engaged in a big Continental war since 1815, but there is every reason to suppose that the spirit of the burghers who routed the legions of Alva burns undimmed in the Hollanders of today. Moreover, those motorized columns which wrought such speedy havoc in Poland could easily be halted in the Dutch lowlands. Early in November, as soon as the situation became threatening, the Dutch raised the level of their dikes, and it was declared that in a few hours a great stretch of country to the east of the vital ports of Amsterdam and Rotterdam could be flooded with the fresh waters stored in the Zuider Zee and the Yssel Lake. " If the Germans hope to beat the waters in speed, they make a great mistake," said a high Dutch official to the special correspondent of the " Daily Telegraph " ; " among all the forces of Nature water is the strongest, and nobody in the world knows it better than the Dutch."

If Holland were attacked, Belgium would not necessarily be involved, for however great the mutual interests of the two countries they are not formally allied. If, however, Germany intended not only to secure favourable bases for the attack on England, but also to deliver a mortal blow at France, then the Nazis might attempt to turn the flank of the Maginot Line by a sudden onslaught through Belgium, thus repeating the strategy of 1914. But the result would be far different. Belgium, as King Leopold said in his speech of October 27, is ten times stronger than she was in 1914. The forts of Liège have been completely modernized, and between Liège and Antwerp now runs the strongly fortified Albert Canal. The Ardennes, too, are honeycombed with forts.

Belgium's neutrality has been guaranteed not only by France and Britain, but by Germany. Always in her people's minds, however, are bitter memories of 1914, and it was with poignant emotion that, on Nov. 10, they paid a last tribute to that heroic figure, Burgomaster Max, whose courage sustained them in the dark days of the German occupation.

This map shows the defences which the Germans would have to face in an invasion of Holland or Belgium. The areas south of the reclaimed Zuider Zee that can be flooded are lightly shaded, but Holland's first line of defence is the rivers Yssel and Maas. Both the Yssel and the Albert Canal afford further flood defences. Belgium is defended on the S.E. by the line of forts from Liège to Dinant, and N. of Brussels by forts on the Albert Canal.
Map, courtesy of the " News Chronicle "

Should the Nazis attempt to invade Holland they must find a terrible obstacle in the flooding of a large area which the Dutch Government is determined to carry out. So far all that has been done is to allow the water of some of the canals to rise, as seen in the photograph, left. Belgium is ready as she was in 1914, and, right, is a gun in a concrete emplacement, part of the defences of a frontier village.
Photos, Sport & General and Central Press

When These Great Guns Begin to Spea

This coastal battery is "somewhere in England." The men who man these batteries have had a long training, and the photograph shows some of them at target practice before the war. The guns, of large calibre, are mounted on revolving platforms and are screened by earthworks, while both guns and mounting are camouflaged. Britain's coastal defence guns are similar to the big guns of the Royal Navy.

n May Well Bid Defiance to Her Foes

There may not be the same danger of raids on the British coast that there was in the last war, when ships of the German High Seas Fleet made "tip-and-run" raids on several East Coast towns. Britain's coastal defences are now much stronger and any enemy ship would have to face powerful shore batteries as well as overwhelming strength in ships. The coast defences are kept fully manned both by day and by night.

WORDS THAT HISTORY WILL REMEMBER

Wednesday, October 25, 1939

LEOPOLD, King of the Belgians in a broadcast to the United States :

In 1937 Belgium proclaimed her policy of independence. Our large neighbours acknowledged this declaration, and even went further by committing themselves to respect Belgian territory.

Belgium is one of the smallest and most densely populated countries in Europe. She is thus dependent on her own activities and on the free extension of her commerce and industry abroad. Belgium has no territorial ambitions.

Neutrality is vital to us. Peace is for the Belgian people a matter of life and death.

If we were to become involved in the fray, it would be on our soil that the issue would be fought out. That would spell utter destruction for Belgium, whatever the issue of the war.

Side by side with Holland, Belgium stands for a pacific island in the interests of all. A strong neutral Belgium constitutes a stronghold of peace and an element of conciliation which can alone save our civilization from the abyss into which a world war would throw it.

We fully know our rights and our duties. We await the future with steadfast serenity and a clear conscience which nothing can perturb. We are prepared to exert our entire strength in order to uphold our independence.

Exactly 25 years ago, day for day, the Belgian army, under the command of my father, King Albert, checked after a hard battle the progress of a cruel invasion.

If we were attacked—and I pray God this may not happen—in violation of the solemn and definite undertakings that were given us in 1937, and were renewed at the outset of the present war, we would not hesitate to fight with the same conviction, but with forces ten times stronger.

Once again a single-minded nation would support its army.

Let me express the hope that the American nation, to whom we seem so closely drawn, will encourage and support the attitude we have adopted for the good of peace in the service of civilization.

COLONEL DENEYS REITZ, South African Minister of Native Affairs, in a broadcast from London :

In the past we fought two bitter wars against the British. I myself served for three years under arms against the British Empire, and I went into exile in a strange land rather than live under the British flag.

But Great Britain, after defeating us in war, treated us with a generosity unknown in history and conferred on us an even greater measure of liberty than we had enjoyed under our own former Republics.

Today, as a voluntary partner in the British Commonwealth, we are not only free, but far safer than we could hope to be if we were on our own with the smash and grab policy which is now trying to dominate the world.

Tuesday, October 31

M. MOLOTOV in an address to the Supreme Soviet Council :

The ruling circles of Britain and France have been lately attempting to depict themselves as champions of the democratic rights of nations against Hitlerism, and the British Government has announced that its aim in the war with Germany is nothing more nor less than the " destruction of Hitlerism."

It amounts to this, that the British, and with them the French supporters of the war, have declared something in the nature of an " ideological " war on Germany reminiscent of the religious wars of olden times.

A Select Record from Week to Week of Important War Declarations and Statements

(Continued from page 306)

In fact the religious wars against heretics and religious dissenters were once the fashion. As we know they led to dire results for the masses, to economic ruin and the cultural deterioration of nations.

But there is absolutely no justification for war of this kind. One may accept or reject the ideology of Hitlerism as well as any other ideological system. That is a matter of political views.

But everybody should understand that ideology cannot be destroyed by force, that it cannot be eliminated by war. It is therefore not only senseless but criminal to wage such a war as a war for the " destruction of Hitlerism," camouflaged as a fight for " democracy " . . . .

The real cause of the Anglo-French war with Germany was not that Britain and France had vowed to restore the old Poland, nor that they had decided to undertake a fight for democracy.

The ruling circles of Britain and France have, of course, other and more actual motives for going to war with Germany. These motives do not lie in any ideology but in their profoundly material interests as mighty Colonial Powers.

The possession of these colonies, which makes possible the exploitation of hundreds of millions of people, is the foundation of the world supremacy of Great Britain and France . . .

It is fear of losing world supremacy that dictates to the ruling circles of Great Britain and France the policy of fomenting war with Germany . . . .

The non-aggression pact concluded between the Soviet Union and Germany bound us to maintain neutrality in the case of Germany participating in war. We have consistently pursued this course, which was in no wise contradicted by the entry of our troops into the territory of the former Poland which began on September 17.

It will be sufficient to recall the fact that on the same day, September 17, the Soviet Government sent a special note to all states with which it maintains diplomatic relations, declaring that the Soviet would continue its policy of neutrality in its relations with them.

It is known that our troops entered the territory of Poland only after the Polish State had collapsed and actually ceased to exist. Naturally we could not remain neutral towards these facts, since as a result of these events we were confronted with urgent problems concerning the security of our State.

Friday, November 3

Hon. T. A. CRERAR, Canadian Minister for Mines and Natural Resources, in a broadcast from London :

We now see a Britain at war, but, as always, a Britain calm and resolute, not to be shaken from a high resolve which has not been lightly taken, and which will be carried through to the end.

May I pay a tribute here to the spirit of this ancient people and to that tribute add the firm conviction that once again, as so often in the story of these islands, this spirit will triumph over the difficulties and dangers of the hour ?

In this war we in Canada are with you, as you are with us, to the end, but we are fighting not merely because of a sentimental impulse to come to the help of the Mother Country.

That feeling, of course, is strong among us, but it could not alone account for the dedication of the strength and spirit of Canada to meet the challenge of this conflict.

Remember that to a great part of Canada the United Kingdom is not a mother country, as approximately half the people of the Dominion are of non-Anglo-Saxon stock.

We are made up of every race—even German-Canadians, who are now loyal to the best that is in Germany and are for that reason joining with other Canadians in the fight against the debasing creed of Nazism.

In this struggle we are as one . . . because we are conscious that we are fighting for our own ideals and for our own existence.

Monday, November 6

Hon. R. G. CASEY, Australian Minister of Supply, in a broadcast from London :

Many foreigners find it hard to understand why a remote self-governing country like Australia goes to war, without any pressure being brought to bear on her, just because your little island, on the other side of the world to us, is at war. The answer is, of course, that we are all of the same British race and we belong, and willingly and gladly belong, to the same British Empire—and that when the King is at war we are all at war.

Although we in Australia are 13,000 miles away, we have seen, as clearly as you, the systematic destruction of three small European countries one after another, and, like you, we realise that if this gangster business is not stopped normal life will become impossible for half the world, including ourselves.

OUR WAR GAZETTEER

Ankara (or Angora). Capital city of Turkey, in heart of Asia Minor ; seat of govt. moved here by Mustafa Kemal in 1923 ; pop. 135,000.

Godesberg, Bad. German health resort on left bank of Rhine, 4 m. S. of Bonn ; scene of second conference between Hitler and Chamberlain, Sept. 24, 1938 ; now German Army H.Q. ; pop. 20,000.

Hague, The (Dutch 's Gravenhage). Capital city of Netherlands, 14 m. N.W. of Rotterdam and 2½ m. from North Sea ; royal palace ; modern buildings include Palace of Peace, built by A. Carnegie for Court of International Arbitration ; first Hague Conference in 1899 ; pop. 486,750.

Hango (Finnish Hankoriemi). Seaport of S. Finland, at entry to Gulf of Finland ; terminus of rly. from Leningrad ; pop. 8,000.

Haugesund. Seaport of Norway ; on W. coast near S. extremity of isl. of Karmö, 60 m. from Bergen ; pop. 17,000.

Murmansk. Seaport of U.S.S.R. within Arctic Circle, at head of Kola Inlet ; developed in 1915 as Arctic terminus of Murman rly. ; occupied by Allies, 1918-19 ; only ice-free port in Russia (except new Baltic bases) ; pop. 117,000.

Petsamo. Seaport of Finland ; that country's only port in Far North ; centre for " midnight sun " excursions.

Tromsö. Seaport of Norway, on an island in far N.W. ; chief port for Spitsbergen ; pop. 10,000.

Venlo. Town of the Netherlands ; on right bank of Maas, immediately adjoining German Rhineland ; railway junction ; pop. 27,000.

Despite the War Paris is Not So Gloomy

Here is an impression of the changes wrought by war in the traditionally gay captial of France. The war is only 200 miles away by direct aeroplane flight, but Paris resolutely refuses to be blacked-out.

ANYONE who visited Paris in the early days of the war would have had some difficulty in believing that this was the city which boasted of being, above all others, the city of light and laughter. In those early days Paris was as dark and gloomy as London—it is difficult to say more.

As the days and weeks passed, however, the blanket of gloom was slowly lifted. So many lamp standards were knocked down in front of the little luxury shops in the Rue de Rivoli that the City Fathers resolved to re-light the extinguished street lamps. There was not, of course, a return to the brilliant illumination of pre-war days ; but the lamps, carefully shaded or provided with blue bulbs, gave sufficient light for reading one's evening paper as one strolled along the boulevards. Traffic was slowed up, but pedestrians did not have to take their lives in their hands every time they crossed the road, nor were hand-torches necessary for feeling one's way along the pavement.

Today Paris displays few ugly piles of sandbags such as litter nearly all the streets of London. Few of the shop-windows are protected by sandbags or boards, though here and there are some crisscrossed with paper : with typical native taste these strips are applied so as to make an artistic design. The public A.R.P. shelters are not so conspicuous by their ugliness as with us, and in many districts they have been rendered almost unnecessary owing to the large cellars with which the big blocks of flats, in which so

many Parisian families live, are provided. Those amusements on which the fame and prosperity of Paris so largely depend were at first severely curtailed ; but ere long something of the old gaiety crept back. In the warm autumn evenings crowds of boulevardiers still sipped their coffee at the little tables beneath the gaily striped awnings, and the cinemas and a handful of the music-halls reopened. Not, however, the expensive stage shows of artistic nudity ; the Bal Tabarin, for instance, was converted into a cut-price restaurant for out-of-work artistes.

So far as the general aspect of the city is concerned the chief difference between August and today is the almost entire

absence of men below middle age. Mobilization in France makes practically a clean sweep of the nation's manhood. Fortunately, however, Frenchwomen are excellent business managers, and in Paris today vast numbers of married women by going out to work manage to keep together those homes which could not possibly be maintained on a French soldier's pay. French women in uniform, however, are hardly ever seen.

In one respect, at least, France is very much better off than Britain : she is practically self-supporting. Up to the present there has been no lack of food-stuffs, and in Paris living is reported to be extraordinarily cheap. So far there

have been no signs of rationing beyond the fact that no meat dishes are served in the restaurants on Mondays and no beef is obtainable on Tuesdays.

Paris had its evacuations, and, like London, its evacuees have been returning in a steady stream. The call of central heating brought many back from the country, but to their deep disgust some found, when they arrived back in their flats, that the landlord was refusing to " keep the home fires burning," on the ground that so many of his tenants had been mobilized—and in France a mobilized man does not have to pay rent.

So the life of the great city goes on. Whether in the gross darkness that followed the declaration of war or in the subdued light in which they move today, the Parisian people—the city clerk and the concierge, the charlady and the charming midinette—all display unbroken their traditional spirit, that combination of valour and vivacity, good taste and good living, which has made them famed for centuries and throughout the world.

Though sandbagging of business premises has not been carried out to the same extent in Paris as it has in London, the public monuments of Paris have been carefully guarded. In the top photograph is a huge heap of sandbags ready to be piled against the Arc de Triomphe. In the lower photograph is a group of midinettes, each carrying her gas mask.

They Have Come Back to Blighty Already

Entertainment for the troops has naturally been extended to the hospitals at home, and the photographs above and below were taken at a hospital "somewhere in England" where soldiers were being entertained. There we see nurses and soldiers joining in community singing, while below is the "front row of the stalls" absorbed in the entertainment.

Photo, L.N.A.

So far all the men killed and wounded in action have been in the Royal Air Force and the Royal Navy, the latter having naturally the greater list of casualties due to the loss of capital ships. It was, however, inevitable that there should be a number of casualties among the men of the British Field Force due to accidents, many of them of the kind that might have overtaken the sufferers in civil life, and there have also been the cases of illness, these again of the kind that might be contracted in ordinary life. Two hospital train-loads of such cases arrived in England early in November, and the arrangements for dealing with them worked perfectly even to the provision of entertainments for the convalescents.

This nursing sister is helping men, who have each an arm in a sling, to a light. Adjoining, patients are at exercise in the hospital grounds. The man on the left has fought before and wears a long row of medal ribbons.

Photos, L.N.A. and Associated Press

Smoothing the Way of the Wounded

The carriage-works of the four great railway companies have been busy building ambulance trains. Above at the L.M.S. works a red cross is being painted on a hospital train. *Photo, Fox*

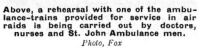

Above, a rehearsal with one of the ambulance-trains provided for service in air raids is being carried out by doctors, nurses and St. John Ambulance men.
Photo, Fox

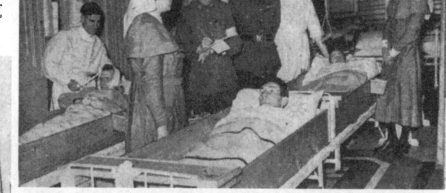

What is practically a hospital ward afloat is here seen. The medical officer is conducting a practice to ensure that when wounded men are brought on board everything shall work without a hitch. Each bunk is occupied by a man with imaginary wounds, and the M.O. is taking down particulars.

So far from being camouflaged, hospital-ships are made as conspicuous as possible. Like that seen centre left in a British port, they are painted white with a broad green or red stripe along the side and fly a Red Cross flag, but even this was not sufficient in the last war to save them from attack by German submarines. Hospital-ships carry a large staff of doctors and nurses and are in every respect floating hospitals. Above are some of the nurses on the bridge of a hospital-ship that has accommodation for 170 patients.
Photos, Planet News and Central Press

Great Guns that Make Our Coasts Secure

Here the gun crew of one of the coastal batteries are seen at their battle stations. In peacetime such heavy guns are seldom fired for practice owing to the heavy cost of the shells, but in wartime, when training has to be intensified, this consideration must be ignored

The muzzle of a big coastal defence gun seen at close quarters is an impressive threat to all enemy raiders.

DURING the last war there was a danger that Germany might attempt to land troops on the East Coast; and though that danger is now almost non-existent, the coastal defences are much stronger and even a solitary raider would have difficulty in getting sufficiently close in shore to do serious damage. Some idea of the strength of these defences is given by the photographs in this page, and those in pages 321 and 336–7. These powerful batteries form a strange contrast to the Martello towers dotted along the south-east coast which formed Britain's coastal defences when Napoleon's threat of invasion was an ever-present menace.

This photograph of a gun of a coastal battery was taken a few seconds before the gun was fired. The gun has been sighted and the artilleryman with his hand upraised is waiting the signal to fire. On the left is a man ready to sponge out the gun when it has been fired. The shells of such guns are too heavy to be handled and on the left is the hoist used to place them in the breech.
Photos. British Official. Crown Copyright

In Wartime ' Q ' is Big Business

We marvel, and rightly, at that wonderful piece of business organization, a big departmental stores. But the work of supplying the wants of even a large section of the civilian buying public is almost child's play compared with that of meeting a great army's every need.

SPIDERS are helping to win the war against the Nazis. In instrument factories in all parts of the country groups of spiders are housed in most comfortable quarters, regularly fed on selected rations and encouraged in their penchant for web-making when the needs of the country require. For their webs, wound on frames as they are spun, are used in the making of lens sights.

It was the Director of Ammunition Production, Ministry of Supply, Eng. Vice-Adml. Sir Harold Brown, who called attention to the patriotic labours of British spiders, and the story may be taken as an indication of the extraordinary ramifications of the supply system of the modern British Army.

as April 1939, with Mr. Leslie Burgin as its head ; but in the first month of war it distributed orders to the value of more than £110,000,000 sterling, and over 10,000 civilian firms are on its books as direct contractors. The number of firms indirectly engaged in war work for the Ministry is beyond computation.

Wherever the soldier may be, whether he is wearing out his boots on the parade ground at the depot or firing off ammunition on the ranges, whether he is on the march to the port of embarkation or is in tents, hutments or billets beyond the Channel ; whether his arm bears not even a solitary stripe or whether there are red tabs to his tunic—he is never out of the charge of the vast " Q " organization.

The task of organizing the transport of the British Field Force to France fell upon Lieut.-General Sir W. G. Lindsell. With such accuracy was it planned that there was not a single casualty.
Photo, Vandyk

With an army of nearly 200,000 men in France, some 90,000 tons of supplies of all sorts have to be provided and transported every month. From the factories under the Ministry of Supply's control the goods are sent by road or rail to the collecting depot, or perhaps direct to the port of embarkation. Conveyed across the Channel, they are sorted at huge base camps which may have an area of, say, 15 square miles, and then dispatched by special trains to the different railheads, whence they are collected by the transport of the corps or divisions and then distributed direct to the troops ; or they may be stored in reserve depots spaced out on the lines of communication.

Without a doubt the British soldier at the front is better fed, better clothed and generally better looked after than any other soldier in the world—now or in the past. He has three good meals a day—sometimes four ; he gets fresh meat and newly-baked bread, his diet is varied ; he is to have two blankets, whereas the *poilu* shares one with a comrade.

Since the Field Force took up its positions 46 days' reserve of food and 38 days' reserve of everything else have been built up in France—of everything except ammunition. Of that the stores are very much larger ; the Q.M.G. knows just how large, but he won't tell. . . .

The task of feeding the Army rests with the Quartermaster-General, Lieut.-General Sir Walter Venning. He is here seen at the War Office with Lieut.-General D. S. Collins, Controller of Engineer Services, and Major-General T. S. Riddell-Webster, Deputy Quartermaster-General.
Photo, Topical.

An army, whether it be at home or in the field, is in need of a thousand and one things, ranging from boots to big guns, from tinned milk to petrol, from bully-beef to flea-powder. So far as the soldiers are concerned, these supplies come through the Royal Army Service Corps and the Royal Army Ordnance Corps, the former being responsible for food and transport and the latter for most of the other paraphernalia of modern war.

At the head of the Army " Q " department is H.M. Quartermaster-General, Lieut.-Gen. Sir Walter Venning, whose job it is to see that the British Army, whether at home or in the field, gets all the supplies it needs. The Q.M.G. in France is Lieut.-Gen. Lindsell. At home is a vast organization of civilian firms whose activities are called into being and directed by the Ministry of Supply. This Ministry was established only so recently

The transport of food and other stores from the railheads in France to the forward positions necessitates the use of many hundreds of motor lorries. Here a convoy is drawn up in a French town ready to set off. The French roads have withstood the strain well.
Photo, British Official, Crown Copyright

'IN THE END WE SHALL BREAK THEIR HEARTS'

In his second statement to the House of Commons on the work of the Royal Navy made
on November 8, Mr. Winston Churchill, First Lord of the Admiralty, described the loss of
the "Royal Oak" and made an encouraging survey of the U-boat campaign.

"IT is now established that the Royal
Oak was sunk in the early hours of
October 14 by a German U-boat,
which penetrated the defences of the
land-locked anchorage of Scapa Flow."
This was the dramatic opening of Mr.
Churchill's masterly survey. Then he
proceeded :

These defences were of two kinds. First,
the physical obstructions by nets, booms and
block ships, and, secondly, by small patrolling
craft upon the approaches to the various en-
trances or sounds, which are seven in number.

Neither the physical obstructions nor the
patrolling craft were in that state of strength
and efficiency required to make the anchorage
absolutely proof as it should have been. It
was not proof against the attack of a U-boat on
the surface or half-submerged at high water.

Measures had been taken and were being taken
to improve the physical obstructions, and the
last block ship required reached Scapa Flow only
on the day after the disaster had occurred.

All the more was it necessary while these
defences were incomplete that the patrolling
craft should have been particularly numerous,
but from a variety of causes connected with
the movements of the Fleet, which was not at
that time using the anchorage, these patrolling
craft were reduced below what was required.

I am unable to enter into details, because
a full explanation—and no explanation is
worth giving unless it is full—would reveal

to the enemy matters which would throw a
light upon our methods of defence. . . .

I must content myself by saying that the
long and famed immunity which Scapa Flow,
with its currents and defences, had gained in
the last war had led to a too-easy valuation of
the dangers which were present.

An undue degree of risk was accepted both
at the Admiralty and in the Fleet. At the
same time I must point out that many risks are
being accepted inevitably by the Fleet and by
the Admiralty as part of the regular routine of
keeping the seas, and these risks which were
inadvisedly run at Scapa Flow seemed to highly
competent persons to be no greater than many
others. . . .

Paying the Forfeit

THUS the forfeit has been claimed, and we
mourn the loss of eight hundred gallant
officers and men, and of a ship which, although
very old, was of undoubted military value.

The inquiries which have been completed
have brought out all the knowable facts to our
attention.

The Admiralty, upon whom the broad
responsibility rests, are resolved to learn this
bitter lesson, namely, that in this new war,
with its many novel complications, nothing
must be taken for granted ; and that every
joint in our harness must be tested and strengthened so far as our resources and ingenuity
allow. . . .

**During this opening phase of the war the
Royal Navy has suffered a greater loss of life
than all the other forces, French and British,
on sea, on land and in the air combined.**

Every loss inflicted on us by the enemy has
been at once announced.

In addition, since the outbreak of war, one
of our submarines, H.M.S. "Oxley," has been
destroyed by an accidental explosion in circumstances which made its publication inadvisable
at the time. These are the only three losses
we have had of H.M. ships of war, but they are,
of course, serious losses.

What I told the House under much reserve
six weeks ago, I can now repeat with more
assurance—**namely that we are gaining a
definite mastery over the U-boat attack. . . .**

During the first eight weeks of war our
net loss of tonnage has been less than one-third
of one per cent. This takes no account of the
important chartering operations from neutrals
which are now in progress.

It is interesting to note that one of the most
valuable of recent prizes was captured from the
enemy by the 'Ark Royal,' which the German
wireless has sunk so many times.

When I recall the absurd claims that they
have shouted round the world I cannot resist
saying, **we should be quite content to engage
the entire German navy, using only the vessels
which at one time and another they have declared
they have destroyed.**

A not less favourable balance is presented
when we turn from the tonnage of ships to that
of cargo. More than 10,000,000 tons of cargo
were brought into this country in British and
neutral ships in the first eight weeks of the war ;
less than 250,000 tons have been lost.

But over 400,000 tons of cargo consigned
to Germany have been captured. Even taking
into account 50,000 tons of exports which were
lost, there remains a balance of over 100,000
tons in our favour. . . .

When we contemplate the difficulty of
carrying on in full activity our vast processes of
commerce, and the need of being prepared at
100 points and on 1,000 occasions in the teeth
of the kind of severe attack to which we are
being subjected, I feel that credit is due to the
many thousands of persons who in every quarter
of the globe are contributing to the achievement,
and especially to the central machinery and
direction which is in fact holding the seas free
as they have never been at any time in any
war in which we have been engaged.

Confidence in the U-Boat War

NOW I turn to the offensive against the
U-boats. It is very difficult to give
assured figures, because many a marauder who
is sunk in deep water leaves no trace behind.
There must be a doubt and a dispute about
every case in which we have not a survivor,
or a corpse, or a wreck to show.

**But I think it would be a fairly sound con-
servative estimate that the losses of U-boats lie
between two and four in every week according to
the activity that prevails.**

Of course, when many are out there are more
losses to commerce and more U-boats are killed.

But the other side must also be considered.
I have not hitherto mentioned to the House the
German building. We must assume that
perhaps two new U-boats are added every
week to the hostile strength, and in ten weeks
of war this would be twenty.

At any rate, our expectation is that we
must face a hundred U-boats available in
January, less whatever sinkings have occurred
in the interval. It will be seen, therefore, that,
although we are making headway, a long and
unrelenting struggle lies before us.

For this our preparations are moving forward
on the largest scale. Three times as many
hunting craft are now at work as at the outbreak
of the war, and very large reinforcements of
vessels, specially adapted to this task, will
flow in increasingly from the spring of 1940
onwards. Therefore it would seem that,
judged upon the material basis alone, we may
face the future with confidence.

But it is not only the material basis which
will decide this struggle. Training the crews
and especially providing the skilled officers will
be the hardest part of the enemy's task.

Moreover, a conflict from which perhaps
one in four of each excursion never returns,
and the others with grievous experience, is one
which must have in it many deterrent factors.
We are exposed to a form of attack justly
considered abominable, but we are making
successful head against it.

I must warn the House again that continual

The close contact between Great Britain and France in all naval and military matters was
emphasized by the visit of Mr. Winston Churchill to Paris which ended on November 5 after
he had discussed the problems confronting the British and French Navies. He is here seen
at the Ministry of Marine, Paris, with General Gamelin and Admiral Darlan, Commander-
in-Chief of the French Navy.
Photo, The Times

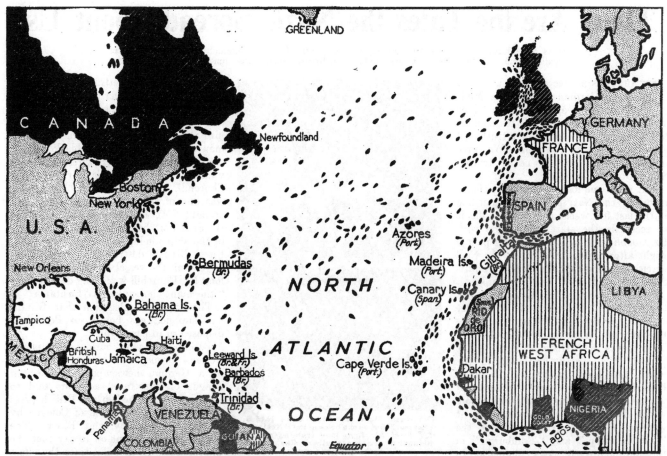

The chief danger to British shipping from U-boats lies in the North Atlantic. When war broke out there were 18,500,000 tons of British shipping at sea, and Britain, in the first eight weeks, had a net loss of less than one-third of 1 per cent. This map, based on an Admiralty Chart, shows the approximate position and number of British merchant ships at sea in the North Atlantic on an average day before the outbreak of war, and demonstrates clearly the enormous target available to the U-boats. About 2,500 vessels are now constantly at sea in wartime.

Courtesy of the " News Chronicle "

losses must be expected. No immunity can be guaranteed at any time.

There will not be in this war any period where the seas will be completely safe; but neither will there be, I believe, any period when the full necessary traffic of the Allies cannot be carried on.

We shall suffer and we shall suffer continually, but by perseverance, and by taking measures on the largest scale, I feel no doubt that in the end we shall break their hearts.

In addition to the U-boat menace, we have to face the attack of the surface raider. It is certain that one, and possibly two, of the so-called pocket battleships has been out upon the Atlantic trade routes during the last six weeks. . . .

The Sea Attack is Controlled

BUT what is remarkable is that, although these powerful vessels have been lying athwart the stream of convoys and individual vessels crossing the Atlantic, they have not been able, or have not dared, so far—and I speak under the greatest reserve—to make any captures worth considering. Only two ships, aggregating 10,000 tons, have been sunk so far by surface action, compared to 212,000 by the U-boats. . . .

On the other hand, let me again strike the note of warning, because the element of risk is never absent from us or indeed from the enemy. Thus, up to the present not only has the U-boat campaign been controlled, but also the attack by surface raiders both by warships and by armed merchantmen has not developed in any serious way.

At this point I must speak of the remarkable contribution of the French Navy, which has not for many generations been so powerful or so efficient. Under the long care of Admiral Darlan and the Minister of Marine, M. Campinchi, a magnificent fighting and seafaring force has been created.

Not only have we been assisted in every way agreed upon before the war, but besides a

whole set of burdens have been lifted off our shoulders by the loyal and ever-increasingly vigorous co-operation of the French Fleet. It seems to me a wonderful thing that when France is making so great an effort upon land she should at the same time offer to the Allied cause so powerful a reinforcement upon the seas.

The House must not underrate the extreme exertions that are required from our sailors and our officers, both in the Royal Navy and in the merchant service, in carrying forward almost uninterruptedly the whole world-wide business of British and Allied commerce.

Happily the reinforcements which are coming to the fleets and to the flotillas will give an easement which is greatly needed both by men and machinery. We must indeed pay our tribute both to the composure and coolness with which risks are taken and warded off in the great ships and to the hitherto unexhausted energies of the flotilla service.

At the Admiralty we are now in a position to consider some mitigation of these severe conditions; and without indulging in any over-confident opinion, I feel,

after the ninth week of the war, that so far as the sea is concerned—and the sea has often proved decisive in the end—we may cherish good hopes that all will be well.

CREDITS	DEBITS
Nine Weeks, Sept. 3rd-Nov. 4th	*Nine Weeks, Sept. 3rd-Nov. 4th*
U-BOATS sunk	MERCHANTMEN sunk
16	
6 damaged, believed sunk.	British Tons 238,793 56 Ships
GOODS captured	French Tons 47,933 6 Ships
	Neutral Tons 93,820 32 Ships
Tons 500,000	
Each symbol = 10,000 tons, except U-Boats	

This statistical chart, based on official figures, shows the results of British operations at sea up to November 4. "Goods captured" represent the work of the Contraband Control and captures by the Royal Navy.

These Are the Tales the Nazis Spread About Us

It is a difficult task to keep abreast of the flood of Nazi mendacity, but this chapter recalls some of the most extraordinary Anti-British allegations made by their wireless.

"THERE is no necessity for us," said the German Propaganda Minister in a speech to the Hitler Youth on November 5, "to counter lies with lies. We know that truth will always come out on top. We give nothing, then, but the naked truth." So Dr. Joseph Goebbels.

But when one looks through the claims made by the Nazi propaganda machine in the last few weeks it is rather difficult to reconcile the statements made with Dr. Goebbels' lofty declaration of policy. Night after night, for instance, the Nazi wireless claimed that the British aircraft-carrier "Ark Royal" had been sunk.

"Where is the 'Ark Royal'?" was the refrain; "Mr. Churchill had better send a diver down to find out." A little later it was "Where is the 'Repulse'?" Then it was the "Hood's" turn. "The 'Hood,' the largest battleship in the world, has been hit by two 250 kilo. bombs dropped by German 'planes and will be six or eight months in dock before it can be repaired." Heavy damage, it was said, had been inflicted on the "Southampton" and "Edinburgh" in the raid on Rosyth. As a culmination to these claims concerning individual ships came the boast that: "The losses which the British Home Fleet has sustained are so enormous that all British ships have disappeared from the North Sea."

The Nazis claim to have sunk H.M.S. "Kestrel," but as can be seen the "Kestrel" is a Fleet Air Arm land training station named, as are several others, like a ship!
Photo, Sport and General

In vain did the British Admiralty declare that the "Ark Royal," the "Hood," the "Repulse," "Southampton," and the rest had suffered not the slightest damage.

Despite every denial, the stream of fantastic claims was maintained. Perhaps the most curious was the broadcast claim that H. M. S. "Kestrel" was sunk. Kestrel is, in fact, the name given to a Fleet Air Arm land training establishment in Hampshire.

German propaganda concerning life in wartime Britain revealed a similar detachment from the truth. Thus the German wireless station told the Poles that "London is already practically starving on the tenth day of the war. Rich women who are still able to purchase what food there is are robbed of their parcels by the poor. There has not been a drop of milk in the capital for the last three days, and women are standing in queues to obtain their household

supplies which are getting scantier every day." The announcer went on to say that all the big British banks had removed their safes with money and valuables into the country—as there had been so many robberies during the blackouts!

According to the Nazi wireless the real villain of the piece is Mr. Winston Churchill. The sinking of the "Athenia" was one of the first charges laid to his account. At first it was alleged that the First Lord had arranged for explosions in the ship's hold, but in a later version, three British destroyers were said to have sunk the vessel by gunfire. Before long Mr. Churchill was being described as "the man who sank the 'Lusitania'"!

The atrocious allegation that Britain had supplied gas bombs to Poland is disposed of in page 276.

Perhaps the most curious example of German propaganda was a description in a German newspaper published in Prague of illustrated accounts said to have been published in the British press of the partial destruction of Cologne by bombs dropped by the R.A.F. The Nazi newspaper went on to say that the photographs did not illustrate the effect of British bombs, but showed demolitions undertaken in the course of rebuilding schemes. As no account of the alleged bombardment and no photographs of the "destruction" had ever been published in the British press, and indeed no claims had been made concerning the bombing of any German town by British 'planes, we have the Nazis attributing a boast to Britain of having done something which she has never claimed to do, in order that they might have the pleasure of denouncing it as a fabrication!

One important aim before the German propagandists is to stir up the neutrals against Britain. The iniquity of the Allied system of contraband control has been bitterly described by Nazi writers. Thus on the morning when their papers carried the announcement of big increases in taxes, Danish citizens all over the country received a Nazi leaflet showing on one side a picture of a folded umbrella, and on the other the umbrella without its cover, revealing a dagger. Printed in Danish, the leaflet bore the statement: "If your cars remain in garages, if you have no petrol, if you are cold and have no coat, if you queue up for rations, you have only Britain to thank. This umbrella is supposed to be used against rain, but it is really a weapon of war."

Then the most determined efforts have been made by the Nazis to drive in a wedge between France and Britain. French troops on the Western Front have been entertained with broadcast exhortations to refuse to fight for the British.

This remarkable map was published by the Munich "Neuester Nachrichten" to show the Nazi mastery of the North Sea. For propaganda purposes the sinking of the "Courageous" has been transferred to the North Sea. The key to map is: black star, British war harbours; white cross, torpedoes; white star, bombarded British ships.

Our Ships Fought Back at the U-Boats

On many occasions when attacked by U-boats, merchant vessels fought back—sometimes with surprising success. Three such encounters, described by members of the merchant crews, are here printed by courtesy of the "Sunday Times" and "Daily Telegraph."

THE following story was told by Antonio Cutajar, a Maltese seaman on a British armed merchant ship, when he arrived at an English port.

"We had left Bristol bound for South America," Mr. Cutajar said, "and were only a few days out when, at seven o'clock in the morning, we saw the submarine come up. It signalled us to stop.

"At once the captain ordered the gun to be brought into action and our reply was a shot which landed so close that the U-boat immediately dived.

"A few minutes later, however, it came up again, this time a bit farther away, and in its turn opened fire.

"We returned it, and our gun was handled so efficiently by the gunner—a naval man—and a fireman who acted as his assistant—an ex-naval man—that the U-boat had to keep at a greater distance than it would have wished.

"But there were times when it was still near enough for us to see clearly the members of its crew manning the gun against us. There was a repeated gun duel at intervals for more than seven hours. The U-boat fired at us and we fired back.

"The submarine got home only one shot amongst us, when one of our lifeboats was smashed by a shell. The only casualty was a member of the crew who was struck on the head by a splinter, but his injury was not serious.

"All the time our captain was keeping the ship on its journey, but he was handling it so skilfully that the submarine could not get into position to sink us or even to damage us.

"All the time we were sending out S O S signals while the fight went on."

Mr. Cutajar said that during one of the final duels the ship's gunner was able to hole the submarine above the waterline.

"This, of course, meant," he added, "that the U-boat could not submerge again, as it had done so often during the time that it had been fighting and following us. Then, at about half-past two in the afternoon, two warships appeared on the horizon in answer to our signals, and we knew that the U-boat was done for.

"The submarine crew tried to put up something of a fight against the warships by directing its gunfire, but it was

hopeless, and soon it was sent to the bottom. The crew was saved by the warships.

"We were certainly pleased that we had been able to put up such a fight against the U-boat, and that we had damaged it so badly that it could not escape the warships."

ON reaching a home port the crew of a British cargo ship reported that they had sunk a U-boat which attacked them after a two-hour engagement in which shell was exchanged for shell.

"The U-boat surfaced almost under our starboard bow," one of the officers said, "the conning-tower opened and men on watch could see distinctly a number of figures running to man the guns.

"They fired eight shells which whistled harmlessly through the rigging.

"Then, with our gun trained on the U-boat we let go. I can't remember the actual details of the battle, but it raged fast and thick."

Another member of the crew said: "When the U-boat fired her first shot we were ready waiting. The word was given and our gun answered every fusillade.

"The shells burst so close to the U-boat that great water spouts cascaded over her deck.

"Suddenly the men on her deck made a scramble for the conning-tower and tumbled inside, the hatch snapped down, and the submarine dived.

"For the time being we had scared the Germans, though we knew we had not sunk them. Close watch was kept on the surrounding sea. We knew the U-boat would strike again.

"She broke surface about three miles away. We were going full speed ahead. She resumed the contest and for every shell she fired we fired one back.

"Our shells were falling thick around her and after a running fight lasting an hour and a half a sheet of white foamy water spread wide around the submarine and she vanished."

THE twenty-five officers and men of the freighter "Sea Venture," 2,327 tons, of Dover, which was sunk in the North Sea after a running fight with a German submarine, arrived at a Scottish port on September 26.

When the "Sea Venture" was attacked her crew pluckily returned fire with their only gun, and for fully half an hour a dogged battle ensued.

Mr. Winston Churchill, in his November 8 speech in the House of Commons on the position of the war at sea, said that some of the delays that had been caused in the shipping of foodstuffs were due to the fact that during the past two months several hundreds of our largest ships had been withdrawn in order to give them defensive arms against submarines. Here we see one of the guns being hoisted on to a liner.
Photo, Topical

Between forty and fifty shells were fired by the submarine before the defenders, their vessel having been hit at least five times, gave up the unequal struggle and took to their only seaworthy boat.

One of the shells went straight through the "Sea Venture's" galley at the time the cook, Mr. L. Pollard, of Sunderland, was cutting up pieces of bread, and he had a lucky escape.

"The submarine set up a regular bombardment," he said. "I heard the whistle of a shell and ran through the door just in time, for the shell landed plumb inside. It blew everything in the galley to bits."

A warning shell screaming across her bows told of the submarine's presence.

"We fired back," another member of the crew said, "and at least five of the submarine's shells struck our ship.

"It was exciting enough while it lasted. Shells seemed to be flying all around us. We put on all steam and put up as good a show as we could, but we had to give up. Our gun could not make the submarine's range.

"When we took to our small boat the submarine torpedoed our ship. For twenty hours we were in the boat. At last we reached an island in the North of Scotland.

"After the scrap the submarine made off," another seaman said. "It had sighted a British seaplane. The pilot brought the 'plane down on the water. He told us he had wirelessed for a lifeboat to come to our assistance."

Captain Joseph H. Gainard, Master of the United States steamer "City of Flint," who tells his story in this page, is seen above.
Photo, Associated Press

I Commanded the Captured 'City of Flint'

Great interest was taken all over the world in the adventures of the American freighter " City of Flint," which was captured by the German pocket battleship " Deutschland " and later released by the Norwegian authorities. The master of the steamer, Captain Gainard, broadcast his story from Bergen to the United States on November 6.

"WHEN we sailed from New York on October 3," said Captain Gainard, " all precautions were taken to ensure the neutrality of the 'City of Flint.' We had one British passenger— the radio operator. But he had been replaced by an American operator.

"On October 9 we were halted by flag signals from the 'Deutschland.' She fired a warning shot. We thought at first that she was French, not German.

"Three officers and 14 men came alongside in a boat. ' We don't want your ship. We want to see the manifest,' they told us. When they found the ' City of Flint' could carry passengers they put 39 members of the 'Stonegate's' crew aboard. [The " Stonegate " a British ship, was sunk by the " Deutschland."]

"Eighteen of a prize crew came on board with 60 hand grenades, 12 rifles with bayonets, 20 pistols and one machinegun. They were not used and finally turned over to the Norwegians at Haugesund. "Lieutenant Hans Pussbach, as captain of the prize crew, addressed the crew in good English. ' We are proceeding as a prize to Germany. You obey your own captain. My soldiers will obey me. Attend to the safety of the ship.

" ' If you interfere I'll put you in the boats and sink the ship.'

"He then told the members of the ' Stonegate's ' crew that the Americans would take care of them and that they were to obey me.

"We proceeded by various courses until October 18. The Germans painted out all the American insignia and painted in the name ' Alf.' The Danish flag was painted on canvas, but was never flown.

"On October 22 the German flag was hoisted and we entered Tromsoe. We

moored under the directions of a Norwegian pilot and I was left in charge overnight. The ' Stonegate's ' crew were set ashore. We then sailed for Murmansk, where the German flag was again hoisted," continued Captain Gainard. "I tried for six days to get in touch with our Ambassador, but never succeeded.

"Eventually we were told that the ship was a German prize, and we must leave at once. The condition of my crew was good. We proceeded and took on fresh water at Tromsoe.

"We were stopped outside Trondhjem by two Norwegian destroyers, one of which was later replaced by the minesweeper ' Olav Tryggvas;on.'

"Lieutenant Pussbach got orders from the ' Schwaben,' which met us outside Bergen. The orders were shouted over the side, as soon as the two ships were near enough for him to answer, to anchor at Haugesund.

"Then the Norwegian officers came on board and took off the German prize crew. They returned the ship to me."

I Saw Hitler's Rout at Munich

November 8 is celebrated by the Nazi Party as the anniversary of their first " putsch " in Munich in 1923. The following dramatic story, told by Elizabeth Castonier, who witnessed the rout of Hitler and his followers, is reproduced from the " Evening Standard."

NOBODY in Munich took much notice of a man called Adolf Hitler in 1923. I used to see him marching through the streets followed by a straggling band of youngsters. These boys and a few disgruntled men were the only people who would listen to his harangues, chiefly against the Jews. . . .

Friends of mine in Munich had a son who joined the Hitler party. It was called the Nazionalsozialistische Deutsche Arbeiterpartei. He was sixteen, and had a party card of which he was very proud. He was a nice boy, not very strong, but filled with idealism. . . .

I remember one day, early in November, 1923, he came home and told his mother that he needed a new pair of shoes. Very strong shoes, he said. Also he would need some hard-boiled eggs, a loaf of bread and a great sausage.

"Are you going away for the weekend, ski-ing?" asked his mother.

The boy answered seriously : " No, not this time. We are marching to Berlin, to upset the Government and to kill the Jews!"

"Silly boy——" his mother replied. But she promised him all he asked, for she thought he was going on some boyish excursion with the other youngsters of the Hitler party. . . .

A day or two later, it was November 8, we were returning home about ten o'clock in the evening. The most important street of Munich, Ludwigstrasse, was empty. But from the distance we could hear singing and the tramp of marching feet. And suddenly, from a side street, there emerged a group of young men with flags, rucksacks, sticks and carrying old-fashioned rifles.

They marched right up to the Ministry of War . . . . The door opened. A very old man, the porter, put his head out.

Yelling and shouting, the boys poured

The Whole World Watched the Odyssey of this Ship

The " City of Flint " is seen above as she lay in Bergen harbour while her fate was being determined by the Norwegian Government. Here her cargo was eventually unloaded, prior to her
re-sailing. Right is the harbour of Bergen seen from the top of Floien Mountain, 1,050 feet.

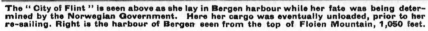

After she had been freed by the Norwegian Government at Haugesund the " City of Flint " was
conducted by the Norwegian minelayer " Olav Tryggvasson " (seen left and right) to Bergen.
The stern view, right, shows the traps through which the mines are dropped. Right, the route
of the " City of Flint."

Photo, R. W. Davidson, Map courtesy of the "Daily Telegraph"

The remarkable story of the capture of
the American ship " City of Flint "
is told by her captain in the opposite page.
The Norwegian Government issued the
following explanation of its action in
releasing the ship and interning the
Nazi prize crew.

A Royal decree of May 13th, 1938, established
that a captured ship of foreign nationality
could not be taken to a Norwegian port except
for reasons of unseaworthiness, bad weather,
or lack of fuel. Any ship so seeking shelter
must leave Norwegian waters again as soon as
the reason for its seeking shelter had been
removed. This decree was violated by the
German prize crew on the " City of Flint," and
the Norwegian authorities therefore intervened.

This is the port of Haugesund, into which the German prize crew brought the " City of Flint,"
although the Norwegian authorities had forbidden the ship to anchor. She was consequently freed.

350   *The War Illustrated*   *November 25th, 1939*

IIIIIIIIIIIIIIIIIIIIIIIIIIIIIIIIIIIIIIIIIIIIIIIIIIIIIIIIIIIIIIIIIIIIIIIII **I WAS THERE!** IIIIIIIIIIIIIIIIIIIIIIIIIIIIIIIIIIIIIIIIIIIIIIIIIIIIIIIIIIIIIIIIIIIIIIIII

in. While we watched, some of them were posted in the entrance, others, dragging an old rusty machine-gun, barred our side of the road ; but most of them surrounded the building and stood motionless, sticks or guns across their shoulders. We tried to find out what was happening.

"The party has overthrown the Bavarian Government," one of the older ones told us. "Adolf Hitler has ordered us to take over the Ministry and to guard it against enemies."

We shrugged our shoulders and went home. Nobody in Munich could believe that all this was serious. . . .

At mid-day Hitler and his followers marched bravely through Munich. There were youngsters, young men and older men, carrying banners, sticks and rifles.

In the forefront marched General Ludendorff. Next came Hitler, Goering, Hess, all shouting commands. It was supposed to be The March on Berlin.

But they had forgotten the German army. As Ludendorff approached the Feldherrnhalle, he saw the troops drawn up. Machine-guns and a tank.

"Halt !" came the command to the Nazis. "Halt, or we fire !" The mob marched on. The soldiers and the armed police fired. The procession fell flat on the ground, some of them dead.

A few minutes later three figures got up and fled, leaving their followers to themselves ; they were Hitler, Goering and Hess. Only Ludendorff marched on.

There was panic. We saw those bewildered children, some only 15 years old, rush the steps of the Feldherrnhalle ; some tried to break through the line of

Each year since he has established himself in power, Hitler has held a meeting at the beer house in Munich where the unsuccessful rising of 1923 was planned by the Nazis. He is here seen (centre) among old party comrades at the meeting in 1938. On the right is Rudolf Hess whom Hitler has nominated as next in succession to him after Goering.
Photo, Topical

death-spitting machine-guns and were killed ; some tried to get into the Palace, but found the gates closed in their faces.

In a few minutes the soldiers had cleared the whole place. Only the dead were left. . . .

It was not yet all over. There were still those left in the " conquered " War Office. Half a dozen of them, from 16 to 20 years old, and half dead with fatigue, were still holding out on their posts. They did not know their leader had quit. . . .

From a side street a tank appeared. An elderly officer with many medals climbed out and walked towards the boys, ignoring the old machine-gun they had posted in front of the building.

"Gentlemen," he said, "it is no use trying to resist. An old machine-gun— let me see—O, my God, the oldest model —can't fight against a tank. You are very brave men. Come along. Your leader has fled, has run away. The whole joke is over. Resistance useless. Go home to your parents."

The man who spoke was General von Epp. Years later he was to be Governor of Bavaria under Hitler.

My friend's son got home in the late afternoon. He did not say where he had been. Never again did he mention this " March on Berlin." He was disgusted that the man who had promised them honour had run away.

We Found a German 'Plane on the Hill

When a German reconnaissance 'plane was brought down in the Lammermoor Hills on October 28, Mr. John K. Irvine of Long Newton Farm was on the spot within a few minutes. His graphic account of the incident was broadcast by the B.B.C.

"I AM the grieve at Longnewton farm, close beside the Lammerlaw Hill.

"I was filling up sacks of barley about a quarter past ten when I heard a noise like the hurling of a barrow. That's what I thought it was at first, but it went on and on and came nearer, and then I knew it was the noise of guns. Then we saw a big black machine with two engines coming over the trees from the north-west. There were four British machines with it. They were circling all round and rattling bullets into the German as hard as they could do it.

"I thought we ought to take cover — there were women workers there. But curiosity brought us out again—whiles we were running in and whiles we were running out—so that we saw the German go over the houses, so low that it almost touched the chimneys. Then they all went out of sight up over the hill, and a few minutes later I saw our fighters going back—all four of them. They seemed to

be finished with their job. So we ran up the hill to see what had happened.

"Two of the crew were dead. I expect they would be the gunners, and they must have been shot before they came my length because I never saw them firing at our 'planes. The machine had scraped its tail over a dyke and come down on the moor on an even keel. One of the crew wasn't hurt at all. He was pulling out his mate. By the time we got up he had him drawn out and lying on the ground.

"We tried to talk to the unwounded man, but he didn't know what we were saying. But he spoke a little English. The wounded man wanted a drink, but the doctor said he ought not to have one. He had two bullet-wounds in the back.

"The police took the unwounded man away. Before he went he shook hands with his mate. We got a gate off one of the fences and carried the wounded man down to the road, and waited there till the ambulance came for him."

After the failure of his first revolution at Munich in 1923, Hitler was imprisoned. Here he is seen leaving the Landsberg fortress on his release in December 1924.
Photo, Planet News

Who Was the Guy Fawkes in the Munich Cellar?

Several attempts are believed to have been made on Herr Hitler's life, but none more
publicized and mysterious than the bomb explosion in the famous beer cellar at
Munich on November 8, 1939.

"A MAN must have luck," Herr Hitler is reported to have said when he was told of the bomb explosion in the hall at Munich. Lucky, indeed, was the Fuehrer, for his escape was entirely due to the fact that he left the hall a little earlier than had been expected. As it was, only fifteen minutes after Hitler and many of his most prominent supporters had gone to the station, an "infernal machine" exploded in the ceiling, and in the resulting crash the platform on which the Fuehrer had just been standing was buried beneath ten feet of débris. Nine people were killed, including two long-standing members of the S.S., and more than sixty injured.

The meeting was held in the famous beer hall in Munich—the Buergerbrau—from which Hitler marched on the occasion of his *putsch* in 1923, and all the thousand persons present were carefully hand-picked members of the Nazi "Old Guard"—each one of them must have carried a party membership card with a number below 10,000—assembled on the occasion of their annual reunion to celebrate the march that initiated their movement.

Following the explosion there was a scene of great confusion. The Black Guards flung a cordon round the place, and in order to facilitate the work of rescue the lights were turned on in the immediate neighbourhood. This sudden raising of the black-out gave rise to the spread of rumours that the war had ended, and in the beer halls and in the streets excited crowds started noisy peace celebrations until they were silenced by the angry police and Black Guards.

Jews and the British Again!

For several hours no official comment on the outrage was available. Then every German commentator brazenly declared that the attempt on the Fuehrer's life was the work of British Secret Service agents; and in a short time, too, the Jews were being bracketed in the accusation. Outside official circles, however, there were doubts. How was it that a bomb could be placed in position in a building which had been most thoroughly searched by the Nazi Black Guards just before the meeting? And what a strange thing it was that Hitler, on this one occasion, should not only have delivered a speech which had not been previously advertised, but, most extraordinary of happenings, had put a stop to his eloquence earlier than was expected!

Soon rumours got around that the attempt had been made by men of the Nazi Party—sympathizers with that Captain Roehm and his followers who had

been slaughtered in the "blood purge" of 1934 because they advocated a radical policy very much on the same lines as that now favoured by Herr Hitler himself. Some spoke knowingly of the Reichstag fire which occurred, or was made to occur, so opportunely on the eve of the 1933 vital election. Might it not be possible that the bomb in the Buergerbrau cellar had been similarly conveniently timed to go off when the German people needed some evidence of British devilish malignity in order to develop a really first-class war-fever?

The anti-Nazi movement in Germany, however, claimed that a real attempt had been made on the Fuehrer's life. "In Munich," declared the announcer from the German Freedom station, broadcast-

Above is the hall in Munich where every year Hitler addresses a meeting of the old fighters of the Nazi party. This photograph was taken at the meeting in 1938, but the scene this year, which was followed by the bomb explosion, was almost exactly the same.
Photo, Associated Press

ing on November 9, "the first bomb against German Dictatorship has exploded; many will follow. Though Hitler has eluded once more the punishment he deserves, he will not escape from his fate. Already the myths of Hitlerism have been smashed by that infernal machine. There is nobody in Germany who will not help the heroes of Munich to flee, who will not give them shelter and assist them in hiding, so that they will be able next time to strike Hitler himself."

The theory that British Secret Service agents, acting on the instructions of Mr. Chamberlain, were responsible for the explosion appeared to be discarded when Himmler, the Chief of the Secret Police, announced on November 11 that "preparations for the unsuccessful outrage in the Buergerbrau cellar were begun as early as last August. Suspicion falls on a person who came frequently to do work

in the gallery of the hall at that time." This mysterious individual was described as a man about 5 ft. 9 in., 30 to 35 years old, wearing workman's yellowish clothes with knee-breeches and a peaked cap.

The Gestapo Worried

This claim was received even in Germany with some misgiving—it would be a very remarkable time-fuse which produced an explosion accurately after some two-and-a-half months!

The occasion gave the Nazi authorities a welcome opportunity for stimulating public loyalty to Hitler, and led to a great round-up of all groups in Germany suspected of hostility to the Nazi regime. The Gestapo asked for information to be given of any suspicious remarks over-heard after the broadcast of the Buergerbrau meeting, such as surprise at the shortness of Hitler's speech. Following the offer of a reward of £45,000 for "information that might throw light on the outrage," special offices had to be set up to deal with the flood of denunciations which poured in. Police raids and house-to-house searches continued day and night, and thousands of arrests were made of Jews, Monarchists (including many army officers), Social Democrats, and even members of the police—but not, apparently, Communists.

The Gestapo itself was uneasy following numerous arrests within its own sacrosanct body. Perhaps the most pointed comment was the German Freedom Station's announcement on November 10: "Our illegal Front Group which knew how to enter the Munich beer cellar will also push open the door of Germany's future."

OUR DIARY OF THE WAR

Monday, November 6

French High Command announced that in a violent fight over the Western Front between 27 German and nine French fighters, **nine enemy machines were brought down,** seven behind the French lines. The French suffered no loss.

Molotov, in a speech at Moscow, re-affirmed that the Soviet policy was one of peace, and denounced the capitalist Powers for striving to extend the war.

The Communist International issued a manifesto in which it classed the German Government with those of Great Britain and France as being hostile to the workers.

King Leopold, accompanied by M. Spaak, Belgian Foreign Minister, **arrived at The Hague** just before midnight, and conferred with Queen Wilhelmina and her Foreign Minister, M. van Kleffens.

Air Ministry reported that R.A.F. aircraft carried out successful reconnaissance flights over Western Germany and secured valuable photographs. One aircraft had not returned.

Diplomatic representations were made in Norway regarding the fate of the " City of Flint," which is still at Bergen.

Finnish talks in Moscow delayed.

During September 37 British merchant ships, total tonnage about 155,000, were lost through enemy action ; during October these had dropped to 19 ships, of about 83,000 tons.

Burgomaster Max died.

Tuesday, November 7

Queen Wilhelmina and King Leopold issued a **joint appeal for peace,** with an offer of good offices to the belligerent Powers.

Admiralty announced that, in the southern part of the North Sea, certain of our light forces, including two Polish destroyers, were in action with German aircraft. No damage was done to any ship.

Air Ministry announced that a number of air actions took place over the North Sea. An enemy aircraft approaching the Shetlands was driven off by anti-aircraft fire and then chased away by British aircraft. Other enemy aircraft were sighted and two were engaged by R.A.F. patrols many miles out over the North Sea, but escaped in cloud.

Further photographic and visual recon-naissances over north-west Germany were made by R.A.F. aircraft. One machine failed to return.

Lord Halifax made a world broadcast on Britain's war aims.

Wednesday, November 8

In a speech in the Buergerbraeu beer cellar, Munich, Hitler made a violent attack on Britain.

An **attempt was made on Hitler's life,** a bomb explosion taking place shortly after he left the cellar. Nine persons were killed and more than 60 injured.

A single-handed action was fought by a New Zealand pilot at a height of five miles over an R.A.F. aerodrome in France, and a German reconnaissance machine was brought down.

Air Ministry announced that three German aircraft were engaged in combat over the North Sea by two reconnaissance aircraft of R.A.F. Coastal Command. One of the enemy aircraft, a **Heinkel seaplane, crashed** on the water **and sank.** Another was seen to fall partially out of control.

Three German attacks on the Western Front were repulsed.

Further disquieting reports of German activity on the Dutch frontier were received. Dutch military authorities decided to extend the safety inundation area.

It was reported that the German supply ship " Uhrenfels " had been captured and taken to Freetown, Sierra Leone.

Thursday, November 9

Nazi press and radio accused Britain of being responsible for the Munich bomb explosion. Hundreds of arrests were made throughout Germany.

THE POETS & THE WAR
VII
THE SHROUD OF GOLD
A New Poem
By HUMBERT WOLFE

All wars are fought in the spirit. Vain
   the trust
  in the mastery of steel. Like him, who
   makes it,
this is no more than a fiction of the dust,
  which blows on the first wind that
   overtakes it.
The struggle is in the heart, and they
   who thrust
  for truth unmoved when heaven itself
   forsakes it
see Liberty—the captain of the just—
  bright in the battle-line before he
   breaks it.
And terrible death itself is here defeated
  by stronger weapons than its own,
   whose might
is bounded by the grave's pretension.
   They
who fall with freedom are not lost nor
   cheated,
  for they become the essence of the light
which in a shroud of gold lays death
   away.

" The Second Great War."
World copyright

Anxiety was caused by **movements of German cavalry** and supplies of petrol **on the Dutch frontier.**

Paris reported increased activity on the front between the Rhine and the Moselle.

Russo-Finnish talks resumed in Moscow.

It was decided that the cargo of the " City of Flint " should be unloaded at Bergen and put up for sale.

The Union Information Officer, **South Africa,** revealed the existence of a **Nazi plot** for the arming of Blackshirt troops to march on Johannesburg and Pretoria and sabotage vital industries.

Armed clash took place on the Dutch frontier

Friday, November 10

at Venlo, in Limburg, one man, believed to be Dutch, being killed.

Paris reported increased air activity in Eastern and North-Eastern France in the preceding 24 hours.

On the Western Front two local enemy attacks were repulsed by infantry and artillery fire. Reinforcements were moving up to the Siegfried Line.

R.A.F. Coastal Command fighters **des-troyed an enemy flying-boat** off the East Coast. A second 'plane was engaged but escaped.

The Admiralty announced that H.M.S. Rover, a small auxiliary vessel, was con-siderably overdue and must be presumed lost, with her crew of four officers and 23 men.

Dutch military authorities started **flooding the main inundation areas** and taking other precautions against invasion.

There was a further hitch in the Finnish-Soviet negotiations.

Empire envoys, accompanied by Mr. Anthony Eden, met M. Daladier and General Gamelin in Paris.

Saturday, November 11

Armistice Day messages were exchanged between the King and the French President.

The Queen broadcast a message to the women of the Empire.

R.A.F. made successful reconnaissance flights the preceding night over towns in South-West Germany, including Stuttgart, Mannheim and Nuremberg. One aircraft failed to return.

Paris reported a quiet day on the Western Front. During the night enemy aircraft flew over North-Eastern France.

Wilhelmstrasse repeated the assurance that the neutrality of Holland and Belgium would be respected.

Empire envoys who are visiting France reached G.H.Q.

Sunday, November 12

The King and the President of the French Republic replied to the offer of good services made by Queen Wilhelmina and King Leopold.

On the Western Front attempts by the enemy to gain ground were repulsed.

Soviet Government issued a statement expressing dissatisfaction at the results hitherto reached in the Finnish negotiations.

Mr. Churchill broadcast a speech on the situation at the end of ten weeks of war.

Among the thousands of persons arrested following the Munich bomb explosion are said to be Monarchists, Jews, Social Demo-crats and members of the Gestapo itself.

It Is Said That . . .

Germany has boasted that she will destroy the British Fleet within six months.

Nazi levy on Jewish fortunes is increased from 20 to 25 per cent as from November 15.

The French liner " Normandie " might be taken to Canada and converted into a 'plane carrier.

Jews in Poland are now forbidden to trade in textiles or leather.

Copies of " Mein Kampf " and anti-communist literature have been confiscated by German police in Prague.

Berlin bookshops report demand for popular science and 19th-century novelists rather than for " dynamic " literature.

Czech steel workers, back in their own country, report great bitterness and disillu-sionment among German workers.

Jews in Austria may not obtain rations until the rest of the population has been served. By then most of the food has gone.

German spies are rife in Scandinavia. Many have been arrested when photographing docks and other strategic points.

Thousands of unemployed Poles are being taken into Russia to work Soviet industries.

Cows are to be used for draught work on German farms.

A wave of suicides was reported in Berlin newspapers.

Germany may send Czechs to Russia and replace them by Germans from S.E. Europe.

Goebbels has given 1,500 radio sets for distribution among the armed forces.

Corks are to be shorter by order of the Reich Bureau for Control of Miscellaneous Wares.

Gangs of Polish prisoners under armed guard have been put to agricultural work in Germany.

Swim-suits are being bought in Germany for underwear, as they are not yet included in rationed articles.

German prisoners in France are amazed at the abundance and quality of the French army food provided for them.

THE WAR ILLUSTRATED

Vol. 1   A Permanent Picture Record of the Second Great War   No. 12

Watched by a few inhabitants, a Scottish regiment is marching into a French village behind the lines where they are to be billeted. On the right the pipe band that has played them in is drawn up. Billeting officers have preceded the troops and arranged quarters. In the last war the Highland regiments wore kilts, but it has now been decided that, for their own comfort, the kilted regiments in the fighting zone are to wear battle-dress similar to that of other infantry regiments.

Photo, British Official: Crown Copyright

'Planes in Action Above the Halted War

Although on the ground the War on the West had entered upon a phase of virtual inactivity, in the air there was an occasional battle between Nazi reconnaissance machines, more venturesome than most, and the warplanes of the Allies.

FOLLOWING the French withdrawal from their tactical excursion into "No-man's land," activity on the Western Front subsided once again. For weeks the war communiqués had nothing to report but quiet nights and empty days. But if fighting there was none, there was along the whole front from Holland to Switzerland an attitude of tense expectancy. Wherever the soldiers were congregated they maintained the utmost vigilance. Fingers were ever, as it were, on the trigger; men were always standing by ready to fire the guns.

Many were the grumbles at the enemy's inactivity, and in many parts of the line only the anti-aircraft gunners could boast of having been in action. Occasionally an enemy raider dared to appear in the sky overhead, and then the military machine sprang to life with a vengeance.

One of these exciting incidents was reported by Mr. Harold Cardozo, " Daily Mail " special correspondent with the French Army, who told of a fight on November 5 between a German twin-engined 'plane and British chasers. He was being shown round the aerial defence of a vital part of north-east France when the rehearsal suddenly became the real thing. A red-tabbed artillery lieutenant arrived, went straight to the battery commander and saluted: " ' German 'plane reported south of X, sir.' The men ran to their battery positions. The predictor glasses swung round the whole arc of the horizon. The German 'planes—there were two of them, it appeared—were not lost sight of for a moment. ' Guns into alert position,' came the order. The ugly long barrels swung up into the sky from their greeny-camouflaged nets. ' Direction south-east,' was the next order. The great guns swung with a wickedly easy movement to the direction given. Events followed swiftly. Wind and temperature corrections were given and checked. The great eyes of the battery position, huge twin telescopes, moved nervously over the whole front, with its patches of mist, of dark rain-squalls and of sunlit clouds."

Then there came a roar of engines in the air, and three 'planes, British Hurricanes, were reported from the observation

This French infantry battalion, marching along one of the level, straight roads of north-eastern France, is just about to pass one of the windmills which are so familiar a feature of the landscape. At once half-forgotten memories of Don Quixote are stirred—but these knights of today are not, like the knight of old, tilting against the imaginary enmity of windmills : their foe is the very real malignity of Hitlerism. In the top photograph young Nazi conscripts are learning how to camouflage trenches.

Photos, Wide World and Topical

Invention Gives Accuracy to the Gunners' Aim

French soldiers are here operating a range-finder for aircraft in front of an artillery position. They are wearing the latest type of French steel helmet, which has a visor.

Photo, Courtesy of French Embassy

post. "Batteries note, British 'planes in air. British 'planes in air. German 'planes to south. German 'planes to south."

Shortly afterwards the observers gave a warning of the approach of the Nazi raider : "Enemy 'plane in sight. Flying south to north, crossing from X to Y. Altitude estimated 6,000 feet. All batteries ready for action." Staccato replies came from gun after gun. "Number one gun ready." "Number two gun ready," and so on.

With his glasses Mr. Cardozo was able to pick up the German machine, a large reconnaissance 'plane with the black and white signs and the Nazi swastika clearly visible. "Orders, with a medley of figures, corrections, came from the central observation posts. They were passed up

Above right is a most unusual view of a big gun taken on the Western Front. The breech block has been opened preparatory to inserting a shell, and this affords a clear view to the distance through the barrel. Guns as well as men are dug in at advance positions, and in the photograph immediately above, British anti-aircraft artillery have completed emplacements for the predictors, those uncanny, elaborate instruments that permit the gunner to follow his target with automatic accuracy. Amidst this warlike scene a French farmer, seen left, still carries on.

Photos, British Official : Crown Copyright

Play and Dance Banish the Poilus' Boredom

The Poilus, like the British, have their entertainments behind the lines. In one of these photographs is a theatre for soldiers at a base camp ; in the other a professional French dance band plays to the troops in a sandbagged shelter.

Photos, Planet News and Courtesy of the French Embassy

and repeated automatically in the form of fingers, red and green, over dials. ' One, two, three, four,' the robot said. The guns roared out. It was grey enough to see the flashes from the batteries, and I could hear the shells swish skywards. The German 'plane was still flying on a straight line. It was obviously, however, defending itself with two machine-guns, one in a turret firing upwards and one firing across its tail. The Hurricanes

soared and swooped like falcons, their guns spitting angrily. One of them shot through the clouds and disappeared. The other I could still see clinging to the Heinkel's tail. As we were about to leave an officer came up with the final message of the fight by British chasers. ' German 'plane brought down 20 miles away. Pilot and observer seriously wounded, two other prisoners.' "

Such exciting interludes as this were

few and far between. For the most part of their daily and nightly vigil the observers turned their glasses on an empty sky. Very, very rarely did the whistle blow which brought the crews to their stations, lifted the muzzles of the guns and plastered the sky with puffs of white smoke. Very likely the Germans on their side of the line similarly complained of the slowness of the war, but over their lines must have brooded, too, a spirit of expectancy. But not the private or his company commander, not the divisional general or the member of the High Command, could know when or where the great stroke was to be delivered. Not even Hitler . . .

Now this would-be Napoleon of the twentieth century turned his eyes on Switzerland, and without a shiver of apprehension the Swiss tested afresh their frontier defences. From Switzerland he swept his gaze towards Holland, and the Dutch, while refusing to admit that any nation could be so wicked, or so silly, as to attempt a violation of their country, raised the level of their dikes and kept their army at full strength. He looked at Belgium, but King Leopold had already declared that his country was far more ready to resist aggression than she was in 1914. He threatened England with secret weapons—and then, when a bomb wrecked the Munich beer cellar, his satellites complained that only a short time before the British had boasted of having a secret weapon ! Like Kaiser Wilhelm, like Napoleon, like Philip of Spain, he saw in England the enemy, but as yet he chafed in impotence.

Empire Pilot's Unique Feat in the Aerial War

The terrific force with which the enemy 'plane, brought down from a height of 27,000 ft., crashed in the street of a French village can be judged from this photograph, taken immediately after it fell. A large area of road surface has been destroyed and parts of the aeroplane are still burning fiercely.

Photo, British Paramount News Reel

THE remarkable achievement of the young New Zealander who brought down a German Dornier bomber from a height of 27,000 ft. was, as regards height, a unique feat in aerial warfare. The young pilot (who had just celebrated his 21st birthday) was up on patrol, when he realized that a raider was above him, and he then climbed up and up until he came within range. In vain the German pilot endeavoured to escape his pursuer. Both aircraft kept up a sustained fire, and the Dornier did its best to dodge the little British 'plane. The German dived towards a bank of clouds, but before he could reach it the New Zealander, as he said, "gave him the works." The results of "the works" are seen in this photograph. During its attack on the enemy bomber the British 'plane had swooped down at about 400 miles an hour and then straightened out—magnificent airmanship.

Some of the wreckage was blown a considerable distance, and here a fragment is lodged in a tree. Right, French soldiers are examining the wreckage.

Photos, Associated Press

Dutchmen Refuse to be Rattled

Faced with the problem of breaking the grip of the blockade, Hitler
is believed to have contemplated seizing Holland in order to establish
air and submarine bases for his war against Britain. But the Dutch
kept calm—and on the alert.

broadcast a most reassuring message to the nation. "The Government have found," he said, "that in the last few days rumours of disaster for our country have caused alarm in many quarters. I am here now to tell you that there is not a single reason to be alarmed." The rumours, he went on, had been caused by statements in the foreign press, wireless reports, and certain measures taken by the Dutch Government—measures which had been widely misinterpreted. Increasing tension in the west had caused the Dutch to make changes in the nature and intensity of their mobilization, but it was a great mistake to conclude that their frontiers were therefore more seriously threatened. "We mobilized in

September this year, not because we distrusted our neighbours, but because it was our duty to be prepared for any emergency. . . . We must never allow the impression to be created abroad that our mobilization is only symbolic ; others as well as ourselves should be convinced that it is effective. Therefore its intensity has to be changed in accordance with the tension near our frontier."

The Prime Minister concluded by saying that he hoped his words would restore the peace of mind of those who had been showing signs of nervousness. Such nervousness was surely not unwarranted, however. Although the "main water line " of defence had not yet been flooded, it was understood that the dike

This remarkably clever piece of camouflage
conceals the trench that leads to a gun
emplacement on the Dutch coast.

KING LEOPOLD of the Belgians makes a night dash to see Queen Wilhelmina of Holland—German troops massing on the Dutch frontier—Holland ready to open her dikes. With these headlines in their morning papers small wonder that people thought that the week-end following Armistice Day might well see an invasion of Holland, and perhaps Belgium as well, by the Nazi legions. But the week-end came and went, and the little countries were still permitted to preserve their neutrality.

On the Monday, November 13, the Dutch Prime Minister, Jonkheer de Geer,

gates were ready to be opened at any moment. Work on the construction of fortifications in the Maastricht Appendix went on day and night. Dutch troops were moved to the frontier, and defence talks were entered into with the Belgian ministers. From the coast came reports that certain lighthouses had been extinguished and lightships recalled to port.

Yet, in spite of all, Jan and Grietje went out on their bicycles as usual for their Sunday excursion along the roads above the brimming dikes ; only the soldiers confined to barracks were unable to keep the appointments they had made for the afternoon. The churches were full—but they usually are in Holland ; the cinemas and theatres put up their house-full boards—again as usual. When night fell the lights of the cities and towns shone brightly, and many a worthy Hollander, listening to the radio as he sipped his schnapps, must have wondered what all the pother was about. After all, how many times was Holland on the eve of invasion in the last war?

Though the last war in which the Dutch army fought was a campaign against a native tribe
in the East Indies in 1906, it has kept in touch with all the latest developments of warfare,
and no possible means of defence against aggression has been omitted. Centre, right, are
steel gates erected on a bridge over the river Maas, near the frontier. Explosives to blow up
the bridge in the last resort are in place. Above is a Dutch anti-aircraft gun fully manned
just inside the frontier. Even the steel helmets are camouflaged.

Photos, Central Press and Planet News

France Has a 'Silent' Navy Too

In the course of his speech on the naval aspect of the War in the House
of Commons on November 8, Mr. Winston Churchill, First Lord
of the Admiralty, paid a high tribute to the work of the French Navy.

THE fame of the French army is
world-wide, and everyone appre-
ciates to the full France's magnificent efforts in producing and maintaining that great body of men which is
now standing to arms in the Maginot Line.
It is perhaps not so generally realized,
however, that France has also a powerful
and highly efficient navy which in this
war, as in the last, is making a most
valuable contribution to the ultimate
success of the common cause.

Shortly before the war France had
seven battleships (the "Strasbourg,"
launched in 1936 ; the "Dunkerque,"
launched in 1936, and five pre-1914),
19 cruisers, 37 escort and patrol vessels,
59 flotilla leaders and destroyers, 12
torpedo boats and 77 submarines. There
is also one aircraft carrier. Most of the
smaller craft are of recent design and
construction. Many vessels are in course
of construction, including the 35,000-
ton battleships "Richelieu," "Jean
Bart" (nearly completed), "Clemenceau" and "Gascogne" ; 2 aircraft
carriers and 9 cruisers.

Perhaps the most important of the
French Navy's activities in the war to
date has been in connexion with the
transportation of the British Field Force
to France. In British waters and for the
greater part of the crossing the transports
were in the custody of the Royal Navy,
but towards the end of the crossing and
until they actually arrived safely in
harbour it was the French Navy which
undertook their protection.

In this operation a large fleet of ships
of many kinds was constantly engaged.
Out at sea patrol vessels and minesweepers
were seeking and destroying mines which
may have been laid by the enemy fathoms
below the surface; reconnaissance vessels,
police boats from the harbours, and pilot
boats had to stand by at all hours to
receive the transports. This work went
on day and night.

The French Navy also ensured the
actual defence of the ports and the coast.
Defence and anti-aircraft batteries had
to be maintained in a state of high
efficiency, and look-out and signalling
stations were constantly on the alert.
Protective nets had to be placed into
position and minefields laid. All this
prosaic, but very necessary, work was
carried out by a crowd of small craft
constantly at sea.

Several hundred transports arrived in
French ports in a single month. For the
most part they did so at night with lights
extinguished and their decks crowded
with troops and war material. The lamps
in the lighthouses having been extinguished, the ships were piloted through
French waters with the help of a modified
system of buoys. One by one the transports drew alongside the quays, gangways
were lowered, and the soldiers filed ashore.
As soon as the ship was empty tugs pulled
it away from the quay; another transport
came alongside and a new crowd of
soldiers fell in and marched away into the
night. At least three convoys crossed
each night during the period of greatest

This typical seaman of the French Navy is
on sentry duty. The personnel of the French
Navy is recruited very largely from Brittany,
the Bretons being among the world's
finest sailors.

Photo, Pierre Boucher

The French Navy maintains the highest standard of efficiency, and both in the Channel and in the Mediterranean fleet exercises and gun
practice were carried out regularly in peacetime. Here a French man-of-war has just fired the big guns of her forward turret, and the smoke
of the propelling charge is still pouring out of the muzzle. The biggest guns carried by French battleships are the 13·4-in. weapons of
battleships completed before the last war.

Photo, Planet News

activity, and every ship arrived intact without the loss of a single man.

Those who were in certain French ports at the time and saw perhaps ten transports discharging simultaneously on to the blue-lit quays, have testified how completely successful was the collaboration between the French Navy and Army and the British headquarters.

In many other ways the French Navy has rendered our own most valuable assistance—in submarine chasing, for instance, and in the protection of the mercantile marine. It is stated that the French Navy has accounted for at least five submarines, and has captured 225,000 tons of contraband. "Not for many generations," said Mr. Winston Churchill in his speech in the House of Commons on November 8, "has the French Navy been so powerful or so efficient. Under the long care of Admiral Darlan and M. Campinchi, the Minister of Marine, a magnificent fighting and seafaring force has been developed." Not only had the French Navy assisted in every way agreed upon before the war, but it had also lifted off our shoulders a whole set of burdens. "It seems to me a wonderful thing," concluded Mr. Churchill, "that when France is making so great an effort upon land, she should at the same time offer to the Allied cause so powerful a reinforcement by sea."

From the bridge of a French warship orders are being transmitted to the engine-room by ratings, on whose accuracy the safety of the ship depends.

This man on a French warship is on the look-out on the bridge, and is endeavouring to identify some suspicious object sighted on the far-distant horizon.

France, like Great Britain, has immense overseas possessions—in North Africa, on the shores of the Mediterranean, in West and Central Africa, besides Madagascar and its dependencies and the large French territories in the East Indies. For this reason a powerful navy to patrol her trade routes is essential to France, and above French warships are seen at sea on this duty. Besides keeping up the patrol, the destroyers of the French Navy have joined those of the British Navy in submarine hunting with conspicuous success.

Photos, Courtesy of the French Embassy

Mighty Symbol of the Naval Strength of France

The French Navy, like the British Navy, has to guard the communications between France and an immense Colonial Empire. One of the ships engaged in this work is the cruiser "Algérie," here seen in port with one of her guns being hoisted out. Just below it can be seen a paravane, the great safeguard against mines that has now been adopted by both the Allied Navies. The "Algérie" is a cruiser of 10,000 tons, launched in 1932, carrying eight 8-in. guns and twelve 3·9-in. anti-aircraft guns.

Photo, Pierre Boucher

French Flyers in Spectacular Air Battle

In the history of aerial warfare it is difficult to find a more conclusive victory against heavy odds than that achieved by nine French fighters over twenty-seven of the foe in the course of a fierce battle above the Western Front.

O N a November day somewhere behind the Maginot Line, several French air pilots are standing stiffly erect before their fighter 'planes. Facing them is a little group of sombrely-clad civilians, set in a frame of glittering staff officers.

One of the civilians, a sturdy, thick-set figure, steps forward and salutes on each cheek the pilots, as one by one they advance to meet him. A handclasp, a perfectly executed salute, and the pilot steps back into the rank. But now on his breast there hangs from a red and green ribbon the bronze *Croix de Guerre*.

Thus M. Daladier, Premier of wartime France, rewards the French pilots who a few days before had been engaged in the biggest air battle of the war on the Western Front. The first announcement of the engagement was given in a French communiqué issued on November 6:

During a violent fight nine French fighters attacked a group of 27 German fighters. Nine of the latter were brought down, of which seven fell within our territory. Every one of our 'planes engaged in this encounter returned safely.

These three sentences hardly do justice to a really sensational and most significant victory. The story opens with a French squadron of nine fighters making a reconnaissance above the German lines. They were high above the clouds, so high that they did not see at first that flying below them were three squadrons of German Messerschmitts.

Putting down the noses of their 'planes the French nine, without a moment of hesitation, valiantly charged down on the twenty-seven. The Germans, soon made aware of the enemy's approach, fought back with desperate bravery, and so, watched by the men of the two armies in the lines below, there developed a fierce dog-fight in the skies.

Though the French fighters were outnumbered so heavily they displayed their manœuvrability and fire power in such excellent fashion that in a very short time the twenty-seven German 'planes were retiring over their own lines.

They were not allowed to get away so easily, however. Dodging here and there among the bursts of anti-aircraft shrapnel, doing their best to escape from the French fighters whose every gun was blazing death, the German raiders were completely routed. Seven of the twenty-seven crashed on French soil, and two others fell just across the line in German territory. It was believed that several of the remaining 'planes were severely damaged.

Flushed with their victory, two of the French 'planes proceeded to fly over the Saar, where they routed nine more Messerschmitts, and in another part of the front on the same day four French fighters successfully engaged nine Nazi 'planes. The German High Command, it may be noted, in its communiqué on the day's happenings, made no mention of the battle with the French 'planes.

With good reason the French rejoiced in a glorious victory. So one-sided was it, indeed, that some experts suggested

that the Messerschmitts engaged must have been obsolescent types; but it is unlikely that such would be used on the Western Front. "It not only brings additional proof of the quality of French pilots," said one semi-official commentary, "but also confirms all that has been said of the technical qualities of French material. In straight-line flying the German Messerschmitts may perhaps have a slight advantage in speed, but as soon as it becomes a question of aerobatics—a vital factor in fighter machines—the French aeroplanes have the upper hand."

Later it was reported on reliable authority that the nine French 'planes were American Curtiss fighters, machines with a speed exceeding 300 miles per hour. With the removal of the American arms embargo, the supply of these and other American machines has been greatly facilitated, and the splendid results of a combination of French dash with American technical efficiency must become ever more marked as the struggle proceeds.

These two remarkable photographs, exclusive to THE WAR ILLUSTRATED, show stages in the great aerial fight between nine French fighter aircraft and 27 Nazi fighters which ended in the astonishing victory for the French described in this page. In the top photograph the heroic nine Frenchmen are going out to meet the foe in formation as perfect as it would have been in manœuvres. Below, is one of the Messerschmitts brought to earth, with French soldiers standing guard round it.

Photos, Courtesy of Pathé Gazette

Solitary Watchers of the Skies

" Some must watch, while some must sleep," to quote Shakespeare ; but all too seldom do we remember the unceasing vigil of Britain's civilian Observer Corps, on whom we rely for the first notification of the appearance of enemy raiders.

W HEN in the early eighteen-hundreds Napoleon mustered his fleet of flat-bottomed boats at Boulogne, the coasts of England were patrolled by pig-tailed Jack tars. Up and down the cliffs they marched, stopping every now and then to raise their telescopes to their eyes, eager to catch the first glimpse of " Boney."

Today an organized band watch afresh the coasts of Britain, or rather not the coasts so much as the air, by which in the twentieth century the enemy is much more likely to come than by the sea.

This army of some 15,000 watchers, occupying isolated posts in those districts of Britain most likely to be crossed by enemy raiders, constitutes the Observer

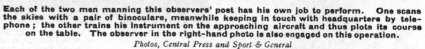

Each of the two men manning this observers' post has his own job to perform. One scans the skies with a pair of binoculars, meanwhile keeping in touch with headquarters by telephone ; the other trains his instrument on the approaching aircraft and thus plots its course on the table. The observer in the right-hand photo is also engaged on this operation.

Photos, Central Press and Sport & General

Above is an observer in his well sandbagged post, telephoning his report of passing aircraft back to headquarters.

Photo, Central Press

Corps, which since the outbreak of war has been placed under the control of the Air Ministry. Its members are, however, civilians enrolled as special constables, and they wear no uniform ; their only distinguishing mark is their " Special's " armlet. Some are full-time " professionals," but the great majority are unpaid volunteers drawn from among the residents in the neighbouring villages. After their periods of duty, involving at regular intervals an unsleeping night, they have to go to work as usual.

Working on four- or eight-hour shifts, two or more observers are on duty beside their sound locator, maintaining a constant watch for the approach of aircraft. Whether hostile or not, every aeroplane that passes within range is carefully scrutinized and reported. If the carefully-trained hearing of the observers recognizes the engine note of an enemy raider, the alarm is at once passed on by telephone from the observers' isolated posts on the coast or inland to their headquarters, and thence to the successive lines of defence.

First the searchlight and sound locator detachments spring into action. Operating their sound locators, the men determine the position of the hostile aircraft by means of the sound of their motors, due

allowance being made for the " sound lag." As soon as the position has been determined the searchlights cease their haphazard probing of the sky and speedily pick up the individual raider. As soon as one has got on to the target two others at once concentrate on it, and this conjunction of lights is a signal to the interceptor fighters, who immediately race to make their attack out of the darkness upon the brilliantly illuminated 'plane. The anti-aircraft batteries also come into action.

But, like that of an air-raid warden, the observer's period of duty is usually unmarked by any such eventful happening as that just described. From his post he surveys a large tract of peaceful countryside, where even the thought of war seems quite out of place. From long experience he has learnt to know and distinguish the distant factory hooter, the noise of passing trains, the hum of the electricity works, and the sirens of boats on the river far away.

Dull work it is for the most part— but, should the enemy bombers come, the Observer Corps is in the very front line of the country's defence, for on the alert hearing of these lonely watchers may depend the safety of vital communications and centres of civilian life.

British Science Is Helping to Win the War

In this war, to a greater extent even than in 1914-1918, scientists are being mobilized
to play their part in the nation's effort. Below is given some indication of the ways
in which their assistance is vital.

THE stimulus of the last war on invention and scientific research produced the tank, the anti-aircraft gun, gas warfare, the extra-ordinarily rapid development of wireless and aviation. To cope with these and kindred developments, three great departments of Government research were founded: Agriculture and Fisheries, Medical and Scientific and Industrial.

The first is essentially devoted to the supply of food, whereas the latter are the concern of the Medical Director-General and the Ministry of Supply respectively. In 1914 the civilian staff of scientists at the War Department numbered less than 40. Today there is a staff of about 800, including specialists in every branch of applied physics, chemistry, and engineering, working in the five laboratories of the Ministry of Supply.

The research carried out in these establishments deals with the application of existing scientific principles to the vast array of weapons, instruments, machines, equipment and stores required by the three fighting services.

to most of it. Some idea can be gained, however, of the type of research that is behind all our weapons by studying some of their requirements and achievements.

Every time a gun is fired and a shell hurled accurately through the air to burst in fragments dead on its objective,

this instrument has to pick out the sound of a particular enemy gun or battery and report its position quickly. Each of the sound-ranging microphones spaced along our front pick up the sound of the enemy gun, transform that into an electrical impulse which is sent by wire to head-

The predictor, as used by anti-aircraft batteries (above), is one of the most wonderful of all the new military equipment. It is a most complicated type of calculating machine, and tells the gun-layer where his weapon should be aimed so that the shell and target will meet.
Photo, British Official : Crown Copyright

This huge searchlight, mounted on a mobile carriage, is of the latest pattern, and spells danger to any raider should its great beam be successfully trained " on target." The projector controller (on the right) can alter both the traversing and elevation of the light.
Photo, Keystone

Seventeen distinguished scientists with fourteen assistants are devoting their full time to speeding up research. A reserve of 140 scientists and assistants, arranged in 27 balanced teams, have been organized to tackle urgent problems the moment they arise. And a further 35 distinguished consultants have been earmarked for service when required.

This scheme is the most comprehensive mobilization of scientists in national service that has ever been attempted, and a really full account of their work is impossible owing to the secrecy attached

is detonated by an elaborate mechanism inside the shell, a clockwork time fuse.

If we can imagine what would happen to an alarm clock when fired out of a gun, we may realize that a fuse is no ordinary piece of clockwork. It has to function accurately, but yet not be damaged by the shock of discharge, although that shock is used to set it in motion.

The sound-ranger for finding the position of enemy guns is highly scientific and the result of much research. Amidst all the indescribable din of battle

the results of long and arduous chemical and physical research are being put to the test. The explosive propelling the shell must be designed to burn slowly, in, say, one-hundredth of a second or so, but the shell itself has to have a high explosive filling burning at a far greater rate. So this filling

quarters, where it is recorded photographically on a special moving strip of cinematograph film. The interval between the impulses received at two neighbouring microphones can then be calculated, and from this the direction of the gun is found. Other pairs of microphones provide several bearings intersecting at the exact position of the gun.

Among the problems successfully dealt with in this connexion is the correction that has to be applied for the drift of sound down wind. Since the last war this has reached a high state of perfection,

Again, the problem of throwing a searchlight beam on to a modern bomber travelling at high speed is not solved by sound-locators. These only indicate where the target *was*, not where it *will be* when the anti-aircraft gun is fired: An intricate mechanism incorporated in the sound-locator unit predicts semi-automatically the line of sight for an accurate hit.

War certainly stimulates inventions, for some 300 or so arrive at the Ministry of Supply each week. But it is considered fortunate if even one in a hundred is useful. Among the less inspired suggestions are death rays that disregard any and every simple scientific principle.

'Battle Practice' Oils the A.R.P. Machine

Above, dealing with an "unexploded bomb" from a "crashed German raider," and right, "Nazi airmen under arrest"—incidents from a Bethnal Green mock air raid.

THE "stand-by" atmosphere of the first few weeks of war may be lost at any moment in the urgency of the "real thing," when the training of Civil Defence personnel will prove the deciding factor in preserving the Home Front unbroken. Realizing this, the local authorities in some districts have staged practice exercises as being the only way of keeping their services on the alert and at the full pitch of efficiency. The photographs in this page illustrate various exercises in the London area carried out when the war was still young.

On the right is another realistic scene during the mock air raid held at Bethnal Green. The remains of the "German raider" burn fiercely while A.F.S. men and rescue squads rush up to attend to the victims and extinguish the fire. Above, in the City of Westminster, another fully-equipped rescue squad show how they deal with a casualty.

Photos, Planet News and Associated Press

'Royal Ordnance' Won't Let the Soldiers Down

With Britain getting into her wartime stride, all her ordnance factories are working at full pressure. Here we have a few impressions of one of the most famous of these, gathered by a Special Correspondent of THE WAR ILLUSTRATED who was privileged to pay it a visit by courtesy of the Ministry of Supply.

IN the days of antiquity the temples of the War God were pillared halls, bare and cool, across whose marble floors moved white-robed priests with silent tread. The temples of the War God in modern Britain are very different. They are huge structures of cement and steel and corrugated iron. Their darkness is shot with the flaming fires of mighty furnaces. They resound with the clang of monstrous hammers crashing down on masses of half-molten iron. They are dim, and through their murk move big-framed men on whose heads are perched little round caps which once were white, whose uniform is blue dungarees, and whose feet are encased in mighty heat-resisting clogs.

Here in this great shed in one of Britain's innumerable ordnance factories are being brought to birth a vast multitude of shells. In the centre is a battery of furnaces with flames licking round the edges of the doors. Now and again a door is opened to reveal a white-hot inferno in which a great lump of iron is being raised to a terrific temperature. A man like some gnome of the underworld, sweat pouring off his brow and hairy chest, pushes into the heart of the furnace a long pair of pincers and drags out into the cool the glowing mass. Then from the roof, from amid a cluster of chains and ropes and wires, a great clamp reaches down, grips the billet and drops it into a hole, sizzling as it goes. Now a kind of giant ramrod descends and bores its irresistible way through the centre of the red hot cylinder. The ramrod is withdrawn, the clamp descends again, raises the billet and drops it on the concrete floor. One of the hovering gnomes deftly lays it on the floor with a single lift of a narrow bar, and then, with a few contemptuous kicks of his mighty boot, rolls it across the floor. Another swift movement with the rod, and the shell in embryo, still glowing pink, is put to stand beside the rest of the morning's batch. One more shell has been born.

Steel for the Guns

In the next great shop there is a magnificent display of fireworks, which would much more than compensate any small boy for the ban on this year's Guy Fawkes celebrations. They are splashed out from a huge cauldron set high above the ground in which molten iron is boiling like soup. Now and again manganese and other metal ingredients are dropped into the seething liquid, and so the iron is converted into high-grade steel. Not far away in another vast shop red-hot billets are being sliced with the ease and cleanness of butter on the grocer's counter. In yet another great shop molten masses are pressed into shape with a pressure of 3,000 tons.

Now we leave the forge and foundry— taking care not to trip over that naval gun, 60 ft. or so in length—and move over to shops devoted to the manufacture of shells and small-arm ammuni- tion. Here there is the same wonder of machinery, the same exactness of working, the same devoted labour, the same care that the ammunition for our soldiers' guns and rifles, for their machine-guns, anti-tank rifles, and so on, shall all be of the most perfect reliability. Every shell is weighed and gauged, checked for this and tested for that; little electric lamps are lowered into its interior to make sure that its surface is not belied by what is within; its base is carefully tapped with little hammers for that false note which would indicate a flaw; on a bench it is passed from hand to hand as each inspector contributes of his skill and experience to the making of a perfect job.

Now we come to the firing butts, where a tremendous naval 14-in. gun is mounted ready for firing. The breech is opened and the gun is loaded with a proof shot. Then the gun crew retires to a safe distance and the monster is left in solitary grandeur.

Suddenly there is an earth-shaking roar and a vast tongue of flame spits out from the barrel. The gunners run from their shelter, open the breech, from which now belches a cloud of white fumes, and a small army of inspectors make a most careful examination of the way in which the barrel has stood up to the discharge.

With the biggest guns, as with weapons, shells and ammunition of every kind, the aim of the ordnance factories is to produce something which will never let the soldier, sailor or airman down.

Destined for one of Britain's capital ships, this great 14-in. naval gun has just fired its first round—not on the sea, but in the proof butts of an ordnance factory somewhere in England. The proof shot is of solid steel weighing about two-thirds of a ton; at present it is buried in the sand at the far end of the range, but at the close of the day it will be dug out and used again. The man with the rod is retrieving portions of the proofing material. Before the Navy accepts delivery, these mighty guns are subjected to the most careful testing and examination.

Photo, Fox

Fiery Particles Streaming from War's Cauldron

Taken in the murk of one of Britain's great Royal Ordnance factories, this photograph shows, not, as might perhaps be supposed at a casual glance, an incendiary bomb blazing its way through the roof, but a great steel converter in which iron, by the addition of certain materials and the application of terrific heat, is converted into steel. Working all unconcerned beneath the shower of sparks, the men in the foreground are handling a new batch of bombs and shells.

Photo, Fox

Lord Gort Gets To Know His Men by Day and Night

Viscount Gort, the Commander-in-Chief of the British Field Force, has been frequently in the battle zone, not only to inspect the work going on there, but to become better acquainted with the officers and men of his Army. Above, he is watching men of a Highland regiment digging in and sandbagging the parapet of their trench. For the men with whom Viscount Gort comes in contact personally he has words of kindly encouragement, as he takes a personal interest in every detail of the Army's work.

Photo, British Official : Crown Copyright

It is not only the work of the soldiers that Lord Gort is interested in, but he has also made their comfort and well-being his concern. He has recognized, too, their need for recreation, and was present at the first entertainment for soldiers given somewhere in France on November 12. In this photograph he is seen leaving a French farmhouse after inspecting the men's quarters. The front of the house is camouflaged with straw. An informal Guard of Honour salutes the C.-in-C. as he leaves. *Photo, British Official : Crown Copyright*

The Commander-in-Chief Watches Every Detail

The closest contact is maintained between the British and French High Commands. Relations between the Army chiefs have been most cordial, and there has been complete unanimity as to all plans. Above is a scene at the British headquarters during a visit by General Gamelin, the French Commander-in-Chief, to Lord Gort. General Gamelin is in conversation with Sir John Dill, commanding the British 1st Corps. Lord Gort is on the left. His large camouflaged car is a familiar sight to the troops.

Photo, British Official : Crown Copyright

Unlike most of the commanders in the last war, Lord Gort has had much experience as a fighting soldier in the front line. His intimate knowledge of the real thing is very much in evidence on his tours of inspection. Above we see him with the Duke of Gloucester, chief liaison officer of the British Army, in conversation with General Sir John Dill, commanding the 1st Corps; and in the centre Lieutenant-General Sir Alan Brooke, commanding the 2nd Corps.

Photo : Associated Press

WORDS THAT HISTORY WILL REMEMBER

Monday, November 6, 1939

M. MOLOTOV, Soviet Prime Minister, at a meeting of the Moscow Soviet in honour of the 22nd anniversary of the Bolshevist Revolution :

The Capitalist Powers, unable to find any other way out of their internal difficulties, have driven more than half the world's population into a murderous war, which they are trying to extend and spread over the whole world. . . . .

Britain and France are doing everything to foster and prolong the war in order to exploit it for the strengthening of their domination of the world and their colonial empires. If they are successful, the number of neutral Powers is bound to decline and that of the belligerent Powers is bound to increase.

It is also well known that some Powers are only using the pretext of neutrality as a mask for shielding their attempts to foster the war, from which they expect to derive huge profits at the expense of the belligerent peoples, and their sufferings, sacrifices, and impoverishments.

Today we are facing the danger of the European war and the Asiatic war expanding into a world-wide conflict if nothing is done to prevent it. This is the point that the Capitalist world today has reached. . . .

The power and the authority of the Soviet Union are becoming more and more evident. The annexation of Eastern Poland has been one of the greatest successes of the Soviet Union's foreign policy. The Soviet Union will be proud of these successes and will remain faithful to the principles of its policy of peace and of proletarian internationalism.

Sins of the Capitalists

We must bear in mind that nine-tenths of the world's population are still living under Capitalism. Yet the Capitalist world has been forced to retrench itself and to retire. We, on the other hand, have added 13,000,000 to our population. . . .

The Capitalists and their Socialist assistants cannot be expected to renounce the war voluntarily. On the contrary, they must be expected to attempt the expansion of the European conflict into a world-wide slaughter. The Soviet Union with its desire to bring the war to an early end is opposed to this policy. . . .

The Capitalist world begins to realize that the Soviet Union is not what they wanted us to be. They wanted to see our country weak, yielding easily to pressure from abroad. The contrary is the case. The Soviet Union is strong, solidly built, and unshakable.

We know that our successful policy of peace is the best policy for the Soviet Union. We must continue this policy without any deviation. This is the will of the people of the Soviet Union, and in the twenty-third year of our revolution we shall continue along the road of Lenin which will lead us to the final victory— the victory of the Soviet regime.

Tuesday, November 7

QUEEN WILHELMINA and KING LEOPOLD in a joint appeal for Peace, issued in a communiqué by the Dutch Foreign Office :

At this hour of anxiety for the whole world before the war breaks out in Western Europe in all its violence, we have the conviction that it is our duty once again to raise our voice.

Some time ago the belligerent parties declared that they would not be unwilling to examine a reasonable and well-founded basis for an equitable peace.

It seems to us that in the present circumstances it is difficult for them to come into contact in order to state their standpoints with greater precision and to bring them nearer to one another.

If this were agreeable to them, we are disposed, by every means at our disposal that they might care to suggest to us, and in a spirit of friendly understanding, to facilitate the ascertaining of the elements of an agreement to be arrived at.

This, it seems to us, is the task we have to fulfil for the good of our people and in the interests of the whole world.

We hope that our offer will be accepted, and that thus a first step will be taken towards the establishment of a durable peace.

Tuesday, November 7

LORD HALIFAX, Foreign Secretary, in a broadcast :

. . . We are fighting in defence of freedom ; we are fighting for peace ; we are meeting a challenge to our own security and that of others ; we are defending the rights of all nations to live their own lives.

We are fighting against the substitution of brute force for law as the arbiter between nations, against the violation of the sanctity of treaties and disregard for the pledged word.

We have learned that there can be no opportunity for Europe to cultivate the arts of peace until Germany is brought to realize that recurrent acts of aggression will not be tolerated.

It must accordingly be our resolve not only to protect the future from the repetition of the same injuries that German aggression has inflicted on Europe in these last few years, but also so far as we can to repair the damage successively wrought by Germany upon her weaker neighbours.

The British are particularly reluctant to interfere in other peoples' business, provided always that other people do not seek to interfere in theirs.

But when the challenge in the sphere of international relations is sharpened, as today in Germany, by the denial to men and women of elementary human rights, that challenge is at once extended to something instinctive and profound in the universal conscience of mankind.

We are, therefore, fighting to maintain the rule of law and the quality of mercy in dealings between man and man, and in the great society of civilized states.

As I look back to those days in which we all walked in the dark valley of decision I can feel no doubt in my own conscience that only with supreme dishonour could we in fact have averted war.

Now supreme dishonour, as well as the supreme folly, lie with the aggressor. The supreme dishonour of the German Government is laid open to the world.

The Prime Minister has stated that we seek no vindictive peace, that we have no territorial ambitions for ourselves, and that we should feel the future to hold little hope unless the new peace settlement might be reached through the method of negotiation and agreement.

But we are determined, so far as it is humanly possible, to see to it that Europe shall not again be subjected to repetition of this tragedy.

The new world that we seek will enlist the co-operation of all peoples on a basis of human equality, self-respect and mutual tolerance.

We need not deny the limitations set to what physical force alone can do, but the recognition of this truth should never blind us to the fact that if, for fear of the tragedy of war, measured in human lives broken and destroyed, we rest inert before action which we hold evil, we are surely surrendering to annihilation the expression of spiritual values which have inspired and guided all human progress.

A Select Record from Week to Week of Important War Declarations and Statements

(Continued from page 338)

Wednesday, November 8

HITLER in a speech in the Buergerbraeu Beer Cellar, Munich :

. . . . It has been said that the British are not fighting the German people at all, but only the regime which speaks for the German people. It is Britain's task, they say, to liberate the German people from this regime and to make it happy. Britain is fighting to free the German people from militarism. . . .

For 300 years Britain has conquered people after people. Now she is satisfied ; now there must be peace.

Today a British Minister appears and says : " We would only be too glad to come to an agreement with Germany if only we could trust the words of the German Government."

I could say exactly the same myself. How gladly we would come to an understanding with Britain if only we could trust the word of her leaders. Has ever an enemy been deceived in a more infamous manner than the German people by British statesmen during the last twenty years ?

Our colonies were taken away, our trade was destroyed, our Navy was taken from us. Millions of Germans were torn from Germany and maltreated. The German people were plundered. Reparations were imposed upon them which could not have been paid in 100 years and which threw the German people into the deepest misery. Since then Germany has become a world Power, thanks to our movement. . . .

You know the efforts that I have made for many years to come to an understanding with Great Britain. We have renounced a great deal, but there is no Government which can renounce the right to live, and the National-Socialist Government naturally does not think of making such a renunciation.

It is my intention to safeguard the life and security of the German people. I have not the slightest intention of making such renunciation. Germany of today, at any rate, is ready and determined to defend and re-establish her frontiers and her *Lebensraum*.

Nazis' ' Fanatical Will Power '

We have built up an army of which there is no equal in the world, and this army is backed by a people of such compact unity as is unparalleled in history ; and above this army and this people there is a Government with fanatical will power similarly without precedent.

There is only war because the British wanted war. . . . At the bottom of this matter there is really nothing except their profound hatred of National-Socialist Germany. What they hate is the Germany which constitutes a bad example. They hate a *soziale* (communal) Germany. They hate the Germany of Social Welfare. They hate the Germany of the abolition of class distinction. They hate the Germany which has achieved all this. They hate the Germany which during the past seven years has made every effort to create for her nationals an adequate standard of living. They hate that Germany. They hate the Germany which provides her sailors with decent accommodation in ships. They hate it because they feel that their own people might be infected by it.

They hate the Germany of welfare for the younger generation. They hate the strong Germany which marches forward. They hate the Germany of the Four-Year Plan. . . . Their struggle is a struggle against a free and sound Germany, and our struggle is a struggle for the establishment of a sound and strong community of people and for the security of this community against the rest of the world. . . .

The Navy, Too, Fights in the Air

The first training of the gunners of fighting 'planes is given with a camera gun which registers on a photographic film the hits made by the gun.

After the camera gun has enabled them to become fairly expert with photographic "shots," the recruits receive training on the butts and fire live ammunition through their guns instead of films.

In the Fleet Air Arm the wireless operator plays an important part; here is a naval rating under instruction.

DURING the greater part of the last war the Royal Naval Air Service and the Royal Flying Corps were two distinct forces, but in 1918 they were combined as the Royal Air Force. The combination was not altogether successful, for when the naval machines were at sea, operating from aircraft-carriers or other warships, they were under naval command, and when they were on land they were under the Royal Air Force. The separation of the two forces gradually became inevitable, but it was not until 1937 that it was finally decided upon, and it was two years before it was completed. This change necessitated the appointment of a Fifth Sea Lord of the Admiralty as chief of the air branch, which is known as the Fleet Air Arm. The uniforms are those general in the Royal Navy, but officers are distinguished by the letter A in the curl of their sleeve stripes.

Photos, Planet News, Fox, Photopress and G.P.U.

This wireless rating is making his notes after one of his first flights. The operator wears the same equipment as the pilot.

Recruits for the Fleet Air Arm, each carrying his notebook, are here moving off for their daily course. They are being trained at a station officially named H.M.S. "Kestrel"—alleged by the Nazi wireless to have been sunk!—for all the training stations of the Fleet Air Arm, like those for sailors undergoing other special courses, are "His Majesty's Ships," though they may actually be islands or even land aerodromes. The aeroplane, a Blackburn Shark, is one of those on which they may later receive even more practical instruction.

One More Convoy Safe Home in Port

Sometime in November a party of British journalists were enabled
to see for themselves what life in a convoy is really like. Here is
an impression of a convoy's progress through North Sea waters.

The lookout man on every ship of a convoy scans the sea for any sign of hostile craft.

"FALL in and follow me" has become a very popular game in British waters since the war began. What with minefields and drifting or ruthlessly sown mines, submarines, and raiding 'planes, the lot of the ship which prefers to be a Garbo is far from enviable. Nowadays there is safety in numbers, particularly when those numbers are guarded and conveyed by ships of the Royal Navy.

At many places off the British coasts you may see the strangely assorted armadas assemble. There are big liners which up to a few months ago were the paradise of the holiday "cruisers"; there are rusty oil tankers, ugly tramps battered by all the seven seas for many a long year, even a sprinkling of grimy colliers. In peacetime they would hardly be on speaking terms, but silly ideas about superiority are soon washed overboard in time of war.

When all the ships of the convoy have arrived at their trysting-place their captains are signalled ashore to hold conference with the naval officers who are to be responsible for the convoy's safety. Charts are studied and carefully explained, and orders are given; there is

not, in fact, much to say beyond impressing on the captains the absolute necessity of maintaining the order in which their ships are placed in the convoy, i.e. to keep station, and not to alter course except at the order of the commodore of the convoy. He is chosen by the masters of the ships themselves; he may be the captain of a big liner or the master of a humble tramp. In his selection only one thing matters—his experience of convoy work.

Now all is quiet until at the prearranged signal the ships up-anchor. With a little manoeuvring that secures their correct position in the line, the ships steam away from their harbourage. As yet, probably, no British warship is to be seen; the nearness of the ships to the coast is protection enough.

When night has fallen, however, signals

Types of the fine seamen of his Majesty's Merchant Navy who are so gallantly defying the menace of submarine and mine are seen in the two centre photographs. Left, Fireman William Bruce wears a smile, though the stokehold is the danger spot of the ship. Right, the Captain and the First Officer of a merchant ship are studying the sealed sailing orders that are issued to all ships at the port at which a convoy assembles. Immediately above an escorting warship is passing the bluff bows of a small steamer in the convoy.

Photos, G.P.U.

Though the Sun Goes Down the Convoy is Unafraid

When the sun sets on a convoy the ships draw near together between the lines of escorting warships on which the duty of protecting them from lurking enemies depends. This convoy of 24 ships in the North Sea is closing in at the end of day. In the stern of the ship in the foreground can be seen the twin Lewis gun mounted against air attack. A number of the ships of the convoy are in ballast, and as without cargoes they draw less water they are not such an easy target for U-boats.   *Photo, G.P.U.*

flash to port and starboard, and an occasional sinister shape moving swiftly past in the gloom, indicate that the British Navy is on the job. Destroyers, cruisers, escort vessels of one kind and another, they keep in close touch with their charge. When dawn breaks they are still there, and the men on the exposed decks of the cargo ships feel freshly confident as they exchange greetings with the cheery sailors.

Never do the escort ships lose sight of their convoy. Occasionally a destroyer dashes into the mist, and then perchance there comes the dull boom of a depth charge dropped where a daring submarine was believed to lurk. Occasionally, too,

the escorting fleet have drawn about the convoy like a hen covering her chickens under her wing, and from their many guns they have shown the enemy raiders that in modern war there is nothing more dangerous than to attack a convoy under the Navy's shepherding.

So the days and nights go by, and in due course, well on time, the convoy comes within hail of its destination. Then the Navy vessels exchange a last greeting and forge away across the water ready to take on their next job of convoy work.

Just how splendidly efficient is their work may be gathered from the statement

made by Sir John Gilmour, Minister of Shipping, in the House of Commons on November 14. "There have been," he said, " 3,070 ships convoyed, and only seven out of that number have been lost. That is a striking example of the co-operation between the Navy and the Mercantile Marine."

Moreover, said Sir John, the convoy system would be greatly improved and speeded up by separate treatment of slow ships as more escort vessels could be furnished, and arrangements are already being made for a substantial increase in the number of convoys. So Britain's lifeline is, and will remain, unbroken.

'THE GERMAN MENACE WILL BE BROKEN'

Broadcasting on Sunday evening, November 12, Mr. Winston Churchill reviewed the profits and losses of the first ten weeks of war. Listeners must have felt encouraged by his forthright manner and clear-sighted estimate of the situation.

'I THOUGHT," said Mr. Churchill, "it would be a good thing for me to tell you tonight how well the war has turned for the Allies during the first ten weeks. It is quite plain that the power of the British Empire and the French Republic to restore and revive the life of the Polish, Czech and Slovak people as well as to do a few other things which I will mention later, has been growing every day." Then he proceeded :

Peaceful parliamentary countries, which aim at freedom for the individual and abundance for the mass, start with a heavy handicap against a dictatorship whose sole theme has been war, the preparation for war, and the grinding up of everything and everybody into their military machine.

In our island, particularly, we are very easy-going in time of peace. We should like to share the blessings of peace with every nation, and to go on enjoying them ourselves. It is only after many vain attempts to remain at peace that we have been at last forced to go

and everybody had better make up their minds to that solid, sombre fact.

Nowadays we are assailed by a chorus of horrid threats. The Nazi Government exudes them through every neutral State. They give inside information of **the frightful vengeance they are going to wreak upon us, and they also bawl it around the world by their leather-lunged propaganda machine. If words could kill we should be dead already.**

B**UT we are not disturbed by these blood-**curdling threats. Indeed, we take them as a sign of weakness in our foes. We do not make threats in time of war. If at any time we should have some ideas of an offensive character we should not talk about them ; we should try to see how they worked out in action.

We do not at all underrate the power and malignity of our enemies. We are prepared to endure tribulation. But we made up our minds about all this ten weeks ago and everything that has happened since has made us feel that we were right then and are still right now.

No one in the British Isles supposed this was going to be a short or easy war. Nothing has ever impressed me so much as the calm, steady,

Our Air Raid Precautions are very different from what they were at the outbreak of war.

The attack of the U-boats has been controlled and they have paid a heavy toll. Nearly all the German ocean-going ships are hiding and rusting in neutral harbours, while our world-wide trade steadily proceeds in 4,000 vessels, of which 2,500 are constantly at sea.

The superior quality of our Air Force has been proved both in pilots and machines over the enemy. Our aircraft have shot down 15 German oversea raiders without losing one machine in the combats. Now the mists and storms of winter wrap our island and make continuous bombing attack of military objectives far more difficult. . . .

'Time is On Our Side'

I DO not doubt myself that time is on our side. I go so far as to say that if we come through the winter without any large or important event occurring **we shall, in fact, have gained the first campaign of the war,** and we shall be able to set about our task in the spring far stronger, better organized and better armed than ever before.

Let us, therefore, bear discomfort and many minor—and even, perhaps, needless—vexations with patience—with understanding patience—because we are all the time moving forward towards greater war strength, and because Nazi Germany is all the time under the grip of our economic warfare falling back in oil and other essential war supplies.

It may be, of course, that at any time violent and dire events will open. If so, we shall confront them with fortitude. If not, we shall profit to the full by the time at our disposal. As you may have noticed, General Goering—I beg pardon, Field-Marshal Goering—who is one of the few Germans who have been having a pretty good time for the last few years—says that we have been spared so far because Nazi Germany is so humane.

They cannot bear to do anything to hurt anybody. **All they ask for is the right to live and to be let alone to conquer and kill the weak. Their humanity forbids them to apply severities to the strong.**

Well, it may be true, but when we remember the bestial atrocities they have committed in Poland we do not feel we wish to ask for any favours to be shown to us. We shall do our duty as long as we have life and strength.

A long succession of important events has moved in our favour since the beginning of the war. Italy, which we feared would be drawn from her historic partnership with Britain and France in the Mediterranean—a partnership which will become increasingly fruitful—has adopted a wise policy of peace.

'Twin Contortionists'

N**O quarrel has developed between us and**Japan. These two great Powers, which had joined Nazi Germany in the Anti-Comintern Pact, find it difficult to accommodate themselves to the change of front towards Bolshevism which Herr Hitler and his bad adviser, Herr von Ribbentrop, both marvellous twin contortionists, have perpetrated.

No one can underrate the importance of the Treaty of Alliance between Britain and France with Turkey.

The Russian Soviet Government, embodied in the formidable figure of Stalin, has barred off once and for ever, all Nazi dreams of an advance in the East. **The left paw of the bear bars Germany from the Black Sea ; the right paw disputes with her the control of the Baltic.**

Whatever history may record about these events, the fact with which we have to reckon is perfectly plain. Nazi Germany is barred off from the East, and has to conquer the British Empire and the French Republic or perish in the attempt.

The close co-operation between the French and British Navies was emphasized when Mr. Winston Churchill arrived in Paris on November 2 to discuss Allied Naval dispositions. He is here seen in Paris with Admiral Darlan inspecting a Guard of Honour. Mr. Churchill's subsequent visit to Lord Gort at British G.H.Q. in France is shown opposite.

Photo, Keystone

to war. We tried again and again to prevent this war, and for the sake of peace we put up with a lot of things happening which ought not to have happened.

But now we are at war, and we are going to make war, and persevere in making war, until the other side have had enough of it. We are going to persevere as far as we can to the best of our ability, which is not small and always growing. You know I have not always agreed with Mr. Chamberlain, though we have always been personal friends ; but he is a man of very tough fibre, and I can tell you that he is going to fight as obstinately for victory as he did for peace. Can I say more ?

You may take it absolutely for certain that either all that Britain and France stand for in the modern world will go down or that Hitler, the Nazi regime, and the recurring German or Prussian menace to Europe will be broken and destroyed. That is the way the matter lies

businesslike resolution with which the masses of our wage-earning folk and ordinary people in our great cities faced what they imagined would be a fearful storm about to fall on them and their families at the very first moment. They all prepared themselves to have the worst happen to them at once, and they braced themselves for the ordeal. They did not see what else there was to do.

We have been agreeably surprised that ten weeks have been allotted to us, so far, to get into fighting trim. We are in a very different position from what we were ten weeks ago ; we are far stronger than we were ten weeks ago : we are far better prepared to endure the worst malice of Hitler and his Huns than we were at the beginning of September.

Our Navy is stronger. Our anti-U-boat forces are three times as numerous. Our Air Force is much stronger. Our Army is growing in numbers and improving in training every day.

So now these boastful and bullying Nazi personages are looking with hungry eyes for some small countries in the West which they can trample down and loot, as they have trampled down and looted Austria, Czecho-Slovakia and Poland. Now they turn their fierce, but also, as it seems, hesitating glare upon the ancient civilized and unoffending Dutch and Belgian nations.

They have not chosen to molest the British Fleet, which has awaited their attack in the Firth of Forth during the last week ; they recoil from the steel front of the French Army along the Maginot Line ;· but their docile conscripts are being crowded in vast numbers upon the frontiers of Holland and Belgium.

A Grave Situation Despite Guarantees

To both these States the Nazis have given the most recent and solemn guarantees. That explains why the anxiety of these countries is so great. No one believes one word Herr Hitler and the Nazi party say, and therefore we must regard that situation as grave.

I shall not attempt to prophesy—that is always dangerous—whether the frenzy of a cornered maniac will drive Herr Hitler into the worst of all his crimes ; but this I will say without a doubt, that the fate of Holland and Belgium, like that of Poland, Czecho-Slovakia and Austria, will be decided by the victory of the British Empire and the French Republic.

If we are conquered all will be enslaved, and the United States will be left single-handed to guard the rights of man. If we are not destroyed all these countries will be rescued, and after being rescued will be restored to life and freedom.

It is indeed a solemn moment when I speak to you on this tenth Sunday after the outbreak of war. Solemn ; but it is also a moment sustained by resolve and hope. I am in the singular position of having lived through the early months of the last German war upon Europe in the same position, in charge of the British Admiralty, as I am now. I am therefore very careful not to say anything of an overconfident or unduly sanguine nature.

I am sure we have very rough weather ahead, but I have this feeling that the Germany which assaults us all today is a far less stronglybuilt and solidly-founded organism than that which the Allies and the United States forced to beg for armistice 21 years ago.

I have the sensation and also the conviction, that that evil man over there and his cluster of confederates are not sure of themselves, as we are sure of ourselves, that they are harassed in their guilty souls by the thought and by the fear of an ever-approaching retribution for their crimes, and for the orgy of destruction in which they have plunged us all.

As they look out tonight from their blatant, clattering, panoplied Nazi Germany, they cannot find one single friendly eye in the whole circumference of the globe. Not one.

Russia returns them a flinty glare ; Italy averts her gaze ; Japan is puzzled and thinks herself betrayed.

Turkey and the whole of Islam have ranged themselves instinctively but decisively on the side of progress.

The hundreds of millions of people in India and in China, whatever their other feelings, would regard with undisguised dread a Nazi triumph, well knowing what their fate would soon be.

The World Against Hitler

THE great English-speaking Republic across the Atlantic Ocean makes no secret of its sympathies or of its self-questionings, and it translates these sentiments into action of a character which anyone may judge for himself.

The whole world is against Hitler and Hitlerism. Men of every race and clime feel that this monstrous apparition stands between them and the forward move which is their due, and for which the age and time are ripe.

Even in Germany itself there are millions who stand aloof from the seething mass of criminality and corruption constituted by the Nazi party machine. Let them, then, take courage amid perplexities and perils, for it may well be that the final extinction of a baleful domination will pave the way to a broader solidarity of all the men in all the lands than we ever could have planned, if we had not marched together through the fire.

As is natural in a descendant of that great British general who became the first Duke of Marlborough, Mr. Winston Churchill' was in his early days a keen and proficient soldier, while among the many offices he has held is that of Secretary of State for War from 1918 to 1921. He naturally took advantage of his visit to the French Admiralty in Paris to go on to the British Army headquarters in France. In an ornate room of an old French château, where the British Commander-in-Chief lives and works, Mr. Churchill, in a characteristic position, with a cigar in his hand, discusses the military situation with Lord Gort, on whose right Lieut.-General Pownall, the Commander-in-Chief's Chief of Staff, listens to the conversation, while he meditatively fills his pipe.
Photo, British Official: Crown Copyright

ODD FACTS ABOUT THE WAR

Worth Noting Today and Re-reading in Years to Come

Safe Deposit for Radium

Westminster Hospital's store of radium is valued at nearly £40,000. In the event of an air raid it will be deposited inside a steel tube, 15 inches in diameter and 50 feet in length, which has been sunk into the Thames gravel beneath the hospital.

"Faithful Ally"

The Air Council is to allocate the gift of £100,000 from the Nizam of Hyderabad towards the cost of a new fighter squadron to be known as the "Hyderabad Squadron," with the motto "Faithful Ally" on its crest.

Cameras in the Firing Line

A number of German war correspondents and cine-photographers have been awarded the Iron Cross. During the Polish campaign they were allowed to take part in fighting and air raids, and news reels now exhibited in Germany show the bombardment of Warsaw from very close quarters, and an attack on Polish machine-guns filmed from the inside of a tank.

"Col. Bramble" Resurrected

André Maurois, official French correspondent with the British Army, is to resume in "Figaro" the adventures of this famous hero of the Great War. Colonel Bramble has now reached the rank of general, and has a grandson in the R.A.F.

Mustn't Tell the Truth

The German newspaper "Schwarze Korps" has been suspended because it published an article dealing with the effectiveness of the Allied blockade of Germany.

From a Former Enemy

Among the many pairs of binoculars sent to the "Daily Telegraph" office, in response to the War Office appeal, was a telescope of German manufacture and ownership. The donor, a refugee living in Britain, enclosed a note which said : "This glass has been used by a former German officer who fought for a country which was not worth fighting for."

British Preferred

United States shipping lines, advertising vacancies for personnel in certain vessels sailing between the British Isles, France, and the U.S.A., specified that applicants should be of British nationality.

When the Ban was Lifted

The first consignment of war materials to leave the U.S.A. for England after the repeal of the arms embargo consisted of equipment for Imperial Airways, part of an order for 56 aeroplane engines and accessories.

Turncoats Entertained

On November 7, Field-Marshal Goering and Herr von Ribbentrop were guests of honour at a reception given by the Soviet Ambassador in Berlin to celebrate the 22nd anniversary of the Bolshevist Revolution.

Orange for Peace

Neutral aeroplanes are to be painted orange. This arrangement was made between Dutch, Belgian, Danish and Swedish air lines, and approved by the belligerent countries.

The Stripe that Failed

The scheme for preserving the New Forest ponies by marking them with zebra-like stripes has proved useless owing to the reduced lighting on vehicles. Moreover, the foals were frightened of their mothers, and fled. So the ponies have either been moved to enclosed pastures or sold.

International Gratitude

The Royal Lifeboat Institution, which has rendered such good service round our coasts to the crews of ships sunk by enemy action, has received expressions of thanks from Dutch, French and Greek shipping companies.

Mutton on the Way

The inhabitants of Jansenville and district, Cape Province, South Africa, have offered 1,000 head of sheep as a war gift to this country. The Minister of Food has gratefully accepted, subject to suitable shipping facilities being available.

Biggest Joke so Far

Britain has listened with amusement to German broadcasters "sinking" her battleships one by one, but the greatest laugh of the war was caused by the solemn announcement, early in November, that H.M.S. "Kestrel" had been sunk. "Kestrel" is the official name of the Fleet Air Arm establishment at Worthing Down, Hants !

One-Seventh

The same day that British householders were officially told that they might burn the same amount of fuel as they did last year, the Mayor of Berlin announced that during November German households and small businesses would be permitted only one-seventh of the fuel they purchased in the same period in 1938.

LEBENSRAUM !

From the Cartoon by Armstrong. By permission of the Proprietors of the Melbourne "Argus"

New Air Service

Hardy and enterprising are the men of the North. The beginning of winter in wartime has been chosen as the appropriate moment to inaugurate an air service, which operates once a week in both directions, between Finland and Scotland.

Bargains in Old Masters

So short is Germany of foreign currency that she is prepared to sell a number of Old Masters from her galleries in order to obtain it. They are going cheap, but in the purchase agreement there is a proviso that they may be bought back again at a 20 per cent increase after Germany has won the war.

Marriage at a Distance

By a special decree, a German soldier and his sweetheart may be declared married, provided that the former gives written notice, through his battalion commander, to the registrar at the bride's home town. The bride goes to the register office and gives a similar notice of her intention. This concludes the ceremony.

Oldest Colony Ever Loyal

Newfoundland, Britain's first colony, is recruiting 1,275 men to form a unit for service overseas. As soon as enlistment is complete the unit will proceed to Britain for military training.

Poppies at the Front

On Armistice Day poppies were distributed to British troops behind the lines as well as to those in advanced posts. Tank guns were hung with poppies. Every one of the British cemeteries in France received poppies. Homage was paid by the R.A.F. to British and French lying side by side. While groups of 'planes dipped in salute, a fighter flew over this cemetery and dropped there a wreath of Flanders poppies and French cornflowers.

Watch-Pigs

Pigs are being used in No-Man's-Land to give warning by their squeals of alarm at the approach of enemy patrols.

Dogs on Service

At the annual military parade in Moscow in honour of the foundation of the Soviet Republic there was a battalion of military cyclists each with a dog running at the wheel. Dogs may not be exported from Russia unless certified to be unfit for military service.

Rooms With a View

In South Queensferry, overlooking the Forth, landladies have obtained premiums for rooms which are taken at week-ends in the hope of seeing further air-raids.

Thanks to the Fuehrer

Vienna's housewives are courageous women. Some of them have paraded the streets with empty shopping baskets on which they have pinned notices which read : "We thank our Fuehrer."

Bonds of Steel

German wives are being encouraged to relinquish their gold wedding rings and replace them by rings of steel. "These," states a German broadcaster, "have a fine and noble effect."

The First Anniversary in the Second Great War

The Cenotaph in Whitehall was unveiled by King George V on November 11, 1920, and after the ceremony the burial of the Unknown Warrior in Westminster Abbey took place. Each year since then there has been a religious ceremony, and wreaths have been laid on the memorial by the King or a member of the Royal Family, and by representatives of the Dominions and ex-servicemen's societies. On the first anniversary of the Armistice of 1918 to be celebrated during the present war there was no set ceremonial, but the men who gave their lives between 1914 and 1918 were not forgotten.

In this page are scenes at the Cenotaph in 1939. Wreaths were laid at intervals, the first being that of the King and Queen. Top, left, Admiral Sir Dudley Pound, First Sea Lord of the Admiralty, lays the tribute of the senior service at the foot of the memorial. Top, centre, General Sir Edmund Ironside, Chief of the Imperial General Staff, offers the Army's tribute; and right, Air Chief Marshal Sir Cyril Newall deposits that of the Royal Air Force. Below, left, a representative of the Polish Military Mission is laying a wreath, while bottom, right, a French matelot pays tribute in the name of France.

Officially, there was no two minutes' silence, but on the first stroke of eleven traffic came to a voluntary standstill and passers-by stood bareheaded till two minutes had elapsed.

Photos, Central Press and Planet News

Yet Another Sea Crime in the Nazi Score

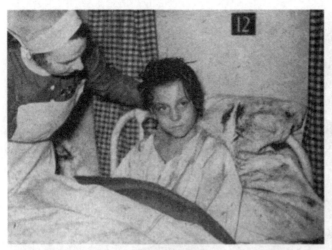

Cristina Wensvoort, left, is seen in a London hospital after her rescue. Her hair is still matted with the ship's oil. Right, one of the lifeboats that stood by all night is returning to port.

THE sinking of the Dutch liner "Simon Bolivar" in the North Sea on November 18 with heavy loss of life, was described by the Admiralty as being "a further example of the total disregard of international law and the dictates of humanity shown by the present German Government." With astonishing effrontery and an almost insane belief in the credulity of neutral nations, the Nazis endeavoured to clear themselves of the guilt for this piratical crime by stating the ship must have been sunk by a British mine. That mines were strewn widely about the open seas by the Nazis is proved by the fact that by midday on November 20 it was announced that seven ships had been destroyed by mines and two others damaged.

Those not needing treatment were taken to London hotels, outside one of which Joan Tresteill is standing.

At an East Coast port many pathetic scenes were observed. Here a survivor carries a small baby who has not been claimed.

The "Simon Bolivar," which was sunk 18 miles from the English coast by a German mine (probably laid by a submarine minelayer), was a liner of 8,309 tons. She was outward bound from Holland to the West Indies and had on board about 400 persons, of whom 140 were landed at an East Coast port. Of the eighty British subjects among the passengers a number were included in the list of over a hundred missing.

Photo, G.P.U., Planet News

I WAS THERE!

Eye Witness Stories of Episodes and Adventures in the Second Great War

The Fuehrer Had Just Left Us When . . .

Early in the morning of Friday, November 10, a few hours after the explosion in the Buergerbrau keller at Munich, what purported to be an eye-witness account of the incident was broadcast from all the German wireless stations.

OPENING his broadcast, the announcer declared that the microphone was standing inside the shattered beer-cellar, on the very spot where Hitler had stood to make his speech twenty minutes before the "infernal machine" went off.

The speaker was said to be a "member of the Nazi Old Guard" who had been present at the reunion.

"About 100 of the Old Guard," he said, "were in the room, and I myself was about a yard away from the door. Suddenly there was a flash overhead and a sudden pressure pushed me out of the door. Almost immediately afterwards came a thundering sound, and then everything was over before we could think what had happened.

"The air was so full of dust we could neither see nor breathe. We held our handkerchiefs over our mouths and got into fresh air. When the dust settled, we went back and found that the ceiling had fallen in.

"There were about 50 of the Old Guard in the hall uninjured and we set about rescue work. It was dangerous work because at any moment more of the ceiling might have fallen in. We worked for some time getting out injured and dead."

He then explained that the explosion was definitely overhead because he had seen a flash come from a spot in the gallery close to the pillar. The charge, he said, must have been in the floor near the pillar or underneath the walls close by.

Here is evidence of the extraordinary force of the explosion that wrecked the Buergerbrau, or beer hall, in Munich just after Hitler left, as explained in page 351. The building was a substantial one, but the roof and ceiling almost entirely collapsed. Those parts which did not fall to the floor were hastily propped up with timber, while the search for the bodies buried beneath the debris was carried out. In the upper photograph firemen and men of the Gestapo are searching the ruins for bodies.

Photos, Wide World

We Saw the Jewish Pogrom in Germany

Among the reports in the White Paper concerning the treatment of Jews in Germany (see page 312) was one from Mr. R. T. Smallbones, formerly H.M. Consul-General in Frankfort-on-Main. Mr. Smallbones and his daughter, who witnessed the terrible effects of the pogrom of November, 1938, told the following story to Mr. E. P. Montgomery of the " News Chronicle."

DURING the first weeks of the terror, said Mr. Smallbones, we gave sanctuary in the Consulate to hundreds of people who would have been safe nowhere else. Men and women who did not dare to show their faces in the light would hide in the woods by day and creep into the Consulate at night for food and shelter.

They slept in the hall, in the dining-room, in the kitchen, on the stairs. My wife and daughter, my staff of 11, even my servants, turned to and helped to give them what food and comfort we could.

Some of us who had seen the sufferings of the people in Germany persuaded the British Government to allow us to grant " transmigration visas," which would enable refugees to get out of Germany quickly and to stay two years in the United Kingdom while, awaiting an opportunity to emigrate to the United States and other countries.

This was provided their maintenance was guaranteed by friends, relatives or charitable organizations.

I worked closely with my American colleague in Stuttgart, and as soon as the formalities for immigration into the United States were complete I would issue a " Letter of Promise," which gave the refugee a promise of a British visa when he could obtain his German pass-port.

These " Letters of Promise " were regarded almost as talismans, for with them the relatives of men in the concentration camps could obtain their release, and possession of them made the holders safe against further molestation by the police and the S.S.

During the worst of the terror we were besieged with applicants for the letters, often trying to deal with as many as 800 to 1,000 a day.

People would begin to gather in the Consulate garden long before dawn, and by 9 o'clock, when we opened the doors, there would be hundreds waiting.

Miss Turnbull, a 23-year-old English teacher who had come in to help, would stand on a table in the hall to deal with the first rush.

We instituted a system of numbered metal disks, which Miss Turnbull handed out in order to save people from standing drearily in a queue for hours. Each one knew his turn and could go away and come back when his time drew near.

One day she had to hand out a number to her own fiancé, a German who was trying to get out.

In the main, the people who came to us were mostly women with husbands, sons or brothers in the concentration camps. Some had to bring their children with them, not daring to leave them alone at home.

All of us had to work long hours to keep abreast of the rush. In addition to the hundreds of interviews daily we had to deal with 200 or 300 applications a day by post.

" My own record, I think, was four days at my desk with six and a half hours' sleep. And the others on my staff worked just as hard, or harder.

All through November, December and January the persecutions—and our work—went on. Then things became a little easier, because the German-Jewish Aid Committee took over some of the work of investigation into means of subsistence and ultimate destination.

Even so, we continued right up to noon on September 1, forty-eight hours before war was declared, with our job of trying to give those frightened, distressed and suffering people our help. If I may say so—England's help.

Mr. R. T. Smallbones, who tells in this page the story of the pogrom of November, 1938, has been in the Consular Service since 1910.

Photo, " News Chronicle "

For weeks Mr. Smallbones' wife and daughter helped in the work, calming the fears of hysterical refugees and serving them with coffee, soup and bread when they came pleading for sanctuary in the Consulate.

They turned their sitting-room, drawing-room and hall into offices for interviewing the victims.

THE first few days of the pogrom were terrible, said Miss Smallbones. Women whose husbands had been beaten up and taken off to concentration camps, and women whose husbands had committed suicide rather than be arrested, came clamouring for shelter.

Some of them were frantic in their despair—their faces unrecognizably swollen with weeping. Their gratitude for what we did was pathetic.

They offered us little articles of jewellery and trinkets—which, of course, we could not accept—in expression of their thanks.

One old man who had maintained stoical calm broke down and wept when we gave him coffee and bread.

There was one awful scene when a woman in the Consulate saw her husband, who was waiting outside, seized and manhandled by a band of Nazi hooligans.

Miss Smallbones emphasized that the masses of the ordinary German people had no sympathy with and took no part in the pogrom.

" Nazi hooligans alone were responsible," she said.

" More than one German apologized to me for what was happening, using such phrases as ' I am ashamed to be a German when I see such things happening.' "

Miss Irene Smallbones, who worked with her father to alleviate the sufferings of the Jews, is the only daughter of Mr. Smallbones.

Photo, " News Chronicle "

||||||||||||||||||||||||||||||||||||||||||||||||||||||||||||||||||||||||| **I WAS THERE!** |||||||||||||||||||||||||||||||||||||||||||||||||||||||||||||||||||||||||||

We Tried to Save Our Mined Destroyer

On November 14 it was learnt that a British destroyer had struck a
German mine, probably laid by a submarine. Although every effort
was made to save the ship she sank. The gallant behaviour of the
crew is described in the following eye-witness stories from the
" Daily Mirror " and the " Star."

AFTER a vain struggle to save their ship,
most of the crew were picked up
by passing craft. Able-Seaman Hoyle,
of Craven Park, N.W., one of the rescued
men, told this graphic story :

" I was on deck. A terrific explosion
shook the ship. I saw a man blown
right past me over the side of the ship
into the water. At the same moment the
mast snapped and crashed down.

" As a lifeboat was lowered to rescue the
man the ship was already listing badly.
Our first thought was for the men
trapped below near the explosion.

" We forced our way through the
wreckage to rescue them. The cook in
the galley was badly injured, and an
officer who was having a bath was
bleeding badly.

" There was no panic. The injured
men were brought up and laid on the
deck while we tended to their injuries.
The man who was blown overboard had
been safely picked up, though he was
hurt by the blast of the explosion.

" We were sinking by the stern, but
there was no order to abandon ship.
Every man was eager to save her. They
worked hard shoring up the bulkheads
and manning the pumps. By this time
the quarter deck was awash.

" Some of the men were so badly
injured that they had to be tied to the
stretchers. We carried them to the other
side of the ship away from the list.

" Our radio and engines were out of
action. Then a tug arrived on the
scene, and actually got a line to us and
began to tow us. The ship had practically
righted herself, and everybody thought
she would hold.

" But a few minutes later she turned
quickly over to port and lay on her side.
Our first thought was for the injured.

" I saw the captain, who had no lifebelt himself, unstrapping one of the
injured from the stretchers.

" We put lifebelts on the injured, and
as the ship was sinking slid them into the
water. I saw one man take off his own
lifebelt and throw it to one of the injured
men as he floated in the water.

" There was a lot of oil floating on the
surface and this made swimming difficult.
A friend of mine who cannot swim a
stroke, held one of the injured men's
head above the water.

" The captain swam around encouraging
the men. Gradually the tug picked up
most of us, and then a trawler and a little
pleasure boat came out and picked up the
rest.

" While they were in the water some
of the men were singing and cracking

jokes. I saw one man who had stayed on
the bow of the sinking ship rolling a
cigarette, and jokingly remarking that
he had no matches.

" Most of the men had only one complaint. That was that they were unable
to save their ship. While we were
sinking we saw an explosion in a merchant
ship not far away."

One of the first boats on the scene
was a motor-boat with Mr. Jack Pocock,
the owner, and Mr. Ben Richards, the
engineer, on board.

" We were within a quarter of a mile
of the destroyer," said Mr. Pocock,
" when we saw her heel over and go

down stern first. Men were pouring
over the side, and the sea seemed full of
swimming sailors and oil.

" I shall never forget the courage of
those men. One swam round singing
' Even Hitler had a Mother,' and another
I tried to pick out of the water refused my
hand, saying there were other men in a
worse plight. I saw one sailor push a
piece of wreckage into the hands of a
boy and swim away.

" The 70 we picked up included the
captain and two petty officers, and we
put them aboard a tug.

" We were on our way home after this
rescue when we saw great founts of water
round the bows of the merchant ship.

" She drifted for an hour and a half
before she sank, and all the crew escaped
in their own lifeboats."

Mr. Ben Richards said :

" We heard an explosion beside a
destroyer which appeared to be under
tow by a tug. We thought they were
deliberately exploding mines and went
on with our fishing until another destroyer dashed up and told us to take
part in a rescue.

" I made our boat go as she has never
gone before and we were within a quarter
of a mile when I saw the destroyer heel
over and go down stern first.

" In the summer our fishing boat takes
50 holiday makers for trips to sea, and
yesterday we crammed 60 into it. They
were covered with oil and few of them had

One of the "happy endings" that sometimes occur when ships are lost at sea and there is a
long list of men missing is seen above. Five of the men who were missing when a British
destroyer was sunk in November were afterwards found to be among those saved. Here one
of them, Ordinary Seaman Gospell, is at his home in the North of England with his mother.

the strength to climb into the boat without
help.

" After transferring them to a tug we
picked up ten more from a rowing boat
that was so full it could not move. Many
of the men had broken limbs and other
injuries.

The engineer of a trawler which landed
six survivors said :

" One man was floating in a sea of
oil for an hour. He was nearly finished
when we pulled him aboard.

" We picked up four men in a Carley
float " (life-saving apparatus).

We Spent Five Days in the 'Deutschland'

After three weeks as prisoners on the pocket battleship " Deutsch-
land " and on the famous " City of Flint," the crew of the British
" Stonegate " arrived home on a Norwegian ship on October 30.
Here is their story as told to the " News Chronicle."

" WE were homeward bound from
South America when, about
11.15 a.m., on October 5, the 'Deutschland' appeared and fired a shot across
our bows.

" We were told to take to our boats.
There were enormous seas running.

" The 'Deutschland' then opened fire,

and within a few minutes the 'Stonegate'
was in flames and soon sank.

" We were taken aboard the 'Deutschland' and placed in cabins on a lower
deck, where constant guard was kept over
us. We were treated very fairly and got
plenty of food, but were only allowed on
deck for a half-hour at dusk for exercise.

"On the fifth day, just before we were due to go for exercise, we saw through the porthole a ship which proved to be the 'City of Flint.'

"The American captain was asked whether he would prefer to have his vessel sunk or taken to Germany. He replied that he would rather have the vessel taken to Germany.

"A boarding party of 18 German soldiers was placed on the 'City of Flint,' armed with hand grenades and revolvers.

"The 37 of us were placed under the fo'c'sle, where we were herded for days, having to sleep in the cold on wet boards. Although the American crew were prisoners they were eventually given full liberty, and did their best to provide us with food and clothing.

"We were told, however, by the German officers that if we moved over the step of the lazaret hand grenades would be thrown among us.

"Before we arrived at Tromsö the American at the wheel told the Norwegian pilot that the ship was the 'City of Flint' and that there was an English crew of prisoners on board.

"The pilot apparently informed the authorities, and a Norwegian destroyer came off and an armed guard boarded the vessel and disarmed the German prize crew.

"The Norwegians maintained control of the 'City of Flint' after we were put ashore. Then the American ship, having taken water aboard, was escorted outside the Norwegian territorial limit, and that was the last we knew of her."

Captain F. C. P. Harris, Master of the "Clement," is here seen on his way to the Admiralty with his chief engineer, Mr. W. Bryant. They established the identity of the "Admiral Scheer."

Our Ship was Sunk by a Pocket Battleship

It was the pocket battleship "Admiral Scheer" which sank the British cargo steamer "Clement" in the South Atlantic on September 30. This news was established when the "Clement's" master, Capt. F. C. P. Harris, eventually arrived in London, and his story as reported in the "Daily Telegraph" is given below.

CAPT. HARRIS, who was accompanied by the chief engineer, Mr. W. Bryant, stated. "That when making for Bahia, Brazil, he saw a battleship a long way off. When she was between four and five miles away a seaplane took off from her. The 'plane circled over us," he continued, "and, without any warning, spattered the bridge with machine-gun fire. Then I knew that she must be a German raider.

"Three times the 'plane circled round us, sending machine-gun bullets into the bridge at each turn. I do not know how I escaped, but the only one hit was my chief officer. He was slightly wounded in the hand.

"Believing that we would be shelled I ordered my crew of fifty to the boats, and had gone into one myself when a picket boat from the German battleship came alongside. They told me and Mr. Bryant to get into the picket boat, and our boats were allowed to go.

"The Germans then carried a number of bombs from the picket boat on to the 'Clement,' but for some reason they did not explode.

"We were taken on board the battleship, and I recognized her at once as the 'Admiral Scheer.'

"When the bombs failed to explode, the 'Admiral Scheer' sank the 'Clement' by shell fire from about a mile off. We

were quite well treated while on board her. We were asked to give our word of honour that we would not attempt sabotage or espionage, but, strangely enough, they did not ask us any questions, and I said very little.

"We were only five hours on board the 'Admiral Scheer.' They then overtook the Greek vessel 'Papalemos,' 3,748 tons, and transferred us to her."

Capt. Harris and Mr. Bryant were landed at St. Vincent, and after seventeen days' wait there were taken to Le Havre by a Dutch boat. The "Clement's" crew was landed in Brazil.

Left are some of the crew of the Booth liner "Clement" on board the Brazilian steamer which rescued them. Right is the "Admiral Scheer," the German "pocket" battleship which turned commerce raider. Though only of cruiser tonnage—that is, 10,000 tons—she carries six 11-in. guns as against the twelve 6-in. guns carried by British cruisers of equal tonnage.

Photos, Associated Press and Planet News

First Bombs Dropped on Britain in This War

Although bombs fell in the waters of the Firth of Forth in the German raid of October 16,
the first bombs actually to fall on British soil were those dropped from the Nazi warplanes
which raided the Shetland Islands on Monday, November 13. In the one raid, as in the
other, the results, militarily speaking, were insignificant.

THE Shetlands in November. Heavy rain, thick mist, poor visibility. Suddenly out of the haze a German bomber sweeps in from the sea, almost skimming the waves as he comes. Passing over a seaplane base he fires unsuccessfully at a British seaplane in

From the nearest point on the German coast to the Shetland Isles the distance is approximately 550 miles. Thus, there and back, Nazi raiders would have to travel at least 1,100 miles.

250 lb. were dropped during the raid. Some fell in the sea and did no damage; of those that dropped on land, four buried themselves in a deep peat moor and failed to explode; and the others, though they made craters up to 20 feet wide and 9 or 10 feet deep, were equally harmless in their results. Quantities of earth and stones were hurled 150 feet into the air, and as they fell the stones were buried in the ground for several hundred yards around. One 7-lb. fragment hit a small house 400 yards away. An empty house near the shore had its roof lifted and windows broken. Crofters' houses in the neighbourhood also had their windows broken by the concussion.

In the village school a young teacher kept her class of five children singing through the clatter of gunfire and bombs without. Fragments from anti-aircraft shells fell round the school, but there were no casualties.

An exultant bulletin was issued by the German official news agency after the raid. "Our reconnaissance machines," read the statement, "discovered two

able weather during which the German reconnaissance aircraft had undertaken flights across the North Sea "deep into enemy air territory," the agency went on to claim that "the new attack against the Shetland Islands adds to the successful actions by the German air force in the northern part of the North Sea, and in attacks against British war harbours. These activities against the Firth of Forth, Scapa Flow and the Shetland Islands are only at the very beginning."

To these claims and boasts the British Air Ministry made a brief but sufficient reply : "No British aircraft were destroyed during the raid," while the Admiralty announced that : "Two attacks on the Shetlands were made today by enemy aircraft, which were driven off by anti-aircraft gunfire. The bombs dropped did no damage."

However, it is not quite true to say that there were no casualties. Careful inspection of the area involved in the raid revealed the corpse of one rabbit who, there is reason to believe, died as the result of enemy action.

Here is the scene of the German raid on the Shetlands on November 13. In the foreground not far removed from the row of crofters' cottages is one of the craters formed by the bombs dropped : A and B mark its limits, and it is about 20 ft. in diameter. Little damage was done, but on the right is one of the windows broken by the concussion.
Photos, Associated Press

the air. Then, when above a number of war vessels at a height of about 1,000 feet, he drops four bombs, or they may have been aerial torpedoes. Again he fails to make a hit.

By now other Nazi raiders have followed in his wake. More bombs are dropped, and then, speeded by terrific anti-aircraft fire, the raiders disappear into the mist as quickly as they came.

At least sixteen bombs—some of them armour-piercing—said to weigh about

cruisers, several smaller units, nine flying boats, several cargo boats and a large passenger ship in Sullom Voe. They decided on the cruiser and the flying-boats as their objectives. Despite firing from anti-aircraft guns, coastal batteries and ships, our flyers dived from the clouds. Two flying-boats were destroyed by fifty-kilogram bombs. It is believed that a heavy bomb struck the cruiser, for flames and smoke were noted by the airmen." After stressing the unfavour-

OUR DIARY OF THE WAR

Monday, November 13, 1939

R.A.F. fighter aircraft repulsed a German raider over the East Coast.

Two attacks on the Shetlands were made by enemy aircraft, which were driven off by anti-aircraft gunfire. Bombs were dropped, the first time in this war on British soil, but did no damage.

Air Ministry announced that an attack on a U-boat was made on Sunday by a British reconnaissance aircraft of the Coastal Command.

German reconnaissance machines reached the outskirts of Paris and were met by anti-aircraft fire.

Activity of aircraft on both sides was reported from the Western Front.

Finnish delegation left Moscow for Helsinki **without an agreement** having been reached.

British steamer " Ponzano " reported sunk by a U-boat.

Admiralty announced that two German steamers, " Mecklenburg " and " Parana," intercepted by British warships, had been scuttled by their crews. After rescuing the crews, the warships finally sank the ships by gunfire to prevent their being dangerous to navigation.

Formation of a South African seaward defence force officially announced.

Tuesday, November 14

Hitler's reply to the offer of mediation by Queen Wilhelmina and King Leopold was reported to have been communicated to the Dutch Minister and the Belgian Ambassador in Berlin, and to be unfavourable.

Admiralty announced the **loss of a destroyer** through striking a German mine.

Survivors of the Fleetwood trawler " Cresswell," sunk by U-boat shell-fire off the North of Scotland, were landed by another trawler after spending over six hours in the submarine.

Norwegian tanker " Arne Kjode " reported sunk by a U-boat.

Polish Prime Minister, General Sikorski, and the Foreign Minister, M. Zaleski, arrived in London.

Medals of the Military Division of the Order of the British Empire were awarded to two airmen for gallantry in helping comrades.

Trade negotiations in Stockholm between Sweden and Germany were broken off.

Czech police broke up a Czech Fascist demonstration in Prague, 12 persons being injured.

Wednesday, November 15

Von Ribbentrop received the Belgian Ambassador and Dutch Minister in Berlin and informed them that as a result of the " blunt rejection " of the peace appeal by Great Britain and France, the German Government considered the matter closed.

Dr. Paasikivi, head of the Finnish delegation, which had returned to Helsinki, stated that **Russia had made military demands** which could not be granted.

Violent propaganda against Finland was broadcast from Moscow.

It was reported that recent daylight reconnaissance flights by R.A.F. machines over Germany had yielded valuable photographs of military objectives.

The King received General Sikorski and other members of the Polish Government.

Mr. Eden and the Empire envoys returned to London after their tour of the Western Front.

M. Paul Reynaud, French Finance Minister, who had paid a two-day visit to London at the invitation of Sir John Simon, returned to Paris.

British steamer " Woodtown " reported blown up, with the loss of nine lives.

Thursday, November 16

Paris reported that formidable defences in front of the Maginot Line had been completed.

German aeroplane which flew over Dunkirk on November 11 now known to have been shot down by French batteries there.

THE POETS & THE WAR

VIII

TO THE DEAD

(NOVEMBER 11, 1918-1939)

BY SIR JOHN SQUIRE

Your Peace, she never came of age,
  That Peace you bought with bitter price ;
Nor now survives in this dull rage
  One sign of all your sacrifice.

Your sons must arm again to do
  What all you, dying, thought you'd done ;
How shall they doubt that rumour true
  Of Vanity beneath the sun ?

A risen Fiend ! A faded goal !
  These trampled lands, this wasted sky
Keep no surprises for the soul
  Either of hope or agony !

*   *   *   *   *

Last night, in cold and smothering dark,
  A memory of your courage came,
And burned, a pure and patient spark
  Which yet may light a world to flame :

Still calmly summoning, as when
  You took it with unquestioning trust
From legions of defeated men
  Who sang revelly from the dust.

O, if we fail in this mischance,
  Not you alone we shall betray,
But all our long inheritance
  Since the first dreamers lost the day !

—*The Times*

German steamer " Leander " was brought into a West Country port after the crew had prevented the captain from scuttling her.

British ship " Africa Shell " sunk by German raider off Portuguese East Africa.

French Minister of Economic Warfare stated that from the outbreak of war to November 10 the French Navy had seized 223,297 tons of contraband goods.

Cost of living officially stated to have gone up by 2½ per cent during October.

General Sikorski discussed with Mr. Burgin, Minister of Supply, proposals for the equipment of Polish forces designed to co-operate with the Allied forces.

German reply to the offer of mediation was considered by the Dutch Cabinet. Later it was announced that the Netherlands Government would communicate with the Belgian Government on the matter.

Friday, November 17

Meeting of the Allied Supreme War Council was held in London.

An **enemy reconnaissance 'plane flew over South-west Lancs, Cheshire and North Wales,** and another over the Shetlands. No bombs were dropped. Anti-aircraft guns were in action.

Air Ministry announced that daylight reconnaissances over North-west Germany were carried out and an important naval base successfully photographed.

Enemy reconnaissance 'planes dropped leaflets over towns in Central and South-east France.

Nine Czech students executed and many demonstrators arrested following **riots in Bohemia.** Czech universities closed down for three years.

Violent attack on Russia, warning her not to interfere in the Balkans, broadcast from Rome in Russian.

General Sikorski, Polish Prime Minister, visited Scotland and presented war decorations to members of Polish naval units.

Saturday, November 18

Martial law declared in Prague and other big Czech towns. Further executions took place.

Dr. Hacha, President of the Protectorate, broadcast an appeal to the Czechs to refrain from disturbance or resistance to authority.

Dutch liner " Simon Bolivar " sunk by German mine in North Sea. About 140 persons reported missing.

German aircraft, sighted in Dutch territorial waters, returned the fire of Dutch 'planes which went in pursuit.

Enemy aircraft reported off the East Coast and the Firth of Forth area. They disappeared when British fighters went up.

Members of the crew of " Africa Shell " identified the raider which sunk her off the East African coast as the German " pocket " battleship " Admiral Scheer."

It Is Said That . . .

Dogs are being used for food in Warsaw.

Acts of sabotage have occurred at the Erzberg iron ore works, Austria.

Salisbury Cathedral, it was stated by a Nazi broadcaster, has been looted.

German farmers and peasants are asked to develop fishing in inland waters.

It has been found that " Buna," German synthetic rubber, is useless for gas masks.

The price of Christmas trees in Germany is to be fixed by Reich Regulations Bureau.

Hitler has practised revolver shooting at moving targets every day since war started.

German shoemenders convert summer shoes into winter ones by applying strong soles and heels.

Prince von Starhemberg, formerly leader of the Austrian Heimwehr, has been deprived of German citizenship.

Rumania prayed for rain to turn her frontier districts into bogs, and so hamper or preclude military operations.

In Germany stockings and socks are rationed, except for children under three.

The German Finance Minister has forbidden women to smoke in Bohemia and Moravia.

An order for 200,000 tons of Argentine meat was placed by Great Britain and France.

Shampoo lotion is used in Berlin in the absence of soap, by those who can afford it.

Von Schirach, militant Nazi Youth Leader, has been rejected by an army medical board.

" Slave of Stalin " was inscribed on the walls of Von Ribbentrop's Berlin house one night.

German schoolchildren aid Nazi propaganda by writing persuasive letters to French children.

Zeal in tell-tale spying in some German towns reached such heights that the authorities had to discourage it.

German minorities in Yugoslavia and Hungary are resorting to desperate expedients to avoid returning to the Reich.

Vol. 1   A Permanent Picture Record of the Second Great War   No. 13

" Be Prepared " is the watchword of the armies on the Western Front, both British and French, and even in the long lull that followed the declaration of war no possible precaution against a sudden onslaught by the German army was neglected. Here in some of the underground fortifications on the sector of the front line occupied by the British troops an officer is going his rounds inspecting the sentries. Both officer and sentry are wearing gas masks—further preparation for the " real thing."

Photo, British Official : Crown Copyright

Once More the Great Adventure is Delayed

Indecision is still the order of the day in Hitler's camp. To attack on the West, or
not to attack? Hungrily he spied out his enemy's line, and once again retired to his
Chancellery, the great question unresolved.

NOVEMBER 11, the anniversary of the day in 1918 on which Germany was handed the humiliating cup of the Armistice, was chosen by Hitler to be the day on which Nazi Germany should deliver a smashing blow against her enemies on the West.

With almost absolute certainty the French High Command have been able to announce that between November 11 and November 14 the Germans had planned to attack along a front extending from Holland to the Upper Rhine. Over a million men were massed in and behind

the Siegfried Line. The time of zero hour had been fixed. Every commander had received his orders; the mechanized columns, the fleets of tanks, had been instructed as to their line of route; the batteries had their targets plotted; the airmen were standing by. Everything was ready for the opening of the "Blitzkrieg" on the West. Only one thing was lacking—the word of the Fuehrer which should launch this mighty armament into the flames of battle. But Hitler let "I dare not, wait upon I would," and the moment chosen for the great adventure passed.

Why was it that, for the first time in his career of bluster and aggression, Hitler halted his army when in effect it had been given the order to march? Perchance it was because his generals counselled caution and delay. According to details of the plan which trickled into publicity, Holland and Belgium were to be invaded and overrun by vastly superior forces equipped with all the latest machinery of modern war. One version has it that Holland was to be attacked first, in order that the Nazis might establish aerodromes and submarine bases for the better prosecution

The last outpost of a French town which lies only a few hundred metres from the German frontier is seen immediately above. The town has been evacuated and the houses are empty, while across the street, once a busy thoroughfare, a sandbag fortification has been built and is guarded night and day by sentries. The deep cellars of the houses have been used as dug-outs for the men who man the position. The top photograph is a close-up and shows the soldier seen right in the lower photograph, lying prone on the look-out, while another emerges from a cellar converted into a machine-gun post.

Photos, Courtesy of the French Embassy

French Forts Held by the Men in Khaki

The deep dug-outs which the warring armies occupied in the last war were a late development, and even then they were primitive shelters compared with the vast network of underground works of today. After the Franco-German war, 70 years ago, France built strong forts on her Western Front and they are once more being used. Some of these forts are now held by the British Army, and, above, British soldiers are entering one of these great structures of brick and earth. Below, British soldiers are being inspected in one of the passages of the fort.

Photos, British Official : Crown Copyright

of their war against England. It was confidently expected that Belgium would not go to the help of her little neighbour, and that if Britain and France attempted to do so across Belgian territory, this violation of Belgian neutrality would meet with armed resistance on the part of the Belgian army.

But on the very eve of the day chosen for the lightning stroke—on November 10, that is—the German ambassador in Brussels telephoned his Government in Berlin to the effect that the Belgian Cabinet, under the Presidency of King Leopold himself, had just resolved that if the German advance through Holland was directed south of Nijmegen, and especially across Dutch Brabant, Belgium would order immediate general mobilization and declare that her own security was threatened.

In the light of this report it is easy to believe that the German High Command may have asked for further consideration of the plan of campaign. To overrun Holland was one thing; but to have to meet not only the Dutch army,

As the winter draws on the British soldiers who were [town dwellers have found amidst much that is unfamiliar in French towns one figure that reminded them of home—the roast-chestnut man. He finds good customers in these soldiers.

Many French farmers and their wives remember the last war. Once more there are strange objects in French farmyards, and here in an outbuilding the British Army has made a small ammunition dump, but it may be taken that it no more perturbs the people of the farm than it does the ducks on their way home from the pond.
Photos, Keystone, British Official: Crown Copyright

supported by sea and air from Britain, but the Belgian army, would be quite another. Moreover, if Belgium came in, the door would be open to the march of French and, more particularly, British armies across the Low Countries. It was well known that the British Expeditionary Force was assembled behind the Maginot Line ready to be dispatched at a moment's notice to the zone of active operations.

Again, the hesitation of the generals may have been buttressed by the advice of the diplomats. Unprovoked aggression against Holland, let alone Belgium, would arouse the fiercest hostility in the United States, in whose national fibre Dutch elements are so conspicuously worked.

Yet another reason for the delay may be advanced—cracks in the façade of the Nazi mansion. Only two days before there had been the extraordinary episode of the bomb in the Munich beer cellar; there was barely-contained insurrection in Czecho-Slovakia; there was grumbling in Austria, and many evidences of deep-seated hatred in Poland. In spite of all the efforts of Himmler's men, criticism of Hitler and his policy was making itself heard. Only a military check might be required to unloose boundless stores of simmering revolt.

Whatever the reason, the chosen day passed as uneventfully as any of its predecessors. Once again the communiqués reported nothing but inactivity on the Western Front. Hitler, it was becoming increasingly apparent, had lost the initiative. Gone were the days of lightning strokes against little peoples far from effectual aid. Now every step was filled with danger, and vast hosts, called into existence by Nazi aggression, waited in easy confidence for the delivery of the onslaught.

'Vivent les Guards!' as They March Through Paris

In the photograph top left a flower girl is pinning a flower to the tunic of a man of a detachment of Welsh Guards marching through Paris. His embarrassment is due to the fact that the wearing of emblems by soldiers without permission is strictly against King's Regulations. Grenadier Guards took part in the Armistice Day celebrations at the Arc de Triomphe this year, and in the photograph top right the French Minister of Pensions is in conversation with a British officer. Below, the Grenadiers are marching past the church of La Madeleine.

Photos, Associated Press and Sport & General

Young France Prepares for Air Battle

This French pilot is typical of the gallant airmen who, in the greatest air battle of the war so far, engaged 27 enemy aircraft with only nine 'planes and brought down nine of the enemy machines (see page 362).

As in the British Air Force, the young French airman in training first learns his marksmanship with a photographic gun which records the "hits" he has made. The learner, above right, is making such a flight with a camera-gun. Immediately above a beginner is being flagged away.

In the photograph immediately above, an instructor is pointing out the features of a big 12-cylinder aero-engine to officers under training. It was to a similar type of French engine that the first successful "motor-cannon," or shell gun, firing between the arms of the "V," was fitted. These guns are now standard armament on many Continental aircraft.

Photos, Robert Capa

THE French Air Force (L'Armée de l'Air) has made remarkable strides during the past year. The crisis of 1938 revealed that while the personnel showed the same gallant spirit as that of 1914–1918, the output of machines had fallen behind. Many military aircraft on which the pilots were trained were out of date, and they were not being rapidly replaced.

As soon, however, as the workers in the aircraft factories realized what their country needed, they set to with a will. All differences were forgotten, and hundreds of aircraft characterized by the fine workmanship and engineering skill of French mechanics were soon being turned out. Now French machines are among the best in the world, and the men who fly them have proved their prowess over and over again.

An official announcement on Nov. 15 was to the effect that French airmen had carried out 260 reconnaissance flights, besides 100 other missions in the air, and had shot down 24 enemy 'planes with the loss of only eight.

Bombers of the New French 'Army of the Air'

Though French airmen were, and are, famed as dashing pilots of fighter aircraft, they are just as efficient when they fly the big bombers of the French Air Force. Above is a scene in the capacious pilot's cabin of such a machine, with one young Frenchman, map in hand, at the controls, and two of his comrades on the "ground floor" also at work. Early in the war a decree lowered the minimum age limit for recruits to the Armée de l'Air from 18 years to 17 years.

Photo, Robert Capa

Poland Tastes the Bitterness of Defeat

No longer a belligerent, Poland remained the war's most tragic victim.   Under the invader's heel a brave people writhed—and stored up vengeance for the morrow.

AFTER the fire and sword of the battle there came in Poland the officially-directed looting and ravaging, the sneaking of the spy, the inquisition of the Gestapo, the crack of the overseer's whip, the clanging of the fast closing door in the dungeon of fortress and prison.   "We Germans," said Herr Forster, the Danzig Nazi leader in a speech at Torun, " we Germans will take revenge for all that Poles have done to us.   We shall never repeat our old mistake of being guided by toleration and sentimentality.   We shall act ruthlessly."

Certainly it was with a ruthless brutality even surpassing that shown by the Kaiser's bullies a generation earlier that the Nazis set about the systematic suppression of everything in Poland that savoured of independence.   There was the deliberate organization of human misery on a huge scale.   Tens of thousands of innocent folk were driven from their homes without compensation and on the eve of winter in order that room might be made for those Germans who had been " called home " by the Fuehrer from the Baltic States.   The " apathetic Poles " who showed no eagerness to co-operate with the Nazis were driven to work by force.   On the heads of the Jews —and there are many Jews in Poland— contumely of the most foul and humiliating kind was heaped ; the Poles were treated as a conquered people, but the Jews as pariahs hardly worthy of the human name.

In the former capital terrible conditions still reigned.   Now reduced to the status of a provincial town, Warsaw bore on every hand the indelible traces of its siege. Most of the principal streets were partly in ruins, and amongst the places largely destroyed were the opera and two other theatres, the National Museum, the royal palace and the chief railway stations. On the pavements sinister crosses marked the burial places of persons killed in the bombardment, and gardens, too, had been transformed into graveyards.   A curfew at seven o'clock in the evening drove the population into homes from which wireless sets and telephones had been seized by the Nazi authorities.   Food was scarce and of poor quality, and the Polish population, and still more the Jewish, were suffering from privation if not from actual starvation.

Expelled at Three Days' Notice

Conditions in Gdynia—renamed by the Nazis Gotenhafen—were even worse, for this model city on the Baltic, proudly looked upon by the Poles as a monument of their regained nationhood after the Great War, was now compulsorily emptied of its Polish population and turned over to the use of German immigrants from the Baltic States.   Three days' notice was given to the Poles to leave the city, and no householder was allowed to take away anything more than personal belongings.   The houses and flats had to be left in good order with the keys in the doors ready for the arrival of the new occupants.   It may be noted, however, that before the newcomers arrived, agents of the Gestapo made a thorough search of the dwellings and removed therefrom practically everything of value over and above the bare furniture and hangings. Most of the Poles were taken to places in the interior of the country, though some who could find nowhere to go were herded in barracks outside the city.

In Russian Poland conditions were on the whole rather better.   No whisper of Polish or Ukrainian nationalism was permitted to be heard, but the Poles, if they were regarded as Russians, were at least treated as such.   Furthermore, there was no such shocking discrimination against the Jews as was witnessed in Nazi Poland. The process of Sovietization was carried

out gradually and the Russian officials exerted themselves to win the good will of the populace.

Strange as it may seem, guerilla fighting was still going on in various parts of the country.   In some places German soldiers and officials took good care not to go out alone after dark for fear of being ambushed.   Occasionally Polish bands of irregulars successfully attacked detachments of Nazis on the march.   In the mountainous country of the Carpathians, Polish troops still refused to submit to the invader, whether German or Russian. Even in the completely occupied territory there was underground activity—that activity of a conspiratorial nature in which the Poles have been perfected during more than a century of repression. Whatever the appearance to the contrary, then, the Polish spirit was still unbroken.

The Communist cyclist canvassers in the top photograph are parading the streets of Bialystok, a town of that part of Poland occupied by Russia, before the plebiscite held to decide whether White Russia should be included in the U.S.S.R.   Immediately above, Polish soldiers taken prisoner during the German campaign are at work on the land under an armed guard.

Photos, Wide World and E.N.A.

Prague under the Bully's Bludgeon

Hard indeed is the lot of the people of Czecho-Slovakia, who, after but twenty years of freedom, are now subjected to a tyranny far worse than that of the Austrian Kaiser. Yet they are not without hope.

Dr. Emil Hacha was chosen President of Czecho-Slovakia on November 30, 1938, immediately after the Nazis had declared the country to be a German Protectorate.

Photo, Planet News

FOR twenty years October 28—the anniversary of the day in 1918 on which the national Council of the Czechs and Slovaks took over the government of Bohemia, Moravia, and Silesia, on the collapse of Austria-Hungary—was celebrated in Czecho-Slovakia as a day of national thanksgiving and rejoicing. Even in 1938, when the humiliation of the Munich Conference was so recent, the celebration was marked by the usual ceremonies and festivities.

Came 1939, and now Czecho-Slovakia was no more. Moravia and Bohemia had been overrun by the Nazi armies and declared German Protectorates—part of the German people's "lebensraum." Prague, the ancient centre of the Czech people, was no longer a capital but a provincial city all too obviously dominated by German might.

As in previous years, the day was set apart for visiting the national monuments and the tombs of the heroes of Czech history. The public vehicles went empty along the streets, and the shops, too, had hardly a customer. In spite of the order that absence from work would be considered as an act of sabotage punishable by German military law, large numbers of the workers left their factories and assembled for the usual parade.

At noon a crowd of many thousands had gathered in the central boulevard of Prague. The demonstration was entirely peaceful, and the Czech police had the situation well in hand. A little later, however, a band of Sudeten German youths started a scuffle with a procession of young Czechs wearing tricolour badges and peaked riding caps such as President Masaryk used to wear. Members of the crowd joined in the fray, and German armoured cars, held in readiness, were rushed into the streets. Soon the place was littered with wounded. A number of

prisoners were taken to the Gestapo headquarters and, judging from the cries heard by those waiting in the street, were brutally treated.

As evening came on curtains were pulled back, blinds remained undrawn, in order that the lamps in the houses should shine forth into the darkness, as is the custom of the Czech people on days of mourning and national distress. Patriotic fervour was still further stimulated when some thousands gathered before the church of St. Mary in the Snow and sang the Czech national anthem. Again there was shooting in the streets, and again gangs of Sudeten Germans, under the direction of the Nazi State Secretary, Karl Hermann Frank, did their best to stir up trouble by way of deliberate provocation, particularly in the park of Karlovo Nemesti, where revolvers, whips and the butt ends of rifles were employed with savage effect. A score or so of Czechs were killed in the street brawls, and 3,500 were estimated to have been taken away to the city prisons.

Despite the shootings and imprisonments, however, the Czech demonstrations continued, and there was a further great expression of national feeling on November 15, when Jan Opletal, a 22-year-old medical student who had died of the six revolver bullets he received on October 28, was carried in honour to the grave. Thousands of his fellow students assembled in procession, funeral flares were lit, defiant speeches made, and the Czech and Slovak anthems sung to the tune of cries of "Death to the Murderers" and "Long live Liberty."

Some of the demonstrators assembled in the square where stands the Czech Unknown Warrior's tomb, and there sang the patriotic anthems. The Sudeten Germans were once again in evidence as agents provocateurs, doing their best to embroil the Czech police with their fellow nationals. Accompanied by German police, bands of Sudeten "specials" raided the University and the Czech societies, and many persons were taken away to the Gestapo headquarters. Here, with or without the mockery of a trial, many of the captives were shot.

The shootings were confirmed by the official German News Agency, which announced on November 17 that nine Czech students—in reality many more—had been executed, a number of demonstrators arrested, and the Czech universities had been closed for three years.

The Puppet at the Microphone

While the arrests and the executions were still going on, Dr. Hacha, the puppet President of the Protectorate, delivered a broadcast address to the Czech people. In his speech, which bore obvious traces of Nazi composition, he pointed out that, as the Czech people had been incorporated in Germany's "living space" and Germany was at war, it should be understood that Germany must take all the measures necessary for victory. . . .

Shortly afterwards it was announced that Hacha had left the city, and von Neurath, the Nazi "Protector," was summoned to Berlin to report. Only six months had elapsed since Hitler marched into Czecho-Slovakia—to restore order!

From the very beginning of the Nazi entry into Czecho-Slovakia there was unrest among the people, and months before the war there were public demonstrations against alien rule. Above is a scene early in the summer when students openly held an anti-Nazi parade. Many arrests were made at these meetings, and, as can be seen above, the police handled those arrested anything but gently.

Photo, Planet News

Round the Clock in a Prison Camp

Written by a non-Nazi German who was interned in England, this sympathetic study of life in a British prison camp may well be compared with the account of the treatment of German nationals by the Nazi Government given in page 312.

One of the guards at a prison camp for Germans in the North of England is this private soldier, formerly in the Coldstream Guards, who stands 6 ft. 3 in. in height.

Photo, Fox

L ET us try to watch Fritz Schmidt or Hans Müller—one of those young Nazis who have fallen into British hands—during a day in his life as a prisoner-of-war. It may be somewhere on the coast, in the pleasant surroundings of a former holiday camp, or farther north in the grounds of an imposing country house. He may live in a large room where pairs of barrack-room beds, one on top of the other, are arranged in orderly rows, or he may share a seaside " chalet " with two of his comrades. In any case his life is ruled by a series of well-thought-out, strict, but humane ordinances.

He has to get up early—at 5.30 in summer, at 6.30 in winter—to air and arrange his bedding, consisting, as the case may be, of a mattress or a palliasse, perhaps a cushion and two or three woollen blankets, and to make his toilet. As a prisoner-of-war he is distinguished by a large round label which he wears on his back directly under the collar of his coat. As a simple " internee "—if, for instance, he was a member of the crew of a mer-

chantman prize—he wears no such badge.

In summer at 7 a.m., in winter at 8, the prisoners, arranged in groups under their own chosen leaders, are marched into the dining-hall for their first meal. The breakfast consists of porridge, tea with milk, and a plentiful supply of bread with margarine ; those who can afford it supplement their meals with jam, marmalade, fruit and, of course, the inevitable consolation of soldiers, in captivity as well as in the field—tobacco in every form. A canteen attached to the camp stocks these and other essentials at regular prices, but as the prisoners are not allowed any cash their purchases are settled by way of a " clearing." They are not allowed many other things, such as knives, scissors, razors, matches, lighters —anything, in fact, which might be used to do harm to the owner or his guards.

The Freedom of the Camp

That, and the barbed wire surrounding the camp, are, however, the most palpable signs of captivity. After the first roll-call following breakfast, and an inspection by the camp's physician with his aides, Fritz Schmidt is free to do mostly as he likes : to play cards with his comrades, to read, to learn English, or to listen to one of the other lessons usually arranged by the prisoners themselves and smiled upon by the British authorities. There are also daily working parties—filling sandbags, digging A.R.P. trenches, gardening or doing other work on the improvement of the " compound," and in keeping it clean and tidy. For hard work the squad are issued with overalls and rubber boots, and are rewarded by extra rations · of food.

Food is a main concern of the prisoners, most of whom are young and healthy youths, and they are glad to be permitted to prepare it themselves according to their national taste. At noon, the principal meal consists of a substantial dish of meat, vegetables and potatoes,

followed by a sweet, often rice pudding or baked apple with custard. A distribution of letters—which come only sparsely and with great delays, while only one per month may be dispatched—or a radio performance may follow, and half an hour later begins the compulsory two hours of recreation. Football and other games are played in the large grass-covered square provided in each camp.

After that they are mostly free again. Perhaps mending their socks and clothes, perhaps—mostly on the obligatory weekly bathing day—doing their modest laundry, playing " skat," chess, or taking part in a choir practice, they fill the hours before and after their third, the evening, meal. This takes place at 5.30 or 6 p.m., and consists of a nourishing vegetable soup, tea, bread and margarine once more. Where possible half an hour of broadcasting performances are given ; and a remarkable sight it was to see the astonishment on the faces of the young disciples of Hitler when they heard their first B.B.C. news in German : incredulity, anger, sneers—then doubt, confusion, sometimes even shame passed over their features. Prisoners though they were, they had at last the chance to catch a glimpse of the real world, the truth that was hidden from them by the soul-crushing machinery of a dictator.

Football has gained a hold on the young manhood of Germany, and these prisoners taken from U-boats and merchant ships are spending a happy hour kicking the ball about. Neither the ground nor the goalposts are " regulation," and an armed guard stands by, but not to protect the " ref."

Photo, Associated Press

Theirs is an Easy Fate—in England

The prisons in which German prisoners of war are confined are ringed round with barbed wire and are guarded by sentries day and night. Right, prisoners are being interrogated. The two men in the foreground speak English and are acting as interpreters. These men have on their backs and knees the circle of cloth that marks them as prisoners of war.

Some places in the North of England have seen unusual passers-by lately. Prisoners have been taken from German ships, and have marched under armed escort to the prison camp which will be their home for the rest of the war. As they pass to the prison camps they are watched with curiosity by the civilians and in not one case have there been hostile demonstrations against the captives, such as were all too frequent against British prisoners in Germany during the last war.

The lot of German prisoners in Britain is by no means a hard one, as these two photographs, taken at a North British internment camp, show. Officers taken from the U-boats are interned in an old country house, and, left, some of them are seen round a log fire enjoying their favourite recreation of reading; but outside there are barbed wire and sentries. Right, seamen from U-boats and captured merchant ships are at their midday meal—plain wholesome fare such as no civilian in Germany gets.

Photos, Fox, Associated Press, G.P.U.

Their Majesties' Lead in Our War Effort

In this war, as in the last, Britain's Royal House is giving the Nation and the Empire a splendid example of devotion and willing readiness to shoulder all the day's fresh burdens and responsibilities.

The Queen during one of her many visits to war charities examining woollen articles at a sale at the Mansion House, London, on behalf of the British Red Cross.
Photo, Topical

In that broadcast to the women of the Empire which the Queen delivered on the night of Armistice Day from a room in Buckingham Palace—in that broadcast so intimate, so filled with understanding—there was one passage which must have made a particularly strong appeal to those whom her Majesty had most in mind. "The King and I know," she said, "what it means to be parted from our children, and we can sympathize with those of you who have bravely consented to the separation for the sake of your little ones."

Amongst the great multitude who heard those words there must have been many who remembered the picture of the Royal couple bidding farewell to their children on the eve of their visit to Canada, and they must have remembered, too, with what joy the young princesses greeted their parents on their return to England after seven weeks' absence in the great Dominion across the seas.

Even then Britain's Royal Family was not long reunited, for on the outbreak of war the children were left in the security of Balmoral Castle in the remote Highlands, while their Majesties returned to London to play their part in the hour of the Empire's crisis.

The King, for his part, displayed the keenest and most intelligent interest in the work of the three Services. It should be remembered that, like his elder brother, the Duke of Windsor, King George has had actual experience of modern warfare. During the Great War he served in the Royal Navy, and was actually present in H.M.S. "Collingwood"

at the battle of Jutland in May, 1916. Since he came to the throne he has given many indications that his headship of the Army, Navy and R.A.F. is no mere titular distinction, but is the expression of a very solid fact. Shortly before the war began he reviewed the Reserve Fleet at Weymouth, and since the opening of hostilities he has paid many a visit to units of the Army and squadrons of the R.A.F.

Getting to Know the Facts

Nor has he forgotten the civilian effort. Long remarkable for his deep interest in social and economic problems—the camps that he organized as Duke of York blazed the trail in the achievement of a deeper understanding between the boys of the public and elementary schools, and the industrial welfare movement owes much to his constant interest—the King is now frequently to be seen inspecting civilian establishments engaged in the production of the munitions of war and the defence posts of the A.R.P. Their Majesties' unremitting interest in the work and welfare of the Dominions has also been illustrated since the outbreak of war by the visits which the King and his Consort have paid to the headquarters of the Dominions in this country. As always, the King likes to get his facts for himself, straight from the men who know them best.

In wartime the Queen's life as wife and mother, Royal hostess and mistress of a large establishment is made ever more busy by the exacting demands of these crowded days. Early in September it was announced that the Queen had been appointed Commandant-in-Chief of the Women's Royal Naval Service, the Auxiliary Territorial Service, and the Women's Auxiliary Air Force, and she is also President of the British Red Cross Society, in addition to being Colonel-in-Chief of several regiments of the Army. Like her husband, she manages to perform in the course of every day a vast variety of service. The daily round begins at 8 a.m., when she sits down with her secretary to run through the morning's post. Her diary, arranged since the war began on a day-to-day basis, may take her to some factory or hospital, to visit mothers in their homes or evacuated children in their billets. At lunch she may preside over an official gathering, and dinner, too, will probably see her still playing her part in the State machine.

Twice a week she presides at Buckingham Palace over a sewing circle composed of the senior palace servants and wives of

palace officers. As a result of the efforts of the Royal sewing party, many a soldier at the Front, many a patient in our hospitals, is enabled to enjoy knitted comforts of one kind or another.

Sometimes, but very seldom, the King and Queen so manage their respective time-tables that they can go out together. On November 13 it was revealed that they went to their first cinema since war began. Even then they had still to see their first wartime play, and to attend their first wartime dance. It is not surprising that with such a round of eventful days, carrying the load of such a burden of responsibility, their Majesties should welcome a quiet evening at home.

The King in the Service uniform of a Field-Marshal, photographed in October 1939. His Majesty has his gas mask slung over his shoulder.
Photo, Speaight Ltd.

The King and Queen Inspect the Home Front

In the course of a tour of military camps in the Home Counties, the King inspects the kit of young soldiers undergoing training.

Photo, Keystone

Here their Majesties are seen after inspecting a unit of the Balloon Barrage—one of those in the vicinity of London.

Photo, Topical

The Queen's Message to the Empire's Women

" War has at all times called for the fortitude of women. Even in other days, when it was an affair of the fighting forces only, wives and mothers at home suffered constant anxiety for their dear ones, and too often the misery of bereavement. . . .

" Now this is all changed, for we, no less than men, have real and vital work to do. To us also is given the proud privilege of serving our country in her hour of need.

. " The call has come, and from my heart I thank you, the women of our great Empire, for the way that you have answered it. . . .

" Many of you have had to see your family life broken up, your husband going off to his allotted task, your children evacuated to places of greater safety.

" The King and I know what it means to be parted from our children, and we can sympathize with those of you who have bravely consented to this separation for the sake of your little ones.

" Equally do we appreciate the hospitality shown by those of you who have opened your homes to strangers and to children sent from places of special danger.

" All this, I know, has meant sacrifice, and I would say to those who are feeling the strain: Be assured that in carrying on your home duties and meeting all these worries cheerfully, you are giving real service to the country. You are taking your part in keeping the home front, which will have dangers of its own, stable and strong. . . ."

From a Broadcast, November 11, 1939.

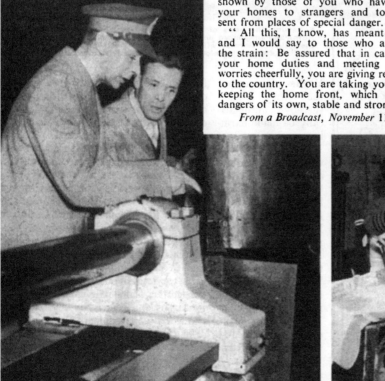

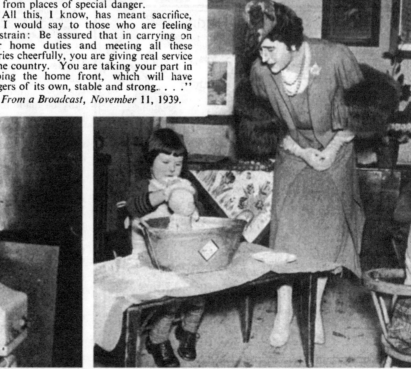

Since the outbreak of war the King and Queen have been tireless in their war work. Even amidst the pressing calls of State duties the King has found time to visit the Navy, the Army, the Air Force and munition factories. Left, his Majesty, who is keenly interested and expert in the use of tools and machinery, is examining work in an ordnance factory. Right, a charmingly natural photograph of the Queen taken during a visit to an evacuation area. Top, her Majesty at the microphone during her broadcast to the women of the Empire on Armistice Day.

Photos, Associated Press and " The Times "

New Nazi Frightfulness Off Britain's Coasts

A number of neutral ships sunk by German mines close into the English shore marked
the opening of another terrible chapter in the history of German frightfulness. But
the repetition with whatever novel features of the horrors of 1917 clearly cannot fail to
have the most disastrous consequences—for Germany.

REALIZING that their submarine campaign against England was not going too well, Germany resorted to the indiscriminate laying of mines in the channels used by ships calling at British ports.

The first victim was the Dutch crack liner "Simon Bolivar," which struck a German mine in the North Sea on November 18 and rapidly sank with the loss of more than 80 lives. "This mining," said an official statement issued from the Admiralty, "is a further example of the utter disregard of international law and the dictates of humanity shown by the present German Government. The mines were laid without any notification in the channel followed by merchant shipping both British and neutral, and there is no doubt that they were laid for the specific purpose of destroying such shipping."

In accordance with the Hague Convention of 1907, the British Government has publicly notified the position of minefields laid by the British Navy outside territorial waters (*see* chart below), and since the war began Germany also has given notification of the areas being strewn with German mines. The mines which caused the loss of the "Simon Bolivar" and the number of other victims which speedily followed were laid by German submarines off the British east coast without any notification and in reckless disregard of the consequences.

At first authoritative Nazi circles maintained that the Dutch liner had sunk at a point where no German minefields existed, and that it was impossible for any German mine to have drifted to the point in question. The suggestion was made, indeed, that it was a British mine that was responsible for the disaster. But not only have no British mines been laid in the particular area— why should they be laid in a channel used continuously by British merchant ships and neutral vessels bringing goods to our ports ?—but any British mines which break adrift from their moorings, as frequently happens in stormy weather, comply with a further requirement of the

neutral vessels have taken place was the inscription in German : "Gott strafe Churchill. When this goes up, up goes Churchill." (See also page 403.)

In view of the recent Nazi hints concerning a "secret weapon," it seemed clear that the losses were due to a new mine of a magnetic type, i.e. which explodes not on contact, but on the approach of a ship which operates the magnetic installation (consisting in principle of a delicately-balanced magnetized needle) and fires the charge. Most of these mines would be laid by submarine minelayers, but an Admiralty report stated that German aircraft had laid mines at five different localities on the East Coast on the nights of Nov. 20 and Nov. 21.

One seaplane was seen to alight on the sea off the East Coast and remain there

Following the news of the sinking of the "Simon Bolivar," the Admiralty announced on November 20 the loss of five other ships by the action of German mines. One of these was the steamer "Blackhill" (2,492 tons), which is seen above as it made its last plunge.

Photo, Keystone

Keeping to the rules of the International Hague Convention of 1907, the positions of the three minefields shown roughly in this map were immediately notified to all governments. Not so the new German minefield off the East Coast of Britain, laid in a crowded seaway used by peaceful merchant ships.

Map by courtesy of "The Times"

Hague Convention that they should thereby automatically be made harmless.

Unfortunately for the Nazi contention, a writer, said to be a naval expert, boasted on November 21 in Field-Marshal Goering's paper, the "Essener National Zeitung" that Germany was "now striking hard blows at shipping right under the English coast"—an obvious reference to the sinking of the "Simon Bolivar" and her fellow victims. Moreover, on a German mine captured in the area where sinkings of

for some time as if it were sowing mines or working in conjunction with a U-boat, and people on the shore of the Thames estuary who watched the raiders on the night of November 22, declared that these were flying very low, and that they saw two or three objects fall from one of the machines and make a big splash.

It may be recalled that on the day that the "Simon Bolivar" sank, the captain of the Danish steamer "Canada," which was lost on November 4, was telling a Court of Inquiry in Copenhagen that his ship was sunk by a "magnetic mine." Magnetic mines of a primitive kind were tried out by the Germans in the last war, and it is reasonable to suppose that the Nazis have not forgotten those early experiments.

The resort to indiscriminate sinkings, indeed, is proof positive of the desperate straits to which Nazi Germany already finds herself. Faced with a deadlock on land, and fearing to take the offensive in the air because of reprisals, only the sea offers a field for what a French writer calls the luxury of ruthlessness.

The Menace of the Hidden Mine

When what was, perhaps, Hitler's boasted " secret weapon " was revealed in a new campaign of indiscriminate sinking of merchant shipping (see opposite page), the whole subject of minelaying and sweeping immediately became of paramount importance.

THE sailors who man the mine-sweepers—small trawlers equipped with special gear or shallow-draught sloops, but a little larger—have what is, perhaps, the most dangerous and yet least spectacular job in the Royal Navy. Just how dangerous was emphasized when, soon after the sinking of the " Simon Bolivar " and other ships in Germany's new campaign of " frightfulness," H.M. minesweeper " Mastiff " was reported lost with seven valuable lives. Yet a few days later Grimsby fishermen queued up outside the Board of Trade office in answer to the Admiralty's call for men for the minesweepers.

In the last war, when the war at sea had reached its grimmest pitch, one sweeper was lost for every two mines swept up—and each time half the crew was killed or wounded. The enemy laid altogether 43,636 mines, and of these our sweepers found and destroyed 23,873 ; over 700 fully-equipped sweeping vessels were engaged in the work.

The work of a minelayer is equally dangerous and arduous. To enable their mines to be sown effectively, the Germans are thought to be using relays of U-boats. Even the smallest of these can carry up to a dozen " eggs," and in all probability specially-built submarine mine-layers, with mine-wells in the bottom of their hulls, are now in service. A fast surface layer can put down more than 200 mines " at a sitting." Moreover, instead of the usual straight-line method of laying (which simplifies the sweepers' task), the U-boat commanders drop their mines in irregular zigzag fashion— say six here, five there, then another six farther on—forming a large area that may keep the sweepers at work for days on end before they can signal

" all clear." Unlike a U-boat, a mine cannot be detected in advance by any apparatus, and the minesweeping crews pit their wits and their lives in a warfare where chance may tip the scales against them. The principal feature of the submarine mine is the unpleasant-looking horns projecting from its steel casing. These are made of soft lead, and are filled with tubes of acid. Any vessel striking one of these horns causes the acid to detonate the deadly explosive inside the mine.

The mine, on a long mooring cable, is laid by dropping its heavy anchor or sinker to the sea-bottom after which it settles at the correct depth.

Minesweepers work in pairs, with each unit 300 to 500 yards apart. Between them, sometimes suspended from two sets of apparatus called Oropesa floats, is drawn the sweep wire, which has a series of steel cutters. Should this come into contact with a mooring cable, the mine will rise to the surface and it can then be destroyed by gunfire. The paravane (see page 119) is a form of mine protection hung in the sea from the bows of a warship when the presence of a minefield is suspected.

The tragic toll of the German minefield laid off England's East Coast in November called forth much speculation as to whether the enemy were using " magnetic mines " such as are described opposite. Some at least of these may have been dropped from aircraft, with parachutes attached to reduce the shock when they hit the water. If they are laid on the sea bottom, normal mine-sweeping methods are ineffective.

The extent of the German minelaying activity is illustrated by the fact that more than 200 mines were washed up on the Yorkshire coast, quite apart from those picked up by trawlers.

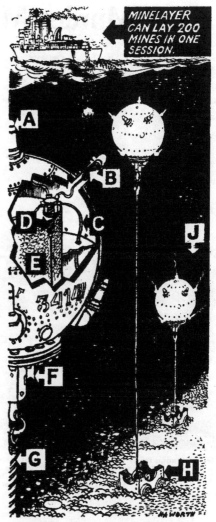

MINELAYER CAN LAY 200 MINES IN ONE SESSION.

The diagram above shows constructional features of the moored contact mine. The soft lead horn (A) contains tubes of acid (B), and a ship hitting the horn breaks the tubes, the acid acts on the wire, (C) and the detonator (D) fires the explosive (E). The spring plunger (F) comes into action to render the mine harmless if it should break from its cable (G) attached to the wheeled sinker (H). Mines to trap submarines (J) are moored deeper and have feelers.

Courtesy of the " Daily Mail "

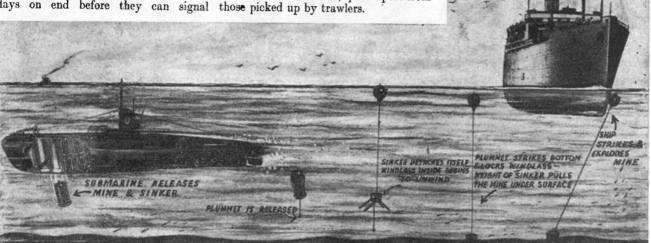

SUBMARINE RELEASES MINE & SINKER

PLUMMET IS RELEASED

SINKER DETACHES ITSELF WINDLASS INSIDE BEGINS TO UNWIND

PLUMMET STRIKES BOTTOM BLOCKS WINDLASS WEIGHT OF SINKER PULLS THE MINE UNDER SURFACE

SHIP STRIKES & EXPLODES MINE

There is little doubt that, as German surface minelayers would hardly cross the North Sea unnoticed and unchallenged by the Royal Navy, recourse was had to submarines for sowing the new illegal minefields off the British coast. Above is a graphic artist's impression of the series of events leading up to the final success of the mine's evil mission with a merchant ship striking and exploding it.

Courtesy of " Daily Sketch "

The Murder Mines: Three Ships Sent to Their D[o

By a strange irony of fate, among the first victims of Germany's new sea crime of laying mines in the open sea without disclosing their position were ships belonging to the two "Axis" powers which Nazis once fondly hoped would be their allies in the war. They were the Italian steamer "Gazia," 5,857 tons, and the crack Japanese liner "Terukuni Maru," of 11,930 tons. The above remarkable photograph, exclusive to this work, was taken by one of the passengers rescued from the ship just as she turned over and sank.

The sinking of ships, both British and neutral, by what is believed to be Hitler's "new weapon," the magnetic mine, is said to be possible only in shallow waters in which the mines, magnetically released, rise quickly to the surface. The "Simon Bolivar," the Dutch liner, one of the first victims of this new form of frightfulness, sank in shallow water, as this photograph shows. She rests on an even keel, and at low water her masts and funnels stand out high above the water.

Photo, " Daily Mirror "; Exclusive to THE WAR ILLUSTRATED

the 'Latest Abomination of German Savagery'

The ship's lifeboats are rowing away laden with survivors. It speaks well for the seamanship and discipline of the Japanese crew that all the 206 persons on board were got away within 42 minutes of the ship striking the mine. Within a quarter of an hour they had all been picked up. The ships seen close at hand in the photograph prove that the mine was laid in a much-used fairway. Note also the Japanese flag painted on the side of the ship as a protection against submarine attack.

On November 21 the destroyer "Gipsy" struck one of the magnetic mines dropped by German aircraft off the East Coast, but was subsequently beached. Good was requited with ill by a remarkable chance, for earlier in the day the "Gipsy" had rescued from their rubber boat the crew of a German flying-boat that had come down in the sea. She had to put to sea again after landing them when she struck the mine, with the loss of 40 men.

Photo, Associated Press

WORDS THAT HISTORY WILL REMEMBER

(*Continued from page* 370)

Observations Upon This Strangest of Wars

Thursday, November 9, 1939

Mr. CHAMBERLAIN in a speech read at the Mansion House luncheon :

I should like to make a few observations upon this strangest of wars which, in the form in which it has hitherto been waged, must seem to many who remember the 1914-1918 conflict to be no war at all, but rather a sort of siege.

We do not know how long this phase will last or whether at any moment it may not be changed into violent conflict. But we can see at any rate that the position of the Allies has, as the weeks have gone by, rather strengthened than deteriorated.

The treaty we and our French allies have concluded with Turkey will be a powerful instrument for the peace of South-Eastern Europe. On the other hand the pact between Germany and the Soviet Union has gained, indeed. great advantages for the Soviet, but has brought only humiliation and loss for Germany.

The repeal of the Neutrality Act in the U.S.A. is a momentous event, for while it affords America the means of maintaining her neutrality it re-opens for the Allies the doors of the greatest storehouse of supplies in the world.

We may be thankful that our successes in hunting down the submarines, and in numerous conflicts in the air, have as yet been unclouded by the terrible casualty lists that were only too familiar to us in the last great war. And we may be proud of the fact that the British Expeditionary Force has been transported to France without the loss of a single man or a single piece of equipment. . . . .

One thing that stands out before everything in these first weeks of war is the essential and fundamental unity of our people. . . .

Peace Without Hatred One War Aim

Friday, November 10

Sir NEVILE HENDERSON in a speech at the Press Club, London :

. . . . My mission ended in a tragic failure, and I think probably it could not have ended in any other way. The ambitions and appetites of a dictator grow as the need for dictatorship diminishes and as the fear of a dictator and of his small extremist minority—the fear of losing their power—becomes more pressing. In the end the megalomania of one man defeated the Prime Minister and defeated me also. You can leave the verdict to history.

I have a very vast respect for the power and influence of the British Press, a very deep appreciation of the absolute necessity for its complete freedom, but also a certain apprehension as to the uses to which it may put its great power. In spite of all the bitterness of failure I still assert that the Nazi case at its beginning had a certain measure of justification, and that the too-sweeping condemnation in England of everything to do with it was not fair. Some people say that there is no distinction between Nazism and Germans. That I submit is a standpoint of despair. This war will have been fought in vain if at the end of it we have not helped to teach the German people themselves that distinction. Hitler himself was the mere creation of a general feeling—felt by every German—against the injustice of Versailles.

It was at least a reasonable view—it was one I held when I went out there—that Nazism could only be destroyed from within, and that the legitimate German grievances had to be eliminated before the German people themselves could eliminate the hateful features of Nazism. I still believe that is the correct standpoint. Had Hitler stopped at Munich, co-operation even with Hitler might still have been possible. Germans for Germany was a perfectly comprehensible view, and a not unworthy conception.

There is only one way in my humble opinion to look upon this war, and that is as a crusade—a crusade based on the ideals of the British Commonwealth of nations undertaken in order to vindicate the highest principles of humanity, to ensure that brute force shall not be the prime and ultimate arbiter in international affairs, and to see that aggression does not pay and that aggression will not pay in the future.

What I would like to say this afternoon is that, in my opinion, the responsibility of the Press in this hateful war is every bit as great as its power, and may perhaps be even still greater when the blessed hour of peace comes. Germany may be incorrigible, but she certainly will be incorrigible if the British Press does not play its responsible part in helping the British people—and after all, it is the British people which ultimately directs British policy—both to see that this war is fought and won and to see that the ensuing peace in the interests of future generations is negotiated and won in accordance with the highest principles of morality and fair play. I am not sure that the second will not be the more difficult victory of the two, and I am quite sure that we will not negotiate it if the British Press does not largely contribute. We are crusaders, and we have got to prove that we are worthy of victory.

We have got to make adjustments. We must end the war in such a way that the only grievances which the Germans have are against their own rulers, against their leader, and against the system which has again brought them to defeat. The problem thereafter will be to see whether Germany can ever be brought to the same standard of civilization as we are fighting for today. If the peace has been a just one we can safely leave that to the coming generation. . . .

There has been a lot of talk about war aims. It seems to me that one of our war aims should be that at the end of this war there should be no hatred left on either side. The British Press in my opinion can render a supreme service to the coming generation, to civilization, and to the world if it can think for the British people in terms which are purely moral and fair-minded, to the exclusion of fear, hatred, and prejudice.

Rulers of Allied Nations State Their Case

Sunday, November 12

Reply of KING GEORGE to the peace appeal of QUEEN WILHELMINA and KING LEOPOLD :

. . . . My Governments deeply appreciate the spirit of your Majesties' offer and they would always be willing to examine a reasonable and assured basis for an equitable peace.

It is, as it has always been, my desire that the war should not last one day longer than is absolutely necessary, and I can therefore at once reply to that part of your Majesties' appeal in which you state your willingness to facilitate the ascertaining of the elements of an agreement to be reached.

The essential conditions upon which we are determined that an honourable peace must be secured have already been plainly stated.

The documents which have been published since the beginning of the war clearly explain its origin and establish the responsibility for its outbreak. My peoples took up arms only after every effort had been made to save peace.

The immediate occasion leading to our decision to enter the war was Germany's aggression against Poland. But this aggression was only a fresh instance of German policy towards her neighbours.

The larger purposes for which my peoples are now fighting are to secure that Europe may be redeemed, in the words of my Prime Minister in the United Kingdom, " from perpetually recurring fear of German aggression so as to enable the peoples of Europe to preserve their independence and their liberties," and to prevent for the future, resort to force instead of to pacific means in settlement of international disputes. . . . .

Should your Majesties be able to communicate to me any proposals from Germany of such a character as to afford real prospect of achieving the purpose I have described above, I can say at once that my Governments would give them their most earnest consideration.

Reply of PRESIDENT LEBRUN to the peace appeal :

. . . . Only a peace founded on justice really endures. France has taken up arms to put a definite end to the methods of violence and force which for the past two years, in defiance of the most solemn engagements and in violation of the pledged word, have already enslaved or destroyed three nations in Europe and today menace the security of all nations. . . . .

Any solution which legalized the triumph of injustice would only secure for Europe a precarious truce bearing no relation to the just and stable peace to which your Majesties look forward.

Today it is the duty of Germany rather than of France to declare herself for or against this kind of peace for which every country, menaced as it is in its security and independence, is waiting.

Why the Dutch Government Took Precautions

Monday, November 13

JONKHEER DE GEER, Prime Minister of Holland, in a broadcast :

We mobilized in September this year, not because we distrusted our neighbours, but because it was our duty to be prepared for any emergency. It was our duty towards those who want to respect our neutrality and who had less confidence in the pledges of their enemies than we had. Our mobilization means protection for all ; but if it is to remain a protection it has to keep pace with changing conditions. We must never allow the impression to be created abroad that our mobilization is only symbolic ; others as well as ourselves should be convinced that it is effective. Therefore its intensity has to be changed in accordance with the tension near our frontier.

This is the meaning of the measures recently taken. I hope that these words may restore the peace of mind of those who have been showing signs of nervousness. We should thank God for the blessings He has vouchsafed us until now and we should consider it our duty to promote peace and thus to serve others. Every neutral nation is a light in the darkness which has fallen upon Europe ; our neutrality is therefore a matter of high importance, and of its maintenance we have not the right to despair. Our future is in the hands of God ; perhaps we shall have to face affliction, which we cannot yet foresee, but even then we shall not allow despair to dominate our spirit. We do our duty leaving the decision to God. However high the waves may come we know that our Father is at the helm and our spirits are quiet and cheerful.

Hitler's 'Secret Weapon' is a Secret No More

The destroyer "Gipsy" sunk by a mine on November 21 is here seen a few hours before she met with disaster. In page 401 she is seen beached after disaster had overtaken her.

Ships Sunk in German Minefield Campaign
November 18–26, 1939

			Dead or Missing	Date Nov.
SIMON BOLIVAR	(Dutch)	8,309 tons	83	18
B. O. BORJESSEN	(Swedish)	1,586 tons	6	18?
BLACKHILL	(British)	2,492 tons	—	18?
GRAZIA	(Italian)	5,857 tons	5	18?
CARICA MILICA	(Yugoslav)	6,871 tons	—	18?
KAUNAS	(Lithuanian)	1,566 tons	—	18?
TORCHBEARER	(British)	1,267 tons	4	19?
WIGMORE	(British)	345 tons	16	19?
SAINT-CLAIRE	(French)	?	9	20
H.M.S. MASTIFF	(minesweeper)	520 tons	6	20
TERUKUNI MARU	(Japanese)	11,930 tons	—	21
FIANONA*	(Italian)	6,660 tons	—	21
H.M.S. GIPSY	(destroyer)	1,335 tons	30	21
ELENA R.	(Greek)	4,576 tons	—	22
GERALDUS	(British)	2,494 tons	—	22
H.M.S. ARAGONITE	(minesweeper)	315 tons	—	22
LOWLAND	(British)	974 tons	10	22?
—	(British steamer)	?	3	23
HOOKWOOD	(British)	926 tons	2	23
SUSSEX*	(British)	11,066 tons	—	24
MANGALORE	(British)	8,886 tons	—	24
GUSTAF E. REUTER*	(Swedish)	6,336 tons	—	25

*Mined, but not sunk.

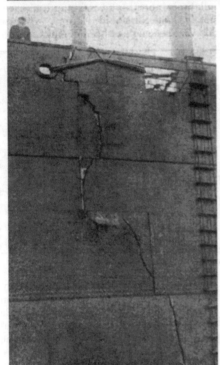

Part of the damage done by the mine that the Italian steamer "Fianona" struck was to split her starboard (right) side in the middle as seen above. Though leaking badly, she was eventually towed into port.

Photo, British International Photos

The effect of minesweeping is to cut the cable by which the mine is moored and bring it to the surface where it is destroyed by gunfire. A photograph of a rating firing at a floating mine is reproduced in page 119.

Photo, Central Press

The "Mastiff," seen left, was a loss caused to the Royal Navy by "magnetic" mines. She was formerly in the North Sea Fishery Protection Flotilla, but was later used as a minesweeper. Right, one of the injured crew is being attended to in the lifeboat. Centre is a portion of the unit used in laying the German mines in the North Sea. The words painted on it read : "If I make a good journey then Churchill will meet with a great disaster."

Photos, Central Press and British International Photos

Europe's Mastery is Germany's Dominant Aim

Based on an article in " The Daily Telegraph " by that journal's Diplomatic Correspondent, Mr. Victor Gordon Lennox, what follows is a revelation of a constant quality
in German political aims.

ON the surface there is much to distinguish the Nazi Reich from the Germany of the Kaiser. On one point, however, the Pan-Germans and the Nazis would be at one—the belief in an inevitable struggle between Germany on the one hand and Britain and France on the other, and coupled with this belief, the conviction that out of such a struggle one side or the other will emerge so overwhelmingly triumphant as to crush the vanquished out of existence.

If the theory of a persistent strain in German politico-military thought be accepted, the maps reproduced in this of the picture. The Allies have won the war, and have imposed the sort of peace the Germans apparently thought fair and reasonable in the circumstances. Germany has been reduced to a state half the size of Switzerland, situated in Thuringia. Belgium—observe the subtle propaganda aimed at retaining Dutch benevolence—has absorbed Holland. England has become once again a Continental Power, having taken over all Germany north of Frankfort-on-Main and Dresden, and stretching as far east as the Oder; furthermore, all Denmark except Jutland, with indisputable control over circulation among the Sudeten Germans giving a series of maps indicating the successive stages in the march of Nazi conquest. Each map is provided with its date : Spring, 1938, Austria ; Autumn, 1938, Czechoslovakia ; Spring, 1939, Hungary ; Autumn, 1939, Poland. In the following spring Jugoslavia, and in the autumn of 1940, Rumania, Bulgaria, and Turkey in Europe are to be absorbed ; and 1941 is to see the incorporation of Denmark, Belgium, Holland, Switzerland, all France north of Lyons, and approximately half Russia in Europe. When this vast scheme has been completed the

German maps circulated in Holland during the Great War : (left) if Germany had won ; (right) if she had lost.

page which were printed in Germany in 1915 and freely distributed in Holland during the Great War, not only illustrate graphically the state of mind then existent in Berlin, but they provide interesting material for consideration in 1939 by Germany's friends and foes alike.

Look first at the map on the left, which shows the sort of Europe which the Germans hoped to establish on the morrow of victory. What would the Russia of today think of the quaint conception that had the Central Powers won the war of 1914-1918, her total European territories were to be limited to the Crimea ? Germany's eastern frontier, it will be seen, was to be carried far beyond that which Poland had achieved in 1772, and a huge Austro-Hungarian state was to extend even beyond this. Belgium was to be obliterated, and so, too, was France, with the exception of a tiny Basque province. The British Isles were to become German and Austrian colonies. Turkey was to gain the restoration of her territories in Europe, and that the map was drawn early in 1915 is obvious from the fact that no retribution against Italy or Rumania for entering the war on the Allied side is indicated.

In the other map we have the reverse the entrance to the Baltic, also falls to her share. France is still more swollen, occupying all south-west Germany, Austria, and a large part of northern Italy— a broad warning to the third member of the Triple Alliance. Tsarist Russia receives eastern Germany, and the Balkans plus Hungary are handed over to the domination of the Serbs.

This fantasy of Imperial Germany may be compared with that of the Nazi Reich. At the time of the Munich Crisis in 1938 a leaflet was published by the Nazis for subjugation of Britain is to be undertaken.

We may judge from the assault on Poland that an attempt is being made to follow this programme, though something seems to have gone wrong in the case of Hungary. But it may be observed that the whole plan breaks down if Britain enters the war before 1942. Thus, that little miscalculation of Von Ribbentrop may have put a stop to what is surely one of the most ambitious, most fantastic plans of conquest formulated in the history of the world.

Britain's War Aims Stated by the Premier

ALTHOUGH the time has not yet come for a definitive statement of the Allies' war aims, Mr. Chamberlain has several times declared the objects for which we are fighting. Thus, in the House of Commons on September 13, he said : " The people of France and the people of Great Britain are alike determined not only to honour to the full their obligations to Poland, but also to put an end once for all to the intolerable strain of living under the perpetual threat of Nazi aggression. Our French allies are, like ourselves, a peace-loving people, but they are no less convinced than are we that there can be no peace until the menace of Hitlerism has been finally removed. *Il faut en finir.*"

Two months later in his broadcast on November 26, the Premier declared that our war aim is to " defeat our enemy "—not merely his military forces, but " that aggressive, bullying mentality which seeks continually to dominate other peoples by force, which finds a brutal satisfaction in the persecution and the torture of inoffensive citizens, and in the name of the interests of the State justifies the repudiation of its own pledged word whenever it finds it convenient."

Why Germans Don't See the War as We Do

The super-optimist will find little to his taste in this article, but all the same it expresses a point of view shared by many who are intimately acquainted with Nazi mentality and the German people.

HARDLY a day goes by without our newspapers carrying some report of dissensions between the Nazi leaders or Hitler and his military advisers. But it may be suggested that the hope of a German collapse as the result of such dissensions is but an example of " wishful thinking " on our part.

Sure of the righteousness of our cause, convinced of the utter iniquity of Hitler and his " evil men," we like to think that in Germany there must be many who share our views and who are looking forward with eagerness to the collapse of the Nazi system. But if we " put ourselves in the other fellow's place," if we endeavour to slip into a German's skin and share his very thoughts, we shall probably find that Hitler and Nazism, Germany's cause and the likely outcome of the war, are one and all very different from what they appeared when we looked at them from this side of the Maginot Line.

To the great mass of Germans Hitler may well appear as one of the greatest statesmen and conquerors of all time. Germany, which before his advent was an outcast among the nations, is now at the very pinnacle of material might. Austria, Czechoslovakia, Memel, Danzig, half Poland—all have been incorporated within the bounds of the Reich. The German army, whose very existence had been denied by those who dictated the Versailles Treaty, now swaggers across the Continent as the instrument of the greatest power in Europe. True, the people hoped and believed that war

would not come, but here again Hitler's deal with the Soviet has removed the menace of war on two fronts, and after three months the soil of the Fatherland has been cleared of the French invaders.

On the home front, too, the German worker may be lulled by the blandishments of the Nazi spokesmen. Listen to Dr. Ley, leader of the Labour Front, as he addresses the German people over the wireless. The war is going so well that rations have been increased. Unemployment has vanished, production has vastly increased. Wages are to be maintained. The eight-hour working day is to be increased to a maximum of ten hours, it is true, but hot meals are to be served in canteens established in every factory. There will be bonuses at Christmas, extra money for night and holiday work, and holidays will be granted again as from the beginning of next year.

Assured of employment and a reasonable standard of living, guaranteed against invasion, and tasting in anticipation the fruits of the alliance with Russia, why should the German people, it may well be asked, consider for a moment a return to the days of the monarchy ?

Even if the seeds of disaffection and revolt were present on a large scale in Germany it is difficult to think of a way in which the revolution could be prepared for and actually begun. " In order to stage anything of the kind," wrote the Munich correspondent of the Belgian paper " La Libre Belgique " on September 20, " malcontents would first have to get together. But if three Germans who dislike the present regime wanted to confer, they would have to feel absolutely sure of one another, which is just what nobody is . . . Is anyone going to believe that a few German men and women, armed with halberds and banking on the chance that their numbers will swell en route, are going to march on the Reich Chancellery to demand the abdication of the Fuehrer ? The German, on the other hand, who would publicly declare that ' il faut en finir with this regime ' would be considered as either delirious, demented, dead drunk or out to commit suicide in a novel way. Bound and gagged, he would be handed over to the police, or his audience would take to their heels in a panic."

Reports of monarchist tendencies, of serious disaffection, of the clash of rivalries in the Nazi Party, may be said to play into the hands of Dr. Goebbels, even if they are not directly inspired by him—as has, indeed, been suggested. The spies of the Gestapo, it must be remembered, are everywhere, and the surest way of preventing a monarchist or an anti-Hitler rising is surely to let Goebbels and Himmler know who are those who are thinking along those lines, when the concentration camp, the bullet, or the headsman's axe, will then do the rest.

To quote the Belgian writer again, " the state of mind of the German civilian is best summed up in the maxim: ' Obey and live ; but obey, too, in order to live.' "

These two photographs recently smuggled out of Germany throw an interesting light on the internal condition of the country. In the top photograph a queue of respectable working-class folk are waiting to obtain the bare means of subsistence at a public welfare station. Immediately above is a German railway fenced with barbed wire, not against foreign enemies, but against sabotage from within. Hundreds of miles of track are thus protected.
Photos. Keystone and E.N.A.

'THE BIG LIE'

And Also Some Lesser Falsities of Nazi Propaganda

By The Editor

SOME of the most sinister passages in "Mein Kampf" expound its author's unswerving belief in deceiving the masses of the people for whom he has the same contemptuous disregard as his even more practised partner in organized oppression, M. Stalin.

The S.S. Athenia sunk by three British Destroyers

This lying "official" leaflet is one of the hundreds of thousands mentioned in this page that have been sent by Nazi propaganda to English-speaking people throughout the world. The original is almost the same size as the page on which this is printed. The text on the reverse is longer than that on the front.

on a large scale" since the war began was the incredible assertion that the British ship "Athenia" was torpedoed by the orders of the British Admiralty to bring about a state of mind in U.S.A. similar to that which followed the sinking of the "Lusitania." No human being in the whole Western world other than a German or an inmate of a mad-house—which for all practical purposes many Germans in Germany are today—could have believed in such villainy even for a doubting moment. The noisome abyss of the bestial minds of the Hitler Huns that conceived and shaped the idea reaches the lowest depths to which any beings of human guise have regressed since a million years ago ape-man began to evolve a mind.

We need not recapitulate the circumstances of the sinking of the "Athenia," known to all intelligent persons in

from "Mein Kampf" just quoted. The paragraph runs thus :

The terrible crime of which Mr. Winston Churchill is accused before the whole world has now found its irrefutable proof. There is now laid bare before the whole world the criminal outrage perpetrated on the British ship S.S. Athenia regardless of the lives of almost 1,500 persons, which had as its sole object the drawing of America into the war against Germany by means of a lie alleging a German submarine attack. This monstrous crime was proved by an official investigation carried out in the United States of America.

That is "untruthfulness on the large scale," and millions of pounds of money that ought to be buying food for their people are being spent in circulating it and other lies, both big and small, throughout the world. For the Hitler propagandists do not despise the small lies for which their master expresses contempt.

The final paragraph from the Nazi leaflets reads :

The British steamer Athenia was sunk by order of the First Lord of the Admiralty, Mr. Winston Churchill. The idea originated in his own mind as he caused this most shocking crime ever devised by human brain to be carried out systematically. Can the British people, in the name of their country, continue to back this criminal?

All who have read the strange wild book of the semi-literate agitator which Germany has accepted as its new bible will remember this atrocious example of his callous candour :

The masses will fall victims to a big lie more readily than to a small one, for they themselves only tell small lies, being ashamed to tell big ones. Untruthfulness on a large scale does not occur to them, and they do not believe in the possibility of such amazing impudence, such scandalous falsification, on the part of others. Some part of even the most glaring lie will always remain behind, a fact which all associations of liars in this world know only too well.

A more brutal contempt of "the masses"—especially the mobs of poor deluded youth—who have bowed the knee to this inhuman scourge could not be conceived, and pitiful contempt for such serfs should be the only feeling in those who look upon them objectively. For they too must have read that paragraph. Never did a bandit more truthfully announce his intentions. Rooted in lying and dishonour this evil man's dishonour truthfully stands.

First of his efforts at "untruthfulness

the world and to all in Germany in their insensate hate of Britain who have not lost the capacity for thinking. But the dynamic determination of Hitler's propagandists in adhering to the written counsel of their tyrant is exhibited once again in the faithfulness with which they are still spreading the great "Athenia" lie on the "Mein Kampf" formula :

If once a propagandist allows even the slightest glimmer of right to be seen upon the other side, he is raising doubt in the mind of the masses. The masses are not able to decide where justice ends and injustice begins. There must be no gradations, only positive and negative; love and hate; right and wrong; truth and lie; never the half and half.

Within the last week or two many persons in Britain, and unknown thousands who can read English throughout the world, but particularly in neutral countries, have been receiving envelopes from Stockholm containing leaflets in which the lie about the "Athenia" is brazenly reiterated. We reproduce specimens of both in this page. Read the first paragraph and see how neatly it fits in with the devilish commandment

The "Athenia" went down by the stern, as is shown in the two photographs in the opposite page. Here her bow rises high above the water as she makes her last plunge.
Photo, G. E. Withams. Exclusive to THE WAR ILLUSTRATED

How Athenia Sank: Subject of Crude Nazi Lies

The sinking of the "Athenia," a 13,000-ton ship of the Donaldson Line, 250 miles off the coast of Ireland, was the first piratical act of the Nazis at sea, and though it happened on September 3, the day on which war was declared, the Nazis are still trying, more than two months after, to exculpate themselves by such propaganda as is described opposite. Above, the ship is seen shortly before she sank by the stern, which is already awash. Other photographs of the "Athenia" and the survivors appear in pages 50 and 51.

Apart from the tragedy of the loss of life, the sinking of such a gallant ship as the "Athenia" is an awe-inspiring spectacle. Above is a close-up view of her as she went to her doom. This photograph, showing nearly the whole of that side of the ship on which she was struck, demonstrates beyond a shadow of doubt the falsity of the Nazi lie that she was sunk by shell fire from British destroyers. There is no sign of her having been shelled, and it is evident that she was struck far below the water line.

Photos, G. E. Withams, exclusive to THE WAR ILLUSTRATED.

'Untruthfulness on a Large Scale' Exemplified

The ridiculous question repeatedly addressed to Mr. Churchill by Nazi propagandists during their broadcasts, "Where is the Ark Royal?" is fully answered by the photograph, above, of the famous aircraft carrier (seen on the right) taken at sea weeks after her alleged destruction. Although even the camera can be made to lie, an artist at work in his studio can more easily imagine scenes which bear only the remotest resemblance to the actualities of war, either at sea or on land. The illustration below shows the futile attempt of a Nazi artist in the German paper "Leipziger Illustrierte Zeitung" to prove with his paint-box and brushes that the "Ark Royal" was sunk.

Into the category of small lies come certain aerial photos of the raid on the Forth Bridge in which the "Edinburgh" was a target. Taking advantage of the curious lighting effect produced by the level rays of the afternoon sun, the propagandists have had this reproduced "the wrong way up," and, so distributed throughout the neutral press, the ingeniously inaccurate marking of certain details on the prints has induced even certain British newspapers, and even War journals, to print it "wrong-way-up."

By this device the little rocky islet of Inchgarvie, which lies on the immediate east of the central span of the bridge and on the shelving rock of which some of the supports of the bridge are embedded, becomes in the description "a bomb which is exploding not far from the bridge"! "Small lies," indeed, but they may have deceived many simple souls who haven't a large-scale map of the scene to check up the photographic details. So far as H.M.S. "Edinburgh" is concerned, THE WAR ILLUSTRATED published an exclusive photo in page 297, where the vessel is clearly undamaged, and that photo was taken when the attackers were flying away!

Yet again, faithful to their instructions never to allow a glimmer of truth to be seen on the other side, the ludicrous lie about the sinking of the "Ark Royal" is still in vigorous life. We reproduce a very recent photo of that aircraft carrier taken at sea weeks after its alleged destruction, together with an admirable picture by a Nazi artist showing how the deed was done—this being just another proof that an artist in his studio can see what no camera on the spot could register!

How the Nazis Make Even the Camera Lie

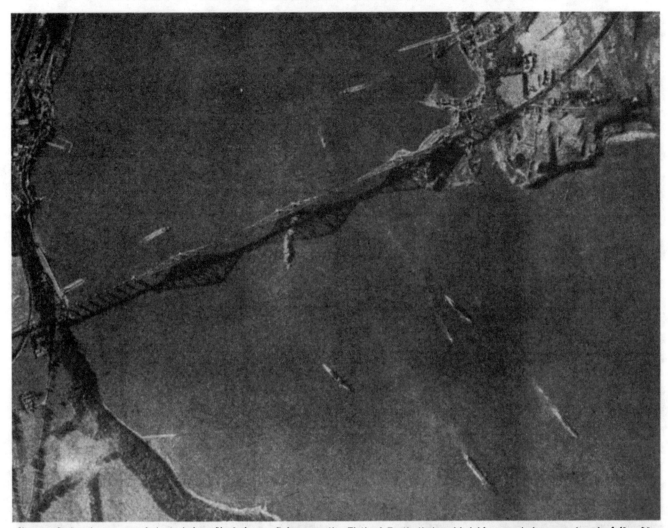

It was a fortunate camera shot, made by a Nazi airman flying over the Firth of Forth, that enabled him merely by wrongly orientating his photograph, to produce evidence that a bomb almost hit the Forth Bridge. At the top of this page is the photograph as it was reproduced in the "Berliner Illustrierte Zeitung," and repeated in many British journals, with what looks like a column of smoke rising from the bridge. Below is the explanation of this astute photographic lie, achieved by turning the photograph wrong way up. Below, right, is the photograph as it should be reproduced, with the north at the top and the island of Inchgarvie beneath the bridge bearing no resemblance whatever to a column of smoke. The map of the area, left, proves that this is the correct position for the photograph.

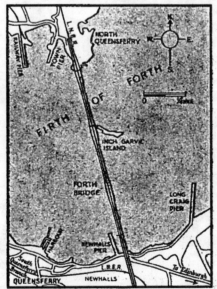

To us the Goebbels propaganda is futile and funny, but it must be realized that the Berlin Ministry of Propaganda has secured its object since it has inspired among the majority of Germans a flaming hatred of Britain where a year ago little was evident. What we are really up against today is the most evil system of police-spy government known to history. Hitler and his criminal associates impose their will upon their own people—enclosed as they are in an hermetically sealed censorship—both by terror and by a perpetual and consistent stream of large-scale lies which our "confetti raids," as the Nazis term them, have counteracted to a limited extent.

We have attempted no more than to touch very briefly on these few examples of the way in which Hitler's vast and impressive (if somewhat comic) propaganda machine does its work. But it would be no difficult matter to fill many pages of THE WAR ILLUSTRATED with pictures of the splendid fleet of British war vessels that the hysterical little rascal Goebbels has "sunk" to cheer Hitler's blind and faithful serfs "who themselves tell only small lies, being ashamed to tell big ones." And with that "sunken" fleet alone, as Mr. Churchill has well said Britain would be well content to meet the entire Nazi Navy and have a fight to a finish!

First Favourites With French and British

There were famous names among the audience as well as on the stage at the Anglo-French concert and vaudeville show for British and French soldiers given on November 12. Viscount Gort, seen above, was present, and with him were the Duke of Gloucester and the Dominion Ministers. Right, is M. Maurice Chevalier, a "star" as welcome to the British as to the French, singing during the evening.

In the first concert arranged by Ensa—to use the by now generally adopted abbreviation of Entertainments National Service Association—to be given in France, the outstanding "star turn" was Gracie Fields, who, in spite of ill-health and against her doctor's orders, insisted on appearing, and sang twice in one day. Left, is the famous comedienne during one of her turns. Right, is the long queue of British soldiers that waited outside the theatre to hear their favourite.

Photos, British Official: Crown Copyright

We Were On the Mined 'Simon Bolivar'

One of the most shocking tragedies of the war occurred on November 18, 1939, when the Dutch liner "Simon Bolivar" struck a German mine in the North Sea, and sank with the loss of over 120 lives, including women and children. Poignant stories told by survivors are here reprinted from "The Daily Telegraph."

MR. L. VELTMAN, of Amsterdam, a Dutch ministry official in Curaçao, had had experience of mines during the last war. He was so sure that a mine might strike the "Simon Bolivar" that he kept his wife and daughters with him throughout the whole journey. When the first explosion came they were all sitting in the smoking-room on the upper deck. Mr. Veltman said :

"I hustled my wife and daughters into a lifeboat and followed them in as we drew away from the boat-side.

"When we were about 100 yards off, some quarter of an hour after the first explosion, another mine blew up, right amidships. This explosion shattered three lifeboats still swinging on the davits. Glass showered on hurrying passengers, and many were badly cut by flying fragments. Others were flung to the deck by the force of the explosion and suffered broken legs, ankles and ribs.

"I saw a steward flung against the superstructure so violently that he broke his back and died immediately.

"My impression was that this second mine was linked to the first, and that the explosions were caused by a twin mine.

I came across examples of this during the last war. The passengers were amazingly calm. The only sign of panic was the screaming of children, but that was natural.

"Three boats were lowered within three minutes of the first explosion.

"Shortly afterwards we and three other lifeboats were picked up by a British patrol steamer. Later they rescued a nun who was blown out of one of the lifeboats with the second explosion and had been drifting on a piece of wood for nearly three hours.

"There were nine seriously wounded in our lifeboats. In our boat was a man with a broken back.

"The wounded were laid on the deck of the rescue ship, and a middle-aged nurse, who was rescued from another lifeboat, made rough splints and dressed wounds with strips of cloth which the crew tore from their clean clothing.

"After she had attended to the wounded she made us cups of cocoa and cheered us up all the way to port.

"There the railway station was turned into a casualty clearing station. Those who were not wounded were given coffee and sandwiches. Blankets were provided.

"Shortly after we were landed an air-raid warning sounded, and we had just recovered from the first shock of our experience when we had to crowd into a bombproof shelter under the station restaurant. We were there for about 20 minutes.

"While I was helping emigration officers to sort out the passengers I saw many of my acquaintances seriously wounded. I saw husbands with their wives and children missing, and wives with their husbands and families gone.

"One man on board had with him his wife and five children, the eldest of whom was only seven and the youngest four weeks. He was holding the hands of two of his children, aged about five and three years. His wife and three other children were missing. As far as we know they have not been found."

MISS ELLA LIEUTENANT, a shorthand-writer from The Hague, a girl in her early twenties who was on her way to the West Indies to become engaged to an officer on an oil tanker, said to me :

"I was in my bunk when the first explosion came. I rushed out into the gangway and said to a steward : 'Has it happened ?' He replied : 'Yes, miss, it's happened.' We both knew what the other meant, because we had been expecting it.

"Never have I seen anything like the scene on the deck. Men, women and

The destroyers are the handy ships of the Royal Navy and are called upon to undertake work, often terribly dangerous, that could not be performed by larger warships. Here is such an occasion. A destroyer is approaching the sinking Dutch liner " Simon Bolivar " to help in the rescue work. The photograph was taken from a ship to which the destroyer had just signalled " Keep clear, danger of mines," while she herself dashed full speed ahead on her errand of mercy. See also page 400.　　　*Photo, Associated Press*

children were hurled to the deck ; wood and glass splinters flew everywhere.

"The first lifeboat I went to was swinging from a single davit. I clambered into a second, and we had just touched the surface of the water when the second explosion occurred.

"I was thrown high into the air and expected to land in the sea. Instead I hit the bottom of the boat I had been flung out of and sprained my back.

"I have had some training as a nurse, and helped the ship's surgeon, Dr. Ebes, to tend to the injured. One was a child of seven months who was held down by a heavy plank of wood. There was so much oil smeared over everything that we could not get a grip on the wood, and it was some time before we could ease the child's suffering. The child's parents were both dead.

"I ripped off pieces of my clothing and helped Dr. Ebes to bind the wounds.

"Eventually we were picked up by a rescue ship. After we were landed there was an air-raid warning, and we were immediately hustled into a shelter. In the darkness I heard a German shouting in German : ' Fritz, Fritz, are you there?' Then he dashed into a corner, where he found his little boy."

Mr. J. H. WISTERS, first-class cloakroom steward, said :

"It was as if the ship was lifted out of the water. The master, Capt. H. Voorspuiy was killed instantly on the bridge. It seemed as if the explosion was immediately underneath him. All the oil-pipes burst and people in the cabins were smothered.

"Some of the lifeboats could not be lowered properly and others were affected by the second explosion, which came within 15 minutes. I saw about 80 people in the water, and the sea was covered with oil. The wireless apparatus was smashed.

"We were almost stationary when the explosion occurred, and were in shallow water. Even when the boat went down her upper structure was still showing."

George Anches, ship's fireman, said that after the explosion steam poured out of the sides and deck of the ship. He added :

"I was dazed, and it was several minutes before I could collect my thoughts. Then I ran up to the bridge where the captain was lying covered with blood. I saw at once that he had been badly injured. He did not move or make a sound and I knelt down and examined him. He was dead."

As the boat Anches was in was drawing away he saw another boat being lowered. "It was crowded with women and children," he said. "Then there was another explosion which shattered this lifeboat, throwing them into the oily water. Those who were not killed instantly were stunned and drowned."

Mr. WILLIAM COWEN, of Ilford, Essex, an A.R.P. worker, told of a West Indian who, having lost his wife and two children in the disaster, rescued a white child about three years old.

"He was a huge man over six feet tall and wearing a blanket," said Mr. Cowen. "He was carrying the little child and was in tears when I assisted him by taking the child from him.

"He told me that he had lost his wife and children aboard, and burst into tears as he said that he intends to adopt the child he had rescued."

Dr. William Besson's life was saved by his strong white teeth after he had drifted in the water for four hours with a broken spine and a shattered right arm after a vain effort to save his six-year-old son.

Dr. Besson, a medical officer, was sailing back to his post. His wife, four-year-old daughter and son were all drowned.

He said : "I was thrown high into the air by the explosion as the ship struck the first mine. I smashed my spine and my arm as I landed on the deck. The ship's boat we clambered into capsized and I was thrown into the water.

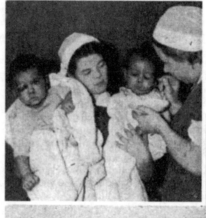

"Clinging to wreckage I drifted for four hours. Then I saw a rope trailing from the side of a British destroyer. I caught hold of it with my teeth and clung to it.

"Then using my teeth and my good arm I gradually hauled myself up. I was too weak to shout for help."

Dr. Besson did not mention how after receiving his terrible injuries he directed rescue operations as he lay in agony on the deck, how he helped his wife and daughter to some drifting wreckage when the ship's boat turned over, how he left their side to plunge to the rescue of his son, who had been swept away by a wave, and how with injuries that would have rendered any man completely helpless in normal circumstances, he swam after the little boy until he could swim no longer.

These things were told by his brother-in-law, Mr. John Davis, a Liverpool University dental student. "His behaviour was heroic and his endurance miraculous," Mr. Davis said.

Dr. Besson, it was stated at the hospital last night, will be from two to three months recovering from his injuries.

ONE of the most remarkable escapes was that of a father and his three-year-old daughter, whom he saved by putting her in a wooden box and swimming behind it for nearly an hour in the oil-covered, icy water.

The father is Mr. Sydney G. Preece,

Scenes of extraordinary pathos were witnessed after the " Simon Bolivar " was mined. The sufferings of those thrown into the icy water were terribly increased owing to the fact that they were steeped in oil. Immediately above, a crowded lifeboat is seen bringing passengers ashore. Top are two piccaninnies in a London Hospital who lost their parents.
Photo, " Daily Mirror," exclusive to THE WAR ILLUSTRATED

December 9th, 1939   *The War Illustrated*   413

|||||||||||||||||||||||||||||||||||||||||||||||||||||||||||||||||| **I WAS THERE!** |||||||||||||||||||||||||||||||||||||||||||||||||||||||||||||||||||||||||||||||||

who lives at Maidenhead, Berks. He was returning to Trinidad, where he is agent for two English firms.

Yesterday Mr. Preece's face was still stained brown and his hair matted with oil which he had encountered in his desperate swim. He and his daughter were picked up by a British minesweeper.

"The first explosion," he said, "blew me a couple of feet in the air. My child Elizabeth, who had been playing on a rocking horse on the promenade deck, was also thrown on to the deck. My chauffeur, Henry Samuel Batt, tried to help me in finding a place in one of the boats for my child, but passengers were jumping on to each other in these boats, and I decided to wait.

"After the second explosion the ship began to founder, and Batt and I seized a 'bull board,' which is used in a deck game and is like a box. We placed the child inside and pushed the box into the water.

"I jumped in after it and I thought Batt was going to do the same, but I have not seen him since and I do not know whether he is alive.

"I pushed the box with one hand and tried to swim with the other, but the oil which had come from the tanks after the explosion had saturated my clothes and I was being dragged under. At that moment I seized a drifting raft with loops on it. Placing one arm through a loop I was able to hold myself up and steady the box in front of me.

"After about an hour we were picked up by a minesweeper. During the whole time my child behaved remarkably. She was not at all perturbed and at one time she said to me, 'Are we going to Trinidad in this, Daddy?' meaning the box.

Sunk—But We Didn't Get Our Feet Wet

During the week-end of November 18–21 six neutral ships were sunk by German mines off the English coast. The largest of these was the 12,000-ton Japanese liner, "Terukuni Maru," but—in happy contrast to the tragedy of the "Simon Bolivar"—all her passengers and crew were saved. The following stories are reprinted from the "Daily Telegraph" and "Daily Express."

On his arrival in London on November 21, Capt. B. Matukura, of the "Terukuni Maru," said:

"My ship arrived at the Downs at 10 o'clock on Sunday morning, and I waited for a naval officer to come on board to give us our contraband clearance.

"At three o'clock that day two officers came aboard and delivered the clearance papers. On them was written: 'Hold you until northbound route is declared clear.'

"This was in consequence of the sinking of the 'Simon Bolivar,' for ships were still sweeping mines away to give us a clear route.

"I waited for the pilot to take me into London, but it was not until yesterday afternoon, about three o'clock, that two naval officers again came on board and once more gave me permission to fly the special clearance signal, and also route instructions.

"Again I waited for a pilot, and felt it was getting rather late for us to proceed from the Downs to London, as we wished to navigate only during daytime, owing to the danger from floating mines.

"The pilot did not come until this morning, when, about 8 o'clock, I signalled for him to come aboard. He immediately joined my ship. We left the anchorage at about half past eight, following the route as instructed.

"I stationed five men as special lookouts for floating mines, and steamed at my ordinary speed of 15 knots.

"We never saw a mine, but at 12.53 we struck one and there was a terrific explosion, Nos. 2 and 3 holds being damaged. It was the first-class passengers' lunch-time. and three out of the total of 28 were slightly injured by the dishes striking their faces. I was standing on the bridge and was unhurt.

"Out of my crew of 177, only three or four were slightly injured. Including the pilot, there was a total of 206 aboard.

"The pilot immediately suggested to me that we should beach the ship, as we were in a narrow deep passage between two shallows. I agreed, but the explosion had been so heavy that water had come into the engine-room and we could not use the engines any more.

"Forty-two minutes later, at 1.35, all eight boats which I had ordered to leave the ship were away. All the passengers and crew and even a passenger's pet dog were safe.

"I think there is no doubt that our look-out system was so good that had there been any floating mines we should have seen them, and it must have been an anchored mine which we struck. The weather was calm and visibility good. Nobody panicked, and when I left the ship, the last to do so, everyone was safely in the boats."

Captain Matukura is here seen telephoning from a London hotel after the disaster to his ship. It was his proud boast that nobody even got his feet wet.

Photo, Keystone

Here the stern of the mined liner is seen a few minutes before she sank. She went down by the bows, her stern rising high above the sea, and the propellers are already out of water. One of the ship's lifeboats, on the left, is still alongside, while on the right are boats that have come out from the shore and taken off some of the passengers.

Photo, Associated Press

I WAS THERE!

Every British sailor will pay tribute to the captain, officers and crew of the " Terukuni Maru " for having maintained the highest traditions of the sea when their ship, bound for London and so close to her destination that the pilot was on board, struck a mine and sank. It was instantly obvious when the explosion occurred that passengers and crew must take to the boats, but there was not a suggestion of disorderly scramble. As can be seen in this photograph, the boat's crews lined up as if they were at boat drill before going to their stations.

Photo, Associated Press

Mrs. Helen Swailes, wife of a chief petty officer, who lives in Aberdare, said :

" I was pacing the deck with my dog Nutty, thinking that if we were struck I was at least safe on the upper deck, when there was a shattering explosion in the forward part of the ship. Nutty jumped and yapped with excitement.

" We were immediately ordered to our stations. There was no panic whatever. The oldest British passenger on board, Mrs. Huntley, aged 70, was magnificent. To all the passengers she said, ' We must remain calm.'

" While she was waiting to enter a lifeboat she carefully adjusted her hair.

" Major Ferguson, who had come from Singapore, asked me where my lifebelt was. I said, ' It is below, in my cabin.' He rushed downstairs and forced his way into a water-logged cabin and got one for me.

" Nutty was the first to leap into the lifeboat. We were under the care of a Japanese coxswain. I shall never forget that man's behaviour. Although blood was streaming down his face, he gave all his orders quietly and calmly.

" Within a few minutes we were taken aboard a drifter. The crew gave us rum and coffee. Nutty wagged his tail in delight when he was given some meat.

" Among those injured was a member of the Japanese Embassy. As he passed me on a stretcher he smiled and said, ' I am so sorry, madam.'

" Mr. Whiteway, of the Colonial Office, was also injured. Twenty-five minutes after the liner was struck every boat was clear of the wreck. We watched her heel over on her side."

Kawasima, junior second engineer, said :

" The explosion flung me into the air about a foot and knocked me over. The whole time the captain stood on the bridge while the stern of the ship rose in the air and the bows went beneath the water, until the sea lapped the foot of the bridge.

" Fuel oil flowed all over the engine-room, and sea water began to pour in. I just had time to go to my cabin and grab my overcoat and a few belongings before getting into one of the boats. The sea was quite calm."

The lifeboats of the " Terukuni Maru " were lowered with commendable promptitude, for when a sinking ship has a pronounced list to either side the launching of them becomes extremely difficult, or even impossible. Here it has been successfully accomplished, and the boats are taking on board the last of their complement.

Photo. Associated Press

Badges of Proficiency and Trades in the Forces

Specialists of the Royal Navy

Gunner's Mate

Gunlayer 1st Class

Captain of the Gun, 1st Class

Rangetaker, 1st Class

Torpedo Gunner's Mate

Torpedo Coxswain

Gunlayer 2nd Class, same as Gunlayer 1st Class, but with top star only. Seaman Gunner same as Captain of the Gun, but with top star only.

Rangetaker 2nd Class has the same badge as Rangetaker 1st Class but with top star only; Rangetaker 3rd Class has no star.

Leading Torpedoman

Seaman Torpedoman

So many and so varied are the occupations represented in the ranks of the Army, Navy, and Air Force that it is impossible in this page to give more than a selection. Those chosen, however, are among those which are most commonly encountered, and concerning which, therefore, the layman is usually in need of guidance. A distinction may be drawn between badges of proficiency, in which there is often an indication of the superior qualifications of the holder, and those badges which indicate a specialist in a particular line of professional activity.

Diver

Leading Telegraphist

Petty Officer Telegraphist's badge has a crown above instead of stars. Telegraphist's badge is the same as Leading Telegraphist's, but with one (upper) star only.

The Army—Skill and Proficiency

Best Swordsman in each squadron

1st Prize Gunner

Bugler

Gunlayer

1st Prize Driver

Best shot of Warrant Officers (Class 2), Sergeants and Lance-Sergeants of a Battalion

Armourer - Sergeant; Machinery Artificer; Machinery Gunner and Smith

Driver in Royal Tank Regiment

Wheeler and Carpenter

Pioneer in Light Infantry and Rifles

2nd Prize Gunner has a star instead of a crown. Buglers in rifle regiments have a badge of two interlocked bugles. Lewis Gunners wear Gunlayer's badges with L.G. Pioneers in Grenadier Guards and Fusiliers have a grenade instead of a bugle; in Coldstream Guards, a rose, and in Scots and Irish Guards, a star.

Specialists of the Royal Air Force

Wireless Operator

Physical Training Instructor

Air Gunner

Apprentices and Boy Entrants

Member of Central Band of R.A.F.

OUR DIARY OF THE WAR

Sunday, November 19

Reported that 120 Czech students had been executed by the Gestapo, and many thousands transported, following riots on Independence Day.

Six enemy aircraft sighted off South-East Coast, and unidentified machines over Firth of Forth area.

Grenade attacks on the Western Front.

Five more ships reported sunk by German mines off the East Coast, namely, Swedish "B. O. Borjesson," "British "Blackhill," Italian "Grazia," British "Torchbearer," and Jugoslav "Carica Milica."

British steamer "Pensilva" torpedoed.

Lithuanian vessel "Kaunas" reported sunk by mine near Zeebrugge.

Both Dutch and Belgian Governments protested at flights of belligerent 'planes over their territories.

Paris announced that in the last four weeks the tonnage of German merchandise captured exceeded by several thousand tons that of French merchantmen lost through enemy action.

Mr. Eden broadcast a speech in French on his visit with Dominion Ministers to France.

Capt. Knudsen, master of Danish vessel "Canada," sunk on November 4 near the Humber, declared that this was due to a "magnetic" mine.

Monday, November 20

S.S. guards reported to be in control of Prague.

Admiralty announced that German aircraft made an unsuccessful attack on British destroyer in southern North Sea.

German aircraft, seen over Kent, Essex and Thames Estuary, chased out to sea by British fighters. One, a Heinkel bomber, was later proved to have been shot down. No bombs were dropped.

Enemy aeroplane appeared over the Orkneys and was beaten off by anti-aircraft fire.

German reconnaissance 'planes made a number of flights over France, including Normandy and Rhone Valley.

Twenty-two survivors of British steamer "Arlington Court," torpedoed off Irish coast on November 16, were landed.

British trawler "Wigmore" reported sunk.

German aeroplane shot down over Holland by Dutch Air Patrol.

Reported by London agents of Royal Netherlands Steamship Co. that the number of those lost in the "Simon Bolivar" totals 83.

Reported from Capetown that the German liner "Windhuk" had slipped out of Lobito, Portuguese East Africa, refitted with full armament of a raider.

Tuesday, November 21

Gestapo announces arrest of man alleged to be responsible for Munich bomb explosion, and also of two British "confederates."

H. M. Destroyer "Gipsy" struck a mine off East Coast and was later beached. There were 40 casualties.

Japanese liner "Terukuni Maru" sunk off East Coast by German mine.

Premier announced that, as reprisals to German violations of international marine law, exports of German origin or ownership will be subject to seizure on the high seas.

R.A.F. fighters shot down a Dornier 17 reconnaissance bomber off Deal.

Enemy aircraft appeared about 7 p.m. over East Coast. Fighter aircraft went up and anti-aircraft batteries engaged them. Coastal defences and a German seaplane fought a machine-gun duel. No bombs were dropped.

German Heinkel bomber sighted over Sutherland. Enemy machines were seen over the smaller islands of the Orkneys.

Admiralty announced loss off East Coast of minesweeper trawler "Mastiff" by German mine.

Paris reported air engagements on Western Front. German reconnaissance 'plane brought down over French lines. Two fighters brought down in flames over enemy lines. Heinkel bomber pursued out to sea and brought down by British fighter.

THE POETS & THE WAR

IX

THE SECRET WEAPON

By "LUCIO" (GORDON PHILLIPS)

I have a weapon, he said, that none shall use
    As we shall use it, unmoved by mercy or ruth ;
Be ours the devices of darkness that blind and bemuse—
    Let us make war on Truth.

Mangle their bodies if so it will serve our aim,
    March them away to their doom in its various kinds.
We shall survive ; for our further shelter and shame
    Let us mangle their minds.

Let the lie be their master ; in action as speech
    Let falsehood be now and for ever our weapon of worth ;
Let it ring round the world with our shadow and reach
    To the ends of the earth.

Let us hector and bully, forswear and denounce and accuse,
    Till the hearts of all peoples are sickened and darkened in sooth.
I have a weapon, he said, that none other shall use—
    Let us make war on Truth.
        —*Manchester Guardian.*

Three Fleetwood trawlers, "Thomas Hankins," "Delphine" and "Sea Sweeper," reported sunk by enemy action.

Finnish steamer "Asta" seized by German warship near Aaland Islands. This was the 16th Finnish ship detained by Germany.

German cargo steamer "Rheingold" brought as naval prize into Scottish port.

Wednesday, November 22

France decided to take measures of reprisals against German breach of mines law similar to those announced by British Government.

Six German aircraft made a bombing attack on the Shetlands. An R.A.F. seaplane lying at its moorings was set on fire. No British casualties.

Enemy aircraft appeared during the day over East Coast and Thames Estuary. One raider driven almost on housetops by R.A.F. fighters.

During Wednesday night enemy aircraft approached South-East Coast ; one shot down over the sea by anti-aircraft fire.

Six German aircraft shot down by Allied aircraft over French territory, including three Messerschmitts. Another Messerschmitt was shot down by anti-aircraft guns.

Air Ministry announced that R.A.F. aircraft made successful flights on Monday and Tuesday over Stuttgart, Frankfurt, Hamburg and Bremen.

Italian steamer "Fianona" struck by mine during Tuesday night off S.E. coast of England, but did not sink.

Paris announced that two U-boats had been sunk by French torpedo-boat.

Admiralty announced that German freighter "Bertha Fisser," which had been masquerading as "Emden I" and also as Norwegian ship "Ada," had been intercepted near Iceland. Her crew tried to scuttle her, the ship ran on the rocks, and her crew were picked up by the intercepting warship.

Sir John Simon broadcast an appeal to the British public to save and lend to the Government.

Thursday, November 23

Admiralty announced that H.M. minesweeper "Aragonite" had been sunk by a mine.

Proved that **magnetic mines had been dropped by parachute from German seaplanes** over Thames Estuary and S.E. coastal waters.

Six vessels reported sunk by mine or U-boat action around British coasts : British steamers "Geraldus," "Lowland," "Darino," and trawler "Sulby." ; Greek steamer "Elena R." ; French trawler "Saint-Claire."

Air Ministry announced that **R.A.F. in France brought down seven enemy bombers.**

Unidentified aircraft passed over North Scotland.

Rumanian Cabinet resigned.

Dutch Government lodged a protest against British and French blockade.

Total of dead in Bohemia and Moravia following suppression of Czecho-Slovak demonstration said to be 1,700.

It Is Said That . . .

Only five Germans in 100 are allowed rubber or substitute rubber overshoes.

Ten thousand Rumanian Iron Guards have recanted in writing.

Goebbels recently appeared before a Berlin tribunal, charged with breaches of discipline.

There is now in Germany an official list of those allowed telephone communications with foreign countries.

"Britain has now become the field of war, and this is only fair, because this is Britain's war." (German broadcast.)

Eighty women were imprisoned at Eger, Bohemia, for complaining in the streets that they had no food for their families.

A 3-oz. tablet of soap substitute, obtainable by ration card, must last an adult German for one month.

Hitler's weight is going down. Is it through worry or slimming ?

Russia's interests may soon clash with Germany's as regards Baltic trade.

American popular opinion has linked Hitlerism and Stalinism as common enemies.

German authorities tried to prevent the arrival in Poland of the International Red Cross.

"Fascism remains anti-Communist, but it also remains obstinately anti-democratic." (Signor Gayda.)

Nazis are deporting 2,000 Jews a day to the Jewish reserve which it is intended to establish in Poland.

The percentage of sick men from the Siegfried Line is causing anxiety to the German military authorities.

Vol. 1   A Permanent Picture Record of the Second Great War   No. 14

The first victim of Soviet Russia's attack on Finland was Helsinki, the little Republic's beautiful capital. Soviet bombing 'planes appeared over the city at 9.15 in the morning of November 30, the first day of the war, and in the course of that day and the next their visit of devastation was repeated many times. A number of innocent civilians, including many women and children, were slaughtered, and many more were wounded. This photograph, flown from Stockholm to London, is one of the first from the scene of horror. Direct hits have been made by incendiary bombs and the city's fire brigade is working at fever heat to control the conflagration.

Photo, Associated Press

Raid and Reconnaissance in a Wintry Scene

Still on the Western Front the siege war, as it has been fittingly styled, went on. Winter
made a large-scale offensive ever more improbable, and only in the air was there
activity. In that element, however, Britain and France again showed their superiority.

As November drew to its close, wretched weather reduced activity on the Western front, both on the ground and in the air, to a minimum. When the word was used, it was only in such sentences as " Patrol activities during the night in the region of the Vosges " or, to quote a German bulletin, " On the Western front slight artillery activity." Snow whitened the heights of the Vosges and the Jura, and in the basin of the Rhine the rivers were swollen with the almost continuous rains. In the Siegfried Line numerous gangs of workmen were noticed reconstructing trenches and fortifications, and many of the posts in No-man's Land were rendered untenable by the rising waters.

From time to time patrols were pushed out from one side and the other, and occasionally there was a brisk fight as the nocturnal prowlers made contact, intentionally or otherwise, with their opposite numbers. In this close-range fighting the French were able to prove the effectiveness of their automatic pistols.

Several raids were reported a few miles east of the Moselle, and one of these was notable in that in the course of it the Germans used a smoke screen for the first time in the fighting on the Western Front. Preluded by heavy artillery fire lasting about an hour, some 200 German infantry moved to attack a French outpost, and their advance was supported by a barrage fire and by a screen of smoke shells. The use of the latter masked to some extent the defensive fire of the adjoining posts, but smoke is a difficult substance to control and in a very short time the French had forced the Germans to return to their own lines.

Occasionally, however, the skies cleared, and then the duels in the air were resumed. In one period of three days Allied fighters were believed to have brought down 19 enemy aircraft. In one day, November 23, the Royal Air Force in France shot down seven 'planes—six on the Allied side of the line and one in the Siegfried zone. This with no casualties to the R.A.F. personnel, although one of our 'planes was forced to land.

Listeners to the Nazi broadcasts were surprised to hear that German reconnaissances had been carried out over a very large part of France ; in fact, such raids as there were, were made by individual 'planes flying at a great height, and the results obtained must have been negligible.

Taking a leaf out of Britain's book, the Germans dropped a number of pamphlets in these flights—little red booklets containing photographs of the Siegfried Line, cartoons, quotations from British and French statements intended to show the " treachery " of the British, and diagrams and figures purporting to show that Germany's economic position and resources are far superior to those of the Allies. Technically, the booklets were described as being quite good, but the Nazi propaganda department was unfortunate in choosing compilers whose acquaintance with French was not of the best. And poor propaganda in bad French is something which makes the Frenchman shrug his shoulders with disdain.

The artillery duels so frequently mentioned in the communiqués from the Western Front have inevitably resulted in the destruction of villages in the area separating the two armies, but there was no loss of life among the civil population, for this had been evacuated. Top, are the ruins of a village, with the railway bridge crashed in the street. In contrast to this is another scene in a French village. Triumphantly borne through the streets on an army lorry are the remains of a German bomber that has crashed and is being taken away for expert examination.

Photos, Associated Press and courtesy of British Movietone News

Where the Allies and the Nazis Stand to Arms

The whole of the frontier between France and Germany is shown in this contour map. The details are so complete and the undulations of the ground are so close to scale that it would be valuable even for military purposes. From Basle to Karlsruhe the Maginot and Siegfried Lines are separated by the Rhine, and from Karlsruhe to the frontier of Luxemburg the two lines run almost due west over broken and, in parts, wooded country.

From a relief map modelled for THE WAR ILLUSTRATED *by Felix Gardon*

Above Ground and Below in Germany's 'Westwall'

There are guns of many types and sizes in the Siegfried Line, and above is a field gun, mounted on a reinforced concrete base, ready for action. The observer is looking out through his binoculars towards the Allied line. Right is one of the machine-guns that are dotted about between the concrete strong points.

Photos, Mondiale, E.N.A. and International Graphic Press

THE 125 miles along which the frontier between France and Germany is formed by the Rhine, a most formidable military obstacle, is defended by a series of concrete forts intended to prevent any attempt to cross the river rather than to meet an advancing army. Farther north, where there is no river dividing the two armies is the Siegfried Line proper, though " Line " is really a misnomer ; a more correct description would be the Siegfried Zone, for the main position is actually in some places two miles deep. In front of it is the first protecting position of barbed wire entanglements and concrete anti-tank defences, while the main defence consists of concrete forts scattered over a wide area. In some parts of the line there are as many as 50 of these to the square mile. All these works were built by conscripted labour.

The Siegfried Line was not finished at the outbreak of war, and in the photograph, centre right, men are still at work upon it. The two bottom photographs—coming from a German engineering paper —show sections of the line constructed deep underground.

Such a Trench as the 'Old Soldiers' Dreamt Of

How very different is this trench from those which were hurriedly dug under fire in the last Great War ! Scottish soldiers are revetting the trench face—essential work, for the sides must be nearly upright, and in order that falls of earth may not happen, some form of support is necessary. Revetting consists of wire-netting or expanded metal held in position by wooden stakes ; more permanently, of sandbags.

Photo, British Official : Crown Copyright

Swastika Over Britain: A Tale of Failure

Just how far the Nazi boasts that their air attacks had destroyed Britain's age-old immunity as an island, may be gathered from this review of the raids and reconnaissance flights delivered up to the end of November.

THOUGH every man, woman and child in Britain expected and was prepared for air raids as soon as war broke out, almost six weeks elapsed before a single enemy machine crossed our coasts. Then there was the sudden and dramatic attack on the naval base of Rosyth and the Forth Bridge, obviously intended both as a reprisal for the R.A.F. Kiel Canal raid of September 4 and a small-scale testing of our defence strength in the Forth area.

Since that first raid on October 16, military (or rather, naval) objectives in Scotland have continued to receive marked attention from the German Air Force. However, Scapa Flow and other anchorages in the Orkneys provided an obvious target for the enemy, for even if no damage were done to ships in the harbour, at least valuable information of naval movements might be obtained.

The first raids on the Orkneys and the far north of Scotland, which took place on October 17, showed the Nazis that they would have to expect heavy losses if their aircraft attempted to penetrate our keen anti-aircraft and fighter defences. On that day four German raiders were shot down, and—whatever the Nazi propaganda announced afterwards—our only damage was to the old "Iron Duke."

During the next few days the only alarms were when German reconnaissance aircraft, flying at a great height, were detected over Scapa and the Forth. A single raider that rashly flew low over the Forth district on October 28 fell a very easy prey to our fighter pilots.

As November opened, enemy aircraft were reported from time to time off the

---

German Air Raids on Britain
Oct. 16—Nov. 29.

Oct. 16. Firth of Forth. Reconnaissance, followed by bombing attacks on Rosyth and bridge. 37 casualties in H.M.S. "Mohawk" and other warships. Four bombers out of 12 or 14 shot down.

Oct 17. Orkneys. Raid by four aircraft, one of which was shot down. Slight damage to H.M.S. "Iron Duke" in Scapa Flow. Three other enemy 'planes brought down off Scotland.

Oct. 18. Orkneys. One raider shot down.

Oct. 22. S.E. Scotland. One raider shot down.

Oct. 28. Firth of Forth. Single raider forced down near Dalkeith.

Nov. 13. Shetlands. Raid by four bombers, 12 bombs falling harmlessly on land.

Nov. 20. S.E. England. Reconnaissance near London by single machine, chased out to sea and shot down.

Nov. 21. Kent. Bomber brought down after battle with fighters near Deal.

Nov. 22. Shetlands. Raid by six bombers. An R.A.F. flying-boat set on fire.

Nov. 29. Northumberland. Raider shot down in sea.

N.B. This table only includes raids in which damage was done either to the objective or to the raiders themselves. It is computed that, all told, there were 29 flights to Scotland and approximately 20 to England up to November 29.

East coast of England—Yorkshire, Norfolk, and Essex. They sheered off as soon as they were discovered, and it is doubtful if the photographs or other information they obtained were of much value. Certainly, however, such long flights are of importance in training crews in piloting and navigation, and also interrupting daily life where the raid warnings are sounded.

The next development was the arrival on November 13 of enemy 'planes over the Shetlands—Britain's farthest north— a journey of nearly 600 miles from the nearest point on the German mainland (*see* page 383). Here the sheltered fiord-like roadsteads were scoured for shipping and aircraft, and 20 bombs were dropped by four raiders, though without result.

On November 17 more raiders appeared, and more bombs were dropped without result. In the next ten days the Shetlands were visited eight times, but the only time on which the bombers drew blood was on November 22, when an R.A.F. flying-boat was set on fire.

Air Raid Alarms in England

As a change from the day-to-day reports of small-scale raids and reconnaissances over Scotland and abortive dive-bombing on convoys and units of our Fleet, there was a report of a disturber of the peace one day over South Lancashire, and then over the Thames estuary and the south-east coast things began to liven up.

First of all, on November 20, a Heinkel appeared over Sussex and flew in towards London. While still on the distant outskirts, it was engaged by R.A.F. fighters, forced out to sea, and shot down. Whatever Goebbels and his propagandists might say, this was the nearest any enemy aircraft had come to London.

In the evening there was a raid warning in East Kent; this was the first time German aircraft approached our coasts in the black-out. The next morning, in broad daylight, a Dornier bomber was shot down off Deal by three R.A.F. fighters after a thrilling fight. It was later reliably reported that seaplanes had been seen dropping "bubble" mines.

The aircraft used (both landplanes and seaplanes) in every raid to date have been of well-tried Dornier and Heinkel types (except that the new Junkers JU 88 was reported over the Forth in the first raid). These are well known and easily recognized by defence forces.

Whether or not such flights are, as a German newspaper put it, "merely a prelude," the results (with *at least* 20 Nazi planes shot down over or near our coasts in just over a month) indicate that the long-heralded Blitzkrieg, if and when it comes, will not succeed. A very significant interview with a German airman who had taken part in flights over the Shetlands and Orkneys was published on November 28 by the official German agency. He said: "The Englishmen shot damned well. . . . The enemy can shoot and he is no slight enemy. That should be known at home."

This remarkable photograph is the first to be published of a raid by Nazi aircraft over the Shetland Islands. High up in the sky can be seen two of the six 'planes that attacked shipping during the raid on November 22. Bombs set fire to an R.A.F. seaplane, the smoke from which is rising above the houses.

These Are the Fighters That Routed the Raiders

Left is the Vickers-Supermarine " Spitfire," the fastest fighter in service in any numbers in any Air Force. Designed by the man who conceived the Schneider Trophy seaplanes, R. J. Mitchell, it has an official maximum speed of 362 m.p.h. The Hawker " Hurricane " (right) was the first of the R.A.F.'s " eight-gun " fighters. It is officially capable of 335 m.p.h., but this may be taken as a conservative estimate. It is a larger, heavier machine than the " Spitfire," with a deeper fuselage. The tank-shaped object under the wing is the radiator. The wheels, unlike those of the " Spitfire," retract inwards.

Photos in this page, Charles E. Brown, " Flight " and Photopress

In this page are close-ups of every type of fighter aircraft at present in first-line service with the R.A.F. With the help of these photographs, identification of friendly machines should be made easier. As explained in page 332, the principal duty of the fighter is to intercept raiding bombers with machine-gun fire, and already the great majority of the many enemy 'planes shot down have been worsted in air battle with our fighters. An " unsolicited testimonial " to the respect accorded these machines by the enemy was the comment by a vanquished German airman as he watched his conqueror overhead—" So it's one of *those*." A British departure in the tactics of air fighting is indicated by the inclusion here of the " Blenheim." Famous as a bombing type, it has been adapted as a long-range fighter.

The famous Bristol " Blenheim " (above), although primarily a bomber, can also be used as a twin-engined fighter. The later " long-nosed " type is seen in page 286.

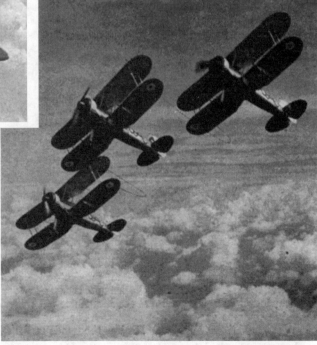

Very little information has yet been released about the Boulton Paul " Defiant " (left). The first two-seater fighter to be ordered as standard equipment for the R.A.F. for some years, its speed is estimated to approach that of the " Spitfire," while its field of fire (with the rear gunner in an enclosed turret) is greater. The engine is the same as that of the " Hurricane " and " Spitfire "—the Rolls-Royce " Merlin," of over 1,000 h.p. Right is a flight of three Gloster " Gladiators " demonstrating their exceptional manœuvrability in close formation flying.

Warsaw is Now a 'City of Dreadful Night'

An eye-witness not only of the bombardment of Warsaw but of its occupation by the German troops, the writer of this vivid account of a great city's calvary is a French-woman who managed to escape at the beginning of November. Reprinted from " Le Petit Parisien," here is a selection from her tale in all its grisly horror.

WARSAW is still alive . . . but who, among those who knew the city as it was, would recognize it now ?

One house in two still stands, but this survivor is riddled with shell-holes and frequently gutted, losing its entrails in the roadway. The streets are full of wreckage, and strewn with shell-holes and bomb-craters.

There is no mechanical transport now. In more than five thousand places the tramlines have been torn up. There are just two services of buses which run at a snail's pace. So the whole city is reduced to walking unceasingly amid the ruins.

It is the nightmare march-past of a drab crowd, as grey as the dust which still floats over the demolished houses. Where is the joy of former days ? Where are the smart costumes of old ? The women go about hatless, their heads covered with a handkerchief ; the men are bareheaded. No more furs and smart coats ; only odds and ends saved from the disaster, only rags and tatters, clothe this multitude of the sick and starving.

With nightfall the streets empty. From

so that the passer-by can see the gaping rooms. Not, however, empty rooms, for even this wall-less wing is a godsend in a city destroyed, and in it the seriously wounded, the trepanned and the amputated, are looked after in the open air.

Here is the old Town Hall, its tottering walls blackened by fire. Opposite, traces of an immense brazier : the Opera House.

In the main thoroughfares in the centre of the city it is still almost impossible to find a trace of the side streets, so littered

are they with débris. Some streets have completely disappeared, gone for ever.

Ten theatres out of thirteen have been completely destroyed. There is not a cinema left. The concert-halls have gone up in flames. There is no means of distraction left—but who could think of distractions in this city ?

There is no news ; and that is more serious, for everyone is anxious to know. The only newspaper published in the city is printed by the Germans in Polish, but nobody buys it ; all wireless sets belonging to Poles have been confiscated. To communicate with each other, these hundreds of thousands of people have only one resource left : handbills.

The crumbling walls are covered with thousands of little bills and tiny posters. So-and-so, living at such-and-such an address, begs for help. Somebody offers " An overcoat for sale," or states " I

would like to buy an overcoat." Another asks for news : " What has become of X—— ? " " Have you any news of Z—— ? " A vast and silent conversation, as though, in this city stricken to death, all had lost the use of speech.

Everywhere, over the ruined gardens, the streets, the suburbs, floats the dreadful smell of the charnel house.

Dr. Goebbels' department has distributed in many neutral countries films showing warm-hearted Germans dis-

tributing soup and bread to the starving of Warsaw. But this is the reality. Long queues form up in different parts of the town. After many hours of waiting, one approaches the open-air stall. There each one is offered a bowl of almost undrinkable soup and a piece of grey bread as hard as an old biscuit. A man stretches out his hand, but before handing it to him the German functionary says to him : " Now repeat the slogan you and your compatriots were so fond of using when you floated the loan for your aerial defence six months ago—' We are ready, we are united, we are strong.' "

The man recoils, this derision striking him as surely as a physical blow. Usually he remains silent. Then he is turned away and goes off with hunger gnawing at his entrails. This comedy is repeated as each man comes up in turn. Nearly always the man renounces his pittance.

At the end of each week the municipality of Warsaw has to pay the German authorities several thousand zlotys as the price of this distribution. German charity !

Since the end of October the Gestapo has come into action. Every night it operates, and at dawn official posters are stuck up on the walls, informing the population that so-and-so has been shot for carrying arms, for having insulted the Fuehrer, or spoken ill of the Reich.

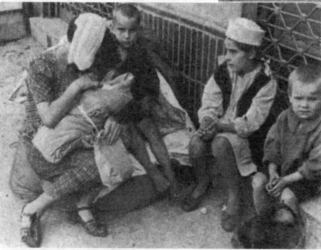

The children immediately above, forlorn and pitiful amid the ruins of Warsaw, have lost their homes and have nowhere to lay their heads. In the top photograph, men and women on foot with some of the household goods they have salved piled on bicycles, are crossing one of Warsaw's bridges in search of new homes.

Photos, Central Press

seven o'clock all traffic is forbidden in the city. The spectacle changes. Torches blaze in the ruins. It is the sinister hour of the gravediggers in this city of dreadful night. One by one the little cemeteries in the streets, courtyards and squares—the September cemeteries—are opened and cleared. By torchlight begins the exhumation of 40,000 dead and their reburial in common graves.

Here is the Military Hospital. Hit by bombs and pulverized by shells, all the central part of the building has collapsed. One wing still stands, minus its façade,

Poland Still Lives and Fights in France

Left, General Sikorski is visiting officers of the newly-formed Polish Army in France. Above, Polish Infantry in training.

THERE is a new Poland now, but it is in France, near the town of Angers, about 200 miles south-west of Paris. There the Polish Government has taken a lease of a château with four acres of ground, and the French Government has granted it full extra-territorial rights with a lease of 99 years. This is the same procedure as was followed when the Belgian Government took refuge in France during the last war. At the end of it the little piece of Belgium in France was surrendered, and the same will happen in the case of Poland. At the first meeting of the Polish Cabinet at Angers the Prime Minister, General Sikorski, said : " I declare that Poland, to-day in distress, will emerge from this catastrophe purified and strengthened. In our deliberations we shall never forget that we are responsible for a nation of 34,000,000 inhabitants who are suffering and still struggling against the enemy." The formation of a Polish contingent to fight in France was one of the first activities of the new Government.

Early in October it was announced that three Polish destroyers had joined the British Navy after a hazardous voyage through the Baltic. They are here seen in a British port, and warm praise has been bestowed on the zeal and efficiency of their officers and crews. General Sikorski is seen, right, with the Duke of Kent during a visit to the Home Fleet. Centre, General Sikorski is leaving Paris for Angers.

Photos, Planet News, Topical, Courtesy of French Embassy, and Pathé Gazette

Inside a Citadel of the Static War

One of the Bastions of Maginot's Mighty Line

ANTI-AIRCRAFT

CONCRETE PROTECTION FOR WATER TANK

PERISCOPE

FIRE CONTROL TOWER

MEDIUM ARTILLERY

HEAVY ARTILLERY

MEDIUM ARTILLERY

75 M·M·GUN

MORTAR

MACHINE GUN

ANTI-TANK

GALLERY

INFANTRY TRAP

MINES

TANK TRAP

LIGHT RAILWAY

ESCALATOR

MINE

MAGAZINE

LIFTS

OFFICERS MESS

KITCHEN

RECREATION ROOM

AIR PLANT

LIGHTING PLANT

FOOD STORE

MAIN CONTROL ROOM

MAIN MAGAZINE

WATER TANK

MAGAZINE

HOSPITAL

MAIN GALLERY

MAGAZINE

WORKSHOP

BARRACKS

MAIN ENTRANCE

ESCALATOR

Haworth

ARMOURED POSITIONS IN GALLERIES

MAIN FORT

TANK TRAP

ANTI-AIRCRAFT GUN

ANTI-TANK GUN

TANK TRAP

MINE

MACHINE GUN

ANTI-TANK ASPARAGUS

LISTENING POSTS

BARBED WIRE

MINES

These two diagrams show the principal features of the French frontier defence known as the Maginot Line. Above is a section of one of the main forts, each of which is a completely self-contained unit. There is, further, a labyrinth of tunnels joining the forts. In the lower drawing such a fort is seen on the right, while in front of it are the obstacles and forward main defences that the enemy would have to overcome before reaching the main defences.

They consist of machine-guns mounted in concrete "pill boxes," anti-tank "asparagus," which consists of railway lines set in concrete at an angle of 45 degrees pointing towards the enemy lines and in some cases with high-explosive caps. There are also special tank traps—deep concrete ditches from which a tank would have no chance of escape. In the very forefront of the fortress are listening posts.

Specially prepared from French semi-official sources for THE WAR ILLUSTRATED by Haworth

'EVERYWHERE ACTIVITY, EVERYWHERE MUD'

Most encouraging was the report of the British Expeditionary Force given by the
Secretary for War, Mr. Hore-Belisha, in the House of Commons on November 22.
Below we reproduce his words in full.

MR. HORE-BELISHA began his statement with a tribute to the Polish Army which, he said, by interposing a delay of several weeks, had facilitated the concentration of the French and British Armies. He went on:

When I last spoke to the House we had 158,000 men in France. Since then some thousands each week have followed them. By the spring of next year they will have been reinforced again by no inconsiderable armament. So will it continue till the cause is won. Although there is no distinction remaining, it must be said that we could not have completed our formations in France without the assistance of the Territorial Army, whose peacetime training has adequately justified the generous sacrifice of leisure which it entailed. Territorial units reached France at a very much earlier stage and in greater numbers than in 1914.

Do not, however, let this country pretend that within a proximate time Britain can furnish an army of Continental dimensions.

The first men to be called up under obligatory service were summoned to the Colours on July 15 this year. It was a timely innovation in our military practice and we shall owe to it the smooth and steady expansion of our effort. Nearly a million men are under intensive training in Great Britain.

Our own defences by sea, land and air, and the barriers against aggression long since established by the prevision and provision of the French Republic, give safe cover to our preparations. **The Maginot Line is some measure of the debt which free nations owe to the vindicated caution of a country which, even when beset with financial troubles, did not hesitate to divert to its construction an unstinted proportion of its economic resources.**

France Has an 800-Mile Line

THE major system of the Maginot Line— with its subterranean railways, its underground accommodation, and its ingeniously emplaced batteries of guns—extends along the frontier which divides France from our enemy. That frontier is 200 miles in extent.

But the low esteem in which the given word of Germany is held, illustrated, as it has repeatedly been, by the world-wide credence that so spontaneously attaches to the slightest rumour of designs upon a neutral country, has necessitated that the defences of France should extend far beyond these limits.

Indeed, whereas Germany has to defend 200 miles of frontier against the possibility of attack by the Allies, France has had to envisage the possibility of aggression by Germany along 800 miles, from the North Sea to the Alps. We now share the task with them. **There are French troops in the British part of the line, and British troops in the French part of the line. Understanding and good relations are complete.**

The sector at present allotted to the British Army, while not comparable with the major system of the Maginot Line, was thus fortunately provided in advance with field works. The task which fell to our soldiers on arrival was to add to and improve upon these, and this task they are undertaking with a will.

This is a fortress war. The House can see, in its mind's eye, the busy work of our soldiers, digging and building. Under their hands blockhouses and pill boxes take shape, and with digging machines and with squelching spades they throw up breastworks or carve out entrenchments. They are making battery positions, skilfully concealed, and obstacles to tank attack.

Everywhere there is activity and everywhere there is mud.

OVER hundreds of square miles of this bleak scene, British troops pursue their avocations.

An organization of almost inconceivably great dimensions has been established—a world within a world. The food, the clothing, the equipment, the correspondence, the amusements of a whole community are brought and are distributed over a distance of hundreds of miles.

Some idea of the ground to be covered can be vividly represented by a single figure. In the initial stages the B.E.F. consumed 500 tons of petrol a day. Now alternative bases have been established, additional locomotives will be imported and permanent-way laid down.

But still it is a question of vehicles, vehicles and more vehicles. We have already sent to France over 1,000 tons of spare parts and accessories.

If a letter is sometimes delayed in course of post, it will be recollected that in Britain communications pass through long-established channels with post offices, machinery for sorting and static staffs. The B.E.F. has an improvised organization and is dealing with 270,000 letters and 17,000 parcels a day—in proportion nearly double the quantity handled in 1918.

When one occasionally hears that a man in whom one is interested has not received a second blanket, it will be borne in mind that this is the first war which we have waged in which more than one blanket has been issued. The soldier, of course, must travel light.

On November 19 Mr. Hore-Belisha concluded a two days' visit to the Allied Armies in France, and spent a day in the British front area. He is here seen with General Viscount Gort during an inspection of earthworks.
Photo, British Official, Crown Copyright

A soldier's life, while he is campaigning, is never an easy one, and while everything practicable is being done to alleviate his lot, nothing can avoid the discomforts which are the inevitable accompaniment of active service conditions.

No man from personal experience understands better than the present Commander-in-Chief the circumstances of warfare and the requirements of his troops. His presence, inspiring confidence, is familiar in every part of the line.

THE ground which our Army occupies is also well known to him, and it is inspiring, as one stands upon some famous bridge or some hill once designated by a number, to hear his vivid description of a well-remembered exploit or encounter.

On the visit from which I have just returned I traversed with him almost the whole of the front, and came into the closest possible contact with officers and men of many different units. I can render at first hand an encouraging account of the fortitude and good temper of the troops.

Their health is exceptionally good, the sickness rate actually being lower than the peacetime rate at home.

The billets are mainly in farmhouses and village buildings, but we have sent to France enough huts to house 36,000 men. We are building great hangars and depots for the accommodation of stores, and I hope that the House will realize that the organizing ability of the Army in tasks having no parallel by their magnitude and variety in civil life is illustrated by those exceptional defects which prove the rule. Meanwhile, our Army grows. We dispatch arms and equipment to other parts of the world. We are preparing for all eventualities.

The Army at Home

AT home our anti-aircraft and coast defences remain continuously manned by personnel whose conditions of service in many cases are as hard as, and more lonely than, those in France, and whose duty is as important.

We have taken, besides the Militia classes which have been called up, over 85,000 voluntary recruits since the war began. Every week we have absorbed over 300 officers from the Emergency Reserve. Over 7,000 men from the ranks have been recommended for commissions, of whom 2,500 have already been posted to officer cadet training units.

Those fit for active service in the divisions at home will be progressively relieved from duty at vulnerable points as the county home defence battalions are formed. There is room in these battalions, as in the pioneer battalions, for men past middle age.

Thus the Army offers occupation in patriotic national service to old and young. The raising to 40,000 of the numbers of the A.T.S.—that admirable regiment of women—is another means of releasing active men for active service.

Those in munition factories are doing equally valuable work, for on them depends the speed with which additional contingents can participate in the war theatre.

Thus the war proceeds. **It is a war of endurance, a quality for which the British people is renowned. Every day that passes finds us stronger.** On the economy of the enemy the passage of time has not the same effect. To win he would have to break through the Allied defences. An assault upon these is awaited with confidence by the French Supreme Commander.

On our side we can afford to choose our opportunity. There is no dissension in our ranks; there are no conflicting counsels. Our strategy is predetermined, and so is the issue of this struggle.

Stalin Makes Foul War on Gallant Finland

After his easy victory over the Baltic States, Stalin made demands on Finland. But the Finns stood up for their heritage, and so on November 30 Soviet troops and 'planes swept across the frontier to punish what was quaintly styled " provocation."

AFTER weeks of goings and comings between Helsinki and Moscow, of negotiations behind closed doors in the Kremlin, of speeches and declarations, consultations with this country and with that, the controversy between Finland and Soviet Russia took a new and much more dangerous turn during the last week-end of November.

On the evening of Sunday, November 26, the Leningrad district High Command issued a communiqué accusing the Finns of having shelled during the afternoon Red Army troops on the Soviet-Finnish frontier. A little later Moscow announced that M. Molotov, Prime Minister and Commissar for Foreign Affairs for the Soviet Union, had handed a note of protest to the Finnish Minister in Moscow, Baron Koskinen. The note stated that the Soviet troops had not returned the fire of the Finnish artillery because they had been ordered not to react to provocation, and recalled that during the recent negotiations with the Finnish delegation the Soviet Government had pointed out the danger created by the presence of Finnish concentrations near Leningrad. This " provocative shelling " now showed that those concentrations not only represented a danger to Leningrad, but constituted a hostile act against the Soviet Union inasmuch as they had led to a direct attack on Soviet troops. Hence the Soviet Government asked that Finland should immediately withdraw all her troops in the frontier district on the Karelian Isthmus to a line twelve to sixteen miles from the frontier. On receipt of M. Molotov's note the Finnish Minister stated that he would communicate with his Government without delay, but the feeling between the two countries was hardly improved by such outbursts as that contained in the Moscow newspaper " Pravda," which referred to the Finnish Prime Minister, M. Cajander, as " a buffoon, jackanapes, perfidious and lecherous reptile without sharp teeth," and alleged that he and the Government were agents of British imperialism.

The Finnish General Staff asserted that not a single shot had been fired by the Finns, and it was pointed out that if the Finnish forces were withdrawn the distance required by the Soviet, it would mean the evacuation of Finland's " Maginot Line " on the Karelian Isthmus facing Leningrad. In view of reports of Soviet military and naval moves, Field-Marshal Mannerheim, Finland's Liberator in the war of 1918, went to the frontier to inspect the defences.

The Finnish reply to the Soviet note was presented on the evening of the next day, November 27 ; it rejected the Soviet Government's protest and declared that no hostile act against the Soviet Union had been committed. The seven shots mentioned by M. Molotov had been fired, it was stated, from guns on the Soviet side of the frontier.

The next day the Soviet military authorities reported two further frontier

Above, right, is Field-Marshal Baron Carl Gustav Mannerheim, who was appointed by President Kallio " Defender of Finland," and Commander-in-Chief when fighting began on November 30. Right is Lieut.-General Osterman, Commander-in-Chief of the Finnish Army. Above is a Finnish anti-aircraft battery.

Finland's Cavalry the Flower of Her Little Army

Finland, like Poland, has not completely mechanized her army and the peacetime establishment includes one cavalry brigade. A Finnish Cavalry regiment, magnificently mounted, is seen here. Every man in Finland from the age of 17 to the age of 60 is liable for military service, and all young men when they reach the age of 21 years are summoned to the colours, the term of service for those who do not intend to make the Army their career being 350 days. All were mobilized in the hour of Finland's desperate emergency.

Photo, Denise Bellon

The bridge at Terijoki, 10 miles from the frontier, where the new puppet Government was established by the Soviet invaders.

This map shows the principal area in which Russia struck at Finland on November 30, by air, sea, and land. The country as a whole is shown in the map opposite. (See also map in page 234.)

which the Finnish Government bears full responsibility." Went on M. Molotov: "The High Command of the Red Army has ordered the Army and Navy to b in readiness for any eventuality in o der to prevent possible fresh provocation by the Finnish military" These measures had not been taken, as was alleged abroad, with a view to violating Finland's independence or annexing Finnish territory— "this is a perfidious calumny. We have no such intentions . . . we regard Finland as an independent and sovereign State whatever her regime may be. . . . This matter must be solved by the Soviet Union in friendly co-operation with the Finnish people."

Such words were obviously intended for home consumption only. The world

with utter recklessness. Invective, which is even cheaper than the German brand, is poured with a ladle on the heads of the Finnish Government out of the apparently inexhaustible sewers of the Kremlin." Through Mr. Cordell Hull, Secretary of State, it was made known that the United States Government was ready to extend its good offices to help to find a settlement of the dispute.

But just as in August Hitler wanted no reasonable settlement with Poland, so in November Stalin rejected every overture. Nothing, it seemed, was to be allowed to stop the march of the steam-roller of the new Russian Imperialism.

On November 30 Finland was invaded by land, sea, and air. The blow which the little country had dreaded so long had fallen at last, and it was part of the irony of things that at the very moment when Stalin's bombers were raining down death on Finland's cities, President Roosevelt's offer of American mediation was being handed in at the Kremlin.

Above is the modern airport at Helsinki on which the Russians dropped incendiary bombs soon after their ultimatum expired. Not all the bombs, however, were aimed at such military objectives as this, and many civilians perished in the ruins of their homes.
Photos, E.N.A. and Associated Press

incidents, and in the evening came the news that Russia had denounced the 1932 Pact of Non-aggression with Finland in view of Finland's denial of the shootings on the preceding Sunday, her refusal to withdraw troops from the frontier unless Russia did the same, and because her troops threatened the safety of Leningrad!

Before the Finnish Minister in Moscow had had an opportunity of delivering his Government's reply to the Soviet measure, M. Molotov announced that Russia had severed diplomatic relations with Finland. He declared that there had been "abominable provocation" by the Finns, and throughout the negotiations the Finnish Government had adopted an "irreconcilable attitude towards our country, acting in the interests of foreign imperialists and warmongers who are the enemies of the Soviet Union. We can no longer tolerate the present situation, for

without watched with increasing disgust Stalin's attempt to cast little Finland for the role of aggressive bully. In America sympathy with Finland was most marked. As the "New York Times" wrote: "It has been left to those self-righteous people, the Government of Russia, so quick to rebuke imagined warmongering in others, to show the world what warmongering really meant in practice.... Hatred is preached

The Finns are immensely proud of their capital Helsinki, formerly known as Helsingfors. It contains many fine specimens of modern architecture, one of the most remarkable being the railway station seen above, standing in an open space in the centre of the city. The walls and the clock tower are of granite.
Photo, Derek Wordley

Finland Defies the Russian Bully

That Stalin had perfected himself in the Hitlerian technique of
aggression was made manifest when, after denouncing the Finns as
warmongers and aggressors, he sent the Red Army to overwhelm a
gallant little people who wanted only to be free.

Dr. Risto Ryti, the new Finnish Prime
Minister, was Governor of the Bank of
Finland until he undertook to form a
Government on December 2nd, 1939.
Photo, Topical

WITHOUT any formal declaration
of war Soviet troops and
aeroplanes crossed the Finnish
frontier on the morning of November 30.
On land the three main attacks were
directed against the Finnish " Maginot
Line " on the Karelian isthmus, north
of Lake Ladoga, and on the Ribachi
peninsula on the Arctic coast. At the
same time the Soviet navy left Kronstadt
and bombarded several of the Finnish
ports in the Gulf of Finland.

The Finns claimed that their army,
now under the command of Baron
C. G. Mannerheim, the Father of Finnish
independence, was able to hold up the
invaders at most points, but they could
do little or nothing against the onslaught
from the air. Several times during the
first day of war Helsinki (Helsingfors),
the Finnish capital, was the victim of
deadly air-raids. In the first, at 9.15
a.m., a number of incendiary bombs
were dropped from three Soviet 'planes,
and about two hours later four raiders
were sighted over Helsinki harbour, and
bombs were dropped on Malm aerodrome.
So far the casualties and the damage
had been almost negligible, but at 2.45
in the afternoon Soviet bombers
approached the capital again from the
sea. Apparently the raiders' objective
was the airport, but the incendiary
bombs went wide and several fires were
started in the centre of the city. Some
heavy bombs, presumably intended for
the railway station, also fell wide. A big
apartment house was almost destroyed,
and a bomb falling in the street almost
wiped out a crowded motorbus.

There was no panic, although the
first bombs dropped barely a minute
after the warning sirens had sounded.
Many people seemed to be too dazed
to take refuge in the cellars, and stood
gazing as if stupefied up into the sky.
As night fell the city was illumined by
the flames of the burning buildings, in
the light of which firemen dug furiously
in the debris to recover the bodies of

the wounded and the dead. Although
the shops reopened and the evening
newspapers came out as usual, thousands
of people made a hurried exodus from
the capital into the snow-covered woods
beyond the suburbs.

At nine in the evening the deadly
silence was broken again by the sirens,
followed swiftly by the noise of crashing
bombs. Still more fires lit up the sky,
and a pitiful procession of women and
children and old people poured in a
constant stream along the roads which
led to the comparative safety of the
countryside. Mothers were carrying
babies or leading young children ; others
staggered beneath bundles of supplies and
rolled-up blankets ; none knew where they
would find safety, if indeed they might
find it at all. They trudged on through
the night, stunned by the calamity which
had come so suddenly upon them.

Many other towns in South Finland
received a similar visitation, but the
Finns were able to bring down at least
24 of the Russian machines. In the
land fighting the
Finns fought stub-
bornly and gave but
little ground. The
Russians were able
to advance their lines
somewhere in the
Karelian isthmus,
and also succeeded in
occupying several of
the islands in the Gulf
of Finland. Their
attacks on Hanko
were repulsed, how-
ever, and after an
initial victory at
Petsamo they were
driven out in a fierce
hand-to-hand fight.
The Russian losses
were heavy both in
men and material ;
the Finns claimed
to have destroyed
between 30 and 40
tanks in the first two
days' fighting. Win-
try conditions pre-
vailed everywhere,
from the far north at
Petsamo where the
war was waged in a
region in which the
sun had set for the
two months' winter
night, to the south
where hundreds of
the invaders were
drowned as they at-
tempted to cross the

ice on the frozen marshes north of Lake
Ladoga.

Mannerheim issued an Order of the
Day to his troops calling on them to
" fulfil their duty even unto death. We
fight for our homes, our faith, our fatherland " ; and in Helsinki the new Government of National Union under M. Ryti
reaffirmed the country's will to resist,
although at the same time they declared
their readiness to negotiate on honourable
terms.

The Russians, however, refused to
acknowledge the new Government, and
set up a puppet creation of their own at
Terijoki, just within the frontier, under
the presidency of Otto Kuusinen, a Finnish revolutionary leader of the civil war
of 1918. This " Government " accepted
a treaty with the Soviet Union in which
all the latter's demands were granted.

Meanwhile, M. Ryti's Government appealed to the League of Nations, and in
every corner of the civilized world Finland's brave fight was watched with
sympathetic indignation.

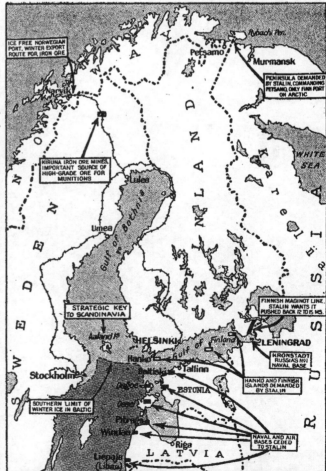

This map shows the concessions that had already been made to
Russia by the Baltic States when the Soviet's demands upon Finland
led to war. Other points of interest in Baltic and Scandinavian
countries are also indicated.
Courtesy of the " Evening Standard "

Dawn Patrol: Britain's Fighters on the Win

Meet the Challenge of a New Day

THIS is not only a beautiful photograph of cloudscape and mounting sun, but also an inspiring study of the Royal Air Force on active service. From its station, lost far below the clouds, a squadron of fighters has taken off, each manned by a lone pilot conscious of his mastery of the machine put in his charge. Now each flight of three keeps perfect squadron formation as it thunders on to its service ceiling, somewhere near 20,000 feet up. The latest "Hurricane" is now disclosed as being capable of climbing to this height in less than nine minutes—and more modern aircraft than the "Hurricane" are already in service.

Photo, Planet News

WORDS THAT HISTORY WILL REMEMBER

(Continued from page 402)

Courage and Discipline of Allied Workers

Tuesday, November 14, 1939

M. PAUL REYNAUD, French Minister of Finance, in a broadcast :

Returning two years ago from a visit to Germany, I said to my fellow-countrymen : " Hurry up and arm. You have already entered the bloodless period of the war." And now we are at war. And again I say, our enemy is formidable. He is making frantic preparation. Time will be on our side if we use it. We must make freely an effort superior to that imposed by force on the German people. Our enemy is convinced that democratic peoples will not submit to such great sacrifices as they themselves. In that they are mistaken. After a few hours spent in this country I am impressed by the unanimous determination of the British people to conquer and to obtain at last the peace which will be really peace. The people of this country are as individualistic as our own, and still they have courageously accepted the discipline which is necessary in time of war. Industry has adapted itself to the necessity of arming the nation. To increase production, the workers have agreed to the relaxation of the rules of the Trade Unions. The sacrifice the taxation demanded is without precedent. All these things bear witness to the determination of the British people.

Now you will ask, what about the French people ? Imagine a country in which one in every eight inhabitants is in the army ; a country in which women have replaced men in the factories and in the fields. Nearly all the horses and the lorries have been commandeered. Very often there remains in a village only one horse, which is used by all in turn. The women whose husbands have left for the front guide the plough. . . .

Everyone has bravely faced the disaster. Our magnificent working-class is working sixty hours a week and more, and they are not only working overtime but they are giving up 40 per cent of their overtime pay. In addition to this, those under forty-nine who, by their age, are eligible for the army, are paying another 15 per cent of their salaries. Beside this, food restrictions have already started. Not only have the French people accepted these sacrifices with courage, but in spite of all this difficulty the financial recovery has not been interrupted. The rich continue to bring their money back into their country, for there are today greater gold and foreign exchange reserves than at the beginning of the war. The poor are making their money available to their country by increasing their savings in the banks. Everyone in France is confident in his country. . . .

Reprisals Against Germany's Acts of Piracy

Tuesday, November 21

Mr. CHAMBERLAIN in the House of Commons :

The House will be aware that during the last three days upwards of ten ships, six of which were neutral, were sunk, with a serious loss of life, by German mines.

The Hague Convention, to which Germany is a party and which she announced her intention of observing as recently as September 17 last, provides that when anchored mines are used every possible precaution must be taken for the security of peaceful navigation. This is the very essence of the Convention, as the mines cannot discriminate between warship and merchant ship or between belligerent and neutral.

The Convention particularly requires that the danger zone must be notified, as soon as military exigencies permit, once the mines cease to be under the observation of those who laid them. None of these provisions has been observed by the German Government in laying mines which caused the losses I have mentioned, and this fresh outrage is only the culmination of a series of violations of the agreements to which Germany had set her hand.

I need only recall the sinking of the Athenia with the loss of 112 lives and subsequently the destruction of British, Allied and neutral vessels by mine, torpedo or gunfire. These attacks have been made often without warning and to an increasing extent with complete disregard of the rules laid down in the Submarine Protocol to which Germany subscribed or of the most elementary dictates of humanity.

His Majesty's Government are not prepared to allow these methods of conducting warfare to continue without retaliation. I may remind the House that in the last war, as a measure of justified reprisal for submarine attacks on merchant ships, exports of German origin or ownership were made subject to seizure on the High Seas.

The many violations of international law and the ruthless brutality of German methods have decided us to follow a similar course now, and an Order in Council will shortly be issued giving effect to this decision.

" Save Your Way to Victory "

Wednesday, November 22

Sir JOHN SIMON, Chancellor of the Exchequer, in a broadcast :

Paying for the war is the business of every one of us. This is the most expensive war ever fought. It is already costing this country at least £6,000,000 a day. . . . We must all save every penny we possibly can, in order that we may have it to lend. Everyone who spends

unnecessarily on himself is making it more difficult to carry on the war. If a man saves all he can and lends it to the Government he is not only making a useful provision for himself, but is himself helping to fight the war and hastening the day of victory. . . .

There is another reason why everybody should limit their spending and instead save all they can. The Government is bound to spend vast sums on supplies for carrying on the war, and there cannot be at the same time the same plentiful supplies for the people to spend their money on as in peacetime. Productive power, which would in peacetime be supplying our ordinary needs, has to be diverted to war production. In wartime our imports from abroad have to be cut down. There is inevitably a reduction in the supplies of some things to which we have become accustomed. There is, therefore, a special need for restraint in outlay, for if supplies are restricted and at the same time the public, instead of saving, tries to buy as much as or more than in peacetime, all this helps to raise prices unnecessarily.

You have been reading in your newspapers today of this latest abomination of German savagery—the magnetic mine secretly deposited in the channels of the sea in order to blow up without warning neutral and British shipping alike ; and to destroy innocent lives—women children, and unarmed men—in breach of rules of war which Germany only two months ago had expressly promised to obey. Not even the inventiveness of Herr Goebbels can suggest that these sinkings have been contrived by the perverse ingenuity of Mr. Churchill in order to throw the blame on Germany ! By this ruthless brutality the enemy hopes to sap the strength of our island fortress and to cut off our supplies. Meanwhile, the brave crews of our mine-sweepers are risking danger for their country's sake, our incomparable Navy is on the watch, the Air Force keeps ceaseless vigil, the Mercantile Marine continues its perpetual service, and all that skill and science can devise is devoted to meeting the new danger. We are confident that their efforts will be successful. Everyone can do his utmost to strengthen and support the country by saving all he can and putting his savings at the service of Britain.

THINGS YOU MAY NOT KNOW

U-Boat is short for *Unterseeboot*, literally " under-sea boat." In this war, as in the last, German submarines bear the letter U followed by a number, e.g. U 35. In the Great War, when the number in commission ran into several hundred, they were named UA, UB, UC, followed by a number.

Blue Book. Although the term " Blue Book " used to be applied only to British parliamentary and consular reports bound in blue paper wrappers and issued in folio form, it is now used to include many other official publications. One of the best-sellers of recent years has been the Blue Book whose official title is : " Documents concerning German-Polish Relations and the Outbreak of Hostilities between Great Britain and Germany on September 3, 1939." Official documents referring to foreign affairs are known as **White Papers**, e.g. Sir Nevile Henderson's " Final Report " and the " Papers concerning the Treatment of German Nationals in Germany." Each Blue Book and White Paper bears a number, e.g. Cmd. 6115, in which Cmd. is short for " command," as the publication is " Presented by the Secretary of State for Foreign Affairs to Parliament by command of his Majesty." Government publications of foreign coun-

tries also have distinctive colours, e.g. Belgium, grey ; France, yellow ; Germany, white ; Italy, green, etc.

Blockade. Although the term may be employed as a convenient one for describing economic warfare based on the exercise of belligerent rights at sea, Britain has declared no blockade of Germany. Blockading in the naval sense is the control of an enemy port or series of ports and coastline, so that not only may none of the enemy ships enter or leave, but no neutral ships may have intercourse with the blockaded area. In February, 1915, Germany declared a blockade of the United Kingdom, and in the following month Britain replied by declaring Germany to be in a state of blockade. At the outbreak of war in 1939 it was considered sufficient to institute a system of **Contraband Control** in the course of which goods consigned to Germany directly or indirectly which might be used in the carrying on of the war were declared to be liable to seizure as absolute or conditional contraband. The " **State of Siege** " referred to by Hitler would seem to be but another term for blockade. Siege really means the " sitting down " of an army, etc., before a fortified place for the purpose of taking it either by direct military attack or by starving it out.

Britain Hits Back at the Mine-Laying 'Planes

Here is the thrilling story of the raid by British warplanes made on November 28 on the German seaplane base at Borkum. They had been looking for the mine-layers—and they had found them.

This map shows the position of Borkum, one of the Friesian Islands, 250 miles from the English coast, on which the raid described in this page was made.

FLYING had finished for the day at the German seaplane base on the windswept island of Borkum. It was almost dark, and the seaplanes had been drawn up on the slipways ready to be put to bed in the hangars.

Perhaps these very 'planes were among those which a week before had been seen by observers on the East Coast of Britain dropping objects by parachute, and also alighting on the water and then taking off again—in other words, laying mines either of the submarine magnetic type or of the floating bubble variety, parachutes being used to lessen the shock of the mine striking the water. If such indeed they were, their nefarious activities were over, for suddenly there swooped down from among the clouds that lay low above the water a squadron of British long-range fighters.

The defence was taken completely by surprise, and the utmost confusion reigned. In what one of the British pilots described as "a few glorious moments of low strafing," five German seaplanes were machine-gunned, three out of four machine-gun posts on the Mole were probably put out of action, and several enemy patrol boats were riddled with bullets.

Flying Ten Feet Above the Guns

The 'planes flew so low—according to the German account some of them were at a height of no more than nine or ten feet—that the defenders found great difficulty in bringing their machine-guns and pom-poms into action. The raiders could see men running in all directions, and some gunners occupying a post on top of a hangar were apparently hit. After a few minutes the anti-aircraft guns and the coastal patrol boats started firing, but by this time the British 'planes had reached their objectives.

Quickly the squadron re-formed and disappeared into the mist. All the twelve returned safely to their base in England, the last 200 miles of the journey being covered in complete darkness. No enemy fighters had spotted their approach in time to come up to engage them, and no enemy aircraft were observed on the return flight. In spite of the intense barrage the British raiding party suffered no casualties, and not one of the dozen aircraft was hit. Later it was disclosed that the 'planes were twin-engined Blenheims, and of the pilots six were R.A.F. regulars and six members of the Auxiliary Air Force. Not one of the intrepid attackers had been under fire before.

Naturally enough, the Germans sought to disparage the results achieved. No serious damage was done, they claimed; but at the same time they admitted that it was "undoubtedly a daring exploit." And away back across the North Sea thirty-six airmen went in to dinner conscious of a day's work well done.

DORNIER Do. 18
FLYING BOAT WITH 2
JUNKER DIESEL ENGINES

HOW MAGNETIC MINES ARE LAID FROM FLYING BOATS
A. Magnetic mines being released. B. Parachutes prevent the mines from striking the sea with damaging force. C. Mines are coupled in pairs. D. Decoy planes fly at a great height to attract the defenders while the mine-laying machines fly just above the sea. Left is a bullet hole in an East Coast pier window made by machine-gun fire from a mine-laying 'plane.

Diagram specially drawn for THE WAR ILLUSTRATED *by Haworth*

'TO DEFEND FREEDOM & TO ESTABLISH PEACE'

On the evening of Sunday, November 26, the Prime Minister came to the microphone
and with many a trenchant phrase reviewed the course of the war and stated anew the
Allies' war aims. Below are the most important passages from his speech.

"THE last time I broadcast to you," the Premier began, "was on September 3, and it was to tell you that we were at war with Germany. Now after just twelve weeks of war I am speaking to you again, with full confidence in our ultimate victory."

Up to the present (he went on) the war has been carried on in a way very different from what we expected. We need not attribute the reluctance of the Germans to begin a great land offensive or to attempt a series of mass attacks from the air upon this country to their humanity. We have had plenty of evidence that no considerations of humanity deter them from any form of warfare that they think will bring them some advantage. . . .

THE latest of these methods as you all know is the sowing of a new kind of mine indiscriminately in our home waters. It matters nothing to them that what they are doing is contrary to international agreements, to which they have subscribed. It matters nothing to them that they are daily blowing up neutral ships as well as British, and thereby drowning or mutilating citizens of countries with which they are not at war. They hope by these barbarous weapons to cut off our supplies from overseas and so squeeze or starve us into submission.

We Shall Master the Mine

YOU need have no fear that this attempt will succeed. **Already we know the secrets of the magnetic mine, and we shall soon master the magnetic mine as we have already mastered the U-boat.** And in the meantime, despite some losses, our convoys are still moving steadily in and out of our ports, and they will continue to do so, thanks to the courage and skill of the men in our Merchant Navy and in the warships which escort them.

It may be that some of you who are listening to me are yourselves serving at sea in H.M. ships or in the vessels which maintain our supplies from oversea. I would like you to know that we are thinking of you, and of the perils of storms and of a ruthless enemy that you are facing day and night . . .

OTHERS of my listeners may be serving in the Army, some in distant garrisons oversea, some in France, some again keeping perpetual vigil over their guns on the Home Front. For you the time for conflict has not yet arrived, but we know that you are cheerfully enduring the monotony and discomforts that inevitably attend the routine of preparation, and that when the day of battle comes you will be ready as your fathers were before you.

And as for you who are serving in the Air Force, our youngest fighting Service, you too have an important part to play in the defence of the homeland as well as in the defeat of the enemy's forces. We have watched with pride and admiration your gallant exploits in those aerial combats in which you have already taken part. . . .

I do not forget that I have tonight a still wider audience and that my voice will travel to all the peoples of the British Empire. I wish that I could speak to each and thank them for their support so freely and so swiftly given. **We entered the war to defend freedom and to establish peace ; those are the two vital principles of our Empire, and the Empire's unity today gives us the moral as well as the material strength to win them.**

AND now I want to speak to those among you who are listening to me from your homes in the towns and villages of Great Britain. Many of you are engaged on one form or another of National Service, often at great sacrifice to yourselves ; others are serving your country no less usefully, on the land, in mines and factories, in hospitals, in offices, in your own homes, and in numberless other ways . . .

THERE must be few to whom it has not meant anxiety or disturbance of mind, discomfort, material loss, or even severe hardship. Husbands and wives have been separated from one another or from their children. Home arrangements have been upset by having to billet strangers or children accustomed to different ways of living. Businesses have been dislocated, hard-earned practices have had to be abandoned. Buildings have been commandeered at short notice and at great inconvenience to their owners and occupants. Heavy taxation has cut into incomes and imposed severe restriction upon expenditure.

Then again there are the daily irritating inconveniences of restrictions of various kinds, not forgetting the black-out and the difficulty and discomfort of travelling. Most of these hardships and inconveniences have been brought about by the necessity of providing against attacks from the air. Some of them may seem now to have been unnecessary since the air raids have not taken place. But if they had come, as every one expected, and had found us unprepared, you would have rightly blamed the Government for its neglect. Even now we cannot assume that the Germans will not change their tactics and make a sudden attack from the air upon this country . . .

I SAID a little while ago that this was a different kind of war from what we expected. Perhaps you may sometimes wonder why we ourselves are not attacking the enemy with more vigour. Well, I would remind you that the art of war consists in bringing the greatest possible force to bear at the right place and at the right time. In our case the place and time will be decided by those who are responsible for the strategy of the Allies. But in the meanwhile we are not losing anything by delay, for time is on our side. **Every week that passes by intensifies the pressure upon Germany of the Allies' blockade, which is slowly but surely depriving her of those materials which are essential to the successful prosecution of a modern war and which she cannot produce within her own borders.**

War Aims and Peace Aims

WHAT is the purpose for which we are today standing side by side with our French and Polish allies ? . . . In my own mind I make a distinction between war aims and peace aims. Our war aim can be stated very shortly. It is to defeat our enemy; and by that I do not merely mean the defeat of the enemy's military forces. I mean the **defeat of that aggressive bullying mentality which seeks continually to dominate other peoples by force, which finds a brutal satisfaction in the persecution and torture of inoffensive citizens, and in the name of the interests of the State justifies the repudiation of its own pledged word whenever it finds it convenient.** If the German people can be convinced that that spirit is as bad for themselves as for the rest of the world they will abandon it. If we can secure that they do abandon it without bloodshed, so much the better ; but abandoned it must be. That is our war aim, and we shall persevere in this struggle until we have attained it.

When we come to peace aims we are dealing with something to be achieved in conditions we cannot at present foresee. Our definition of them can, therefore, only be in the most general terms, but there can be no harm in declaring the broad principles on which we should desire to found them.

OUR desire, then, when we have achieved our war aim, would be to **establish a new Europe ; not new in the sense of tearing up all the old frontier posts and re-drawing the map according to the ideas of the victors, but a Europe with a new spirit in which the nations which inhabit it will approach their difficulties with good will and mutual tolerance.** In such a Europe fear of aggression would have ceased to exist, and such adjustment of boundaries as would be necessary would be thrashed out between neighbours sitting on equal terms round a table, with the help of disinterested third parties if it were so desired.

In such a Europe, it would be recognized that there can be no lasting peace unless there is a full and constant flow of trade between the nations concerned, for only by increased interchange of goods and services can the standard of living be improved. In such a Europe each country would have the unfettered right to choose its own form of internal government, so long as that government did not pursue an external policy injurious to its neighbours. Lastly, in such a Europe armaments would gradually be dropped as a useless expense, except in so far as they were needed for the preservation of internal law and order.

LET us then gird up our loins, confident in our own tenacity and resolute in our determination. Let us keep clear before our eyes the necessity that **this reign of terror instituted under the present German Government should come to an end, in order that we may build a new and better Europe.** We know that in this great struggle we are fighting for the right and against the wrong. Let us then go forward with God's blessing on our arms, and we shall prevail.

In this portion of a recent photograph of the whole War Cabinet, Mr. Chamberlain, whose vigorous second war broadcast is condensed in this page, is seen with Mr. Churchill and Sir Kingsley Wood.
Photo, B.I.P.P.A.

'Rawalpindi' Went Down With Colours Flying

On November 23, 1939, the " Rawalpindi " wrote another glorious page in British sea history when she fought single-handed the German pocket battleship " Deutschland."

This map shows approximately the position, south-east of Iceland, in which the " Rawalpindi " fought her great fight against the " Deutschland " and a ship that it was not possible to identify.

O N a raw November afternoon the " Rawalpindi " was keeping her course in the cold, tempestuous Atlantic somewhere between Iceland and Norway. Only a few months before she had been sailing the tropic seas as one of the crack liners of the P. and O. passenger fleet ; now and since the war began she was forming a part of the Northern Patrol, that flotilla of armed merchant cruisers, large vessels of good sea-keeping qualities and capable of enduring frequent storms, which enforce the contraband control of German trade.

At 3.30 p.m., when it was already dusk, she sighted an enemy ship. What followed may be best related in the words of the Admiralty official account :

Captain Kennedy, having examined this vessel through his glasses, said : " It's the ' Deutschland ' all right," and the crew were immediately ordered to action stations. Course was altered to bring the enemy on the starboard quarter. Smoke-floats were lit and cast overboard to enable the " Rawalpindi " to escape. However, a second enemy ship was seen to starboard.

The " Deutschland," approaching, signalled to the " Rawalpindi " to stop, and when she continued her course fired a shot across her bows.

As this warning was rejected, the first salvo was fired by the 11-in. guns of the " Deutschland " a little after 3.45 p.m. at a range of 11,000 yards. The " Rawalpindi " replied with all her four starboard 6-in. guns. The third salvo from the " Deutschland " put out all the lights and broke the electric winches of the ammunition supply. The fourth salvo shot away the whole of the bridge and wireless room.

Both the German ships were now closing rapidly, and by this time the second had gone round the " Rawalpindi's " stern and was firing from the port side. The " Rawalpindi " maintained the fight until every gun was put out of action and the whole ship ablaze except the forecastle and the poop.

After about 30 to 40 minutes of this unequal combat, about 4.15 to 4.25 p.m., the enemy ceased firing, and three boats which were not shattered by shell-fire, one of which became waterlogged, were lowered. Two of these boats, containing over 30 men, were, it is believed, picked up by one of the German ships.

The 11 survivors, who have been brought in by the " Chitral," swam to the waterlogged lifeboat, and would probably have been picked up, but for the fact that at about 6.15 p.m. the approach of a British cruiser caused the enemy immediately to withdraw.

The " Rawalpindi " continued to burn amidships until 8 o'clock, when she turned turtle to starboard and foundered with all remaining hands. Meanwhile the British cruiser attempted to shadow the German ships, but in a sudden heavy rainstorm and the darkness of the night, they made their escape from the scene.

So the Admiralty statement. The German statement was far less detailed. " German naval forces," it ran, " commanded by Rear-Admiral Marschall, carried out scouting operations in the North Atlantic between the Faroe Islands and Greenland. Near Iceland, the British merchant cruiser ' Rawalpindi '

KEY TO DIAGRAM OF THE "DEUTSCHLAND"

A Forward turret of three 11-in. guns.
B Gun crew at action stations.
C Gun-layers and range-finders at work.
D Forward conning-tower and range-finder.
E Two 3-pounder anti-aircraft guns.
F Control tower.
G One of six 44-in. searchlights.
H Main fire-direction tower.
J The foremast.
K The admiral's barge.
L Two of the eight 5·9-in. guns.
M Crane for hoisting aircraft aboard.
N Twin 4·1-in. anti-aircraft guns.
O Lifeboat.
P Seaplane on catapult.
Q The aft direction tower.
R Second twin 4·1-in. anti-aircraft guns.
S Aft turret of three 11-in. guns.
T Two sets of four 21-in. torpedo tubes.
U Officers' mess.
V Sailors' mess.
W Pantry.
Y Workshops.
I Ammunition hoist.
2 Stores.
3 One of the eight 6,750 h.p. Diesel engines.
4 Anti-torpedo protection bulge.
X Cabins.
Z Bathroom.

The main points of the " Deutschland " are seen in this diagram. It represents the vessel as she was when she was launched in 1931. As her design was more or less experimental some slight alterations may since have been made. The diagram, together with the photograph in page 279, gives a very complete conception of the construction and appearance of the ship.

Courtesy of the " Daily Mail "

DAWORTH.

'A Most Gallant Fight Against Overwhelming Odds'

Above, the 11-in. guns of the "Deutschland" are firing a salvo. She carries six guns of that calibre, a remarkable armament for a ship of only 10,000 tons.
Photos, Planet News

was met and sunk after a short battle. Only 26 of her crew could be rescued owing to the rough sea."

Eleven more of the "Rawalpindi's" complement of some 300 were landed at a Scottish port by the "Chitral." One had clung to a lifeboat for 23 hours.

One of the "Chitral" ratings who had heard the stories of these survivors gave the "News Chronicle" a résumé of what happened. According to his account, the "Rawalpindi" was battered to pulp before the crew had much chance of getting into the boats. "The 'Deutschland,' as the 'Rawalpindi' was going down for the final plunge, put on full speed past the lifeboat, almost swamping it. Sailors on the deck of the 'Deutschland' shouted to the men in the lifeboat in English: 'Is it cold down there?' Some of them spat at the men.

"The survivors were very bitter at this treatment, and when we heard of what had happened there was a good deal of ill-feeling on board between us and the German prisoners we had picked up three days before.

"It was even worse when we realized the suffering of the man who was rescued from the upturned lifeboat. He was with other members of the crew when the boat capsized and all but himself were drowned. We got him about three o'clock on Friday afternoon, 23 hours after the 'Rawalpindi' was sunk. For hours he was crouching on the keel of the boat and was half dead from cold when we spotted him."

To return to the Admiralty account, "the 'Rawalpindi' made a most gallant fight against overwhelming odds, and went down with her colours flying. The search for the two enemy warships is continuing in tempestuous weather both by night and in the brief hours of daylight."

The "Rawalpindi" was in peacetime one of the crack liners of the P. & O. Company plying between England and Japan. At the outbreak of war she was converted into an armed merchant cruiser and thus became a ship of the Royal Navy flying the White Ensign. She was manned chiefly by men of the Royal Naval Reserve and the Royal Naval Volunteer Reserve.

Nelson Would Have Said 'Well Done'

These two survivors of the crew of the " Rawalpindi " are taking tickets at a northern station. On the left is one of the ship's boys who could not swim, but by clinging to an oar managed to reach a lifeboat. The man on the right held on to a capsized boat for 19 hours. *Photo, G.P.U.*

The Enemy Could Not Forbear to Cheer

On board a German warship.

It is late afternoon. We are south-east of Iceland. The sun is just beginning to dip behind the clouds on the horizon.

There. A signal. "A large steamer sighted." The Admiral orders, "Halt, steamer." Suddenly the Briton moves away from us. With full steam ahead, we follow the foe, who is evidently seeking to escape. Does he hope, with his fast engines, to escape destruction in the dusk ?

Alarm ! In a moment our ship is ready to take on any opponent. The commander goes to the bridge. I stand near him and witness an action which, in dramatic power and grandiose beauty, cannot be surpassed.

The outline of the enemy ship, which is recognized as an auxiliary cruiser, is silhouetted sharply against the skyline.

A mighty burst of firing is unleashed from our ship ; a thick cloud of smoke follows. It places a warning shot before the stranger's bows. What's that ? A burst of firing flashes over there. The steamer is answering us. Is he trying to hold us off until help arrives ?

Suddenly there is a mighty roar on our ship. The bridge trembles. Have we ourselves been hit ? No. Our ship has only let its guns speak.

Then follows salvo upon salvo. After a few minutes hits can be discerned on the enemy. But he is still defending himself. Amidships something whistles over the heads of our anti-aircraft guns. Several hundred yards behind us the enemy's six-inch shells crash into the water. Now a couple of salvos in front of us. Detonation on the enemy. Now he is burning astern and amidships—and he ceases firing. We silence our guns.

A great black pall of smoke hangs over the burning ship. Suddenly he lurches heavily forward. A roar and crackling reach us. Explosion follows explosion. The magazine has caught fire.

In a minute the sky is lit up as if with silver stars. The tracer ammunition of the anti-aircraft guns has gone up ! He is a tough fellow ! The explosions last one hour while the whole ship is a mass of flames, but is still afloat.

A boatload of survivors was picked up. The Admiral ordered that the wrecked crew should be taken on board. Desperately the British clung to lines helpfully thrown to them and to lowered rope ladders, still in danger of being crushed by the wildly-rolling boats.

From the German official statement.

Captain E. O. Kennedy, R.N., who fought his ship in the spirit of Sir Richard Grenville, had retired, but at the age of 60 rejoined the R.N. and was given command of the " Rawalpindi." *Photo, " Daily Mirror "*

'They Were Great'

The following fine tribute to his mates was paid by a survivor of the " Rawalpindi " :

Against terrific fire from two enemy warships the poor old " Rawalpindi " had no chance at all. Soon the whole ship was in flames. Yet our men fought their guns to the very last as though they were on manœuvres. They were great—every man of them. Maybe some people think that the British Navy tradition is a kind of fairy story. Now that I have watched the Navy fight, I know better. The tradition of the British Navy is something far greater than can be imagined by anyone who has never seen the Navy in action.

And here is what the Premier said :

These men must have known as soon as they sighted their enemy that there was no chance for them, but they had no thought of surrender. They fought their guns until they could be fought no longer. Many of them went to their deaths carrying on the great traditions of the Royal Navy. Their example will be an inspiration to others . . .

On Wednesday, November 29, ten of the survivors of the " Rawalpindi " were inspected on the Horse Guards Parade by Admiral Sir Charles Little, Chief of Naval Personnel. The party was led by Petty Officer Percy Harris ; just behind him, right, is Able-Seaman F. Russell. *Photo, Associated Press*

They Watch and Wait for Endless Hours

"They're fine men whose trying job it is to wait and watch for endless hours in all
weathers," wrote Mr. Trevor Allen in the "Star," after a night-time visit to a balloon
barrage station. Here is his description of what he saw.

A BLEAK black-out night somewhere beyond London's East End. For all I know it might be the end of the world. . . .

In the gloom R.A.F. boys are close-hauling a barrage balloon. It yaws in the bitter wind, looms overhead like some monstrous elephant. The Flight Officer beside me says: "They can be the devil sometimes. Bounce half a dozen hefty men about and make them feel almost as helpless as children. When it's rough you may have to give a balloon a rest every thousand feet to steady it." He leads the way to a dark building a few yards off, pushes open a door. "Come into the office . . ."

I find myself in a saloon bar: Business as Usual, it seems. Two or three of the boys off-duty are "having one." Upstairs, within sound of the revelry and clinking glasses, is the Orderly Room, with telephone, records, Orders of the Day, and beds for the orderlies.

A Service lorry brings to a balloon barrage station a supply of hydrogen gas. It is contained in cylinders filled under very high pressure.

An adjoining room is the officers' bed-room, looking as near as possible like home. An Orderly Room in a public-house! Yes, it's a strange war.

Nicely fortified against the cold wind, we groped across the waste bit again to the side-quarters; a bell-tent with sandbagged brailing, a bunkhouse with earth floor like a Klondyke miner's.

The men had built the bunkhouse themselves, mostly from material scrounged from kind-hearted folk who know how the wind can whistle over those river flats on winter nights and make you think longingly of Home, Sweet Home.

Food in 'Hay-boxes'

All the meals for the isolated balloon sites in a Flight are cooked at Flight H.Q., and distributed in thermostatic "hay-boxes." So picture the orderlies, in some cases, man-handling the boxes across muddy marshes and ditches even in the dark; savour their dulcet R.A.F. murmurings as one comes a cropper in the mire and his mate slides shin-deep at least into a dyke. Far, far away now across a black no-man's land is that friendly, cosy tavern. There's a wind howling, and maybe the rain teeming down. They know of a better 'ole but they can't go to it.

Some boxes must be carted to a tug which takes them to barges way out over the chill, bleak river—say, an hour's journey. They carry "love and kisses" from a two-bob-a-day cook who was cook in a submarine in the last war and rose to 14s. 6d. a day C.P.O. rank.

And they smell good when you're living the life of a bargee with something high and mighty to look after which tries to make your days a nightmare when gales be blowin', and induced a

new aircraftman to say, as he tugged at the silver brute: "Lumme! I'd rather deal with the missus any day!"

Squadron H.Q. comprises an infants' school where the Lilliputian sanitary fixtures move hefty aircraftmen to mirth. There I meet the keen-as-mustard O.C., who charts all his balloons on maps and blackboards and knows at a glance at any given moment the state of his brave barrage, its gadgets and hydrogen supply. He was formerly a Cavalry officer; and, believe me, where bucking broncs are concerned, he'd rather deal with the most temperamental 'osses any day.

Like the 'osses, these balloons have to be "groomed, fed and watered" daily in systematic rotation, so that no dangerous gaps are left in the barrage at any one time. Hydrogen constantly leaks out, air enters under pressure, causing loss of lift. Rigging must be adjusted, valves overhauled.

There is fire-danger from thunder-storms; tricky air-currents may entangle two balloons. If one breaks loose—and how the site-corporal loves losing his balloon!—off goes a 'phone flash to an aerodrome, and up goes a pilot to chase it and shoot it down.

So it's not as simple as it looks, this balloon-nursing. But it gives London and other cities and vital points reasonable security from swooping raiders and precision-bombing; it compels attacking aircraft to fly high and take pot-luck where fighters and anti-aircraft can best deal with them—so near the "ceiling" that they may have to use oxygen-gear.

An officer commanding a German Balloon Barrage, speaking from Berlin, declared that "aircraft will definitely avoid attacking an objective protected by balloon barrage." He ought to know.

The men who are in charge of the balloon barrage lead lonely lives, even though their stations are in the heart of a great city. They do their best to while away their long watches with cards and the radio, as the two men above are doing, but some of them can put up a notice outside their canteen such as that seen (right).
Photos, Fox

These 'Babies of the Sky' Are Lusty Infants

If and when the test comes, there is no reason to suppose that the usefulness of the balloon barrage in defence will be any less than that of the fighters or anti-aircraft guns, already proved in action. The balloons are manned by personnel of the Auxiliary Air Force, and some of these volunteers are seen above man-handling a fully-inflated balloon. This has a capacity of 20,000 cubic feet of hydrogen, and the envelope is made of two-ply rubber-proofed cotton with an aluminium powder finish to reflect the heat of the sun.

Photo, Fox

'Mail Up!' is the Call Soldiers Like Most to Hear

Bоth at home and in France the huge mail that goes to troops is handled by the postal section of the Royal Engineers. There is an Army post office "Somewhere in England" to which the Post Office delivers the Army post and whence the letters are sent on to the serving men both at home and abroad. The task of the sorters in the Army Post Office is a particularly arduous one, for the units in which the men to whom the letters are addressed are serving are often on the move. They cannot give notice of "change of address," but the Army Post Office knows where they are and their letters follow them with scarcely any delay. Some 4,500 bags of letters and 13,000 bags of parcels are now sent to the B.E.F. every week.

Photos, "Daily Mirror"

Top, a post office van is being loaded. Below, a parcel that has become a casualty is receiving treatment.

Above, sorters are at work in an Army post office dealing with letters for the troops in France as well as for those at home. Most of them have had previous experience of Post Office work.

Wherever there are British soldiers, in France, in camps or hospitals at home, the arrival of the mail is a "high spot" of the day. In the photograph on the left eager hands are stretched out to a nurse who is making the rounds just after the postman has called.

Photos, Keystone and Planet News

I WAS THERE!

We Scanned the Sea for Mines and U-Boats

In co-operation with the Navy, reconnaissance aircraft of the R.A.F.
Coastal Command patrol the seas daily, watching for U-boats and
floating mines and protecting convoys. One of these reconnaissance
flights from an aerodrome in the East of Scotland is here described
by an eye-witness.

IT was still dark as we crossed from the mess to the aerodrome intelligence-room, where crews studied the secret files and orders relating to the flight.

Each member of every crew signed a form certifying that he was carrying nothing that would, if found, convey information to the enemy.

A basket of carrier-pigeons for use in emergency was handed into our machine, and we climbed in. Greatcoats were unnecessary, for a mechanical heater kept the temperature warm, but over our uniforms we wore the air-filled life-jackets known familiarly among pilots by the name of an American film-star of ample curves.

A few minutes later we were off the ground, crossing the misty coast of Scotland, and heading for the open sea.

Wedged in the nose of the aircraft, surrounded on all sides by toughened glass, the navigator lay flat taking bearings through the transparent floor. He rose, sat at a light table on which was spread a chart, consulted his instruments, and made a few calculations. Presently he handed the pilot a slip of paper on which was written : " Set course . . . degrees." The pilot adjusted the compass, turned the machine slightly and set it on its course.

In front of the pilot some 36 needles danced upon their dials as the engines roared their steady, deep cruising note. He glanced over his instrument board with approval, selected one of the 28 small handles and knobs around him, and moved it upwards. It clicked home like the gear-lever of a sports car.

"George has her now," he said, releasing the controls and relaxing (" George " is the automatic gyroscopic pilot which keeps a machine flying steadily on the course set).

In a few moments we saw a tiny, dark smudge on the sea ahead. It was a cargo vessel ploughing towards Britain.

" We will have a look at her," said the pilot, resuming personal control.

We swept down like an express lift to a few feet above the waves, and roared past the ship. She was a Swedish tramp, with sides that needed painting, but with well-scrubbed deck and superstructure.

A sailor was swabbing the deck in the morning sunshine, and two more members of the crew tumbled up from below as we flashed past. We had a glimpse of the skipper, pipe in mouth, as he strolled out of the wheel-house to wave us a cheery salute.

A moment later and we were hundreds of feet away, looking down on a toy ship seemingly stationary in a flat sea.

All the time we were scanning the sea for U-boats or mines. Often a white flurry in the water would resemble the feather of spray from a periscope, and an occasional piece of floating jetsam looked like a mine. We had bombs for the U-boats and machine-gun bullets for the mines. . . .

So the flight went on, with ships to inspect here and there, until we had

The Coastal Command of the R.A.F. has done valuable work not only in submarine spotting but in saving life. This photograph, taken from a coastal patrol flying boat, shows a torpedoed merchant ship in flames. The seaplane, though it cannot itself take off the crew, sends out SOS messages to destroyers and other ships in the vicinity to come to the rescue.
Photo, British Official, Crown Copyright

444   *The War Illustrated*   December 16th, 1939

IIIIIIIIIIIIIIIIIIIIIIIIIIIIIIIIIIIIIIIIIIIIIIIIIIIIIIIII **I WAS THERE!** IIIIIIIIIIIIIIIIIIIIIIIIIIIIIIIIIIIIIIIIIIIIIIIIIIIIIIIIIIIIIII

Though the flying-boats of the R.A.F. carry radio—part of the aerial can be seen on the right—they also have on board a basket of carrier pigeons. Above, an observer is releasing his pigeons, as he would if the flying-boat was in difficulties and he wished to send a message for help without attracting attention.
Photo, British Official : Crown Copyright

reached the limit of our patrol. After the navigator had been once more prostrate on the floor, we re-set our course in the direction of Britain, this time combing a different section of sea.

Some score of miles from the coast we released our pigeons one by one to give them exercise and training. Scotland was a welcome sight after the long hours of grey sea and cloud.

The pilot stepped out and saluted his senior officer. "Nothing sensational to-day, sir," he reported. It had been just another day's routine work.

Our Ship Could Not Sail Home

An 11,000-ton Polish liner, the "Chrobry," set out from Gdynia on her maiden voyage to South America before the Germans invaded Poland. After roaming the seas for more than three months, she reached an English port—a ship without a home.

WHEN the Polish ship "Chrobry" berthed at an English port in the middle of November, her crew—264 officers, men and women—were homeless. They had no country. They did not know what had happened to their wives, children, sweethearts, and relatives.

There were twenty women and fourteen boy apprentices, between sixteen and eighteen, from a Polish sea school, among the party.

There was a pretty, twenty-two-year-old woman doctor's assistant, three nurses, and a young girl who took charge of the shop in the ship. All but one of the rest were stewardesses. That one was a tall, handsome girl of twenty-two, Bronislawa Wernik, a college art school mistress.

Miss Wernik bought a £100 ticket for the round voyage of the ship to Buenos Aires, back to Poland. She sold a piece of land she owned to pay for the trip.

Every night until Warsaw fell they all listened to the Polish broadcasts on the ship's radio. Loudspeakers were fixed up so that all might hear.

That was their only contact with their country since they sailed one bright day at the end of July, with bands playing on the pier.

One of the girls, Jadwiga Mickiewicz, was to have taken her final examination for a doctor's degree.

She said : "I have made these trips to sea for the last three years to gain experience. If only I had stayed in Poland ! My degree would probably have been granted to me by now."

Ignacy Kollupailo, one of the officers, said : "We sailed on July 29. Our ship was the newest and finest in Poland, and we carried 1,167 passengers.

"The trip was uneventful until we reached Buenos Aires on August 19. Then we knew by the radio that the war clouds were blowing up.

"When we left five days later, authorities warned us two unknown submarines had been sighted outside Uruguay waters.

"We were twelve hours out from Pernambuco when we heard over the radio that Germany had invaded Poland. There was great excitement when we arrived, for nine German ships were already hiding in the harbour.

"The British consul advised us to stay. From that moment we felt we were under British protection.

"The Brazilian authorities had to fix a frontier between our ship and the Germans. It seemed that a fight would break out at any moment.

"Then Warsaw fell. We placed more guards on our ship in case the six hundred German sailors who were there sabotaged us.

"The Brazilians heard of this and said, 'Don't worry, there won't be a German house left that isn't in flames if anything happens.'

"We stayed forty days there. We repainted the ship, the women lent a hand, and then one night we crept out of harbour, with all lights out.

"For three more weeks we wandered round the seas. At last we were directed into a British port by one of your warships."

Above are four of the Polish subjects, the strange and tragic end of whose pleasure cruise in the Polish ship "Chrobry" is told in this page, walking in a London park. Left to right are Mr. Ignacy Kollupailo, one of the ship's officers, Miss Jadwiga Mickiewicz, Nurse Helena Rutkowska and Miss Bronislawa Wernik.
Photo, Associated Press

IIIIIIIIIIIIIIIIIIIIIIIIIIIIIIIIIIIIIIIIIIIIIIIIIII **I WAS THERE!** IIIIIIIIIIIIIIIIIIIIIIIIIIIIIIIIIIIIIIIIIIIIIIIIIII

We Weathered A Gale in Open Boats

When the British steamer "Arlington Court" was torpedoed in the Atlantic, twenty-two of the crew were in an open boat for four days and seven others for six days before being picked up. Their stories, as printed below, were issued by the Press Association and "Daily Telegraph."

TWENTY-TWO survivors of the 5,000-ton "Arlington Court" were landed at an Irish port on November 21, after a terrible ordeal in an Atlantic gale. All showed the effects of their ordeal; their feet, legs and hands were terribly swollen. There were two stretcher cases.

Second-Officer Claude Boothby stated that, as he was talking to the radio

operator on Thursday afternoon (November 16), and saying that it would be almost impossible for a submarine to attack them in such a heavy sea, there was a terrific explosion which sent pieces of the hatch into the air. Their radio was wrecked, preventing their sending out messages.

"After the first explosion," said Mr. Boothby, "Third Engineer McKissock ran below to the engine room and shut off steam to prevent the possibility of the revolving propeller striking us. Captain Hurst received injuries to his chest getting into the lifeboat.

"We had to roll away as the ship was drifting down upon us and throughout the night we rowed continually to keep the boat's head to the wind and prevent being swamped. Our provisions consisted of sea biscuits, a few tins of condensed milk and bully beef and fresh water. Our daily ration was two biscuits and two dippers of water—about a glassful—together."

Several vessels were sighted. Flares were lit, but the lifeboat, tossing about in the huge waves, was not seen. A chance of rescue seemed hopeless.

On Friday morning they hoisted sail and set a course for Land's End, more than 300 miles away. They had covered about 180 miles when picked up by the "Algenib."

Before the rescuing vessel reached them the exhausted survivors saw the chief engineer—H. Pearson, aged 60—

die from exposure. He was unable to stand the change of the heat of the engine-room to the bitter cold of the open boat. Pearson was buried at sea.

SEVEN more members of the crew of the "Arlington Court," rescued exhausted after drifting in an open boat in the Atlantic for six days, were landed at a South Coast town on November 24. Four were taken to hospital suffering from frost-bite and exposure.

George Partridge, who was in charge of the boat from which the men were rescued, said that after the steamer was torpedoed and sunk they waited near the spot, thinking an S O S must have been sent out. After waiting 28 hours they hoisted sail and set off, hoping to strike a Channel port.

"There were only two barrels of water in the boat," he said. "One was ruined by sea-water, the other was only half full. I rationed the men to half a glass a day.

"Our only provisions were biscuits, which we had to break with an axe, and condensed milk. We had no rockets and no means of making a smoke screen.

"It was extremely cold at night, and some of us had only our underclothes. We had four blankets, but they were soon soaked. Waves broke over the boat, and two of the boys were bailing constantly.

"Our plight was becoming desperate, water was running low, and we could only touch it with our lips.

"On the fifth day we sighted a British ship which was standing by. I tried to light a flare of crude oil, but it was no use. Matches were running short. At seven on the morning of the sixth day we were picked up by the Norwegian motor-vessel 'Spinanger.'"

In the top photograph is the "Arlington Court" belonging to the Court Lines, whose ship the "Kensington Court" was also torpedoed on September 18. Immediately above are five members of the "Arlington Court's" crew sitting round the fire in a seaman's mission hall after the terrible experience of being six days in an open boat, narrated in this page.
Photos, B.I.P. and courtesy of Court Lines

'U-Boat Men Not All Heartless Murderers'

Seven survivors of the trawler "Cresswell" landed at Fleetwood on November 14, and told how they were picked up by the German submarine. This story is reprinted from the Glasgow "Bulletin."

WHEN the "Cresswell" was shelled by a German submarine off the north of Scotland, the crew of thirteen escaped from the sinking trawler, ten on a raft, two clinging to the smashed lifeboat, and one with a lifebelt. The two on the lifeboat and the man with the lifebelt were

drowned, and, despite the efforts of their comrades to keep them above water, three of the men on the raft became exhausted by the buffeting of the waves and let go their hold. On arriving at Fleetwood the survivors told the following dramatic story of their adventures.

I WAS THERE!

Here a German submarine, U39, is seen submerging, and her bow is already awash. It is thus that many crews have seen the last of their enemy as, after destroying the ship, she disappears for fear that Allied destroyers may be responding to the ship's S O S.

Photo, Kosmos

The 17-year-old deck boy, Frederick Lee, youngest member of the crew, said : " There was no warning before the submarine began shelling the trawler. We did not know a submarine was near until shells began whizzing all round us. We had not time to launch the boat, but, in any case, it would have made no difference because it was smashed by gunfire.

" The submarine sent at least 20 shots at the trawler."

Another member of the crew stated that it was just getting daylight when they heard the gunfire. There was only the watch on, and it was every man for himself.

William Faussett, the mate, said he saw Boatswain Andrews jump overboard with a lifebelt.

" Ten of us threw the raft into the water and clung to it. We were all crushed together, the water was icy cold, and rain pelted down on us unmercifully.

" After the firing the submarine disappeared, and we thought she had left us for good.

" The raft was tossed about, and it needed a great effort to hold on. At times it submerged, and this made our plight worse."

Faussett then went on to tell how Gateley was the first to go under.

" The men did their best in turns to help me to keep his head above the surface. Our legs were numbed with cold and our arms ached, and it was from sheer exhaustion that we had to let go. He disappeared below. He was all in."

The next, he said, was Lazenby. He had withstood a terrible buffeting. After that they never saw Laerte again. In the distance they could see Killey and Kirby clinging to an upturned boat.

" I never saw them go down, but at the end of an hour we could not find them," he added.

They had been in the water for nearly two and a half hours when the U-boat reappeared. She hailed the men clinging to the raft, and then they were hauled aboard.

" After that the U-boat crew did every-thing to make us comfortable. They gave us clothing, hot food, brandy, and other drinks," said the mate.

They then learned that the submarine had left them to find a neutral ship which could take them aboard.

Faussett said they were in the submarine for more than six hours cruising about until they sighted the Fleetwood trawler " Phyllisia."

While on the submarine they saw the " Cresswell " sink after being shelled again by the submarine.

They were put aboard the " Phyllisia " and taken home.

The U-boat commander's parting words to Mr. George Bull, the skipper of the " Cresswell," were : " Tell Mr. Churchill that the German U-boat men are not the heartless murderers you are led to believe."

Some of the officers and crew of U36 are seen on the conning tower when the submarine is at rest on the surface. She is flying the Nazi war flag. U39 (seen at the top of the page) is one of the newest and largest class of German submarines, being of 750 tons. The U36 is an older vessel of 500 tons, completed in 1936.

Photo, Pictorial Press

Mr. Briton'll See It Through

A detachment of steel-helmeted soldiers in the West End of London take a surprised glance at a horse-drawn vehicle that has now come into its own again. Such four-wheeler cabs almost disappeared when taxi-cabs came into use.

The white walls of England have been put to a new use at Ramsgate, which suffered severely from air raids during the last war, for a large shelter has been dug in the cliffs 90 feet below the ground. Here is its entrance.

One of the devices for overcoming the rationing of petrol is the substitution for short journeys of an electric motor for the internal-combustion engine.

The basis of most of portable camouflage is string netting, and above girls in a North Shields factory usually employed in making fishing nets are busy on this most useful adjunct to the safety of the Army. One of the uses to which similar netting is put in France can be seen in the photograph in page 259. Right, a fishmonger at Bicester combines the win-the-war spirit with the sale of herrings.

OUR DIARY OF THE WAR

Friday, November 24, 1939

Over 200 drifting mines washed up on Yorkshire coast.

Enemy aircraft made two raids over **Shetlands.** No bombs were dropped.

Admiralty announced that the cruiser "Belfast" was damaged on November 21 by torpedo or mine in Firth of Forth.

British steamer "Mangalore" sunk by mine off East Coast.

Five survivors of Dutch tanker "Sliedrecht," sunk by U-boat in Atlantic, picked up after 7½ days in open boat.

Paris announced that a small French submarine chaser had sunk a U-boat.

Belgian Government addressed a Note to Britain on subject of British reprisals against mine-laying.

Stated that two British subjects, Mr. Best and Major Stevens, kidnapped at Dutch frontier on November 21 by Gestapo for alleged complicity in Munich bomb explosion, are believed to have been authorized by British Government to inquire into genuineness of certain German peace proposals.

German liner "Watussi," thought to be a supply ship for the raider in East African waters, left Mozambique on Thursday night.

First R.A.F. man to be decorated by France for gallantry in this war died in hospital : Sergeant-Observer J. Vickers, awarded the Médaille Militaire.

Saturday, November 25

Italy, Japan, Denmark and Sweden made representations to British Foreign Office with regard to policy of reprisals.

Two bombing attacks by German aircraft made **on H.M. ships in North Sea.** No hits were obtained and there were no British casualties.

Enemy aircraft seen over Orkneys and Shetlands.

R.A.F. carried out successful flights over North-West Germany, including Wilhelmshaven and Heligoland.

British refrigerator ship "Sussex," damaged by mine in English Channel, reached port.

German liner "Adolph Woermann" scuttled by crew in South Atlantic in order to avoid capture.

Swedish tanker "Gustaf E. Reuter" struck a mine off Scottish coast and was badly damaged.

Nazi mine-layer sank after striking a mine near Danish island of Langeland.

New Rumanian Cabinet, with smaller pro-German element, formed by M. Tatarescu.

Sunday, November 26

Reported that Germans have laid mines within Swedish four-mile zone at southern entrance of the Sound, leaving a channel only 16 feet deep.

Admiralty announced that **British armed merchant cruiser "Rawalpindi"** had been **sunk.**

Polish liner "Pilsudski," under charter to British Navy, **sunk by U-boat.**

Reported that British steamer "Hookwood" was sunk by mine on Thursday.

Paris reported patrol activities during night in region of the Vosges.

Prime Minister broadcast an address on Britain's war and peace aims.

Soviet Government alleged that Finnish artillery fired on Red Army troops on Soviet-Finnish frontier, and demanded that troops should be withdrawn from frontier district on the Karelian Isthmus.

Danish steamer "Cyril," carrying coal from Britain to Stockholm, seized by Germans. This was thought to be the first capture by Nazis of a neutral ship sailing from Britain to a neutral port

Monday, November 27

Admiralty announced that the sinking of the "Rawalpindi" on November 23 off coast of Iceland was due to overwhelming attack by the "Deutschland" and another enemy warship.

Two enemy merchantmen, "Borkum" and "Konsul Hendrik Fisser," **captured.** The latter was brought into port ; the former was sighted and shelled by a U-boat, killing four Germans but none of the prize crew. The ship was abandoned.

Dutch liner "Spaarndam" mined off Thames Estuary.

Paris reported local infantry and artillery engagement east of the Moselle.

Finnish Government issued denial that shots had been fired from Finnish side of frontier, but suggested to Soviet mutual withdrawal of troops.

Reprisal Order-in-Council signed by the King.

Overwhelming response to Admiralty's appeal for drifters to assist in mine-sweeping.

Two corporations formed in United States to enable Americans to contribute towards war relief in Great Britain and France.

Tuesday, November 28

Announced that British and French reprisals on German export trade come into force on December 4.

R.A.F. fighter patrol **attacked five seaplanes** lying at mine-laying seaplane base at Borkum, one of the Friesian Islands. Attack was made at a low altitude with machine-guns. All British aircraft returned safely.

Air Ministry announced that R.A.F. machines carried out a successful flight over North-West Germany during Monday night.

Soviet Government denounced their **Treaty of Non-Aggression with Finland,** and alleged two more "incidents" on the Karelian Isthmus, Soviet-Finnish frontier.

Quiet day reported on the Western Front.

British steamer "Rubislaw" sunk by a mine off South-East Coast.

British steamer "Uskmouth" sunk by U-boat in Bay of Biscay.

Paris announced that two German freighters, "Trifels" and "Santa Fé," had been captured by French warships.

Eleven survivors of the "Rawalpindi" landed from merchant cruiser "Chitral."

The King opened a new Session of Parliament.

Three R.A.F. pilots were awarded the Distinguished Flying Cross.

Cargo of "City of Flint" has been bought by Norway.

Wednesday, Nov. 29

Unidentified aeroplane seen over the Shetlands.

Enemy bomber shot down by a British fighter in an air duel off the Northumbrian coast.

Two British patrol aircraft shot down Dornier seaplane over North Sea.

Russia severed diplomatic relations with Finland before receiving the Finnish reply to the Soviet Note of Tuesday.

Mr. Cordell Hull, U.S. Secretary of State, announced his Government's willingness to intervene in the dispute between Russia and Finland.

Paris reported two successful reconnaissances by French troops into territory held by the Germans in the Vosges.

British steamer "Ionian" sunk off East Coast.

Government of Eire decided to put into commission some motor torpedo boats and armed trawlers.

During week ending November 25, British Contraband Control intercepted and detained 21,500 tons of contraband goods suspected of being destined for Germany.

Thursday, November 30

Two R.A.F. fighters encountered an enemy aircraft north of Firth of Forth and chased it out to sea.

Soviet Union attacked Finland by land, sea, and air. Helsinki, Viborg, Petsamo and other towns were bombed. Soviet warships shelled Finnish coast and strategic islands were seized.

Finnish Government resigned at midnight.

Paris reported that a French torpedo boat had sunk an enemy submarine.

British steamer "Sheaf Crest" mined off South-East Coast.

Six survivors of a Greek steamer sunk west of Ireland were picked up after four days in their lifeboat.

Reported that two British destroyers, one towing a damaged submarine, had anchored off Mastrafjord, near Stavanger. The destroyers left later, and the submarine was taken to a shipyard for repair.

Admiralty announced the names of 39 officers and 226 ratings missing as result of loss of H.M.S. "Rawalpindi."

THE POETS & THE WAR

—X—

SHADOWS ON THE LAKE

By George Shelley

For long the lake had lain within those bounds,
  Unruffled and serene with quiet grace,
Unmoved, whatever challenged her command
  Or sought by means of force to shake her place.
There men had come, their hearts aflame with hope,
  With wills that seemed to brook no alien mind,
To work, and work the ways of certain peace
  That would the path to certain glory find.

"No war," they said. "The nations shall not fight
  And tear each other piecemeal yet again,
No war, and ours the watch, that they who died
  Shall not cry out that they had died in vain."
No war, the echoes rang with hollow sound—
  No war, but while those haunts were strangely still,
Across the peaceful beauty of the lake
  Moved once again that darkening cloud of ill.

With sullen force the storm from slumber rose
  Destroying all within its awful reach,
And breaking will with vain insensate rage
  Till hate and passion found the widening breach
What means Geneva now, her life and peace ?
  For death usurps her place and by his side
Is war, red war, and men who seek to slay
  The hopes for which far nobler men have died

Is there no power to break this chain of crime
  Will not the golden dawn of peace awake
When gentle reason takes the place of hate
  And shadows cloud no more Geneva's lake ?

Copyright

Vol. 1   A Permanent Picture Record of the Second Great War   No. 15

Though communiqués of the French Army have generally been brief and have referred chiefly to artillery activity, French infantry have been in frequent contact with the enemy in small actions, as this photograph shows.   A farmhouse in the area between the Maginot and Siegfried Lines has been under artillery fire, and is so badly damaged that only parts of the walls are left standing. In the vantage point thus created French infantry are cautiously creeping forward.

Photo, " The Times "

Over the Top and Down Below with the Nazis

In the last war the Germans were the first of the fighting armies to use very deep shelters, and again they appreciate the importance of shell-and bomb-proof positions deep under ground. Below is a mess-room 200 feet below ground in solid rock. That they are not ill-provided with liquor is proved by the array of bottles on the table.

Photo, Keystone

When the French moved back from their advance posts in the Saar they kept up a heavy bombardment of the area they had evacuated. Above, German infantry are running through a village under fire.

I N Germany the might of the Army is regarded as being, potentially, as decisive a factor in the war as we hold the British Navy to be. Raised by compulsory service (on a two-year basis), it was estimated that by the end of November 1939 its mobilized strength stood at about 150 divisions—say about 2,000,000 men. The infantry is still the backbone of the Nazi Army, though the artillery, the tanks and the armoured cars (used so extensively in Poland) are of highly-boasted excellence.

Germany's Army is well equipped with big guns, and, like the Allies, she is using such big naval guns as those that proved effective against concrete defences in the last war. Here a big gun on a railway mounting is in position on a single line of railway. Behind both the Allied and enemy lines there are many miles of single-track railway which sometimes carry supplies and sometimes guns.

Photo, E.N.A.

Three Months of War and Now Comes Winter

With the end of November the war completed its first three months, and the time
seems opportune for an investigation into the position and outlook as they may appear
to those responsible for the policy of the belligerents and of the European neutrals.

THREE months have passed since that first day of September when the world learnt with horror and alarm that Nazi 'planes had bombed Warsaw. Those three months have been rich in the material of history. There have been great changes in the map. There have been moves that were expected, and moves, far more, that were unexpected. To the man in the street in all countries this war is, indeed, as the Prime Minister has described it, "the strangest of all wars." But how does or how may it appear when looked at from the eyrie of Berchtesgaden, the inner sanctum in the Kremlin, and the Cabinet room at No. 10 Downing Street?

Let us look over the shoulder of Herr Hitler as he studies the map of Central Europe. If he is in one of his magniloquent moods he may well feel fortified in the belief that he is the greatest of all Germans when he puts his finger on this country and that which since his advent to power have been included in the bounds of Greater Germany. Austria, Czecho-Slovakia, Memel-land, and now more than half Poland. What a galaxy of conquests! Never was Germany so great as now. Never were there so many millions within the Nazi Reich.

Yet perhaps he sees another picture in his hours of solitary reflection. He sees those millions of Poles added to his already large minorities of dissidents; he thinks of the coming winter when even Poles and Jews must be fed in a countryside which has been blackened and ravaged by his *blitzkrieg*. He tries to cheer himself with the thought that his pact with Russia has removed the spectre of starvation; and then he recalls the other side of the bargain—that long common frontier with the country whose ideology and whose leaders he has for years until but the other day denounced with all the fury of his richly-stored vocabulary.

Russia's Westward Drive

As he bends again over the map, the Fuehrer's finger moves northward to those Baltic States which again since September have become satellites of the Soviet power, and, still moving forward, it arrives at last at the Gulf of Finland, now on both sides grasped by the Russian bear, and ruefully indeed he must reflect that the Baltic is no longer a German lake. . .

Nor does he find much consolation if he lifts his eyes to that corner of the map where the British Isles lie separated from the mainland by seas which his bombers find it difficult to cross, and his submarines and even his mines of latest pattern cannot deny to the ships of the Allies.

We may leave Hitler to his thoughts. Let us now interview the dictator of Russia as he sits at his bureau in the Kremlin. From Russia's point of view the war, it would seem, is going excellently. White Russia and the Western Ukraine, those provinces of the Tsardom which were lost after the Revolution, have been won back with the loss of but a few hundred men, and the process of Sovietization is proceeding without a hitch. Estonia, Latvia, and Lithuania, also lost in the Tsarist débâcle, have been converted into satellite states. Finland, which dared to resist the most reasonable demands, is now being brought to heel. There remains Bessarabia; Bessarabia has not been forgotten. Then Russia will indeed be safe from foreign attack. . . .

Time Favours the Allies

Very different is the outlook from the windows of Downing Street and the Quai d'Orsay. The Maginot Line has done all and more than all that it was expected to do. Up to date such fighting as there has been on the Western Front has been done on German soil. Not an inch of French ground has been taken by the enemy. Losses in man-power have been inconsiderable. In the air the superiority of the Allies is plain for all to see. The entente between Britain and France is more cordial even than during the last war, and already nearly 200,000 British troops, splendidly equipped with all the latest weapons of war, have arrived in France, and many of these are already in the firing line. Every month, every week, every day that passes sees further increase of the Allies' strength.

At home in Britain the country mourns the losses of many a gallant ship and of a host of brave men, but still the British Navy is mistress of the seas. In three months German shipping, with the exception of submarines and a few raiders, has been driven into harbour, while the mercantile marine of Britain sails in every ocean. The submarines have been tackled in so effective a way that they no longer constitute a really dangerous menace. The mine will be mastered in the same way as the submarine. Air attacks have been numerous, but the results have been negligible. Despite

During the first three months the war was fought in autumn weather, but with the coming of winter the situation was transformed. Rains and floods, heavy snowfalls, frozen surfaces of land and water—all have their reactions in the military sphere. In some cases they favour the defence, in others they may facilitate offensive operations. Here in this map the possible influence of the weather is pictorially displayed.   "*News Review*"

Out In No-Man's Land a Mine Goes Up

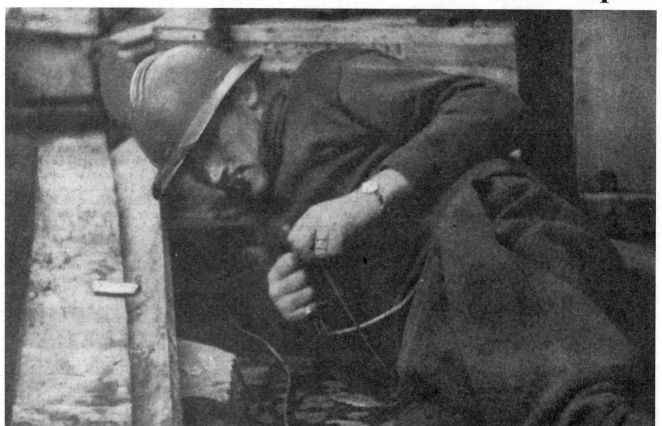

One of the minor incidents in the outposts between the Maginot and Siegfried Lines is shown in the photographs in this page and that opposite. It has been notified from headquarters that a certain road is to be blown up to obstruct an enemy advance. In the top photograph a French soldier is connecting up the mine which will do the work with the igniter. The photograph immediately above, taken a few minutes later, shows the mine exploding and the road cut.

French Official photographs

So on This Road Too 'They Shall Not Pass'

Continuing the story from the opposite page, directly after the explosion a wave of French infantry goes forward to consolidate the position and hold the broken road (top). A few hours later a new forward position has been established, as seen in the lower photograph. A barrier of timber and bricks, proof against rifle fire, has been erected, and from behind it French infantrymen can direct a deadly fire against the advancing enemy and make them pay heavily for any attempted advance.

French Official photographs

France is Always on the Qui Vive

This anti-aircraft gun, set amidst the sand dunes on the French side of the Channel, has painted camouflage that makes it tone with the sand and tufts of marram grass.
Photo, Associated Press

stalemate on the Western Front have been ended ? Will Hitler have sent hundreds of thousands to their death in a mass assault on the Maginot Line ? Will Holland and Belgium be no longer neutral as a result of a Nazi invasion intended to turn the flank of the Allies' defence ? Will Mussolini still content himself with words ? Will Rumania still guard her oil ? Will the groans of the tortured Czechs and the starving Poles still rise to heaven ? Will Russia have met no check in her career of imperialist aggression ? Will Britain's breakfast-tables still be well spread, and her towns still unpitted by the craters of Nazi bombs ? These are some of the questions posed at the coming of winter, which may be answered with the flowers of spring.

all the Nazi boasts Britain is still assured of her principal means of life.

Coming now to the neutrals, we find on every hand apprehension, nervousness, and deep concern. Norway, Sweden, and Denmark watch with horror the unprovoked assault on their fellow Scandinavian State, and they find it difficult to fit themselves into a world in which their best customers are at war. The Low Countries and Switzerland hope for the best and prepare for the worst. Spain and Italy are alike in regarding with rising disgust the growth of the Soviet power. In the Balkans, from Hungary to the Bosporus, there is not a country which does not fear for her own security.

Such, then, is the state of Europe after three months of war. Now winter is knocking at the door, and before its fogs and rains and snows have cleared away what further changes will have been wrought in the European scene ? Will what some commentators have called the

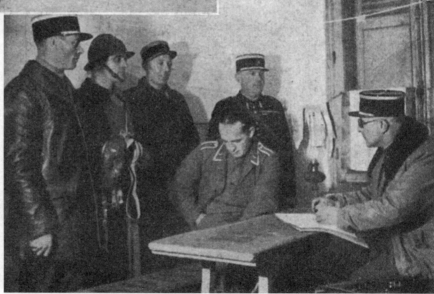

Prisoners often unwittingly give away much valuable information. In the upper photograph are two young German prisoners, one of them hiding his face from the photographer with his hand. Immediately above, a German prisoner is undergoing what the other two will soon have to experience—a close examination from a German-speaking French officer.
Photos, Associated Press and Wide World

Finland Fights On in Snow and Ice

Yet another little country of Europe was savagely attacked by a neighbour vastly superior in size and resources. But Finland refused to be intimidated, and put up a most gallant resistance to the Soviet onslaught.

THE twenty-second anniversary of Finland's Declaration of Independence found the little country engaged in a struggle for life with her great neighbour on the east. A few days before, the Red Army had crossed the frontier at several places, Soviet 'planes had rained down incendiary bombs on Helsinki and other towns in south Finland, and ships of the Red Navy had bombarded Hanko and seized some of the islands in the Gulf.

Although to the outside world the conflict took on the aspect of a struggle between Lilliput and Brobdingnag, the Finns put up a stout resistance. Despite their overwhelming superiority in men and mechanized armament, the invaders made but slow progress in the Karelian Isthmus in front of Leningrad, and their shock troops and artillery came to grief when trying to advance over the frozen marshes north of Lake Ladoga, many being drowned as the ice broke beneath their weight. In the far north the Russians were able to claim that they had succeeded in occupying the Ribachi peninsula, but their attack on Petsamo developed into a ding-dong battle in which first one side and then the other claimed the victory. Yet a third advance was made in the direction of Kuolajaervi in the "waist" of Finland, with a view to severing her land connexion with Sweden. Here again the attackers made little progress, for not only was there a most vigorous defence,

but the heavy falls of snow hampered the movements of the invaders who may well have been unaccustomed to movement in such an Arctic scene. The Finnish troops, specially trained for snow fighting, moved swiftly here and there on their skis, and sorely harassed the Russian soldiers, who were blinded by the driving snow and, moreover, walked in ever-present dread of the mines which they had good reason to believe were hidden in every snowdrift.

War correspondents of the Moscow newspapers complained bitterly of the fact that the Finns had laid land-mines everywhere, that they shot from behind trees and even from among the snowdrifts, that they fought in small mobile

M. Vaino Tanner (above) held the portfolio of Foreign Minister in the newly formed Government of Finland.
Photo, Keystone

groups instead of coming out into the open and attacking in large formations such as were employed by the Red Army. "Pravda's" correspondent said that "the Finns hide in heaps of pine branches and in snowdrifts. They are as wicked as wolves, hungry and in rags, and shoot from behind . . . Our Red soldiers shout 'You filthy snakes' as they bring them toppling down out of trees."

Another correspondent reported with undisguised wrath that the Finns had attached mines to things which could not but tempt the Muscovites—alarm clocks, for instance! "Izvestia's" correspondent denounced the Finns for using poisoned sweets, cigarettes, and water attached to booby traps; "these mad dogs," he averred, "must be destroyed."

Bad weather was supposed to have been responsible for Helsinki's immunity from air raids beyond those carried out in the first few days of war. But in the far north the skies cleared sufficiently for the Finns to be able to launch a surprise air

The Finnish Army is fairly well provided with tanks, and above two soldiers are camouflaging one with branches of trees before the invasion. Above right, two Finnish soldiers are using their skis to prevent their machine-gun sinking into the snow.
Photos, New Age and Wide World

Finns and Russians Plod to Battle Across the Snows

Winter weather, accompanied by heavy snow, has added to the difficulties of the war between Russia and Finland, and in both armies soldiers on skis have come into action. The Finnish ski-riflemen are all picked marksmen, and with the speed in manoeuvre that the skis give them they can seriously harry much larger numbers of the enemy. Those on skis seen on the left above are wearing white cloaks as camouflage against a background of snow. Russia also has a few soldiers equipped with skis, and on the right some of them are on the march.

Photos, Associated Press and Planet News

attack on the Soviet air base at Murmansk. The Finnish airmen, returning in triumph, claimed that they had destroyed as many as sixty Russian machines by means of small incendiary bombs. Red warplanes were reported to have bombed Salmijaervi, the nickel mining centre, but one of the Russian bombing squadrons was stated to have met disaster in a snowstorm in the Lake Ladoga region.

So dogged a resistance seems to have been entirely unexpected by the Soviet chiefs. Unfortunately for the success of their plans they had not profited by Hitler's example in preparing the way for their aggression by fostering sedition in the ranks of their proposed victim. The Finnish people as a whole rallied behind the new Government of M. Ryti, and displayed nothing but contempt for the puppet government established by the Soviet invaders at Terijoki. As the Finnish wireless declared, "this so-called government exercises its powers in a vacuum—in a completely depopulated area."

A woman's body taken from a Russian aircraft that bombed Helsinki, showed that Russian women took part in this dastardly work. These three women of the Russian Air Force flew from Moscow to the Far East in record time in 1938. Left to right, Captain Polena Osipenko, Soviet Deputy, Valentina Grizodubova, and Senior Lieut. Marina Raskova.
Photo, Planet News

On November 30 President Kallio proclaimed Finland to be in a state of war, and at a Council meeting Field-Marshal Baron Carl Mannerheim was appointed Commander-in-Chief of all the Finnish Forces. He is here seen (left) at a review with two of his staff. Left to right are Géneral Ostermann, Commander-in-Chief the Army, General Ohqvist, and Marshal Mannerheim.
Photo, Associated Press

Here is a stretch of barren shore line near Petsamo, the Finnish Port which was bombed by seven Soviet aircraft. The main road which connects it with the town of Enare was also bombed and an omnibus machine-gunned. Petsamo is in the extreme north, and is Finland's only outlet to the Arctic Ocean.
Photo, Derek Wordley

The Russian newspapers printed many sneers at little Finland, pointing out how small was the Finnish army, how deficient in 'planes, heavy artillery, and tanks—in other words, how easy it must prove to exterminate her. Time after time they asserted that the Red Army was invading Finland solely as a liberator—to free the "real working people" of Finland from the "bankrupt politicians of the Finnish bourgeoisie."

Compared with such nauseous rodomontade, M. Ryti's broadcast to the United States was refreshing indeed. "The strength of Finland," he declared, "lies in the unity of the Finnish people." In defending her own liberty Finland believed that she was defending the liberty of every nation. "Our only hope," he said, "is that it will not prove too great for the powers of a small nation. But whatever our fate may be, I am deeply convinced that through our fight and our sufferings we are helping to further the creation of a better world."

Germany the Real Betrayer of Finland

Written by an anti-Nazi German, this article provides some of the background necessary for the understanding of the Russian attack upon Finland. Not long ago a protégée of Germany, Finland, since the Moscow Pact, has been left to the mercy of the Soviet.

EARLY in the last Great War the German newspapers were full of pictures of fair, tall, " Nordic " lads of the 27th Battalion of Riflemen training in the Lockstedt Camp near Hamburg. They were Finnish students and Boy Scouts, young and ardent patriots whose one desire was to rid their country of the Russian yoke to which it had been subjected, with interruptions, for more than 200 years. After the Russian revolution of November 1917 this band went home to fight for an independent Finland, joining the " White Guards " formed by Baron Mannerheim. After severe fighting in Viborg and elsewhere, the Finns finally mastered the Reds.

Mannerheim—a Finn by birth, a Swede by descent and a Russian cavalry general by profession—could not have won that fight, even with the help of these German-trained and equipped soldiers, had not Germany herself taken a hand in that struggle. Not from any altruistic motive —the Kaiser wanted his relatives to rule the Baltic States ; indeed, his brother-in-law, Prince Frederick Charles of Hesse, was actually " elected " King of Finland a month before the Armistice. So a German division under General Count von der Goltz, a nephew of the famous Marshal of that name, set out in February 1918 and, with a small fleet and 12 troop-carriers, broke through the ice of the Baltic and the Gulf of Finland to land the army which subsequently took the mainland, including Helsinki, the capital of Finland, from the Russians. Hangoe, the naval port at the entrance of the Gulf, went up in flames. (Incidentally, it was Von der Goltz's fighters who, on their return became the backbone of the German Free Corps and later of the Nazi Party.)

Since then Finland has been extremely popular in Germany. Her decorations have been proudly worn by many German officers, and many Finnish soldiers boasted the Iron Cross.

German 'Double-Dealing'

How these men must have blushed when they learned of the German-Russian treaty engineered by Ribbentrop, and witnessed the abandonment of Finland to her Russian oppressors without so much as a word of regret appearing in the Goebbels press ! Whether they saw this German betrayal of her " adopted child " in the North as a sign of pitiful weakness, or as the price of a disgraceful bargain, they could not but feel ashamed of the Nazi successors of General Ludendorff, who had launched upon Russia and the world Lenin and Trotsky, the Communist fanatics. With the same treachery as the Nazis now show, Ludendorff, only a few weeks after he had dispatched the Bolshevik revolutionists in a sealed car through Germany, had ordered the German fleet and army to fight them in Finland. He then posed as the liberator of a small nation, which his successors have now flung to the wolves.

This is the outcome of the Russian dilemma : having called in the Russian bear in her own defence, Germany now sees it swallow up all her strategic outposts on the Baltic seaboard, and finally her own " protégée," the Republic of Finland. And Ribbentrop's blunder in signing the Nazi-Soviet pact is reacting against him at home. The German army —and not only the army but the Brownshirts and Blackshirts as well, and with them the mass of the civilian population —have always been and still are genuinely anti-Bolshevist. They can see that this new crusade of the hammer and sickle will also prevent the formation of a defensive " bloc " in the Balkans and thus interfere with Nazi Germany's " Drang nach Osten " policy ; they see it for what it is—a direct menace to the very existence of Germany.

Ideologies at a Discount

Russia's invasion of Finland with the tacit consent of Germany has finally disposed of any ideological differences between the two dictatorships. Not much is now left of Hitler's ideals—state-directed capitalism, leadership of the élite, " protection of the priest at the altar," and a racially pure nation. Nor have Communist ideals stood any firmer. Where are the Bolshevist's disdain for Tsarist ambitions and " Imperialist " wars, where are " collective security " and " peace indivisible " ? The Russian method is identical with that used by the Nazis in the rape of Austria and Czecho-Slovakia—the campaign of slander, the fabricated incident, the open menaces, and the final onslaught on an inoffensive and weak neighbour. Hitler's propaganda had to resort to the clumsy and transparent lie that Britain has fostered anti-Russian " aggression " among the 3¾ million people of Finland, but that will not distract the mind of the German people from the fact that, one day, 90 million Germans will find it hard to resist 183 million Russians. Whatever the Nazi propagandists may say, the present Nazi-Soviet arrangement is only a repetition of what frequently enough happened in American cities in pre-G-men days : two gangsters have temporarily joined hands to plunder the wealthier citizens, on the understanding that they will " shoot it out " between them later. When it comes to a " show-down " the bigger gang wins.

This photograph illustrates not only an interesting incident in Finland's recent history, but also the complete volte face which Germany has made under the Nazi regime in her relations with Russia. General von der Goltz is seen on a visit to Baron Carl Mannerheim at his headquarters in 1918 when, with German help, he was resisting the Bolsheviks.

Photo. E.N.A.

Red Russia : Weak at Sea, Strong in the Air

Though Russia is weak in ships some unusual attempts to make its personnel efficient have been made. Left, Russian sailors in full uniform are swimming in military formation in the Khimi Reservoir, Moscow. Right is the Kirov, one of Russia's 8,000-ton cruisers. She is believed to have been badly damaged by the Finns.
Photos, Planet News

Described as modern heavy bombers, these 'planes of the Red Air Fleet are certainly larger than any standard bomber in the British Air Force, but they can equally certainly not be described as modern. Although later aircraft are now in use, these four-engined TB3 or ANT6 machines are believed still to form the bulk of the Soviet offensive air force. The type was designed by A. N. Toupolev, Russia's most eminent aeronautical engineer, and was one of the first home-designed machines to supplement and replace foreign products.
Photo, E.N.A.

Red Tsar of the Kremlin

What sort of man is he who, since the war began, has seized half Poland, dominated the Baltic States, and now invaded Finland? Here are the main facts of Stalin's career, and a brief inquiry into his dominating motive.

Smiling amiably, the Red Tsar of the Kremlin is seated side by side with Marshal Klement Voroshilov, who since 1925 has been the Soviet Commissar for War. When Stalin considered that the time had come to teach the Finns a lesson, it was Voroshilov who was entrusted with the campaign.
Photo, E.N.A.

TWENTY-ONE years have passed since the last of the Tsars fell riddled with bullets in the ghastly shambles in the cellar at Ekaterinburg. But today a new tsar walks the corridors of the Kremlin, and from his bureau wields autocratic sway over nearly two hundred millions, inhabitants of a vast realm stretching from the Baltic to the Sea of Japan, from the tundras of Arctic Siberia to the borders of Afghanistan.

When Stalin was born in the little Georgian town of Gori, near the Black Sea, Alexander II held sway as Tsar of All the Russias. Josef Vissarionovich Djugashvilli—he was not called Stalin until years later—was the son of a poor shoemaker, and as a youth of fifteen he entered the Orthodox theological seminary in Tiflis. Very soon, however, he found that the books of Darwin, Marx and Engels were far more to his taste than theological manuals, and he was expelled for his revolutionary sympathies. Abandoning all idea of entering the priesthood he joined a group of Social Democrats, keeping himself the while as a book-keeper, and wrote for a number of working-class papers under several pseudonyms, including that of Stalin—" man of steel "—by which he is now universally known.

When nineteen he became known to the authorities as the organizer of a strike of Tiflis railway-workers, and not long afterwards he was sentenced to the first of many periods of imprisonment and exile. His last spell in Siberia was ended by the revolution of February 1917. From a tiny village within the Arctic Circle he hurried back to Europe and became one of Lenin's colleagues.

During the civil war between the Reds and Whites in 1919 and 1920, and in the war against Poland, he played quite a distinguished part, and became editor of " Pravda." In 1922 he was appointed General Secretary of the Central Committee of the Communist Party, and after Lenin's death in 1924

became the dominant personality in the Soviet State. It was Stalin who captained the Five Years' Plans, which from 1928 worked a complete transformation of the Russian industrial and agricultural scene. Although his position is still nominally that of Secretary, Stalin is today, as he has been for many years, virtual Tsar of Russia.

For the ten years required for the working out of the First and Second Five Years' Plans, Stalin seemed to be fully occupied with the internal development of the Soviet realm. In Europe it was confidently asserted that Bolshevik Russia had " gone Asiatic," as indeed might be expected from the fact that Stalin himself was of Asiatic origin.

Stalin's Westward Drive

From time to time, however, pronouncements from the Kremlin showed that the inner circles of the Bolshevik party were not altogether blind to what was happening in the outside world, and in the summer of 1939 Russian policy took an altogether new turn. Turning his eyes from the Far East and from the home front, Stalin looked across his western frontier to that Central Europe whose state system was collapsing under the strain of Nazi aggression.

During that last pre-war summer Stalin was wooed assiduously by France and Britain, who were anxious to include the U.S.S.R. in their Peace Front of nations pledged to resist further Nazi demands. Ultimately, however, it was Germany that made the deal. On August 23 Germany and Soviet Russia signed the Pact of Non-Aggression in the Kremlin.

Von Ribbentrop as he appended his signature to the document may well have thought that Britain and France would now be intimidated from going to Poland's assistance; Stalin's motives are more a matter of

conjecture. Some would have it that he was attracted by the prospect of easy loot. It seems that Germany and Russia agreed on a partition of Poland between them, and Russia's entry into the war on September 17 was according to the pre-arranged plan. Certainly as a result of that " stab in the back " Russia was enabled to occupy nearly half Poland without having to fight anything more than a few skirmishes. Nor was this all. As made clear in other pages of this work, Stalin, in a few days in October, converted the Baltic States into vassals, and at the end of November invaded Finland to enforce his demands.

Restoring the Tsar's Empire

Thus in December 1939 Russia, under Stalin's leadership, had regained in large measure the territory lost in the period 1917–1920; only Finland and Bessarabia remained to be re-won.

If Stalin be, then, the Bolshevik Imperialist that some would assert, then he may claim to have repeated the triumphs of even the greatest of the Romanoffs. There are others, however, who believe that he is inspired by no mere imperialist urge, by no desire to regain the empire of the Tsars, but that he continues to be what he has been from the days of his early youth—a sincere Bolshevik. If this be the case, then his support of Germany in her war against Britain and France may be due to a belief that the war of 1939 will leave the western nations as ripe for the Bolshevik virus as was Russia in 1917.

Imperialist or Red Revolutionary? Only history can supply the answer.

PEACE BY PIECE
Cartoon by Zec, by courtesy of the " Daily Mirror "

No Indiscriminate Air-Raids On Civilians—Yet

Here Major-General C. H. Foulkes, C.B., C.M.G., D.S.O., gives his reasons for believing that Nazi air attacks on our great cities are not an immediate danger. In the Great War Major-General Foulkes was Gas Advisor to the C.-in-C. An amplification of his present subject will be found in his book " Common Sense and A.R.P."

AFTER three months of war our A.R.P. services have not yet been called upon to perform the duties for which they have been trained. So far only half-hearted air attacks have been made on our shipping and on our fleet, but soon Hitler must risk something more.

In the first place, an attack on the Western Front may be forced on him ; in this case he may not be able to afford the use of bombers with which to carry out major raids against this country, because the German war technique, based on the success of the method in Poland, appears to be to mass mechanized forces in the attack of a defensive position, to push them forward regardless of loss, and to support them with the whole strength of his air force.

Or he might shrink from the losses which such an attack would involve and concentrate on the use of his air force against this country in particular ; in such an event he would probably confine his attacks to military and naval objectives, as he would refrain from raiding our cities because of the inevitable retaliation on his own. He can ill afford to add to the hardship and suffering— and, possibly, the political unrest—which already exist in Germany.

It is probable, therefore, that there will be no indiscriminate air raids on the civil populations of this country, such as we have been led to expect—at any rate for the present. The common sense of the situation is that air raids on a civil population which solidly supports its own Government are not worth while.

We have already had some experience of them in the last war, and the results were then insignificant. Only 1,414 people were killed and 3,416 wounded during a period of nearly four years, while 8,500 bombs big and small were dropped—that is, 2 bombs were necessary for each casualty. In 1938 alone, 881 persons were killed in this country by falling downstairs ; 1,352 by falling down somewhere in their houses : and 87 simply by falling out of bed ! And the total material damage caused amounted to less than three millions sterling.

This was a paltry result in comparison with the effort expended and the losses sustained by the raiders, especially as at first anti-aircraft guns were mounted only in St. James's Park, London.

Costly Daylight Raids of 1918

As our defensive organization developed aeroplanes were largely used instead of Zeppelins, and daylight raids, which are necessary in wartime for navigation and for accurate bombing, gave place to raids by moonlight ; even these proved so costly that during the last six months of the war no raids took place over London.

The indirect effects of these raids were, of course, far from negligible, as not only was the output of munitions restricted, but a substantial part of our available air and anti-aircraft equipment was retained for home defence.

Since that time, bombing technique has improved and the range, speed, and carrying capacity of aircraft has been increased. But these advantages have probably been more than offset by the greater accuracy of modern anti-aircraft fire and the efficiency of fighter 'planes.

In September 1938 the Spanish Ambassador, speaking at Geneva, stated that the casualties sustained by Spanish civilians up to that date, were less than one for each bomb dropped. A great deal of private property was, of course, destroyed, but although terrifying, the bombing raids had no appreciable influence on the conduct of the civil war, while the moral effect produced by them was opposite to that intended.

Similarly in China : the figures compiled and published by the Shanghai Publicity Committee revealed that in one year, up to June 1938, a little more than one casualty was caused by each of the 33,000 bombs that had been dropped on Chinese cities. In both cases the raids were against communities that were very poorly equipped to resist attack.

Futility of Civilian Raiding

In view of these results it would be surprising if belief in the omnipotence of the bomber was not shaken, and the futility of air raids on civil populations was not generally recognized. They have not succeeded anywhere in the past in provoking revolutions.

Since, therefore, it is unwise to assume that an enemy is going to misapply any of the forces at his disposal in time of war, it is probable that if raids are carried out against this country only objects of real naval and military importance will be sought out and attacked—at any rate at first. Where one side considers itself predominant it will strive to maintain its superiority by annihilating the enemy's aerodromes, factories, and ground organizations, and as many as possible of the key establishments on which his fighting strength and ability to wage war depend. When the defending air force has been crippled, munitions works have been destroyed, and food supplies cut off, attention might then be turned to the civil population, regardless of world opinion.

When the war began there was a clash of opinion between those who believed that air raids on cities might be expected at any moment and those who maintained that the first attacks would be on places of real military and naval importance. Even in country districts every precaution was taken against air raiders, as seen in the above photograph showing villager members of the A.F.S. going into action.   *Photo, Keystone*

Stocking the Nation's Wartime Larder

As in the last war so in this, a Ministry of Food strives to ensure that the people's food shall be adequate in supply and fairly distributed. Here some of the steps taken in this direction since war began are described.

Mr. W. S. Morrison, Chancellor of the Duchy of Lancaster, was appointed Minister in charge of the Food (Defence Plans) Department on April 11, 1939, and became Minister of Food in the War Cabinet.
Photo, Central Press

AMONG the most important of the steps taken at the outbreak of war was the placing of the nation's food supply under Government control. Bulk purchase of staple foods was undertaken by the Government through its agents abroad, and at home bulk stocks were taken over and the prices of most of the essential foods strictly regulated. The object of these measures was to prevent any great rise of prices and anything in the nature of speculation in the nation's food, and also to ensure that the available supplies were fairly distributed.

Immense difficulties were encountered in the tremendous task of providing the wherewithal of existence for 45,000,000 human beings, but the experience gained in the last war stood the administrators in good stead. At the outset, of course, there were muddles, large and small. When the war began the authorities believed that large-scale air raids on London were to be expected at any moment, and so the metropolitan fish and meat markets at Billingsgate and Smithfield were decentralized—with such disastrous results on the smooth working of the distributive machinery, however, that it was not long before they were restored to London.

Evacuation created constant difficulties. Some milk distributors found that their "round" had dropped by 20 per cent, while others soon realized that there had been such a big influx of population into their area that their milk supplies were quite insufficient.

Supplies of butter and bacon—the two foods which it was announced were to be the first subjects of rationing—were also difficult to allocate to the evacuated and reception areas. The supplies to the retailers of butter, controlled from about September 23, were based on the supplies

of a datum period consisting of the preceding June and July, when the population in the areas was at its peacetime level. The datum period fixed for the supply of bacon, controlled on September 9, was the four weeks ending August 19, when large numbers of people were away on holiday. Thus, when bacon control was instituted, the holiday resorts found themselves granted liberal supplies, while those districts to which the holiday-makers had now returned were short.

Another difficulty concerning bacon is that normally four-fifths of Britain's bacon supplies come from overseas, principally from Denmark, Eire, Canada and

Thousands of tins of food are being stored in this London warehouse. High medical authorities have declared that tinned food loses none of its nutritive value.
Photo, Keystone

the Baltic countries. With the development of the Nazi submarine and mines campaign, supplies from Denmark and the Baltic became decidedly erratic, and so the country became specially dependent upon home-cured and Irish bacon.

Butter was included in the rationing scheme, because, like bacon, supplies are lower than in peacetime owing to reduced shipments from North European countries from which normally large supplies are obtained. Like bacon, butter is too perishable to be suitable for inclusion in the reserves of food supplies which the Government were building up even before the war; but the main raw material of margarine was stored in large quantities, and since the outbreak of war the Ministry of Food has stimulated the production of margarine. For a few weeks all margarine produced was of standard quality, retailed at a standard price of 6d. per pound, but ere long the branded

supplies were again on sale. There was no blending of butter with margarine and no mixing of butters.

There was more than a storm in a teacup when it was announced that all the tea stocks in the country were to be pooled, and that the tea drinkers who had become addicted to one particular blend were to be compelled in future to take a cup that would neither inebriate nor cheer them. So great was the public outcry that it was soon announced that, although the Ministry of Food had requisitioned the existing stocks of tea, taken control of future arrivals and of its marketing, pooling had been abandoned.

There was a sigh of relief, too, when it was announced that there is no likelihood of a shortage of sugar. Large reserves of sugar are available, and the Ministry purchased in September a whole year's requirements, that is, more than 1,000,000 tons of Empire sugar. There is, moreover, a home crop from East Anglian beet.

So the story could be continued as regards meat, bread, flour, eggs, condensed milk, potatoes and canned salmon. Even dried fruits have not been forgotten, and well in time for Christmas the Ministry made arrangements for securing ample supplies of currants and sultanas for the festive pies and puddings.

This wartime scene in an English port shows one of the ships brought safely home by convoy, unloading its cargo of food from one of the Dominions.
Photo, L.N.A.

When a Convoy Comes Safe to Port

Great quantities of food are still arriving at the Port of London, but the routine of dealing with cargoes has changed. As a rule ships come in on every flood tide and very soon lighters are alongside into which cargoes are unloaded to be carried farther up the river. They are got away at once. Since the convoy system has been in operation the flow of shipping is less regular, and large numbers of ships come in together. Before they arrive such a great fleet of lighters as is seen here is got together to take off the cargoes.

Photo, Central Press

Finland's Cap

OF the Baltic capitals none is laid out on more spacious and more modern lines than Helsinki, or, to use the Swedish form, Helsingfors. Yet by a cruel fate it was this city which was bombed time and again by the Russian warplanes, and here in these pages are illustrated some of the results of this exhibition of Soviet frightfulness. The earliest scene in point of time is that on the left (1) where pedestrians are searching the débris resulting from some of the first explosions which have wrought havoc in a block of shops and tenements. Below (2) is a street in which move firemen and A.R.P. helpers in their work of succour. Below on the right (4) a boarding-house has been shattered by a bomb. One photograph (3) shows one of the flights of Red bombers actually above the city; the bottom 'plane is in difficulties, probably as a result of the defenders' anti-aircraft fire.

Photos, Associated Press

Receives a Lesson in Soviet 'Frightfulness'

WORDS THAT HISTORY WILL REMEMBER

(Continued from page 434)

Soil from which Spring Roots of War

Monday, November 27, 1939

MR. HERBERT MORRISON, M.P., Leader of the London County Council, in a broadcast :

Stage by stage Hitler built up his power. Piece by piece he swallowed up his neighbours. Each time, like the drunkard, he swore it would be the last. Each time he set about preparing the next daylight robbery. In Poland he used force instead of merely threatening it ; but having seized what he wanted he made the old promise that now he would turn over a new leaf and settle down.

Today we stand, with France, prepared for what may come ; today, owing to Poland's terrible martyrdom, the Allies have had time to make ready. Germany has missed the aggressor's best chance—a flying start.

But suppose we made peace now ? How do we know that, when his strength was renewed and our preparations were dissipated, Hitler would not launch his Blitzkrieg out of a clear sky, and crush us before we could start ?

Some seem to hope that Russia has Hitler pinned down and will not allow him to start a new war in the west. But has Russia ever said so ? And what other guarantee of safety and freedom for Europe have we besides the word of Adolf Hitler ?

Poisonous Growth of Nazism

The Nazi regime is, as it always has been, a poisonous growth, a wholly evil thing. A leopard of this kind cannot change its spots. It must dominate, or die. And what would happen if it did dominate, and if the threat of military defeat—which was drawing very near to us this summer—became a realized fact ? A victorious Nazi Germany insists upon setting up in its conquered territories governments of its own kidney . . .

If we are fighting only to end the Nazi threat to our future, if we have no aim but to get back to pre-Nazi Europe, we are chasing a will-o'-the-wisp, and we shall fall into the mire. The roots of Nazism are not all to be found in the original sin of the Prussian temperament ; the roots of war lie deep in our present ways of living, and we have the chance now to dig some of them out.

If we really mean to build a clean, ordered, secure world after this war, we must be ready for sacrifice as individuals, as classes, as a nation. While we must be ready to surrender a measure of national sovereignty, we must maintain the cultural freedom of nations and a proper measure of independence in their political life. We must cling to an ideal of government, whatever its actual form, as something which exists to serve peoples, not to dominate them . . .

War Aims Must Precede Peace Aims

Tuesday, November 28

MR. CHAMBERLAIN in the House of Commons :

There is one observation I should like to make on the subject of peace aims which I do not think has been made before. This idea of building a better world does not require a war to bring it into men's minds. Every statesman who has any right to such a name has been hoping and trying to improve the general condition of the world whenever he had any opportunity of doing so, but the condition in which Europe has been kept for such a long

period by the policy of Germany has made it absolutely impossible to make any progress in this task of improving world conditions on the scale which we should have liked to see. . . .

When I spoke on this subject on Sunday I said that the conditions in which peace aims could be achieved could not at present be foreseen. I did not say that they were remote. I do not know. I said that they could not be foreseen, and I say now that none of us knows how long this war will last, none of us knows in what directions it will develop, none of us knows when it is ended who will be standing by our side and who will be against us, and I say that in those circumstances it would be absolutely futile—indeed it would be worse than futile, it would be mischievous—if we were to attempt to lay down today the conditions in which the new world is to be created . . .

First of all, we must put an end to this menace under which Europe has lain for so many years. If we can really do that, confidence will be established throughout Europe, and while I am not excluding the necessity for dealing with other parts of the world as well, I feel that Europe is the key of the situation and that if Europe could be settled the rest of the world would not prove so difficult a problem. If we can establish that confidence, then many things which have seemed difficult or impossible in the past might prove to be, if not easy, at any rate attainable . . .

We shall need all our courage, all our tenacity, all our patriotism to achieve our war aim, for let us not make the mistake of underrating the strength of our enemy. When we have achieved that aim, then indeed we may find that we may require an even greater vision, an even greater will to win the peace than it has taken to win the war. I do not doubt that when that time comes there will be those who will have that vision and that will.

British Courage and Skill Will Win the War

Tuesday, November 28

SIR SAMUEL HOARE, Lord Privy Seal, in a speech to the Chelsea Conservative Association :

We were prepared for a sudden, a swift and staggering climax. In its place there have been three months of watching and waiting. People are saying that we are suffering from boredom. I believe myself that this feeling is altogether superficial. If we look impartially upon the story of the last three months we shall come to the conclusion that so far from nothing

having happened things have happened that will leave for all time their mark upon the course of events in the world . . .

In the early days of September the German Government believed that the Russian agreement meant a preponderance, or at least a balance, of force in the world. Yet throughout these three months the German Army has been pinned to its muddy trenches on the Western Front. Hitler has been foiled of his knock-out blow, although it was the very essence of his strategy. Instead, there have been endless discussions at his headquarters. There have been rumours of wrangling with his advisers ; there have been ominous outbreaks in Poland and Czecho-Slovakia ; there have been murmurs of discontent in Germany itself. I do not exaggerate the importance of these reports. I do not suggest that morale is likely to break in Germany. But what I do say is that whilst Hitler was determined to finish his quick war in a few months, these twelve weeks have left him weaker and not stronger, and they have enabled the French and ourselves greatly to strengthen our military position in the world. The knock-out blow can never be delivered.

Hitler's Secret Weapon

Only in one direction has Hitler attempted to act. Violating all treaties and agreements, contrary to every dictate of humanity, he launched his U-boat campaign and has followed it with the ruthless use of his much vaunted secret weapon, the mine that is dropped from the air. These inhuman attacks have led to the sinking of many ships and the loss of many lives.

We are beating the submarine, and so it will be with the new mine. We shall suffer losses and we shall bear them with resolution. They will lead to even greater efforts, and this new effort will show that Hitler's secret weapon will end by doing him more injury than it will ever inflict upon us.

If we hold firm, we are sure of victory, and look where I will I see every evidence to show that we shall hold firm . . .

If I describe our economic policy in a single sentence, I would say that it is to interfere with the intricate machine of trade and industry as little as the circumstances of war allow and to obtain as much co-operation as we can between the Government on the one hand and industrialists and labour on the other.

It is co-operation that we need everywhere if we are to have a 100-per-cent war effort. So far as I am concerned as a member of the Cabinet, I can say that we welcome the help of any citizen, be he a member of the Opposition, or of our own party, or of no party at all if the result of the help is to make our effort more fully effective. For in all these things we are determined to win the war ; that is our first and over-ruling war aim.

OUR WAR GAZETTEER

Angers. City of France, 212 m. by railway S.W. of Paris ; the medieval capital of Anjou ; junction of roads and railways ; cathedral ; educ. centre ; new seat of Polish Government ; pop. 87,000.

Borkum. German island in the Frisian group, only 9 m. from coast of Holland ; nearest German territory to England ; in peacetime a favourite seaside resort ; 5 m. long and 2½ broad ; pop. about 3,000.

Karelia. (*Ka-ray-lya.*) Autonomous republic of U.S.S.R. within the R.S.F.S.R. (Russia proper) ; capital, Petrosavodsk ; lies E. of Finnish frontier from White Sea to L. Ladoga ; narrow tongue between latter and Gulf of Finland called Karelian Isthmus ; a. 53,000 sq. m. ; pop. 342,000 ; Karelia is in Finland.

Ladoga, Lake. Between U.S.S.R. and Finland, the largest lake in Europe ; 125 m. long and 80 wide ; contains many islands, mostly Finnish.

Rybachi. The "Fishermen's Peninsula" in far N. of Finland, on which Arctic port of Petsamo stands.

Salmijaervi (*Salmi-vair-vi*). Town of Arctic Finland ; near by, at Kolosjoki, is important nickel mining centre.

Terijoki (*Teri-yo-ki*). Small town on Karelian Isthmus, within Finnish side of frontier ; seat of puppet "Finnish People's Government" set up by Russia Dec. 1, 1939.

Viipuri (or Viborg). Town of Finland, in W. Karelia ; on Gulf of Finland, 75 m. N.W. of Leningrad ; pop. 73,000.

Small Arms Great in Quality and Performance

W̶HEREAS in 1914 the rifle was almost the only instrument of fire-power, it is now supplemented to a tremendous extent by automatic weapons of various types. Vickers, Lewis, and Hotchkiss are names veterans of the Great War will remember, but Bren is a newcomer to the nomenclature of armament. But whether it be an old-established weapon or one which is a comparatively new invention, in the manufacture of British small arms only the best is good enough, and so our soldiers know that their weapons will never let them down.

A Bren gun is here being tested on the range for correct working of the mechanism and accuracy of shooting. If the gun fails to pass the tests, it is at once sent back to the factory for correction.   *Photo, Planet News*

Above, the moulded steel ingot that will form the barrel of a Bren gun is being tempered by making it red-hot and then plunging it into a bath of oil. Only steel of the finest quality can withstand the pressure to which such guns are put during the tests.

Photo, Planet News

One of the tasks of the small arms factory is to deal with the repair and reconditioning of rifles and to send them out equal to new. Here rifles in various stages of reconstruction are being stacked ready to go through the next stage towards complete renovation.   *Photo, Fox*

The ordnance factories make not only Bren guns but rifles and revolvers, and those Vickers machine - guns which were so familiar a weapon in the last war, and which are once more being issued to the Army in large numbers. Right, a scene in a shop where the Vickers are assembled.

Photo, Planet News

How the British Soldier of 1939 Goes to War

STEEL HELMET
2½ lbs.

ANTI-GAS CAPE
3½ lbs.

RESPIRATOR
(in "ALERT" Position)
3½ lbs.

HAVERSACK
& CONTENTS
5 lbs.

STRAPS, BELT etc.
3½ lbs.

POUCHES
(Each containing
60 Rounds Bren
Gun ammunition)
10 lbs each.

BAYONET
& SCABBARD
1¾ lbs.

RIFLE
8 lbs 10½ ozs.

THE "battle dress" of the British Army was finally approved in April 1939, and is now worn by both men and officers. It is a two-piece garment of khaki serge, consisting of a blouse and trousers buckling at the wrists and ankles, the ankles also being protected by web anklets. The weight of the uniform is about 12 lb. This soldier is wearing battle dress, but is not completely equipped. When wearing full marching order, the infantryman carries a valise (or pack) on his back in place of the haversack seen here, the latter being transferred to the left hip above the bayonet and counterbalanced on the right by a water-bottle.

The valise holds the great-coat, cardigan when not worn, and such other personal effects as individual skill in packing can get into it; while in the haversack are a hold-all with comb, tooth-brush, shaving outfit, fitted housewife, socks, mess tin, emergency ration, etc. The large patch pocket on the trousers is to hold maps and papers. Though officers carry some additional articles of equipment, such as revolvers and binoculars and compasses, there is nothing in their uniform to distinguish them from the men except the shoulder badge.

ANKLE BOOTS
4¾ lbs.

Specially photographed for THE WAR ILLUSTRATED *under War Office supervision*

The Winged Lion Soars Over Heligoland

As if to show that the Nazi air raids on Scotland were but amateurish efforts, the R.A.F.
delivered a full-scale attack on Heligoland, one of the most strongly fortified places to
be found anywhere on the map. After dropping their bombs, every 'plane returned.

NEARLY 300 miles from the English
East Coast lies the little island of
Heligoland. During most of the
nineteenth century it belonged to England,
but in 1890 it was ceded to Germany in
return for concessions in East Africa, and
by the time of the Great War it had been
converted into a great outlying bastion of
the Kaiser's realm. The treaty-makers at
Versailles decreed its de-fortification. and
for some years it became again what it had
been before the Kaiser dreamed of world
power—a mile-long rocky bank whose
grassy slopes provided grazing ground for
sheep and cows, and whose beaches were
the summer playground of thousands of
holiday-making Hamburgers. Came Hitler,
who ordered the island's re-fortification—
in secret at first, and later, when he felt
sure of his position, openly. So to-day it
is once again one of Germany's most
strongly fortified areas defended with
16-inch and 11-inch guns, themselves
protected by heavy anti-aircraft batteries. This was the place which was
chosen by the R.A.F. for their raid of
December 3—the latest of their audacious
assaults on the strongholds of the enemy.

A week before British machines had
flown over and photographed the island,
and to these pioneers must some of the
credit for the success of the raid be attributed. Nor should we forget those who
took part in the raid of September 29, from
which some of our aircraft did not return.

It was in perfect weather that on that
first Sunday morning in December the
British 'planes roared up into the sky
when the order for action was given.
They were within sight of Heligoland
about 11.45, and riding high in the blue,
their crews gazed down on the island
and its near neighbour, Sandy Island, and
the roadstead in between where lay two
Nazi warships and several smaller craft,
probably minelayers. From that immense
height the ships and the islands themselves
had the appearance of toys set out on a
blue nursery carpet.

On receiving radio orders from the
squadron leader, the bombers poised miles
high over their objectives dipped sharply,
then with engines screaming in a power
dive, they went hurtling down. The
" nursery carpet " became grim reality—
an inferno of bomb concussions and anti-
aircraft barrages.

Nazi Warships Under Fire

Arrived above their objectives, the
pilots pulled their 'planes out of the
plunge and started bombing systematically. The pilot of one machine reported
that three of his bombs straddled a warship and he was quite sure that he had
registered a hit. Another pilot dropped
a bomb directly on a warship, and a
third reported that one of his bombs fell
so close to a ship that it must have caused
considerable damage.

According to the German communiqué
the British 'planes were able to drop only
a few bombs owing to the heavy anti-
aircraft fire, but in fact the anti-aircraft
shells exploded high above the British
'planes when they began to dive, and
by the time the Germans had shortened
their range the bombers had climbed
again above the exploding shells. In
spite of the anti-aircraft fire Heligoland
was circled twice, as on the first occasion
clouds obscured the target.

One British 'plane which became temporarily isolated from the rest was attacked
by a Messerschmidt fighter—the only
enemy 'plane encountered during the
operation. But the British machine-
gunner returned its fire to such good
effect that the German fighter was sent
down out of control with smoke and
flames belching from its fuselage. The
British gunner was hit by a bullet, but
it struck the buckle of his parachute
and he returned home uninjured. He
kept the bullet as a memento of his
escape.

After many hours in the air the bombers all returned safely to their base.
There were no casualties to the personnel
and only one 'plane was damaged, being
hit in its tail by a shrapnel splinter from
the barrage. As a result of this hit the
pilot was fifteen minutes late on the
return flight. It may be hoped that they
kept his tea for him in the mess !

This photograph from the air shows Heligoland over which aircraft of the Royal Air Force made a daring raid on December 3. In the
foreground is the harbour. Heligoland, which lies about 29 miles from the nearest point on the German coast, has an area of only 130 acres,
about one-third of that of Hyde Park. Really it consists of an island—Rock Island—and an islet, Dünen-Insel.
Photo, Keystone

'CARRY ON AND DREAD NOUGHT!'

Magnificently confident, the First Lord of the Admiralty in his survey of the first three months of the sea war, given to Parliament on December 6, made clear the relative inefficacy of mine and U-boat warfare, but stressed the need for sustained effort.

MR. Churchill opened his inspiriting review by remarking that the main attack of the enemy had been concentrated upon the Royal Navy and the seaborne commerce upon which the British Islands and the British Empire depend. He continued :

We have always over 2,000 ships at sea, and between 100 and 150 ships move every day in and out of our harbours in the United Kingdom alone. This immense traffic has to be maintained in the teeth of a constant U-boat attack, **which never hesitates to break the conventions of civilized warfare to which Germany so recently subscribed.**

We have been frequently attacked from the air. Mining on a large scale has been practised against us, and latterly magnetic mines have been dropped from aeroplanes or laid by submarines on the approaches to our harbours, with the intention of destroying British, and still more neutral, commerce under conditions contrary to the accepted rules of sea warfare and to German engagements in regard to them.

Besides this, two of the so-called pocket battleships and certainly one other cruiser have been loose for many weeks past in the North and South Atlantic, or near Madagascar.

The Admiralty's task has been to bring in our immense world-wide traffic in spite of this position. Besides this, we have to cleanse the seas of all German commerce and to arrest every German vessel and every scrap of cargo in which Germany is interested. . . .

THE destruction of the U-boats is proceeding normally and in accordance with the estimate I gave to the House of between two and four a week. That is to say at a rate superior to what we believe to be the German power of replacing U-boats and of replacing completely trained captains and crews.

When I see statements, as I have done lately, that the Germans during 1940 will have as many as 400 U-boats in commission, and that they are producing these vessels "by the chain-belt system," I wonder if they are producing the U-boat captains and crews by a similar method. If so, it seems likely that our rate of destruction might well have to undergo a similar expansion.

I must again repeat the warning which I gave to the House in September, that a steady flow of losses must be expected, that occasional disasters will occur. . . .

It is, however, my sure belief that we are getting the better of this menace to our life. We are buffeted by the waves, but the ocean tides flow steady and strong in our favour.

The convoy system is now in full operation. Very few ships have been attacked in convoy ; less than one in 750 has been sunk. Nevertheless, we must remember that convoy involves a certain definite loss of carrying power, since

the ships must wait during the assembly of the convoy and the convoy must travel at the speed of the slowest ship. This loss is being steadily reduced by the institution of slow and fast convoys and by other appropriate measures.

In consequence of these processes the U-boats have found it easier to attack neutral shipping than the vessels of Britain and France. The figures are really remarkable.

The losses of British merchant ships in October were half what they were in September, and in November they were only two-thirds of what they were in October.

Quite contrary has been the case with the neutrals. They lost half as much again in the second month as they did in the first, and double as much in the third month as they did in the second. . . .

In the last few weeks the German U-boats have largely abandoned the gun for the torpedo, have descended from the torpedo to the mine. This is about the lowest form of warfare that can be imagined. **It is the warfare of the I.R.A., leaving the bomb in the parcels office of the railway stations.**

THE magnetic mine, deposited secretly by the U-boat under the cloak of darkness in the approaches to our harbours, or dropped from parachuting aircraft, may perhaps be Hitler's much-vaunted secret weapon. . . .

More than half our losses in the last month have been due to the magnetic mine, but more than two-thirds of the total losses from the use of this mine have fallen not upon belligerents but upon neutrals.

In fact, in the third month of the war neutral losses by mine were twice as great as British losses, and neutral losses of all kinds one-third greater than belligerent losses.

So far as the sea war is concerned, German friendship has proved far more poisonous than German enmity.

The magnetic mine is neither new nor mysterious. As the Prime Minister announced in his broadcast, its secrets are known to us. Indeed,

the preparation of counter-measures was already far advanced before the first magnetic mine was laid in British waters. . . .

The recklessness of this latest attack upon neutrals, and the breach of international agreements which it involves, have led us to place a retaliatory embargo upon the export of all goods of German ownership or origin.

This measure was taken in the late war, when it worked with surprising smoothness and efficiency. German oversea exporting power was rapidly destroyed, and with it perished all power of building up new credits abroad.

It is satisfactory to learn from German sources that goods for export are already piling up on the German quays and in their warehouses to such an extent that, we are told, they hamper the handling of incoming merchandise.

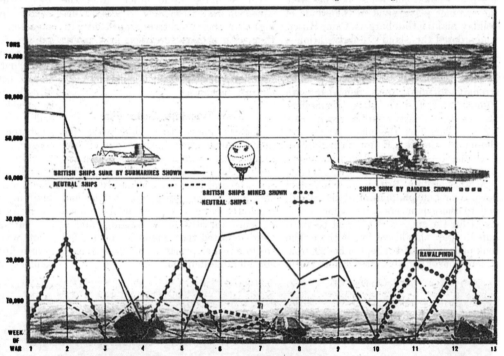

In the House of Commons on December 6, Mr. Winston Churchill stated that the British Empire entered the war with 21,000,000 tons of shipping, and that the total loss up to the time he spoke was 340,000 tons. Replacements from various sources totalled 280,000 tons ; leaving a net loss of 60,000 tons. Above, the losses of British and neutral ships are shown diagrammatically.

Courtesy of the " Daily Mail "

The service of mine-sweeping is of peculiar danger, calculated to try the strongest nerves. **All these serious dangers were sufficient to bring forward an overwhelming response from fishermen and crews who were called upon to come to their country's assistance. . . .**

The offices which were open on Saturday night at some of the fishing ports were crowded and thronged, and had to be kept open all night and on into Sunday, and in a very short time full complements were made up by these fisherfolk eager to serve their country in the manner which they felt would be really effective.

WE began the war with 21,000,000 tons of merchant shipping. This figure, of course, included ships on the Great Lakes of North America, and a number of very small coastal vessels.

Out of this total we have lost, during the three months in which we have been subject to severe and concentrated attack by all kinds of methods, fair and foul, by U-boat, by mine, by surface raider, and by the hazards of the sea, about 340,000 tons.

Against this we have gained by transfer from foreign flags, by prizes taken from the enemy, and by the new vessels we are building on a

This badge, approved by the King, is to be issued to officers and men of the Merchant Navy and worn in the left buttonhole.

This photograph shows the Board of Admiralty in session in the Board Room, with a portrait of William IV, the Sailor King, looking down upon their deliberations. Left to right round the table are Mr. Geoffrey Shakespeare, M.P. (Parliamentary and Financial Sec.) ; Rear-Adm. H. M. Burrough, C.B. (Assist. Chief of Naval Staff) ; Vice-Adm. Sir Alexander Ramsay (Fifth Sea Lord ; ret. Nov., 1939) ; Rear-Adm. T. S. V. Phillips (Deputy Chief of Staff) ; Adm. of the Fleet Sir Dudley Pound (First Sea Lord) ; Sir J. Sidney Barnes (Deputy Secretary) ; the First Lord ; Sir Archibald Carter (Secretary) ; Adm. Sir Charles Little (Second Sea Lord) ; Rear-Adm. B. A. Fraser (Third Sea Lord) ; Rear-Adm. G. S. Arbuthnot (Fourth Sea Lord) ; and Capt. A. U. M. Hudson, M.P. (Civil Lord).

Photo, British Official : Crown Copyright

large scale, about 280,000 tons, leaving a net loss of about 60,000 tons.

For every 1,000 tons of British shipping sunk, 110,000 tons have entered the ports of this threatened island, which we are told on the enemy's authority is beleaguered and beset on all sides, in the first three months of war. In the month of November, nearly 250,000 tons of shipping entered or cleared from our harbours for every 1,000 tons lost.

The losses which have fallen upon the protecting warships of the Royal Navy are necessarily heavier in proportion than those which affect the Mercantile Marine. . . . The Navy has never been so many days at sea each month as in this war.

We have lost in these three months of war two great ships, the " Courageous " and the " Royal Oak," two destroyers, and the submarine which was blown up by accident—in all about 50,000 tons.

We have at present building, much of it in an advanced stage, nearly 1,000,000 tons of warships of all classes.

We have also lost one of our 50 armed merchant cruisers, the " Rawalpindi," whose glorious fight against overwhelming odds deserves the respect and honour of the House and of the nation. However, our losses in warships during the first three months of war in 1914 were more than double those we have now suffered.

Of course, war is full of ugly and unpleasant surprises. No one must indulge in easy habits of mind, or relax for one moment the vigilant attention to the fortunes of the State, and that fearless desire to measure the real facts, understand them, and master them, which are incumbent upon all responsible citizens, and still more upon their Parliamentary representatives.

We have the means and we have the opportunity of marshalling the whole vast strength of the British Empire, and of the Mother Country, and directing them steadfastly and unswervingly to the fulfilment of our purposes and the vindication of our cause, and for each and all, as for the Royal Navy, the watchword should be " Carry On and Dread Nought."

DEBITS		EACH SYMBOL = 10.000 TONS	CREDITS
Merchant Ships sunk		EXCEPT U-BOATS **Goods captured by British**	**U-boats sunk by Allies**
BRITISH (Sept., Oct., & Nov.)	**FRENCH**		

Merchant Ships sunk
BRITISH (Sept., Oct., & Nov.) — *Tons 294.673   80 Ships*
FRENCH — *Tons 55.385   11 Ships*
NEUTRAL — *Tons 167.223   46 Ships*

Goods captured by British — *Tons 475.000*

U-boats sunk by Allies — *25*
5 damaged, believed sunk by Allies

In page 302 of this work a diagram is given showing the number of British, French and neutral ships sunk by enemy action up to October 31, 1939. Above, the tale of losses and credits is continued up to November 30. The diagram includes all ships the loss of which had been officially announced at that date. In April, 1917, the worst month of unrestricted submarine warfare in the last war, the total tonnage lost by enemy action was 850,000 tons, of which 515,000 tons was British, nearly twice the total of the three months shown here.

Britain's Answer to Germany's Mine Campaign

While the Nazis were still gloating over the first successes of their indiscriminate mine-laying, the British Government dealt another smashing blow at German commerce by the Order in Council described below,

IF the magnetic mines which sank the "Simon Bolivar" and nineteen other ships in the course of a single week be indeed Hitler's "weapon which is not yet known," he was a little premature when he went on to claim that it was "a weapon against which there was no defence." Only a nation whose naval and mercantile vessels had been driven from the seas would dream of strewing the channels with unanchored mines, but Britain is not left defenceless against this latest development in Germany's campaign of frightfulness.

As Mr. Chamberlain said in his speech in the House of Commons on November 21, the Government is not prepared to allow such methods of conducting warfare to continue without retaliation. "I may remind the House," he said, "that in the last war, as a measure of justified reprisal for submarine attacks on merchant ships, exports of German origin or ownership were made subject to seizure on the high seas. The many violations of international law and the ruthless brutality of German methods have decided us to follow a similar course now, and an Order in Council will shortly be issued giving effect to this decision."

Seizing Germany's Exports

The Order in Council to which the Premier referred was signed by the King on November 27, although it did not come into operation until December 4.

Of the legality of the new stroke there can be no doubt. As the Prime Minister pointed out, a similar measure was adopted in the last war. Moreover, it is generally agreed that if one belligerent breaks the recognized laws of war, the other is justified in his resort to reprisals in order to compel an abandonment of the illegal methods.

In Germany it was claimed that, though the new measure would stop the German import and export trade with countries overseas, the Latin republics of South America in particular, such trade was already reduced to insignificant proportions. Besides, although Britain could effectually shut the sea-door, Germany by her pact with Russia had seen to it that the land-door should remain open. (It may be noted that this rosy view could hardly survive the outspoken article which appeared a few days later in one of Marshal Goering's periodicals. "We must face facts," wrote Emil Helferrich, one of Germany's foremost economic experts; "as in 1914 to 1918 England's power has brought the German overseas trade to a complete standstill. German ships are lying in more than 100 harbours all over the globe. These goods and ships are blockaded by the British Navy, and part of them have already been confiscated.")

The neutral countries, however, professed deep concern, and a number of representations were made to Lord Halifax at the Foreign Office. The Italian Ambassador was believed to have questioned the Order's legality, although in the last war Italy as one of the Allies made not the slightest objection to the British Order in Council which authorized the confiscation of German exports carried in neutral vessels. The Japanese Ambassador stressed the difficult position in which Japan would be placed if her imports from Germany—which include arms and munitions for the war in China—were cut off. The Danish, Belgian, and Dutch Ministers also made protests; and the last-named stressed the hardship and loss which Dutch shippers and agents would suffer if the British intention were carried through.

On the other hand, Government circles in the U.S.A. took up the attitude that the blockade of German exports does not constitute an interference with genuinely neutral trade, although the Isolationists demanded that the U.S.A. should protest against the Allies' reprisal on the ground that it violated neutral rights. The Isolationists did not, however, demand a protest against Germany's indiscriminate minelaying. Admittedly, the British scheme of reprisals may cause grave hardship to innocent neutrals, but it cannot be compared with that method of warfare which makes no discrimination between friend and foe, and sends to the bottom the ships not only of the warring powers, but of the most inoffensive neutrals.

British Concern for Neutrals

Moreover, as Mr. Butler, Under-Secretary for Foreign Affairs, stated in the House of Commons on December 1, His Majesty's Government were doing their best to understand the difficulties of neutrals and to spare them undue hardships—always consistently, of course, with our primary object of exercising our belligerent rights and of winning the war.

In this map the heavy lines show the sea routes by which in peacetime Germany receives her main imports. It will be seen that to reach Germany all the north and south Atlantic routes converge into two lines, both dominated by the British Navy.

Courtesy of the "News Chronicle"

Stockholm Now Lies Under the Shadow of War

Nᴏᴛ since the days of Waterloo has the Swedish Army been in action, but Russia's invasion of Finland brought war very near. Hence it was not surprising that the City Fathers of Stockholm looked afresh at the plans already made for the evacuation of the citizens if the worst came to the worst, and on the same day, December 5, it was announced that Sweden had called a number of her young men to the colours. She lent, moreover, practical aid and moral support to her unhappy neighbour, the Finns, assailed by the brute force of the Soviet armies.

Though an old city, Stockholm is a progressive one. Among its modern developments is the fine Airport, left. In the fashionable street know as Kingsgatan, above, are the first two skyscrapers built in Scandinavia.

Photos, International Graphic Press, and courtesy of Swedish Travel Bureau

In the foreground is old Stockholm, known as the " City within the Bridges," as it stands on an island the approach to which is by bridges. In it are the oldest buildings in Stockholm, and the magnificent Royal Palace, dating from 1754, seen in the photograph. During the conference between the Kings of Sweden, Norway, and Denmark and President Kallio of Finland, which opened on October 18, 1939, the three Kings and the President appeared on the balcony of the Palace during a remarkable demonstration of Scandinavian fellowship.

ODD FACTS ABOUT THE WAR
Worth Noting Today and Re-reading in Years to Come

" Peace " Postcards Banned
The Ministry of Propaganda in Berlin has ordered the confiscation of picture postcards showing Hitler and Mussolini together and inscribed " The Fuehrer and the Duce have decided—Peace." Seals bearing the words " Adolf Hitler, Our Peace Leader," are also banned.

Pocket Mirrors for Pilots
R.A.F. machines on patrol duty along the Western Front have fixed a little mirror inside the cockpit, to be used as a motorist uses a driving mirror. In this way no Nazi machine may take them unawares in the rear.

In England Now
" The British people enter the winter in hunger, cold, and darkness, and in continual fear of German air raids. New and harsh police measures have been introduced, forbidding all criticism of the Government." (Nazi broadcaster.)

Front Line Boating
Flood water from the Rhine has reached part of the Siegfried Line, and the unfortunate troops manning one of the fortresses have their supplies brought to them by boat.

More Vitamin A Needed
One of the by-products of malnutrition is night blindness, a condition which makes its victims helpless in a black-out. German scientists are faced with the problem of finding a remedy other than a liberal diet of butter, eggs and meat.

Factory Hustle in U.S.A.
The American aeroplane industry is now capable of turning out 1,250 aircraft a month. This is a large increase on last year's total production of 3,675 machines, but it is stated that projects are under way which will speed up production still more.

Taking Precautions
Herr Lohse, Nazi District Leader at Kiel, is so apprehensive of an anti-Nazi revolt that he is reported to have turned his house into a sort of fortress, with food, arms and ammunition stored in the cellars.

Aid to Economy
A stonemason in Berne is urging people to order tombstones in advance, as the price of stone and marble is going up. As an inducement, he promises that they shall be stored free of charge until the customer or his relatives request delivery.

Yellow Peril Suspected ?
Japanese papers in Manchukuo published an advertisement offering a reward of 300,000 Manchukuo dollars for information leading to the arrest of those responsible for the Munich bomb explosion.

Headaches for the Censor
In future all scientific theses presented in Germany for doctors' degrees must first pass the censorship. This is to ensure against the introduction of any theory contrary to Nazi doctrines.

Swiss Merchant Service
Switzerland may have no Navy, but she is soon to inaugurate a fleet of merchant vessels flying the Swiss flag, to ensure supplies from overseas.

Nazi Dress Allowance
Under the new clothes rationing scheme each member of a German family has a book of coupons, coloured according to age and sex. As each book has to last a year, considerable judgement will have to be exercised in the choice of apparel. One coupon will obtain a woman's handkerchief, and for 25 she can get either six pairs of quarter-wool stockings or a house frock. Her husband must surrender 25 coupons for a pair of pyjamas, 30 for a sweater and 60 for a suit.

Seamstresses Unemployed
The sale of cotton and other sewing materials has been forbidden in Germany. This is stated to be merely a temporary measure, but even so it must add materially to the difficulties of the orderly Hausfrau.

" Flag Nights " in Berlin
The anti-Hitlerites are getting more daring. During the hours of black-out, not content with pushing leaflets under doors and posting them upon walls, they now spread their propaganda by decorating the overcoats of unsuspecting Berliners with little flags bearing some anti-Nazi message.

When Taking Is Not Looting
The German High Command has its own definition of " looting," an offence which may be punishable by life imprisonment. But the term does not include " the acquisition in case of urgent need of clothing, equipment, provisions (whether necessaries or luxuries), fodder, fuel, vehicles, petrol and other requirements."

Magna Carta in America
The Lincoln Cathedral copy of Magna Carta was sent over to New York as the chief exhibit in the British pavilion of the World's Fair. It has now reached Washington, where, in the Library of Congress, it will remain in safety for the duration of the war.

Eton's Playing Fields Again
The authorities at Eton College have offered 15 acres of the school's famous cricket field, known as Agar's Plough, to the local agricultural committee in answer to the Government's appeal for increased production of home-grown food.

No Common Shelter
The Soviet Embassy in London has built itself a fine air raid shelter. But it is not a Communist one, for in the event of a raid the Ambassador and his secretaries will take refuge in a compartment separated off from the part occupied by the household staff.

Austrian Royalists
At a ceremony in the church of St. Germain les Prés, and in the presence of the Archduke Otto, the Legitimist Austrians in Paris proclaimed themselves allies of the Western Powers. Along the nave and outside the church French and Austrian flags were draped together.

War Against Nazism
Nazi propaganda is being combated in South Africa by a legion known as " The Knights of Truth." It is to consist eventually of 50,000 men and women, and one battalion of the legion, under its own officers, will be established in every district of the Union.

Pitiless
In Hamburg there is a 1914-1918 war memorial surmounted by a weeping mother holding a child. By order of the Nazi authorities, these figures are to be replaced by an eagle, " for such tears are unworthy of a German woman."

Now Hospital Ships
Germany's " Strength Through Joy " ships have been equipped for war service. Repainted in accordance with the Geneva regulations, they are fitted out as Red Cross hospital ships.

Metal Harvest
All metal which is not essential to daily activities is being collected throughout Germany, and garden owners in Berlin are ruefully watching the removal of the iron railings enclosing their properties. Perhaps they do not mind so much now that the growing of foodstuffs instead of flowers has been made compulsory.

Soft Hearts—Hard Labour
The proprietor of a large shoe-shop at Tilsit and his wife were each sentenced to four years' hard labour, a heavy fine and loss of civil rights for five years for illegally selling shoes to people without ration cards.

Shaming the Drunkard
Himmler has given orders that habitual drunkards are to be excluded from public-houses in the Reich. Not only that, but their names and the fact of this exclusion will be published in the local newspaper, and the offender thus held up to execration.

THE OLD STORY.
"You gave me insufferable provocation. When I wanted to rob you I found you had locked the door." *From the cartoon by Sir Bernard Partridge.*
By permission of the Proprietors of " Punch "

We Manned the Guns of the 'Rawalpindi'

The first real naval engagement of the War—the battle between the "Rawalpindi" and the "Deutschland" on November 23—was an epic fight in the finest Naval traditions. Of the crew of 276, only 28 were known to be saved, and the story of some of these gallant survivors is here reprinted from "The Daily Telegraph."

TEN survivors of the "Rawalpindi" were loudly cheered in London on November 29 following their arrival from Scotland. They were marched out, bareheaded, in double file on to the Horse Guards Parade, to await the arrival of the Second Sea Lord and Chief of Naval Personnel, Admiral Sir Charles J. C. Little. The men were led by a stocky gunner with a grey stubble of beard.

Admiral Sir Charles Little came out of the Admiralty buildings to express the Admiralty's thanks and appreciation for their services.

Graphic accounts of the "Rawalpindi's" 40-minutes' fight were given by some of the survivors.

One of them, who was in H.M.S. "Malaya" at the Battle of Jutland and joined the "Rawalpindi" as an A.B. seaman gunner, said that he was on the aft starboard 6-in. gun.

"Action stations were sounded when the enemy were sighted," he went on, "and those of us who were below deck rushed up and manned the guns. In the fading light of the afternoon we could see the enemy ship on the horizon about 10,000 yards away.

"She began to bombard us, and with our 6-in. guns we could see that we would be outranged. We got nearer, however, and shells began to hit us. We were given the order to fire, and we got three rounds off.

"Other guns around me were also firing. We might have hit the enemy. I cannot say, but shell after shell hit us, and before long the 'Rawalpindi' caught fire.

"Another enemy craft began firing at us and a shell fell near my gun. I think several of my mates were hurt. The gun-layer was hit in the knee and was laid out. I do not know what became of him when the order to abandon ship was given. With another chum I jumped into the sea. The ship was burning like a piece of paper. A boat, empty but waterlogged, came near. I think that about 30 of us jumped from the ship's side, and I believe only about 10 got to the boat. How we clung on I do not know. It was getting darker every

Petty Officer Frank Simpson, one of the survivors of the "Rawalpindi," owes his life to the fact that he is a good swimmer. Only a superhuman effort enabled him to reach the only lifeboat that remained intact.
Photo, H. Hearn

minute and it seemed a long time before we were picked up."

Another of the survivors, a first-class petty officer and Royal Marine reservist, who has had 25 years' service, said: "My job was in the aft magazine well below water mark. With three others I opened the magazine and began sending up ammunition. Our guns were firing, and then we felt several hits.

"After one hit, the lights in the magazine went out. Then we realized that a fire had broken out amidships. It was an inferno. I was in charge and realized that there was nothing else to do but to flood the magazine to prevent the ammunition exploding.

"I called for eight men to come up with me to B deck. Live shells and cordite were in the path of sparks and flames shooting from the fire amidships. We began throwing shells overboard.

"Our guns were still firing. I can't remember how we reached the deck. The ship was ablaze all over and was being abandoned.

"About 30 or 40 of us went over the side. We saw a waterlogged boat floating past. It was a thousand-to-one chance of being able to reach it. Some of us did. One of the first men I saw in the boat was an old 'townie' of mine, who was one of the gun-crews.

In page 431 the inspection of the 10 survivors of the "Rawalpindi" by Admiral Sir Charles Little is shown, but here two of the men, Petty Officer Percy Harris and Able Seaman F. Russell, in that photograph are seen exchanging a little friendly "back-chat" before the inspection, while another survivor enjoys the fun. That they are not downhearted is shown by their expressions: that they are fresh from their terrible experience is proved by the fact that neither has had time for a shave. *Photo, Fox*

IIIIIIIIIIIIIIIIIIIIIIIIIIIIIIIIIIIIIIIIIIIIIIIIIIIIIIIIIIIIIIIIIIIIII **I WAS THERE!** IIIIIIIIIIIIIIIIIIIIIIIIIIIIIIIIIIIIIIIIIIIIIIIIIIIIIIIIIIIIIIIIIIIIIIIIIIIIII

Here are some of the survivors of the "Rawalpindi" photographed soon after they had been brought to shore at a northern port. They had just been through one of the most heroic actions in the history of the Royal Navy and had faced "fearful odds." But their demeanour shows that they had taken it in the spirit associated with the finest traditions of the Navy.
Photo, L.N.A.

Royston A. Ledbetter, another of the survivors, arrived at his home at Etruria, Stoke-on-Trent, a week after the action. He said that he and his brother Jack were members of the gun crews in different parts of the ship.

"When my gun was put out of action by a shell," he went on, "it killed practically every member of the gun crew. I escaped only because I had moved away to fetch ammunition."

His brother's gun crew was also put out of action, and he put a lifebelt round him and took him to the boat deck.

"I left him there to search for a friend. I had no clear recollection of what happened after that, but I did not see either my brother or our friend again.

"As the ship was sinking I saw a half-submerged lifeboat about 70 yards away from the ship. Although I could only swim a few strokes I jumped into the water and somehow or other got to the boat. Altogether there were ten of us in this boat and the Germans, having thrust their searchlight on us, told us to go alongside.

"We could not make much progress as we had only three oars, but when we got near the 'Deutschland' members of her crew shouted, 'Is it cold down there?'

"The Germans must by that time have heard that one of our cruisers was coming to the spot, for they never gave us any real chance of going on board. They put on speed and vanished."

"The only thing we could find in the boat was a pocket handkerchief with which to try to attract attention. We tied it on to the end of a boat-hook and hung it up, but the boat was rolling heavily. Then we tried to fix up a jury-rigged sail with oilskins, hoping to make land. We thought that we might make the Hebrides, but, luckily, we were picked up by the 'Chitral.'"

Crowds gathered in Seabright Street, Bethnal Green, E., on Nov. 29, to cheer 21-year-old Harry Fleming, a survivor of the "Rawalpindi," who had just been reunited to his wife, whom he married on September 25. He said that their honeymoon lasted only six days. Then he put to sea as a steward. Describing the fight with the "Deutschland," he said: "The Nazis, I estimate, came to within 200 or 300 yards of us and fired at point-blank range. One of our gunners scored three direct hits before his gun jammed. When he turned round to call on his mates for assistance he found them lying around him dead. He was one of the survivors and it was a great disappointment having to leave his gun.

"Many men were walking or sitting about with severe wounds, refusing to go to the surgeons who were attending to those totally disabled. I saw one man with his arm and shoulder torn off, calmly sitting on a locker smoking. When a burst of flame enveloped him he was too weak to get out of its way.

"The whole ship was ablaze from stem to stern, and I was thrown into the sea trying to launch one of the boats. Four of us scrambled on to an overturned lifeboat, but gradually one by one the

others fell off. I flattened myself against the hull, and when I was picked up unconscious the cold and sea had frozen my body to the shape of the hull. One of my rescuers said they had a job to drag me off the boat, so firmly had I fixed myself rigid with cold."

A Polish Destroyer Rescued Us

Working in co-operation with the British Navy, three Polish destroyers played an active part in patrolling the seas and destroying U-boats, and, as told in this story reprinted from the "Daily Telegraph," it was a Polish destroyer which picked up the crew of the Newcastle collier "Sheaf Crest" after she had been mined.

MEMBERS of the crew of the Newcastle collier "Sheaf Crest," which was mined off the East Coast, arrived in London on December 1.

Several of the men were injured. A

naval rating, on signalling duty, was killed when the explosion occurred.

G. S. Nesworthy, a South Shields man, said in an interview:

"The ship broke in two, the fore part

Above is one of the three Polish destroyers, now acting in co-operation with the British Navy. This photograph was taken in the Atlantic Ocean from the American liner "President Harding" just after she had received an SOS from the French steamer "Emilie Miguel." The Polish destroyer was at this time hunting for the submarine.

I WAS THERE!

Our Polish Allies Are Swift to Rescue of British Seamen

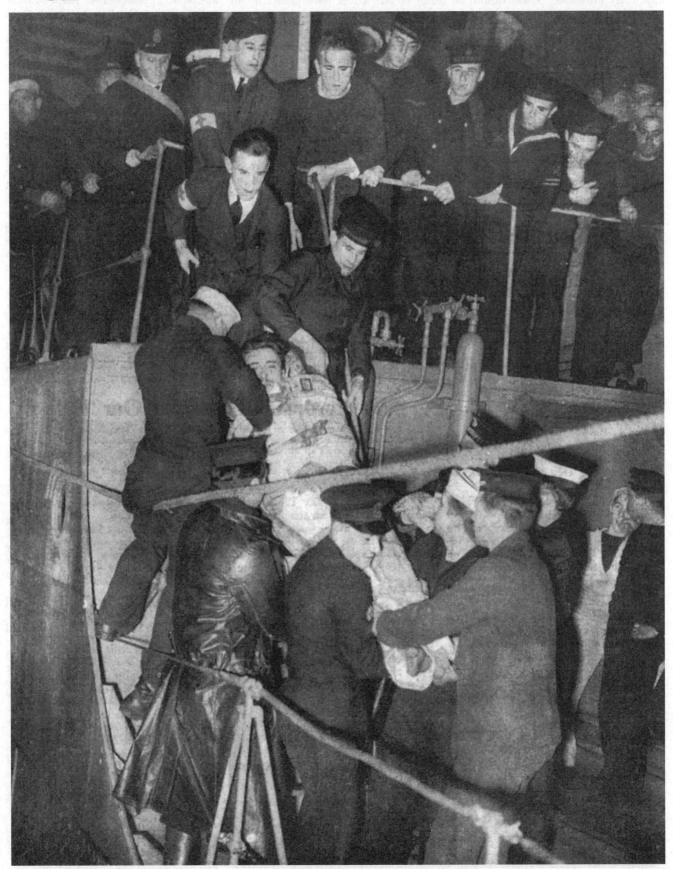

One of the many valuable services rendered by the three Polish destroyers now acting with the Royal Navy was the rescue of the survivors of the Newcastle collier, "Sheaf Crest," a ship of 2,730 tons, which struck a mine in the North Sea and sank. The Polish destroyer picked up the ship's distress signals and was soon on the scene. She saved 17 of the "Sheaf Crest's" crew, some of whom had been seriously injured by the explosion. Here one of the worst cases is being carried ashore in a splint jacket by Polish sailors.

Photo, Keystone

478   *The War Illustrated*   December 18th, 1939

|||||||||||||||||||||||||||||||||||||||||||||||||||||||||||| I WAS THERE ! ||||||||||||||||||||||||||||||||||||||||||||||||||||||||||||

sinking immediately, but the after part apparently grounded. I was thrown on my back and nearly swept overboard by the wash.

"The first boat we tried to launch filled with water, but we managed to lower another, and we helped into it two members of the crew who were wounded. One, a naval rating, had been on the bridge. The explosion had overturned a pile of sandbags on him and his mate. The other man was dead.

"When we had rowed away a bit we saw a Polish destroyer approaching. They took us aboard and also got the dead man off the wreck. There were fourteen of us in the destroyer. I believe some of our mates were picked up by other boats, but we have not seen them."

Nesworthy did not know what had become of the master.

J. J. Baker, the steward of the "Sheaf Crest," who had his arm in a sling, was in the galley cooking dinner when the ship struck the mine. He said :

"I made for the port galley door, but as I was opening it a wash over the ship threw it back and crushed my hand. By this time the galley was filling with water and everything in it was afloat, but I struggled to the starboard door and got out."

We Drifted for a Week Without a Compass

When the Dutch tanker "Sliedrecht" was torpedoed in the Atlantic on November 16, five of her crew drifted for seven days in an open boat before being picked up off the English coast. Here is their story, as told in the "Daily Telegraph."

PETER BRONS, of Vlaardinge, Holland, one of the five survivors of the "Sliedrecht's" crew, stated in hospital that on November 16 the vessel was stopped in the Atlantic by a submarine. It ordered the captain to send over the ship's papers in a small boat for examination.

Brons and four members of the crew rowed to the submarine. After examining the papers the submarine commander said that he would have to sink their ship and gave the crew half an hour to abandon her.

"We told him that we were a neutral ship bound for a neutral port," said Brons, "but it made no difference. He said he would still have to sink us. We then asked him if he would take us on board and transfer us to another ship, but he refused, saying that he had no room.

"Before we returned to our ship he warned us that if we gave any distress signals he would sink us without any further warning. It took us nearly half an hour to return to the 'Sliedrecht' and as we approached we yelled to those on board that the ship was going to be sunk and to man the lifeboat.

"The 26 other members of the crew immediately lowered the boat and scrambled in. Shortly afterwards the submarine fired and there was a terrific explosion. I shall never forget the flame that shot up into the air. In the darkness we lost sight of the other boat.

"We had no compass, but we considered that the wind would blow us towards land. For days the weather was terrible and we were continually bailing water out of the boat. What little food we had quickly disappeared.

"On Wednesday, November 22, the weather improved slightly and we managed to make a sail out of two overcoats. That evening we saw the flash of a lighthouse and knew that at last we were near land.

"We lay off the light during the night in case we were washed against the rocks in the darkness, and in the morning we sighted a trawler. With the little strength that we had left we shouted and attracted the boat's attention. We were taken aboard exhausted and frozen."

An Aeroplane Raced to Our Help

Like many merchant seamen whose ships were torpedoed, the crew of the Norwegian tanker "Arne Kjode" were adrift for many hours in an open boat. More fortunate than some, they were sighted by an aeroplane which sent a ship to their rescue. Their story is here reprinted from the "Star."

WHEN they reached an east coast port on November 20, 12 Norwegian seamen revealed that an aeroplane helped to save them after their vessel, the Norwegian tanker "Arne Kjode," was torpedoed by the Nazis some days ago.

For 55 hours they were adrift in a small open boat which twice capsized. On the second occasion they were left clinging to the sides.

They lost all their food when the boat upset the first time and for two days the 17 men who comprised the original party kept alive on a few drops of water, for there was only a gallon to share between them.

On the third day the boat capsized again, drowning the captain, the steward, and two seamen. The second mate told a vivid story of their sufferings :

"When the boat capsized the second time we were so weak that we could not get in again. Thirteen of us managed to cling to the sides, however, and we were in the water five hours.

"We had given up hope when an aeroplane sighted us and raced back for help.

"I am very hazy about what happened after that because, like all the others, I was 'all in.' I can remember the rescue vessel coming alongside. That would be about two hours after the aeroplane sighted us.

"The bosun let go of the boat and died just as the rescue vessel reached us. That made, with the four drowned earlier five dead out of the 17 who set out."

Twenty-three other survivors of the "Arne Kjode," who escaped in another boat, were landed on November 14.

The Norwegian ship "Arne Kjode" was an oil tanker of 1,600 tons bound from Aruba, West Indies, to Denmark. Above are some of the 23 survivors whose terrible experiences are related in this page. The photograph was taken while they were still on board the Grimsby trawler "Night Hawk" which landed them at a Scottish port.

Photo, Wide World

Skill and Qualification Badges: Navy and Army

The Royal Navy

Chief Yeoman of Signals

Leading Signalman and Signalman

Physical and Recreational Training Instructor 1st Class

Good Shooting Badge

Mechanician

Leading Stoker and Stoker 1st Class

Chief Armourer

Chief Shipwright

Shipwrights and Artisans

Submarine Detector Instructor

Submarine Detector Operator 1st Class

Master at Arms

Writer

Sick Berth Rating

Good Conduct Badges (one to three stripes)

Bugler

Supply Rating

THERE are many more proficiency badges in the Royal Navy than in the Army. The reason is that a warship is a highly complicated piece of machinery for the working of which many skilled men are required. Guns, torpedoes, electrical equipment, signals, the wireless installation and, above all, the engines, can be dealt with only by men with the highest technical qualifications. In recent years, as naval warfare has developed, many new badges have been added, among the most recent being those that are borne by the men engaged in submarine detection. Other proficiency badges are shown in page 415.

The Army

Gunnery Instructor

Drummer of Foot Guards and Bands other than Household Cavalry

Range Finder

Trumpeter

Signaller

Orderly Class I. R.A.M.C.

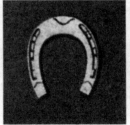

Farrier and Shoeing Smith

Royal Tank Regiment

Riding Instructor

Good Conduct Badges

OUR DIARY OF THE WAR

Friday, December 1, 1939

There were further air raids on Helsinki and other towns.

Finnish communiqué claimed that **all Russian attacks had been repulsed** along the south-eastern frontier, and nearly all on the Karelian Isthmus ; that 1,200 prisoners were captured, a **destroyer sunk by a Finnish coast battery**, 19 tanks destroyed, and at least 16 'planes shot down.

New Finnish Cabinet formed with Dr. Risto Ryti as Prime Minister. Molotov refused to negotiate with it.

Soviet set up a **puppet " Finnish People's Government "** at Terijoki, in the Karelian Isthmus.

President Roosevelt formally condemned the action of Soviet Russia in Finnish territory.

British steamer " Dalryan " mined off South-East Coast.

Finnish steamer " Mercator " mined off Scottish coast.

Norwegian steamer " Realf " reported sunk in North Sea.

Men of third age group liable for service called up.

Announced that a full Royal Australian Air Force squadron would be ready for active service with Coastal Command early in New Year.

Saturday, December 2

Soviet Government signed a Pact of Mutual Assistance and Friendship with the " Finnish People's Government."

Finns claimed that since the invasion **36 Soviet tanks had been destroyed and 19 'planes shot down.**

New Finnish Cabinet submitted an Appeal to the League of Nations.

Anti-Soviet and pro-Finnish demonstrations were made in Rome.

Swedish Government called up reserves.

German Press campaign launched against Sweden.

Reported that a former Grimsby trawler had sunk a U-boat off the East Coast.

British tanker " San Calisto "reported sunk by mine.

German liner " Watussi " was scuttled by her crew after being intercepted by South African Air Force bombers.

Forty-two U-boat prisoners landed at Scottish port.

U.S.A. Government asked for a " moral embargo " on sale by American manufacturers of arms to nations guilty of " unprovoked " bombing from the air.

Sunday, December 3

Finnish resistance to Russian advance continued. Finns claimed that they had **retaken Petsamo.**

Soviet claimed capture of islands of Hogland, Seiskari, Lavansaari and Tytarsaari in Gulf of Finland.

R.A.F. bombers attacked German warships in vicinity of **Heligoland.** Direct hits were obtained with heavy bombs. A Messerschmitt fighter was shot down. All our aircraft returned.

R.A.F. patrol 'plane **destroyed a U-boat** in the North Sea.

Reports were to hand of the destruction of three other U-boats and the capture of a fourth in the Bristol Channel.

Through the Swedish Government the new Finnish Cabinet inquired whether the Soviet Government was prepared to open peace negotiations.

There was minor artillery action on the Western Front.

Swedish steamer " Rudolf" sunk off British coast.

Monday, December 4

The King went to France to make a tour of the British Forces.

Fighting in Finland brought to a standstill by snow.

Finnish Government announced the **decision to fortify the Aaland Islands.**

British Government notified their intention of being represented at the meeting of the League of Nations Council on December 9, when the Finnish Appeal will be considered. Soviet Government refused to attend.

Soviet Government refused Sweden's offer of mediation on grounds that it does not recognize present Finnish Government.

Announced that the British Navy had lost, since the beginning of the war, 4 per cent of her tonnage.

Total number of German merchant ships put out of action from September 3 to December 2 was 33, a total tonnage of 171,390. U-boat losses estimated at a minimum of 30 ; 144 prisoners of war from U-boats interned in this country.

British steamer " Doric Star " sunk by German raider.

Paris reported patrol activity on Western Front.

Tuesday, December 5

The King visited the troops and went up to front line positions.

Helsinki announced that **Finnish 'planes carried out a surprise attack on Soviet air base** at Murmansk, and much damage was done to Russian machines by small incendiary bombs.

It was further claimed that in three days' fighting on the Karelian Isthmus **64 Russian tanks had been taken.** Also that the **Finnish Air Force** had **brought down 24 Russian 'planes** in the past two days.

Evacuation of Helsinki practically complete.

Sweden ordered " partial mobilization."

Germany announced that the former Polish port of Gdynia (called Gotenhafen) is now a naval base.

Report from the Western Front stated that the enemy attempted a number of raids all of which failed.

British steamer " Horsted " sunk by U-boat off East Coast.

Announced that the munitions output had been doubled in past six months and would be doubled again in coming six months.

Wednesday, December 6

Independence Day celebrated by few still in Helsinki. President Roosevelt sent message of sympathy to President Kallio.

Finns retreated slowly to main line of defences in Karelian Isthmus. Elsewhere Soviet troops made little progress.

Fifty aeroplanes have arrived in Finland from Italy. Great Britain and other countries have also dispatched aeroplanes and armaments.

Air Ministry announced **enemy air activity** during preceding night **off East Coast.** Owing to weather conditions, fighter aircraft were unable to make contact.

Wreckage of a Heinkel machine and the body of a German airman were recovered on East Anglian coast.

Enemy machine sighted over Orkneys.

R.A.F. aircraft carried out successful flight over North Germany.

Berlin issued a Note to Foreign Press in which neutral countries, especially Holland, were attacked for lack of resistance to British blockade. Holland later made a semi-official protest against German criticism.

German ship " Ussukuma " captured by British warship in South Atlantic.

Greek steamer " Paralos " sunk in Thames estuary.

Danish steamer " Ove Toft " mined in North Sea.

It Is Said That . . .

Nazis allocated £100,000 to bribe Danish periodicals to turn pro-German.

Old bicycle tires can be used for soling shoes, urged a German broadcaster.

Hitler is taking lessons in strategy, a science of which he is at present ignorant.

" Germany is the only country in Europe where the cost of living has not gone up." (Herr Esser, Nazi State Secretary.)

For every 20 lb. of washing sent to a laundry in Germany, the soap ration card must be delivered.

All church bells in Bavaria have been requisitioned and will be melted down for munitions.

" The effort to unite 15,000,000 German women in one organization has been absolutely successful." (Frau Scholz-Klink, Reich Leader of the German Women.)

" We know that truth will always come out on top. We give nothing, then, but the naked truth." (Goebbels in a speech to Hitler Youth.)

Germany is desperately short of raw materials.

" Every day life seems to become greyer." (Goebbels in a broadcast.)

" The Soviet Government is not at war with Finland." (Molotov, December 4.)

German potato acreage was less this year than in previous years.

The average weight of British child evacuees has increased by about 3½ lb.

Anti-Hitler leaflets are being distributed from some unknown source throughout Bavaria.

German High Command may construct a second Siegfried Line, 40 or 50 miles behind the present one.

Leaflets falling from German 'planes over Luxemburg territory were printed in Arabic as well as French, presumably for soldiers from Tunisia and Algeria.

" Pontius Pilate was the first pacifist because he did not resist evil—the crucifixion of Christ—but washed his hands of it." (Judge Hargreaves.)

Vol. 1   A Permanent Picture Record of the Second Great War   No. 16

Viscount Gort, as Commander-in-Chief of the British Field Force in France, has headquarters of Spartan simplicity. The door of the room in which he works is distinguished only by a piece of card nailed to the door with the letters C.-in-C. on it, and below are the same letters roughly chalked under the panel. Behind that door momentous decisions involving the whole course of the war have been taken—and will continue to be taken as the conflict develops.

Photo, " Match," Paris

Viscount Gort is At Home to His Majesty

Inside the door seen in page 461 Viscount Gort is at work in such plain, matter-of-fact conditions as have been favoured by most of our great generals. His desk is of plain boards supported on trestles. A wire basket for papers, a few books, one of which is the Army List, the carton of a bottle of ink, a rack of notepaper, and a packet and a tin of cigarettes, a few letter clips and a small electric torch—these are the things which may be noted on his desk. The comforts of the room are few and sparse.

Photos, "Match," Paris

THE headquarters of Viscount Gort, Commander-in-Chief of the British Army in France, are at a château just outside a village, and almost hidden from the road by trees. It is in telephonic communication with all parts of the line held by the British Army, with the base and with the French headquarters, so that a constant flow of information comes in that has to be co-ordinated, sifted and made ready for the consideration of the Commander-in-Chief and his staff. Conferences take place there between Lord Gort and his Corps Commanders and between the British and the French Generals, and it is from there that orders emanate regulating the whole routine of the Army.

During the King's visit to France, Viscount Gort accompanied His Majesty on his troop inspections. They are here seen together in the Commander-in-Chief's car setting out for a tour. Right is the entrance to Viscount Gort's headquarters, with an orderly on duty. On the table beside him are the C.-in-C.'s cap and gas mask.

Photo. British Official : Crown Copyright

The King Goes Up The Line

At the beginning of December King George paid a visit to the Front
in France where, as will be seen from this account, he was able to
congratulate the first men of the B.E.F. to be in action.

The King leaving a trench after inspecting
some of the remarkable work that British
troops have done in strengthening the line.

THE Channel was unpleasantly rough
when King George crossed to
France on the afternoon of
December 4, but he remained on the
wave-swept bridge throughout.

The secret of his journey had been well
kept, and when he stepped ashore on
French soil only General Viscount Gort
with a few senior officers, flanked by half
a dozen French soldiers in oilskins and a
handful of gendarmes, were there to meet
him. As he drove away in the C.-in-C.'s
car, a few Frenchwomen waved their
handkerchiefs to cheer him on his way.
It was quite dark when he arrived at
British General Headquarters, where he
was to stay for the next few days as Lord
Gort's guest.

paraded in his honour, and a similarly
vociferous reception was given him as he
drove past troops tramping along the
muddy pavé. That day he lunched in a
corporals' mess established in a village
estaminet, and the *patronne* was all of a
flutter when she learned only just before
the guests arrived that it was the King of
England to whom she was to do the
honours of the house. After a meal of
chicken pie and cheese, His Majesty
continued his tour of inspection until dusk
overtook him while at the quarters of a
Highland regiment. Still wearing their
kilts and with a drum and fife band,
the men presented a fine spectacle, and
they gave the King a wonderful send-off
as he left for the C.-in-C.'s château.

During his visit to the Front the King saw both British and French
troops. Above, a line of British soldiers is cheering His Majesty as
he passes on foot.　Right, he acknowledges the Royal salute of
a guard of French infantry.

Photos, British Official : Crown Copyright

The next day was bitterly cold and
rainy, but the car with the Royal Standard fluttering from the roof drove for
more than 100 miles through the sector
occupied by the British Army. Accompanied by his brother, the Duke of
Gloucester, and Lord Gort, the King
visited an aerodrome, where he chatted
with a group of pilots, many of whom had
just returned from aerial reconnaissances
over Germany. Later in the morning he
visited a 25-pounder battery concealed
under the dripping trees in an orchard,
and tramped through the mud to the gun
pits to meet the crews. Many times during
the day he descended from his car to
walk down the lines of cheering troops

Wednesday,
too, was bitterly
cold, but the sun
came out as the
royal procession
formed up for a
tour of British units. After inspecting long
lines of troops under the command of
Lt.-General A. F. Brooke, he accompanied
Air Vice-Marshal Blount to an R.A.F.
fighter station and chatted some time with
pilots and crews who had recently brought
down German aircraft. Just before lunch
he reviewed a Guards regiment, and took
the salute as they marched past with just
such rigid precision as would be expected
of them on the parade ground close by

Buckingham Palace. After lunch there
were more inspections until darkness fell.

On the next day the King, accompanied by Lord Gort, proceeded to the
zone of the French Army. At lunch in a
little country hotel he was host to M.
Lebrun, President of the French Republic,
and M. Daladier. The afternoon and the
whole of Friday were passed in an
inspection of a sector of the Maginot Line,
in which General Gamelin acted as the

'Somewhere in France' King and President Meet

On December 7, during his visit to the armies in France, King George entertained the President of the French Republic, M. Lebrun, and the French Prime Minister at luncheon. Viscount Gort was also present, and is seen on the right above. Next to him is M. Daladier, and on the King's left is the President. This photograph was taken as the King and President were leaving the hotel in a provincial town in which the luncheon took place. There was no ceremony and no speeches were made, but the King expressed to M. Lebrun his pleasure at being once more on French soil.

Photo, British Official : Crown Copyright

King's guide. King George displayed a keen interest in the fortifications, and at one point spent almost an hour underground ; he rode on one of the trains far below the surface, and watched huge guns being swept into position at the touch of an electric switch.

A little later the King walked to an observation post less than three miles from the German line, and from there looked across at the positions occupied by the enemy. By now it was almost dusk, and the time for the King's visit was drawing to a close. Before he left the French sector, however, he was awarded the Maginot Medal, which is given to all French soldiers who have a part in the defence of France's great fortified line.

So he entered his train on the first stage of his journey back to England, and on the morning of Sunday, December 10, he was once again at his desk in Buckingham Palace. One of his first thoughts was to send a message to Lord Gort.

"I am satisfied from all you have shown me," it read, "that the British soldier of today is at least the equal of his predecessor, both in efficiency and spirit. I send my best wishes to all ranks of the B.E.F. and assure them of the complete and unfailing confidence placed in them by their fellow-countrymen."

It was not until after the King's return that it was revealed that among the troops he had inspected were men who in the last few days had been the first of the British Army to exchange shots with the enemy. They formed part of a force which, under the French High Command, occupied certain forward positions of the Maginot Line. Including battalions from some of the most famous Midland county regiments, this force had already been engaged in one or two skirmishes with the Germans during night patrols.

The men on whom the choice had fallen for this work of active co-operation with our French Allies were justly proud of the honour that had been done them. On the eve of their going into the line the

G.O.C. issued an Order of the Day which deserves to be remembered : " I wish every soldier in this force," it read, " to realize that this moment is an historical occasion. You have been chosen to go into action as the vanguard of the British Army. We shall be in the closest touch with our Allies, who have extended to us the warmest of welcomes. Unless every one of you had done his duty since arrival in France this unique honour would not have been conferred on you. The enemy awaits our arrival with expectancy. The opportunity is yours to maintain and enhance the glorious traditions inscribed on your colours. Be vigilant, keep cool and fire low—to the last round and the last man, and a bit more. The eyes of your country as well as those of your Allies and the whole Empire are on you. With justice on our side, your proud watchwords will be, ' On ne passe pas, on les aura '—' We will stop them, and we will win.' "

All Hands to the Pumps in the Trenches

Day by day since the B.E.F. took over a section of the front line the defences were steadily improved, and many parts of it were changed beyond recognition in the course of a month or two. The work went on regardless of the weather, and though the heavy and continuous rain sometimes made working conditions very unpleasant, the men toiled with unflagging zeal. Here is a typical scene after heavy rain had flooded the excavations, and the water had to be pumped out before work could be resumed.

Photo, British Official: Crown Copyright

Finland's Heroic Resistance Surprises the World

To the surprise of the outside world, but not of the Finnish people themselves, Finland succeeded in putting up a prolonged and desperate resistance to the Russian onslaught. A most effective ally was the winter weather.

WHEN the Russians invaded Finland at the beginning of December they expected a "walk-over." According to a report current in Moscow, it was anticipated that Helsinki would fall in four days, and that the campaign would be over in little more than a week. So confident, indeed, was the Kremlin that the Finns would put up no resistance that M. Molotov, days after the hostilities began, persisted in declaring that there was no war.

Weather and the Finnish will to resist played havoc with the Soviet plans. Long after "President" Kuusinen had hoped to remove his government from Terijoki to Helsinki the bayonets of his supporters had hardly passed the frontier. Nowhere, claimed the Finnish General Staff, did the Russian advance exceed 20

miles, and the Soviet troops were being held all along the line.

In the far north Petsamo was still the scene of a bitter conflict. The weather conditions were terrible. Frost, snow, and ice hampered the attackers, many of whom, so reports ran, were drawn from the warm open regions of central and southern Russia. Miserably clad and ill-equipped, the Red conscripts were blinded by the snow and terrified by the perpetual gloom of the winter forests. As they huddled together for company in the open glades they were mown down by the Finnish machine-gunners, who took advantage of every inch of cover; and when they clustered about their camp fires in the long winter night, they presented an easy target for the Finnish airmen. The Finns for their part were used to such Arctic conditions and they moved across the ground with easy speed on their skis, stopping every now and then to pick off a Russian straggler or to decimate with their automatics little groups of Soviet soldiery.

In central Finland the Russians were able to make some progress by sheer weight of numbers, and fierce fighting developed on the line Kuolajaervi-Suomussalmi-Kuhmo. Here again the Finns had the advantage of defending country whose every inch they knew, and much of the line, too, was based on a string of lakes which proved impassable barriers to the march of the Russian armoured forces. Farther to the south, in the neighbourhood of Lake Ladoga, the Russians made repeated efforts to carry the Finnish positions and so permit of a flanking movement against industrial regions and Helsinki itself, but

In the first two days of war Helsinki suffered heavily from attacks by Russian bombers, but the Finnish anti-aircraft fire was so steady and accurate that the raiders soon desisted. At a conservative estimate they were said to have lost forty aircraft either from anti-aircraft fire or from the activities of the Finnish fighter 'planes. Some of the Russian casualties are illustrated in this page; all the photographs are of Russian bombers brought down in flames in or near Helsinki. Finland's first line air force numbered only 230 warplanes in peacetime, but these included Fokkers, and British Blenheims and Gladiators.   *Photos, G.P.U. & International Graphic Press*

This map shows the physical features of the southern half of Finland, and in particular shows how truly it is called the Land of the Thousand Lakes. The central plateau of the country has an elevation of from 300 to 500 ft. Off the southern coast are many islands of widely differing sizes. Both the rivers and lakes are frozen from December to May.

Specially drawn for THE WAR ILLUSTRATED *by Felix Gardon*

the most violent assault was delivered against the Finnish " Maginot Line,"—the Mannerheim line of defence stretching across the Karelian Isthmus from the Gulf of Finland to Lake Ladoga. Based on some twenty lakes and numerous rivers, this presented a whole series of problems to the Russian tacticians, and so strong was the resistance put up by the defenders that the Russian onset was definitely halted. Far in front of their main defence lines the Finns had constructed a range of movable obstacles which were let down until the tanks had passed, when they were raised so as to cut off their retreat. The tanks were then surrounded and destroyed piecemeal, while the infantry following some way in the rear were dismayed at the loss of their tank supports.

In the course of a few days' fighting more than 100 Russian tanks were put out of action. The Russian infantry attacked time after time in mass formation, but despite their overwhelming superiority in numbers they made little progress. So desperate was the conflict that the Russians were alleged to have used gas in the fighting on the banks of Lake Ladoga, a form of warfare for which the Finns were unprepared. Hurriedly a supply of 60,000 gas masks was ordered from Britain, and it was a distinct relief to find that the snow and cold so condensed the gas as to make it ineffective.

In the air there was no repetition of the attacks on Helsinki, but the Finns —who were now believed to have obtained delivery of a number of British

This photograph adds one more piece of evidence to that given in pages 496 and 497 that Russians bombed Helsinki with complete indifference to where the bombs fell. Here is a small church that has been half-wrecked by a bomb through the roof.   *Photo, G.P.U.*

and Italian warplanes—bombarded Leningrad with leaflets stating the Finnish case, and also dropped bombs on the Soviet aerodrome at Murmansk and on the newly established base at Paldiski in Estonia.

On the air there was a fierce battle between Helsinki and Moscow. Russians were adjured " not to believe what your Bolshevik leaders tell you. Eighteen years ago Lenin promised to respect our frontiers, but Stalin has broken that

on because they know they are fighting for their independence, for the lives of their dear ones, and for their whole future."

While her armies were contesting stubbornly on every front Finland appealed to the League to take notice of the unprovoked attack that had been made upon her by another member of the League. Special sessions were held at Geneva, and from the representatives of almost every State there came expressions of sincerest sympathy.

promise." Swift came the reply from the mouth of Moscow's woman announcer: " Give yourselves up, Finnish soldiers. Revolt against the tyrants. Stab them in the back. Destroy them." Then across the ether came the voice of M. Ryti, Finland's Premier : " Soviet soldiers may kill women and children. They may use poison gas, but the Finnish people will fight

The baby seen top right is being carried into an air raid shelter during one of the Russian raids on Helsinki, while above, children are huddled together as bombs explode outside. Right, is a typical Finnish woman with children evacuated from Helsinki.

The Russian pretence that they were not making war against women and children is shown to be yet another " Red " lie by the photographs in this page. In that immediately above, people of Helsinki, chiefly women, are seeking some sort of protection from the bombs by standing close to a creeper-clad wall. The position they have taken up is probably as safe as any that could be found in the open. Russian airwomen were stated to have taken part in the bombing of the women and children of Helsinki.

Photos, Associated Press and Topical

Close Up to the War with French Patrols

The French Army is now almost completely mechanized, and is particularly strong in tanks. These range from such imposing landships as those seen in page 108 to such small wasps of war as that above. These small landships are manned by one man. This driver is standing on the top of his little landship to look ahead.

Photo, Wide World

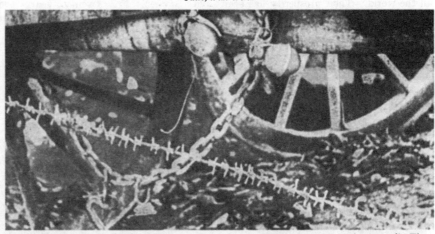

In this war as in the last the Germans have made extensive use of "booby traps." The photograph above actually shows such a trap found by the French, but it has been reproduced by the Nazis as an example of Allied methods of warfare.

This is among the first few photographs of actual fighting by the French Army to be issued for publication. A French soldier with his rifle at the ready keeps watch in a ruined building. He is a veritable "poilu," for he is bearded, and "poilu" means hairy. Most of the French soldiers of today are, however, clean-shaven.

Photo, Keystone

In addition to reporting artillery duels the French communiqués have frequently recorded activity by patrols. Right, a French patrol is making its way through barbed wire doing its dangerous duty of observing the enemy positions. Since the French retired from their advance positions in the Saar sector most of the infantry activity has been of this nature.

Scandinavia is Shaken by War's Thunder

However remote at first the Scandinavian countries might seem from the quarrel, it was not long before even they began to fear that they might become the victims of just such an attack as was delivered on Finland. In this article their concern is analysed.

Not so long ago Scandinavia was the one corner of Europe in which wars never seemed to occur, and to which even the rumours of war hardly seemed to penetrate. It was as peaceful as the Balkans in the opposite corner of the Continent was generally distracted. Today, however, a great change has come about. Neutrals though they be, Norway, Sweden, and Denmark have already suffered heavy losses as a result of the war, and they have watched with undisguised concern the march of Soviet Russia as, not content with seizing half Poland and dominating the Baltic States, she launched an attack on the little cousin of the Scandinavian brotherhood.

All the Scandinavian countries want nothing so much as to live in peace with all the world. Their prosperity has been built up on peaceful commerce; they have never a trace of imperialism, and have kept aloof from the ideological

Now they find themselves threatened not only by Germany but by Soviet Russia. Sweden in particular is apprehensive following the invasion of Finland, and the embers of the age-old hostility of Swede for Russian are being stirred into fresh life. If Finland goes down, then the Russian power will be entrenched on the farther side of the Gulf of Bothnia, and, moreover, the Russian armies will be brought within striking distance of Sweden's rich iron mines behind Lulea. Within the space of a few weeks Russia has seized the control of the Gulf of Finland, and must be turning longing eyes on the Aaland Islands—that archipelago of some 5,000 islands at the north end of the Baltic Sea which might easily constitute a stepping-stone between Finland and Sweden. For twenty years the islands have been in the possession of Finland, and by an international convention they remained unfortified; since

the crisis of 1938, however, the Finns are understood to have begun the work of fortification. If Russia were to occupy the Aaland Islands, then her bombing 'planes would be within a few minutes' flight of Stockholm, Sweden's capital; the shipments of iron ore from Lulea to Germany might easily be interrupted; and Boden, Sweden's Gibraltar at the head of the Gulf of Bothnia, would be in effect outflanked. It was not surprising, then, that when the Finnish territorial waters west of Abo through the Aaland Islands up to the Swedish territorial limits were mined by the Finns, the Swedish naval authorities promptly extended the minefield up to their own coast.

Within sight of Sweden across the Sound is little Denmark, who, still more so than Sweden, is concerned for her fate in a world at war. In the past she has prided herself on being the larder of

Lulea, at the head of the Gulf of Bothnia, is the port from which Sweden's iron ore and lumber are chiefly exported. Its harbour is one of the finest in the North.

conflict. They managed to retain their neutrality during the Great War, but they are finding things far more difficult in 1939.

Although it is probably true to say that the great mass of Scandinavian people, democrats as they are, would like to see the Allies triumph, they fully realize that they live next door to Germany. On the one hand, they are most anxious to maintain their vast trade with the British Isles and the world beyond, but that trade has been made both difficult and dangerous by the Nazi submarines and mines. On the other hand, they have a very considerable trade with Germany and hesitate to do anything to risk a quarrel. Already they have been told by Germany that their neutrality is suspect, and that if they wish to remain in her good graces they must see to it that their ships have no intercourse with blockaded Britain.

For many centuries Sweden has been one of the biggest producers of iron ore in Europe, and in 1937 nearly 15,000,000 tons were extracted. Almost the whole of this was exported, largely to Germany; indeed, Germany would be unable to carry on the war if her supplies of Swedish iron ore were stopped. Among the principal mines are the Kirunavara (seen above), which dominate the town of Kiruna in Swedish Lapland.   *Photos, E.N.A.*

Sweden is one of the most peaceloving of nations, but when Finland was attacked shortly before Christmas in 1939 the Swedes felt that the time had come to put their defences into an efficient state. On the right above, soldiers of the Swedish first line forces are digging trenches on the frontier, and on the left is a car displaying samples of gas masks which formed part of an A.R.P. procession through the streets of Stockholm.
Photos, Keystone and International Graphic Press

Europe, but it does not tend to peace of mind to know that one has the reputation of being fat and well-fed while a great and powerful neighbour is on rations ! Time and again Denmark has protested her complete and utter neutrality, but so long as she endeavours to keep Britain's breakfast tables supplied with butter and eggs and bacon, she is likely to be threatened, and perhaps coerced, by Germany.

Then, to complete the Scandinavian trinity, there is Norway. Of the three she has perhaps the least to fear, but as the owner of one of the world's largest mercantile marines she is subjected to all the strain and stress of the economic war. Moreover, though she faces away from Europe on to the vast open spaces of the Atlantic, the Norwegian peasants in the far north have heard and seen the fighting round Petsamo, and a glance at the map will show that her coast is such as a submarine commander must dream of.

At the beginning of December a bitter attack was made by the official German

News Agency on the Scandinavian countries, who were accused of having not only supported the Versailles Treaty and the League of Nations, but of having fallen more and more under British influence and given many evidences of anti-German sentiment.

In the light of such an attack war became no " far off thing " but a very present possibility. The Stockholm crowds clamoured for action in support of Finland against Russia, the traditional foe of their people, but the military chiefs of the Scandinavian countries had a greater regard for reality. Sweden has an army of about 35,000 men, Norway can muster some 12,500, Denmark has under arms only about 7,000. War material and aeroplanes are on an equally small scale. The total population of the three countries does not amount to 13,000,000. What could these do if it comes to war, in an age in which, even more than in the days of Frederick the Great, " God is on the side of the big battalions " ?

Next door to Germany, Denmark may be excused for feeling decidedly uncomfortable. Above is a camouflaged anti-aircraft gun on the Danish frontier —part of Denmark's preparations to defend her neutrality should she be attacked.

The beautiful photograph on the right shows a vessel of the Norwegian navy moving through an ice-flecked sea. It is one of a little fleet which strives to maintain the neutrality of Norwegian waters.

Photos, International Graphic Press.

This Nazi 'Plane Will Drop No More Mines

The wreckage of the Nazi 'plane which came down (left) off Sheringham on December 6 is being examined by officers of the Royal Air Force after it had been brought up from the beach. The remains of the 'plane were at once surrounded by troops to prevent the activities of souvenir hunters.

When every bit of material had been collected the remains were carried some distance in shore. Below we see soldiers removing all that remained of the fuselage.

Photos, Fox and Associated Press

THE Air Ministry's announcement of the crash of the Nazi raider on the East Coast near Sheringham on December 6 stated : " The wreckage of a German aircraft and the body of a German airman were recovered on the coast of East Anglia early this morning. This aircraft crashed during the night. It is presumed that it had been engaged on mine-laying operations." The aeroplane was heard in the neighbourhood at about 3 a.m., and was over the land just before it crashed. It was a Heinkel reconnaissance aircraft. The body of the pilot, still wearing his helmet, was washed ashore soon after the machine was found, but the other members of the crew were missing.

Above is the aeroplane as it was revealed when daylight came and the tide receded. The coast here is sandy and shelves gradually, so that the machine was in very shallow water. When it crashed the whole of the undercarriage was, in airmen's parlance, "written off." Both engines were missing. They had probably been torn off and sank in deeper water before the wings and fuselage were submerged. The machine was broken in two, but no bullet marks were discovered. It is presumed that engine-trouble was the cause of the crash.

Photo, " Daily Mirror "

Taking the Sting Out of the 'Devil Fish'

Left is a mine that has buried itself in the sands on a Yorkshire beach. The footprints of the man who found it can be seen. Above, the end of a mine. After the detonators have been removed it is exploded from a safe distance.

As soon as a mine is washed ashore, precautions are taken to prevent it being accidentally exploded. Here naval men have performed the delicate task of removing the detonators. After this the charge will be withdrawn and exploded separately. In bad weather and heavy gales even mines properly anchored are liable to break adrift and be washed ashore, and often a large number are adrift.

Photos, top, "News Chronicle"; above, P. Stevens

"Devil Fish" (to Mr. Winston Churchill on his 65th birthday).

Cartoon by Sir Bernard Partridge, by permission of the Proprietors of "Punch"

Unravelling the Tangle of the Balkan Pattern

Not so long ago the Balkans were a byword for disunity, fierce national rivalries, and bitter racial feuds. That time is past. Today the countries of the Balkan peninsula have to put in the background every thought of internecine war through fear of the aggressive designs of their great neighbours.

O N the surface, at least, the political alignment of the Balkan States seems simple enough. First, there is the Balkan Entente, consisting of Rumania, Yugoslavia, Greece, and Turkey, which is primarily concerned with the maintenance of the status quo resulting from the settlement of 1919. Then there is the Peace Front established by Britain and France in the summer of 1939, which includes Rumania, Turkey, and Greece. Outside both these groups is Bulgaria. Then, finally, there is Hungary, which, though geographically not a Balkan country, has many close links with the countries to the south-east.

But this system of alliances conceals a multitude of problems, any one of which in days not long distant might well have given rise to war. Each of the Balkan States has claims to make and claims to resist. To start with the country on the Balkan fringe, Hungary has revisionist aspirations against Rumania; in other words, she hopes that Rumania may agree to a revision of the peace settlement of 1919 that would result in her recovering some at least of the immense territory—Transylvania, Bukovina, and the Banat of Temesvar—which she was compelled to cede following the collapse of the Austro-Hungarian empire. Hungary's claims against Czecho-Slovakia were settled at the time of the Munich Conference, but her satisfaction at the return of Ruthenia was considerably diminished when a year later the Russians occupied the adjoining districts of Poland.

In addition to the territories obtained from Hungary, Rumania at the close of the Great War occupied Bessarabia, a large slice of Russian territory bordering on the Ukraine and reaching from the Black Sea to Poland. There is still further cause for nervousness in that Bulgaria acquiesced with very bad grace in the loss of the Dobruja—that Black Sea region which was seized by the Rumanians in 1913, was restored to Bulgaria in 1918 following Rumania's defeat by the Central Powers, and then later in the year passed into Rumania's possession.

Bulgaria (always inclined to a pro-Russian and Pan-Slav policy) has thus a territorial grievance against Rumania, and there is, moreover, abundant fuel for friction with Greece in the feuds of the Macedonian tribes of the borderland, not to mention Bulgarian aspirations for the establishment of a territorial "corridor" reaching to the Aegean.

Of Greece and Turkey it may be said that they are more or less satisfied with the present distribution of territory, and so, too, is Yugoslavia.

Italy's Growing Influence

There remains Albania—and Albania since Good Friday, 1939, has been an Italian possession. Indeed, it is regarded in the Balkans as the spearhead of Italian aggression, and most of the countries live in dread of further efforts at Italian expansion, military, economic, and political. Italian influence is manifested as far north as Hungary, and in December 1939 the suggestion was mooted that the "Kingdom without a king" should be placed under the aegis of the Italian crown. About the same time Marshal Balbo made the definite claim that the Balkan peninsula, historically and geographically, enters into the Italian sphere of influence. Russia and Germany were thus both alike "warned off," but Balbo went on to make it plain that "Bucharest must meet Hungarian needs" as the price of Italian support against the Soviet.

Rumania, it will be seen, finds herself in an intensely difficult position; with so many offers of protection she may well fear for her national integrity. For years past Germany has openly coveted her oil and wheat, and now that the bayonets of Red Russia have put a stop to the German advance on the Ukraine, it is not surprising that the Nazis are turning their attention to the route to the Black Sea. The assassination of M. Calinescu by Iron Guards on September 21, 1939 (*see* page 136), was generally believed to have been staged so as to afford Germany an excuse for armed intervention. Fortunately for Rumania, the Reich had its hands full at the time with the Polish question; and it was distinctly naïve on the part of the Nazi propagandists to discover that the murder was the work of members of the British Intelligence Service! At the same time there was no slackening in the pressure designed to wring from Rumania economic concessions.

Nervous as she was of Germany, Rumania might feel even deeper concern over the intentions of Soviet Russia, particularly when the organ of the Communist International in Moscow declared that Rumania must immediately sign a pact of mutual aid with the U.S.S.R. on the same lines as those recently concluded with the Baltic States. It was easy to imagine the kind of demands which Russia would make as the price of her friendship; almost certainly they would include the cession of Bessarabia with control over the mouth of the Danube, and possibly the right to establish naval bases on the Rumanian coast. "Conditions in Bessarabia are unbearable," declared the Comintern organ, "therefore there is a possible Soviet claim to rescue her oppressed brothers." The paper went on to insist that there was popular discontent not only in Bessarabia, but also in Transylvania and the Dobruja, which formerly belonged to Hungary and Bulgaria respectively. Rumanian official circles declared that there was no change in the situation, but the fact remained that from the borders of Hungary to the Bosporus there was deep apprehension of what the morrow might bring.

"WHAT, ME? NO, I NEVER TOUCH GOLDFISH"
Cartoon by Illingworth. Courtesy of the "Daily Mail"

There's a Place in the Line for the Air Cadets

Above, model aircraft of a very advanced type are being constructed by a group of Air Defence Cadets ; right, another detachment of volunteers, who have changed their smart uniforms for serviceable overalls ; learn the principles and working of a big radial aero-engine in the workshop.
Photos, Fox

Pride of squadron is shown by every one of these lads on parade.   Down the lines is carried their newly dedicated colour, borne by an R.A.F. officer marching with an escort of Air Cadet sergeants. The similarity of the Cadets' uniform to that of the R.A.F. will be noted ; the belt, however, incorporates a special buckle, and on the forage cap is a badge.   *Photo, John Topham*

THE credit for the inception of the Air Defence Cadet Corps goes to the Secretary-General of the Air League of the British Empire, Air Commodore J. A. Chamier, who realized the demand existing amongst the air-minded youth of Britain for an organization which would combine service to the country with practical instruction. Although formed less than two years before the war, such was the immediate success of the new Corps that it numbered at the beginning of December 1939 more than 20,000 boys, all between the ages of 14 and 18.

The cadets are organized in 174 squadrons raised locally at centres all over the country. The importance of the service done by the lads in assisting at R.A.F. aerodromes, doing guard duty, acting as A.R.P. messengers and the like, led to the taking over of some of the squadrons by the R.A.F., which now feeds, transports and pays them. Previously the Air Defence Cadet Corps had been an entirely non-Government organization—although its work had always met with the approval of the Air Ministry—and its members had to contribute towards its funds. The training includes airmanship, drill, and discipline, with technical instruction wherever possible.

Helsinki Feels the Force of the So

The two photographs above were taken immediately after the raids of Russian bombers on Helsinki, on Thursday, November 30, 1939. That at the top of the page shows a street scene in the Finnish capital. Incendiary bombs have been dropped and motor-cars set on fire. Petrol tanks have been blown up, and sheets of flame arise from the streets. In the lower photograph men and women are coming out into the streets once more to find them blocked by the debris resulting from the dropping of high-explosive bombs.

gan: 'Workers of the World Unite!'

This is a close-up view of one of the cars set on fire by an incendiary bomb. Most of the bombs dropped were incendiary, and it was fortunate indeed that many of the buildings in Helsinki are constructed of fire-resisting materials.

The effect of Russian bombs is seen again in the photograph above. One building has been demolished and another is in flames. The heat engendered by the incendiary bombs kindles a fire so fierce that it is difficult to extinguish. Following the raids on Helsinki on November 30 and the following day, it was officially announced that 80 people, mostly women and children, had been killed. Many of the bombs dropped by Russian aircraft on Helsinki and other Finnish towns fell on the homes of working people.

WORDS THAT HISTORY WILL REMEMBER

(Continued from page 466)

Finland's Proposal to Submit to Arbitration

Tuesday, November 28, 1939

Reply of FINNISH GOVERNMENT to Russian demand for withdrawal of troops from frontier near Leningrad.

It is established that the discharge of cannon shots mentioned in your communication did not take place on the Finnish side. Investigation showed instead that on November 26 between 3.45 p.m. and 4.5 p.m. firing occurred on the Russian side of the frontier in the vicinity of Mainila, the place mentioned by you. . . .

Therefore it is our duty to deny, protest and establish the fact that from the Finnish side no hostile action towards the Soviet Union has taken place. It should be pointed out that on the Finnish side of the frontier only frontier guards are stationed, and there is no artillery whose range would reach the other side of the frontier.

Consequently, although this is no concrete reason to remove our troops from the frontier line in the manner you suggested, the Government is nevertheless ready to negotiate with the Soviet Union on the proposal with the intention that troops be removed from both sides to a fixed distance from the frontier.

The Finnish Government has noted with satisfaction your intimation that the Soviet Government does not intend to exaggerate the importance of the frontier incident which they, according to your communication, believed at the time had taken place.

In order that no obscurity whatever may remain in any circumstances, the Finnish Government suggests that the Karelian Isthmus Frontier Commission be instructed jointly to investigate in the manner regulated by the treaty of October 24, 1938, concerning frontier demarcation.

Soviet Premier Bitterly Attacks Finnish Leaders

Wednesday, November 29

M. MOLOTOV in a broadcast to the Soviet peoples :

The hostile policy of the present Finnish Government compels us to take immediate steps to safeguard the external security of our State. You all know that the Soviet Government had patiently negotiated on certain proposals which, in view of the present international tension, the Soviet considered to be the minimum guarantee for the safety of our country, and in particular Leningrad. During these negotiations the Finnish Government adopted an irreconcilable attitude towards our country. Instead of attempting to find a friendly basis for an understanding, the present leaders, acting in the interests of foreign imperialists and warmongers, who are the enemies of the Soviet Union, elected to take a different course.

It is well known where this has led. There has been abominable provocation by the Finnish military on the Finnish-Soviet frontier during the past few days. Our soldiers were even shelled by artillery near Leningrad, and heavy casualties were caused among the Red troops. Our efforts to prevent a repetition of such provocations by practical proposals put to Finland have met with no response, and even evoked a hostile attitude in Finnish leading circles.

As you all know from yesterday's Soviet Note, the Finns have replied by rejecting our proposals and by denying established facts. They have even jeered at our victims. Their reply shows their undisguised desire to continue their threat to Leningrad. All this has made it quite clear that the present Finnish Government, who are entangled in anti-Soviet commitments to foreign imperialists, do not wish to maintain normal relations with the Soviet Union. They show no desire to comply with the provisions of the Non-Aggression Pact, and want to keep our glorious Leningrad under military threat.

From such a militarist Government we can expect nothing but fresh impertinent provocation. The Soviet Government were therefore compelled yesterday to declare that they do not consider themselves any longer bound by the Non-Aggression Pact.

In view of fresh attacks by Finnish troops on the frontier our Government found themselves compelled to take new decisions. We can no longer tolerate the present situation, for which the Finnish Government bear full responsibility. Our Government have decided that they can no longer maintain normal relations with Finland and have considered it necessary to recall their diplomatic representatives. Furthermore, the High Command of the Red Army has ordered the Army and Navy to be in readiness for any eventuality in order to prevent possible fresh provocation by the Finnish military.

These measures have not been taken, as has been alleged abroad, with a view to violating Finnish independence or annexing Finnish territory. This is a perfidious calumny. We have no such intentions. . . .

It has also been alleged that our measures are directed against Finnish independence, and that they constitute an interference with Finnish domestic and foreign policy. This is also a malicious calumny. We regard Finland as an independent and sovereign State, whatever her regime may be.

We consider that the Finnish people are entitled to decide themselves all matters of foreign and domestic policy in the way they deem necessary. The peoples of the Soviet Union have done what was necessary for the independence of Finland. The peoples of our country are prepared to assist the Finnish people in securing a free and independent development. . . . The only aim of our nation is to safeguard the security of the Soviet Union, and in particular of Leningrad, with its population of 3,500,000.

In view of the present international situation, which is extremely tense as a result of the war, we could not make the solution of this vital and urgent question conditional upon the bad faith of the present Finnish leaders. This matter must be solved by the Soviet Union in friendly co-operation with the Finnish people. Only the successful solution of the problem of the safety of Leningrad can lead to a new era of friendship between the Soviet Union and Finland.

Russia's Indefensible Act of Aggression

Thursday, November 30

Mr. CHAMBERLAIN in the House of Commons :

The House will be aware that for some time past there has been an exchange of views between the Soviet Government and the Finnish Government on certain questions, mainly of a strategic character, raised by the former. Some apprehension had been expressed by the Soviet Government at the proximity of Leningrad to the Finnish frontier, which is, in fact, only some 20 miles distant, and a proposal was made by them for the relinquishment of that part of the frontier in exchange for territorial compensation farther north.

Further claims were also made for the acquisition of certain Finnish islands in the Gulf of Finland and of a Finnish port at the entrance of the gulf in order, it was stated, to assure the position of the Soviet Union in the Gulf of Finland. . . .

The attitude of the Finnish Government was from the outset unprovocative, though governed by the determination to do nothing which would impair their country's sovereign status. It is known that the Finnish note delivered in Moscow immediately before the announcement of the rupture of diplomatic relations was of a most conciliatory character.

The Finnish Government proposed to submit the dispute to arbitration and offered meanwhile to withdraw all troops from the Finnish frontier in the Karelian Isthmus with the exception of the ordinary frontier guards and Customs forces. Nevertheless the Soviet Government on Tuesday night denounced the Soviet-Finland non-aggression pact, which had been expressly designed to ensure the settlement of disputes such as this by peaceful means.

His Majesty's Government have observed this development with increasing concern and have found it difficult to believe that strategic measures of such scope and importance as were suggested should have been considered necessary to protect the Soviet Government against a country as small as Finland.

Late last night M. Molotov broadcast a statement, in the course of which he is officially reported as having denied the suggestion, which he attributed to the foreign Press, that a Soviet attempt on Finland was intended. Yet only a few hours after this broadcast it is understood that Soviet forces have invaded Finnish territory on several sections of the frontier and have dropped bombs in the vicinity of Helsinki. It is later reported that Helsinki, Viborg and other centres have been bombed, in some cases with loss of life.

His Majesty's Government warmly welcomed the offer of mediation made by the United States Secretary of State, because in their opinion the questions at issue between Finland and the Soviet were not of a nature to justify warlike measures. They deeply regret this attack on a small independent nation, which must result in fresh suffering and loss of life to innocent people.

Words of Condemnation from U.S.A.

Friday, December 1

PRESIDENT ROOSEVELT in a statement at a Press Conference :

The news of the Soviet naval and military bombings within Finnish territory comes as a profound shock to the Government and people of the United States.

Despite efforts made to solve the dispute by peaceful methods to which no reasonable objection could be offered, one Power has chosen to resort to force of arms. It is tragic to see the policy of force spreading and to realize that wanton disregard for the law is still on the march.

All peace-loving peoples, those nations that are still hoping for a continuance of relations throughout the world on the basis of law and order, will unanimously condemn this new resort to military force as the arbiter of international differences.

To the great misfortune of the world the present trend towards force makes insecure the independent existence of the small nations of every continent and jeopardizes the rights of mankind to self-government.

The people and Government of Finland have a long, honourable, and wholly peaceful record which has won for them the respect and warm regard of the people and Government of the United States.

The Christmas Spirit: in '39 as in '14

The British Expeditionary Force of 1939 is better fed than any British Army has ever been, and every man will have a first-rate Christmas dinner. Besides that, there will be the little extras from home, and above, left, sweets, biscuits, tobacco and other small comforts are being packed. Right, Christmas puddings are being packed at a depot at Reading. *Photos, Topical*

ONE of the most remarkable incidents of the last war was the unofficial truce observed between the British Army and the German Army at Christmas 1914. This year there can be no fraternization with the Nazi Army, but Christmas will be kept up in the real British way under far better conditions than in 1914. An idea of what sort of Christmas it is to be for the men can be gathered from this typical menu for the R.A.F. The dinner includes: Crême of tomato soup; fried fillet of sole and lemon; roast turkey; roast pork and apple sauce; roast potatoes; cauliflower; Christmas pudding with brandy sauce.

The Christmas spirit of 1914 is shown in the centre photograph, where a British soldier gives an old lady the traditional salute under mistletoe gathered in an orchard near by. For the first Christmas of the last War Princess Mary, now the Princess Royal, inaugurated a fund to send chocolates and cigarettes to men at the Front, and above, right, the Princess's gifts are being distributed. King George and Queen Mary sent Christmas cards to all the troops as the King and Queen are doing this year. Left, the cards of 1914 are being handed to the recipients. *Photos, L.N.A.*

The Wartime Theatre Defies the Black-out

One of the unexpected happenings of the war has been the early discovery of the tonic value of theatrical entertainment both at home and at the Front. The theatre's triumphant assertion against every sort of difficulty is strangely in contrast with the state of affairs in 1914-1918.

MORE effective than the most gorgeous gala performance was the informal visit of the King and Queen to "Black Velvet" at the London Hippodrome, and their cheery "send-off" at a Drury Lane rehearsal of companies bound for "Somewhere in France." These gave royal sanction to the living drama as a wartime necessity, and so happy a gesture could hardly have been more timely or better deserved. Alike, the vitality of the theatre and the popular need for it have come as a surprise in more than one official quarter.

London Theatres Crowded Again!

The greatest surprise of all has been in London itself. There seemed little hope for the stage anywhere when the order went out, on the declaration of war, that "every place of public assembly" was to be closed. Whatever happened, one felt that this was going to be the end of the West End theatres. The gradual withdrawal of restrictions has proved all such prophecy false. In spite of darkness, "staggered" hours, shut tube-stations and empty homes and offices—not to mention the still valid air-raid threat— what do we find? Here, after three months, are thirty London theatres welcoming crowded audiences, twenty-three of them in the West End! This is not merely "back to normal," but considerably better—generally there is a lull just at this time on the brink of the holiday season. Where the folk come

from, and how they get back, is their own secret. Enough that there they are, filling every seat at the favoured shows both for evening and matinée performances, or twice nightly. The queues have been lengthened as the promised Christmas leave began to operate, and husbands, brothers, and sweethearts came back from France eager for charm and jollity.

In the provincial towns, both large and small, the record is much the same. It is true there is not the same reason for astonishment. To hosts of evacuees, who have not had time to make many new friends, a lively and inspiring play is a godsend. Already over eighty companies touring drama, comedy, musical plays and revues are doing their best to keep the wartime public in heart. So also are at least thirty resident repertory companies. The preference is undoubtedly for light musical shows. For the time being, at any rate, it is only natural that most people should want to forget their anxieties. But trivialities have by no means a monopoly. Mr. Priestley's "Music at Night" at the Westminster— the first serious play to be presented in wartime—has done remarkably well. "Julius Caesar" (in modern dress), the Old Vic company in "Romeo and Juliet," "The Corn is Green," "Dear Octopus," "Design for Living," "Lady Precious Stream," "Whiteoaks," "Robert's Wife," and "The Importance of Being Earnest" —plays like these, already running or in prospect, show that there are plenty of

people whose taste is by no means confined to what the late Henry Arthur Jones used to call "legs and tomfoolery."

There remains the greatest achievement of all—the sending out by "N.A.A.F.I." (Navy, Army and Air Force Institutes) and "E.N.S.A." (Entertainments National Service Association) of a score of companies to play to the troops in France. It is good to know that the number is to be increased each week until every member of His Majesty's Forces is in reach of the mental relief and invigoration that only a good theatrical performance can give. This is not counting the shows that "N.A.A.F.I." has presented, and "E.N.S.A." produced for camps and ports at home. Up to the end of 1939 Mr. Basil Dean, who has converted Drury Lane into a hive of theatrical industry under "N.A.A.F.I.'s" auspices, calculates that a million men have been entertained.

The Theatre Goes to the Forces

The productions are of every kind, from Mr. Ralph Reader and his "Gang" of Scouts, who go right up the line, to the mixed concert-parties of "stars" under Mr. Leslie Henson and Sir Seymour Hicks, and, last of all, the dramas and comedies. Of these "Eight Bells," "Who Killed the Count?" "Almost a Honeymoon," and "Heroes Don't Care" are the first choice. They do not exactly compare, perhaps, with the offerings of the Comedie Française to the French war-theatre. But they are a beginning.

All these productions are, it should be said, sent out from Drury Lane complete, with scenery, lighting apparatus and, if necessary, the actual stage. Before Christmas the Drury Lane scene-dock was bright with some highly-coloured Chinese settings destined for a war-pantomime of "Aladdin," which was prepared by Mr. Leslie Henson for France.

Altogether, our stage has proved itself far more alive than it was twenty-five years ago. Then there was no immediate suppression, no "black-out," no competition of films and radio. Yet, so far as the general public were concerned, the first season just petered out; and the whole four years gave us little else but "Chu Chin Chow," "The Passing Show," and "The Bing Boys." As for the troops, it was not until the splendid endeavours of Miss Lena Ashwell and Mr. Basil Dean himself bore fruit in 1915–1916, that anything regular was done. Meanwhile, we have learned the truth of what Matthew Arnold said when Bernhardt came over during the Franco-Prussian war: "The theatre is irresistible; organize the theatre."

In the wartime theatre a particularly bright spot is the work of E.N.S.A. (Entertainments National Service Association), which has its headquarters at Drury Lane Theatre. When this photograph was taken on the stage of this famous old London theatre, the King and Queen were being introduced to members of Mr. Leslie Henson's Gaieties, who were busily rehearsing just before leaving for France. Her Majesty is talking to Miss Binnie Hale (left) and Miss Violet Lorraine.   *Photo, L.N.A.*

Over Thirty-five but Not Too Old to Serve!

These men who have answered their country's call are too old for the fighting line, but as their medal ribbons show they have fought before and know that the soldier's first duty is to keep his rifle clean. The soldier right was the oldest man present at a parade of the A.M.P.C. He is W. H. Drewett, from South Wales, and still is as smart a soldier as men half his age.

ON November 10, 1939, recruiting was opened for a new Corps—the Auxiliary Military Pioneer Corps, consisting of men from 35 to 50 years of age, to take part in such work as bridge-building, the construction of railways, trenches and fortifications. The response was excellent, and by December more than a thousand men trained at an East Coast resort were ready for service overseas.

The over 35's undergo their training at what was once a holiday camp on the East Coast, and in the centre photograph some of them are setting out on a route march, proud to show that they have lost none of the soldierly qualities that they carried with them into civilian life in 1918. In the lower photograph is the Sergeants' Mess in what was once the cocktail bar of the holiday camp. The yarns that are exchanged there are chiefly reminiscences of the last war.

Photos, Fox

WE HAVE THE MEN—WE HAVE THE 'PLANES

When he spoke in the House of Commons on December 12, the Air Minister, Sir
Kingsley Wood, had a very encouraging report to make on the opening of what he
called the second chapter of the war in the air.

"WHEN I made my last statement to the House on October 10," said Sir Kingsley Wood, "we had not yet been able to test out in actual operations the state of preparedness of our air defences. But already this first chapter of the war in the air was drawing to its close, and I should date the beginning of the second chapter with the raid on warships in the Firth of Forth by German aircraft on October 16." Sir Kingsley went on:

Since that date, though we have still had no great aerial battles, no encounter of armadas in the air, there has been steadily increasing activity. We have had to deal with a series of reconnaissances and raids over this country—some by single aircraft, and some in force—and we have thus been able to test out the strength of our defences and the efficiency of our organization.

We have also, both in this country and in France, been able to try out our aircraft in combat with the enemy.

The results, and the conclusions which we have been able to draw from them, though of necessity provisional, are certainly encouraging.

We have been able to satisfy ourselves by actual operations that the various elements of our air defences, the anti-aircraft guns and searchlights, the fighter squadrons, the balloon barrages for close defence, and the units of the observer corps have been successfully welded into an efficient and adaptable system under the operational control and command of one Commander-in-Chief. . . .

In this great organization every element is manfully playing its part—the Territorial units manning the guns and searchlights and, by no means least, if I may single them out for special mention, the personnel of the balloon barrage and of the observer corps. . . .

Superiority Over German Fighters

OUR fighter squadrons, Regular and Auxiliary alike, have taken a heavy toll of such of the enemy as have tried to cross our air defences, and **we can, I am certain, justifiably claim a definite superiority in our aircraft over the Germans.** Our Hurricanes and Spitfires have been in contact with Dornier, Junkers, and Heinkel bombers, and there can be no doubt that they possess a decisive margin of advantage.

Even more encouraging, I think, is the knowledge of the superiority that they have shown over the German fighters. Not only have they twice the gun-power of the Messerschmitt, but they have markedly better flying characteristics, and are superior both in control and manoeuvrability at high speeds.

At sea the ceaseless watch of the Coastal Command continues in the freezing winds and sleet of winter. . . . Every day they escort the many convoys which are constantly on the move, and in the course of their flights they have on many occasions encountered and shot down enemy aircraft.

They have carried out attacks on submarines on 57 occasions, and in 19 cases we can be sure that substantial damage has been caused. **Every month over 1,000,000 miles are flown! Every day a distance that is greater than the circumference of the globe.**

Perhaps I could instance the achievements of one squadron which are typical of many. Since the outbreak of war this squadron—No. 269—though only formed just three years ago, has flown 3,000 hours on long-distance tasks over the sea by day and by night.

Its aircraft have already travelled nearly 500,000 miles, an average of 6,700 miles a day

since the start of hostilities. They have brought in detailed reports for safety and contraband purposes on some 700 merchant vessels; they have sighted seven enemy submarines and carried out attacks on five occasions. Their motto is "Omnia Videmus" (We see everything)—a motto that is fully justified. . . .

In the Bomber Command, too, the units have added to their laurels, and **the recent attack on German warships at Heligoland was yet another of the fine offensive actions of the war. It was a particularly difficult and dangerous operation, requiring skill, daring, and resolution,** but our bombers reached their objectives successfully, registered direct hits with heavy bombs on the enemy, and returned safely.

It is significant that in the course of this flight the aircraft were engaged by some 20 Messerschmitt fighters, and the two of these which pressed home their attack were driven down and one of them certainly destroyed. This, I think, is a very striking tribute to the formidable gun defences of our bombers.

Over Germany Again and Again

RECONNAISSANCES over Germany have been continued, and our aircraft have visited Hamburg, Bremen, the Ruhr, Berlin, Munich and Nurnberg in succession, and in many cases on more than one occasion. Conditions are more difficult now, but our men have stood up to the elements in the same spirit of daring as they have faced the fire of anti-aircraft batteries and the fighters sent up by the enemy. Of the value of these flights there can be no doubt, and the Germans have paid us the significant compliment of copying our ideas.

The Royal Air Force units in France have been greatly encouraged by the visit of his Majesty the King, and are carrying out yeoman service. They have adapted themselves with

the greatest cheerfulness to the very different conditions of service, and they are working everywhere in the closest comradeship with the French.

Everywhere the morale of our Air Force is magnificent. **We have a definite superiority over the Germans in the initiative and skill of our pilots,** and it is, I am sure, no cause for surprise that nearly one-third of the men who are now registering are expressing a preference for service in the air.

AFTER referring to the contributions to the Empire's air strength that are being made by and in the Dominions, the Air Minister proceeded:

As regards the important matter of production, I am glad to say that the mere numerical output today is more than twice what it was a year ago, and that the types that are now passing from the factories to units represent not only in man hours of construction but also in their efficiency as weapons of war not a twofold but a manifold accretion of strength.

I said at the beginning of my account today that we were now in the second chapter of the war in the air. That in its turn may be drawing to a close, and we must be prepared to face, perhaps soon, perhaps in the spring, another and more strenuous and difficult chapter.

It is clear that we must continue unceasingly in all our efforts and extend them; and we must not for a moment relax the state of our preparedness.

But we can be confident that our air defence system is sound, that our personnel and aircraft are superior to the enemy's, and that our strength, defensive and offensive, is growing steadily so that every day we are in a better position to establish our ascendancy in the air.

This remarkable photograph was obtained by a coastguard watching from the shores of the Thames Estuary. A German minelaying aircraft, apparently a large Dornier DO24 flying boat, has been caught full in the powerful beam of one of the defensive searchlights. Always alert, our defences give short shrift to any marauder that does not immediately turn tail.
Photo, G.P.U.

Picture-Diagram of a Heligoland Bomber-Raider

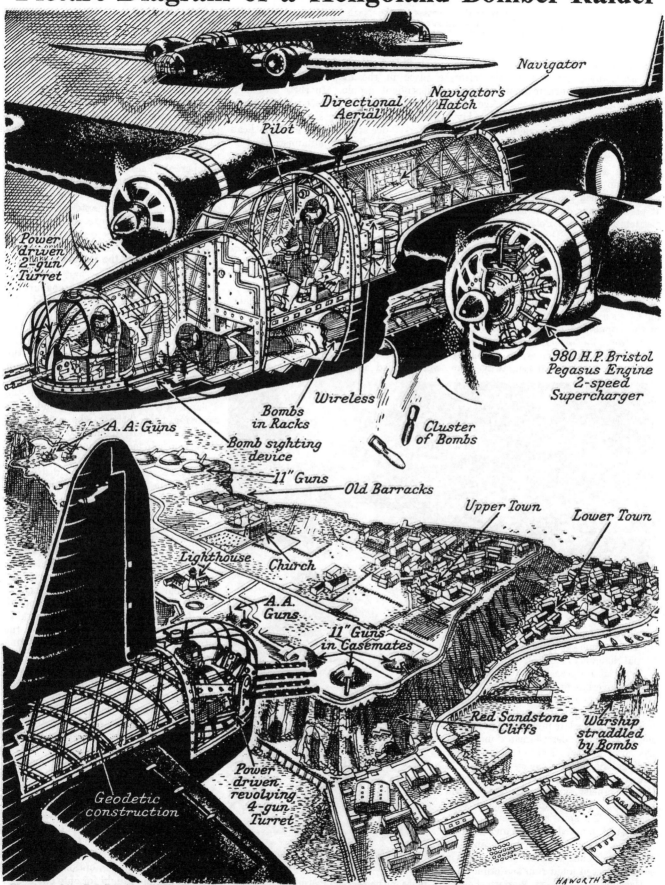

Navigator

Navigator's Hatch

Directional Aerial

Pilot

Power driven 2-gun Turret

Wireless

980 H.P. Bristol Pegasus Engine 2-speed Supercharger

Bombs in Racks

Cluster of Bombs

A.A. Guns

Bomb sighting device

11" Guns

Old Barracks

Upper Town

Lower Town

Lighthouse

Church

A.A. Guns

11" Guns in Casemates

Red Sandstone Cliffs

Warship straddled by Bombs

Geodetic construction

Power driven revolving 4-gun Turret

HAWORTH

The story of the R.A.F. raid on Heligoland (December 3) shows it to have been the most successful offensive air operation yet carried out during the war. The aircraft employed were of the twin-engined Vickers-Armstrongs "Wellington" type, already famed for its part in the September 4 raid on the Kiel bases. The "Wellington" is one of the largest of R.A.F. aircraft, yet its speed—a maximum of 265 m.p.h.—compares favourably with any of the world's bombers, and it can fly up to 3,240 miles non-stop. Beneath the cutaway diagram specially prepared for THE WAR ILLUSTRATED of the "Wellingtons" may be seen features of their objective, the island base of Heligoland.

Specially drawn by Haworth

'We are Masters: As Masters We Behave'

So foul were the excesses of the Nazis in German-occupied Poland that even the Prussian officers entrusted with the military occupation of the country were reported to have been filled with disgust. Below we mention some of the features of the Terror that aroused almost universal reprobation.

IN the history of the Polish people there are many chapters filled with terror and gloom, but there is not one which can compare with that whose pages are being written in the Poland of today. "Never before in modern history," declared General Sikorski, the Prime Minister of the Polish Government in Exile, in a statement to Lord Halifax, "not even during periods of the fiercest wars, have such grim events occurred as at present occur daily in Poland. In all districts of Western Poland leading citizens in the life of the nation are being shot one after the other, and their names are whispered throughout the horrified country over their silent graves.

"From all parts of the country occupied by Germany reports are arriving which fill us with horror. While the property of the population is being seized on the spot from its owners who are being evicted from their homes, so the entire population is being driven away from

vast and ancient Polish areas, and human life has become the sport of ferocious and bestial hangmen."

At a later date, he continued, "The Polish Government will publish a White Book tabulating the cruelties which have come to its cognizance, but it considers it its duty to declare immediately that the soil of Poland under German domination has become the soil of martyrdom. National Socialist savagery is writing a new and ominous page in the history of German cruelty, which by slaughter of the helpless outdoes the darkest memories of the past. The spirit of conquest and robbery which marked in blood and destruction the march of Germany throughout the centuries has come to life again and is sowing its seed amid ruin and crime."

Germany's object in Western Poland is obviously so to crush out all Polish national sentiment and destroy every focus of Polish culture that it will be

impossible for the Poles ever again to find a place in the map of Europe as an independent people. In their own land the Poles are now reduced to the condition of serfs, if not slaves. "We are masters," declared Herr Uebelhör, head of the Nazi district administration at Lodz; "as masters we must behave. The Pole is a servant here and must only serve. Blind obedience and ruthless fulfilment of orders must be enforced. We must inject a dose of iron into our spinal columns, and never admit the idea that Poland may ever arise again here."

To convince his hearers that the glory of Poland was departed, and departed for ever, the monument of the Polish national hero Kosciusko which stood in Liberty Square (now Adolf Hitler-Platz) in Lodz was blown up by Nazi engineers, and other Polish historical monuments were treated with similar contumely.

Some 300,000 Polish prisoners of war were carried away into Germany to be

In the top photograph Polish prisoners are being marched off to East Prussia, where they will work practically as slaves for Nazi masters. Above is Dr. Frank, the organizer of this new form of white slavery.

Photos, E.N.A. and International Graphic Press

formed into agricultural labour-gangs for work on the land, and it was given out in Germany that at least 4,000,000 Germans were to be settled in the provinces seized from Poland and incorporated in the Reich. As the territories in question were already over-populated, it was obvious that a corresponding number of Poles would have to be got rid of some way or another, and soon the victors had embarked upon a process of expropriation and extermination of the landowning classes recalling the worst days of the Bolshevik revolution.

Enslaving the Populace

Dr. Hans Frank, the first Governor-General of German Poland, took up his quarters in Cracow on November 11, the day which is celebrated in Poland as Independence Day. Not content with this exhibition of tactlessness, Dr. Frank delivered to the Poles gathered in the Royal Chamber of the castle an oration in which he condemned the "barbarous persecutions" of the Germans in the Poland of yesterday, and concluded by asserting that "those who oppose our creative work are doomed to perish, but those who help may live quietly and work."

One of the new Governor-General's first decrees made a sharp distinction between the Germans and the native Poles; the former were given privileges of every kind, while the latter were stigmatized as belonging to an inferior and altogether subject race. A dual police control was instituted, for Poles and Germans respectively; and another decree introduced a universal labour service for the whole Polish population, women as well as men, between the ages of 17 and 45.

A few days after Dr. Frank's installation a special tribunal was set up in the city to deal with cases of Poles resisting the Germanization of the country, and large numbers of Gestapo inquisitors and spies were let loose on the population. Priests, professional men, officers and prominent landowners were arrested wholesale. At the same time the campaign of systematic looting and seizure of plant and materials was intensified.

What Germanization means may be gathered from the steps which were taken in Lodz. There the names of the streets were Germanized, Polish shop signs were taken down, and Polish newspapers forbidden to appear. Polish schools were abolished, all Polish text books were withdrawn from circulation, and the Polish language was made an optional subject in the curriculum, taught for only one hour a week. So in 1939 the apostles of Nazi Kultur repeated the worst excesses of the Tsarist tyranny of generations before.

'Graf Spee' is Brought to Bay

On December 8, 1914, "Admiral Graf von Spee" went down with his flagship at the Falkland Is. Twenty-five years later the "Admiral Graf Spee" badly battered was driven into port on the same coast.

The scene of the first considerable sea battle of the second Great War, fought in the same waters as those in which Von Spee went down twenty-five years earlier.

FOR a hundred days of war the pocket battleships that were the pride of Nazi Germany's fleet sailed the vast open spaces of the ocean, and the only news of their voyagings was contained in the brief messages which stated that yet another merchant ship had been sent to a watery grave. Now it was the "Deutschland" that set the cables buzzing; then it was the "Admiral Scheer"; then, but more rarely, the newest of the "pocket battleship" trio, "Admiral Graf Spee." All the world knew that these ships, amongst the eight most powerful war vessels in existence, were at large; all the world knew that they were being hunted night and day with the most relentless persistency by the ships of the British Navy. At last, one of the quarry was sighted, and after a few hours of dramatic combat "went to earth" in a neutral harbour.

On December 13 she was making her course along the Uruguayan coast— "Admiral Graf Spee," third and newest of the "pocket battleships." It was already dawn when at 6 a.m. the German warship was spotted by a British cruiser and "Formose," a French merchantman. Within two hours the cruiser, with her speed of over thirty knots as compared

The "Exeter" is a cruiser of 8,390 tons, completed in May, 1931. She carries six 8-in. guns, eight 4-in. anti-aircraft guns, six 21-in. torpedo tubes, and two aircraft with catapults. Like the "Ajax" and the "Achilles," which formed part of Commodore Harwood's squadron, she has a speed of 32·5 knots.
Photo, Wide World

with the German ship's twenty-seven, had come within range, and both ships opened fire. No doubt the "Graf Spee" hoped that with her vast superiority of armament she would be able to repel the attack, and possibly sink her opponent But now another British warship, the "Exeter," appeared over the horizon.

Natives on the shore at Punta del Este, who had rushed from their homes at the sound of firing and were watching with eager eyes the flashes of flame as the great guns went into action, heard twelve shots fired in quick succession. At the same time the first British cruiser, supposed to have been "Ajax," poured out a vast smoke screen.

Now, the "Graf Spee" headed for the open sea, but the second cruiser began to close in, and a running fight developed which continued within sight of shore at intervals throughout the day. As fast as her engines could take her the German ship made for the refuge of the River Plate, and as hard

and as fast as their guns could fire, the British cruisers—by now a third, the "Achilles," had come up—were doing their utmost to sink her, or at least put her out of action before she could reach territorial waters.

In a later stage of the engagement one of the British cruisers, the 8-inch gun "Exeter" was damaged, and in consequence forced to reduce her speed and drop behind. The other two cruisers, "Ajax" and "Achilles," both small ships mounting 6-inch guns only, continued the chase and scored repeated hits. They were unable, however, to bring the hunted ship to bay, and as dark fell the "Graf Spee's" searchlights played on the shore of Montevideo as she searched for the opening of the harbour. Maritime police put off in a tug and guided the ship to her anchorage. Ambulances were rushed to the quay as soon as she moored, and thirty-six dead and some sixty wounded were taken off. Her captain was among the wounded, having been injured in the arm. A Uruguayan spokesman was reported to have said that the badly-damaged battleship would be allowed to remain in the port up to thirty days in order to effect necessary repairs.

So the day ended, and in the outer harbour or in the estuary all three ships of Commodore Harwood's squadron—for, despite her damage, the "Exeter" had succeeded in coming up—maintained an unsleeping vigil. "Graf Spee" was trapped.

The "Admiral Graf Spee" is the last of the three "pocket battleships" of the Deutschland class with six 11-in. guns to be completed, having been launched in 1934. She has a displacement of 10,000 tons and a crew of about 950.
Photo, Keystone

Outfought and Outsailed She Fled to Safety

With the coming of the morning light the battered ship showed her gaping wounds to the crowds which packed the quays. There were three shell holes on the water-line on the starboard quarter, and through a huge hole on the port quarter one could see into the crew's sleeping compartments. The plates were bent outwards, indicating a terrific explosion inside the vessel. On deck a mass of wreckage was all that was left of an aeroplane which had suffered a direct hit from a British shell. A shell had gone right through the control tower, and another tremendous hole had been torn in the fighting tower, where were most of the 36 men who were killed. The gun tower on the port side had been torn from its foundations.

Nearly Blown out of the Water

As one observer said, the British did everything but blow "Graf Spee" out of the water. It was obvious that she would need the most extensive repairs, and there were many who believed that she would never put to sea again, particularly in view of the fact that outside the harbour the three cruisers which had chased her so gallantly had now been strongly reinforced.

The news of the battle electrified the world. Perhaps the most dramatic account of the battle was that given by the six British captains of merchantmen who had been kept as prisoners in the "Graf Spee" since their vessels were sunk by the raider. Said Captain Dove

after a tribute to the courteous conduct of the German commander, "When the battle started yesterday they bolted the door, and I did not know what was happening until I heard the 'Graf Spee' guns and felt the impact of the British shells. According to our reckoning the 'Graf Spee' was hit sixteen times. We played cards, including bridge, throughout the battle. One shot exploded near us, and we kept splinters of it as souvenirs."

Everywhere the fight was hailed as a British triumph—everywhere, that is, but in Germany where it was claimed that the "Graf Spee" in an heroic battle had won a great victory. Said one German paper, the British had fired gas grenades, and "as there was a danger that foodstuffs might have been affected by poison gas the commander of the 'Graf Spee' put to anchor in the harbour for fresh supplies"!

Naval experts were amazed at the success of the three comparatively small British cruisers in driving from the seas one of the most formidable of modern battleships. The British cruisers' gun range is only 18,000 to 25,000 yards as compared with the 30,000 yards of the German ship, and their biggest guns fired shells of only 250 lb. as against the 670 lb. shells belched from the "Graf Spee."

Speaking in the House of Commons, the Prime Minister referred to the "very gallant action which has been fought by three comparatively small British ships against a much more heavily armed

adversary"; and in the House of Lords, Lord Chatfield spoke of the "brilliant and successful fight in the South Atlantic." He went on, "we had been hunting for the 'Graf Spee' for some time. It could be assumed that any ship that got into touch with her was not going to lose touch. That is the spirit which animates the Navy today, as it has animated the Navy of past days." Lord Chatfield concluded by saying that he had no doubt that the "Graf Spee" would soon put out to sea again"—and added grimly—"for a short time."

Commodore H. H. Harwood, in command, hoisted Nelson's immortal signal on his flagship as he went into action.

The foolish boast of the Nazis that the "Graf Spee" showed no battle scars is utterly disproved by these two remarkable photographs taken in Montevideo harbour and transmitted to London by wireless. Above is the catapult apparatus, with a seaplane badly damaged by shell fire. Left, the "Graf Spee" in harbour. Circles and arrow mark where direct hits were made.

Associated Press

I Saw Horrible Sights in Helsinki

Air raids were launched on Helsinki, the Finnish capital, on November 30, at the outset of the Russian attack on Finland. Accounts of the first raids on the city, given by eye-witnesses, are here reprinted by permission of the " Daily Telegraph " and British United Press.

MRS. CHOLERTON, wife of the "Daily Telegraph's" Moscow correspondent, arrived in Stockholm on September 2 with her small daughter from Abo, the large Finnish port near the entrance of the Gulf of Finland, on board the Swedish steamer " Brynhild." She stated : " My little girl was in school at the other end of Helsinki from where I was when the first air raid alarm in the city was sounded on Thursday morning (November 30). Imagine the feelings of a mother in this situation."

The little girl interrupted : " Our teacher helped us to reach home safely."

Mrs. Cholerton continued : " The machine-gunning was worse than the bombs. I saw horrible sights when the tack-tacking of the machine-guns started from the Soviet 'planes.

" Owing to the spy situation all foreigners need a police permit to leave Finland. As I tried to get mine at police headquarters a second raid occurred, and the office was closed. Bombs fell all around and a building collapsed in the street, blocking my way at first.

" On December 1st I succeeded in leaving by train while the Russian attacks were stopped to permit Russians and Germans to evacuate the city. The ' Brynhild,' which was meant to hold 150, was crammed with 300 people.

" We were escorted by two Finnish destroyers, but near the Aaland Islands Russian warplanes were reported and all passengers were sent below decks. We heard afterwards that the destroyers engaged the 'planes and that Soviet submarines were also seen."

A British press correspondent at Helsinki, describing the effects of one of the Soviet air raids on the city, said :

" When the first bomb was dropped I was thrown to the floor. All the windows of the hotel were shattered.

" Being none the worse for my fall, I telephoned

A non-combatant victim of the Red raids on Helsinki on November 30, being carried to hospital by two civilians.
Photo, Wide World

The scenes of horror which the dropping of incendiary and high-explosive bombs can produce in a great city are shown in these two photographs. They were certainly not military objectives; above, left, is the motor omnibus mentioned in the eye-witness's account of the bombing in the next page. Right, are buildings in Helsinki after being bombed—one razed to the ground, the other burning fiercely.
Photos, Wide World and Planet News

the City Exchange in order to get a trunk call. The telephone girl was still at her post, and quite coolly got me my number.

" I counted at least a dozen bombs, two of which were huge and shattered windows over a radius of about half a mile. Incendiary bombs were dropped, evidently aimed at the airport. They went wide and started several fires in the centre of the city.

" The heavy bombs were presumably for the railway station, but a motor-bus got the worst of one of them and a number of people in it were killed.

" There was pandemonium from the continuous anti-aircraft gun-fire. From my window I could see three blazing buildings. There seemed to be numerous casualties in the street.

" The huge glass dome of the Hotel Torni crashed into the lobby. There was complete calm, and the guests were calmly shepherded into the cellars. The offices of the Great Northern Tele-graph Company were hit by a bomb. No one was hurt.

" The raid had come practically with-out warning. The first bombs dropped barely one minute after the sirens were sounded. There was no panic, but many people appeared too dazed to make for the cellars and stood stupefied, staring up into the sky. City transport was paralysed.

" In one area the fire department took charge, and the firemen began digging in the débris to recover bodies. Large blocks of flats suffered badly and several were burning fiercely.

" Scores of persons are believed to have been killed when a heavy bomb landed on an apartment house and destroyed it. .

" The darkness which came down at 4 p.m. was broken by winking flashlights of citizens picking their way through the rubble, and by the glare from burning buildings where rescue work was still going on."

A Nazi Tank Slew My Wife in Poland

This eye-witness account of terrible happenings in conquered Poland was told to a correspondent of the " Daily Telegraph " by Count Joseph Michalowski, who succeeded in reaching Paris at the end of November.

WHEN war broke out I was mobilized and fought in an army group commanded by Gen. Kleberg. I became a Bolshevik prisoner of war on September 20. But after a few days I succeeded in escaping and started a search through Poland to try and find my wife and my three children. . . . I had no idea at that time that my wife and my eldest son, a boy of 17, had been shot by the Germans.

I went to Poznan to find out among my friends if they knew anything about my family.

Poznan is in the grip of the wildest form of German terror. The Poles are being ejected from their properties and businesses. Polish shops bear notices " Deutsches Geschaeft " — " German shop." All streets in Poznan are being renamed by German names. The hotels bear inscriptions : " Polen und Juden Eintritt verboten "—" Poles and Jews forbidden to enter."

The population of Poznan is terrorized and haunted. The streets are empty, and only those who have urgent calls leave their houses.

FROM Poznan I followed the tracks indicated to me as the direction which my wife had gone and stopped in the little town of Szamotuly. There, I think it was on October 20, I witnessed the following terrible scene :

It was market day and the market was crowded with people. Suddenly a group of German soldiers arrived, pushed the whole crowd, of whom I was one, into one end of the market and drew a cordon separating us from the other part of the market place.

After having cleared that space from the public the German soldiers led into it five young men who were all keeping their hands crossed behind their heads. The five young men kneeled down and prayed aloud in Polish.

One of them exclaimed in Polish, " Long live Poland "—" Niech zyje Pol-ska." Another cursed the Germans in German. The crowd where I stood was crying, women were weeping aloud and many were kneeling, praying and ex-claiming, " Where are you, our Lord ? "

The five young men were executed. The S.S. chief personally shot each of them in the head with his revolver.

The five young Poles came from the village of Otorow, which is near by. One of them was the local hairdresser. They were shot because the Hitler flag had been torn from the local town hall. The five men had been kept as hostages and hostages are being executed publicly.

THE search for my wife led as far as Sochaczew, about 30 miles west of Warsaw. Along the road I came across numerous common graves.

I was able to ascertain that my wife was driven on that road in a hackney-carriage with two other women, friends of hers, and a devoted servant girl. A second hackney-carriage was behind them with other women evacuating towards Warsaw.

I found the driver of that second hackney-carriage, and he took me to a spot near the village of Tulowice, where the first hackney-carriage, containing my wife, had crossed the River Bzural.

Some distance away, on the other side of the river, a few yards off the road, I discovered the hackney-carriage, which I recognized as one from my estate. There among the panels I found one shoe which belonged to my wife. On a common grave near by we found the relic-image of the Saint Teresa. It belonged to my wife's servant girl. Local peasants gave me the following dramatic report :

A German tank approached the hack-ney-carriage on which the four women were seated and riddled it with machine-gun bullets.

There were no Polish soldiers in the vicinity, and the hackney-carriage was at the moment standing abandoned in the road with only the four unhappy women in it. The Germans deliberately killed the four women. My wife was not killed outright, but fatally wounded. As she was an American—her maiden name was Crosby—she probably cried in English for help.

My wife was brought in a coma to the nearest hospital at Blonie, where she died after the Germans had refused to give her any help. They pretended that she was not a woman but an English officer masquerading as a woman.

I learned further that my son, who with some other friends was being motored to Warsaw a few days before my wife was killed, was killed also. The car was shot at by German colonists acting as spies.

We Escaped Torpedo, Fire and Shipwreck

Passengers and crew of the Dutch motor-vessel " Tajadoen " had a thrilling experience on December 7. When their ship was tor-pedoed they were picked up by the Belgian steamer " Louis Scheid," which was herself wrecked on a hidden rock a few hours later. This story is reprinted from columns of the " Evening Standard " and the " Manchester Guardian."

WHEN the Dutch motor-vessel " Tajadoen " was torpedoed in the North Sea on December 7 the ex-plosion set fire to oil floating on the sea, and the survivors in lifeboats had to race away from a spreading sea of fire which crept upon them.

The captain of the ship, Mr. J. B. Roederink, revealed this when he and 62 of the crew and passengers (including five women and two children) were landed at an English south-west port.

The Belgian ship, the " Louis Scheid " (6,057 tons), which rescued them, was herself wrecked on a hidden rock near the coast and the survivors took to boats for a second time within a few hours.

Captain J. B. Roederink said :

I WAS THERE!

" All the passengers of the ' Tajandoen ' and a number of the crew were in their bunks when the explosion occurred. It was a terrific explosion and the ship went down in a quarter of an hour.

" We got all the passengers and crew away with the exception of two engineers and four seamen. Then began a grim race for safety.

" The explosion had allowed our fuel oil to escape on to the sea, and had ignited it. The surface around the vessel was soon a huge blazing lake which spread away from the sinking vessel.

" As it spread the lifeboat crews worked desperately to keep their boats ahead of the blazing oil and, fortunately for all in the boats, they won the race."

The first intimation that the Belgian rescue ship had hit a rock was when rockets rent the black-out.

Coastguards saw the vessel brilliantly lit from bow to stern, and called help. The vessel came on to the beach within about 100 yards of an hotel.

Several times the lifeboats made gallant efforts to get alongside, but their work was hampered by the heavy seas.

The coxswain of one of the lifeboats said :

" We had a very rough trip in lashing rain. It was terrible. The first time we went along to the port side of the ' Louis Scheid ' we took off 40 ; the second time we took off 22 more of the Dutch crew and passengers. All but five are thus accounted for.

" They had to jump with ropes round them. It was with the utmost difficulty we got them all on board."

A small boat carried the survivors from the lifeboat to land and then they were half-carried up a steep cliff.

The officers and crew of the " Louis Scheid," who remained on their vessel after the removal of the survivors of the " Tajandoen," were later rescued by breeches buoy.

Although it was foggy, a rocket carrying a lifeline was shot across the steamer, and the breeches buoy apparatus brought

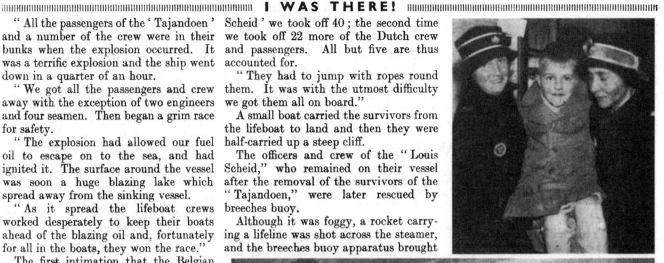

Here are scenes in the double tragedy that befell the survivors of the Dutch motor-ship " Tajandoen," 8,159 tons, which was torpedoed in the Channel on December 7. The Belgian ship " Louis Scheid," 6,057 tons, by which the passengers and crew were rescued, afterwards ran ashore on the coast of Devon through one of the ordinary hazards of the sea, but all the survivors of the " Tajandoen " were rescued by the rocket apparatus. At the top is one of them—Rudy van Essen, aged 6 years—being looked after by English nurses. Centre, one of the crew of the " Louis Scheid " is being brought ashore in the breeches buoy. Bottom, the Belgian ship on the rocks.
Photos. G.P.A. and Associated Press

into operation. In a short time all the officers and men had been brought ashore.

Spectators could see the seamen bobbing over a choppy sea as they were hauled through mist and driving rain on to the sands.

A lifeboat and a tug stood by off the rocky shore. Police and villagers for miles around hurried to the beach to aid in the laborious work of rescue.

One man said :

"It has been a terrible night. There was no respite from the lashing rain and tide. We had to rush the apparatus to another point two miles away to bring the vessel within length of the rope."

The Maire Who Welcomed the King

In the course of his tour of the British positions in France, the King was welcomed one December morning by the maire of a little village. Mr. E. A. Montague, Special Correspondent of the " Manchester Guardian " here describes the event.

A TINY French village, huddled in a field in the downs, heard that it was to be visited by the King of England. The news was delightful but overwhelming, and most of all to the maire. For a unit of the Guards had its headquarters at his farm, and the King was to inspect them. The maire must do the honours not only of his village but also of his own house. Hastily he sent the news out through the village, and decreed a holiday for the school children. Then he shut himself indoors and set about the writing of a speech. He was conscious of the occasion. He had fought through the last war as an N.C.O. in the artillery, commanding his men on the Somme, on the Marne, in Belgium, and the horrors of Verdun, while his wife kept the farm going within the sound of the guns, but for both of them this was the most important and daunting day of their lives.

An hour or two later some of us came into the village, half an hour or so ahead of the King's party. We found twenty or thirty children, very small and excited, shuffling their feet at the cross-roads, while the elderly schoolmistress tried in vain to explain to a willing but baffled military policeman that she wanted to take them where they could see the King.

We arranged matters for her, and she said how sorry she was that she had not known earlier about the visit ; she would have taught the children to sing " God Save the Queen." We reminded her that it was a King who ruled over us nowadays. "Ah, yes, of course ; I was thinking of the song they taught me when I was a girl."

We went on to the maire's house, and found a detachment of about a hundred Guardsmen drawn up in three ranks along one side of the farmyard. In front of the house stood a group of officers, and at the end of it, next to the front door, the maire and his wife, in ceremonial black. At the gate was posted a guard of four men with tin hats and fixed bayonets, and beside them stood a bugler.

A sudden command froze everybody into a silence which made the farmyard sounds of ducks and hens and pigeons seem magically louder. The guard presented arms with a smacking accuracy which must have impressed the old soldier standing outside his front door nervously fingering a sheet of paper in black-gloved hands, and the bugler blew the royal salute as the King and his officers came through the gate.

After shaking hands with the commanding officer the King moved towards the other officers and was immediately menaced by a lolloping terrier pup, who rushed towards him barking, thought better of it, and scuttled away again. The King was introduced to the officers of the unit, and at last the maire's proud, dreaded moment had come.

He did not tempt fortune by trying to remember his speech. He produced his piece of paper and read from it in a steady voice the result of his meditations on how a Frenchman should speak for France. It was thus :

" Your Majesty,—In the name of my country I thank your Majesty, I thank your people, I thank your splendid Army, so closely united with the French Army on our borders for the defence of this sublime and noble cause, for the defence of humanity."

And then, raising his eyes from the paper and lifting his voice to the tone which must have rallied his gunners outside Verdun, he ended, " Vive le Roi, vive l'Angleterre, et vive la France ! "

They shook hands, the King of England and the little man in black gloves, and then the King passed on to review the Guards' parade in the yard.

Again the guard at the gate presented arms, again the bugler blew the royal salute, and the commanding officer called for three cheers for the King. As he paused before leading the first cheer one of the maire's hens gave him the note with a hoarse, triumphant uproar which signified that the Allied food supply had been increased by one egg, and the sound of the cheering set all the geese stretching their necks and hissing.

The King and his party passed out of the farmyard, and the maire's great day was over. We found him afterwards in his house, and took wine with him, while the puppy which had tried to assault a King rolled about under the table.

He was composed and content in the knowledge of having carried himself worthily. We congratulated him from our hearts on his speech, and he gave me the sheet of paper on which he had laboriously written it. I shall keep it as a memento of one of the humble men out of whose characters have been built up the greatness and glory of France.

During his visit to France the King saw troops under many conditions. Here His Majesty, walking on duckboards laid in a rain-flooded French farmyard, is cheered by British troops as he leaves after an inspection of their quarters. Immediately behind him is the British C.-in-C., Viscount Gort. It was amidst such surroundings as this that the King heard the simple yet moving address recorded in this page. *Photo. British Official : Crown Copyright*

NOW IT CAN BE TOLD: EPIC STORY OF THE 'ORZEL'

Here we have the first of what it is to be hoped will be a number of accounts of exciting
and heroic incidents, the full story of which was not revealed for one reason or another
at the time of their happening.

WHEN General Sikorski, the Polish Premier, visited England in November, 1939, he conferred decorations on Lieutenant Grudzinski and all the members of the crew of the Polish submarine "Orzel." Following this public recognition the full story of a most remarkable feat of heroic seamanship was given to the world.

When Hitler's men marched into Poland at the beginning of September, the "Orzel" (which means Eagle) was trapped in port at

Above is the scene at the launching of the Dutch-built Polish submarine "Orzel," whose amazing adventures are told in this page. She has a displacement of 1,473 tons, and carries a normal complement of 56 men. Fitted as a minelayer, she has a radius of 3,500 miles and a speed of 10 knots on the surface.

Gdynia. But the 60 daring men on board declined to surrender their ship, and took her to sea in spite of an attack from the Nazi fleet.

The commander was sick and should have been in hospital. For four days he cruised, submerged in the Gulf of Danzig, watching through his periscope the aerial attacks sweeping over the Polish coast towns at ten-minute intervals.

He was sighted and bombed. A cordon of German submarine hunters was spread across the Gulf and the commander sought the wider waters of the Baltic.

Put Under Arrest

FOR a week he searched for a sister submarine which had signalled for help. By now he was so ill that he had to be hauled up the conning tower on a rope's end, and on the thirteenth day he was so ill that his second in command decided to land him in a neutral country, and chose Estonia. They put into Tallinn on September 15.

The submarine was secured alongside by four wires to the jetty, by another to a destroyer and a sixth held his bow to an anchor in the

harbour. The sick captain was landed, and the first lieutenant, Lt. Cdr. John Grudzinski, took command. One German merchant ship in the harbour was to leave shortly, so the Estonian authorities refused permission for the "Orzel" to proceed for another 24 hours.

At the end of this time officials arrived on board with the astonishing announcement that, as "Orzel" had exceeded the time allowed in a neutral port to belligerents by international law, the submarine was under arrest. They were asked for no parole, but the breech blocks of the guns were removed, all charts and small arms taken out of the ship, and preparations made to hoist out the torpedoes with a crane. Two guards were mounted, one in the control-room on board and the other on the jetty ashore.

By the time 15 torpedoes had been hoisted out the second in command had contrived, unseen by the guard, to file through the wire of the hoisting apparatus. It broke, leaving five torpedoes on board. In the meanwhile the captain was unobtrusively busy with a hacksaw cutting the wires, until only a few strands held them to the jetty.

The only aid to navigation left on board was a list of lighthouses and lightships in the Baltic. The second engineer, who had been promoted to navigator, got a piece of squared paper and contrived to plot their approximate positions on it, thus reconstructing a crude chart of the Baltic.

This could be done only in odd moments when the guard climbed on deck to smoke or talk to his confrère on the jetty.

At such moments the escape was planned. It was decided that when midnight came they would overpower the guards, break the strands of wire that secured the submarine and get away as quickly as they could. The chief difficulty was the gyroscopic compass, which has to be run for some hours before it is serviceable. To drown the hum of the gyro they increased the speed of the ventilating fans, complaining to the guard that they were being deprived of fresh air. Then they all turned in.

At midnight two burly members of the crew went on deck on the plea that they wanted a smoke. The guard ashore had been joined by a friend who stayed chatting with him. At intervals the Polish sailors returned to the upper deck. The Estonians had an overhead searchlight shining down on the submarine and jetty. There was also a telephone within reach of the guard. At 2 a.m. the visitor left. The two Polish sailors offered the guard a cigarette, which he declined. To attract him nearer to the gangway they drew his attention to a peculiarity of their gun-mounting. This appeared to interest him and he leaned over the side of the jetty. The Poles immediately seized, gagged and bound him and bundled him into the submarine. At the same moment his confrère below was seized, and an officer ran

ashore and cut the wires of the searchlight and telephone. The stranded wires that held them to the wharf were carried away. The sound of their capstan revealed their intentions, and destroyers switched on searchlights, and opened fire on them with rifles.

They made for the entrance, blinded by searchlights, with bullets spattering all round them. There was a general fusillade from every direction. They blew their tanks, went full speed astern, and slid off the rocks. Then they went ahead again, and this time succeeded in slipping through the entrance out into the night—and freedom.

The story goes on to describe how the men went on through the night, submerged, steering blindly, with no chart. At dawn they lay on the bottom. Next day they heard the hunters passing to and fro; and depth charges burst around till they lost count of the explosions. About 9 p.m. there was a lull and at midnight they rose cautiously. There was nothing in sight.

It must be remembered that their sole armament was five torpedoes. Their guns were out of action; they had no rifles or revolvers. The captain decided to cruise in the Baltic in search of German ships as long as his torpedoes lasted and then make for England.

Hunted and Harried for Three Weeks

HE found a sanctuary and charged his batteries. He also ran ashore about five times on shoals and rocks, getting more and more damaged. By this time they were getting tired of their prisoners, who kept up a ceaseless lamentation and speculation on how their families were faring. They learned from the German wireless—which was the only news they had—that they were being denounced to the world as the murderers of their guards.

Accordingly, one fine night, in a flat calm, they stopped off an island, launched their boat, put their two Estonian prisoners into it with money, cigarettes and a bottle of whisky and watched them row to the shore. Then these men who had lost their country and their families made a wireless signal to announce that the Estonians were safe so that their relations might have no further anxiety. This was the 22nd day.

For a fortnight they cruised in the Baltic. Every night they were hunted to prevent them from charging batteries; by day they cruised submerged, never knowing when they would strike a rock, or they lay on the bottom. By this time their water was running low and the cook had a scratch that was causing blood-poisoning. On the thirty-eighth day they decided to try to reach England.

In spite of lack of charts, constant attacks by German destroyers, and further damage by grounding, they threaded the intricate channels of the exits from the Baltic and gained the North Sea. Once there every man's hand was against them; they were fair game for German and British alike, menaced from the air, by surface patrols, and by submarines; their wireless apparatus had been damaged by rifle fire. But the first lieutenant Piasecki could speak English.

On October 14 a faint message reached a British wireless station : "Supposed position from 0630 on appointed place for Polish Navy. Beg permission entrance and pilot. But have no chart.—' Orzel.'"

A few hours later a British destroyer found them and led them triumphantly into harbour. They learned then that their sister submarine was also safe. They had only three requests : to land the sick cook, to replenish their water supplies, and to be given breech blocks for their guns. They were then prepared to go to sea forthwith on whatever patrol it pleased the British Navy to employ them. They were received with hearty cheers when they joined the British fleet.

OUR DIARY OF THE WAR

Thursday, December 7, 1939

Finns maintained defence of Karelian isthmus and denied that Russians had broken through. Russian attacks in the north were repulsed. Fierce fighting in Petsamo district.

Nine enemy aircraft driven off by R.A.F. fighters from Firth of Forth area, five being hit.

Two enemy machines were engaged off North-East Coast by R.A.F. fighters and pursued out to sea ; one was hit.

Air Ministry announced that in an engagement over the North Sea on Dec. 6 **two Dornier seaplanes were attacked and damaged** by aircraft of the Coastal Command. One British aircraft failed to return.

Patrol activity was reported from the Western Front, German raiding parties showing great persistence.

H.M.S. " Jersey " damaged by torpedo, but reached port. Attacking U-boat reported sunk.

Two **Polish submarines, " Wilk " and " Orzel,"** escaped from the Baltic and joined the British Navy.

Reported that H.M. trawler " Washington " was sunk by mine in North Sea on Dec. 6.

Dutch freighter " Tajandoen " torpedoed in English Channel. Survivors taken off by Belgian cargo boat " Louis Scheid," which later ran aground on Devon coast.

Norwegian tanker " Britta " sunk off West Coast of England.

British steamer " Thomas Walton " sunk, probably by torpedo, off Norway.

Friday, December 8

The King, in the course of his tour of the B.E.F., visited aircraft units, and decorated Flying-Officer R. C. Graveley and Sergeant F. H. Gardiner.

Coastal Command aircraft **sank a U-boat by bombing.** Another was attacked.

Enemy aircraft reported off East Coast during preceding night. R.A.F. aircraft went up to intercept them. One enemy machine approached Thames estuary and was driven off by anti-aircraft fire.

British cargo-boat " Merel " mined off South-East Coast.

British cargo-steamer " Navasota " torpedoed in Atlantic.

German naval launch mined in German minefield off Langeland.

Russia declared a blockade of Finnish coast along Gulf of Bothnia.

Saturday, December 9

The King visited troops on the frontier and inspected a sector of the Maginot Line.

Announced that **British troops had taken up their positions in the Maginot Line** and had been in action against the enemy.

Finns repulsed new attacks on Karelian isthmus. Soviet bombers raided Hangoe.

Fierce fighting along the line Kuolajaervi-Suomussalmi-Kuhmo, where Russians claimed an advance.

British ship " Brandon " sunk off West Coast. British steamer " Corea " sunk off East Coast.

German steamer " Henning Oldendorff " brought into port as naval prize.

League of Nations Council held private meetings to discuss Finland's appeal against Russian aggression.

Sunday, December 10

The King returned to London after his tour of the Western Front.

Russian troops reported to be in contact with Finnish main line defences. Farther north the attack designed to cut Finland in two was said to be making slow progress.

Western Front reported that there were patrol encounters at various points.

Soviet Government handed a Note to the British Ambassador in Moscow protesting against Britain's two-way blockade.

Sweden appointed General Thoernell Commander-in-Chief of Swedish Defences.

H.M. drifter " Ray of Hope " sunk by mine.

Four neutral ships reported sunk : Swedish steamer " Vinga," Dutch motor-ship " Immingham," Danish collier " Scotia," Norwegian steamer " Gimle."

THE POETS & THE WAR

XII

PAR NOBILE FRATRUM

By A. A. Milne

Press fury (well controlled), a " hostile act,"
" Exhausted patience "—and the broken pact.
Which is the prettier ? Stalin, tongue in cheek,
Or Hitler thinking proudly "My technique " ?

—*The Observer*

Estonian steamer " Kassa " torpedoed in Gulf of Finland.

Von Papen, German envoy to Turkey, summoned to Berlin.

Department of Public Prosecutions in Istanbul began an inquiry into the activity of the German Embassy's Press Service.

Soviet Government refused offer of service of International **Red Cross Committee in Geneva** on grounds that Russia is not at war with Finland.

Monday, December 11

Renewed Russian attacks in Karelian isthmus were repulsed. On the central " bottle-neck " front the Finns claimed the recapture of Suomussalmi. Fighting continued in the Petsamo area.

League of Nations urged Soviet Union to cease from hostilities within the next 24 hours.

Officially stated that four British steamships— "Ashlea," " Newton Beech," " Huntsman " and Trevanion "—were now long overdue and must be considered lost.

British steamer "Willowpool " mined in North Sea.

Greek steamer " Garoufalia " torpedoed off Norway.

German aircraft seen off South-East Coast and over Yorkshire Coast.

German barrage balloon came down in Shetlands.

Tuesday, December 12

Soviet Government refused League of Nations offer to mediate in the Russo-Finnish conflict.

Russians gained ground in central Finland and threatened lines of communication between North and South. Finns lost Salla, Kirovsk and Kandalaksja. Russian advance in Karelian isthmus held up.

Enemy attacks on Western Front were repulsed.

British vessel " King Egbert " sunk in North Sea.

British collier " Marwick Head " mined off East Coast.

Swedish steamer " Toroe " mined off Falsterbo.

German steamer " Bolheim " sunk in Gulf of Bothnia by gunfire from submarine, believed to be Russian.

German liner **" Bremen " arrived in German port** from Murmansk after having been sighted by British submarine which, by rules of sea warfare, was precluded from torpedoing her without warning.

Wednesday, December 13

Finns alleged to have recaptured Salla. They were also successful in heavy fighting north of Lake Ladoga.

H.M. cruisers " Exeter," " Ajax " and " Achilles " **attacked German " pocket " battleship " Graf Spee "** in South Atlantic. " Exeter " received damage and fell out ; the other cruisers continued the fight, the enemy ship was hit repeatedly and sought shelter in Montevideo harbour.

Air Ministry announced that two aircraft of Coastal Command attacked two Dornier flying-boats over North Sea and damaged them.

R.A.F. fighters went up to intercept enemy raiders off east coast of Scotland.

U-boat sunk and enemy cruiser torpedoed by British submarine that sighted the " Bremen " during voyage from Murmansk.

Air Ministry disclosed that R.A.F. security patrols maintain a dusk-to-dawn watch over enemy mine-laying aircraft bases in Heligoland Bight.

German raids and patrols increased on Western Front, but were all repulsed by French.

League of Nations Assembly adopted a resolution condemning Russian aggression and calling on League members to help Finland.

House of Commons held secret sitting to debate questions concerning supply.

German liner " New York " reached Hamburg from Murmansk.

TREASURE ISLAND
" How do we stand when we get it ? Do we share—or do we fight ? "
From the cartoon by Sir Bernard Partridge by permission of the Proprietors of " Punch "

The WAR ILLUSTRATED

Vol. 1   A Permanent Picture Record of the Second Great War   No. 17

The gallant fight of the three British cruisers, "Achilles," "Ajax," and "Exeter," against the "Admiral Graf Spee" turned the eyes of the world upon three of those ships of the British Navy whose part in sea warfare is no less important, no less hazardous, yet generally far less spectacular than that of the capital ships that fight fleet actions. The cruisers, ranging from 4,000 to 10,000 tons, keep the Seven Seas for the Allies and are scattered all over the world. Here is the scene on the deck of one of them engaged in patrolling the North Sea at sunset. In the distance is another cruiser, and overhead speeds a flight of R.A.F. reconnaissance aircraft.

Photo. Planet News

Britain's Army Is in the Front Line Again

Shortly before Christmas there came the news that the British Army in France was not only "in the line" but had suffered its first casualties in patrol action against the foe.

ALMOST twenty-one years after they fired their last shot in the Great War—it was just before eleven on the morning of November 11, 1918, just outside Mons—the British were in action again against the same foe, although under very different circumstances. In 1918 they were engaged in open warfare pursuing the defeated and demoralized invader. Now they had their places in the greatest system of permanent fortifications which the world has ever seen—that Maginot Line which marks the impregnable front of the defenders of civilization and culture in the West.

The fact that British troops were actually in the front line and had exchanged shots with the enemy came out in connexion with King George's visit to France early in December. Shortly after he had arrived back in London, it was announced that his Majesty had inspected troops who had only just come in from the forward positions in which they had been in fighting contact with the enemy. The names of no regiments were mentioned, but it was understood that the men were drawn from some of the most famous of the Midland units.

It is not to be understood that the British were occupying any of the great underground fortresses of the Line; that responsibility falls to the French fortress troops who have been specially chosen for the task. Those fortresses are like battleships, and the men who man them must first be subjected to years of training and arduous preparation.

But in between the forts and far out in the "No-man's land" which stretches right up to the wire in front of the Siegfried Line, there is a complicated network of outposts and a stretch of territory of varying width which is systematically patrolled. It is in this area, in between sectors held by French troops, that the advance guard of the British Army in France has now taken up its position. British troops have their eyes glued to their periscopes in the most advanced observation posts; British soldiers have their guns mounted and ready to fire in the concrete machine-gun posts; at dawn and dusk they stand to at the parapet; when night falls British patrols move out into the dark and dangerous zone in search of prisoners and information.

Occasionally in these nocturnal perambulations they have come into contact with German patrols making a similar reconnaissance. It was in such a clash on the front at Buschdorf, near the Luxemburg frontier that—according to a French report—these hardy Midlanders first used rifle and bomb against the enemy. A night or two later there was a similar clash. Attacks were driven off or frustrated, bombs thrown, shots exchanged, and the information brought back was of the greatest value.

First British Casualties

On December 17 the first casualties of the B.E.F. since they took over a sector of the Maginot Line were announced officially in the words: "The British now have their wounded and even their dead on French soil once again."

One of the casualties was an infantry sergeant-major of sixteen years' service,

If as a last desperate throw Hitler should attempt a break-through on the Western Front, he will have many formidable obstacles to overcome before he can even approach the outworks of the Maginot Line. Here is a typical one, a battery of French 105-mm. guns, equivalent to 3½-in. The man with his hand raised has just fired the gun. The guns of the French artillery, most of which are built at the famous Schneider-Creusot works, are second to none in design and workmanship.

Photo, Planet News

Taking the Discomfort of War in Their Stride

These three men of the British Expeditionary Force are taking the mud, as they take all other discomforts, in their stride.   Rain has been
as heavy and constant in the opening months of this war as it was in the autumn of 1914, but it has not caused quite the same acute discomfort
to the troops as it did then, for they are occupying carefully prepared positions and the ground is not pitted with shell holes that quickly
become quagmires as it was twenty-five years ago.

Photo, British Official : Crown Copyright

That great range of linked fortresses which is known as the Maginot Line is to the greatest possible extent self-contained and self-supporting, so that the troops who man it have only the discomforts of comparatively confined space and constant artificial light to contend with. There are ample stores of food and well-equipped kitchens are provided. Left, the midday meal is being served many feet underground. Right, a Poilu is taking it easy in his rest-time lying on the top of an underground log cabin which has been named "Cabin—All's Well."
Photo, Planet News

who was visited in hospital somewhere behind the line by Mr. Douglas Williams, War Correspondent of the "Daily Telegraph." The sergeant-major had been instructed to take a small party from a well-known Midland county regiment out on patrol. The night was bitterly cold with occasional flurries of snow, and pitch dark. The little band set out on its reconnaissance into "No-man's land," worming its way over rough ground, sometimes crawling through holes half filled with water or cutting its way through old rusty wire.

All went well until they approached a gully. Then all of a sudden a mine went up—under their very feet it seemed

—and several were wounded, including the sergeant-major. Though bleeding profusely from his arm wounds the latter rallied his men and pushed on through the darkness in the hope of catching any Germans that there might be about. A volley was fired into the unknown, but there was no reply and the party returned to attend to its wounded. These were then carried back across two miles of broken ground, and before dawn the party arrived in safety and tumbled into our lines.

So Christmas 1939 repeats in some measure those four war Christmases of 1914 to 1917. British troops are once again in the front line.

Day by day and night by night the French Army far in front of the Maginot Line keeps a watch on every movement of the German Army, so that a surprise attack at any time is impossible. Centre left is a French observation post equipped with the latest instruments looking out towards the German lines. The taking of prisoners is one of the main objects of the patrols. It is work of extreme danger and the French troops who volunteer for it are known as "Groupes Francs." Above, some of them are in training. *Photos, Planet News and Courtesy of French Embassy*

First to Arrive for Christmas in 'Blighty'

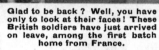

Glad to be back ? Well, you have only to look at their faces ! These British soldiers have just arrived on leave, among the first batch home from France.

The bus driver greets this soldier of the B.E.F. with a hearty handshake and wishes him a Merry Christmas. London may be dark, but it's a welcome sight to him and no blacker than the forward areas in France.

A soldier of the B.E.F. greeting his little daughter on arrival home. He has even got a sprig of mistletoe fastened to his rifle, so the wife will get a greeting, too.

Photo, Topical

One of many happy scenes as the leave men arrived. A sergeant leaves the station with his kit, while the lady shoulders the rifle happily. To older readers such scenes will be reminiscent of leave trains twenty-five years ago, but with the vital difference that these men have not come from scenes of slaughter and filth.

Photos, Fox

Here are some of the first arrivals for Christmas leave, and there's no mistaking the way they feel about it. Won't they be glad to get all that kit off! Anyhow it is not clogged with mud as their fathers' was. Like the B.E.F. of the last war leave is a delight, but fortunately it is without the haunting fear of a quick return to war's worst horrors.

Here's To a Day's Good Deed Well Done!

THE British soldiers in France during the last war won the affectionate admiration of the French civilian population by their readiness to lend a hand in any task in which their help was needed. So again the soldiers of 1939 are giving practical proof of the fact that the alliance has something more than military significance. Here we have an instance. A French wine merchant's van has overturned in a ditch. Some British light tanks have come along and at once take the job in hand. Three of them are harnessed to the van to begin the work of salvage (right).

SUCH a change as this from the ordinary routine is very welcome to the Tommies, and all traffic is held up while the work of salvage is in progress. Above left, the tanks are ready to give the long pull, the strong pull, and the pull together that should prove irresistible. Successful it was, and the wine merchant's van is back on the road with neither bottles nor bones broken. It is now his turn to do his day's good deed — by depleting his stock with no niggardly hand (left).

Finland Was Not Stalin's Birthday Present

Still little Finland fought on against what might well have seemed irresistible odds. Weather and native valour kept the invader at bay—for the time being.

STALIN'S sixtieth birthday fell on December 21, and the Commissars in the Kremlin had planned, it would seem, a birthday present of much more than ordinary magnitude—nothing less, in fact, than a conquered Finland. Their kindly intention was defeated, however, by the Finns, who to the Russians' surprise protested in the strongest and most unmistakable fashion against their incorporation in the Soviet sphere. When the anniversary of Stalin's natal day dawned, it found his troops fighting desperately to retain those frontier territories which were all they had so far managed to seize.

The Red Army started the invasion with an immense superiority of men, 'planes, tanks, and all the other material of war. Three weeks later their advance beyond their own border nowhere exceeded twenty miles, and much of the territory occupied had been abandoned by the Finns for tactical reasons. Neither Helsinki nor any of the towns in the industrial region in the south had been taken ; even the bombing of the first two days of the war was not repeated till Dec. 19—owing, perhaps, to the discovery that the bombing of civilians was an activity in which both parties could engage. The propaganda leaflet raids carried out by Finnish 'planes on Leningrad may also have played their part in Helsinki's lengthy immunity.

In the Karelian Isthmus the main forces of the Red Army made little progress, and despite the claims of the Moscow wireless, the Mannerheim Line was not breached in any spot. Offensive after offensive was launched by the

Russians in the isthmus and north of Lake Ladoga, but each in turn failed to break the Finnish lines. Thousands of casualties were incurred, and in one day 14 of the Soviet tanks were destroyed.

In the far north, where the winter night was almost continuous, Petsamo changed hands time and again, until eventually the Finns left it as a burning ruin. Salmijaervi, where are the famous Anglo-American nickel mines, was the scene of fierce fighting, and although the Finns were ultimately compelled to withdraw, they had time to put the mining machinery out of action. To the south, the Russian drive across the " waist " of Finland with a view to reaching the shores of the Gulf of Bothnia and the railway at Oulu (Uleaborg), seemed to be halted after an initial success.

A special correspondent of the " Daily Telegraph," writing from Rovaniemi on this front on December 15, said that the shooting of the Finnish marksmen was deadly. The weather, moreover, was terrible. " If the Russians do not huddle

When the Red Army has been driven back by the Finns after an attempted advance, the Finnish Army has acquired many trophies. This young Finn has secured a Russian sword as a souvenir.
Photos, Associated Press

The Finns have not hesitated to lay waste their country to check the Russian advance. Left, a Finnish soldier is preparing to blow up a house that might provide useful cover for the enemy. Above are tank traps in front of the Mannerheim Line. It has been stated that the Finns have destroyed or captured 250 Russian tanks.

War's Tempest Blows Fiercely in the North

This map of Finland indicates all the sectors in which land operations are now in progress and the towns and villages prominent in the war news. The Russian strategic plan of cutting off the northern Finnish forces from those in the south by striking across the "waist" is explained. The Karelian Isthmus where the fighting has been fiercest, is shown in the small inset.

Above, a Soviet bomber of the twin-engined SB type brought down by Finnish gunfire. It displays the five-pointed Red Star.
Photo, Keystone

together," he said, " they die of cold. If they do crowd together round their camp fires, Finnish sentries pick them off one at a time without wasting a single shot." He talked with some of the miserably-clad Russian prisoners in the Petsamo area. " One of them," he wrote, " had only trousers and jacket. Only officers have vests and pants. Many corpses have been found clad in women's underclothes, looted from a co-operative store outside Petsamo. A captured Russian lieutenant showed me with pride a pair of corsets he was wearing. ' They keep me warm.' he said."

War in the Arctic

Fighting in a winter-blasted desert with a temperature of 20 degrees below freezing, and every building burnt to the ground, the plight of the invaders—many of whom were reported to have come from Soviet Asia—was pitiable. Their difficulties may have been enhanced by errors in leadership. Not only were the officers unused to warfare under such conditions, but they were said to be under the control of civilian political commissars, who assumed responsibility not only for the political morale of the troops but for the actual conduct of operations. This arrangement can hardly have conduced to success in battle; and, furthermore, the officers of the Red Army have been so purged and re-purged of recent years that their fighting efficiency may well have been affected.

In the war of words, Moscow still maintained its quaint attitude that the Soviet Union was not at war with Finland. This was true if Finland indeed consisted of that little corner of " No-man's land " which was alleged to be under the control of " President " Kuusinen and his " People's Government of the Democratic Republic of Finland." That Finland which was defending itself so resolutely —that Finland which, as President Kallio declared in his broadcast to the

No 'Picnic' in Finland for the Red Army

Finnish Army, preferred death to Bolshevism—was not, so Moscow declared, the real Finland, but the "clique of Mannerheim and Tanner."

Such an assertion carried little weight with the outside world, which watched with unconcealed admiration a little people fighting to maintain its independence. The League of Nations on December 14 took the unprecedented step of declaring that " by its action against the Finnish State the Union of Soviet Socialist Republics has placed itself outside the League of Nations. It follows that the U.S.S.R. is no longer a member of the League."

Passers-by in Moscow are listening to the wireless of a car broadcasting the officially garbled story of a Russian advance in Finland.

Photos, Planet News, Central Press and Keystone

Considerable material assistance was rendered, but, as a Finnish spokesman declared, " a small land like Finland with 3,000,000 people cannot be expected for ever to hold Russia with 180,000,000. Finland is fighting desperately for her life—a life which may last several months, possibly several years. But the big Russian bear is after the small Finnish dog, and though the dog may escape for a time, the bear must win in the end. Will all countries of the world stand by and see Finland slowly devoured . . . ?

On the first day of the Russian campaign Viipuri was among the towns on which bombs were dropped by the Red Air Force. They struck houses and street traffic. Above is a tramcar set on fire by a Russian incendiary bomb.

The Finns have found a trusty ally in Winter. Temperatures as low as 20 degrees below zero and heavy falls of snow have presented considerable difficulties to the Russians. Snow has, moreover, been most useful as camouflage. Left is a Finnish gun in a wood with the ordinary camouflage such as is to be found on the Western Front. Right is such camouflage as snow provides. In the centre of this photograph is a Finnish soldier wearing one of the white camouflage coats seen in page 456. His face, waist belt and a glove alone are visible.

British Submarines' Best Week-–So Far

The successes achieved by British submarines in the course of the previous week were disclosed on Monday evening, December 18, in a broadcast by Mr. Winston Churchill and statements issued by the Admiralty. The full story of the " Graf Spee," including Mr. Churchill's comments, appears in pages 526-530.

MR. CHURCHILL began his broadcast by expressing the satisfaction felt at the news that the pocket battleship " Graf Spee " had met her doom. He then proceeded :

Here at home in the North Sea our British submarines have had the best week I can remember in this or the last war. British submarines suffer from the serious disadvantage that they have very few targets to attack. They are not allowed by the custom of the sea and by the conventions to which we have subscribed to sink merchant ships without warning, or without being able to provide for the safety of the merchant crews. British submarines do not wage war on neutral vessels. They do not attack humble fishing boats. They have to work for the most part among the minefields and in the strongly defended waters of the Heligoland Bight. It is only when a German warship is sighted that they are able to use their power and skill.

AFTER giving an account of the exploits of the British submarines " Salmon " and " Ursula " (both of which are illustrated opposite) Mr. Churchill went on :

The Nazi Navy and Air Force are venting their wrath for these heavy blows by redoubling their efforts to sink the fishing-smacks and drown the fishermen in the North Sea ; and all yesterday and today their Air Force has been trying to bomb individual unarmed merchant ships, including an Italian ship, which were moving up and down the East Coast of Britain. They have even in some cases machine-gunned the sailors on the decks of these unarmed merchant ships and fishing-boats. I am glad to tell you that the heat of their fury has far exceeded the accuracy of their aim. Out of twenty-four ships attacked by bombs yesterday and today, only six small boats engaged in fishing and one small coasting vessel have been sunk, and the bulk of the others, including the Italian, have not even been hit by the many bombs cast upon them.

These outrages are the tactics of a guilty regime which feels the long arm of sea power laid upon its shoulder.

Although German mines of all kinds are being scattered profusely upon the approaches to our island, I am able to tell you tonight that the whole vast movement of British traffic is proceeding, I will not say unimpeded, but uninterrupted ; and that yesterday the leading division of the Canadian Army, strongly escorted across the ocean and guarded by our main Battle Fleet, disembarked safely and smoothly in one of our harbours, for a period of intensive training in England before joining their British and French comrades on the Western Front.

MR. CHURCHILL then paid a tribute to the work of the First Sea Lord, Admiral of the Fleet Sir Dudley Pound, the Naval Staff at the Admiralty, and Sir Charles Forbes, Commander-in-Chief of the Main Fleet, and concluded :

But, after all, no leadership or expert naval direction could be successful unless it was supported by the whole body of officers and men of the Navy. It is upon these faithful, trusty servants in the great ships and cruisers that the burden falls directly day after day. In particular the flotillas of destroyers, of submarines watching in the throat of the Elbe, of anti-submarine craft, of minesweepers multiplying on all our coasts, all these have undergone and are undergoing a toil and strain which only those who are informed in detail of their efforts can understand. The chance of honour came

suddenly to the three cruisers engaged in the South Atlantic. . . . But if the call had come elsewhere in the oceans or in the narrow seas, skill and courage of equal quality would have been forthcoming. . . .

THE Admiralty's communiqué on the feat of the small submarine " Ursula " briefly stated that :

H.M. Submarine " Ursula " reports that she sank one Koeln class cruiser at the mouth of the Elbe on Thursday, December 14.

The cruiser was screened by six German destroyers.

What 'Salmon' Did to the German Cruisers

A FORTNIGHT'S adventures of the submarine " Salmon " were described in a longer statement :

The submarine had not long been in her patrol area before she sighted a big-type U-boat. The U-boat was steaming fast on the surface, with all the self-assurance of a newly painted vessel outward bound in search of Iron Crosses.

She was a trifle too self-confident. The British submarine manoeuvred quickly to the attack. A few minutes later the torpedoes were fired. In the British submarine there were a few moments of agonizing suspense. Then there came a shattering explosion.

Through his periscope the commander of the British submarine saw a blinding flash. This was followed by a deafening explosion, and the wreckage was thrown at least 200 feet into the air.

A few days of routine patrol followed. Then one morning the engines of a large ship were heard on the hydrophones. The submarine came to periscope depth to investigate—and found the " Bremen," pride of the German mercantile marine, steaming past.

Here is a small fishing vessel of the type which have been attacked by Nazi airmen, who dropped bombs and machine-gunned the crews.   *Photo, Fox*

In fact, it would have been impossible for the captain of the submarine to have missed such a great target—had he decided to fire at it ; but he did not so decide.

He knew that under International Law merchant ships must not be sunk except in the case of persistent refusal to stop when summoned ; and he had definite orders from the Admiralty that war at sea was to be conducted in strict accordance with International Law.

Having surfaced, the submarine signalled by daylight lamp, " Stop instantly." That is the international code signal " K." The " Bremen " took no notice. The commander of the submarine at once gave the order for his gun to be loaded so that a shot could be fired across the bows of the " Bremen " . . . .

The warning shot was never fired. German aircraft appeared overhead and forced the submarine to dive. In spite of being forced to dive the submarine could easily have fired six torpedoes into the " Bremen " as she dived, for she was already on the attacking course.

But in that case the dictates of International Law would not have been complied with. So the " Bremen " was allowed to proceed on her way unharmed.

Rather less than 24 hours after the " Bremen " had passed, the submarine was again cruising submerged, keeping a look-out through the periscope, when ships were sighted. On closer investigation these proved to be the two German battle-cruisers, " Scharnhorst " and " Gneisenau," and one of the pocket-battleships, with three cruisers in company.

At first it appeared that the British submarine would be unable to do more than report the fact that the enemy was at sea, his strength, position and course ; for the enemy ships were steering so that they would pass a long way from the submarine.

Just as the submarine commander was giving up all hope of being able to attack, however, the enemy cruisers altered course so as to pass within torpedo range of the submarine.

A few minutes later the sights of the unseen and unsuspected submarine came on. She fired six torpedoes, on slightly different courses.

It would have been an easy matter for her to have fired all torpedoes at one cruiser, and thus made certain of sinking one ship. But she fired them at different angles, hoping thereby to disable more than one ship and thus do more towards provoking the fleet action for which the British Navy is for ever hoping.

The first torpedo hit the cruiser " Leipzig." There was a pause of only a minute. Then two more terrific explosions told that two other torpedoes had found their mark—almost certainly upon the second heavy cruiser of the " Bluecher " class.

The submarine, however, could not wait to determine the exact result of her attack. The enemy were after her. She had to dive deep and try to elude her pursuers by steering a zigzag course at high speed at a considerable depth.

Though the submarine was hunted and depth-charged for two hours, these tactics proved successful. It was not until after dark that the British submarine returned to the scene of her kill. Then she found an area of nearly four square miles of sea thickly coated in oil fuel . . . .

It seems certain that at least one heavy cruiser, in addition to the " Leipzig," was badly damaged and that at least one of the ships might well have failed to reach port.

The officers and crew of the " Salmon " were amazed when their entry into harbour was the occasion for the sounding of the sirens of every ship present.

They had had an amazingly eventful fortnight on the enemy's " front doorstep " in which, emulating the feats of Drake, they had effectively singed the Fuehrer's moustache.

They Singed the Fuehrer's Moustache!

Lieut.-Commander E. O. B. Bickford, who was in command of H.M. Submarine "Salmon."

Photo, Russell, Southsea

Here are two submarines whose exploits are described in the Admiralty statements opposite. The "Salmon" (above) was completed in 1936 and her surface displacement is 670 tons. She carries 40 men and one 3-in. gun, one machine-gun, and six 8-in. torpedo tubes. The 540-ton "Ursula" (below), launched in February 1938, is one of the smallest of British submarines.

Photos, Fox and Central Press

Lieut.-Commander G. C. Phillips, who was in command of H.M. Submarine "Ursula."

In his broadcast on December 18, Mr. Winston Churchill said : " The exploits of H.M. Submarine ' Salmon ' last week are remarkable and praiseworthy in the highest degree. First, she blew to pieces by a volley of torpedoes one of the larger German U-boats which was going out upon a raiding foray. Secondly, she rightly abstained from torpedoing the ' Bremen ' when that enormous ship was at her mercy. Her third encounter was the most important. On Thursday last she observed through her periscope the German Fleet proceeding to sea on one of its rare excursions. She fired six torpedoes at the cruiser squadron which was accompanying the German battle-cruisers, and hit one 6,000-ton cruiser with one torpedo, and a second cruiser of equal size with two. These cruisers may have been able to limp home—although that is by no means certain in the case of one—where they will be out of action for many a long month,"

After his remarks about the " Salmon " quoted above, Mr. Winston Churchill spoke of another exploit scarcely less meritorious.

" Now, today," said Mr. Churchill, " H.M. Submarine ' Ursula ' reports that on the 14th she sank a 6,000-ton cruiser of the ' Koeln' class, although it was surrounded by German destroyers. A considerable proportion of the total German cruiser strength has been sunk or put out of action in a single week, and that the same week in which almost on the other side of the globe the pocket battleship 'Graf Spee' met her inglorious end."

The Admiralty communiqué announcing this success is printed in the opposite page.

Photos, Central Press and Russell, Southsea

The German cruiser sunk by the " Ursula " in the Heligoland Bight was either the " Koeln," the " Koenigsberg," or the " Karlsruhe." They are cruisers of 6,000 tons, with nine 5.9 guns and twelve 21-in. torpedo tubes. They each carry two catapult aircraft. Above is the " Koeln."

'Taken in Wartime'—At Least So They Said!

Nummer 48 · 30. November 1939   45. Jahrgang · Preis 20 Pfennig

Berliner
Illustrirte Zeitung

In diesem Heft einzigartiger Bildbericht:
Wie deutsche Flieger England sehen

German photograph reproduced as " a coastal fort at the mouth of Moray Firth. The batteries are marked A and the barracks B."

THE photographs in this page and in that opposite have been widely published in Germany as Nazi propaganda to prove Germany's superiority in the air. The line of reasoning is that if German aeroplanes can fly at will over places in Britain our air defences must be impotent and our fighters useless against the vastly superior German air force. How totally devoid of truth is such a statement has been proved repeatedly by the comparative ease with which all the raids of bombers have been beaten off.

This issue of Germany's foremost illustrated paper (The Berlin Illustrated Journal), whose cover is seen top left, contains reproductions of photographs taken over England, and purporting to show how " Germany's air-weapon overcomes England's war preparations." Above is one said to show Thames Haven, with A, oil refineries, and B tankers.

Photo-Propaganda to Cheer the Nazi Home Front

THESE photographs *may* have been taken by German airmen since war began. They are, however, remarkably clear and bright considering the great height from which they must have been taken, for if they were not taken in the first month of the war—which is hardly probable—there have since been very few days in which atmospheric conditions were sufficiently good to allow of such results. It has, moreover, been pointed out by experts that the shadows are hardly long enough to have been made by autumn sunlight.

The photograph above, of Liverpool, is thus described by the Nazis. "Entrance to the commercial harbour at Birkenhead (A), opposite which, on the farther bank of the Mersey, stretch the wharves (B) of the City of Liverpool with the landing-stages for passenger-boats at (C). The ships (D) are motor-boats, part of the city's river traffic. Across the Mersey runs the underwater-way (tunnel) shown by the broken line."

The photograph above is described as "Kinloss Aerodrome in North Scotland. Barracks (A) and characteristic layout of the hangars with camouflage painting (B). The locality is in the immediate neighbourhood of a big city. Camouflage (C) is intended to deceive the enemy. A row of machines ready to take off from the aerodrome (D)." Actually the nearest town to Kinloss is Inverness, about 25 miles distant.

Right is Dover harbour as a Nazi airman claims to have photographed it. The caption given when it was published in Germany read: "(A) The railway station. (B) The breakwater. (C) Sidemole. (D) Entrance to the harbour. (E) Coastal defence batteries. (F) Forts. (G) The Citadel." The last named is Dover Castle, which though a prized historical relic is of no military value.

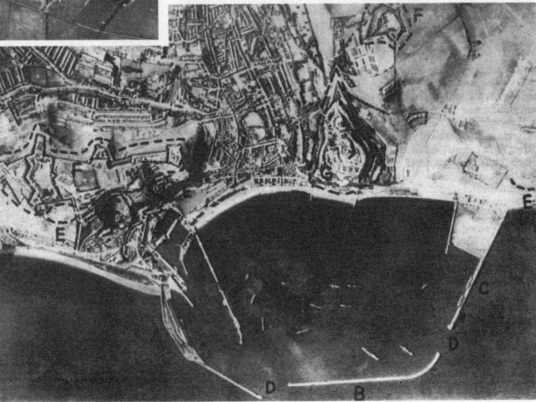

'The Glorious Battle of the River Plate'

Lord Chatfield was right when he expressed the opinion in the House of Lords that the "Graf Spee" would soon put out to sea again—for a short time. On December 17, after days of frenzied preparation, she left Montevideo, and two hours later was scuttled in the fairway by her own crew. The story of what has been well styled "Ignominy to order" is given below.

I**T was late at night on Wednesday, December 13, when the German pocket battleship "Admiral Graf Spee" limped into the neutral harbour of Montevideo.

For fourteen hours she had been engaged in a running fight with three British cruisers—"Ajax," "Achilles," and "Exeter." All three were small ships of their class, and against the "Graf Spee's" six 11-inch guns and eight 6-inch guns, the "Exeter" mounted only six 8-inch guns and her two consorts eight 6-inch guns apiece. A broadside fired by

most gallantly they tackled it. They took every advantage of their superior speed, attacking the enemy from ever-changing angles. When they made their final dash, closing in at full speed from opposite directions to almost point-blank range, completing their destructive work, the spirit of their naval forefathers must indeed have cried 'Well done!' Here was no necessity to hoist Nelson's favourite signal 'Engage the enemy more closely'; it was a perfectly working team of gallant fellows each knowing what he had to do and doing it."

So it was that, sorely battered, with holes gaping in her superstructure, and riddled by shells just above the waterline, the much-vaunted pocket battleship just

managed to limp into harbour. Close on her tracks went "Ajax" and "Achilles," ready and eager to renew the battle, while the "Exeter" came up through the night ready to take part in a fresh attack. Not until the "Cumberland" arrived did the crippled ship depart to care for her wounded and injuries.

For three days the "Graf Spee" swung at anchor in Montevideo harbour; for three days her men toiled desperately to repair the damage and plug the holes which had been torn by the British shells. Mr. E. Millington Drake, the British Minister at Montevideo, urged that the battleship should be required to put to sea at once or be interned for the duration of the war; a battleship which could travel so fast as did the "Graf Spee" when seeking refuge must, he pointed out, be perfectly navigable. Captain Dietrich, German Naval Attaché at Buenos Aires, and a German civilian expert, also examined the battleship and, so it was believed, reported that she was navigable.

According to international law a warship that is seaworthy may be compelled to leave a neutral harbour, and the Uruguayan Cabinet decreed that the "Graf Spee" must leave Montevideo within 72 hours—by 8 p.m. on Sunday evening, December 17 (11.30 p.m. Greenwich mean time)—or be interned.

Afterwards it transpired that Captain Langsdorf protested strongly against the time limit. He wanted fifteen days in which to repair the damage that had been done, for, so he maintained, although the fighting capacity of his ship had been

the "Graf Spee" was half as much again as the total broadside of the three British cruisers, and the disparity was still further increased by the fact that early in the action the "Exeter" was hit by a German salvo which knocked out two of her four turrets, smashed three of her 8-inch guns, and inflicted nearly a hundred casualties. Though she was able to continue in the chase, the "Exeter" was forced to drop behind, and it was the two comparatively small British cruisers "Ajax" and "Achilles" which finally drove the "Graf Spee" off the seas.

Well might Captain Langsdorf talk of the "inconceivable audacity" displayed by "Achilles" and "Ajax"—of that "incredible manoeuvre" which brought the two cruisers dashing through the smoke screen to within a mile of the "Graf Spee," firing salvo after salvo into the German ship at close range.

"When the 'Exeter' dropped out of the action," wrote Admiral Sir Howard Kelly in the "Daily Telegraph," "the two small cruisers had a tremendous task in front of them, and

The superstructure of the "Admiral Graf Spee" is seen in these two photographs as it was before the action, top, and above, when she lay in Montevideo harbour. The points at which hits were scored are ringed round. The superstructure is the nerve centre of the ship from which she is navigated and her gunfire controlled.

Photos, Associated Press and Central Press

'Incredible Audacity' Wins the Day for Britain

practically unaffected by the battle, certain repairs would have to be done to the hull in order to make the ship seaworthy.

As the hours drew on activity on the great ship was intensified. The German cargo boat "Tacoma" came alongside and fuelled her with oil, and a number of steel plates and cylinders of oxygen for welding were taken aboard. Several local firms refused to have any hand in the repair work, and amongst the ship-workers anti-Nazi feeling was so strong that the police had difficulty in controlling the crowds who, marching up and down the quay, shouted "Down with Germany!"

Nevertheless, the work went on and as yet there were no indications of the ignominious climax which was being prepared. Sunday dawned, and crowds of Montevideans flocked to the harbour and lined the shore in the hope of catching a glimpse of the wounded ship. All day long launches went to and fro between the "Graf Spee" and the quay, while her sailors continued their repair work. Some of them were noticed to be busy polishing the ship's guns.

Intense diplomatic activity continued, as on the one hand Mr. Millington Drake urged that the ship should be compelled to leave port at once in view of the claim that she was perfectly seaworthy, while on the other hand Dr. Otto Langman, his German opposite number, made desperate efforts to persuade the Uruguayan Government to extend the time limit.

Shortly after five in the evening the "Graf Spee" weighed one anchor, and a quarter of an hour later the second. At six o'clock the tens of thousands of onlookers were surprised to see that the

Outmanoeuvred by British ships far inferior in gun power, the German pocket battleship "Graf Spee" was obliged to seek refuge in the harbour of Montevideo, seen here.
Photo, Associated Press

bulk of the battleship's crew were being transferred to the "Tacoma," and they realized that something strange was afoot when at 6,19 the ship left the inner harbour with only a skeleton crew.

Slowly she sailed down the fairway, followed by several launches. At 6.40 she turned west as if making for Buenos Aires, then a few minutes later turned again and moved slowly towards the open sea. At seven the ship halted in the middle of the estuary; most of the onlookers thought that her captain was waiting for complete darkness before making his dash through the British line.

The moment of the great drama had come—but it was a drama of defeat and ignominy, not of bravery and defiance. Precisely at 7.50 p.m. (11.20 G.M.T.) there was a terrific explosion. A great column of smoke rose up into the darkening sky, and flames leaped and ran along the whole length of the ship. As the special correspondent of the "Daily Telegraph" wrote: "At that moment the sun was just sinking below the horizon, flooding the sky in which small grey clouds floated lazily, a brilliant blood red. It was a perfect Wagnerian setting for this amazing Hitlerian drama."

At first it was thought that Captain Langsdorf and his crew had gone up with the ship, but soon the amazed and terrified spectators saw boats proceeding from the scene. The captain had indeed left the ship a few minutes before the fuses fired the several tons of explosives placed in the ship's magazine. He was taken on a launch to the "Tacoma," which had followed the "Graf Spee" down the river. There, leaning on the rail with bowed shoulders, tears streaming

Above is a photograph, wirelessed from South America, showing the funeral of the 36 men killed on the "Graf Spee" in her encounter with the British cruisers "Exeter," "Ajax" and "Achilles." Above, Commodore Henry Harwood, who was in charge of the British cruisers. He was promoted Rear-Admiral and made K.C.B. immediately after the battle.
Photos, Planet News and G.P.U.

'The Nelson Touch': The Most Aud

The Pride of the Nazi Navy Sails to Her Ignominious End After Being Sha

The scuttling of the "Admiral Graf Spee" was described in an American newspaper as "a spectacular admission of defeat." The last moments of the
seen in this historic photograph which, sent by radio across the world, was received in London only a few hours after she left Montevideo harbour
steaming out to meet her self-appointed fate, and go up in a blaze, the very reverse of glorious. With characteristic disregard for the neutrals the

Photos, Keystone, Wright & Logan, Photopress and Topical

Sea Fight in Modern Naval History

Cornered by British Light Cruisers

Above is the "Exeter," an 8,000 ton cruiser completed in 1931 and re-commissioned at the outbreak of war. At the battle of the Plate she was commanded by Captain F. S. Bell, who, at the beginning of the last war, served as a midshipman in the "Cumberland" and "Challenger." At the battle of Jutland he served in H.M.S. "Canada."

Captain C. H. L. Woodhouse, centre right, served as a lieutenant in H.M.S. "Malaya," at the battle of Jutland. Above, the "Ajax," which he commanded at the fight with the "Graf Spee." Right, Captain Parry, who commanded the "Achilles," seen below, served as torpedo officer in the "Birmingham" in the last war. All three captains were given the C.B.

chose to sink his ship in the chief anchorage of Montevideo in such water that she remained a menace to shipping until she could be destroyed. On the right is seen the German tanker "Tacoma."

The Shameful Suicide of Hitler's Proud Warship

In this sketch map the place of the " Graf Spee's " inglorious sinking is indicated by X ; it is not far beyond the 3-mile limit (shown by the dotted line).   On the extreme right is Punta del Este, from where observers had a grandstand view of the battle.

from his eyes, he watched his ship blaze and smoke into ruin.

Later, reports were current that there had been insubordination among the " Graf Spee's " crew as soon as they learned on the Saturday evening that their vessel was to be scuttled, and there seems to be little doubt that although in his letter to Dr. Langman Captain Langsdorf said that " in the circumstances there remains no solution but to sink my ship by blowing her up near the coast," this decision was dictated by the Fuehrer himself. Furious because his ship was trapped,

Hitler in a moment of passion issued the order to scuttle—thus revealing to the world in the plainest fashion his doubts concerning the ultimate victory. For if the ship had been interned and Germany won the war she would have been returned to the triumphant Reich. . . .

" The news," said Mr. Churchill in his broadcast to the nation on December 18, " which has come from Montevideo has been received with thankfulness in our islands and with unconcealed satisfaction throughout the greater part of the world. . . .

" The German pocket battleship, in spite of her far heavier metal and commanding range, was driven to take refuge in a neutral harbour

by the three British cruisers whose names are on every lip. Once in harbour she had the choice of submitting in the ordinary manner to internment, which would have been unfortunate for her, or of coming out to fight and going down in battle like the 'Rawalpindi,' which would have been honourable to her.

" She discovered a third alternative. She came out not to fight but to sink herself in the fairway of a neutral State from whom she had received such shelter and succour as international law prescribes.

" At that time the pocket battleship 'Graf Spee' knew that the British heavy ships 'Renown' and 'Ark Royal' were still a thousand miles away, oiling at Rio. All that awaited her outside the harbour were the two six-inch gun cruisers 'Ajax' and 'Achilles,' who had chased her in, and the eight-inch gun cruiser 'Cumberland,' which had arrived to take the place of the 'Exeter.' "

The world heard the news with amazement mingled with contempt. " Incredible," said Rome ; " she might as well have fired upon the enemy first," said Japan. " But," as the " Daily Telegraph " pertinently said, " When it takes orders from Hitler, the German Navy has to ' leave honour out of the question ' . . . when the ' Graf Spee ' was sunk by her captain in the channel of the neutral harbour of Montevideo, he wrote the last line of an immortal epic of ignominy."

This amazingly realistic photograph transmitted to London by radio shows Germany's pocket battleship " Admiral Graf Spee " burning furiously shortly after her scuttling by her commander at Hitler's orders.   The spot chosen is right in the fairway of shipping going to and coming from Montevideo, one of the greatest of South American ports, and its selection is petty spitefulness—in the true Nazi vein—against the little neutral country which had refused to accept Germany's demand for an extension of the time limit.

Photo, Planet News

At £2,000 a Shot Torpedoes Must Be Accurate

The head of a torpedo practically complete is being filled with water ballast preparatory to undergoing trials. This is equivalent to the weight of the explosive to be inserted.

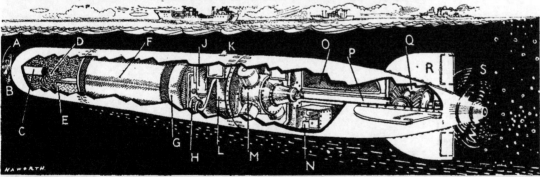

One more torpedo case is being added to those in stock before undergoing the severe tests which precede issue to the Navy.

TORPEDOES are by far the most costly of all the missiles of war costing about £2,000 each. The largest are 21 ft. long and 21 in. in diameter. Their speed is between 40 and 50 knots; their maximum range is about 10,000 yards. They are driven by a remarkably ingenious miniature engine, water-cooled, and actuated by compressed air at a pressure of 2,500 lbs. to the sq. in. The head contains about 500 lbs. of high explosive.

Below is a scene at a testing station where torpedoes are discharged from the land in exactly the same way as they would be from a warship. During the test the torpedo carries no high explosive, but a dummy head such as is used for practice in the Royal Navy.

Photos, Keystone

A modern torpedo contains about 6,000 working parts, and much of the mechanism is extremely delicate, so that its construction calls for the most skilled craftsmanship.

Key to the Diagram—

A, Firing pin; B, Safety fan; C, Detonator; D, 500 lb. explosive; E, Water ballast; F, Compressed Air at 2,500 lb. sq. in.; G, Water chamber; H, Steering Control for horizontal rudders; J, Depth control; K, Trigger Starter; L, Paraffin bottle; M, 4-cyl. Engine (hot air); N, Gyroscopic rudder control; O, Buoyancy chamber; P, Propeller shaft; Q, Gear box; R, 2 vertical and 2 horizontal fins and rudders; S, 2 Propellers.

Some Secrets of the Convoys Revealed

Written by an ex-officer of the Merchant Service, this article gives a " behind the scenes " account of the organization, skill and daring involved in wartime convoy work.

In bitter winds and often lashed by ice-cold rain and spray such British sailors as this are winning the war at sea.
Photo, Fox

CONVOYS work to carefully-prepared plans, and those plans are drawn up by officers of the Royal Navy who are stationed at the ports especially for this purpose. The ships which are to form a convoy assemble slowly in the haven or roadstead which has been chosen for the rendezvous. The ships have to make their way there from the various ports at which they have been lying, and as some have farther to go than others, and may not be able to catch the same tides, it is quite possible that days may pass before the convoy is ready to set out on its mass voyage.

The speed of a convoy is necessarily the speed of the slowest ship, and for this reason it is important that all the ships comprising any particular convoy should be able to maintain a uniform speed. So we have fast convoys and slow convoys, in order to cater for the fifteen-knot cargo-liner or the nine-knot tramp respectively.

'Blacking-Out' at Sea

All the vessels have previously been fitted with various contrivances, which, although seemingly unimportant, are nevertheless essential for convoy work. For instance, in addition to ordinary black-out precautions, such as the screening of all portholes and deck-lights, each outside cabin door is fitted with a special type of contact switch which is arranged so that the mere act of opening the door automatically extinguishes the light within.

The bridge and wheelhouse and other vital spots are protected by sandbags. The master and mates are provided with tin hats, and the whole crew have gas masks and are equipped in every way to deal with incendiary bombs and other dangers from the air.

In all cases the ship's name is painted over on both bow and stern; in order that port officials and others may be able to identify the ships whilst they are in dock, the name is displayed on a blackboard which is removed immediately the ship sails.

Each ship that is to sail in convoy must be equipped with a special type of alarm clock, the face of which is fitted with a number of adjustable stops.

These stops can be so adjusted that a bell will ring every ten minutes, or at any desired interval. The clocks of the whole convoy are synchronized, so that when the convoy is zigzagging, each captain is warned by his alarm clock of the exact moment to change course. By this means, the difficult manoeuvre of making dozens of ships twist and turn whilst bunched close together, is accomplished without any of them colliding or falling out of line.

In foggy weather it is impossible for any of the ships to see even the one immediately ahead, and there is a very real danger of collisions occurring unless the ships of the convoy can manage to keep their proper distance behind each other. To help in doing this, every ship tows from the stern on the end of a long line a brightly-painted wooden cask, which is known as a fog-buoy.

The boat that is following tries to keep close to the fog-buoy of the next ship in the line, and thus keep its allotted station in relation to the other invisible members of the fog-enshrouded convoy. That is no easy task, it must be admitted, but the officers on the bridge are keyed up by the knowledge that, should they get separated from the rest, their solitary ship would offer a very tempting target to any prowling U-boat.

In contrast to the fog-buoys are the special smoke flares which are carried on the deck of each ship. When dropped overboard, they set up a dense smoke behind which they can give the enemy the slip.

The convoy is nearly always protected by a number of destroyers or other escort vessels, which circle around, ready to dart away at terrific speed and drop their deadly depth-charges whenever there is a sign of a periscope. As a unit, the convoy presents a much bigger target to the enemy than might seem prudent, but this is more than balanced by other considerations and the fact that powerfully armed escorts can be provided for nearly every convoy, whereas it would be impossible to give such protection to single ships.

Answering the U-Boats

Certain of our merchant ships are defensively armed. Together with the guns of the escort vessels, the ships of a convoy can put up such a terrific aerial barrage as to make it impossible for enemy bombers to reach the one position necessary for the scoring of a direct hit. It is for this reason that many experts consider that the convoy system has provided the answer not only to the U-boat menace, but also to the peril of attack from the air.

From the bridge of an escorting warship, officers clad for the North Sea are keeping watch on the convoy of whose escort their ship forms part. Besides looking out for enemy submarines they have to shepherd their flock of ships, making sure that stations are correctly kept and the prescribed speed maintained.
Photo, Fox

Guardian Wings Above the Convoy's Course

Here in this diagram-sketch we look down on a convoy from one of the flying boats of the R.A.F. Coastal Command. The machine is a Short "Sunderland," the Service version of the famous Empire marine air-liners. It is the largest type of aircraft known to be in use in our Air Force today. Details are indicated as follows : (A) One of two pilots. (B) Life-saving neck belt. (C) Navigator plotting course at right angles to convoy. (D) Engineer controlling four "Pegasus" engines. (E) Radio operator in touch with warships. (F) Signal flares. (G) Gangway to lower decks. (H) Entrance to fire turret. (J) Messroom. (K) Reserve pilot resting. (L) Engine down below on the surface. (M) Escort vessel. (N) Armed minesweeper. (O) One of the coloured buoys which are towed by ships to enable them to keep station in fog. The course of the convoy is frequently changed, and it is here shown altering course to port, as seen at (Q). In order that all the ships may turn together alarm clocks (P), synchronized to ring at certain intervals as a warning to change course, are carried in all convoy ships.

Specially drawn for THE WAR ILLUSTRATED *by Haworth*

The Commonsense View of Gas Attacks

In this article Major-General C. H. Foulkes, C.B., C.M.G., who was Gas Adviser to
British G.H.Q. in the Great War and is today one of the leading A.R.P. consultants,
discusses the question of gas attacks on civilians. He is author of " Gas ! The Story
of the Special Brigade " and " Commonsense and A.R.P."

A PROFOUND change in the degree of security enjoyed by the civil population of this country in time of war has been brought about by the development of the aeroplane. With a supreme Navy ruling the seas there has been no risk of an invasion of our shores for generations past ; but with the advent of the bombing aeroplane our cities are now exposed to attack. That attack may take several forms—incendiary bombs, high-explosive bombs, and gas.

Of these gas, we have been told, is the chief danger in an air raid, and much of the effort expended on the instruction of the public in A.R.P. has been devoted to it. Indeed, exaggerated importance has been given to it by the Government. In May 1938 a prominent Home Office official went so far as to tell a London audience that " cows, hens, and other farm stock should have gas-proof barns provided for them," and, emulating this example, a beekeepers' magazine published an article showing how beehives could be protected by charcoal-packed quilts. I have even read an account of how to protect goldfish in bowls.

Expert opinion is now almost unanimous in believing that gas is very unlikely to be used, not because of its supposed inhumanity, but because, although it would be effective, it would be less so, weight for weight, than high explosives.

In the last war the conditions were very different in the chaos of the battlefield. Men had necessarily to occupy gas-contaminated ground for days at a time, and guns had to be served and ration and working parties were compelled to expose themselves in the open. Decontamination of scores of square miles of scarred surface was an obvious impossibility, and the air in a bombarded area remained dangerous for days, while contaminated mud was often carried unwittingly into sleeping quarters with disastrous results. Men's bodies and equipment also came into contact with the ground, especially during the last six months of the struggle, when semi-open conditions of warfare prevailed.

Gas will probably still find its uses on the battlefield, and it has been used in Abyssinia and by the Japanese, but not by the latter against Chinese cities ; nor was it used in Spain in the Civil War. There is good authority for saying that

it is unlikely that any " new " effective gas has been discovered since the last war, and efforts to find more effective ways of using known chemical agents are more likely to be profitable than any attempts to discover more powerful compounds. For instance, it has been determined that about two-thirds of a teaspoonful of mustard gas absorbed into a man's lungs, will cause his death ; so that there is enough potential poison in a ton of this substance to kill 45,000,000 persons. But in the last war only 33 casualties

were caused, on an average, by each ton of it released on the battlefield, and only one of these proved fatal.

Rumours are being constantly circulated of the discovery of some new gas of incredible potency ; one of these substances, if released from a bomb in Piccadilly Circus, would, according to one writer, destroy all life between Regent's Park and the Thames—perhaps a million persons. Another, according to an American report, would make millions of people unconscious. This started another scare, and when investigations were made it was found that this terrible new substance was ethanol. This is the scientific name for alcohol, which is sometimes found in beer.

Gas and the poisonous smokes, without the accompaniment of incendiary and high-explosive bombs, would, in the writer's opinion, have little physical effect

on an organized community sheltered, or partly sheltered, in buildings ; and the casualties caused by them would be less severe in nature, and they would fall far short of the number estimated in some of the fantastic forecasts that have been published in recent years by persons seeking notoriety or aiming at sensationalism.

When a volatile gas like phosgene is released from a bomb it may be thrown a hundred feet up into the air, but it would quickly settle down, and unless the cloud was steadily reinforced by other bombs in the same neighbourhood it would drift away. It would be most effective in such circumstances as exist in the City of London, where lofty buildings and narrow courts would not favour rapid dispersion, but even there immense quantities would be required.

As regards poisonous smokes, these are much more difficult to release from aerial bombs than cloud gas, although buildings and masks give somewhat less protection against them. However, they are not usually lethal.

Persistent gases sprayed from an aeroplane would fall on roofs, walls and open spaces, and people under cover should not be affected. Danger, however, would arise if the liquid was allowed to lie and vaporize on the ground.

Mustard gas liberated as a spray from a great height would vaporize and much of it be blown away as it fell. To be really effective, mustard gas would have to be released from an aeroplane flying at the dangerous height of only a few hundred feet from the ground. Very little of the spray would reach the ground, and in any case it might take half an hour to do so.

It is true that asphalt and bituminous road surfaces absorb mustard gas rapidly and retain it for some length of time, but there would be little risk in walking along roads so contaminated, and there would be no risk at all in frosty weather. The spray would be most effective in delaying rescue work and repairs in the open.

If people are provided with masks of the standard approved by the Government, masks which have been fitted individually and tested in a gas chamber, there should be no casualties at all in a gas attack, except in the immediate neighbourhood of the explosion of a bomb, where the concentration of gas would be, of course, very high.

SILENCE AND THE BLACKOUT

A New Poem

by

HUMBERT WOLFE

●

Why must you cry the Sunday news? If good,
  it well can wait; if evil, all too soon
it will be known. For my part, if I could,
  I would be far and quiet as the moon,
whose only sound is light on the long cruise
  through the deep seas of interstellar space,
and in whose orbit all the argent news
  is the sun changing gold to silver grace.
Nor is it craven, newsboys, to implore
  one day for silence. With her fingers cool
laid to the Sunday streets even in war
  she makes them hallowed, hushed and beautiful,
as in the evening dark she builds in them
the half-seen turrets of Jerusalem.

Copyright reserved

Mr. Briton'll See It Through

Some schools in the neighbourhood of London have been re-opened for those children who were evacuated but whose parents have insisted on bringing them back before the danger is over. But they are still well looked after and do gas-mask drill in class. Above right, grandfather does his bit by knitting comforts for the troops.

Photos, Keystone, F. R. Winstone, Fox and Topical

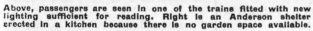

Above, passengers are seen in one of the trains fitted with new lighting sufficient for reading. Right is an Anderson shelter erected in a kitchen because there is no garden space available.

Two important factors in winning the economic warfare are the reduction of our imports to the minimum and the careful use of all material generally regarded as waste. Left is a motor-bus with a gas-producing trailer burning anthracite, to lessen petroleum imports. Right is a scene during the big drive to save every bit of scrap metal. At the tram depot at Kingswood, Bristol, old cars are being scrapped at the rate of one a day for the sake of the metal. Above, the motor and bogie of a tram-car are being broken up while another awaits its fate.

Poland is the Nazis' Jig-Saw

Based on information contained in "Free Europe," a newly-established journal devoted to Central and East European affairs, this article gives facts and figures concerning the fate of Poland under the Nazi yoke.

Arthur Greiser, who is Governor of one of the provinces into which Germany's share of Poland is divided, was a Danzig business man who held several offices in the Danzig government. *Photo, Wide World*

FOR some 125 years Poland as an independent State was banished from the map of Europe. In 1918 it was restored, and after a mere twenty years it has once again disappeared. Between them the Nazis and the Russians have effected yet another partition of Poland, which, so far as the conquerors can ensure it, is intended to be irrevocable. Poland, indeed, has been so savagely mutilated, her people have been so redistributed, that the partitions of the eighteenth century, horrible as they were, have been quite put into the shade.

By this most recent division of the spoils little short of half Poland was allocated to Germany. Of this area of roughly 187,000 square kilometres, with a population of 21,200,000, the western provinces have now been incorporated in Germany as the *Reichsgebiet* (Reich region), while the central districts are to form a Polish "reserve" the *Reststaat*.

Incorporated in the Reich

The incorporated area comprises the three Polish voivodships (provinces) of Pomerania, Poznania, and Silesia. The first two have been converted into *Reichsgaue* (Reich provinces), Westpreussen, and Posen or Wartheland, with their capitals at Danzig and Poznan, and their respective *Reichsstatthalters* (provincial governors), Herr Forster and Herr Greiser, both of whom were prominent in Danzig before the war. Polish Silesia has been simply tacked on to the existing *Gau Schlesien*, i.e. German Silesia. Although these three western voivodships are claimed by Nazi propagandists to be *urdeutsch* (German-from-the-beginning), of their population of 5,520,000 only 389,000, i.e. 7 per cent, were Germans according to the Polish census of 1931.

German Territorial Greed

These changes were made in October, and in the next month there were further alterations in the map. Suwalki, wedged between Lithuania, East Prussia, and the new Soviet frontier, was incorporated in the *Gau Ostpreussen*, and Posen's frontier was carried right up to and including Lodz, thus taking in a number of districts which were popularly known as the *Gau Warthe*. This extension brought the German frontier to where it had been in 1918 following the collapse of Russia. Arthur Greiser, *Reichsstatthalter* of Posen, sent a telegram to Hitler saying that he was keeping watch on the Warthe, to which Hitler replied: "The age-old river Warthe will remain German for ever." Slight adjustments were also made in the frontier adjoining the former Czecho-Slovakia. These additions increased the territory of the *Reichsgebiet* by 17,000 sq. km., with a population of 2,110,000.

No sooner was the *Reichsgebiet* established than the work of Germanization was prosecuted with the utmost vigour. Poles who were not born in the western provinces, including most of the population of Gdynia, were forcibly removed to the *Reststaat*, while those who did happen to be natives were declared to be German citizens.

There can be no two opinions about the difficult task which confronts the German administration in the *Reichsgebiet*. According to the "Frankfurter Zeitung," 4,000,000 Germans are to be settled in this region, in which the average density of population under Polish rule was 73 per sq. km. in Pomerania, 83 in Poznan, and 307 in Polish Silesia. Well may "Free Europe" hold up to reprobation "the monstrous crime which is about to be committed against the Polish peasants and shopkeepers who are to be hounded from their homes to make room for this lighthearted experiment in juggling with populations."

The spirit in which this juggling is being done was indicated in the speech made by Forster at a meeting of Germans in Torun. "Our country," he said, referring to Polish Pomerania, "is beautiful and fertile, but there have been too few of us living in it. Now that Germans from other countries are flocking here, our numbers will increase. In a few years' time Polish will no longer be heard in the streets of this town."

Central Poland, including the provinces of Warsaw, Lodz, Kielce, Lublin and Cracow, were joined to form the *Reststaat* (remaining territory), with Hans Frank as Governor-General. Its area is barely 112,000 sq. km., with a population of 13,570,000. Semi-military administration was introduced for the time being, for no Poles could be found who would undertake to form a government under the conquerors.

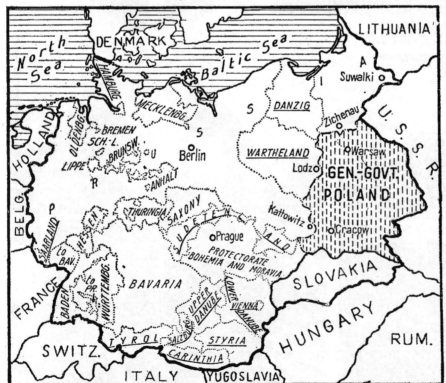

The whole area of Greater Germany as it was in November 1939 is shown in this map. The names of the provinces directly governed by the Reich are underlined. The shaded area shows the "Reststaat," that area in Central Poland which is a Nazi "protectorate." The other Polish areas are described in the accompanying article.

Courtesy, Keesing's "Contemporary Archives"

One of the Seven of a Single Day's Bag

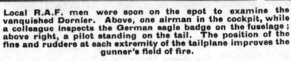

Local R.A.F. men were soon on the spot to examine the vanquished Dornier. Above, one airman in the cockpit, while a colleague inspects the German eagle badge on the fuselage; above right, a pilot standing on the tail. The position of the fins and rudders at each extremity of the tailplane improves the gunner's field of fire.

SEVEN raiders were shot down on the Western Front in one day—that was the achievement of the R.A.F. on November 23, 1939. The unhappy end of one of the victims—a Dornier DO 17, of the "flying pencil" type—is pictured in this page. In the fight the enemy pilot was left alone in his machine to combat a flight of R.A.F. fighters, and he adopted the clever ruse of feigning death. Seeing him slump over the controls, a British "Hurricane" flew past him unsuspecting. When in a favourable position, the German sprang to life and peppered it from his front gun. However, the odds were too great, and the Dornier was forced down. Such was the admiration of the R.A.F. for this pilot that he was entertained to dinner in the Squadron Mess. He broke down during the meal, overwhelmed by the kindness shown him.

Very naturally and properly interested in its prizes of war is the R.A.F. The technicians especially take the opportunity of examining the details of modern German construction when, as in this particular case, the enemy is brought down in our own lines. In the circle, a group are studying one of the engines, a 9-cylinder B.M.W. radial; below left, one of the cameras carried on board the Dornier; and right, the bullet-scarred fuselage and tail.

Photos, British Movietonenews

WORDS THAT HISTORY WILL REMEMBER

(Continued from page 498)

Appeal to the League by Finland

Saturday, December 2, 1939

Letter addressed by M. RUDOLF HOLSTI, Permanent Finnish Delegate, to M. Avenol, Secretary-General of the League of Nations :

The Union of Soviet Socialist Republics, with which Finland, since the signature of the treaty of peace at Tartu in 1920, has maintained neighbourly relations, and signed a pact of non-aggression which should have expired in 1945, unexpectedly attacked on the morning of November 30, not only frontier positions, but also open Finnish towns, spreading death and destruction among the civil population, more particularly by attacks from the air.

Finland has never engaged in any undertaking directed against her powerful neighbour. She has continuously made every effort to live at peace with her.

Nevertheless, alleging so-called frontier incidents and adducing the alleged refusal of Finland to acquiesce in strengthening the security of Leningrad, the Union of Soviet Socialist Republics first denounced the above-mentioned pact of non-aggression, and then refused the Finnish Government's proposal to have recourse to the mediation of a neutral Power.

In consequence, acting on the instructions of my Government, I have the honour to bring the foregoing facts to your knowledge, and to request you, in virtue of Articles 11 and 15 of the Covenant, forthwith to summon a meeting of the Council and Assembly, and ask them to take the necessary measures to put an end to this aggression.

I will forward in due course a complete statement of the reasons and circumstances which led my Government to request the intervention of the League of Nations on the dispute which has brought two of its members into conflict with one another.

Churlish Attitude of the Soviet Premier

Monday, December 4

Reply of M. MOLOTOV to League of Nations :

In the name of the Soviet Government, I have the honour to reply that the convocation of the Council on M. Holsti's initiative is considered as unwarranted by my Government. The Soviet Government is not at war with Finland and does not threaten it, so that the reference to Article XI of the Covenant of the League is incorrect.

The Soviet Union has a pact with the People's Democratic Republic of Finland which regulates all questions which negotiations with the former Finnish Government failed to achieve.

The People's Democratic Government appealed to the Soviet Union for military assistance to liquidate the war danger created by the Former Finnish Government. M. Holsti's application lacks a legal basis for calling the Council, since M. Holsti and his superiors do not represent the Finnish people.

The Soviet Union will not take part if the Council is convoked for December 9. . . .

Russian Aggression Inspired by Germany

Tuesday, December 5

LORD HALIFAX in a speech in the House of Lords :

. . . The toll of evil flowing from the German example and practice of aggression has grown, and we have witnessed what has been universally condemned as an inexcusable act of aggression by one of the largest upon one of the smallest but most highly civilized nations of Europe—their open towns bombarded, their women and children mutilated and done to death—on the pretext that a nation of under 4,000,000 had hostile designs against 180,000,000. The British people . . . have profoundly admired the magnificent resistance of the Finns.

The Russian attack on Finland seems to me to be a direct consequence of German policy. By the agreement which he thought would give him a free hand to attack Poland it would seem that Herr Hitler bartered what was not his property to barter—the liberties of the Baltic peoples. The sequence of events has shown how wide is the damage once the floodgates are opened.

Earlier in the year we tried to improve our relations with Russia, but always maintained the position that rights of third parties must remain intact and unaffected by our negotiations.

I think that events have shown that the judgement and instinct of the British Government in refusing agreement with the Soviet Government on the terms of formulae covering cases of indirect aggression on the Baltic States were right, for it is now claimed that these formulae might well have been the cloak of ulterior designs, and I have little doubt that the people of this country would prefer to face difficulties and embarrassments rather than feel that we had compromised the honour of this country and the Commonwealth on such issues. . . .

Finland Protests Against Illegal Blockade

Friday, December 8

Statement issued by FINNISH GOVERNMENT on the Russian blockade :

After the aggression against Finland the Soviet Union declared that a state of war did not exist. She has therefore no right now to take blockade measures, which involve not only Finland but other nations.

A blockade in time of peace is permissible only against countries which have violated certain stipulations of the League of Nations —as indeed Russia has done by invading Finland. To be legal, moreover, a blockade must be effective, as was stipulated by the Declaration of Paris of 1856, signed by all civilized countries, including Russia.

As far as is known Russia has no ship at the moment in the Gulf of Bothnia ; and no ship can enter, since the Aaland Sea has been closed by mines. Hence, if the blockade concerns the Gulf of Bothnia, it is obviously without legal as well as without practical significance.

It is unlikely also that Russia will be able to blockade the Gulf of Finland effectively considering the length of its coast and the inadequacy of the Russian Fleet to carry out such an operation. Finland, thanks to her coastal defences, aviation, service vessels, and mines, can take effective measures to prevent Russia from carrying out the blockade

---

THINGS YOU MAY NOT KNOW

Swastika. Known universally nowadays as the symbol of the Nazi Party, and hence of National Socialist Germany, the swastika (Ger. *Hakenkreuz*) was originally a religious sign of great antiquity. Hitler borrowed it from the German Free Corps which helped the Baltic States to obtain independence from Soviet Russia in 1919. It is also incorporated in the national markings of Finnish and Latvian military aircraft coloured blue and red respectively.

Fricordin. A term applied to the Germans by the French soldiers who took part in the occupation of the Rhineland after the last war. It corresponds to the German Christian name "Fritz."

Blimp. The term "blimp" originated in the last war, when British lighter-than-air aircraft were divided into A—rigid, and B—limp (i.e. without rigid internal framework). The modern barrage balloon may therefore be classed as a blimp. The name was borrowed by Low, the cartoonist, for his famous "die-hard" character, Colonel Blimp.

Boche. The word Boche written on the side of the German aeroplane seen in page 418 was the term used by French soldiers for the Germans in the last war, but it is less often heard today. Its origin is doubtful. One suggestion is that it derives from Alboche, a Parisian slang version of the word *Allemand*. Another explanation is that it is an abbreviation of the slang word "Caboche," meaning much the same as the slang expression "napper" for a head.

Oropesa. As explained in page 399, a type of minesweeping float. The name originated from that of a trawler in which the newly-invented gear was first tested.

Fifth Column. A phrase which dates from the siege of Madrid during the Spanish Civil War when General Franco boasted that he had four columns marching on the city and a fifth secret one inside.

Navicert. A name invented by Mr. R. P. Skinner, United States Consul-General in London during the last war. It was a system whereby particulars of all shipments from the United States to Scandinavia were first submitted to the Trade Department of the British Embassy, who immediately cabled the details to London, a decision being reached before the consignment left American shores.

Squadron. A term adopted by the R.A.F. from the Navy and the Cavalry, a Squadron in the R.A.F. corresponds to a regiment in the Army. It is the basic tactical unit, a number of Squadrons forming a Wing, so many Wings a Group, and so to the Command. The Squadron itself is usually divided into two or three Flights, each of at least three machines. If in squadron formation a Squadron of fighters or bombers will fly in a "vee" with three Flights of three machines each.

Artillery Ties. Few people know the meaning of the zigzag red stripe on the Royal Artillery tie ; it is derived from the legend in which the pagan father of St. Barbara (patron saint of artillerymen) was killed by lightning for martyring his daughter. The Honourable Artillery Company tie has additional red bars across the zigzag.

Asdic. This word, mentioned by Mr. Churchill in one of his speeches, is an abbreviation for Anti-Submarine Detector Indicator Committee, which invented a type of secret apparatus now used by the Navy.

We Flew from Germany on Clipped Wings

The brief official reports of reconnaissances by British aircraft over
Germany hardly did justice to the hazards to which our airmen were
often exposed. A broadcast by a New Zealand pilot describing
one adventurous flight into enemy territory is here reproduced.

WE took off from our base in
England at nine o'clock in the
evening and settled down on
our course for the target at a steady climb,
leaving behind us a beautiful moonlight
night. In half an hour we were at a height
of fifteen thousand feet, where there were
72 degrees of frost. We were now flying
along between towering clouds which
stretched below us to the sea. We were
going to do a reconnaissance of parts of
North-West Germany.

About two hours from home we had
calculated that we should be near our
objectives so we started coming down
through the clouds, which now thickened
up and were becoming very black.
Gunners who had been working their
turrets and guns to keep them fit, now
reported queer flashes of blue flame
playing around the muzzles of their guns,
and we could see the same blue flames
on our wing tips—lightning.

As the temperature, increasing with our
descent, approached freezing-point, a
snowy type of ice grew on the control
column, on the inside of the windows,
and on the instrument panel. When we
reached two thousand feet and wiped the
stuff from the windows we found that
we were just below the clouds—over
Germany, a few miles inland. The navigator had done well.

Heading towards our objective a
searchlight beam snapped us, but was
soon put off as we popped up into the
clouds again. We came out of them and
flew along at varying low heights to see
what we could. The visibility was bad

and the black clouds were still there, so
I opened my window to see better. It
was snowing. The navigator table and
the instruments were soon covered again
with half an inch of snow and ice. The
front gunner could see nothing from his
cockpit but white snow—when he came
back to see us his helmet and shoulders
were buried beneath an inch of the stuff.
Shortly afterwards a blinding flash, and
a bump bigger than the others, took away
our trailing aerial—and knocked all the
snow off the instruments.

Realising that with conditions as they
were we should see nothing more of value
here—the tail gunner had already collected some pretty useful information—
we set our course for another objective,
climbing and circling to avoid a heavy
cloud.

At ten thousand feet, our gyro-horizon
froze, and the tail gunner reported
"Fighters on our tail," so we decided

to go straight through the cloud. Gradually we climbed to nineteen thousand five
hundred feet, when the aeroplane, which
had been behaving queerly, became un-
controllable and dropped like a stone to
one thousand five hundred feet.

We thought we should have to land
on the sea, so the navigator went back
to prepare the rubber dinghy and collect
the rest of the crew. However, as we got
down to five hundred feet the engines
began to pick up, and when the navigator
returned to report "All O.K. for a landing"
we were maintaining height at one hundred
and ten miles an hour and it seemed that
we might be able to make England.

A small winking light shone on the sea
and we circled this, turning left. The
moon shone through in patches to reveal
a choppy sea whipped up by a forty-mile-
an-hour gale. The left wing seemed
definitely odd, and it was most difficult
to straighten up on our course. I mentioned this to the navigator, who said:
"Oh yes—when I was getting the dinghy
ready I noticed that a bit of fabric had
come off the wing."

Later I learned that he had wisely kept
to himself the full extent of the damage

These photographs illustrate the dramatic story told in this page by a New Zealander serving in the R.A.F. Taken after the safe return of
the aeroplane—an Armstrong-Whitworth "Whitley" heavy bomber—one wonders anew how any flying machine with wings thus battered
could stay in the air, let alone reach its base. Fortunately the aileron control flaps on each trailing edge appear undamaged, but even so it
was a fine feat of airmanship that brought the "Whitley" home from over enemy territory.
Photos, British Official, Crown Copyright

540   *The War Illustrated*   *December 29th,* 1939

|||||||||||||||||||||||||||||||||||||||||||||||||||||||||||||||||||||||||||| I WAS THERE! |||||||||||||||||||||||||||||||||||||||||||||||||||||||||||||||||||

which must have horrified him at the time—the port wing was almost completely stripped of fabric, and there was a large lump missing from the starboard one. This did not stop him working out a careful course for home. Three hundred and fifty miles to go. Flying at five hundred feet to avoid the high wind and to make things safer for a possible landing, we encountered a couple of rain-storms which we could not go under or around.

After two-and-a-half hours of this the wireless operator obtained three good bearings from a station near the East Coast before our wireless ceased to function. Nearly an hour later we sighted land ahead and clear weather. It was not long before we found an aerodrome and landed at half-past three in the morning, never before so pleased to set our feet on the earth. There we had a look at the wings and almost died of fright.

However, the experience had not all been ours. We were soon talking with others who had been on the same trip: in one machine the tail gunner's eyebrows became frozen up when the aircraft was at twenty-one thousand feet, where there were 72 degrees of frost. They had also run into this electrical storm and had seen the weird blue flashes playing around the wing tips and guns, and some bigger flashes which lit up the whole aircraft.

Two of the gunners of the other machines suffered from frostbitten fingers and another pilot described what he called a firework display, such as was seen by pilots in the last war : " flaming onions "—green balls of fire coming up from the ground as though someone were throwing cricket balls up at a terrific speed. He was able to avoid these and watch them fly harmlessly by into the clouds. This particular machine encountered terrific headwinds at the height it was flying—up to eighty miles an hour from the west. Because of this it took many hours to reach home. They landed in daylight with a broken wireless, having navigated the whole of the way back with a sextant.

Captain Stubbs was in command of the 10,000 ton refrigerator ship " Doric Star," which was the largest of the " Graf Spee's " victims. His own story is told in page 541.
Photo, G.P.U.

I Saw The ' Admiral Graf Spee ' Attacked

The first big naval engagement of the war was the battle of the River Plate, fought on December 13 between the German pocket battleship " Graf Spee " and the British cruisers " Exeter," " Ajax," and " Achilles " (see pages 526–530). The following actual eyewitness account of the action is reprinted from " The Star."

A DRAMATIC account of the battle between the " Graf Spee " and the British cruisers was given by a director of the Havas News Agency, who was on board the French liner " Formose."

" I left Le Havre on November 11 for Rio Plata," he said.

" As we entered the last stage of the voyage the ' Formose ' intercepted a message from the ' Graf Spee ' warning the cruiser ' Ajax ' to pick up the crew of a British cargo boat she had just sunk. The message did not give the position where the sinking had taken place.

" A few minutes later a neutral ship signalled the position of the ' Graf Spee.' The German warship was apparently then only 30 miles from the ' Formose,' travelling at some 24 knots.

" Our commander, Captain Baton, immediately changed our course and sought the shelter of the coast. The danger was kept a strict secret from the passengers.

" The ' Graf Spee's ' position was again signalled three hours later at 1 p.m., this time approaching the coast at a reduced speed, apparently making for Montevideo.

" At 6 p.m. we were within sight of the Uruguayan coast. Almost at the same moment we sighted the ' Graf Spee.' She was sailing parallel with us, and soon afterwards fired four shots—at whom we could not see. She continued parallel with us for some 10 miles, reducing her speed and seeming to watch the ' Formose.'

" Most of the passengers were still unaware of the nationality of the ship and thought she was having gunnery practice.

" At 7.30 p.m. we saw another warship a long way out to sea, but approaching at a great speed. She was a British cruiser, and she opened fire on the German.

" The first shell missed the ' Graf Spee,' but the range was then rectified, and the second shot took her fair and square in the stern. The cruiser then threw out a smoke screen to hide herself, and took up the chase at full speed.

" The ' Graf Spee,' surprised by the sudden attack, increased her speed and replied with a volley of four shots, all of which fell wide. Taking advantage of her hesitation, the cruiser pressed the attack without allowing her the slightest breathing space.

" When night fell, about 8.30, the Graf Spee ' was still firing shells, seemingly at random, and she disappeared into the darkness still pursued.

" At 10.15 a.m. on December 14 we sailed in to the quayside at Montevideo, passing within 100 yards of the damaged ' Graf Spee.' "

Captain Langsdorff, of the " Admiral Graf Spee," scuttled his ship in accordance with orders received from Berlin. He is seen above, wearing his Iron Cross, on a tug at Buenos Aires, surrounded by members of his crew. His cheerful demeanour does not suggest that he had heard the opinion of Naval men of many nations on his ship's end.
Photo, Associated Press

We Were Prisoners On the ' Graf Spee '

On board the " Graf Spee " as prisoners were the captains of six
British merchant ships, who were uncomfortably aware of the action
although they saw nothing of it. These accounts are due to the
" Daily Express," Reuters, and British United Press.

CAPTAIN STUBBS, of the " Doric Star,"
said : " It was about six o'clock in
the morning when a German officer came
down and said, ' Gentlemen, I'm afraid
we'll have to leave you to your own
devices.' We didn't know what he
meant.

" Our quarters were pretty cramped,
right under one of the ' Graf Spee's ' gun
turrets.

" Then we heard the roar of guns in
the distance and we knew that our lads
had spotted the Nazi battleship.

" Next minute the ' Graf Spee ' rolled
drunkenly. There was a tremendous
crash over our heads. She had opened
fire.

" We thought it would never end. W
counted 17 hits altogether o the ' Graf
Spee.' Did we cheer and sing ?

" It was the strangest position I've ever
known in my 40 years at sea.

" Some fellows were cool. They had
begun shaving before the battle started—
and they went on shaving.

" I had a sore throat and was gargling
when a fragment of shell tore into our
quarters. It did not hurt anyone, but it
made me swallow my gargle.

" The worst part of all was when the
' Graf Spee's ' guns just overhead fired.
It was like an earthquake.

" The best part was when the German
officer finally came down and said,
' Gentlemen, the war is over for you.
We have just entered Montevideo harbour.'

" That, we knew, meant a British
victory."

Captain Charles Pottinger, of the
steamer " Ashlea," which was captured
on October 7, said :

We were treated fine on board the
" Graf Spee." Once her commander told
me he was proud to say that not a single
British life had been lost by his exploits.

Mostly we prisoners played rummy
and sat around, talked and smoked.
The Germans let us keep our money when
we were captured, and allowed us to buy
cigarettes from their ship's stores.

Late on Tuesday (December 12), while
I was exercising with Captain Stubbs, of
the " Doric Star," I noticed an atmosphere of unusual tension on board.
Officers began hurriedly inspecting gun
stations and controls.

Captain Charles Dove, master of the sunk
British tanker " Africa Shell " was on the
" Graf Spee " during the battle (see p. 542).

Moving out of Montevideo harbour goes the " Graf Spee " on what was to prove her last journey. In the foreground of this remarkable photograph, wirelessed across the world, is
the " Graf Spee," while behind is the " Tacoma " which had just refuelled her. To the left
is a quay packed with spectators.

Captain Pottinger of the " Ashlea," another
of the " Graf Spee's " victims also heard the
battle from within the German ship.
Photos. G.P.U. and Planet News

IIIIIIIIIIIIIIIIIIIIIIIIIIIIIIIIIIIIIIIIIIIIIIIIIIIIIIIIIIIIIIIIIIIIIIIII **I WAS THERE!** IIIIIIIIIIIIIIIIIIIIIIIIIIIIIIIIIIIIIIIIIIIIIIIIIIIIIIIIIIIIIIIIIIIIIIIIIIIIIIIII

A young lieutenant who had been particularly friendly to us all walked by at that moment, and, while I never expected a reply, I asked him what was the matter. Turning and eyeing me severely, he observed, " We are expecting an attack, and I admire the courage of men who plan to attack the ' Graf Spee ' with such little ships."

About five o'clock on Wednesday morning the hurry and scurry stopped. Most of the prisoners thought that the sudden lull was due to the fact that the danger was past, and many of us dozed. I must have slept several hours, but it seemed like five minutes later when a roar woke me.

Commands began to come through the loudspeaker. The " Graf Spee's " engine revolutions changed from a steady thud to an almost continuous roar .... Suddenly I felt the ship shudder slightly, and a great roar of orders broke out again. This must have been the " Exeter's " first hit.

For the next forty minutes there was pandemonium. We listened, counting the roars as the " Graf Spee " fired. When the count went past twenty we knew the Germans had run into something big.

We felt the dull thuds that followed every time the British shells found a mark. I don't know whether any of us was afraid to die. I do know that if ever I was afraid of death it was then. It's one thing to pass out during illness ; it's different when you feel fit and strong to be faced with the prospect of drowning slowly behind a locked steel cabin door.

The firing stopped as suddenly as it had started. It seemed obvious that the " Graf Spee " must have sunk whatever enemy he had faced.

Although normally I am not very religious, I dropped on my knees to pray. I couldn't say what I prayed for—whether it was for my own safety or for the poor lads I thought must have gone down.

Captain Dove, of the " Africa Shell," revealed a tribute that one German had paid to the British.

" After the battle," he said, " Captain Hans Langsdorff, commander of the ' Graf Spee,' called me to the bridge and said, ' Your cruisers made a very gallant fight. When people fight like that, all personal enmity is lost. Those British are hard.' "

Captain Dove added that another officer said to him : " You fellows have been prisoners here for quite a while. Now it looks as if it's our turn."

" I was treated all right on board," Captain Dove added. " I even struck up a friendship with the commander, who instructed a tailor to make me heavier clothes owing to the cold weather.

" When the battle started yesterday they bolted the door, and I did not know what was happening until I heard the ' Graf Spee's ' guns and felt the impact of the British shells upon the ship's hull.

" It was a funny feeling. We wanted the ' Graf Spee ' to be sunk, but we couldn't help wondering what would happen to us."

Captain Dove said that the German battleship thought she was near some cargo ships when she sighted the cruiser " Exeter."

" The order to man action stations was sounded. I and my colleagues were locked up in the mess deck. The ' Graf Spee ' opened fire and the ' Exeter ' immediately replied. According to our reckoning the ' Graf Spee ' was hit at least 16 times.

" We played cards, including bridge, throughout the battle. One shell exploded near us, and we kept splinters of it as souvenirs."

I Scuttled My Ship to Avoid Capture

When stopped on the high seas by British warships or 'planes many German merchant ships were scuttled to avoid capture. The graphic story of one such incident among many that have astonished the world is here reproduced by arrangement with Reuter's Agency

On December 2 the 9,500-ton German liner " Watussi " was scuttled by her captain after being intercepted by 'planes of the South African Sea Defence Force.

Captain Stamer, who is now a prisoner in South Africa, said that his ship was not bound for Germany when she was sighted.

The reason he fired the ship was that " It is the unwritten law of the sea that a captain never allows his command to fall into enemy hands."

When a South African military aeroplane demanded the name of the ship he realized that there was no chance of escape and played for time, meanwhile provisioning lifeboats with two weeks' supplies and mustering the passengers on deck.

The passengers' quarters were then set on fire, the seacocks opened, the Nazi flag run up and the crew and passengers swung out in their lifeboats.

" I knew from the experience of the French liner ' Paris ' that the best place to set fire to the liner was in the wood-panelled passengers cabins and the corridors," said Captain Stamer.

" When the aeroplane ordered me to recall the boats or take the consequences it was too late to turn back as the ship was blazing below decks.

" In any case I would not have turned back as I was determined that my ship should not be captured.

" We were only in the lifeboats an hour before we were all picked up by a British warship. We could not have been better treated by the Royal Navy. The captain gave me a much-needed drink and the passengers were given coffee and food. My crew also received every attention.

" The lifeboats made good speed in the stiff wind ; we must have looked like a Saturday afternoon regatta," concluded Captain Stamer with a laugh.

Above is the 9,500-ton German liner " Watussi," whose end is described by her captain in this page, as she was seen after her sea-cocks had been open and the fire, started by her captain's orders, was blazing fiercely. The " Watussi " was the seventeenth German merchant ship to be scuttled to avoid capture. When the sinking of the " Columbus " on December 19 brought the number up to 18, the total tonnage lost by the Nazis in this way was 124,637.   *Photo. Central Press*

Russia Unmasked by the Cartoonist's Pencil

"Our Ambassador Can't Come—Will I Do?"
From the " Daily Mirror "

THE well-nigh universal horror which the invasion of Finland by Russia engendered is reflected by the cartoons that appeared in newspapers all over the world. Two, typical of hundreds of others, are reproduced in this page, while the third of our selection shows with biting truth the only court in which Hitler could get a verdict of " Not guilty."

"NOT GUILTY!"

'MEIN VERDICT'
From the " Melbourne Argus "

UNDER NEW MANAGEMENT   *From the " Evening Standard "*

OUR DIARY OF THE WAR

Thursday, December 14, 1939

German pocket battleship " Admiral Graf Spee," badly damaged, took refuge the preceding night in Montevideo harbour, and was granted permission to stay for 48 hours. Five British cruisers waited outside harbour.

Five Messerschmitt fighters shot down in air battle over Heligoland Bight. German warships joined in attack on British aircraft. R.A.F. lost three machines.

Admiralty announced loss of H.M. destroyer " Duchess " by collision with another British warship.

H.M. trawler " William Hallett " sunk by mine.

Soviet Union expelled from League of Nations.

New Russian drive reported in Petsamo region. Finns claimed success in central " waistline " area.

French communiqué announced sharp engagements between reconnaissance units in the Vosges and along the Blies.

Premier stated that approximately 2,100 officers and other ranks lost their lives in first three months of war. During the same time there were 2,975 road deaths in Great Britain.

Friday, December 15

British forces off Montevideo joined by French battleship " Dunkerque." The " Graf Spee " reported to have been given until 11.30 p.m. on Saturday to leave.

R.A.F. machines bombed enemy seaplane bases of Borkum, Norderney and Sylt during night of 14-15.

Finns withdrew from Salmijaervi in Arctic after blowing up nickel mines. Red armies said to be routed north of Lake Ladoga.

Paris announced encounters between advanced units in regions immediately west of the Vosges.

Prime Minister went to France to visit the B.E.F.

H.M. trawler " James Ludford " mined.

British tanker " Inverlane " reported mined.

Belgian steamer " Rosa " sunk off North-East Coast.

Norwegian steamer " Foeina " sunk by mine off Scotland.

British tanker " Atheltemplar " damaged by enemy action.

German ships " Duesseldorf " and " Adolf Leonhardt " scuttled by their crews.

Saturday, December 16

Reported from Montevideo that the " Graf Spee " was getting up steam. Time limit allowed by Uruguay said to have been extended.

Finns continued to hold their own except in extreme north. There was a successful Finnish counter-drive in Suomossalmi district and area immediately north of Lake Ladoga.

French communiqué reported repulse of enemy raid on French post east of the Moselle.

One British and four neutral ships reported mined : British steamer " Amble," Norwegian steamers " Ragni " and " H. C. Flood," Swedish vessel " Ursis," Greek steamer " Germaine."

German merchant ship " Teneriffe " scuttled after being intercepted.

Count Ciano spoke in the Italian Chamber on Italian foreign policy.

Sunday, December 17

Mr. Chamberlain continued his tour of the British area in France.

" Graf Spee " scuttled, by Hitler's orders, five miles outside Montevideo. Crew previously taken off by German tanker " Tacoma " and launches.

Reported that there had been an increase in activity of German reconnaissance parties

on the Western Front, and that **British troops in Maginot Line had suffered their first casualties.**

Enemy aircraft appeared at several points off British coast. Anti-aircraft guns opened fire in Humber district and fighters were seen to engage the enemy.

R.A.F. carried out further raids on German seaplane bases of Norderney and Sylt.

Finns standing fast on two fronts : Karelian isthmus and central " waistline " area.

First contingent of Canadian Forces landed in Britain.

British motor-ship " Serenity " and trawler " New Choice " sunk off East Coast by bombs and machine-guns from Nazi 'planes. British aircraft drove off raiders.

Admiralty announced that five officers and 56 ratings of H.M.S. " Exeter " were killed in action on December 13.

Commodore Harwood, in command of British action against " Graf Spee," awarded K.C.B. and promoted Rear-Admiral. Captains of " Ajax," " Achilles " and " Exeter " appointed C.B.

Battle-cruiser " Renown " and aircraft-carrier " Ark Royal " arrived at Rio de Janeiro.

Moscow issued long and abusive reply to League's resolution expelling Russia.

Monday, Dec. 18

Captain and some of crew of " Graf Spee " landed at Buenos Aires. Four others arrested by Uruguayan authorities, charged with blowing up their ship.

Fierce air battle over Heligoland Bight. Twelve Messerschmitt fighters shot down. Seven British bombers failed to return.

Admiralty announced that a **German cruiser** of Koeln class had been **sunk** off mouth of Elbe by H.M. submarine " Ursula."

Russians made sudden advance on

Arctic front with massed infantry, tanks and bombers, and reached Pitkaejaervi. New Soviet attack on Karelian isthmus also reported.

German troops reported to be massing on Luxemburg frontier.

Admiralty supplied details of exploits of H.M. submarine " Salmon," announced on December 13. Besides one enemy cruiser sunk, two were damaged.

Announced that only **10 ships out of 1,109** entering or leaving ports had been **lost** round British coasts during first ten days of December.

Confirmed that German steamer " Antiochia " was scuttled during November.

Admiralty and Air Ministry issued joint statement on attacks by enemy aircraft with bombs and machine-gun fire on merchant and fishing vessels in North Sea.

Tuesday, December 19

Prime Minister returned from visit to B.E.F., after meeting of Supreme War Council in Paris.

Further Russian advance in north-east of Finland, threatening highway to Arctic and rearguard of Finnish troops near Petsamo.

Helsinki and other coastal towns bombed by Soviet aircraft.

Russian battleship reported sunk by Finnish batteries at Koivisto.

German liner " Columbia " scuttled 300 miles off U.S. coast.

Marked activity of contact units reported from Western Front.

Eleven more cases of bombing and machine-gunning of fishing trawlers made known. Of these, " Active " and " Zealous " were sunk.

British steamer " City of Kobe " sunk by mine after surviving bombs and bullets from aircraft.

Three neutral ships reported sunk through enemy action : Norwegian steamer " Glitrejell " ; Danish steamers " Jytte " and " Bogoe."

COMRADESHIP " Go forth and preach the Brotherhood of Mankind to the workers of the world ! "

From the cartoon by Sir Bernard Partridge. By permission of the Proprietors of " Punch "

The War Illustrated

Vol. 1   A Permanent Picture Record of the Second Great War   **No. 18**

This scene is in a forward listening post of the French defences in front of the Maginot Line. Very notable is the strong brushwood and timber revetting of the trench. Here there is no chance of the parapet collapsing, as it sometimes did in the hastily dug trenches during the last war. The officer in the centre of the photograph is on a round of inspection. In page 426 is a diagram that shows the position of such a listening post in regard to the main defences of the Maginot Line itself.

Photo, Wide World

'Brains Trust' of the R.A.F. in France

Belying the simple nature of the decoration, the room seen above is the Operations Room of the R.A.F. on the Western Front. Grouped round the table are staff officers, including an Army liaison officer. On the right is an officer attached from the Intelligence Corps.

A message comes through the headphones to an R.A.F. wireless operator as he sits in a tender not far from the front line.
Photos, British Official : Crown Copyright

Air Vice-Marshal P. H. L. Playfair, Air Officer Commanding, Royal Air Force in France, gives an order by telephone.

Such is the confidence reposed in their leaders by our airmen on the Western Front that no one today hears sarcastic references to "brass hats," the traditional term for the staff officers of the High Command. Similar feelings of confidence and appreciation are expressed by the officers regarding the men they lead. As the Air Minister said : "The Royal Air Force units in France . . . are carrying out yeoman service . . . Everywhere the morale of our Air Force is magnificent." The illustrations in this page show glimpses of the work of headquarters and of the great Force they direct. Co-operation between the Allied Armies in matters affecting the air war is always of the closest nature.

A Fairey "Battle" bomber—with its camouflage blending effectively with the aerodrome surface—stands waiting with two of its crew aboard and its engine ticking over, while the third member runs out to take his place. In a few seconds all will be ready, and the "Battle" will take off for yet another reconnaissance flight over the German lines. *Photo. Associated Press*

Britain Greets the New Year with a Cheer

None can tell what the year that has just dawned will bring in its train, but there
is no need to look far for a guiding motto. " We are in this war to win . . ."

NINETEEN-FORTY dawns on a world in which the dogs of war have been once again unleashed. The rosy dreams of a world whose ways are ways of pleasantness, whose paths are paths of peace, have been shattered. Germany, her destinies guided by a man driven mad by lust for power, intoxicated by his own megalomaniac ravings, has for the second time in a quarter of a century outraged the conscience and aroused the resistance of the civilized world.

No countries have striven more earnestly for peace than those which today are meeting the challenge of Nazi aggression. Since that day of Armistice of 21 years ago Britain in particular has given every indication of seeking peace, has striven most earnestly to ensue it. Not until the clangour of martial preparation resounded to high heaven in Hitler's Reich was Britain's war machine refurbished and reinforced. For months and years her statesmen strove to appease the ravenous appetite of totalitarian Germany. Only when fair words were met with brutal defiance, only when the choice lay between the sword and the sacrifice of honour, did Britain make the unhesitating choice. On September 3 she picked up the gauge which a swaggering Germany had flung into the bloodstained dust of Poland, when Hitler, blinded by a malign fate, had stopped his ears to the warning that Britain would fight in defence of her plighted word.

Armed to Defend the Right

Thus it is that now Britain and the British Commonwealth of Nations stand ranged in the very forefront of the peoples who have armed to defend the right and what may be salvaged of international decency. A million men are already under arms, and across the Channel, linked arm-in-arm with their French allies, are ranked nearly 100,000 soldiers drawn from the cities, towns and villages of the homeland. Shortly before Christmas British troops were in action for the first time on the Western Front since the " Cease Fire " on November 11, 1918, and now day by day the newspapers contain the names of those who have been wounded or have given their all in defence of their Country and their King. Britain herself is a hive of war

industry, and millions are now engaged in producing guns and munitions and stores for the army that already is, and for the armies that will shortly be. Vast reserves have been built up, and a thousand lines of communication run across the narrow seas to that front where there is no " thin red line tipped with steel," but a khaki host entrenched in what is the greatest system of fortifications the world has ever seen.

In the air and on the sea huge navies fly the British flag. For the men who man the fighting 'planes and ships this has been no war of waiting, but one in which, from the very first, difficulty and danger and the menace of imminent death have been ever-present companions. Many a warplane has flamed to its end, many a ship has gone to the bottom, carrying with them lives whose self-sacrifice and devotion remain as an inspiration to those who come after. Heavy, indeed, is the price which has to be paid for superiority in the air and on the waves, but that price is being paid and will continue to be paid without a murmur of hesitation. At sea, despite all the efforts of the lurking submarines, wandering mines, and hit-and-run surface raiders, the stream of commerce to the ports of the Allies is uninterrupted.

Great and ever-growing as are her own resources, Britain's power and Britain's confidence are immensely strengthened by the help which the Dominions and Colonies —indeed, every member of the British Commonwealth—has rushed to afford.

No miscalculation of the Nazis was more gross than that which enabled them to believe, against all the evidence, that Britain's Dominions would fight shy of

Symbolical of the spirit with which Britain enters the New Year is this photograph of soldiers of the B.E.F. cheering the Prime Minister during his visit to the Front just before Christmas. Surprises may be in store, but on land and sea and in the air the British Commonwealth and her great French ally are ready. And meanwhile, there's time for a " gasper " (top).

Photos. " Match." Paris, and British Official: Crown Copyright

On the Western Front in the Depths of Winter

becoming involved in another European quarrel. On the eve of war the true voice of the Empire rang out loud and clear : "We stand with Britain," said Mr. Menzies, Prime Minister of the Australian Commonwealth, in a broadcast to his people, and a few hours later his emphatic declaration was re-echoed in Canada, New Zealand and South Africa—everywhere, indeed, where flies the British flag.

The resolve of the Empire's peoples was translated swiftly into action. In even the earliest of the air battles Canadians, Australians, New Zealanders, and South Africans covered themselves with glory, while at home contingents of air force and army were swiftly raised. A week before Christmas it was announced that

From every quarter of the Empire comes evidence of the realization that, as Mr. Menzies said on December 20, "the winning of this war and the success of our noble cause are just as much the business of Australians as of Englishmen, of New Zealanders as of Scotsmen, of Canadians as of Irishmen. Scattered though we may be over the seven seas of the world, living in different countries, governing our own affairs, conducting our own international discussions, and handling our own trade, we are still one people." In the light of so forthright a declaration Britain needs no encouragement to be of good cheer. All her history—and she can look back on a thousand years and more of freedom-loving and freedom-maintaining existence

Birds are very sensitive to gas and are taken into the workings of coal mines to detect its presence. This small bird on the Maginot Line may one day give warning of a gas attack and save many lives.
Photo Courtesy of French Embassy

—makes her staunch in the belief that "naught shall make us rue, if England to itself do rest but true."

Yet today it is not in the glorious past, even in the England of Shakespeare and Drake and Elizabeth, that we may best seek inspiration and courage to face the morrow. We may find it in such freshly uttered words as those of the Empire statesman whom we have quoted. "We are in this war to win," said Mr. Menzies. "We did not enter it lightly, and we will not depart from it except as victors."

Snow has fallen on the Siegfried Line, and the uniforms of the soldiers, moving amidst the powdered pines and the mass of wire, stand out black against it.
Photo, International Graphic Press

the first contingent of the Canadian Active Service Force had arrived in Britain, and the whole British people shared in the words of the King when he declared that : "The British Army will be proud to have as comrades in arms the successors of those who came from Canada in the Great War and fought with a heroism that has never been forgotten."

Only a day or two before, not Britain only, but the whole world had been electrified by the story of the magnificent sea fight off the Plate—and "Achilles," one of the three ships which for fourteen hours maintained the fight from dawn till dark with an "incredible audacity" to which the "Graf Spee's" captain paid tribute —was manned for the most part by sailors drawn from New Zealand. Well might Lord Galway, Governor-General of the Dominion, telegraph that "the ship's bravery and audacity are worthy of the highest traditions of the British Navy."

Though this war is in most ways strangely different from the last, there are scenes on the Western Front which vividly recall those which were witnessed by the men who fought from 1914 to 1918—for instance, that shown in this photo of a German patrol advancing very cautiously through a village that has been heavily shelled. *Photo, E.N.A.*

'All Members of the Great Family of Nations'

In a broadcast to the nation on December 18, 1939, Mr. Winston Churchill gave out the first news of the arrival of the Canadians in England. Above is a scene on the quayside as a transport filled with men of the Canadian Active Service Force berthed at a British port.

Photo, Associated Press

"THE people of Canada have reposed in us their trust to defend the cause of justice and of liberty against oppression and aggression. In this cause we are to stand in battle beside our comrades-in-arms from the British Commonwealth and France, and we carry an obligation of honour to live up to the proud traditions established by the Canadian Corps. It is for us to prove ourselves worthy of this inheritance."

From Major-General A. G. L. McNaughton's Order of the Day.

THE KING'S MESSAGE TO THE EMPIRE
(Broadcast Christmas Day, 1939)

THE festival which we know as Christmas is above all the festival of peace and of the home. Among all free peoples the love of peace is profound, for this alone gives security to the home.

But true peace is in the hearts of men, and it is the tragedy of this time that there are powerful countries whose whole direction and policy are based on aggression and the suppression of all that we hold dear for mankind.

It is this that has stirred our peoples and given them a unity unknown in any previous war. We feel in our hearts that we are fighting against wickedness, and this conviction will give us strength from day to day to persevere until victory is assured.

At home we are, as it were, taking the strain for what may lie ahead of us, resolved and confident. We look with pride and thankfulness on the never-failing courage and devotion of the Royal Navy upon which, throughout the last four months, has burst the storm of ruthless and unceasing war.

And when I speak of our Navy today, I mean all the men of our Empire who go down to the sea in ships, the Mercantile Marine, the minesweepers, the trawlers and drifters from the senior officers to the last boy who has joined up. To every one in this great fleet I send a message of gratitude and greeting, from myself as from all my peoples.

The same message I send to the gallant Air Force, which, in co-operation with the Navy is our sure shield of defence. They are daily adding laurels to those that their fathers won.

I would send a special word of greeting to the armies of the Empire, to those who have come from afar, and in particular to the British Expeditionary Force.

Their task is hard. They are waiting, and waiting is a trial of nerve and discipline. But I know that when the moment comes for action they will prove themselves worthy of the highest traditions of their great Service.

And to all who are preparing themselves to serve their country, on sea or land or in the air, I send my greeting at this time. The men and women of our far-flung Empire, working in their several vocations, with the one same purpose, all are members of the great family of nations which is prepared to sacrifice everything that freedom of spirit may be saved to the world.

A new year is at hand. We cannot tell what it will bring. If it brings peace, how thankful we shall all be. If it brings us continued struggle we shall remain undaunted.

In the meantime, I feel that we may all find a message of encouragement in the lines which, in my closing words, I would like to say to you.

"I said to the man who stood at the gate of the year: 'Give me a light that I may tread safely into the unknown.'

"And he replied, 'Go out into the darkness, and put your hand into the hand of God. That shall be to you better than light, and safer than a known way.'" [*From " The Desert," by Miss M. L. Haskins.*]

May that Almighty hand guide and uphold us all.

During the war of 1914-18 the first convoy of the Canadian Army arrived at Plymouth on October 14, 1914. Twenty-five years later another Canadian force has come to Britain's aid. Here the men of the vanguard of this new Canadian Active Service Force, safely convoyed across the Atlantic by the Royal Navy, are seen on the quayside after disembarkation.

Photo, G.P.U.

Finland's Vantage in Arctic War

According to all the rules little Finland should have been swamped long ere now, but after a month of war it seems that she may prolong her resistance until the melting snows of spring. And by then much may have happened on the other fronts of war.

In a land of intense winter cold the Finnish soldiers are protected, like the sentinel above, by a coat of reindeer skin.
Photo, Planet News

O**N** the morning of December 21, Stalin's birthday, the Moscow newspapers contained column after column of the most fulsome adulation of the man whom one described as the "greatest man of all humanity; genius's leader; creator and architect of the new life." No mention was made of the war in Finland, where at that very moment soldiers of the Red Army were reddening the snows with their blood.

The day had been chosen by the Russian High Command as one to be marked by a great and glorious victory in the central zone, and as they went over the top the soldiers were spurred on from behind by a number of political commissars. As they floundered on, however, they encountered a vigorous counter-attack and soon were swept away in complete rout. For fourteen miles the Finns continued the pursuit and in their retreat the invaders left behind machine-guns, field artillery, and armoured cars, while their dead and wounded were estimated to total some 20,000. The retreat had become a rout.

At the same time the repeated Russian assaults on the Mannerheim Line in the Karelian Isthmus were also repulsed with heavy losses. Here the fight was watched by an American journalist, Mr. Leland Stowe, who declared that the troops which the Kremlin had sent into the field in this sector of the front were "probably the most miserable-looking beings in uniform which this part of Europe has seen since Napoleon's half-starved and ragged men retreated from Moscow."

More and more it became obvious that Moscow had miscalculated badly, having underestimated not only the fighting qualities of the Finns, but the conditions in which the war must be waged during the Arctic winter. The "waist" of Fin-

Here is a rifle pit in a trench in Finland's system of defence—the Mannerheim Line, named after her famous marshal.
Photo, Associated Press

land, in which the most dangerous of the Russian attacks was developed, lies roughly on the Arctic Circle, where the temperature may fall to 50 degrees below zero. Unprotected hands and faces become frostbitten in a few minutes; it is impossible to touch the metal of a rifle with the bare flesh; leather boots are of no avail to keep out the cold. Yet observer after observer reported from the front that the Russians engaged in this region of terrible cold were clad in uniforms of cotton stuff and had on their feet ordinary shoes made of such poor material that after a short time the toes

Stubborn fighting took place from the outbreak of the Russo-Finnish war on the Karelian Isthmus which joins Finland to Russia. Despite desperate and heavy onslaughts by the Soviet mechanized forces, the Finns held their own and inflicted heavy losses on the Russians. Above are three prisoners taken by the Finns during the fighting. *Photo, British Movietone News*

Finland's Peasant-President in the Trenches

President Kallio, once a peasant farmer and now Finland's leader in her astounding fight for freedom, is here seen during his recent visit to the Finnish Army in the south. Accompanied by officers of the High Command, he is inspecting a gun emplacement in the Mannerheim Line. He has followed the magnificent work of the Finnish Army with intense pride, and at the close of a broadcast to the Army that has withstood the onrush of the Red hordes he said : " Together with the Fatherland and sorrowing relatives we salute with you in all solemnity those heroes who have fallen in the defence of our country."

Photo, Planet News

Real Arctic Weather Aids a Gallant Defence

The Finns are experts on skis, and these ski-soldiers in white uniform must present a very difficult target to the Russians.
Photo, Central Press

stuck out. And bad as were the weather conditions, worse still might be expected, for the really intense cold in this region does not begin until about the middle of January.

Some have argued that the Russians have such an enormous preponderance of men and war material that it is only a question of time before they swamp the Finnish defences. Such a view, however, pays insufficient regard to climatic conditions and to the all-important question of communications. In the Karelian Isthmus the invaders are fighting within but a few miles of the frontier and of their great base at Leningrad. Yet even here they were held up for weeks by the Finnish defences. In their campaigning in the centre of Finland and in the far north they are entirely dependent upon a single railway which runs from Leningrad to ports on the White Sea and thence to Murmansk. This line was hurriedly built in 1916 during the last war, and it is believed to be still only single-track. A few well-directed bombs might, therefore, completely sever this most vital line of communication, and the Russian armies would then be marooned in a country which is completely frostbound and even in summer produces little but timber.

Nor could succour be rendered by water, for the White Sea from Archangel westwards is now frozen over, and, although Murmansk is still open, it would

Not unlike choirboys in white surplices are these Finns in white cloaks, who are manning a similarly camouflaged gun.
Photo, Wide World

be no easy matter to ship vast quantities of supplies through the Baltic and round Norway and the North Cape. Even if winter enforces a truce, life in these frozen lands must become terrible in the extreme, for the towns are so small and far apart that next to no shelter would be available. The natives find it impossible to work out of doors in wintertime.

It is not surprising that the main Russian attack was directed across the Karelian Isthmus, and that perhaps 150,000 men were flung into the battle in the hope of reaching a decision before the weather worsened. It was no doubt with the same intent of finishing the war as soon as possible that the air attacks on the southern cities of Finland were renewed after the middle of December. Not by such methods, however, is Finland's resistance likely to be overcome.

Judging from this photo of the feet of a Russian taken prisoner by the Finns, Soviet equipment is hardly of the first class, and quite inadequate for Arctic war.
Photo, Planet News

WHO IS FIGHTING WHOM?
Some Passing Thoughts on the German People and the Nazis
By The Editor

FROM the start of this strange war one of the expressed desires of those having authority in Great Britain has been that journalists should be mindful to distinguish between the Government based upon the dictatorship of the Nazi Party and the German people themselves. In this we have one more example of how our leaders, with the best intentions, may still contrive to mislead.

A like attempt was made in the war of 1914–18 to drive a wedge between the Kaiserism of that day, so much milder and decenter than Nazism and the German people, who still enjoyed a modest measure of personal and political freedom, as witness the various liberal-minded groups that were allowed to thrive, despite the frequent enforcement of *lèse-majesté*. There were no concentration camps, where outspoken objectors to the ruling power languished and rotted : the Kaiser's Germany had no Siberia.

Yet the attempt was made from 1914 onwards to effect a cleavage between Kaiserism and the Kaiser's people. An ineffectual attempt. Be it remembered that not until the British blockade and the sacrifice of more than two millions of British and French lives had beaten Germany's monstrous hosts of fighting men, long nurtured to conquer France and Britain, and to stretch the gimcrack German Empire from the Baltic to the Black Sea, did the rift appear between the starveling people and the Prussian Imperialists who led them, all in varying degrees of compliance and willingness. And be it also remembered that even their leading scientists and men of letters, their religious leaders (notably excepting Einstein), did not hesitate to back their Prussian war lords in the long-planned effort to place " Deutschland über Alles."

An Illusion Dispelled

Internationally - minded writers may vainly argue that there is no such thing as national characteristics, that the common people of all lands are all tarred with the one brush, or painted with the same whitewash ; that only the dominant leaders, using the common people for their own selfish ends in their lust for power, have qualities that are " national " or " individual." But the whole book of world history proves any such generalization unwarrantable.

Anyone who has had the opportunity to study at first hand, as I have had, the characteristics of the Latin Americans, for example, is astonished at the sharply defined national differences between Argentines and Chileans, between Brazilians and Peruvians, indeed between the peoples of all the ten republics who have derived from one original stock. It is true

that these national characteristics can be traced in large measure to the crossing of the original Iberian peoples with native races of distinct tribal and ethnographical origins, resulting in physical and mental differences so obvious that they leave no room for " illusion." Indeed, certain of these Latin American peoples differ from their remoter Iberian progenitors as much as the Spaniards today differ from the Finns.

The thesis is too expansive to be pursued in a sentence or two, but it can be asserted that the real illusion is to

---

THE GERMANS THROUGH TWENTY CENTURIES

The Germans are out for plunder.
VELLEIUS PATERCULUS, Roman Historian, 19 B.C.–A.D. 31

The Germans impute mercy to fear, and the more you forgive them the more audacious they become.
PETRARCH, Italian Poet, 1304–1374

The Germans have no pity if they have the upper hand, and are hard and evil handlers of their prisoners.
FROISSART, French Historian, 1338–1404

The Berlin public is so utterly despicable that it can be well compared with the herd of swine in the Gospels.
FICHTE, German Philosopher, 1762–1814

Barbarians from old time, rendered more barbarous by hard work, science and even religion, profoundly incapable of any God-like emotion.
HOLDERLIN, German Poet, 1770–1843

Personal distinction was the virtue of antiquity. Submission, obedience, whether public or private—such is German virtue.
NIETZSCHE, German Philosopher, 1844–1900

The Germans have arrived too late with their claim to political hegemony. With such a claim they can no longer conquer the world ; they can only lay it waste.
ERICH KAHLER, German Publicist, writing in 1937

---

suppose that the qualities of the German people and the British and French peoples are all of a piece. They are not, any more than the characteristics of the Moors and the Scottish Highlanders are akin.

The German tribes have been the scourge of Europe and the world ever since the ancient days of Goth and Hun. " The good German God " so often invoked by both Kaiser and Nazis is merely a nebulous tribal deity, whose conception has modified the outlook of the German people, imbuing them with a sense of racial superiority surpassing even that which the Jews have derived from the God of Israel, whom so many have made pretence to worship.

The modern history of Germanic ideals and aspirations suggests that a spirit of brutal heroics has been breathed into the common people, and has developed in them a sense of their being " chosen " by

their " good German God " as a superior race, destined to rule the world.

How, then, shall the common people escape from this illusion ? They have not escaped — all their triumphs in the humaner arts notwithstanding. As a race they are distinguished by a willingness to suffer so that their national greatness may be made a reality before the world. Their subservience to their accepted leaders, their lack of independent courage —so greatly at variance with their mass courage—is the first and final proof of their radical differences from their remoter kinsmen, the French and British.

Free Peoples are Fighting Slaves

Now, all this brings me to the one thing of which we as a nation of free men, like our allies the French, should take heed : there can be no greater futility of thought than the supposition that the Germanic people, derived from groups of aggressive and predatory tribes, do other than rejoice to follow the leadership of those among them who promise rich spoils from their neighbours. Nothing can be farther from reality than the belief that there is at present a considerable body of Germans ready and willing to break with Hitlerism. If there were, Hitler would have been assassinated long ago.

That the free peoples of Europe are today fighting the slave peoples is the stark and demonstrable truth. Britain and France are now engaged in a life and death struggle with the Germanic slave peoples, and not until that struggle has been decided by the destruction of the " evil thing " that has made Germany the home of the horrors that free men everywhere have fought against for ages—not until this has been eradicated will there be a hope of making them see the light.

All Germans—not merely their war-lusting leaders—must be held responsible for originating these horrors of modern warfare : (1) Poison Gas, (2) slaughter of thousands of innocent men, women and children at sea, (3) aerial bombing of open cities with immense destruction of good and harmless lives, and (4) the poisoning of world thought with a flood of lying propaganda the effect of which will endure for centuries.

That they themselves have been poisoned in the process is hardly to their credit, and it is undeniable that nationally considered they are our enemies, whether it be Treitschke or Hitler that has made them so. We British must be realists, and until we have proved to the German people by every means in our power that their age-old business of aggression and inhuman assault upon their peace-loving neighbours doesn't pay, there will be no peace in Europe or the world.

Greatest Air Battle in History

What was the biggest air battle of the war to date was fought in the
skies near Heligoland on December 18, 1939.   There were losses on
both sides, but Germany's newest fighters gave no indication of
their much-vaunted superiority.

**This smiling young man, wearing his full
flying kit, is one of the pilots who took part
in the great aerial battle of Heligoland on
December 18, 1939.   The photograph was
taken on December 21.**

In mid-December H.M. Submarine
"Salmon" and units of the Royal
Air Force observed several ships
of the German Fleet venturing for the
first time outside their naval strongholds,
and it was at once decided to send a
force of British heavy bombers to search
for and attack any enemy warships found
at sea.   So in the afternoon of December 18
a squadron of big Vickers "Wellingtons"
flew out to carry the fight once again
far into the enemy's territory.

Reaching the Heligoland Bight area,
there was not a warship to be seen outside the harbours, but the Germans on
this occasion seemed determined to teach
their aerial gate-crashers a lesson, and
sent up a fleet of fighters to engage
the "Wellingtons" when they approached
their objective at Wilhelmshaven.

The leader of the British formation
said afterwards: "I could see them
collecting like flies waiting to attack us.

"This was, in fact, the biggest aerial battle
ever fought.   At a hazard I should think that
there were about 80 to 100 aircraft engaged.
We were greatly outnumbered and out-
manœuvred because of the higher speed of the
fighters.   The crews fired shot for shot and
gave better than they got.   Most of our crews
were under fire for the first time, and they
have returned confident that on the next
occasion the enemy will suffer a far heavier
blow.   That occasion, they hope, will not be
too distant.

"There is no doubt whatever that we were
attacked by the best fighters of the German
Command.   Ours was just a normal team.
All the crews were surprised at the performance
of the German aircraft and their determination
to press home the attack.   We felt that they
were worthy opponents."

The famous single-engined Messerschmitt ME 109 formed part of the
defending force, but a large proportion
consisted of the new Messerschmitt ME
110 type, used in Poland but not hitherto
met with by the R.A.F.   These formidable "air destroyers," as the Germans
have dubbed them, are heavily armed
twin-engined fighters said to be capable
of 370 miles per hour—a nominally
higher speed even than our own "Spitfire" single-seater can attain.   The armament is believed to consist of two shell-
firing guns as well as four rifle-calibre
machine-guns.   Our own modern fighters,
like the "Hurricane" and "Spitfire"
employ very successfully eight of the
latter class of weapon.

In the Heligoland Bight battle the
"Wellingtons"—100 miles per hour

slower than their adversaries, but with
five separate machine-gun positions, including two in power-operated turrets—
were undaunted by the appearance of
the ME 110, but were, on the contrary,
eager to match themselves against the
enemy's new weapon.   The gunners of the
British machines sent more than twelve
Messerschmitts, including at least six
of the new type and representing in
all about half of the defence forces,
crashing down to destruction.   The concentrated fire of the Messerschmitts also
told on the attacking squadron, for seven
of our aircraft and their daring crews
failed to reach home and their unfortunate loss was immediately admitted by
the Air Ministry.

This is anticipating, however.   Let us
return to the official story of the battle.

The fighting quickly became intense as the
crack fighter squadrons strained every nerve
to find means to break down our close and
tightly-packed sections.   Then, as the bombers
came over Wilhelmshaven, they were exposed
to the full blast of the anti-aircraft defences of
the naval base.   The Germans hoped in this
way to force the formations to open out, so
that their fighters might then be able to deal
with them individually, and it was after our
bombers had completed their task and turned
away from their objective on the return journey
that the main attack of the enemy fighters
developed.

As this phase of the action developed
casualties on both sides began to mount up.
The heavy concentrated fire of the formations
had resulted in so many losses to the Messerschmitts that, in a last desperate attempt to
break down the ordered array of bomber sections,
the Messerschmitts 110 attempted the most
spectacular attacks at great speed on the beam
of the formations, trying to sweep the formations
with fire from stem to stern.

**Here are some of the British pilots who took part in the great aerial battle of Heligoland.   Smiles and thumbs up show that they know they
had by far the best of it.   The official report of the Heligoland battle stated that : "The laurels go to the Wellington bombers, which resisted
the most desperate, and, it may be said also, the most courageous and dashing efforts of the enemy's crack fighters to break them up."**

They Were 'Like Flies Waiting to Attack Us'

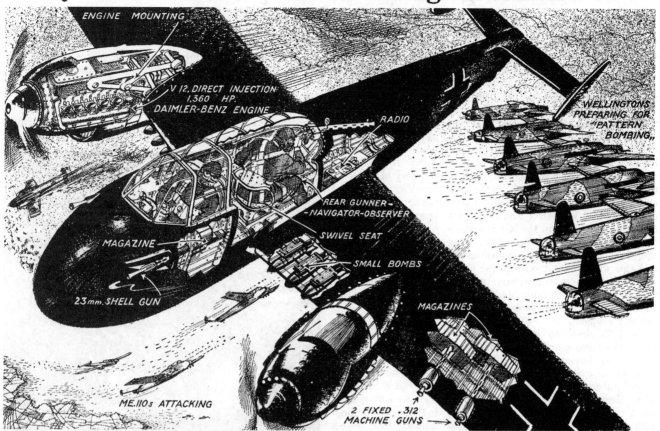

ENGINE MOUNTING

V 12, DIRECT INJECTION
1,360 H.P.
DAIMLER-BENZ ENGINE

RADIO

WELLINGTONS
PREPARING FOR
"PATTERN
BOMBING"

REAR GUNNER—
—NAVIGATOR-OBSERVER

MAGAZINE

SWIVEL SEAT

SMALL BOMBS

23 mm. SHELL GUN

MAGAZINES

ME.110s ATTACKING

2 FIXED .312
MACHINE GUNS →

The Messerschmitt ME110, shown here in sectioned diagram, is a new design of fighter aircraft that was used by the Nazis in the Polish campaign, and machines of this type have now reinforced the defence forces on the north-west coast of Germany. Coming into the twin-engined two-seater class, it is exceptionally fast and well armed. The drawing indicates the position of the six forward guns ; there may be also a rear gun for the observer, and this is shown. In the great air battle near Heligoland on December 18, an ME110 was employed as an interceptor fighter against the R.A.F. "Wellingtons," but its value for bomber escort, ground attack, or reconnaissance has not been overlooked.

Specially drawn for The War Illustrated *by Haworth*

But even this manœuvre had little success and many of their aircraft were shot down. The defeat of this final effort was the last phase of the action, and our air gunners, excited and tired, had the satisfaction of seeing the last remaining fighters disappearing towards their own shore.

Flying wing-tip to wing-tip, the "Wellington" bombers had held together in spite of anti-aircraft fire and continuous attacks. Again and again the enemy fighters, daring to come in too close, were shot down, and the bombers continued on their course unchecked and unshaken.

Where single aircraft were forced by hits to fall away from their section formation they were still by no means an easy proposition for the enemy fighters. Some of these aircraft were lost fighting to the end, with a gallantry to which the Germans themselves bear witness. Others fought their formidable opponents off single-handed, and ultimately succeeded in crossing 300 miles of sea, even though maimed and with fighting turrets out of action.

One of the bombers shot down no fewer than five fighters, and although the crew were attacked continuously for nearly forty minutes, closely followed 60 miles out to sea by a swarm of fighters, they succeeded in driving them off and bringing their aircraft back safely. This exploit testifies to the tremendous fighting power of the "Wellington" and to the dogged determination and courage of its crew.

Now for some first-hand narratives. The pilot of the 'plane which "drew first blood" said :

"When we were near Heligoland, and before the main fight had begun, we were attacked by a solitary fighter. He chose my aircraft out of the formation, and in a few seconds my rear gunner had the satisfaction of seeing his enemy crash into the sea.

"Later, when the battle had developed on a large scale, and when the formation was steadily penetrating over German waters, a Messerschmitt 110 singled us out and sat on our tail for about twenty minutes.

"We certainly hit him, but I am not sure whether he was actually brought down. We last saw him flying towards the sea. Perhaps he was one of the few casualties which the Germans admitted. They claimed, I think, that two of their fighters had landed on the water.

"We were busily engaged with another Messerschmitt 110 when a Messerschmitt 109 suddenly flew straight into our cross-fire and blew up in the air.

"The enemy attack was sustained and most persistent throughout. All our gunners were kept fully occupied by their enemy's method of employing about five fighters to each bomber. If at any time during the battle we were able to get a fifteen-seconds rest we were more than grateful."

The Gunner Was Dangling Over the Sea

One aircraft had to leave the formation and descend into the sea some distance off the English coast through a petrol leak. This aircraft had been severely shot at in the action. All its guns had been put out of action by shells and machine-gun bullets, and the bottom of the front turret had been blown out by shells and set on fire.

"My gunner," the pilot said, "was very prompt with the fire, and put it out with his gloved hand. But for him the aircraft would have been set alight within a few seconds. His quick action saved our lives.

"When the bottom of the gun turret was blown away the gunner found that one of his legs was dangling in the air over the water, but his huddled position kept him from falling into the sea."

This young - gunner expressed the greatest admiration for his sergeant pilot. "We shall never know how the pilot managed to control his aircraft through such difficulties," he said.

The German Propaganda Ministry, true to tradition, immediately fastened on this air fight as a suitable reply for the defeat at sea of the "Graf Spee." So the German public had it impressed upon them that their airmen had achieved a truly *kolossal* victory. Forty-four R.A.F. 'planes ventured near Germany, they said, but only eight lived to tell the tale—yet, as the British Air Ministry dryly commented, our total forces of aircraft engaged were less than the losses alleged !

Wing Commander Schumacher, of the German Air Force, stated that as leader of the fighter squadrons in that area he sent up every available machine to attack the invaders, and that the rout of the latter was complete and shattering. The German losses were (at least, so he said) only two Messerschmitts of the ME 109 type, and not one of the men was a serious casualty. Furthermore, Goering had decorated him with the Iron Cross (1st Class) for his part in the "victory."

'Non-Belligerency' Is Italy's Name For It

What will be Italy's attitude to the war during 1940 ? This article, while not pretending to give anything in the nature of a definitive answer to the question, at least suggests some of the considerations which must be borne in mind.

WHEN on September 1 Italy decided to keep out of the war—for the time being, at least—there was hardly an Italian who did not breathe a deep sigh of relief. Although the man in the street had gradually come to regard France as his country's rival and possible enemy, he had little desire to fight Britain, between whom and Italy there had been a feeling of friendship since the days of the Risorgimento ; nor was he in the least enthusiastic to march at the side of German troops in a quarrel which was not really his. Besides, in the last few years Italy has had her fill of war. After every war there comes a period of disillusion, and this was true not only of the Great War, but of those comparatively small affairs in Libya, Abyssinia, and Spain in which Italian troops have been more recently engaged.

As 1939 drew to its close Italians found more and more occasion for gratification in having "kept out of it." Fascism has ever regarded Bolshevism as its natural foe, and Hitler's cynical pact with Moscow came as a tremendous shock to Italian political feeling. It was with disgust and horror that the Italians learnt the news of the rape of Poland—a Catholic country like their own ; and they were still further perturbed when Russia, not content with having seized half Poland, proceeded to dominate the Baltic States and finally to make an altogether unwarranted attack on Finland. When the Red Army invaded the territory of the little republic crowds of young Italians demonstrated in favour of Finland, and it was reported on good authority that a number of Italian 'planes had been dispatched to the scene of war.

When on October 31 Signor Mussolini subjected his cabinet to drastic overhaul, it was noticed that many of those ministers who were most in favour of the Nazi alliance had been dropped, while their places were taken by men, some of them comparatively untried and newcomers so far as the public was concerned, who had made no disguise of their opposition to Bolshevism.

Still, however, the Duce was careful to insist that there was nothing in the

Here is thirty-six-year-old Count Galeazzo Ciano, Mussolini's son-in-law, who since 1936 has been Foreign Minister of Italy.
Photo, Wide World

nature of a break in the Rome-Berlin axis. "The relations between Italy and Germany," the Fascist Grand Council put on record after its meeting of December 7, "remain such as they were fixed by the Treaty of Alliance and by the exchanges of views that took place in turn at Milan, Salzburg, and Berlin."

A few days later, on December 16, Count Ciano, the Italian Foreign Minister, in a speech to the Chamber of Fascios and Corporations in Rome, gave a review of the situation which was interesting if not altogether illuminating. "The position assumed by Italy on September 1," he said, "was a position of non-belligerency strictly in conformity with the German intention of localizing the conflict, and directly ensuing from the Pact and collateral undertakings existing between Italy and Germany." Italy had made it known to Germany shortly before the war, he went on, that a minimum period of three years was necessary to bring the preparations of her war equipment up to the desired maximum level. Not that Italy feared war. "The Italian people are so little afraid of war that since 1911 to this day they have spent more years at war than in peace."

Nevertheless, at the close of the year Italy found herself at the parting of the ways. Three courses lay open. In the first place she might maintain her present

Since the Great War Italy has tended to regard the Balkans as being her own particular sphere of influence, but she has now to meet in ever-increasing measure the rivalry of Germany and Russia. How complex is the state system of this uneasy corner of Europe will be plain from this map. Also indicated are the principal rail and water lines of communication. Turkey's key position will be manifest.

But Mussolini Still Has His Dreams of Empire

In the war of ideologies Fascism has declared itself to be firmly opposed to Bolshevism, and it was hardly surprising that when the U.S.S.R. made its attack upon Finland the sympathies of the Italian people were shown to be most obviously with the latter. Above we see Italian students gathered in vociferous sympathy outside the Finnish Legation in Rome.

Photo, Wide World

attitude of " non-belligerency " which, she claimed, had up to now averted an extension of the conflict to south-eastern Europe. This was the attitude confirmed by the Grand Council.

Alternatively, Italy might definitely enter the war as an active partner of Germany. Such a course would seem to be natural on the part of a member of the Axis, and before the war it was openly suggested that Italy was to be given a free hand by Germany in the Balkans, while the Nazis made their drive towards the Ukraine. The pact with Moscow upset this calculation, however, and it is almost certain that the signing of the pact was the decisive factor which induced Signor Mussolini to refrain from declaring war in September.

Interest in the Balkans

As suggested in an earlier article (*see* page 213), the Duce may well be sincere in that detestation of Bolshevism which he has often expressed, and the developments of recent weeks may have fortified him in his attitude of hostility. Not only have most of the political and territorial gains accrued to Russia, but Italy's hopes in the Balkans are likely to be affected by the revived interest of Russia in Bessarabia and the Black Sea. Furthermore, now that the road to the Ukraine is effectively barred by Soviet bayonets, the Nazis cannot but feel attracted by that alternative road to the south—that road which runs through Rumania and the heart of the Balkans.

In the light of this eventuality, Italian spokesmen made frequent reaffirmations of Italy's profound interest in the political

and economic situation of the Balkans; for instance, in the speech quoted above, Count Ciano denounced any scheme for the formation of a Balkan bloc.

As a last alternative Italy might decide to repeat her step of 1915 when she broke with her partners of the Triple Alliance and entered the war against them as the ally of France and Britain. It may seem unlikely that 1915 will be repeated in 1940, but the Duce, realist as he is, may come to the conclusion that he has little to gain from his present allies, who, after all, can do little more than encourage him to seize from the " fat democracies " Tunis, Corsica, or North Africa. . . .

But though Mussolini may hesitate to draw the sword, it would be dangerous to infer from his hesitancy that he has decided to forgo his claims. " A new Europe can be built only when Italy's territorial claims have been satisfied," says Signor Gayda, the Duce's mouthpiece.

As the year closed it was far from certain which of these courses Italy would pursue. Perhaps on the whole it was most likely that she would continue to preserve that position which in the language of current diplomacy is styled as " non-belligerency," but is perhaps only another word for that very old thing called " sitting on the fence." Italy will come down from the fence when she sees the way clear to the satisfaction of those colonial demands which are still in the very forefront of the Fascist programme.

Signor Mussolini's skill in keeping his country out of war has still further enhanced his popularity amongst his people, and when the seventeenth anniversary of the March on Rome was commemorated the Duce was the centre of enthusiastic demonstrations. This photograph shows men of the Fascist militia saluting him with upraised daggers. Behind the Duce is General Starace, recently-appointed Chief of Staff of the Militia.

Photo, Planet News

The King Honours the Brave and the Fair

Five men were decorated by the King on December 19 at a Naval depot in recognition of their remarkable bravery in dismantling a German magnetic mine that had come ashore. Four are seen above: left to right, Chief Petty Officer C. E. Baldwin, D.S.M.; Lieutenant J. E. M. Glenny, D.S.C.; Lieutenant R. C. Lewis, D.S.O.; Lieut.-Commander J. G. D. Ouvry, D.S.O. Right, the King is decorating the fifth, Able Seaman A. L. Vearncombe with the D.S.M.

T HE men whom the King decorated were from the chief torpedo and mine school of the Royal Navy, which, though it is on land, is officially known as H.M.S. "Vernon." They opened and examined the first mine dropped by Nazi aircraft to drift ashore, so that its secrets might be known and the necessary counter-measures taken. As the exact nature of the mechanism was unknown the mine might have exploded at any moment, and the work called for skill and bravery of the highest order.

During his tour of Naval depots in the South of England the King inspected a number of "ratings" of the Women's Royal Naval Service on the Parade Ground of Marines' Barracks. Left, his Majesty is passing down the line while recruits, not yet in uniform, stand rigidly to attention. At all Naval depots "Wrens" are now doing work as clerks, cooks and in many other capacities, thus relieving men for more active work.

Photos, Keystone

The King has lost no opportunity in expressing his admiration of the work of the men who man the minesweepers, and his Majesty is here seen during his tour of Naval depots inspecting the crews of minesweepers whose work, though unspectacular, is fraught with the utmost danger. The minesweepers are manned chiefly by fishermen, and when, at the end of November, the call was made for 2,000 to form the crews of the additional trawlers needed to meet the new Nazi frightfulness on the sea, more men than were needed immediately volunteered.

Photo, Keystone

They Were Targets of the Nazi Air Murderers

On December 19 Nazi airmen made another attack on defenceless British trawlers. Two were sunk and one, the "Etruria," badly damaged. Three of the "Etruria's" crew were killed, and above are the survivors after landing at a British port. Below is the fore deck of the "Etruria" with the bow practically torn away.   *Photos, Topical*

IN his broadcast on December 18, after speaking of German losses at sea, Mr. Winston Churchill said: "The Nazi Navy and Air Force are venting their wrath for these heavy blows by re-doubling their efforts and sinking fishing smacks and drowning fishermen in the North Sea. . . . These outrages are the tactics of a guilty regime which feels the long arm of sea-power laid upon its shoulder." During the attack in which the "Etruria" was sunk 15 of these defenceless little ships were bombed, an act of savagery scarcely ever equalled in the annals of the sea. Two of them were sunk.

Looming Silent and Shadowy in the Night

These impressive photographs were taken at night in gun-pits in France. Left, a big gun, screened from prying eyes by a curtain of camouflage, is ready to be fired, and a member of its crew is checking the lay by the light of a pocket torch. Camouflage in warfare is more necessary today than ever in the past, for enemy aircraft take great pains to photograph their opponents' positions as often and as completely as possible, and what is not easily visible to the naked eye from ground level may be spotted by the camera from the air.

Work of remarkable ingenuity has been done in the Allied line in camouflaging gun emplacements, aerodromes and other positions that might be spotted from the air. Artificial camouflage has had many clever extensions since the last war, but the best of all is still that which Nature herself provides. Here, in a hollow such as is often to be found in the neighbourhood of willow-trees, a British 18-pounder field gun has been placed. The gas-masked gun crew are ready for all eventualities.

Britain's Guns Are Made Ready to Roar

Crouched in this war's equivalent of a "dug-out," the British officer and his staff, seen in the upper photograph, are taking directions for their battery from a forward observation post. The eerie scene in the lower photograph is of a big gun just about to be fired ; its crew stand round—gas masks donned, for a barrage of gas-shells is an ever-present possibility—ready to go into action as the uplifted hand indicates.

Photos, British Official : Crown Copyright

WORDS THAT HISTORY WILL REMEMBER

(*Continued from page* 538)

What Russia Demanded from Finland

Monday, December 11, 1939

Extracts from WHITE BOOK issued by FINNISH GOVERNMENT, outlining the Soviet's demands :

To make possible the blocking of the Gulf of Finland by artillery from both coasts to prevent enemy warships or transports entering the Gulf of Finland.

To make it possible to prevent any enemy gaining access to those islands in the Gulf of Finland situated west and north-west of the entrance to Leningrad.

To move the Finnish frontier along the Karelian Isthmus, now 20 miles from Leningrad —that is, within the range of big guns—to positions farther north and north-west.

To adjust the frontier in the north in the Petsamo region, where the frontier was badly and artificially drawn.

The following questions of common interest should be settled by mutual arrangement :

First : Leasing to the Soviet Union for 30 years the port of Hangoe and the territory adjoining situated within a radius of five to six nautical miles to the south and east, and three to the north and west, for the purpose of establishing a naval base with coastal artillery capable, in conjunction with the naval base at Paldiski (Estonia), of blocking access to the Gulf of Finland.

For the protection of the naval base the Finnish Government should permit the Soviet Union to maintain in the port of Hangoe the following : One infantry regiment, two anti-aircraft batteries, three Air Force regiments, one battalion of armoured cars—the total not to exceed 5,000 men.

Finland, in exchange for other territories, should grant the following : The islands of Suursaari, Sriskara, Lavanskari, Tytarskari and Koivisto, part of the Karelian Isthmus to a total of about 1,066 square miles.

Germany Shifts War Guilt on to Britain

Tuesday, December 12

HERR VON RIBBENTROP in the preface to German White Book " Documents for the Period Preceding the War.":

Since enemy propaganda is busy misleading the world about the causes of the war, it is important to prove beyond all doubt, with the help of official documents, that Britain alone caused the war, and desired it in order to destroy Germany.

This collection of 482 documents deals with all the most important of the events from which the war with Poland, and then with Britain and France, developed. The documents show the systematic struggle conducted by the Poles, ever since the Great War, against Danzig and to destroy everything German in Poland. They prove the unlimited and gracious patience of the Fuehrer, and his statesmanlike endeavours to put German-Polish relations on a permanent basis that would do justice to the interests of both sides. They prove, on the other side, the short-sightedness and lack of understanding of the Polish rulers, who destroyed the possibility of reaching a final settlement that was offered again and again by Germany.

Above all, one can see from them how, immediately after Munich, Britain's will to war became more and more obvious, and how the British Government finally used the blind-ness of the Polish Government—which Britain had deliberately brought about—to unleash against Germany a war that had been planned long ago.

It would be necessary to give the history of the whole post-war period fully to unmask the hypocritical policy of Britain, whereby she opposed any attempt by Germany to free herself from the chains of Versailles, and stopped any possibility of a revision of those dictates at the conference table.

But it is sufficient to look at the short period since the autumn of 1930, on the basis of the documents in this White Book, to recognize that Britain had determined beforehand to meet the progress of the Fuehrer with force—the Fuehrer, whose statesmanship had removed the worst crimes of Versailles without bloodshed, and who would have succeeded in the same way in finding a peaceful solution of the German-Polish question if Britain had not misused Poland as a tool in her desire for war.

This historic fact is confirmed by Britain's insulting challenge to Germany in answer to the final magnanimous offer of peace which the Fuehrer made in his Reichstag speech on October 6. . . .

No Peace for Europe on Hitler's Terms

Wednesday, December 13

LORD HALIFAX, Foreign Secretary, in the House of Lords :

. . . We are blamed . . . for not having made sufficient effort to conciliate Germany. I am not aware that Germany has exhausted herself in efforts to conciliate us, and I entirely decline to see this country put into the dock in international affairs and held in any way to blame comparably with Germany for the tragedy into which the world has moved. . . .

I am quite certain Hitler is very anxious for peace on his own terms. I cannot be sure that he is anxious for peace on terms that would make for the peace of Europe in later generations.

Nobody can feel more strongly than I do the horror and tragedy of war. Nobody can feel more strongly than any one of your lordships about how criminally wrong it would be to miss any opportunity for peace.

But do not you come back to the fundamental question : Were you or were you not right to make a stand for the cause which led you into this war three months ago ? I could understand the pacifist saying you were wrong, but if you were right, would it not be wrong to stop until you had done your utmost to secure the cause for which you went to war ? . . .

Unity and Self-Sacrifice will Win the War

M. PAUL REYNAUD, French Finance Minister, in the Chamber of Deputies :

This is the language of sacrifice. . . . I consider victory to be certain if Frenchmen will show themselves worthy of the great hours of their history. The war potential of the Allies is immense because the freedom of the sea, though disturbed, is still maintained.

After six years of the Nazi regime the German people are undergoing a nervous strain comparable with that which they underwent at the beginning of 1918 after three and a half years of war. Nazi leaders know that a military check would set in motion factors leading to the collapse of the regime drawing its sustenance from prestige and terrorism.

We must prepare ourselves against the dangers of prolonged military inaction. Hitler, who is a revolutionary agitator, has watched German democracy fall to pieces. He has always since 1933 placed his hope in the weakness of democracy, and he is still playing this card, believing that internal dissension will come as time passes. . . .

It is possible that this war, which began in a sort of apathy, may finish in a general conflagration. Perhaps in the darkest days our idea of liberty and of prosperity will exist only in our hearts, but it will be there ready to blossom forth after the days of trial.

That day is upon us, but we shall win. We shall conquer the enemy if first of all we conquer ourselves.

Russia Ignominiously Expelled from the League

Resolution of LEAGUE OF NATIONS on Russian Invasion of Finland :

The Assembly of the League, having determined that by the aggression which she has committed against Finland the Soviet Union has violated all its agreements and special political accords with Finland, as well as the Pact of Paris (the Kellogg-Briand pact) and Article 12 of the Covenant of the League : and inasmuch as it has proceeded to a denunciation without legal right of the treaty of non-aggression concluded with Finland in 1932 which should have remained in force until the end of 1945 ;

Solemnly condemns the action of the Soviet Union against the Finnish State, addresses the present appeal to each member of the League, so that it might furnish such material and humanitarian aid to Finland which it is able to do, and might abstain from any act which might diminish Finland's power of defending herself, authorizes the Secretary-General to give all the aid of the League's technical services to the assistance of Finland. . . .

Considering that the Soviet Union, in spite of the invitation extended to it, and which it rejected before the Council and the Assembly could make an inquiry into the conflict with Finland.

That by virtue of the fact that it has violated its most essential obligations towards the League and its guarantees for the peace and security of nations, and has acted in this affair as if the conditions outlined in Article 15 of the Covenant did not apply to itself,

That it has vainly tried to justify its rejection by pretending to be in relations with a Government which does not exist, either legally or in fact, and has ignored the Government of the Finnish people which represents Finland's free institutions.

That the Soviet Union is not only guilty of violation of its obligations under the Covenant, but by this very fact is placed beyond the jurisdiction of the Covenant. . . .

Thursday, December 14

Resolution expelling Russia from League of Nations :

The Council, having taken cognizance of the resolution adopted by the Assembly on December 14, 1939, regarding the appeal of the Finnish Government, (1) associates itself with the condemnation by the Assembly of the action of the Union of Soviet Socialist Republics against the Finnish State, and (2) for the reasons set forth in the resolution of the Assembly, in virtue of Article 16, paragraph 4, of the Covenant, finds that, by its act, the Union of Soviet Socialist Republics has placed itself outside the League of Nations. It follows that the Union of Soviet Socialist Republics is no longer a member of the League.

'Tin Hats' for the Heads of Britain's Defenders

The raw material of steel helmets is seen above. Blanks from which they are stamped out are being piled on a truck which carries them to the press room.

IT was not until February 1916 that the first steel helmets were issued to the British troops in the last war, but in this war they are an essential part not only of the soldiers' equipment but of that of the police, the A.F.S. and A.R.P. workers. The steel helmet of today has been evolved by the patient research of scientists and can now be considered to have been perfected In the factory where these photos were taken about 300 men are employed and 50,000 helmets a week are produced.

When the blank has been pressed into shape the next process is fitting the stainless steel rim. It is welded in position and then clinched home by the impressively powerful machine seen above.

Above left, a helmet has just been stamped out of a blank and the operator holds in his hand the surplus metal. When once the helmet has taken its final shape it is painted inside and outside before the linings are put in. Right, a man is spraying on the paint. He wears a mask over his mouth and nose to guard against inhaling particles of paint, while his hair is protected from the spray by bandages. After being painted, the helmets are passed on a conveyer through drying furnaces.

Photos, Pictorial Press

They 'Scuttle'—Because That's the Nazi Way

THE most remarkable evidence of the plight in which the Nazi rulers of Germany find themselves is afforded by the policy of scuttle adopted for the German Mercantile Marine. From the outbreak of war up to Christmas eighteen German merchant ships were sunk to prevent them becoming prizes of the Allies. They are the following :

" Adolf Leonhardt," 2,989 tons	" Inn," 2,867 tons
" Adolf Woermann," 8,577 tons	" Johannes Molkenbuhr," 5,294 tons
" Antiochia," 3,106 tons	" Mecklenburg," 7,892 tons
" Bertha Fisser," 4,110 tons	" Minden," 4,165 tons
" Carl Fritzen," 6,594 tons	" Parana," 6,038 tons
" Columbus," 32,581 tons	" Poseidon," 5,864 tons
" Emmy Friedrich," 4,327 tons	" Tenerife," 4,996 tons
	" Ussukuma," 7,834 tons
" Gonzenheim," 4,574 tons	" Watussi," 9,521 tons
" Halle," 5,889 tons	

The scuttling of the " Columbus," Germany's third largest liner, off the coast of Virginia on December 19, was the climax of this astounding series of incidents, unique in the history of the sea.

" The Order of the Silver Scuttle "   *Cartoon by Illingworth, by courtesy of the " Daily Mail."*

In the photograph (left) the 32,581-ton German liner " Columbus " is seen at anchor off Campeche shortly after she sought refuge on the outbreak of war, September 3. The Nazis continued their policy of scuttle by sinking her and setting her on fire after she had been challenged by a British warship on December 19. Below is " Columbus " burning, with some of the survivors rowing away.

Photos, Wide World and Planet News

Ursula's Exploit in 'Hitler's Cabbage Patch'

Seen here returning to port in triumph, the "Ursula" is one of the Unity class of submarines, called "Babies" in the Navy because of their small tonnage. They are primarily intended for coastal work in home waters. "Ursula's" tonnage is 540, and her crew normally 27. See also photograph in page 523.

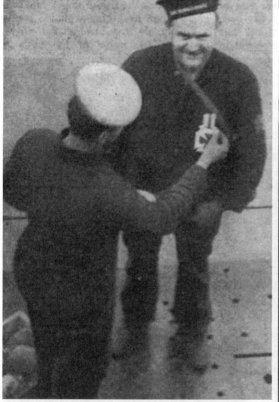

Here a member of the "Ursula's" crew decorates a shipmate with a cardboard "Iron Cross" which was specially cut for the occasion.

The warmest of welcomes awaited the men of the "Ursula" as they came ashore (above). Centre right, Lieut.-Com. G. C. Phillips, bearded and happy, being congratulated by Captain Bethell.
Photos, Topical Press

By skill and daring the little submarine "Ursula" was manoeuvred through the thickly-sown minefield known to our submarine service as "Hitler's cabbage patch." Now it was December 14, and her captain was closely watching through the periscope a number of German patrol vessels. Then a cruiser of the Köln class came in sight at a range of about four miles. The German cruiser was screened by six destroyers, and in order to reach a firing position "Ursula" had to dive beneath them. As she did so, their propellers were clearly heard overhead.

Snatching a quick look at the German cruiser through his periscope, "Ursula's" captain, Lt.-Com. G. C. Phillips, gave the order to fire. Those in the submarine waited, counting the seconds to see if they had scored a hit. They had. "Ursula" was shaken by a tremendous explosion. The first torpedo had found its mark. A few seconds later there was another great explosion, proving that the second torpedo had also hit, possibly a magazine. Both explosions shook the submarine badly and the second

one broke the electric light bulbs. At the time the torpedoes were fired, the noise of the propellers of the enemy cruiser could be clearly heard in the submarine. With the first explosion these ceased abruptly and after the second explosion the noises of rending metal and of a ship breaking up were heard.

Four of the destroyers at once turned towards the submarine, and attacked "Ursula" with depth charges. She skilfully avoided the attack, however, and after a time came to periscope depth to have a look round.

Two destroyers were standing by where the enemy cruiser had been, as if searching for survivors. There was no sign at all of the cruiser, which had obviously broken up and sunk. Satisfied with her work, "Ursula" left an area which was still very unhealthy, and arrived home in port just in time for Christmas.

Her captain's "Christmas present" was a D.S.O. and promotion to Commander, and two D.S.C.'s, seven D.S.M.'s, and ten Mention in Dispatches were granted to other members of a very gallant ship's company.

Bombs are the Real Danger in Air Raids

In this article the famous gas and A.R.P. authority, Major-General C. H. Foulkes, C.B., C.M.G., discusses the menace of bombs dropped from enemy 'planes, and concludes with some remarks on air-raid precautions in general. More information on the subject will be found in the author's "Commonsense and A.R.P." (Pearson).

London's only experience of air raids has so far been practice by A.R.P. workers. These temporary casualties at such a rehearsal are contriving to look their parts.
Photo, Topical Press

UNDOUBTEDLY the chief danger in an air raid is from *high-explosive bombs*. It is estimated that to give adequate protection against direct hits from medium (500 lb.) and heavy (1 ton) projectiles fitted with delay action fuses, it would be necessary to construct shelters 50 or more feet below ground or to provide them with reinforced concrete roofs 10 or 15 feet in thickness. Such measures would not be generally considered reasonable or practicable, and they have been rightly rejected by the Government.

Fortunately, the risk of a direct hit is not too great. In an area within 15 miles of Charing Cross, containing a population of 8½ millions, the odds against a bomb falling within 50 feet of any particular spot are 2¼ millions to 1, and the odds against its striking any particular Anderson shelter is more than 650 million to 1. Two-thirds of the bombs dropped on London during the last war caused no casualties at all, and it has been calculated from air photographs that 90 per cent of the London area is open space, so that only one bomb in every ten would fall on any building.

Many more bombs may, therefore, be expected to fall near a building than directly on it, so that the blast and fragmentation resulting from them constitute the most frequent and serious risks of an air raid ; and since these effects are produced, in the case of bombs that explode on contact, more or less in a horizontal direction from the point of impact, any shelter below ground—even a shallow open trench—will give substantial, if not complete, protection against them.

We now come to the third of the principal forms which air attack may take—*incendiary bombs*. It is the 2 lb. thermit magnesium bomb which, according to official expectation, is likely to be used in considerable numbers, with a view to achieving the most widespread effects in relation to the number of aircraft employed.

But incendiary bombs have not proved very effective in practice. Ninety per cent of the bombs that were used in some of the raids on this country in 1914–18 were of this nature, and 258 fell in London in one night ; but they proved to be so disappointing to the Germans in the results achieved that their use was almost entirely abandoned towards the end of the war. This type of bomb has been much improved since that time, but incendiaries were not very successful in Spain, where, no doubt, the Powers that were engaged in what was termed " non-intervention " were trying out their experimental equipment. Many such bombs were used, especially in Madrid, but they are reported to have done little damage. Nevertheless, particular attention has been rightly given to fire-fighting in A.R.P., as the risk of direct hits is far greater than from high-explosive bombs.

Finally, we may mention *anti-aircraft fragments*. In some of the raids on

Here is the real thing—a scene in Helsinki during one of the Red Air Force's raids in the opening days of the war in Finland. An high-explosive bomb has been dropped on a four-storey house. Three of the walls have collapsed, and on that which still stands are the shattered remains of a staircase. Men are at work searching the debris.
Photo, Wide World

Air Raids on Britain: This War and the Last

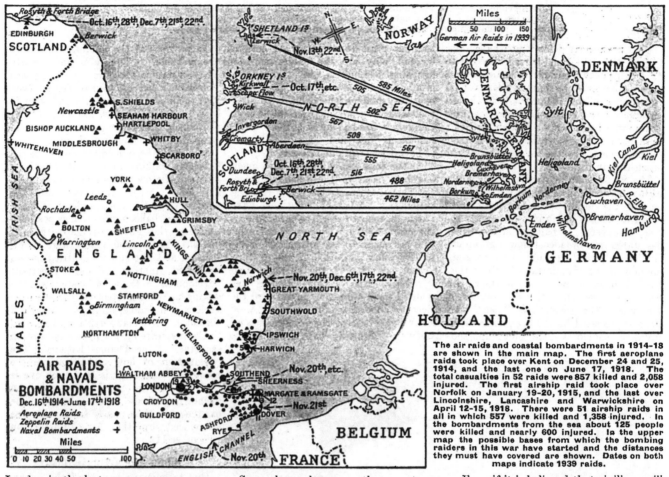

The air raids and coastal bombardments in 1914-18 are shown in the main map. The first aeroplane raids took place over Kent on December 24 and 25, 1914, and the last one on June 17, 1918. The total casualties in 52 raids were 857 killed and 2,058 injured. The first airship raid took place over Norfolk on January 19-20, 1915, and the last over Lincolnshire, Lancashire and Warwickshire on April 12-15, 1918. There were 51 airship raids in all in which 557 were killed and 1,358 injured. In the bombardments from the sea about 125 people were killed and nearly 600 injured. In the upper map the possible bases from which the bombing raiders in this war have started and the distances they must have covered are shown. Dates on both maps indicate 1939 raids.

London in the last war as many as one-third of the total casualties were caused by fragments from our own anti-aircraft fire. This was due chiefly to the foolhardiness of spectators in the streets, and it can be prevented by avoiding unnecessary exposure in the open and at windows. A much higher percentage of shells fired from anti-aircraft guns is now high-explosive, and as these break up into smaller fragments than shrapnel they will not be so dangerous as formerly, as they can penetrate only light roof coverings and glass sky-lights and windows.

If it be asked what precautions should be taken to guard against these various risks, some people adopt the attitude that nothing much can be done about it ; if a bomb comes, one is " for it," so what is the use of distressing oneself unnecessarily or, indeed, of taking any precautions at all ? Some have refused to be fitted with gas-masks because they regard them as part of the paraphernalia of war ; others fall an easy prey to the purveyors of all the air raid gadgets on sale ; and yet others have insisted on the absolute necessity for the construction, at a cost of hundreds of millions sterling, of tunnelled or reinforced concrete shelters for everybody, which are calculated to give complete protection even in the event of direct hits with high-explosive bombs.

Somewhere between these extreme views a commonsense solution must be found, and in our preparations a sense of proportion should be observed and a proper balance must be struck between expenditure on bombers to destroy the enemy's aerodromes and industries, on fighter 'planes, anti-aircraft guns and balloon barrages to weaken the attacking forces in the air and to make their task more difficult, and on shelters, evacuation, and all the other passive defence measures known as air raid precautions.

Cost of Protection Must be Reasonable

Some preparations must, of course, be made for minimizing the effects of air attacks, but their cost should be reduced to reasonable proportions. The risk of direct hits with high-explosive bombs has got to be accepted, and reasonably safe protection against their splinter and blast effects, and against incendiary bombs and gas can be provided at no great expense. The streets should be cleared at all costs, and at least 75 per cent. of casualties should be avoided if shelter is taken in buildings of some sort.

Our main defensive effort ought to be concentrated on the protection of the many small areas which contain ports and dockyards, arsenals, aerodromes, food and oil depots, munitions works and other objectives of real military importance.

Even if it is believed that civilians will be made definite military objectives, there should be discrimination between some centres of population and others. An air raid over London, for example, would be a costly adventure, though the City, as the nerve centre of the Empire, and the dock area, in which one third of the food supply of the whole country is handled in normal times, are tempting targets. The important manufacturing centres in the Midlands and the North are also legitimate objectives, but the danger from chance bombs in villages and small towns and, in fact, in about nine-tenths of the whole country is negligible, and the issue of gas masks to the inhabitants of rural districts was an absurdity matched only by the precautions which we are told are being taken in the Gambia, our West African colony, where the sacks used for packing ground nuts are being used for sand-bag protection and intensive training is being carried out in decontamination.

Of course, we must not assume that air raids are not a very real source of danger to this country. But public attention was, for a long time, confined to how they might be endured rather than how they might be met and defeated—an attitude which is not in harmony with the spirit that the nation has shown in its past history.

Balloons Now Float Above Britain's Seas

In previous pages (see 185 and 441) we have illustrated various features of the balloon barrage, now so familiar a sight in Britain. Some of the difficulties surmounted and developments simultaneously pressed forward are discussed below.

AFTER nearly four months of war the balloon barrage raised to protect our cities has not once been challenged by enemy raiders. Its destructive effect, however, has been unhappily proved on at least three occasions, when straying British aircraft have been brought crashing down, their wings severed by the steel cables of the death-trap in the sky.

The work of the Auxiliary Air Force balloon squadrons might be regarded as one of the more unexciting forms of warfare. This is by no means always the case, however. A balloon aircraftman has stated in a broadcast how a group of civilian helpers "all had a very revised opinion of the 'comfortable' job of the balloon barrage men" when their job was over; certainly the difficulties of "playing" the great silver "fish" are little appreciated by the lay public. For instance, should a gale blow up, the

balloons must immediately be lowered, for not only are the cables notorious lightning conductors, but the dangers of a truant balloon are very real. Moreover, the pull on the cable is so strong that on more than one occasion in a gale the heavy five-ton lorry to which every balloon is "earthed" has been known to be moved bodily and disastrously.

As the weeks have passed not so much has been seen of the London barrage, but this is certainly no sign of relaxing vigilance. Weather conditions have partly accounted for the grounding of the craft, and in any case each balloon can be raised to its operational ceiling in a very few minutes.

The extension of the barrage system to other cities besides London was decided upon only early in 1939, and the officers and men who came forward were mostly ignorant of the idiosyncrasies of balloons. Starting thus from scratch,

the progress of the units has been truly remarkable. There are now nearly 40,000 men in the service, yet there was no balloon barrage in existence, not even for London, until towards the end of 1938. Up to the outbreak of war none of the provincial crews had enjoyed any practical experience of their clumsy charges.

As one of the immediate results of the German bombing raid on the Firth of Forth on October 16—a very useful test in many other respects, also—the Auxiliary Air Force was ordered to move a number of balloon units to new positions guarding the Forth Bridge within 24 hours. Five special trains were requisitioned and the job was carried out to schedule. Another and most important development of the whole system was the setting up of a protective barrage over various vulnerable strategic points off the coast, particular attention being paid to the favourite areas of the mine-sowing seaplanes in the Thames Estuary. The explanation of how a balloon can be moored *off* the coast is that each one is sent up on the usual cable from an anchored (though mobile) barge. The existence of these newly-sited units was announced by the Air Ministry on December 11.

Blown Here from Germany

Our technicians have had the opportunity of examining similar balloons used by the Germans in their defensive scheme, for two balloons obligingly came to rest in these islands after war began. The standard German type, which is of a more angular shape than ours, has the cable attached near its tail, so that the nose rides high. More doubtful at first of the usefulness of the balloon barrage, Germany has a smaller and less highly-developed system. France has no such barrage, but, unlike Britain, she still uses captive balloons for army observation purposes.

It is an open secret that our own barrage is now equipped with a weapon that adds to its lethal potentialities, but its nature is, of course, entirely "hush-hush."

The institution and maintenance of the barrage is no negligible item in the nation's war budget. About a thirtieth of a balloon's hydrogen gas capacity is lost per day, so that in that short time 6s. 8d. must come from the taxpayers' pockets to provide for its upkeep. But the psychological effect of these innocent-looking craft, both on the enemy—forced either to keep clear above the barrage where the guns can "pot" at them, or to take a chance by diving among the cables—and on our own people, is incalculable.

Above is one of the first photographs taken of the new balloon barrage over the Thames Estuary which may upset the nerves of the Nazi airmen attempting to lay "murder mines" in the way of British and neutral shipping. In this case the anchorage of the balloon is a motor barge.
Photo, Associated Press

'Silver Fish' Provide Work for Clever Hands

The work of manufacturing barrage balloons needs the finest workmanship and special training is given to the "hands." Left, girls are attending a course in which a small model of a balloon is being used to show the general construction. Above, air is being pumped into the stabilizer during a final test of a balloon.

THE balloon factories have now to supply the new demand of the balloon barrages that have been set up to protect such vulnerable points as the Firth of Forth and the Thames Estuary. The Thames balloon barrage, one of the units of which is seen in page 568, is worked from mobile barges. The men of the R.A.F. who man these balloon sections have arduous work to do, for they have to face the bitter winds and rough water that winter brings to the North Sea area. Normally the crews do turns of 48 hours straight off, but in case it should be impossible to relieve them within that time the barrage barges are provisioned for six days. Each vessel carries a balloon crew of four men in addition to the crew of the barge. On each vessel are a balloon platform, winch, and a stack of hydrogen tubes. The work of land balloon stations is illustrated in pages 440–41.

The girl workers take great pride in their work, and in the centre photograph they form an admiring group at what is practically the launching of the balloon, for it is being fully inflated for the first time. In the photograph immediately above, Air Vice-Marshal Owen Tudor Boyd, officer in charge of the Balloon Command, is inspecting some of the R.A.F. men who are working the balloon barrage in the Thames Estuary. They are clothed against the bitter weather that they must encounter, and are wearing the lifebelts, oilskins, and sou'-westers essential for all whose duties are performed afloat.

Photos, Topical and Associated Press

Workers Who Put Our Fighters Into Khaki

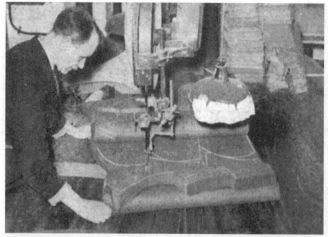

Thanks to many mechanical devices Army clothing can now be made very quickly. This man is cutting out uniforms with a mechanical cutter that enables him to work with great speed and accuracy.
Photo, Keystone

There was at one time a shortage of overcoats for men called up, but it was soon made good. Here, in a factory employing over 2,000 hands, overcoats are being made in large numbers.

The first requirement for the soldier is his battledress, the new uniform that has the great advantage of doing away with puttees. Here women are at work in an Army clothing factory sewing uniforms with batteries of mechanically driven sewing machines. Centre left is a girl with a big pile of forage caps. The Royal Army Ordnance Corps is responsible for supplying every requirement of the Army, from guns and shells to clothes and boots, with the exception of food and transport, which fall within the province of the R.A.S.C.
Photos, Central Press, Sport & General and Fox

We Saw The Canadians Land in England

It was for most people a dramatic surprise when Mr. Churchill
announced in his broadcast on December 18 that contingents of the
Canadian Army had just arrived in England. Here the scene at one
of the ports where they disembarked is described by a special
correspondent of the " Manchester Guardian."

IT was a cold, grey day. The water,
the sky and the farther shore were
all cold and grey. One transport was
already at anchor, and the journalists
who had been let into the secret that
the Canadians were coming stood on the
little pier at noon and stamped their
cold feet as the other grey ships came
stealing into harbour.

They came in one by one, the transports
looking high and heavy beside the rakish
warships that escorted them. They
came up the middle of the channel, so
that the cheering from them seemed
faint ; but we heard it, and the sound of
bagpipes from one ship and shrill
" Yippees " from another. That was
the Westerners, the Canadian pressmen
told us. On other ships some men were
singing " Pack Up Your Troubles."
There were not many of us to cheer
back, for this was a secret till the troops
and the ships were clear and safe from
German bombings, and even the people
of the port knew nothing.

There were the journalists, a few
soldiers and the dozen or so local folk
who made a daily visit to the pier, and
this time had found something worth
watching. Some of them, though,
miraculously knew what it was all about.
A tired-looking, middle-aged woman
went up to a young lady of fashion, all
furs and lipstick, to ask her. " It's the
Canadians," the younger woman told her
in a bored, know-all voice, and then she
thawed and grinned as though it were a
lark that the Canadians were coming.

It was mid-afternoon before the
Canadian G.O.C., Major-General Mc-
Naughton, came ashore at another pier,
with Mr. Eden and Mr. Vincent Massey.
The troops had told the Dominions
Secretary that the crossing had been
" dandy," and the General told us the
same thing. The officers had been in
suites and the men in first-class cabins.
When he came over in 1914 they had been
cramped in hammocks for twenty-eight
days. He had been a major then ; now he
was in command, with many on his staff
and among his N.C.O.s who had been with
him twenty-five years ago.

There was more of a crowd on this
pier, some naval officers and a few
hundred of the local people. " The story

gets about," said a policeman. The
civilians were let on to the pier and
kept behind barricades.

There was nothing to do for a time
but watch the warships winking their
semaphore lights to the signallers on
shore, and the aeroplanes manœuvring
overhead. At last three machines
swooped low over one of the transports,
startling the gulls that had been rocking
on the water. It must have been a
special salute, for soon a black and white
tender came puffing to the shore, over-
flowing with khaki. The Canadians
were here, cheering wildly and waving
their rifles above their heads, their
bugle band blowing like mad. The
sailors on the little warship at the pier
cheered them as they passed.

We could see what they looked like
now as they came alongside, singing :
thick-set, open-faced boys in the same
battle-kit that the British Army wears,
but with a maple-leaf badge in their fore-
and-aft caps. . . .

The men fell in on the pier, their
officers hurrying them off the boat.

" Tiny " Wilson, one of the cooks of the first
Canadian contingent to come ashore in
Britain, carried not only his kit, but odds and
ends of his kitchen utensils stuck in his belt.
Photo, " Daily Mirror "

The first contingent of Canada's Army to arrive in England was described by the Commanding
Officer, Major-General McNaughton, as " a broad cross section of the Canadian people."
They had the friendliest of greetings from the spectators as they first set foot on British soil.
Photos, British Official : Crown Copyright

Some of the Canadian troops who landed so " secretly " in England on December 17th, are here seen coming down the gangway from one of the transports directly after it had tied up at the quay. Their safe arrival was a significant event in the war.

They formed up in ranks and came to attention, and the local area's general officer commanding read them the King's message. . . .

Then they stood easy and smoked and talked, and we walked among them in the fading light, admiring their physique and moved to think of the journey they had made and the journeys they had still to make. They had seen only the speech-makers on the pier and the little crowd, but they were off again now, on to the troop train that was to take them through a blacked-out Britain.

We Had Scuttling Drill on the 'Columbus'

Following the scuttling of the " Graf Spee " on December 17 came the news of the loss of the 32,000-ton North German Lloyd steamer " Columbus." She left Vera Cruz on December 14, and on December 19 was stopped by a British warship. The story of her scuttling as told by her master, Captain Daehne, is here reprinted from the " Daily Express " and " Daily Telegraph."

THE only two casualties in the scuttling of the crack German liner "Columbus" were two "happy-go-lucky firemen," according to Captain Wilhelm Daehne, master of the ship.

He said that they must have thought he was "kidding" when he ordered the ship's suicide to avoid capture by a British warship.

United States destroyers, said Captain Daehne, followed his ship all the way from Vera Cruz until Monday, December 18, when the United States cruiser, "Tuscaloosa," took up the escort.

Captain Daehne said that he sighted the British warship about 2.30 in the afternoon. "I could make out the British flag at 2.55," he said, "and I sounded the general alarm for the crew—stand by, scuttle, burn. I had drilled the crew for a month for this task and they knew what to do.

"I radioed all ships of our position, saying we were ready to scuttle. At 2.57 we got flag signals from the warship, 'Stop immediately.' At 3.5 she fired two shots across our bows.

"At the same time we lowered the life-boats, and one minute later we opened the seacocks."

By 3.14 all the boats except the two left for the scuttling crew and fire brigade had been lowered. At 3.16 the chief engineer reported that the men had left the engine-room. At 3.39 all the boats were away except the captain's motor-boat.

"When the whole ship was ablaze," said Capt. Daehne, "I slid down the rope and circled the 'Columbus' in a motor-boat. The destroyer was about 50 feet away, but I could not make out her name."

The captain said there were originally twelve women aboard. When he got orders to leave Vera Cruz he said to them : "I'll leave you behind. The trip is too dangerous for a woman." Nine of them refused to be left behind.

Asked what were his reactions to the order sending the "Columbus" out of her refuge, he said, "When you get an order you don't ask questions."

This photograph was taken from one of the boats of the "Columbus" after she had been set on fire and scuttled. She is still sending up clouds of smoke and sheets of flame, but soon afterwards took her last plunge. The young sailor who just comes into the photograph shows his sorrow at seeing the tragic end of a fine ship. *Photos, " Daily Mirror," "Keystone.*

IIIIIIIIIIIIIIIIIIIIIIIIIIIIIIIIIIIIIIIIIIIIIIIIIIIIIIIIIIIIIIIIIIIIIIIIIIIIIIIIII **I WAS THERE!** IIIIIIIIIIIIIIIIIIIIIIIIIIIIIIIIIIIIIIIIIIIIIIIIIIIIIIIIIIIIIIIIIIIIIIIIIIIIIIIIIIIII

Our Trawlers Were Bombed From the Air

A new campaign of terror by German warplanes began on December 17, when a number of unarmed fishing trawlers were bombed and machine-gunned in the North Sea. Graphic stories by members of the crews of some of the first vessels to be attacked are reproduced from the " Daily Telegraph " and " Daily Mail."

" I NEVER thought white men would do what these German airmen did to us," said Mr. John Robb, skipper of the trawler " Craigie Lea."

" They gave us no warning before they started to bomb and machine-gun us. They circled round us repeatedly and sprayed the vessel with bullets. The crew were on deck when they made their first attack, and I told my men to take cover immediately. We had an amazing escape."

Five bombs were dropped on the " Craigie Lea," but only one hit the ship. This crashed through the engine-room skylight to the engine-room near the chief engineer, Lewis MacDonald, but did not explode. Two men were wounded by machine-gun fire—William Innes, fireman, and Alexander Murray, second fisherman.

Capt. Robb said that two German aeroplanes came from the north-west and flew about 100 feet above the ship. The leading 'plane started machine-gunning them.

The second aeroplane dropped a bomb about five yards from their starboard quarter, rocking the ship. Another bomb dropped in the water about six yards away.

" I signalled to the aeroplanes to allow the crew to get away in the small boat, but the only reply was more bursts of machine-gun fire and more bombs, one of which crashed through the engine-room skylight but did not explode," said Capt. Robb.

Machine-gun bullets entered the store-room in which Innes and Murray were sheltering. Innes was struck on the back and head, and Murray in the back. Soon afterwards the German aeroplanes made off.

When the trawler " Isabella Greig " was bombed and sunk, two of the crew of ten, Andrew Banks and Ronald Tweedie, both of Granton, were injured.

As the crew were being taken aboard another trawler the Nazi 'planes again swooped down and machine-gunned them.

John Tweedie, engineer of the " Isabella Greig," said : " A fleet of trawlers were at the fishing grounds when two German bombers appeared. One of the 'planes was about two or three hundred yards away when it opened fire, and swept the decks of the trawlers.

" The crews dashed below, and I counted about twenty bombs being dropped round the vessels.

" The last bomb hit our ship and the deck collapsed. As we were getting our lifeboat ready the 'plane came back again

and machine-gunned us, hitting another member of the crew and myself. The two German 'planes then attacked some of the other trawlers, and the ' Compaganus ' was sunk.

" Again one of the 'planes returned to attack our ship, and, as we were lowering the lifeboat, we were fired upon once more. One of the crew waved a white sheet, hoping that the airmen would have mercy, but they paid no attention, and it was not until some British 'planes appeared that the Germans made off.

" One of our own 'planes saw our plight and signalled to a trawler to come to our aid."

Three other trawlers, the " Eileen Wray," " Compaganus," and " Pearl,"

were similarly attacked. The " Eileen Wray " was towed into a north-east port. One member of the crew of the " Compaganus," James Swanney, was killed and another wounded by machine-gun fire, and three of the " Pearl's " crew were wounded, the ship being abandoned in a sinking condition.

When the Nazi 'planes made their attack on the " Eileen Wray " they circled the trawler one behind the other, the first dropping eight bombs and the second following up with bursts of machine-gun fire.

As the crew made efforts to lower the lifeboats the 'planes swooped again and again, and no fewer than sixteen times the men had to leap for cover. Only the last of the eight bombs fell near its mark. It struck the water a few yards from the vessel and damaged the engine-room.

As the 'planes made off, water began to leak into the hull. Capt. Hartley, the skipper, said that the attack occurred after the trawler had been fishing for twelve hours.

" I could see the track of tracer bullets each time the 'plane swept round," he said, " but as in the case of the bombs the markmanship was bad. Not a man was injured. As we made attempts to lower the boat, we were jumping in and out of cover like Jacks-in-the-box."

The crew of the " Compaganus," which was struck by a bomb, were rescued and landed by the trawler " Colleague." A member of the crew said that they were fishing when they were attacked by machine-gun fire and bombs from two German aeroplanes. Four bombs were dropped, but they did not strike the ship. The crew rushed for shelter.

James Swanney, who was killed, was struck by machine-gun bullets while running along the deck. The attack lasted half an hour.

About an hour and a half later two 'planes reappeared and resumed the attack. Ten bombs were dropped on this occasion, and one struck the vessel and passed right through into the engine-

On the same day as the attacks described in this page, the unarmed collier " Serenity " was bombed, machine-gunned and sunk by Nazi seaplanes. Here are skipper and crew cheerfully ready to sail again as soon as another boat is available.
Photo, Topical Press Agency

room. Their small boat was riddled with bullets.

Samuel Buck, of Edinburgh, the mate of the " Compaganus," said that Swanney was killed within five minutes of the start of the attack at 10.20 a.m. They were trying to get away the fishing gear, and he shouted to Swanney to run when the attack came.

Their wireless was put out of action by the gunfire. After the attack they steamed for about two hours with the " Colleague " as escort, and at about 12.30 p.m. the second attack was made.

" We tried to get to our small boat, but it was riddled with bullets. We signalled to the ' Colleague,' which came alongside, and we got on board her, carrying the cook with us," he added.

" The vessel was badly damaged and there was a number of holes on the water-line. When we last saw her she was going down by the stern. The 'planes fired several bursts of machine-gun fire at the ' Colleague,' hitting the vessel, but no one on board was hurt."

Why the Nazis Want to 'Deify' Hitler

Strange as are most of the manifestations of Nazism, nothing perhaps is so strange as
the building up of an extraordinary farrago of myth, in which ancient Teutonic paganism
mingles with racial absurdities and the more extreme of modern German philosophies.

PERHAPS the most damaging revelation of the true character of the Nazi ideal is that associated with its expressed intention of destroying the Christian faith in the Fatherland and substituting for it a modern form of the spirit of ancient German paganism as it is found in Teutonic myths and hero-tales. That this is no mere fantastic rumour or alarmist invention, but a definite and carefully designed policy is plainly apparent from the writings and speeches of Nazi officials of high rank and the actual dissemination of literature inspired by a pagan spirit and philosophy of life published with the approval and at the expense of the Nazi Government.

In order to clear the ground for the popular acceptance of this new " Nordic " creed the Christian Churches of all denominations in Germany have been subjected to a gradual but purposeful process of persecution and demolition, their clergy have been partially disbanded or imprisoned in concentration camps, and the conduct of their affairs, both spiritual and financial, has been placed under Nazi control.

Rosenberg's Pagan Teaching

This is the result of a campaign which has been directed against Christian life and endeavour in Germany since the year 1920. Herr Alfred Rosenberg, a journalist of Russo-Baltic origin and a close intimate of Herr Hitler, who was appointed Director of Philosophical Outlook for the Reich on the Nazi Party's advent to power, from that time onward has been steadily engaged in broadcasting the propaganda of a new doctrine among the German people, the main principle of which is the restoration of habits of thought derived from pagan sources.

In a bulky volume entitled " The Mythus of the Twentieth Century," which has enjoyed a vast circulation throughout all parts of Germany, he has appealed to the folk of the Reich to abandon the " Jewish " ideals embraced in the Scriptures and to return to those Nordic traditions of "masculine" paganism which he declares are those best fitted to fortify and encourage a conquering race.

The Founder of the Christian faith, he asserts, was of "Aryan" not Jewish descent and encouraged a manly and war-like way of life and ethical behaviour. But the later " infection " of Christianity by " degenerate " Jewish ideals, such as the doctrines of humility, gentleness and universal love, are " slavish " and " nauseous to German virility " and must be abandoned by the German people if it desires to achieve conquest of the world.

Above all, he avers, it is impossible to distinguish between the idea of God and the racial soul of the German folk, which must be substituted for that idea. Germany should, indeed, worship herself or the great prophets and heroes who have most saliently represented her throughout the ages. The Christian doctrine of redemption and the ideals inculcated in the Sermon on the Mount must be abandoned in favour of the old Germanic virtues of bravery and " sacrificial heroism," which can alone redeem the Fatherland from the " demoralizing " influences of Christianity.

'Good Old German' Gods

The youth of Germany must be nurtured upon the myths and sagas of the Teutonic past, the legends of Odin and Thor, the tale of the Nibelungs and the Eddas of Scandinavia, which illustrate the stark and powerful ideals of soldierly might implicit in the German nature. Along with these it must be fortified with the philosophies of Nietzsche, Wagner and Hitler, the true prophets and apostles of German thought and culture.

In order to give practical expression to this doctrine, a Nazi " Church " was founded. Its chief apostle is Julius Streicher, the notorious Jew-baiter and terrorist, who, in 1937 and in the following year, celebrated its rites on the Hesselberg, a mountain declared to be sacred by Herr Hitler. On both occasions, on the festival of the Summer Solstice in June, he addressed vast meetings which gathered round great balefires lit on the slopes of the height, and after denouncing and ridiculing the Christian faith,

appealed to them to turn their thoughts backward through the ages to the ideals and outlook of their pagan ancestors.

Parallel with this departure is manifest a growing movement to " deify " the personality of Herr Hitler, to confer upon the Fuehrer a kind of Messiahship of a semi-religious character. This has been given public expression by Dr. Robert Ley, who, addressing the Hitler Youth, has said : " We believe in Adolf Hitler alone in this world. . . . We believe that the Lord God has sent us Adolf Hitler."

The advent of the new paganism has aroused the deepest concern and unrest in responsible quarters throughout Germany, yet it has behind it the full force of the more fanatical elements in the Nazi caucus, while others regard it with complacency, or fear to oppose it. But that it has its origin in the mentality of Hitler and his supporters alone and that their downfall will assuredly imply its total disappearance is only too manifest.

Alfred Rosenberg is the chief apostle of the new paganism, the religion of force and brutality which Hitler is imposing on Germany. Immediately above is a Hitler youth at the heathen Midsummer festival held on the Baltic coast in connexion with a Congress of the Nordic Association in 1935. He is standing beside one of the fires that are part of the pagan ritual.
Photos, Wide World and Keystone

Last Scenes of All in the Battle of the River Plate

This extraordinarily dramatic photograph sent from Montevideo by wireless was taken as the "Admiral Graf Spee" was sinking in flames. She was destroyed by a number of bombs placed in different parts of the hull. They exploded with terrific force, columns of flames and clouds of smoke arose from the ship and five minutes later there was another explosion when the flames reached the magazine. For a week she continued to burn and smoulder until only a broken hulk remained of the once proud ship.

Photo, British Official : Crown Copyright

A GREAT "naval occasion" was the dramatic engagement between the "Admiral Graf Spee" and the British cruisers on December 13, in which the British ships, though outclassed, showed a seamanship and fighting spirit worthy of the best traditions of the British Navy. The gallant "Exeter" was hit from 40 to 50 times by shells three times the weight of those she could herself discharge. Nevertheless, she returned shot for shot till three of her 8-in. guns were smashed and only one could be fired, and that by hand. Her steering gear was damaged, she sustained nearly a hundred casualties and numerous fires broke out on board, but she continued in the wake of the speeding battle and took up station at the mouth of the estuary until relieved by the arrival of the "Cumberland." Officers and men were, in the words of her captain, "superb."

Captain Langsdorf committed suicide on December 20 and was buried on the following day. During the night his body lay in state in the Buenos Aires Arsenal guarded by members of the crew of the "Graf Spee." The Nazi flag, as can be seen in the photograph, hung in the background, and another draped the coffin.

Photo, Planet News

DRAMATIC as was the end of the "Graf Spee," yet another sensational element was added to the story by the suicide of her commander, Captain Hans Langsdorf, on December 20. He was found shot dead in the naval arsenal at Buenos Aires, and a significant fact is that, according to reports from reliable sources, he was discovered lying on the German Imperial flag, not the Swastika of Hitler, whose instructions were "Scuttle, don't fight." He was buried the next day with full naval honours, and his funeral was attended by Captain Pottinger, of the steamer "Ashlea," as representative of the British merchant seamen released from the "Graf Spee" before her end. When the news of the suicide was released in Germany the Nazi propaganda machine was hard put to it to explain what all the world realized was a gallant seamen's protest against the Fuehrer's order.

Shortly before he committed suicide Captain Langsdorf addressed his men, more than a thousand in number, in the grounds of the Buenos Aires Arsenal. All but the crew of the "Graf Spee" were excluded from the meeting, seen above.

Photo, Planet News

OUR DIARY OF THE WAR

Wednesday, December 20, 1939

Reported that Captain Langsdorf, who commanded " Graf Spee," committed suicide on Tuesday night.

Heavy Russian attack in Karelian Isthmus was **repulsed.** In the north Soviet troops checked by snowstorms.

U.S. cruiser " Tuscaloosa " arrived at New York with 579 survivors from scuttled German liner " Columbus."

Unidentified aircraft appeared over Eastern counties.

Paris announced that two more U-boats had been sunk by French Fleet.

Swedish steamers " Mars " and " Adolf Bratt " sunk by mines.

Admiralty announced sinking by enemy aircraft of fishing trawlers " Pearl " on December 17 and " Trinity " on December 18. H.M. trawlers " Evelyn " and " Sedgefly " were overdue and presumed lost.

Reported that British troopship collided in fog with liner " Samaria," the latter being damaged.

Thursday, December 21

Enemy bombers twice raided Helsinki and did damage in the hospital quarter. Other open towns were also bombed.

Finns counter-attacked against Russian advance on Kemijaervi **and drove enemy back 20 miles.** Successes also claimed in area north of Lake Ladoga. Enemy attacks in Karelian Isthmus repulsed.

Western Front reported renewed air activity over Lorraine and Alsace.

R.A.F. Coastal Command machine co-operated with British warship in rescue of Swedish sailors adrift on raft in North Sea.

Lieut.-Commander Bickford of H.M. Submarine " Salmon " awarded D.S.O.

Italian ship " Comitas " mined off North Holland.

French Government issued Yellow Book containing French diplomatic documents of pre-war period.

Newly arrived Canadian division had their first ceremonial parade at Aldershot.

Friday, December 22

Helsinki raided by three Soviet bombers, which damaged the outskirts of the city.

Finns compelled Russians to retreat in Petsamo and Salla districts. They also launched successful counter-attack along a 12-mile front in the Karelian Isthmus. Russians repulsed on other fronts, with heavy loss of men and material.

Enemy aircraft engaged by British fighters off the Firth of Forth.

Enemy aeroplane reported over Suffolk coast, and two machines, thought to be Heinkel bombers, sighted at another point on East Coast.

Air Ministry reported that on the Western Front four Messerschmitt fighters attacked three Hurricane fighters. Two British and one German machine were shot down.

Reported that the British trawler " River Annan," which on December 17 had rescued the crew of the mined Danish steamer " Boge," was sunk on December 19 by German bombers. Both crews were picked up by a Swedish steamer.

M. Daladier announced that the Maginot Line had been extended on the Northern and Jura frontiers.

Saturday, December 23

Paris reported intense air activity on Western Front. Allied 'planes were busy photographing German lines.

Russian troops were in retreat in Karelian Isthmus, in Petsamo region, and also in the Salla sector, where the Finns were again in command of the Kemi River valley, an important strategic position.

Russian aeroplanes bombed towns on southern coast of Finland, and dropped leaflets over Helsinki with a message from the " puppet " Prime Minister.

Admiralty announced intention of laying a mine barrage of nearly the full length of the East Coast as a reply to German action.

League of Nations received favourable replies from a number of member countries, including South Africa, in regard to helping Finland.

U.S.A. and 20 other American Republics made a protest, in the form of a joint

---

THE POETS & THE WAR

XIV
DACHAU
By Humbert Wolfe

I thought of the concentration camps
  and the tortured men,
and, as I began to dream of vengeance
  and dark reprisal,
of the shocking retort that, being
  denied by life, denies all,
a voice whispered deep in my heart,
  " Have they triumphed again ? "

—*The Observer*

---

neutrality declaration, against the activities of belligerent warships in American waters.

Sunday, December 24

Finns claimed to have shot down at least 14 Russian aircraft.

North of Lake Ladoga, **Finnish storm battalions crossed the Russian frontier** near Lieksa after routing Russian troops in Tolmojaervi and Aglajaervi districts.

On the northern sector Finnish troops approached Salla.

After blazing for a week, the hulk of the " Graf Spee " burnt out.

Monday, December 25

The King broadcast a Christmas message to the peoples of the Empire.

Finnish advance in Russian territory was maintained.

Twenty-three Russian bombers attempted to raid Helsinki but were driven off by anti-aircraft guns. Other large flotillas of

bombers attacked Viborg, inflicting considerable damage. There were also raids over Borga, Tampere and Turku.

Enemy 'planes bombed Koivisto coastal batteries repeatedly. Koivisto was also shelled by Russian warship " Marat."

Finland claimed that during the day her naval and air forces combined **destroyed at least 23 enemy 'planes.**

R.A.F. aircraft, patrolling the North Sea to protect fishing vessels, were attacked by German patrol ships.

British steamer " Stanholme " torpedoed off West Coast of Britain.

Tuesday, December 26

Finns maintained their positions on the outskirts of Salla.

Enemy attacked at various points on the Karelian Isthmus, but were repulsed, and large numbers of Russian guns and prisoners were captured.

Christmas week-end was reported to have been generally quiet on the Western Front.

First squadron of the Royal Australian Air Force to reach England for active service landed at a South Coast port.

Reported that three more neutral ships were sunk during the week-end : Swedish vessel " Carl Henkel " ; Norwegian cargo-boat " Lappen " ; and Spanish steamer " Perez."

Swedish reservists were called up.

Wednesday, December 27

Finns continued their advance from Lieksa into Russian territory, and reached Lake Ruua. In Suomussalmi sector they advanced in direction of Raate, about 15 miles from Russian frontier.

On Salla front Finns pressed enemy back some 50 miles towards the frontier. Three heavy assaults on the Mannerheim Line were repulsed.

Russian losses on Finnish front were estimated to be 30,000.

Viborg seriously damaged by shells from long-distance guns.

More leaflets dropped over Helsinki by Russian bombers.

R.A.F. Coastal Command machines were **engaged in a series of fights** over the North Sea with German air and surface craft. One Nazi patrol ship disabled by a bomb from a British 'plane which attacked two destroyers and 11 patrol vessels.

Reported that Indian troops had arrived in France.

Nearly 7,000 tons of contraband seized during week ended December 23.

It Is Said That . . .

" I have not sacrificed my millions for Bolshevism but against it." (Herr Thyssen to Hitler.)

Von Ribbentrop has been given the Lenin order, the highest Russian decoration.

" We Germans will take revenge for all that the Poles have done to us." (Herr Forster, Danzig Nazi leader.)

" Patched trousers seats get more and more fashionable in Germany." (Nazi broadcaster.)

Hitler is planning a Siegfried Line in the East as a defence against his new Russian ally.

Austrians distrust German newspapers and there is a great demand for the Hungarian " Pester Lloyd," printed in German.

German soldiers in Poland are very depressed and are buying civilian clothes preparatory to deserting.

Blitzkrieg : Sudden and terrifying German attack which never strikes at the same place once. (" Peterborough " in the " Daily Telegraph.")

German food rations may be still further curtailed during the winter months.

Most Zoo animals are immune to tear gas, though monkeys may be slightly affected.

The Germans have no present intention of recognizing Molotov's " Finnish People's Government."

Old gramophone records are collected in Germany for melting down, owing to shortage of shellac.

Jewish property in Austria taken over by Nazis is valued at about £190,000,000 at pre-war rates.

Delegates avoided shaking hands with Soviet representative at League of Nations committee on December 6.

Berlin censor stopped description of miniature A.A. gun seen in toyshop sent by American correspondent to U.S. paper.

" The force of arms will ensure that even the last remnants of British hopes are destroyed." (" Deutsche Allgemeine Zeitung.")

Vol. 1   A Permanent Picture Record of the Second Great War   No. 19

The Soviet Air Force has found the Finnish anti-aircraft gunfire surprisingly and unpleasantly effective. Here in the winter snows a member of a Finnish anti-aircraft gun crew is observing Soviet machines with a range-finder. Fighter aeroplanes, as well as guns, have taken part in meeting the Red menace from the air with remarkable results. On December 27 the official Finnish communiqué announced that "during the day our air force and anti-aircraft guns destroyed 12 enemy 'planes, mostly bombers." When to these were added the aircraft brought down by the Finnish naval units the total amounted to at least 23 destroyed in a single day.

What is the Front Line Really Like?

One of the most realistic descriptions of the real front line that have passed the Censor, this article is drawn from a contribution made by M. Alexandre Arnoux to " La Revue de Paris." M. Arnoux's vivid word-picture may be taken as being equally true of that portion of the front held by British troops.

From Viscount Gort, V.C., Commander-in-Chief of the British Field Force :

ONCE more within the memory of many of us a British Expeditionary Force is spending Christmas in France, and once again, under the leadership of a great soldier of France, the Allied Armies stand united to resist aggression.

In the year that lies ahead difficulties and dangers will undoubtedly arise, as they have done in the wars of the past, but they will be surmounted owing, on the one hand, to the close understanding which today exists between the French nation and ourselves and, on the other hand, to the knowledge that your thoughts are with us at all times, whether the weather be fair or foul.

In whatever part of the Empire you may dwell, I extend to you all cordial good wishes for Christmas and the New Year. *December 23, 1939*

IF we wish to meet the fighting soldiers in this war we shall find them in front of the Maginot Line between the Rhine and the Moselle. No continuous line of trenches is there, for it would be impossible to consolidate them where the spongy land exudes water and each shell-hole is quickly transformed into a swamp; nor can there be any battle in the usual sense of the word—only an infinity of skirmishes, patrols, raids, and ambushes, hazardous nocturnal reconnaissances and probings across an obscure desert tangled and slimy with mud. Here in the night traps are more important than artillery or assault, and each soldier becomes in turn a hunter of men or a trapped beast, often both at once.

Deciding one day to go up to the advanced positions, I took the road of the rations. From the army butchery I travelled to the dump where the meat was distributed to the army cooks. There I attached myself to one of the field kitchens which was going to take a hot meal to men in the front line.

We left the main road and branched off up a winding lane on the flank of a wooded hill. When we got near to the crest of the hill we had to stop, otherwise the "Fridolins" [Fritzes] would catch sight of us, my companion informed me,

as they held the ridge on the other side of the valley.

A stretch of grassy downland separated us from the French troops. They saw us coming, and the ration party came out of the wood at the top of the hill, running down with their mess tins, their canvas buckets, their dishes and their billie-cans. The two rear men were pushing perambulators, looking like khaki nurses. It is a good way of transporting the rations.

I walked up the slope behind them. We crept into the undergrowth across a colonnade of grey trunks, tramping over the sodden leaf-mould. There is no means of digging a dug-out here. They sleep, whenever they can snatch an hour's repose, on the ground, protected by the disjointed planks taken from some farm building and a scrap of corrugated iron or tarred felt.

The only guard against a surprise attack is a few strands of wire, strung between trees, to which are attached as a primitive form of alarm, empty sardine and bully-beef tins. A kitchen range, dragged out of an evacuated farm, serves to warm up the food and the coffee, but it can be lit only when a favourable breeze will dissipate the smoke.

' Rations Up ! '

The ration party unloaded the billies and the dixies, placed the bucket of wine on the ground, unwrapped the cheese and pâté, and apportioned the bread. From time to time a shell whistled over our heads. The odour of the stew mingled with that of the cold fermenting of the forest, through which passed a chilly breeze, impregnated with mist.

The noise of mastication, slow and methodical, filled this corner of the wood. Conversation was rare. These men, who have held this position for many days, have already become old campaigners, with no distractions save an occasional brief nap. They have not had their clothes or boots off for days, and have kept an unceasing guard with eye and ear, even in their dreams. They ate their food standing up, taciturn.

An officer agreed to take me with him on his tour of inspection of the advanced posts. We set off, surrounded by three or four men with loaded rifles at their hips. It was growing dusk. On the edge of the wood a sentinel was gazing through the branches with his field-glasses. "Nothing fresh," reported the look-out, whose face was muffled in a thick scarf, "except for some smoke on the right, and the passing of shadows. They have certainly posted observers between those two big oaks."

We continued our rounds, skirting the woods. We could now see quite clearly the little hamlet that was to be the scene of tonight's expedition. It lay there silent, without a movement, absolutely deserted in appearance.

We reached the machine-gun post. In the distance could be heard the lowing of a cow, left there after its masters had departed. Pigs, too, wandered about in the fields, coveted by the soldiers of both sides, grunting their way between a French death and a German death, not knowing whether they would become democratic black-pudding or totalitarian sausage.

There was the hoot of an owl. The machine-gunner pricked up his ears. Then a faint metallic sound struck the ear, so feeble that it might have been a ghost bell. Everyone listened and peered out. Nothing more could be heard. One of the men affirmed that the cry of an owl and the bell have already been used as a rallying signal.

The men of a reconnaissance group emerged from the middle of a lake of mud of the consistency of syrup. The captain welcomed us. We slopped along in his wake, past " Destruction 5," where the mined roadway formed a yawning crater, past the barrier of trunks and branches.

The advanced posts were all alike on this sector of the front : alert sentinels, machine-gunners, the watching of the tracks of the German nightly infiltration, large woods guarded by a handful of men dispersed in little groups, the temporary occupation of the barns and hamlets in

While leading a patrol, Corporal Thomas William Priday (above) was killed on Dec. 9 —the first British soldier to be killed in the war. His funeral in a military cemetery was attended by the French G.O.O.

Ready to Fire Six Hundred Rounds a Minute

Well camouflaged in a snow-clad wood, this Bren gun, manned by British infantrymen, is ready to spit a veritable hailstorm of bullets at the enemy, for it fires 600 or more rounds a minute. In the Army of 1914 there were only four machine-guns to a battalion, but now there are fifty Bren guns in the armament of each battalion.   Four men are needed for each gun, two to work it and two to bring up the ammunition. This gun is being fired from a tripod, but Bren guns can also be fired from the shoulder.   Their weight is 21 lb.

Photo, British Official : Crown Copyright

Friend and Foe as Near as the Rifle Speaks

The men who joined the forces "for the duration" of the last war were known as the "New Army." Today there is another "New Army," for men who were little more than infants when the "war to end war" was fought have responded to their country's call in her hour of need in a spirit that must put to shame those who decried the younger generation. It is difficult to imagine a happier band of warriors than these young Britons marching through a wood towards the front line in France. *Photo, G.P.U.*

Above are two scenes with the German Army somewhere in front of the Siegfried Line. The top photograph shows a camouflaged German artillery observation post, looking out towards the Maginot Line. In the lower photograph German soldiers are carrying up rations in metal containers to the front line through a wood where undergrowth makes heavy going.
Photos, Planet News and International Graphic Press

No-man's land, and the always perilous search for German mines. Certain of the men seem to have developed a special flair for this work, and have become, as it were, "diviners" of these hidden traps.

"Marsan," said a sergeant to me, "can smell the things. You see that greenhouse over there, on the edge of the stream? I was just going to step on the doormat when Marsan caught me by the shoulders and stopped me. I would have been a 'goner,' otherwise. We investigated, and there was the fuse, sure enough. I tell you, he smells them. We have to keep our wits about us. The door-handle trick is an old one; we are not caught by that one any more. But we have to look out for the bell rope in the church, the canary's cage, the false corpse and the watch chain. Naturally, we give as good as we receive."

There are all types of men here: plebeians and aristocrats, the austere and the irrepressible, the snobs and the mixers, all working together in perfect union. France remains today one of the few countries that cannot be reduced to a grey uniformity, where a commander of a reconnaissance group can still keep his spurs, and where a humble private is ready to die but obstinately refuses to have his hair cut!

And this, then, is the kind of war they are carrying on; strenuous, sleepless, full of constant anxiety, calling for stubborn physical resistance, watchfulness without repose, well-conditioned reflexes, the firmest courage, the suppleness of an Indian on the warpath, tenacity, a constant tension, and a sang-froid which neither fatigue nor nerve-strain nor isolation in the woods can destroy.

Air Heroes of Two Wars Now Sleep Side by Side

This headstone marks the grave of 2nd Lt. Pollock of the R.A.F. killed July 20, 1918, and buried in the Charmes Military Cemetery at Essegny, Vosges. Right, a cross in the same cemetery on the grave of A Sgt. C. Thomas, a British airman killed in 1939.

THE great British cemeteries in France have once more opened their gates for the burial of British soldiers who have laid down their lives in the fight for freedom, thus giving the lie to the Nazi gibe that England will fight to the last Frenchman. A writer in "France Magazine" commented thus on these photographs: "British soldiers who lost their lives in the present conflict lie side by side with their elder brethren in the same historic ground that is the soil of our country. Germany is wasting her time in denying this." Here are the British and French casualties as published in Paris late in December 1939:

		Navy	Air	Army	Total
British	...	2,070	438	3	2,511
French	...	256	42	1,135	1,433

The three photographs in this page appeared originally in a French illustrated paper, "France Magazine." Each of them was described in terms emphasizing the solidarity of Britain and France in their fight against Nazism and the equality of their sacrifice. Beneath the photograph reproduced above were these words. "Somewhere on the French front two British soldiers have just been taken to their last resting-place. In this solemn hour their comrades and those who bore them there stand in silent homage before the graves strewn with autumn flowers gathered in a garden of Lorraine."

Brains Triumph over Brute Masses in Finnish War

With dramatic suddenness the Finns turned the tables on the Russians in the last days
of 1939, when not only did they halt the Red Army's offensive, but they themselves
crossed into enemy territory at several points. Swiftly they pursued their advantage,
hoping to force the issue before Russia's millions were flung into the fight.

CHRISTMAS brought no armistice in the war which is being fought in the "Land of a Thousand Lakes." On Christmas Day, indeed, most of the people of Helsinki who had not been evacuated spent much of the morning and afternoon in the air-raid shelters as Russian bombers passed across the sky. Some 20 or 30 bombs were dropped on the outskirts, but little damage was done. More than forty other Finnish towns were also bombed, and Viipuri (Viborg) in particular suffered considerable damage, although no objects of military importance were hit. Viipuri was also bombarded by Russian howitzers from a distance of twenty miles or so, and by midnight several hundred shells had fallen in the town and a number of fires had been started in the wooden buildings.

If in the air the Russians resumed the offensive, on the land there was a very different tale to report. The force of the onrush which at the opening of the war had carried the Soviet hordes across the frontier was now spent, and in a fierce counter-attack the Finns swiftly recaptured most of the ground which had been lost.

In the Karelian Isthmus the fighting was of the fiercest description, but although the Russians were reported to be employing more than 100,000 men they were unable to breach the Mannerheim Line. Wave after wave of shock troops were sent across the frozen lakes, but, repeating Napoleon's famous stroke at Austerlitz, the Finnish artillery blew holes in the ice, with the result that many hundreds of the attackers were drowned. After firing a million shells and employing hundreds of tanks and warplanes, the Russians were forced to recoil, baffled afresh. Here it was reported that the Finns were making history in fighting on skates.

North of Lake Ladoga near Tolvajärvi and Aglajärvi a battle which lasted for several days ended on December 23 in the

Weather conditions in Finland make mechanical transport extremely difficult, and the Red Army has employed many horse- and mule-drawn vehicles. Above is the pitiable scene after a Soviet supply train had been ambushed and completely wiped out by a party of Finnish machine-gunners.

Photo, Planet News

A large number of Russians, both officers and men, unable to endure the conditions under which they are fighting, have given themselves up to the Finns. Above, a Red Army officer is caught by the camera in the act. Right, General Wallenius, in command of the Northern Finnish Army, is questioning a Russian prisoner.

Photos. Keystone

Disaster Overtakes the Columns of the Invader

complete rout of the invaders. The Russian troops were driven back to the frontier and even in some places beyond it, and the Finns claimed to have killed 2,000 and to have captured 600 prisoners.

In the "waist" of Finland, in the war's central zone, the invading columns of the Red Army were similarly unsuccessful. First, the column moving on Suomussalmi was driven back, and then those troops which had moved from Salla in the direction of Kemijaervi and Rovaniemi were taken by surprise and completely routed. Here in a wilderness of forest and lake, in a world of perpetual twilight and the most bitter cold, the invaders found themselves assailed on every side by hardy fighters who knew every inch of the country and were, moreover, thoroughly acclimatized to the terrible weather conditions. After a week's struggle the Finns scored a decisive victory. The 163rd Russian division of 18,000 men, their powers of resistance sapped by the bitter cold and by shortage of food, was almost annihilated, and huge quantities of guns and war material were captured. The Finns' only complaint was over the scarcity of their ammunition. "There are more Russians in this sector," said one, "than we have cartridges."

So complete was the reversal of fortune that by the end of the year General Wallenius, Commander of the Finnish Northern Army, revealed that his troops

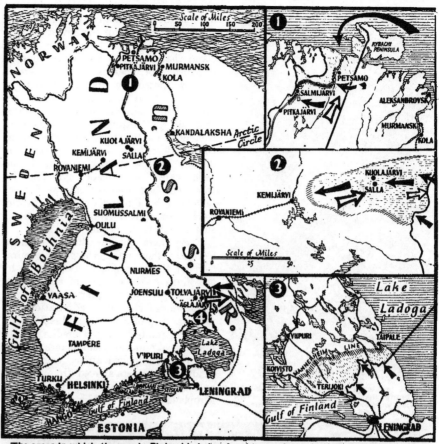

The areas in which the war in Finland is being fought are shown in these four maps. The black! arrows indicate the direction of the Russian attacks, while the white arrows refer to the Finnish counter-attacks. Three of the battle areas are shown in more detail in the smaller maps inset on the right.   *By courtesy of "News Chronicle"*

Here is a scene with the Finnish Army in the southern war area. Troops are deploying to take up positions in which to meet an advance of the Red Army. The thickly wooded country, now deep in snow, is typical of that through which the Russians have attempted to advance towards the Mannerheim Line.   *Photo, Wide World*

were now operating in enemy territory. The woods which extended across the frontier were filled with Russian dead and wounded, and there was not a spot, he declared, between the frontier and Kandalaksha, the Russian advanced base on Kandalaksk Bay, an arm of the White Sea, where the Russians were safe from attack. "We don't let them rest," he said, "we don't let them sleep. This is a war of numbers against brains. We train our men to fight individually and they can do it, whereas the Russian soldier can never rid himself of his natural gregarious instincts."

Even in the extreme north, where the Russians were able to land troops and munitions from the sea, they were so harried by the Finnish sharp-shooters moving invisibly on their skis across the snow, that they retreated on Petsamo, leaving behind them a miniature railroad and some Diesel tractors and trucks which the Finns promptly turned round and used to bring up their supplies.

None can tell what were the real losses in this campaign where the corpses of the fallen were swiftly covered by white snow and the sombre waters of the lakes. Moscow professed that the Red Army casualties were only some 1,800 killed and 7,000 wounded, but the Finns put the enemy killed, wounded, taken prisoner and incapacitated by frostbite

Incendiary Bombs Illumine the Wintry Scene

Fierce fires were caused in Turku (Aabo) by the bombs dropped by Red bombers. Here A.R.P. workers are fighting the flames in the bitter cold of the Northern winter.

at some 100,000. In any case, the casualties were too great for the Soviet authorities to be able to "put over" their claim that this was not a war but an expedition of liberation. Observers in Moscow noted an increasing tension, and there were signs of increasing war fever. In Leningrad it was rumoured that all the hospitals were filled with wounded and that schools were being commandeered as hospitals. Even in distant Moscow it was understood that beds were being made available for those who had been laid low by Finnish bullets or by Finland's climate. Stories were afoot of Red Army generals being shot for their ill-success.

Everywhere outside Russia, even in Germany, there was nothing but admiration for the magnificent stand made by the Finns in the defence of their homeland. From many quarters there was forthcoming not only admiration but material help of the most valuable kind. America granted Finland credits for the purchase of munitions and 'planes, Britain and France supplied arms; some thousands of volunteers arrived from Sweden and Italy; and South Africa released aeroplanes for the Finnish front.

Many scenes of such pathos were witnessed during the bombing of Helsinki. A Finnish mother with her baby in a basket is fleeing during the air attack on Christmas Day.

The scenes in this page would have to be multiplied many times over to give an idea of what Christmas week meant to the Finns. Above are houses in Viipuri, the Finnish port on the Gulf of Finland, which were set on fire by bombs dropped by Red aircraft on Christmas Day. Viipuri is only a little over 70 miles from Leningrad, and therefore within easy reach of bombers. Besides being bombed from the air it has been bombarded by Russian long-range guns.

Photos. Wide World, Keystone and Associated Press

Cameos of Destruction in Raided Helsinki

Another Soviet 'plane has come to grief in the snows of Finland during the course of an air raid. Its remains are being examined with interest by Finnish airmen.

Photo, Fox

Above, a Finnish radio commentator, microphone in hand, is describing to listeners a Soviet air raider shot down by the Finnish defences. The red star of the Soviet Union is plainly marked on the fuselage.

Photo, Fox

Right, a house in Helsinki after a Russian air raid. The upper storeys were completely destroyed and the entrance was wrecked by bombs, so that the only means of escape for those who were sheltering within the building was by climbing down this wooden pole.

Photo, Fox

This children's hospital in Helsinki was badly damaged by incendiary bombs, and firemen are seen throwing down debris from the roof. Luckily the patients had been evacuated in time. In the circle, a Finnish air raid warden is standing by a notice which reads : "Stop ! Unexploded bomb."

Photos, Keystone

Finland Has Her 'Lawrence of the North'

In the epic story of the war in Finland, in which a veritable Goliath of a Russia is hard
put to it to maintain its attack against the Finnish David, there is no more heroic
episode to record than that of the " Suicide Squad " operating in enemy territory.

O F all the famous figures thrown up
by the Great War there was
none more spectacular than
"Lawrence of Arabia," the young
archaeologist who exchanged his search
for inscriptions and potsherds for the
organizing of dare-devil dashes against
the Turkish lines of communication in
Palestine and Syria. Today Finland is
acclaiming the man whom she is proud
to call the "Lawrence of the North."
Just as Lawrence and his Arabs tore up
the Turks' railway lines, so General
Tavela has succeeded in severing the railway which is the only link between Lenin-

grad and Russia's northern army of some
10,000 men based on Murmansk.

Himself a champion ski-runner, General
Tavela picked 250 of the most expert ski-
runners available to compose what, considering the danger and difficulty of the
enterprise in which they were about to
be engaged, was not inaptly called the
"Suicide Squad." They were armed with
pistols and 250 rounds of ammunition
apiece. They wore white coats and white
helmets so as to render them invisible
against the snow, and carried on their
backs concentrated food for ten days
and a lamb-skin sleeping sack. Even

means of which they were able to keep
in touch with the Finnish headquarters.
Nerved to do or die by the realization
of their country's distress, the "Suicide
Squad" attacked any and every Russian
force with which they could make contact.
By day they raided the marching columns,
seizing the moment when, perhaps, a
waggon had slipped off the track and the
men in the column had no eyes for the
ghostly figures which flitted here and
there among the sombre trees. With
deliberate aim the intrepid ski-runners
picked off man after man, until the scene
was wrapped once more in a dark silence.

Those men who formed the "Suicide Squad," whose activities are
described in this article, were dressed very much as are the Finnish
soldiers seen in the top photograph. So clad they must have been
invisible against the white landscape. Our other photograph is of a
Russian light tank which has come to grief on one of the tracks—they
can hardly be called roads—followed by the invaders. By the end of
the first month's fighting the Finns claimed that they had disposed
of 250 enemy tanks.   *Photos, Keystone and Planet News*

their skis and boots
were specially
treated to make
them noiseless.

Their objective
was to attack the
Russian flanks and
supply columns
and to destroy the
railways and roads.
Shortly after leav-
ing their head-
quarters the squad
split up into small
groups each charged
with a different
task. General
Tavela with fifty
men chose the most
difficult of the ob-
jectives—the attack
on the Leningrad-
Murmansk railway.

Swiftly the pat-
rols went about
their work. They
sped across the
snows invisible and
silent, for they com-
municated not by
words but by signs.
In each party the
youngest carried a
portable radio
transmitter, by

By night, too, they kept up the fight,
and many a shivering wretch, cursing the
inefficiency of the Soviet commissariat,
crashed into the embers of his camp fire
with a Finnish bullet in his brain.

Meanwhile, Tavela and his chosen fifty
pushed on as fast as they could travel
across the hundreds of miles which
separated the Finnish front from their
objective near the shores of the White
Sea. Threading the well-nigh trackless
forest, they crossed the frontier into
Russia and pushed on through enemy
country until at last they came in sight
of their goal. Then, having waited their
opportunity, they descended on the thin
black line of steel and tore up the railway,
flinging the metals into some inaccessible
gulley. Some reports stated that the
" Suicide Patrol " reached Kandalaksha,
the Russian base on the White Sea.

As the Turks found in Syria in 1917, so
the Russians must find it in 1940 a difficult
task to repair the line, when new rails
have to be brought from Leningrad and
work has to be done when the barometer
registers 50 degrees below freezing. Yet
until the repairs have been effected, the
Red Army operating in the Arctic is
completely cut off from Leningrad and
the Russian interior. Murmansk, too,
must be deprived of its supplies, and
following the success of the " Suicide
Squad" there were reports of food riots in
this northern outpost of the Soviet realm.

New Zealand Hastens to Help the Motherland

Above, recruits for the New Zealand Expeditionary Force undergoing intensive training in their own country.

A LTHOUGH New Zealand lies at the other end of the world—so far away that her people have no need of black-outs, gas masks, or air-raid shelters—she is playing her full part in the Empire's war effort. New Zealand pilots have distinguished themselves in the air fights over the North Sea, and the "Achilles," in the glorious battle of the Plate, was manned very largely by New Zealanders. Moreover, the Dominion is raising a large force for service overseas, to be commanded by Major-General B. C. Freyberg, V.C., who played such a gallant part in the Great War, both on Gallipoli and in France.

There is work for those pilots of the New Zealand Air Force who are still at home, for a constant coastal reconnaissance patrol is kept up to watch for raiding enemy warships. Above left, New Zealand airmen making a flight on this service. Right are some of the New Zealanders resident in Great Britain who are now training to be ready to join the main contingent when it arrives from their homeland. A gas mask inspection is in progress.

Photos, L.N.A., International Graphic Press and Fox

Britain's Shipwrights Are Outpacing the Nazis

WHILE British shipyards are hard at work replacing the ships destroyed by Nazi submarines and mines—the losses numbered 112 up to the end of 1939—Germany has already made a most unwilling contribution to the Allied merchant fleets in the shape of some 20 of her ships captured by the Royal Navy.

Here a man is riveting a deck plate. Riveting was once done by hand, but now, whenever the position allows, either pneumatic hammers or hydraulic machines are used.

The long steel bar which the man is drawing out of the furnace in the top photograph will eventually be shaped to form one of the ribs of a new ship. Above, workmen are punching rivet holes in steel plates which form the sheathing of the big vessel.

Right is a cargo steamer on the stocks. Only on the lower part of the hull have the plates been riveted in position, but within a few weeks the ship will be launched and ready for the engines to be fitted. In the foreground are the concrete air-raid shelters for the shipwrights.

Photos, Fox

Another Stout Ship for Britain's Merchant Navy

Besides warships many merchant ships are being built at top speed in Britain's yards to replace the losses caused by Nazi submarines.
Here is a merchant ship in the first stage of construction. In his speech on September 26, Mr. Winston Churchill stated that, " If we are losing
tonnage we are also taking steps to replace it on a much larger scale. Old ships which were laid up are being refitted and prepared for sea.
An enormous building programme of new ships of a simple character, capable of being rapidly built, is already in full career."   *Photo, Fox*

Terrible Things are Happening Under the Nazis

Taken from the columns of " Free Europe," the paragraphs given below throw some light on what is happening in Western Poland and Czecho-Slovakia under German rule. Strict as is the Nazi censorship, these whispers of things shocking to endure and to contemplate have filtered to the wider world.

IN spite of his assurances that he does not want any foreign peoples in the German Reich, Hitler, as the result of his policy of unprincipled aggression, now oppresses over thirty millions who are not German by race or sentiment. This total is made up as follows :

Poles	19,700,000
Czechs	7,000,000
Jews	3,600,000
Yugoslavs	150,000
Lusatians (Wends)	130,000
Lithuanians	78,000
Danes	12,000
Other nationalities	30,000

No doubt if he could have had his own way many more millions would have been incorporated in what the Fuehrer is pleased to call the German "Lebensraum." In the east, however, he has now come up against Stalin; and a line of Soviet bayonets and tanks prevents further expansion towards the much coveted Ukraine, while along the Baltic he has even been compelled to " bring home " members of the German colonies who have lived in the Baltic States for centuries.

It is in Poland that the Nazi terror is seen at its height, and the following paragraphs give an indication of a truly shocking state of affairs.

Reliable information has been received as to the circumstances in which all the professors and lecturers of the Cracow University were arrested. The Germans issued invitations to all the members of the teaching staff of the University, requesting them to attend a lecture given by a German professor. The German lecturer began by reviling Polish scholars and Polish science in most abusive language, whereupon the professors and lecturers left the hall.

In front of the University large lorries were already waiting. All the 160 professors were arrested and severely manhandled. All the arrested professors, of whom many are over seventy, were at once taken to the military barracks, where they had to spend the night on the bare floors of unheated rooms. Next day they were all deported to Germany and interned in a concentration camp. Furthermore, all the professors of the Cracow Mining Academy and all the headmasters of the secondary and primary schools in Cracow were arrested. Simultaneously mass arrests were carried out among the general population of the city. A number of streets were closed, and all men found in these streets were arrested. Women who accompanied many of the men and protested were slapped in the face.

At Gdynia, 300 of the 350 hostages seized after the occupation of the town from among priests, industrialists, and intellectuals were shot in batches, in conditions of bestial cruelty. Before being shot the victims were forced to dig their own graves, after which Gestapo men dispatched them one by one with revolvers, while those who were to be murdered later were obliged to look on. All these executions were carried out without even the semblance of a trial.

Polish Executions by Day and Night

At Szamotuly, a small town in Poznania, five young Poles were executed publicly in the market-place on market day. They had been kept as hostages because in a neighbouring village the Nazi flag was torn down and the guilty could not be traced. As the German soldiers fired at them, the five Poles exclaimed : " Long live Poland ! " S.S. men then walked up to the dying men and fired further revolver shots at them. Several Polish professional men, including doctors and solicitors, were then ordered to place the dead bodies in a lorry and take them to a place outside the cemetery, where they had to dig graves and bury them. At Koscian, the local priest and 48 other Poles were executed in a public square. At Wolsztyn, 20 Poles were shot at night, the scene being illuminated by military searchlights. The inhabitants of the neighbouring houses were

called from their beds and forced to witness the executions.

In Pomorze Polish priests, many of them of advanced age, are forced by the Germans to perform heavy manual labour. In Torun a prelate, respected by all, was forced by the Germans to undertake the heavy work of reconstructing a bridge on the Vistula. When the old priest, overcome by fatigue, fell into the water, his fellow-workmen were about to rescue him, but the S.S. men shot him dead in the river.

Everything is being done to remove all traces of things Polish. Already Polish street names and shop signs have been replaced by German ones. The Polish language is banned in the schools. In the city of Poznan, all the large Polish business houses, firms and factories have been seized from Poles and handed over to Germans or to German institutions.

Murder in Czecho-Slovakia

IN Czecho-Slovakia, too, the Nazi terror flourishes, and in earlier pages we have described some of its most hateful manifestations. The position was summed up by M. Jan Masaryk, son of the Republic's founder, in a broadcast in Czech under the auspices of the B.B.C. :

Our innocent boys are being murdered for not having forgotten quickly enough the meaning of freedom. Our glorious " Alma Mater," the famous Charles University, and all the other high seats of learning have been closed under the order of two treacherous satanic disciples, Karl Hermann Frank and Neurath. They will open their gates again, and it will not be three years before they will be opened by the free people of Prague and Czecho-Slovakia. The blood of our young martyrs, so wantonly spilt, binds all who believe in the freedom of thought to dedicate all their efforts to the most pressing task of all, to the task of destroying and damning for all times to come the gospel of a demented Austrian corporal. Over the fresh graves of our martyrs I solemnly promise that we shall continue our struggle until the final rebirth of a free Europe.

In the reign of terror which is now proceeding in Nazi-occupied Poland house-to-house visitations by detachments of German troops and their Gestapo allies are everyday occurrences. When this photograph was published in the "Munich Illustrated Press" it was given the heading, "Stopping the little game of the Polish Rebel Battalions," and it purports to show Nazi soldiery entering a house suspected of being a "store of hidden weapons and stolen goods."

'Graf Spee' Pays the Full Price of Defeat

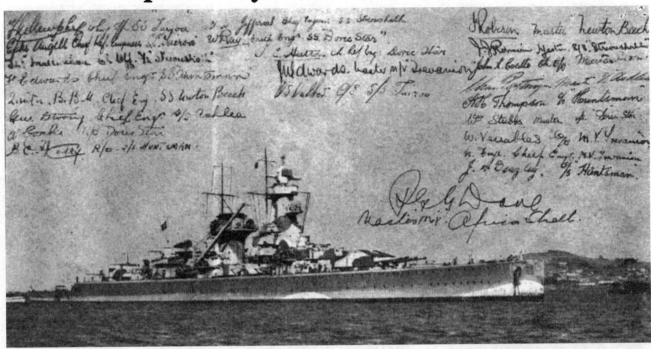

This remarkable picture of Germany's pocket battleship " Admiral Graf Spee " as she lay in the harbour of Montevideo into which she had been chased by the British cruisers was taken by Captain Henry Daniel, Special Correspondent of the " Daily Telegraph," on the morning of the day on which she sailed to her doom. The photograph bears the signatures of 23 masters and officers of British merchantmen who had been captured during the " Graf Spee's " career of depredation and were actually in the battleship during the battle of the River Plate.

ALL Montevideo's quays, piers, breakwaters, and adjacent coastline were densely crowded with people breathlessly watching the German corsair. The crowds stood silent as the great ship passed to sea. Suddenly she turned, not as they expected to seaward where the ships of Britain watched, but westward towards the setting sun. . . Her speed dropped to dead slow, then she stuck her nose into a mudbank and stopped and her anchor was dropped.

The hour was 8 p.m. and the sun was dipping below the river's western rim. Suddenly there was a flash of flame and a double explosion which shook the air, and the centre of the ship was blotted from view by a cloud of dense black smoke. The concussion had not died away before a blinding burst of flame shot from the after part of the ship high above her masthead, and a thunderous roar deafened the ears of the watching crowds. The whole ship seemed to lift and crumple as though inferno itself had burst forth from her vitals. . . .

Out to seaward could be seen the flicker of a Morse lamp and the distant flash of a searchlight from a British cruiser going about her business.

From a message to the " Daily Telegraph " by a Special Correspondent in Montevideo, Captain Henry Daniel, D.S.C.

Aflame from bow to stern, the " Graf Spee " is slowly sinking into the waters of the Plate. This dramatic photograph was taken, like that above, by Captain Henry Daniel. The white funnel has collapsed in dense clouds of smoke. " Sheets of flame spread over the tranquil sea," wrote Captain Daniel, " as the oil from the bunkers of the riven ship came to the surface and caught fire. Dense clouds of smoke rose in the air, and soon the wreck was a blazing inferno from stem to stern. It was the end of the tragedy."   *Photos, Courtesy of the " Daily Telegraph "*

Frozen Finland Was Scorched With the Fla

In Helsinki the celebration of the birth of the Prince of Peace was interrupted by the air-raid warnings, and those people who remained in the capital after the evacuation spent hours in the shelters or, like these youths, in trenches just outside the city.   *Photo, Keystone*

Here is a scene in one of the streets of Helsinki after a squadron of Russian bombers had passed over the city scattering their deadly cargo with regard for where the bombs descended.   A high-explosive bomb has dropped in the street, making a big crater.   The building in front of which is an apartment house, and every window in it and the house next door was blown in, while the walls were heavily scarred with flying fragm Twenty of the inhabitants, mostly women and children, were killed.

Photo, K

War on the Birthday of the Prince of Peace

he murderous onslaught of the Red aircraft on Finland was directed not only upon the big towns, but also upon remote villages. In these the houses
ere so inflammable that a single incendiary bomb might set fire to a whole village and leave the inhabitants without shelter in the rigour of a
orthern winter. In the photograph above a Finnish village is seen on fire from end to end after incendiary bombs have been dropped upon it. Below
a scene from the fighting front : Finnish Red Cross men are carrying in wounded comrades near Lake Ladoga. *Photos, Keystone*

WORDS THAT HISTORY WILL REMEMBER

Extracted from Authoritative War Speeches and Statements Week by Week

(Continued from page 562)

'The Cause of All Nations Who Love. Freedom'

Thursday, December 14, 1939

Mr. G. A. GRIPENBERG, Finnish Minister, at a meeting at the House of Lords:

I stand before you as a representative of a small, democratic, peace-loving country which overnight, without warning and without any declaration of war, has become the victim of the most ruthless aggression. Finland has striven unceasingly for agreement. We were willing to go very far in order to avoid what has now happened, but the Russian Government would not have it.

There was no reason for Finland to refuse to discuss any question that the Soviet Government wanted to discuss. To give some conception of what the Russian demands clearly meant, I will make a comparison. Think what it would mean to Great Britain if some neighbour about forty times bigger than this country demanded the Channel Islands, the Isle of Wight, the port of Southampton, the port of Liverpool, and part of the county of Kent, and also asked to be allowed to keep garrisons in some ports and enter into a military alliance which would make it possible for the bigger country to direct the foreign and home policies of the smaller country....

We went so far as to accept two-thirds of the Russian terms, but there was one condition we had to stick to. We could not accept anything which would have jeopardized our right to live as free men and women in the land of our fathers.... While discussing this the Russian Government suddenly started the so-called incidents....

Even after the beginning of the war, after hundreds of casualties among the civil population, our Government let it be known to Russia that we were still willing to come to terms on condition that a life of liberty and independence would be recognized. Molotov said he would not have any negotiations at all, and so we fight. The Finnish Prime Minister has said "We will hold out, but if we perish, then we believe that our fight has been an inspiration to the whole world." And so I believe it is, for ours is the cause of all nations who love freedom.

Britain's Immediate Aid to Finland

Mr. CHAMBERLAIN in the House of Commons:

It was generally agreed during the deliberations at Geneva in September of last year that each member of the League should decide for itself, in the light of its own position and conscience, on the nature of the sanctions which it would apply under Article XVI of the Covenant against an aggressor State. His Majesty's Government for their part have always held the view that no member State ought to remain indifferent to a clear case of aggression of the sort with which we are now faced. At the outset of the attack on Finland, and before the question had been raised at Geneva, they decided to permit the release and immediate delivery to Finland by the manufacturers concerned of a number of fighter aircraft of which the Finnish Government stood in urgent need, and they intended similarly to release other material which will be of assistance to the Finnish Government....

The opportunity provided by this conflict has been eagerly seized upon by the German propaganda machine, and by many people acting consciously or unconsciously in its service, to deflect attention from the primary objective of the Allied war effort, which is the defeat of Nazi Germany. We must never lose sight of that objective. We must never forget that it was German aggression which paved the way for the Soviet attack on Poland and Finland, and that Germany, alone among the nations, is even now abetting by word and deed the Russian aggressor. We must all give what help and support we can spare to the latest victim of these destructive forces; but meanwhile it is only by concentrating on our task of resistance to German aggression, and thus attacking the evil at its root, that we can hope to save the nations of Europe from the fate which must otherwise overtake them.

Italy's Foreign Minister on Neutrality

Saturday, December 16

COUNT CIANO, Italian Foreign Minister, in a speech to the Chamber of Fascios and Corporations:

... The singular importance of the decision taken by the Governments of Moscow and Berlin to sign a mutual pact of non-aggression was emphasized by the sense of surprise which the communication aroused throughout the world.

For many months France and Britain attempted a policy of close collaboration with Russia which should have led to a much-heralded pact, and which, according to press reports, might even have reached the point of military collaboration. True, the slowness with which the negotiations went on and the existence of certain problems with regard to which a fundamental divergence of views between Russia and the western democracies had arisen had induced scepticism as to the possibility of arriving at a speedy and favourable conclusion.

Few people, however, were expecting an epilogue such as the one experienced with the conclusion of the German-Russian Pact. The truth is that Russia was going through a bitter crisis due to the pitiless purge of Lenin's Old Guard conducted in three memorable trials, following which dozens of death sentences against leaders of the Revolution, Army field-marshals, admirals and ambassadors had been carried out. The country was now being readmitted into the prestige of international politics by the great democracies, whose envoys had for five months been filling the waiting-rooms of that inaccessible fortress known as the Kremlin. If the great democracies had only ignored Russia, Germany would have had good reason to want to do likewise.

The question had been broached with the German Government as far back as April and May. At that time we had agreed to proceed to a policy of détente with regard to Russia. Our object was to obtain the neutralization of Russia and to keep her from entering the system of encirclement planned by the great democracies—an action therefore of limited scope. In any case it appeared to us impossible to reach any more distant goal in view of the fundamentally hostile attitude which Nazi Germany had always assumed with regard to Russia....

Once hostilities had begun and the Franco-British decision to assist Poland had been made known, the Fascist Government in its communiqué issued on September 1, following a meeting of the Cabinet, stated that Italy would not take any initiative of a military character. This decision was previously known to the German Government and to the German Government alone. It defined the Italian attitude with regard to which there existed a full accordance of views with the German Government.

The position assumed by Italy on September 1 was a position of non-belligerence, strictly in conformity with the German intention of localizing the conflict and strictly ensuing from the pact and collateral undertakings existing between Italy and Germany. These and no other are the reasons for Italy's statement that she would not assume any initiative of a military character. ...

It is universally recognized that the realistic attitude of Italy has prevented a generalization of the conflict, which is in the interest of our country and of all States. I wish to make it clear that no initiative has been taken by the Fascist Government so far, nor is it our intention, as things stand, to take any.

I would add that Italy reaffirms her desire to maintain and consolidate order and peace in the Danube and Baltic region. At the same time she does not believe that the formation of any kind of bloc can be of use to the countries which would take part in it, nor would such a bloc serve the higher purpose of hastening the re-establishment of peace. ...

Fascist Italy continues to follow with a vigilant spirit the development of events, ever ready, if it be possible, once again to make her contribution towards world peace, but equally determined to protect with inflexible firmness her interests and her traffic on land, at sea and in the air, as well as her prestige and her future as a Great Power.

The Empire is Still One People

Wednesday, December 20

Mr. R. G. MENZIES, Prime Minister of Australia, in a broadcast:

... Some of the ingenious gentlemen who broadcast from Berlin are feverishly engaged from day to day trying to explain to you that a country like Australia is really not involved in this war, that Australia will simply sell foodstuffs to Great Britain and hope to make some profit, but that otherwise she will take care to risk no soldiers or ships or airmen or seamen in the conflict.

This silly falsehood has done service before. It overlooks the record of Australia in the last war; it overlooks the contribution of Australia made in blood as well as in treasure towards the winning of that war. It ignores the fighting Australian spirit. It seeks to reduce a race of free and vigorous and courageous men and women to the level of mere bargainers.

I say this to you without mental reservation and without ambiguity. If Australia were to do what the German propaganda says she proposes to do, she would be no more than a benevolent neutral. But because, in truth, she is not only furnishing Great Britain with material supplies, but is in course of providing for active service thousands of airmen and soldiers and thousands of sailors, I am able to say we are not benevolent neutrals We are belligerent partners. We are in this war to win. We did not enter it lightly and we will not depart from it except as victors.

Germany need encourage herself with no false hopes. She will discover to her cost that the winning of this war and the success of our noble cause are just as much the business of Australians as of Englishmen, of New Zealanders as of Scotsmen, of Canadians as of Irishmen. Scattered though we may be over the seven seas of the world, living in different countries, governing our own affairs, conducting our own international discussions, and handling our own trade, we are still one people. What touches one, touches all; what is vital to one is the supreme business of all.

Land-Ships of Which Britain May Rightly Be Proud

—HAWORTH.

This is a sectional view of a cruiser tank. The vehicle is driven by a high horse-power engine K, through a clutch L and gearbox to a rear axle M. This axle drives two outside sprocket wheels O, which in turn drive the caterpillars. The shock-absorbing mechanism P, enables the tank to move at high speeds over very rough ground. This mechanism is shielded by armour at Q. Direction is controlled by two levers F and J (see also photo below) which act as a brake on the caterpillar on the inside of the turn, while gear is changed by the lever H. The driver G looks forward through two small louvres. The gun-turret A revolves mechanically and the three-pounder gun B is laid by gunner D and loaded by E. There are two half-inch Vickers guns at C and N ; a third is on the other side of the tank corresponding with N.

Specially drawn for THE WAR ILLUSTRATED *by Haworth*

Above, militiamen are undergoing an intensive course of instruction at an Army advanced school for tank training. They become thoroughly efficient tank drivers in about 24 weeks. The pupil has his hands on the two direction control levers F and J.

THE mechanization of the British Army has led to the establishment of the Royal Armoured Corps, in which are included the Royal Tank Regiment and all the Cavalry and Yeomanry regiments that have been mechanized. The tanks of the Cavalry and Yeomanry are of the lighter type, successors of the "whippet tanks" of the last war. These machines are manned by three men, and are not only faster but much easier to handle than those that went into action in 1918. The heavier tanks, sometimes known as "cruisers," are used in conjunction with infantry, preceding an advance not only to machine-gun the enemy but to clear a way through barbed wire entanglements and other obstacles. The future crews for tanks of all types are trained at a special school, a scene in which is shown in this page. The course of instruction the men undergo includes driving, for every man of the crew must be able to drive, and also a thorough technical knowledge of the working of the very complicated piece of mechanism of which they are to have charge.

Striking the Balance of the Blockade

At the opening of the New Year, Germany faces a prospect of increasing scarcity as the Allied blockade becomes ever more effective. On the other hand, her desperate counter-measures are all unavailing. Slowly but surely she is being strangled.

SINCE the war began the navies of Britain and France have been engaged in relentlessly driving the enemy's ships and mercantile marine from off the seas and in strangling Germany's economic life by the stoppage of those supplies which are constituted contraband of war.

The campaign has been strikingly successful. Most of the units of the German navy have hardly gone out of sight of their harbours since hostilities began; while as for her merchant shipping, it plies only in the Baltic and the Black Sea, and for the most part is laid up idle in harbour, or has been scuttled to avoid capture, or has actually been taken.

Seizures of Contraband

Just before Christmas it was announced that the British Contraband Control had intercepted and detained over half a million tons of contraband suspected of being destined for Germany, while in addition the French Contraband Control had detained in the same period a total of approximately 360,000 tons. By the end of the year the total detentions amounted to nearly a million tons. Not a week has passed since the war began, indeed, during which Germany has not been deprived of quantities of petroleum, mineral ores, cotton, oils and fats, rubber, fibres, hides and skins, and foodstuffs.

Thus, to take an actual instance, during the week ending December 30, 1939, the British Contraband Control intercepted 20,800 tons of contraband goods suspected of being destined for Germany. This total included:

17,500 tons of petroleum and allied products
1,450 tons of ores and metals
600 tons of miscellaneous foodstuffs
400 tons of oilseeds
160 tons of cotton
160 tons of gums and resins

In addition to these goods the seizures comprised quantities of rubber, chemical products, tanning materials, timber and hides and skins. When the year closed the British Contraband Control could look back upon seventeen weeks of most successful activity, in the course of which they had prevented Germany from receiving a total of 537,600 tons of goods that could be used in the prosecution of the war.

Translating the joint Allied total into picturesque terms, 600 trains consisting of 30,000 trucks would be required to transport the amount of petroleum seized. Similarly, 640 trains consisting of 32,000 trucks would be needed to carry the various metals detained. To transport by rail all the contraband seized would require 116,500 trucks, which if coupled together into a continuous train would occupy 600 miles of railway track. Taking the British seizures alone, the fibres seized would be sufficient to make 46,000,000 sandbags, and the hides and skins are sufficient for well over 5,000,000 pairs of army boots. The cotton seized would have been sufficient to manufacture enough gun-cotton for 12,000,000 6-in. howitzer rounds, and the petroleum products of various kinds detained amount to over 23,000,000 gallons, which would more than have filled to capacity the tanks of every motor vehicle on the roads in Britain in the last month of 1939.

Germany's Real Losses

Moreover, it should be remembered that these figures are of contraband actually seized; they give no indication of the enormous quantities of goods which would have been dispatched to Germany from the neutral States in normal times. Yet another great blow was dealt to Germany's commercial and industrial

system when it was decided by way of retaliation against the inhuman and illegal mines campaign that the Allied Contraband Control should detain not only Germany's imports, but such of her exports as came under the heading of contraband.

Very different is Britain's position. In the four months of war the Royal Navy has enabled nearly 21,000,000 tons of British shipping to keep the seas, and although the rationing of several of the most important foodstuffs has been instituted, this step has been dictated not by scarcity so much as by the desire to conserve cargo space and foreign credits.

SHIPPING LOST: SEPT.—DEC. 1939

	Vessels	Tons	% Loss of Tonnage
GERMAN			
Lost	22	136,317	
Captured	19	88,218	
Total ...	41	224,535	5·0
BRITISH	112	422,232	2·0
FRENCH	12	56,106	1·9
POLISH	1	14,294	11·7
BELGIAN	3	9,350	2·4
DANISH	9	22,333	1·8
DUTCH	7	39,243	1·3
ESTONIAN	1	396	0·2
FINNISH	5	11,919	1·9
GREEK	9	42,686	2·4
ITALIAN	2	9,339	0·3
JAPANESE	1	11,930	0·2
LITHUANIAN ...	1	1,566	—
NORWEGIAN ...	23	61,903	1·3
PANAMANIAN ...	1	757	0·1
RUSSIAN	1	968	0·1
SWEDISH	19	34,629	2·2
JUGOSLAV	1	6,371	1·5
Totals ...	249	970,557	1·4

Of course, there have been losses, as will be seen from the table printed above reprinted from Lloyds' List. Yet, notwithstanding the activities of U-boats and aircraft in torpedoing ships without warning, notwithstanding the mines laid indiscriminately in traffic channels, in relation to total tonnage the British losses have amounted to only 2 per cent., while the German losses in the same period were 5 per cent.

DEBITS · *Each Symbol represents 10,000 Tons, except U-Boats.* · CREDITS

MERCHANT SHIPS SUNK (SEPT. 3–DEC. 31)

BRITISH 422,232 Tons = 112 SHIPS

FRENCH 56,106 Tons = 12 SHIPS

POLISH 14,294 Tons = 1 SHIP

NEUTRAL 253,390 Tons = 83 SHIPS

U-BOATS SUNK BY BRITISH

U-BOATS SUNK BY FRENCH

GERMAN MERCHANTMEN CAPTURED OR SCUTTLED
224,535 Tons = 41 SHIPS

GOODS CAPTURED BY BRITISH 517,000 Tons

CAPTURED BY FRENCH 360,000 Tons

This picture diagram continues the story of the Allied blockade from Nov. 30 (p. 471). Covering the last week of 1939 it includes all ships officially then stated as lost and, in addition to enemy goods captured by the British Contraband Control those by the French Control. Figures for the week ending Dec. 30, received while printing, were British, 20,800 tons (total 537,600 tons); French, 69,000 tons (total 429,000 tons).

Lifeboatmen Rise to the New Challenge of War

The signalman of the Southend lifeboat, seen above, is flagging a signal to a ship that the rocket apparatus will be used for the rescue. When the lifeboat is tossed by heavy seas he is steadied by a rope tied round his waist and held by two men. Right is Coxswain S. H. Page, of the Southend lifeboat, who in 1938 twice won the bronze medal of the R.N.L.I. for gallantry.

THE lifeboatmen are too often the "forgotten men" of this war. In peacetime we tend to take as a matter of course their bravery and self-sacrifice in fulfilling the duties of the great service to which they belong. In time of war their duties are even more arduous, for besides helping ships in difficulties through stress of weather, they are called upon to succour the crews of those vessels that have struck mines or been torpedoed by enemy submarines. Since the war began lifeboats of the Royal National Lifeboat Institution have been launched over 400 times and have saved over 1,000 lives. In the last war the average number of lives saved every week was 21; in the present war, up to the end of 1939, it was no less than 64.

When it is impossible for a lifeboat to go alongside a ship a rocket apparatus similar to that used from the shore, but on a smaller scale, is used by the lifeboat. In the two photographs above the apparatus is in use. Right, the rocket that will carry the first thin line to the ship is being fired. It enables the crew of the ship in distress to pull aboard the stouter rope, left, from which is suspended the breeches buoy, in which a man is being hauled on board the lifeboat.   *Photos, Topical*

Without Oil the Wheels of War Must Stop

As long ago as 1904 Lord Fisher declared that the countries which control oil supplies will control the world. Today, during a war of petrol- and oil-driven machines, the advantage possessed by the Allies, who have not only huge oil resources of their own but may draw on the resources of the whole world, must become ever more apparent.

If it be true to say that civilization could not continue without oil, it is still more true to say that without oil, war as it is waged in the twentieth century would be quite impossible. Aeroplanes, tanks, armoured cars, mechanical transport, ships of war—all are dependent on the oils extracted from the bowels of the earth. In 1938 the world production of crude petroleum was over 270,000,000 metric tons.

Nature has greatly favoured the democratic powers in the distribution of petroleum. By far the greatest producer is the United States, which is responsible for some 60 per cent of the world's present supplies. In 1938 Germany and Austria produced only 615,000 tons, Italy 140,000 tons (127,000 from Albania), Poland (507,000) and Japan 356,000. Compare with these figures the production of the U.S.A. of over 164,000,000 tons, and even of Canada, which in 1938 produced 940,000 tons.

Next largest producer to the U.S.A. is the U.S.S.R. In 1913 Russia's extraction of petroleum was over 9,000,000 tons; from 1920 to 1925 it oscillated between 3,000,000 and 8,000,000 tons, and since then has shown a steady increase, mounting in 1938 to about 29,000,000 tons. At present the Russian refineries are capable of dealing with the output, but many of them are out of date. Moreover, the industry produces only sufficient to satisfy the country's own requirements, as is shown by the fact that between 1932 and 1938 Russian exports of mineral oils fell from just over 6,000,000 tons to 600,000 tons. Russia might increase her petroleum exports by intensifying her production, and this would seem feasible enough seeing that she has vast deposits of oils still unexploited. But it would take time, and it would necessitate a thorough overhaul of her present very defective transport organization.

Only a very little short of Russia's production is that of Venezuela, which in 1938 produced just under 28,000,000 tons; as recently as 1935 her production was under 3,000,000 tons. There are indications that oil might be tapped right along the Andes to the south of Argentina.

Britain's Huge Oil Base in Iran

Next on the list is Iran, where in 1938 the production of crude petroleum was over 10,000,000 tons. Its exploitation is in the hands of the Anglo-Iranian Oil Company, which possesses at Abadan one of the three largest oil refineries in the world. Its storage capacity is nearly a million tons. Abadan is the refuelling centre of the British Navy in the East.

Of the other producer-countries the most important are the Netherlands Indies, which produced over 7,000,000 tons in 1938; Rumania (6,600,000 tons), Mexico (4,800,000 tons), Irak (4,250,000 tons), the British West Indian island of Trinidad (2,470,000 tons), Argentina (2,370,000 tons), Peru (2,100,000 tons) and British Burma (1,060,000 tons).

At the present time interest centres on Germany's hopes of obtaining large quantities of petroleum from Russia and Rumania. During 1938 the Reich imported nearly 5,000,000 tons of petroleum, motor fuel and lubricating oils, but in time of war her requirements must be far greater. As just stated, Rumania's production in 1938 was under 7,000,000 tons, and it would seem to be hardly likely that Russia could set aside for export 5,000,000 to 10,000,000 tons of petroleum annually. Even if she could produce it, how could it be delivered to Germany, seeing that all the existing Soviet pipe-lines have their outlets either on the Black Sea or the Caspian? Rail would be the only means available.

It is true that Germany has made immense efforts to assure her self-sufficiency in the matter of petroleum supplies by seeking oil beneath her soil and by the synthetic preparation of motor fuels. With regard to the former, soundings have so far been unsatisfactory, and it seems that the maximum production cannot exceed 700,000 tons even if Austria be included. As to synthetic fuels, the Reich does not seem capable of producing more than 3,000,000 tons annually of petrol and gas oil.

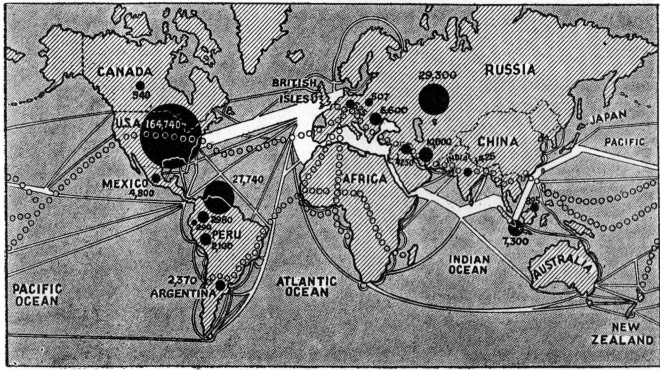

In this sketch map are indicated the principal oil-producing centres of the world and the routes by which petroleum is conveyed to the principal areas of consumption. The black disks give some indication by their comparative sizes of the petroleum deposits. The broad and narrow white lines mark the main commercial traffic routes. The chains of circles mark the main lines of distribution of petroleum products by oil tankers, pipe lines, rail and other methods.

In Uniform and Overalls British Women Serve

These "ratings" of the Women's Royal Naval Service are attending a course before taking commissions. Right, two volunteers of the First Aid Nursing Yeomanry, known as "Fanys," are cleaning their ambulance.

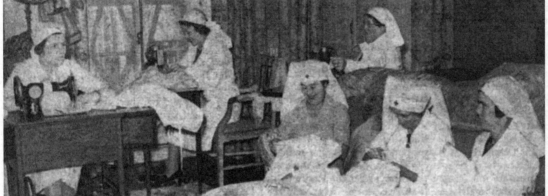

Australian women in London have thrown themselves whole-heartedly into work that may help the Empire in wartime. Left, workers of the Australian Women's Voluntary Service are at work in Australia House under the leadership of Lady McCann, left, wife of Sir Charles McCann, Agent-General for South Australia. The headquarters of the organization were recently visited by the Queen.

Photos, Wide World, Planet News, Fox and Kosmos

In the factory and warehouse of the Navy, Army and Air Force Institutes in South London, food and many other things to stock the canteens are prepared and stored; above left, girls are making meat pies. Right is Miss Mona Friedlander, one of the eight women pilots who were appointed to a special section of the wartime organization known as Air Transport Auxiliary, whose duties are to assist in flying light trainer aircraft from the factories to R.A.F. aerodromes.

Germany's 'Gates' Are Closing One by One

As the blockade of the Allies is intensified, the economic position of the Nazi Reich
must become ever more precarious. Just how difficult is the position may be gathered
from this article and the accompanying map on which it is based.

IN 1917, when Britain began to apply the weapon of the blockade in real earnest, Imperial Germany was at the height of her power on the continent of Europe. The Kaiser's writ ran from Lille to Constantinople and beyond to the borders of Persia, and under his control were not only Germany and her Austro-Hungarian ally, but Belgium and north-eastern France, Russian Poland, Rumania, Serbia, Bulgaria and Turkey.

At that time five "gates" were open through which supplies could reach the Central Powers, viz., the Baltic, Holland, Switzerland, Turkey and Russia. Yet in spite of this vast concentration of political and economic power, within a year Imperial Germany crashed into ruin—very largely as a result of the strangle-hold applied by the Allies' blockade.

In 1940 Germany is again beleaguered, but this time the territory under her control is far smaller, both in size and resources. It is true that there are seven main "gates," but several of these, as will be seen, are little more than ajar, and all are being slowly but surely closed. Let us look at them in turn.

First there is the northern "gate" opening from the Scandinavian countries. Germany is dependent on Swedish iron-ore for the maintenance of the war; from Sweden, Norway and Finland she gets timber, and from Denmark large supplies of foodstuffs. Since war began she has put strong pressure on these countries to cease their exports to Britain and to send all their surplus produce to the Reich. Naturally enough, the Scandinavian countries are not eager to

abandon that profitable trade with this country which has been built up through the centuries, more particularly as they obtain from Britain manufactured goods which they cannot obtain elsewhere. Despite the activities of the German submarines and minelaying 'planes, the Scandinavian ships still cross the North Sea, and probably nothing short of a German invasion of Scandinavia is likely to prevent their voyaging.

The Russian war with Finland has also closed the Scandinavian "gate" a little more, as it has put an end to Finnish timber exports, and has rendered precarious the supplies of iron-ore coming from the mines at the head of the Gulf of Bothnia. Another repercussion of the Russo-Finnish war is the retention within the Scandinavian States of supplies which in normal times they would export.

The next "gate" is Holland, and this, too, is closing as the Allied blockade prevents the entrance of goods which have been declared to be contraband. True, Holland may supply Germany with home-produced food, but at the best of times the little country has no large export surplus of the goods which Germany most vitally needs.

Not far away is the Belgian "gate" through which Germany receives considerable quantities of iron, but these supplies are now being reduced owing to the Belgians' own armament.

Leaping over the length of the Maginot Line we come next to the "gate" through which Swiss condensed milk, cheese, and meat pour into the Nazi realm. But Switzerland is a very small

country, and what she produces cannot be relied upon to stock the German breakfast-tables.

Italy's "gate" through the Alpine passes is a very important one, for Italy is still a member of the Axis. As the war goes on and the blockade by sea is intensified, this gate will become ever more crowded, for it gives on the rich plains of northern Italy, and not far away lie all those Italian ports to which come cargo ships from every corner of the world. Yet the Allied contraband control is active in the Mediterranean as well as in the North Sea, and so this "gate," too, is showing signs of closing.

All-important Balkan 'Gate'

The sixth "gate" is in Hungary, and through it move the lorries of wheat from the plains of Hungary and Transylvania and barges and railway-tanks filled with Rumanian oil. For years Hitler and his Nazis have turned longing eyes on these lands, flowing with the modern equivalents of milk and honey, and since the war began Rumania in particular has been subjected to a policy of threats and cajoleries all intended to secure from her ever larger supplies of food to fill German bellies, and oil to fill the tanks of Germany's 'planes.

In the past Germany has received through this "gate" vast supplies from the Balkan countries, but she has now little manufactured goods and machinery wherewith to make payment. Now, moreover, her buyers have to meet the competition in the Balkan market-places and exchanges of the commercial representatives of the Allies, and it really is not surprising that the Balkan producer should prefer to take the Allies' cash and let Germany's credit go.

Now we come to the last of the "gates," that which connects the Nazi portion of conquered Poland with the portion which is now subject to Soviet rule. One would think that through this "gate" would move vast convoys of raw materials and food supplies produced on the boundless plains of European and Asiatic Russia. But convoys cannot move without wheels —the day of the horse is really past—the Russian transport system is elementary, to say the least, and the lines in Poland have been blasted by the devastation of war. Now by a miscalculation of the Kremlin the Soviet is engaged in a first-class war with Finland, and we may be sure that much of the supplies that were originally earmarked for a pressing Germany are now being diverted to the use of the Red Army in the frozen north.

Seven "gates," but how long will all or any of them remain open?

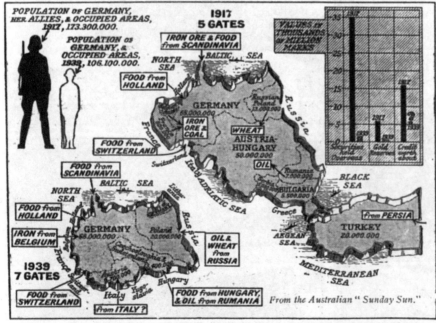

From the Australian "Sunday Sun."

Above are illustrated in diagram form the "gates" of Germany in the last war and in this; explanatory details of the seven "gates" now open are given in the accompanying text. Population and financial resources are also represented for the two periods under review.

War Honours Won by Sea and Air in 1939

River Plate ("Graf Spee") Action

Rear-Adm. Sir H. Harwood, in command of the squadron (Dec. 13). Awarded K.C.B.

Capt. W. E. Parry, of H.M.S. "Achilles." Awarded C.B.

Capt. C. H. Woodhouse, of H.M.S. "Ajax." Awarded C.B.

Lt.-Cmdr. (now Cmdr.) R. B. Jennings, of H.M.S. "Exeter" Promoted.

Cmdr. (now Capt.) D. H. Everett, of H.M.S. "Ajax." Promoted.

For Submarine and Other Actions

Cmdr. E. O. Bickford, of H.M. Submarine "Salmon" (Dec. 14). Awarded D.S.O.

Lt. M. F. Wykeham-Martin, of H.M.S. "Salmon." Given D.S.C.

Cmdr. G. C. Phillips, of H.M. Submarine "Ursula" (Dec. 14). Awarded D.S.O.

Cmdr. R. F. Jolly, of H.M.S. "Mohawk" (Oct. 16). Posthumous E.G.M.

Sgt. Obs. J. Vickers, W. Front air action. Awarded Médaille Militaire on deathbed.

Pioneers in Magnetic Mine Destruction

A.B. A L. Vearncombe. Given D.S.M.

C.P.O. C. E. Baldwin. D.S.M.

Lt. J. E. M. Glenny. D.S.C.

Lt. Cmdr. R. C. Lewis. Awarded D.S.O.

Lt. Cmdr. J. G. D. Ouvry. Awarded D.S.O.

For Air Actions at Sea

A/Sqn. Ldr. K. C. Doran, led Kiel raid (Sept. 4). D.F.C.

Sgt. Pilot W. E. Willits, North Sea action. D.F.M.

F/O A. Macpherson, Kiel reconnaissance. D.F.C.

F/O T. M. W. Smith, "Kensington Court" rescue (Sept. 18). D.F.C.

F/O J. Barrett, "Kensington Court" rescue. D.F.C.

For Fighter Actions

Wg. Cmdr. P. R. Barwell. D.F.C.

Sqn. Ldr. P. Gifford. D.F.C.

Sqn. Ldr. H. Broadhurst D.F.C.

Sqn. Ldr. G. C. Pinkerton. D.F.C.

F/O. R. C. Graveley, gallantry when shot down. E.G.M.

The 'Bloodstained Criminals' Court Each Other

For years no term of abuse was too foul for Hitler to apply to the "Bolshevik scum,"
and Stalin for his part returned the vilification in good measure. Then came the
Berlin-Moscow pact, consummated for the reasons suggested in this article by a German
Anti-Nazi resident in this country.

WHEN Hitler, ever since he wrote "Mein Kampf," spoke of his Moscow counterparts as being "bloodstained criminals," and "scum of humanity"—when he asserted that an agreement between Russia and Germany would mean the end of his own country, he was insincere as always. He may have despised the Bolsheviks, he may have hated them, but in his profound cynicism he wanted to use them for his own ambitions. That much is clear now, after we have heard from his former confidants, such as Dr. Hermann Rauschning, what he told them within four walls.

It was the same with Stalin. Whatever importance one may attach to the disclosures of W. G. Krivitsky, the former Red General and Intelligence Officer, they fit in marvellously with the picture of the two deadly enemies, afraid of each

"*The latest edition of
Hitler's 'Mein Kampf'
omits all reference to
Stalin*"
NEWS ITEM

"**It's a thinner story now!**"
Cartoon by Zec, by Courtesy of the "Daily Mirror"

other, and willing to set aside all their high-sounding principles in order to neutralize each other's power, if possible to win each other's help. It is the story of American gang and racket leaders all over again, who decide to bury the hatchet for the time being in order to rob with united forces the "fat and lazy bourgeois" who bow before their guns.

After all, it is not so astonishing. For had not Germany and Russia co-operated for long years in circumventing the former's Treaty obligations? The Western Democracies, while officially insisting that the weak German Republic should conform with every letter of the Versailles peace document, permitted this clandestine evasion in the teeth of evidence. While official Germany dis-

armed according to orders, she had since 1922 established armament works in Soviet Russia, evolved new models of guns, tanks and aeroplanes in Russian engineering centres, experimented with them on Russian training fields, and imported shells, arms and other finished products from there. Officers of the Reichswehr went to and fro mostly with double passports; pilots, who later on were to form the nucleus of the Nazi Air Force, were trained in Moscow.

Was a Russian Alliance Inevitable?

True, all that came to a sudden end when Hitler's rise to power forced him to give the flood of spite and hate, which had borne him upwards, some definite outlets. The Jews were not enough; for France and Britain he was not ready. Thus it had to be Soviet Russia, who, he knew, could bear a fair amount of mudslinging. Yet, as far back as 1934, if we can believe Rausch-ning, Hitler complained to him about the premature init-iative of his East Prussian provincial leader Koch, who tried to persuade him into an alliance with Russia against Poland. "Perhaps I shall not be able," so he said, "to avoid an alliance with Russia. I shall keep that as a trump card. Perhaps it will be the decisive gamble of my life." And a little later: "I could at any time come to an agreement with Soviet Russia. I could partition Poland when and how I pleased. But I don't want to. I need Poland so long as I am still menaced by the West."

Is that clear enough? And at the same time Stalin, in a speech before his Party Congress on January 26, 1934, carefully offered his hand to Hitler, deciding to enter the game of Geneva only after this hand had been disdained. Yet, even then he won the first round in his fight with that other fellow who had had the courage to shoot his own most intimate friends and the most valuable collaborators of his early days; in spring, 1935, Russia was granted a long-term loan of 200 million gold marks from Berlin. Litvinov's hypocritical speeches about Democracy in Geneva and else-

where, the Russian succour for the Spanish Republic by tanks, aeroplanes and men—even the fulminating protests against the inhuman treatment of Communists in German concentration camps, were just dust in the eyes of the world, pressure upon Hitler to come to terms.

Many people in this country disapproved of the way in which the great Eastern "Democracy" had been neglected and offended when the fate of unhappy Czecho-Slovakia was settled in September 1938. For had not Russia's foreign minister Litvinov reiterated with a glib tongue that Russia, of course, would fulfil her Treaty obligations to her Slavonic brother if France fulfilled hers?

With his tongue in his cheek evidently! For shortly afterwards Stalin pledged himself not to sell his oil—life-blood of the war machine!—to others than Germany and Italy, and Hitler, at the same time, openly held a friendly conversation with the new Soviet Ambassador. He may have prepared the field for his subsequent wholesale swallowing of Czecho-Slovakia, and for many other things which the world witnessed during the summer of 1939, without being fully aware of their portent. They led to the conclusion of the Russo-German Treaty on the eve of the war, to the sealing of the fate of Poland, Estonia, Latvia, Lithuania.

Hitler's Dream of Vast Conquests

It is a marriage of convenience, however, which could not survive either defeat or overwhelming success of either of the partners. Hitler goes on dreaming of his ultimate conquests in the vast eastern plains, of transferring the Czechs and all other Slavs from Central Europe to Volhynia or Siberia, and of getting Ukrainia as his future granary.

To quote Hitler again, according to Rauschning: "The end of such a pact would be the decisive battle that cannot be escaped. Only *one* can rule. If we want to rule, we must first conquer Russia." Alluding to that great "gamble," he states: "It will never stop me from firmly retracing my steps, and attacking Russia when my aims in the West have been achieved."

Stalin's ruthless war upon the valiant Finns has taxed even docile Nazi Germany's allegiance to her unscrupulous leader to the uttermost. Hitler had to permit some help to be given Finland and thereby to enrage Moscow. But he did it with an understanding nod to Stalin, who will forgive it, as he forgave the blood-curdling speeches and slandering attacks. For there are still bourgeois to be jointly plundered; the racketeering business is still good enough for two.

I WAS THERE!

We Tried to Save Half Our Ship

When the 17,000-ton London tanker " San Alberto " was torpedoed
on December 9, the vessel broke in half. Members of the crew
who had escaped in boats returned to their ship and raised steam,
in the hope of getting the floating half to port. Their eventual
rescue, as described by one of the officers, is here reprinted from the
pages of " News Chronicle."

THE " San Alberto " was hit at 6.15 in
the morning. The explosion blew
the skipper into the air and in
falling he broke his wrist. He was the
only one injured.

" The torpedo tore up 60 ft. of deck,
and the fore part of the ship was totally
isolated from the after part. All the
officers were in the fore part where their
quarters were, and the men were in the
after part.

" This resulted in there being no officers
aft to direct the manning of lifeboats.
The bo'sun, Malcolm Bain, of Greenock,
as senior petty officer, took charge, and
his splendid work in seeing that the men
all got away safely cost him his life.

" He was a first-class seaman and a
man of unflinching courage and discipline.
He left himself until last ; unfortunately
there was not much time left, and in
jumping into the last boat he missed and
was lost.

" When daylight came we discovered
that one of the boats containing three of
the crew and a passenger had got lost.
This boat we never saw again.

" Actually it was adrift for five days
and four nights, and though the men had
plenty of food all were suffering from
exposure and trench feet when they
landed at a South Coast port.

" All are now recovering. The rest
of us, after 10 or 12 hours in the boats,
decided that the after part of the ship
would probably remain afloat a long time,
so the whole of the crew returned.

" The engineers broke up accommodation fittings to raise steam in the auxiliary
boilers so that they could get the main
motor started. They did a magnificent
job of work throughout.

" By keeping the engines going slow
astern the crew prevented the seas from
tearing the front part of the ' San
Alberto's ' remains to bits, but every time
she came head to sea great strips of
plating were torn away.

" We had lights and heating in the
accommodation and hot meals all in a
mere fragment of a ship. We made a
fire on the poop in the hope of attracting
a patrolling aeroplane, but after a time
this was put out in case it should only
bring another submarine.

" There was no radio, of course, and
when the Belgian steamer ' Alexandra
Andre ' came along we signalled to her
with a pocket torch. They sent out a
boat, but the sea was too rough for it to
get near.

doned until the morning, and the ' Alexandra Andre ' began a vain search for the
missing boat.

" She stood by all next day until a
destroyer came in response to her radio
call. The sea was still too rough for
rescue efforts, and the destroyer stood by
all the second night, and it was eventually
decided that the only way to transfer
the crew was by Carley Float.

" The ship was sinking rapidly, and
there was not a minute to spare when the
last of the men had been transferred.

" They all had to jump into the icy

The " San Alberto " was the second tanker belonging to the same owners to be sunk by enemy
action. The first was the " San Calisto," which struck two mines off the south-east coast of
England, and in this photograph is seen going down by the bow.
Photo, British International Photos

" Two men did jump. The first landed
safely, but the other missed and in a
few minutes he had drifted fully a mile
away.

" Then the skipper of the Belgian ship
showed the man he was. He backed up
his ship and picked the man directly out
of the water without the assistance of a
small boat. In such a gale, it was a
superb piece of seamanship.

" All rescue efforts were then aban-

water and be dragged on to the float. It
was bitterly cold and the gale was blowing
even worse. Yet three of these men were
at sea for the first time in their lives and
could not swim a stroke.

" There was another passenger who
had originally got away from the ship
in the captain's boat. He, too, like
everyone, behaved as though sailing
in the remnant of a sinking ship was
quite an everyday occurrence."

How I Bombed A German Submarine

For nearly two months the parents of Lieut. G. B. K. Griffiths,
a naval airman, mourned him as dead when he failed to return
from a flight. Then they received a letter from Germany describing
his adventures and his capture by a German submarine. His story
is here reprinted by permission of the " Daily Express."

WHEN Lieut. Griffiths reached Germany he was imprisoned in a
castle, and he wrote from there : " The
castle moat is filled with wild boars to
prevent prisoners escaping. . . .

" I went out in my machine to look for

a submarine which was supposed to have
sunk one of our merchant ships. I could
not find it, so started back.

" My observer suddenly shouted,
' There's a merchant ship on the horizon.
Let's look at it.' When we were almost

604　　　　　*The War Illustrated*　　　　　*January 12th,* 1940

IIIIIIIIIIIIIIIIIIIIIIIIIIIIIIIIIIIIIIIIIIIIIIIIIIIIIIIIIIIIIIIIIII **I WAS THERE!** IIIIIIIIIIIIIIIIIIIIIIIIIIIIIIIIIIIIIIIIIIIIIIIIIIIIIIIIIIIIIIIIIII

Lieutenant G. B. K. Griffiths, Royal Marines, whose remarkable adventures after bombing a U-boat are told in the accompanying narrative.
Photo, " Daily Express "

on it my chap said, ' Go low so that I can see its name.' So I went to sea level and slowed down. Just as I got alongside I spotted the submarine on the far side of the ship.

" Up I went, but the U-boat had already got half submerged, leaving me no time to get to a safe height to bomb from. So I took a chance and bombed from a low height in order to hit.

" My first bomb missed by about twenty feet and I hit the sea at 200 m.p.h. at a steep dive. I went straight down without stopping.

" I tried to get out of the cockpit, but was jammed in with a stuck roof. When I was almost out of breath I managed to break free and came to the surface. My observer must have been killed at once. I never saw him again. I looked for him, but with no luck.

" I then found I was nearly a mile away from the merchant ship, in very cold water, with flying clothes on and not a little knocked about. Somehow I got there, and clambered aboard.

" Some of the submarine's crew were collecting the ship's papers, and I was taken prisoner. A few minutes later up came the submarine, the ship was torpedoed almost at once, and once more I was submerged. I also had to swim to the submarine.

" I spent a fortnight in that submarine before it returned to Germany. I was then lodged at the local gaol for a fortnight, followed by a fortnight elsewhere, and then moved to this place."

Although his bomb had missed the submarine which captured him, it was so badly shaken that during the fortnight he was aboard the commander carefully avoided battle.

I Drove Over a Finnish Field of Victory

In the war in Finland the mass movements of Russian troops were harassed and broken up by comparatively small bodies of Finns armed with rifles and machine-guns. The scene of havoc following a battle on the Northern Front is vividly described here by the " Daily Express " correspondent, Geoffrey Cox.

O N a forest road near Salla, on the Finnish Arctic front, I stood to-day among the bodies of a Russian column struck on the flank by the Finns.

To make this attack the Finns marched all night through the woods on skis.

For more than a mile both sides of the narrow snow-covered roads were choked with lorries, some smashed, some whole, with carcases of horses, overturned carts, masses of clothing, rifles, equipment and foodstuffs.

Amid this at every turn lay the crumpled figures of the dead.

This was where a supply column preparing to encamp for the night had been trapped. The Finns waited in pits by the roadside to fire into them practically at point blank range.

But the main battlefield was half a mile back. There, strewn across the road, lying on the stunted pine trees, were bodies in their drab Soviet khaki and with peaked caps carrying the red star in front.

There, too, were Finns in their white snow capes and grey fur caps fallen in the attack. They were easily identifiable. Their comrades had always covered their faces, sometimes with a cloth, sometimes just with a pine brush.

Here, the Soviet infantry, marching up in columns towards what they thought was a safe camping ground, suddenly met a double belt of machine-gun fire. This was where the Finns made their flank attack.

Lying in position in the woods the Finns kept up their fire as the Russians

A Soviet 'plane is flying over a house in the town of Salla in North Finland. Smoke is rising from an incendiary bomb dropped on a building just behind the house.

Some idea of the men who make up the vaunted Red Army can be obtained from this photograph of Russian prisoners taken by the Finns. Dejected, ill-clad and worse shod they are far from being the sort of men who go to make an invincible army.
Photos. Central Press and Planet News

After the Battle the Grim Silence of Death and Captivity

This transport wagon captured from the Russians by the Finns carried a miscellaneous load, among it being a portrait of Stalin. In many convoys that have fallen into Finnish hands were found material obviously destined as propaganda to make new subjects of the U.S.S.R. familiar with their ruler.

Some of the dead men seen by Mr. Geoffrey Cox are lying here as they fell in their fruitless defence of the convoy. This photograph shows the head of the column, while that on the right, shows the centre of the convoy. The Finns used automatic pistols and hand grenades as well as machine-guns.

Above is the scene when a Russian convoy was ambushed by Finnish troops in one of the fiercely fought actions on the Arctic front. This long line of lorries fell as booty to the Finns after the remarkable action fought in the Salla region.

Photos, Keystone and Planet News

The Russian prisoners, left, were photographed on January 1, 1940, after they had surrendered to the Finns. In the action in which they held up their hands a small Finnish force on the Suomussalmi front routed 18,000 men of the 163rd Russian Division. In their defeat, as in others, the weather was a good ally of the Finns.

A Russian motor-lorry has been overturned on its way to the front, and Finnish soldiers are examining its load, a pile of black bread, the principal fare of the Russian troops. Every such loss is a serious one to the Red Army, for difficulties of transport on each of the northern fronts have caused a shortage of food.

Photo, Planet News

disentangled themselves and got into position to fight back.

You could see clearly how the fight had gone. In one place a small group of Soviet soldiers lay around a machine-gun. They had fought to the end, for Finnish losses in the snow ahead were heavy.

At another place the Russian infantry, apparently retreating, had been wiped out from the back. They bodies lay in a long line across the road.

In a small clearing were a dozen Soviet guns. Their horses were dead in their traces fifty yards behind. The men were piled around a gun wheel. There had been hand-to-hand fighting, for many of the dead had died from bayonet wounds. This battle had lasted forty-eight hours.

The Russians, superior in numbers, had fought hard, but they never recovered from the shock of the first attack.

Now we came on the first traces of the battle as we drove out of a forest village of scattered wooden houses.

By the roadside three men approached us. Two were Finns with rifles in their hands, the third a Russian prisoner, his hands held high. He looked grey with exhaustion. He had been wandering in the woods for two days.

Beyond, in the snow, looking like bundles of rags from the distance, were the bodies of the advance guard of Finns and Russians.

We motored across a frozen river to the woods on the other side. Suddenly we came on the smashed column. At first

sight it looked like a great junk heap on the outskirts of the wood.

More than twenty lorries lay deep in the ditch, others were overturned or had missing wheels. Three of them had been caught when their drivers were trying to turn to escape. Beside them the Finnish troops and peasants were carrying the dead into a big yellow van.

The Russians' horses had been mown down where they were tethered in a big circle under the trees. Their carcases lay in a great heap. There was gear of every description—telephone wires, mattresses, clothes, kettles, blankets, boots, shovels, ammunition, stacks of rifles, mostly with bayonets fixed, haversacks and gas-masks.

It seemed impossible in the winter afternoon silence, with the sky a soft gold behind the pine trees, to think what this battle meant, to realise how many of these people had been husbands, lovers, sons and fathers.

I could feel more easily about the Finns, because I have lived among them and am surrounded every day by these men in grey uniforms. But the Russians I do not know as individuals.

Then suddenly I saw lying in a pile of telephone material a broken plaster doll. It had come from a small suitcase in which was a child's pair of gym shoes and some woollen clothes. It was not hard to realise how they came there.

A Russian soldier, thinking of his child, had picked them up in some evacuated Finnish village. He had probably looked forward to the day when he would go back to his village and his child.

Now the doll and the clothes lay here in the snow.

I picked up a book lying on the road. Out of it fell two photographs. One was of a young Russian lieutenant with an open face, a solid man. The other showed a group of Red Army men photographed under a tree like an old group of some rowing crew. I looked at the book again. In its Russian lettering I spelled out the title—"The Principles of Leninism, by J. Stalin."

My Ship Broke Clean in Half

On Dec. 6, 1939, a tremendous explosion destroyed the Greek steamer "Paralos" in the Thames Estuary. Three of the crew of 27 were killed and ten injured, and the ship, her back broken, sank in ten minutes. Captain Cotomatis, master of the "Paralos," told the following story to the "Star."

CAPTAIN COTOMATIS believes he is a very lucky man to be alive.

"After the explosion, which was right amidships," he said, "the ship broke clean in half.

"I was on the bridge when the funnel came crashing down, missing me by a hair's breadth.

"Then down came the masts, together with a shower of debris.

"After the explosion only one lifeboat was left. The others were smashed to matchwood.

"This boat was loaded in orderly fashion, very special care being taken of the injured.

"Waist deep in water and clinging to a stay I had to crawl round the opposite side of the boat before I could be taken off.

"We were all very happy to see the British boat which picked us up."

Captain Cotomatis said that he could not say with any certainty whether his ship struck a mine or was hit by a torpedo. He thinks it was a mine.

The 10 injured men were taken to hospital, but only five were detained.

The remainder of the crew were sent to boarding houses. Most of them were in a state of collapse through fatigue.

The radio operator said :

"The explosion occurred after about three-quarters of an hour's steaming. We had been at anchor previously because we were not quite certain of our position.

"We found the skipper clinging to one of the funnel guys and took him off. We had already rescued the injured men and that was indeed a tough job."

Horse and Mule Keep Going When Motors Stop!

The training of horses and mules for transport work, in case rain and shell fire should make the Western Front a morass such as it was in the last war, goes on constantly. Above, horses of an Animal Transport Company of the R.A.S.C. are being exercised.

Photo, Central Press

The horse transport of the R.A.S.C. is learning the lessons of the last war. One of them is the art of camouflage. This man with a packhorse has camouflaged it cleverly enough—rather to the surprise of the horse!

Tʜᴇ British Army is perhaps more mechanized than any other in the world. Nevertheless, the experience of the last few months, when autumn and early winter rains and snow have been exceptionally heavy, has made it apparent that there must be a reserve of animal transport when the big guns get going and No-man's Land is churned into a sea of mud. Already a large number of horses and mules are being trained in Great Britain and France to meet such an emergency, and there is a call for still more.

Many veterans of the last war will have mixed memories of the mules—stubborn beasts that sometimes made life almost unbearable to their drivers, but whose surefootedness rendered them invaluable in places where horses would have been useless. These men, in training for the Animal Transport of the R.A.S.C., have named their two mules "Hitler" and "Goering," a stroke of humour that is evidently appreciated far more by the men than by the mules, to judge from the expressions.
Photos, Fox, Keystone

OUR DIARY OF THE WAR

Thursday, December 28, 1939

Censorship of Press messages from Moscow reimposed.

Fierce hand-to-hand fighting on frozen Suvanto river near Mannerheim Line. Finns claimed to have **wiped out two Russian companies.**

Reported that Russians have brought up picked Ogpu troops into Karelian Isthmus.

Air Ministry announced successful reconnaissance of north-west Germany on Dec. 27. One aircraft failed to return.

R.A.F. fighters chased unidentified 'plane above Scottish coast.

Admiralty announced that H.M. trawler "Loch Doon" must be considered lost with crew of 15.

Danish steamer "Hanne" sunk by mine.

Eight survivors (out of 43) of British freighter "Navasota" torpedoed early in December, landed at Capetown.

French Senate accepted Budget of £450,000,000 after stirring speech by M. Reynaud, Finance Minister.

Nazi authorities announced that entire population (70,000) of Polish town of Kalisz were to be deported to make room for German Balts.

Friday, December 29

Soviet troops in Salla section said to be in revolt.

Detachment of **Finnish troops reached and damaged Leningrad-Murmansk railway** at three points.

Finnish "**Suicide Company**" of 250 picked ski troops, first sent forward to attack railway, reported to have **penetrated as far as Kandalaksha,** an important Russian base on arm of White Sea.

Russians maintained pressure in Karelian Isthmus where they now have 9 divisions.

Finnish Government protested to Estonia against presence of Russian destroyers in Tallinn harbour.

British battleship, torpedoed by U-boat on Dec. 28, reached port under own steam.

Paris reported renewal of air activity on Western Front.

British trawler "Resercho" sunk by mine in North Sea.

British steamer "Moortoft" reported sunk.

Fishing trawler "Adam" reported having been bombed and machine-gunned by German seaplanes.

Saturday, December 30

Russian troops launched new attack against Mannerheim Line.

Finnish northern army virtually **destroyed Russian division** of 15,000 men near Lake Kianta, in Finland's "waist-line." Great quantity of war material and many tanks captured. Victory was culmination of battle raging in this sector for a week.

Patrol activity between Moselle and Saar, despite intense cold.

Paris reported sinking of U-boat by French warship off coast of Spain.

Air raid made on Hangoe, during which 60 bombs were dropped.

Sunday, December 31

Russian aircraft raided at least 11 Finnish towns, including Helsinki.

Successful Finnish counter-attack launched in Salla sector. Continuous heavy fighting in Karelian Isthmus.

Second contingent of Canadian troops arrived at a West Coast port.

German steamer "Tacoma," aboard which "Graf Spee" crew had been transferred on Dec. 18, left Montevideo by order of Uruguayan Government, and anchored outside harbour.

Monday, January 1, 1940

Royal Proclamation issued extending liability of men for military service up to age of 27.

Violent attack by Soviet forces in Taipale sector of Karelian Isthmus repulsed.

North of Suomussalmi Finnish troops were in pursuit of defeated Russians.

Bombing raid made on Turku (Aabo), with result that historic castle was burnt down.

German 'planes raided Shetlands; **one bomber shot down. Heinkel seaplane brought down** in North Sea by machines of Coastal Command.

British steamer "Box Hill" sunk.

Norwegian steamer "Luna" torpedoed without warning.

Reply to League of Nations stated that British Government would give all possible help to Finland, and was already taking steps to do so.

German steamer "Tacoma" returned to Montevideo and was interned.

Italy recalled her ambassador in Moscow in reply to Soviet's action in recalling its new ambassador in Rome, following anti-Soviet demonstrations in that city.

Tuesday, January 2

Nazi aeroplane sighted over Shetlands.

Russians launched attack on Mannerheim Line, but a blizzard over southern Finland brought fighting to a standstill.

Finnish successes at Lake Kianta and other points on eastern front have relieved pressure on railway line from Joensuu to Nurmes and Oulu, of great strategic importance to Finland.

Details were published of great Finnish victory in region of Lake Tolva, north of Lake Ladoga, where fighting raged from Dec. 13-23. Soviet division annihilated, and vast quantities of war material destroyed or captured.

Report from Berlin stated that Stalin had applied to German Government for 200,000 experts to reorganise Russian economy. Later denied.

The King visited an Army Division in the Southern Command and made an 80 mile tour of the various units.

Fight over North Sea near German coast **between three R.A.F. bombers and 12 Messerschmitt long-range fighters.** One fighter shot down in flames; two others driven down and probably lost. One British machine shot down and another missing.

Survivors of crew of Swedish steamers "Lars Magnus Trozelli," sunk by enemy action, landed at Haugesund.

Estonian steamer "Mina" reported missing.

Freezing of Danube has cut off Germany from over three-quarters of products supplied to her by Balkans.

Prague announced that new wave of arrests had swept over Protectorate, victims including ex-officers of Czecho-Slovak army and journalists.

Wednesday, January 3

H.M.S. "Ajax" arrived at Montevideo, and H.M.S. "Achilles" at Buenos Aires, for refuelling and provisioning. Both ships received a tumultuous welcome.

During five weeks of war **Finns** claim to have **destroyed 400 Russian tanks and** brought down at least **150 'planes.**

Finnish air force raided Soviet base at Uhtua, opposite Finnish "waistline," and also Murmansk and Russian base at Liinahamari, port in Petsamo region. Machines used were fast bombers.

Reported that Arctic weather conditions were responsible for as many Russian deaths as were the Finns.

R.A.F. reconnaissance machine forced down in Belgian territory after being engaged by three enemy fighters in neighbourhood of frontier between Germany and Belgium.

Paris reported that patrols and reconnaissance parties were active on Western Front. French fighters **brought down two enemy 'planes.**

President Roosevelt, opening third session of Congress, warned Americans that isolation was impossible and that the mission of U.S.A. was to promote peace by means of trade co-operation.

Swedish steamer "Svarton" sunk by U-boat off north coast of Scotland.

M. Daladier stated that France would help Finland by every means in her power.

British Contraband Control announced that 20,800 tons of goods were intercepted during week ended December 30.

Germany said to have warned Scandinavian countries that if Allies gain advantages there "under pretence of" helping Finland, she will interfere.

From the cartoon by Sir Bernard Partridge, by permission of the proprietors of "Punch."

Vol. 1   A Permanent Picture Record of the Second Great War   No. 20

A most impressive suggestion of power is afforded by these 9·2-in. howitzers lined up " somewhere in England." As a result of the strange changes that the mechanization of the Army has brought about, they are now manned by Yeomanry. Their great weight makes it impossible to move them as a whole, so for transport they can be divided into three parts, the barrel, the bed and breech, and the recoil apparatus.

Photo, Fox

Europe's Map Saw Many Changes in 1939

So swift-moving is the march of events that we sometimes tend to forget the changes
which have been wrought in the course of but a few weeks and months. In this chapter
the contributions made by 1939 to a changed and changing Europe are reviewed.

At the beginning of 1939 the peoples of Europe were congratulating themselves on having turned a very nasty and highly dangerous corner.

Much, very much, had happened in the space of less than a year. The Anschluss of Austria with Germany had been effected, and the man who had left Austria as a poor craftsman returned to Vienna as the triumphant Fuehrer of the German race. Then, the Sudeten Germans, encouraged by the success of the Nazis in Austria, inflamed by Hitler's demagogy and financed by Hitler's gold, clamoured first for autonomy and a little later for full

On this sketch-map of Europe are indicated the principal changes
that occurred in the eventful year of 1939, principally the result of
the territorial ambitions of the Fuehrer of the Nazi Reich.

union with the Reich. For a few weeks in the early autumn Europe had been on the very brink of war. Only at Munich at the eleventh hour was the menace lifted, and then at the price of Czecho-Slovakia's independence and of the prestige of the democracies. At the end of the year Germany was inflamed with her easily-won victories, her ranks were swollen by the millions of Austrians and Sudeten Germans who had " returned " to a fold from which in fact they had never strayed.

But Hitler had declared that after Munich he wanted no more Czechs; he had professed with his hand on his heart that he had no further territorial aims in Europe. Those in every country who both hated war and feared it were hopeful that the new year would introduce an era of peaceful accommodation amongst the great Powers. They took comfort in the thought that the nations, armed to

the teeth though they were, had come to the very edge of the precipice of war, and looking down had shrunk with horror from precipitating themselves and their neighbours into the fearsome abyss. Particularly in Britain and in France the advocates of a policy of appeasement were —somewhat ruefully, be it admitted— taking credit for the even limited success of their untiring efforts.

But history was to prove once again that tigers cannot be appeased. At the very moment when the spokesmen of the democracies were extolling the fruits of " appeasement," the dictators who held in their hands the destinies of the enslaved millions of the totalitarian States were meditating further aggressions, planning still more extensive encroachments, preparing for another onslaught on those peoples whom they envied for their riches and hated because of their independence. Thus it was that in the event 1939 brought even more changes to the map of Europe than its predecessor.

The first blow fell on the rump State of Czecho-Slovakia. At six o'clock on the morning of March 15 the German troops invaded the little republic in overwhelming strength, and the same evening the Fuehrer drove into Prague as a conqueror. Henceforth, so ran his fiat, the republic of Czecho-Slovakia ceased to exist. Bohemia and Moravia were taken under the aegis of the Reich as a protectorate, and a little later Slovakia was confirmed in a similarly puppet status.

Hitler Shocks the World

Europe shivered at the stroke; the whole democratic world was aghast at this latest demonstration of the Fuehrer's innate mendacity, his irrepressible propensity for double-dealing. But Hitler cared for none of these things. Looking about him on the long lines of German tanks, the endless columns of German infantry, the roaring squadrons of German 'planes, he found it easy to believe that his Rubicon had not yet come within sight, and that bluster, backed by irresistible force, was a

card which, in his opinion, the democracies could never trump.

So, only a week after Prague, he told the Memellanders in person that they had returned home to the Reich, and already he was setting in motion his well-tried technique of aggression against yet another destined victim — this time Poland. But now the limelight shifted for a week or two to Mussolini, who chose Good Friday for the invasion of Albania, the little kingdom just across the Adriatic with which for years Italy had professed to be on terms of sincerest friendship. What small resistance there was, was soon overcome, and the King of Italy received from Mussolini the crown of Albania.

Poland's New Partition

Through the summer the tempo kept on rising. The question of Danzig and the Polish Corridor was ever on the front pages of the newspapers, and behind the scenes the statesmen and diplomats wrangled and wrought. At last on the first day of September the simmering cauldron boiled over, and German troops invaded Poland at a dozen points. Two days later Britain and France declared war on the German aggressor.

A fortnight went by, and Russia, too, invaded Poland. Her stab in the back was effective. The republic's resistance was at an end. On September 29 Nazi Germany and Soviet Russia obliterated the independent State of Poland, and divided her territories between them in a fourth partition even more infamous and horrible in its aftermath of murder and oppression than its predecessors of the 18th century.

Hardly had the ink dried on this pact between wolf and jackal, when Russia proceeded to reduce the three Baltic States, Estonia, Latvia, and Lithuania, into satellites of her power. True, they still have their places on the map, but independence can be but a name when each little country contains the garrisons of another Power. Still not satisfied, Stalin reached out towards Finland, and when his demands were refused, dispatched the Red Army to " liberate " the Finns from the oppression of their rulers.

But at last one of the dictators had overreached himself. The Finns were so inconsiderate as to greet the "liberators" with bullet and bomb, and at the year's end the long-blown-up bubble of Soviet efficiency seemed about to be pricked.

Here, then, 1939 took its leave and 1940 made entrance. Looking at the changes which one short year has brought to the map of Europe, who shall say what will be its appearance when another year of violent change has passed ?

Once Again the Stern Vow---'They Shall Not Pass!'

These French soldiers are grouped together in front of a concrete pill box on the Western Front. They have inscribed on it words immortal in the history of the last war, "On ne passe pas"—"They shall not pass." This was the motto that inspired the heroic defenders of the fortress of Verdun, whose amazing stand against the Kaiser's hordes was one of the most glorious feats of arms in the history of the French Army.

During the last days of 1939 and the first days of 1940 a large part of the Western Front was mantled with hoar-frost and the whole countryside was turned into a fairyland suggesting anything but warfare. This French patrol is marching out through frost-bound woods to make contact with the enemy. It is the beginning of one of those incidents described in the French communiqués as "some patrol activity."

Photos, Planet News

Germany Lost That War: How Can She Win This?

In 1918 Imperial Germany reached the zenith of her conquests, and in a few brief months crashed into stupendous ruin and defeat. In 1939 Nazi Germany set out on the same trail, yet (as this article and the accompanying maps show) with a much smaller territory as a jumping-off ground.

MAPS can be eloquent things, and the two appearing in this page are indeed eloquent. They may afford some relief to those who, oppressed

Belgium stands outside the conflict; France's soil is inviolate; Italy boasts of her attitude of non-belligerency; Hungary, Yugoslavia, and Bulgaria are all neutral

and may be expected to remain neutral as long as they are permitted to do so. Greece, Rumania, and Turkey have placed themselves under the wing of Britain and France. On the east, Soviet Russia is Nazi Germany's ally, but the alliance is economic rather than military, and up to the end of 1939, at least, Russia seemed to have had the best of the bargain. Half Poland and the three Baltic States might be held to constitute a striking justification of Stalin's foreign policy, if Finland had not to be counted in the other side of the scale.

In 1918, at the time of the conclusion of the Treaty of Brest-Litovsk between Germany and the Bolsheviks, the Germans controlled a vast area with a population of 230,000,000, of whom 83,000,000 were in the occupied territory. At the end of 1939 the Germans controlled some 110,000,000 people, of whom 42,000,000 live in the occupied territories. In 1918 Germany held the oilfields of Rumania and of Poland, the great wheat-lands of the Ukraine, the fertile plains of Hungary and Rumania, the coal mines of Belgium. In 1939 she controlled none of these sources of the vital materials of war.

Germany lost the first Great War in 1918; we may well ask ourselves whether she has any real chance of winning the second Great War in 1940.

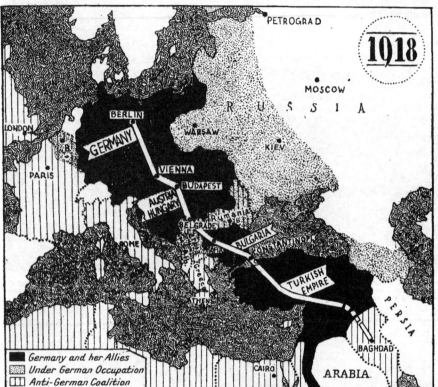

Germany and her Allies
Under German Occupation
Anti-German Coalition

by a consciousness of Germany's military might and of the unthinking subservience of the German masses, fear that Hitler's Germany may be able to put up a vigorous and prolonged resistance both on the economic and military fronts.

Look first at that which is labelled 1918. Across it sprawls the black shape of Germany and the German-controlled realm of the last year of the Great War. It stretched for 2,000 miles from the North Sea to the mountains of Asia Minor. Germany, Austria-Hungary, Bulgaria, and Turkey were actual allies in the war, and their troops had overrun nearly all Belgium and much of north-eastern France, Serbia, Montenegro, Rumania, White Russia, and the Baltic provinces, the Ukraine and the Caucasus. Against this mighty congeries of allied and dependent countries were ranged the Powers of Western Europe—Britain, France, and Italy, with Greece as a rather unwilling ally.

Now turn to the companion map which illustrates the ranging of the Powers at the end of 1939. As in 1918 Central Europe is either German or under German occupation, but the limits of Hitler's realm are drawn much more narrowly than were those of the Kaiser.

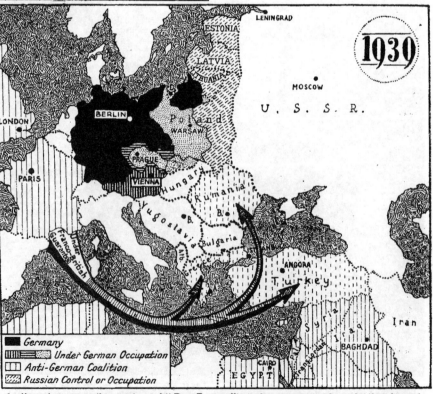

Germany
Under German Occupation
Anti-German Coalition
Russian Control or Occupation

In these two maps (by courtesy of " Free Europe ") we have a comparison, in the clearest possible form, of the extent of Germany's power in 1918, when she made her last desperate bid for victory in the Great War, and in 1939, when under the Nazis she for the second time raised up against herself a ring of enemies.

Unsleeping Watch on the German Side of the Rhine

Where two huge armies face each other unceasing vigilance must be maintained, and foggy wintry weather calls for increased watchfulness. Above, a German sentry on duty in front of the Siegfried Line, where barbed wire barriers wind in and out of the concrete anti-tank defences, is peering at a village in No-man's land, nebulous in the winter mist.

Photo, Associated Press

In Finland's Snows Stalin's 'Comrades' Perish

So complete was the rout of the Russians in certain sectors of the Finnish war that it was suggested on every hand that the Red Army was far less formidable in equipment, if not in the native quality of its men, than had been generally supposed. For the present, at least, its ill-success had deprived it of much of its prestige.

WHEN the Red Army invaded Finland on the last day of November, 1939, all the world except the Finns themselves believed that the "Russian steam-roller" would have little difficulty in swiftly crushing the Finnish resistance.

But the days and weeks went by, and

This Finn, whose house at Borgaa has been wrecked by Soviet bombers, despondently obeys a well-known Biblical injunction.

at the opening of the New Year it was Finland's gallant little army which had won all the laurels of the war. In a number of engagements they had worsted the invaders and at not one point of the whole 750-mile front could the Russians claim to have made any real progress. Indeed, such gains as they had been able to make in the early days of the war were almost entirely wiped out by the counter-offensive, and in some places the Finnish ski patrols were operating well behind the enemy lines in Russian territory.

Russia's Huge Losses

In a campaign of five weeks eight divisions of the Red Army were held at bay on the Karelian Isthmus, and seven more divisions were thrown back on the central and northern fronts. Moscow was reported to have sent to the front more than 300,000 men, and it was estimated that their losses in dead and wounded certainly exceeded 100,000 men. Many more were taken prisoner. (Some of these were in a terrible state of nerves, for the poor fellows had been told by their political commissars that if captured by the Finns they would be flayed alive!) On the other hand, the Finnish casualties, despite the immense disparity of numbers, were very small.

A very large proportion of the casualties on both sides were caused by the intense cold. "I have felt extreme cold in many parts of the world," writes Mr. Hamilton Fyfe, the veteran war correspondent. "but never did I feel it more than in Finland. Thirty below is harder to bear there than elsewhere because there are so many lakes and marshes. Forty below is hell." So severe was the weather that some even of the Finnish ski patrols, men who were well equipped for the rigours of the Arctic winter, and who were hardened by a lifetime spent in the far north, fell victims to its effects.

A vivid picture of the awful conditions in which the rival armies conducted their operations was given by a Special Correspondent of the "Daily Telegraph," who early in January visited the forest which constitutes the battlefield of Lake Tolva, where between Dec. 13 and Dec. 23 the Finns almost annihilated a division of Russian shock troops. Driving along the road that leads from Tolva to Agla he saw the shattered tanks, broken supply lorries, and heaped debris left behind by the Soviet division in its flight. All along the roadway he noticed strange shapes bulging beneath the snow among the trees. Sometimes the shapes might have been logs. Sometimes they looked like

The intense cold of the winter months in Finland had an important bearing on the Russo-Finnish war, for many of the ill-clad Soviet soldiers perished in the snow. Above left, Finnish soldiers are investigating weather conditions by sending up a weather balloon. The Finnish troops made several successful raids upon the Murmansk railway, the main line of transport between Leningrad and the Arctic Ocean. Above is the railway at Kandalaksha, Russia's base on the White Sea.

Photos, Associated Press, Central Press and A. B. Howse

Hungry Reds Leave Even Their Food Behind

In this photograph of part of the great Russian convoy captured in a forest at Salla (seen also in page 605), a Finnish soldier is happily contemplating a string of sausages hanging from a captured Russian sword. The loss of the convoy—which included, as will be observed, foodstuffs received from overseas—must have been a serious blow to the Russians, whose lines of communication are precarious in the extreme.

Photo, Planet News

Spoils of War Add to Finland's Armaments

This young Finnish soldier takes a justifiable pleasure in turning a rifle (with fine telescopic sights), one of thousands captured from the Red Army, against the invaders of his beloved country.

These rifles and machine-guns on wheels were among the great quantity of munitions captured from the Red Army by the Finns. During the rout of the Russians at Lake Tolva between December 13 and 23 alone nearly a hundred light machine-guns and over 1,500 rifles were taken.

Photos, Central Press

crooked limbs cast into the discard by the woodsman's axe.

"Sometimes," he wrote, "heavy felt boots, bared of snow by the stumbling contact of some passing Finnish soldier, protruded suddenly and revealed the truth. Sometimes, too, we saw soldiers dragging frozen shapes like pieces of cord wood from the forest—and here and there bodies lay in crude, contorted heaps waiting for a common grave. But for the most part the snow had cloaked these forms in the immaculate anonymity of the far northern winter. Nature had done her charitable best. But it still did not seem quite possible that these had been human beings only a few days ago, or that the mask of the snow around Lake Tolva concealed more and more hundreds of dead."

Then he climbed on to the crest of a ridge and followed his guide into the forest on the left. "There are many of them here," he was told, "they were all wiped out by our machine-gun fire. . . . Suddenly we found ourselves among whole groups of white-covered figures. Some lay straight on the ground, but mostly the arms were drawn convulsively upward or projected stiffly above the shoulder. Their legs were bent or doubled. Sometimes one body, curiously oversized with its two-inch coating of snow, lay grotesquely like a cross against the sur-

rounding white. These were the Russian dead. All carried gas masks. All about us lay featureless human shapes, their masks of snow making them more anonymous than death itself. Beside one of these I paused. Slowly I brushed the snow away. An unshaven face with an alabaster forehead emerged and then the stubble of close-cut black hair."

On every hand men in steel helmets painted with a slender red star lay where they had fallen. From pockets protruded letters, newspaper clippings, and membership cards of Bolshevik organizations, and in the snow were pitiful little packets of letters from home. . . .

After a month and more of war the Soviet troops had consolidated their advance in one sector only—in the far

and frozen north at Petsamo. Their drive in the direction of the Gulf of Bothnia was completely halted, and the invaders were driven back almost to their own frontier. North of Lake Ladoga they were defeated as we have seen, with heavy loss. Even on the Karelian Isthmus, where they were able to employ their masses of troops to the best advantage and where their base was within easy reach, they failed completely in their repeated onslaughts on the Mannerheim Line. From many points on the far-flung front there were reports of the Russians digging in—the trenches had to be blasted by dynamite— as if they were intending to rest their offensive until spring should have brought with it melting of the snows and the thawing of the frozen ground.

The Hardy Finns Don't Mind the Arctic Weather

These Finnish soldiers are sleeping in a shelter behind the lines in a battlefield where the temperature is often below zero. They are huddled together for warmth, but obviously they are well clad and well shod.

In the photograph centre left a Finnish soldier is holding up, for the benefit of the photographer, a pair of Russian military trousers carefully camouflaged. The boots below them are wholly unsuitable for winter warfare. Above, Finnish soldiers have just had a boiling hot bath and are cooling themselves by dressing amidst the snow. This sort of bath, known as " Tauna," is usual among the hardy Finns.

Photos, Planet News & Press Topics

Stalin's Grip on the Baltic is Tightened

Although the subject of Soviet Russia's subjection of the three little Baltic republics has been dealt with in earlier chapters (*see* pages 170 and 233), this summary of what has been effected by the various agreements may prove helpful to an understanding of the Hitler-Stalin Axis in the New Year.

"IT must make Hitler sick to see what is happening to the Russian army in Finland," declares the "New York World-Telegram"; "he gave Russia half Poland and control of the Baltic—prizes which she was too weak to win for herself." Whether we agree or not with the American newspaper's almost contemptuous view of the Red Army, there can be no two opinions about Russia's dominant position in the Baltic.

Within a fortnight from the end of September, 1939 the three Baltic States were induced or compelled to sign treaties of mutual assistance with the U.S.S.R. Estonia was the first to be tackled, and on September 28 her Foreign Minister, M. Karel Selter, and Molotov, Russia's Foreign Commissar, signed an agreement under which Soviet Russia was granted military, naval, and air bases on the islands of Dagö and Ösel, and at the port of Paldiski (Baltiski), and also two inland air bases at Kechtna and Kuzika. Shortly afterwards Russia was granted the right to maintain three garrisons on the Estonian coast opposite Dagö and Ösel.

A week later M. Munters, Latvia's Foreign Minister, put his signature to a pact by which the Soviet Union was entitled to establish naval bases at Libau (Liepaja) and Windau (Ventspils), artillery bases on the coast between Windau and Petragge (Pitrags), and several airfields at places inland.

Then, on October 10, M. Urbsys, Lithuania's Foreign Minister, agreed that Wilno air-field should become a base for the Soviet air force, and four Russian garrisons should be stationed on Lithuanian territory. In return for these concessions Wilno, Lithuania's ancient capital, which for twenty years had been in Polish hands, and the surrounding district were transferred to Lithuania.

Pacts of Mutual Assistance

All three treaties contained an identical clause stating that the contracting parties would render each other every assistance, including military assistance, in the event of aggression or the menace of aggression against one or the other, as well as in the event of aggression or the menace of aggression against the Soviet Union by any European power over the territory of any of the three Baltic States. Furthermore, the Soviet Union expressed its willingness to render assistance in armaments to its new satellites, and the contracting parties undertook not to conclude any alliances or to take part in any coalitions directed against one or the other.

When it is noted that the Estonian army numbers 10,000, the Latvian 25,000, and the Lithuanian 23,000, it will be possible to value at its true worth the clause contained in all the treaties which declares that: "the realization of this treaty should not affect in any way the sovereign rights of the contracting parties, in particular their State organization, economic and social system, military measures, and generally the principle of non-intervention in internal affairs."

Up to the present the spirit of the agreement would seem to have been kept.

From this sketch-map (taken from "Free Europe"), on which are marked the new bases secured by Soviet Russia in the Baltic States, the measure of the grip already exercised by Stalin in the Baltic will be manifest.

SOVIET BALTIC BASES
- ○ Air Bases
- ▢ Army Bases
- △ Naval Bases
- ✴ Army, Naval and Air Bases

Now that their commerce with Britain and the West has been interrupted by the war, the Baltic States must become more and more dependent on Russia for raw materials, and recently barter agreements were entered into between them and the Soviet Union whereby the bulk of their agricultural, dairy, and leather produce is to be exchanged for Russian coal, oil, and iron-ore.

Ties of Race and Culture

Besides these economic ties there is a racial bond, in that in each of the three countries there is a considerable Russian element. It is true that in large measure the Baltic Russians are well-to-do bourgeois, and even "White" émigrés, but the revival of Russian imperialism strikes a responsive chord in their breasts. On the other hand, at the other end of the social scale there are many Balts who harbour pro-Communist sentiments.

Then, there can be no doubt that the majority of the Baltic peoples, if they had to choose between Russian and German overlords, would prefer the former. The German "Baltic Barons" had a bad reputation because of their treatment of the local Letts and Estonians, whereas under the Tsarist tyranny, brutal and cruel as it often was, quite a number of these races attained to power and influence in the State.

But although the little countries still have their place on the map of Europe and have political, social and economic systems which are widely at variance with those of Soviet Russia, it may be feared that 1939 brought to an end their brief period of independence.

If Stalin had had his way, the same year would have seen the end of Finnish independence, for in early October he made demands on Finland very similar to those which had already been granted at the pistol's point by the three Baltic States, thus making it clear that he was aiming at securing control of both sides of the Gulf of Finland. The negotiations dragged on for several weeks, until at last it would seem that Moscow's patience was exhausted. A frontier incident happened in suspiciously convenient fashion, and on November 30 the advance guard of the Red Army crossed the frontier in what Moscow obviously expected would be a mere "walk-over." But the commissars of the Kremlin had not allowed for the independent spirit and natural valour of the Finnish people—nor for the rigours of an Arctic winter.

Thus it came about that when his programme of expansion in the Baltic was almost complete, Stalin was nonplussed by Finland's heroic stand.

Women Work and Die for Finland

Miss Fanni Luukkonen has been at the head of the Lotta Svard for ten years, and in that time its membership has grown from 50,000 to its present strength of over 100,000.

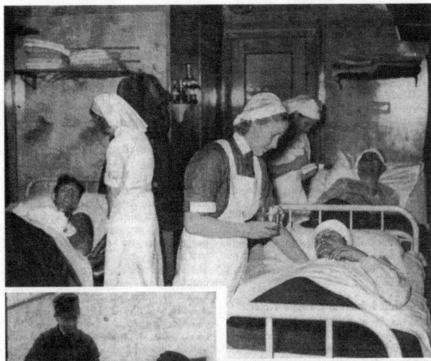

Finland has made a wonderful effort to meet the needs of the wounded. Above, nurses are at work in a hospital train made up of ordinary coaches in which beds have been placed.

L OTTA SVARD, the Finnish women's national service organization, has over 100,000 members who undertake every sort of non-combatant duty in support of the army. Service is voluntary and unpaid, while the women even provide their own uniforms. The name is derived from a woman whose heroism during the war of 1808-9, in which Sweden lost Finland to Russia, made her one of the most popular characters in the poems of J. L. Runeberg, Finland's national poet.

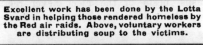

Excellent work has been done by the Lotta Svard in helping those rendered homeless by the Red air raids. Above, voluntary workers are distributing soup to the victims.

First members of the Lotta Svard to be killed in action were three women employed as look-outs, who were shot dead at their posts by Soviet machine-gunners. " In the name of the Army," said Marshal Mannerheim, " I pay tribute to their memory, and at the same time I thank members of the Lotta organization for their faith, courage and devotion to duty." Above right, women observers on a Helsinki roof; left, the wife of a Helsinki doctor setting out as a Fire Guard.

Photos, Associated Press, Planet News, and Lubinski

Come Aboard One of Our Aircraft Carriers!

Written by Capt. H. C. Biard, the famous test pilot and winner in 1922 of the Schneider Trophy air race, this article gives much hitherto unpublished information concerning those great floating aerodromes, our aircraft carriers, of which, thanks partly to Nazi mendacity, the " Ark Royal " is the most famous.

ONE of the puzzles of the earlier part of this war concerned the British aircraft carrier " Ark Royal." The Germans claimed to have sunk her; we denied the claim. Come aboard her with me, and I will show you round the ship which the enemy claim is now in Davy Jones's Locker.

The latest type of aircraft carrier has a flying deck 65,000 square feet in area. This protects about seventy modern naval aeroplanes that shelter in hangars beneath.

On the deck is a landing-space of about two acres. It is fitted with wires, hooks, springs and other apparatus to grab aircraft as they land and bring them to a standstill. Some 130-feet width is none too much for putting down a fast and powerful machine whose wingspan may exceed 50 feet. A big white line is marked on which descending machines should land; but gusts of smoke and pockets of hot air from the funnels, as well as the movements of the ship itself, make the task one for a skilled pilot.

Britain has those skilled flyers. During two months' tests at sea recently, 1,500 flights and landings were made on one aircraft carrier without a single mishap. On one occasion 10 machines landed in just under 11 minutes, all quite safely.

Our latest carriers are so steady that even in a Bay of Biscay gale the angle of roll does not exceed 5 degrees from the horizontal. Elaborate precautions are taken against fire. Two great steel fire-curtains, each about 70 feet wide, can be dropped in a few seconds to subdivide each of the hangars where the machines are housed,

thus localizing any fire outbreak. Four smaller fire-curtains, half the width of the others, can be dropped round the open wells of lifts, to stop flames going up or down. About 600 automatic sprinklers are fitted in vital parts of the vessel. The four pumps operating them have a delivery of 150 tons a minute. Scores of chemical fire extinguishers are placed ready to hand round the hangar walls, and every man aboard is trained and practised in fire drill.

Electrical equipment aboard includes 620 motors, 240 miles of cable, and 3,500 lamps. About 65 per cent of the hull of the ship is welded, with a saving of weight, through the absence of rivets, of about 500 tons.

Isolated from the Battle's Noise

There is a " silence room " aboard, where officers of the watch can receive orders from the bridge; it is enclosed by sound-insulated walls through which the roar of bombs, the rattle of quick-firers and the boom of great naval guns cannot penetrate.

Down in the bowels of the ship there are repair sheds manned by skilled mechanics who can carry out work of all sorts on the dive-bombers, deck-fighters, reconnaissance machines and other types now used for naval flying.

The funnels, superstructure and controls of an aircraft carrier are all jammed over to one side, out of the pilot's way.

And, believe me, some of these carriers have very good teeth of their own! Slim, long-muzzled anti-aircraft guns, heavy machine-guns with long range and terrific

delivery of high-explosive bullets, and lighter machine-guns stick up in blobs and groups like asparagus sticks at a flower show.

Moreover, the mother-ship would be guarded by 350 m.p.h. fighters that would zoom up into the skies about her on the first hint of danger, like angry wasps when someone has thrown a stone into the nest. Blackburn Skuas, Blackburn Rocs, Fairey Swordfishes, Fairey Seafoxes, Avro Ansons, Hawker Nimrods, and all sorts of other deadly types will be seen in the air when the first guns thunder out the overture to the next great naval battle. They will be joined by enormous Short Sunderlands, torpedo carriers, dive-bombers, and all sorts of other types, many of them operating from land bases.

Each side will try, first, to destroy the enemy aircraft carriers. They cost £3,000,000 to build, and a single bomb, with a lucky hit, might disable one—the bomb would cost perhaps £150.

Once the wasps' nests of a fleet were destroyed, the wasps would be rendered largely powerless, after their first attack, and one of the factors of naval battle now most feared by all experts would be removed.

As the German Fleet prefers to sail about its own harbours, our aircraft carriers are doing splendid work helping to guard trade routes and act as bases for the hundreds of aircraft that patrol the skies searching for submarines and mines.

Many a thousand tons of food for Britain has been saved because these wasps' nests of the Fleet never relax from their everlasting humming activity.

Landing on and taking off from the deck of one of the Navy's aircraft carriers is never an easy matter for any pilot. With the introduction into the Fleet Air Arm of high-performance monoplanes like the Blackburn " Skua " fleet-fighter dive-bomber, seen in the above photograph, a new technique had to be studied. With wheels and landing flaps lowered, the pilot makes his approach. In a few seconds the arrester gear will engage with the wires stretched across the deck, and the " Skua " will be brought to a halt.

Photo, Fox

Where is the Ark Royal?—Why, Here She Is!

The "Ark Royal" is here seen alongside a quay at Cape Town during her recent cruise in the South Atlantic. At the outbreak of war she was the largest aircraft carrier in any fleet. She was also the only ship in the Navy specially built for this purpose.

NOTHING has done more to expose the stupidity of Nazi propaganda than the persistence in the absurd lie that the "Ark Royal" had been sunk. During her cruise to the South Atlantic the great aircraft carrier was sighted by a number of neutral ships, many of whom were close enough to read her name with binoculars. The first suggestion that she might be bound for South American waters appeared in a New York paper which stated that an American ship had sighted in mid-ocean small aircraft that could have come only from a carrier.

After leaving Cape Town the "Ark Royal" crossed the South Atlantic, and on December 17, just before the battle on the River Plate, she was at Rio de Janeiro refuelling. Above we see her moored in that port, and the remarkable construction of her hull is clearly visible. There could be no mistaking her identity as her name-plate, in the photograph left centre, shows. In the photograph right she is taking oil on board.

Photos, Associated Press

We Shan't Win the War by 'Wishful Thinking'!

"What is called the 'lull' of the past four months," says Sir John Anderson, Home Secretary and Minister of Home Security, "may be the lull before a great storm . . ." So he, too, finds a danger in that "wishful thinking," discussed in this article by E. Royston Pike of THE WAR ILLUSTRATED Editorial Staff.

FIVE months of war, and not a single British civilian killed by an enemy bomb! Five months of war, and only a handful of British soldiers killed on the Western Front! Five months of war in which the German fleet has not once dared to come out in strength—such strength as it has—to meet the Royal Navy!

Such remarks as these are to be heard every day over the breakfast-table and in the smoking-room at the club, on the top of the bus, and over the evening's hand of bridge. They are cheering; and in these weeks of natural and artificial black-out, who can blame us for seeking cheer where we may find it?

Although Britain has not yet been subjected to an aerial "Blitzkrieg," the North Sea has been crossed many times by enemy raiders. This German photo claims to show a Nazi 'plane on its way to the Scottish coast over German minesweepers in the North Sea. *Berliner Illustrierter Zeitung*

Sometimes, too, our spirits are uplifted by what we hear of happenings, or supposed happenings, in Germany. We smile when we hear that the poor old Fritzes are getting rheumatism because the water seeps through the badly-constructed Siegfried Line. We smile again—some people even permit themselves a gibe—when we hear that the "hausfrauen" are being told how to make tea from blackberry leaves, that the Germans must go dirty because one 3-oz. tablet of soap has to last a month, and that a hundred-point rationing system has been introduced in respect of German clothing. Surely it is obvious, we argue, that if rationing has been carried to such lengths in Germany so early in the struggle, the front of our enemies must already be cracking!

Rumours of political changes are also singularly comforting. Hardly a day goes by but we hear that Hitler has lost all interest in the war, or is dying of cancer, or that he is shortly to be superseded by Goering and the generals, or that Goering and the generals are about to be purged by the Fuehrer. Then there are stories about German warplanes being nothing like so numerous nor so dangerous as we had been led to believe. The German soldier, too, is not to be compared with his father, for not only does he lack training, but his stamina has been undermined by the hard years which have been Germany's since Versailles.

Indulging in such thoughts as these, opening our ears to the flood-tide of cheerful rumour, noting the facts and figures purveyed by our official and unofficial propagandists, we may well feel that the title of the Ministry of Information's most recently published booklet is thoroughly well chosen. "Assurance of Victory"—that indeed is ours!

But if we turn to the other side of the picture we may have to admit that some at least of our ardent hopes and fondest expectations of an easy victory — a victory which will be won not by hard fighting, but by the collapse into chaos of the German social and economic system or by a revolution which will sweep Hitler from the stage and put in his stead a government of generals or of monarchists —are just so much "wishful thinking."

Perhaps the most foolish of these expectations is that a sure and permanent peace would inevitably come to Europe and the world if Hitler were to fall from power. Charming as they appear in retrospect, the petty German principalities of a century and more ago were really rendered an anachronism by the thunder of Napoleon's guns; and if we think of a monarchist Germany let us not forget that it is on the shoulders of the last of the Kaisers that history has placed the responsibility for plunging the world into the first Great War. As for a government of generals, that could only mean a government dreaming of military victory and planning for it. What else, indeed, can the members of a military caste be expected to dream of and plan?

On the morrow of Hitler's downfall the military camarilla might indeed profess with their hands on their hearts that they wanted nothing more than a long period of peace, but it is surely obvious that that period of peace would be but an interlude between this struggle and one greater far.

Nor can the realist derive much comfort from the fact that up to the present the German air force has had such little success in its raids upon Britain's shores. In Poland the story was very different, and it is surely not unreasonable to suggest that the Nazi warlords have not yet seen fit to give an exhibition of the aerial "blitzkrieg." If we have been spared so far it is not because the enemy is too humane to bomb crowded cities: Poland must ever be an object lesson to the contrary. Rather it is because a few minutes after the first bomb is dropped on London or Sheffield, a hail of bombs will be descending on Germany's vital arteries in the Ruhr and the Rhineland. Not humanity but cold, hard calculation have we to thank for our immunity to date. Air raids may come—some would say must come—though perhaps they will be delayed until Hitler and his Nazis stand on the very brink of destruction. Then they will launch their aerial armadas in the resolve to take down with them into the pit all that can be smashed and destroyed of Western civilization.

Rationing a Sign of Strength?

But, it may be said, surely the extensive rationing in Germany is proof positive of economic shortage and approaching collapse? It may be so, but the German people have long been accustomed to short rations, and they have long gone to bed with hardship. Now they are told by the man whom millions of Germans still regard with an almost ecstatic worship as the saviour of their country that further hardships and a continued shortage are the price they have to pay if they would save themselves and their country from the "extinction" with which (so the Nazi propagandists allege) they are threatened by the Allies.

But more important still is the thought that Germany's rationing may be a sign not of weakness, not even of undue shortage, but of the determination to employ the available supplies to the best advantage and so to husband the resources that victory may be won.

Germany, in a word, knows that she is at war, and is ready for every sacrifice necessary for its winning. Britain is at war, too, and, like Germany, is fighting for the existence of herself and her Allies and of everything that makes life dear. But does she realize it?

Heroes of Wartime Black-out—Unseen & Unsung

IN broad terms their name is legion, not forgetting the newsvendor who still stands shivering at his wintry pitch, lustily shouting " the latest " when you can only discern him dimly by the glow of his cigarette. But chief of the unknown heroes to whom town dwellers are so indebted when the pall of blackness enfolds the city and suburbs are the bus drivers and the taxi-men ; all of them. Few men would willingly become drivers of either cabs or omnibuses under the nerve-racking conditions that prevail in the many thousand miles of Metropolitan highways and byways after night falls on the unillumined thoroughfares. For even the new .00024 lights seem only to make the darkness more profound.

But War caught these essential transport toilers at their job, and in the good British spirit they—not perhaps without an excusable grumble—felt they could but " carry on." And nobly have most of them done so. To be stopped on your taxi in the Strand and asked to drive to Streatham Hill or Wimbledon in the inky night, with no more than a hooded headlight and the tiniest of twinkling signals at the cross roads, is a job to daunt even the stoutest heart. Yet the taxi drivers are rarely known to refuse even so distant a fare, except when restricted petrol supply might fail them.

Terrifying as their job may be, it is even less formidable than that of the heroes who pilot the mighty omnibuses, those veritable overland cruisers, on their long and frequent-stopping journeys from ten to twenty miles at a stretch. The success with which they are carrying on is one more evidence of the astonishing capacity of the human being quickly to adapt himself to new, strange and frightening conditions of activity.

Even in the best of times a London bus driver is not one to be envied, but how much more difficult is his task when he has to pilot his vehicle through a darkness thick enough to be felt !

Photo, specially taken for THE WAR ILLUSTRATED

In Paris, as in London, policemen on point duty during the black-out have been issued with white cloaks so as to make them a little more visible to those dangerous Jehus, the Paris taxi drivers.

Photo, Keystone

Old Homer tells us that one of the lands to which Odysseus came in his long journeying was that of the Cimmerians, who lived in a place where the sun never shone. If the fabled voyager could now come to life and take his stand in the heart of London near the plinth where Eros used to look down on the flower-sellers, he might well imagine himself back in the Cimmerian realm. A gross darkness enwraps the scene, pierced now and again by the beams of bus lamps and by the erratic flickerings of pocket torches.

Photo, specially taken for THE WAR ILLUSTRATED

Intimate Pictures of Daily Life in the R.A.F

These men in their quarters at a British aerodrome in France are upholding the belief that the English are a nation of tea-drinkers. Besides the boiling kettle, the teapot and the tin mugs being always in request, innumerable cups of tea are supplied at the many NAAFI canteens in France.

After a cup of tea may come an impromptu sing-song such as these men are enjoying. The word "hot" is painted on the stove as kindly advi visitors to keep their hands off. In the photograph, top right, a Fairey Battle Bomber is parked in the open. The snow forms a natural camou but the Royal Air Force has also used special camouflage for autumn and for winter when the trees are bare.

Photos, British Official : Crown Copyright, and " Match," Paris

a British Aerodrome on the Western Front

bove, the tea welcomed in the photograph, top left, is being
rried up from a dug-out. Right, a pilot, just returned from
long flight, has thrown off his kit and, after a shower-bath,
has put on his football boots for a game.

WORDS THAT HISTORY WILL REMEMBER

Extracted from Authoritative War Speeches and Statements Week by Week

(Continued from page 594)

Nazi Contempt for Legal Code of Sea Warfare

Wednesday, December 20, 1939

ADMIRAL LORD CHATFIELD in a broadcast :

Whatever she may say, Germany needs a short war, and so her hope is to break the British Navy's grip on her supplies and to endeavour to defeat us rapidly where we are indeed most vulnerable, yet where we are strongest—namely, on the sea.

Now that the Royal Navy has broken the back of her submarine attack Germany has started to use a new type of mine, not laid according to international law in defined places, but strewed promiscuously over the sea routes to terrify the merchant seamen of the world from approaching our shores. Her latest effort is to machine-gun and bomb our fishing-vessels and their crews employed on their ordinary daily work.

There is a third sea weapon she is using, the surface warship and the armed raider. To find a needle in a bundle of hay is an easy task compared to finding a single raider free to roam the seven seas—those vast ocean spaces in which British trade moves. It would be hard enough if you had perpetual daylight, permanently clear weather, and a vast number of warships to hunt each quarry. While we therefore are justly proud of what the Navy has done to bring honour on this country and itself, let us remember that the dispositions of our hunting forces were mainly the difficult and anxious responsibility of the Admiralty from the First Lord downwards. Naval warfare is full of disappointments, but luck is bound to turn up if it is skilfully worked for. . . .

France Branded with Britain in Equal Guilt

Friday, December 22

DR. GOEBBELS, Reich Minister of Propaganda, in a speech at a political Christmas Party :

This is a " war Christmas " celebrated by a determined people. There is hardly anybody in Germany who is not suffering from difficulties and hardships, and there is certainly nobody who does not want to suffer.

Germany's very existence is at stake. Utterances from London and Paris provide clearer and clearer evidence of this fact. If, during the first weeks of the war, the Allied politicians tried to persuade the world that they were waging a war against Hitlerism without wanting to injure the German people, nobody is trying to conceal today that it is their goal to strike Germany down, to dismember her as a nation, and to split her up, thereby bringing her back to her former political and economic impotence. Either we resign as a great Power or we win this war.

It is of little significance for our national future who in particular among our enemies wanted this war or whether the British and French peoples are waging it joyfully and willingly. The great fact is that we are waging war. It would be wrong to assume that the warmongers in Paris would be more inclined to spare us than those in London. Both of them are just as brutal and cynical in their openly proclaimed war aims. This means that the whole plutocratic world has risen against the German people and its social community and wants to smash and destroy it. . . .

We celebrate this Christmas with that profound faith which is always the prerequisite of victory. There is among us no lack of that optimism essential to living and fighting. In this hour, we are not moved by grief and mourning but by pride and confidence. Our people are united as one great family and they are determined to bear the burden of fighting and working. We promise those at the front to see that the home front does its duty.

Wherever burdens and sacrifices can be mitigated, we have done so and shall continue to do so. But wherever they are inevitable, we will bear them together in order to make them lighter. Although peace is the real meaning of Christmas, we shall talk of peace only after victory.

Great Religious Leader's Five Peace Points

Sunday, December 24

HIS HOLINESS THE POPE, in an address to the College of Cardinals :

All nations, great and small, strong and weak, have a right to life and independence. When this equality of rights has been destroyed or damaged or imperilled the juridical order calls for reparation based on justice.

The nations must be freed from the burden of armament races, and from the danger that material forces may become not the defender but the tyrannical violator of right. Peace must be founded upon disarmament. . . .

Lessons must be drawn from past experience. This applies also to the creation or reconstitution of international institutions. And, since it is difficult, if not impossible, to foresee and safeguard everything at the moment of the peace negotiations, the constitution of juridical institutions which may serve to ensure the loyal and faithful application of the agreements and, where the need is recognized, to revise and correct them, is of decisive importance for the honourable acceptance of a peace treaty and for the avoidance of arbitrary and unilateral infringements and interpretations of the terms of the treaties.

In particular, attention must be paid to the true needs and just demands of the nations and peoples, and of the ethnical minorities. . . .

Rulers of the peoples and the peoples themselves must become imbued with that spirit of moral justice which alone can breathe life into the dead letter of international instruments. . . .

Culture and Ideals of the Finnish Nation

Tuesday, December 26

MR. G. A. GRIPENBERG, Finnish Minister in London, in a broadcast :

Although the English people and the Finns are very much alike in both ideals and culture, many Englishmen know very little about my country. We are a long way away and rather off the beaten track. I should like to tell you, therefore, that we are quite ordinary people, and our cities are quite ordinary cities. We have large modern buildings, universities, theatres, cinemas, and all the wonderful amenities of modern civilized life.

In the years since we gained our complete independence we have built up a State where there is no unemployment, where every man and woman has the right and privilege to take part in the shaping of the destinies of the State, where the youth of all classes can proceed to the highest education and where, thanks to a far-reaching social legislation, the poorer classes are in every respect assisted and supported as far as our economic means will permit.

We have built a State with one hundred and fifty thousand new independent landowners, with new schools, new hospitals, and new welfare organizations, a State where every man, no matter what his origin, can reach the highest office, a State in which every man has the right to think and to speak freely, to worship as he pleases, and to follow whatever vocation or occupation he prefers. You will understand, therefore, why we are now standing and fighting to resist the Russian attempt to destroy us. All these things which we—and indeed you—love and cherish are now at stake ; our heritage from past generations, our freedom, the very lives of our women and children.

THINGS YOU MAY NOT KNOW

Knot. The word knot is a nautical measure of speed, and is so called from the knots in the log line by which a ship's speed used to be calculated. A vessel is said to travel at so many nautical miles per hour, a nautical mile being usually 6,080 feet. One must never speak of so many knots or at so many knots per hour.

Scuttling. A ship is scuttled by letting the sea in to fill her, usually by leaving open the sea-cocks or valves and all watertight bulkheads.

Battle-Cruiser. There is often some confusion between the terms battle-cruiser and battleship, but the difference is very simple. Battle-cruisers are in most respects the same as battleships, except that in their case some of the heavy armour belting has been sacrificed to give them greater speed. They are not smaller than battleships. The three British battle-cruisers in commission at the outbreak of war were the "Hood," "Renown " and " Repulse," the first-named of 42,000 tons with an armoured belt of 12 ins., while the other two are of 32,000 tons with a 6-in.

armour belt. The "Hood" has a speed of 32 knots, and the "Renown " and " Repulse " a speed of 29 knots. The two most modern **Battleships** in commission in the Royal Navy at the outbreak of war, " Nelson " and " Rodney," are of 33,000 tons with an armour belt of 14 ins., but a speed of only 23 knots. Compare with these the **Pocket Battleship** " Deutschland," which, though only of 10,000 tons, has six 11-in. guns. Her speed is 26 knots, which would enable her to escape from all heavily-armed British ships except the three battle-cruisers.

Armed Merchant Cruisers. These are for the most part liners which have been taken over by the Royal Navy and converted into warships, e.g. the " Rawalpindi," sunk by the " Deutschland " on Nov. 23. They have a broadside armament of guns of not more than 6 ins. intended for attack as well as defence, while **Armed Merchant-Ships** carry only stern guns and anti-aircraft guns—purely defensive armament for use against submarines and aircraft.

Photo-Story of the Life and Death of a U-Boat

Left is the conning-tower of a U-boat putting to sea in search of British merchant-ships. In the centre photograph she is out in the North Sea, and a keen look-out is being kept for any ship that may become her prey—and for one whose prey she may become. As soon as a ship is sighted the submarine is submerged from the engine-room, right, and only the periscope shows above water.

The ship eventually sighted was a small coasting steamer, an easy victim as its slow speed made escape impossible. The U-boat commander chooses to use one of his few precious torpedoes and, left, a cloud of smoke is rising as it strikes the defenceless hull. Right is the scene a few minutes later. The crew have taken to their boats, and the little ship plunges stern first to the bottom.

Quite frequently it is the U-boat's worst enemy, a British destroyer, that is sighted. The result is seen above. Depth charges have been dropped, and later a part of the shattered hull came to the surface, left. Above, a boat has put off from the destroyer to look for survivors.

Photos, Topical and G.P.U.

Hunter and Hunted in the Submarine War

Based on an article in " The Navy," the monthly organ of the Navy League, this
account by Mr. Maurice Prendergast of recent development of the U-boats and the
British counter-measures has a very topical interest.

IN the autumn of 1918 the U-boats were held at bay, but had by no means been mastered. Ample evidence existed that, in the spring of 1919, they were prepared to deliver a third and yet more terrific onslaught. However, thanks to the introduction of convoying, the establishment of great mine-barrages across the North Sea, and a vastly increased output of anti-submarine equipment and other expedients, our mercantile losses had been brought down, by the autumn of 1918, to the level of about 140,000 tons per month. This rate was tolerable, as the output of new shipping exceeded the scale of losses.

So much for matters from our own point of view. How did they look from the enemy's ? On this score we have first-hand testimony at command, in the shape of reminiscences of commanding officers of the old U-boats.

They are unanimous in the opinion that the depth charge is a terrible weapon for the crew of any submarine to face. They declare that it was extremely difficult to make a successful attack upon a convoy, if that convoy was accompanied by fast, numerous and well-armed escort vessels. They admit that our introduction of the paravane was a bad blow to them, for it nullified the war value of that half of the German submarine force which had been devoted to minelaying craft. They admit that the unfinished Anglo-American mine-fields between Scotland and Norway were becoming " a formidable obstacle " to their operations. They had an exaggerated notion of the efficiency of our anti-submarine detecting hydrophones. They hated and dreaded the English " Q ships," but our aircraft, in those days, did not worry them much.

Between the fateful November of 1918 and September of last year, there is an intervening span of nigh on twenty-one years. During that interregnum of peace submarine and anti-submarine were arming for the renewal of the fight.

Evading the Versailles Ban

The disarmament of Germany under the Versailles Treaty included a strict injunction that she should not build or acquire any further submarines for her fleet. Despite the prohibition, submarines continued to be built to German designs and by German labour—but in shipyards outside the Third Reich !

First of all, there was established in Holland a concern known as the " Nederlandsche Ingenieurskantoor voor Scheepsbouw " (Dutch Technical Centre for Shipbuilding). Outwardly it was a Dutch organization, but inwardly it contained a strong assembly of German

naval architects and technicians, all proficient in the designing and building of war vessels. Most significant was the fact that the presiding genius of the N.I.V.S. was no other than the famous Dr. Techel, who, during the war of 1914–18 had been Chief of the Submarine Building Branch of the great Krupp-Germania shipyard at Kiel.

In 1927 a Dutch firm produced, under the auspices of the N.I.V.S., two submarines for the Turkish Navy. They were pretty well replicas of the " UB.III Type," which had been built for the Kaiser's Navy in 1916–18. Next came the acquisition of a large share in the Crichton shipyard at Abo, Finland, by the German Vulkan A.G. of Stettin, whereupon the production of submarines for the Finnish Navy was begun. It was the N.I.V.S. at The Hague which provided the necessary plans and technical knowledge ; the requisite skilled labour and plant were transferred from Germany.

In 1935 the Crichton-Vulkan firm began to build a small submarine to the order of nobody in particular. Following this came news that the firm of Echavarrieta y Larrinaga at Cadiz, in Spain, was building a mysterious underwater vessel which had not been ordered by any Government. For her building " plans and material were being imported from Holland." The designs, once again, were the product of the N.I.V.S. It was suspected that these Finnish and Spanish vessels were actually " pattern boats " which were being created to serve two purposes. The first was to test the rapidity with which identical vessels could be assembled in German shipyards ; the second was to prove the sea performance of new types before they were put into production.

After this, large contracts were placed with German marine engine builders for sets of high-speed Diesel engines, and the outside world was told that such machinery was required for " new coastal ship-

ping." Sectional parts for construction of submarine hulls were quietly collected in the German yards—and then all disguise was dropped. Germany declared that she had resumed the construction of U-boats.

And what was happening on the British side in all the years that separate 1918 from 1939 ? We emerged from the last war with one bitter experience branded indelibly on our memories. It was the knowledge that, in the spring of 1917, the ghastly slaughter of our shipping had brought us to the brink of ruin, starvation and surrender. We were determined that the like should never happen again in any future war we undertook. In the depth charge, we had certainly discovered a most potent weapon against hostile submarines, if—and always if !—it was applied in the

The Finnish submarine, " Iku-Turso," was one of three built at the Turku (Abo) shipyard in 1930 and 1931. In this yard, largely the creation of German experts, other warships for Finland have been built.   *Photo, Derek Wordley*

right place and at the right moment. " Location " of the target is, was, and always will be the crux of the problem in offensive operations against that invisible antagonist, the submerged submarine. Accordingly, as soon as our Navy had settled down to its post-war organization, we concentrated our scientific knowledge, technical abilities and engineering resources upon intensive research for the perfection of the anti-submarine directional hydrophone. That would find the submarine for us—and then we could depth-charge it !

At last, after the most laborious and patient work, we got what we wanted. Details of the modern British anti-submarine directional hydrophone are, most properly, kept in the closest secrecy. It has been declared in Parliament that, in this branch of naval equipment, we have resources far in advance of any employed by any foreign Navy. That this declaration is true, the modern U-boats know.

So Foch's prediction that " the next war will begin where the last one ended " has come true, so far at least as the U-boat war is concerned.

How a Submarine of the 'Ursula' Class is Operated

Vertical Rudder

Propellers

Hydroplane or Horizontal Rudder

Oil Fuel

Control Room

Water Ballast

Oil Fuel

Periscope Well

Detachable Keel in Emergency

HAWORTH

This submarine is one of the same class as the gallant "Ursula" (see p. 565). Known as the Coastal Type, they displace only 540-730 tons. Their armament is six 21-in. torpedoes, and the surface speed 11·25 knots. They carry a crew of 27.

The sectional drawing shows the boat cruising just below the surface with a foot or so of periscope A above water. To get into this position the wireless mast B is lowered and all outside gear stowed and hatches C closed. The commander climbs down ladder D into control-room and takes his place at eye-piece of periscope E. Water is run into ballast tanks F, and boat is trimmed. Diesel engine G is stopped and electric motor H started from battery tank J. As boat moves forward

men at K move fore and aft hydroplanes into correct position to make boat dive slightly and stay there. L steers by vertical rudder.

When the boat is required to rise, the water is forced from the ballast tanks by compressed air, which is stored in bottles M. When torpedoes N are to be fired, crew in torpedo storage O slide torpedoes into firing tubes P, open watertight door Q by means of mechanism R. Torpedo can then be fired by compressed air stored at 2,000 lb. pressure in tanks S. Actual firing is done by cylinders T, at 500 lb. pressure. Torpedoes can also be fired from amidships or from stern.

Picture-diagram specially prepared for THE WAR ILLUSTRATED *by Haworth*

The Modern Mine is a Double-Edged Weapon

Contributed by Mr. Frank C. Bowen, the well-known writer on Naval affairs, this
article gives much interesting information concerning the mines which have become
so important a weapon in the war at sea.

ALTHOUGH it was regarded for generations as being a purely defensive weapon, and as such perfectly legal within the limitations laid down by the Hague Convention of 1907, the Germans proved during the late war that the mine could also be an offensive one. In that role, however, it is difficult to keep it within the rules of international law and humanity, and the Germans have made little effort to do so in any case.

The first minefields laid in the North Sea are shown in page 398 ; this sketch map shows the British East Coast minefield, whose existence was announced on December 27. Also indicated is the area off Heligoland Bight, systematically patrolled by the R.A.F.

The necessity for controlling the use of mines comes from their inability to select their victims. The man in charge of the gun or torpedo has the opportunity of identifying his target before he fires, and if he sinks a neutral ship it is deliberate. Mines will detonate under any vessel, and it was therefore agreed by all nations at The Hague that they should not be laid where they could sink harmless neutrals who could not avoid them and that they should automatically become innocuous as soon as they broke from their moorings and drifted away from their published position.

The new British minefield, covering practically the whole east coast of Great Britain, is perfectly legal because its exact limits have been clearly published to the whole world, and neutral ships on their lawful occasions can pass round either end without the least danger from it. If they try to pass through it, there can be no doubt that their purpose is unneutral and that they are working for

Germany. The same thing applies to the published German minefield.

But mines laid in the open sea without any warning, which is the essence of the employment of the minelaying submarine and the magnetic mine, are in quite a different class and offend against all the promises given by the German Government in 1907 and confirmed by Hitler before, and Grand Admiral Raeder at the outbreak, of the war. The secrecy of their position is the reason of their success, and neutrals cannot avoid them unless they stay in port.

These secretly laid minefields are an essential part of the German submarine campaign ; the U-boats which lay them are also fitted with torpedoes and guns against commerce. While many magnetic mines have been laid by 'planes, this was probably only intended to be a temporary measure while the submarine minelayers were being completed, and once the first surprise was past the R.A.F. Security Patrol made an excellent antidote.

The submarine is the most dangerous layer of mines in narrow waters, and the mine is her most dangerous enemy. Of the British submarines lost in the late war, nine are known to have been sunk by mine, no other weapon securing more than four, and probably most of the 21 which " went missing " were due to the same cause. Forty of the 199 U-boats which did not return are known to have been mine victims, and again there were many whose loss was unexplained but probably due to the same cause.

The two great fields which " contained " the German submarine fleet were those in the Straits of Dover, laid at the outbreak of war but not made fully effective until 1918, and the Great Northern Barrage between Norway and the Orkneys, into which the British and American navies put 63,117 mines in the last few months of hostilities. Being legally laid and notified, this stopped short at the edge of Norwegian territorial waters, and the Germans took advantage of them.

In those days it was necessary, in order to make a field reasonably proof against submerged submarines, to lay an enormous number of mines at various depths.

A modern field would generally—with many exceptions owing to local conditions—consist of contact mines laid just below the surface to catch raiding or bombarding men-of-war and mines at various depths for submerged submarines. The latter, it must be remembered, are very much more susceptible to explosion close to them than a surface warship. They do not possess the same margins of stability or buoyancy, so that the shock which would be merely uncomfortable to

One of the chief differences between the German and British mines is that the latter are automatically rendered harmless in the event of their breaking adrift. One such vagrant is seen in this photograph being recaptured.

Photos, Sport and General

an ordinary ship, and perhaps cause leaks with which the pumps can deal without difficulty, is often disastrous to a submarine. In many cases they have been rolled right over, and in many more the lighting circuit has been destroyed. The slightest leak is serious, not only because their small reserve of buoyancy will force them to come to the surface, but because sea water getting to their accumulators will generate the deadly chlorine gas.

And then there is the terrible nerve strain of passing in a submerged submarine through an area known to have been sown with mines.

Australia's Airmen Now Comrades of the R.A.F.

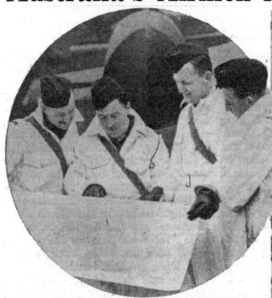

Australian airmen who have just arrived in England
will have their first experience of war service with the
Coastal Command. Above, pilots are studying charts
before going on one of their first patrols.
Photo, Fox

The first squadron of the R.A.A.F. came
ashore on December 26, 1939. Besides
pilots there were gunners, observers and
ground staff.   *Photo, Associated Press*

IN a message to the first Australian
squadron to land in Britain, Mr.
J. V. Fairbairn, Australian Minister for
Air, said : " A great responsibility rests
upon you as members of the first Australian Air Force squadron to come on
active service in this country. You will
be comrades in a great and just campaign with the men of the R.A.F., and
Australia is confident that you will play
your part in whatever spheres you may
be called upon to serve."

Two airmen of the Royal Australian Air
Force squadron now serving with the R.A.F.
Coastal Command are seen here at the two
gun positions amidships in the hull of a
" Sunderland " flying boat.
Photo, Fox

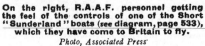
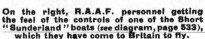

On the right, R.A.A.F. personnel getting
the feel of the controls of one of the Short
"Sunderland" boats (see diagram, page 533),
which they have come to Britain to fly.
Photo, Associated Press

How Big a Threat is Germany's Air Force?

Following some account of the pre-war organization of the German Air Force, this article goes on to introduce us to the uncertain mathematics of German aeroplane production and first-line strength of 'planes.

ALTHOUGH it was only in the spring of 1935 that the German Air Force—the Luftwaffe, " air arm" —was officially constituted, it has since been built up into an instrument of national policy of the most impressive size and formidability. One great advantage it has had is the fact that it is the favourite child of Field Marshal Goering, who was a German air ace in the Great War.

Not the least important of the many offices which Goering has collected is that of Air Minister, and his position as industrial dictator of the Reich has led to a state of affairs in which Germany's Air Ministry is an almost autonomous power in the Nazi State. Not only is the whole of the German aeronautical industry under its (or his) authority ; not only are all the aerial forces of whatever kind—bombers, fighters, reconnaissance and co-operation 'planes, etc.—all the aerodromes, the recruiting and instruction of airmen and ground staff, at its immediate disposal, but, in addition, the whole of the anti-aircraft defence and even the whole system of passive defence —that which we know as A.R.P.

In February 1938 the Air Force was reorganized on lines which were still in force when the war started, and, so far as we can tell, are still in force today. The territory of the Reich is divided into four huge Air Commands, each under an Air Fleet Commander who has under his control all the means necessary for the conduct of an aerial war, both offensive and defensive, in his particular area.

To feed this vast concentration of offensive and defensive air power there is an aircraft industry which has been brought to a high level of efficiency. In May 1939 " Aircraft Engineering " stated that it comprised some 29 firms with 51 factories, not counting a very large number of sub-contractors and manufacturers of accessories. None of these factories, be it noted, was situated near a dangerous frontier, but were distributed in central Germany and along the Baltic coast. One peculiarity of the German system is the separation of the factories in which the original types are designed from those devoted to mass production. Thus at Warnemuende, near Luebeck, is the vast array of flying grounds, hangars, and workshops where Heinkel types are built and tested, while the firm's main production is centred at Oranienburg, just north of Berlin.

The Junkers firm has five groups of factories for airframes in central Germany, besides three for complete aircraft ; even in peacetime its personnel exceeded 25,000 workmen. The former Zeppelin works at Friedrichshafen are used by the Dornier company. The Messerschmitts are produced at Augsburg.

No one can say with certainty what was—still less, what is—the strength of Germany's Air Force. In October 1938 M. Paul Rives, official reporter of the air estimates of the French Chamber, estimated the first line strength of the German Air Force at between 4,500 and 5,000 'planes. He went on to state that the German aim was to create an air

force between 8,000 and 10,000 machines by 1940 at the latest. Before the war Germany's 750 aerodromes had an estimated capacity of between 10,000 and 12,000 machines, and no doubt many more flying fields have since been constructed. Then the American journalist, Mr. Garrison Villard, on returning from a visit to Germany in November 1939 stated that he had heard there the most astounding figures as to the size of the air fleet that was being accumulated for a spring attack on Britain. Even if those assertions were heavily discounted, he said, " there still remains the figure of 30,000 machines to be available when good flying weather returns."

It is only fair to say that many authorities regard such figures with high suspicion ; a force of 30,000 aeroplanes would require a ground staff to maintain them of about 300,000 men, and it is improbable that Germany has either men or material on this colossal scale.

Besides, as Dr. Brinkmann, then Vice-Director of the Reichsbank, is reported to have asked at a meeting of Nazi chiefs in February 1939 : " What is the use of all these aeroplanes if we have no oil for them—and we still are short in that respect ? " But when every allowance has been made for the exuberance of Nazi propaganda, the fact remains that over a period of several years Germany has devoted a very large proportion of her national effort to the building up of an Air Force second to none. Just how far she has succeeded only the grim trial of war will be able to determine.

Though many have alleged that the Messerschmitt single-seater fighter (type ME 109) has shown grave failings in the testing time of war, there is little doubt that it is, in fact, efficient and of high-class workmanship. Moreover, a special version holds the present world's speed record at 469·2 m.p.h. Above is a pilot climbing into his Messerschmitt, one of the newer machines with the 1,000 h.p. Daimler-Benz engine.

Photo, International Graphic Press

Are They Practising for a 'Blitzkrieg' in the Air ?

Young Nazi airmen are put through an intensive course of training. They are here learning the far from gentle art of bombing. In this ingenious apparatus a map on rollers passes beneath the pupil showing a stretch of country as nearly as possible as it would appear seen from an aeroplane flying at a great height and speed. When the lever releasing the bomb is pulled the aim is automatically registered on the map.

Photo, Dorien Leigh

'WHAT ARE WE TO DO TO WIN THIS WAR?'

At the opening of a year which must be fateful in the history not only of our own country
but of the whole of Western civilization, Britain's Prime Minister delivered at the Mansion
House, London, on January 9, a speech which was at once a warning of the grim things
which may be in store and an encouragement in the path that must be followed to victory.

MR. CHAMBERLAIN opened his
speech by saying that since
war broke out, his sole thought
and all his actions had been directed to
doing all he could, in the closest collaboration with France, to bring the war to a
successful conclusion. He went on :

Once again, as twenty-five years ago, the
historic buildings and the ancient streets of
Britain are looking upon the faces of the
King's subjects who have come here from all
parts of the world of their own free will, far
away from their homes and their families, to
take their part side by side with us in the great
struggle that is before us.

Their presence here and the profound conviction of the necessity of putting an end to the
German policy of constant aggression—which
alone could have induced them to undertake
such sacrifices—has brought to the aid of the
Allies not only a most welcome addition to their
fighting strength, but what is perhaps even more
valuable, the moral support of their unanimous
approval of our cause.

**This New Year, which will probably be a fateful
one in the history of the world, has opened quietly,
but it is the quiet of the calm before the storm.
We are at war.**

It is only on the sea that the war may be
said to be in full operation, and it is on the
sea that we can discern most clearly the trend
of hostilities in the first four months of war.

AFTER surveying the respective gains
and losses of the belligerents at
sea, Mr. Chamberlain said that inexorable
pressure of sea power acting upon the
enemy was producing ever-increasing
difficulties for her whole economy and for
her ability to carry on the war.

Germany (he went on) used her brute force
upon unhappy Poland, and today we can see how
she is treating the Poles and the Czechs—ex-
ploiting their resources, carrying off their food,
starving and shooting the people, tearing and
uprooting them from their homes to make way
for Germans who, in their turn, have been forced
to leave the lands where they and their families
have been settled for generations.

And now it is the turn of Finland to be
attacked by that Power with whom Germany
made an unholy pact and to whom she set the
example of aggression.

Finland today, amidst her snows and her
frozen lakes, is fighting against the forces of
unscrupulous violence, just as we are ourselves.

Our Close Association With France

MR. CHAMBERLAIN then referred to the
assistance given by the British
and French governments to the victims
of the Turkish earthquakes, and continued :

This collaboration between France and ourselves for humanitarian purposes is only just
another instance of that close, that even
intimate, association between us which now
covers every aspect of the war—military,
political, financial and economic.

**I cannot help thinking that our experience of
this association during the war will prove it to be
so valuable that when the war is over neither of
us will want to give it up.**

It might even develop into something wider
and deeper, because there is nothing which
would do more to facilitate the task of peaceful
reconstruction which has got to be undertaken
at some time—there is nothing which would
contribute more towards the permanence of

its results—than the extension of Anglo-
French collaboration in finance and economics
to other nations in Europe and, indeed, perhaps,
to the whole world."

Mr. Chamberlain spoke of our mobilization as prodigious, and, dealing with the
civil defences, said :

Whilst we have already reviewed all our
different precautions and modified and amended
them where we thought that we could do so
without disregarding the important factor of
safety, **I do not consider that the risk of air raids
is over or even that it has diminished.**

And as long as that is so I am certain that we
should make a capital mistake if we were to
reverse the policy that we have hitherto
followed—the policy which I may sum up by
saying that it is the evacuation, while the
evacuation can be carried out free from bombs
and machine-guns, of all who can be evacuated
without the serious loss of efficiency.

PAYING a tribute to the British people's
willingness to make sacrifices to
win the war, Mr. Chamberlain said :

**What I am not quite so sure of is that
they understand what they are up against,
or that we shall have to face a phase of this war
much grimmer than anything we have seen yet.**

We have got to do without a lot of things
that we shall miss very much, and I am going

Mr. Chamberlain delivering his speech on
January 9, 1940, at the Mansion House—
that speech which, as one New York paper
had it, "crackled with determination."

to try to show you why. Although we are not
yet actually fighting on land, we are making
preparations to enable us to do so with the
greatest effect whenever the right moment
comes.

For that purpose, we are devoting more
and more of our man-power to the production of
armaments. That must mean that there is less
and less of our man-power available to produce
civilian goods.

Even supposing we had ample supplies
of labour we should still have to curtail our
imports of goods which are not necessary for
the prosecution of the war, so as to leave
available our resources of foreign exchange and
of shipping to purchase and to bring home in
ships imports of those things which we cannot
do without.

Saying that he did not think anyone
at home would complain of the necessary
sacrifices, the Premier continued :

Nearly a year ago, speaking in the House of
Commons, I warned the country that it was the
intention of the Government, on the outbreak
of a major war, that direct taxes, already so
heavy as to constitute conscription of wealth,
would be still further increased.

That prediction was fulfilled when my heavy-
handed friend and colleague [Sir John Simon]
last September placed his little finger upon the
shoulder of the income-tax payer.

Already, the wealthier classes have suffered
a very heavy reduction in their income, and we
have left them mighty little prospect of being
able to increase it again.

I don't say that we have come to the end of
our demands upon them, but . . . it is
not possible for them alone to solve the problem
of how to reduce consumption of unnecessary
articles, because two-thirds of the consumption
of the people of this country is by those who
only have small incomes ; and, therefore, I say
that it is necessary that they too should make
their sacrifice as is done, not only in totalitarian
Germany, but also in the great democracy of
France.

'We Must Save, and Do Without'

WHAT are we to do to win, and, if
possible, to shorten this war ?

**We must save, we must control imports, we
must do without commodities that are not
necessary, we must, if required, ration them so
that all may share and share alike.**

" If you find that you cannot buy the woollen
goods that you have been accustomed to,
remember that wool is wanted for the clothing
of the Army. If you are asked to lessen your
consumption of bacon and sugar, remember
that you are making available space in ships
which can be used for iron ore or machine tools.
If you are asked to put your savings into
Savings Certificates, instead of spending them,
remember that you are giving help to the
Chancellor in his Herculean task in finding the
wherewithal for our unprecedented expenditure.

It is becoming increasingly clear that the
German Government has long planned the
successive stages of a programme of conquest,
and that its appetite grows by what it feeds
upon. Today the members of that Government
do not hesitate to say that they desire to achieve
the ruin of the British Empire, and no doubt
they would rejoice if they could treat us as they
are treating the victims already within their
grip. We on our side have no such vindictive
designs.

But, on the other hand, the German people
must realize that the responsibility for the pro-
longation of this war, and all the suffering
that it may bring in the coming year, is theirs,
as well as that of the tyrants who stand over
them. They must realize that the desire of the
Allies for a social, human, just, Christian settlement cannot be satisfied by assurances which
experience has proved to be worthless.

In his recent message to the Pope the President
of the United States declared that only by the
friendly association of the seekers of light and
the seekers of peace everywhere can the forces
of evil be overcome.

I profoundly agree. But I would add that,
**if the forces of right are to prevail, we must not
hesitate to risk our blood and our treasure for so
great an end.**

Against such a combination as that, the
powers of wickedness will fight in vain, and we,
at the beginning of this New Year, can await
the future with unshaken confidence in the
strength of our arms and in the righteousness
of our cause.

We Saw Our 'Planes Bomb a U-Boat

Attacked by a submarine in the Atlantic, crew and passengers of the freighter "Fanad Head" took to their boats, and before being rescued by a destroyer were spectators of a battle between the U-boat and British aircraft. This broadcast eye witness story by K. E. Halnan is illustrated with photographs (later developed on the "Ark Royal") taken by his brother, who was on board.

Eye Witness Stories of Episodes and Adventures in the Second Great War

I WAS a passenger on board a large freighter, the "Fanad Head," bound for Belfast from Montreal with a cargo of grain : there were nine passengers altogether. The first part of the voyage passed uneventfully. Then one morning, as I was sitting in the saloon after break-fast, I heard somebody running to his cabin and there was a continuous ringing of the ship's bells. The captain had sighted a submarine about five miles away on the starboard bow, approaching us at full speed.

I rushed to my cabin, put on my mack-intosh and lifebelt, stuffed a few of my most treasured possessions in my pockets, and went on deck. There I found the other passengers assembled near the lifeboats. The ship had altered course and the submarine was dead astern, visible as a black speck surrounded by large white bow-waves and with dense black smoke pouring from it—evidently German engines as well as British were being driven to their utmost capacity.

With her superior speed the submarine gradually but surely overhauled us, and after an hour - and - a - half's chase the captain decided to abandon ship. While the boats were being made ready for lowering, the bos'un suddenly shouted "He's going to fire," and everyone took cover as we heard the noise of the shell. The shell passed clear of the ship and we resumed our preparations for departure.

During all this time the wireless operator had been at his post, sending out an S O S, and had got in touch with an American ship. In addition, although we did not know it at the time, the Navy had also got our S O S.

The boats were launched and we all got into them. After we had rowed a short distance from the ship the submarine came alongside the boat I was in and the commander spoke to our captain. The submarine was a modern type, painted a dirty yellowish green except for the con-ning tower which was dark green, with an armament consisting of a machine-gun similar to the Bren gun, and a small gun firing shells weighing a few pounds, which we had already seen and heard in action. The commander asked us in perfect English what our cargo was, appeared somewhat disappointed when he found

it was grain, told us an American steamer was coming to pick us up, and then gave us a tow to our No. 2 lifeboat which was about four hundred yards away. He then cast off our painter and told us he was going off to sink the ship, after which he would come back and give us a tow. We made fast our No. 2 lifeboat, threw overboard a sea anchor, and stood by to watch events. The submarine partially submerged and went towards the ship, standing off for a little while before finally going alongside, where it remained some considerable time.

Meanwhile the lifeboats were rocking about badly in the swell and more and more of the passengers and crew were

becoming sea-sick. After waiting mono-tonously for some time, we suddenly got the surprise of our lives. In the distance beyond the ship we heard a low hum and saw a dark speck that resolved itself into an aeroplane. At first we thought it was a transatlantic flying boat, but as it rapidly approached we saw that it was a monoplane of the Fleet Air Arm fully loaded with bombs. As soon as it came near the ship it dived on to the sub-marine and released four bombs. The submarine crash-dived and the mono-plane turned, released three more bombs and then disappeared behind the ship. About ten minutes later another 'plane flew over the boats and flashed us a message by signal lamp, "help coming."

By this time we were all excited and sea-sickness was forgotten. Then, just as we had decided that the submarine must have been sunk, she reappeared and again approached our ship. Soon after this the monoplane reappeared and dived towards

As related in this page, the survivors of the British freighter "Fanad Head," who had taken to their boats when the ship was attacked by a German submarine, had the thrill of seeing the U-boat attacked and bombed by a British aeroplane. A companion 'plane is here seen diving low over one lifeboat, cheered by the crew (see *also* photos in page 637). *Photo, G. A. Halnan*

the submarine. This time the submarine made no attempt to submerge and we heard a crackle of fire as though heavy machine-guns were operating. Soon afterwards six biplanes appeared in sight and circled over the area as if searching for the submarine which had again submerged. Suddenly a tremendous vertical explosion occurred on the starboard side of our ship, and immediately the six planes swooped down on an area of the sea about half-a-mile from the ship—swooped down just like a lot of hungry gulls after bread —and dropped many bombs. We could easily see the explosions. Evidently the submarine had torpedoed the ship and the track of the torpedo had given the submarine's position away to the hunting aircraft.

Having completed their task the aeroplanes flew over the lifeboats and were wildly cheered by all of us, then went off. Meanwhile our late ship, badly hit by the explosion, began slowly to break up. First the masts slowly canted towards each other, then the funnel gradually sank in the water, then the two boilers exploded one after the other, the bow and stern slowly rose in the water and finally disappeared from view almost touching each other as the ship finally sank from view.

We now saw a slight smoke haze on the horizon and soon we could distinguish the masts of two destroyers approaching us. While the first destroyer that reached us circled round, evidently still seeking the enemy, the second by clever manoeuvring came to a standstill near enough for us to row alongside and to make fast to lines thrown to us from her deck. Two days later we were landed at a fishing village in the North of Scotland.

A new twin-engined Messerschmitt 110 long-range fighter, also shown sectioned in page 555. This was the German type engaged in the battle described below.
Photo, "The Aeroplane"

Our Three Bombers Fought Twelve Fighters

In an air battle off the German coast on January 2, three British bombers were engaged by twelve Messerschmitt fighters. One of the German 'planes went down in flames and two others were driven down, while of the British 'planes one was shot down and one was missing. The story of the pilot who returned is here reprinted from the "Evening Standard."

"WE gave as good as we got," was the comment of the pilot of an R.A.F. bomber which alone returned from a battle between three bombers and twelve Messerschmitt long-range fighters near the German coast on January 2.

At a point about eighty miles northwest of Heligoland and about eighty miles north of Borkum, when our bombers were on close formation and flying at about 10,000 feet, they were suddenly attacked by the Messerschmitt 110 Squadron.

The pilot of the aircraft which returned said :

"We were going south when suddenly the look-out man shouted 'Fighters!'

"Almost before he had given the warning I saw their streams of white tracer bullets flashing past on one side.

"I then realized this was a serious battle. We had not seen the enemy because they came straight out of the sun.

"The first burst of enemy fire penetrated our fuselage but did no material damage.

"We found ourselves fighting about twelve of the enemy. More bullets entered our aircraft, and some of them missed us by a few inches."

Six Messerschmitts made three dual attacks on the bomber, which escaped after bringing down two of its attackers.

We Were Torpedoed on Christmas Day

On December 25, 1939, while members of the crew were celebrating Christmas below decks, the London steamer "Stanholme" was sunk without warning by a German submarine and fourteen lives were lost. The stories of two of the eleven survivors are here reprinted from the "News Chronicle" and "Manchester Guardian."

THE U-boat was sighted by a deckhand too late to raise an effective alarm. Within five minutes the "Stanholme" had disappeared.

The ship's boats were smashed by the explosion of two torpedoes, but two of the hands lowered a raft. For a quarter of an hour they were rowing around the spot where the "Stanholme" had disappeared and were able to assist those still in the water. For nearly an hour 11 people remained on the raft. It had, however, been damaged by the explosions, and when a lifeboat from a Norwegian steamer arrived on the scene the raft was sinking.

Among the survivors was Mrs. Jenvy, wife of the chief engineer, who said :

"The captain had poured us out drinks in his cabin and had wished us all a merry Christmas, when a terrible explosion occurred which threw us to the floor.

"We rushed on deck as the vessel began to heel over, and a second explosion shook us.

"My husband ran to the lifebelts, put one over my head and threw me into the water.

"That was the last I saw of him, for he went down with the ship.

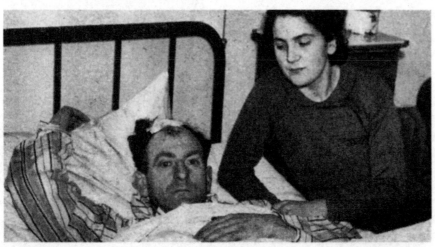

After the sinking of the steamer "Stanholme" described by eye witnesses in this and the following page, the survivors were landed at Cardiff. Above, the first officer, Mr. T. G. Phillips, who was injured in the head, is being visited by his wife in the Seamen's Hospital.
Photo, Fox

Victims See Swift Revenge on the U-Boat that Sank Their Ship

The group of passengers, top left, on board the S.S. "Fanad Head" sunk on September 15 have been told that a U-boat is chasing their ship and is slowly overhauling it. They are awaiting without a sign of panic whatever Fate may have in store for them. Meanwhile, the crew are launching the life-boats, above, for the U-boat has fired a warning shell. A little later the passengers and crew took to the boats.

Centre is the last close up view of the ship, taken from one of the boats as it pulled away from her. Soon afterwards the U-boat fired a torpedo and, above, a cloud of smoke arose as the ship was struck. But a few minutes later the victims saw British aeroplanes approaching (*see* p. 635), and while their ship was still afloat a rain of depth charges, seen in the photograph right, sealed the fate of the submarine.

Photos, Copyright G. A. Halnan

"I could not swim, but the lifebelt kept me floating in the coal-dust-covered sea, until a Norwegian vessel picked me up.

"The captain of the Norwegian boat was very kind and gave us clothes, food and hot drinks."

Seaman E. L. Evans said : "We left port early on Christmas morning and were torpedoed less than three hours later. We were having breakfast when suddenly there was a terrific explosion, followed by another a second later. We had no warning and no time to launch the lifeboat, but I pushed a small raft we had on deck into the water and scrambled on to it.

"One of my shipmates told me that the radio operator was blown to pieces. The ship started to go down in four minutes. The crew jumped overboard and were all struggling in the water and we managed to pull several on board, until there were eleven of us there.

"Eventually we were picked up by the lifeboat of a Norwegian steamer which was lying some distance off and whose crew had heard the explosion and saw the ship sinking."

How We Escorted a Merchant Convoy

In the protection of convoys the Royal Air Force Coastal Command co-operates with the Royal Navy as shown in page 533. A typical flight on escort duty is here described by an occupant of one of the aircraft.

OUR flight started from the East Coast. Taking off in a haze of smoke blown over the countryside from factories farther north, we were soon out at sea. Looking back, we saw the land, half obscured by a grey mist like a layer of dirty cotton wool.

In a few minutes we had reached the convoy. The toy-like ships followed steadily in each other's wake, while destroyers zigzagged on each side and ahead. Guarded by sea and air, the convoy was a formidable formation for any U-boat to tackle. Indeed, there could be little doubt that bombs and depth-charges would send a pirate to his account.

The aircraft which we were relieving on escort duty flew alongside us, while the two pilots, who came from the same station and were due for a game of squash together later in the day, waved their arms and grinned. Then the other banked away and dropped astern of us, setting a course for home. The changing of the air guard was complete.

At a height of a few hundred feet, we made a round of the convoy, looking down on grey-painted hulls and funnels, and yellowish-brown decks. From above, the ships seemed hardly to be moving, but splashes of white spray around plunging bows showed that they were really making good headway.

Every ship must keep her station. To leave the formation is to invite danger from mines. We saw a small but fast steamer try to make use of her superior speed and draw ahead. She looked exactly like a motorist trying to cut out of a queue to get into the lead.

The offender was soon spotted by one of the destroyers ahead of the convoy. Turning sharply the warship raced back with a high plume of spray rising from her bows. She signalled the delinquent to move back into line. We, from our position in the "gallery," could follow the whole comedy. We saw the cargo boat's bow wave disappear as she fell back to take her proper place. Soon she was in line again and the destroyer was back at her station. We flew ahead to patrol the route.

Suddenly a light winked intermittently at us from the bridge of one of the destroyers. Our wireless operator, still wearing his headphones, picked up his signalling lamp and pointed it through a window towards the destroyer. Moving his finger on a trigger like that of a pistol, he clicked out an acknowledgement. Again the distant light flashed, following us as we circled the destroyer. The operator wrote the message as he watched the signals. He handed a slip to the pilot. It read : "Am going to let off some practice rounds."

We flew off to a safe distance, and saw the flash of an anti-aircraft gun as the destroyer fired a target shell. A tiny puff of smoke appeared high against the blue sky. A powerful salvo followed. In the aircraft we could hear the boom of the guns above the roar of our engines. In a few seconds the sky was spotted with smoke-puffs, and from our "ringside" seats in the air, we saw a spectacle which made us heartily glad it was not our duty to attack a British warship !

In due course we were on the look-out for the aircraft which was to relieve us. Dead on the minute it arrived. Once again greetings were exchanged, and on this occasion it was our turn to hand over. We waved our arms, banked away, and sped homewards.

In page 533 appeared a sectional diagram of a Short "Sunderland" flying boat on convoy patrol. Here is a photograph from another aircraft of one of these great machines—the largest in the R.A.F.—alighting off the coast. "Sunderlands" were concerned in the famous "Kensington Court" rescue, described in page 156.

Photo. Fox

Cartoonists on Red Aggression

Gulliver's Travails!
By Zec, courtesy of the " Daily Mirror."

Racketeer.
" New York Journal, American."

Honour Among Thieves?   **(Stalin is said to have asked for German help.)**
From the cartoon by Sir Bernard Partridge. By permission of the proprietors of " Punch."

The Sportsman.
" Saginaw News" (U.S.A.).

OUR DIARY OF THE WAR

Thursday, January 4, 1940

Russian air force active in region bordering railway line to Swedish frontier.

Finns isolated a Soviet battalion, part of a force sent to make contact with Russian troops at Suojaervi, north of Lake Ladoga.

Finnish warplanes dropped 3,000,000 pamphlets over Leningrad on January 3, and carried out **bombing raids on Soviet island bases** at Oesel and Dagoe.

R.A.F. made successful reconnaissance flights over north-west Germany, and patrols over seaplane bases in Heligoland Bight.

Goering assumed supreme control of German war industries and all Government departments concerned with economic side of war.

Paris reported that in Lower Vosges enemy detachment of 100 was surprised and machine-gunned by French patrol.

British trawler " Daneden " feared lost with crew of nine.

Reported that British liner " Tuscan Star " had been bombed and machine-gunned by German aeroplane shortly after leaving England. Raider driven off by ship's anti-aircraft guns.

Friday, January 5

Russians reported to be digging themselves in opposite middle of Mannerheim Line.

Soviet warship " Kiroff," damaged by Finnish coastal batteries, towed into port for repairs.

Mr. Hore-Belisha, Minister of War, **resigned from the Government,** and Mr. Oliver Stanley was appointed in his place.

Sir John Reith became Minister of Information in place of Lord Macmillan.

Paris reported intense artillery activity along 125 miles of the Western Front.

Announced that part of the first Indian contingent to join the B.E.F. had reached the British forward zone.

Swedish steamer " Fenris " shelled and sunk by Soviet submarine in Gulf of Bothnia.

Saturday, January 6

Helsinki reported that fighting was continuing near Suomussalmi, and that on the Karelian Isthmus artillery fire had intensified.

Battle on five " fronts " in progress in Salla sector.

Finns said to have **made contact with new Russian division** near frontier north of Kiantajaervi.

Russians lost eight 'planes in raid on Utti, 60 miles north-east of Helsinki.

British trawler " Eta " sunk by mine in North Sea.

British liner " City of Marseilles " struck a mine off east coast of Scotland, but was safely towed into port.

Dutch Government issued formal declaration that Holland would defend her integrity against any attack.

Discussions took place at Venice between Count Ciano and Count Csaky, Foreign Ministers of Italy and Hungary.

Sunday, January 7

Mr. Churchill in France visiting British Forces.

Attempt by Russian ski detachment to outflank Finns in Salla sector was defeated.

Russian 'planes again bombed Turku and also raided town of Kuopie.

Paris reported patrol activity at different points of the front. Artillery action east of the Blies.

British collier " Towneley " mined off South-East Coast.

British ship " Cedrington Court " sunk off South-East Coast.

Monday, January 8

Fight on Karelian Isthmus continued in desultory fashion.

During week-end **Finns won great victory** in " waistline " area. **Russian 44th Division destroyed,** 1,000 prisoners and large quantity of war material captured.

Successes were also reported from farther north, engagements on Salla and Petsamo fronts yielding much valuable booty.

Paris reported patrol activity in region west of Vosges.

New German Army H.Q. said to have been established at Recklingshausen, 10 miles from Dutch frontier.

Reported that British liner " Highland Patriot " was attacked by U-boat on December 29, but beat enemy off with 4-in. gun.

British tanker reached Amsterdam after being attacked by Heinkel bomber in North Sea.

Sir Edmund Ironside and Lord Gort decorated with Grand Cross of Legion of Honour by General Gamelin.

Rationing scheme came into operation, foods affected being sugar, butter, bacon and ham.

Tuesday, January 9

Nazi aeroplanes attacked, with bombs and machine-guns, merchant ships, fishing craft and Trinity House vessel off East Coast. British steamers " Gowrie," " Oakgrove " and " Upminster " sunk; steamer " Northwood " attacked and trawler " Chrystalite " disabled. Danish ships " Ivan Kondrup " and " Feddy " also attacked but reached port.

Union-Castle **liner " Dunbar Castle " sunk by mine** off South-East Coast.

British tanker " British Liberty " sunk.

Dutch steamer " Truida " mined.

British trawler " River Earn " reported sunk by Nazi bomber in North Sea.

Russian communiqué admitted that Red troops had retreated several kilometres east of Suomussalmi.

Soviet aircraft raided six small towns in Finland.

Reported that Leningrad-Murmansk railway had again been cut by patrols.

Announced that out of 5,911 ships—British, Allied and neutral—convoyed by British Navy, only 12 were sunk while in convoy.

First Colonial contingent—from Cyprus—landed in France to join B.E.F.

Creation of a Royal Air Force Command in France announced, with Air-Marshal A. S. Barratt as Commander-in-Chief.

Reported that Italy had made representations to Germany concerning detention in German ports of war supplies sent by Italy to Finland.

Wednesday, January 10

Artillery action and air activity reported from Western Front.

R.A.F. made **bombing raid on German seaplane base of Sylt ;** reported that Hindenburg Dam, connecting island with mainland, was damaged.

R.A.F. aircraft had **running fight with Messerschmitts** over North Sea. One enemy fighter destroyed and at least one disabled. One British machine lost.

Helsinki reported battle in progress north-east of Lake Ladoga. In Suomussalmi region **Finns drove Russians back over frontier.**

Russians attacking in Salla sector with fresh troops.

Finns reported that 700 out of 1,000 Soviet bombers ranged on eastern frontier were snowbound and frozen up.

Norwegian steamer " Manx " mined in North Sea.

Sweden passed emergency laws giving Government wide powers in case of war.

He Leaves—But His Work Lives On

WITH dramatic suddenness Mr. Leslie Hore-Belisha resigned his post as Secretary for War on January 5. In the pages of " The War Illustrated " we are not concerned with politics, nor with the reasons, whatever they may be, which led to Mr. Hore-Belisha's resignation. But his great work at the War Office should not pass unrecorded in our pages.

Comparatively young himself, he has seen to it that the young men got their chance, and in particular his selection of Lord Gort for the post of Chief of the Imperial General Staff, from which he proceeded in due course to the command of the British Field Force in France, was recognized as a welcome break with traditional ideas. To the rank and file he gave not only raised pay and improved marriage allowances, but facilities for promotion to commission rank ; as he has said, " the star is within every private soldier's reach." History will remember him, too, as the Minister who was in office when Britain introduced conscription for the first time in peacetime, doubled the Territorial Army, and sent to France at the beginning of the war the largest Expeditionary Force which Great Britain has ever put into the field as a complete fighting unit.

Leaving the War Office on January 6 after his resignation, Mr. Hore-Belisha, cheerful as ever, returns the commissionaire's salute.